COUNTRIES
AND THEIR
CULTURES

EDITORIAL BOARD

Countries and Their Cultures was prepared under the auspices and with the support of the Human Relations Area Files, Inc. (HRAF) at Yale University. The foremost international research organization in the field of cultural anthropology, HRAF is a not-for-profit consortium of 19 Sponsoring Member institutions and more than 400 active and inactive Associate Member institutions in nearly 40 countries. The mission of HRAF is to provide information that facilitates the cross-cultural study of human behavior, society, and culture. The HRAF Collection of Ethnography, which has been building since 1949, contains nearly one million pages of information, indexed according to more than 700 subject categories, on the cultures of the world. An increasing portion of the Collection of Ethnography, which now covers more than 365 cultures, is accessible via the World Wide Web to member institutions. The HRAF Collection of Archaeology, the first installment of which appeared in 1999, is also accessible on the Web to those member institutions opting to receive it.

COUNTRIES
AND THEIR
CULTURES

LAOS
TO
RWANDA

Melvin Ember and Carol R. Ember, Editors

Macmillan Reference USA
an imprint of the Gale Group
New York • Detroit • San Francisco • London • Boston • Woodbridge, CT

Countries and Their Cultures

Copyright © 2001 Macmillan Reference USA, an imprint of Gale Group

Macmillan Reference USA
1633 Broadway
New York, NY 10019

Macmillan Reference USA
27500 Drake Rd.
Farmington Hills, MI 48331-3535

Library of Congress Cataloging-in-Publication Data
Countries and their cultures / Melvin Ember and Carol R. Ember, editors.
  p.cm.
  Includes bibliographical references and index.
  ISBN 0-02-864950-8 (set : hc.)
1. Ethnology-Encyclopedias. I. Ember, Melvin. II. Ember, Carol R.
GN307 .C68 2001
306'.03-dc21
                     2001030188

Volume 1: 0-02-864947-8
Volume 2: 0-02-864948-6
Volume 3: 0-02-864949-4
Volume 4: 0-02-864946-X

Printed in the United States of America

Printing number
 2 3 4 5 6 7 8 9 10

Front cover photos (clockwise from top): Aymara man with llamas © Gian Berto Vanni/Corbis; Japanese kindergarten students © Don Stevenson/Mira; Hooded men at Oaxaca Festival © Liba Taylor/Corbis; Kava Ceremony, Fiji © Charles & Josette Lenars/Corbis; Wedding service in a Russian Orthodox church © Dean Conger/Corbis; Egyptian ranger battalion demonstration © Corbis; Boy eating lobster at Friendship Regatta festivities © Dean Conger/Corbis; Akha villagers perform a Chi Ji Tsi ritual © Michael Freeman/Corbis. Background: Desert Rose block print by Arlinka Blair © Jonathan Blair/Corbis.

LAOS

CULTURE NAME

Lao

ORIENTATION

Identification. The ethnic Lao in Laos account for 50 to 60 percent of the population, depending on how some subgroups are classified. The way people self-identify ethnically is often contextual. Related groups include the so-called tribal Tai, Black Tai, White Tai, and Red Tai. These groups are not Buddhists and are influenced by the neighboring Sino-Vietnamese culture. The country contained forty-three ethnic groups in 1995 according to the official classification, mostly in the countryside and mountains. The cities contain significant ethnic Chinese and Vietnamese populations.

Location and Geography. Laos is a landlocked Southeast Asian country surrounded by Thailand, Vietnam, Cambodia, Myanmar (Burma), and China. It has an area of about 91,400 square miles (236,800 square kilometer). A key physical feature is the Annamese Cordillera mountain range that runs from north to south, along the eastern border with Vietnam. There are other secondary ranges, and to the north of the capital, Vientiane, is the highest peak, Mount Bia. Out of these ranges all the main rivers flow from east to west into the Mekong River. In the north, the Mekong forms a short border with Burma and most of the border with Thailand. Along the rivers there are floodplains suitable for rice paddies. There are no extensive lowland plains. Upland soils are much less fertile, but there are two plains areas: the Plain of Jars, and the Boloven Plateau in Champassak Province. Most of the country is covered by monsoon forests with varied wildlife. A tropical monsoon climate is modified by the mountains. The wet season runs from May to October.

Vientiane was the capital of earlier Lao kingdoms. It was destroyed by the Siamese early in the nineteenth century, but the French reestablished Vientaine as the capital in 1893, when Laos became part of French Indochina. A royal capital existed in Luang Prabang until the fall of the monarchy in 1975. The two other main cities, Savannakhet and Pakse, are also on the Mekong.

Demography. In 1998, the population was 5,261,000. Urban dwellers made up 23 percent of the population. Close to 70 percent of the population is under 30 years old. Laos is one of the least densely populated countries in Asia.

Linguistic Affiliation. Lao is the language of government, education, and mass communications. Lao belongs to the Tai language family. There are variations in pronunciation and vocabulary from north to south. Most Lao understand and speak Thai. Lao has many borrowings from Pali and Sanskrit, particularly in its literary forms.

Among the minorities, there is the Miao-Yao (Hmong-Iu Mien) language group, mostly spoken in the north. Among the Hmong, Chinese characters are used in religious rituals. Many Hmong are fully literate in an orthography developed by missionaries, and there is a Hmong messianic script. Among the Iu-Mien (Yao), literate individuals use Chinese characters to write histories. Tibeto-Burman speakers, mainly in the north, also make use of Chinese characters for ritual purposes. Austronesian and Mon-Khmer speakers live in the north but are most heavily represented in the south. These groups have no indigenous tradition of literacy. Illiteracy is as high as 40 percent, primarily among older people and women. Because of the use of Lao as a lingua franca, most people have some knowledge of it, particularly for purposes of trading. Vietnamese and Chinese in urban areas have autonomous traditions of literacy, and have their own schools. The majority of them are also fluent in Lao.

Laos

Symbolism. The key national symbols are Buddhist, despite the fact that only around 60 percent of the population is Buddhist. Before the revolution in 1975, Buddhism and the monarchy were linked as key symbols. The Communist regime tried to substitute purely secular national symbols, and a calendar of mostly secular holidays was instituted. The flag of the first independence movement in 1945, the Lao Issara, replaced that of the Royal Lao Government (RLG). With the collapse of communism, the state has reverted to purely nationalist symbols; this "retraditionalizing" of the regime has meant a greater prominence for Buddhism. The national day of December 2 was celebrated after the revolution, but has been eclipsed by the celebration of the That Luang Festival. The That Luang stupa in Vientiane, built by the revered King Sethathirat, is one of the most sacred spaces and is recognized by all groups. Other national icons are also Buddhist, but some, such as the megalithic jars from the Plain of Jars, point to complex origins. Much of this iconography was pioneered by the RLG, including that associated with "hill tribes," who are typically presented in their "national dress." In general, national culture symbols are drawn fro Lao culture, suggesting that other ethnic groups are required to assimilate these symbols. This is a source of low-key contention in the country. The appropriation of "old regime" symbols has muted some of the conflict between refugee Lao and the LPDR (Lao People's Democratic Republic), but has led to debates over how much of the past to "revive."

Nowhere is this conflict clearer than in the declaration of the old royal capital as a national heritage city by UNESCO, thus making Luang Prabang a symbol of Lao culture and a tourist attraction. This dual use has led to debates about how much of the royal ("feudal") past should be revived. The communist government tried to promote a cult around the communist leader Kaysone Phomvihane after his death, and statues of him were erected all over the country.

HISTORY AND ETHNIC RELATIONS

Emergence of the Nation. The main parameters of the modern state were established by French colonialism between 1893 and 1954: The French delineated the borders and wrote the first national history of Laos. It was also the French who began restoring monuments and constructing a "national" literature. This work was continued by a small group of intellectuals under the RLG associated with the Literature Committee and by the Royal Academy. The LPDR has added little to this stock of national markers. A nationalist movement was encouraged by the French during World War II, and became an independence movement, the Lao Issara. This movement is a claimed by both Communists and anti-Communists. The current regime claims to be the true nationalist heir, but it came to power and survived only with the military assistance of the Vietnamese. This reliance tarnished its nationalist credentials after 1975, but declining reliance on Vietnam in the 1990s boosted those credentials.

National Identity. More people of Lao ethnic origin live in Thailand than in Laos. Laos was almost absorbed into Siam and that has tinged Lao national identity with fears of disappearance. The fact that most ethnic Lao in the Thai northeast do not identify themselves with the Lao nation-state is a source of confusion, blurring the cultural boundary between Laos and Thailand. Although Lao and Thai languages are very close, central Thai is the key cultural marker of the difference. However, many Lao consider Thai to be more developed than Lao.

Lao identity may have been more clearly demarcated when it had a monarchy of its own. Now, many Lao follow the itineraries of Thai royalty as if to fill a cultural absence at home.

Ethnic Relations. An ethnic hierarchy exists, placing ethnic Lao at the apex. Many urban Chinese have assimilated into Lao culture, and even those who have not are considered to represent a major civilization. Vietnamese also have assimilated, and those who have not are situated just below the Chinese, though they are more disliked. A small Indian population lives in the urban areas, and dislike for them usually focuses on their dark skin, smell, and alleged deviousness. There is little intermarriage between them and Lao. The term "ethnic minorities" normally refers to the hill tribes. This initial bipolar categorization of ethnic Lao and minorities gives way to a threefold categorization of the population into Lao Lum (lowland, [ethnic,] Lao), Lao Theung (literally midland Lao), and Lao Soung (literally highland Lao). The government has attempted to come up with a comprehensive classification of the ethnic groups, which ranged in number from sixty-eight to forty-three in 1995. Ordinary Lao are likely to use the tripartite classification or even derogatory terms for those designated Lao Theung and Meo. Most disrespect is reserved for the Austronesian groups in the south, whose pipe-smoking women are singled out for comment. LPDR attempts at resettlement of minorities for political control, ecological preservation of forests, and delivery of social services have been poorly executed and have caused resentment. In the south, this has led to the breakup of matrilineal longhouses as groups are moved into standard housing. In the north, Hmong groups, have resisted these attempts at control, sometimes violently. In its early years the communist government highlighted its alleged respect for minority cultures, but today there is a greater emphasis on Lao culture.

URBANISM, ARCHITECTURE, AND THE USE OF SPACE

Laos is one of the least urbanized countries in Southeast Asia. Vientiane has around 500,000 people, many in rural districts. Savannakhet and Pakse are the next most important cities, while Luang Prabang is the most important historical city.

All these cities have a mixture of French colonial architecture, Buddhist architecture in temples, traditional Lao houses raised on stilts, American-style houses built in the 1950s and 1960s, and new large houses that imitate Thai styles. All these cities are built alongside rivers whose banks provide major recreational spaces.

Most Lao people live in rural villages clustered around a temple. Lao, Tai, and groups such as the Khmu live in houses raised off the ground on stilts. In Khmu villages, instead of a temple, there may be a communal house for meetings, usually used by men. Hmong, Iu Mien, and some other groups in the north build large sturdy houses on the ground. In the south, among the Ta Oi, there are still villages with matrilineally organized longhouses. The temple in most Lao villages remains the main center for social and recreational activities, usually associated with religious celebrations.

FOOD AND ECONOMY

Food in Daily Life. Sticky rice is the staple. Chinese, Vietnamese, Hmong, and some other groups favor nonsticky varieties that can be eaten with chopsticks or spoons rather than with fingers. Spoons and forks are used to manipulate the dishes that accompany the rice, while sticky rice may be dipped directly into condiments of chili paste and fish paste. Soup is a regular feature of meals. In the countryside, people eat chopped raw meat and foods gathered from the surrounding forests. Hygiene campaigns have caused a decline in the eating of raw foods in cities. *Laab*, finely chopped meat with spices, is a favorite dish that can be eaten raw or cooked. For most lowland Lao, fish dishes are a central part of the diet. Relatively little pork is eaten, and chicken, buffalo, or beef is more common. An important culinary change in the main cities since the revolution is a spread of dog eating, which previously was associated with Vietnamese and Sino-Viet groups. Dog meat is considered a "strong" male dish and is accompanied by strong liquor. Rice whisky often accompanies snack eating among males, and heavy drinking usually occurs on ceremonial occasions. At the New Year heavy female drinking also occurs. In the countryside and mountains, fermented rice "beer" is drunk from jars using bamboo straws. In the cities, beer consumption is widespread.

Influenced by the French, many Lao in cities and small market towns drink coffee and eat bread at breakfast, which strikes Thai visitors as exotic. In the cities there are French, Indian, and Chinese restaurants that cater mainly to foreigners. The dish ordinary Lao most commonly consume in roadside restaurants is *feu*, a soup-noodle dish imported from Vietnam.

Cars on a busy street. Laos is one of the least urbanized countries in Southeast Asia.

Food Customs at Ceremonial Occasions. Lao do not reserve special foods for the New Year or other occasions, and foods generally do not have special meanings. *Khao poun*, a fermented rice vermicelli, signifies life piling up over the years, while *aab* means luck. Celebrations involve more food and a greater variety of foods, with more sweets, desserts and alcohol. These are occasions for reinforcing village reciprocity and solidarity. End of harvest celebrations are similar.

Buddhists make offerings of food to monks from the local temple. Usually this is done when the monks file through the village or city early in the morning. Among some southern minority groups large buffalo sacrifices take place, but they have been discouraged by the government. Less spectacular sacrificing of buffaloes and other animals occurs among all the ethnic groups.

Basic Economy. Paddy rice and rice grown in swiddens (slash-and-burn agriculture) in hilly areas provides subsistence for the majority of the population. Maize is important for some upland groups. The rural population consumes most of the food it produces, but Laos is a net importer of food, primarily from Thailand. Market exchange for food occurs in occasional markets and small market towns for most rural people. These towns are also conduits for industrially produced commodities for households and farms. In more remote areas, industrially produced cloth and clothing gives way to home-produced clothes. Market gardening increases near large towns and cities.

Land Tenure and Property. Under the RLG, land that was not freehold was technically Crown Land. However, there was a commercial market for land in the towns and some freehold titles were granted to people in the countryside. After the revolution property was nationalized. Only after the economic reforms of the 1990s was private ownership recognized and a foreign-assisted land-titling program now grants ninety-nine year leases and allows for commercial transfer. Most land is subject to recognition of rights through use. In the upland Tai areas there is still a traditional system of mixed communal and family land ownership. Rights to swiddens are based on use. Customary rights are exercised over rivers, streams and ponds, and communal rights apply to some forests.

Commercial Activities. After the revolution, there was a massive contraction of commercial activity, especially in services. The liberalization of the 1990s led to the re-emergence of private banking and legal and commercial consultants and an expansion of private restaurants and retail outlets that sell handicrafts such as weaving.

Major Industries. Logging and timber have been the major industries and are run by the state and army-controlled companies. In the 1990s, there was a rapid expansion of foreign-owned garment-making factories. Hydroelectric power generation is another major industry.

Trade. The main items traded internationally are hydroelectricity sold to Thailand, timber, and garments. Imports include gasoline, vehicles, heavy industrial equipment, and most goods related to light manufacturing. The economy has a chronic trade deficit.

Division of Labor. Beyond gender, there is no marked or customary division of labor. Because Laos remains an overwhelmingly peasant society and because there is little manufacturing or industry in and around the cities, a modern, elaborate division of labor remains rudimentary. There are a small number of professionals, such as lawyers, operating in the capital, but most indigenous expertise is located in the state. Besides this, there is a significant foreign aid community that provides a body of professionals across the board. Historically, the Vietnamese have functioned as tradesmen and laborers in the cities, which they still do to some extent.

SOCIAL STRATIFICATION

Classes and Castes. Since the abolition of the aristocracy in 1975, there have been no hereditary castelike groups. Many members of the aristocracy fled after the revolution, as did members of the state-based elite, such as army generals, and capitalists and commercial traders, many of whom were Chinese or Vietnamese. The new elite was composed of the upper echelons of the communist state apparatus. With liberalization, this access to power has allowed these groups to branch out into private enterprise. Foreign investment and foreign aid led to corruption in the upper echelons of the state, which then became pervasive throughout. A very small urban-based middle class has begun to form, but most people belong to the peasantry and are powerless and poor.

Symbols of Social Stratification. Before the revolution, some styles of dress and fabrics were reserved for the king and his court. Formal dress for all groups imitated courtly style and included the *sampot* for men and the *sinh* skirt for women. The sampot is a traditional form of dress not unlike the Indian *dhoti* in which the corner of cloth is drawn up between the legs and tucked in at the back, thus forming a kind of billowing short trousers. The sinh is a long traditional skirt that is usually made of silk and that features a wide and often elaborately woven section at the foot. Minorities, especially women, wore Lao dress or traditional dress. After the revolution egalitarian dress was emphasized. In the 1990s much of the older dress style came back as the new rich elite publicly flaunted their wealth, and elite men now wear business suits. In everyday life dress styles have diversified.

Courtly language was abolished after 1975, and egalitarian forms such as "comrade" became widespread. Deferential forms continued to be used with Buddhist monks and in the family. With the formation of the new elite and liberalization, these deferential forms have reemerged in public life.

POLITICAL LIFE

Government. Until 1975, the RLG attempted to maintain a fragile liberal democracy, but it was undermined by the conditions of war. Since 1975 the country has been a communist one-party state. Until the proclamation of a constitution in 1991, the Communist Party ruled by decree. The constitution provides for a National Assembly that is elected for terms of five years. While seats are contested and contestants do not have to be members of the Communist Party, they must be approved by that party before running for office. No other parties are allowed. The country is administratively divided into sixteen provinces, and key positions in the provincial administration are held by party members. A judicial system was reestablished in the 1990s, partly because of the demands of foreign investors, but judicial decisions are not independent of the ruling party. A major instrument of government is the Lao Front for National Reconstruction, which controls all the major social and cultural organizations, such as the Buddhist Sangha, the Lao Womens' Union, the Trade Unions, and youth organizations.

Leadership and Political Officials. The key to political advancement is a membership in of the Lao Peoples' Revolutionary Party. In the early years of the regime, political criteria for membership were paramount, including "class background." As a new elite has consolidated itself, family politics and connections have come to play a prominent role in gaining access to the party and the privileges that flow from it. Members of the old grand families have gradually been able, through intermarriage with the emerging communist elite, to "cancel out"

A group of Buddhist monks visit houses at dawn to collect alms in Vientiane.

their class background for political purposes while trading on their possession of cultural and economic capital. This elite has gravitated toward deeply rooted symbolic practices of power, such as sponsoring temple rebuilding and the casting of Buddha images. With the growing economic power of these new elite families, more conventional entourages have gathered around "big men," who demand deference, which was frowned upon in the egalitarian aftermath of the revolution.

Social Problems and Control. After the revolution, socially undesirable people such as prostitutes were sent to "reeducation" camps and the army and party exerted social control. Movement was restricted, and visitors had to be reported to the village head. Permission had to be sought for celebrations such as marriages and housewarmings. After the 1990s, restrictions on domestic and international travel were eased. The liberalization that occurred in the 1990s has seen the opening of discos and bars in urban centers and the reemergence of prostitution, drug use, and petty crime. This is the product of an inadequate education system and a lack of economic opportunities for youth. To deal with this and "spiritual pollution," the authorities occasionally crack down on bars and insist that women wear traditional dress, men not grow their hair long, and less foreign music be played. In rural

villages, disputes are handled as much as possible by village committees, usually made up of senior men. Intravillage disputes are handled by the district administration, with attempts to follow party guidelines and local customs. In general, the aim is to achieve a consensus.

Military Activity. The government that came to power in 1975 was largely oriented toward military activity, and military norms were dominant in its early years. However, the leadership of the Communist Party was primarily made up of professional politicians. In the 1990s, this changed as professional soldiers took key positions of power in the state and the party. The current government combines elements of an orthodox communist state and a military dictatorship. The rise of the military is partly a product of the waning of orthodox communism, but the military also has come to play an important economic role.

SOCIAL WELFARE AND CHANGE PROGRAMS

Social welfare is orientated toward state and party officials, with the amount of benefit varying according to rank. Housing is one of the most important benefits. Health care was once important but has become increasingly privatized. Other welfare and change programs, such as child care, AIDS, and

A house in the small northern town of Xiang Kok. Most Lao people live in rural villages clustered around a temple.

women's education programs, are financed and partly run by bilateral aid donors and international organizations.

Nongovernmental Organizations and Other Associations

Nongovernment Organizations (NGOs) established by Lao nationals are not permitted. International NGOs have been allowed to operate since the early 1990s, but they have to be connected to a particular ministry or government organization so their activities can be monitored. Relations between some NGOs and the government have been strained, particularly over the issues of dam building and the relocation of minorities. Attempts to establish an informal NGO forum to discuss development issues have failed. Nevertheless, their presence has seen the emergence of discussions of politically related social and cultural issues, in which Lao employees participate.

Gender Roles and Statuses

Division of Labor by Gender. Besides age, gender is the main way in which social roles and practices are organized. In Buddhism, men are the main religious leaders as monks, and while women can become nuns, it does not entail a sacred transforma-

tion. Women are the main everyday supporters of Buddhism. Shamanism among Lao is usually a prerogative of women. There are male shamans, but monks often traffic in magic and preempt their role. Among non-Lao groups, men play the main role as religious practitioners, usually practicing a form of shamanism. In rural areas there is no separation of tasks by gender, except for weaving, and, among the Hmong, sewing. There is a tendency for women to be concerned with household chores and 'lighter' work. Women have played a major role in petty trade, and recently in long-distance trade. Men predominate in public political positions, but this is slowly changing.

The Relative Status of Women and Men. Women were given full citizenship rights in 1957 when they received the right to vote, ten years after men attained that right. Since that time they have been formally equal in the eyes of the state. Socially and culturally, their status has been ambiguous. Among the Lao, women have considerable social and cultural status by virtue of the tendency toward matrilocality. This gathers together groups of related females and unrelated males and thus potentially strengthens female solidarity and influence. While men are considered culturally superior because of their ability to become monks this status is affected by social class. Men have status because they occupy key positions in the public realm. Women have relatively high standing in the private and civic realms. Among patrilineal groups such as the Hmong, women have less influence socially and culturally; among the matrilineal groups in the south, such as the Ta Oy, they have relatively high status. As these groups are resettled, however, that status rapidly collapses.

MARRIAGE, FAMILY, AND KINSHIP

Marriage. Ethnic Lao partners have a considerable degree of freedom in choosing a spouse, although there is some preference for cousins. Parents may propose a potential spouse and must be consulted about potential marriage partners. A payment like a brideprice is made, and its value varies considerably. The marriage ceremony usually takes place in the bride's family home. At the center of the ritual is a spirit-calling ceremony. Groups were allowed before 1975, when they were outlawed, and re-emerged unofficially in the 1990s. Divorce can be initiated by either party and is not uncommon. Among patrilineal groups, parents play a much more active role in choosing spouses for their children. Among the Hmong, there has been some practice of so-called marriage by capture. Residence in these cases is patrilocal. Polygyny is found among some highland groups.

Domestic Unit. A tendency toward matrilocality among ethnic Lao means that the main house at the center of a group of related women almost always contains a stem family. The oldest daughter and her husband move out after the marriage of the next daughter but try to live nearby or in the same compound. The main house usually is inherited by the youngest daughter, who is responsible for the care of aging parents. The proximity of nuclear households and their continued relationship with the main house creates the appearance of a modified extended family. However, these new units move eventually, separate from the original main house and become main houses. Among highland patrilineal groups, there are large houses containing extended families of related brothers, while in the southern highlands, there are extended families of related women. Men generally are recognized as the household head for religious and political purposes.

Inheritance. Aside from the inheritance of the main house by the youngest daughter among ethnic Lao, inheritance tends to be equal between sons and daughters. Residential practices determine what is inherited, with those moving away, most often

sons, selling land to their sisters or leaving it in their care. The passing on of a house and productive land signals the passing of authority from one generation to another. Jewelry and woven cloth pass from mothers to daughters. Among patrilineal highlanders, houses and land, if they are held by residentially stable groups, are passed through sons, usually the eldest, while daughters are given a substantial dowry.

Kin Groups. Kinship among the Lao is reckoned bilaterally, and there is little genealogical consciousness beyond two generations except among the former aristocracy. Patrilineal clans and lineages can be found among the Hmong, Iu Mien, Khmu, and others; these clans are exogamous.

SOCIALIZATION

Infant Care. Little research has been done on infant care among all groups in Laos. Among ethnic Lao, babies are constantly in the care of the mother and are fed on demand. With babies and children, separation is avoided and crying is actively discouraged. Usually the whole family sleeps together until the children reach puberty. Even in modern homes where children may have a separate room, they all sleep together. Older children are responsible for the care of younger children.

Child Rearing and Education. Hierarchical interdependence is the central value instilled in children. Parents raise and support their children, and the children reciprocate as soon as they can. This creates strong family bonds. It is assumed that elders have the best interests of their children at heart; if they instruct a child to engage in a particular activity or marry, it is assumed that their motives are benign. A key rite of passage for Buddhist males is to enter the monastery, but no similar public event is available to women. Marriage and having children are their key rite of passage. In the past boys would receive their first education in the temples, but the temple has been eclipsed by government-run primary schools.

Higher Education. Esoteric Buddhist knowledge is highly valued, but an awareness of the importance of higher education is increasing. Children from Sino-Lao or Vietnamese-Lao backgrounds are reputed to be the best scholars. They have special schools in the main cities. Similar attitudes can be found among Sinicized highlanders, such as the Hmong. Most higher education is pursued abroad. A national university was established in the early 1970s, but it was dismantled by the revolution.

A Laotian dancer performs at Pha That Luang, the country's largest Buddhist Stupa, during the That Luang, or "Full Moon," Festival.

Only in the mid-1990s was a national university reestablished. Restrictions on reading material and censorship by the government have discouraged the emergence of a culture of reading among adults.

ETIQUETTE

Among all groups, but particularly among the ethnic Lao, a high value is placed on the avoidance of conflict and actions likely to cause emotional discomfort. Careful attention to one's place in the social hierarchy is important, with inattention or deliberate flouting of the hierarchy being a major cause of conflict. The greeting of superiors by clasping one's hands in a prayerful motion combined with a slight bow was discouraged after the revolution, but has made a come-back in social interaction. Hierarchical interaction also involves polite forms of speech and body movements. Public body contact, especially between men and women, is avoided.

RELIGION

Religious Beliefs. The ethnic Lao and some Tai groups are Theravada Buddhists. There are also beliefs usually labeled animistic and beliefs associated with shamanism that involve house spirits, village spirits, district spirits, city spirits, and spirits of the realm. At the higher levels these spirits overlap strongly with Buddhism and are embodied in stupas and temples. These beliefs in territorial spirits also are held by the non-Buddhist Tai. The majority of the population has various beliefs concerning sacred places and objects. Ancestor worship is strong among lineally organized groups. Christianity has made inroads among nonethnic Lao, with the Khmu, Hmong, Vietnamese, and Chinese most often being converts.

Religious Practitioners. Monks are the main religious practitioners among Lao, and most young men are expected to become a monk for a short period to prepare them for marriage. This practice is also crucial for the transfer of merit from son to mother and is the source of a special bond between them. After 1975, entry into the temples was discouraged, but the practice is flourishing again. Most men enter the temple for not more than a month. Young men who stay longer are from poor families and are there to receive an education; some, however, stay for life. Older men sometimes retreat into the temple, as do a few older women. The monks not only are in charge of Buddhist religious ceremonies but function as dream interpreters, traditional medical practitioners, and counselors. Other religious practitioners include spirit mediums and shamans, most of whom are women. Shamans and mediums also are found among all the minorities. A ubiquitous ritual is the *sou khouan* or *baci*, which is a spirit-calling ceremony used at rites of passage and other threshold occasions. Among the Lao the officiant is usually an ex-monk who has attained considerable esoteric knowledge of the ritual language of the ceremony. Among non-Lao these ceremonies draw less on such Indic referents.

Rituals and Holy Places. For ethnic Lao, the Buddhist lunar calendar marks the major annual rituals. At the full moon every month there is a festival (*boun*), the most important of which are the Buddha's enlightenment in the sixth month (May), the beginning and end of lent (July and October), and New Year (15 April). Sacred stupas and temples have special festivals. The most important is the festival held at the That Luang stupa in Vientiane in November. Syncretistic festivals that combine Buddhism and non-Buddhist beliefs are the Rocket Festival (a fertility festival) and boat races. The New Year is a key festival for most minorities, but is determined according to their own calendars.

Death and the Afterlife. Among the Lao, cremation is practiced except for those who have anomalous deaths, such as women who die in childbirth. Although Buddhists desire the ending of the cycle of rebirths and the achievement of nirvana, the aim of most death rituals is to speed the soul of the deceased through the various hells and into rebirth through the transference of merit from the living to the dead. The remains normally are placed in a small stupa inside the temple fence. The remains are powerful magically, and offerings to them may channel that power into the fulfillment of one's wishes. This stops short of ancestor worship, which is found among the Chinese, Vietnamese, and non-Buddhist Tai. For them, burial rather than cremation is the norm and the ancestors are believed to be present and active in the affairs of their descendants; offerings are made to them on a regular basis.

MEDICINE AND HEALTH CARE

Modern health care remains rudimentary, but since the French colonial period, biomedical ideas about disease have spread and modern medicines are used even in the most remote villages. Depending on a person's level of education and exposure, biomedical ideas compete with or combine with folk ideas.

Those ideas include spirit loss and the balance and imbalance of humors that can be remedied by diet and by herbal medicines. For spirit loss, a baci, or a shamanistic ceremony may be performed. The indigenous medical tradition that draws on Indian knowledge is paralleled by Sinitic folk medical traditions in the towns.

SECULAR CELEBRATIONS

Since 1975 the main secular celebrations have been associated with the party and state. The most important are National Day on 2 December, Freedom from the French Day on 12 October, Liberation Day on 23 August, Free Lao Day on 13 August, Children's Day on 1 June, Labor Day on 1 May, People's Party Day 22 March, Women's Day 8 March, Army Day on 20 January, and Pathet Lao Day on 6 January. The Lao New Year is a religious event, but is becoming secularized.

THE ARTS AND HUMANITIES

Support for the Arts. Since the revolution, the arts have been under state patronage and direction. In the 1990s, some writers began to publish stories in Thailand for money, but publication inside Laos requires state approval. The reading audience is very small, and it is hard for artists to find an audience. Traditional performers can make a living independently from state patronage.

Literature. Traditional literature draws on Indian epics such as the Ramayana but also includes indigenous forms such as *Sinxay*. There are no important modern novels, although a short story tradition developed under the RLG. Poetry has been a very important form. After 1975 the demand for socialist realist literature produced dreary propaganda, but in the 1990s less politically motivated literature and poems were published.

Graphic Arts. Graphic arts are almost totally dependent on traditional Buddhist themes, which are expressed in an architectural form as murals or carvings on temple doors and window shutters. There is no developed practice of the fine arts, and cartooning disappeared after 1975. The other main form of visual art is silk and cotton woven cloth with elaborate and subtle patterns and colors.

Performance Arts. Before 1975, performances of the Ramayana were patronized by the king, and there were some attempts at privately sponsored modern theater. After 1975, there were attempts to produce revolutionary theater. As the state tried to

An elephant pulls teak and rosewood logs at the Pak Lay Sawmill. Logging is a major state-run industry.

retraditionalize itself in the 1990s, it revived performances of the Ramayana. The actors and dancers are trained at the school for fine arts in Vientiane, and a similar school has been established in Luang Prabang. Puppetry and shadow plays have almost disappeared. Performances in which a male or female singer improvises or sings standard songs accompanied by an instrumental orchestra are still employed at important local celebrations. Popular songs leave politics aside and often deal with romantic love.

THE STATE OF THE PHYSICAL AND SOCIAL SCIENCES

A College of Pedagogy and a Royal Institute of Law and Administration were established in the 1950s, and the Royal College of Medicine was established in 1969. Those institutions were brought together as the foundation faculties of Sisavangvong University in 1972, but the university closed in 1976. Higher education was reoriented toward the socialist bloc, and students went to study in Vietnam, the Soviet Union, and other Eastern Bloc countries. In some cases, institutes were established within ministries and charged with doing research, but few people participated and in the physical sciences there was a lack of modern equipment. In the mid-1980s,

there was an attempt to establish a Committee for Social Sciences along Vietnamese lines, but it was dissolved in 1993 and the different institutes were relocated.

Some Lao began to study for higher degrees in Thailand, Australia, the United States, and France. A National University was established in 1996, but its facilities are poor and it is not research-oriented. Research in most fields is rudimentary, although significant joint research papers have been written on dengue fever and malaria by the Institute of Epidemiology in the Ministry of Health. In the social sciences nothing of significance has been produced since 1975.

BIBLIOGRAPHY

Archaimbault, Charles. *Structures Religeuses Lao (Rites et Mythes)*, 1973.

Chazee, Laurent. *Atlas des Ethnies et des Sous-Ethnies du Laos*, 1995.

De Berval, René. ed. *Kingdom of Laos. The Land of the Million Elephants and of the White Parasol*, 1959.

Evans, Grant. *The Politics of Ritual and Remembrance: Laos Since 1975*, 1998.

———, ed. *Laos: Culture and Society*, 1999.

Ireson, Carol J. *Field, Forest, and Family: Women's Work and Power in Rural Laos*, 1996.

Koret, Peter. "Contemporary Lao Literature," in *Contemporary Southeast Asian Short Stories*, 1997.

Ovesen, Jan. *A Minority Enters the Nation State: A Case Study of a Hmong Community in Vientiane Province, Laos*, 1995.

Proschan, Frank. "'We Are All Kmhmu, Just the Same': Ethnonyms, Ethnic Identities, and Ethnic Groups," *American Ethnologist*, 24, 1: 1997.

Sahai, Sachchidanand. *The Ramayana in Laos (A Study in the Gvay Dvorahbi)*, 1976.

Savada, Andreas Matles, Ed. *Laos: A Country Study*, 1994.

Stuart-Fox, Martin. *Laos—Politics, Economics and Society*, 1986.

———. *A History of Laos.* 1997.

Walker, Andrew. *The Legend of the Golden Boat*, 1999.

Zago, Marcel. *Rites et Ceremonies en Milieu Bouddhiste Lao*, 1972.

—GRANT EVANS

LATVIA

CULTURE NAME
Latvian

ALTERNATIVE NAMES
Latvija, Latviešu Kultūra, Lettiņi (German; when Latvians use this to refer to themselves, it is always in a tone of caricature or self-depreciation)

ORIENTATION

Identification. Baltic tribes arrived in what is now Latvia from the Pripet marshes around 1000 B.C.E. These included the Lettgalians, and the term *Latvju* derives from the peoples and province of *Latgale*. The most important minority group was the Baltic Germans, who settled there in the thirteenth century. Jews arrived in the seventeenth century. A sizable Russian community moved to the cities, particularly Riga. The polarization of cultural identification in terms of Latvian and Russian is primarily a rural-urban divide.

Location and Geography. Latvia lies on the eastern shores of the Baltic sea, with an area of some 25,100 square miles (65,000 square kilometers). The capital, Rīga, lies at the mouth of the Daugava River. Latvian lands form an extension of the great plains of Russia. Latvia's importance as a mediator between east and west was recognized in 1710, when the capture of Rīga afforded the tsar Peter the Great "a window on the west."

Demography. Urbanization, war, and the Soviet occupation have been the major sources of demographic change. Until the Soviet occupation Latvia was a predominantly rural society. World War II and Soviet occupation brought about massive changes. The German occupation resulted in the extermination of the Jewish population as well as thousands of Latvians. The Soviet occupation led to the loss of 250,000 Latvians through exile and death. At present ethnic Latvians account for 56 percent of the population.

Linguistic Affiliation. Latvian belongs to the Baltic group of languages. Livonian, a Finno-Ugric language is now almost extinct but is experiencing a revival. By the twelfth century a common language was spoken. Russian has had a strong influence on religious vocabulary, while German has influenced the domestic vocabulary.

Written Latvian bore little relationship to the spoken language until 1638. Spelling followed German orthographic traditions until the foundation of an independent state. Russian linguistic influence is also noticeable.

In the nineteenth century most educated Latvians spoke German. In the second half of the nineteenth and the early twentieth centuries the educated segments of the population became fluent in Russian. During the Soviet period Russian was a compulsory subject at school. In the post-independence period parents can have their children educated in Latvian or Russian.

Symbolism. Folk songs (*dainas*) are the most potent symbol of national identity. These songs construct a vision in which the natural, human, and supernatural worlds are intertwined. Oak and lime trees symbolize men and women. The apple tree is frequently associated with orphanhood, a state that symbolically represents the Latvian nation.

The rural character of the national identity was promoted by the role of landscape in art and literature. An association of Latvian artists founded in 1929 argued "for art with a Latvian content and form," primarily in landscape painting. The result of this cultural policy was to include not only the recently emerged intellegentsia and middle classes but also those who lived in the countryside and worked the land.

The repression of the Soviet period contributed symbols of national identity and introduced new

Latvia

days of commemoration and mourning in the national calendar.

HISTORY AND ETHNIC RELATIONS

Emergence of the Nation. The abolition of serfdom in the Baltic provinces between 1817 and 1861 and the removal of restrictions on residence in 1863 opened up opportunities for travel and education. The second half of the nineteenth century saw an enormous increase in Latvian publications, many of them dealing with nationality issues. The revolutions of 1905 and 1917 channelled the disaffection of the peasantry and led eventually to the founding of the state in 1918.

National Identity. In the second half of the nineteenth century many novels and plays dealt with the hardships of serfdom and helped shape a histori-

cally rooted ethnic identity, but national identity was consolidated largely through the collection of folk songs after the 1870s. Many of those songs describe the harshness of German masters and the hardness of work. In the period of independence from 1918 to 1940, farmers were supported by government loans and the redistribution of land, the extension of free schooling, and support for the arts. The undermining of national and cultural identity was a prime goal of the Soviet occupation.

Ethnic Relations. Ethnic relations have been shaped by twentieth-century historical events. The early period of independence was characterized by a tolerance of cultural diversity. The constitution of 1922 safeguarded the rights of all citizens and protected the rights of minorities. The climate became increasingly nationalistic after 1934, and various

Women at Baltic Sea Beach in Jurmala, near Rīga.

government policies were introduced to promote Latvian culture.

URBANISM, ARCHITECTURE, AND THE USE OF SPACE

Until World War II Latvia was essentially a rural society, with two-thirds of the population living in the countryside. Centuries of serfdom contributed to the longing for one's own piece of land. In the eastern province of Latgale the dominant type of settlement was the village, but in the rest of the country separate individual farms predominated. The establishment of the Ethnographic Museum in 1922 transformed the farmstead into an art form. The farmstead consisted of a set of buildings grouped around a yard: the living dwelling faced the cowshed and the storehouse while the threshing house and steam bath house were set at a further distance. The adjoining farm buildings were often of a similar size and featured a more substantial and elaborate construction. The use of space by farmstead householders changed with the seasons. In winter the occupants would retreat to the warmth of the hearth. In summer, they would disperse to sleep in the various outbuildings.

The growth of the population of Rīga in the late nineteenth century led to a huge expansion in the building of apartment houses whose architectural style expressed the social aspirations and ethnic membership of their owners. With the growth of the urban population, summer houses became popular. Brick was the preferred medium, but wood houses were built in imitation of the rural style. The Soviet occupation after 1940 resulted in the expropriation of property and a dramatic contraction in the entitlement to space. Rural dwellings were expropriated and state-sponsored immigration from the Soviet Union led to the building of high-rise blocks to house the incoming labor force.

FOOD AND ECONOMY

Food in Daily Life. The staples of the diet are rye, wheat, and potatoes. Dairy products are valued for their purity and health-giving qualities. Milk, butter, sour cream, and curd cheese were traditionally highly prized additions to the diet. Pork is the most commonly eaten meat. Smoked fish are particularly popular in Rīga and the coastal areas. A huge variety of bread is available in markets and shops. During the Soviet period the main meal of the day was eaten outside the home in a canteen attached to the workplace or school. The evening meal usually was not cooked and consisted of bread and cheese or sausage and possibly salad. There has been a diversification of foods and eating habits, and pizza and Chinese food have found ready acceptance.

Food Customs at Ceremonial Occasions. Yeast breads are an essential ingredient of all family celebrations and religious festivities. Birthdays and namedays call for *klingeris*, a saffron-scented bread made of yeast dough with dried fruits into the shape of a figure eight and decorated with flowers. Christmas and other religious and ceremonial occasions call for home-baked *pīrāgi* bread parcels stuffed with bacon and onion. Beer and *šnabs* are drunk. A special cheese made with caraway seeds, *jāṇa siers*, is made expressly for the midsummer solstice festival of *Jāṇi* and drunk with specially brewed beer.

Basic Economy. Historically, the economy was dominated by transit trade and agriculture, although Rīga has been an important seaport and trading center since the Middle Ages. Many peasants lived in isolated farmsteads, but villages and strip landholdings existed in the eastern province of Latgale. Agrarian reform after World War I led to a prevalence of small family farms. During the Soviet occupation, collective and state-run farms dominated this sector, although small family farms were tolerated. Industry was concentrated in urban centers after the nineteenth century, a pattern that continued under Soviet rule.

Land Tenure and Property. Before the formation of the republic in 1918, land ownership was divided between peasant smallholders and the Baltic German nobility. The distribution of land to the peasantry after World War I was reversed under the Soviet occupation as land was collectivized and put under the control of the state.

Major Industries. In the czarist period, Rīga, Liepāja (Libau), and Ventspils (Windau) became major transit centers for trade between Russia and Western Europe. Flax, timber, hides, rye, butter, and eggs moved west in exchange for rubber, steel, and coal. Rīga became a major export and processing center for timber at that time. In the 1920s and 1930s, industry was restructured, with an orientation toward internal resources and markets. Later, rapid industrialization and ubranization caused a major shift in the economy. Since independence, there has been a decline in agriculture and heavy industry and growth in the financial and service sectors.

SOCIAL STRATIFICATION

Classes and Castes. In the nineteenth century, social mobility depended on education and the ability to speak German. The period of independence after World War I led to the formation of a middle class of professionals and businesspeople. Under the Soviet occupation, professional positions were filled primarily by Russian immigrants. Social mobility was linked to ethnicity and membership in the Community Party. Since 1990, although wages have not kept up with inflation, creating new types of poverty, education has remained the route to professional success and high social status.

POLITICAL LIFE

Government. Under the constitution of 1991, the highest legislative authority is vested in the parliament (*saeima*), which includes one hundred members elected in general multiparty elections every four years (before 1998, it was every three years). The parliament elects the president and prime min-

Architectural view of the old town center in Rīga.

ister. The prime minister is responsible for forming the government, while the president has primarily nominal powers, such as nominating the prime minister, declaring war, and dissolving the parliament. The main power lies with the prime minister and the cabinet of ministers. Only the citizens of Latvia can elect members of parliament and local councils or hold elected positions.

GENDER ROLES AND STATUSES

Division of Labor by Gender. Women's employment is primarily in lower-paid occupations, such as teaching, nursing, and culture management. Although employment levels are roughly equal for men and women, men are four times more likely to be employers. Women are under represented in political and legislative institutions. In the home women spend nearly twice as much time on housework as do men. Traditionally, women have been responsible for family maintenance, and this conferred a privileged role on the male members of the household.

The Relative Status of Women and Men. Literacy rates are equivalent between women and men. Half of secondary school graduates are women, and there are more female than male university graduates. The acceptance of gender inequality in the 1990s may be a reaction to the imposed gender equality of the Soviet period. Latvian culture lacks cultural examples of female leadership and entrepreneurship. The image of woman as a caring mother and loyal and supportive wife in folk songs has led to the perception of women as occupying a secondary role in the public field and a primary role in the domestic sphere.

MARRIAGE, FAMILY, AND KINSHIP

Marriage. Traditionally, marriage in the Baltic provinces was virilocal (meaning women moved away from their families to live in the husband's farmstead), and descent was traced patrilineally. The patrilineal kin group (*dzimta*) consisted of a man and his brothers and their wives and children. However, the household also contained male and female servants, shepherds, orphans, and foster children. Today, marriage is viewed as the natural outcome of emotional and sexual maturation, and a prolonged single status is stigmatizing for women. In 1998, 37 percent of children were born outside wedlock.

A vendor handles baked goods at a stall in the Rīga Municipal Market.

Domestic Unit. Cramped living conditions are both a reason for seeking the independence marriage promises and its consequence, as forced residence with in-laws intensifies the need for space.

SOCIALIZATION

Child Rearing and Education. Gentleness in caring for infants and teaching children by example are highly valued. Traditional child-rearing practices emphasize the importance of work and respect for nature. Grandparents play an important part in child care. Until recently early retirement for women allowed grandmothers to look after young children while the mothers worked. Summers in the countryside with grandparents are highly valued.

Higher Education. Higher education traditionally provided an escape from a deeply stigmatized identity. The loss of a familiar social landscape and the financial hardship suffered by the professional classes in the post-Soviet era has led to diminished demand, if not respect, for higher education.

ETIQUETTE

Restrained behavior, including lowered voices and the avoidance of eye contact, is expected in public places. Self-control, particularly with regard to an-

ger, is highly valued. Until the identity of strangers is established, Latvians try to avoid acknowledging the presence of others. Relationships between same-sex friends and family members are characterized by a high degree of intimacy, body contact and the use of affectionate diminutives.

RELIGION

Religious Beliefs. The Christianization of Latvia occurred through contact with Germans and Russians. The Orthodox Church arrived before the twelfth century, and the Catholic religion was brought by the knights of the Teutonic order. The Moravians who arrived in Rīga in 1729 and founded a seminary in Valmiera quickly attracted a following. This movement evoked ecstatic responses and acquired a strong nationalistic streak. Baptists who arrived in the mid-nineteenth century also succeeded in awakening the interest of the indigenous population. The Lutheran and Catholic religions were identified with the oppressive Baltic German presence.

Traces of traditional earlier beliefs have been assimilated within the local understanding of Christianity, and influence everyday attitudes and conversation. The continued celebration of the midsummer solstice *Jāņi* is a reminder of the power of earlier beliefs and practices and has come to symbolize national identity.

Religious activity was repressed during the period of Soviet occupation, and many ministers were imprisoned. However, funerals and commemorative days of the dead were highly elaborate affairs and came to provide an indirect vehicle for the expression of national sentiment. The post-Soviet era has witnessed a revival of religious practice and the introduction of a large number of new religious movements.

MEDICINE AND HEALTH CARE

Soviet Latvia was well provided for in terms of medical and psychiatric care. However, there was an absence of family practitioners, and this led to an extensive use of emergency ambulance services. Post-Soviet attempts to privatize health care have met with resistance. Latvia has a strong tradition of folk remedies and treatments which is undergoing a revival.

SECULAR CELEBRATIONS

Commemorations of the Molotov-Ribbentropl Act (23 August) and forced collectivization under Soviet rule (15 June and 25 March) are now days of national mourning.

THE ARTS AND HUMANITIES

Support for the Arts. During the period of independence the government generously supported visual, literary, and performance arts. Founded exactly two years after the declaration of independence, the Cultural Foundation was established in 1920 to promote and give financial support to the arts; its self-avowed rationale was closely linked to the development of national identity.

During the Soviet period, artists and writers were kept under surveillance and their work was heavily censored. This was done largely through state sponsorship. Artists who were approved by the state were given superior accommodation and the state purchased their work.

During the post-Soviet period, government support of the arts has been severely curtailed. Even the National Opera House, whose restoration has come to symbolize the reemergence of an independent cultural identity, has had difficulty securing funds from the government.

Performance Arts. The first song festival took place in 1872 and involved the coming together of local choirs from different parts of the country. These early festivals played an important role in the emergence of national identity and attracted large numbers. During the Soviet period the festivals were repressed or used as vehicles of propaganda. During the movement toward independence from the Soviet Union, folk songs again became a powerful vehicle of social criticism and national sentiment.

BIBLIOGRAPHY

Bunkse, Edmunds Valdemars. "Landscape Symbolism in the Latvian Drive for Independence." *Geografiska Notiser* 4: 170–178, 1990.

Eglīte, P. and Zariņa, I.B.,eds. *Time Use by Gender in Latvia*, 1999.

Gimbutas, Marija. *The Balts*, 1963.

Grosa, Silvija. *Art Nouveau Time and Space: The Baltic Countries at the Turn of the Century*, 1999.

Hiden, John and P. Salmon. *The Baltic Nations and Europe*, 1996.

Karklins, Rasma. "Ethnic Integration and School Policies in Latvia." *Nationalities Papers* 26 (2): 283–302, 1998.

Kundzins, Pauls. *Latvju Seta: The Latvian Farmstead*, 1974.

Lieven, Anatol. *The Baltic Revolution*, 1993.

Plakans, Andrejs. "Peasant Farmsteads and Households in the Baltic Littoral, 1797." *Comparative Studies in Society and History* 17: 2–35, 1975.

———. *A Historical Dictionary of Latvia*, 1997.

Silins, Janis. *Latvijas Maksla 1915-1940*, 1990.

Skujenieks, Margers. *Atlas Statistique de la Lettonie*, 1938.

Skultans, Vieda. *The Testimony of Lives: Narrative and Memory in Post Soviet Latvia*, 1998.

Svabe, Arveds. *Agrarian History of Latvia*, 1930.

Vikis-Freibergs, Vaira, ed. *Linguistics and Poetics of Latvian Folk Songs*, 1998.

—VIEDA SKULTANS
AND ROBERTS ĶĪLIS

LEBANON

CULTURE NAME
Lebanese

ALTERNATIVE NAMES
The Republic of Lebanon

ORIENTATION

Identification. *Loubnan* derives from the Phoenician for "white mountain" and denotes Lebanon's mountains, some parts of which remain snow-covered all year.

Location and Geography. Lebanon is bounded on the north and east by Syria, on the west by the Mediterranean, and on the south by Israel.

Lebanon consists of two mountain chains, the Lebanon and the ante-Lebanon; a narrow coastal strip, where all the major cities lie; and a fertile plain, the Bekaa valley, which lies between the two mountain chains and provides most of the local agricultural produce.

The capital, Beirut, was chosen for its ideal location on the Mediterranean and acts as the heart of Lebanon's banking industry, tourism, and trade. The port of Beirut is the busiest and most important in the country.

Demography. As of 1994, the population of Lebanon was estimated to be 3,620,345. Ninety-five percent of the population is Arab, 4 percent is Armenian, and other ethnic backgrounds comprise the remaining 1 percent. The birth rate is 27.69 per thousand and the death rate is 6.55 per thousand. The average life expectancy for those born at the end of the twentieth century was 69.35 years.

Whereas at independence, gained in 1943, the population was one-half Christian and one-half Muslim, a higher birth rate among Shiite Muslims upset this balance and was one of the causes of the civil war. Estimates in the 1990s reveal a population composed of nearly 70 percent Muslims and 30 percent Christians.

Linguistic Affiliation. Languages spoken include Arabic, French, English, and Armenian. There are many accents in Lebanon. The Beirut accent is the mellowest and most highly regarded, while country accents are harsher. Accents are a much higher indicator of social status than they are in the United States.

Lebanon has seen many invasions, which introduced new cultures and languages. The Canaanites, the first known settlers in the country, spoke a Semitic language. In the Hellenistic era Greek was introduced and spoken along with Aramaic. Latin later became common, and finally the Arab invasion in the eighth century introduced and assured the hegemony of Arabic. Today, all Lebanese speak Arabic; most of them, especially the upper and middle classes, speak French; recently, English has become increasingly important.

Symbolism. The cedar in the center of the Lebanese flag is the symbol of six thousand years of history: the cedar was Lebanon's chief export in ancient times. The location of the cedar tree in the middle of the flag touching the upper and lower red stripes is also a reminder of Lebanon's constant troubles because the red stripes represent the blood spilt by the Lebanese throughout their history.

The country's religious diversity has led to the transformation of many religious holidays into national ones. Additionally, the new government has placed much emphasis on secular holidays, particularly *Id Il-Jaysh*, which celebrates the accomplishments of the Lebanese Army.

HISTORY AND ETHNIC RELATIONS

Emergence of the Nation. The first cities to emerge in Lebanon were built by a maritime people, the Phoenicians, who determined the cultural land-

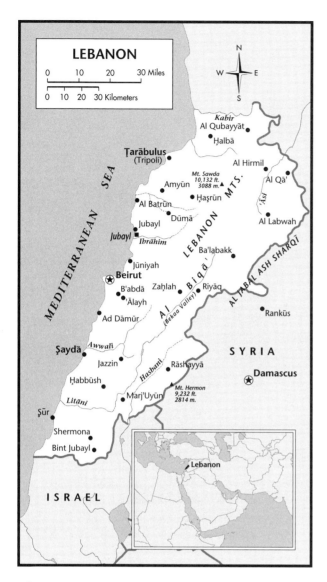

Lebanon

scape of the country from about 2500 to 400 B.C.E. and absorbed aspects of the many other cultures around them. The Phoenicians are celebrated today in the government-supervised history books as the inventors of the alphabet and as the symbol of Lebanon's golden past.

In the medieval period, Christian minorities often helped the Crusaders. This created a close relationship between Lebanese Christians, particularly the Maronites, and Europe, particularly France. These ties persisted and grew stronger, especially in the eighteenth century, and were a major factor in the creation of the modern Lebanon.

After World War II, Lebanon was placed under French mandate. Later, France gave Lebanon a parliamentary system and, for the first time in the Middle East, created a nation where Christians had a

strong political presence: each government office was apportioned to a representative of the country's main sects, with the presidency reserved for the Maronite Christians. The privileging of Christians in governmental positions was one of the main reasons for the civil war, when the population percentage shifted in favor of the Muslims.

National Identity. Although the various communities in Lebanon share a similar ethnic background, the fact that they are of different religions and they define their cultural and often geographical boundaries through religious affiliation has always been a source of discord. On numerous occasions religious diversity has eclipsed the sense of belonging to a common state. When the civil war erupted in the mid-1970s, all formerly suppressed differences and incongruent loyalties emerged and came to dominate the political arena, fuel hatred, and provide an easy ground for outside powers to interfere in the country's affairs.

A tired Lebanon emerged in the early 1990s. Under the *Ta'if* agreement the civil war ended, the Christians lost some of their political power, and a new government of technocrats came into power with reconstruction highest on its agenda.

Today the new moderate government is seeking to secularize political offices and fight corruption.

Ethnic Relations. There is a feeling today that most Lebanese are tired of the war and are trying to put their differences behind them as they reconstruct their country, which is currently under Syrian hegemony.

Lebanese are present throughout the world. Since they have always been at the border between East and West, they often blend easily with the societies to which they migrate.

URBANISM, ARCHITECTURE, AND THE USE OF SPACE

Most of Lebanon's population lives in the main cities of Beirut, Tripoli, and Sidon which are densely populated.

Cities in Lebanon suffer from a lack of space. Most people live in apartments. Furniture is often a mixture of Arabic, Italian, European, and American styles. Apartments are usually decorated in western style: couches are placed against the walls, end tables are common, and walls are often adorned with framed paintings and tapestries.

Lebanese people gather for sports, political events, and concerts. The Lebanese prefer to hold

A market in the war-ravaged capital city of Beirut, circa mid-1980s.

public gatherings in open-air and historical locations.

Government buildings are generally simple and do not display reliefs, paintings, or slogans. Government buildings are often surrounded with small flowerbeds and/or trees.

FOOD AND ECONOMY

Food in Daily Life. Lebanese cuisine is Mediterranean. Pita bread is a staple. The Lebanese enjoy *hummus* (a chick pea dip), *fool* (a fava bean dip), and other bean dishes. Rice is nearly a staple, and pasta is very popular. Salted yogurt is common in many dishes. Red meat and chicken are common but are usually eaten as part of a dish. Pork is less popular, since it is forbidden under Islamic law.

Eating in Lebanon is tied to family: people almost never eat alone. The Lebanese consider eating out a social and almost aesthetic experience. Hence, restaurants usually have a pleasant view, of which Lebanon's geography affords many.

Food Customs at Ceremonial Occasions. *Ramadan*, the Muslim month of fasting, is the occasion for large meals at sundown. Soup, *fatteh* (a

chick pea and yogurt dish), and *karbooj* (a nut-rich pastry) are especially eaten during Ramadan.

During Lent, Christians eat meatless dishes and at Barbara (Halloween) they eat a variety of wheat-based dishes.

Basic Economy. Although Lebanon produces and exports much of its agricultural produce, it still imports much of what its inhabitants consume, such as rice and some vegetables. Since most people live in city apartments, the only Lebanese who grow their own food live in mountain villages and some coastal towns.

Land Tenure and Property. Private property is very common and encouraged in Lebanon, although the government still owns most public services. Land laws are similar to those in France and the United States, but both religious and secular courts govern land inheritance.

Commercial Activities. Lebanon produces and sells oranges, apples, and other fruits, as well as a variety of beans and vegetables. It is also becoming a Middle East hub for a number of computer software and hardware manufacturers. The banking industry, which was very prominent before the war, is once again rising to occupy a privileged place in the region.

Major Industries. The major industry is the manufacture of concrete and building material, to serve local needs. There are also some small factories that produce clothing and fabrics.

Trade. Lebanon sells fruits and vegetables to neighboring Arab countries as well as to Italy, France, and the United States. Wine is produced in the Bekaa and exported to France. Lebanon imports fruits and vegetables from Europe, North Africa and the Middle East; crude oil from Saudi Arabia and Kuwait; and electric and electronic gadgets and cars from Europe, Japan, and North America.

Division of Labor. Adolescents in Lebanon rarely work. The working population is usually 18 years and older. Lebanon is mainly a capitalist country, and the price of living is quite high. Lebanon is rebuilding itself; construction sites are everywhere.

Construction companies prefer to hire workers from Syria or Egypt, who will accept a wage of about $100 (U.S.) a month, an insufficient wage for a Lebanese.

SOCIAL STRATIFICATION

Classes and Castes. There is no caste system in Lebanon. Money is now the most important factor in determining class lines. The middle class suffered a great loss of wealth during the war, and the gap between the very rich upper class and the lower class has widened. As a result, there have been numerous strikes and demonstrations. Differences in wealth and status often occur along religious and family lines.

Symbols of Social Stratification. All Christians and most Muslims who live in the cities wear European style clothes. In poorer Muslim towns and in some Muslim areas in the main cities, one may still find the Muslim *chador* (the veil traditional Muslim women wear). In the countryside, women sometimes wear traditional colorful skirts and men wear a traditional *serwal* (baggy trousers).

POLITICAL LIFE

Government. Lebanon is a democratic republic with a parliament, a cabinet, and a president, although power is divided along religious lines. The President (a Maronite Catholic), who lost part of his executive power after the war, is the head of state; the Prime Minister (a Sunni Muslim) is the head of government and chairs the Cabinet; the Speaker of the House (a Shiite Muslim) presides over Parliament, which passes the Cabinet's bills and elects the President.

Leadership and Political Officials. There is much nepotism in Lebanon. However, the political spectrum is very wide: Lebanon boasts a strong communist party, the Syrian Nationalist Party, and the last Phalange party is still in existence.

Each party has its own newspaper and, at least during the civil war, its own television station.

Social Problems and Control. Lebanese civil law is based on the French Napoleonic law. Police as well as the Forces of General Security uphold the law on the streets. People rarely take the law into their own hands, except when it came to opposing ideologies during the civil war. As a result, the crime rate in Lebanon is very low.

Military Activity. The Lebanese Army was highly divided along religious lines during the civil war. Today, the government is rebuilding the army and trying to modernize it.

SOCIAL WELFARE AND CHANGE PROGRAMS

Lebanon has a relatively good health care program and some free hospitals.

Unemployment is high in Lebanon and, at least according to the IMF and other international organizations, the government, which is struggling to rebuild the country's infrastructure, does not offer sufficient help for the unemployed.

NONGOVERNMENTAL ORGANIZATIONS AND OTHER ASSOCIATIONS

There is a considerable number of nongovernmental organizations in Lebanon, many of which, such as Friends of the Disabled, welcome members from all religions. A number of independent organizations help the poor.

Many international organizations, such as the World Health Organization (WHO), have offices and activities in Lebanon.

GENDER ROLES AND STATUSES

Division of Labor by Gender. The marketplace traditionally has favored men, and more women stay at home than men. Women are allowed to vote, work, attend school, and participate in all forms of public life, but they tend to occupy tradi-

View from Crusader Castle of the Port of Sidon.

tionally female jobs such as secretaries and school-teachers.

The Relative Status of Women and Men. Men hold higher social status than women because of the omnipresence of patriarchal religions in Lebanese life. Family is still stressed, as is the woman's role as a nurturing mother. However, many women have broken traditional boundaries and entered the polit-ical, artistic, and literary environment, especially in Beirut and other major cities.

MARRIAGE, FAMILY, AND KINSHIP

Marriage. Arranged marriages are rare, although they still exist. The country's present economic crisis has rendered money, a secure job, and a home big factors in contracting marriages.

Polygamy is legal among Muslims; however, it holds a social stigma, and very few people choose this lifestyle.

Religious courts decide on issues of marriage and divorce. Divorce is easy among Muslims, harder for Orthodox Christians, and most difficult in Maronite communities. The divorce rate remains very low.

Domestic Unit. Most household units are made up of a nuclear family. However, the extended family is also very important and often functions as a social security system.

In the household, the husband and wife share authority, although wives usually wield more influence over children and in various household matters.

Inheritance. Inheritance laws are the affair of the various religious courts, which usually favor male heirs. In villages, land is the most important inheritance, whereas apartments, money, and privately-owned shops constitute the bulk of inheritance in the cities.

Kin Groups. After the family, a person's loyalty is usually with members of his/her own religion who inhabit the same town. However, marriage between different religious groups has become frequent, and at the end of the twentieth century there was an effort to pass a law legalizing civil marriages which may undermine the traditional religious and communal boundaries.

SOCIALIZATION

Infant Care. Infants are usually placed in cribs and playpens, and they have their own small bedrooms. Kindergartens and babysitters are becoming more common as many women today work outside the house. Quite often grandparents or members of the extended family will help care for a baby.

Child Rearing and Education. Education is very important in Lebanon. Many parents prefer to place their children in the more expensive religious private schools, where they may receive moral guidance.

Children are encouraged to learn and to be quiet. Parents are usually strict and demand great devotion. Lebanese children grow up with deep respect for their parents.

Higher Education. Higher education is highly encouraged in Lebanon, which still has some of the

Agricultural fields occupy a stretch of countryside. Lebanon produces and exports much of its agricultural produce.

best universities in the region. However, there are very few jobs awaiting young graduates.

ETIQUETTE

The Lebanese are very gregarious. The *souks* (markets) are always crowded; shopping downtown is very popular, as is strolling with friends along the busy streets. Lebanese people usually sit close together and interact vivaciously.

Manners are important and are highly influenced by French etiquette, especially in matters of dress, address, and eating. Strangers as well as acquaintances greet each other respectfully, usually using French terms, such as *bonjour*, *bon soir*, and *pardon*.

Hospitality is very important. Travelers to Lebanon are received genially.

RELIGION

Religious Beliefs. Most people in Lebanon are religious and monotheistic. Lebanon is made up of Muslim and Christian sects which escaped persecution throughout history by seeking shelter in its mountains. No one religion is dominant. The country has Muslim Shiites, Sunnis, Druzes and Christian Maronites, and Greek Orthodox and Armenian Orthodox.

Religious Practitioners. Religious figures have a lot of authority in Lebanon since religious courts decide on many issues concerning individuals' rights and privileges. This authority has been slightly undermined by the civil war.

Death and the Afterlife. Funerals are usually very elaborate; people are encouraged to express their feelings of loss openly and to follow funeral processions.

All the religions in Lebanon place much emphasis on the afterlife. Individuals are constantly exhorted to live righteous lives in the present, which will allow them to enter a beauteous paradise.

MEDICINE AND HEALTH CARE

Health care is highly developed in Lebanon. Very little belief in the efficacy of traditional medicine remains. Lebanon has more doctors than it actually needs, and hospitals are constantly trying to modernize.

SECULAR CELEBRATIONS

Independence Day celebrates the country's independence from France. Army Day celebrates the accomplishments of the Lebanese army. Christmas is celebrated by all Christian denominations but Muslims also participate. Id Il-Mouled celebrates the birth of the Muslim prophet Muhammad.

THE ARTS AND HUMANITIES

Support for the Arts. Artists are usually self-supporting, although some do receive contributions from patrons of the arts. There is no official government allocation of monies for the arts, although art schools sometimes receive government aid.

Literature. Lebanon has a long history of excellent poets and novelists. In the early years of the twentieth century, Lebanese authors took the lead in defending Arabic and its use in literary creation. Today, Lebanon still has many authors who write in Arabic as well as French and sometimes English.

Oral literature is preserved in villages, where the *zajal*, a form of poetic contest in the Lebanese dialect, is alive and enjoyed by everyone.

Graphic Arts. Painting is very varied and encouraged in Lebanon. French surrealists, cubists, and impressionists mostly influence Lebanese artists, who add an oriental touch to the French technique and subject matter. Many exhibits are held throughout the country, including the recently reopened Lebanese Museum in Beirut.

Traditional pottery-making is still popular in the coastal towns, such as Al-Minaa in the north, and Sidon in the south.

Local crafts are encouraged and many souks specialize in selling traditional objets d'art to tourists.

Performance Arts. Oriental and Western music are both popular. International festivals are once again very popular and offer an array of symphonies, classical and modern ballets, foreign and local dance troupes, and opera and pop singers. These festivals are usually held in open air on historic sites, such as the Roman temples of Baalbek, Byblos' crusader ruins, or Beirut's central district. Because of the diversity of the programs such festivals offer, people from all walks of life attend and interact.

THE STATE OF THE PHYSICAL AND SOCIAL SCIENCES

Schools of engineering are highly developed in Lebanon. However, they produce more engineers than the country needs, and many engineers find themselves unemployed or forced to accept menial jobs.

Social sciences are taught at the major universities; however, students are not encouraged to pursue them as they are less lucrative than other careers.

The Lebanese are encouraged to learn foreign languages and are usually bilingual.

BIBLIOGRAPHY

Abukhalil As'ad. *Historical Dictionary of Lebanon*, 1998.

Abul-Husn, Latif. *The Lebanese Conflict: Looking Inward*, 1998.

Brody, Aaron Jed. *Each Man Cried out to his God: The specialized religion of Canaanite and Phoenician Seafarers*, 1998.

Dagher, Carole. *Bring Down the Walls: Lebanon's Postwar Challenge*, 2000.

Edde, Michel. *The First Colloquium on Popular Culture in Lebanon*, 1993.

Mardam-Bey, Farouk. *Liban: Figures contemporaines*, 1999.

Mouzoune, Abdekrim. *Les transformations du paysage spatio-communautaire de Beyrouth*, 1999.

Shehadeh, Lamia. *Women and War in Lebanon*, 1999.

Uvezian, Sonia. *Recipes and Remembrances from an Eastern Mediterranean Kitchen*, 1999.

Various authors. *Political Studies Dedicated to Joseph Moughayzel*, 1996.

Ziser, Eyal. *Lebanon: The Challenge of Independence*, 2000.

—FRANK DARWICHE

LESOTHO

CULTURE NAME
Mosotho (singular); Basotho (plural)

ALTERNATIVE NAMES
Kingdom of Lesotho; formerly known as Basutoland

ORIENTATION

Identification. The area now called The Kingdom of Lesotho (pronounced le-Soo-too) was originally Basutoland. Both names derive from the common language, Sotho, which was spoken by the many groups which united to form the nation in the early 1800s. Lesotho is often referred to as "The Kingdom in the Sky" or "The Switzerland of southern Africa" because of the stark beauty of its rugged mountainous terrain. It is also described as "The Hostage State" due to the unfortunate situation of being completely surrounded by and dependent upon the Republic of South Africa.

Location and Geography. Covering 11,718 square miles (30,355 square kilometers), the Kingdom of Lesotho is approximately the size of Maryland. The area is ruggedly mountainous, landlocked, and completely surrounded by The Republic of South Africa. It lies between latitudes 28 degrees and 31 degrees south and longitudes 27 degrees and 30 degrees east. The lowlands in the west and south rise from forty-five hundred feet (fifteen-hundred meters) to the highlands of the Maluti and Drakensberg mountain ranges whose highest point, Thabana Ntlenyana, is approximately 10,400 feet (thirty-five hundred meters). Lesotho is unique as being the only nation in the world with all of its land situated more than 3,280 feet (one thousand meters) above sea level. The terrain consists of high veld, plateau, and mountains. The climate is temperate with hot summers and cool to cold winters. A long rainy season during the summer months (December to February) combined with freezing conditions in the winter (June to August) creates adverse travel conditions which isolate much of the highland areas. A wealth of rivers and waterfalls makes Lesotho valuable to the surrounding arid industrial areas of South Africa. The soils are poor, a result of over-grazing, over-cropping, and serious erosion, with only one-eighth of the land being arable.

Demography. The population of Lesotho, in 1998, was estimated to be 2,089,289 with a growth rate of 1.9 percent. At the end of the twentieth century these figures could alter rapidly as the HIV/AIDS crisis impacts the general population. The people of Lesotho are called *Basotho* (plural) and *Mosotho* (singular). The culture is cohesive, with Basotho comprising over 99 percent of the country's population, the remainder being of Asian of European origin. Most Asians are traders while the Europeans are businessmen, technicians, government officials, missionaries, and teachers. The highlands are sparsely populated with most of the administrative headquarters and towns located in the lowlands area.

Linguistic Affiliations. Sesotho, or Southern Sotho, is spoken in Lesotho as well as in parts of South Africa. Sesotho was one of the first African languages to develop a written form and it has an extensive literature. English is the second official language, dating back to 1868 when Lesotho was placed under the British for protection against South African aggression. Zulu and Xhosa are spoken by a small minority.

Symbolism. The spectacular scenery of Lesotho's rugged mountains, massive gullies (called *dongas*), and sparkling waterfalls create a tourist's dream destination. Picturesque villages, herdboys with their flocks, men on horseback, and women wearing the national dress of Moshoeshoe depicted in the

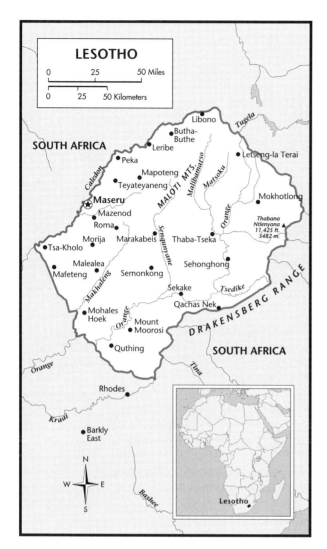

Lesotho

(*nala*). A shield that is part of the country's coat of arms appears in the upper left diagonal space. The national anthem is ''Lesotho, Land of our Fathers'' (*Lesotho fatse la bontat'a rona*).

HISTORY AND ETHNIC RELATIONS

Emergence of the Nation. Lesotho was originally inhabited by the Bushmen who roamed southern Africa, as evidenced by the Bushmen drawings and paintings in the river gorges. During the 1700s and 1800s, tribal wars in southern Africa decimated many tribes. Survivors of the wars fled into the highlands of what is now Lesotho and, under the leadership of an African chief named Moshoeshoe, formed the current Basotho ethnic group. Moshoeshoe established fortresses in the mountains and consolidated the Sotho-speaking inhabitants into a nation in the early 1800s. During the middle of the 1800s, the Basotho nation lost much of its territory to the Boers in a series of wars. Moshoeshoe appealed to Great Britain for protection and the remaining area became a British protectorate. In 1966 the nation gained independence and the constitutional monarchy of Lesotho was established. Moshoeshoe II, great-grandson of Moshoeshoe I, was installed as king and head of state, and Leabua Jonathan served as prime minister and head of government. Although Lesotho has undergone politic strife and change during the past thirty years, the Basotho are bonded by a deep reverence for the royal family and a fierce determination to remain an independent nation.

National Identity. Lesotho is a very homogenous nation, both in terms of the ethnic makeup of its population as well as religion and culture. Lesotho's strong cultural identity does not translate into a strong national identity, however, since its location deep in the heart of South Africa has historically forced the small country into dependence on its much larger neighbor.

Ethnic Relations. The Sotho ethnic group comprises almost 100 percent of Lesotho's population. The homogeneous makeup of the country has allowed Lesotho to avoid much of the civil unrest that has plagued other African nations with more ethnically diverse populations.

URBANISM, ARCHITECTURE, AND THE USE OF SPACE

Over 80 percent of the population live in the lowlands where soil conditions are more favorable

angora wool wall hangings and rugs of Basotho fame.

The Basotho hat, a conical woven hat with a distinctive topknot, is a symbol of Lesotho's unification. It depicts a mountaintop, conical and topknotted, which is visible from the fortress and tomb of Moshoeshoe I (pronounced mo-SHWAY-shway) near Masaru. Both men and women invariably wear the wool Basotho blanket as a cloak, regardless of the season. The careful selection of color and pattern allows for individual expression.

Everywhere in Lesotho one will see the small, sturdy Sotho pony, adept at negotiating the steep mountains and gullies and indispensable for carrying the grain to the mill for grinding. The nation's flag, adopted in 1987, has diagonal stripes of white, blue, and green. White is symbolic for peace (*khotso*), blue for rain (*pula*), and green for plenty for agriculture. The western border of Lesotho has one of the highest population densities in Africa. Maseru (ma-SAY-roo), population of 400,000, is the capital city, located in this western border area. Political strife in 1998 resulted in a frenzy of looting and burning which destroyed the main thoroughfare and infrastructure of Maseru. Although much rebuilding has occurred, many historical buildings were lost. Other semi-urban areas are called "camptowns" and are very rustic in appearance. The main camptowns are Teyateyaneng, population twenty-four thousand; Leribe, population three-hundred thousand; Mafeteng, population 212,000; Mohale's Hoek, population 184,000. Most Basotho live in villages of fewer than 250 people.

The cattle pen (krall) is the nucleus of family groups who build their huts in a spaced fashion around the pen. Traditional huts are constructed of mud and dung walls with thatched roofs. These round houses (rondovals) are often decorated with bright designs. Each village has a meeting place (khotla) where business is conducted. The areas around the villages are owned in common by the people and the land is assigned by the chief for family farming.

FOOD AND ECONOMY

Food in Daily Life. A three-stone fireplace in the courtyard is the focal point of the Basotho women's daily activity. Here they prepare the pot of cornmeal porridge (pap-pap) which is the staple of the Basotho. Usually a sauce of peas, chopped greens, or other vegetables accompanies the thick porridge, and on special occasions a chicken is added to the pot. During the summer season, local peaches, and small, hard fruits add variety to the diet. In the winter, family members sit around the three-stone fireplace and roast ears of dried corn.

A local beer (joale) is brewed in a large vat placed on the three-stone fireplace. This beer is the center of informal neighborhood gatherings and provides a small income for the family. Milk is often served as a soured drink.

Maseru has a number of modern restaurants that are mostly patronized by business and professional people and tourists.

Food Customs at Ceremonial Occasions. In the villages, cultural rites are predominately centered around the sacrifice of a cow. Funerals often drain a poor family's assets as a cow must be purchased at great expense. A family's honor is dependent on the quality and quantity of food at wedding and funeral gatherings—spit-roasted cow and chicken are mandatory.

Basic Economy. Lesotho is a developing country with a free-market economy. It boasts few natural resources and is dependent on imported food and materials to meet the basic needs of the population. Nearly all families engage in subsistence farming, consisting mostly of corn, wheat, peas, and beans, but the depleted soil does not yield sufficient crops to feed them. Lesotho's economy is fragile, even with the benefits it derives from South Africa which include a partially shared customs union, a single currency (the South African rand is used interchangeably with the Lesotho loti), and an integrated communications system. A major sustaining factor in the country's economy is employment found in South African mines, farms, and industries. Approximately 35 percent of active male wage earners work most of the year in surrounding South Africa, resulting in family income but having a detrimental effect on family life. In the United Nations Development Program's ranking of countries of the world in 2000, which considers the factors of life expectancy, income, education, and health care, Lesotho ranked 127th out of 174 countries.

Land Tenure and Property. All land is held in trust for the Basotho nation by the king and may not be alienated. The local chiefs allocate farmland to individuals, and user rights are generally available to married males. A 1979 act increases security of tenure by recording rights of inheritance and allowing mortgaging and subletting of land.

Commercial Activities. Lesotho's abundance of cattle, sheep, and goats provides a basis for a wool and mohair industry. Although there are no other large industries, small industries and businesses are supported by national and foreign assistance and are having some success. Perhaps the most promising, although highly controversial, effort to improve the economy is the Highlands Water Project which is designed to utilize the nation's valuable resource of water to provide electricity, employment, and economic development for the general population. The project involves the construction of a series of six dams and hundreds of miles of tunnels to funnel water into the arid industrial areas of nearby South Africa, for which Lesotho will receive monetary compensation. The controversy arising from the project revolves around the detrimental effect of the relocation of area communities, the delayed compensation for the loss of ancestral lands,

Women roll barrels and carry buckets containing materials needed for the construction of a reservoir.

and the social problems associated with large construction sites.

Major Industries. Lesotho has a wide variety of light industries, which include tire retreading, tapestry weaving, diamond processing, and production of textiles, electric lighting, candles, ceramics, explosives, furniture, and fertilizers.

Trade. Lesotho has trade relations with South Africa, Botswana, Swaziland, Namibia, North America, and Europe. Imported items are primarily corn, clothing, building materials, vehicles, petroleum products, machinery, and medicines. Exports include clothing, furniture, footwear, and wool products.

SOCIAL STRATIFICATION

Symbols of Social Stratification. Cattle represent wealth in Lesotho and the Basotho value cows above money. The wealthy villager usually lives in a concrete block house with a metal roof instead of a rondoval, and usually has two outdoor bathrooms as opposed to the single outhouse other families possess and often share. The very wealthy send their children to private schools and often to the one university in Lesotho at Roma, or to England or Canada for further education. In the villages, an automobile is an unusual and significant symbol of upper social status.

Government. The government of Lesotho is a constitutional monarchy with the capital in Maseru. The country is divided into ten administrative districts. The legal system is based on English common law and Roman Dutch law. The executive branch has a king as chief of state and since 1996 King Letsie III has filled this position. The legislative branch is composed of a bicameral parliament with a senate appointed by the ruling party and an assembly chosen by popular vote. The judicial branch is the high court, with a chief justice appointed by the monarch. The monarchy is hereditary and is a living symbol of national unity with no executive legislative powers. In January 1993 Lesotho became a democracy. The constitution was adopted on 2 April 1993.

Leadership and Political Officials. There are three major political parties: The Basotho National Party (BNP), the Basotho Congress Party (BCP), and the Marematlou Freedom Party (MFP). The BNP was the major force behind Lesotho's drive for independence and became the government's ruling party following independence in 1966. The BNP maintained control of the government by suspending elections and the constitution in 1970 and re-

A woman standing by a row of thatched houses. Over 80 percent of Lesotho's population lives in the country's lowland area.

mained in power with strong military backing until multiparty elections finally became a reality in 1993. The BCP, the major opposition party, is more Pan-Africanist than the BNP, and assumed power following the 1993 elections. The MFP was formed in 1965 by the merger of two parties that had supported the chieftaincy.

Social Problems and Controls. Traditional authority is the basis of village government. The system of chieftaincy follows the progression of paramount chief (the king), senior chiefs, sub-chiefs, headmen and sub-headmen. Their primary role is the authority to distribute the land of the nation to the people. Many political affiliations are passed down through the chain, with entire villages voting in accord during an election. Village crimes of a minor nature are judged in the village court, often a grassy area under a tree. Local groups mete out the punishments that are handed down. Serious crimes of theft or murder are removed from the village to the regional and national courts and institutions of imprisonment.

Military Activity. The Lesotho Defense Force (LDF) and the Lesotho Mounted Police comprise the nation's security forces. These two factions have developed an antagonistic relationship since 1997 when the army was called upon to put down a serious police mutiny.

SOCIAL WELFARE AND CHANGE PROGRAMS

Lesotho has received economic and social welfare aid from a number of countries including the United States, the United Kingdom, the European Union, and Germany. The escalating crisis of HIV/AIDS has mobilized assistance from a variety of sources including UNAIDS/WHO. The United States Peace Corps has been active in Lesotho since 1966. The volunteers are involved in working in the fields of agriculture, education, rural development, women's issues, and the environment. In 2000, specially trained volunteers were enlisted to address the HIV/AIDS issue in this and other African nations.

GENDER ROLES AND STATUSES

Division of Labor by Gender. Most of the agriculture and home building is done by the women. They hoe, plant, and weed, and harvest the crops. They walk great distances to obtain firewood and carry the load home on their backs, often with an infant wedged between the tree branches. Water must be carried from the village pump for cooking, drink-

A Lesothan man in a traditional costume.

ing, washing, and laundry. Clothing is scrubbed and hung on bushes to dry.

Men are primarily responsible for the livestock. Boys begin training for herding at age five or six. In the highlands, where pasture is scarce, herdboys often spend months alone with their flocks in a mountain valley some distance from their home. Girls similarly begin life-role training as soon as they are able to carry a sibling on their back and a pail of water on their head.

The Relative Status of Women and Men. As in most African countries, a female has no power, authority, right, or privilege, unless it is granted by a male. A wife is the property of her husband. However, women play a powerful role through their religious organizations and societies and have attained suffrage.

MARRIAGE, FAMILY, AND KINSHIP

Marriage. Lesotho is a blend of past and present, traditional and modern beliefs and practices. While church ceremonies are customary for weddings, the practice of extracting brideswealth from the man's family continues, making a family of daughters a lucrative situation. In turn, the bride becomes the property of the man, and leaves her family to live with the family of her husband.

Domestic Unit. The domestic unit consists of any number of the extended family. Often second or third cousins become "brothers" or "sisters." Grandmothers become official mothers. By tribal custom, widows become a wife of the brother or other male member of her deceased husband's family.

Kin Groups. The clans of the Sotho are often named for animals such as crocodiles and bears. The line of descendants is through the male, and members of the same clan are allowed to marry relatives as close as cousins.

SOCIALIZATION

Infant Care. Compared to western standards, infant care in Lesotho is casual. The infant and young child spend much of their first two years bound to their mother's backs as she performs her household chores, hoes the fields, and markets or travels. Babies usually nurse for up to two years of age or until a new baby is born. At that time, an older sister usually assumes the caretaker role.

Child Rearing and Education. "It takes a village to raise a child" is a well-known and accurate description of African practices. Every village woman is eligible to correct an erring child, to rescue one in difficulty, and to encourage all. When a child is able to begin school (age varies from five to ten years) the mandatory school dress or shirt is passed from one family to another. Many boys do not attend school for years because they begin at age five or six to herd and care for the livestock.

Higher Education. There are two major institutions of higher learning in Lesotho: the National University of Lesotho and the Lesotho Agricultural College. A very small percentage of the population reaches this level of education. Very wealthy families send their children to higher education in England.

RELIGION

Religious Beliefs. Religion in Lesotho is a mix of traditionally based ancestor worship and Christianity (about 80 percent), with a small representation of Islam. The main church groups are Catholic, Anglican, and Dutch Reformed. The dominance of the Catholic religion reflects the church's involvement in education, with over 75 percent of all primary and secondary schools being owned and managed by Catholics. Many church services include traditional Lesotho rituals such as chanting, drumming, and cultural costumes.

MEDICINE AND HEALTH CARE

Lesotho is essentially a healthy country. A good climate eliminates the widespread African problem of malaria. The primary diseases are chronic rheumatism, respiratory tract infections, malnutrition, and venereal diseases in addition to an escalating number of HIV/AIDS cases. Health centers, mountain dispensaries, and traditional medical practitioners are available and primarily used by the village population.

SECULAR CELEBRATIONS

The two days which all of Lesotho celebrates are Moshoeshoe's Day (12 March) and Independence Day (4 October). Moshoeshoe's Day is for the nation's school children, who prepare throughout the year for choir and sports competitions. Independence Day is a time for formal state ceremonies, speeches, and traditional dance group performances.

THE ARTS AND HUMANITIES

Literature. Sotho literature is dominated by folktales and praise poems. Early in the 1900s a Masotho named Thomas Mofolo wrote the famous and widely read novel *Chaka*.

Performance Arts. Traditional music, dance, and literature combine in Sotho cultural performances. Storytellers, dancers, and musicians join with audience chanting, clapping, and singing to retell ancient folktales. The involvement with mining has produced a unique tradition of singing and dancing males, with high-kicking group dances. Many handmade instruments include whistles, drums, rattles, and stringed instruments.

BIBLIOGRAPHY

Africa South of the Sahara 1999, 1998.

Ashton, Hugh. *The Basuto*, 1952.

Central Intelligence Agency. ''Lesotho.'' *World Fact Book*, 1995.

Hull, Richard. *Modern Africa*, 1980.

Johnson, D. ''Lesotho,'' *World Biographical Series*, 1996.

''Lesotho,'' *Epidemiological Fact Sheet on HIV/AIDS and Sexually Transmitted Infections. UNAIDS/World Health Organization*, 2000.

''Lesotho,'' *The New Book of Knowledge*, 1996.

Web Sites

''Sesotho-Southern Sotho.'' 2000. http://www.cyberserv.co.za/users/~jako/sesotho.html

U.S. Department of State Annual. ''Lesotho,'' *Report on International Religious Freedom for 1999* http://www.state.gov/www/global/human_rights/irf/irf_rpt/1999/

—PATRICIA OSBORN STODDARD

LIBERIA

CULTURE NAME

Liberian

ORIENTATION

Identification. Liberia lies on the west coast of Africa. The name comes from the English word "liberty" and refers to the nation's origin as a colony of free blacks repatriated to Africa from the United States in the early nineteenth century. Although the settlers and their descendants, known as Americo-Liberians, defined the boundaries of the nation-state, made English the official language, and dominated the government and economy for almost one hundred fifty years, they have never constituted as much as 5 percent of the population. The remaining people belong to sixteen broadly defined ethnolinguistic groups of the Niger-Congo family. The Mel (West Atlantic) group consists of the Gola and Kissi, who are believed to be the oldest inhabitants. The Mande group, made up of Mandingo, Vai, Gbandi, Kpelle, Loma, Mende, Gio, and Mano peoples, is believed to have entered the area from the northern savannahs in the fifteenth century. The southern and eastern areas are inhabited by people who speak Kruan (Kwa) languages; the Bassa, Dei (Dey), Grebo, Kru, Belle (Kuwaa), Krahn, and Gbee are linguistically related to the peoples of the Niger delta far to the east.

All these groups were present in the territory when the American settlers arrived in 1822. Although Liberia has been independent since 1847, making it the oldest republic in Africa, most of its citizens have never felt allegiance to the nation-state. With most government institutions concentrated in coastal cities, many inhabitants of the interior had little sense of being Liberian until the second half of the twentieth century.

Location and Geography. Liberia lies on the western "bulge" of Africa. About half the country is covered by primary tropical rain forest containing valuable hardwoods. A monsoon climate of alternating wet and dry seasons characterizes the weather. Plateaus and mountain ranges in the northern region are rich in iron ore, gold, and diamonds. The Atlantic coastline of 353 miles (568 kilometers) has no natural deep-water harbors and is pounded by heavy surf.

The capital, Monrovia, was named for the United States president James Monroe and is situated near the original landing site of the American settlers. The area had been known as the Grain Coast, in reference to the malagueta pepper that was the primary export. Negotiations with the Bassa and Dei to "purchase" land for the settlers apparently were carried out at gunpoint, and the indigenous people probably believed they were entering into a trade agreement with the newcomers rather than giving up ownership of their territory. The rest of the country was acquired though similar "purchases," conquest, and negotiation with British and French colonizers.

Demography. The population was 2,893,800 in 1994. A disastrous civil war from late 1989 to 1997 is believed to have cost at least 200,000 lives, and many Liberians live as refugees in neighboring countries and elsewhere in the world. The relative distribution of the population among the sixteen recognized ethnic groups has remained relatively constant. The Kpelle are the largest with 20 percent of the population, followed by the Bassa with 14 percent. All the other groups number less than 10 percent of the total.

Linguistic Affiliation. The official language is English, which is used for instruction in all public and mission schools and in university education. A significant portion of the population is bilingual and often competent in several indigenous languages as well as English. Those in the regions bordering Ivory Coast and Guinea are often conversational in French. The English spoken in most common, informal settings is "Liberian English," a creole form.

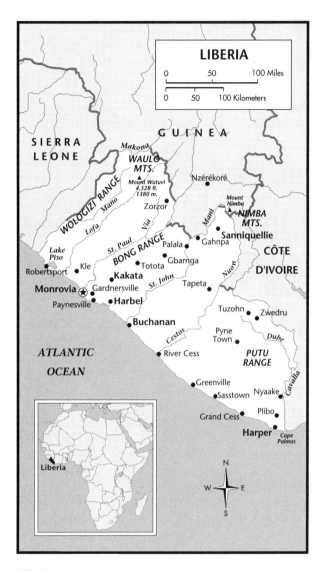

Liberia

Educated people frequently switch between the creole form and the more standard English promoted by schools. Men tend to have more facility with both standard and creole English than do women, reflecting men's greater access to formal education and urban mores.

Symbolism. The official national symbols, such as the official language, reflect the American origin of the nation-state. The flag is a replica of the American flag, but with a single large white star on a blue field representing Liberia's long history as the "Lone Star," the only independent republic in Africa during the colonial period. The Great Seal depicts a sailing ship like that which carried the American settlers to Africa, a palm tree, and a plow and ax with the motto "The Love of Liberty Brought Us Here."

HISTORY AND ETHNIC RELATIONS

Emergence as a Nation. The nation's origin as a nation-state lies in a paradox of United States history. Even before the end of the war for American independence, public figures such as Thomas Jefferson were concerned about the status of free people of African descent and their integration into a free society. The American Colonization Society (ACS), dedicated to the resettlement of free people of color outside the United States, was founded in 1816. The ACS used private funds donated by wealthy white contributors to "purchase" land in west Africa and recruit African-American settlers, the first group of whom arrived in 1822. Most of the earliest immigrants had been born free; they were relatively well educated and belonged to an emerging class of free black professionals and businessmen. Although white administrators appointed by the ACS governed the colony in the early years, in 1847 the settlers declared independence and became the first sovereign black republic in Africa.

National Identity. The first settlers were augmented by recently manumitted slaves from the United States and "recaptured Africans" or "Congos" taken from smugglers after the slave trade was abolished in 1808. Over time, these disparate groups merged to become Americo-Liberians. The early history of the republic was characterized by struggles between political parties representing "mulattoes" (lighter-skinned, upper-class businessmen or "merchant princes") and "true blacks" (poorer ex-slaves and recaptives). In 1877, the True Whig Party (TWP), identified with the "blacks" and with agricultural rather than trading interests, came to power. The TWP remained dominant for almost a hundred years, making Liberia essentially a one-party state. It also created links with indigenous elites in the interior, and membership in the TWP was synonymous with national identity for most of the twentieth century.

The lack of racial difference between the colonized and the colonizers allowed individuals to "pass" into the Americo-Liberian group. Institutions such as adoption, wardship, informal polygyny, and apprenticeship brought many indigenous children into settler homes. Within a generation, they had entered the Americo-Liberian group and forgotten their "tribal" origins. Another recognizable social group, the so-called civilized natives, consisted of those who had been educated and Christianized in mission schools while maintaining their indigenous identity. This group was often a vocal source of criticism of the settler elite.

Ethnic Relations. Liberia's sixteen ethnolinguistic groups, although characterized as tribes, have never constituted unified, historically continuous political entities. In the northwestern section, Mande-speaking groups formed multiethnic chiefdoms and confederacies that coordinated trade and warfare, especially during the period of the slave trade. Although there were no precolonial states, the northwestern peoples were united in two panethnic secret societies: Poro (for men) and Sande (for women). The linked ''chapter'' structure of Poro and Sande lodges could in theory mobilize the entire population under the authority of elders.

South and east of the Saint John River, Kwa-speaking peoples who migrated from the east lived in smaller, less stratified communities. As the Americo-Liberians attempted to extend their control from the coast to the interior, they created administrative units that were thought to be coterminous with existing ''tribes.'' For example, Maryland County in the southeast was treated as the home of the ''Grebo tribe,'' even though the people there did not recognize a common identity or history beyond speaking dialects of the same language.

For most of Liberia's history, the primary meaningful division on the national level was between the tribal majority and the settler minority; with few exceptions, one's tribe made little difference in terms of life chances and upward mobility. After the military coup of 1980, however, a new tribalism or politically strategic ethnicity began to emerge. Samuel Kanyon Doe, the leader of the military government and a Krahn from Grand Gedeh county, systematically filled the elite military units and government positions with members of his ethnolinguistic group. As opposition to his autocratic and repressive regime grew during the 1980s, it took the form of ethnically identified armed factions that attacked civilians on the basis of their presumed tribal affiliation. Western journalists attributed the violence to ''ancient tribal hatreds'' even though these ethnically identified groups had emerged only in the previous ten years.

URBANISM, ARCHITECTURE, AND THE USE OF SPACE

Before the civil war of 1989–1997, Liberia was predominantly rural, with the majority of the population involved in subsistence agriculture; small-scale market production of cash crops such as rubber, sugar, palm oil, and citrus fruits; or producing primary products for export (iron ore, rubber, and tropical hardwoods). Monrovia had a population of about two hundred thousand, and other coastal cities had less than one hundred thousand. Areas of resource exploitation operated by foreign-owned concessions were the primary population centers in the interior. During the war, the population of Monrovia swelled to over three hundred thousand as refugees attempted to escape from the fighting in the interior.

While rural communities still contain examples of traditional round huts with thatched conical roofs, most newer houses have a rectangular floor plan and are roofed with sheets of corrugated zinc or tin. Wattle and daub construction, in which a lattice of sticks is packed with mud and covered with clay or cement, is the most common building method regardless of the shape of the structure, but many people aspire to a house built of cement cinder blocks and may spend years acquiring the blocks. Rural communities have a ''palaver hut,'' an open-sided roofed structure that functions as a town hall for public discussions and the hearing of court cases.

In the cities, especially Monrovia, imposing public buildings from the prewar period were built mostly in the post-World War II International Style, including the Executive Mansion, which became an armed fortress during the civil war. Houses from the nineteenth century are similar to antebellum architecture of the American South, with verandas and classical columns. The civil war reduced many buildings to ruins and left others occupied by homeless refugees.

FOOD AND ECONOMY

Food in Daily Life. The primary staple is rice. This complex carbohydrate forms the centerpiece of the meal, and savory sauces provide flavor. Meat or fish is used as a garnish or ingredient in the sauce rather than being the focus of the meal. In rural areas, people begin the day with a small meal of leftover rice or boiled cassava dipped in the sauce from the day before. Depending on the time of year and the work schedule, the main meal may be served at midday or in the evening. Snacks of mangoes, bananas, sugarcane, coconut, fried plantain or cassava, and citrus fruits may be consumed throughout the day.

In the countryside, rice is produced by a system of rain-fed swidden (slash and burn) horticulture. Men clear an area of the forest and burn the dried brush, and women and children do most of the planting, weeding, and harvesting. Rice is used ceremonially to make offerings to ancestors and the recently dead and is offered to social superiors when one is asking for favors or initiating a patron-client relationship. Use rights to land are acquired

A wall painting on a house near Robertsport depicts the motif of a mask dance of the Kru people.

through patrilineal descent; men and women have the right to use land claimed by their father's lineage in the vicinity of the town in which he is a citizen. Because tropical soils are fragile, fields must be moved every year and, once harvested, allowed to rest for seven to twelve years. This system requires a large amount of available land and a low population density. Some areas have been overfarmed, with resulting damage to the tropical forest ecosystem, but the greatest constraint on agriculture is a shortage of labor.

This system is capable of providing for family subsistence but not of producing a large surplus for sale. Urban areas have depended on imported rice, mostly from the United States. Locally produced vegetables, including eggplant, peppers, pumpkins, and greens, are sold in outdoor markets. It is a sign of Western sophistication and wealth to be able to afford imported processed foods such as corn flakes, canned goods, and snack foods. During the civil war, agricultural production was almost completely disrupted and the entire population was dependent on donations of food.

Basic Economy. The prewar economy was heavily dependent on a few primary products or raw materials. In 1975, 75 percent of the value of exports came from iron ore alone; iron ore and rubber to-

gether amounted to over 80 percent. This dependence on a few income earners left the country vulnerable to the worldwide economic recession of the 1970s. There was almost no growth in the annual value of the economy between 1976 and 1980, and many workers in the mining industry lost their jobs. This economic crisis was one of the factors that led to the military coup of 1980.

SOCIAL STRATIFICATION

Classes and Castes. There is a status division between the minority claiming descent from the American settlers and the indigenous majority. The settler group contains people at all class levels, from rich to poor, who continue to maintain a sense of prestige and entitlement. In the indigenous community, a distinction between "civilized" and "native" people emerged early in the nineteenth century as a result of mission education and labor migration along the coast. Civilized ("kwi") status implies facility with English, a nominal allegiance to Christianity, a degree of literacy, and involvement with the cash rather than the subsistence sector. Although kwi people maintain their ethnic identities as Grebo, Kru, Vai, or Kpelle, an undeniable prestige difference separates them from their native neighbors and kin.

Symbols of Social Stratification. Civilized people, especially women, are distinguished by Western-style clothing and household furnishings. The association is so strong that native women are also known as "lappa women," a reference to the two pieces of cloth (lappas) that constitute native female dress.

POLITICAL LIFE

Government. The constitution of 1847 was patterned on the American constitution and provided for a separation of powers among the executive, legislative, and judicial branches. The legislature is bicameral with an upper house based on equal representation of the thirteen counties with two senators each and a lower house based on population. This structure was retained in the revised constitution of 1986, which was intended to prevent the abuses of one-party rule that had characterized most of the nation's history. At the local level, each county is administered by a superintendent appointed by the president and further divided into districts, chiefdoms, and clans. The system of "native" administration retains much of the older system of indirect rule in which local chiefs are empowered by the central government to collect taxes and judge minor court cases.

Leadership and Political Officials. Politics has tended toward the autocratic, with the constitution more a symbol of democracy than a guide for action. Although elections were held regularly, the absence of opposition parties made them largely nationalist pageants rather than expressions of the people's will. The True Whig Party's patronage system ensured that the president never faced opposition from the other branches of government, and as a result, the executive branch was overwhelmingly dominant. The personality cult around the presidency reached its height with W. V. S. Tubman, who served from 1944 to 1971. Tubman was widely popular for creating the illusion of broad participation in national life but was extremely repressive: jailing, executing, and exiling his opponents. This tradition of concentrated power in the hands of the president has continued in the administration of Charles Taylor, who was elected in 1997.

Social Problems and Control. Liberia has long had a system of multiple and often overlapping judicial structures. A separate judiciary with hierarchically arranged statutory courts was established in 1847 but rarely has been independent of the executive branch. The statutory courts delegated most local-level social control to "chiefs' courts," where a modified version of "native law" was codified and applied in cases ranging from divorce to petty theft. Liberians who are Muslims can settle disputes in Imam's courts where judgments are based on Islamic law. Individuals in search of a favorable verdict have been known to try their luck in all three kinds of courts, claiming to be "civilized" in the statutory court, "native" in the chief's court, and Muslim in the Islamic court.

Indigenous methods of trial by ordeal have long been used in rural communities. Ordeals include the testing of suspects with hot knives, hot oil, or the drinking of poison. In the poison ("sasswood") ordeal, suspects drink a decoction of tree bark; the innocent vomit the poison and live, while the guilty die of its effects; this system combines the determination of guilt and the administration of punishment. The sasswood trial was outlawed by the central government early in the twentieth century; other forms of ordeal were tolerated through the 1960s.

During the civil war, all legal and social control institutions experienced complete breakdown. Random massacres were conducted by armed fighters as young as nine years old in the service of warlords with no political agenda beyond survival and profit. Since 1997, Liberian legal institutions have been slowly reestablished, but many abuses of civil rights have continued.

Military Activity. Since 1980, politics has been dominated by armed men. In the early years of the republic, a Frontier Force of indigenous conscripts was used to "pacify" the peoples of the hinterland and enforce the collection of taxes and corvee (unpaid) labor. In late 1970s, the ethnic split between the officer corps (made up of Americo-Liberians) and the rank and file created tension, with soldiers often used as unpaid laborers on the farms and building projects of their superiors. The men who led the coup which brought down the True Whig Party government in 1980 were all non-commissioned soldiers of indigenous background. The first military coup provided a model for many future attempts. Master Sergeant Samuel K. Doe was threatened by ambitious young men like himself, leading him to institute increasingly repressive policies. Foreign aid from the United States, especially during the Reagan administration, took the form of a vast military buildup. This lethal equipment was later turned against the Liberian people during the civil war. Under the current administration, the armed forces and other security agencies

At the Liberia National Commemoration, women wear dresses depicting the Liberian flag and political leaders.

continue to absorb the bulk of the national budget. According to the peace accords that led to the 1997 election, the national military was supposed to have been restructured by the West African intervention force (ECOMOG) to reflect all the parties that contested the war. Once elected, however, Charles Taylor claimed his constitutional role as commander in chief to essentially remake the armed forces along the lines of his faction, the National Patriotic Front for Liberia (NPFL). Tensions in the armed forces and among demobilized combatants remain a destabilizing factor in national life.

SOCIAL WELFARE PROGRAMS

Most social welfare institutions, including those for the provision of education and medical care, remain in the hands of religious organizations and international aid agencies. Liberia was one of the earliest host countries for the United States Peace Corps.

NONGOVERNMENTAL ORGANIZATIONS AND OTHER ASSOCIATIONS

During the worst period of the civil war, networks of concerned Americans and Liberians living in the United States lobbied for protected status for refugees, increases in humanitarian aid, and diplomatic pressure to restore human rights. Within Liberia, a number of local organizations, such as the Catholic Justice and Peace Commission, have monitored human rights issues and spoken out against repression. During the siege of Monrovia in 1990, a local group called SELF (Special Emergency Life Food) organized distribution centers for relief food.

GENDER ROLES AND STATUSES

Division of Labor by Gender. All of the indigenous groups are patrilineal and have ideologies of male dominance. The nineteenth-century domestic ideology brought with the American settlers also was highly patriarchal, with women assigned to roles as homemakers and nurturers of children. However, the sexual division of labor in indigenous agriculture affords women a great deal of power, if not formal authority. Women's labor is extremely valuable, as seen in the institution of bridewealth that accompanies marriage. Among "civilized people" of indigenous or Americo-Liberian background, women's domestic role in caring for clothing, household decoration, and the other symbolic means by which the status of the household is communicated has great importance. While it is acceptable for an educated woman to hold a white-collar job outside the home, she cannot participate in the most common activities of native women—farming, marketing, and carrying loads of wood and water—without threatening her status.

The Relative Status of Women and Men. Indigenous constructions of gender usually emphasize the breadwinner or productive role for women and the warrior role for men. Indigenous political structures have a "dual-sex" organization, that is, parallel systems of offices for men and women. Among the northwestern peoples, this takes the form of the dual organization of the Poro and Sande secret societies. In the south and east, female councils of elders use a series of checks and balances on official male power. On the national level, the last transitional leader before the 1997 election was also the first female head of state in Africa, Ruth Sando Perry. The presidential candidate who came in second to Charles Taylor was also a woman.

MARRIAGE, FAMILY, AND KINSHIP

Marriage. Among the indigenous majority, marriage is ideally polygynous and patrilocal, with the bride moving to her husband's compound to live with his extended family. Probably less than 30 percent of men actually have more than one wife at a time, and those marriages often fail because of conflicts between co-wives. Marriage is a process rather than an event, with bridewealth payments made over many years and solidified by the birth of children. The increasing access of women to cash through the marketing of foodstuffs has resulted in some women freeing themselves from unwanted marriages by paying back the bridewealth. Bridewealth establishes the right of a husband to claim any children born to his wife regardless of their biological father. The great value placed on women as agricultural workers and childbearers ensures that no woman who wants a husband is without one for long. Among the civilized native and Americo-Liberian communities, statutory marriages are limited by the Christian insistence on monogamy. Most successful men, however, have one or more "country wives" who have been married through bridewealth in addition to the "ring wife" who shares their primary residence. Children from secondary marriages often are raised by the father and his official wife and form junior lines within important families in Monrovia and other coastal cities. Before 1980, the most prominent settler families practiced formal endogamy, resulting in a situation in which most important government officials were related by kinship and intermarriage.

Kin Groups. Among the indigenous people, groups in the northwest are organized into ranked lineages of "land owners," "commoners," and "slaves." Kinship is crucial in determining social status among these groups. The ranking of lineages is mirrored in the Poro and Sande societies and dictates the "secrets" that may be learned by initiates. Chieftaincy belongs to particular families, although succession does not follow a strict father-to-son transmission. Among the less stratified peoples of the southeast, kinship determines less in terms of individual life chances but remains crucial in regard to citizenship, identity, and access to land.

SOCIALIZATION

Child Rearing and Education. Children are highly valued as potential workers and supporters of their parents in old age. Babies are constantly carried, tied to the back of the mothers or another care giver. Children take on chores at an early age and are expec-

Historically, mining—especially for precious gems such as diamonds—played a large role in Liberia's economy.

ted to learn through observation and imitation rather than through formal verbal instruction and the asking of questions. In the Poro and Sande "bush schools" for initiates, formal instruction in local history and genealogy is provided in addition to specialized training in herbalism and midwifery. Formal Western educational institutions originated with mission schools whose primary aim was conversion to Christianity; in areas of Muslim conversion, Koranic schools offer literacy training in Arabic.

Higher Education. Access to higher education at the University of Liberia was limited, especially for those of "tribal" background, until large numbers of the elite began taking advantage of foreign scholarships to send their children to Europe and the United States in the 1960s. Many of the current leaders, including President Charles Taylor, received their education in the United States.

RELIGION

Pre-coup Liberia often characterized itself as a "Christian nation," but a number of shifting religious identities and practices were and still are available. Active membership in a Christian denomination probably involves less than 20 percent of the population. Twenty to 30 percent of the population is at least nominally Muslim, and the remainder practices indigenous religious systems surrounding ancestor worship and secret society membership. Even in areas of widespread Christian or Muslim conversion, indigenous institutions such as polygyny, belief in witchcraft, and trial by ordeal persist. Many individuals combine elements from all three systems. Funerals are very important in all religions and are as elaborate as a family can afford, often going on for days or weeks.

MEDICINE AND HEALTH CARE

A number of serious diseases afflict the population, including malaria, tuberculosis, and cholera. Health care facilities generally are located in or near major cities, and the majority of people have no access to Western medicine. There is a widespread belief that illness and death are caused by the evil intentions of other people. A great deal of effort is expended on the local level in the hearing of witchcraft cases. Liberians are happy to combine Western and indigenous health care systems; they eagerly seek access to Western drugs for the relief of symptoms and make heroic efforts to get family members to clinics and hospitals. The root cause of misfortune, however, is sought in disrupted social relations, often between family members who have quarreled. Much of the medical infrastructure outside

Monrovia was destroyed during the civil war, and restoring at least some services remains a challenge for the new government.

SECULAR CELEBRATIONS

National holidays include 26 July, marking the anniversary of independence; Flag Day; and the birthdays of important presidents such as Joseph Jenkins Roberts (the first president) and W. V. S. Tubman. After the 1980 military coup, an Armed Forces Day was instituted. Images of an armed soldier were introduced as national symbols on coins, statues, and monuments. Attempts to supplant the earlier symbolism, including the flag and motto, were popularly rejected.

THE ARTS AND HUMANITIES

Graphic Arts. Liberia is known as the home of the "classical" African mask. The artistic ability of its wood carvers is widely recognized. Many masks are commissioned by the Poro and Sande societies for use in their initiation rituals; some powerfully charged masks may be seen only by initiates, while others are used in public masquerades. The range of forms produced by carvers is impressive as is the continuity of some styles over time. Other indigenous art forms include murals painted on the exterior walls of buildings, pottery, weaving, music, and dance. A small community of creative writers led by Bai T. Moore existed before the war.

BIBLIOGRAPHY

Anderson, Benjamine. *Narrative of the Expedition Dispatched to Musardu by the Liberian Government in 1874*, 1971.

Bellman, Beryl L. *Village of Cureres and Assassins: On the Production of Fala Kpelle Cosmological Catagories*, 1975.

Bledsoe, Caroline H. *Women and Marriage in Kpelle Society*, 1980.

Burrowes, Carl Patrick. "The Americo-Liberian Ruling Class and Other Myths: A Critique of Political Science in the Liberian Context." *Temple University Occasional Papers* no. 3, 1989.

Carter, Jeanette, and Joyce Mends-Cole. *Liberian Women: Their Role in Food Production and Their Educational and Legal Status*, 1982.

Clower, Robert W., George Dalton, Mitchell Harwitz, and A. A. Walters. *Growth without Development: An Economic Survey of Liberia*, 1966.

d'Azevedo, Warren L. "Some Historical Problems in the Delineation of a Central West Atlantic Region." *Annals of the New York Academy of Science* 96: 512–538, 1962.

Dunn, D. Elwood, and Svend E. Holsoe. *Historical Dictionary of Liberia*, 1985.

—— and S. Byron Tarr. *Liberia: A National Polity in Transition*, 1988.

Fraenkel, Merran. *Tribe and Class in Monrovia*, 1964.

Gay, John. *Red Dust on the Green Leaves: A Kpelle Twins' Childhood*, 1973.

Gershoni, Yekutiel. *Black Colonialism: The Americo-Liberian Scramble for the Hinterland*, 1985.

Hasselman, Karl H. *Liberia: Geographical Mosaics of the Land and the People*, 1979.

Hlophe, Stephen. *Class, Ethnicity, and Politics in Liberia*, 1987.

Holloway, Joseph E. *Liberian Diplomacy in Africa: A Study of Inter-African Relations*, 1981.

Holsoe, Svend E., and Bernard L. Herman. *A Land and Life Remembered: Americo-Liberian Folk Architecture*, 1988.

Huband, Mark. *The Liberian Civil War*, 1998.

Huberich, C. H. *The Political and Legislative History of Liberia*, 1947.

Johnson, Barbara C. *Four Dan Sculptors: Continuity and Change*, 1986.

Liebenow, J. Gus. *Liberia: The Quest for Democracy*, 1987.

Lowenkopf, M. "Liberia: Putting the State Back Together. In I. William Zartman, ed., *Collapsed States: The Disintegration and Restoration of Legitimate Authority*, 1995.

McDaniel, Antonio. *Swing Low, Sweet Chariot: The Mortality Cost of Colonizing Liberia in the Nineteenth Century*, 1995.

Moran, Mary H. *Civilized Women: Gender and Prestige in Southeastern Liberia*, 1990.

Reno, William. *Warlord Politics and African States*, 1999.

Republic of Liberia. *Planning and Development Atlas*, 1983.

Sawyer, Amos. *The Emergence of Autocracy in Liberia: Tragedy and Challenge*, 1992.

Shick, Tom. *Behold the Promised Land: A History of Afro-American Settler Society in Nineteenth-Century Liberia*, 1984.

Staudenraus, P. J. *The African Colonization Movement, 1816–1865*, 1961.

Stone, Ruth. *Dried Millet Breaking: Time, Words, and Song in the Woi Epic of the Kpelle*, 1988.

Sundiata, I. K. *Black Scandal: America and the Liberian Labor Crisis, 1929–36*, 1980.

Wiley, Bell I., ed. *Slaves No More: Letters from Liberia, 1833–1869*, 1980.

—MARY H. MORAN

LIBYA

CULTURE NAME

Libyan

ALTERNATIVE NAMES

The Socialist Popular Libyan Arab Jamahiriya

ORIENTATION

Identification. The Socialist Popular Libyan Arab Jamahiriya—literally, "state of the masses," is a nation that has been undergoing a radical social experiment over the last thirty years. This experiment has been underwritten by massive oil revenues and directed by the revolutionary government of Muammar Qaddafi.

Location and Geography. Situated on the coast of North Africa, nearly all of the nation's land mass is within the Sahara Desert. The country is bounded to the north by the Mediterranean Sea, to the west by Tunisia and Algeria, and to the south by Chad and Niger. Egypt borders Libya to the east and Sudan is to the southeast. The landmass of 679,500 square miles (1,760,000 square kilometers) makes Libya the fourth largest country in Africa.

Each of the three provinces of Libya—Tripolitania on the western coast, Cyrenaica to the east, and Fezzan in the south—are influenced by the great Sahara in different ways. Tripolitania is sheltered by barrier mountains, the Jabal Nafusa, south of the coast. While the mountains create a favorable environment for agriculture, the coastal littoral, protected from the Sahara, is still arid and requires irrigation. The capital of Libya, Tripoli, is an oasis on the Tripolitanian coast and its inhabitants rely on aquifers to meet most of their water requirements. The coastal mountain range of Cyrenaica, the Jabal Akhdar, rises to a high plateau, which breaks precipitously down to the sea. There are five distinct ecological zones in this region, from a high plateau in the north to desert in the south, each with different combinations of pastoralism and agriculture. There are large towns in Cyrenaica, but until recently the nomadic Bedouins dominated the countryside.

The Gulf of Sirte is between eastern Tripolitania and the mountain chains in Cyrenaica. Primarily steppe country, it is suited to pastoral pursuits and historically has been a major seasonal grazing ground for some of the powerful tribes who spend winters in the interior of the desert.

South of the two mountain chains and the Gulf of Sirte lies the Sahara Desert and the province of Fezzan. The area is vast, extremely dry, and barren. It is characterized by large sand seas, eroded mountain ranges, and upland mesas. Aridity is a fact of existence in Libya. There is not a single permanent waterway in the whole country.

Permanent settlement in the south is limited to a number of depressions where irrigated agriculture may be pursued due to easily accessible supplies of fresh water from deep aquifers. These oases produce a wide variety of fruits and vegetables and support extensive date plantations. While these areas contain highly productive agricultural systems, they are restricted in population size due to the limitation on amounts of water available for irrigation.

Demography. This vast land has an extremely small population, estimated at 5.1 million in 2000, including approximately 163,000 non-nationals. The indigenous population is homogeneous, with 90 percent claiming to be of Arab ancestry. While largely rural, the massive oil wealth beginning in the 1960s changed the economic and residential profile of the population. For instance, between 1954 and 1964, the citizen population of Tripoli grew by 58 percent, while Benghazi grew by 66 percent. A five-year plan introduced in the 1960s was geared to bring prosperity to rural areas. Its success slowed the migration to the urban areas and made paid employment widely available throughout the country. The oil industry brought large

Libya

numbers of European and North American workers to the country. Oil revenues allowed the state to greatly expand its work force while the wealth stimulated the private sector. Thus, over the years large numbers of guest workers have found their way to Libya from Eastern Europe and the surrounding Mediterranean and Arab states.

Linguistic Affiliation. The Bedouin invasion of North Africa in the eleventh century brought the Arabic language to Libya. In the western mountains of Libya, the Berber language is still spoken in places and remnants of it remain in the southern oases. Still, Libya is culturally homogeneous. Its citizens speak a distinctive dialect of Arabic in public while

1291

modern standard Arabic is taught in the schools and used in government and business. In culture, language, and religion, Libya forms a part of the greater Arab world.

HISTORY AND ETHNIC RELATIONS

Emergence of the Nation. In Libya, as in most of the Middle East and North Africa, the modern concept of the territorially discreet nation is a recent development. Historically, Libya was characterized by sets of connections between relatively autonomous polities. Even under Turkish rule in the nineteenth century, the city of Tripoli was more of a city–state with commercial links to a politically autonomous countryside rather than a center of integrated rule. A large tented population of pastoral nomads, independent and aggressively autonomous, resided in the steppe and desert to the southeast and to the west. Smaller towns, some similar in commerce, trade, and political aspiration to Tripoli, occupied the shores of the Mediterranean to the west and east. The town of Misarata, with the support of the powerful Bedouin tribal allies of the Wafallah confederacy, challenged Tripoli's hegemony. To the south, the richly endowed agricultural communities of the Jabal Nafusa Mountains maintained an opposition to the coastal powers. With abundant rainfall and a temperate climate, crops were plentiful; citrus and olive groves abounded. Communities maintained independence, some supported by their kin among the powerful camel herding tribes to the south. Everyone was aware of the military prowess and political autonomy of the tribes.

Cyrenaica had a similar but more distinct antagonism between the desert and the town, and between pastoral tribal and sedentary agricultural society. Important towns like Ajadabya and Benghazi were isolated from a countryside occupied by Bedouin tribes who numbered over 90 percent of the province's population. The country was divided among the so-called noble tribes (i.e., landowners), all linked to one another through a common genealogical pedigree from a common ancestress, Sa-ada. In the south, there was a similar opposition between the oasis communities and the tribes.

Much of Libya was organized into agricultural centers surrounded by tribally-organized Bedouin nomads. There was no sense of nation; instead there was a series of social structures bound by the material conditions of trade in both practical and luxury goods. The only nineteenth-century institution that might be considered a defining characteristic of the country was the presence of a Turkish administration (the Porte). Even here the Porte was at a loss to exert its influence outside of the administrative centers.

The nascent strides toward a national identity began with the Italian invasion in the early twentieth century. The first Italian invasion in 1911 focused on the fertile coastal plain of Tripolitania and the city of Tripoli where political fragmentation gave the Italians an easy victory. Libyan allies were easy to gain if not to maintain. Having secured a foothold on the coast, the Italians mistakenly turned their attention to the Fezzan. They marched south through the Al Jufrah oases to Sebha, the modern capital of Fezzan, securing towns on their way. Once in Sebha, the tribes rallied, cut off the garrison and harassed the Italians as they tried to fight their way back to the coast. A decisive battle was fought in Sirte where the tribes under the Ulad Sleman defeated the Italians who then withdrew from the countryside.

In 1934, a more determined Italian force invaded. This time the primary opposition came from Cyrenaica where the tribes rallied under the banner of the Sanussi religious order and the leadership of such national heroes such as Umar al Mukhtar. A brutal and bloody ten-year guerilla war followed, pitting the modern military might of the Italians against a largely subsistence-based nomadic society. It is claimed that nearly 50 percent of the population of Cyrenaica perished during the struggle. The guerilla war represents an historic struggle in the minds of the Libyan people and its leader Umar al Mukhtar became Libya's first national hero.

The future king of Libya, Idris, the head of the Sanussi order (an ascetic Muslim sect), remained in exile during the colonial period, a symbol of regional if not national opposition to the Italians. He lent his support and that of his forces to the allied war effort in World War II, in exchange for a promise of national independence. The United Nations awarded Libya independence in 1951 and economic stability was assured by grants in aid from the United States and several European countries.

National Identity. In 1969, Libya underwent a revolution with far reaching consequences for the country both nationally and internationally. Muammar Qaddafi emerged as leader of the country. Under this regime, a series of far reaching social experiments have been tried, producing a somewhat unique political system. Internationally the pan-Arab and leftist leanings of the regime have had an impact, as the immense oil wealth of the country

A man using a camel to plough a field along the Tunisia-Libya border.

has allowed the leadership a position on the international stage disproportionate to the country's size. The majority of Libyans have a pride in nation. The birth of the nation, the heroics of Umar al Mukhtar, and the 1969 revolution are commemorated in annual national celebrations as are the major religious events on the Islamic calendar.

Ethnic Relations. Although the Libyan people are in culture, language, and religion largely homogeneous, there have been and still are significant cultural minorities. Until the last half of the twentieth century there were relatively large Jewish and Italian communities in the country. Members of the Jewish community began to emigrate to Israel in 1948 and several anti-Israeli riots in 1948, 1956, 1967, and 1973 encouraged further emigration. In 1973, the revolutionary regime of Muammar Qaddafi confiscated all property owned by non-resident Jews. Also in 1973, Qaddafi's regime "invited" forty-five thousand Italian residents who remained from the Italian colonial era to leave the country, and all Italian properties were confiscated by the State.

Black Libyans are descendants of slaves brought to the country during the days of the slave trade. Some worked the gardens in the southern oases and on the farms along the coast. Others were taken in by Bedouin tribes or merchant families as retainers and domestics.

Berber peoples form a large, but less distinguishable minority in the Libyan population. The original inhabitants in most of North Africa, they were overrun in the eleventh and twelfth centuries by the Bedouin Arab armies of the expanding Islamic empire. Over the centuries, the Berber population largely fused with the conquering Arabs. Evidence of Berber culture still remains. The herdsmen and traders of the great Tuareg confederation are found in the south. Known as the "Blue Men of the Desert," their distinctive blue dress and the practice of men veiling distinguish them culturally from the rest of the population. Historically autonomous and fiercely independent, they stand apart from other Libyans and maintain links to their homelands in the Tibesti and Ahaggar mountain retreats of the central Sahara.

URBANISM, ARCHITECTURE, AND THE USE OF SPACE

Modern Libyan architecture throughout the country reflects the impact of the spectacular oil wealth. Modern apartment buildings and government and private office complexes abound in the major urban centers, while government (peoples') housing is a

A man walking along a covered street in Tripoli. Walled fortifications dominate the old section of the city.

characteristic of the countryside. However, the distribution of political power among the sectors of Libyan society, to some degree, is reflected, still, in traditional forms of architecture. Walled fortifications, a testimony to tribal power as well as a reminder of the past as a piratical state, dominate the old section of Tripoli. Similar concerns for security characterized other ancient Libyan towns. In the mountains of Tripolitania, some settlements were constructed completely underground on hillsides. These towns of troglodytes maintained security by having only one entrance. Further south, the con-

cern for defense also was a characteristic of architecture. Most oasis communities were walled and fortified. In the Sawknah oasis of Al Jufrah, for instance, the fortified wall extended around the entire residential area. There were only two gated entrances to the community, and the wall had parapets at intervals of twenty yards to allow defenders to catch the enemy in crossfire. In the center of the walled town stood a large fort whose ramparts commanded a line of fire on all sections of the outer wall. It stood as the last line and a sanctuary should the town be overrun. In many towns the traditional pattern of residence was a dense settlement of domestic units inside a fortified perimeter with agricultural lands lying at some distance from the residential areas.

Libyan towns are characterized by a strict distinction between public and private use of space. The streets, cafés, mosques, and shops are a man's world, while the domestic compound is the woman's world. The gardens, usually worked by families, are sanctuaries, not to be entered by strangers. The compact nature of fortified residential centers gives them a distinctive character. Streets are narrow and twisting. In some areas, kin groups, looking to extend the space available to developing extended families, have joined houses at the second-story level over the street to extend living quarters. This bridging effect produces long canopied cul-de-sacs, where kin groups may convert public to private space by gating the residential quarter. Whole communities may extend this concept of the privacy of space to the reception of strangers.

The use of space in relation to social distance is a major feature of Libyan custom. Public space is a busy, bustling, man's world. Private space is as rigidly defined for men as is public space for women. Traditional house design presents no windows at the first-floor level. Houses may have windows at the second-story level, but they are barred, sometimes with elaborate iron filigree. There is usually only one entrance, through a heavy wooden door. Some of the more luxurious homes have a large rectangular courtyard with elaborate gardens and fountains. The courtyard is completely enclosed, as is the private world of the immediate family. A wide balcony runs the full length and width of the second story and is accessed by one or two elegantly designed staircases. As the residence of a large extended family, rooms and apartments lead off from the center of the house on all sides and on both levels.

In the houses of prominent persons and local notables, another set of stairs is located immediately inside the front door without a view of the inner sanctuary of the courtyard. These stairs lead to the guestroom or *marabour*, a quasi-public space within the confines of the intensely private home. The head of the household entertains friends, business associates, clients, political supporters, and delegates in the marabour. Some of these rooms may accommodate as many as fifty guests. The marabour is almost always rectangular with mattresses lining the walls to provide seating and bedding for guests. Guests who are strangers are confined to this chamber and will not meet the women of the household.

In tented societies, spatial use and the distinction between public and private spaces are similar to that observed in the towns. Pastoral society has less of a problem defining public space. Bedouin camps consist of closely-related kin, and the physical distance between family groups in the same tribal section reinforces privacy. For most of the year, Bedouin camps spread across the countryside with groups separated from each other by several miles. Camps consist of discreet domestic units residing in tents that are placed in a single line.

Camps are organized to meet the complex demands of herd management and cottage industry. Individual male herd owners cooperate to accomplish the difficult task of managing several different herds with varied grazing and maintenance requirements. Male cooperation also extends to producing charcoal and to planting and harvesting cereal crops in years of plentiful rainfall. Women aid each other in weaving and spinning the wool and hair from the flocks; making tent tops, blankets, and storage bags; and milking and processing the products from the herds. Although members of the camp cooperate in daily activities, each married male member of the camp is an independent herd owner, with sons receiving their share of the family herd upon marriage.

FOOD AND ECONOMY

Food in Daily Life. Food in normal daily life reflects the simplicity of peasant and nomadic life styles. Libyan cooking styles are similar whether rural or urban, sedentary or nomadic. Main courses are almost always one–pot dishes. *Couscous* (cracked wheat), the national dish, is prepared in a spicy sauce of hot peppers, tomatoes, chick peas, and vegetables in season. All meals are eaten out of a communal bowl. Meals are of great symbolic importance; in the houses or the tents of prominent men, the major meal of the day rarely is taken without invited guests.

Most meals are frugal and simple with the daily consumption of meat kept to a minimum. The Bedouin rarely consume meat more than once a month. Agriculturists always seem to have adequate supplies of fruit, vegetables, and grain. Nomads have an abundance of milk, dates, and grain in most seasons. In both town and desert, meals are ended with three glasses of green tea, preparation and consumption of which is a distinct ritual.

Food Customs at Ceremonial Occasions. Meals are prepared by the women of the household and served to guests by the young men of the household. Food is served on long low tables, tall enough to allow guests to sit cross legged and to belly up to the edge.

Meals served in the tented society vary slightly from presentation in towns. In tented society, important guests are honored with a sacrificial slaughter of a goat or sheep. In towns, sacrifice is not as frequent because there usually is easy access to daily markets. The animal is butchered, and the flesh is boiled to form the essential ingredient of a stew to be served over *couscous*. Sometimes various types of pasta may be used as a substitute for *couscous*. The main course usually is preceded by dried dates, milk, and buttermilk. Each liquid is served in a large communal bowl. Libyans drink green tea after all meals and throughout the day.

Lavish meals are prepared for almost all ritual occasions. Special and elaborate meals are prepared daily during the month of Ramadan when the daily fast is broken by a meal after sunset.

Basic Economy. The two major components of the traditional Libyan economy were agriculture and pastoralism, both largely subsistence activities. Most agricultural communities were kin-based, organized through patrilineal descent. Differences in wealth produced a class of local notables who relied upon the community for their influence and power. There was a tendency for communities to view themselves as corporate groups rather than agricultural communities or pastoral hinterlands. There were influential trading families in the larger commercial centers, but their power in the hinterland was limited. Communities tended to be self-contained and were based on subsistence activities in which families provided for most of their needs from their own labor. Surpluses were traded in local markets and exchanged in networks of pastoral families.

The economic specialization of pastoral and agricultural communities fostered cooperation as town and country sought each other's products. The Bedouin supplied the towns with meat, wool, hides, clarified butter, and security; markets in the towns provided necessary and luxury goods from artisans and traders (guns and ammunition) and agricultural products.

Land Tenure and Property. Traditionally, property was occasionally held communally, but most agricultural land was held privately. Land fragmentation led to a degree of local social stratification in which sharecropping developed. Generally, agriculture expanded onto marginal lands, mixing agriculture with herding. These communities were largely egalitarian, and less fortunate members of the community could count on support from their kinsmen.

In the pastoral realm, families owned their herds individually and secured land for grazing and watering rights as members of patrilineally-based corporations. Powerful tribes claimed ownership of discrete blocks of territory. A tribe is composed of a number of corporate land-owning groups who define relationships between themselves according to their relative position on the tribal genealogy. Tribal territory was subdivided between tribal sections following a genealogical charter. This charter of descent links the ancestors of the living corporate land-owning descent groups to each other in clearly defined measures of genealogical closeness or distance. Thus the members of one corporate land-owning group see the members of an adjacent group as having rights to their territory by virtue of their descent from the brother of the founder of their own group.

Major Industries. Libya has been described as a "hydrocarbon state" since oil sales have an all pervasive role in the Libyan economy, politics, and social structure The discovery of oil in the late 1950s radically altered development and ushered in a period of massive economic redirection. In the first phase of exploration, the oil companies spent large sums and expenditures increased rapidly.

The first substantial oil revenues were paid to the government in 1962 and these revenues increased dramatically during the 1960s, providing rapid expansion in both the private and public sectors.

Two other industries that grew rapidly during the late 1950s and in the 1960s were construction and transportation. Construction, particularly in the cities, increased dramatically. Whole sections of Tripoli were built during this time. Construction was undertaken to provide suitable quarters for the many new local and foreign companies that grew in Libya. There also was an increase in construction of private dwellings in this period. New construction provided accommodations for the increased population and thriving business community in Tripoli.

Trade. Today, crude oil refined petroleum products and natural gas constitute nearly all Libya's exports, totaling $6 billion (U.S. dollars) in 1989. Major export partners were Italy, Germany, Spain, France, Sudan, and the United Kingdom. Major im-

Men gather with carts of melons near the Roman arch dedicated to Marcus Aurelius in Tripoli.

ports include machinery, transportation equipment, food, and manufactured goods. In 1989, Libya's major import partners were Italy, Germany, the United Kingdom, France, Tunisia, and Belgium.

Division of Labor. The increase in prosperity brought about a large-scale change in occupation. There was a major decline in persons working in agriculture but there was a sharp increase in laborers and clerical, sports and recreation, and transportation workers. The oil boom had massively changed the occupational and residential structure

of the population in just a few years. In the countryside, the five-year plan of the 1960s ushered into existence a period of rural prosperity when many nomadic families became sedentary in order to take advantage of steady wage employment. A wide-scale patronage system developed that was administered through local political structures. Thus, "lamb barrel" politics, in a situation of radical economic change, reinforced family, lineage, tribal, and village structures. The traditional Libyan economy has continued to shrink as the oil economy has grown. By 1997, agriculture accounted for only 7 percent of the economic sector, while industry and services accounted for 47 percent and 46 percent respectively. But not even a revolution could dismantle the national lamb barrel.

POLITICAL LIFE

Government. On 1 September 1969, a group of army officers staged a successful bloodless coup that forced the king into exile and abolished the existing form of government. Muammar Qaddafi quickly emerged as the undisputed leader. The group of young officers considered themselves revolutionaries, but none of them had a background in revolutionary activity or schooling in radical politics. They aligned themselves with Gamal Abdul Nasser, leader of Egypt. Domestically, the conservative nature of the officers' policies became clear when they permanently closed nightclubs and prohibited the consumption of alcohol. They declared themselves to be socialist in politics and conservative in Islamic religious practices.

Once consolidated in power, the Revolutionary Command Council (RCC) undertook a series of radical initiatives to transform the economic, social, and political organization of Libya. Begun in 1973, this transformation was guided by the *Green Book* written by Qaddafi. The thesis of this book is a critique of participatory democracy in which it is argued that no man should represent another, but that the people should represent themselves directly. A contradictory argument of Qaddafi's is that the building blocks of society are family, tribe, and nation.

In the early 1970s, radical reform of the political process was undertaken to bring about direct participation of the people in the national democratic process. The municipalities in the country were reorganized territorially and their management was placed in the hands of locally elected peoples' committees. These committees were responsible for local government and the development of local budgets. Representatives of local committees presented budgets and other matters through a people's congress, which met once a year to discuss matters of concern and to deliver fiscal demands. This became one mechanism through which Libya redistributed some of the national wealth, and involved its citizens in a democratic process.

In 1975, a crisis developed in the ruling RCC and in the army concerning the course that the revolution should take. There was an attempted coup that was not successful; the army was purged and the RCC disbanded. The five remaining loyal RCC members were assigned to ministerial posts. Qaddafi,

A Muammar Qaddafi banner hangs over a street in Tripoli. Qaddafi assumed leadership of Libya in 1969.

now firmly in control of the country, set a course that was enormously disruptive for the country and the international community.

Internally, Qaddafi unleashed the young zealots of the revolution, urging them to form revolutionary committees to instruct the people on the goals of the revolution. A rein of terror followed that was to last for over a decade. Revolutionary courts were soon established and nearly all institutions of government and commerce were put under the scrutiny of these committees. Only the institutions of banking and the oil industry were kept from their reach. Enemies of the revolution were ferreted out, tried secretly in revolutionary courts, jailed, tortured, and subjected to long prison sentences or death. Furor developed on the university campuses and on at least one occasion the student body witnessed the public hanging of fellow students who had been tried by students belonging to the revolutionary committee. There were numerous public hangings of citizens for crimes committed against the revolution, many of which were broadcast on national television. These measures were followed by other "reforms" which tore at the fabric of Libyan society. Private enterprise was abolished and all privately-owned shops were closed and replaced by government run Peoples' Markets. The regime nationalized all non-owner occupied housing and confirmed ownership on the occupants. Bureaucrats were sacked from government ministries and, in 1980, Qaddafi demonetized the currency, severely restricting the amounts of old money that citizens could convert to the new currency. There were reports of outraged citizens burning large piles of currency outside of the National Bank. These measures were adopted at a time when the world price for oil dropped severely, thus ushering in a decade of austerity in Libya. Qaddafi also canceled the stipends of thousands of Libyan students studying abroad and ordered them to return home. Many chose not to return and large numbers of citizens joined them in exile, most from the better-educated classes. By the mid 1980s, as many as 100,000 Libyans were living abroad, many joining political groups opposed to the revolution.

During the 1980s, the consequences of the revolution were being felt abroad. Qaddafi urged that revolutionary committees replace the diplomatic corps in Libyan embassies, renaming them "Peoples' Bureaus." In London a young female constable was shot dead outside the Peoples' Bureau where an anti-Qaddafi rally was under way. Qaddafi stepped up pressure on dissidents and called for the obligatory repatriation of all Libyan exiles. Noncompliance was to result in death. There were gang style executions of Libyan nationals in several European cities.

Internationally, Qaddafi played a controversial role. He fought a war with Chad, skirmished with Egypt, and trained a commando group which attacked a city in southern Tunisia. There were well-publicized financial contributions to Pakistan to aid in building the "Islamic Bomb," and to the Irish Republican Army, the Palestinian Liberation Organization, and other revolutionary organizations.

There was also growing suspicion in the international community that the Qaddafi regime was involved directly in terrorism itself. These suspicions resulted in the United States and Britain severing diplomatic relations with Libya, putting in place severe economic sanctions and bombing the cities of Tripoli and Benghazi. Subsequently the Pan American Airline explosion over Lockerbie, Scotland was blamed on Libyan agents and the United Nations banned all air travel to Libya until the government was prepared to turn its agents over the Scottish government for trial. By late 1980s, Libya was thoroughly isolated by the international community.

This same period (1986–1987) marked a turning point in the revolution internally. The revolutionary committees were chastised for excesses. Qaddafi released prisoners from jail, personally supervising the destruction of one prison. He invited dissidents to return home without penalty; allowed citizens to travel freely, giving family members $1,000 (U.S.) each for the journey; and restored free enterprise. The liberalization has resulted in free market conditions with satellite dishes springing up everywhere, cell phones in use, and a full array of goods in the shops. But it does not appear that the liberalization has met with entrepreneurial fervor among the citizens. They seem to know that their mercurial government could change course at a moment's notice.

Libya has many characteristics which distinguish it organizationally from other states. Most importantly, the state does not rely upon taxation of its citizens for revenues. State budgets remain out of the realm of public discussion because those in power do not combine finance with politics. The central power seeks other means to gain compliance from its citizens. While direct democracy is a mechanism for distribution of some of the national wealth to the citizens, most of the national wealth remains to be used by those in power beyond public accountability. For instance, the budget for the military, one of the most important elements of Libya's new elite, is simply not published.

Military. The Libyan military has had a critical role in maintaining the Qaddafi regime in power. This support seems to have functioned from three perspectives. First, the military is extremely well funded. Although exact figures are difficult to obtain, Libya has spent at least $5 billion (U.S.) for military procurements every year since the late 1970s, with occasional military expenditures exceeding 40 percent of total government expenditures. The country spent $1,360 (U.S.) per capita in

1984. These figures are about twice the average per capita spending on defense for the North Atlantic Treaty Organization and are rivaled only by Israel, Saudi Arabia, and a few oil rich Gulf Emirates. Second, these figures reflect an enormous procurement process in which the senior military seem to have profited greatly. There are accounts of senior officers living opulent life styles, building stately villas, and acquiring properties outside of normal channels. There is a suggestion here that Qaddafi has bought their loyalty. Third, there is hard evidence that tribalism has a role in the army. Qaddafi, during the revolutionary furor that he unleashed, appointed his family members as his bodyguards, trained his tribal kin as his elite army unit and, during the Revolutionary Committee period, appointed members of his tribe to the committee in the army. Thus opulent economic favor, nepotism, and tribal loyalty combined to assure that the most powerful institution in Libyan society continued to support the revolution and its leader.

GENDER ROLES AND STATUSES

The Relative Status of Women and Men. Purdah, the custom of secluding and veiling women, is a traditional feature of Libyan cultural life. Groups of veiled women are still found in markets in the company of kinsmen but they are infrequent visitors to mosques and absent entirely from café life. Women were traditionally placed in seclusion at puberty and appear in public veiled. They are only freed from this custom at menopause. The push toward female emancipation, as exhibited in the opening of public space to women, may be repealed at any time by either domestic male prerogative or national decree. Qaddafi established a military academy for females and, occasionally, has arrived at international meetings accompanied by female bodyguards dressed in battle fatigues.

Qaddifi claims that men and women are radically different in biology and nature. His view is that the nature of woman is to nurture and her role as mother and domestic is part of a natural order.

Where social life outside of the compound may be limiting for women due to the institution of *purdah*, within the household, the movements of women are not constrained. All are close kin and many are descendants of a common ancestor. As such they share a common daily social life. The movements of women are not restricted within the compound and both sexes may freely enter each other's abodes without invitation.

MARRIAGE, FAMILY, AND KINSHIP

Marriage. Descent kinship and marriage are major organizing factors in social, economic, and political life. Patrilineal descent defines group membership, while kinship is largely the product of marriage arrangements. Where the collective interests of descent groups are clearly defined, the patterns of kinship and marriage will reflect these interests. Marriages are arranged by the parents in consultation with members of the extended family and lineage. Libyan society, like much of the Arab world, places a premium on father's brother's daughter's marriage. This rule of "first right" is so important that in strongly-focused descent groups the male first cousin must waive his right to the girl before she is allowed to take a more socially distant spouse. Girls may marry at age fourteen, while men must usually wait until they are in their mid-to-late twenties. The age qualification for marriage between cousins thus restricts this form of marriage.

Approximately 20 percent of all marriages are "first right." Such arrangements give many descent groups a second set of social relationships. Since the father's brother's daughter's marriage removes the rule against group endogamy found in other societies, people are free to arrange marriages within the group outside the range of siblings and within generation. Thus, multiple strands of kinship crosscut group structure and further reinforce the corporate descent group.

Although groups may strive toward endogamy, other interests of the family and corporate group may lead to marriages being contracted between distant relations. In Bedouin society it is normal for groups to contract marriage with groups in distant ecological zones. Failure of the rains in one territory may lead to an invitation by more fortunate kin to visit and graze and water one's animals on their territory for the season.

Occasionally, there are marriages between the Bedouin and families of trading partners in oases. Marriages between adversaries in a feud may occur at the conclusion of the peace agreement. Marriages also are a way of binding groups in alliance since the offspring of successful unions will have close kin in two different groups. Thus marriage reflects family and group interests, and the patterns weave a web of mutual interest between families, lineages, and tribes.

Marriage arrangements require that siblings are married sequentially according to age. For a man to marry, he must be able to pay a "bride price" to the bride's family. Weddings may tax family resources because the more distantly related the bride, the

Libyans tending an urban vegetable patch.

higher the "bride price." Groups of brothers work together to gather the resources necessary for marriage. In Bedouin society, the resources used to marry come from the family herds. In towns, men contribute a portion of their pay to a brother's bride price.

Indications that in the urban areas some of the structures described above have been modified are manifest in several ways. Many women are now seen unveiled in public. A recent report now claims that there are more female than male university students. And the Qaddafi regime has prohibited the admission of foreign women into the country unaccompanied by senior male kinsmen, as the bride price for mail-order brides from surrounding Arab states is significantly less than for Libyan women. These suggestions of social transformation have not been adequately analyzed as yet.

Domestic Unit. The social makeup of Bedouin camps almost always consists of closely-related patrilineal relatives and their wives. A camp may consist of a large central tent housing a couple and their unmarried sons and daughters. Adjacent tents will house married sons and their wives and children. Occasionally a distant relative or friend and his family may join the camp for a season. In the line of tents, social solidarities are expressed by the proximity of tents in the line. Close kin, brothers, and fathers position their tents so that the tent pegs overlap and the guide ropes of the tents cross one another. The tent of a more remotely related member of the camp will be at the end of the line, a few yards from his neighbor, without guide ropes crossing.

Kin Groups. Descent groups with clearly-focused interests usually reside in contiguous residential structures, marry endogamously, cooperate in all social, economic, and political matters, and have a highly ramified social life within the group. For the most part, life is extremely comfortable.

The tribal land-owning corporations are themselves patrilineal descent groups or lineages whose members acquire rights by virtue of being the sons and daughters of a particular man. In theory all members of the group are patrilineal descendants of the founder. Members are said to be of one flesh and bone with equal rights to territorial resources. Equal rights also implies equal obligations. Members have the obligation to defend the territory against the encroachment of neighboring corporations. Liability is not an individual matter, but a matter between groups. Injury leads to a "state of feud" between groups in which all members of the offended group are required to take revenge against any male member of the offending group; this can lead to anarchy with a continual cycle of killings. Feuds have rules of conduct in which groups may decide to end the matter by a payment of a "blood price" whereby the offending group must compensate the offended group for the loss of life with payment. The members of the offending corporation must all contribute to the blood price, while all members of the offended group share in the compensation.

The institution of the feud makes possible a fairly orderly set of relations between competing groups where there are no institutions of government. While feuds may lead to peace through settlement, the relationships between groups defined through the genealogy will lead to a stand-off of equal numbers through opposition. The tribal segmentary system thus fosters an ethic of egalitarianism with its expression found in the members of the corporate patrilineal descent groups.

Nicknaming within tribes is prevalent as an expression of individual personality. The descent group is an institution that gives pride of place to its members, demands extreme loyalty of them, and provides a warm, nurturing support system to men and women of all ages.

The oil wealth has radically transformed the Libyan economy and its demography with widespread urbanization and wage employment. This process has only partially undermined traditional social structures as they were first reinforced by the pre-Revolutionary patronage system and then by the post-revolution political system. In the urban areas the constraints of family, lineage, and tribe have no doubt loosened. While the upper level bureaucrats—a second major section of the new elite—may answer to Qaddafi and his ruling clique, this is not true for the rural areas. There, ties of family, lineage, tribe, and residence still remain the dominant forms of organization. This striking feature of Libyan life is partially the result of the implementation of the political structures described by Qaddafi in the *Green Book*. Local committee members and bureaucrats are themselves members of local kin-based groups whose loyalty they must retain and whose wishes they must consider. While this is a society where immense oil wealth might lead to radical social transformation, in the rural areas, at least, this has not happened. There, cultural traditions have been slow to change as the political and economic institutions of government are refracted through family, lineage, and tribal interests.

SOCIALIZATION

Higher Education. Libya has two universities, several technical schools, and a well developed primary and secondary school system. By the mid 1980s, there were 1,245,000 students enrolled in primary and secondary education: 54 percent were males and 46 percent were females. During this period the government claimed to have constructed 32,000 new classrooms while the number of teachers increased from about 19,000 to 79,000.

University enrollments also show dramatic increases from 3,000 students in 1969 to more than 25,000 during the 1980s with female enrollments numbering about 25 percent. Education is free and university students receive generous stipends. Even though large strides have been made in Libyan education, the country still lacks technical expertise in many areas. The military lacks the skilled personnel to adequately maintain its weapons systems. Most doctors, dentists, and pharmacists are foreign nationals, while 60 percent of Libya's top bureaucrats and 40 percent of the work force are expatriates.

ETIQUETTE

A polite stranger, when approaching a camp, will pause about one hundred yards from the line of tents. A series of activities converting private into public space begins. Either one tent in the line will be vacated and converted into a guest tent, or the large tent of the oldest male will be divided down the middle to produce a guest compartment separated from the domestic section. Entertainment of guests in tented society is similar to towns. One difference in tented society is that a guest will not be asked his social identity until after the meal when the breaking of bread has placed the guest under his host's protection. This rule of sanctuary ensures that members of rival groups or those in a feuding relationship may travel the desert in relative safety.

RELIGION

Religious Beliefs. Most traditional Libyans are devout Muslims and practice a simple and deeply personal religion. Adults follow the strictures of Islam; they pray five times a day, give alms to the poor, and fast for the month of Ramadan. There is a certain austerity to Libyan Islam shaped by the harshness of traditional life. This asceticism was reinforced by the Sanussi order, which was abolished by the Qaddafi regime for political reasons. In its place, the regime instituted fundamentalist practices with very little impact on rural life, where the Libyan version of an ascetic Islam is still practiced.

Religious Practitioners. The Ulama, or religious scholars, have been upstaged by the regime, but in the countryside mosques are well attended. The folk religion of the people subscribes, in part, to a deviation from traditional Islam. In Libya, as in other parts of North Africa, the cult of saints is highly developed. There are individual living saints, *marabout*, whose miracles are widely reported and whose services in a curative capacity are sought. People also visit the tombs of men of reputation, seeking cures for illness, success in business, and luck in passing an examination. There are small tribes whose members are said to have inherited *baraka*, the quality of goodness or holiness, and minister to local people. There are also lineages who are said to be descendants of the prophet Mohammed. They are given the title of *sharif*.

BIBLIOGRAPHY

Allan, J. A. *Libya. The Experience of Oil*, 1981.

———. *Libya Since Independence: Economic and Social Development*, 1982.

Anderson, L. *The State and Social Transformation in Tunisia and Libya*, 1986.

Arnold, G. *The Maverick State. Gaddafi and the New World Order*, 1996.

Behnke, R. H., Jr. "The Herders of Cyrenaica: Economy and Kinship Among the Bedouin of Eastern Libya," *Illinois Studies in Anthropology*, 12; 1980.

Blundy, D. and A. Lycett. *Qaddafi and the Libyan Revolution*, 1987.

Cockburn, A. "Libya," *National Geographic Magazine*, March 2001: 2-32.

Cooley, J. K. *Libyan Sandstorm: The Complete Account of Qaddafi's Revolution*, 1983.

Dalton, W. G. "Economic Change and Political Continuity in a Saharan Oasis Community," *Man*, 1973.

———. "Lunch with Abdullah: An Account of Politics in the Fezzan Region of Libya." Proceeding of the African Studies Association, Brandeis University, 1978.

———. "Sedentarization of Nomads: The Libyan Case." In Salzman and Galaty, ed. *Nomads in a Changing World*, 1990.

Davis, J. *Libyan Politics: Tribe and Revolution*, 1987.

Evans-Pritcharsd, E. E. *The Sanusi of Cyrenaica*, 1949.

Farley, R. *Planning for Development in Libya: The Exceptional Economy in the Developing Word*, 1971.

El-Fathaly, O. and Palmer, M. "Institutional Development in Qaddafi's Libya." In Vanderwalle, D. ed., *Qaddafi's Libya 1969-1994*.

———. *Political Development and Bureaucracy in Libya*, 1997.

First, R. *Libya: The Elusive Revolution*, 1975.

Khadduri, M. *Modern Libya: A Study in Political Development*, 1963.

Khouri, P. and J. Kostiner eds. *Tribes and State Formation in the Middle East*, 1990.

Library of Congress. *Libya*, 1987.

National Salvation Front. *Libya Under Qaddafi and the NFSL Challenge*, 1992.

Pelt, A. *Libyan Independence and the United Nations*, 1970.

Peters, E. L. "Aspects of the Family Among the Bedouin of Cyrenaica," In M. F. Nomkoff, ed. *Comparative Family Systems*, 1965.

———. "Some Structural Aspects of the Feud Among the Camel-Herding Bedouin of Cyrenaica," *Africa* 37: 261-82, 1967.

———. "The Tied and the Free: An Account of a Type of Patron-Client Relationship Among the Bedouin Pastoralists of Cyrenaica." In J. G. Peristiany, ed. *Contributions to Mediterranean Sociology* 167-88, 1968.

———. "The Proliferation of Segments in the Lineages of the Bedouin of Cyrenaica." In L. M. Sweet, ed. *Peoples and Cultures of the Middle East*: 363-98, 1970.

Roumani, J. "From Republic to Jamahiriya: Libya's Search for Political Community," *Middle East Journal* 37 2: 151-68, 1983.

Vandewalle, D. *Libya Since Independence*, 1998.

Wright, J. *Libya: A Modern History*, 1982.

—WILLIAM G. DALTON

LITHUANIA

CULTURE NAME

Lithuanian

ORIENTATION

Identification. Lithuanians are fond of nature and have a strong feeling of a shared culture that begins as early as primary school, where folk music, national traditions, and holidays play an important role. Among those who remember life under the Soviet regime, pride in surviving a period of repression and difficulty is a focal point of the national culture.

The most noticeable distinction between regions is the change in dialects as one travels across the country. To an outsider, a different dialect can sound like a completely different language and in some cases—particularly in border towns—may incorporate elements of the neighboring country's language.

Location and Geography. Lithuania is on the coast of the Baltic Sea. Just over 40,500 square miles (65,000 square kilometers) in area, it shares borders with Poland and Kaliningrad (Russian Federation) in the southwest, Belarus in the east, and Latvia in the north. The country is divided into four regions: Aukštaitija, the highlands in the northeast and central portion of the country; Žemaitija, the lowlands in the west, stretching from the Baltic coast to the Nevėžis river; Dzūkija, in the southeast; and Suvalkija, in the southwest. The climate is maritime along the coast and continental in other areas. The physical environment varies from sandy terrain spotted with pine trees on the coast and the Curonian Spit, to flatlands and low, rolling hills farther inland. There are more than eight thousand lakes, mostly in the uplands.

The capital, Vilnius, lies in the southwestern part of the country at the confluence of the Neris and Vilnia rivers. Vilnius has been the capital since the fourteenth century, except for the period from 1919 to 1939 during Poland's annexation of southern Lithuania, when it was temporarily moved to Kaunas.

Demography. In 2000, the population was 3.8 million, of which approximately 80 percent were ethnic Lithuanians, 9 percent Russians, 7 percent Poles, 2 percent Belarussians, and 2 percent were of other nationalities. Lithuania is 70 percent urban, with the largest cities being Vilnius (population 600,000), Kaunas (population 430,000), Klaipėda (population 210,000), Šiauliai (population 150,000), and Panevėžys (population 130,000).

Linguistic Affiliation. The official language is Lithuanian, one of two remaining languages in the Baltic branch of the Indo-European languages. Dialects vary by region, and their distinctiveness often depends on the distance from the nearest big city or the proximity to borders, where incorporation of neighboring countries' words is common. The language has survived despite a history of domination by foreign powers and serves as a focal point of cultural identity.

Lithuanian is spoken by nearly everyone in the country except for a few Russians and Poles in Vilnius and in the extreme east and south. It is a language with many words to describe a single idea. There is an abundance of nature words, probably because the people are so fond of the outdoors. This is particularly evident in traditional personal names such as Rūta (''Rue''), Aušra (''Dawn''), and Giedrius (''Dew''). Lithuanian often makes use of diminutives to soften the connotation of words or make them more personal.

Symbolism. The national symbol is Vytis, the white knight, sitting astride his horse and brandishing a sword; he symbolizes the nation's struggle to defend itself from intruders. The national plant is rue, and the national bird is the stork. The flag consists of horizontal stripes in yellow, green, and red; the colors symbolize nature (sun and trees)

Lithuania

and traditional values such as solidarity and national pride.

HISTORY AND ETHNIC RELATIONS

Emergence of the Nation. The origin of the nation and the development of its culture were strongly influenced by foreign occupation of the country and are the result of the perceived need of the people to preserve something of their own. Even when the national language was banned and reading or writing of books in the native tongue was forbidden, people were determined to spread their heritage and share their traditions.

The first Lithuanian state was established in 1230 after Duke Mindaugas united the tribes and lands in the area. His crowning in 1252 marked the beginning of a cultural identity focused on solidarity. Further credit for the early development of this character goes to Gediminas, the principal unifier of the territory from the Baltic to the Black Sea. He was one of the first leaders to instill in the people the spirit of nationhood, and the main street of Vilnius, with the parliament building at one end and the national cathedral at the other, bears his name. In the fourteenth and fifteenth centuries, the marriage of Jogaila, the grand duke of Lithuania, to Queen Jadvyga of Poland created the formal confederation Rzeczpospolita; extensive development of the Lithuanian cultural identity took place during that period. While at several points in history this camaraderie could not overcome the presence of occupiers (in 1569 an attempt to defend against an expanding Russian state failed, and attempts at independence in 1795, 1830–1831, and 1863 were also unsuccessful), the resolute nature of the national character was not undermined.

National Identity. In the late nineteenth and early twentieth centuries, literacy became a valuable tool in the development of cultural and national identity. Although it was illegal, people continued to read the literature of the national movement. Literacy rates were considerably higher than those in Russia and contributed greatly to the rise of a national identity.

In 1905, when over two thousand delegates representing different sectors of the society gathered at the Great Lithuanian Assembly to discuss the Lithuanian nation, representatives of different political backgrounds agreed that the country should fight for and be granted autonomy, whether within Czarist Russia or independent of it. The intelligentsia, with help from the Lithuanian Academy of Sciences, drafted a document making demands for the future of the Lithuanian state. Among those demands were autonomy, equal rights for aliens within Russia, the construction of Lithuanian schools, freedom of worship, and the return of Suvalkija, which was controlled by the Poles.

In 1918, Lithuania formally declared independence, which was granted by both Germany and the Soviet Union. While lasting independence would not come until nearly a century later (the Soviet Union occupied the nation in 1940, and the Nazis in 1941), the fact that schools resumed teaching in Lithuanian, folk dance groups began meeting more freely, and people around the country assembled more readily to discuss their views was significant.

The period from 1941 to 1944 saw the countryside destroyed and almost all of the Jewish population (up to 250,000) annihilated. The period under Stalin, from 1945 to 1953, made the people more determined to put an end to the repression their country had experienced for so long. Tens of thousands of people, including most intellectuals, were deported to Siberia for being educated or being involved in intellectual circles, and many others fled. Those who remained were determined to change the system. Groups of "forest fighters" fled to the woods to avoid deportation and maintain nationalist resistance. It is said that some of these fighters remained in the forests until 1960, seven years after Stalin's reign ended.

At the beginning of 1989, the popular movement Sajūdis announced a platform for the complete restoration of Lithuanian sovereignty. This led to closer monitoring by the Soviet Union and increased Soviet troop movements in Lithuania in an effort to maintain order. The remainder of 1989 and most of 1990 were marked by deliberations both between the Soviet government and the Lithuanian popular movement and among different parties within those constituencies. In March 1990, Lithuania declared full reestablishment of independence from the Soviet Union, based on the argument that the occupation and annexation of the country by the Soviet Union was a result of the Molotov-Ribbentrop Pact of 1939 and its secret protocols and thus were illegal. In response, the Soviet Union imposed an economic blockade.

In late 1990 a popularist rally to help Lithuanians evade the Red Army draft was organized, and the Soviet government decided to deal with "the Lithuanian problem" once and for all. The Lithuanian Communist Party secretary had claimed that the human rights of non-Lithuanian citizens in the country were being violated and encouraged Soviet intervention. In January 1991, KGB plants posing as Russian workers stormed the parliament. A few days later, in what were described as precautionary measures to protect the human rights of Soviet citizens, Soviet troops gathered around the Parliament, the Lithuanian Press House, and the Vilnius television tower. Soldiers abused bystanders with little or no provocation, and several people were wounded.

The culmination of the Soviet campaign occurred on 13 January at the base of the Vilnius television tower, where thousands of nonviolent protestors had gathered. Irritated by Lithuanian persistence, Soviet forces attacked the crowd. Tanks crushed those who got in the way, and soldiers fired into the crowd. Thirteen people died at the television tower.

Two weeks after the episode, Mikhail Gorbachev appointed a delegation to negotiate with Baltic leaders. Although troop movements continued for much of the year, especially in Vilnius and along the border with Kaliningrad, it was obvious that the Soviet presence was finished. In September 1991, the Soviet Union recognized Lithuania as an independent republic. Later that month, Lithuania became a member of the United Nations—three months before the demise of the Soviet Union. In 1993, the first directly elected president, Algirdas

Vehicles dot a highway in the Lithuanian capital of Vilnius in 1975.

Brazauskas, was chosen; the last Russian soldiers left the country; and Lithuania became a member of the Council of Europe.

Ethnic Relations. Historically, relations with other ethnic groups have been amicable; this is perhaps because over 80 percent of citizens are ethnic Lithuanians. While relations with minority groups, especially Russians, were strained during the period immediately preceding the reestablishment of independence, ethnic strife is not a matter of grave concern.

URBANISM, ARCHITECTURE, AND THE USE OF SPACE

Styles of architecture reflect the sociopolitical and religious past of the country. While most people in urban areas live in Soviet-era blocks of concrete apartment buildings, the countryside is dotted with traditional wooden churches and houses. Also present are fortlike structures and castles built in the sixteenth and seventeenth centuries as residences for the local nobility. The Old Town of Vilnius has been restored and was named a UNESCO World Heritage Monument.

Present-day government buildings are often old brick edifices left over from the Soviet period. The propagandistic statues in many of the main squares were removed in the early 1990s and have been replaced with more nationalistic monuments.

Among the 70 percent of people who reside in urban areas, many live in small two- or three-room apartments with sitting rooms that double as bedrooms. Kitchens are generally small, and toilets are often separate from washrooms. Most of these apartments were distributed during the Soviet period, and many are owned or rented by the original recipients.

Among those who live in towns, it is common to have a garden just outside the city limits, often as part of a collective. In the summer, families tend these gardens and grow produce to be canned and consumed in the winter. Many families live in garden houses for extended periods during the summer to escape cramped accommodations at home.

FOOD AND ECONOMY

Food in Daily Life. The typical diet consists of items that are readily available and not expensive. National dishes reflect the economic situation and the fact that the weather is cold for much of the year, creating a shortage of vegetables in the winter and a desire to prepare and eat warm, wholesome food. Pork, smoked meats, cabbage, beets, and pota-

The Vilnius City Square. Lithuanian architecture reflects the sociopolitical and religious past of the country.

toes are staples. Two favorite traditional dishes are *šaltibarščiai*, cold beet soup with buttermilk, and *cepelinai*, boiled potato dumplings filled with meat or curd and served with fried pork fat or sour cream. Eating in restaurants has become more popular, and there are many different types of restaurants in the larger cities; how frequently a family dines out is determined by its income.

Food Customs at Ceremonial Occasions. Food plays an important role in celebrations, and a long table full of tasty fare is considered a sign of hospitality and affluence. It is customary for all guests to sit at a common table that fills most of the room, and for the hosts to ensure that no guest leaves the table hungry. These meals start with salads, cold meats, and bread, accompanied by *kompotas* (cold fruit tea) or juice, vodka, wine, or *gira*, a carbonated soft drink made from grain. This is followed by a hot course, singing and conversation, and perhaps dessert and coffee.

The Christmas Eve meal, *kučios*, is the most symbolic meal of the year. Twelve meatless dishes are prepared, including several types of herring, grain porridge, and often pickled mushrooms. Hay sometimes is sprinkled under the tablecloth to represent the manger where Jesus was born. People often eat *kučiukai* (bite-sized biscuitlike cakes) with

poppy milk (poppy seeds boiled with water and sugar) for dessert. They also break symbolic Christmas wafers (*Dievo pyragai*) which were once acquired in churches but are now available in local shops at Christmas, to bring the family closer together and wish for a healthy and successful year. If a family member has died in the past year, a plate and chair are placed at the table, along with a small candle, to welcome the spirit to participate in one last family gathering.

Basic Economy. The economy is mainly agricultural, but in recent years the government has attempted to distribute commercial activity. Light industry, metalworking, and woodworking, along with petroleum refining, are part of the commercial profile. Livestock breeding, primarily pigs, and dairy farming are an important sector of the economy, and cereals, flax, beets, and potatoes are the primary crops. Lithuania's unit of currency is the *litas*, pegged at four *litas* per U.S. dollar.

Lithuania is dependent on other nations for fuel and raw materials. The main economic problems are job insecurity, high unemployment, and poor labor protection laws.

Land Tenure and Property. Reestablishment of independence in 1991 led to the abandonment of the strict Soviet system of property and land allocation, and a need for new laws on restoration of ownership rights. There is has been a movement to accelerate the restoration process, clarify the property registration system and the role of government ministries therein, and develop a national strategy on property security and management.

Commercial Activities. Commercial activity is determined largely by geography. On the coast, where tourism and fishing are prevalent, fish products and the shipping of equipment are the major commercial endeavors. In the south, where the soil is fertile and mineral springs are predominant, wild mushrooms and farm products are the major products. The east is known for wooden handicrafts and metalworking, and the north for wheat, flax, and beets.

Major Industries. Metalworking, manufacturing, woodworking, and light industry are widespread in the east; water power, metalworking, manufacturing, food processing, farming, and livestock rearing are predominate in the south; and shipbuilding, fish processing, and tourism in the West. The north does not have any major industries.

Trade. In the past, Lithuania traded mainly with Russia, exporting foodstuffs, especially dairy products, and textiles. It also exported machinery and light industrial products to other countries of the former Soviet Union. Since 1991, exports have shifted more to the west, and close to 50 percent of exports are to the European Union. Major imports are fuel and raw materials, primarily from the European Union and Russia.

Division of Labor. The division of labor is by law determined by ability, certification, education, and training, but age, gender, and social connections continue to play a role in career advancement. The coming of independence ended the institutional guarantee of a job.

SOCIAL STRATIFICATION

Classes and Castes. There is not a highly defined caste system in Lithuania. Society is primarily middle class, and there is a large income gap between the wealthy and the very poor. Low salaries, high unemployment rates, and a poor social security system make it difficult for pensioners to meet their basic needs.

Symbols of Social Stratification. Owning a private home or new car is a symbol of wealth, but there is not a traditional system of social stratification in Lithuania.

POLITICAL LIFE

Government. Lithuania is a parliamentary democracy, with a constitution that was adopted in 1992. The Parliament, or Seimas, is unicameral with 141 seats and is the highest legislative body. Seventy-one members are elected directly by popular vote, and seventy by proportional representation from single seat districts, to four-year terms.

The head of state is the president, who is elected to a five-year term by universal, equal, direct suffrage. The president is responsible for approving and publishing laws adopted by the Seimas and appoints and dismisses the prime minister with approval of the Seimas. Ministers are appointed by the president upon recommendation by the prime minister.

The government is actively involved with international organizations, including the United Nations and the World Trade Organization, and its continual membership in both the European Union and the North Atlantic Treaty Organization.

Leadership and Political Officials. The political system includes a central government, and forty-four regions with eleven municipalities. Public opinion toward political officials and their effectiveness and trustworthiness is mixed, and corruption is a problem in some governmental bodies.

The major political parties are the conservative Homeland Union Party, the Christian Democrat Party, the New Union Party, the Center Party, the Social Democrat Party, the Liberal Party, the Democratic Labor Party, and the Lithuanian Women's Party. All major parties promote integration into the European Union and NATO. The constitution provides "guarantees for the activities of political parties and political organizations" and mandates that state personnel, judges, prosecutors, and investigators may not be active members of political parties.

Social Problems and Control. The judicial branch of the government includes the Constitutional Court and Supreme Court, plus district and local courts whose judges are all appointed directly or indirectly by the Seimas. The most common crimes are theft, domestic and public violence, and corruption.

Public opinion of social control often reflects dissatisfaction with the system. Bribery, which has been present since the Soviet era and may stem from the low salaries of public servants, is widespread among police officers. Some people argue that "taking of the law into one's own hands" is a

A Lithuanian railroad worker takes a break. Commercial activity in Lithuania is largely determined by geographical region.

natural response to and means of closing the gap between public sector salary levels and the value of the public sector's contribution to the national economy.

Military Activity. The military is composed of ground forces, air and air defense forces, a navy, security forces (internal forces and border guards), and a national guard. All male citizens over the age of eighteen are required to complete one year of mandatory military service unless exempted for ac-

ademic or professional reasons. Alternative service is available.

SOCIAL WELFARE AND CHANGE PROGRAMS

There are social welfare and change programs at all levels of society, including several national youth clubs and peer support groups, as well as societies for recovering alcoholics and members of marginalized groups. Local and national environmental and conservation groups have begun participating in international projects to reduce pollution in the Baltic Sea and the region as a whole.

The involvement of governmental and nongovernmental organizations is a key factor in the success of these programs. While many social programs are in the beginning stages because only scientific organizations could legitimately address "controversial" issues in the Soviet era, increased interest in schools and by the international donor community has contributed to social progress.

NONGOVERNMENTAL ORGANIZATIONS AND OTHER ASSOCIATIONS

There are several thousands of organizations and associations, which by law are divided into four distinct types: societal organizations, associations, charity and sponsorship funds, and public institutions. Regulations regarding the establishment of and guidelines for various organizations are confusing.

The Vilnius NGO Information and Support Centre serves as a central clearinghouse for nongovernmental organizations (NGOs), provides links to other organizations around the world, and attempts to establish dialog between the two groups. Also, 1998 amendments to NGO laws, which resulted from cooperation among NGOs, the government, the United Nations Development Programme, the Information Centre for Not-for-Profit Law, and the NGO Information and Support Centre, have brought in outside help for this sector. Current policies endorse tax breaks for NGOs, further clarification of NGO laws, and the redefinition of charity versus sponsorship, along with greater flexibility in administrative matters.

GENDER ROLES AND STATUSES

Division of Labor by Gender. Gender discrimination in employment is illegal, and control mechanisms and ombudsman institutions ensure that the law is observed. Nevertheless, while the workforce has seen an increase in female participation, division of labor by gender still exists. Jobs traditionally done by women are often lower-paid positions such as teaching and public service jobs. The majority of doctors are women because of the low salaries for public servants; the health, social service, and education sector also are characterized by high concentrations of female employees. Although women now constitute 50 percent of the labor force and close to 90 percent of working-age women work or study, this female presence is not reflected in pay

rates. As the private sector becomes more prominent, the workforce is shrinking, and women are being squeezed out regardless of their educational level.

The Relative Status of Women and Men. Obvious discrepancies exist with regard to pay rates, and increased unemployment and decreased real wages affect women in particular.

MARRIAGE, FAMILY, AND KINSHIP

Marriage. Marriages typically have two components: religious and legal. Couples must register at the municipal wedding hall and often have a religious union in a church, followed by an elaborate party that can last for three days. While on the average people marry younger than do their Western counterparts, this has changed with the increasing popularity among women of higher education. There has been a sharp decrease in the number of marriages since the Soviet period. The ending of a woman's surname changes to reflect her marital status, and people may look skeptically upon older women who have never married.

Domestic Unit. The primary domestic unit is the nuclear family based on a marital relationship. Households are often run by women, who have traditionally been the cooks and cleaners. This has changed because more women are discovering that if they stay home, they miss out on opportunities to make money and can lose their competitive status in the job market.

Families usually have close ties with parents and immediate relatives, and much of everyday life focuses on this relationship. Lithuanians often use the term "acquaintance" and grant the title of "friend" only to someone who is very close and like a member of the family.

Kin Groups. Membership in groups helps some people improve their standard of living. Strong social networks and extended relationships with family and friends are an important part of life. Often family members are assisted by relatives who live abroad and send money, clothing, and other goods.

SOCIALIZATION

Infant Care. Infants usually are cared for by their mothers or grandmothers. Children go to nursery school or kindergarten as early as three years old and stay until they start elementary school. Younger children with working parents often stay at nursery school or kindergarten until the early evening.

Child Rearing and Education. Child rearing is traditionally the responsibility of the mother. Although the law allows fathers to take paternal leave and receive paternal pay, it is not common for men to do this. Children are required to complete nine years of formal schooling, but most finish twelve grades. The number of specialized schools has increased as higher education has become more popular. Many children also attend music, art, or athletics schools.

Higher Education. There are fifteen institutions of higher education: six universities, seven academies, and two institutes. Most higher education is free or very inexpensive, as the state subsidizes 75 percent of university education. A university education is becoming increasingly important for getting a good job.

Studying abroad has become very popular, although complications with visas and high foreign tuition present problems for many students. Foreign donor programs make it possible for many students to overcome these financial difficulties.

The largest universities are Vilnius University, Vytautas Didysis University, Kaunas Technological University, Klaipėda University, Klaipėda Christian College, and Šiauliai University. Vilnius University, established in 1579, is the oldest university in Central Europe and the most prestigious in the country. The majority of university students are women, primarily majoring in education. Male students are more likely to study business or computers.

ETIQUETTE

Lithuanians are a reserved people with respect for tradition. They generally will not go out of their way to greet someone they do not know; people on public conveyances do not look directly at someone else unless they are friends and generally give up their seats to their elders.

People often bring a small gift of candy or flowers when they visit someone (always an odd number of flowers unless someone has passed away). Hosts are generous and do anything they can to make a guest comfortable.

Men always shake the hands of male friends when they meet in a café or on the street but never inside a door. This is one of many superstitions, which include not whistling indoors for fear of call-

ing little devils and not sitting at the corner of a table if one wishes to marry soon.

RELIGION

Religious Beliefs. Lithuania is mainly Roman Catholic (90 percent), with some Lutherans and a few members of other churches. The Jewish population, was almost completely erased between 1941 and 1944.

Religious Practitioners. The Catholic Studies Academy has over eight hundred members in Lithuania, and there are several seminaries and monasteries. Klaipėda University has a Lutheran Evangelical Theology Center that hosts about thirty monks. The Lithuanian Lutheran Youth Center and various Bible studies organizations serve religious practitioners and their patrons.

Rituals and Holy Places. One of the most significant holy places is the Hill of Crosses just north of Šiauliai on the road to Rīga, Latvia. The hill has hundreds of thousands of crosses brought by believers from throughout the country and around the world. Although the Soviets bulldozed the hill several times for its open violation of their anti-religious policy, the crosses always reappeared.

MEDICINE AND HEALTH CARE

The health care system, many of whose elements are left over from the Soviet regime, is a system of state hospitals, clinics, and smaller doctors' offices, with a growing number of private practitioners. People who go to public health clinics often face long lines and complain about the high prices of prescription drugs, but visits to the doctor are free.

Economic conditions have a significant influence on health; some families cannot afford to buy healthy foods or pay for prescription medicines. Doctors often are not paid on time because of lack of funds or cutbacks. While there are many doctors, they often face the problem of scarce resources. As a result, it is customary for patients to take a "gift" to the doctor to thank him for his services and ensure that he makes an effort to get the patient what he or she needs.

Many people prefer to use traditional home remedies that have been passed down for generations. Hot tea with honey or lemon, vodka, chamomile, and mustard plasters on the back are considered a sure cure for the common cold or the flu and cost far less than products available in phar-

A group of Lithuanians demonstrate for independence from the Soviet Union in 1989.

macies. Doctors make house calls, especially for older people and those living on the countryside.

SECULAR CELEBRATIONS

The Day of Remembrance of the Television Tower incident is celebrated on 13 January. Shrove Tuesday (*Užgavėnės*), the second Tuesday in February, is a Catholic feast day forty days before Easter, that has become popular with the nonreligious and is the Lithuanian equivalent of trick or treating. Children wear masks and go door to door singing a song that asks for pancakes and coffee. More elaborate celebrations involve the burning of an effigy of winter to welcome the spring. Independence Day is celebrated on 16 February. Saint Kazimier's Day on 4 March, originally was a religious holiday but now provides a reason to hold annual fairs at which vendors sell handicrafts. Every five years a national folk music festival takes place in honor of Saint Kazimier's Day. Reestablishment of Independence Day is celebrated on 11 March. Midsummer's Eve (Saint John's Day) on 24 June, celebrates the arrival of summer. The tradition includes running into the forest at night to search for fern blossoms. Legend holds that Midsummer's Eve is a night for young people to find a mate, and finding a fern blossom is a sign of great luck. Women and girls make wreaths

of flowers to be worn on their heads or floated down the river with candles. Celebrants dance around a campfire and jump over it to bid farewell to the cold season. Crowning of Mindaugas Day occurs on 6 July. The Day of Remembrance of the Molotov-Ribbentrop Pact is celebrated on 23 August.

Death and the Afterlife. Funeral practices in Lithuania take place in three phases. First, the deceased is formally dressed and laid out for a three-day, three-night viewing either at home or in a public venue. Family and friends keep watch and ensure that candles stay lit as people come to bring flowers—always in even numbers—and pay their respects. This is followed by a burial ceremony at a cemetery (cremation is not common), and a sit-down luncheon for all funeral attendants. The luncheon is a time for friends and family to share their memories of the deceased. It is common to visit the graves of loved ones at birthdays and on 1 November (All Souls' Day), when most cemeteries overflow with flowers and burning candles.

THE ARTS AND HUMANITIES

Support for the Arts. Many artists are self-supporting, but limited funding is available from the government. Some apply for foreign grant money,

A group of Lithuanian folk dancers and musicians perform in a Vilnius public square.

and many spend time in foreign countries studying or practicing their trade. There are strict laws on exporting cultural properties, and anyone who wishes to purchase or move cultural properties more than fifty years old must follow a detailed registration procedure.

Literature. *Chronicles of the Grand Duchy of Lithuania*, a historical treatise, marks the beginning of the national literature. Works in the Middle Ages were primarily religious, the first in Lithuanian being *Katekizmas* (the catechism). From the sixteenth to the eighteenth century, literature increased in popularity; Konstantinas Sirvydas printed the first Lithuanian language dictionary, and the Bible was translated into Lithuanian during that period.

Secular literature became more widespread in the eighteenth century. Kristijonas Donelaitis, considered the founder of Lithuanian literature, wrote *Metų Laikai (Seasons)*. at that time.

Literature in the early twentieth century was linked to the national independence movement. Writings were characterized by symbolism, romanticism, and existentialism. The Soviet occupation undermined the creativity of writers, many of whom fled to the West and wrote in secret. After World War II, there emerged a collection of literature describing experiences during the war. The most famous is *Dievų Miskas (Forest of the Gods)* by Balys Sruoga,which describes life in a concentration camp.

Poetry has also served as a means of expressing and sharing cultural heritage and has played a role in preserving the national identity.

Graphic Arts. Graphic and decorative art have been part of the cultural heritage for centuries. The Vilnius School of Art was established at the end of the eighteenth century, but handicrafts and religious art date much further back. Large carved wooden crosses and statues are seen throughout the countryside. They sometimes mark the boundaries of towns but often are set up for decoration or to mark the spot of the death of a loved one. Large collections of wooden statues appear in sculpture parks across the country.

Many towns have art galleries, museums, and handicraft shops to exhibit or sell works. Several international artist unions have Lithuanian branches, and artists often arrange personal shows outside the country.

Performance Arts. There are thirteen professional theaters, a National Opera Theater, several youth theaters, puppet theaters, state orchestras, and hundreds of choral groups. The Vilnius Quartet and the Rinkevičius Orchestra are well known throughout the country, and the Nekrošius Theater has won international acclaim. Folk music and dancing are the most popular performance arts, and there are thousands of folklore groups. Often schools and towns have their own groups that dress in traditional costume, travel, and perform or compete with groups from other locations. Attending theatrical and musical events is a reasonably priced and popular cultural activity.

THE STATE OF PHYSICAL AND SOCIAL SCIENCES

The Lithuanian Academy of Science is a major force in the physical and social sciences and was actively involved in the preservation of the national identity when scientific organizations were the only groups permitted to investigate and criticize existing social policies. It was a principal agent in the fight against opening an additional nuclear reactor at the Ignalina Power Plant in eastern Lithuania. The Academy of Science promotes physical and social science around the country. Twenty-four of the country's twenty-nine scientific institutes were founded by the academy, and scientists trained there work in all scientific fields.

Institutes of higher education play an important role in the development of the physical and social sciences and provide training and instruction for scientists. The Academy of Science and other institutions of higher learning receive funding from the state, but have become increasingly reliant on foreign grants and foundations.

BIBLIOGRAPHY

Ashbourne, Alexandra. *Lithuania: The Rebirth of a Nation, 1991–1994*, 1999.

Dawson, Jane I. *Eco-Nationalism: Anti-Nuclear Activism and National Identity in Russia, Lithuania, and Ukraine*, 1996.

Gerner, Kristian, and Stefan Hedlund. *The Baltic States and the End of the Soviet Empire*, 1993.

Girnius, Kestutis. "The Party and Popular Movements in the Baltic." In Jans Arves Trapans, ed. *Toward Independence: The Baltic Popular Movements*, 1991.

Hiden, John, and Patricia Salmon. *The Baltic Nations and Europe: Estonia, Latvia and Lithuania in the Twentieth Century*, 1991.

Krickus, Richard J. *Showdown: The Lithuanian Rebellion and the Breakup of the Soviet Empire*, 1997.

LaFont, Suzanne. *Women in Transition: Voices from Lithuania*, 1998.

Lithuanian Institute of Philosophy and Sociology. *Everday Life in the Baltic States*, 1997.

Norgaard, Ole, and Lars Johannsen with Mette Skak and Rene Hauge Sorensen. *The Baltic States after Independence*, 1996.

Oleszczuk, Thomas A. *Political Justice in the USSR: Dissent and Repression in Lithuania, 1969–1987*, 1988.

Suziedelis, Saulius. *Historical Dictionary of Lithuania*, 1997.

Vardys, V. Stanley, and Judith B. Sedaitis. *Lithuania: The Rebel Nation*, 1997.

Web Sites

Lithuanian Institute of Mathematics and Informatics. Lithuanian Homepage, http://neris.mii.lt

Ministry of Foreign Affairs of Lithuania "Welcome to the Ministry of Foreign Affairs of Lithuania," http://www.urm.lt, 2000.

United States Department of State. *Background Notes: Lithuania*, http://www.state.gov/www/background_notes/lithuania_0697_bgn.html

—COLEEN NICOL

LUXEMBOURG

CULTURE NAME

Luxembourger

ORIENTATION

Identification. The name of the nation derives from *Lucilinburhuc,* which in the local Germanic dialect meant "Little Fortress," referring to a small Roman castle on a rocky promontory overlooking the Alzette River.

Location and Geography. Luxembourg is one of the world's smallest sovereign states at 999 square miles (2,586 square kilometers). The triangle-shaped country borders Germany to the east, France to the south, and Belgium to the west. The most important influence on the nation's cultural traditions is its location between the French and Germanic culture realms.

The southern two-thirds, known as "the Good Land" (*Bon Pays* in French and *Gutland* in German), has rich sandy soil and one of Europe's major iron ore deposits, the basis of the country's wealth. The capital, Luxembourg City, where one-fifth of the people live, is in the *Bon Pays.* The northern third, called Eisléck (*Oesling* in French and *Osling* in German), is hilly and heavily forested and contains only 15 percent of the population.

Demography. The population increased from 281,000 in 1947 to 420,000 in 1997, a growth rate of about 1 percent per year. Underlying that growth was a dramatic shift in the ethnic composition of the population. The number of native-born Luxembourgers increased modestly from 262,000 in 1947 to 280,000 in 1997, because Luxembourgers have one of the world's lowest fertility rates, but the number of immigrants increased from 29,000 to 140,000.

The largest groups of immigrants came from Italy in the 1950s and 1960s and from Portugal beginning in the 1970s. In 1997, Portuguese ac-

counted for 13 percent of the population, Italians 5 percent, French 4 percent, Belgians 3 percent, Germans 2 percent, citizens of other European Union countries 3 percent, and citizens of other countries 3 percent. The percentage of native-born residents declined from 93 percent in 1947 to 67 percent in 1997.

Linguistic Affiliation. Language is the most important element of cultural identity for the native-born. Those residents speak, read, and write in French, German, and Luxembourgish (Lëtzebuergesch), switching between them effortlessly. The major newspaper publishes most international news in German, cultural features in French, and classified advertisements in Luxembourgish. The simultaneous use of three languages derives from a combination of historical tradition and economic necessity.

Native residents speak Luxembourgish to each other, and that is the first language infants learn to speak at home. Classified as a Moselle-Franconian dialect of German, Luxembourgish was enriched during the Middle Ages with so many French words and phrases that it is no longer understood by Germans. Traditionally, Luxembourgish was rarely written, and no official rules of spelling and grammar existed until they were established by the government in 1984. Older Luxembourgers suddenly found themselves accused of making spelling and grammatical errors.

As the major language most easily understood by native Luxembourgers, German is the principal language of instruction in elementary school, although children speak Luxembourgish in the playground. Beginning in the second grade, French is taught as a subject, although instruction is still principally in German. Over the years, French becomes more important and by high school replaces German as the language of instruction, with German limited to specialized courses in language and literature.

Luxembourg

the language of school instruction in higher grades, using German can be taken as a sign of limited education. Also, older Luxembourgers recall the German occupation during World War II, when they were forced to speak German, and have passed on their memories to later generations. However, in their homes, Luxembourgers are more likely to watch television programs in German than those in French.

Symbolism. The national motto, *Mir wëlle bleiwe, war mir sin,* means "We want to remain what we are." That accurately captures the two dominant goals of contemporary society: protection from linguistic or other imperialism on the part of its more powerful French and German neighbors and protection from economic and political instability that would threaten the country's prosperity and extremely high standard of living.

The national anthem consists of the first and last verses of the song *Ons Heemecht* ("Our Fatherland"). Written in 1864, immediately before the nation gained full sovereignty, the anthem calls for peace.

The flag has three horizontal stripes of red (on the top), white, and blue (on the bottom). It is virtually identical to the flag of the Netherlands except for a slightly different blue shading (sky blue instead of ultramarine). In the nineteenth century, Luxembourg and the Netherlands had the same monarch.

HISTORY AND ETHNIC RELATIONS

Emergence of the Nation. The modern independent state is a nineteenth-century creation, but national identity developed when Luxembourg was an independent duchy between 963 and 1443 C.E. Sigefroi (Siegfried), count of Ardennes, bought the area in 963 from the Abbey of Saint Maximin in Trier and built a fortress on the site of the Roman castle. The nation's links with Germanic culture strengthened during the five centuries of independence, especially in the fourteenth century, when Luxembourg's dukes also ruled the German-centered Holy Roman Empire and the national territory extended as far east as the present-day Czech Republic.

Luxembourg was conquered in 1443 by Philip the Good, duke of Burgundy. That conquest brought Luxembourgers closer to French culture and severed their links with Germany. French became the language of official business and the one preferred by the elite. Luxembourg experienced four

French is the principal language for government legislation and speeches. Street names, shop signs, and menus are written in French, and it is preferred by the more educated, intellectual elite. French is also the lingua franca used to communicate with immigrants, most of whom already know another Romance language.

Although their language is closer to German than to French, Luxembourgers are reluctant to speak German. Because French replaces German as

centuries of foreign occupation, primarily by Spain, Austria, and France. The fortress was coveted for its strategic position.

The 1815 Congress of Vienna, ending the Napoleonic wars, designated Luxembourg a grand duchy, and awarded it to William I, prince of Orange-Nassau, who was also made the first king of the Netherlands. Luxembourg's territory was reduced to its current size when the Congress of Vienna transferred the land east of the Our, Sûre, and Moselle rivers to Prussia and the western half joined Belgium in a successful revolt against the Netherlands in 1830. The portion remaining under William's control was forced to join the German Confederation, a union of monarchies dominated by Austria and Prussia, and to let Prussian soldiers occupy its fortress.

Luxembourg gained independence during the 1860s. The German Confederation was dissolved in 1866, and after the 1867 Treaty of London, Prussia withdrew from the fortress and accepted Luxembourg as a neutral country.

The final step in the emergence of a fully independent country was the accession of different monarchs for Luxembourg and the Netherlands in 1890. William I (r. 1815–1840), William II (1840–1849), and William III (1849–1890) ruled both countries, but when William III died, his only child, Wilhemina, became queen only of the Netherlands, whereas Adolphe, head of another branch of the house of Nassau, became grand duke of Luxembourg. In 1783, the Nassau family had agreed that no woman would become a monarch, and in 1815, the Congress of Vienna decided to apply that rule to Luxembourg but not to the Netherlands. In the twentieth century, though, Luxembourg had two female monarchs: Marie-Adelïde (1912–1919), who was the granddaughter of Adolphe (1890–1905) and the only daughter of William IV (1905–1912) and Charlotte (1919–1964).

National Identity. A strong national identity beyond speaking Luxembourgish resulted primarily from two German invasions in the twentieth century. During World War I, Grand Duchess Marie-Adelaïde incurred the wrath of her subjects by tolerating the occupation. In 1919, she was forced to abdicate in favor of her sister, Grand Duchess Charlotte. A few months later, Luxembourgers voted to retain the monarchy while extending democratic privileges, including universal suffrage.

When Germany again invaded in 1940, Grand Duchess Charlotte instilled national unity by refus-

ing to collaborate with the Nazis, instead fleeing to London until the Allies liberated the country in September 1944. The last major German offensive of World War II, the Battle of the Bulge, was fought largely in Luxembourg. Charlotte abdicated in favor of her son, Grand Duke Jean, 1964, and she died in 1985.

Ethnic Relations. Ethnic relations are dominated by large-scale immigration from southern Europe. The earlier Italian immigrants are well integrated into society, and many families have hyphenated last names that combine Italian and Luxembourgish names. The more recent Portuguese immigrants are less well integrated, although Luxembourg has not had the level of ethnic tensions seen in neighboring countries.

URBANISM, ARCHITECTURE, AND THE USE OF SPACE

The dominant public space is the medieval fortress built on Bock promontory. Portions remain of Sigefroi's castle built in 963, as well as archaeological evidence from ancient Gallic encampments and Roman outposts. In the seventeenth and eighteenth centuries, when the nation was occupied by the Spanish, French, and Austrians, increasingly elaborate fortifications were constructed on the promontory, and Luxembourg became known as the "Gibraltar of the North." Carved inside the cliff was a fourteen-mile (twenty-three-kilometer) maze of tunnels for underground defense, known as casemates.

When the Prussians withdrew in 1867, the fortifications were larger than the city of Luxembourg. No longer serving a military purpose, most of the fortifications were demolished in the late nineteenth century. During the 1930s though, eleven miles (seventeen kilometers) of casemates and some of the aboveground fortifications were restored as parks and museums. The restored fortifications are the most prominent feature in contemporary "skyline" photographs of the city.

Homes in the historic, central area are typically narrow two- or three-story row houses. Those originally built for wealthier families are more ornate than those originally occupied by working-class families. Older homes in smaller towns and villages, and newer ones in the suburbs, are freestanding, but relatively close together. Outside these houses are well-kept gardens, as well as space to park cars.

The Echternach marketplace in Luxembourg.

FOOD AND ECONOMY

Food in Daily Life. Luxembourg cuisine is said to combine the finesse of French cooking with the heartiness of German food. More recently, it has been inspired by the cuisine of Italian and Portuguese immigrants. Traditional Luxembourgers consume a small French-style breakfast and large meals at midday and in the evening.

Food Customs at Ceremonial Occasions. Specialties include *Judd matt Gaardeboùnen* (smoked collar of pork with broad beans), *thuringer* (small sausages), Luxembourg ham (smoke-cured), *friture de la Moselle* (small deep-fried river fish), pike in Riesling sauce, *gromper keeschelche* (potato pancakes), *kach keis* (soft melted cheese), paté, and *quetsche tort* (plum tart). Special dishes are consumed on national and religious holidays, as well as on Sunday afternoons. After consuming these large meals, Luxembourgers are fond of taking walks in the country, along well-marked trails.

Well-regarded dry white wine is produced from Reisling grapes grown on the east-facing slopes of the Moselle River, across from Germany. Luxembourg also produces *eaux-de-vie*, or plum brandies, made from *mirabelle* (yellow plums) and *quetsch* (purple plums).

Basic Economy. Luxembourgers have a saying, "Just as Egypt is a gift of the Nile, Luxembourg is a gift of iron." For centuries, the country sat atop a large field of iron ore that contained too much phosphorous to be made into high-quality steel, but in 1877 the British engineer Thomas Gilchrist invented a method of removing phosphorous during the smelting process. Steel production dominated the economy for nearly a century and transformed a very poor, mostly agricultural society into one of the world's wealthiest industrialized countries. At its peak, the steel industry employed one-fourth of the workforce and generated two-thirds of exports, but when world demand for steel plummeted in the 1970s, three-fourths of the steelworkers were laid off. The iron ore fields were closed in 1981, and the surviving steel industry makes specialized products with imported ore.

The loss of the steel industry did not plunge Luxembourg into economic disaster. In the 1970s and 1980s, the country became one of Europe's most important financial services centers. Luxembourg had two hundred thirty-three banks in the 1990s—compared with only seventeen in 1960—as well as seven thousand holding companies and 1,300 investment fund operations. Financial institutions were attracted by the low tax rates and strict privacy laws. Luxembourg also houses a number of European organizations, including the general secretariat of the European Parliament, the European Union's statistical and publications offices and court of justice, the European Investment Bank, and the European Court of Auditors.

Land Tenure and Property. Luxembourgers place a high value on owning property and the protection of private property rights.

Commercial Activities. With the large decline in the steel industry and the growth in financial and European institutions since the 1970s, most citizens are now employed in services. In 1993, 68 percent of the workforce was in services, 29 percent in manufacturing, and 3 percent in agriculture.

Major Industries. The major steel producer Arbed (Acieries Réunies de Burbach-Eich-Dudelange) is a transnational corporation with headquarters in Luxembourg City and factories in seven other countries. Somewhat offsetting the loss of steel jobs, several transnational corporations have built factories. The manufacture of chemicals, rubber, and plastic products has increased.

Trade. Because of its large number of financial services, Luxembourg has a strongly positive international trade balance. Other European Union countries—primarily the three neighboring countries of Belgium, France, and Germany—account for 61 percent of exports and 74 percent of imports.

Division of Labor. One-half of the workers are foreign, about equally divided among immigrants living in the country and commuters from Belgium, France, and Germany. Immigrants hold a large percentage of jobs in construction and minimally skilled services, whereas commuters work in financial services and international institutions.

SOCIAL STRATIFICATION

Classes and Castes. The most fundamental social division is between native Luxembourgers and foreign-born residents. Portuguese immigrants are likely to hold lower-status jobs such as street cleaning, bus driving, and restaurant waiting.

Symbols of Social Stratification. The major symbol of social class difference is the language spoken and understood at home. Native Luxembourgers address each other and their families in Luxembourgish but switch to French, German, or English to talk with foreigners.

POLITICAL LIFE

Government. Luxembourg is a representative democracy within a constitutional hereditary monarchy. The grand duke or duchess, the ceremonial head of state, appoints the prime minister, who is responsible to a sixty-member Chamber of Deputies that is popularly elected every five years.

Leadership and Political Officials. The three principal political parties are the right-leaning Christian Social Party (PCS), the left-leaning Socialist Workers' Party (POSL), and the centrist Democratic Party (PD). The government is nearly always a coalition of the conservative PCS and one of the two more progressive parties.

The most influential informal decision-making bodies are three councils: *le Conseil d'Etat* (council of state), *le Conseil économique et social* (economic and social council), and *les chambres professionnelles* (confederation of employers and unions). Former ministers and business, labor, and other civic leaders are appointed to these councils, which are consulted before legislation is enacted affecting their areas of national life.

Social Problems and Control. The legal system is strongly influenced by French practice. The highest court is the *Cour Superieure de Justice* (Superior Court of Justice). Judges are appointed for life by the grand duke. The crime rate is extremely low, and civil disorders are unknown.

Military Activity. Luxembourg is an active member of the North Atlantic Treaty Organization (NATO). It spends 0.8 percent of the gross domestic (GDP) on defense and has a volunteer army of about eight hundred active soldiers.

SOCIAL WELFARE AND CHANGE PROGRAMS

About one-third of GDP is spent on social welfare programs; this is one of the world's most generous systems. About half that spending is on pensions, one-fourth on health insurance, and one-fourth on disability payments. With only five thousand unemployed people, spending for unemployment compensation is low.

GENDER ROLES AND STATUSES

Division of Labor by Gender. In principle, women have full political and economic equality. The percentage of women active in the labor force has increased rapidly, but the country has a lower female labor force participation rate than do other

Two men harvest potatoes on a farm. Luxembourgers place a high value on owning property and protecting property rights.

developed countries: only 43 percent among citizens and 54 percent among foreigners.

Few women are compelled by economic necessity to seek employment, and housework is counted as employment in determining social security and other benefits. Because of the very low birthrate, women citizens are torn between child rearing and working outside the home. The main impetus for the growth in female labor force participation is a desire for more independence and equality and less social isolation.

The Relative Status of Women and Men. Older women wield considerable informal authority, in part because they constitute a high percentage of the population: About 12 percent of native-born Luxembourgers are women over age 65. Older women have a large percentage of the national wealth and provide their middle-aged children with considerable financial support, such as assistance in buying a house. In the afternoon, the streets are filled with older women heading for the bakeries to consume coffee and pastry with friends.

MARRIAGE, FAMILY, AND KINSHIP

Marriage. Marriage rates have dropped sharply in recent years. One-third of couples who live together are unmarried, one-seventh of the children are born to unmarried mothers, and one-third of marriages end in divorce. All these practices were rare a generation ago.

Domestic Unit. Although the older generation controls much of the family wealth, three-generation households have become much less common than they were in the past. Older women who cannot live independently are more likely to move into expensive, comfortable retirement homes than to move in with one of their children.

Inheritance. Inheritance laws do not induce early divesting of an estate to heirs, and so older people hold on to their wealth until they die. Because Luxembourg has had a very low birthrate for a long time, an inheritance is typically divided among a small number of children, but with high life expectancy, most middle-aged and even retired people have living parents.

SOCIALIZATION

Infant Care. Among the native-born, the birth of a baby is a relatively rare event at about three thousand per year, several hundred less than the number of deaths. An extensive publicly supported network of day care centers is available for the 50 percent of

Harvesters pick wine grapes in a vineyard in Wellenstein.

mothers who work outside the home. Nearly half the babies are born to foreigners, and they are entitled to the same maternity and day care as the native-born population.

Child Rearing and Education. People are taught to be prudent, careful, responsible, and practical. Creativity and expressiveness are not emphasized. An infant is not a constant center of attention, and parents are not obsessed with twenty-four-hour catering to a child's whims. Regular mealtimes and other activities are not disrupted by the arrival of a child.

Higher Education. There is no university. Because French is the principal language of instruction in secondary school, Luxembourgers are more likely to attend a university in France or Belgium than in Germany.

ETIQUETTE

Luxembourgers regard their cultural values as deriving primarily from their French rather than their German neighbors. However, they do not admire the spontaneity of Latin culture. Punctuality is expected at meetings, social activities, and cultural events.

RELIGION

Religious Beliefs. About 97 percent of the people are Roman Catholics. Native-born Luxembourgers are overwhelmingly Roman Catholic, as are most immigrants from Italy and Portugal.

MEDICINE AND HEALTH CARE

Like other European countries, Luxembourg has a free and universal national health insurance system.

SECULAR CELEBRATIONS

The public holidays are a mix of Christian and secular dates, such as Christmas, New Year's, and May Day. Luxembourg celebrates National Day on 23 June as the sovereign's official birthday. The night before (22 June) is festive, with torchlight parades, fireworks, music, and parties. National Day is more ceremonial, including military parades, cannonades, and a "Te Deum" sung in the national cathedral.

THE ARTS AND HUMANITIES

Support for the Arts. The major supporter of the arts is the Grand Ducal Institute, which promotes work in languages and folklore, arts and literature, history, natural science, medicine, and moral and political sciences.

Literature. Luxembourg lacks a distinctive literary tradition because of the absence of spelling and grammatical rules and the limited vocabulary and grammar constructions of Luxembourgish. Thus, writers are more likely to work in genres, such as poetry and plays, that are meant to be spoken rather than read silently. The major writers, including the essayist Marcel Noppeney (1877–1966) and the poet Michel Rodange (1827–1876), have invariably used French or German.

French books and publications are widely read, and Luxembourg's periodicals, literary reviews, and magazines aimed at intellectuals are almost always written in French. Luxembourgers writing in French are better able to compose essays and scientific tracts than to write novels.

Because Luxembourgish is essentially a German dialect, writers in German are able to weave in local phrases and sentiments that are meaningful in Luxembourgish, although "pure" German would discourage such colloquialisms. However, the discomfort of Luxembourgers with the German language discourages its widespread use.

Graphic Arts. Luxembourg lacks internationally prominent graphic artists, and its principal museums—the National Museum of History and Art and the Museum of History of the City of Luxembourg—emphasize history and artifacts rather than graphic arts. Contemporary artists are represented at the Musée d'Art Moderne Grand-Duc Jean.

Performance Arts. Luxembourg has had a degree of influence in modern communications media. Radiotelevision Luxembourg (RTL), a privately owned company, transmits radio programs in five languages and television programs in French and German. RTL first developed a large audience in the 1960s, when it was the only major station in Europe that played pop music. RTL also supports the major orchestra, the Grand Orchestra of Radiotelevision Luxembourg.

BIBLIOGRAPHY

Als, Georges. *Les femmes et l'économie*, 1983.

———. *Luxembourg Historical, Geographical and Economic Profile*, 1980.

———. *Les mutations de l'économie luxembourgeoise*, 1983.

Barteau, Harry C. *Historical dictionary of Luxembourg*, 1996.

A Brief Survey of the City of Luxembourg, 1982.

Christophory, Jul. *Who's Afraid of Luxembourgish? Lëtzebuergesch? Qui a peur du Luxembourgeois?* 1979.

——— and Emile Thoma. *Luxembourg*, 1997.

Clark, Peter. *Luxembourg*, 1994.

Glaesener, Jean-Pierre. *Le Grand-Duchy de Luxembourg, historique et pittoresque*, 1985.

Maertz, Joseph. *Luxemburg in der Ardennenoffensive, 1944/45*, 1981.

Margue, P., et al. *Luxembourg*, 1984.

Newcomer, James. *The Grand Duchy of Luxembourg: The Evolution of Nationhood, 963 A.D. to 1983*, 1984.

Newton, Gerald, ed. *Luxembourg & Lëtzebuergesch: Language and Communication at the Crossroads of Europe*, 1996.

—JAMES M. RUBENSTEIN

MACAU

CULTURE NAME

Macanese

ALTERNATIVE NAMES

Macao, Aomen, Haijing Ao

ORIENTATION

Identification. Macau is a city in southern China's Guangdong province, and was until 20 December 1999 an overseas Portuguese territory, founded in 1557. It is now a special administrative region within the People's Republic of China, which agreed to recognize the city's special social and economic system for a period of fifty years.

Macau's status as an outpost of European settlement and commerce in China and its air of isolation gave it a special historical identity. Its population, while politically dominated by the Portuguese and their descendants, was always marked by an admixture of groups and by a steady influx of Chinese migrants. Since the early nineteenth century the majority of the population was Chinese. Macau was located on the old "silk route" and emerged as a major *entrepôt* (intermediary) trading center in Southeast Asia in the seventeenth and eighteenth centuries.

The name Macau is derived from the Chinese A-ma-gao Bay of A-Ma. A-ma was the name of a Chinese goddess, popular with the Chinese seafarers and fishermen who had a temple on the peninsula when the Portuguese first anchored there in 1513.

As a creation of the Portuguese, Macau represents a peculiar blend of Oriental and Western influences. This has given rise to a unique and hybrid urban culture, which gives the city an air of romance and nostalgia. At present, it is a rich commercial and industrialized city. Macau also has a reputation, dating from the 1920s and 1930s, as a place of smuggling, gambling, prostitution, and crime controlled by Chinese "triads" (crime syndicates). Macau's gambling houses were (and are) famous across Asia and still form a popular (Chinese) tourist destination.

Location and Geography. Macau is located on a small peninsula and lies at the western shore of the great Pearl River Delta, opposite Hong Kong. Together with its two islands, Taipa and Coloane (connected to the peninsula by large bridges), it measures only some 8.5 square miles (22 square kilometers). Before inclusion into China in December 1999, Macau was separated from the mainland by the Barrier Gate (Portas do Cêrco) frontier. The city has good air links, and ferry and hydrofoil service to the neighboring islands, the mainland, and Hong Kong. A large international airport was opened in 1995.

There is no flora and fauna to speak of, as buildings have filled up most of the available space, and most primeval forest was used for construction and industrial purposes. Some pine forest remains on Coloane. In the late twentieth century significant land reclamation projects were carried out around the peninsula, creating space for new housing and industries, thus doubling the surface area of the city. The climate of Macau is subtropical and humid.

Demography. The city's population is about 465,000 (1999), with 95 percent ethnic Chinese. The Portuguese comprise about 3 percent of the population, with the rest including other Europeans, Indians, and various other groups, such as Filipinos. Immigration from China's mainland has always been significant, fueled by the opportunities of Macau's international trade and dynamic urban economy (especially in the twentieth century there was an exponential growth of immigration). At present, population growth is about 1.8 percent annually. Fertility (1.27 children per woman) is low according to Asian standards. Almost 50 percent of the ethnic Chinese population was born outside

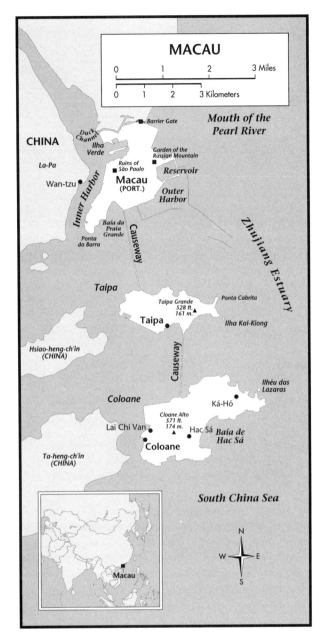

MACAU

0   1   2   3 Miles

0   1   2   3 Kilometers

CHINA

Duck Channel

Ilha Verde

Barrier Gate

Mouth of the Pearl River

La-Pa

Garden of the Russian Mountain

Ruins of São Paulo

Macau (PORT.)

Reservoir

Wan-tzu

Outer Harbor

Inner Harbor

Baía da Praia Grande

Ponta da Barra

Causeway

Zhujiang Estuary

Taipa

Taipa Grande 528 ft. 161 m.

Ponta Cabrita

Taipa

Ilha Kai-Kiong

Hsiao-heng-ch'in (CHINA)

Causeway

Ilhéu das Lazaras

Coloane

Ká-Hó

Cloane Alto 571 ft. 174 m.

Lai Chi Van

Hac Sá

Baía de Hac Sá

Coloane

Ta-heng-ch'in (CHINA)

South China Sea

N
W   E
S

Macau

Macau

Macau, but about 90 percent of the Portuguese were born in Macau.

Linguistic Affiliation. Indigenous languages spoken are Chinese-Cantonese (Yue dialect and Min dialects, about 96 percent of the population) and Portuguese (about 4 percent). Beijing-Chinese (Putonghua dialect) is a second language and growing in influence (for example, it is used in education). English is also expanding as a language in commerce and tourism. The old Macanese language (Patuá, or Makista) was a typical Creole language, based on Portuguese but heavily influenced by vari-

ous Chinese dialects and by Malay. It has now virtually died out.

Symbolism. The coat of arms of Macau shows two angels around a shield with a crown, one holding a cross and one holding a globe. Beneath is the motto; ''City of the Name of God, there is none more loyal,'' which refers to Macau's Catholic identity and bond with the Portuguese motherland. What the status of this coat of arms will be under Chinese rule is unclear.

As unofficial emblems or symbols of the town one might see the casino as the emblem of ''modernity'' (giving the city its main income), and the lone facade of Saint Paul's Cathedral as an apt symbol of Macau's past. This façade, a typical Portuguese structure, is the only remnant of an impressive Catholic church destroyed by fire in the eighteenth century. It may symbolize the near token presence of Portuguese culture in a now predominantly Chinese city that owes the larger part of its wealth to the Chinese fascination with gambling and to the efforts of Chinese businessmen and laborers.

HISTORY AND ETHNIC RELATIONS

Emergence of the Nation. Although Portuguese sailors first anchored in 1513 and started using the peninsula for provisioning, Macau as a town was founded in 1557. It was a fixed point on the trade route to the Far East.

Macau always self-consciously maintained its bond with Portugal, even in times of war and turbulence. Religious identity played a great part in this. The city was a foothold for the Jesuits in their efforts to spread the gospel in Japan and China, though without much success. Beginning in the sixteenth century, other groups such as British Protestants, Japanese, and Indians also settled in Macau in small numbers.

Macau thus emerged as a Portuguese colonial settlement with a European-Christian identity, but as a result of its allowing Chinese immigration and settlement from early on, acquired a mixed character. Due to its open, commercial character and its weak military position vis-à-vis China, there was never any exclusivist policy or national identity, though its political adherence was to Portugal.

Macau-Chinese relations were occasionally tense but never violent. Macau's historical status contrasts with that of Hong Kong, which was forced by Britain from China in an unfair treaty and under the threat of violence.

In 1887, Portugal by treaty received full sovereignty over Macau from China. This was reversed exactly one century later by a new treaty, ceding Macau to China.

National Identity. Macau is a peculiar amalgam of Portuguese and Chinese culture. This is evident in its rich and remarkable architecture, economic activities, and demography, as well as its political culture. Imperial, and later communist, China never gave up its claims to Macau as ultimately a part of China, but its relations toward Macau (and the Portuguese-Macanese attitude toward the Chinese) were marked by pragmatism, laissez-faire, and cooperation, a policy that was in tune with Macau's exceptional position as a hub of economic and commercial activity on the frontier of two worlds. The Chinese in Macau never clamored for inclusion into China (indeed, many came to Macau from the mainland as political and economic refugees) but did not protest when it became inevitable. They acquired, however, a distinguishable identity as Macanese-Chinese vis-à-vis the rest of China's people, though this will inevitably fade after the handing over of Macau.

Ethnic Relations. Ethnic relations in Macau, though hierarchical and rooted in a colonial relationship, developed into a largely harmonious and relaxed pattern. Major tensions did occur when China interfered in the internal affairs of the city, as happened occasionally in the nineteenth century and in 1966, during the Cultural Revolution, when there were Chinese-inspired pro-communist riots.

Throughout its history, Macau always received people from many places, either forced (slaves from Africa) or voluntary (Indians, Malay, Filipinos). It also was a hospitable place for refugees, as most evident before and during World War II, when the Japanese offensives drove some 160,000 people (mainly Chinese) to the city, and after 1949, when the communists took over in China.

URBANISM, ARCHITECTURE, AND THE USE OF SPACE

The old urban architecture of Macau is one of the most attractive features of the city. Macau was built by the Portuguese, but the Mediterranean-European designs were always given an Oriental slant in actual building, and the Chinese made their own contribution in the form of shrines, temples, and Chinese gardens. The combination has charmed almost all visitors to the place; Macau's historical old city, its churches, forts, statues, parks, monuments, and government palaces give the city a ro-

A woman working on a toy car. The toy industry plays a prominent role in Macau's economy.

mantic character. But this unique architecture is now also under threat, because massive modernization, population growth, and urban renewal have led to the demolishing and crowding out of many old buildings and neighborhoods. Before and after the handover of Macau to China, several statues and landmarks disappeared (some of them were even shipped to Portugal). Macau is one of the most densely built-up urban areas in the world. Environmental pollution is a growing problem.

FOOD AND ECONOMY

Food in Daily Life. The Macanese cuisine is a much-praised mixture of Portuguese and Mediterranean cooking with some Indian and African influence (as people from Portugal's African colonies also came to Macau). Chinese influence was not pervasive. Macanese cuisine is popular among the Chinese population, and also outside Macau's boundaries, such as in Hong Kong.

Basic Economy. Macau is a rich city, with per capita gross domestic product (GDP) of US$17,500. It was built on entrepôt trade, gambling, and port services. These activities are still very important, despite the fact that the city also has developed into a major industrial center. Of growing significance is

Macau's role as a center of financial services, both legal and illegal. Its status as a free port, its low taxes, the absence of foreign exchange controls, its flexible corporate laws, and its long experience in commerce and financial dealing make it an ideal place for uncontrolled, often criminal business schemes. Its relaxed system of governance has traditionally condoned this. There is a large "informal" unregistered sector.

Macau's economy has always been strongly dependent on ties with China and especially Hong Kong. Macau imports virtually all its food items (and even its water) from the Chinese mainland. China in turn derives great benefit from Macau, using it as a gateway to the capitalist world through which it imports and launders huge sums of unregistered money. This aspect of Macau's economy makes it a growing concern for global financial institutions and for the United States, which has identified Macau as a major center of money laundering and financial crime. Organized crime groups have a significant, but not clearly recorded, hold on Macau's economy. Corruption and bureaucratic red tape are a problem.

Land Tenure and Property. Most land is private property and owned by large business syndicates and individuals. Land prices are high due to great scarcity. The Chinese were allowed to acquire property in 1793. Since the 1920s there have been ongoing efforts at land reclamation, financed by both the government and private capital.

Commercial Activities. Macau's economy is based on commerce, import-export, tourism, and gambling (the latter accounting for about 25 percent of GDP), and expanding industrial production. Gambling brings in some 55 percent of the city government's revenue. Still, Macau has an aura of a city not only of casinos but also of shady business deals and financial crime. There are strong indications that China uses Macau as a major conduit of money laundering and unrecorded import-export transactions. Other tourist-related activities are horse, dog, and car races (the Grand Prix of Macau).

Major Industries. After the decline of its port, Macau succeeded in quickly reorienting its economy towards industrialization. Prominent industries include textiles, footwear, toys, incense, machinery, enamel, firecrackers, wooden furniture, Chinese wines, and electronic goods. Small and medium-sized businesses play a remarkably large role.

The tourism industry, centered around the twenty four-hour-a-day casinos, is of great impor-

tance, as are prostitution and racketeering. Through these activities the city had already become notorious in the late eighteenth century, with an upsurge in the 1920s and 1930s. Tourism declined somewhat in the late twentieth century.

Trade. International trade was the mainstay of Macau as a free port, and has been important until recently. Its first fortunes were made on the Europe-Japan trade route. Macau is a major importer of goods from China (food, textiles, clothing, electronics, and cheap consumer goods). Some of these are reexported.

Division of Labor. The Portuguese were active in the political administration, the higher civil service, and the army and police; the Macanese were mainly in the professions, in trade, and in some businesses; and the Chinese in business, casinos, fishing, crafts, manual labor, and other trade activities.

SOCIAL STRATIFICATION

Classes and Castes. Macau is largely a Chinese society, though significantly influenced by the specific urban culture and its Portuguese elite. During colonial times, there was a basic stratification in three groups: Portuguese (a small minority of "pure" Portuguese, often immigrants sent or appointed from Portugal), Macanese (a Creole group, some claiming descent from the original Portuguese-Malay unions), and Chinese (within this group there was a complex substratification). There was a prestige ranking of these groups and a certain amount of ethnic-"racial" prejudice, evident at critical social moments, such as choosing a marriage partner.

Economically speaking, the Portuguese were the original dominant class in Macau, although the Chinese, by virtue of their business success and connections with the mainland, soon came to form a powerful stratum. Following the December 1999 handover, the Portuguese political elite has been receding from the administration and government services. Chinese are becoming more prominent in the leading strata of Macanese society. The Portuguese have seemed to close their ranks, although the Macanese are in a more vulnerable position due to the pull of Chinese culture. Business and financial institutions are largely controlled by a small Chinese elite. In Macau's strongly commercial-capitalist economy there is a definite class structure based on wealth and business interests.

Symbols of Social Stratification. Dress, diet, and leisure activities distinguished the various groups from each other. According to social and community background (Portugese, Chinese and Macanese), people of the city visibly differentiate themselves by their religious behavior, leisure activities, and manner of dress, but wealth and social status have cut across any easy "ethnic" identification. Elite groups tend more to resemble each other, sharing smart western clothing, choice of the better residential areas, and leisure activities like attending horse and greyhound races and clubs, literary-cultural activities, and international traveling. In terms of diet, Portugese and other culinary traditions have to some extent mingled in Macau, but their essentials remained distinct and are still a mark of difference if not "identity" among the various communities.

POLITICAL LIFE

Government. Until December 1999, Macau was ruled by a Portuguese governor, appointed from Lisbon, and assisted by a Legislative Assembly of twenty-three members (citizens and officials). One-third of these were directly elected by the populace, and the rest were either appointed or "chosen" by business interest groups. There was also a ten-member Consultative Council, an advisory body.

Under Chinese rule and the new Basic Law (a temporary constitution, promulgated by the China's National People's Congress in 1993, and instituted in Macau in 1999), there is a chief executive, chosen in a complicated procedure. The Legislative Assembly remained, and was by law accorded sole legislative power. In practice, however, the chief executive has the decisive role. The Basic Law also gave citizens a large number of civic, social, and economic rights. But there was no significant expansion of democratic political rights.

Portuguese law codes still are at the basis of Macau's legal system, and the judiciary is held to be independent. There is a three-tier court system topped by a Supreme Court.

Leadership and Political Officials. The last Portuguese-appointed governor was general Vasco J. Rocha Vieira. In December 1999, Edmundo Ho Hau-Wah (a prominent and well-connected businessman, educated in Canada) assumed the top post of chief executive of Macau. There are no political parties.

Social Problems and Control. There are problems of organized crime, prostitution, trafficking in women, gang wars, and financial crime. Such crimes as assault, rape, and burglary are rare, but kidnappings, stabbings, and homicides frequently occur in the criminal world of the competing triads. The legal environment of Macau is not tight enough to allow the effective combating of organized crime—the traditional attractiveness of the city (and its wealth) is explained by its record of condoning loopholes in economic and financial laws.

Military Activity. Macau was a fortified city, with its own Portuguese army and city forts, that were built in the seventeenth century after a 1622 Dutch naval attack and reinforced after Chinese and British threats to the city. The army was also active against Chinese pirates that infested the Pearl River Delta beginning in the late sixteenth century. In 1975 the military were withdrawn and an internal security force of forty-six hundred men took its place. Since the 1999 handover, a Chinese army garrison of one thousand has been stationed in Macau, but it officially has no role to play in internal security.

SOCIAL WELFARE AND CHANGE PROGRAMS

Existing programs in this field—support for orphans, the handicapped, and the aged; refugee care; social work—all have their origins in Christian religions institutions and missionary societies. In addition to the Church foundations, the government has also developed social safety-net provisions.

NONGOVERNMENTAL ORGANIZATIONS AND OTHER ASSOCIATIONS

There are many cultural and nongovernmental organizations in Macau, devoted to charity, public monuments, heritage preservation, and cultural life. Some of these are financed by prominent businessmen.

GENDER ROLES AND STATUSES

Division of Labor by Gender. Women are more and more active in business (forming about 43 percent of the workforce), but are not well-represented in political life. Chinese women in particular are taking their place in public and business life.

The Relative Status of Women and Men. Women and men are equal before the law, and in all private and public organizations must receive equal pay for equal work. In recent years, there were no court cases concerning sex discrimination. There are no significant social or cultural barriers to the partici-

A family relaxing on a rooftop overlooking the cityscape. Despite continued Chinese dependence on larger, extended families, the nuclear family is most pervasive in Macau.

pation of women in society. Violence against women is not reported much. Among the Chinese and other Asian groups, women were subject to many more restrictions than among the Portuguese and other European groups, but this has changed due to economic developments.

MARRIAGE, FAMILY, AND KINSHIP

Marriage. The three subcommunities of Macau—the Portuguese, Macanese, and Chinese—have traditionally intermingled, but as the population grew and the Chinese population became more predominant, intermarriage declined. The Portuguese and Macanese had formal monogamous marriage, while the Chinese also engaged in polygamous unions until the 1940s (depending on the economic situation of the husband). Weddings are important and costly occasions for celebration in both the Portuguese and Chinese communities.

Domestic Unit. Among the Chinese, the extended family, based on lineage connections, remains important; among Portuguese and Macanese, the nuclear family is the common domestic unit. Macau's capitalist economic development contributed to the nuclear family becoming the dominant form of domestic unit among all groups. In recent years, many young people live alone and/or marry late.

Inheritance. Inheritance still follows an adapted form of Portuguese law, but recognition is given to Chinese customary law on succession and family matters. Under Chinese rule, only laws approved by Macau's legislative and legal bodies are accepted, not Portuguese "imported" laws.

Kin Groups. Among the Chinese, lineage membership (with an emphasis on the father's side), and occasionally clan identity, remain important elements in social and ritual life. Lineages and extended kin (with some relatives often remaining in the Chinese area of origin) provided the moral framework of economic activity for the Chinese migrants. In Chinese business careers in Macau, the role of relatives on the mother's side has increased, indicating a development away from patrilineal orientation towards bilateral relationships: appealing to relatives from both father's and mother's as a resource.

SOCIALIZATION

Infant Care. Children are cared for in the family tradition of their community. In the Chinese community, this means the extended family participates in child rearing.

Child Rearing and Education. Formal schooling is growing in importance as a framework of socialization. The school system is partly run by the government and partly in private hands (also subsidized by the city government). Education levels in Macau are still relatively low. About 25 percent of the population has secondary education, and less than 5 percent go to college. Education is compulsory up to only five years of primary school, though nine years of state education are provided free of charge. Parents show high levels of ambition for their children. There is an increasing demand for schooling, which has led to overcrowding. The overall literacy rate is about 90 percent (slightly less for women). About thirty thousand children (including many Chinese) are educated in Christian schools.

Higher Education. Higher education in Macau is well-developed, with two universities: the University of Macau (before 1991 called the University of East Asia) and the Macau Polytechnic. There are also various nonuniversity institutions, such as the Institute of Tourism Education, the Armed Forces College, and the International Institute of Software Technology.

ETIQUETTE

Chinese culture emphasizes family integrity, lineage solidarity, reserved public behavior toward the powerful, and respect for parents and elder persons (that is, filial piety, or *xiao*). These values are also largely maintained in Macau's urban culture. The Portuguese and the Macanese form relatively cohesive subsocieties of Catholics with their distinct values and preferences.

RELIGION

Religious Beliefs. According to 1996 census figures, a majority of the population (some 60 percent) claimed to have no religion. Buddhism is adhered to by some 17 to 20 percent of the population. There are minorities of Roman Catholics (7 percent), and of followers of Taoism and Confucianism (14 percent). There were also several popular Chinese spirit cults in Macau. Other religions such as Islam and Hinduism are adhered to by tiny minorities. In the late 1990s there also emerged a small but growing group of Falun Gong practitioners (although this is not considered a religion).

Notable in Macau's history is the great degree of tolerance and relaxed coexistence of the various religious communities. This is also reflected in the mixed architecture of the town, showing churches, temples, and other places of worship close to each other. The 1998 Religious Freedom Ordinance, which codified freedom of religion, is still in force after the handover to China.

Religious Practitioners. Macau has a Roman Catholic bishop and Buddhist dignitaries. The other religions do not have notable community leaders. Catholic and Buddhist officials often appear together at public functions in the city. Among the Chinese, many geomancers (i.e., diviners interpreting the [in]auspiciousness of lines and figures on the ground) are found.

Rituals and Holy Places. There are many churches and temples in Macau. The oldest religious structure is probably the Ma Kok Miu temple, dating back to a thirteenth century shrine. The most important churches are the Macau Cathedral, the Saint Joseph Seminary, and the Saint Laurence. Saint Paul's Church, of which only the facade remains, was built in the seventeenth century and was the largest church.

Death and the Afterlife. Attitudes toward death and belief in an afterlife differ according to the various religious doctrines. Many Chinese have domestic shrines for ancestor worship.

MEDICINE AND HEALTH CARE

Medicine and health care are well-developed in Macau, with thirty-four hospitals and a doctor density of 1.5 per thousand inhabitants. The health-care system has its origins in Catholic Church institutions. There is a good disease- and epidemic-control system, which is important in a densely populated city with high rates of mobility. Health authorities are on alert for imported diseases brought by Chinese immigrants, such as hepatitis B and tuberculosis.

SECULAR CELEBRATIONS

The Chinese and Christian New Year are major holidays. An important Chinese festivity is the Dragon Boat festival.

THE ARTS AND HUMANITIES

Support for the Arts. Before the handover, the city government designated Macau as a "city of cul-

Macau's urban architecture, as seen in Leal Senado Square (above), combines Portuguese and Chinese influences, which lend a romantic character to the city.

ture.'' It supported various arts foundations, such as the Fundação Macau and the Fundação Oriente. There are also private cultural foundations, such as the Instituto Português de Oriente. Since the mid-1990s, several new museums have opened, including the Chinese Robert Ho Tung Museum, the Luis de Camões Museum, and the Museum of Art. There is also a National Library. The tourist market and local people have created a demand for contemporary art.

Literature. There is a long Portuguese-Macanese literary tradition in the city, which likes to take inspiration from the myth that the famous seventeenth-century Portuguese poet Luis de Camões spent some time in Macau. The most famous writer in the Macau *patois* was José dos Santos Ferreira (d. 1993). Macau also inspired many local Chinese poets and authors (such as seventeenth-century poet Wu Li, and twentieth-century author Liang Piyun). The local Chinese and Portuguese literary traditions have remained relatively separate. Chinese Macanese literature is as a rule more political in content.

Graphic Arts. The Chinese graphic arts emerged as landscape painting, Chinese calligraphy, and book illustration. Some European painters (such as George Chinnery, d. 1852, and A. Borget, d. 1877) lived in Macau and depicted life and landscapes of Macau in many drawings, watercolors, and paintings. Notable local painters in nineteenth-century Macau were M. Baptista and Guan Qiaochang. Several Chinese painters in Macau show a creative mix of Chinese and European styles. There are also Portuguese-Macanese artists. The contemporary graphic arts scene (among both Portuguese and Chinese artists) is alive and well, supported by cultural foundations.

Performance Arts. In hotels and clubs one finds traditional Portuguese dance performances, *fado* singers, Chinese dance groups and foreign artists. The theater scene in Macau is relatively unimportant.

THE STATE OF THE PHYSICAL AND SOCIAL SCIENCES

The University of Macau is a notable center for technology studies, ICT, science and social studies. There is also the Inter-University Institute of Macau, which is active in ICT and technology studies. In the sciences, however, Macau stands in the shadow of Hong Kong, which has more institutions and research facilities.

BIBLIOGRAPHY

Chaves, Jonathan. *Singing of the Source: Nature and God in the Poetry of the Chinese Painter Wu Li*, 1993.

Cremer, Rolf D., ed. *Macau: City of Commerce and Culture*, 2nd ed., 1991.

Batalha, Graciete Nogueira. *Lingua de Macau*, 1974.

Boxer, Charles R. "Macao as a Religious and Commercial Entrepôt in the sixteenth and seventeenth Centuries." *Acta Asiatica*, 26: 64–90, 1974.

———, ed. and trans. *Seventeenth Century Macau in Contemporary Documents and Illustrations*, 1984.

Gunn, Geoffrey C. *Encountering Macau: A Portuguese City-State on the Periphery of China, 1557–1999*, 1996.

Hing, Lo Shiu. *Political Development in Macau*, 1995.

Miu Bing Cheng, Christina. *Macau: a Cultural Janus*, 1999.

Porter, Jonathan. *Macau: The Imaginary City*, 1996.

Roberts, Elfed Vaughan, Sum Ngai Ling, and Peter Bradshaw. *Historical Dictionary of Hong Kong and Macau*, 1992.

Shipp, Steve. *Macau, China: A Political History of the Portuguese Colony's Transition to Chinese Rule*, 1997.

—JON G. ABBINK

MACEDONIA

CULTURE NAME

Macedonian

ALTERNATIVE NAMES

Makedonski, Slavo-Macedonian, Skopia

ORIENTATION

Identification. The ancient Macedonians were considered non-Greek but are claimed as co-nationals by the modern Greeks. Modern Macedonians are Slavs descended from the peoples who arrived in the Balkans in the sixth and seventh centuries. There are six ethnic groups: Miyak, Brsyak, Southern, Struma-Mesta, Macedo-Shop, and Upper Vardar.

Location and Geography. Macedonia is a landlocked nation located in southeastern Europe. The current border runs along mountain chains that separate the republic from Bulgaria, Greece, Albania, and Kosovo and Serbia. Macedonia is slightly larger than the state of Vermont with a total area of 9,781 square miles (25,333 square kilometers). The country consists mostly of mountains separated by flat river valleys. The capital, Skopje, is the largest city.

Demography. In 1994, the population was 1,945,932. The population in that year was 67 percent Macedonian, 22 percent Albanian, and 4 percent Turkish, with smaller numbers of Roms (Gypsies), Vlahs (Aromanians), Serbs, Muslims, and others. The number of Macedonians in neighboring states is difficult to determine.

Linguistic Affiliation. Macedonian is a South Slavic language in the Indo-European family whose closest relatives are Bulgarian and Serbian. There is a major east-west dialectal division and about twenty subdivisions. Macedonian evolved in contact with non-Slavic languages such as Greek, Albanian, Aromanian, and Turkish. During the Ottoman period, multilingualism was the norm, but today young Macedonian speakers are more likely to know English than the other national languages. Multilingualism is common in urban areas but is less common in rural areas.

Symbolism. The unsuccessful Saint Elijah's Day (Ilinden) uprising of 1903 is the organizing metaphor of statehood. The Macedonian Peoples Republic (with Macedonian as the official language) was established in 1944. The sarcophagus of Gotse Delchev in a church in Skopje is near the site of a ceremonial commemoration that includes fireworks, picnics, and folk dancing. The national anthem refers to the sun of freedom, the struggle for rights, and the heroes of Ilinden. The first flag used after independence, featuring a yellow sixteen-pointed symbol in the center of a red field, was based on a symbol found at the presumed burial site of Philip of Macedon in Greek Macedonia in 1977. The use of this symbol infuriated the Greeks, and in 1995 the Macedonian parliament adopted a flag with a yellow circle with eight rays projecting to the edge of a red field. Other metaphors of community include "Mother Macedonia," "heart of the Balkans," and "oasis of peace."

HISTORY AND ETHNIC RELATIONS

Emergence of the Nation. Byzantine documents indicate that the Slavs of Macedonia were a distinct group in the early medieval period, and Slavic dialects from Macedonia are identifiable from early Slavic documents. The modern national movement emerged in the nineteenth century. Although many Macedonians self-identified as Greeks, Bulgarians, or Serbs, a distinct sense of national identity developed from a sense of linguistic difference from Bulgarian and Serbian. Owing to Greek, Serbian, and Bulgarian territorial claims, Macedonian claims to nationhood were ignored until the end of World War II, when a Macedonian republic was established within the Yugoslav federation. That republic adopted an independent constitution on 17 November 1991.

Macedonia

National Identity. At the beginning of the nineteenth century the primary source of identity was religion, but the focus shifted to language before the end of the century. As the modern Bulgarian and Serbian literary languages took shape, Macedonians attempted to create a literary language based on their speech, but Macedonian did not receive official recognition until 1944. It is claimed that a Macedonian national identity arose during World War II to keep Yugoslavian Macedonia separate from Bulgaria, but there is documentation that the development of a national identity was indigenous in the nineteenth century.

Ethnic Relations. Ethnic Macedonians live in contiguous parts of Bulgaria, Greece, and Albania, and Muslim speakers of Slavic dialects classifiable as Macedonian who consider themselves to have a separate ethnicity (Goran) live in Kosovo and Albania. Albania recognizes as Macedonian only the Christians living in its southeast, omitting the Macedonian-speaking Muslim and Christian population of

the eastern highlands and the Gorans. In 1999, Bulgaria recognized the independent existence of the Macedonian literary language, but in return Macedonia has renounced support for the Macedonian minority in Bulgaria. Greece claims to have no national minorities and thus does not recognize the existence of its Macedonian minority. In Greek EU-funded minority language projects, Macedonian has never been included. Within Macedonia, religion is as important an organizing principle as language: Most Macedonians, Serbs, and Aromanians (Vlahs) are Christian, and most Albanians, Turks, and Rom are Muslim. The national culture is identified with the Macedonian Orthodox Church, and Macedonian-speaking Muslims are divided among those who self-identify as Macedonians on the basis of language and those who self-identify as Muslims.

URBANISM, ARCHITECTURE, AND THE USE OF SPACE

The traditional culture is rural, but today more than 60 percent of the population is urban, with a quarter of the national residents living in metropolitan Skopje. Traditional architectural influences are Mediterranean, Byzantine, and Ottoman. Modern high-rise apartment blocks have a balcony, which often is used for storage and clothes drying. A traditional Muslim household has separate rooms for male and female guests, whereas a Christian house has a single room. In older urban neighborhoods, individual single-story rooms open into a central courtyard. Wealthier traditional urban houses have one or more upper stories projecting over the street. Urban areas are characterized by a historical center with an open bazaar. Skopje was almost entirely destroyed by an earthquake in 1963. The old main train station, torn in half with its clock stopped at the moment of the quake, was reinforced and left standing as a monument to the disaster. Many public monuments commemorate those fallen in World War II or Ilinden. Since 1991, many villages have restored or built new churches or mosques.

FOOD AND ECONOMY

Food in Daily Life. Breakfast is eaten around nine a.m. by workers in offices, but earlier by factory workers, and in the field in the country. Dinner is the main meal and is eaten at around two p.m. Supper is eaten later after the afternoon siesta. Meals are prepared immediately before consumption, although they may include leftovers. Hot food often is allowed to cool to room temperature. Breakfast can consist of bread and cheese, sometimes with eggs. Other meals

1335

can begin with *meze* (appetizers) served with *rakia* (fruit brandy). Bean casserole *(tavche-gravche)* is the national dish, and bread is considered the most basic food. In restaurants, pizza is especially popular. Hotel restaurants are popular venues for banquets, and there are many private restaurants. There are no food taboos other than those associated with religion, but folk beliefs about food abound.

Food Customs at Ceremonial Occasions. Among Christians, a bird is eaten for Christmas, and lamb for Easter. Among Muslims, a lamb is slaughtered for Kurban Bayram. At Christmas Eve dinner it is traditional to serve a cake with a coin in it. Sweet desserts are associated with religious holidays, New Year's Day, births, weddings, and funerals and commemorations. *Blaga rakia* (hot sugared fruit brandy) is served by the parents of the groom the morning after the wedding night if the bride is found to have been a virgin.

Basic Economy. The traditional economy was agricultural and pastoral. The nation is now industrialized and has been integrated in international trade.

Land Tenure and Property. Traditionally, land was held in common by the extended family, which was patrilocal and was defined patrilineally. After the division of property, wells and threshing floors often continued to be used collectively. Each village has a boundary that is the basic level of property division above that of the family. During the communist period, private property rights were restricted.

Commercial Activities. Cash crops include sugar beets, sunflowers, cotton, rice, tobacco, grains, fruits and vegetables, opium poppies, wine, livestock, dairy products, fish, and hardwoods. There is a tourist industry and a traditional crafts industry.

Major Industries. Steel, cement, mining, textiles, pharmaceuticals, petroleum products, and furniture making are the largest industries.

Trade. Exports include food products, tobacco, pharmaceuticals, and textiles. Serbia was the major trading partner before the imposition of international sanctions. Other important major trading partners include the former Yugoslav republics, other Balkan states, and the European Union.

Division of Labor. Labor is primarily based on agriculture, mining, and light industry. There were about one million persons in the labor force in 1998. In 1996, 38.8 percent of the labor force could not find employment. The minimum age of employment is fifteen years.

SOCIAL STRATIFICATION

Classes and Castes. Differences in the distribution of wealth have increased since 1991, with Roms at the bottom. Other social differences result from differences between urban and rural populations. Serbs and Aromanians are well integrated into the economy, while Albanians are underrepresented in the state sector.

Symbols of Social Stratification. Ethnicity is more important than class. Dress and behavior are likely to follow ethnic lines, although national costumes and articles of clothing have become less common as a result of increasing urbanization and modernization.

POLITICAL LIFE

Government. Macedonia is a parliamentary democracy. Macedonia's unicameral assembly of one-hundred twenty seats is called the *Sobranje*. The executive branch consists of the President (elected by popular vote) and the Council of Ministers (elected by the majority vote of all the deputies in the Sobranje).

Leadership and Political Officials. Political parties tend to follow ethnic lines and draw their leaders from educated elites. The main exceptions are parties led by former communists, which tend to be multiethnic. Personal connections are an important aspect of political life.

Social Problems and Control. The revision of the legal system after the communist period is not complete. Police brutality can take on ethnic overtones. Albanians are significantly underrepresented in the upper ranks of the security structure. The lack of independence of the judiciary from the political system is a perceived problem. Informal social control involves the family, gossip, saving face, and the threat of vengeance. Violent crime is rare.

Military Activity. The army is small and has outdated equipment, although it is in the process of modernizing, especially since 1999. Macedonia's security has been guaranteed by international troops since January 1993. The most important military activity is protecting the country's borders.

SOCIAL WELFARE AND CHANGE PROGRAMS

The state provides social welfare to needy families and grants pensions to retirees.

A minaret overlooks a Macedonian town. Thirty percent of Macedonia's population is Muslim.

NONGOVERNMENTAL ORGANIZATIONS AND OTHER ASSOCIATIONS

Macedonia has numerous foreign and domestic nongovernmental organizations. The boundaries between local organizations, cultural associations, and political parties is fluid.

GENDER ROLES AND STATUSES

Division of Labor by Gender. Men and women work outside the home, but women are responsible for most domestic labor. In academia, men dominate in the sciences and engineering, whereas women are more visible in the humanities.

The Relative Status of Women and Men. In principle, the genders are equal. In practice, men have higher status, and women are likely to manage the household. Women occupy some positions of power but their representation is not in proportion to their numbers.

MARRIAGE, FAMILY, AND KINSHIP

Marriage. Traditionally, marriages were arranged by the parents, but today young people are likely to choose their own partners. Pregnancy often leads to marriage among urban youth, but in the traditional culture the bride is expected to be a virgin. Traditional marriages usually do not cross religious lines. Polygyny occasionally occurs among Muslims. Marriage is the norm, and adults who have never been married are rare. Divorce and remarriage are regulated by civil law.

Domestic Unit. The traditional unit is the patrilocal extended family consisting of a married couple, their unmarried daughters, and their sons with their own spouses and children. This is becoming increasingly less common in urban areas. Children tend to live with their parents until they are married.

Inheritance. Traditionally, inheritance goes through the male line except for what women take with them as a dowry. Today children inherit equally or by assignment.

Kin Groups. Traditionally, above the level of the family or extended family there was the exogamous clan. In rural areas, a clan often constituted a hamlet within a village. The church, however, allows intraclan marriage after three generations.

SOCIALIZATION

Infant Care. Infants are swaddled and carried, and sleep in cradles. They do not have separate play

Drying tobacco in a Macedonian village. Although the nation is now industrialized, tobacco continues to be a major cash crop in Macedonia.

spaces. In urban areas, sleeping and playing arrangements depend on the space available.

Child Rearing and Education. Children are looked after by their mothers, grandmothers, neighbors, or older siblings. Children play freely at an early age. Boys are expected to be more active than girls. In urban areas there are also nursery schools and kindergartens. Eight-year elementary education is compulsory.

Higher Education. Society places a high value on higher education, but ethnic minorities are under-represented. Approximately 87 percent of those holding university degrees are ethnic Macedonians.

ETIQUETTE

In the traditional culture, the young show deference to the old. It is normal for male friends to shake hands and for women to kiss when meeting and saying good-bye. A person entering a room where others are seated will shake hands with each person. Physical contact among friends of the same gender is considered normal. Although staring at strangers was once common, it became relatively rare in the 1990s. It once was the norm to remove one's shoes at the entrance of a home, but this practice is receding among urban Christians.

RELIGION

Religious Beliefs. The major religions are Orthodox Christianity (66 percent) and Islam (30 percent), with small groups of Roman Catholics, Protestants, and atheists. Most Jews were deported and killed by the Nazis, but a few still live in Macedonia. Belief in the evil eye is widespread, and religious practices in rural areas often reflect folk beliefs.

Rituals and Holy Places. Rituals take place at the church or mosque, at the cemetery, in the village, and at home. The most important holidays are Christmas and Easter for Christians and Ramadan and Kurban Bayram for Muslims. Among the Rom, Saint George's Day on 6 May is the major holiday. The Aromanians celebrate 20 May as the Day of the Vlahs, to commemorate the Ottoman recognition of a separate Aromanian church (and therefore millet "nationality") in 1905. Among the customs still practiced are the lighting of bonfires and the singing of special songs on Christmas Eve. Traditionally on the Feast of the Epiphany, a cross is thrown into a major body of water to bless it for the new year.

Death and the Afterlife. Relatives visit the grave on the third, ninth, and fortieth days after the burial; after six months; and after the first year to mourn, give out food, light candles and incense, and pour libations of water or wine. An unmarried young person is buried dressed for a wedding. Among folk beliefs are various practices to prevent a corpse from becoming a vampire.

MEDICINE AND HEALTH CARE

Medicine is modern, but there are also the traditional folk healers, normally old women, who deal with mysterious illnesses such as warts and maladies caused by the evil eye.

SECULAR CELEBRATIONS

Official holidays include the New Year on 1 and 2 January, Orthodox Christmas on 7 January, Easter Monday, the International Day of Labor on 1 and 2

Traditional dress follows ethnic lines but, due to increasing modernization, it has become less common in recent years.

May, Saint Elijah's Day on 2 August, Macedonian Independence Day on 8 September, and the Day of the Uprising of the Macedonian People on 11 October to commemorate World War II.

THE ARTS AND HUMANITIES

Support for the Arts. The arts are supported by the state through the Macedonian Academy of Arts and Sciences, institutions of higher learning, and public theaters. Despite its small size, Macedonia boasts thirteen active professional theater groups that average over sixteen hundred total performances per year, a philharmonic orchestra (established in 1944), six chamber ensembles, and a host of annual folk music festivals.

Literature. Modern Macedonian literature made its appearance during the late 1800s with the poetry of the brothers Dimitar and Konstantin Miladinov, whose works are still recited by students. The growing literary collection grounded in the current, or codified, standards of the Macedonian language, on the other hand, marks its beginning with the 1939 publication of Kosta Racin's programmatic collection of poems entitled *Beli Mugri* (White Dawns). While most of the distinguished nineteenth and early twentieth century literary figures were poets, since the end of World War II there has been an increase in the number of prose writers and playwrights.

Graphic Arts. Villagers in Macedonia are known for their weaving of colorful blankets and carpets. Gold and silversmiths are plentiful in the bazaars of larger cities, and *stomnari*, or urn-makers, still produce glazed terra cotta utensils such as urns, pitchers, cups, and bowls.

Performance Arts. Since gaining independence, Macedonia has produced a number of promising film directors whose pictures have acquired international recognition and praise. The film *Before the Rain*, for example, was nominated in 1994 by the American Film Academy for the Best Foreign Language Film Award. It had already won the Golden Lion award at the Venice Film Festival.

THE STATE OF THE PHYSICAL AND SOCIAL SCIENCES

The Macedonian Academy of Sciences and Arts, founded in 1967 at Skopje, has sections of biological and medical sciences and of mathematical and technical sciences. The country also has an Association of the Sciences and Arts, founded in 1960 at Bitola, as well as specialized learned societies concerned with physics, pharmacy, geology, medicine, mathematics and computers, veterinary surgery, engineering, forestry, and agriculture. Macedonia has research institutes dealing with geology, natural history, cotton, animal breeding, tobacco, animal husbandry, and water development.

The University of Skopje (founded in 1949) has faculties of civil engineering, agriculture, veterinary medicine, forestry, medicine, pharmacy, mechanical engineering, electrotechnical engineering, technology and metallurgy, natural and mathematical sciences, stomatology, and geology and mining. Between 1987 and 1997 science and engineering students accounted for 47 percent of university enrollment. During that same period, Macedonia had 1,335 scientists and engineers and 546 technicians per million people engaged in research and development. The Natural History Museum of Macedonia (founded 1926) is located in Skopje.

BIBLIOGRAPHY

Arbatski, Yuriy. *Beathing the Tapan*, 1953.

Barker, Elizabeth. *Macedonia: Its Place in Balkan Power Politics*, 1950.

Borden, Anthony, and Ibrahim Mehmeti, eds. *Reporting Macedonia: The New Accommodation*, 1998.

Brailsford, H. N. *Macedonia: Its Races and Their Future*, 1906.

Brown, Keith S. "Of Meanings and Memories: The National Imagination in Macedonia." Ph.D. dissertation, University of Chicago, Chicago, 1995.

Byrnes, R. F. ed. *Communal Families in the Balkans: The Zadruga*, 1976.

Chashule, Vangja ed. *From Recognition to Repudiation: Bulgarian Attitudes on the Macedonian Question*, 1972.

Danforth, Loring. *The Macedonian Conflict: Ethnic Nationalism in a Transnational World*, 1995.

Ford, George H. "Networks, Ritual, and 'Vrski': A Study of Urban Adjustment in Macedonia." Ph.D. dissertation, Arizona State University, Tempe, 1982.

Friedman, Victor A. "Macedonian Language and Nationalism during the Nineteenth and Early Twentieth Centuries." *Balkanistica* 2: 83–98, 1975. (Reprinted in *Macedonian Review* 16 (3): 280–292, 1984.)

———. "The Sociolinguistics of Literary Macedonian." *International Journal of the Sociology of Language* 52: 31–57, 1985.

Hall, Jonathan M. *Ethnic Identity in Greek Antiquity*, 1997.

Ilievski, Petar. "The Position of the Ancient Macedonian Language and the Modern Name *Makedonski*." *Balkanistika* 10: 227–240, 1997.

Kramer, Christina. *Macedonian: A Course for Beginning and Intermediate Students*, 1999.

Lazarov, Risto. *This Is the Republic of Macedonia*, 1993.

Liebman, Robert. "Wedding Customs in the Ohrid Village of Peshtani." *Makedonski Folklor* 9–10: 125–240.

Lunt, Horace. "Some Socio-Linguistic Aspects of Macedonian and Bulgarian." In: B. Stolz, I. Titunik, and L. Dolezel, eds., *Language and Literary Theory*, 1984.

———. "On Macedonian Nationality." *Slavic Review* 45: 729–734, 1986.

Miloslavlevski, Slavko. *Fakti za Makedonija*, 1996.

Perry, Duncan M. *The Politics of Terror: The Macedonian Revolutionary Movements 1893–1903*, 1988.

Poulton, Hugh. *Who Are the Macedonians?*, 1995.

Radin, A. Michael. *IMRO and the Macedonian Question*, 1993.

Rossos, Andrew. "The British Foreign Office and Macedonian National Identity 1918–41." *Slavic Review* 53: 369–394, 1994.

———. "Incompatible Allies: Greek Communism and Macedonian Nationalism in the Civil War in Greece,1943–49." *Journal of Modern History* 69: 42–76, 1997.

Roudometoff, Victor, ed. *The Macedonian Question: Culture, Historiography, Politics*, 1999.

Rubin, Barnett, ed. *Toward Comprehensive Peace in South-eastern Europe: Conflict Prevention in the South Balkans,* 1996.

Sachs, Nahoma. ''Music and Meaning: Musical Symbolism in a Macedonian Village.'' Ph.D. dissertation, University of Indiana, Bloomington, 1975.

Stardelov, Georgi, Cvetan Grozdanov, and Blazhe Ristevski, eds. *Macedonia and Its Relations with Greece,* 1993.

Statistical Office of Macedonia. *The 1994 Census of Population, Households, Dwellings and Agricultural Holdings in the Republic of Macedonia,* 1996–1997.

Tomovski, Krum, Galaba Palikrusheva, and Angelina Krsteva, eds. *Ethnology of the Macedonians,* 1996.

Wilkinson, H. R. *Maps and Politics: A Review of the Ethnographic Cartography of Macedonia,* 1951.

—Victor A. Friedman

MADAGASCAR

CULTURE NAME

Malagasy

ALTERNATIVE NAMES

Malagasy refer to themselves and their language as Malagasy and their country as Madagasikara. French speakers refer to the people and the language as Malgache and the nation as Madagascar.

ORIENTATION

Identification. The official name of the country is the Republic of Madagascar (*Repoblikan'i Madagasikara*). The extent to which Malagasy from different regions view themselves as sharing a unified culture is context dependent. In terms of international politics, they see themselves as Malagasy unless they are recent immigrants or members of one of the minority populations (i.e., Chinese, Indo-Pakistani, and Comorian). Domestically, however, in the political arena, there is a significant degree of regionalism that is loosely based on ethnicity.

A common regional division is between those ethnic groups living on the high plateau and the *côtiers*, who inhabit coastal areas (or live outside of the high plateau region). Historically, the largest ethnic group is the Merina located on the high plateau. The traditions of this group (e.g., turning the bones of the dead) represent many Malagasy, and are often portrayed in tourist documents as the primary island traditions. However, people who live in some outlying coastal regions do not identify with or observe these traditions. The highland/ côtier division can be understood in terms of the historical domination by the Merina Empire, which was originally centered on Imerina (the current capital Antananarivo).

There are some common cultural practices that all Malagasy share. Consulting with, and reflecting upon, dead ancestors (*razana*) guides the living in making choices about social, moral, and religious aspects of everyday life. The building and maintenance of tombs and observance of religious ceremonies related to ancestors are central to the way of life for most Malagasy. Another important commonality is that kinship terminology is consistent across different ethnic groups.

Location and Geography. Madagascar is located off the eastern coast of southern Africa in the Indian Ocean along the Mozambique Channel. It is the fourth largest island in the world with a landmass of 226,498 square miles (586,889 square kilometers) which includes its offshore islands. It is one thousand miles long (1,609 kilometers).

Regional ethnic divisions loosely coincide with geographically distinct locations. To some extent internal migration has resulted in sharing some customs such as spirit possession (*tromba*). The West Coast is characterized by deciduous trees on dry, open savanna grassland sloping toward the sea. It was once, like much of the island, thickly forested. Sakalava is the dominant ethnic group in this region. They are involved in agriculture fishing, and cattle herding. The East Coast consists of several narrow bands of lowlands that lead to an intermediate zone of steep bluffs and ravines abutting a 1650 foot escarpment which provides access to the central highlands. The Betsimisaraka, the second largest ethnic group, is the most numerous group pursuing trading, seafaring, fishing, and cultivation. The Southwest is defined by the Ivakoany Massif to the east and by the Isala Roiniforme Massif to the north and includes the Mahafaly Plateau and the desert region. The arid southwest is inhabited by Antandroy and Mahafaly who pursue cattle raising and limited cultivation. The northern end of the island features the Tsaratanana Massif with an elevation of 9,500 feet. The coastline is very irregular. The Antankarana inhabiting this region are involved in cattle raising and tropical horticulture. The High Plateau (Central Highlands) contains a wide range of topographies: round eroded hills,

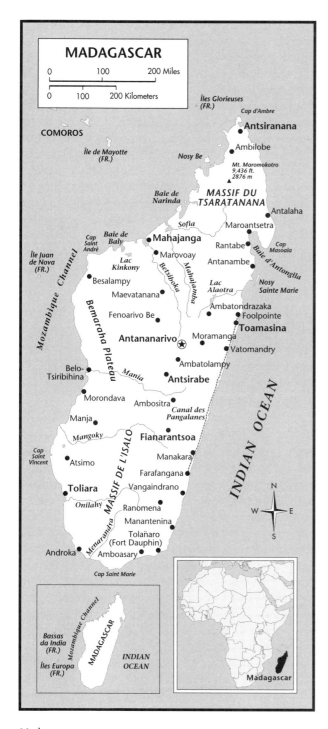

Madagascar

and are considered the best rice farmers in Madagascar.

Demography. Madagascar's total estimated population in 1998 was 14,462,509. In 1998, the age structure of the population was 45 percent between 0-14 years; 52 percent 15-64 years; and 3 percent over 65 years. The annual population growth rate is 2.81 percent. Life expectancy at birth is 51.7 years for men and 54.1 years for women. The fertility rate is 5.76 children born per woman. The average population density is 36 inhabitants per square mile. Over 18 ethnic groups live on the island including: Merina 26.1 percent; Betsimisaraka 14.9 percent; Betsileo 12.0 percent; Tsimihety 7.2 percent; Sakalava 5.8 percent; Antandroy 5.3 percent; Antaisaka 5.0 percent; Tanala 3.8 percent; Antaimoro 3.4 percent; Bara 3.3 percent; Sihanaka 2.4 percent; Antanosy 2.3 percent; and Mahafaly, Antaifasy, Makoa, Bezanozano, Antakarana, Antambahoaka (less than 2 percent each).

Linguistic Affiliation. The official language of Madagascar is Standard Malagasy (Malagasy Official). This language can be traced to the Malayo-Polynesian language family. Standard Malagasy taken from the Merina dialect was the first dialect to be written in Latin characters and is considered the literary dialect. The most similar language found outside of Madagascar is Ma'anyan, a language spoken in Borneo. Both Malagasy and Ma'anyan are similar to languages spoken on the western Indonesian archipelago. There are twenty-two dialects of Malagasy. Many of the dialects borrow from Bantu languages, Swahili, Arabic, English, and French. The government claims that all Malagasy can speak the Standard dialect because that is what is taught in schools. However, given the multiple array of dialects, and varying levels of literacy depending on the degree of isolation of an area, one cannot assume that the Malagasy from one region can understand the dialects spoken in other regions.

French emerged as the dominant language during the colonial period (1896–1960) and Malagasy became secondary. In 1972 Malagasy returned to prominence in education and related cultural changes led to the rejection of French influence. However, by 1982 it was evident that the "Malagachization" of society was failing and the government began to use French again. Today both Malagasy and French are used in government publications. Comorian, Hindi, and Chinese are also spoken by some immigrants.

granite outcroppings, extinct volcanoes, and alluvial plains and marshes. It is defined by an escarpment along the east coast and a more gradual slope along the west coast. The predominant ethnic groups are the Merina and the Betsileo. The capital, Antananarivo, located in this region, is the largest town, with over one million people, and is an ethnic melting pot. The Betsileo live south of the Merina

Symbolism. The flag, divided into three colors, is considered a national symbol and is found in all government buildings. A white rectangle, representing purity, is located on the left horizontal axis. Smaller red and green rectangles, signifying sovereignty and spirit, are placed on the horizontal axis, red over green. The motto is "Fatherland, Revolution, Freedom." The president is a symbol of national unity or *ray aman-dreny* (father and mother of the nation). The national anthem, *Ry tanindrazanay malala* ("Oh, My Beautiful Country that I Love"), is written in Malagasy Official. The song is intended to inspire sentiment and loyalty.

HISTORY AND ETHNIC RELATIONS

Emergence of the Nation. The Malagasy people are of mixed Malayo-Indonesian and African-Arab ancestry. It is generally accepted that the first migrants appeared between 1,500 and 2,100 years ago. One migration theory asserts that what is considered the Malagasy mix arrived already blended having followed a coastal route over a long period with stops in India, the Arab peninsula, and eastern Africa. Another theory contends that the common elements the people share were developed from interactions over a period of time after the arrival of various immigrants groups.

National Identity. Malagasy history has been marked by both international and domestic tensions, some of which are present in contemporary society. During the eighteenth and nineteenth century there were four main kingdoms: Merina, Betsileo, Betsimisaraka, and Sakalava. Friction between the Merinas, the largest ethnic group, and the other ethnic groups during the pre-colonial period eventually resulted in domination by the Merina Empire. Ethnic groups that controlled regions outside of the high plateau were classified as a single group called *côtiers* even though they were made up of unaligned kingdoms. Two Merina monarchs were responsible for establishing political dominance over the island: King Andrianampoinimerina (reigned 1797-1810) and his son Radama I (r. 1810-1828) who succeeded him upon his death. Radama I was forward-thinking with an interest in modernizing along western lines. He organized a cabinet and invited the London Missionary Society to establish schools. The latter action was to have far-reaching effects. Successive Merina rulers embraced or rejected advances made by France to control the island. In 1894 France declared Madagascar a protectorate, and a colony in 1896. The colonial period was marked by the vacillating popularity of French influence over Merina elites. Nationalist sentiments against the French emerged resulting in various concessions made by France to give the Malagasy people greater control. This eventually led to independence on 20 June 1960. Political tensions between the main Malagasy groups (high plateau and côtier) still exists today and are characterized by the perception that the central government does not meet the needs of the côtiers. Each of Madagascar's presidents has struggled to achieve a viable cultural balance between the acceptance of western ways of life, most notably French, and the safeguarding of traditional Malagasy customs. That which has emerged as quintessentially Malagasy in the national sense is a constantly evolving product of all of these influences.

URBANISM, ARCHITECTURE, AND THE USE OF SPACE

Madagascar has a primarily rural population, with fewer people living on the west coast and more in the high plateau. The most crowded city is the capital, Antananarivo.

There are several distinct styles of architecture. A vast majority of government buildings in the capital and regional urban centers were built during the colonial period showing a French influence. However, there are two distinct traditional architectural styles evident in the country. The style of homes built on the high plateau differs markedly from homes found elsewhere due to a heavy reliance on local materials. Homes on the high plateau tend to be multistoried and are constructed of mud bricks that are plastered with a hard drying mud coat that is then painted. Verandas are often made of elaborate scrolled woodwork. The countryside in this region has homes enclosed by ancient mud walls and newly constructed brick walls. Homes in coastal regions are often built on a raised platform in areas with high rainfall and on the ground in drier areas. These homes tend to be much smaller with one or two rooms and are made of bamboo-like materials. The type of materials used signifies a past or present economic status. In most cases, manmade materials such as corrugated metal or cement are more desirable than natural materials as they last longer and signify greater prestige.

The situational aspect of homes and important buildings are considered very important. The most desirable direction for the primary roof line is north-south. Homes, cattle pens, family tombs, and the village are aligned in relation to this orientation. As recently as the 1950s it was common to find the

Rice terraces line a river in central Madagascar. In addition to being an important food source, rice is Madagascar's greatest export.

interior furnishings of homes arranged in a traditional fashion in keeping with the Malagasy cosmological conception of the world being square and horizontal. For example, the bed was located in the northeast, the greeting place for guests in the northwest corner, and the cooking hearth in the middle of the western side of the house. Although some people still follow traditional customs of the placement of objects, the practice is in decline. Those in coastal regions that can afford to buy furniture tend to acquire a bed frame or sofa and wooden table. A single room serves multiple functions.

Food and Economy

Food in Daily Life. Rice is the staple of the Malagasy diet. It is usually accompanied by some form of *kabaka* (a protein dish such as fish, meat, chicken, or beans). In some parts of the island a side dish (*romazava*) made of green leafy vegetables in broth is common. Generally, side dishes serve to add flavor to the rice rather than provide nutrients. Most Malagasy entrees are prepared in one of four ways: fried, grilled, boiled in water, or cooked with coconut juice. A spicy condiment known as *lasary* in Malagasy and made of chili peppers, green mangos, or lemons can be added to enhance flavor. Food is

generally prepared in a kitchen that is physically separated from the main house for fire safety. Meals are served in the house, on the veranda, or on mats placed on the ground outside the house. Lunch and dinner leftovers are warmed for breakfast the following morning. Breakfast consists of rice and a tea made of local herbs or leaves and sweetened with sugar. Some alternate breakfast foods include boiled manioc, maize porridge, or fried cakes made of rice flour. Water is the usual beverage served with meals. *Rano ampango* (water boiled in the rice cooking pot) is sometimes served.

Food taboos (*fady*) tend to be passed down within family groups and along ethnic lines. Some fady apply to daily life and some are observed during special circumstances such as pregnancy and lactation. *Fady indrazana*, taboos related to ancestral lineage, link Malagasy to their ethnic groups. For example, it is fady for most Sakalava to eat pork or eel. For Antandroy, sea turtle and cows without horns are taboo. When a man and woman from different ethnic groups marry, it is common for a woman to observe both her and her husband's fady indrazana as well as the fady which apply to both ethnic groups during pregnancy and lactation.

Vegetables such as carrots, cauliflower, cabbage, potatoes, peppers, and zucchini are available year round. Fruit such as pineapples, coconuts, oranges, mangoes, bananas, apples, and leeche are subject to seasonal availability. Although improved transportation in recent years has increased the availability of such foods to isolated regions, they are generally unaffordable on a regular basis. Therefore, although a wide variety of foods is available, a significant portion of the population remains undernourished.

Traditional Malagasy restaurants (*hotely*) offer a plate of rice with a scoop of one of several kinds of stews. The geographical location of the hotely is often an indicator of what is offered. For example, hotelys along the coast will offer fish more frequently than those in the highlands. Restaurants in most major urban centers serve European-style Malagasy, French, Chinese, and Italian cuisine. French-style baguettes, pasta, and other non-traditional Malagasy cuisine can be found in villages near urban centers.

Food Customs at Ceremonial Occasions. For ceremonial meals and special occasions, extra meat is added to stews. Depending on a family's financial ability, traditional ceremonies such as burials, reburials, circumcision, tomb building, first hair cutting, and the coming out of the house of a newborn often involve the sacrifice of at least one zebu, a local breed of hump-back cow. Many families will serve one of several local alcoholic beverages such as palm wine, grain alcohol, rum, or beer. Family and friends assemble and participate in some aspect of ceremonial preparations. A person or family's adherence to ceremonial protocol pays respect to one's ancestors. The ultimate show of prestige is the ability to provide sacrificial cattle for ceremonies. The number of cattle slaughtered indicates the level of prosperity and the intent of honoring ancestors.

Catholics attempt to observe traditional practices and Muslims observe Ramadan.

Basic Economy. Agriculture is the basis of the economy providing approximately 80 percent of exports in 1993, which in turn constitutes 33 percent of the gross domestic product (GDP). The other two-thirds of the GDP were comprised of industry at 15 percent and services at 52 percent. Eighty percent of the labor force was employed in the agricultural sector in 1993. The majority of the population exists at subsistence level growing rice. Just over one-half of the total landmass supports livestock but only 16 percent of land under cultivation is irrigated.

Imports from France, Japan, Hong Kong, Singapore, and the United States included intermediate manufactures, capital goods, petroleum, consumer goods, and food.

Land Tenure and Property. There are two types of land tenure regimes in Madagascar: a customary system and a state system. Customary tenure systems are generally comprised of holdings and commons. Holdings consist of rice paddies or agricultural land, individual trees, and irrigation canals. Commons include pastureland, water resources (in some instances irrigation canals), and selected forest lands. State tenure systems are governed by written laws and regulations. Communities have clearly defined rules and procedures which resolve civil conflicts as well as disagreements over access to and control of resources. It is common in some places for customary and state tenure systems to be simultaneously applied. A right of passage law gives people the right to pass through private land. Recently there has been government movement toward creating local security teams to supervise adherence to land tenure laws.

Only Malagasy may own land. It is possible to lease land through either formal or informal channels. A formal lease can be short or long term and confer the indefinite right to occupy and use the land. Informal leasing commonly consists of a verbal agreement giving the user rights to the land. In return, the lessee gives one-third of the harvest or something of equivalent value to the owner. In 1984–1985, the average farm size was three acres.

Commercial Activities. Commercial activities in Madagascar vary by region. Although a significant proportion of the population lives at the subsistence level, many of these people sell modest surpluses of agricultural produce to purchase basic necessities, such as matches, soap, and petrol. Agrarian production includes coffee, vanilla, sugarcane, cloves, cocoa, rice, cassava, beans, bananas, peanuts, and livestock.

Major Industries. A European embargo on shrimp and fin fish production in 1997, resulting from concerns about adherence to internationally approved standards of hygiene, had a devastating impact on this relatively new and growing industry.

Major industries include meat processing, soap, beer, leather, sugar, textiles, glassware, cement, automobile assembly, paper, petroleum, and tourism. Tourism was one of the fastest growing industries in the 1990s with a significant increase in the number of hotel beds available in the capital, Antananarivo, and tourist destinations. Natural resources include graphite, chromite, coal, bauxite,

In rural areas people must rely on local materials when building homes and walls. This oven is constructed of mud bricks and a plaster made of hard drying mud.

salt, quartz, tar sands, semiprecious stones, mica, and fish.

Trade. Commodities exports to France, the United States, Japan, and Italy include coffee, vanilla, cloves, shellfish, sugar; and petroleum products.

Division of Labor. The division of labor by formal sector relative to gross domestic product is agriculture, 33 percent; industry, 15 percent; and services, 52 percent. The informal sector is focused primarily in agriculture.

SOCIAL STRATIFICATION

Classes and Castes. Society consists of a small elite class whose wealth, power, and influence is several generations old; a small bourgeois class; and a large lower class. The gross national product per capita was $250 in 1997. Madagascar experienced a negative growth rate in the latter part of the twentieth century which resulted in its decline in World Bank ranking based on GNP from the thirtieth poorest country in 1979 ($290 per capita) to the tenth poorest in 1991.

Changes in society since independence have resulted in the establishment of an elite class that overlaps with the pre-independence elite (based on connections to royal lineage and French patronage). Increased importance has been placed recently on access to state power for self-enrichment, resulting in an increase in the number of people who have acquired wealth through association with government. Distinctions between the old Merina elite whose wealth was generated from private industry and the new state based côtier elite is becoming blurred.

Malagasy identify themselves in large part by their ancestry. Numerous kingdoms populated the island prior to colonization by the French. Early Merina society was divided into four cast groups: *andriana* (nobles), *hova* (commoners), and *mainty* and *andevo* (slave groups). The Sakalava kingdom included a royal caste (*ampanzaka*) and descendants of African slaves (*makoa*). During French colonial rule attempts were made to undermine the royal power of the Merina and Sakalava. Prior to colonial influences, hereditary leaders had both social and political power, but this has softened in the post-colonial period. Although living royalty is recognized in some ethnic groups such as the Sakalava, their power is now limited to the local social sphere with political power managed by state-appointed functionaries. There is a basic split within most ethnic groups between those who are descended

1 3 4 7

from free men and from slaves. The closeness of specific clan groups to royalty is a highly valued form of social prestige.

The differential access to education found in Madagascar dates back to imperial times. Descendants of nobles and key common families who controlled their land, slaves, and trade dominated nineteenth century Merina society. This "Merina bourgeoisie" has been perpetuated in contemporary society as slaves became sharecroppers, investments were made in land and small business, and favored access to education was transformed to preferred placement in high government position in colonial and post-colonial governments. This bourgeois class now includes the families of highly-placed politicians of non-Merina ethnic groups involved in post-colonial politics. A key focus of the 1972 uprising was reform of the educational system. Discontent focused on a structure of privilege. Some attacked the principle of privilege while others objected to being excluded from it.

Symbols of Social Stratification. Styles of dress vary by region but primarily follow western norms with males wearing pants and shirts and females wearing dresses or skirts and blouses. It is common for women to cover their lower outer garments with a traditional wrap (*lamba*). Often an additional matching cloth will be used as a shawl to cover shoulders and head. Men may also wrap their lower half with a lamba rather than pants. A distinguishing feature of people of the high plateau is a white wrap worn for special occasions that both men and women drape over outer garments on their shoulders. Straw hats vary in style, indicating either where the hat was made or where the wearer is from.

POLITICAL LIFE

Government. Since independence from France in 1960, Madagascar has been a democratic republic. Since independence, while the country has struggled with economic and political insecurity, Madagascar has moved from post-colonial democracy, to a transitional military government, to a socialist regime, to a parliamentary democracy. The current constitutional framework was approved on 19 August 1992. Currently the president is elected by universal suffrage to a five-year term with a two-term limit. The bicameral parliament is comprised of a senate and national assembly. The prime minister is nominate by the parliament and approved by the president. The system is one of proportional representation which has resulted in many indepen-

A woman decorates a large sheet of paper with pressed flowers. The paper industry plays a significant role in the nation's economy.

dent parties. In the 1993 elections more than one hundred twenty political parties supported four thousand candidates for one hundred thirty-eight seats.

An unwritten law regarding government relates back to the *côtier*-high plateau split. It is understood that when a president is elected from one group, then the prime minister will be appointed from the opposing group.

The country is divided into six provinces (*faritany*) which serve as administrative subdivisions. The provinces are further divided into counties (*fivondronana*), which in turn are divided into villages (*fokontany*). The village is the smallest administrative unit, with a state-appointed president (usually already a state functionary such as a schoolteacher or nurse). The village president serves with locally appointed village elders (*rayamandreny antana*) on a local security committee. This system of government is called the *fokonolona* and handles all matter of civil concerns allowing for a limited degree of self rule. Tension continues between those wanting to maintain a centralized government and those wishing to give greater power to provincial administrators in an effort to decentralize.

Contemporary political connections can be traced back to pre-colonial monarchies ruled by Merina and Sakalava kings and queens. The only kings and queens who ruled over all of Madagascar, as compared to regional kingdoms, were Merina. This "old" power was confronted with the "new" post-colonial authority of Madagascar's three presidents since independence, all of whom are *côtiers* born of one of the minority ethnic groups found along the coast. This resulted from a political maneuver originally influenced by the French and Merina politicians who believed that a Merina president would never survive long in office given the historical ethnic tensions between Merina and most other ethnic groups which when combined outnumber the Merina population.

Leadership and Political Officials. There are two established parties that have adequate infrastructure and financial support to gain island-wide influence. The Vanguard of the Malagasy Revolution (AREMA) was initially represented as a coalition of pro-government parties. The Committee of Living Forces (CFV) is an opposition group composed of approximately sixteen parties.

Social Problems and Control. The Malagasy Penal Code is based on the French system and has been influenced by Malagasy customary law. The most severe punishments are death and forced labor for life.

There are three levels of courts. The lower courts oversee civil and criminal cases with limited fines and sentences. The supreme court is the highest court. The court of appeals is responsible for criminal cases with sentences of five or greater years. The constitutional high court reviews laws and monitors elections. A military court oversees cases involving national security.

Conditions in the national prison system are harsh. Cells that were built for one house as many as eight prisoners. The families of prisoners must augment insufficient food rations. Street crime in larger cities, including muggings and purse snatching, is on the rise. Penalties for drug trafficking are strict and involve jail sentences and fines. Local security counsels are the focal point of smaller village level crimes where self-policing is important.

Military Activity. In 1994 the military budget was an estimated $37.6 million (U.S.) which represented approximately 1 percent of the gross domestic product (GDP). The military consists of about twenty thousand army, five hundred navy, one hundred marine, and five hundred air force personnel. Military service begins at 20 years of age.

SOCIAL WELFARE AND CHANGE PROGRAMS

A social security system reserves a portion of earned income for the retirement of every person who participates. Unfortunately, due to the subsistence nature of the economy, 96 percent of the labor force does not receive money wages, and only a small percentage of the population participates.

NONGOVERNMENTAL ORGANIZATIONS AND OTHER ASSOCIATIONS

Since the liberalization of the economy and the strengthening of ties to the West in the early 1990s, there has been a noticeable increase in the number of foreign aid programs. A vast array of organizations have focused on environmental, health, and development issues. Environmental organizations such as Conservation International and the World Wildlife Fund have dealt with the loss of habitat and species extinction through educational programs and improvements to the management of protected areas. Social welfare organizations such as Care International, Catholic Relief Services, and the Red Cross have focused on educational efforts to improve, for example, the utilization of oral rehydration salts and family planning, and provide feeding programs to the nutritionally vulnerable. Bilateral organizations such as the United States Agency for International Development (USAID) and other foreign agencies as well as multilateral organizations such as those funded by United Nations programs (e.g., UNICEF, UNDP, and UNESCO) are also involved in similar efforts.

GENDER ROLES AND STATUSES

The Relative Status of Women and Men. Recent laws have begun to emphasize the importance of equal treatment of men and women in certain spheres. Women are to receive the same wages as their male counterparts for the same work. In the political arena, an increasing number of women from the high plateau are entering politics. Although new laws improve the rights of women, men are still given greater consideration in social and religious roles. Men are generally the primary money earners. Although women frequently engage in petty commerce to supplement their household budget, they rely upon their husband's earnings. Even though men and women are capable of participating in all forms of activities, men focus

A general store in Antananarivo. The nation's capital, Antananarivo, is its most populous city, with over one million residents.

their efforts on economic and women on household and familial activities.

MARRIAGE, FAMILY, AND KINSHIP

Marriage. Traditional, civil, and church-sanctioned marriages are recognized, with one or more types applying in any given case. Regardless of the form of marriage, most unions today are formed by joint consent with the institution of arranged marriage decreasing in frequency. When a family does arrange a marriage, it is generally with the purpose of securing or strengthening familial and social relationships. Marriage patterns vary according to socioeconomic status and have political implications in that they are intended to preserve or increase wealth, power, and prestige. However, the majority of marriages are traditional in nature as are most divorces. Long after a union may have dissolved the children of that union give continued meaning to familial obligation.

Specific customs may differ by ethnic group. The Betsileo, for example, will arrange a marriage only after scrutinizing at least three generations of the family of the potential spouse. If satisfied with their findings, the family will then consult an as-

trologer to set a date. In the Bara, where it is common for cousins to marry, a grandmother can arrange a marriage by decree between the children of her children. Once she has died this marriage must be performed to avoid angering ancestors. For Bara a marriage is established after the sacrifice of one cow. Among some Sakalava in the northwest there is no ceremony to mark the marriage aside from moving in together.

In precolonial times polygyny was viewed as a sign of success. The institution of men maintaining more than one wife and household varies across the island and is generally refereed to as *deuxieme bureau* (second office) or *vady aro*, *telo*, or *efetra* (second, third, or fourth wife). It is estimated in some areas that more than 50 percent of adult men simultaneously maintain two or more wives and households at some point in their lives.

Divorce is a common occurrence. By the age of forty, most Malagasy have been involved in several successive marital unions. Reasons for the dissolution of marriages are fairly specific, including the infidelity of either spouse (although this does not always lead to divorce); neglect of duties as a husband (he does not provide adequate food); or neglect of duties as a wife (she does not care adequately for those in her charge or does not spend household money wisely). All property acquired during a marriage is considered the property of both and is divided equally if the union terminates.

Domestic Unit. Nuclear households usually are comprised of a male and female household head and the children from their union as well as any children fostered by either the man or woman. It is common to find single female-headed households but single male-headed households are extremely uncommon. Extended family households usually are comprised of an elder male and/or female household head, their unmarried children, and any number of grandchildren who are fostered to grandparents. When marrying, a woman tends to leave her natal home to live with her husband and his family. Some extended families may live in fenced compounds or clustered housing arrangements that house multiple family units.

The division of labor within a household is determined by age and, to some extent, by gender. Children begin playing at doing household tasks such as carrying water and collecting firewood at an early age and generally begin making modest contributions to household work by the time they reach age five. Both men and women learn to do all household tasks; however, women tend to dominate the domestic sphere, caring for family, meals, laundry, and shopping, while men dominate the professional sphere, often farming or fishing away from the home.

Inheritance. Customary inheritance practices pass land and household to male children and the contents of the household such as furnishings and jewelry along to female children. Although current law states that male and female children have equal rights to all of the family resources the cost of taking this to court is too prohibitive for most.

Customary land tenure practices traditionally resulted in land being passed from father to son. Daughters and other relatives inherited land only in the absence of sons. Although current law states that male and female children have equal rights of inheritance, it is still common for land to be given to male children.

SOCIALIZATION

Infant Care. Although child-rearing practices may vary somewhat by region, there are common themes between most ethnic groups. Newborn children are kept inside the house for a period of approximately seven days after birth, at which time a small ceremony is performed to celebrate the "coming out" of the child. It is common for mothers to provide foods such as tea to supplement their breast milk. To facilitate easy feedings, an infant sleeps with or near his mother and father until they are completely weaned. At that time the child begins to sleep with siblings. Children are carried on the back of their caregiver, attached by a traditional cloth (*lamba*).

Child Rearing and Education. Primary caregivers for small children are the mother and/or father. However, many children will be fostered to other family members such as a grandparent, an aunt, or an uncle from a few months to a few years or for the child's whole life. Older children in a household are generally assigned the task of looking after younger children when an adult is not available. Children are taught from an early age what they are not allowed to do. They are told stories of disobedient children who are cursed by their parents. This preserves ancestral understanding in future generations.

Ceremonies specific to childhood that are focused on life events include the first hair cutting and circumcision. An astrologer will be consulted to choose an auspicious date for these ceremonies.

Education is compulsory from age 6 to 14. This can be difficult to enforce in more remote areas where children make important contributions to the agricultural work force of the household. Education is not seen as separate from other aspects of life. Learning the wisdom of one's elders is often as highly valued, if not more so, as school-based knowledge. Children are expected to be respectful of their elders and their ancestral customs (*fomba*). Parents frequently attribute children's personality, particularly when misbehaving, to nature. Destiny, or *vintana*, a form of cosmology, is used to explain certain aspects of one's personality or future. It is dependent on time, days of the week, and month for interpretation. If one is born with a bad destiny, a diviner must be called upon to change it.

Higher Education. The degree to which higher education is emphasized is relative to its attainability and usefulness. There has historically been an unequal distribution of educational resources over the island which results in unequal representation in administrative and professional positions. The gradual expansion of educational opportunities has resulted in a rise in literacy from 38 percent in 1966 to 80 percent in 1991. Prior to the educational reform resulting from the 1972 uprising, a stratified educational system allowed a small proportion of students to attain a university education. Of these, many were not able to find work. As of the early 1990s, about 5 percent of the student population was able to pursue higher education. In spite of basic improvements, national spending on education has declined from 33 percent in the early 1980s to less than 20 percent in 1993, 95 percent of which was devoted to salaries.

ETIQUETTE

There is some variation in etiquette between ethnic groups but there are idealized behaviors shared by many ethnic groups. With the exception of honored guests, when male and female family members eat together elder men are served first and tend to be given the choicest food. If male and female family members eat in separate groups, the eldest member of each group will be served first. These behaviors are easily identified during ceremonial meals but are much more relaxed in daily practice. Often the youngest children are served before older more dexterous children, so that they will have adequate food. Traditional social norms for interaction such as eating from a common pot that were prevalent as recently as the 1960s are beginning to give way to more Western behavior.

Washing clothes in the Ikopa River, Antananarivo. Men and women share responsibility for domestic tasks, although women often manage meal preparation, shopping, and laundry.

RELIGION

Religious Beliefs. An estimated 52 percent of the people hold indigenous beliefs; 41 percent are Christian (evenly divided between Roman Catholic and Protestant); and 7 percent are Muslim. However, many people hold a combination of indigenous and Christian or Muslim beliefs. The traditionally accepted supreme god is *Zanahary* (God on High) while *Andriamanitra* (the King of Heaven) is the Christian god. At the most fundamental level of traditional beliefs and social values is the relationship between the living and dead.

Religious Practitioners. A variety of traditional practitioners provide the functions of diviner, traditional healer, and/or astrologer. Clergy from either the Catholic or Protestant church are consulted alongside traditional practitioners. Illness, misfortune, financial hardships, and relationship problems are frequently connected to the discontent of ancestral spirits, making healers of all traditional practitioners.

Rituals and Holy Places. Burial tombs are a prominent feature of the landscape. The materials

used vary depending on region, but the time and money used to construct and maintain them is significant and in many cases more costly than one's own household. The degree of elaboration of tombs reflects the level of privilege of the dead. People often live and work quite a distance from their ancestral tombs (*tanindrazana*) with the latter maintaining strong sentimental attachment and a desire to be buried in their natal tombs. Among the Merina and the Betsileo of the high plateau, the ceremony of *famadihana* is an opportunity to reaffirm one's link with ancestors. Often the deceased are buried temporarily near where they lived. Later, sometimes after many years of planning, the bones are removed from the tomb, wrapped in a new shroud, and transferred to the ancestral tomb. At that time the family decides whether to place the bones in the tomb of the mother or the father depending on group allegiance regarding descent.

Ancestral tombs are considered sacred places—particularly royal tombs. In the northwest, as elsewhere in the country, sacred places are abundant. Most villages have a sacred tree or other sacred place nearby.

Death and the Afterlife. Ancestral spirits are regarded as intermediaries between the living and either of the two supreme gods. The dead are viewed as having the power to affect the lives of the living. They are considered the most important members of the family, influencing lives on a day-to-day basis. *Razana* (ancestors) are the pulse of the life force and the creators of customs (*fomba*).

MEDICINE AND HEALTH CARE

There is one major government hospital and at least one private hospital in each of the main provincial cities. There are health clinics staffed by nurse midwives in rural areas. In 1993, the average distance to a health clinic was at least three miles; consequently, UNICEF determined that 35 percent of the population did not have adequate access to health resources. Although there were a number of new hospitals and health care centers built during the 1970s and 1980s, economic decline has lead to a deterioration of services between the late 1980s and early 1990s. As of 1994, only 2 percent of the national budget was allocated to health care. The decline in the adequacy of the health care system, coupled with a resurgence in some traditional healing practices due to the post-colonial Malagachization movement, has resulted in increased popularity of traditional healers, particularly in rural areas. Reliance on traditional healers is further motivated by economics because their fees are generally a fraction of the cost of Western treatment.

Traditional herbalists provide a wide array of local remedies for the treatment of specific illnesses. In cities, the local pharmacists may serve this niche. Many Western-trained doctors attempt to support the use of traditional healers, sometimes simultaneously with Western medicine, and focus on educating their patients to recognize when Western medical treatment would be most beneficial. For many Malagasy there is often a connection between ill health and ancestral discontent. A diviner may evoke the power of the ancestors to effect a cure. Sorcerers use amulets, stones, and other objects to cure. Astrologers understand destiny (*vintana*) so they are consulted to establish auspicious dates for important activities. There are also witch doctors who practice a form of black magic involving poisons and misfortune for one's enemies.

SECULAR CELEBRATIONS

The first of January is New Year's Day. Memorial Day is celebrated 29 March for those who died in the French Malagasy War of 1949. International Women's Day, when women are honored for their contributions, is 30 March. The third Thursday in May is Labor Day, an important holiday for workers. The unity of the Organization of United African Countries is celebrated on 25 May. Madagascar's independence from France in 1960 is celebrated on 26 June. The Celebration of the Dead is held on 1 November and is a day devoted to ancestors and their burial grounds that can involve the building of elaborate tombs. The Anniversary of the II Republic, which began in 1975, is celebrated on 30 December.

THE ARTS AND HUMANITIES

Support for the arts is understandably limited due to the poor economic conditions of the country. *The Centre de Culture Albert Camus* in Antananarivo hosts local and international performances and exhibits in the fine arts. Although there is little public funding for the fine arts there are many excellent individual artists. There is a growing market both internally and internationally for artisan goods. Hand-crafted objects are made in wood, leather, horn, metal, stone, mineral, clay, cloth, and feathers. *Kabary* is an elaborate and poetic form of discourse in which the speaker makes a critical point in a indirect fashion.

THE STATE OF THE PHYSICAL AND SOCIAL SCIENCES

The unique flora and fauna, coupled with a rapid rate of environmental degradation resulting in loss of habitat, has made Madagascar a popular focus for international physical and social scientists from the United States, France, and other European countries. The University of Madagascar has six main independent branches in Antananarivo, Antsiranana, Fianarantsoa, Toamasina, Toliara, and Mahajunga. Degrees are offered in law, economics, sciences, and letters and human sciences. Of importance is the *Institute de Civilisations–MusJe d'Art et d'Archeologie* at the University of Antananarivo. The Institute publishes the journal *Taloha* which includes articles by Malagasy and international social scientists. In addition, there are numerous schools that specialize public administration, management, medicine, social welfare, public works, and agronomy. An excessive number of university students in relation to capacity has resulted in an increasing number of degrees attained at foreign universities for those who can afford it.

BIBLIOGRAPHY

Astuti, Rita. *People of the Sea: Identity and Descent Among the Vezo of Madagascar*, 1995.

Bare, Jean Francois. *Sable Rouge: une monarchie du nord-ouest malgache dans l'histoire*, 1980.

Bloch, Maurice. *Ritual, History, and Power: Selected Papers in Anthropology*, 1989.

Bradt, Hilary. *Guide to Madagascar*, 1992.

Brown, Mervyn. *A History of Madagascar*, 1995.

Covell, Maureen. *Madagascar: Politics, Economic, and Society*, 1987.

Descheemaeker, Anre. *Plantes Medicinales Malgaches*, 1990.

Feeley-Harnik, Gillian. *A Green Estate: Restoring Independence in Madagascar*, 1991.

Grimes, Barbara F., ed. *Ethnologue*, 1996.

Huntington, Richard. *Gender and Social Structure in Madagascar*, 1988.

Jaovelo-Dzao, Robert. *Mythes, rites et transes B Madagascar*, 1996.

Keenan, Edward Louis and Elinor Ochs. "Becoming a Competent Speaker of Malagasy." In *Language and Their Speakers*, Timothy Shopen ed., 1987.

Kottak, Conrad Phillip. *The Past in the Present: History, Ecology, and Cultural Variation in Highland Madagascar*, 1980.

———, Jean-Aime Rakotoarisoa, Aidan Southall, Pierre Verin, eds. *Madagascar: Society and History*, 1986.

Leisz, Stephen et al *Land and Natural Resource Tenure and Security Madagascar*, 1995.

Metz, Helen C., ed. *Indian Ocean: Five Island Countries*, 1995.

Ministere de l' Economie et du Plan. *Image Regionale de l'Economie Malgache, 1989*, 1989.

Raharilalao, Hilaire Aurelien-Marie. *Eglise et Fihavanana: a Madagascar*, 1991.

Ruud, Jorgen. *Taboo: A Study of Malagasy Customs and Beliefs*, 1960.

Sharp, Lesley. *The Possessed and the Dispossessed: Spirits, Identity, and Power in a Madagascar Migrant Town*, 1993.

Viloteau, Nicole. *Les sorciers de la pleine lune*, 1990.

Wilson, Peter J. *Freedom by a Hair's Breath: Tsimihety in Madagascar*, 1992.

—LISA L. COLBURN

MALAWI

CULTURE NAME
Malawian

ORIENTATION

Identification. Malawians are part of the large Bantu population that migrated northward from South Africa at around the turn of the twentieth century.

Location and Geography. Malawi is a landlocked country that lies east of Zambia, north and west of Mozambique, and south of Tanzania. Its area is 45,747 square miles (118,500 square kilometers). The major topographic feature is Lake Malawi, a freshwater lake that is home to hundreds of fish species found nowhere else in the world. Twenty percent of the landmass consists of water. The topography varies from the high Nyika plateau in the north to the Shire River valley in the south that is an extension of the Great Rift Valley. In the far southeast corner is Mount Mulanje, which is among the highest mountains in Africa.

The capital, Lilongwe, is roughly in the center of the country. However, the major commercial center is Blantyre, named after the birthplace in Scotland of the first European to discover Lake Malawi, the English explorer Livingston. Access to the Indian Ocean is normally by rail to the port of Beira in Mozambique.

Demography. In 1999, the estimated population was ten million, with 45 percent of the population under age 14, and 3 percent over age 65. The population density is one of the highest in Africa. Among the major ethnic groups are Chewa, Nyanja, Tumbuko, Yao, Lomwe, Sena, Tonga, Ngoni, Ngonde, Asians, and Europeans.

Linguistic Affiliation. The most widely spoken language (60 percent of the population) is Chewa, which originated among the Bantu tribes of South Africa. Five percent of the people speak Yao, and 30 percent speak Arabic. The language of government, industry, and commerce is English, which every schoolchild studies. English is spoken in cities but rarely in rural areas.

HISTORY AND ETHNIC RELATIONS

Emergence of the Nation. Evidence of Stone Age and Iron Age settlements has been found around Lake Nyasa. Bantu peoples moved into the territory in the first millennium C.E. By the sixteenth century, a Malawi kingdom had trade relations with the coastal areas of Mozambique.

Jesuit missionaries from Portugal visited the territory near Lake Nyasa in the seventeenth century, but the lake probably was not known to Europeans until the Scottish missionary and explorer David Livingstone reached its shores in 1859. European involvement began in 1875 and 1876, when Scottish church missions were established, and a British consul was stationed in the country in 1883. In 1891, treaties that had been negotiated with indigenous rulers resulted in the formal declaration of a British protectorate called the Nyasaland Districts Protectorate. Beginning in 1893, it was known as the British Central Africa Protectorate, and in 1907, the area was officially designated the Nyasaland Protectorate. In 1915, John Chilembwe, an African preacher, staged a short, bloody uprising in response to the treatment of Africans by British colonists.

After World War II, nationalist movements gained strength. After 1953, the protectorate was joined for ten years in a federation with Northern Rhodesia and Southern Rhodesia (now Zambia and Zimbabwe) called the Federation of Rhodesia and Nyasaland. That federation was opposed by nationalists who advocated political freedom from British rule. After the federation's dissolution in 1963, Nyasaland achieved internal self-government, with Hastings Kamuzu Banda as the first prime minister. The protectorate gained independence in 1964 under

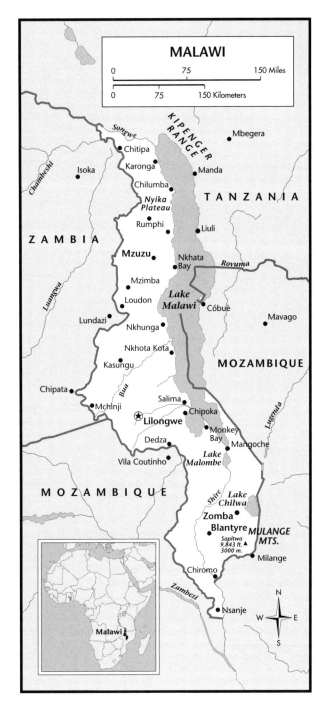

Malawi

its new name, Malawi. It was declared a republic in 1966, and Prime Minister Banda was elected president by the National Assembly.

Under the Banda regime, the country embarked on a vigorous program of economic development. In international affairs, Banda maintained a policy of neutrality in the dispute between Great Britain and the government of Rhodesia (known as Southern Rhodesia before 1964), maintaining extensive

trade relations with Rhodesia's rebellious white minority government. He also maintained friendly relations with Mozambique (until 1975 governed by Portugal) and in 1967 signed a trade pact with South Africa.

In November 1970, the constitution was amended to make Banda president for life. Maintaining good relations with white-dominated South Africa, he became the first black African head of state to visit that country. His policy toward South Africa brought criticism from other black African countries, and his influence in continental affairs was minimal.

The first parliamentary elections were held in 1978. Although only the Malawi Congress Party participated, a majority of the incumbent members were defeated; participation in the 1983, 1987, and 1992 elections also was restricted to that party. The economy performed sluggishly in the early 1990s, burdened by foreign debt and an influx of Mozambican refugees. Meanwhile, Banda faced rising domestic discontent and international criticism of his human rights record.

In May 1994, a new constitution was approved, and then the first multiparty elections took place. Bakili Muluzi, the leader of the United Democratic Front and a former federal cabinet member, defeated Banda for the presidency and formed a government dominated by that party. In keeping with the new constitution, which established a human rights commission, Muluzi freed political prisoners and closed three prisons where tortures was said to have taken place. In early 1995, Banda and a top deputy were tried for the 1983 killings of four government officials. Both were acquitted.

Dr. Hastings Kamuzu Banda, called *Ngwazi*, or ("Fearless Warrior,") had strong ties with and feelings for Britain. He modeled his government on the British Parliament and built Kamuzu Academy as a private school patterned after Eton. Only the brightest and wealthiest were able to attend; students were required to wear uniforms with straw boater hats and played cricket and rugby. The British influence still can be seen in driving on the left side of the road, roundabouts, speed bumps, and school uniforms.

Banda was revered by the general population, but most of the intelligentsia wanted him removed. Every government office had his picture on the wall. When he traveled within the country, streets would be closed and would be lined with schoolchildren waving flags and singing national songs. An audience with Banda would be extremely deferential, and servants were expected to enter and leave the

A row of laundry hangs to dry on a washing line in Malawi. Water is obtained from lakes, rivers, and wells and must be carried over great distances.

room on their hands and knees, facing the president. A *mbumba*, a ceremonial group of women dancers accompanied him to all state functions.

Ethnic Relations. The many tribes generally have gotten along well. However, there is a feeling that people from the north are more intelligent than their southern counterparts, and Banda mistrusted northerners, attempting to keep them out of public office and curtail their enrollment in Kamuzu Academy. Citizens feel a kinship with the neighboring countries and during the civil war in Mozambique created many refugee camps along the borders and fed the refugees with the country's reserves of corn. At that time, Malawi was one of the few African countries that could feed itself.

URBANISM, ARCHITECTURE, AND THE USE OF SPACE

Malawi has an agricultural economy, and even in urban areas, each home generally has a small plot of corn. There are three main cities. Blantyre, the commercial center, Lilongwe, the new capital, replacing Zomba; and Mzuzu in the far north. In 1990, the tallest building in the country was seven stories and the country had only four traffic signals. The vast

majority of homes are constructed of sticks and mud with either a thatched roof or a roof of corrugated iron held down by stones. Families tend to build their homes close to each other in a small compound.

A typical home might consist of such a house with separate rooms for sleeping, eating, and storage. Cooking is done over a wood or charcoal fire in a separate building with a smoke hole in the roof. Furnishings are very simple, often homemade, with few decorations. Cow dung often is used to create the floor of the house. Bathing is done outside, often within a circular thatched shield with an open roof. Water is carried, often over great distances, from a lake, river, or well for cooking and bathing. In the larger cities, the water is potable.

FOOD AND ECONOMY

Food in Daily Life. Chickens, goats, and an occasional pig are used to supplement the standard dish of boiled cornmeal called *nsima*. *Nsima* is eaten twice a day, usually at lunch and dinner, and is preferred by most people to rice or potatoes. Fruits are plentiful, including mangoes, melons, oranges, bananas, and pineapples. Vegetables are cultivated but are not popular.

Soft drinks are quite prevalent, especially Coca-Cola. Alcoholic beverages are mainly beer (there is a large brewery in Blantyre), a homemade brew called *chibuku*, that is usually produced by women and served in cut-off milk cartons, and a more potent distilled liquor that often causes severe health problems.

Food Customs at Ceremonial Occasions. Most weddings and funerals involve the consumption of alcoholic beverages.

Basic Economy. In the last decade, the economy has gone downhill, the value of the *kwacha* has declined, and the rate of inflation is high. Malawi relies heavily on foodstuffs supplied by Western nations.

Land Tenure and Property. Land is treated as part of the public domain. A person may settle on a piece of ground, build a home, and grow crops as long as he gets the approval of his neighbors. After a certain period, he is permitted to register the plot with the government and is given legal title.

Commerical Activities. Malawi's economy is based largely on agriculture, which accounts for more than 90 percent of its export earnings, contributes 45 percent of gross domestic product (GDP), and supports 90 percent of the population. Malawi has some of the most fertile land in the region. Almost 70 percent of agricultural produce comes from smalholder farmers. However, land distribution is unequal with more than 40 percent of smallholder households cultivating very small plots. The country's export trade is dominated by tobacco, tea, cotton, coffee, and sugar. There is very little import trade. Tourism is beginning to build after the collapse of the repressive government of Dr. Banda, and plans are in place to build more resorts and restore the roads.

Major Industries. The organizations that produce coffee, tea, and tobacco, such as the British-American Tobacco Company, are replacing their British managers with Malawians. The country produces no manufactured goods for export; thus, the economy depends heavily on agricultural staples. During the years of apartheid, Malawi was the only country in Africa that had diplomatic relations with South Africa. Many South Africans visited the country, and a basic tourism infrastructure was developed. Today there are tourists from many countries, but the country does not have an abundance of wildlife and there are no game parks. However, there is a potential for increased tourism because of the natural beauty and varied topography and because the country is unspoiled and inexpensive.

Trade. The major exports are tobacco, coffee, and tea. The country imports electrical appliances, small machinery, and automobiles, primarily Japanese. The balance of trade is favorable. The major trading partners are Germany, the United Kingdom, the United States, Zimbabwe, Japan, and South Africa.

SOCIAL STRATIFICATION

Classes and Castes. People from the northern region have a reputation for being better educated and more skilled in business. For this reason, they are mistrusted by people from the southern two-thirds of the country and efforts are made to keep them out of government positions. Men dress in a Western style, wearing shirts and trousers, women often wear traditional costumes consisting of two or three *chitenjes*, which are large pieces of colored fabric used as a skirt, a headdress, and a saronglike wrap that holds a small infant on the woman's back. One way to distinguish between the three regions is by the color of the dress; red, blue, and green represent the north, central, and southern regions, respectively.

Symbols of Social Stratification. Shoes are expensive and often the local people are barefoot even in the cities.

POLITICAL LIFE

Government. Malawi is now a multiparty democracy, instead of a dictatorship with one party. Citizens and those resident for more than seven years can vote. The president is both the chief of state and the head of the government. He appoints a twenty-eight-member cabinet. The judicial branch consists of a Supreme Court of Appeal, a High Court, a chief justice appointed by the president, additional judges appointed on the advice of the Judicial Service Commission, and magistrate's courts. The legislative branch is made up of the National Assembly with 177 members elected by plurality vote from single-seat constituencies for a five-year term. The Senate contains eighty members, all elected. Local government consists of twenty-four districts.

Leadership and Political Officials. The three major political parties are the Malawi Congress Party (MCP), the Alliance for Democracy (AFORD), and the United Democratic Front (UDF). The most recent elections were held in 1999; Bakali Muluzi of

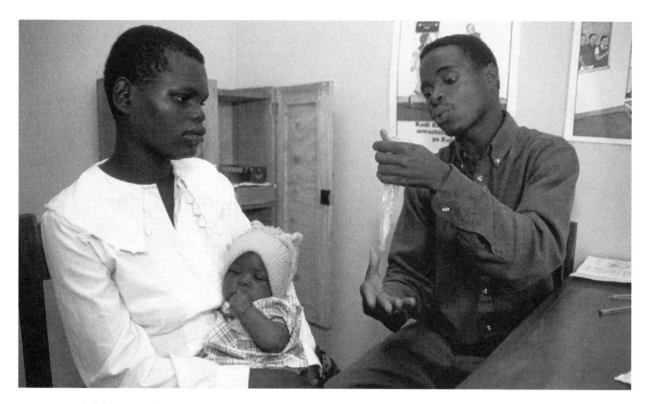

A woman and child visit a family planning clinic in Malawi. The average woman will bear five to six children, but fewer than half survive beyond five years of age.

the UDF won the presidency with over 51 percent of the vote.

Social Problems and Control. The most serious crime is robbery, which generally occurs in the major cities and in tourist areas, although murder is not unknown. The police are conspicuous by their lack of weapons and vehicles. Local justice often is meted out on the spot. If a criminal is caught by local residents, he often is taken to the police station and beaten on the way while those around him sing and mock him. These beatings have caused death on occasion. During Banda's rule, there was a youth group that could turn violent. Its purpose was to intimidate the people into joining Banda's political party. The group members would stand at bus stations and prevent people from boarding until a membership card was produced or purchased.

Military Activity. The armed forces total about ten thousand, plus a paramilitary police force of about fifteen thousand. The army is by far the largest branch; the air force is small, and the navy is practically nonexistent. During World War I, Malawi sent a substantial number of troops to serve as part of the Kings African Rifles. There is monument to that unit in the former capital of Zomba.

SOCIAL WELFARE AND CHANGE PROGRAMS

International fraternal groups such as the Rotary Club, Lions Club, and Kiwanis have a presence in the country. In the agricultural sector, there are large, well-organized growers' associations for tea and tobacco.

NONGOVERNMENTAL ORGANIZATIONS AND OTHER ASSOCIATIONS

In one of the world's poorest nations, many foreign nongovernmental organizations are present. Among them are *Medicins sans Frontieres*, Save the Children, World Vision, and several United Nations organizations, such as the United Nations High Commission for Refugees. There are volunteer organizations such as United States Peace Corps and similar groups from England, Canada, Japan, and Germany. The World Food Program helps with food distribution.

GENDER ROLES AND STATUSES

Division of Labor by Gender. In a patriarchal society, men do most work outside the home. However, with help from Western countries, women are being encouraged to start their own businesses.

A thatched grain store in a Malawian village. Because Malawi produces no manufactured goods for export, it has an agricultural economy.

There are a few women in governmental positions. Inside the home, women dominate.

The Relative Status of Women and Men. When a family returns from the market or from gathering firewood or drawing water, women and children carry the burdens. The man leads the way, smoking if he can afford tobacco, with the rest of the family trailing behind. In a culture that separates the sexes in most aspects of life, three-quarters of literate persons are men. Usually, men eat separately from women, using the only table in the house. The woman serves the meal to the man, often on her knees. At weddings, it is customary for the bride to serve food to the husband's parents in that position.

MARRIAGE, FAMILY, AND KINSHIP

Marriage. Marriages often are arranged, particularly in rural areas. Dowries are presented by the bride's parents to the husband to be and play a significant role in the selection of a partner. Dowries are usually in the form of livestock, such as cattle, goats, or chickens, but may consists of grain or land. Larger women often are favored as brides because they appear to come from a well-to-do family

that can provide a significant dowry and seem strong enough to carry heavy loads. Polygamy is practiced occasionally by those who can afford it. On occasion, the co-wives will share the same house with the husband.

Females undergo an initiation ceremony at the onset of puberty or menstruation and just before marriage. It often consists of very explicit instructions on the sexual aspect of marriage. Divorce is becoming more common and is very difficult on the wife, who must go back to her family and hope it will take her in. The husband receives all the couple's possessions.

Domestic Unit. Families are quite close and often live in adjoining houses. Elderly persons are taken care of by their children, and usually the oldest members of a family have a strong voice in running the household and raising the children. Especially important is the uncle; male adolescents ask advice first of the uncle, who is also influential in the selection of a bride.

SOCIALIZATION

Infant Care. Infants usually are carried on the mother's back, facing inward. Mothers conduct many activities with their babies in attendance: shopping, carrying water, hoeing a garden, and dancing in a ceremony. Separate rooms or cribs for infants are almost nonexistent because most houses are small and include many family and extended family members.

Child Rearing and Education. The average woman will bear five to six children, less than half of whom will live past the age of five years. Children are raised under strict family control, usually by the mother, until they leave home. They are expected to help with the chores of daily living. Most tasks are done by female children, such as carrying water, cleaning the home and washing dishes, and going to the market. Half the population over the age of fifteen can read and write, but education is reserved for those who can afford school fees and uniforms. Most children have to end their education before high school to help tend the fields or care for younger siblings.

Higher Education. College or even vocational training is rare, although Chancellor College has a good reputation and Queen Victoria Hospital, the largest in the country, has a school of nursing. Recently, a medical school was opened in Blantyre. However, those able to afford it usually send their

A medicine man selling herbs at a market in Blantyre. Medicine men are sought out to cure illness and to aid in such tasks as finding a wife.

children abroad for higher education. The preferred destinations are the United Kingdom, the United States, and Germany. Advanced degrees often are obtained overseas with financial help from Western organizations.

ETIQUETTE

Verbal greetings are accompanied by a handshake. This is done with the right hand, with the left hand gripping the right forearm to show that one is not armed. Stopping to talk on the street is customary, and the conversation continues even after the parties go their separate ways. Although residents are gregarious, they respect other people's privacy in a crowded country where private space is at a premium. A person approaching someone's house will often cry *Odi, Odi* to announce his or her presence. Any visitor almost always is offered a drink and perhaps something to eat. Eating usually is done without utensils, but only with the right hand, because the left hand is considered "dirty."

RELIGION

Religious Beliefs. Fifty-five percent of the people belong to the Church of England but there are also Methodists, Baptists and Seventh Day Adventists. Twenty percent of the population are Muslim, and 20 percent are Catholic. There is a small Hindu presence.

Rituals and Holy Places. Most larger towns have a Christian church and a Muslim mosque. Most major cities also have a Hindu temple. In rural areas, animistic religion is practiced.

Death and the Afterlife. Because of the short life expectancy, the growing incidence of AIDS and other diseases, and the high infant mortality rate, death is a constant presence. Employers give workers time off for funerals, and funerals and mourning can last several days.

MEDICINE AND HEALTH CARE

There are hospitals as well as a school of Medicine and several schools of nursing. The best hospital is probably the Seventh-Day Adventist Hospital in Blantyre, which also has a dental clinic. Queen Elizabeth Hospital in Blantyre is the largest in the country but is not particularly sanitary.

Medicine men and women provide health care for many people, especially in rural areas, using traditional or folk medicine. Sometimes called

Women collecting water. While men commonly dress in a Western style, women tend to wear chitenjes, *large pieces of colorful fabric.*

singanas, they work out of the home or from a clinic, using natural medicines such as roots, herbs, and potions. Medicine men base their healing on the assumption that most illnesses are caused by supernatural powers and that supernatural powers are required to cure them. The individual may fall ill after offending one of the gods, through witchcraft or sorcery, or through the unprovoked attack of an evil spirit. The task of the curer is to diagnose the disease and then apply the spiritual remedy, such as retrieving a lost soul, removing a disease-causing object, or exorcising an evil spirit. Often medicine men are called on to help in areas not considered medical problems in the West, such as finding a wife or lover, conceiving a child, and helping in business matters.

Yellow fever and malaria are prevalent, and the country has one of the highest incidences of AIDS in the world. Despite some efforts by the government, it has been difficult to lower the rate of AIDS because of long-standing social mores.

SECULAR CELEBRATIONS

The three major national holidays are Independence Day, 6 July; Republic Day, 6 July; and Constitution Day, 18 May. Independence Day celebrates the end of the British colonial status in 1964, Republic Day commemorates the formal declaration of the republic in 1966, and Constitution Day celebrates the drafting of the first constitution as a democratic society in 1995.

THE ARTS AND HUMANITIES

Support for the Arts. Malawi has built a National Dance Troupe over the past few years which has been well received. It is partially subsidized by the government and receives the only governmental financial support to the arts in the country.

Literature. There is a long tradition of oral artistry. Before the spread of literacy in the twentieth century, texts were preserved in memory and performed or recited. Those traditional texts provided entertainment, instruction, and commemoration. However, no distinctions were made between works composed for enjoyment and works with a more utilitarian function. Those works were primarily, myths, legends, and folktales.

Performance Arts. The performing arts are not highly developed. Local bands, that use primarily native instruments play throughout the country at festivals and celebrations but seldom travel abroad. Dance troupes are becoming more popular; their performances relate stories of everyday life. Some of the most popular are episodes involve a policeman, with uniform and whistle, who directs people by alternating verbal and whistle commands.

Graphic Arts. Wood carving and pottery making account the items most frequently purchased by tourists and Africans. Every home has one or more wood statues, generally of people or animals, along with elaborately carved tables and chairs. Every large town has carvings for sale, even in the supermarkets. The best pottery is said to come from Dedza on the Mozambique border. These pieces are often hand-painted with scenes, such as fishing boats on Lake Malawi at sunset.

THE STATE OF THE PHYSICAL AND SOCIAL SCIENCES

Lack funding has constrained the development of the physical and social sciences. The University of Malawi (also known as Chancellor College) has a good reputation, but the staff is poorly paid and the facilities are not kept up to date. The Polytechnic University in Blantyre relies on highly paid foreign professors.

BIBLIOGRAPHY

Chanock, Martin. *Law, Custom and Social Order: The Colonial Experience in Malawi and Zambia*, 1998.

Crosby, Cynthia A. *Historical Dictionary of Malawi*, 1993.

Glagow, Manfred, et al. *Non-Governmental Organizations in Malawi: The Contribution to Development and Democratization*, 1997.

Hanna, A. J. *The Beginnings of Nyasaland and Northern Rhodesia, 1859–1895*, 1982.

Mandala, Elias C. *Work and Control in a Peasant Economy: A History of the Lower Tchiri Valley in Malawi, 1859–1960*, 1990.

Michie, W. D. et al. *The Lands and Peoples of Central Africa*, 1981.

Mtewa, Mekki. *Malawi Democratic Theory and Public Policy*, 1986.

Muyebe, Stanslaus C. *The Catholic Missionaries Within and Beyond the Politics of Exclusivity in Colonial Malawi, 1901–1945*, 1999.

Needham, D. E. *From Iron Age to Independence: A History of Central Africa*, 1984.

O'Toole, Thomas. *Malawi in Pictures*, 1988.

Rotberg, Robert I. *Rise of Nationalism in Central Africa: The Making of Malawi and Zambia, 1873–1964*, 1965.

Schoffeleers, J. Matthew. *River of Blood: The Genesis of a Martyr Cult in Southern Malawi, c. A.D. 1600*, 1992.

Shepperson, George, and Thomas Price. *Independent African: John Chilembwe and the Origins, Setting and Significance of the Nyasaland Native Rising 1915*, 1987.

Sindima, Harvey J. *The Legacy of Scottish Missionaries in Malawi*, 1992.

Sweeney, Mary E. *The Proper Care of Malawi Cichlids*, 1993.

Williams, T. David. *Malawi: The Politics of Despair*, 1978.

Wills, Alfred John. *An Introduction to the History of Central Africa: Zambia, Malawi and Zimbabwe*, 1985.

Woods, Anthony, and Melvin E. Page. *The Creation of Modern Malawi*, 2000.

—BRUCE H. DOLPH

MALAYSIA

CULTURE NAME
Malaysian

ALTERNATIVE NAMES
Outsiders often mistakenly refer to things Malaysian as simply "Malay," reflecting only one of the ethnic groups in the society. Malaysians refer to their national culture as *kebudayaan Malaysia* in the national language.

ORIENTATION

Identification. Within Malaysian society there is a Malay culture, a Chinese culture, an Indian culture, a Eurasian culture, along with the cultures of the indigenous groups of the peninsula and north Borneo. A unified Malaysian culture is something only emerging in the country. The important social distinction in the emergent national culture is between Malay and non-Malay, represented by two groups: the Malay elite that dominates the country's politics, and the largely Chinese middle class whose prosperous lifestyle leads Malaysia's shift to a consumer society. The two groups mostly live in the urban areas of the Malay Peninsula's west coast, and their sometimes competing, sometimes parallel influences shape the shared life of Malaysia's citizens. Sarawak and Sabah, the two Malaysian states located in north Borneo, tend to be less a influential part of the national culture, and their vibrant local cultures are shrouded by the bigger, wealthier peninsular society.

Location and Geography. Malaysia is physically split between west and east, parts united into one country in 1963. Western Malaysia is on the southern tip of the Malay peninsula, and stretches from the Thai border to the island of Singapore. Eastern Malaysia includes the territories of Sabah and Sarawak on the north end of Borneo, separated by the country of Brunei. Peninsular Malaysia is divided into west and east by a central mountain range called the Banjaran Titiwangsa. Most large cities, heavy industry, and immigrant groups are concentrated on the west coast; the east coast is less populated, more agrarian, and demographically more Malay. The federal capital is in the old tin-mining center of Kuala Lumpur, located in the middle of the western immigrant belt, but its move to the new Kuala Lumpur suburb of Putra Jaya will soon be complete.

Demography. Malaysia's population comprises twenty-three million people, and throughout its history the territory has been sparsely populated relative to its land area. The government aims for increasing the national population to seventy million by the year 2100. Eighty percent of the population lives on the peninsula. The most important Malaysian demographic statistics are of ethnicity: 60 percent are classified as Malay, 25 percent as of Chinese descent, 10 percent of Indian descent, and 5 percent as others. These population figures have an important place in peninsular history, because Malaysia as a country was created with demography in mind. Malay leaders in the 1930s and 1940s organized their community around the issue of curbing immigration. After independence, Malaysia was created when the Borneo territories with their substantial indigenous populations were added to Malaya as a means of exceeding the great number of Chinese and Indians in the country.

Linguistic Affiliation. Malay became Malaysia's sole national language in 1967 and has been institutionalized with a modest degree of success. The Austronesian language has an illustrious history as a lingua franca throughout the region, though English is also widely spoken because it was the administrative language of the British colonizers. Along with Malay and English other languages are popular: many Chinese Malaysians speak some combination of Cantonese, Hokkien, and/or Mandarin; most Indian Malaysians speak Tamil; and

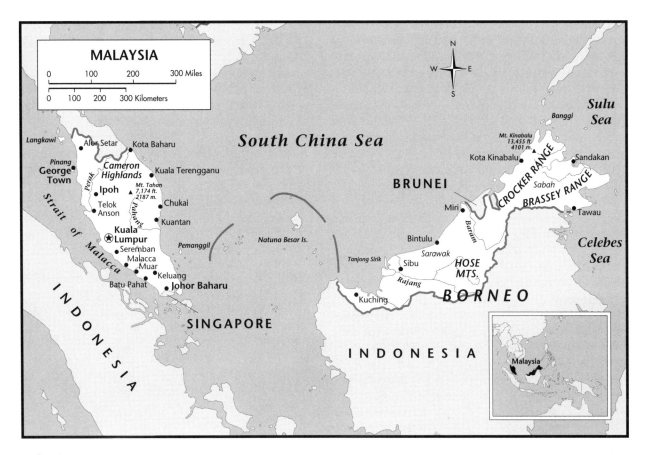

Malaysia

numerous languages flourish among aboriginal groups in the peninsula, especially in Sarawak and Sabah. The Malaysian government acknowledges this multilingualism through such things as television news broadcasts in Malay, English, Mandarin, and Tamil. Given their country's linguistic heterogeneity, Malaysians are adept at learning languages, and knowing multiple languages is commonplace. Rapid industrialization has sustained the importance of English and solidified it as the language of business.

Symbolism. The selection of official cultural symbols is a source of tension. In such a diverse society, any national emblem risks privileging one group over another. For example, the king is the symbol of the state, as well as a sign of Malay political hegemony. Since ethnic diversity rules out the use of kin or blood metaphors to stand for Malaysia, the society often emphasizes natural symbols, including the sea turtle, the hibiscus flower, and the orangutan. The country's economic products and infrastructure also provide national logos for Malaysia; the national car (Proton), Malaysia Airlines, and the Petronas Towers (the world's tallest build-

ings) have all come to symbolize modern Malaysia. The government slogan "Malaysia Boleh!" (Malaysia Can!) is meant to encourage even greater accomplishments. A more humble, informal symbol for society is a salad called *rojak*, a favorite Malaysian snack, whose eclectic mix of ingredients evokes the population's diversity.

HISTORY AND ETHNIC RELATIONS

Emergence of the Nation. The name Malaysia comes from an old term for the entire Malay archipelago. A geographically truncated Malaysia emerged out of the territories colonized by Britain in the late nineteenth and early twentieth centuries. Britain's representatives gained varying degrees of control through agreements with the Malay rulers of the peninsular states, often made by deceit or force. Britain was attracted to the Malay peninsula by its vast reserves of tin, and later found that the rich soil was also highly productive for growing rubber trees. Immigrants from south China and south India came to British Malaya as labor, while the Malay population worked in small holdings and rice cultivation. What was to become East Malaysia had different colonial administrations: Sarawak was governed by a British family, the Brookes (styled as the "White Rajas"), and Sabah was run by the British North Borneo Company. Together the cosmopolitan hub of British interests was Singapore, the central port and center of publishing, commerce, education, and administration. The climactic event in forming Malaysia was the Japanese occupation of Southeast Asia from 1942-1945. Japanese rule helped to invigorate a growing anti-colonial movement, which flourished following the British return after the war. When the British attempted to organize their administration of Malaya into one unit to be called the Malayan Union, strong Malay protests to what seemed to usurp their historical claim to the territory forced the British to modify the plan. The other crucial event was the largely Chinese communist rebellion in 1948 that remained strong to the mid-1950s. To address Malay criticisms and to promote counter-insurgency, the British undertook a vast range of nation-building efforts. Local conservatives and radicals alike developed their own attempts to foster unity among the disparate Malayan population. These grew into the Federation of Malaya, which gained independence in 1957. In 1963, with the addition of Singapore and the north Borneo territories, this federation became Malaysia. Difficulties of integrating the predominately Chinese population of Singapore into Malaysia remained, and under Malaysian directive Singapore became an independent republic in 1965.

National Identity. Throughout Malaysia's brief history, the shape of its national identity has been a crucial question: should the national culture be essentially Malay, a hybrid, or separate ethnic entities? The question reflects the tension between the indigenous claims of the Malay population and the cultural and citizenship rights of the immigrant groups. A tentative solution came when the Malay, Chinese, and Indian elites who negotiated independence struck what has been called "the bargain." Their informal deal exchanged Malay political dominance for immigrant citizenship and unfettered economic pursuit. Some provisions of independence were more formal, and the constitution granted several Malay "special rights" concerning land, language, the place of the Malay Rulers, and Islam, based on their indigenous status. Including the Borneo territories and Singapore in Malaysia revealed the fragility of "the bargain." Many Malays remained poor; some Chinese politicians wanted greater political power. These fractures in Malaysian society prompted Singapore's expulsion and

produced the watershed of contemporary Malaysian life, the May 1969 urban unrest in Kuala Lumpur. Violence left hundreds dead; parliament was suspended for two years. As a result of this experience the government placed tight curbs on political debate of national cultural issues and began a comprehensive program of affirmative action for the Malay population. This history hangs over all subsequent attempts to encourage official integration of Malaysian society. In the 1990s a government plan to blend the population into a single group called "Bangsa Malaysia" has generated excitement and criticism from different constituencies of the population. Continuing debates demonstrate that Malaysian national identity remains unsettled.

Ethnic Relations. Malaysia's ethnic diversity is both a blessing and a source of stress. The melange makes Malaysia one of the most cosmopolitan places on earth, as it helps sustain international relationships with the many societies represented in Malaysia: the Indonesian archipelago, the Islamic world, India, China, and Europe. Malaysians easily exchange ideas and techniques with the rest of the world, and have an influence in global affairs. The same diversity presents seemingly intractable problems of social cohesion, and the threat of ethnic violence adds considerable tension to Malaysian politics.

URBANISM, ARCHITECTURE, AND THE USE OF SPACE

Urban and rural divisions are reinforced by ethnic diversity with agricultural areas populated primarily by indigenous Malays and immigrants mostly in cities. Chinese dominance of commerce means that most towns, especially on the west coast of the peninsula, have a central road lined by Chinese shops. Other ethnic features influence geography: a substantial part of the Indian population was brought in to work on the rubber plantations, and many are still on the rural estates; some Chinese, as a part of counter-insurgency, were rounded up into what were called "new villages." A key part of the 1970s affirmative action policy has been to increase the number of Malays living in the urban areas, especially Kuala Lumpur. Governmental use of Malay and Islamic architectural aesthetics in new buildings also adds to the Malay urban presence. Given the tensions of ethnicity, the social use of space carries strong political dimensions. Public gatherings of five or more people require a police permit, and a ban on political rallies successfully limits the appearance of crowds in Malaysia. It is therefore understandable that Malaysians mark a

A house on Langkawi Island. Land ownership is a controversial issue in Malaysia, where indigenous groups are struggling to protect their claims from commercial interests.

sharp difference between space inside the home and outside the home, with domestic space carefully managed to receive outsiders: even many modest dwellings have a set of chairs for guests in a front room of the house.

FOOD AND ECONOMY

Food in Daily Life. Malaysia's diversity has blessed the country with one of the most exquisite cuisines in the world, and elements of Malay, Chinese, and Indian cooking are both distinct and blended together. Rice and noodles are common to all cuisine; spicy dishes are also favorites. Tropical fruits grow in abundance, and a local favorite is the durian, known by its spiked shell and fermented flesh whose pungent aroma and taste often separates locals from foreigners. Malaysia's affluence means that increasing amounts of meat and processed foods supplement the country's diet, and concerns about the health risks of their high-fat content are prominent in the press. This increased affluence also allows Malaysians to eat outside the home more often; small hawker stalls offer prepared food twenty-four hours a day in urban areas. Malaysia's ethnic diversity is apparent in food prohibitions: Muslims are forbidden to eat pork which

is a favorite of the Chinese population; Hindus do not eat beef; some Buddhists are vegetarian. Alcohol consumption also separates non-Muslims from Muslims.

Food Customs at Ceremonial Occasions. When Malaysians have guests they tend to be very fastidious about hospitality, and an offer of food is a critical etiquette requirement. Tea or coffee is usually prepared along with small snacks for visitors. These refreshments sit in front of the guest until the host signals for them to be eaten. As a sign of accepting the host's hospitality the guest must at least sip the beverage and taste the food offered. These dynamics occur on a grander scale during a holiday open house. At celebrations marking important ethnic and religious holidays, many Malaysian families host friends and neighbors to visit and eat holiday delicacies. The visits of people from other ethnic groups and religions on these occasions are taken as evidence of Malaysian national amity.

Basic Economy. Malaysia has long been integrated into the global economy. Through the early decades of the twentieth century, the Malay peninsula was a world leader in the production of tin (sparked by the Western demand for canned food) and natural rubber (needed to make automobile tires). The expansion of Malaysia's industrialization heightened its dependence on imports for food and other necessities.

Land Tenure and Property. Land ownership is a controversial issue in Malaysia. Following the rubber boom the British colonial government, eager to placate the Malay population, designated portions of land as Malay reservations. Since this land could only be sold to other Malays, planters and speculators were limited in what they could purchase. Malay reserve land made ethnicity a state concern because land disputes could only be settled with a legal definition of who was considered Malay. These land tenure arrangements are still in effect and are crucial to Malay identity. In fact the Malay claim to political dominance is that they are *bumiputera* (sons of the soil). Similar struggles exist in east Malaysia, where the land rights of indigenous groups are bitterly disputed with loggers eager to harvest the timber for export. Due to their different colonial heritage, indigenous groups in Sarawak and Sabah have been less successful in maintaining their territorial claims.

Commercial Activities. Basic necessities in Malaysia have fixed prices and, like many developing countries, banking, retail, and other services are tightly regulated. The country's commerce correlates with ethnicity, and government involvement has helped Malays to compete in commercial activities long dominated by ethnic Chinese. Liberalization of business and finance proceeds with these ethnic dynamics in mind.

Major Industries. The boom and bust in primary commodities such as rubber and tin have given Malaysian society a cyclical rhythm tied to fickle external demand. In the 1970s the government began to diversify the economy (helped by an increase in oil exports) and Malaysia is now well on its way to becoming an industrial country. The country has a growing automotive industry, a substantial light-manufacturing sector (textiles, air conditioners, televisions, and VCRs), and an expanding high technology capacity (especially semi-conductors).

Trade. Malaysia's prominent place in the global economy as one of the world's twenty largest trading nations is an important part of its identity as a society. Primary trading partners include Japan, Singapore, and the United States, with Malaysia importing industrial components and exporting finished products. Palm oil, rubber, tropical hardwoods, and petroleum products are important commodities.

Division of Labor. The old ethnic division of labor (Malays in agriculture, Indians in the professions and plantations, and Chinese in mining and commerce) has steadily eroded. In its place, the Malaysian workforce is increasingly divided by class and citizenship. Educated urban professionals fill the offices of large companies in a multi-ethnic blend. Those without educational qualifications work in factories, petty trade, and agricultural small holdings. As much as 20 percent of the workforce is foreign, many from Indonesia and the Philippines, and dominate sectors such as construction work and domestic service.

SOCIAL STRATIFICATION

Classes and Castes. Class position in Malaysia depends on a combination of political connections, specialized skills, ability in English, and family money. The Malaysian elite, trained in overseas universities, is highly cosmopolitan and continues to grow in dominance as Malaysia's middle class expands. Even with the substantial stratification of society by ethnicity, similar class experiences in business and lifestyle are bridging old barriers.

Symbols of Social Stratification. In Malaysia's market economy, consumption provides the primary symbols of stratification. Newly wealthy Malaysians learn how to consume by following the lead of the Malay royalty and the prosperous business families of Chinese descent. A mobile phone, gold jewelry, and fashionable clothing all indicate one's high rank in the Malaysian social order. Given the striking mobility of Malaysian society, one's vehicle marks class position even more than home ownership. Most Malaysians can distinguish the difference between makes of cars, and access to at least a motor scooter is a requirement for participation in contemporary Malaysian social life. Kuala Lumpur has more motor vehicles than people. Skin color, often indicative of less or more time working in the hot tropical sun, further marks class position. Distinct class differences also appear in speech. Knowledge of English is vital to elevated class status, and a person's fluency in that language indexes their social background.

POLITICAL LIFE

Government. Malaysia's government is nominally headed by the king whose position rotates among the nine hereditary Malay rulers every five years. The king selects the prime minister from the leading coalition in parliament, a body which is further

Beginning in the 1970s, the government has attempted to increase the number of Malays living in urban areas like Kuala Lumpur (above).

divided into the elected representatives of the Dewan Rakyat and the appointed senators of the Dewan Negara. Since independence Malaysian national elections have been won by a coalition of ethnic-based political parties. Known first as the Alliance, and, following the 1969 unrest, as the National Front, this coalition is itself dominated by the United Malays National Organization (UMNO), a party composed of Malay moderates. UMNO rule is aided by the gerrymandered parliamentary districts that over-represent rural Malay constituencies. The UMNO president has always become Malaysia's prime minister, so the two thousand delegates at the biannual UMNO General Assembly are the real electoral force in the country, choosing the party leadership that in turn leads the country.

Leadership and Political Officials. Malaysian political leaders demand a great deal of deference from the public. The Malay term for government, *kerajaan*, refers to the *raja* who ruled from the pre-colonial courts. High-ranking politicians are referred to as *yang berhormat* (he who is honored), and sustain remarkable resiliency in office. Their longevity is due to the fact that successful politicians are great patrons, with considerable influence over the allocation of social benefits such as scholarships, tenders, and permits. Clients, in return, show deference and give appropriate electoral support. The mainstream press are also among the most consistent and most important boosters of the ruling coalition's politicians. Even with the substantial power of the political elite, corruption remains informal, and one can negotiate the lower levels of the state bureaucracy without paying bribes. However, endless stories circulate of how appropriate payments can oil a sometimes creaky process.

Social Problems and Control. Through its colonial history, British Malaya had one of the largest per capita police forces of all British colonies. Police power increased during the communist rebellion (the "Emergency") begun in 1948, which was fought primarily as a police action. The Emergency also expanded the influence of the police Special Branch intelligence division. Malaysia retains aspects of a police state. Emergency regulations for such things as detention without trial (called the Internal Security Act) remain in use; the police are a federal rather than local institution; and police quarters (especially in more isolated rural areas) still have the bunker-like design necessary for confronting an armed insurgency. Even in urban areas police carry considerable firepower. Officers with M-16s are not a rarity and guards at jewelry shops often have long-barrel shotguns. Criminals tend to be audacious given the fact that possession of an illegal firearm carries a mandatory death sentence. Since the police focus more on protecting commercial than residential property, people in housing estates and rural areas will sometimes apprehend criminals themselves. The most elaborate crime network is composed of Chinese triads who extend back in lineage to the colonial period. Malaysia is close to the opium producing areas of the "Golden Triangle" where Burma, Thailand, and Laos meet. Drug possession carries a mandatory death sentence.

Military Activity. The Malaysian military's most striking characteristic is that, unlike its neighbors, there has never been a military coup in the country. One reason is the important social function of the military to insure Malay political dominance. The highest ranks of the military are composed of ethnic Malays, as are a majority of those who serve under them. The military's controversial role in establishing order following the May 1969 urban rebellion further emphasizes the political function of the institution as one supporting the Malay-dominated ruling coalition. The Malaysian armed forces, though small in number, have been very active in

United Nations peace-keeping, including the Congo, Namibia, Somalia, and Bosnia.

SOCIAL WELFARE AND CHANGE PROGRAMS

The Malaysian government has promoted rapid social change to integrate a national society from its ethnic divisions. Its grandest program was originally called the New Economic Policy (NEP), implemented between 1971 and 1990 and continued in modified form as the National Development Policy (NDP). Since poverty eradication was an aim of the NEP a considerable amount of energy has gone to social welfare efforts. The consequences of these programs disseminate across the social landscape: home mortgages feature two rates, a lower one for Malays and a higher one for others; university admissions promote Malay enrollment; mundane government functions such as allocating hawker licenses have an ethnic component. But the government has also tried to ethnically integrate Malaysia's wealthy class; therefore many NEP-inspired ethnic preferences have allowed prosperous Malays to accrue even greater wealth. The dream of creating an affluent Malaysia continues in the government's 1991 plan of Vision 2020, which projects that the country will be "fully developed" by the year 2020. This new vision places faith in high technology, including the creation of a "Multi-Media Super Corridor" outside of Kuala Lumpur, as the means for Malaysia to join the ranks of wealthy industrialized countries, and to develop a more unified society.

NONGOVERNMENTAL ORGANIZATIONS AND OTHER ASSOCIATIONS

Through its welfare policies the government jealously guards its stewardship over social issues, and nongovernmental organizations (NGOs) work under its close surveillance. The state requires that all associations be registered, and failure to register can effectively cripple an organization. NGO life is especially active in urban areas, addressing problems peripheral to the state's priorities of ethnic redistribution and rapid industrialization. Many prominent NGOs are affiliated with religious organizations, and others congregate around issues of the environment, gender and sexuality, worker's rights, and consumers' interests.

GENDER ROLES AND STATUSES

Division of Labor by Gender. Malaysia's affluence has changed the gender divide in the public sphere of work while maintaining the gendered di-

Young people are instructed at an early age to socialize primarily with kin.

vision of labor in the household. Most conspicuous among the new developments are the burgeoning factories that employ legions of women workers on the assembly lines. Domestic labor is a different matter, with cooking and cleaning still deemed to be female responsibilities. In wealthier families where both men and women work outside the home there has been an increase in hiring domestic servants. Since Malaysian women have other opportunities, nearly all of this domestic work goes to female foreign maids.

The Relative Status of Women and Men. Generally men have more power than women in Malaysian society. Male dominance is codified in laws over such things as the guardianship of children. The top politicians, business leaders, and religious practitioners are predominately male. Yet Malaysian society shows considerable suppleness in its gender divisions with prominent women emerging in many different fields. Most of the major political parties have an active women's wing which provides access to political power. Though opportunities for men and women differ by ethnic group and social class, strict gender segregation has not been a part of modern Malaysian life.

MARRIAGE, FAMILY, AND KINSHIP

Marriage. Even with significant changes in marriage practices, weddings reveal the sharp differences in Malaysian society. There are two ways to marry: registering the union with the government; and joining in marriage before a religious authority. Christian Malaysians may marry Buddhists or Hindus answering only to their families and beliefs; Muslim Malaysians who marry non-Muslims risk government sanction unless their partner converts to Islam. Marriage practices emphasize Malaysia's separate ethnic customs. Indians and Chinese undertake divination rites in search of compatibility and auspicious dates, while Malays have elaborate gift exchanges. Malay wedding feasts are often held in the home, and feature a large banquet with several dishes eaten over rice prepared in oil (to say one is going to eat oiled rice means that a wedding is imminent). Many Chinese weddings feature a multiple-course meal in a restaurant or public hall, and most Indian ceremonies include intricate rituals. Since married partners join families as well as individuals, the meeting between prospective in-laws is crucial to the success of the union. For most Malaysians marriage is a crucial step toward adulthood. Although the average age for marriage continues to increase, being single into one's thirties generates concern for families and individuals alike. The social importance of the institution makes interethnic marriage an issue of considerable stress.

Domestic Unit. Malaysian households have undergone a tremendous transformation following the changes in the economy. The shift from agricultural commodities to industrial production has made it difficult for extended families to live together. Yet as family mobility expands, as a result of modern schedules, efforts to maintain kin ties also increase. Improved telecommunications keep distant kin in contact, as does the efficient transportation network. A dramatic example of this occurs on the major holidays when millions return to hometowns for kin reunions.

Inheritance. The critical issue of inheritance is land. With the importance Malays place on land ownership, it is rarely viewed as a commodity for sale, and the numerous empty houses that dot the Malaysian landscape are testament to their absentee-owners unwillingness to sell. Gold is also a valuable inheritance; Malaysians from all groups readily turn extra cash into gold as a form of insurance for the future.

Kin Groups. The crucial kin distinctions in Malaysian culture are between ethnic groups, which tend to limit intermarriage. Among the majority of Malays, kin groups are more horizontal than vertical, meaning that siblings are more important than ancestors. Those considered Malay make appropriate marriage partners; non-Malays do not. These distinctions are somewhat flexible, however, and those that embrace Islam and follow Malay customs are admitted as potential Malay marriage partners. Greater flexibility in kinship practices also appears among immigrant groups amid the fresh possibilities created by diasporic life. A striking example is the Baba community, Chinese who immigrated prior to British rule and intermarried with locals, developing their own hybrid language and cultural style. These dynamics point to the varied kinship arrangements possible between the different ethnic communities in Malaysian society.

SOCIALIZATION

Infant Care. Malaysian babies are lavished with considerable care. Most are born in hospitals, though midwives still provide their services in more remote areas. Careful prohibitions are rigidly followed for both the infant and the mother, according to the various cultural customs. New mothers wear special clothes, eat foods to supplement their strength, and refrain from performing tasks that might bring bad luck to their babies. Grandmothers often live with their new grandchildren for the first few months of their new life.

Child Rearing and Education. Malaysian child rearing practices and educational experiences sustain the differences among the population. Most Malaysian children learn the importance of age hierarchy, especially the proper use of titles to address their elders. The family also teaches that kin are the appropriate source of friendly companionship. The frequent presence of siblings and cousins provides familiarity with the extended family and a preferred source of playmates. In turn, many families teach that strangers are a source of suspicion. The school experience reinforces the ethnic differences in the population, since the schools are divided into separate systems with Malay-medium, Mandarin-medium, and Tamil-medium instruction. Yet the schools do provide common experiences, the most important of which is measuring progress by examination, which helps to emphasize mastery of accumulated knowledge as the point of education. Outside of school, adolescents who mix freely with others or spend significant time away from home are considered "social," a disparaging remark that suggests involvement in illicit activity. A good Malaysian child re-

A textile worker creates a batik in Kota Bharu. Outside of northern peninsular Malaysia, batik designs are usually produced in factories.

spects hierarchy, stays close to kin, follows past examples, and is demure among strangers. These lessons teach Malaysian children how to fit into a diverse society.

Higher Education. Higher education is a vital part of Malaysian life, though the universities that are the most influential in the society are located outside the country. Hundreds of thousands of students have been educated in Britain, Australia, and the United States; the experience of leaving Malaysia for training abroad is an important rite of passage for many of the elite. Malaysia boasts a growing local university system that supplements the foreign universities. The quality of local faculty, often higher than that of the second- and third-tier foreign universities that many Malaysians attend, is rarely sufficient to offset the cachet of gaining one's degree abroad.

ETIQUETTE

Malaysian society is remarkable due to its openness to diversity. The blunders of an outsider are tolerated, a charming dividend of Malaysia's cosmopolitan heritage. Yet this same diversity can present challenges for Malaysians when interacting in public. Because there is no single dominant cultural paradigm, social sanctions for transgressing the rights of others are reduced. Maintaining public facilities is a source of constant public concern, as is the proper etiquette for driving a motor vehicle. Malaysian sociability instead works through finding points of connection. When Malaysians meet strangers, they seek to fit them into a hierarchy via guesses about one's religion (Muslims use the familiar Arabic greetings only to other Muslims); inquiries into one's organization (as an initial question many Malaysians will ask, "who are you attached to?"); and estimations of age (unknown older men are addressed by the honorific "uncle," women as "auntie" in the appropriate language). Strangers shake hands, and handshaking continues after the first meeting (Malays often raise the hand to their heart after shaking), though it is sometimes frowned upon between men and women. Greetings are always expressed with the right hand, which is the dominant hand in Malaysian life. Since the left hand is used to cleanse the body, it is considered inappropriate for use in receiving gifts, giving money, pointing directions, or passing objects.

RELIGION

Religious Beliefs. Nearly all the world religions, including Islam, Buddhism, Hinduism, and Christianity are present in Malaysia. Religion correlates strongly with ethnicity, with most Muslims Malay, most Hindus Indian, and most Buddhists Chinese. The presence of such diversity heightens the importance of religious identity, and most Malaysians have a strong sense of how their religious practice differs from that of others (therefore a Malaysian Christian also identifies as a non-Muslim). Religious holidays, especially those celebrated with open houses, further blend the interreligious experience of the population. Tension between religious communities is modest. The government is most concerned with the practices of the Muslim majority, since Islam is the official religion (60 percent of the population is Muslim). Debates form most often over the government's role in religious life, such as whether the state should further promote Islam and Muslim practices (limits on gambling, pork-rearing, availability of alcohol, and the use of state funds for building mosques) or whether greater religious expression for non-Muslims should be allowed.

Religious Practitioners. The government regulates religious policy for Malaysia's Muslims, while the local mosque organizes opportunities for religious instruction and expression. Outside these institutions, Islam has an important part in electoral politics as Malay parties promote their Muslim credentials. Hindu, Christian, and Buddhist clergy often have a presence in Malaysian life through cooperative ventures, and their joint work helps to ameliorate their minority status. Religious missionaries work freely proselytizing to non-Muslims, but evangelists interested in converting Muslims are strictly forbidden by the state.

Rituals and Holy Places. Malaysia's most prominent holy place is the National Mosque, built in the heart of Kuala Lumpur in 1965. Its strategic position emphasizes the country's Islamic identity. Countrywide, the daily call to prayer from the mosques amplifies the rhythm of Islamic rituals in the country, as does the procession of the faithful to fulfill their prayers. Reminders of prayer times are included in television programs and further highlight the centrality of Islam in Malaysia. Important holidays include the birth of the Prophet and the pilgrimage to Mecca, all of which hold a conspicuous place in the media. The month of fasting, Ramadan, includes acts of piety beyond the customary refraining from food and drink during daylight hours and is followed by a great celebration. Non-Muslim religious buildings, practices, and holidays have a smaller public life in Malaysia. Part of this is due to fewer believers in the country, and part is due

to public policy which limits the building of churches and temples along with the broadcasting of non-Muslim religious services. The important non-Muslim holidays include Christmas, Deepavali (the Hindu festival of light), and Wesak day (which celebrates the life of the Buddha). The Hindu holiday of Thaipussam merits special attention, because devotees undergo spectacular rites of penance before vast numbers of spectators, most dramatically at the famous Batu Caves, located in the bluffs outside of Kuala Lumpur.

Death and the Afterlife. Malaysians have a strong interest in the metaphysical, and stories about spirits and ghosts whether told in conversation, read in books, or seen on television gain rapt attention. Many of these stories sustain a relationship with people who have passed away, whether as a form of comfort or of fear. Cemeteries, including vast fields of Chinese tombs marked with family characters and Muslim graves with the distinctive twin stones, are sites of mystery. The real estate that surrounds them carries only a modest price due to the reputed dangers of living nearby. Muslim funerals tend to be community events, and an entire neighborhood will gather at the home of the deceased to prepare the body for burial and say the requisite prayers. Corpses are buried soon after death, following Muslim custom, and mourners display a minimum of emotion lest they appear to reject the divine's decision. The ancestor memorials maintained by Chinese clans are a common site in Malaysia, and the familiar small red shrines containing offerings of oranges and joss sticks appear on neighborhood street corners and in the rear of Chinese-owned shops. Faith in the efficacy of the afterlife generates considerable public respect for religious graves and shrines even from non-adherents.

MEDICINE AND HEALTH CARE

Malaysia boasts a sophisticated system of modern health care with doctors trained in advanced biomedicine. These services are concentrated in the large cities and radiate out in decreasing availability. Customary practitioners, including Chinese herbalists and Malay healers, supplement the services offered in clinics and hospitals and boast diverse clientele.

SECULAR CELEBRATIONS

Given the large number of local and religious holidays observed in Malaysia, few national secular celebrations fit into the calendar. Two important ones

Farm workers harvesting tea leaves. Ethnic division of labor, in which Malays work almost entirely in agriculture, has eroded in recent years.

include the king's birthday, and the nation's independence day, 31 August. The strong Malaysian interest in sports makes victories for the national team, especially in badminton, a cause for revelry.

THE ARTS AND THE HUMANITIES

Support for the Arts. Public support for the arts is meager. Malaysian society for the past century has been so heavily geared toward economic development that the arts have suffered, and many practitioners of Malaysia's aesthetic traditions mourn the lack of apprentices to carry them on. The possibility exists for a Malaysian arts renaissance amid the country's growing affluence.

Literature. The pre-colonial Malay rulers supported a rich variety of literary figures who produced court chronicles, fables, and legends that form a prominent part of the contemporary Malaysian cultural imagination. Developing a more contemporary national literature has been a struggle because of language, with controversies over whether Malaysian fiction should be composed solely in Malay or in other languages as well. Though adult literacy is nearly 90 percent, the well-read newspapers lament that the national belief in the importance of reading is stronger than the practice.

Graphic Arts. A small but vibrant group of graphic artists are productive in Malaysia. Practitioners of batik, the art of painting textiles with wax followed by dying to bring out the pattern, still work in northern peninsular Malaysia. Batik-inspired designs are often produced in factories on shirts, sarongs, table cloths, or dresses forming an iconic Malaysian aesthetic.

Performance Arts. Artistic performance in Malaysia is limited by the state's controls over public assembly and expression. The requirement that the government approve all scripts effectively limits what might be said in plays, films, and television. The preferred performance genre in Malaysia is popular music, and concerts of the top Malay pop singers have great followings in person and on television. Musical stars from Bombay and Hong Kong also have substantial numbers of very committed fans, whose devotion makes Malaysia an overseas stop on the tours of many performers. The favorite Malaysian entertainment medium is television, as most homes have television sets. Malaysians watch diverse programming: the standard export American fare, Japanese animation, Hong Kong martial arts, Hindi musicals, and Malay drama. The advent of the video cassette and the Internet was made for Malaysia's diverse society, allowing Malaysians to make expressive choices that often defeat the state's censorship.

THE STATE OF THE PHYSICAL AND SOCIAL SCIENCES

Given the Malaysian government's considerable support for rapid industrialization, scientific research is high on the list of its priorities. Malaysian universities produce sophisticated research, though they are sapped for funds by the huge expenditure of sending students overseas for their degrees. Malaysian scientists have made substantial contributions in rubber and palm oil research, and this work will likely continue to increase the productivity of these sectors. Government monitoring of social science research increases the risks of critical scholarship though some academicians are quite outspoken and carry considerable prestige in society.

BIBLIOGRAPHY

Alwi Bin Sheikh Alhady. *Malay Customs and Traditions*, 1962.

Amir Muhammad, Kam Raslan, and Sheryll Stothard. *Generation: A Collection of Contemporary Malaysian Ideas*, 1998.

Andaya, Barbara Watson, and Leonard Y. Andaya. *A History of Malaysia*, 1982.

Ariffin Omar. *Bangsa Melayu: Malay Concepts of Democracy and Community 1945-1950*, 1993.

Carsten, Janet. *The Heat of the Hearth*, 1997.

Chandra Muzaffar. *Protector? An Analysis of the Concept and Practice of Loyalty in Leader-Led Relationships within Malay Society*, 1979.

Cheah Boon Kheng. *Red Star Over Malaya*, 1983.

Collins, Elizabeth. *Pierced by Murugan's Lance: Ritual, Power, and Moral Redemption Among Malaysian Hindus*, 1997.

Crouch, Harold. *Government and Society in Malaysia*, 1996.

Gomez, Edmund Terence and K. S. Jomo. *Malaysia's Political Economy: Politics, Patronage, and Profits*, 1997.

Gullick, John. *Indigenous Political Systems of Western Malaya*, 1958.

Harper, Timothy. *The End of Empire and the Making of Modern Malaya*, 1999.

Jomo, K. S. *A Question of Class: Capital, the State, and Uneven Development in Malaya*, 1986.

Kahn, Joel S., and Francis Loh Kok Wah, ed. *Fragmented Vision: Culture and Politics in Contemporary Malaysia*, 1992.

Kaur, Amarjit. *Economic Change in East Malaysia: Sabah and Sarawak Since 1850*, 1998.

Khoo Boo Teik. *Paradoxes of Mahathirism: An Intellectual Biography of Mahathir Mohamad*, 1995.

Kratoska, Paul. *The Japanese Occupation of Malaya: A Social and Economic History*, 1998.

Loh, Francis K. W. *Beyond the Tin Mines: Coolies, Squatters and New Villagers in the Kinta Valley, c. 1880–1980*, 1980.

Means, Gordon. *Malaysian Politics: The Second Generation*, 1991.

Milner, Anthony. *The Invention of Politics in Colonial Malaya: Contesting Nationalism and the Expansion of the Public Sphere*, 1995.

Mohamed Noordin Sopiee. *From Malayan Union to Singapore Separation*, 1974.

Nagata, Judith. *Malaysian Mosaic: Perspectives from a Poly-Ethnic Society*, 1979.

Ong, Aihwa. *Spirits of Resistance and Capitalist Discipline: Factory Women in Malaysia*, 1987.

Rehman Rashid. *A Malaysian Journey*, 1993.

Roff, William. *The Origins of Malay Nationalism*, 1967.

Shamsul, A. B. *From British to Bumiputera Rule: Local Politics and Rural Development in Peninsular Malaysia*, 1986.

Stenson, Michael. *Class, Race, and Colonialism in West Malaysia: The Indian Case*, 1980.

Strauch, Judith. *Chinese Village Politics in the Malaysian State*, 1981.

Sweeney, Amin. *A Full Hearing: Orality and Literacy in the Malay World*, 1987.

Tan Chee Beng. *The Baba of Melaka: Culture and Identity of a Chinese Peranakan Community in Malaysia*, 1988.

Winzeler, Robert L., ed. *Indigenous Peoples and the State: Politics, Land, and Ethnicity in the Malayan Peninsula and Borneo*, 1997.

—THOMAS WILLIAMSON

MALDIVES

CULTURE NAME
Maldivian

ORIENTATION

Identification. The Maldives is one of the world's poorest developing countries. It is threatened by global warming because of its very low elevation. The main natural resources are fisheries and a marine environment conducive to tourism. The other constraints it faces are small and widely dispersed island communities, limited skilled human resources, and rapid population growth.

Location and Geography. The Republic of Maldives is an archipelago consisting of twenty-six coral atolls, in the northern Indian Ocean. The chain of islands extends 510 miles (820 kilometers), but occupies an area of just 116 square miles (300 square kilometers), roughly 1.5 times the size of Washington D.C. The closest neighbors are India and Sri Lanka. The capital is Malé.

The twenty-six coral atolls contain 1,190 very small islands of which 198 are inhabited. Most of the islands are close to the atoll enclosure reef, and some are still in the process of forming. The longest is Gan in Adu atoll. Because the islands are coral-based, they are flat and low-lying. As a result, the water table is high. However, the islands are protected from the elements by the reef and rarely have major storms. In the older islands a larger layer of topsoil has formed, and these islands are covered with coconut trees, breadfruit, and dense shrubs. Agricultural potential is limited by the high alkalinity of the soil and its poor water retention. However, people grow vegetables, fruits, and yams.

The climate is warm and tropical. Seasonal changes are determined by the two yearly monsoons. The season of the northeast monsoon is characterized by dry, mild winds, and generally extends from December to April. The southwest monsoon, although irregular, extends from May until August and brings heavy rains and wind. The northern atolls are drier, while the southern atolls are wetter. The humidity is fairly high throughout the year.

Demography. In 1996, the population was 256,157, compared with 195,000 in 1986; the estimated population for the year 2000 is 289,117. The annual rate of population growth is almost 3 percent. Almost most half the population is under fifteen years of age, and about 3 percent is sixty five years and older. About 25 percent of the population reside in Malé. The growth rate in Malé atoll has been high as a result of employment opportunities offered by growth in the service sector. Even though income in Malé is significantly higher than that in the atolls, the resulting rural-urban migration has led to increasing unemployment. Emigration from the republic is rare except for educational purposes or to work as a crew member on Maldivian ships.

Linguistic Affiliation. Dhivehi, which is spoken in all parts of the country, is not spoken in any other part of the world. It is considered an Indo-European language related to Singhala, the language spoken in Sri Lanka. The alphabets and writing system are similar to Arabic. English is the second language and is widely used in commerce and in many government schools.

Symbolism. The national flag is red with a large green rectangle in the center bearing a vertical white crescent on the hoist side. The country is associated with the ''maldive fish'' (boiled sun-dried tuna).

HISTORY AND ETHNIC RELATIONS

Emergence of the Nation. The early settlers probably came before 500 B.C.E., from Sri Lanka and southern India. In the twelfth century, sailors from East Africa and Arab countries arrived. Originally, Maldivians were Buddhists, but in the twelfth century Islam was proclaimed the national religion. The

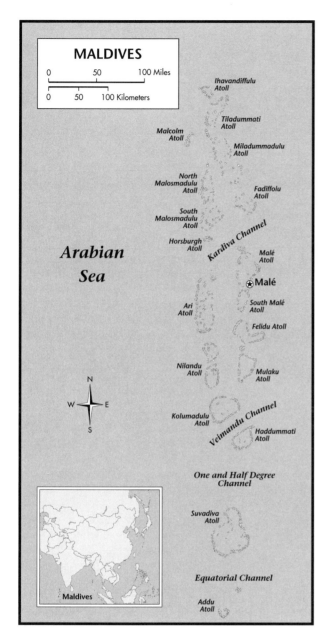

Maldives

Republic of Maldives was created with an elected president. The country joined the British Commonwealth in 1982.

Ethnic Relations. The population consists of a mix of people who trace their descent from Sri Lanka, India, Arab countries, and Africa. Because of religious and linguistic homogeneity, there is stability and unity.

URBANISM, ARCHITECTURE, AND THE USE OF SPACE

Malé is the center of political and economic life. It has a maze of narrow streets with over twenty mosques and markets. Poor people live in houses built from thatched palm with tin roofs, and the more prosperous have houses made of crushed coral with tile roofs. The main attractions are the National Museum, which displays items from Arab, Sri Lankan, and Dravidian cultures; Sultan Park; the Islamic Centre; and the gold-painted Grand Friday mosque. The oldest mosque, Hukuru Miski, is known for its intricate stone carvings.

FOOD AND ECONOMY

Food in Daily Life. Rice and fish are the staple foods. Fish is the most important source of protein in the average diet. Very few vegetables are eaten. Betel leaf with arecanut, cloves, and lime, known as *foh*, is chewed after meals. Old people smoke *guduguda*, an elongated pipe that goes through a trough of water. Most food served in tourist resorts is imported.

Food Customs at Ceremonial Occasions. Meat other than pork is eaten only on special occasions. Alcohol is not permitted except in tourist resorts. The local brew, *raa*, is a sweet toddy made from the crown of the coconut palm.

Basic Economy. All the fish that is consumed locally is from the domestic economy. Basic food commodities such as rice, sugar, and flour are imported. There are over seventy resort islands near the capital.

Land and Tenure and Property. Land belongs to the state and is given free to families in the island of their origin to build houses. The only exception is that public servants lease land where they work. In other islands, where tourist resorts, a cannery, the airport, and other small industries are located, employees are provided with temporary accommodations.

Maldives has always been an independent political entity except when it was under Portuguese control from 1558 to 1573. In 1887, the Maldives agreed to become a protectorate of the British government, allowing the British to take responsibility for it defense and foreign relations while maintaining for itself internal control. The first constitution was ratified by the Sultan in 1932, and the sultanate became an elected rather than hereditary position.

National Identity. The Maldives regained full sovereignty in 1965 and joined the United Nations that year. In 1968, the sultanate was abolished and the republic was declared. On 11 November 1968, the

Young girls gather at a well. Almost half of the country's population is under fifteen years of age.

Commercial Activities. Because of the limited land mass, the main prospect for economic development is the country's marine resources. Fisheries, tourism, trade, and transport (shipping) constitute the principal economic base.

Major Industries. Fisheries and international tourism are the main industries. The economy has changed from a reliance on fisheries to a service-sector-based economy driven by international tourism. The main primary sector is fishing. The secondary sector consists of construction and manufac-

turing. In the tertiary sector, tourism, government administration, and transport are the dominant industries. Manufacturing output consists primarily of processed fish; apparel and clothing; cottage industries such as woven mats, coir rope, and handicrafts; and boat building industries.

Trade. In addition to food, the country imports manufactured goods such as petroleum products and various consumer goods. In 1997, these products were imported primarily from Singapore, India, Sri Lanka, the United Arab Emirates, Malaysia, and the United Kingdom. About 80 percent of exports consist of frozen, dried, and salted skipjack tuna; canned fish; dried shark fins; and fish meal. A small manufacturing export sector exports apparel and clothing accessories. In 1997, the leading destinations for exports were the United Kingdom, the United States, Sri Lanka, Japan, and Singapore.

Division of Labor. There were approximately sixty-four thousand members of the Maldives workforce in 1999, one-third of whom were foreign workers. About 20 percent of the workforce in 1999 worked in the fishing industry; 15 percent in industry; 10 percent in tourism, and 55 percent in other sectors. The minimum working age is fourteen (sixteen for government work).

SOCIAL STRATIFICATION

Class and Castes. A disproportionate share of government expenditures directly benefits Malé and ensures its residents a standard of living that is substantially higher than that in the atolls. Status is derived primarily from wealth rather than family, although family ties and connections are important in determining the availability of opportunities. One's position with the government also confers status, while education is less important.

POLITICAL LIFE

Government. The legislative assembly known as the Majlis is composed of fifty members: two from Malé, two from each of the twenty administrative atolls, and eight appointed by the president. The speaker of the Majlis is not a member of that body and is appointed by the president. Even though all the members have the right to attend sessions and speak at the Majlis, only elected members can vote. The right to vote is universal for those age twenty one years and over. The head of the government is the president who is nominated in a secret ballot by the Majlis, and then elected by a majority vote at a national referendum for a five-year term. The president appoints the ministers and all judges to the courts. The high court consists of a chief justice and four judges.

The executive branch is divided into the president's office, the attorney general's office, and seventeen ministries and associated entities that implement government programs. The ministries of government, the attorney general's office, and the high court all function under the president's office. The current president is also the governor of the central bank.

Leadership and Political Control. The government appoints an atoll chief who exercises the government power. Each island has an island chief appointed by the government who is the administrative head of the island. The atoll offices and the island offices come under the Ministry of Atoll Administration, which is responsible to the president.

Social Problems and Control. Historically, the society has been closely knit and disciplined as a result of unity of religion (Sunni Muslim) and language. Although there was civil unrest in the past, it was mostly related to power struggles within the government, and the stormy relationship between Maldives and the British government prior to the termination of Britain's military presence in the islands in 1976.

Military Activity. The country maintains only one security unit, the National Security Service. This organization has about 1,800 personnel who perform army, police, and maritime duties. Because of the geographic spread of the islands, it is impossible to have a military presence on every island and for the coast guards to protect the area. Since independence, the country has not faced any external threats.

SOCIAL WELFARE AND CHANGE PROGRAMS

The government has focused its spending on social services and preventive health services. There is no organized social welfare system. Assistance is traditionally provided through the extended family. Employees are entitled to medical and maternity leave.

GENDER ROLES AND STATUSES

Division of Labor by Gender. Over 25 percent of women are employed, primarily by the government. The government sector employed 15,862 people in 1996, approximately 64 percent males and 36 percent females. Women in the atolls generally are employed only in domestic or selected duties within the family, such as tending crops and producing general handicraft items such as coir rope and woven coconut palm leaves for domestic use. Women also collect cowrie shells from the shores.

The Relative Status of Women and Men. Women make a significant contribution to social, political and economic affairs. The economic sectors in which women are employed are education, health and welfare, services, tourism, transport, and communication.

A Himmafushi Island man relaxes with his child. Most Maldivian households consist of nuclear families.

MARRIAGE, FAMILY AND KINSHIP

Marriage. The legal age for marriage is eighteen, although half of the women marry by age fifteen. Marriages are not arranged. In accordance with Islamic law, a man can have four wives at any time if he can support them financially, but polygamy is uncommon. Sex before marriage is a punishable offense. Marriages can take place only between Muslims. Maldives has one of the highest divorce rates in the world; according to a 1977 census, nearly half of the women over the age of thirty had been married four times or more.

Domestic Unit. Unlike households in many other Muslim countries, households in Maldives typically do not include extended family members. Nuclear families consisting of a married couple and their children comprise roughly 80 percent of the households, with the father typically recognized as the head of the family. Unmarried persons generally live with their families rather than by themselves.

Inheritance. Both men and women may inherit property.

Kin Groups. The island communities outside of Malé are generally close-knit, self-contained groups in which most everyone is related through generations of intermarriage.

SOCIALIZATION

Child Rearing and Education. Primary level education is for five years and secondary education is in two stages: five years at the lower level and two years at the higher level. Education is not compulsory. There are three streams of Maldivian education: traditional religious schools (makhtabs), which teach the Koran (Qur'an), basic arithmetic, and the ability to read and write Divehi; modern Divehi-language primary schools; and modern English-language schools. Primary and secondary schooling is based on the British educational system.

In 1998 there were 48,895 students enrolled in 228 primary schools, with 1,992 teachers. In the same year, secondary schools had a total of 36,905 students.

Higher Education. Maldivians must go abroad for higher education. Currently the Science Education Centre in Malé provides pre-university courses, and the Centre may evolve into a university.

ETIQUETTE

Maldivians are brought up to respect elders and those who are educated while conforming to an Is-

A group of boys fish in the shallow waters off the Maldives Islands. In addition to being an important food source, fish is the nation's greatest export.

lamic code of conduct. Strong loyalties tie the individual to the extended family.

RELIGION

Religious Beliefs. Islam is the only national religion; no other religions are permitted. All Maldivians belong to the Sunni sect. Only Muslims may become citizens, marry, or own property in Maldives, and daily life is regulated according to the tenets of Islam. The widespread belief in *jinns*, or evil spirits, has resulted in a blending of Islam with traditional island beliefs into a magico-religious system known as *fandita*.

Religious Practitioners. The political, judicial, and religious systems in Maldives are so closely intertwined that the political leaders and judges are also the country's religious leaders. The president is considered the primary religious leader, and judges, known as *gazis*, are responsible for interpreting Islamic law in the courts.

Rituals and Holy Places. Most holidays are based on the Islamic lunar calendar. In addition to the Golden Grand Friday mosque, twenty other mosques are scattered around Malé. Mosques are also found in each of the islands. In Malé, a grave-

yard holds the tomb of Abu Al Barakat, a North African Arab who brought the Koran to the Maldives in the twelfth century. He later became the first sultan. Also located in this graveyard are tombstones of all the former sultans.

Death and the Afterlife. In accordance with the Islamic faith, the people of Maldives believe that people go to heaven or hell after death, depending on how faithfully they adhered to the five tenets of Islam while still alive. Believers are considered worthy to enter heaven if they were faithful to repeat the creed "There is no God but Allah, and Muhammad is the prophet of Allah"; fast during the month of Ramadan; pray five times every day; give alms to the poor; and, if possible, make a pilgrimage to the holy city of Mecca sometime during their lifetime.

MEDICINE AND HEALTH CARE

Improved health services have decreased the infant mortality rate and the general death rate. Life expectancy increased to seventy-one years, from sixty-one years between 1986 and 1996. The birth rate per thousand dropped from forty-five in 1986 to twenty-six in 1996.

The minaret of a mosque on the island of Malé, the principal island in the Maldives. Islam is the only religion permitted in the country.

SECULAR CELEBRATIONS

Kudaeid celebrates the sighting of the new moon at the end of Ramadan, and the Prophet Mohamed's birthday is also celebrated. National Day, the day Mohammed Thakurufaan overthrew the Portuguese in 1573, occurs on first day of the third month of the lunar calender. Victory Day on 3 November celebrates the defeat of the Sri Lankan mercenaries who tried to overthrow the govern-ment. Republic Day on 11 November commemorates the foundation of the current republic.

BIBLIOGRAPHY

Adney, M., and W. K. Carr. "The Maldives." In J. M. Ostheimer, ed. *The Politics of the Western Indian Ocean Islands*, 1975.

Anderson, R. C., and A. Hafiz. *The State of the Maldivian Tuna stock: Analysis of Catch and Effort Data and Estimation of Maximum Sustainable Yield*, 1985.

Cole, R. V. "The Island States of the Indian Ocean: A View from the South Pacific." *Pacific Economic Bulletin* 1 (2): 41–46, 1986

Fifth National Development Plan 1997–2000, 1998.

Maniku, H. A. *The Republic of Maldives*, 1980.

Ministry of Planning, Human Resources and Environment. *Statistical Year Book of Maldives*, 1998.

Sathiendrakumar, S. *Development of Resources of the Sea for Regional Cooperation and National Development*, 1983.

——. "Artisanal Fisheries, Tourism and Development: Economic Analysis of the Maldives and Fishing-Boat Mechanisation." Ph. D. Thesis, University of Newcastle, New South Wales, Australia, 1988.

——. "An Appropriate Management Policy for the Tuna fishery in the Maldives." *Asian Fisheries Science* 2: 163–175, 1989.

——. "Marine Areas as Tourist Attractions in the Southern Indian Ocean." In M. L. Miller, and J. Auyong, eds., *Proceedings of the 1990 Congress on Coastal and Marine Tourism*, 1990.

——. "Problems Faced by Indian Ocean Island Economies: The Case of the Maldives." In R. Gabbay, R. N. Gosh, and M. A. B. Siddique eds., *Economics of Small Island Nations*, 1996.

——. "Environmental Management for Sustainable Economic Development in Island Economies: The Maldivian Experience." In K. C. Roy, H. C. Blomqvist, and Hossain Iftekhar, eds., *Development That Lasts*, 1997.

——, and C. A. Tisdell. "Tourism and the Development of the Maldives" *Massey Journal of Asian and Pacific Business* 1 (1): 27–34, 1985.

——. "Fishery Resources and Policies in the Maldives: Trends and Issues for an Island Developing Country." *Marine Policy* 10 (4): 279–293, 1986.

——. "Optimal Economic Fishery Effort in the Maldivian Tuna Fishery: An appropriate Model." *Marine Resource Economics* 4 (1): 15–44, 1987.

——. "Migration from Traditional Rural Communities and Outside Employment: A Study of Maldivian Fishing Villages." *South East Asian Economic Review* 8 (2): 121–63, 1987.

———. ''Towards and Appropriate Effort-Based Fishery Model for the Tuna Fishery of Maldives.'' *Indian Journal of Fisheries* 34 (4): 433–454, 1987.

———. ''The Maldives: Development and Socio-Economic Tensions.'' *South East Asian Economic Review* 9 (2): 125–162, 1988.

———. ''Economic Importance of Tourism for Small Indian Ocean and Pacific States.'' In C. A. Tisdell, C. J. Aislabie, and P. J. Stanton, eds., *Economics of Tourism: Case Studies and Analysis*, 1988.

———. ''International Tourism and the Economic Development of the Maldives.'' *Annals of Tourism Research* 16 (2): 254–264, 1989.

———. ''Determinants of Relative Wealth in Maldivian Fishing Villages.'' *Asian Profile* 17 (2): 155–168, 1989.

———. ''International Tourism and the Economic Importance of an Archipelago: The Case of the Maldives.'' In J. L. Kaminarides, Briguglio, and H. Hoogendonk, eds., *The Economic Development of Small Countries: Problems, Strategies and Policies*, 1989.

———. ''Technological Change and Income Distribution: Findings from Maldivian Fishing Villages.'' *Journal of Economics and International Relations* 3 (3): 217–240, 1990.

World Bank. *The Maldives: An Introductory Economic Report*, 1980.

———. *Fishery: Sector Policy Paper*, 1982.

—RAJASUNDRAM SATHUENDRAKUMAR

MALI

CULTURE NAME
Malian

ORIENTATION

Identification. Malian national culture can be best defined as a project that was developed with different emphasis and credibility by the governments that led Mali (formerly French Sudan) in the postindependence period (1960 to the present). It is undoubtedly a colonial legacy. As in most postcolonial nations, the territorial and administrative boundaries established by the colonial power, in this case France, remained essentially unchanged long after independence. Westernized Malian politicians and intellectuals reappropriated modern colonial institutions and adapted them to their reinterpretation of local aims and aspirations. For instance, the choice of Mali as the name for this country—harking back to one of the great medieval empires that blossomed in this area—is representative of a wider attempt by Malian politicians to validate a new political order, the postcolonial state, by claiming its derivation from African political formations already in existence prior to colonization. This reappropriation did not occur in a sociocultural vacuum. Indeed, it was affected by transnational economic and political forces as well as by local popular responses to the policies implemented by local governments.

Since independence, the Malian political leadership has pursued the syncretic integration at the national level of various elements deriving from ethnic and regional cultures. Yet this process of cultural syncretism has not been homogeneous. If most regional or ethnic cultures have been implicated, not all have contributed in the same measure. Indeed, a number of scholars of Mali have noted an imbalance in favor of the numerically dominant Mande (a branch of the Niger-Congo language family) people and their traditions in the formation of a national culture. For the most part, the process of national construction has been a relatively peaceful one, given the long traditions of coexistence, cultural exchange, and mutual tolerance between the populations living in this area.

The ongoing project of Malian national construction can also be viewed as a site of contestation insofar as it is viewed and experienced differently by different strata of the Malian population. In other words, the dominant or hegemonic construct of the Malian nation is based on the reflections of the Westernized Malian elite and does not necessarily coincide with the view of peasants or disenfranchised urban populations. A number of studies of rural communities have highlighted both peasants' hope of receiving benefits from the policies implemented by the Malian governments and their periodic disaffection from and resistance to those policies. Even the democratic government's effort in the late twentieth century to decentralize state institutions, that is to give more power and greater economic means to local communities, met with some skepticism and occasional resistance at the level of some local bodies. Nevertheless, this policy of decentralization, however negotiated at the local level, has begun to dramatically transform local geographies of power.

ORIENTATION

Location and Geography. Mali is 478,764 square miles (1,241,278 square kilometers). It is a landlocked country approximately twice the size of Texas. According to late twentieth century estimates, less than 2 percent of the land is arable; 24.6 percent consists of permanent pasture; 5.7 percent of forests and woodlands; and 68 percent of mostly desert land. Ninety percent of Mali's population is concentrated in the southern regions—Kayes, Koulikoro, Sikasso, Ségou, and Mopti. The climate is hot and dry, with some semitropical zones in the far south. The north is semi-desert or desert. Most cities—many of which already existed well before

Mali

colonization—are located along Mali's rivers: the Niger, the Bani (a tributary of the Niger), and the Senegal. Bamako, the capital, is a colonial city. In the seventeenth and eighteenth centuries, prior to the coming of the French, Bamako was only a village at the center of a semi-independent polity on the periphery of the Ségou state. By 1920, Bamako had become the capital and commercial center of the French Sudan (today's Mali). After independence, Bamako's population grew exponentially, from 100,000 in 1960 to approximately 1,000,000 in 1998 (59 percent of Mali's total urban population). This was partly the outcome of the fall in 1960 of the short-lived Mali Federation (uniting Mali and Senegal) and the subsequent forced return of many Malian citizens living in Senegal. Most of all,

Malians were drawn to the city because of its greater job opportunities—indeed, most administrative headquarters and more than half of all Malian factories and enterprises are concentrated in Bamako.

Demography. Mali's population is approximately 10 million (1998 census). Most Malians live in rural areas, with only 18 percent residing in urban centers. Major ethnic groups in Mali are the Mande (e.g., Bamana, Jula, Malinke), who comprise 50 percent of the population; Peul or Fulbe, 17 percent; Voltaic, 12 percent (e.g. Bobo, Senufo, Minyanka); Tuareg and Moor, 10 percent; Songhai, 6 percent; and other, 5 percent. It should be mentioned that the rigidity of such ethnic categories dates back to colonization. In other words, the classification of local populations into neatly defined ethnic groups is the product of the interaction and misunderstandings between locals and colonial administrators as well as some ethnographers. Indeed, the boundaries between these groups are highly permeable and context-related, and their meanings are subject to renegotiation.

Linguistic Affiliation. Most Malians speak several languages and live in a truly multilingual context. The official language of Mali is French. An educated elite speaks French, and it is the dominant language of the administration, formal education, and the media. Bamana has progressively become the lingua franca of Mali and is spoken by 80 percent of the Malian people, although it is the mother tongue of only 38 percent of the population. Various factors have contributed to the spread of the Bamana language in Mali. Under colonization Bamana became the vernacular of the French colonial army, but it was also used in other institutional contexts such as schooling by the White Sisters, a Catholic women's missionary organization. The development of a written literature in Bamana (e.g., Bamana-French dictionaries, collections of proverbs and stories) and, after independence, the creation of newspapers and television and radio programs in Bamana further contributed to the hegemony of Bamana. The national organization in charge of promoting applied linguistic research, literacy, and education in national languages is the Direction nationale de l'alphabetisation fonctionnelle et de la linguistique appliquée (DNAFLA); created in 1975, it also enforced Bamana as a national language. Other national languages promoted by the DNAFLA include Fulfuldé, Songhai, Senufo, Dogon, Soninké, and Tamasheq.

Symbolism. A number of symbols reinforce and elaborate such central aspects of Malian national culture as the struggle against colonization, the celebration of Mali's rich history, and its long multicultural tradition. The text of Mali's national anthem was composed by an influential politician and novelist, Seydou Badian Kouyaté, at the request of Mali's first president, Modibo Keita. It celebrates the Malian struggle for independence and its newly achieved unity as well as urges Malians to channel their efforts into the process of nation building. Mali's flag uses the color symbolism of the pan-African unity movement—green (hope), gold (a reference to one of Mali's natural resources), and red (the blood sacrificed in the struggle against colonization).

In the late twentieth century the Malian government launched a series of public works, including a remarkable number of monuments (approximately twenty) and a women's museum (Musée Muso Kunda) with an attached research center focusing on women's development. Of these monuments—mostly concentrated in the capital—many have a historical theme and celebrate local and/or regional heroes in the struggle for independence as well as the Malians fallen in the 1991 struggle for democracy. Other monuments celebrate Mali's long multicultural tradition (e.g., the Obelisk) and the tentative peace with the Tuareg population (e.g., the Peace Monument). The Bamana term for "nation" is *faso*, which literally means "the father's house" and by extension refers to one's nation of origin. This reflects the patrilineal skewing of the local kinship system and its impact on the national imagination.

HISTORY AND ETHNIC RELATIONS

Emergence of the Nation. Although this geographic area has been occupied by large empires and states throughout its history (the empires of Ghana, Mali, and Songhai; the Ségou state; and the Omarian state, among others), Mali's current geographic boundaries and, to a large extent, its politico-administrative organization are the result of French colonization (c.1880–1960). The conquest of this area was not without resistance on the part of local populations, such as the fierce resistance to the French by Samory Touré and his troops, and the Tuareg.

After World War II, Africans' growing political demands, the spreading anticolonialist stance at the international level, and the recognition of Africans' participation and sacrifice in the two world wars were all factors that led French colonial subjects to finally gain important political rights. They could create their own political parties and, via their elected representatives, increasingly participate in the political institutions of French West Africa. In 1946 the Rassemblement démocratique africain (RDA)—an inter-territorial party coordinating the pro-independence efforts of most French West African political activists—was created in Bamako. After some uncertain beginnings, the political representatives of the Sudanese branch of the RDA, the US-RDA, were able to win over all opponents and successfully lead Mali to independence. After the dramatic fall of the short-lived Mali Federation (which included Senegal), the French Sudan, under the name of Mali, achieved independence from France on 22 September 1960.

A Peul woman wears large gold earrings and a ring through her nose. Her lips are tattooed in the traditional style.

From 1960 to 1991 Malian politics was primarily organized on the basis of a one-party system. The charismatic Modibo Keita, leader of the single-party, the US-RDA, became Mali's first president. In the aftermath of independence, the Keita government launched an extensive program of national development based on socialist ideas. This included the formation of African cadres, the implementation of a five-year plan of economic development, the politicization of the masses, and the reevaluation of the historical and cultural heritage of the country in light of its socialist option. In particular, the reinterpretation of local traditions was a key step in the effort to legitimize the Malian leadership and justify its political platform. For instance, a number of local griots (a semi-endogamous group of professional bards) composed celebratory songs in honor of Modibo Keita, in which the political leader was depicted as the direct descendent of Sunjata Keita, the founder of the Mali empire. The government's political and economic measures had significant repercussions on the social structure of the Malian society. In particular they favored the transformation of the civil servants into an economic class. The Keita government lost progressively its popularity among various strata of the population. An alliance between the dissatisfied seg-

ments of the Malian population—the peasants, the merchants, and the army (threatened by the growing influence of the party militia)—led to the success of the military coup d'état of 1968.

The first ten years after the coup were characterized by the despotic rule of the Comité militaire de libération nationale (CMLN) under the leadership of Lieutenant Moussa Traoré. The most unpopular of Keita's political measures, such as the obligation of peasants to cultivate collective fields, were removed, and some freedom of trade was established. In the late 1970s Moussa Traoré, after having eliminated all possible rivals, founded Mali's second single party—the Union démocratique du peuple malien (UDPM)—and a number of horizontal organizations (for youth, women, and workers) that granted him and his clique control of the country until 1991. The Traoré period was characterized by a slow liberalization of the economy, progressive political disenchantment, galloping corruption at the administrative level, and a lack of political expression outside the party boundaries.

In 1991, after a series of popular uprisings demanding democratic elections, a military coup led by Colonel Amadou Toumani Touré (popularly known as ATT) brought the Traoré era to an end. An insurgence of grassroots organizations, the opening of new radio stations, and the founding of a large number of newspapers accompanied the advent of democracy. An intermediary government composed of army officials and civilians under the leadership of ATT followed the coup. ATT kept his initial commitment and led the country to its first multiparty elections in 1992. The presidential elections were won by Alpha Oumar Konaré, a distinguished archaeologist and leader of the party ADEMA (Alliance pour la démocratie au Mali).

National Identity. Malian national culture is first and foremost the product of the Malian educated elite and their interpretation of the needs of the general population, which is non-literate to a large extent. Indeed, many postindependence political and economic efforts were geared toward the strengthening of the elite position via the solidification of their economic basis and the broadening of their ranks. People's involvement in state institutions was further expanded by the creation of state-owned enterprises and the recruitment of an increasing number of wage workers, as well as by the predation and redistribution of state resources from the bureaucracy to its clients.

Malian elite have not acted in a vacuum, however, and oftentimes have had to modify their strategies and objectives in accordance with people's responses. This was the case for educated women, who very early on had to postpone the realization of many of their objectives—for instance, the abolition of polygyny—because of a lack of support from their constituencies. In addition, Malian elites have been able to build on established local traditions to foster a sense of a shared nation. Indeed, perhaps one of the secrets of Malian pluralism is the so-called *sinankuya*, or *cousinage*, a pact establishing a joking relationship between certain families, neighboring groups, and ethnic groups. It allows for the free venting of tensions and peaceful overcoming of conflicts.

More generally, the celebration of local cultures and local histories, and their appropriation in national contexts, has been one of the most successful avenues for the construction of the idea of a nation. Consider the organization of the Biennale artistique et culturelle des jeunes du Mali (1962–1988), when artistic troupes that won competitions at the regional level were invited to Bamako to compete at a national level. National holidays and politicians' visits have also been occasion for performances by local troupes. Most of all, theater plays (such as by the Groupe dramatique du Mali), musical events (in particular, griots' performances); radio programs (including the much listened-to stories of Jeli Baba Sissoko), and, in more recent times, television programs, cultural festivals, and the construction of an impressive number of monuments and cultural centers, have constituted important vehicles for the development of a Malian national culture.

Ethnic Relations. Building upon Mali's cultural and linguistic diversity, Malian governments have been able to foster, for the most part, a truly pluralistic society. Complicating this picture somewhat is the history of the difficult relationships between the Tuareg (or Kel Tamasheq), a Berber population living in the north, and the Malian government. Different cultural traditions, issues of race (and in particular Tuareg xenophobia toward the surrounding black populations), the Malian army's cruel retaliations against Tuareg attacks, and the marginality of the Tuareg within state institutions are some of the reasons behind the periodic conflict in the north. In 1994, and after the failure of the Pacte National of April 1992, the Malian government signed a new peace accord with the Tuareg, one that commits the government to the development of all northern populations. The situation in the north continues to be characterized by some instability, but external observers have expressed some confidence in the capacity of the government and the local people to overcome this crisis.

URBANISM ARCHITECTURE, AND THE USE OF SPACE

Typical of this area is the so-called West Sudanese architecture, characterized by the use of sun-baked clay bricks of various shapes. Majestic artistic expressions of this architecture are the beautiful mosques of the northern cities of Djenné and Mopti. The Sudanese style also decorates the facades of many traditional compounds in cities and historic villages. Many rural and urban Malians live in compounds, an enclosed space encompassing a number of two-room houses occupied by an extended family and/or, mostly in the cities, by renters. The first room is typically used for sleeping and receiving guests, while the back room is a more private space and is used for storage and/or sleeping. The use of Western materials, such as tin roofs and cement, is associated with higher social status, and in the cities such materials tend to replace traditional materials. Western materials require less maintenance, but they are more expensive and make for a much hotter space than traditional clay architecture.

The structure of the family is often reflected in the organization of living space. For instance, in the practice of polygyny, each wife is typically allotted her own house, most often within the same compound as the other wives but sometimes elsewhere. The husband either sleeps in his wives' houses on a rotating basis or, if means permit, may build his own individual house, where he receives his wives.

There are significant variations in architecture not only between regions but also within a single region according to people's main source of livelihood. For instance, pastoral groups such as the Fulbe may live not in compounds but in more temporary constructions. From the Mopti region northward, houses are most often two stories, with beautiful terra-cotta pipes for water drainage. In the northern regions people often entertain visitors on their roofs, where they spread colored blankets to take advantage of the occasional breeze. French colonial architecture was inspired by the much-admired local Sudanese style, with French housing and public buildings in Bamako and Ségou showing an interesting mixture of Western, Moroccan, and Sudanese styles. In recent years both local and foreign architects as well as intellectuals, recognizing the aesthetic and functional qualities of baked clay, have been experimenting by mixing it with cement to enhance its durability.

Two Dogon people perform a divination ritual using the prints left in the sand by a jackal. An estimated 19 percent of Mali's population follows traditional religious practices.

FOOD AND ECONOMY

Food in Daily Life. Malian families invest more than half of their household income in food expenditures. In the cities, rice is the preferred dish (40 percent of the daily food intake), followed by cereals (sorghum and millet, 35 percent), peanuts, sugar, and oil (20 percent). In the rural areas where rice is produced, farmers tend to consider rice a luxury item and they sell it. Their basic staples are millet, sorghum, and fonio (a West African cereal) that are consumed in a variety of ways: served with sauces with fish or meat and various vegetables, or in the form of porridge (mixed with water, sugar, and fresh or powdered milk).

Food Customs at Ceremonial Occasions. Malian cuisine varies from region to region, but some dishes and drinks have acquired a national dimension, such as *nsaamè* or *riz au gras* (a rice dish with meat and vegetables), *jinjinbere* (a drink made of water, sugar, lemon, and ginger), and *dabileni* (a drink made of water, sugar, and sorrel).These dishes are often prepared for the celebration of life-cycle rituals (e.g., naming ceremonies, weddings) and other ceremonial events.

Basic Economy. The Malian economy is principally based on the cultivation of cotton (Mali is the second largest producer of cotton in Africa), food crops (rice, millet, sorghum, fonio, peanuts, and corn), and livestock (cattle, sheep, and goats). The primary sector accounts for approximately 46 percent of the gross domestic product (GDP) and is mostly run by small-scale family-run enterprises. Industry, including manufacturing, contributes 20 percent to the GDP, and services approximately 33 percent. According to official statistics, Mali is one of the poorest countries in the world. Solidarity links among family members, neighbors, and coworkers; entrepreneurial skills; and redistributive practices, however, go a long way to ease difficult economic conditions.

Land Tenure and Property. Prior to colonization, land was not a commodity. Among the Bamana agriculturists, access to the land (that is, the right to cultivate a piece of land, not individual ownership) was often mediated by the so-called "land chief" who was often a respected elder from the first family to settle in the area. The land chief was in charge of distributing the land among the various lineages of the village. He was also responsible for the celebration of various sacrifices, in particular to the shrine of the spirits in charge of protecting the village, the so-called *dasiri* (a cluster of trees and shrubs). Lineage members would collectively cultivate the land and the lineage chief would be in charge of the redistribution of resources among individual households according to their perceived needs. However, conflicts among households of the same lineage would periodically erupt and often lead to further fissions within the lineage. Besides collective farming, individuals of both genders could cultivate smaller fields on the side and independently manage their revenues. The colonial conquest has greatly complicated the issue of property. At the present, local systems for the allocation of property, Islamic law, and colonially derived property rules (mostly affecting parcels in urban areas) coexist, but not without conflict, side by side.

Major Industries. The Malian economy is scarcely industrialized despite massive efforts in this direction by the Keita government after independence. Locally operated industries mostly concentrate on processing farm commodities (such as food and fish), construction (e.g. the production of cement), and the production of minor consumer goods such as cigarettes, matches, and batteries. The strict programs of structural adjustment imposed by the World Bank and the International Monetary Fund (IMF) since the late 1980s have forced the Malian government to reduce dramatically the number of state employees, progressively privatize state-owned enterprises, and devalue the local currency (the *franc de la Communauté Financière d'Afrique*, the CFA) by 50 percent. The consequences of these programs have been mixed. Even though official economic indexes show some economic growth, there has also been a neocolonial return of foreign capital. This has been the case for COMATEX, the largest textile factory in Mali, built with Chinese cooperation in the late 1960s. In October 1993 an accord between China and Mali paved the way for the privatization of COMATEX by a Chinese group (the COVEX), despite efforts by a group of Malian entrepreneurs to purchase the enterprise (the Malian state retains 20 percent of the capital).

Similarly, new gold mines have opened, but they remain mostly foreign operated. Given the advanced technology and large amount of capital resources gold mines require, the business is for the most part in the hands of companies such as the South African Randgold Resources and the Canadian IAMGOLD. As a result the revenues of the Malian state have been estimated, at best, to equal 10 percent of the total value of the gold extracted.

A few Tuareg people outside Timbuktu during a dust storm. Conflicts between the Tuareg and the Malian government improved after the signing of a 1994 peace accord.

Trade. Mali's major exports are cotton (50 percent of foreign exchange earnings), gold (17 percent), and livestock products. In 1998, main destinations for exports were Thailand, Italy, Brazil, and Portugal. In the same year, Mail purchased most of its imports (in particular, machinery and petroleum products) from Cte d'Ivoire, France, Belgium and Luxembourg, and Senegal. In general, the Malian economy is extremely vulnerable to fluctuations in prices on international markets. It is also heavily dependent on foreign aid, and in this context benefits from its positive international image as a model African democracy progressing steadily toward the privatization and diversification of its national economy.

Division of Labor. Although the available statistical data are often not reliable, they do give a general picture of labor distribution in Mali. Employment in the formal economy, at best, approximates 6 percent of the total economically active population (the latter estimated at 44.7 percent of the total population). The large majority of the population is involved in the so-called informal sectors of the economy or are unemployed. Unemployment is much higher among the educated elites because of the lack of employment opportunities in the modern sector, and amounts to 13.2 percent of those employed in this sector. Agriculture, forestry, animal husbandry, and fishing employ the large majority (83 percent) of the total active population. Other occupational sectors include the craft industry (5.4 percent) and trade (4.7 percent). In order for Malians to provide for their families, they are often forced to take on several jobs at the same time, a situation rarely expressed by official statistics.

SOCIAL STRATIFICATION

Classes and Castes. In the late 1960s French anthropologist Claude Meillassoux remarked on the complexity of the relations between new and old social milieus in Mali, and his observations still capture an important component of social stratification. Border crossing and mélanges of cultural elements still characterize Malian social distinctions. Some scholars have observed how for many years the Malian bureaucracy did not properly constitute a class; indeed, it established a series of practices modeled after the traditional code of behavior of the Malian aristocracy. For instance, the Malian bureaucracy did not reinvest monetary capital into productive enterprises, but engaged in the predation and redistribution of state resources. Other scholars have highlighted the huge gap between the elites and the mass of the population and have essentially presented Malian post-colonial history as the history of alliances and conflicts between Malian elites, that is, the bureaucracy and the merchants.

Prior to colonization, Mali was a highly stratified and complex society. Most ethnic groups distinguished among *horonw* (free people or nobles), *nyamankalaw* (semiendogamous professional groups such as leather workers, griots, and smiths), and *jonw/wolosow* (first-generation slaves or slaves born in the family). Recent studies have shown a certain flexibility among these social groups, one that allowed for movements and permutations across the different groups. Along the same lines, local people have renegotiated the boundaries of traditional professions. In fact, especially in the cities, the exercise of a given profession is no longer limited to people with the appropriate family background. The Institut national des arts in Bamako has played a major role in this direction, opening *nyamakala* professions (such as sculpture and music) to the rest of the Malian population.

In addition to this fuzziness between group boundaries, individuals are redefining their traditional professions in new directions. This is the case

with very entrepreneurial *jelimusow* (women *jeliw*, or griots) who, from a position of relative marginality vis-à-vis male singers, have come to dominate the cassette market and musical radio programs in today's Mali. Their success is partly linked to people's searches for social recognition in the context of the dislocation brought about by transformations of the political economy since colonization.

At the level of practices, the aristocratic code of behavior translates into the display of modest and controlled manners. On the other hand, nyamakalaw and jonw have traditionally enjoyed a broader freedom of expression. In particular jeliw or griots can afford to voice their opinions openly; that is, according to the occasion they can praise, criticize, or fire up their patrons.

POLITICAL LIFE

Government. Mali is a democratic republic. The democratization of state institutions started under the transition period (1991–1993) with the organization of a national assembly during which a new constitution was drafted and was formally adopted via popular referendum in 1992, and the organization of free and democratic elections (1993). The constitution follows the French model and sanctions the separation of the executive, legislative, and judicial powers.

Leadership and Political Officials. Alpha Oumar Konaré, of the party ADEMA, was the first democratically elected president in the history of post-independence Mali. Konaré was re-elected in 1997, in much discussed elections, and will end his second and last term in 2002. The ruling government coalition includes ADEMA and a few other, minor parties such as the Parti de la renaissance national (Parena). The main opposition alliance is represented by the Collectif des partis politiques de l'opposition (COPPO), which is extremely critical of the Konaré government, accusing it of political monopoly, corruption, and insufficiently integrating dissenting voices into the democratic process. Since 1997, however, COPPO leaders have refused to participate in all elections, thus further marginalizing themselves politically.

Social Problems and Control. Information is scarce on crime in Mali. However, crime is considered to be low compared to other countries in the region. The crime situation in Mali's northern regions is more complex. Due to this area's intermittent political instability, some tourists have occa-

While architectural styles in Mali vary, most buildings are made of sun-baked clay.

sionally experienced banditry and carjackings. The Gendarmerie and local police forces are in charge of internal security. The Malian judiciary system (made independent by the 1992 Constitution) is complicated by the coexistence of traditional, Islamic, judiciary traditions that are often syncretically used by the Malian population.

Military Activity. Military expenditures total approximately 5.5 percent of the national budget. Beside a dispute over the boundaries with Burkina Faso, which led to five days' fighting (25-29 December 1985) and was quickly resolved by dividing up the disputed land between the two countries (in December 1986), Mali has not been involved in any foreign conflicts.

The army has been a major player in domestic politics, for instance via the organization of coups d'état (many of which were unsuccessful) and/or via the participation of military officials in various governments. Military forces have been extensively deployed in the North to control the Tuareg rebellion. According to Amnesty International, the Malian Army has infringed fundamental humanitarian norms. To Tuareg attacks, the Army has responded with reprisal killings of civilians—a situation that generated a spiral of violence from both

sides in the mid 1990s, but since then seems relatively under control. Noteworthy is Mali's more recent peacekeeping efforts, of which president Konaré is a major proponent, in the Western African region. In particular, Mali is involved in trying to reestablish peace along the borders between Guinea, Liberia, and Sierra Leone.

SOCIAL WELFARE AND CHANGE PROGRAMS

Mali, at least on paper, provides an extensive welfare system. Workers are entitled to retirement benefits, health care, sick leave, maternity leave, and other forms of compensation. The actual realization of the welfare program is often significantly hampered by the state's limited resources. Furthermore, many aspects of the social welfare system, even if it were fully operational, would affect only wage workers, who constitute a minority of the overall Malian worker population. However social welfare remains at the center of the government agenda. The Malian government, with the backing of the World Bank and the IMF, is planning to increase spending in health and education. Most Malians work in the so-called informal sector and rely on alternative welfare strategies, such as the development of reliable social networks among kin, friends, neighbors, and coworkers.

NONGOVERNMENTAL ORGANIZATIONS AND OTHER ASSOCIATIONS

Nongovernmental organizations (NGOs) are the expression of a development approach that takes into account the needs and aspirations of the local people and ideally involves them at all stages in the development project. The blossoming of foreign and local NGOs in recent years is in part the result of the implementation of structural adjustment programs and the privatization of the Malian economy. The state was the largest employer in Mali until the mid-1980s, but many people have since lost their jobs or future employment opportunities. NGOs, coordinated by the Comité de coordination des ONG du Mali, have thus become a major provider of employment for the many educated yet unemployed Malians. Funding is provided by the state and foreign partners. NGO projects include literacy programs, health training programs, initiatives to alleviate rural women's work burdens, reforestation programs, and initiatives to support the decentralization of state institutions.

GENDER ROLES AND STATUSES

Division of Labor by Gender. In many Malian farming communities both women and men are actively involved in agricultural activities. Among the Bamana, women, in addition to taking care of many household chores, work most of their lives in the collective fields of their husband's extended family. Once women reach menopause they retire from work in the collective fields and often redirect their efforts in the cultivation of their own fields. Women are also very active in trade activities. Post-menopausal women, as in many other parts in Africa, are freer to engage more extensively in trade activities than are women of child-bearing age. However, women sell mainly food items, both raw and processed, and a few manufactured goods (e.g. cloth), while men engage more often in the sale of manufactured goods. In other words, women's access to market participation tends to be limited to a series of economic activities which are scarcely lucrative, or at least less so if compared to the business in which men engage.

In the cities women continue to take care of most of the household chores as well as to be actively involved in petty trade. Rural girls prior to their marriage are often employed as maids in the cities in order to accumulate goods for the constitution of their own dowry (*konyon minén*). Women are underemployed in the formal economy, although some studies have recently shown that women are well represented in certain professions such as law.

From a political standpoint, under the single-party system, women's associations have experienced some of the same limitations that affected other groups (such as youth associations and workers' associations) and have often had to promote the party's interest over women's own agenda. After the coup of 1991, an impressive number of women's associations were created. They are coordinated by the Ministère pour la Promotion des Femmes, des Enfants, et de la Famille. In a political reshuffling that took place on 21 February 2000, women's representation achieved a historical high—out of twenty-one newly appointed ministers, seven were women.

The Relative Status of Women and Men. In general, women are less represented than men in the more lucrative sectors of the economy; that is state employment, private enterprises, and long-distance trade. However, there are significant differences among women. For instance, women's living conditions in the rural areas often differ from those of urban women. In general, rural women have a much heavier workload and reduced access to health care than city women. Furthermore, there are significant class differences, especially in the cities. There certainly are some common issues that most women are confronted with, such as women's circumcision (practiced by most ethnic groups, with the exception of the Tuareg), a strong emphasis on women's role in the socialization and education of children, and discriminatory inheritance practices (in the absence of state legislation on this issue), to mention only a few. The ways in which a woman is affected by these issues vary significantly, however, depending upon her location, her education, her class, and her relationship with her husband. Studies of urban women show women's entrepreneurial efforts in establishing broad networks of family, friends, and neighbors upon whom they can rely for companionship and mutual help. In addition, some local and foreign aid agencies have increasingly been involved in helping individual women as well as women's groups in setting up small enterprises (e.g. small enterprises of food processing) but much is still to be done in this direction.

MARRIAGE, FAMILY, AND KINSHIP

Marriage. Marriage is the most important ritual of the life cycle and entails numerous celebrations that are spread throughout a period of variable length, up to ten years. It involves major expenses on the part of the bride's and groom's extended families and friends, although the practice of bride-wealth (the transfer of gifts or money from the groom's family to the bride's family) puts more financial pressure on the groom and his family. Three different forms of marriage can be distinguished in Mali today: traditional (which varies greatly from region to region and across ethnic groups), civil, and religious (mostly Muslim). In the cities, many couples see the ideal marriage as one that has been legitimized traditionally, civilly, and religiously. Civil marriage is especially popular among wage workers, for without official sanction by the state, wives and children will not be entitled to social welfare benefits such as pensions. In the rural areas and to some extent in the urban areas, marriages are arranged. This practice reflects the importance of establishing alliances between families over individual preferences.

Although the first years of marriage are frequently quite difficult for women, a woman's position within the household tends to improve over time. Age and children tend to increase a woman's status. Old women are better off, and take up managerial responsibilities in directing other women's work. Noteworthy is the fact that husbands and

Women in rural communities often experience harsher living conditions than urban women.

wives manage their revenues independently. It follows that the management of a household is the outcome of a negotiation between husband and wives as to who is going to assume which responsibilities. However some underlining patterns can be detected—for instance, women tend to take care of the sauce that flavors the meal and men tend to provide the cereals that are the staple for the daily meals, at least in the cities.

Domestic Unit. Most Malian ethnic groups are patrilineal, and residence tends to be patrilocal. In rural areas and to a large extent in the cities, domestic units are rarely limited to the nuclear family. Indeed, most often they consist of an extended patrilineal family (that is, they consist of a father, his wife(ves), his sons, their wives and children, and unmarried daughters). Polygyny is legal, and couples have the option of choosing between monogamy and polygyny when they enter into a civil marriage (although this is not necessarily binding). Among the Mande, relationships between mothers and their children are very intense and affectionate, and children of the same mother tend to rely on each other for help over the years. Traditionally, relationships between half-siblings with different mothers are more tense and competitive. Another area of potential conflict is the relationship between

co-wives, which varies considerably from compound to compound. Yet it is not rare to find co-wives who get along with each other and establish relationships of mutual support—a situation often feared by the husband, who is clearly put in a minority position in the household. In the cities it is not rare to find couples who live independently from their extended families—this typically reflects a higher social standing and Western education. Even in these cases household members are not limited to the nuclear family and may include children from previous marriages, nephews, nieces, or other family members, and clients.

Kin Groups. Many Malian ethnic groups are further divided in several lineages and clans, which are represented at the village level by clusters of households sharing a common section of a village under the leadership of a respected family elder. Traditionally certain clans entertain joking relationships with one another (e.g. the Diarra and the Traoré). Despite the fact that residence is predominantly patrilocal, recent studies show that women maintain close bonds with their family of origin. Women continue to be involved in the lives of their natal family members via periodic visits, and via the exchange of gifts and services throughout their lives. Kinship bonds continue to be important despite geographical dislocation. Malian migrants, both to the city and to foreign destinations, maintain strong links with their extended families and contribute substantially to the local economies by sending home a constant flux of money and gifts. Despite the poverty of the majority of the population, real or fictitious kinship links provide support and comfort for many Malians in times of need.

SOCIALIZATION

Infant Care. Babies are kept in close contact with their mothers and accompany them in most of their activities, usually carried on the mother's back and secured by a tightly wrapped cloth. In the cities, the complex male and female initiation practices found in the rural areas are often reduced to simple circumcision (the removal of the foreskin for boys) and clitoridectomy (the removal of the clitoris for girls)—usually performed on the eighth day of the baby's birth. Traditionally male and female initiation marked the passage from childhood to adulthood (it was a requirement for women to marry, and in some areas it was incorporated within the marriage process) and entailed the passing of traditional and religious knowledge from the old to the new generations. On the other hand urban circumcision tends to be incorporated into another set of rituals, those performed on the occasion of the naming of a child.

Child Rearing and Education. Children's informal education is to a great extent a collective endeavor, with people other than the children's parents participating in their rearing. Small children, up to two or three years, receive much affectionate attention from both family and nonfamily members and are rarely disciplined.

Education is free and compulsory for the first nine years, although private schools, which draw their students from the better-off strata of the population, are expanding. In general, the attitude toward western-style schooling is ambivalent—both because it is viewed as a colonial legacy and also because it is often disconnected from the rural populations' complex realities. In addition, scarce opportunities for employment in the formal sector of the economy, especially in rural areas, may demotivate families and pupils from investing resources and time in formal schooling.

Traditionally, children learned about their future economic responsibilities by observing and helping older same-sex kin, but in the cities boys increasingly have fewer responsibilities, while girls are still expected to help at home.

Higher Education. Since independence the government has devoted more resources to secondary education than to mass primary schooling. Secondary schools are concentrated in urban areas, Bamako in particular. Until very recently the most important objective for the Malian school was the production of administrative cadres, and until 1983 the state guaranteed employment for students with a secondary-school or university diploma. At that time, however, the state had to confront the fact that it could no longer assume this responsibility, and since then, enrollment in state schools has dropped. The numerous student strikes that have occurred in the late twentieth century were an expression of students' anxiety about their uncertain professional future as well as dissatisfaction with the form and quality of education. Statistics from the 1990s suggest a literacy rate of about 38 percent. Students' success rate is also extremely low. In the 1980s only 50 percent of the students who began primary education were likely to complete six years of schooling and go on to secondary education. Female students are underrepresented at all levels of education, and their presence decreases from one educational level to the next; for instance, in 1998 there were 2,737 female students out of a total of 13,824 at the university level.

ETIQUETTE

Malians are very proud of their traditions of hospitality toward local and international visitors, and indeed, hospitality has been raised to the level of a national value. Greetings and salutations for special occasions (births, marriages, deaths, etc.) are the subject of much social regulation. They symbolize an individual's education and his or her concern and respect for others, with younger people typically expected to initiate the greeting as a sign of respect for their elders. Foreign travelers who learn at least a few greetings in Bamana or other local languages have their efforts warmly acknowledged by the local people. The majority of the Malian population is Muslim, and foreign travelers, both men and women, are encouraged to be sensitive to the local dress code (e.g. the wearing of shorts is discouraged for both women and men). Gift-giving and sharing of resources are some of the axioms upon which Malian society is based. Consequently, one's integration in the Malian society requires the learning of the complex grammar of gift-giving. A different set of rules govern people's behavior in market places, where initial prices are typically inflated and bartering is an expected ritual.

RELIGION

Religious Beliefs. An estimated 80 percent of the Malian population is Muslim, with the others practicing Christianity (1 percent) or following traditional religious practices (19 percent). Islam has been present in this area since the eighth century, but until the coming of the French its practice was mostly restricted to merchants, clerics, and the rulers and the elites of the great West African empires that blossomed in this area. Under French colonization Islam's influence greatly expanded in the region. For instance, during the first phases of French colonization, colonial administrators relied upon Islamic representatives to extend their control over the local populations. The French also aided in the establishment of new Islamic tribunals in the region. Finally, transformations of the local economy and people's increased mobility contributed to the spreading of Islam.

Today Mali is a secular state, but religion and in particular national Islamic religious organizations play an important role in the life of the country. Moussa Traoré, Mali's second president, increasingly relied on the display of Islamic devotion and intervened in Islamic affairs to further legitimize his power. President Alpha Oumar Konaré has alternated public displays of faith and expressions

An overview of the city of Bamako, in which a twin-spire mosque can be seen in the background.

of Islamic piety with cautions about religious extremism.

Rituals and Holy Places. There are a number of celebrations that are performed on the occasion of major Islamic events, such as the anniversary of the birth of the Prophet Mohammed and of his baptism. Ramadan (in Bamana, *sunkalo*, literally "the fasting month") is concluded by a religious feast called in Bamana *selijinin*, or "small feast." Forty days after this feast is the time of *seliba* (tabaski), or "big feast," in commemoration of Abraham's sacrifice. This is a time when most families sacrifice a sheep, people wear their best outfits, and everyone busily exchanges gifts of meat and prepared foods as a sign of solidarity. All these Islamic holidays as well as Christian holidays such as Easter and Christmas are officially recognized.

MEDICINE AND HEALTH CARE

Western health care is limited, with one doctor per 18,376 persons. Medical facilities are insufficient, under equipped, and mostly concentrated in urban areas, especially Bamako. In most cases patients need to provide nearly all supplies necessary for their treatment, including medicines, disposable medical equipment, and food. Given both the under funding of the health sector and some corruption among underpaid and under trained health-care personnel, patients must rely on their social network for financial help and to ensure that they receive proper care. This process obviously delays medical treatment and discriminates against the poor. Statistics show that one out of five children in rural areas will die before the age of five; the child mortality rate decreases significantly in urban areas and in Bamako in particular. Average life expectancy increased slightly in the late twentieth century, reaching forty-nine years (however, the increasing spread of AIDS in this region will have a dramatic impact on this figure). Most people utilize both Western and traditional systems of medicine.

An emerging sector of research is the so-called ethnopharmacopeia, which involves the production on a larger scale of traditional medicines of proven efficacy. These medicines are less expensive and stem from medical knowledge already in the hands of the majority of Malians. This sector would offer the possibility of local industrial expansion if training and funding were provided to cooperatives of traditional healers and local researchers.

SECULAR CELEBRATIONS

A major public holiday in Mali, and the occasion of parades, political speeches, and other celebrations, is

22 September, Independence Day. Other public holidays include the commemoration of the overthrow of Moussa Traoré (25 March), Armed Forces Day (20 January), Labor Day (1 May), and Africa Day (25 May).

In addition to the celebrations of the public calendar there are a number of well-known regional festivities, such as the *sogobo* of the Ségou region, the reroofing of the sacred hut in Kangaba, and the *sigui*, a Dogon festival celebrated every sixty years. These celebrations, which attract tourists, often become the occasion of visits by politicians and are thus often reappropriated into a nationalistic rhetoric.

THE ARTS AND HUMANITIES

Literature. Malian oral literature is extremely rich, varied (proverbs, stories, epic poetry), and well researched. The Malian epic tradition (the story of Sunjata) is the most relevant to a discussion of national culture. Since independence, the *jeliw* (griots), masters of words and the holders of the epic tradition, have been essential in the process of nation building, becoming heavily involved in the process of rewriting Mali's history and of conveying political messages to the general population. Some Malian scholars are extremely critical of these recent developments and see the griots' art as having lost its critical wit as it moved into the service of politics and the powerful. But the issue is open to debate, as other studies show the resilience of some of the *jeliw*'s prerogatives of social critique.

In very schematic terms, two underlying trends can be distinguished in Mali's literary tradition. The first is represented by a traditionalist literature oriented toward the reconstruction of the precolonial past and the retrieval of precolonial cultural traditions; the second is involved in the critical analysis of Mali's contemporary social problems, including the long-term consequences of colonization. Representative of the first current are the writings of Amadou Hampaté Bâ and some of the writings of Massa Makan Diabaté. The second perspective is represented by writers such as Yambo Ouologuem (winner of the Renaudot Prize in 1969), Pascal Baba F. Couloubaly, Seydou Badian Kouyaté, Moussa Konaté, Ibrahima Ly, and Ismaila Samba Traoré, just to mention a few. Few well-known Malian writers are women; noteworthy is the political autobiography of Aoua Kéita, *Femme d'Afrique: la Vie d'Aoua Kéita Racontée par elle-même*, an influential political representative. There is also an emerging literature in national languages, predominantly in Bamana.

Graphic Arts. Malian pottery, sculpture, and textile traditions—in particular *bogolanfini*, hand-woven cotton bands decorated with dyes and mud and sewn together to make cloths—are extremely diverse and have been the subject of numerous studies. A visit to the Musée national du Mali, in Bamako, provides visitors with an appreciation of the richness of Malian artistic traditions.

Performance Arts. In terms of the quality and success of Malian music, it suffices to mention stars of international reputation such as Salif Keita, Ali Farka Touré, Oumou Sangare, and Ami Koita. Extremely active—and with significant implication for development—is the (predominantly comic) theater tradition in Mali known as koteba. Finally, Malians artists have also distinguished themselves as film directors, including Souleymane Cissé, Cheick Oumar Sissoko, Adama Drabo, and Kadiatou Konaté.

THE STATE OF THE PHYSICAL AND SOCIAL SCIENCES

The institution in charge of coordinating research in Mali is the Centre national de la recherche scientifique et technologique. It is not directly involved in research activities but coordinates other existing research institutes (such as the Institut des sciences humaines and the Institut national de recherche en santé publique), distributes resources, and sees to the publication of research results. Most research projects in Mali are development-oriented and are concentrated in the areas of agriculture and health. In addition, in the absence of sufficient state funding, Malian researchers are heavily dependent on external aid for training, research, and publication. Assuming it is properly funded, the creation of the Université du Mali, constituted in 1993, has the potential to open up important opportunities for the development of local research.

BIBLIOGRAPHY

Amselle, Jean-Loup. "Le Mali socialiste (1960–1968)." *Cahiers d'Études Africaines* 72 (18, 4): 631–634, 1978.

———. "Socialisme, capitalisme, et précapitalisme au Mali (1960–1982)." In H. Bernstein and B. K. Campbell, eds., *Contradictions of Accumulation in Africa*, 1985.

————. ''Fonctionnaires et hommes d'affaires au Mali.'' Politique Africaine 26: 63–72, 1987.

————. Mestizo Logics: Anthropology of Identity in Africa and Elsewhere, 1998.

———— and Grégoire Emmanuel. ''Complicités et conflits entre bourgeoisies d'état et bourgeoisies d'affaires: Au Mali et au Niger.'' In E. Terray, ed., L'Etat contemporain en Afrique, 1987.

Arnoldi, Mary Jo. ''Political History and Social Commentary in Malian Sogobò Theater,'' Africa Today 2: 39–49, 1994.

————. 1995. Playing with Time: Art and Performance in Central Mali, 1995.

Bâ, Amadou Hampaté., The Fortunes of Wagrin, 2000.

Bagayogo, Shaka. ''L'État au Mali: Représentation, autonomie et mode de fonctionnement.'' In E. Terray, ed., L'État Contemporain en Afrique, 1987.

————. ''Lieux et théorie du pouvoir dans la monde mandé: Passé et présent.'' Cahiers de Sciences Humaines (ORSTOM) 25 (4): 445–460, 1989.

————. ''L'hospitalité dans l'aire culturelle mandingue.'' Études Maliennes, 44: 4–20. 1991.

————. ''Littérature orale et légitimation politique au Mali (1960–1990).'' In Bogumil Jewsiewicki and Jocelyn Létourneau, eds., Constructions identitaires: Questionnements théoriques et études de cas, 1992.

Bailleul, Charles Père. Dictionnaire Bambara-Français, 1996.

Ba Konaré, Adame. ''Rôle et image de la femme dans l'histoire politique du Mali (1960–1991): Perspectives pour une meilleure participation de la femme au processus démocratique.'' Paper presented at the CODESRIA Workshop on Gender Analysis and African Social Science, Dakar, September 1991.

————. Dictionnaire des femmes célèbres du Mali, 1993.

Bazin, Jean. ''À chacun son Bambara.'' In Jean-Loup Amselle and E. M'Bokolo. eds., Au coeur de l'ethnie, 1985.

Bertrand, Monique. ''Un an de transition politique: De la révolte à la troisième république.'' Politique Africaine, 47: 9–22, 1992.

Bingen, R. James, David Robinson, and John M. Staatz. Democracy and Development in Mali, 2000.

Bird, Charles S., and Martha B. Kendall. ''The Mande Hero.'' In Ivan Karp and Charles Bird, eds., Explorations in African Systems of Thought, 1980.

Blonde, Jacques. ''La situation du français au Mali.'' In A. Valdman, ed., Le Français hors de France, 1979.

Brenner, Louis. ''Constructing Muslim Identities in Mali.'' In Louis Brenner, ed., Muslim Identity and Social Change in Sub-Saharan Africa, 1993.

Brenner, Louis, and Sanankoua Bintou. L'enseignement islamique au Mali, 1991.

Calame-Griaule, Geneviève. Ethnologie et language, la parole chez les Dogons, 1996.

Ciminelli, Maria Luisa. Follia del sapere e saperi della follia, 1998.

Cissé, Seydou. L'Enseignement islamique en Afrique noire, 1992.

Conrad, David, and Barbara Frank. Status and Identity in West Africa, 1995.

Cutter, Charles. ''The Politics of Music in Mali,'' African Arts, 1 (3): 38–39, 74–77, 1968.

De Benoist, Joseph Roger. Le Mali, 1968.

De Bruijin, Mirjam, and Han Van Dijk. ''Fulbe Mobility: Migration and Travel into Mande.'' Mande Studies, 1: 41–62, 1999.

De Jorio, Rosa. ''Incontro con le donne bambara.'' Africa e Mediterraneo, 5: 19–28. 1993.

————. ''Modelli competitivi del matrimonio in Mali, Africa occidentale.'' Africa, 51 (4): 518–534, 1996.

————. ''Female Elites, Women's Formal Associations, and Political Practices in Mali (West Africa).'' Ph.D. dissertation, University of Illinois, Urbana-Champaign, 1997.

Delafosse, Maurice. Haut-Sénégal-Niger. 3 vol., 1912.

De Noray, Marie-Laure. ''Mali: Du kotéba traditionnel au théâtre utile.'' Politique Africaine, 66: 134–39, 1997.

Diarrah, Cheick Oumar. Mali: Bilan d'une gestion désastreuse, 1990.

————. Le Défi démocratique au Mali, 1990.

Dieterlen, Germaine, and Youssouf Cisse. Les fondements de la société d'initiation du Komo, 1972.

Djata, Sundiata A. The Bamana Empire by the Niger: Kingdom, Jidad and Colonization, 1712–1920, 1997.

Direction nationale de l'alphabetisation fonctionnelle et de la linguistique appliquée. DNAFLA: Une Institution malienne d'éducation pour le développement, 2nd ed., 1987.

Doumbia, Bréhima, and Yannick Jaffré. ''Lire en langues nationales au Mali.'' Notre Librarie 75–76, 149–153, 1984.

Drisdelle, Rhéal. Mali: A Prospect of Peace? 1997.

Duran, Lucy. ''Jelimusow: The Superwomen of Malian Music.'' In G. Furniss and L. Gunner, eds., Power, Marginality and African Oral Literature,

Echenberg, Myron. Colonial Coscripts: The Tirailleurs Sénégalais in French West Africa, 1857–1960, 1991.

Economist Intelligence Unit. Country Profile: Mali, 2000.

Fay, Claude. ''La démocratie au Mali, ou le pouvoir en pâture.'' Cahiers d' Études Africaines, 137 (35, 1): 19–53. 1995.

Frank, Barbara E. Mande Potters and Leatherworkers: Art and Heritage in West Africa, 1998.

Gaudio, Attilio. Le Mali, 1998.

Gérard, Étienne. ''Entre état et populations: L'École et l'éducation en devenir.'' Politique Africaine 47: 59–69, 1992.

Griaule, Marcel. *Dieu d'eau, entretiens avec Ogotemmêli*, 1966.

Grosz-Ngaté, Maria. "Monetization of Bridewealth and the Abandonment of Kin Roads to Marriage in Sana, Mali." *American Ethnologist* 15: 501–514, 1988.

——— "Hidden Meanings: Explorations into a Bamanan Construction of Gender." *Ethnology*, 28 (2): 167–183, 1989.

Hoffman, Barbara. "Power, Structure, and Mande Jeliw." In David Conrad and Barbara Frank, eds., *Status and Identity in West Africa*, 1995.

Hopkins, Nicholas. "Socialism and Social Change in Mali." *Journal of Modern African Studies* 7 (3): 457–467, 1969.

———. *Popular Government in an African Town: Kita, Mali*, 1972.

Imperato, Pascal James. *Mali: A Search for Direction*, 1989.

———. *Historical Dictionary of Mali*, 1996.

Kaba, Lansiné. *The Wahhabiyya: Islamic Reform and Politics in French West Africa*, 1974.

Keita, Cheick Mahamadou Chérif. "Jaliya in the Modern World: A Tribute to Banzoumana Sissoko and Massa Makan Diabate." *UFAHAMU* 17 (1): 57–67, 1988.

Keita, Mamadou Konoba. "Réflexion sur la presse écrite." *Politique Africaine* 47, 79–90, 1992

Kendall, M. "Getting to Know You." In David Parkin, ed., *Semantic Anthropology*, 1982.

Klimkeit, Dirk. "La Construction d'une culture nationale par l'état au Mali." Résumé du mémoire remis à la Faculté des arts et des lettres de l'Université de Cologne, 1997.

Konaré, Alpha Oumar. "Birth of a Museum at Bamako, Mali." *Museum* 33 (1): 4–8, 1981.

——— "Toward a New Type of 'Ethnographic' Museum in Africa." *Museum* 35 (3): 146–149, 1983.

Konate, Moussa. *Mali: Ils ont assassiné l'espoir*, 1990.

Launay, Robert, and Benjamin F. Soares. "The Formation of an 'Islamic Sphere' in French Colonial West Africa." *Economy and Society* 28 (4): 497–519, 1999.

Levtzion, Nehemia. *Ancient Ghana and Mali*, 1973.

Maas, Pierre. "Djenné: Living Tradition." *Aramco World* 41 (6): 18–29, 1990.

Maharaux, Alain. *L'Industrie au Mali*, 1986.

Mann, Michael, and David Dalby. *A Thesaurus of African Languages*, 1987.

Martin, Guy. "Socialism, Economic Development, and Planning in Mali, 1960–1968," *Canadian Journal of African Studies* 10: 23–47, 1976.

McNaughton, Patrick R. *The Mande Blacksmiths: Knowledge, Power, and Art in West Africa*, 1988.

Meillassoux, Claude. *Urbanization of an African Community: Voluntary Associations in Bamako*, 1968.

———. "A Class Analysis of the Bureaucratic Process in Mali," *Journal of Development Studies* 6 (2): 97–110, 1970.

Ministère de l'économie, des finances, et du plan. *Mali: Profil de la pauvreté*, 1993.

Montel, Charles. *Les Bambara du Ségou et Kaarta*, 1976.

Morgenthau, Ruth Schachter. *Political Parties in French-Speaking West Africa*, 1964.

N'Diaye, Issa. "Les apports récents des littératures en langues nationales." *Notre Librairie* 75–76, 143–145, 1984.

Ouédraogo, Dieudonné, and Victor Piché. *L'Insertion urbaine à Bamako*, 1995.

Ouloguem, Yambo. *Bound to Violence*, 1971.

Perinbam, Marie B. *Family Identity and the State in the Bamako Kafu, c. 1800–c. 1900*, 1997.

Prasse, Karl G. *The Tuaregs: The Blue People*, 1995.

Raghavan, M. "Les ONG au Mali." *Politique Africaine* 47: 91–100, 1992.

Roberts, Richard. *Warriors, Merchants, and Slaves*, 1987.

Rovine, Victoria. "Bogolafini in Bamako: The Biography of a Malian textile." *African Arts* 30 (1): 51, 94, 1997.

Savane, Amadou Sy. "Le roman des indépendances." *Notre Librairie* 75–76, 123–127, 1984.

Schatzberg, Michael. "The Coup and After: Continuity or Change in Malian Politics?" Occasional Paper no. 5, African Studies Program, University of Wisconsin, Madison, 1972.

Schulz, Dorothea Elisabeth. "Praise in Times of Disenchantment: Griots, Radios, and the Politics of Communication in Mali." Ph.D. dissertation, Yale University, 1996.

Silla, Eric. *People Are Not the Same: Leprosy and Identity in Twentieth-Century Mali*, 1998.

Sonfo, Alphamoye, and Urbain Dembele. "De l'oral à l'écrit." *Notre Librairie* 75–76, 77–85, 1984.

Sow, Abdoulaye-Sékou. "Nation, patrie, et symbolisme." *Revue du Citoyen*, 8: 7–11, 1998.

Tauxier, Louis. *La religion Bambara*, 1927.

Turrittin, Jane. "Men, Women, and Market Trade in Rural Mali, West Africa." *Canadian Journal of African Studies*. 32: 583-604, 1988.

———. "Aoua Kéita and the Nascent Women's Movement in the French Soudan." *African Studies Review* 36 (1): 59–89, 1993.

Vaa, M., S. E. Findley, and A. Diallo. "The Gift Economy: A Study of Women Migrants' Survival Strategies in a Low-Income Bamako Neighborhood." *Labour, Capital, and Society* 22 (2): 234–60, 1989.

Zahan, Dominique. *Sociétés d'initiation bambara: le N'Domo et le Koré*, 1960.

—ROSA DE JORIO

MALTA

CULTURE NAME
Maltese

ORIENTATION

Identification. The Maltese archipelago consists of Malta, Gozo, Comino, Cominotto, and Fifla, plus a few minute limestone outcroppings. Over 92 percent of the inhabitants live on Malta, by far the largest island, and the rest live on Gozo except for a few farmers on Comino. Although all residents call themselves Maltese, people on Gozo also are called Gozitans. The earliest written reference to Malta is in the biblical account of Saint Paul's shipwreck.

Location and Geography. Malta is located in the center of the Mediterranean Sea. Sicily is 58 miles (93.3 kilometers) to the north, and Tunisia is 194 miles (312.5 kilometers) to the west. The territory of the three inhabited islands is 94.9 square miles (320 square kilometers).

Gozo has more greenery, and farming there is done on a larger scale. The environment has thin soil and scarce groundwater. Terracing is used to contain erosion in agricultural areas, and herding is confined mostly to Gozo. There is little wildlife besides insects and migratory birds.

Public buses reach large towns on Malta and Gozo, and regular ferry service connects the islands. Beaches, coves, grottoes, and fishing villages lie close to roadways, but in some places, the islands fall abruptly into the sea over rocks and cliffs or look out to it across elaborate medieval fortifications. A rainy season occurs in October through February, but the climate is mild year-round.

The Grand Harbor of Malta is dominated by Valletta, the national capital, whose construction was begun by the Knights of Saint John in 1566, a year after the defeat of the Great Siege by Ottoman Turkey. The capital of Gozo is Victoria.

Demography. The population as of July 1999 was 369,451, of whom 341,906 lived on Malta and 27,545 lived on Gozo except for a handful on Comino. Live births in that year were 4,826 for a birth rate of 13.1 per thousand. The fact that the estimated national population as of July 1999 was 381,603 indicates that it is continuing to grow. In part, this is because the emigration rate has been declining. Singapore is the only country more densely populated than Malta.

Linguistic Affiliation. Maltese is the only European language in the Afro-Asiatic family, which includes Arabic, Hebrew, Berber, and Hausa. Although its closest relationships are with the forms of Arabic spoken in Libya and Tunisia, its vocabulary has been strongly influenced by Sicilian. Written with a twenty-nine-letter alphabet, Maltese is universally understood by citizens and has only minimal dialectical variations. Educated Maltese often speak English, and many understand Italian.

Symbolism. Saint Paul is a powerful national symbol, as he is credited with converting the Maltese to Christianity. It is symbolic that the Maltese, under theocratic governance, fought in Crusades long after most other Europeans had abandoned them. Other symbols are Roman Catholicism, the Maltese cross, a strong European identity, and a siege mentality. Not only did Malta persevere during the Crusades, it was victorious against the Turks in 1565 and survived intense bombardment during World War II. Dolphins are also a national symbol.

HISTORY AND ETHNIC RELATIONS

Emergence of the Nation. Megalithic temples that predate the Egyptian pyramids, Bronze Age archaeological sites, Phoenician inscriptions, and Roman catacombs all contribute to a sense of nationhood. Maltese place particular emphasis on the nation that emerged after Christian conversion. The long-ruling Knights of Malta recruited their members

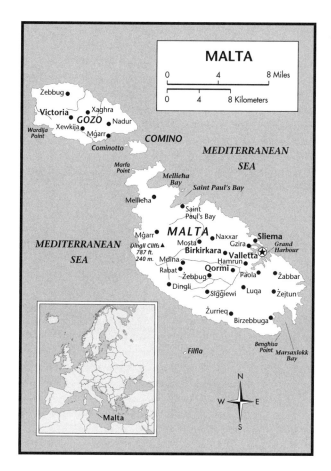

Malta

from noble families throughout Europe while denying the Maltese entry into their ranks. As this order was able to maintain itself in Malta largely by keeping the nation on a continuous war footing, it was anachronistic at a time when Europeans in countries such as England and France were being introduced to the Industrial Revolution. Still, two centuries after Napoleon forced the Knights to leave Malta, chivalry, as well as pride in European and Catholic identity associated with a knightly and crusading heritage, impacts Maltese nationalism in fundamental ways.

National Identity. Maltese people celebrate the contributions to their culture of Phoenicians, Romans, Greeks, Normans, Sicilians, Swabians, Arogonese, Castilian, the Knights, and the British. Maltese claim little knowledge of or are ambivalent about the northern Africans who contributed the foundation of their language, however. The nation became independent in 1964, and became a republic in the British Commonwealth in 1974. Although identification with Europe remains strong, it has been tempered by a strong emphasis on nationalism

and neutrality coupled with the idea of forming a cultural bridge between Europe and northern Africa.

Ethnic Relations. Malta is relatively homogeneous by modern standards. A Jewish community numbers about one hundred twenty, and settlers from India number about sixty. Perhaps six hundred Maltese are married to Arabs, mostly Libyans and Palestinians. There are a few Chinese as well as illegal immigrants from Bulgaria, Albania, and Russia.

URBANISM, ARCHITECTURE, AND THE USE OF SPACE

Most buildings are constructed of limestone from domestic quarries, and many houses are identified by names rather than street addresses. Water is scarce, and residences have flat roofs to capture rainwater. Most houses lack lawns and are attached to each other in rows that nestle close to sidewalks or streets, which are often narrow. Some bedrooms may be entered only by passing through other bedrooms; their doors often are left open, with curtains providing some privacy. In both urban and rural areas, people tend to live in nucleated settlements surrounding a parish church.

FOOD AND ECONOMY

Food in Daily Life. A heavy meal includes pasta, meat and vegetables, and dessert or fruit. Occasionally, a small bowl of soup called *minestra* begins the meal. *Lampuki* pie is a seasonal pastry-covered fish casserole containing spinach, cauliflower, chestnuts, and sultanas. Stuffed octopus, squid, and cuttlefish are served with a tomato sauce, while a roulade of beef known as *bragoli* is served with gravy. Stuffed poultry and baked pasta dishes are common. Among favorite finger foods are hot *pastizzi*, in which ricotta cheese, peas, meat, and anchovies are encased in a crust. The cuisine is seasonal.

Food Customs at Ceremonial Occasions. Rabbit stewed in wine is a specialty, often with some of its sauce served over pasta as a first course. Tender lamb is eaten at Easter.

Basic Economy. The central Mediterranean location, moderate climate, beaches, and ports generate income and employment. Malta's decimal currency has the lira (LM) as its basic unit and one lira is equivalent to 100 cents. Over two-thirds of the population is employed in services, slightly less than one-third in industry, and about 3 percent in agriculture. Parts assembly is also important, and a

View of Grand Harbor, where the Knights of Saint John began construction of the nation's capital, Valletta, in 1566.

single electronics firm produces two-fifths of industrial exports.

Tourism accounts for one-fourth to one-third of the gross national products (GDP) but employs a larger proportion of the population. Such employment peaks in the summer. The country annually attracts tourists equal to almost three times its population and television sets receive programming from abroad, making foreign cultural influences constant.

In the centralized capitalist economy, the state is the largest employer, with monopolistic control of utilities, fuel, the airline, the shipping line, shipyards and many factories and hotels. Agriculture accounts for about 3 percent of employment but about 4 percent of GDP. Despite a perennial trade deficit, the estimated 1998 GDP per capita of $13,000 was higher than that of Turkey, Portugal, and Greece.

Land Tenure and Property. As most houses are adjoined to others, many laws on land tenure and property relate to the competing rights of neighbors. A homeowner may legally compel a neighbor to maintain at joint expense a common wall between two courtyards or gardens, and neighbors are restricted from placing a stove or manure against common walls.

Trade. Important imports are machinery, fuel, and other products vital to the tourist industry, such as transportation equipment, live animals, food, tobacco, and chemicals. Exports also include chemicals and food. The European Community accounts for slightly more than three-quarters of foreign trade and most foreign investment.

SOCIAL STRATIFICATION

Nothing suggesting caste distinctions has existed in Maltese society since the expulsion of the ruling aristocratic knights and the freeing from enslavement of a small non-Maltese segment within the population. Despite traces of marginal variation based on heritage, Maltese society recognizes no entrenched ethnic divisions. Relative stratification is evident along the lines of higher education, economic status, comportment, and styles of dress, especially as found in rural areas.

POLITICAL LIFE

Government. The democratic government is highly centralized. The two major parties are the Nationalist Party, which stresses free enterprise and Christian democratic values, and the Malta Labour Party, which stresses income leveling, a mixed economy, and nonalignment. Until the Local Councils' Act in 1993 provided for limited local government, local authority was largely religious and centered in the parishes. There are sixty-seven local councils, which share power with the national government in social welfare, housing, town planning, sanitation, leisure, and traffic planning.

Social Problems and Control. The crime rate in Malta is low. Typical offenses are growing cannabis, circulating counterfeit money, theft, homicide, and entering the country illegally. The National Prison in Paola has seventy to eighty prisoners. The Juvenile Court is in the Centre for Social Welfare, which also houses the Commission against Drug and Alcohol Abuse and the Action Team on Violence against Women.

Military Activity. The tiny Armed Forces of Malta has land, sea, and air responsibilities for national security, surveillance, and assistance to civil authorities in emergencies. It is organized in a headquarters and three regiments. An amendment to the constitution in 1987 made Malta a "neutral State," and foreign forces may not serve on its territory.

SOCIAL WELFARE AND CHANGE PROGRAMS

A social security system is supported by employee contributions, and benefits are available for injury or disability, surviving spouses, the support of dependent children, and pensions. The system also provides means-tested support for people in financial difficulty through the Social and Family Affairs Department, which also offers crisis intervention and counseling services in areas ranging from probation and rehabilitation to adoption and fostering. It also offers support to citizens who are physically and mentally challenged or abused and to the elderly.

NONGOVERNMENTAL ORGANIZATIONS AND OTHER ASSOCIATIONS

Clubs exist for bands, plant lovers, and religious confraternities. There are also health- and disability-related organizations, single-parents groups, and professional, international, folklore, historical, social, and athletic organizations and teams.

GENDER ROLES AND STATUSES

That the literacy rate is equal for males and females in Maltese society (88 percent) suggests that both genders use education in carrying out their assigned roles in society. In the public domain of gainful employment, however, there exists less equivalence between the roles of married women and men than between those of single women and men. The public sector is where most Maltese are employed and, according to a long-standing tradition, women with government jobs were expected to resign upon getting married. That men as husbands and fathers should be the principal providers of material support for families has long been consistent with traditional Catholic values and has tended to be a status symbol among the middle and upper classes. However, the Constitution gives both genders equal rights in employment and, as there now exists within the Ministry of Social Development an Equal Status for Women department, more married women are employed than previously. The Soroptimist International of Malta has been making these and other changes for women.

The professions have long been open to both men and women in Malta although higher ecclesiastical positions are reserved for men. Women work as professors, physicians, nurses, reporters, editors, and legislators. In fact, approximately 15 percent of all persons elected to local councils nationwide are female.

Males and females are free to circulate in public without sanction. While it is still a common sight to see men gathered in piazzas or public squares near local churches socializing with each other on Sundays, until recently domestic chores restricted the time available to married women for leisure away from home. There continues to be considerable division of labor based on gender in households. For example, while some men may help to dry dishes and some boys take out rugs for spring cleaning, cooking as well as many other domestic chores generally is expected to be performed by females. Fathers are much less involved in the rearing of infants, especially female infants, than mothers, although the former may sometimes now be seen pushing a pram or carrying a child onto a bus.

MARRIAGE, FAMILY, AND KINSHIP

Family connections are reckoned through both parents, but Maltese have closer emotional ties and more frequent contact through the maternal side. Matrilocal residence is considerably more common than patrilocal residence, although neolocal residence is preferred. A wife is legally obliged to obey her husband, reside where he wishes, and accept his surname. Children inherit the father's surname and

A fisherman mending a net in the village of Marsa Xlokk. The Mediterranean Sea surrounds Malta.

often nickname. It is uncommon for single people to quit the parental residence at any age.

Marriage. Marriage is viewed as an opportunity for two groups of people to establish ties, and many status considerations come into play, with each side interested in obtaining prestige. The fact that women traditionally have been married with a dowry means that a family's status can rise and fall with the amount of the dowry. Cousin marriages are not socially preferred. Divorce is still not legal in Malta.

Domestic Unit. There is no tribal or lineage organization in families, although the offspring of the same maternal grandmother are typically friendly while she is still living. However, people often recognize that they are related to other people going back at least five generations when marriage decisions are made. Singlehood is not uncommon, and there are large communities of priests and nuns.

Inheritance. Only a husband and wife can make a joint will. Although spouses, children, and parents have certain rights to inherit, there are extreme cases in which they are deemed unworthy or may be disinherited. Members of religious orders may inherit only small life pensions and cannot dispose of property through wills.

Kin Groups. In ordinary conversation, Maltese do not often refer to family units larger than those descended from a particular grandparent or grandmother unless they are tracing their genealogy. After a mother dies, relations between her children are often not close. It is not uncommon for elderly parents or grandparents with living children to reside in homes for the elderly or infirm.

SOCIALIZATION

Child Rearing and Education. Children sometimes are called by diminutives of their names. Christening takes place in church, usually about a week or two after birth. The parents select as godparents a married couple who are often relatives. A firstborn child may share the parents' bed for two or three years, but if there is an older sister, that child may sleep with her after a year or so. Child rearing is considered more a matter for women than for men. Parents generally prefer that their children attend single-gender schools.

After first communion at about age 6 or 7, a child is taken to church regularly. Confirmation takes place at about age 10, and at that time a child gets a third godparent, always of the same gender as the child. If a child is admitted to a good secondary school, it is considered a tribute to the family. Sex is a taboo subject, and puberty is not discussed in detail. Open courtship is not encouraged before age 18.

Higher Education. The University of Malta goes back to the 1592 founding of the *Collegium Melitense*, a college founded by the Jesuits mainly to educate students not intending to enter the Jesuit order. It has seven thousand students, including four hundred foreigners. Its ten faculties range from architecture and civil engineering to arts and theology. Associated with the university are fourteen institutes. Higher education is also available through the Archbishop's Seminary and the Foundation for Theological Studies.

ETIQUETTE

Maltese culture defines correct behavior and comportment in a variety of ways depending on status, familiarity, age, and social connections. They range from reserved and courtly to warm and expressive.

Men play brilli, a form of bowling often called ninepins, on a narrow street in Gozo, Malta.

Whereas introductions and recommendations can open doors, presumptions of instant familiarity invite rebuff. Even business relationships are sometimes resented as manipulative if they do not unfold in a context of social intercourse. Invitations into homes for tea or dinner are considered special and non-routine occasions.

The wearing of scanty dress away from the beaches is not welcomed, nor is immodest dress inside of churches. Face-saving behavior is important in Maltese society, not only because of decorum and for the sake of maintaining the respect of individuals, but also to protect the honor of families. In contrast to nearby northern Africa, public hand holding among men and the veiling of women do not occur.

RELIGION

Religious Beliefs. Over 98 percent of the population are Roman Catholics, who tend to be highly observant. The year is filled with important religious events, and all localities are identified with patron saints who are celebrated, somewhat competitively, with fireworks and *festa* pageantry, including processions. Numerous pilgrimages take place, including the annual Franciscan pilgrimage to the National Shrine of Our Lady of Mellieha in May. In Valletta, there are a Greek Catholic church, a Greek Orthodox church, an Anglican cathedral, and a Jewish synagogue.

Death and the Afterlife. It is common to pray for the souls of the departed to assist those in Purgatory, and family members openly discuss the kinds of graves they are considering buying. A sharp distinction is made between a common grave and a family grave, which is considered more honorable. The average family grave has compartments for four or five coffins as well as a space below for bones when it is periodically "cleaned" by cemetery workers. It is considered improper to open a grave in less than a year even if another death occurs in the family.

MEDICINE AND HEALTH CARE

The largest hospital is Saint Luke's Hospital with 900 beds; the Gozo General Hospital has 159 beds. There are also midwifery services and government dispensaries.

SECULAR CELEBRATIONS

Most celebrations have at least an indirect relationship to religion. Among those that may be considered secular are the pre-lenten Carnival, Independence Day (21 September), Republic Day (13 December), and the Spring Show of Flowers, Vegetables, and Fruits at San Anton Gardens that were established in the 17th century. Additionally, there are circuses, sports events, and activities associated with the theater as well as orchestral, rock, folkloric, and choral concerts.

THE ARTS AND HUMANITIES

Support for the Arts. A long artistic tradition includes the making of furniture, jewelry in gold and silver, glass, sculpture, lace, tableware, dolls, ceramics, brassware, copperware, and miniature cribs and figurines as well as painting. Government involvement with the Valletta Crafts Centre and the Ta Ciali Crafts Village on Malta and the Ta Dbiegi Crafts Village in Gozo as well as its maintenance of the gilded and brocaded Manoel Theatre is important.

Literature. Oral literature exists in the form of proverbs, folktales, and folk songs. The earliest known written literary work in Maltese is a poem entitled *Cantilena*, which was composed in the fifteenth century; a tradition of written literature emerged in the seventeenth century.

THE STATE OF THE PHYSICAL AND SOCIAL SCIENCES

At the University of Malta, areas of scientific research are numerous and include concentrations as varied as dental surgery, microelectronics, gender relations, religious movements, and linguistics.

BIBLIOGRAPHY

Abela, Anthony M. *Women and Men in the Maltese Islands: Statistics from the Census of Population and Housing,* 1998.

Aquilina, Joseph. *A Comparative Dictionary of Maltese Proverbs,* 1972.

———. *Papers in Maltese Linguistics,* 1970.

Black, Annabel, "Negotiating the Tourist Gaze." In Jeremy Boissevain, ed., *Coping with Tourists: European Reactions to Mass Tourism,* 1996.

Blouet, Brian. *The Story of Malta,* 1972.

Boissevain, Jeremy F. *Hal-Farrug: A Village in Malta,* 1969.

———. *Saints and Fireworks: Religion and Politics in Rural Malta,* 1965.

Callus, Angela, ed. *Il-Mara Maltija wara s-Sena 2000 [The Maltese Woman after 2000],* 1998.

Caruana, Carmen M. *Education's Role in the Socioeconomic Development of Malta,* 1992.

Council of Europe Publishing. *Structure and Operation of Local and Regional Democracy: Malta Situation in 1997,* 1997.

Earle, Peter. *Corsairs of Malta and Barbary,* 1970.

Evans, J. D. *The Prehistoric Antiquities of the Maltese Islands: A Survey,* 1971.

Findlay, Ronald, and Stanislaw Wellisz. "Malta." In Ronald Findlay and Stanislaw Wellisz, eds., *Five Small Open Economies,* 1993.

Galley, Micheline, ed. *Maria Calleja's Gozo,* 1994.

Goodwin, Stefan C. "Dimensions of Social Stratification in the Maltese Islands." In *Proceedings of the Alpha Kappa Delta Sociological Research Symposium,* 1977.

Koster, Adrianus. "Clericals versus Socialists: Toward the 1984 Malta School War." In Eric R. Wolf, ed., *Religious Regimes and State-Formation: Perspectives from European Ethnology,* 1991.

Mahoney, Leonard. *5000 Years of Architecture in Malta,* 1996.

Pons, Connie Attard. *Manjieri Tajba Fis-Socjeta' [Good Manners in Society]*, 1961.

Price, Charles A. *Malta and the Maltese: Study in Nineteenth Century Migration*, 1954.

Sire, H. J. A. *The Knights of Malta*, 1994.

Trump, D. H. *Malta: An Archaeological Guide*, 1972.

—STEFAN CORNELIUS GOODWIN

MARSHALL ISLANDS

CULTURE NAME
Marshallese; Marshall Islander

ALTERNATIVE NAMES
Rālik-Ratak, Marshalls; formally known as the Republic of the Marshall Islands

ORIENTATION

Identification. The Marshall Islands derive their identity from British Captain William Marshall, who explored the area with Captain Thomas Gilbert in 1788. The atolls were not a cohesive entity until Europeans named and mapped them, and Rālik-Ratak, the Marshallese designation for the leeward and windward chains of atolls, was considered an appellation at the time of independence.

Location and Geography. The Marshall Islands occupy a vast expanse of ocean in the west-central Pacific, from 2,000 to 3,000 miles (3,220 to 4,830 kilometers) south and west of Hawaii. With a mere 66 square miles (171 square kilometers) of land, the twenty-nine low-lying atolls and five coral pinnacles that make up the Marshalls are like fine necklaces of reef and sand spits strewn across the 780,000 square miles (1.26 million square kilometers) of ocean that unifies and separates the atolls. The major atolls are located between 160° and 173° E and 4° and 20° N. The surrounding ocean helps maintain an average temperature of 81° F (27° C) with very little diurnal or yearly variation. Rainfall increases as one nears the equator, with around 60 inches (152 centimeters) per year in the north and 180 inches (460 centimeters) per year in the south. The dry part of the year, November through April, is typified by brisk breezes, and the central month of the wet season, August, often has periods with very little wind. For much of the year northeasterly trade winds provide natural air conditioning. Typhoons are not uncommon in the winter months.

Demography. Since World War II the capital of the Marshall Islands has been located on Majuro, in the southern part of the Ratak chain. With a very high rate of population increase, the Marshall Islands has changed rapidly from 43,380 people in 1988 to a projected population of well over 60,000 in 1999. Residents are very mobile, and nearly 80 percent are now urban. Approximately one-half of the population resides on Majuro Atoll where government employment created a post-independence population explosion. The other urban enclave is Ebeye (Epjā islet), Kwajalein Atoll, one of the world's most densely-populated locations, where many residents work on the United States military base on nearby Kwajalein islet. Other Marshall Islanders choose to reside on one of two dozen inhabited outer atolls or coral pinnacles where a more traditional style of life can be maintained.

Linguistic Affiliation. All residents speak Marshallese, an Austronesian language that shares numerous affinities with other Pacific languages, particularly those of eastern Micronesia. Marshallese dialects began to disappear after missionaries from the American Board of Commissioners for Foreign Missions (ABCFM) arrived on Ebon, in the southern Ralik Chain, in 1857 and developed a transcription system. At least three mutually intelligible dialects remain: Ratak, Rālik, and an Enewetak/Ujelang variant. Former eras of Spanish, German, Japanese, and American administration and intermarriage between Marshall Islanders and other Pacific Islanders mean that Marshall Islanders often learn multiple languages. Many residents understand and/or speak a pidgin English, which has become a *lingua franca* in the west-central Pacific.

Symbolism. The independent Marshall Islands is perhaps too new to have developed core symbols, metaphors, or traditions, but the image of the rising and setting sun, emblematic of the Ratak "facing toward the windward" (sunrise) and Rālik "facing toward the leeward" (sunset) symbolism forms a

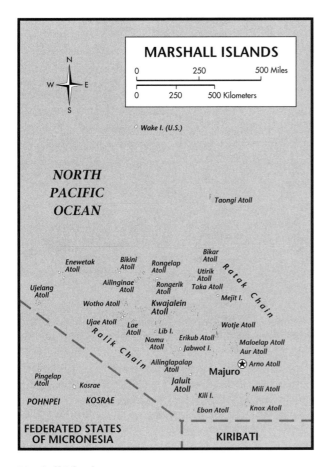

MARSHALL ISLANDS

Marshall Islands

central element of the flag. Stick charts which were once used to instruct novice sailors, outrigger canoes, and finely woven pandanus and coconut fiber art produced by Marshallese women, have assumed extraordinary value as images of national integration. Atoll specific celebrations that recognize the end of World War II and the elaborate celebrations of *Kūrijmōj* (Christmas) are popular communal events.

HISTORY AND ETHNIC RELATIONS

Emergence of the Nation. Beginning with the establishment of the Congress of Micronesia in 1965, local elites representing the various island groups that made up the Trust Territory of the Pacific Islands established the Micronesian Political Status Commission in 1967 to explore political options for the future of the region. The range of options that were discussed with representatives of the United States included total independence, a status of free association with the United States, continuing status as a Trust Territory, and integration with the United States. Even though the original negotia-

tions had posited a common future for the Trust Territory, the United States, based on its own differential interests in the region, soon began to negotiate separately with the Northern Mariana Islands. The United States Department of Defense also wished to maintain special rights of access and use in the Marshall Islands and Belau and, on the basis of these strategic advantages, these two districts were also granted separate opportunities to negotiate their political futures. The remaining districts of the Trust Territory, lacking in special resources or strategic value to the United States, were not granted separate negotiational status. The United States favored commonwealth status for the region in 1970, and in 1975 the Northern Mariana Islands voted to become a commonwealth of the United States. Prior to the formal establishment of the Commonwealth of the Northern Mariana Islands, however, the United States reconsidered its initial rejection of free association as a viable option, and the Marshall Islands, Belau, and the remaining districts of the Trust Territory, now known as the Federated States of Micronesia, began to negotiate constitutional governments that would be linked to the United States by compacts of free association. Most elements of self-government were assumed by the Republic of the Marshall Islands in 1970, with formal statehood in free association with the United States decreed by the United States president in 1986. The Republic of the Marshall Islands was welcomed as a member state of the United Nations in 1991.

National Identity. National identity remains formative due to recent independent status. People often rely on their atolls of birth and residence to ground their identities, but a cohesive identity is forming. Residence in the United States and elsewhere has fostered people's sense of being, first and foremost, Marshall Islanders. Urbanization also contributes to a homogenous identity, but policies that create an unequal distribution of wealth and a glut of new missions act as counter-cohesive forces.

Ethic Relations. While ethnic diversity on most atolls is limited, Majuro is becoming multi-ethnic in character with representatives from many Pacific and Pacific Rim locales. While no distinct ethnic groups exist in the Marshall Islands, people from atolls with substantial colonial contact—notably Ebon, Jaluij, Kwajalein, Majuro and, to some extent, Wotje and Maloelap—have been historically advantaged by these contacts.

URBANIZATION, ARCHITECTURE, AND THE USE OF SPACE

The Marshall Islands have rapidly urbanized since the 1960s, first with employment opportunities on Kwajalein and more recently with rapid population expansion on Majuro. Since independence, radical disparities in wealth have become apparent. Majuro boasts million dollar homes next to dilapidated and overcrowded plywood and rusted tin dwellings. Those who can afford cement homes and automobiles have moved from urban districts (Delap, Uliga, Djarrit) to suburbs that extend from Rairek to Majuro. Public buildings, like the capitol, are elaborate, expensive structures, while equally important buildings such as hospitals are in disrepair.

Sitting on small white paving stones around dwellings kept humans from potentially polluting soil, but imported furniture is becoming commonplace among the wealthy.

FOOD AND ECONOMY

Food in Daily Life. Throughout the Marshall Islands food is not only valued for sustenance, it is used to create and maintain cohesiveness. Meals always balance a drink with a food and use fish or meat to complement the staples. Local staples include breadfruit, arrowroot, pandanus, and taro, and are now supplemented with imported rice, flour, and sugar. Indigenous complements are seafoods, birds, and eggs, supplemented with pig, chicken, and an increasing variety of tinned meats. Coffee and cola have replaced coconut milk as the primary drink. While outer islanders still rely on many indigenous foods from fishing and gathering, overpopulation on Majuro and Ebeye makes residents almost entirely reliant on imports. The limited array of affordable imported foods has resulted in epidemic levels of diabetes, heart disease, hypertension, and other diet-related diseases.

Basic Economy. The Marshall Islands have successfully marketed their strategic location for military purposes, northern Marshall Islanders' incomes have been supplemented through compensation for post World War II nuclear tests, and attempts have been made to revitalize copra production and energize the fishing industry.

Land Tenure and Property. Land in the Marshall Islands is held in perpetuity by members of clans and extended families, and certain lands and fishing waters are held by the entire community. Practices vary from atoll to atoll, but anthropologists have depicted land as passing through matrilines, though

People relaxing on a beach in Majuro, Ratak. The average temperature on the Marshall Islands is 81 degrees.

the offspring of male members of the matriline also have residence rights as workers of the land. Other anthropologists have noted bilateral features of land tenure that allow for flexibility in land transfer. On outlying Enewetak and Ujelang, land is a mark of identity claimed bilaterally. Copra production in the nineteenth century greatly increased the power of Marshallese *iroij* chiefs and *alab* land heads, since Europeans relied on them to oversee the growing, collection, and processing of coconut. Japanese land registration in the 1930s increased the amount of communal land to which the Japanese-controlled government had access. During the American and post-independence eras, pressures have multiplied to create alienable land that can be bought and sold. Long-term land leases have become popular in Majuro, and a lease that allows the United States Army to use large segments of Kwajalein Atoll provides income for chiefs and land-holders of Kwajalein.

Commercial Activities. Whalers from Europe and the United States were originally attracted to Marshall Islands' waters in the 1830s to 1850s but by the 1860s copra (the production of dried coconut) dominated Europeans' interest in the islands. Copra production under German rule (1885–1915) substantially altered Marshallese social relations. Under Japanese control (between World War I and World War II) copra production continued, supplemented by a fishing industry (dominated by Okinawans), and by exports of phosphorus, coconut husk mats, and handicrafts. Following World War II, the United States had a strategic interest in the Marshall Islands with few attempts at development. As copra prices declined on the world market, Marshall Islanders relied more on the meager income from handicrafts to supplement the subsistence economy. By the 1960s and 1970s, financial assistance programs were instituted to make up for United States neglect of the region and became the major source of income. Since independence, United States aid has been supplemented by programs from other Pacific Rim countries.

Major Industries. A small garment manufacturing industry has been started, and many government officials hold out hopes for future tourism.

Trade. Other than the islands' strategic location, which has been marketed to the United States as part of the Compact of Free Association agreement, the main exports include fish and fishing rights in Marshallese waters and products derived from dried coconut. In addition, the re-export of dyes figures prominently in the list of 1990s exports. Foods, fuel, automobiles, machinery and transportation equipment, manufactured goods, materials, and beverages and tobacco make up the bulk of imported goods.

Division of Labor. Division of labor is largely based on gender and age, with special positions held by chiefs, land heads, extended family heads, and by local pastors. In urban areas, an elite made up of chiefs, the descendants of half-caste families, and, increasingly, educated young adults, hold most government positions and public or private sector jobs.

SOCIAL STRATIFICATION

Classes and Castes. In the past highly ranked persons were at the center or windward end of discussion circles and elevated above compatriots or were seated on the ocean side of persons of lesser rank.

Since independence, an emergent class structure has become apparent in urban sectors with radical differences in wealth between the rich and poor. In part, the class structure reflects the distribution of jobs but, at its highest levels, reflects a monopoly of political power among a group of chiefs and a small

set of English-speaking half-caste residents and other elite families. The distinction between chief and commoner is long standing. Until the mid-1800s chiefdoms were small, seldom including more than one or two atolls. With colonial support, the power and influence of the chief increased.

Symbols of Social Stratification. In the past intricate tatoos distinguished men and women of higher class from commoners. Renowned warriors and those respected as navigators and medical specialists also displayed their identities through distinctive tatoos. Restricted speech genres were also used to interact with those of highest rank. Speaking styles are divided into honorific and ordinary styles today. Marshall Islanders commonly wear American-style dress modified it to local norms but elite styles of costly dress and personal adornment are increasing as signs of emergent class distinctions.

POLITICAL LIFE

Government. The Republic of the Marshall Islands (RMI) formed a constitutional government in 1979 and gained formal independence in 1986. Prior to that time, the Marshall Islands was a district within the Trust Territory of the Pacific Islands (TTPI) administered by the United States.

The RMI is governed by a bicameral parliament with a president as the head of state; an upper house of government, the Council of *Iroij* (Chiefs) and a lower house, or *Nitijelā* (legislative body). Thirty-three senators elected from twenty-four atoll districts make up the Nitijelā. Twelve paramount chiefs on the Council of Iroij are advisors to the Cabinet and review land tenure issues and other matters of traditional concern. To date, the two RMI presidents, parallel cousins, were selected by the Nitijelā from the group of high chiefs eligible to sit on the Council of Iroij. Both were born to grandsons of Kabua the Great, renowned paramount chief during German times.

Leadership and Political Officials. Local law enforcement rests in the hands of atoll policemen. The judicial branch of the RMI consists of a supreme court, high court, traditional rights court, and district and community Courts. Questions often arise about the independence of the judiciary, since judges are appointed by the Nitijelā for only two years. On outer islands and atolls, however, most matters are settled internally, with little reliance on the state judicial apparatus.

Men checking a fish trap in Majuro, Ratak. Outer Island citizens still rely heavily on indigenious foods like fish.

Social Problems and Controls. While driving offenses, theft, and even murder are recent urban concerns, most outer island problems have to do with land matters and with drunken behavior, particularly among youth. Since rank within a community and extended family are largely determined by relative age, young males often resort to drunken outbursts to display sublimated disenfranchisements.

Military Activity. There is no standing military force, but many youth have joined the United States military to find careers and increase their ability to attend college.

SOCIAL WELFARE AND CHANGE PROGRAMS

Since the 1960s, numerous social welfare programs have been available, supported by the United States, various religious groups and, since independence, other Pacific Rim nations. United States social welfare programs for education, health and nutrition, and the needs of youth, women, and the aged are particularly visible. Many residents rely on these programs, especially in urban areas.

NONGOVERNMENTAL ORGANIZATIONS AND OTHER ASSOCIATIONS

Economic incentive programs are supported by Australia, New Zealand, Japan, and Taiwan, as well as the United States. International nongovernmental organizations are highly visible, particularly Greenpeace and others concerned with nuclear-related issues.

GENDER ROLES AND STATUSES

Division of Labor by Gender. Males typically perform activities associated with the sea and sky (fishing, canoe building, gathering drinking coconuts, capturing birds) while females dominate activities on the land (digging arrowroot or gathering pandanus fronds). Females also control the domestic sphere and are associated with activities in the village, while men work in the bush lands away from the village and travel freely to foreign countries.

The Relative Status of Women and Men. Females control a great deal of power in the matrilineal social structure so while men are the public performers, women's behind-the-scenes decisions often predominate.

MARRIAGE, FAMILY, AND KINSHIP

Marriage. Marriage is permitted between members of different clans who are related as immediate or extended cross-cousins, but due to internal and trans-national mobility, marriage with non-related foreigners is also frequent. Youths select spouses from the large group of cross-cousin and unrelated potential marriage partners, but many marriages do not last. Once a couple has a stable relationship divorce is infrequent, though not prohibited. Stable couples have typically resided for a period of time on lands of one of the couple's parents, have established ancestral status with the birth of one or two children, and have become recognized members of the community. Polygamy, at one time permitted, was prohibited by missionaries and now is not condoned. Urbanization has created stress in many marriages, and domestic violence is not uncommon. Nevertheless, on the outer atolls, marriage provides an entry into the community exchange system balancing the husband's provisioning tasks with a wife's responsibility to transform raw foods into edibles, combining a woman's ability to transfer core clan identity to offspring with the man's ability to shape the child's physical features, and providing pathways that embed the couple and their offspring in extended families and community of which they are an integral, contributing part.

Domestic Unit. Elevated sleeping platforms have always separated highly ranked family members from others. Members of one to four or five households that are part of the same extended family comprise typical cookhouse groups. The extended family may be from one matri-clan but often cookhouse groups are comprised of residents related through male or male and female ties. One or more respected elder, female or male, heads the cookhouse group, though robust young males and females often do the provisioning and food preparation. Girls and boys from about age five perform household duties, and elders too old to cook or fish weave mats and handicraft or repair tools, dwellings, and watercraft. The irrelevance of this once-integrated extended family task orientation, from more nucleated residence patterns, and from a reliance on cash provisioning rather than sharing, has placed strains on urban families.

Inheritance. The core of one's identity, derived from one's mother, provides the central item of inheritance, though bio-cultural links with one's father determine external features of self. With warfare prohibition and the focus on copra, land holding transmittals were largely restricted to matri-clan pathways, but males in good standing retain worker's rights on the land for one or more generations. On Ujelang and Enewetak atolls, land may be transferred along male or female pathways though, as throughout the Marshall Islands, actively working the land to transform it from bush into living space is a critical way to establish rights to use clan or extended family lands. In ancient times, a person's possessions were burned at his or her death and, until the recent appearance of class distinctions, meager amounts of personal property remained to be distributed. While immediate family members might keep small mementos, all other property is distributed to distant community members.

Kin Groups. Beyond the bounds of cookhouse groups, Marshall Islanders are members of large extended kin groups and remain linked to those relatives through shared companionship, shared land, shared clanship (transmitted through females), or shared blood (transmitted through males). These identity groups often extend beyond the bounds of an atoll. One's position as a member of a village segment, a village, a district, and an atoll are important elements of identity, and one's position in a religious organization, a Christmas–time song-fest group, a handicraft and mat manufacturing circle, or a sailing group may be of equal importance. In the outer island setting, most of these groups interact regularly, creating overlapping networks of close-knit relatives. While identity groups are fairly effective in urban settings, high mobility and the market economy do not provide time or support for shared daily activities that are the substance of such identity groups.

SOCIALIZATION

Infant Care. Infants are indulged, with few restrictions on their activities. They are nursed until two or three years of age, or until the birth of a younger sibling. Infants are fully integrated into daily domestic activities, and are carried on the hip by working mothers or slightly older siblings.

Child Rearing and Education. By the age of four or five, children become nursemaids. They assist with babies, run errands, and attend to small chores around the residence. Young boys are given freedom to explore beyond the village, and they frequently accompany older siblings, fathers, or mother's brothers on fishing and gathering expeditions. While children are given considerable freedom, they are also admonished with strict shouts of *nana!* (bad!) when important social boundaries have been crossed.

The program of socialization in local values and cultural abilities is supplemented with formal schooling. Outer atoll schools include grades one through eight with curricula focused on reading, English, and arithmetic. The most skilled students pass an examination to enter high school in Majuro. Others who can afford schooling beyond grade eight continue in one of several private Majuro high schools. Most are affiliated with religious groups, and attendance often leads to conversion of part or all of a student's family.

Higher Education. Recently, many Marshall Islanders have chosen to pursue higher education, usually in the United States where they are eligible for education loans.

ETIQUETTE

The Marshall Islands is a ranked society in which elders rank above those who are younger and chiefs rank above commoners. Codes of respect and deference are important and Americans are often considered haughty, brash, and irreverent. One should not walk in front of, upwind of, or elevate one's head

Nuclear test bunker in the Bikini Atoll. The United States has a military base on Kwajaleir Atoll.

above the level of one's seniors and, if the relative ranking of persons is unknown, one should always defer to others. Similarly, high ranked persons speak on behalf of others. Persons of lower rank begin public speeches with disclaimers such as "My words have no significance compared to those of other high-ranked persons here . . . . "

RELIGION

Religious Beliefs. In 1857, the American Board of Commissioners for Foreign Missionaries (ABCFM), the ideological offspring of missionaries who traveled to Hawaii in 1819, began to convert residents to Christianity. Catholic conversion soon followed, and these two missionary enterprises have been supplemented by a plethora of new religious groups in the past twenty-five years. Nevertheless, on outer atolls most residents shared a single mission-inspired religion until the late 1980s, when religious competition for souls extended beyond Majuro and Ebeye. In some cases, this competition has proved very disruptive to outer island communities.

Religious Practitioners. Ancient Marshall Islands belief included a pantheon of chief-deities who lived in primordial times and are now represented as constellations. Local religious and medical practitioners

provided access to life-giving powers, though specialists who controlled evil magic were not unknown.

Rituals and Holy Places. Magic continues to be an important factor in the organization of daily life and in many ways characteristics of former deities have been infused in the current Christian deities. Elaborate churches, often the highest and most centrally-located buildings in a village, have replaced the sacred shrines of old, often sacred stones or particular coconut or pandanus trees. Nevertheless, attitudes toward sacred places remain largely unaltered.

Death and the Afterlife. Death does not mark a radical disjunction from life, but simply a passage into another form of existence. Having become an ancestor at the birth of one's first child and having invested one's substance into the soil through years of working certain lands, many visible evidences of a person's being remain at death. Death represents the passage to becoming a non-corporeal ancestor, a being who continues to interact with community members, but one for whom the last vestiges of one's body are "planted" to become a part of the soil which has already been reshaped by the energies of one's lifetime.

MEDICINE AND HEALTH CARE

In addition to local medical practitioners who oversee births and treat illnesses, a system of American-style medicine is available through two underfunded urban hospitals and local health clinics on each atoll. The hospitals are reliant on doctors from abroad, but recently Marshallese doctors have begun to assist local medical officers (similar to United States physician's assistants), nurses, and health aides in staffing the hospitals and clinics.

SECULAR CELEBRATIONS

Throughout the years of the Trust Territory of the Pacific Islands, United Nations day was an important holiday, but that has now been replaced by Marshall Islands independence day. Local atoll rituals that commemorate the end of suffering during World War II and *Kūrijmōj* (Christmas), a ritual event of up to four months in duration, celebrated by all (not only church members), are the other major celebrations.

THE ARTS AND HUMANITIES

Graphic Arts. The Alele Museum and local handicraft shops display artistic endeavors in the Marshall Islands.

Performance Arts. There is a strong oral tradition. Marshall Islanders are great orators and at first birthday celebrations and other public events, elaborate speeches are always given. There is a budding song recording industry, and musical and dance performances are an important part of *Kūrijmōj*. A resurgence of interest in local hula-style dances and in sailing canoe manufacture provide diversity in the arts available.

THE STATE OF THE PHYSICAL AND SOCIAL SCIENCES

Considerable physical and social science research has been conducted but local islanders work largely as assistants on these projects, not as project designers. Beginning with Kotzebue (1817), exploring expeditions maintained an interest in the area, and numerous environmental research projects took place during the post–World War II nuclear testing era. Substantial social scientific study was conducted during post–World War II CIMA (Coordinated Investigation of Micronesian Anthropology) and SIM (Scientific Investigation of Micronesia) projects, and many anthropologists and applied social researchers have worked in the Marshall Islands since that time. The College of the Marshall Islands, formerly part of the College of Micronesia, offers a two-year college program.

BIBLIOGRAPHY

Carucci, Laurence M. "The Source of the Force in Marshallese Cosmology," in L. Lindstrom and G. White, eds., *The Pacific Theatre: Island Representations of World War II*, 1989.

———. "Nudging Her Harshly and Killing Him Softly: Displays of Disenfranchisement on Ujelang Atoll," in Judith Brown, Jacquelyn Campbell, and Dorothy Counts, eds., *Sanctions and Sanctuary*, 1992.

———. *Nuclear Nativity: Rituals of Renewal and Empowerment in the Marshall Islands*, 1997.

Hezel, Francis X., S. J. *The First Taint of Civilization: A History of the Caroline and Marshall Islands in Pre-Colonial Days, 1521–1885*, 1983.

———. *Strangers in Their Own Land: A Century of Colonial Rule in the Caroline and Marshall Islands*, 1995.

Kiste, Robert C. "New Political Statuses in American Micronesia," in Victoria Lockwood, Thomas Harding and Ben Wallace, eds, *Contemporary Pacific Societies: Studies in Development and Change*, 1993.

——— and Michael Rynkiewich "Incest and Exogamy: A Comparative Study of Two Marshall Island Populations," *The Journal of the Polynesian Society* 85: 209–226, 1976.

Mason, Leonard. "Relocation of the Bikini Marshallese: A Study in Group Migrations." Ph.D. dissertation. Department of Anthropology, Yale University. 1954.

———. "Marshallese Nation Emerges from the Political Fragmentation of American Micronesia," *Pacific Studies* 13 (1): 1989.

Spoehr, Alexander. *Majuro, a Village in the Marshall Islands*, 1949.

Tobin, Jack A. "Land Tenure in the Marshall Islands," in *Land Tenure Patterns: Trust Territory of the Pacific Islands*, 1958.

—LAURENCE MARSHALL CARUCCI

MARTINIQUE

CULTURE NAME

Martinican (sometimes spelled Martiniquan)

ALTERNATIVE NAMES

(as part of broader geocultural grouping) French Caribbean, French West Indian, French Antillean, Antillean

ORIENTATION

Identification. Early in his exploration of the New World, the Amerindian inhabitants of Cuba and Hispanola told Christopher Columbus about a smaller island which they called Martinino. Coming to the island in 1502, Columbus gave it the name Martinique. Indigenous Carib islanders called it Madiana or Madinina (''Island of Flowers''), designations still used informally in song and poetry. The Carib Indians of Martinique, however, were eradicated by the French in the seventeenth century and ensuing Martinican history and culture has been the result of creolization between French colonial and African slave societies. Martinicans are French citizens.

Location and Geography. Situated in the Lesser Antilles of the Windward Islands in the Caribbean, with the islands of Dominica to the north and Saint Lucia to the south, Martinique measures 431 square miles (1,120 square kilometers). It is a mountainous, tropical island of volcanic origin. The 1902 explosion of Mount Pelée totally destroyed the major town of Saint Pierre resulting in the capital being relocated to Fort-de-France.

Demography. As of July 1998 the population of Martinique was estimated at 407,284. Another 30 percent of Martinicans currently reside in France. Almost half as many people are born in France of Martinican parents as there are residents of Martinique itself. About 5 percent of the population residing in Martinique hail from France. Only about 2,500 Martinicans on the island are direct descendants of the original French settlers (*békés*). Most of the fewer than five thousand resident foreigners are agricultural laborers from other Caribbean islands.

Linguistic Affiliation. As part of France, the official language of Martinique for its government, schools, newspapers, and media is French. However, the vernacular which is spoken in most informal and family contexts is Creole. Derived mostly from French (with sprinklings from African, Amerindian, and English dialects), Creole is particularly expressive and idiomatic, using a relatively simple grammatical structure. Creole originally developed out of the need for African slaves to communicate among themselves as well as to understand the commands of their French masters. The lack of local Creole literature has prompted many Martinicans to deny that Creole constitutes a language. In Martinique itself, Creole is becoming more and more French as a result of increasing cultural influences from France. Standard French is widely spoken, albeit in a distinctive, lilting French West Indian accent.

Symbolism. *Ile aux Fleurs* (''Island of Flowers'') is one of the island's unofficial nicknames; the other, invoking its magical charm, is *Pays des Revenants* (''Land to Which One Returns''). The *gommier* (wooden fishing boat) symbolizes a society surrounded by the sea while the *bakoua* (a high conical hat woven from the pandanus plant) represents the early predominant peasant culture. *Colibri* (hummingbird) is the island mascot.

Colorful, striped female dress (madras) with a knotted kerchief represents the languorous West Indian woman of the past. Music and dance, especially of a sensuous variety, are distinctly Martinican. Poets and writers have used the mangrove (swamp) as metaphor for Martinique.

Recently, symbolism has been used to commemorate emancipation from slavery. Initially,

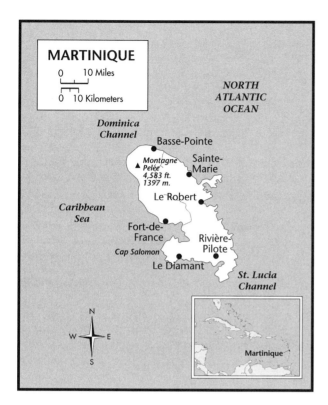

Martinique

credit for the abolition of slavery had gone exclusively to Victor Schoelcher, the "Abraham Lincoln" of the French colonies. In the last two decades Martinican nationalists have campaigned to emphasize the role of slave revolts and *marronage* (escape) in their actual liberation. The combined French and Caribbean Martinican identity has created a complex political symbolism that celebrates the French Bastille Day as well as the Martinican abolition of slavery.

Metissage, the mixing of multiple races and ethnicities (particularly French and African but also East Indian and Chinese) into a composite, multi-racial society, includes the controversial concepts of *négritude* (black consciousness), *antillanité* (West Indianness), and *créolité* (transcultural fusing with a Caribbean emphasis). Doudouism—the image of a tropical island paradise with a French accent, laced with romance and lassitude—usually is regarded as a saccharine stereotype.

HISTORY AND ETHNIC RELATIONS

Emergence of the Nation.
The existence of a Martinican "nation" is a matter of dispute. After the definitive abolition of slavery in 1848 (an earlier emancipation act of the French Revolution was rescinded by Napoleon), the dominant colonial policy

became assimilation: the full extension of French education, language, and civil rights to all those living under the French flag. This policy came to its apogee in 1946 when, at the urging of the representatives of the local populace (especially member of parliament Aimé Césaire), the National Assembly in Paris voted to make Martinique an overseas department of France. As full citizens of France, Martinicans are members of the European community.

National Identity.
Society is more like that of France than on other Caribbean islands. A relatively small group of nationalists demand outright independence for the island while others prefer autonomy within the French Republic. Most Martinicans, while preserving French West Indian cultural identity through Creole language, music, cuisine, and mores prefer not to sever their political ties with the French nation.

Ethnic Relations.
The békés—white descendants of the original French settlers—have long constituted the local élite engendering varying degrees of both envy and resentment. Residual racial preferences within the non-white populace (lighter is preferred to darker skin) still mark marital and other social choices. *Metros* (short for *metropolitans*, whites from France) are regarded as outsiders by all Martinicans. Metros often occupy visible positions in government, civil service, and education, which local nationalists periodically protest. Intermarriage between Martinicans and metropolitans is fairly common.

URBANISM, ARCHITECTURE, AND THE USE OF SPACE

Departmentalization and concomitant economic change have transformed the rural sugar plantation character of the island into one highly dependent on the tertiary sector and urban activity. One-third of the island's population converges daily into Fort-de-France, whose narrow symmetrically squared streets are as congested during the day as they are empty at night. Distinctive colonial-era architecture adapted to the tropics—wood and stone constructions of large, open spaces with verandas and light filtering (but wind porous) windows—is gradually giving way to more "functional," enclosed, air-conditioned construction. Such architectural change, especially in government buildings, projects a less colonial look and feel in favor of a more uniform and efficient French model. An unwalled, conical straw shelter—the carbet—still dots the landscape and is reminiscent of Amerindian days.

1417

In addition to the classic war memorials which dot villages throughout France (and therefore Martinique), monuments to Victor Schoelcher, the leader of the abolitionist movement, are also common. One monument in particular—a statue in the Savanna (central park) of the Fort-de-France of the Empress Josephine, the Martinique-born wife of Napoleon Bonaparte—has been the object of continuous vandalism for those who see it as a symbol of racism and continued colonialism (Napoleon's decision to reinstate slavery is attributed to the influence of Josephine).

FOOD AND ECONOMY

Food in Daily Life. Until supermarkets and imported common cuisine (including steak-and-fries and fast food chains) proliferated, daily Martinican cuisine was characterized by a unique blend of French and Creole cooking, often laced with *piment* (hot pepper). Open air markets still supply locally grown fruits (bananas, coconuts, guava, pineapples, mangoes, love apples, and passion fruit) and vegetables (breadfruit, chinese cabbage, yams, gumbo, and manioc). Much Martinican cuisine is prepared from seafood and shellfish including salted cod, *lambi* (conch), octopus, *blaff* (boiled fish with chives) and the national dish, *court-bouillon* (fish in a spicy tomato sauce). However, one-quarter of the average household food budget is now spent on mostly imported meats and poultry, especially beef. Restaurants have yet to cultivate the same air of sophistication and hospitality as in France.

Food Customs at Ceremonial Occasions. *Boudin*—a fat sausage of spicy pig's blood—is a staple at all holidays. At Easter and on Pentecost a spicy dish of crab and rice, *matoutou*, is always served. Small fried vegetable or fish cakes (*acras*), used to be reserved for saints days but have become a popular appetizer. Special occasions call for a gumbo and vegetable soup with crab or salted meat (*calalou*). East Indian influence is evident in the *colombo*, a mutton, goat, or chicken curry. No social gathering is complete without drinking a *ti-punch* (straight rum with a twist of lemon sweetened with cane sugar) or a *planteur* (fruit juice and rum). *Shrubb* (rum with marinated orange or tangerine rinds) is served at Christmas.

Basic Economy. The economy is linked to that of France. The agricultural basis for the island—banana, sugar, and pineapple plantations—is heavily subsidized by the French economy.

Local islanders called Mauritius Madiana or Madinina, which means "Island of Flowers."

Land Tenure and Property. Nearly one-half of large land holdings were inherited from colonial-era distributions. Land tenancy may be practiced either by share (*colonage*) or cash (*métayage*). Land division for inheritance purposes is supposed to follow normal French legal practice but unresolved plot disputes abound.

Commercial Activities. While the agricultural sector employs only about 10 percent of the population, approximately one-third of workers are in government service. Another one-third of the workforce is chronically unemployed.

Major Industries. Sugar cane processing and tourism are the major industries.

Trade. Imports are equal to more than five times exports. Primary imports are consumer goods and agro-industrial products. Major exports are bananas, pineapples, flowers, and rum. Martinique's principal trading partners include metropolitan France, Great Britain, Germany, and Guadeloupe.

SOCIAL STRATIFICATION

Classes and Castes. Universal suffrage and departmentalization (i.e., statehood) have seen the power of the békés shift from politics almost exclusively to economics. Mulattos (mixed-race persons) still retain a residual social edge over those who are descended more directly from exclusively African forebears.

Symbols of Social Stratification. Western dress, urban outlook, white collar employment, and automobile ownership are all traits of social advancement. However, the most direct hallmark of upper class status besides skin color is the use of the French language rather than Creole and a metropolitan accent rather than a West Indian accent.

POLITICAL LIFE

Government. Martinique is one of one hundred *départements* (states) of the French Republic and one of five overseas departments (DOMs). It sends four deputies (representatives) to the National Assembly in Paris and in turn receives an appointed prefect who serves as the central government's local executive. There are also two locally elected assemblies: the general council with forty-five members, which is responsible for roads, housing, transportation, education and overall infrastructure, and a regional council with forty-one members, which oversees economic, social, sanitary, cultural and scientific development.

Leadership and Political Officials. The establishment and exploitation of patron-client relations are significant means of leadership attainment in this small society. Job and contract distribution is a major criterion for political popularity. Political parties can be classified into three major categories: local affiliates of French parties which are in favor of continued departmental status for Martinique (the gaullist Rassemblement pour la République, the moderate right Union pour la Démocratie Française, and the leftist Fédération de la Martinique); those advocating autonomy for Martinique within the French Republic (the Parti Communiste Martiniquais, Parti Progressiste Martiniquais); and pro-independence parties (Combat Ouvrier, Conseil National des Comités Populaires, Group Révolution Socialiste, Mouvement des Démocrates et Ecologistes pour une Martinique Souveraine, Mouvement Indépendantiste Martiniquais). The major figure in twentieth-century Martinican politics is Aimé Césaire, founder of the Parti Progressiste Martiniquais.

Social Problems and Control. The legal and judicial systems of Martinique are those of France, as are the police force and *gendarmerie*. They are accorded high legitimacy in the eyes of the populace. The most common crime is theft, especially car break-ins and automobile theft. Economic and financial crimes are also common. Social and political protest movements have occasionally resulted in fatalities. Politically motivated vandalism has damaged or destroyed monuments and installations at electricity, telecommunications, police, and court offices.

Military Activity. France's armed forces in Martinique are the third strongest military contingent in the Caribbean after the United States and Cuba. Land, sea, and air units are represented as well as the gendarmerie. Over five thousand officers, sailors, and soldiers serve in Martinique and Guadeloupe, most of whom are from France. A special program of "adapted military service" permits Martinican conscripts to remain in the French Antilles, receiving vocational training and contributing to local development.

SOCIAL WELFARE AND CHANGE PROGRAMS

Martinicans benefit fully from the generous package of welfare programs available to all French citizens, covering health, retirement, widowhood, and large families. Given the high rate of unemployment in Martinique, the workfare program plays an important role in ensuring a minimal income level for the least privileged. A joint commission made up of members of the general and regional councils controls local economic development. As part of France, Martinique is part of the European community, and has benefitted over the years from development funds made available through the community. In anticipation of the 1992 Treaty of Maastricht creating a single European economic

A house in Fort-de-France. One third of the population converges in this city daily.

zone, the European community instituted a special program to ensure that the overseas parts of constituent members not be adversely affected by economic integration.

NONGOVERNMENTAL ORGANIZATIONS AND OTHER ASSOCIATIONS

Local branches of nongovernmental organizations such as Amnesty International, the Red Cross, Doctors of the World, and Catholic Rescue channel Martinican philanthropy throughout the world.

GENDER ROLES AND STATUSES

The Relative Status of Women and Men. Machismo, a long-established tradition within West Indian society, still permeates Martinican society. There is a long matrifocal history of single female-headed households, which since 1975 have been heavily subsidized through government family allowance funds. Women retain power and influence in the private domain but in the more public spheres few women (with some exceptions in the fields of education and culture) occupy positions of high authority. Contraception has created a "fertility revolution," decreasing the child bearing

average from almost six children in the 1950s to slightly over two in the 1990s.

Since the 1980s over one-half of Martinican women have entered the workforce, where they are disproportionately represented as salaried employees in the services sector where they are employed as servants, clerical workers, and teachers. Martinican women are three times as underemployed and more unemployed than men. One-fifth of women have achieved middle class economic status. Despite an evolution among the young and middle class, the combination of large numbers of unmarried women in an economy that creates pressure for marriage puts wives in a vulnerable position within the household, where they must often submit to male chauvinistic attitudes and behavior lest their husbands abandon them and/or take mistresses.

MARRIAGE, FAMILY, AND KINSHIP

Marriage. In principle, Martinican couples marry by mutual consent on the basis of love. Particularly in village society, this typically follows a period of premarital co-residence and, frequently, childbirth. Families often apply subtle pressure to ensure that their eligible children "marry up" or at least do not "marry down" in terms of class and, especially, race as measured by skin color. Strong pressures to maintain endogenous family ties are exercised within the béké community. Legal formalities for marriage and divorce are those of France; declarations of common law marriage (*concubinage*) may be made at town hall. Approximately two thousand marriages are performed yearly in Martinique; between three hundred and four hundred divorces are processed. Little more than one-third of eligible age Martinicans (age 18 for men, age 15 for women) are in fact married.

Domestic Unit. The domestic unit in Martinique has evolved somewhere between the nuclear and extended family. Couples live together with their children without the benefit of formal matrimony, and nearby relatives often assist with child care. Approximately one-third of single mothers are heads of the household and depend on relatives for child care and housework. Feminist challenges notwithstanding, it has been a longstanding practice in Martinican society for men to take mistresses.

Inheritance. Inheritance follows the laws of France. In practice, particularly due to a high frequency of "illegitimate" heirs, following death the division of land and real estate may be subject to dispute and protracted litigation.

SOCIALIZATION

Child Rearing and Education. Child rearing is strict and often includes corporal punishment. In households where the father is present, it is generally he who is in authority. Martinique benefits from the same highly developed child care infrastructure and school system in place in France.

Higher Education. Even before the establishment of the University of the Antilles—French Guiana in Schoelcher pursuing a higher education in France was the goal of upwardly mobile Martinicans. University and professional degrees convey high status in local society. University education and professional training abroad (particularly in France) carry more weight in local eyes than do equivalent educational experiences in Martinique.

ETIQUETTE

Formality and social distancing characterize most interactions between strangers in Martinique. Language is the principal means by which social distance is established and maintained. Even though Creole is the lingua franca it is much more polite to address the other, at least until a sufficiently close relationship is established, in French. It can be considered disrespectful to initiate conversations in public spaces (i.e., government offices, stores) in Creole. If one can speak French, addressing a stranger in Creole is to acknowledge that person as socially inferior. Respecting French language norms of politeness (such as second person usage of the more formal *vous* as opposed to *tu*) is also a must. Shaking hands is part of local etiquette.

Informal interactions call for more intimate social exchanges. These include double (and even triple and quadruple) cheek kissing, even between members of the same sex. While double cheek kissing parallels that of French society in its frequency, it is performed in a distinctly Antillean style: more slowly and with greater head turning for a more perpendicular cheek-to-lip encounter.

RELIGION

Religious Beliefs. Ever since the establishment of French rule Roman Catholicism has been overwhelmingly predominant. In recent years evangelical Protestantism (e.g., Seventh Day Adventists) has been growing in strength as have Jehovah's Witnesses. Bahai, Jewish, and Muslim faiths also have their own sites of religious and cultural congregation.

Throughout and beyond the slave era a parallel system of belief and practice, known as *quimbois*, has existed alongside Christianity. Quimbois encompasses plant and herb remedies, sorcery, and spiritual healing, and is embedded deep within popular culture. A version of nineteenth century Hinduism, brought to the West Indies by south Indian immigrants, still survives in small temples and shrines where the burning of incense, garlanding of statues, and offering of sacrifices are still practiced. Both Hindus and *quimboiseurs* ordinarily consider themselves also to be Catholic while the local Rastafarians—a sect that began in Jamaica and worships the late emperor, Haile Selassie—break more squarely with Western religion.

Religious Practitioners. An archbishop presides over forty-seven parishes and over 60 priests.

Rituals and Holy Places. In addition to the regularly celebrated Catholic holidays (Christmas, Easter, All Saints Day, etc.) each commune (district) organizes an annual celebration in the name of a saint or Catholic holiday. Annual local Catholic pilgrimages include Sacré Coeur in Balata, the Way of the Cross of Mount Vauclin, Notre Dame de la Salette in Sainte-Anne and Saint-Michel in François. Notre Dame de la Délivrande, celebrating the 1851 rescue of Martinique's first bishop from a tropical storm in the Atlantic, has become the patron saint of the island as well as the pilgrimage of Morne-Rouge. A number of Martinicans partake in the cult of miraculous medal of Sainte Catherine Labouré in Paris. In recent years there has been annual revival of the Hindu *mela*.

Death and the Afterlife. Death announcements are a regularly scheduled part of the daily official radio program. Funeral rites invariably follow Roman Catholic practice and, especially in villages, include public funeral processions in which men are uniformly dressed in black suit, white shirt and black tie. *Jour des Morts* (Day of the Dead), when people gather in cemeteries after dusk to light candles at grave sites, is observed 2 November, the day after All Saints' Day.

MEDICINE AND HEALTH CARE

Modern medicine, administered through the Administration of Health and Social Services of France, has supplanted rural medical beliefs and practices relying on herbal cures. Folk or traditional medical practitioners (*guérisseurs*) are no longer common even in villages. Widespread belief in *quimbois* (sorcery) and the associated concepts of the evil eye and

Produce and goods for sale at an open-air market in Saint-Pierre. Traditional meals are a combination of French and Creole cuisines.

devil's work has been supplanted by psychiatric and other scientific explanations of extraordinary behavior.

SECULAR CELEBRATIONS

In addition to all the national holidays of France such as Bastille Day, Armistice Day, and May Day, Martinique observes Emancipation Day (marking the end of slavery) and *Bannzil Kréyol* (the International Day of Creole). Although originally grounded in Catholic ritual (encompassing, in particular, Mardi Gras and Ash Wednesday) Carnival has become a more secular and boisterous festival. Distinctive and often wild costume and behavior are on display, as groups vie in parade for attention and appreciation. On Mardi Gras regalers dress in red; the following day, in black and white. Music and dance "wake the dead." Vaval, a giant puppet, is the symbol of Carnival, and each year personifies a new theme. Vaval's ritual bonfire at Wednesday dusk marks the end of the raucous festivities.

THE ARTS AND THE HUMANITIES

Support for the Arts. Martinique is endowed with an extraordinarily rich infrastructure for the arts:

that of the region (FRAC–Regional Funds for Contemporary Art); the municipality of Fort-de-France (SERMAC–Municipal Service of Cultural Action); and mixed national and departmental (CMAC–Martinican Centre of Cultural Action). Festivals for artists and musicians, competitions and prizes, and concerts and institutional acquisitions support every art genre.

Literature. Explorers and missionaries (Father Labat being the most renowned) introduced seventeenth century Martinique to the world. A rich indigenous oral literature, best represented by the folk tales of the wily rabbit Compère Lapin, developed during the slave and post-slave era. With the publication of *Return to My Native Land* (1939), Aimé Césaire explained *négritude* (black consciousness of Africa and its West Indian diaspora) to the rest of the world; Edouard Glissant (*The Lizard*; *Antillean Discourse*) followed this genre. Psychiatrist Frantz Fanon provided a penetrating analysis of the French West Indian mentality in *Black Skin, White Masks* (1952). Contemporary Martinican writers of note include Patrick Chamoiseau (whose novel *Texaco* won the Prix Goncourt) and Raphaël Confiant (*The Negro and the Admiral*).

Graphic Arts. The most notable graphic arts movements are the 1970s Caribbean Negro School, inspired by apprenticeship in Africa following study in France; and the 1980s Fromajé, steeped in the island's ancestral heritage. Annual artistic events are CMAC displays of paintings and sculptors, pastels and watercolors; SERMAC's Festival of Fort-de-France; and expositions by the Association of Young Martinique Artists (ADJAM) and the Martinican Association of Plastic Artists (AMPC). FRAC hosts artists-in-residence and degree-granting training is offered by the Regional School of Plastic Arts of Martinique (ERAPM). Legacies of Carib Indian culture survive in basket weaving and artisinal pottery from the colonial era continues but the Trois-Ilets Pottery has been modernized.

Performance Arts. Around the world Martinique is popularly known for its music, thanks to such groups as Kassav and Compagnie Créole. Zouk has largely supplanted the *biguine* of the past although the group Malavoi preserves a traditional instrumental style. A distinctive style of drumming is *gwo-ka*. Theater flourishes, especially at the Municipal Theater and Regional Dramatic Center. The Grand Ballet of Martinique maintains the island's folk heritage, mostly for the tourist audience.

THE STATE OF THE PHYSICAL AND SOCIAL SCIENCES

Research institutes of France in Martinique include those for general science and development, geography, agronomy, geology and mineralogy, and oceanography. Demographic and economic studies are conducted through INSEE (National Institute for Statistics and Economic Studies). The Martinican campus of the University of the Antilles-French Guiana offers two tracks of study: law and economics; and letters and social sciences. Training courses for social work, business and management, and nursing and midwifery are also available.

BIBLIOGRAPHY

Bernabé, Jean, Patrick Chamoiseau, and Raphaël Confiant. *Éloge de la Creolité/In Praise of Creoleness*, 1990.

———. "Towards 1992: Political-Cultural Assimilation and Opposition in Contemporary Martinique.*French Cultural Studies* 3: 61–86, 1992.

———, and Fred Reno, eds. *French and West Indian: Martinique, Guadeloupe, and French Guiana Today*, 1995.

Césaire, Aimé. *Return to My Native Land*, 1971.

Chaimoiseu, Patrick. *Creole Folktales*, trans., 1994.

Constant, Fred. "The French Antilles in the 1990s: Between European Unification and Political Territorialization." *Caribbean Studies* 26 (3–4): 293–243, 1993.

Daniel, Justin. "Political Constraints of Economic Dependency: The Case of Guadeloupe and Martinique." *Caribbean Studies* 26 (3–4), 311–334, 1993.

Fanon, Frantz. *Black Skin, White Masks*, trans., 1966.

Guilbault, Jocelyn, et al. *Zouk: World Music in the West Indies*, 1993.

Horowitz, Michael M. *Morne-Paysan. Peasant Village in Martinique*, 1967, reissued 1992.

Lasserre, Guy, and Albert Mabileau. "The French Antilles and Their Status as Overseas Departments." In Hilary Beckles and Verene Shepherd, *Caribbean Freedom: Economy and Society from Emancipation to the Present: A Student Reader*, 1996.

Miles, William F. S. "Abolition, Independence, and Soccer: Premillennial Dilemmas of Martinican Identity." *French Politics and Society* 17 (2): 23–33, 1999.

———. "Deja Vu with a Difference: End of the Mitterrand Era and the McDonaldization of Martinique." *Caribbean Studies* 28 (2): 339–368, 1995.

———. *Elections and Ethnicity in French Martinique. A Paradox in Paradise*, 1986.

Murch, Arvin. *Black Frenchmen. The Political Integration of the French Antilles*, 1971.

—WILLIAM F. S. MILES

MAURITANIA

CULTURE NAME

Mauritanian

ORIENTATION

Identification. The name of the country is derived from the Latin *Mauretania*, meaning "west," which corresponds to the Arab name of North Africa, *Maghreb*. The Romans referred to the Berber people as *Maures*.

The French occupied the country in 1860 in close cooperation with Maur religious leaders. Mauritania became a nation after the destruction of the kingdoms of Fouta Toro and Walo Walo and the Arab-Berber emirats of Trarza, Brakna, Taganet, and Adrar. As a result, the country has two main ethnic groups: black Africans and Arab-Berbers. The black African group includes the Fulani, Soninke, and Bambara. The Maurs include the Arab-Berbers (Beydan) and the black Maurs known as Haratin. The Haratins are black Africans who were enslaved by white Maurs. White and black Maurs consider themselves Arab, whereas black Arabs see themselves as African. The most important common denominator is Sunni Islam.

Location and Geography. Mauritania encompasses 400,385 square miles (1,037,000 square kilometers), more than three quarters of which is made up of the Sahara desert and the semiarid Sahelian zone. The remaining portion lies along the Senegal River Valley in the extreme south and southeast. The terrain consists of a plateau with vast sand dunes. The climate is hot and dry with frequent sandstorms. The country borders Senegal to the south, Mali to the southeast, Algeria to the northeast, and the Western Sahara to the north. In the southern region, most people engage in agriculture and livestock raising. The people in the south are settled black African farmers, whereas in the north the people have a nomadic lifestyle.

The capital, Nouakchott, is on the on the Atlantic coast. It was chosen a year before independence in 1960. Because the French wanted to transfer power to their Arab-Berber allies, the idea of having a major cities such as Rosso or Kaedi as the capital was ruled out.

Demography. As a result of ethnic clashes between pro-arabization groups and black Africans, the authorities have banned discussion of population issues to maintain the myth that Mauritania is the land of the Maurs with a tiny minority of black Africans. The most recent estimate of the population is 2.5 million. Because population growth in the black African communities in the south is much higher, white Arab-Berbers have become a minority. According to the latest estimates of ethnic distribution, the Haratin community accounts for 40 to 45 percent of the total population, while the white Arab-Berbers account for 25 percent and black Africans 30 percent.

Linguistic Affiliation. There are four national languages. Hassaniya is a mixture of Arabic and Berber and is the language of the white Maurs and the Haratin. Pulaar (Fulani) is spoken on the Atlantic coast and across the sahel-savannah zone. Soninke (Sarakolle) is spoken on the borders with Mali and Senegal. Wolof is widely spoken. Bambara is spoken in the southeast. At independence, French became the official language and, in 1965, the Arab-Berber regime made Arabic compulsory in primary and secondary education. This resulted in ethnic confrontation over the national language. The clashes intensified until 1999, when Colonel Maaouiya Ould Sid Ahmed Taya decided to resurrect French and downgrade Arabic. Black Africans' determination to resist Arabization resulted in the official recognition of Fulani, Soninke, and Wolof as national languages in 1980 and the creation of a national institute to teach those languages in public schools. That experiment was sabotaged by a palace coup in 1984.

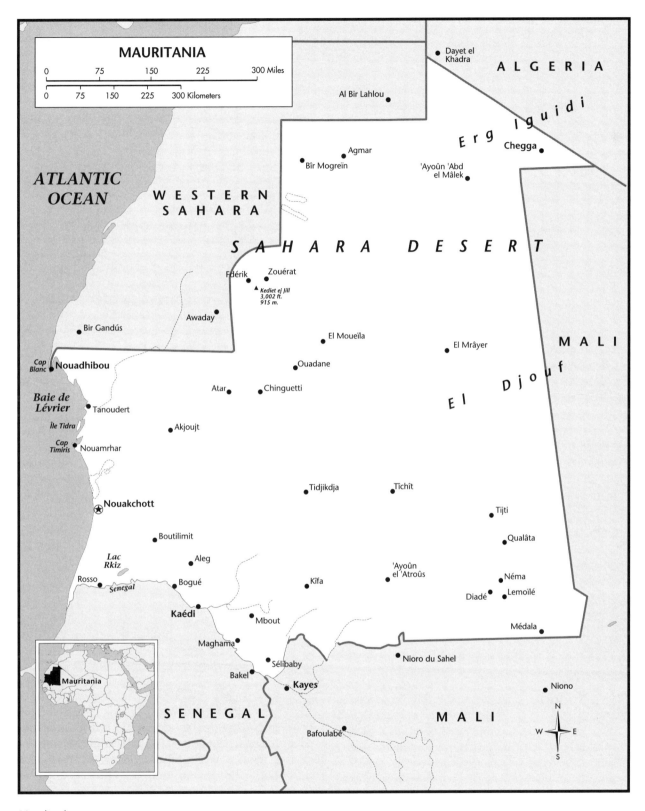

Mauritania

Symbolism. All Mauritanians self-identify themselves as Sunni Muslims of the Malkite rite and believe that their society is the most Islamic in Africa. Mauritania is an Islamic republic whose basic law is the sharia, and the flag (green with a yellow crescent and stars) symbolizes Islam. Mauritanians believe that they have a mission to promote Islam and Islamic values throughout black Africa, and most symbols are linked to Islam.

Religious leaders and people from immigrant families symbolize power, intelligence, respect, and holiness. There are three important religious brotherhoods and subsects whose leaders symbolize supernatural knowledge and insight: the Tijaniya, Qadriya, and Hamaliya. The founders of these brotherhoods are venerated. Ancestors are honored, and cemeteries are respected and feared. There are no national monuments, museums, secular national heroes, poets, or artists. Only the few people who are educated know what the national flag, national anthem, and national day symbolize. Some black intellectuals want the national day to be observed as a day of mourning for the martyrs of ethnic cleansing in 1990 and 1991.

HISTORY AND ETHNIC RELATIONS

Emergence of the Nation. Mauritania did not exist as an independent political unit before 1960. The country was created by colonial France in close alliance with the Arab-Berber theocracy in the Trarza region. The motives for creating the country was to build a bridge between French black West African colonies and Algeria and block the expansionist aspirations of proponents of a greater Morocco.

National Identity. Ethnic conflict has sharpened ethnic, tribal, and caste identities. Because the French conspired to keep political power exclusively in the hands of the Arab-Berber aristocracy, a sense of national identity has not developed.

Ethnic Relations. In the past, ethnic relations were characterized by conflicts, shifting alliances, and some cooperation. The more settled black Africans dominated in the south, whereas the nomadic Arab-Berbers controlled the desert north. The different communities were able to function without contact with each other. Gradually, drought and the ensuing environmental degradation pushed the nomads toward the south, and conflicts over decreasing resources arose. With the creation of the state, competition over political power and access to public funds, jobs, and privileges aggravated this situation. In 1989, when ethnic conflict reached a violent level, West African and black citizens became the target of government pogroms. Mauritania then was drawn into the ethnic conflict between the government in Mali and the Maur and Tuareg tribes. Thus, while Mauritania was deporting its black citizens to Mali and Senegal, it was welcoming Maur and Tuareg refugees from Mali. The main political groups and parties are divided along cultural and ethnic lines. The Arab population is sponsored by Iraq, Libya, and Saudi Arabia, and FLAM, the black political party, is based in Senegal.

URBANISM, ARCHITECTURE, AND THE USE OF SPACE

Without coherent national planning policies, construction in modern towns and cities is anarchic. Thus, architecture in Nouakchott is a mixture of traditional French concrete building with Spanish and Asian influences. Because of the fragile and sandy terrain, buildings are low.

As a result of drought and the attraction of urban centers, most residents have become totally or party urbanized. Colonization, rapid urbanization, modern education, technology, and mass communication have led to the emergence of two cultures. The modern elite live in Western-style houses, which have replaced thatched-roof houses and tents. Houses are used to shelter extended families and guests. Even in modern houses, there is little furniture and few wall decorations. Many houses have colorful traditional pillows and mats, teapots, trays, and carpets. Mattresses are placed along the walls with traditional pillows. Houses are crowded because of strong family bonds. An urban house normally is open to relatives and friends.

Apart from mosques, government buildings follow Western styles. Some Arab-Berbers put up tents in the courtyards of their villas. Normally, there are no plants inside the house.

FOOD AND ECONOMY

Food in Daily Life. Food has important social and psychological functions. People eat together in groups from a large bowl or calabash, using the right hand. People eat first and then drink cold water or sour milk mixed with cold water, juice from the hibiscus flower, or baobab juice. After lunch and dinner, it is customary to drink small glasses of green tea with sugar and mint. The tea is served by younger persons, women, and slaves.

The diet consists mostly of meat, millet, rice, fish, and sweet potatoes and potatoes. The main

A group of women painting a hut. Mauritanian houses have few wall decorations and sparse furniture.

meal is lunch among black Africans, whereas Arab-Berbers have the main meal in the evening. Breakfast consists of milk and cereal with French bread and butter. People use a lot of oil in cooking and sugar in drinks. Eating almost always takes place at home. It is not acceptable to eat with or in the presence of one's in-laws, and eating with the left hand is forbidden.

Food Customs at Ceremonial Occasions. People are expected to slaughter an animal according to the number of wives and the wealth of the husband. At the end of Ramadan and at the sacrificial feast that ends the annual pilgrimage to Mecca, a married man is expected to offer a lamb. The meat must be eaten up within three days or it is thrown away. It is customary to offer an animal in connection with name-giving, initiation, marriage, and funeral ceremonies and when people return from Mecca or other important places. Only circumcised adult men are allowed to slaughter animals.

Basic Economy. While the public and private sectors depend on foreign sources such as development aid and the exportation of iron ore and fish, the vast majority of citizens engage in traditional subsistence agriculture. The informal economic sector is increasing in importance. People do not expect much from the government and rarely pay taxes. Mauritania is one of the largest recipients of foreign aid in the world and is deeply in debt. Despite abundant livestock, one of the world's richest fishing zones, and a huge agriculture potential, the country is not self-sufficient in food and other basic necessities.

Land Tenure and Property. Traditionally, individuals could not own land, which was owned collectively by the community. The head of the clan or community was responsible for the allocation and leasing of communal land. In a society organized according to hierarchical caste, land was controlled by the aristocracy, and the lower classes rented, borrowed, or worked the land according to a sharecropping system. A land ordinance of 1983 stipulated that land belongs to the state and abolished traditional ownership. Black citizens were quick to label the ordinance racist.

Commercial Activities. Animals, meat, and hides are exported to neighboring countries, and iron ore, copper, gypsum, and fish are sent to the European Union nations and Japan. White residents dominate retail trade with the West, and black Africans trade with Central Africa.

Major Industries. Mauritania is one of the least industrialized countries in the world. The few industries involve the production and partial processing of iron ore. There is a fish processing plant and an oil refinery in Nouadhibou and a sugar refinery in Nouakchott as well as a meat processing factory in Kaedi. Traditional crafts are produced in Nouakchott. There is a textile factory in Rosso.

Trade. Iron ore, copper, and fish are sent to the European Union and Japan, and animals are sold to Senegal. Imports consist of food, machinery, and weapons. There is much informal trade with neighboring African countries. Gum arabic and salt also are sold abroad.

Division of Labor. Most people work as farmers, cattle herders, and traders. Regulations regarding child labor are not enforced, and most school-age children work.

SOCIAL STRATIFICATION

Classes and Castes. Society is organized along strict ethnic lines, with a rigid system of castes; every caste has its own internal hierarchy. In both ethnic groups, the division of labor is clear. At the top are the religious and warrior caste, followed by the skilled caste, which consists of smiths, carpenters, weavers, fisherfolk, and leather workers. Historians or court bards, musicians, and court advisers form a lower caste, followed by the theoretically freed slaves and current slaves at the bottom of the social order.

Symbols of Social Stratification. Dress style, comportment, and speech are dictated by the climate and ethnic heritage. Putting on one's best clothing is important in black African communities to express one's social status. Women decorate themselves with gold, silver, and amber to display their wealth and change clothes several times during a party. People in the higher castes to tend to be quiet and generous toward those below them, whereas the lower castes tend to be talkative, outgoing, and "greedy," with less concern about shame. Generally people are kind and hospitable to foreigners.

POLITICAL LIFE

Government. Mauritania is an Islamic republic with a highly centralized government in which power is vested in the executive president as head of state, aided by a prime minister who acts as the head of government and a council of ministers. Since 1992, direct presidential elections have been scheduled every six years. Universal suffrage occurs at age eighteen years. The legal system is derived from Islamic sharia law and modern Western law. The legislative branch includes a bicameral legislature consisting of the fifty-six-seat Senate elected by municipal mayors for six-year terms and a seventy-nine-seat National Assembly elected by popular vote for five-year terms. The judicial branch has lower courts, appeals courts, and a supreme court. Administratively, the country is divided into twelve regions.

A multiparty system functioned from independence until 1965, followed by a one-party civilian regime that was overthrown by the army in 1978. Between 1978 and 1991, the country was ruled by decree, with no citizen participation. With the end of the Cold War and after Mauritania's alliance with Iraq in the Gulf War, the government was forced to transform the military committee into a political party.

There are twenty-two political parties, including the Democratic and Social Republican Party (PRDS), the Union of Democratic Forces–New Era (UFD/EN), and Action for Change (AC). The PRDS is a continuation of the military committee. Parties are tribal and personal rather than ideological. Action for Change is closely linked with the antislavery movement El Hor. Forces de Liberation Africain des Mauritania (FLAM) is illegal and operates from exile in Senegal. Founded in 1983, FLAM works for ethnic equality, social justice, democracy, and development. It has called for federalism and regional autonomy.

Leadership and Political Officials. Ethnicity and caste membership have caused political positions to be monopolized by religious warrior upper-caste clans and families. Gender, age, wealth, and region also are important factors in attaining and maintaining power. No ruling party has ever lost power to the opposition. Individuals are expected to vote for leaders from their ethnic group, clan, family, and region. Ideology and political programs have minimal relevance and people who cross ethnic and tribal lines are considered traitors. People are afraid of government representatives, especially those in uniform.

Social Problems and Control. Apart from Arab-Berber slave raids, Mauritania was relatively free of crime. With the creation of a neocolonial state, formal mechanisms for dealing with crime have been based on the violent colonial system. Crime management is now provided by repressive police forces in the cities and towns and a gendarmerie in the countryside and a national guard in remote areas. People fear men in uniform, who harass, rape, confiscate cattle, and terrorize the population. Informal social control mechanisms are effective because of strong family and kinship ties and the collective shame associated with committing a crime; people tend to punish criminals on the spot. In the past, the most common crimes were kidnapping children from the south for slavery in the north, stealing cattle, and illegal grazing. Today the most common crimes are official corruption, stealing, political murder, and rape.

Military Activity. The military has become a prestigious institution. The army is huge relative to the population and the nation's poverty. The armed forces number 18,500 men divided into an infantry, a navy, an air force, paramilitary forces, border guards, and auxiliary troops of the Interior Ministry. At independence, the army had fewer than one hundred black officers who had served in the colonial army. Arab-Berbers were exempted from military service by the French, who considered them superior to black Africans. After the Saharan war the army mushroomed in size, staffed mainly by black Africans and Harantin abandoned by their white masters, but most of the commanders were white. After the 1978 coup, ethnic and tribal competition plagued the armed forces. A campaign of ethnic purging of black armed personnel, whom the regime accused of belonging to FLAM and plotting a coup began in 1986. The government then passed a blanket amnesty for the armed forces for any crimes committed in the period 1989–1993. As a result, the national army has become an ethnic army of racist repression.

SOCIAL WELFARE AND CHANGE PROGRAMS

Social welfare is provided for within the family and kinship system. Government-supported welfare is nearly nonexistent because of a lack of funds, nepotism, and corruption.

NONGOVERNMENTAL ORGANIZATIONS AND OTHER ASSOCIATIONS

A few nongovernment organizations (NGOs) work on human rights issues. One of the most important is the Association Mauritanienne des Droits de l'Homme (AMDH), which was created in 1991 after a government massacre of more than five hundred black army officers and civilians in custody. Comité de Solidarité avec les Victimes de la Répression en Mauritanie (Solidarity Committee of with Victims of Repression in Mauritania, or CSVRM) was created by the widows, mothers, and sisters of victims of racist extrajudicial killings in 1990 and 1991.

SOS-Esclaves (SOS Slaves) was founded in 1992 by a former slave. SOS fights for the emancipation of the nearly one million former and current slaves of the ruling white Maurs. Ligue Mauritanienne des Droits de l'Homme (Mauritanian Human Rights League, or LMDH) was created when political parties and NGOs were not allowed in the country after the campaign of terror against black intellectuals in 1986. It is considered a front for the government.

GENDER ROLES AND STATUSES

Division of Labor by Gender. Culturally, women's importance is recognized, but men dominate in the economic, political, social, and religious spheres. In the south, men provide for the family and women process and cook food and take care of children. In the Arab-Berber north, women are not

People outside a cinema, Aioun el Atrouss. Open air theater performances are also attended by many people.

supposed to perform physical work, which is seen as degrading. Work there is the domain of slave women.

The Relative Status of Women and Men. Although people honor and obey their mothers, women suffer on the account of their gender. In Islamic-run courts two women count as one witness, polygamy is widespread in the black communities, and female circumcision is practiced by all the ethnic groups except the Wolof. Women inherit half the share that their brothers receive. Children take the father's clan name. When women marry, they tend to join the husband's household. Many marriages are forced or arranged. During racial pogroms, women are targets for rape and terror. There is more illiteracy and unemployment among women than men. Female slaves are sexually exploited. Forced feeding to fatten young girls for marriage is common among the Maurs and Haratin.

MARRIAGE, FAMILY, AND KINSHIP

Marriage. Marriages usually are arranged, especially the first marriage. Illiterate rural individuals have less choice than do people with a modern education. People tend to marry for the sake of their parents and community and usually marry within their community and clan. There is a lot of marriage between cousins, but it is not permissible to marry someone with whom a person has shared breast milk. When it is discovered that a husband and wife shared milk earlier in life, they are obliged to divorce even if they have children. Muslim women are not allowed to marry non-Muslim men, but Muslim men can marry Christian or Jewish women. Polygyny is allowed, but polyandry is forbidden. According to the prevailing value system, all adults must marry and have many children but it is not unusual to find unmarried women, particularly among the white Maurs.

Economic aspects of marriage are very important. Men are responsible for the economic sustenance of their wives and for brideprice, along with lavish gifts to the parents, relatives, friends, and associates of their wives. Divorce is not common, especially in the black communities. Couples are allowed to divorce twice, and the third divorce is final. If divorce is the fault of the man, the wife keeps the brideprice. According to tradition, children follow the father, but small ones remain with the mother and the husband is obliged to support her and the children until they grow up.

Domestic Unit. The basic household unit consists of a husband and his wife or wives plus their children and the family of the husband, but household units in urban centers are getting more compact. The man has authority in the household because the couple lives with his kin and he is normally older and richer than the wife. Even though the household is an extended family, tasks are sharply divided according to gender and age.

Inheritance. Inheritance is based on Islamic law and local "economic calculation." When male and female relatives are equally close to the deceased, the male relatives gets a double portion. Because the woman joins her husband's family, she often is pressured to renounce her inheritance, especially if it consists of land. All kinds of property including slaves are inheritable by relatives. Sometimes a man inherits the wife or wives of his brother because the family wants to keep the children and property within the household.

Kin Groups. In this extremely traditional society, belonging to a group is very important, and the larger the group, the better. People use clan names rather than family names. When the climate and economic conditions allow it, larger kin groups form a village or neighborhood. Clan members interact by sharing land and engaging in interclan marriage. The male leader, normally the oldest and "most competent" man, manages communal property and affairs.

SOCIALIZATION

Infant Care. Child care is provided by the older members of an extended family and the first born child is looked after by the grandmother and aunts. Women, including older sisters and cousins, take care of children, and men come into the picture as a child grows up. Infants are not separated from adults and are nearly always carried.

Child Rearing and Education. Education is based on a combination of three overlapping philosophies: indigenous, Islamic, and Western. In the first system, the objective is to prepare the young to be useful members of the local community. Education is thus inward-oriented and functional and is provided by parents, elder siblings, peers, and specialized traditional teachers. The key values are belief in God, honor, respect, and service to the community, generosity, hospitality, endurance, and patience, Islamic teaching prepares Muslims to serve Allah and the community of believers by learning the Koran and practicing the five pillars of Islam. The most important qualities in a "good" child are respect and service to the parents and the community,

truthfulness, learning, prayer, and politeness. Parents believe that children are what they inherit and learn from their parents. If the mother is of good character, her children will be good.

Higher Education. Before independence, there were few schools and illiteracy was close to 100 percent. Sons of the black aristocracy were sent to a special school established by the French in Senegal. After power was transferred to the Arab-Berbers, the new rulers built schools in their areas and neglected the south.

ETIQUETTE

The upper castes give, and the lower castes serve and obey. Maur women do not shake hands with foreign men, and people do not eat in front of their in-laws or address older persons by name. People stare at passing strangers and greet each other with a handshake and ask about a person's health and wealth. People stand very close to each other.

RELIGION

Religious Beliefs. Mauritania is 100 percent Muslim. The people are Sunni Muslims who belong to the Khadria and Thiyania brotherhoods. Religion is a mixture of Islam and local African beliefs. People believe in supernatural spirits, feeling that everything and being has life and presents potential danger. Taboos are observed, and charms and amulets are used for protection.

Religious Practitioners. Each brotherhood has a founder who acts as a spiritual medium and is venerated and considered to have healing powers. People can receive a blessing through spiritual contact with these spiritual leaders. The founders' power increases with their age. Traditional spiritual medicine men and women have an authority based on the local experience and value system.

Rituals and Holy Places. Rituals often are linked to Islamic prayers. Tombs and graveyards are seen as holy places. People avoid going to those places during certain times of the day and avoid cutting wood near a graveyard. Certain forests and trees are considered holy, and people use them for healing. Daily religious ceremonies take place in a mosque or in open fields. For more important weekly ceremonies, prayers take place in open fields or in the larger mosques in urban centers.

Death and the Afterlife. People believe that after death they will be judged and go to hell or to para-

Women making pasta at a women's cooperative in Walata. Most Mauritanians work as farmers, cattle herders, or traders.

dise. Old people are buried directly in the ground without coffins. Only those who die from a contagious disease are cremated. Among the nomadic Arab-Berbers, only the graves of holy people are marked. After a burial, Berbers leave the area for fear of bad spirits. Black people have fixed graves and venerate the burying places of their ancestors. Funerals often are occasions for celebrations and family reunions. Because of the climate, the deceased are buried almost immediately. Bodies are washed seven times and then wrapped in white cloth and carried to the graveyard. The deceased is placed in a grave facing Mecca. Only men attend funerals. After the burial, the guests do not turn back toward the graveyard. Normally, the personal belongings of the deceased are given to the poor.

MEDICINE AND HEALTH CARE

People believe that disease is caused by destiny, bad magic, or breaking taboos and seek help from traditional and Islamic healers who combine modern medicine with traditional methods. Very few people have access to medical care, which is concentrated in the urban centers. The rudimentary public health care has crumbled, and the rich have set up private health units and pharmacies.

There are many tropical diseases, but there is a low incidence of psychological disorders, and AIDS is almost nonexistent. Life expectancy is low, and infant mortality is high, partly because of a lack of clean water.

Modern doctors are treated as important personalities, especially if they are white. Traditional practitioners are respected and feared. Traditional medicine men and women use herbs and touching as well as healing words.

SECULAR CELEBRATIONS

There are very few secular celebrations with the exception of the national day on 28 November and Constitution Day on 12 July. Some of the Westernized elites celebrate Christmas and the New Year. Farmers celebrate the harvest and marry at that time. Herders' dispersed families gather and celebrate the rainy season with sumptuous meals. The returns of family members from abroad is celebrated.

THE ARTS AND HUMANITIES

Support for the Arts. There is little appreciation of and support for artists. The little support that is given is ethnically biased and oriented toward entertainment. The arts are functional and cannot be distinguished from crafts.

Literature. The oral tradition includes epics, story-telling, riddles, puzzles, and Islamic poetry and prose.

Graphic Arts. Wall drawings, paintings, some sculpture, textiles, and pottery are produced. Artists are thought to have a secret knowledge that they hand down from generation to generation.

Performance Arts. People attend popular and democratic performances held in the open air.

THE STATE OF THE PHYSICAL AND SOCIAL SCIENCES

The state of the physical and social science is deplorable because of the lack of interest among the authorities. A university established in 1981 teaches law, literature, and economics. There are fewer than three thousand students, and the university lacks qualified teachers and researchers, books, facilities, and buildings.

BIBLIOGRAPHY

Ba, Oumar. *Le Fouto Toro au Carrefour des Cultures*, 1976.

Baduel, Pierre Robert. *Mauritanie entre Arabité et Africanité*, 1989.

Boye, Alassane Harouna. *J'Etai a Oualata*, 1999.

Centre d'Etudes d'Afrique Noire. *Introduction a la Mauritanie*, 1979.

Cotton, Samuel. *Silent Terror, A Journey to Modern Day African Slavery*, 1998.

Daure-Setfaty, Christine. *La Mauritanie*, 1993.

FLAM. *Radioscopie d'un Apartheid Méconnu*, 1990

Garba, Diallo. *Maritania: The Other Apartheid*, 1993.

———. *Mauritania: Neither Arab nor African*, 2000.

Human Rights Watch/Africa. *Mauritania's Campaign of Terror: Repression of Black Africans*, 1994.

Leservoisier Olivier. *La Gestion Fonciere en Mauritanie: Terres et Pouvoir dans le Region du Gorgol*, 1995.

Marchesin, Philippe. *Tribus, Ethnies et Pouvoir en Mauritanie*, 1992

Okwudiba, Nnoli, ed. *Ethnic Conflicts in Africa*, 1998.

Oumar, Moussa Ba. *Noirs et Beydanes Mauritaniens, l'Ecole, Creuset de la nation?* 1993.

Pazzanita, Anthony G. *Historical Dictionary of Mauritania*, 2nd ed., 1996.

Robinson, David. "France as Muslim Power." In *Africa Today* 46 (3/5), 1999.

—GARBA DIALLO

MAURITIUS

CULTURE NAME

Mauritian

ORIENTATION

Identification. The island of Mauritius was apparently uninhabited until 1638. It was then that the Dutch, under the Dutch East India Company, made their first attempt to colonize the land, named after the prince of Denmark, Maurice of Nassau. The people of Mauritius are descendants of European (mostly French) settlers, the Franco-Mauritians; African slaves and creoles, the Afro-Mauritians; Chinese traders, the Sino-Maurtians; and Indian laborers, the Indo-Mauritians. Such cultural diversity and geographic isolation have led to a nationalized sense of pride. There is unity in being a Mauritian despite not having a shared language and customs. For this reason Mauritius is often considered a global example of successful cultural integration.

Location and Geography. A total of 790 square miles (2,046 square kilometers) of land cover Mauritius. These include the island of Mauritius, with 720 square miles (1,865 square kilometers); the island of Rodrigues, about 350 miles (563 kilometers) east of Mauritius; the small Agalega Islands, 580 miles (933 kilometers) north; and the Cargados Carajos Shoals, 250 miles (402 kilometers) north.

The island of Mauritius, where the overwhelming majority of the people live, lies 500 miles (805 kilometers) east of Madagascar and 2,500 miles (4,023 kilometers) southwest of India. Mauritius was formed by volcanic activity that left a plateau in the middle of the island rising 2,200 feet (671 meters) above sea level. This plateau slopes downward to the north until it reaches the sea. In the south and west the plateau drops sharply to the coast. The driest part of the island in is the southwest, which receives about 35 inches (89 centimeters) per year. The center can receive up to 200

inches (508 centimeters) a year. The capital is Port Louis, on the northwestern roast of the island of Mauritius.

Demography. The current population is approximately 1.1 million. The majority live in the capital and largest city, Port Louis. The population density is one of the highest in the world. Immigration came in successive and dramatic waves. This is demonstrated through the official census, first published in 1846. In that year the total population was 158,462. The white and colored population was 102,217, and the Indian population was 56,245. In 1861 the total population reached 310,050. The white and colored population increased to 115,864. The Indian population more than tripled, to 192,634, to become the majority, and the Chinese population first registered at 1,552. In 1921 the white and colored population decreased to 104,216, the Indian population increased to 335,327, and the Chinese increased to 6,745, in a total population of 376,485. The next census was in 1952, which showed the total population at 501,415. Whites and coloreds were 148,238; Indians once again increased, to 335,327; and the Chinese moved to 17,850. In 1962 the census combined the whites and coloreds to become the "general population" and separated the Indians into Hindus and Muslims. In 1983 the census stopped ethnic comparisons altogether in favor of religious groupings. This was part of a government-based objective to de-emphasize ethnic differences. Results from the 1990 census are as follows: 535,028 Hindus, 172,047 Muslims, and 343,395 Christians, with 6,190 listed as Other.

Linguistic Affiliation. There is no official language in Mauritius. Government and administrative work is written in English. The press uses French, which is understood by more of the population than English. The majority of people understand a Creole language. There is no agreed-upon written form of this language, however, so it appears unlikely that this would be adapted as a na-

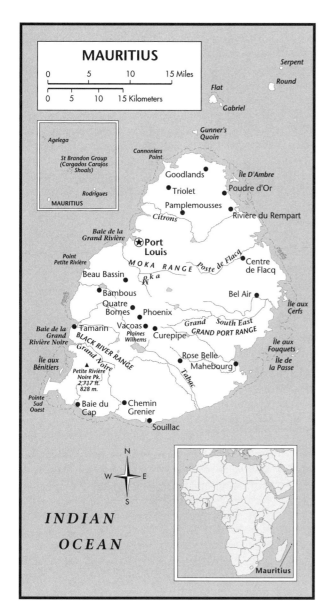

Mauritius

the settlements led to their total abandonment in about 1710.

Five years later, Dusfrene d'Arsel claimed the island for France. The French already had nearby Réunion Island, and with these geographic holds the Mascarene Islands became an important base for attacks on British possessions in wartime. Under French rule Mauritius developed colonial plantation patterns.

The British attacked and captured the strategic islands in 1810. Réunion was given back to the French four years later because of the lack of good harbors. The Mauritius culture saw little change with the English takeover. The Cape of Good Hope was a more prized British possession, and subsequently little capital and effort was put into the Mauritian economy.

In 1825 the preferential West Indian sugar tariff was repealed, and the island transformed itself into a sugar-based economy.

Slavery was abolished in 1835. This led to large-scale demographic changes. The majority of the total population were plantation slaves. With the release of obligatory duty, upwards of half the slaves fled the plantations to live in shantytowns or unoccupied land. To make up for the loss in the workforce, plantation owners imported laborers from India. From 1835 to 1845 the Indian population went from nonexistent to a third of the total population.

Emergence of the Nation. Mauritius started self-government in the 1950s, which led to full independence from Great Britain on 12 March 1968. Sir Seewoosagur Ramgoolam was the leader of this movement and afterward became the first prime minister. He served in that post from 1968 to 1982.

National Identity. The national identity of being a Mauritian is forged early in school and continues in the workplace. The mix of cultures forms the identity of the island. With no defining national cultural traits, the question arises whether Mauritius has a unique culture, or whether one is developing.

Ethnic Relations. The 1980s led to an economic boom for the island. This was fueled mostly by the industrialization of the export business. This led to more interracial mingling as the workplace brought previously separated ethnic factions together. This is mirrored in the school system.

The main ethnic groups have been emphasizing their ethnic roots and have helped to set up the Ministry for Culture and Arts to promote cultural

tional language despite its widespread use. At the school level the official policy is to promote ancestral languages. Thus the true state of languages seems to be genuinely a hybrid affair, and the government finds this the least intrusive of all possible measures.

HISTORY AND ETHNIC RELATIONS

Arab and Swahili sailors knew of Mauritius before the 1500s. Portuguese explorers visited in the early sixteenth century. In 1638 the Dutch made attempts to colonize and inhabit the island. They brought small numbers of African slaves and introduced sugarcane to the island. Trouble maintaining

activities and a better understanding of the different cultures in Mauritius. Cultural centers accomplish this task at the local level. These tend to reinforce cultural identity and strengthen the independent ethnic groups. Many of these centers obtain outside help from the parent cultures.

URBANISM, ARCHITECTURE, AND THE USE OF SPACE

With one of the highest population densities in the world, Mauritius places a high premium on housing. Hindus and Muslims tend to invest their life savings in real estate. Many creoles rent in urban areas. Their unique architecture is known for sharp roofs, long balconies, and canopies. Many of the traditional creole houses have been replaced in places by newer materials and designs. The government, in recognition of the heritage of the older houses, has campaigned to save their designs.

FOOD AND ECONOMY

Food in Daily Life. The foods in Mauritius are as varied as the cultures. Chinese mostly own the restaurants in the cities, and they combine different ethnic foods on the same menu. Street food also is quite common for snacks and includes samosas, roti, curried rolls, soups, and noodles.

At home, rice is the most common staple. This is usually combined with fish, fowl, or red meat and copious spices to form a type of stew. Local vegetables are eaten readily and include chokos, red pumpkins, squash, and greens.

Basic Economy. The Mauritian economy is centered in agriculture and manufacturing. Commerce and services jobs also are evident. The currency is the Mauritian rupee.

Land Tenure and Property. The original Franco-Mauritian families that were given land rights in French colonial times still own more then 50 percent of the sugar fields. Large numbers of Indian planters own the remaining fields. The Chinese own a heavy concentration of commercial property. The creoles have never had any extensive land holdings. The government instituted a sugar tax to deal with the vast inequalities of the sugar industry. In the 1990s the tax was revoked after constant pressure from the sugar estates. However, a program whereby workers could buy shares in the sugar industry was begun.

Tamil celebrations. Religious freedom is constitutionally guaranteed in Mauritius.

Major Industries. Sugar has been the historical base of industry. Until 1979, 90 percent of the national economy was based on it. While not as powerful as they once were, the refined-sugar and molasses industries still hold much importance. Textiles and clothing manufacturing also have become important industries, along with chemicals, metals, and machinery. As with many island nations, tourism is an important source of revenue.

Trade. Because of the relatively small size of the island and scarcity of natural resources, Mauritius must import huge amounts of goods from countries such as France, South Africa, and India. Major imports included textiles, petroleum, machinery, metals, and food.

Major exports include industrial products and sugar. Agricultural products also exported are tea, peanuts, tobacco, potatoes, tomatoes, and bananas. Exports tend to be centered on the United Kingdom, France, and the United States. In 1997 the net export value was $1.616 billion (U.S.) and net imports $2.264 billion (U.S.), for a trade deficient of $648 million (U.S.).

Division of Labor. Traditionally, urban industrialization used mostly the creole women as the workforce. Rural industrialization has brought more of the Indian population, who live in higher numbers in the countryside, into the factories. The boom in industry has opened skilled-labor positions to all ethnicities in Mauritius, leading to very low unemployment rates.

SOCIAL STRATIFICATION

Classes and Castes. The Franco-Mauritians have had land and ownership privileges that the other ethnic groups have not, and they form a small, privileged high class. The Indians and Chinese form subgroups in relation to language, religious branches, and regional origins. Hindi is considered more prestigious among the Indian population, but northern Indian dialects are more commonly used in the countryside. The creoles have had the poorest economic conditions of any group.

POLITICAL LIFE

Government. The British Westminster model of government is the basis for Mauritius. Until 1992 the queen of England was the head of state and queen of Mauritius in a constitutional monarchy, with Mauritius as a commonwealth. In 1992 Mauritius became a republic. The presidency of the republic is a ceremonial office only; the president is appointed by the prime minister and the National Assembly, whose members are chosen via general elections. The prime minister is the leader of the majority in the National Assembly.

In the National Assembly, eight seats in addition to the sixty-two elected seats are awarded to candidates defeated in the general election: four to those candidates who fared the best in relation to the other defeated candidates, and four on a party and community basis. There has been discontent with this system, and a major reworking of the electoral process has been widely discussed.

Leadership and Political Officials. All of Mauritius's prime ministers have been Hindu. The first, Sir Seewoosagur Ramgoolam, led the independence movement in Mauritius.

Social Problems and Control. In February 2000 several days of rioting occurred in Port Louis. A popular creole singer, Kaya, died while in police custody. The creole community suspected the police of misconduct leading to his death and retaliated by protests that spiraled into rioting and violence. Four deaths and fifty million dollars of damage resulted. It was the worst social unrest in Mauritius's history.

Military Activity. The military has an annual budget of $11 million and thirteen hundred active personal. Most of these are trained for internal disputes. Combined with the coast guard they have five hundred boats and aircraft available worth an estimated $87 million.

NONGOVERNMENTAL ORGANIZATIONS AND OTHER ASSOCIATIONS

The first study of nongovernmental organizations (NGO) in Mauritius focused on twenty-six groups as follows: eight, social; five, labor; five, business; four, religious; three, cultural; and one, environmental. Most of these groups have an influential impact on governmental policies.

GENDER ROLES AND STATUSES

Division of Labor by Gender. The economic success of industry has led to low unemployment rates. This has changed the workplace and home life as women joined the workforce. This industrialization also led to women being promoted faster. According to the Minister of Women, Family Welfare, and Child Development, a quarter of all managers are now women.

Women are the traditional homekeepers of the society. Between 1985 and 1991 the numbers of women working outside the home increased from 22 percent to 41 percent. With that trend continuing, hired housekeeping and child care have become relatively new and important industries.

The Relative Status of Women and Men. Historically, women have had subordinate roles in Maurition society. However, the Constitution specifically prohibits discrimination based on sex, and women now have access to education, employment, and governmental services.

In March 1998 the Domestic Violence Act was passed. This gave greater protection and legal authority to combat domestic abuse. In that same year it also became a crime to abandon one's family or pregnant spouse for more than two months, not to pay food support, or to engage in sexual harassment.

Women are underrepresented in the government. The National Assembly has seventy seats, of which women hold five.

The urban view over Port Louis. Mauritius has one of the highest population densities in the world.

MARRIAGE, FAMILY, AND KINSHIP

Marriage. Most marriages in Mauritius occur within the same ethnic group; only about 8 percent of marriages are interethnic. Those couples who do intermarry usually take on a single ethnic identity for their children. Those children in turn usually associate with that ethnic group and marry within it.

Ethnic identification is considered to be more important than class and is the single most examined factor in selecting a mate; group and parental influences also are factors. Marriage outside ethnic lines risks the family's disapproval and sometimes can lead to punishment. This carries additional weight in Mauritius, where families typically live with each other because of high land costs.

SOCIALIZATION

Child Rearing and Education. Education is free from the primary to the tertiary level and is mandatory until age twelve. The government considers education one of its greatest concerns and has an "education for all" policy to ensure fair education to the different socioeconomic groups. Some schools in low-rent areas have large drop out rates, which particularly affects the Creole community.

The greatest amount of interethnic mingling occurs in the schools, and this has the promise of leading to the formation of a national identity.

Higher Education. The University of Mauritius was established in 1971. The original focus was oriented toward agriculture and manufacturing. Since 1989 the university has increased its majors to include the humanities.

ETIQUETTE

Most outsiders think of Mauritians as being aloof at first. Among themselves they are quite social and friendly, and this ultimately prevails with visitors and locals alike. Dress is culturally dependent but somewhat conservative. Lightweight and colored fabrics are usually worn. Attire among women can vary from one-piece bathing suits to complete covering, especially among Muslims. Toplessness and nudity are not condoned for either sex.

RELIGION

Religious Beliefs. Religious freedom is the major key to peace on Mauritius and is a constitutionally guaranteed right. Hindus make up 52 percent of the total population. Christians (28.3 percent), Mus-

Women stand in a narrow canal to wash and rinse clothes on the island of Mauritius. About 40 percent of Mauritian women work outside the home.

lims (16.6 percent), and others (3.1 percent) follow them.

MEDICINE AND HEALTH CARE

Public and private hospitals are on the island. The private hospitals are generally considered to be of better quality and are more expensive than the public hospitals. Both are adequate, if a little below Western standards.

Malaria is very rare and exists only in the rural areas. Hepatitis A is fairly common. The more severe hepatitis B and C are rare.

Men have an average life expectancy of sixty-six years; women, of seventy-five years.

SECULAR CELEBRATIONS

There are thirteen official state holidays. They are: New Year's Day (1 and 2 January); Chinese New Year (January/February); Thaipoosam Cavadee (January/February); Maha Shivaratree (February/March); Republic Day (12 March); Ougadi-Telegy New Year (March/April); Labor Day (1 May); Ind El Fitr (lunar); Ganesh Chaturthi (August/September); Diwali (October/November); All Saints (1 November) and Christmas (25 December).

THE ARTS AND HUMANITIES

Performance Arts. Popular music from the West and from India are widely listened to. The only original music and the national music is *Sega*, a tribal-based drumbeat based on African rhythms. It has a ritualistic dance that is often done in tandem. The women dance in sensual ways to lure partners, but they are not allowed to kiss or touch.

THE STATE OF THE PHYSICAL AND SOCIAL SCIENCES

The sciences have been neglected in Mauritius at different levels since its inception. The University of Mauritius is trying to focus more energy on research and science, and the government has obtained permission and funding for a new technological university.

BIBLIOGRAPHY

Alladin, Ibrahim. *Economic Miracle in the Indian Ocean: Can Mauritius Show the Way?*, 1993.

Allen, Richard. *Slaves, Freedman, and Indentured Laborers in Colonial Mauritius*, 1999.

Carroll, Barbara, and Terrance Carroll. "Accommodating Ethnic Diversity in a Modernizing Democratic State:

Theory and Practice in the Case of Mauritius." *Ethnic and Racial Studies* 23 (1): 120–142, 2000.

Nave, Ari. "Marriage and the Maintenance of Ethnic Groups Boundaries: The Case of Mauritius." *Ethnic and Racial Studies* 23 (2): 329–352, 2000.

Selvon, Sydney. *Historical Dictionary of Mauritius*, 1991.

U.S. Department of State, Bureau of Democracy, Human Rights, and Labor. *1999 Country Reports on Human Rights Practices: Mauritius*, 2000.

Young, Crawford, ed. *The Accommodation of Cultural Diversity*, 1999.

—David Matusky

MAYOTTE

CULTURE NAME
Mahore

ALTERNATIVE NAME
Wamaore (singular, *mmaore*)

ORIENTATION

Identification. The name "Mayotte" comes from the Swahili word for Mahore, *Maote*. The name "Mahore" appears in the French adjective *mahorais*. Mahore identity is based on Comorian, Malagasy, French, and Creole cultural traits. Comorian culture is prevalent on Mayotte, the fourth island in the archipelago, which also has cultural characteristics of its own.

Location and Geography. Mayotte, with an area of 144 square miles (374 square kilometers), is the easternmost island in the Comoros off the coast of southwestern Africa, and geologically the oldest. The coral barrier reef that surrounds it has created one of the largest lagoons in the world. Mayotte is made up of several small islands, including Petite Terre, where the airport is located, and Grande Terre, the main island.

Demography. The population grew from 45,000 in 1975 to 131,000 in 1997, with half the people being under age 20. The population of Mamoudzou is 32,000. In 1841, the island had three thousand inhabitants; twenty years later, there were twelve thousand. These people were mostly Mahorans, African slaves and bondsmen, Malagasy, and Comoreans from other islands in the archipelago. There were also a few dozen Creoles, some Indian merchants and European planters, and a few Arabs.

Linguistic Affiliation. Mahorans speak *Shimaore*, a form of Comorian that is similar to *Shindzuani*, which is spoken on the next island. More than a third of the population speaks *Shibushi* or Mahoran

Malagasy, which is similar to the *Sakalava* spoken on Madagascar. These two languages have influenced each other, principally through borrowings. French is the language of public services, education, and foreign exchange, but sixty percent of the population does not speak it. The majority of children attend a Koranic school to learn Koranic text.

Symbolism. The coat of arms that was adopted in 1982 shows a crescent moon representing Islam and two ylang-ylang flowers, the island's principal agricultural product, against a blue, white, and red background that represents the French flag; the border stands for the coral reef. Two seahorses recall the shape of the island, reposing on the motto *Ra hachiri* ("We are vigilant").

HISTORY AND ETHNIC RELATIONS

Emergence of the Nation. Inhabited in the eighth century and organized into chieftainships and then a sultanate that often was threatened by Nzwani, Mayotte became a French possession in 1841, after a period of Malagasy raids and the violent seizure of power by a succession of usurpers. At the outset a sugar colony and then the administrative center of the archipelago, Mayotte lost that distinction in 1958, when the capital was moved to Moroni (Ngazidja). When the Comoros gained independence in 1975, Mayotte chose to remain French to benefit from French development funds, which residents feared it would no longer receive.

National Identity. There is a common desire to remain French in order to preserve social equality and receive financial aid. However, Mahorans feel that they share in Comorean culture along with certain Malagasy traits and are united by their practice of Islam. This explains their reluctance to abandon their individual status under local (Islamic) law. Their French identity as an overseas collectivity is somewhat precarious: The status of the island

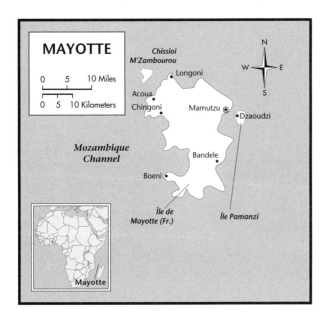

Mayotte

within the French republic is considered provisional and will be reviewed in 2010.

Ethnic Relations. Mahorans, who have family ties to the inhabitants of the other Comorian islands, especially Ndzuani and the northeastern part of Madagascar, are faced with immigration from the neighboring islands (officially 26,000 Comorians and 1,500 Malagasy), where the standard of living is lower. From Ngazidja, men come to marry Mahoran women to obtain French citizenship and gain the right to enter France. Poor farmers from Nzwani arrive clandestinely. Despite this migratory pressure, violent social reactions are rare.

People from France, called *wazungu* (singular, *mzungu*), make up 4 percent of the population. They work mainly in the municipal administration and are in a position of authority. A different lifestyle, a higher economic level, and a lack of understanding of the local languages reinforce their separation from Mahorans.

URBANISM, ARCHITECTURE, AND THE USE OF SPACE

The typical two-room house is built of cob (earth mixed with rice straw), coconut fronds, or raffia. A program of social housing put in place in 1975 encourages the construction of houses made of earthen bricks and cement painted in bright colors: Sixty-five percent of the population lives in houses made out of solid materials and 75 percent of houses have electricity. Televisions are more numerous than refrigerators. The dwellings of bachelors (*banga*), built and occupied by themselves, are decorated with painted murals done by adolescents.

The mosque and the royal tombs from the sixteenth century in Tsingoni, the capital of the sultanate, have been restored. Some sugar factory chimneys from the nineteenth century, a reminder of the colonial period, also have been preserved.

FOOD AND ECONOMY

Food in Daily Life. The food of the common people is similar throughout the Comorian Islands, with rice the staple of the daily diet, along with manioc and other root vegetables, plantains, fresh and dried fish, and milk from grated coconuts. Products imported from France and South Africa are more common in Mayotte, which has several supermarkets.

Food Customs at Ceremonial Occasions. Mayotte follows traditional Comorian practices. Rice, curdled milk, and meat are eaten at celebratory meals.

Basic Economy. The agricultural and food-producing sector has declined (falling from 50 percent to 12 percent of household activity), to the benefit of the cash sector (administration, building, and public works and business). The flow of public funds is the driving force in the economy.

Land Tenure and Property. Any nonregistered land is supposed to be in the public domain. This is the case with many personal and family fields that are held jointly. As in the Comoros, common knowledge or an Islamic property act often takes the place of modern property registration, which is subject to tax. The local administration is conducting a cadastral survey of the island.

Commercial Activities. Because of its remote location, tourism remains underdeveloped.

Major Industries. Agriculture, including livestock raising, and fishing are the major industries. Also important to the economy are industries involving the preparation of plants and spices for export.

Trade. Mayotte imports food and building materials, primarily from France. Exports items, especially to France, include ylang-ylang (perfume extract), coffee, cinnamon, copra, coconuts, and vanilla.

Division of Labor. The wazungu hold the majority of responsible positions in administration and teaching. Work on the land is in disfavor. Most

Mahorans wish for office jobs, and many young people who have finished school lack employment.

SOCIAL STRATIFICATION

Classes and Castes. The primary basis of social distinction is a person's level of education and wealth. The French make up the leisure class, along with local elected officials (among them a number of Creoles descended from planters), merchants, and salaried workers. The older families in villages enjoy the respect of their fellow citizens, as do religious officials (imams and heads of brotherhoods). Indian merchants have a network of relations that are based as much on family ties as on business.

Symbols of Social Stratification. Mahorans dress in both the European style and the Comorian fashion, combining in different ways the business suit, the muslim robe *(kandzu)*, and the embroidered cap *(kofia)*. A veil for the head is part of a well-dressed woman's attire, worn with a dress or the local wrapped garment. Young people follow styles from abroad. Speaking French has contradictory connotations, depending on the context: It is a sign of education in administrative circles but is offensive at the village level, where "acting like a *mzungu*" is considered a sign of a bad attitude.

A woodland ylang-ylang perfume distillery. Ylang-ylang is the island's principal agricultural export.

POLITICAL LIFE

Government. Mayotte, as a territorial collectivity of France, has an administrative organization based on the French *département* with a legislative unicameral General Council, consisting of nineteen seats. Its members are elected by popular vote to serve three-year terms. Mayotte elects one member to the French Senate. The executive power is vested in the prefect, who represents the French government.

Leadership and Political Officials. The Mahoran People's Party, the historical defender of the nationals link to France, is opposed by political groups organized by a younger generation of leaders. The proposal to integrate Mahore with France dominates the political agenda. The village population remains far removed from the political strategies of the local elite.

Social Problems and Control. The police and the French gendarmerie help the European judges who dispense justice in the penal system and constitute the court of appeals for the tribunals of Islamic judges *(cadis)*. Offenses qualified as "outrages and rebellions" are on the rise, as are motor vehicle theft, clandestine employment, and sexual assaults. The authority of the Islamic judges is exercised in civil matters ranging from personal interpretations of local law to the transmission of wealth and property.

The services provided by the state have to a large extent replaced the social control that used to be exercised at the village level. The individualization of social relationships and the pressure to consume are indicative of the transformation of moral values. Strain on the fabric of the family, has made social regulation difficult.

Military Activity. France garrisons a regiment of the Foreign Legion in Mayotte, as well as a naval detachment. Local volunteers may obtain professional training through a program known as *le Service Militaire Adapté*.

SOCIAL WELFARE AND CHANGE PROGRAMS

In recent years, development initiatives have affected health, education, roads, communication, and the construction of new infrastructure. There has been an increase in the number of *wazungu* officials.

NONGOVERNMENTAL ORGANIZATIONS AND OTHER ASSOCIATIONS

Sports, music, and dance are the most common activities sponsored by associations. Local television broadcasts their special events, such as the *deba* or the *wadaha*. The deba is a Muslim prayer that is sung and danced with the head and hands by veiled young girls covered in gold and flowers. The wadaha, the dance of the pestles, is an exercise in manual dexterity and seduction, conducted to a vigorous musical rhythm.

GENDER ROLES AND STATUSES

Division of Labor by Gender. There has been a lot of incorrect commentary about matriarchy in Mayotte because of the activity of women in the inner circle of the Mahoran People's Party, which politicians have exploited to the greatest extent possible. As in Comoros, important and normative public roles are held by men. Women are active groups within the family and in social networks.

The Relative Status of Women and Men. The combination of matrilocal residence and polygamy has produced the same effects that it has in the Comoros. Women have a degree of material and psychological security but suffer complete instability in conjugal relationships. With age, women acquire a position of authority within the family that is comparable to that of men.

MARRIAGE, FAMILY, AND KINSHIP

Marriage. The Great Wedding ceremony *arusi* is a festival. Shorter than they are in Ngazidja, these events reveal the degree to which Mahorans want to preserve their ancient social values and affirm their social position in a way that is specific to the local culture. These ceremonies also provide an opportunity for entertainment (music and dance), as well as social interaction. Separation and remarriage are common.

Domestic Unit. As in the other Comoros, a house is given to a woman by her family at the time of her first marriage. Maternal parents have a strong presence in the domestic unit.

Inheritance. Inheritance is not as exclusively matrilineal as it is in Ngazidja. Family land is handed down to the children either as a whole or after division, and a field is set aside for girls who need one. Houses and jewels are handed down to girls.

Kin Groups. Filiation is bilateral, but as in the Comoros, because the family lives in the mother's house, there is a strong maternal bond. Mahorans pride themselves on having a far-reaching parental affiliation, which remarriages encourage, and maintain those bonds by visiting relatives in other villages.

SOCIALIZATION

Infant Care. Family care habits are the same as in Comoros, where children are cherished, but in Mayotte, health services for mothers and children are of much higher quality and are more accessible.

Child Rearing and Education. Western education encourages individualism, while Comorian education favors obedience and conformity to the group. Children thus are torn between two languages and two cultural systems. Despite spectacular progress in school and preschool facilities, half the students fail when entering high school, can not find an occupation, and lose their competence in French. Some ten thousand youths are members of sports clubs, most of them boys. Girls are sheltered. Pregnancy outside of marriage is always considered dishonorable even though abortion is legal. The mother gladly keeps the child if the father agrees to marry her quickly.

Higher Education. Approximately six hundred Mahorans receive scholarships to study in universities in France, and about the same number of high school students are enrolled there in programs that are unavailable in Mayotte.

ETIQUETTE

Conduct is based on respect for elders and Comorian customs of public appearance, but the Western education that is given in middle school and high school offers alternative values that are sometimes contradictory.

RELIGION

Religious Beliefs. Sunni Islam of the Chafeite rite is the major religious affiliation, accompanied for part of the population by a cult of possession of Mahoran spirits known as *patros* and Malagasy ones known as *trumba*.

Rituals and Holy Places. Islam is practiced in mosques. Worship of spirits takes place in holy places (*ziara*): on sites where houses once stood, in the ruins of former mosques, and at the tombs of

A decorated Banga house. Houses made of earthen brick and cement are encouraged by the government social housing program.

sheikhs. There, spirits of the earth or of ancestors are summoned and partially Islamized rituals are performed.

MEDICINE AND HEALTH CARE

Mayotte has had rapid development of maternal and infant care and health services, with several rural clinics and two hospitals. Intervention by traditional practitioners and rituals of possession by spirits remain the preferred way of dealing with personal or relationship problems that may result in illness. Rapid changes in society have affected school-age adolescent girls in particular.

SECULAR CELEBRATIONS

French as well as Muslim holidays are celebrated.

THE ARTS AND HUMANITIES

Support for the Arts. The Mahoran Center for Cultural Action, which receives public funding, supports artistic endeavors, and encourages the blending of local and metropolitan French culture.

Literature. A body of oral literature is being assembled at the Office of Cultural Affairs and has been partially transcribed. Young Mahoran fiction authors have begun to write in French.

Graphic Arts. Traditional pottery has become scarce, but painting has begun to appear, practiced by wazungu artists and Mahoran youth.

Performance Arts. Theater in native languages (Comorian or Mayotte-Malagasy) is performed in villages, combining humor and social criticism (parent-child relations, marriage, polygamy). Contemporary music blends Comorian and Malagasy styles with Creole and European genres.

THE STATE OF THE PHYSICAL AND SOCIAL SCIENCES

Mayotte has no museums. The Cours Normal School houses a library, but access is restricted.

BIBLIOGRAPHY

Abdou, S. Baco, *Brulante Est Ma Terre*, 1990.

Allibert, Claude. *Mayotte, Plaque Tournante et Microcosme de l'Ocean Indien Occidental*, 1984.

Blanchy, Sophie. *La Vie Quotidienne a Mayotte (Comoros)*, 1990.

———. *Dictionnaire Mahorais-Francais et Francais-Mahorais*, 1996.

———. "Les Mahorais et Leur Terre: Autochtonie, Identite et Politique." In *Droit et Cultures*, 37: 165–185, 1999.

———, and Zaharia Soilihi. *Furukombe et Autres Contes de Mayotte*, 1991.

———, Noel J. Gueunier, and M. Said. *La Maison de la Mere: Contes de Lile de Mayotte*, 1993.

Breslar, John, Bernard Chatain, and Leon Attila Cheyssial. *Habitat Mahorais, Etude Analytique et Perspectives*, 1979.

Brolly, Mabe and Christisan Vaisse. *Mayotte*, 1988.

Gueunier, Noel J. "Lexique du Dialectee Malgache de Mayotte." *Etudes Ocean Indien* 7: 1986.

———. *Contes Comoriens en Dialecte Malgache de l'Ile de Mayotte*, 1994.

Lambek, Michael. *Human Spirit: A Cultural Account of Trance in Mayotte*, 1981.

———. "Virgin Marriage and the Autonomy of Women in Mayotte." In *Signs: Journal of Women in Culture and Society* 9 (2): 264–281, 1983.

———. *Knowledge and Practice in Mayotte: Local Discourses of Islam, Sorcery, and Spirit Possession*, 1993.

Rombi, Marie-Francoise. *Le Shimaore (Ile de Mayotte, Comoros): Premiere Approche d'un Parler de la Langue Comorienne*, 1983.

—SOPHIE BLANCHY

SEE ALSO: COMOROS

MEXICO

CULTURE NAME
Mexican

ALTERNATIVE NAMES
Cultura mexicana (sometimes referred to as mexicanidad)

ORIENTATION

Identification. The word "Mexico" is derived from Mexica (pronounced "Me-shee-ka"), the name for the indigenous group that settled in central Mexico in the early fourteenth century and is best known as the Aztecs.

Mexicans make several cultural subdivisions within the nation. The most common one identifies northern, central, and south or south-eastern Mexico. The extensive and desertlike north was only sparsely populated until the middle of the twentieth century, except for some important cities such as Monterrey. It has traditionally housed only small indigenous populations and is generally regarded as a frontier culture. Densely populated central and western Mexico is the cradle of the nation. Highly developed Indian cultures populated this region in pre-Columbian times and it was also the heart of the colony of New Spain. Many prominent colonial cities are major urban and industrial centers today. Southern Mexico has a tropical or subtropical climate and some rain forest. It is characterized by a strong indigenous heritage and is also the poorest part of the country.

Another relevant cultural division is that between the central template highlands (the altiplano) and the much more humid mountainous regions (the sierras) and coastal plains. In many parts of Mexico this division parallels the relative presence of indigenous populations, with the sierra regions being the most indigenous.

On a smaller scale the Mexican nation has traditionally been characterized by strong provincial and local cultural identities. People identify closely with their own state; stereotypes about people from other places abound. Strong regional and local identities have given rise to the idea that there exist "many Mexicos." Nevertheless, even though Mexican culture is diverse, there is also a strong identification with the nation-state; nationalism is vigorous.

Location and Geography. Mexico is situated in North America, although culturally, it is identified more closely with Central and South American countries. It borders the United States in the north, Guatemala and Belize in the south, the Pacific Ocean in the west, and the Gulf of Mexico in the east. The national territory measures more than 750,000 square miles (nearly two million square kilometers) and contains a wide range of physical environments and natural resources. Two huge mountain chains—the Western Sierra Madre and the Eastern Sierra Madre—run from north to south and meet in central Mexico. East and west of the mountain chains are strips of humid coastal plains. The entirely flat Yucatán peninsula in the southeast is an exception in mountainous Mexico. The possibilities and limitations of this topographic and climatic system have had a strong influence on Mexico's social, economic, and cultural organization.

The national capital is Mexico City, situated in the heart of central Mexico. In pre-Columbian times it was the site of the capital of the Aztec Empire and during the three centuries of colonial rule it was the seat of the viceroys of New Spain. Mexico City today is the second largest city in the world with 17 million inhabitants as of 1995. Most administrative and economic activities are concentrated in Mexico City. A ring of cities—Puebla, Cuernavaca, Toluca, and Querétaro—surrounds the capital. Other major cities are Guadalajara in the west and the industrial city of Monterrey in the north. In the late twentieth

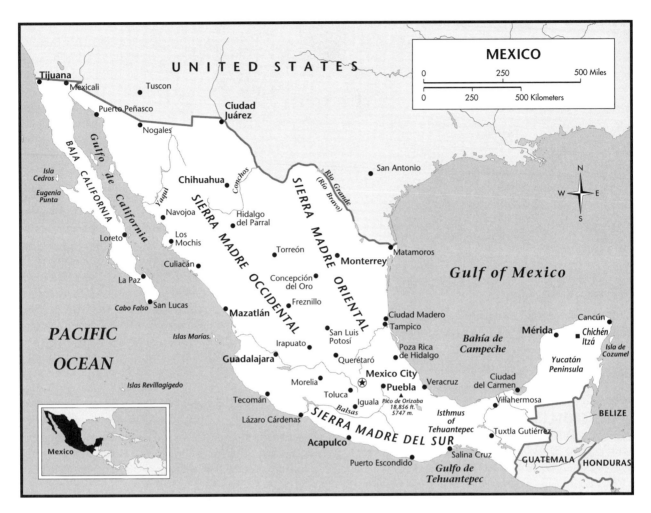

Mexico

century, major urban centers developed along the border with the United States.

Demography. The preliminary results of the 2000 population census calculated the total number of Mexicans as 97,361,711. In 1950, the total population amounted to approximately 25 million, with the figure reaching nearly 50 million in 1970. These numbers demonstrate the rapid rate of demographic growth that was so characteristic of Mexico during the second half of the twentieth century. The growth rate has slowed, but the population is still very young. The average life expectancy in 1999 was estimated at sixty-nine years for men and a little over seventy-five years for women; the infant mortality rate was almost twenty-five per one thousand. In the late twentieth century, emigration to the United States (mainly of the illegal variety) became a significant phenomenon.

Mexico's population still contains many Indian groups. Depending on the definition used, the total number of Indians varied from 6.7 million to 10 million in 1995. The most significant groups are the Nahuas, Otomís, Mayas, Zapotecas, Mixtecos, Tzeltales, and Tzotziles.

Linguistic Affiliation. Spoken by more than 95 percent of the population, Spanish is the official language of Mexico and was introduced through conquest and colonization. Mexican Spanish has its roots in the Spanish of Spain. In terms of grammar, syntax, and spelling there are no important differences between the two, but the pronunciation and sound are different. Certain words from the principal Indian language (Nahuatl) are incorporated into Mexican Spanish, especially in the domains of food and household. Some of these words have also been incorporated into other languages such as the English 'chocolate' from the Nahuatl 'chocolatl'. The national culture of Mexico boasts sixty-two indigenous languages. In 1995 at least 5.5 million people spoke an indigenous language. The level of bilingualism, however, was high at 85 percent.

Symbolism. The most prominent symbols that express and reinforce national culture belong to the domains of state, religion, and popular culture. As a product of the Mexican Revolution (1910–1917), the Mexican state has been an important point of convergence for national identity. Because it was a widely shared process that profoundly refashioned the country's social, political, economic, and cultural characteristics, the revolution itself has become an important source of national identity. The postrevolutionary state has been very active and effective in nurturing national symbols and heroes. Children who attend public schools honor the national flag and sing the national anthem every Monday morning. The flag consists of three vertical strips in the colors green (representing ''hope''), white (''purity'') and red (''blood''). In the central white strip is the image of an eagle standing on a cactus plant and eating a snake. This image represents the myth of the foundation of Tenochtitlán, the capital of the Aztec Empire.

The most important icon of Mexican national culture is the Virgin of Guadalupe, which illustrates the pervasive influence of Roman Catholicism in the national culture. She is viewed as the ''mother'' of all Mexicans. The dark-skinned Virgin is the Mexican version of the Virgin Mary and as such represents national identity as the product of the mixing of European and Meso-American religions and peoples. Her image was used in the struggle for independence against the Spanish.

Mexicans have developed a particular sense of uniqueness, which is expressed in the popular saying *como México no hay dos* (Mexico is second to none). This sense is also expressed in numerous elements of popular culture such as food and music.

HISTORY AND ETHNIC RELATIONS

Emergence of the Nation. Mexican national culture slowly emerged from a process of accommodation between the indigenous cultures and the Spanish colonial domination that lasted three centuries. Mexico gained independence in 1821. In the nineteenth century, the formation of the national culture and polity remained a difficult task mainly due to political instability, military uprisings, and foreign invasions. In these years Mexico lost large portions of its original territory. Most important in this respect was the war with the United States between 1846 and 1848, which broke out when the United States attempted to annex independent Texas. The war ended with U.S. forces defeating the Mexican army. The 1848 peace treaty ceded Texas, Califor-

nia, and New Mexico to the United States and reduced Mexico's territory by half. Despite this tragic loss, the war did contribute to the development of a genuine nationalism for the first time. In 1853, in a contradictory decision, the Mexican government sold present-day southern New Mexico and Arizona to the United States in order to solve budgetary problems. The relationship between Mexico and the United States has remained difficult and ambivalent ever since.

Mexico was invaded again in 1862, this time by the French, who installed a monarchy in coalition with conservative Mexican elites. Civil war ensued until the French were defeated by Mexican liberals in 1867, which inaugurated a new republic that was finally becoming a nation-state. These were years of nascent economic, infrastructural, and political modernization. Political stabilization and economic development were also the hallmarks of the regime of Porfirio Díaz (1876–1910). The years of the Díaz regime were also the time when Mexico became increasingly connected in a railroad network. These processes fostered the political, economic, and social integration of different groups and regions within the nation and strengthened state and nation building. These profound transformations, however, also created many tensions and conflicts between rich and poor, peasants and large landowners, Indians and non-Indians, and the politically influential and the aspiring middle classes. This instability eventually led to the outbreak of the Mexican Revolution in 1910, which drove Díaz out of power and then developed into a harsh and violent civil war. It is estimated that 1 million people were killed during the revolutionary period (of a total population of a little more than 15 million in 1910). Armed struggle formally ended with the adoption of a new Constitution in early 1917, but it still took several decades more before a new nation-state consolidated. Postrevolutionary reconstruction affected all domains of society and gave an entirely new meaning to the nation.

National Identity. The development of Mexican national identity has occurred through distinctive positioning in the international arena and through internal strides towards unity and homogeneity. Mexico's history of complicated relationships with colonial or imperial powers explains its current drive toward a proud and self-conscious identity. Especially after World War II, the nation sought ways to project itself onto the international scene. For example, Mexico hosted major world sporting events on three occasions: the Olympic Games in 1968 and the World Cup world soccer champion-

The National Cathedral in Mexico City, which sits upon the ancient city of Tenochtitlan. The dominant religion in Mexico is Roman Catholicism.

ships in 1970 and 1986—an accomplishment achieved otherwise only by rich countries such as France and Italy.

The development of Mexican national identity has also focused on Mexico's distinctive relationship to the United States. U.S. economic and cultural influence in Mexico is strong. Mexicans resent this situation but at the same time admire the achievements of their northern neighbors.

Internally, the forging of a national identity always revolved around the issue of race. The adoption of liberalism in the nineteenth century implied that all racial groups in Mexico were made legally equal in the framework of the incipient nation-state, although not in social practice. The dominant ideology actively sought to eliminate racial heterogeneity. It was believed that only a racially homogeneous population could develop a national identity, which led to the promotion of racial mixing, or *mestizaje*.

After the revolution, the emphasis shifted from racial to cultural differences. The value ascribed to Mexico's indigenous peoples also changed. The grandeur of pre-Columbian Indian culture was incorporated into the national imagery. At the same time, the ideas and policies that stressed cultural uniformity and homogeneity persisted. In the ideol-ogy of the revolution, the opposition between Indian and European had given rise to a synthesis, the *mestizo*, who was considered the authentic Mexican. In the middle of the twentieth century, the elaboration of the national identity increasingly concentrated on the supposed (psychological) character of the quintessential Mexican mestizo. This gave rise to the mythology of *mexicanidad*, or "the essence of being Mexican."

In recent years, the ideas about Mexican national identity have again changed. Although the absolute majority of the population is mestizo, there is a renewed attention to and appreciation of cultural differences and diversity. The rethinking of the role and meaning of indigenous peoples has given rise to the notion of a pluricultural national identity.

Ethnic Relations. Social policies aimed at the emancipation of Indian groups and the elimination of profound socioeconomic inequalities have been employed since the 1930s. Nevertheless, indigenous populations are among the poorest and most marginalized groups in Mexico. Prejudice among broad sectors of the population toward Indians persists. Elites in provincial towns in predominantly indigenous regions are often openly racist. This situation has strained ethnic relations and there has been a rise of indigenous movements in recent years that demand a new space in the national culture. Most significant has been the outbreak of armed indigenous rebellion in the state of Chiapas, where the Zapatista Army for National Liberation declared war on the government in January 1994.

URBANISM, ARCHITECTURE, AND THE USE OF SPACE

Mexican cities have been built from the central square (*zócalo*) outwards. The main church and the municipal or state palace are invariably to be found on the zócalo, which is the center of a colonial checkerboard pattern of streets. The zócalo with its benches, bandstand, and fountain is a crucial place for citizens to meet for leisure activities, political rallies, civic rituals, and demonstrations. The huge zócalo in Mexico City has become synonymous with a public space appropriated by ordinary people.

In recent decades, Mexican cities have grown at a pace surpassing the capacities of urban planning. Urban growth has been accompanied by squatter settlements and uncontrolled commercial and industrial expansion. This growth has also consumed extreme amounts of space, because low-rise buildings prevail and because priority is given to new and prestigious projects in the outskirts as opposed to urban renewal.

Mexican architecture was heavily influenced by Spanish and French traditions. Nevertheless, local traditions and indigenous crafts always mediated European influences. In the twentieth century, Mexican architecture developed a proper style. Public buildings constructed in the latter half of the century breathe a monumental atmosphere, reminiscent of the great pre-Columbian pyramids.

The houses of well-to-do Mexicans have been inward looking, towards a patio, since colonial times. Their front sides mainly consist of plastered walls and barred windows. This reflects the desire to protect the family from the outside world and underscores the key role of family life in the national culture. Today, wealthy neighborhoods are mosaics of entirely walled residences. The majority of poor Mexicans live in smaller and very modest houses and apartment buildings. Building one's own house is an important cultural imperative. Mexicans like to paint their houses in vivid colors.

An extensive network of highways links Mexican cities and towns. All major highways converge on the capital, which illustrates the national culture's deeply engrained centralist tradition.

The Festival for the Dead, El Dia de Los Muertos, is held each November 2nd to honor the deceased.

FOOD AND ECONOMY

Food in Daily Life. Mexico possesses an extensive and sophisticated culinary culture, with a great variety of regional dishes. Three products constitute the heart of most Mexican dishes: corn, hot peppers (chiles), and beans, products that stem from pre-Columbian times. Corn is consumed in all possible forms: as a cooked or roasted corncob (*elote*), cooked grain of corn, porridge (*atole*), as wrapped and steamed dough with filling (*tamal*), but most importantly as a tortilla, a thin, round "pancake." Tortillas are made from corn dough and come in many sizes, although the traditional tortilla that accompanies most meals has a diameter of approximately six inches (15 centimeters). When tortillas are filled with meat or other ingredients they are called tacos or quesadillas, which are especially popular in central Mexico. Much of the sophistication of Mexican cuisine comes from the use of more than one hundred different types of chiles, which range from the large and "sweet" *chile ancho* to the small and extremely hot *chile habanero*.

Mexicans generally have a light breakfast of coffee and/or fruit before they leave for work or school. Halfway through the morning, people may eat a warm tortilla-based snack or a bread roll. The most important meal of the day is served between two and four in the afternoon (the *comida*) and consists of three or four courses: soup; rice or pasta; meat or chicken—if affordable—accompanied by tortillas and refried beans; and dessert. Dinner is served between eight and ten at night and consists mainly of sweet rolls, coffee, and milk. Mexicans frequently eat outdoors. Homely restaurants serve inexpensive fixed menus known as *comida corrida*. Mexicans drink huge quantities of soft drinks and beer. Although the national liquor is *tequila*, which is produced from the maguey cactus, Mexicans prefer rum with cola during weddings and other celebrations, or fiestas.

Food Customs at Ceremonial Occasions. There are numerous religious and secular occasions in Mexico that are accompanied by special food. A popular religious fiesta is the Día de la Candelaria (Candlemas) on 2 February, which celebrates the purification of Mary and the presentation and blessing of Jesus. After the church ceremony family and close friends join for *tamales*. During the Day of the Dead, 2 November, people consume *pan de muerto* (bread of the dead), a long and flat sweet bread prepared with many eggs and sugar. At Christmas people eat *romeritos*, a plant similar to rosemary served with sauce and potatoes; *bacalao*, dried codfish cooked and served in a sauce of tomatoes, olives, and onions; and all sorts of stuffed turkey. In September people commemorate independence and, in central Mexico, eat a sophisticated dish called *chile en nogada*, a stuffed *chile poblano* dressed with a white walnut sauce, red pomegranate, and green parsley, in a representation of the Mexican flag.

Basic Economy. Mexico has a free-market economy with a mixture of modern and traditional industry and agriculture, increasingly dominated by the private sector. Until the mid-1980s, state regulation of the economy and protectionist policies were influential, but since then the Mexican economy has experienced deregulation, internationalization, and privatization. The number of state-owned companies fell from more than one thousand in 1982 to fewer than two hundred in 1998. Economic restructuring was promoted by national and international interest groups in response to several late twentieth century economic and financial crises.

The gross domestic product (GDP) amounted to $415 billion (U.S.) in 1998. The composition of GDP by sector was as follows: agriculture, a little more than 5 percent; industry, 29 percent; and services, almost 66 percent, of which commerce, restaurants, and hotels accounted for a third. Mexico's external debt amounted to $154 billion (U.S.) in 1997.

Land Tenure and Property. The unequal distribution of land was a key cause of the Mexican Revolution. The struggle for land led to the adoption of a policy of land reform that reached its height in the 1930s but slowed steadily after. Since then Mexico has known three types of land tenure: *pequeña propiedad* (small property), *ejido*, and the *tierra comunal*. The first category refers to privately owned land. Ejido land, which was established after the revolution, is officially owned by the state, which confers usufruct rights to land reform recipients. Legally recognized communal lands, the tierra comunal, belong to particular communities and are distributed according to tradition. In 1992, a controversial constitutional reform put an end to land reform and made possible the privatization of ejido lands.

Commercial Activities. The GDP of commerce, restaurants, and hotels accounted for $77 billion (U.S.) in 1998. Mexicans have a long tradition of acquiring basic goods and foodstuffs in small neighborhood grocery shops (*tienda de abarrote*). These shops may sell very small quantities of certain products. In 1998, more than half of all commercial units belonged to this category and almost a third of all personnel employed in commercial activities worked in these shops. At the same time, in urban areas there is an increasing tendency to shop in huge supermarkets. Mexican merchants own most national supermarket chains, but American and French companies are rapidly gaining influence in this sector.

Major Industries. The gross national product (GNP) of the manufacturing industry in 1998 amounted to almost $82 billion (U.S.). The major manufactured goods were motor vehicles, consumer durables, food, beverages, tobacco, chemicals, textiles, and clothing. After Mexico City, the most important industrial center is Monterrey in the north. Much of recent industry is organized in so-called *maquiladoras* (labor-intensive assembly plants). All sorts of maquiladoras were originally introduced only in a narrow zone along the U.S. border, but they are now allowed throughout Mexico.

Trade. In 1998, Mexico's exports totaled more than $117 billion (U.S.) and its imports amounted to more than $125 billion (U.S.). Although Mexico produces and exports large quantities of oil, the overwhelming majority of exports came from the

A traditional Yucatecan Maya house. Cozumel, Mexico.

manufacturing industry. The most important sectors were, in diminishing order, machinery, automobiles, textiles, and clothing. The United States is by far the most important trading partner, accounting for more than three-quarters of Mexico's imports and exports. Trade with the United States and Canada increased substantially following the implementation in 1994 of the North American Free Trade Agreement. Mexico is pursuing additional trade agreements with countries in Latin America, as well as with Israel and the European Union to lessen its dependence on the United States.

Division of Labor. The labor force consisted of 38,617,500 persons in 1998, of which 20 percent were employed in the primary sector, almost 25 percent in the secondary sector (especially in manufacturing and construction), and 55 percent in the tertiary sector, which includes commerce and services. Although jobs are formally assigned on the basis of qualifications, access to jobs is crucially mediated by personal networks.

SOCIAL STRATIFICATION

Classes and Castes. Mexico has a very unequal distribution of wealth, even compared to other Latin American countries. With the introduction of neoliberal economic policies, inequalities have

sharpened. In 1998, the top 20 percent of income earners accounted for 55 percent of Mexico's income, while an estimated 27 percent of the population was living below the poverty line. The size of the middle classes has shrunk in recent years.

Although poverty and marginalization are widespread, they are particularly strong in central and southern Mexico and especially in rural areas. An official marginalization index that includes income levels and the availability and quality of services (such as drinking water, sewage, and education) indicates that the smallest settlements are the most underprivileged.

There is a correlation between socioeconomic hierarchy and ethnicity. Among the poorest segments of the population a strong presence of Indian groups can be found. In 1995, almost all communities whose populations were comprised of more than 40 percent native language speakers suffered from high degrees of marginalization. This strongly contrasts with the wealthiest segments of the Mexican population, which are predominantly made up of whites.

Symbols of Social Stratification. Class differences are marked in Mexico and are expressed symbolically in numerous ways. Wealthy Mexicans live in neighborhoods that are sealed off by armed private

Scenic view of downtown Mexico City, Mexico. All major highways in Mexico converge in the capital city.

guards. At the same time, conspicuous consumption and grandeur is an important characteristic of Mexican culture. A prominent medium is the possession of new and expensive cars. Members of the lower middle class put in great financial effort to demonstrate to the outside world their aspirations, sometimes to the detriment of elementary needs.

Wealthy people dress elegantly according to international clothing standards and wear expensive watches and jewelry. Dress codes are very strict in Mexico, especially at work and school. In primary and secondary school, students wear uniforms. Since colonial times, the use of sandals has been associated with the countryside, poverty, and Indians.

An important cultural marker of class difference is access to all sorts of private facilities. Whereas wealthy people and members of the upper middle class send their children to private schools and universities, use private means of transportation, and go to private hospitals and sports clubs, the not-so well-off make use of crowded state-subsidized facilities.

Class differences are also confirmed in certain behavioral rules. One such rule involves the ritual of waiting that a person from a lower position in the social hierarchy has to endure when seeking access to someone at a higher level. When class differences coincide with ethnic distinctions, discriminatory practices are not unusual.

POLITICAL LIFE

Government. Mexico is a federal republic—hence its official name *Estados Unidos Mexicanos*—operating under a centralized government. Governmental powers at the federal level are divided between executive, legislative, and judicial branches, but in political practice the executive, that is, the presidency, has had strong control over the legislative branch. Only in recent years has the legislative branch seen its power increase because of the strengthening of the multiparty system. The president is elected by popular vote for a six-year period and is both the chief of state and head of government. The president appoints cabinet members. The legislative branch is a bicameral National Congress consisting of the Chamber of Deputies and the Senate. The Chamber of Deputies has five hundred members, elected for three-year terms; the Senate has 128 members, elected for six-year terms. In the judicial branch the Supreme Court of Justice is the highest tribunal.

The federation is made up of thirty-one states and the Federal District (the capital). Each state has a governor, who serves a six-year term, and a unicameral legislature. Both are elected by popular vote. Before 1997, the chief of the Federal District was appointed by the president, but has since been elected directly by popular vote. The Federal District also has an Assembly of Representatives. The local administrative level is the municipality, which is governed by a popularly elected mayor and a municipal council for three-year terms. Suffrage is universal and mandatory (but not enforced) for those over the age of eighteen.

Leadership and Political Officials. The modern presidency stands in a long tradition of pre-Columbian rulers (*tlatoani*), Spanish colonial viceroys, and nineteenth century and revolutionary *caudillos*. The president holds great discretionary powers. Power and leadership are attained through the management of personal relations, which are ruled by principles of loyalty, trust, and reciprocity. These informal networks are interconnected in a pyramidal way and form the real centers of decision making. Vertical patron-client relations can be found in all segments of society. Interactions between politicians, union leaders, top bureaucrats, and ordinary people also take place through these networks. In recent years, academic credentials and technocratic knowledge have become more important than political and electoral experience.

Besides being chief of state and head of government, the president has traditionally been the leader of the Institutional Revolutionary Party (PRI), which held power from 1929 to 2000. During much of the twentieth century, Mexico was a one-party democracy. The PRI emerged from the revolution and incorporated mass organizations of workers, peasants, and urban middle classes. Because of its particular origins, its longevity in power, and the influence of diverse interest groups, the PRI is difficult to classify ideologically. There are two other significant parties in Mexico. The conservative National Action Party (PAN) began enjoying electoral success at the state level in 1985. The social-democratic Party of the Democratic Revolution (PRD) emerged as a breakaway movement from the PRI in 1987 and began governing Mexico City in 1997. Both the PAN and the PRD aim at democratization, but the PRD also proposes a more equal distribution of wealth. The dominance of the PRI in federal elections was finally broken on 2 July 2000, when the candidate of the PAN won a stunning victory with 43 percent of the vote.

Social Problems and Control. Both petty and organized crime increased in the 1990s. Muggings and burglaries, increasingly violent, became widespread. Drug-related violence constituted another serious cause of concern. Public security has thus become a key issue for ordinary citizens and the authorities. At the same time, the police and the judiciary system are widely believed to be ineffective and lack public credibility, partially due to unresolved high-profile political assassinations and corruption. This has led to incidents of people taking the law into their own hands. Paid neighborhood watches are common wherever people can afford them. Private security guards no longer patrol only at banks and government buildings but also at medium-sized offices and shops. In response, the government founded an additional police force in 1999, the National Preventive Police.

Military Activity. Mexico has had civilian presidents since 1946 and has not been involved in international disputes in recent decades. The primary role of the military is the maintenance of internal order. The Ministry of National Defense (the army and air force) and the marines together comprised an armed force consisting of almost 240,000 members in 1998. Military expenditures have increased substantially in recent years and amounted to $2.5 billion (U.S.) in 1996, accounting for almost 1 percent of the GDP. In recent years the military has been involved in two serious problems: the armed uprising in the state of Chiapas and the struggle against drugs. Mexico is a major supplier of marijuana and heroin to the U.S. market and is the primary transshipment country for cocaine from South America. In 1998 the government spent $147 million (U.S.) to combat drug trafficking, an amount that has increased spectacularly in recent years.

SOCIAL WELFARE AND CHANGE PROGRAMS

As part of its revolutionary heritage, the state provides welfare facilities for most Mexicans. In urban centers, but not in rural areas, health facilities are mostly well equipped. Based on the revolutionary constitution of 1917, education is provided freely by the state. People who have worked in the formal economy receive small pensions after they retire. There are no unemployment benefits. After 1982, the state's ability to uphold social expenditures was seriously undermined by economic crises, the financial burden of external debt, and the adoption of structural adjustment policies. A major government initiative, the National Solidarity Program, was launched at the end of the 1980s to attempt to counteract this development and revitalize social policies. The program was based on a shared obliga-

A scribe works with a client on a sidewalk in Mexico City. Beside them are papier-mache for a Holy Week festival.

tion by the state and local communities to implement projects aimed at improving the standard of living. The National Solidarity Program was practically discontinued with the election of a new president in 1994, and replaced with new, but less ambitious, programs. Given the magnitude of Mexico's problems of poverty, unemployment and underemployment, and deficient social services, the effects of these programs have been modest.

NONGOVERNMENTAL ORGANIZATIONS AND OTHER ASSOCIATIONS

Several political pressure groups in Mexico have founded powerful organizations. Very influential are the national business associations that have sections in all states and major cities. The most important are the Confederation of Employers of the Mexican Republic, the Coordinating Council of Entrepreneurs, and the Confederation of National Chambers of Commerce.

In recent decades, numerous organizations and associations have emerged around particular social issues. They strive to be independent from political parties and openly battle government-controlled organizations. There has also been a tendency to form national alliances of local and regional organizations. Two large networks of peasant organizations are the

National Union of Regional Autonomous Peasant Organizations and the National Coordinating Committee "Plan de Ayala." Nongovernmental organizations (NGOS) have also emerged in urban areas because of the inadequate conditions in housing, transport, public services, and security. The most important of these is the National Coordinating Committee of Urban Popular Movements. In Mexico City, the Association of Neighborhoods emerged after the 1985 earthquake. Indigenous movements have proliferated in recent years, founding the National Indigenous Congress. In the 1990s, NGOs focusing on the defense of human rights have become influential. They are a response to political violence and police brutality. The environmental movement is gradually becoming more active in Mexico.

GENDER ROLES AND STATUSES

Division of Labor by Gender. The degree of economic participation of women was 35 percent in 1995, while that of men was about 75 percent. Nevertheless, female economic participation is increasing rapidly. In addition, it is generally assumed that many women are employed in nonregistered and underpaid informal activities. Women also generally earn less than men and their level of educational is lower. Most women are economically active when they are young (between twenty and twenty-four years of age).

Although the political arena is strongly dominated by men, the presence of women in public space has become more common place. In the early twenty-first century, for example, the leadership of major political parties was in the hands of female politicians, as was the government of Mexico City and the chair of Mexico's largest union. The involvement of women in numerous social movements has also been significant.

The Relative Status of Women and Men. Although women and men are equal before the law, clear differences persist in terms of authority and privileges. Women play crucial roles in the family, but even here the male is "chief of the family" (*jefe de familia*). Women are seen as the caretakers of morality and hence take center stage in the domain of religion.

In assigning males and females to different economic, political, and social roles, Mexicans can make use of complex and sometimes contradictory cultural representations of masculinity and femininity. The two key cultural icons for defining femininity are La Malinche and the Virgin of Guadalupe. The myth of La Malinche refers to the Indian woman who was given to conqueror Hernán Cortés in 1519. During the remaining part of the conquest she was his interpreter and "mistress." La Malinche is the collaborator and traitor, but also the sexually violated who gave birth to an illegitimate son, the first *mestizo*. In contrast to La Malinche, the Virgin of Guadalupe represents suffering and sacrifice. This has given rise to the image of the submissive, self-sacrificing, but virtuous woman (*la abnegada*). Together these myths explain the ambiguity attached to defining females. The key concept for defining masculinity is machismo, which is associated with violence, power, aggressiveness, and sexual assertiveness. These general cultural representations have formed the basis for ideas of "natural" male dominance and power and female suffering and motherhood. They have been influential in the imagery of Mexican men and women, but they are increasingly considered simple stereotypes. Under the influence of profound social and cultural transformations in an increasingly urbanized Mexico, perceptions of masculinity and femininity are shifting continuously.

MARRIAGE, FAMILY AND KINSHIP

Marriage. Mexicans are free to choose their marriage partners. Informally, however, there are rules that constrain choices, most importantly those re-

lated to class and ethnicity. People usually marry after a period of formal engagement that can last several years. In 1995, the average age at marriage for a male was almost twenty-four years; for a woman it was nearly twenty-two years. Out of all Mexicans aged twelve and above, just over half were married or otherwise united. Although the basis for marriage is love, many Mexicans consciously or unconsciously look for a partner who can provide social and economic security or upward mobility. Monogamy is the only marriage form allowed. A marriage ceremony consists of a civil registration and a religious wedding. Afterwards, the couple holds a huge and costly party with family and friends. At the beginning of the 1990s, the divorce rate was a relatively low 6.5 percent. It is legally easy to divorce but the social pressure against it can be formidable.

Domestic Unit. The nuclear family is the common household unit: in 1995, almost three-quarters of all family households were nuclear. Households consisted of an average of 4.6 members. In the same year, almost 6 percent of the households were single-person. At the same time, a significant number of households consist of "extended" nuclear families, which often exist on a temporary basis. Particularly among the urban poor there are households consisting of parents, children, grandparents and sometimes other relatives. Recently married couples may live for a few years with the kin of husband or wife in order to save sufficient money to establish an independent domestic unit. In the countryside different nuclear families might live close to each other and share common resources. In 1995, 82 percent of households were male-headed. Although women generally hold fundamental responsibilities in the household, men are still the principal authority. Domestic violence constitutes a serious problem in Mexico.

Inheritance. Inheritance laws make no distinction between men and women. Each child is legally entitled to an equal share, but in practice male descendants are often privileged. In the countryside land is often distributed only among sons.

Kin Groups. The extended family is of crucial importance to most Mexicans. Although family members generally live dispersed, sometimes very far away due to international migration, they seek opportunities to gather on several occasions. Family members will occasionally get together for a meal during the weekend, but will more typically gather on religious occasions. Fictive kinship relations are established through godfathers (*padrinos*) and godmothers (*madrinas*) at Catholic baptismal ceremonies. The family and larger kin groups are the main locus of trust, solidarity, and support in Mexico. These networks are mobilized with diverse objectives such as finding work, establishing political connections, and evading red tape.

SOCIALIZATION

Infant Care. The average number of children per household has decreased in recent decades and was just over two in 1995. Infants are mostly cared for at the parental home. Some are cared for at a private nursery from the age of three months. At the age of four, children are officially required to attend a kindergarten for two years. Children in Mexico are rapidly integrated into the activities of adults, but they are also strongly protected and not actively encouraged to discover their surroundings on their own.

Child Rearing and Education. After kindergarten, children are required to go to primary school for six years. Nevertheless, in 1995 almost 32 percent of the population over the age of fifteen had not finished primary school. In public and private schools pupils have to wear uniforms. Whereas public schools stress civic values and lay education, the majority of private schools tend to place more emphasis on religious values. There are also more liberal private schools. Relations between teacher and pupils tend to be strict.

Role and rule differentiation between girls and boys begins at an early age and forms key aspects of child rearing until adolescence. Male babies are dressed in blue and female babies in soft pink. There is a tendency to raise boys as "little men" and girls as "little women," thereby preparing them for their future gender roles. Sexual education within the family is still taboo for many Mexicans. Methods of child rearing also show differences according to class. In lower-class households it can be strict and traditional. During the 1990s, the government launched campaigns against the use of corporal punishment.

The most important initiation ceremony for girls is held when they turn fifteen. This *fiesta de quince años* marks the transition from girl to *señorita*, that is, a young virgin. The event also indicates that the young woman is now available for marriage. The ritual includes a holy mass during which the need to maintain purity until marriage is stressed. Afterward, the family holds a large party. There is no comparable ritual for boys.

Higher Education. In Mexico higher education is considered a road to socioeconomic progress and well-being. During several decades, public universi-

ties were recruitment sites for the political and administrative elite. This function has increasingly been taken over by the most prestigious private universities. In 1995, nearly 12 percent of the population over the age of twenty-five enjoyed some degree of higher education. At the beginning of university courses in 1998, there were just over 1.5 million students in the universities (excluding preparatory schools), of which 811,000 were men and 704,000 were women. Half the students studied social and administrative sciences and a third were in engineering and technology.

ETIQUETTE

Mexican etiquette is strongly informed by the culture of social hierarchies and distance. These can exist along the lines of race and gender, but class distinctions regulate social interaction most decisively. It goes without saying that the different social hierarchies frequently run parallel.

Generally speaking, Mexicans shake hands when they meet or in the case of two women meeting or a man and a woman meeting, kiss each other on the cheek once. In the case of close friends and on special occasions, such as New Year's Eve, Mexican men and women embrace each other, pat each other gently on the back, and then shake hands. This *abrazo* expresses confidentiality and the crucial value of trust. Because strangers cannot be placed within the different circles of intimacy and confidentiality they are generally treated with suspicion.

When people of different socioeconomic status meet, the individual with the socially ascribed inferior status will wait for the person with superior status to define the terms of the encounter. Mexicans are very keen on being addressed with their academic or professional title. The most commonly used academic title is that of *licenciado*. The form of address of licenciado is more linked to the position someone holds than to that person's precise academic credentials. People of lower standing will also invariably address a socially superior with the formal you (*usted*), while the latter will most likely use the informal you (*tu*). These forms of address draw boundaries, create distance, and confirm the social hierarchies so characteristic of the national culture.

Mexicans value the art of eloquence. Conversations will mostly begin with polite and informal exchanges and slowly move toward the subject matter. Even then Mexicans remain indirect speakers, avoiding clear-cut statements. Politicians and

This colonial church with two bell towers was built with ancient Maya stones. Spanish and French architectural traditions influenced Mexican buildings.

senior bureaucrats are identified as the masters of this rhetorical style. They have become the object of irony in the hands of the famous comic Cantinflas, who by speaking a lot but saying nothing gave birth to the verb *cantinflar*.

RELIGION

Religious Beliefs. Roman Catholicism is the dominant religion in Mexico. After the conquest by the Spanish, Mexico's indigenous peoples readily ac- cepted Catholic beliefs and practices, but they did so on the basis of their pre-Hispanic religious beliefs. The Virgin of Guadalupe, for example, was associated with the pagan goddess Tonantzin. As a result, Mexican folk Catholicism is frequently described as syncretic. Catholic beliefs pervade the life of ordinary Mexicans. Because the Catholic Church has been a very powerful institution in Mexican history, its relationship with the state has at times been tense and sometimes openly hostile. In recent decades, Protestant missionaries have been particularly active in southern Mexico and among the urban poor.

Religious Practitioners. The most important practitioners are Catholic priests, who conduct regular masses and officiate over events Mexicans consider crucial such as birth, weddings, death, and quince años (the initiation ceremony for girls). Priests also perform more quotidian rituals such as the blessing of new houses or cars. As parish priests are profoundly involved in the social life of local communities, their influence reaches beyond religious matters.

Rituals and Holy Places. Mexico's most significant religious rituals are determined by the Catholic calendar. Easter (*Semana Santa*) is perhaps the most important of all. In different places within Mexico, the reenactment of the crucifixion of Jesus Christ on Good Friday is attended by great crowds. The largest is in Iztapalapa in Mexico City and attracts more than 100,000 believers.

The nation's patron saint, the Virgin of Guadalupe, has her shrine in Mexico City, near the hill of Tepeyac, where she first appeared in 1531. The huge modern basilica there attracts hundreds of thousands of pilgrims from all over the country every year, especially on 12 December, Guadalupe's Day. Every community (rural or urban) has its own patron saint who is honored with processions and fiestas every year.

Death and the Afterlife. Representations and rituals of death play a prominent role in popular culture, art, and religion. It has been suggested that this is related to pre-Columbian indigenous beliefs. Such rituals are most vigorously expressed in the festivities of the Days of the Dead, 1 and 2 November. On this occasion, Mexicans arrange altars for the dead in their homes with food, beverages, and other objects (such as skulls made of sugar or chocolate) to welcome them on their return to earth. Many Mexicans also visit churchyards and adorn the graves with large orange flowers. They will spent some time by the grave praying but also sharing memories about the deceased. The so-called Mexican cult of the dead has attracted much attention abroad.

MEDICINE AND HEALTH CARE

The Mexican health system is sharply divided between public and private facilities, the latter being accessible only to the well-to-do. The overwhelming majority of the population depends on govern-

A Mexican woman prepares tortillas with salsa and beans. Corn, chili peppers, and beans are the main items in most Mexican foods.

ment institutions such as the Mexican Social Security Institute. The national health system consisted of more than seventeen thousand medical units in 1998, of which 885 were hospitals and the rest basic medical service centers in rural areas. The government health sector had a budget of approximately $11 billion (U.S.) in 1999 and employed around 300,000 doctors and nurses. Many doctors from public hospitals also have their own private consultation clinics.

Ordinary Mexicans frequently discuss sickness, health, and medicine and are familiar with self-treatment. Since most medicines can be purchased freely in commercial pharmacies, Mexicans tend to consume medication in considerable quantities. In addition, several folk health-providers exist and have a regular clientele. Herbalists can be found at local markets. *Curanderos* (''healers'') use traditional curing procedures and medicinal plants. Spiritualist healers consider themselves religious practitioners first and alternative health-providers second. Generally, Mexicans do not assume a fundamental inconsistency between folk health-providers and physicians.

SECULAR CELEBRATIONS

The Battle against the French is celebrated on 5 May (*Cinco de Mayo*), remembering the victory of Mexican forces over the French invaders in the hills near the city of Puebla in 1862. It took the French a year to bring reinforcements and take the Mexican capital in 1863. Cinco de Mayo is an important symbol of national sovereignty and parades are held throughout the country.

Independence Day is 16 September and celebrates the start of the struggle for independence in 1810, which began when the Catholic priest Miguel Hidalgo y Castilla rang the church bells in the village of Dolores and called upon the parishioners to drive out the Spanish. This act—the so-called *Grito de Dolores*—is repeated ritually on the night of 15 September by the authorities throughout Mexico and even by ambassadors abroad. The ritual ends with the vigorous shouting of "*Viva México*" three times. On the morning of 16 September there are military parades organized by the government. Independence Day is the most important civic ritual and enjoys broad popular participation. During the whole month of September houses, offices, and public buildings are decorated with the colors of the Mexican flag.

The Day of the Revolution, 20 November, commemorates the planned uprising of Francisco Madero against the dictator Porfirio Díaz in 1910 that marked the beginning of the Mexican Revolution. It is mainly a state-orchestrated event that arouses modest popular participation. The main event is the long sports parade in front of the National Palace in the center of Mexico City.

THE ARTS AND HUMANITIES

Support for the Arts. The most important federal institution active in the field of arts is the National Council for Culture and Arts (CNCA). The CNCA coordinates the activities of more than thirty public institutions in the world of arts; one of them is the National Fund for Culture and Arts, founded in 1989, which provides modest financial support (such as scholarships and project financing) to young and distinguished artists in a wide variety of disciplines. There are also private funds that support the arts.

Literature. The earliest evidence of writing dates back to 600 B.C.E. in the form of Zapotec glyphs, which have not yet been deciphered. Pre-Columbian literature is generally considered to include the scarce writings from before the conquest as well as the poetry and prose in indigenous languages that was recorded in alphabetical writing and produced after the conquest. The former group comprises the codices, pictographic writings on accordion-pleated *amate* ("paper,") most of which were destroyed. Their content is mainly religious and historical. The most important Mayan literary texts, such as the Popol Vuh, belong to the second group. One of the most significant legacies of Aztec culture is the poetry of the king of Texcoco, Nezahualcóyotl (1402–1472).

In colonial New Spain, the seventeenth century produced two most outstanding literary talents: writer and scientist Carlos Sigüenza y Góngora (1645–1700), and Sor Juana Inés de la Cruz (1651–1695), a brilliant woman who became a nun in order to continue her scholarly and literary pursuits. She is best known for her poetry and her theological and secular prose.

After independence, such international literary trends as romanticism, realism, and modernism influenced Mexico's literary achievements. Ignacio Manuel Altamirano (1834–1893) was the foremost representative of Mexican romanticism, which strove to develop a national literature nurtured by the realities of the country. Others include José López Portillo y Rojas (1850–1923) and Amado Nervo (1870–1919).

The Mexican Revolution and its aftermath led to the emergence of a new generation of writers and literary themes. The "novel of the revolution," which started with the 1915 publication of *Los de abajo* ("The underdogs") by Mariano Azuela (1873–1952) and expanded with Martín Luis Guzmán's novels, takes a bitter look at the revolution, the violence, and its leaders. This theme has also inspired other authors, among them Mexico's contemporary literary giant Carlos Fuentes. Juan Rulfo published very little but *Pedro Páramo* (1955) is considered a masterpiece. In poetry, a group centered around the literary journal *Contemporáneos* set new standards in the 1920s. Mexico's most outstanding poet, however was Octavio Paz (1914–1998), who also wrote numerous essays including *El laberinto de la soledad* (1950), a classic essay about Mexico's national character that earned him international recognition. In 1990 he was awarded the Nobel Prize in literature. In recent decades female novelists as Elena Poniatowska, Angeles Mastretta, and Laura Esquivel have gained prestige in Mexico and abroad.

Graphic Arts. Mexico's long tradition of graphic arts goes back to pre-Columbian times. When the different Indian civilizations prospered, they constructed impressive urban centers and religious buildings and produced sophisticated graphic art such as pottery and frescos. In general, pre-Columbian sculptures and images of gods provoke a sense of awe and fear. Pre-Columbian art has acquired a prominent place in the canon of the national culture and is displayed in numerous museums, especially the National Museum of Anthropology in Mexico City. These museums are frequently visited by pupils from primary and secondary schools as part of their history assignments.

After the Spanish conquest, the church and the monasteries were the key contributors in the field of arts. As a consequence, religious architecture became the most important form of creative expression. Although icons and styles were imported, techniques, materials, and forms used by indigenous artisans gradually gave way to a distinctively Mexican style. At the end of the seventeenth century a recognizable Mexican baroque with an abundance of decorative elements flourished. In the eighteenth century, this developed into the even more profuse Churrigueresque style. Sculpture and painting developed along similar lines.

Political instability and recurrent war seriously hampered artistic development in the nineteenth century, with the exception of painting, where there was a hesitant interest in pre-Columbian themes. The most important artists were Pelegrín Clavé and landscape painter José Maria Velasco.

After the Mexican Revolution, a period of intense artistic innovation commenced, giving rise to the most widely acknowledged Mexican art form, the mural. A recognition of artistic independence by the new revolutionary elite and active state support coincided with a renewed interest in popular culture, such as the engravings of José Guadalupe Posada (1851–1913), and in pre-Columbian themes and artistic expressions. Mexico, its history, and its people became the single most important themes of the huge murals that decorate the walls of public buildings. The most well-known exponents of the Mexican Muralist school are Diego Rivera (1886–1957), David Alfaro Siqueiros (1896–1974), and José Clemente Orozco (1883–1949). In recent years, the eccentric paintings of Frida Kahlo (1907–1954) have attracted worldwide attention. Painters of later generations who have gained national and international reputations include José Luis Cuevas, Juan O'Gorman, Rufino Tamayo, and Francisco Toledo.

Mexico's artistic qualities are perhaps best illustrated by the broad variety of popular art and handicrafts. Popular artists can be found throughout Mexico, but regions and even villages specialize in particular trades.

Performance Arts. In classical music the Mexico City–based National Symphony Orchestra and the Philarmonic Orchestra of the National University are most renowned. Mexico's most important composer of the twentieth century was Carlos Chávez (1899–1978). Popular music, such as *mariachi* and *ranchero* music, has acquired fame throughout the world and produced such stars as Vicente Fernández and Juan Gabriel. Mexico also has a native rock scene. Mexico City has become a major recording center for the Spanish-speaking world. The same is true for the production of soap opera series for television. Mexican cinema flourished in the 1940s and 1950s, producing such heroes of popular culture as Jorge Negrete and Pedro Infante. One of Mexico's most important venues for the performance arts is the *Festival Cervantino*, which is held every year in the provincial town of Guanajuato.

THE STATE OF THE PHYSICAL AND SOCIAL SCIENCES

Most scientific research in Mexico is conducted in the public universities, mainly in the National Autonomous University and the Autonomous Metropolitan University, both in Mexico City. The National Polytechnic Institute, also in Mexico City, is the foremost research institute in engineering and technology. In recent years there has been government support for developing research centers outside the capital. There is also an extensive network of specialized autonomous research institutes that are dependent on state finances such as the National Institute of Astrophysics, Optics, and Electronics and the College of Mexico.

Just over half of the almost $2 billion (U.S.) of federal expenditures in science and technology in 1998 was channeled through the Ministry of Public Education and another 34 percent was channeled through the Ministry of Energy. The majority of the latter funds are spent on research into the exploitation of oil. Public policy concentrates on three areas: promotion of quality and quantity of scientific research, establishment of linkages between science and industry, and the promotion of technological innovation.

The National Council of Science and Technology is the most important funding agency for the physical and social sciences. In 1998 it had a budget of $287 million (U.S.), with 47 percent allocated to individual postgraduate grants, 25 percent to scientific research and technological development, and 22 percent to the National System of Researchers (SNI), a program of financial incentives to productive academics. In 1998, more than sixty-five hundred researchers were in the SNI. Information on corporate funding of research and development is unavailable but is estimated to be very modest compared to Mexico's main trading partners.

BIBLIOGRAPHY

Bartra, Roger. *La jaula de la melancolía: Identidad y metamorfosis del mexicano*, 1987.

Basave Benítez, Agustín. *México mestizo: Análisis del nacionalismo mexicano en torno a la mestizofilia de Andrés Molina Enríquez*, 1992.

Bethell, Leslie, ed. *Mexico since Independence*, 1991.

Billeter, Erika, ed. *Images of Mexico: The Contribution of Mexico to twentieth Century Art* (catalogue), 1987.

Bonfil Batalla, Guillermo. *México profundo: Una civilización negada*, 1987.

El Colegio de México (various authors). *Historia de la Revolución Mexicana*, 23 vols., 1978–1979.

Chant, Sylvia. *Women and Survival in Mexican Cities: Perspectives on Gender, Labour Markets, and Low-Income Households*, 1991.

Cornelius, Wayne A., Ann L. Craig, and Jonathan Fox, eds. *Transforming State-Society Relations in Mexico: The National Solidarity Strategy*, 1994.

Cypess, Sandra M. *La Malinche in Mexican Literature: From History to Myth*, 1991.

Dealy, Glen Caudill. *The Latin Americans: Spirit and Ethos*, 1992.

Díaz-Polanco, Héctor. *La rebelión zapatista y la autonomía*, 1997.

Finkler, Kaja. *Spiritualist Healers in Mexico: Success and Failures of Alternative Therapeutics*, 1985.

Florescano, Enrique. *Memoria mexicana*, 1994.

Foster, David William, ed. *Mexican Literature: A History*, 1994.

Foweraker, Joe, and Ann L. Craig, eds. *Popular Movements and Political Change in Mexico*, 1990.

Gamio, Manuel. *Forjando patria*,1916, second ed., 1960, third ed., 1982.

Garrido, Luis Javier. *El Partido de la Revolución Institucionalizada: La formación del nuevo estado en Mexico, 1928–1945*, 1982.

Grayson, George W. *Mexico's Armed Forces: A Factbook*, 1999.

Gruzinski, Serge. *La colonización de lo imaginario: Sociedades indígenas y occidentalización en el México español, Siglos XVI–XVIII*, 1991.

Gutmann, Matthew C. *The Meanings of Macho: Being a Man in Mexico City*, 1996.

Hart, John Mason. *Revolutionary Mexico: The Coming and Process of the Mexican Revolution*, 1987.

Harvey, Neil. *The Chiapas Rebellion: The Struggle for Land and Democracy*, 1998.

Ingham, John M. *Mary, Michael, and Lucifer: Folk Catholicism in Central Mexico*, 1986.

Knight, Alan. *The Mexican Revolution*, 2 vols., 1986.

Loaeza, Soledad. *El Partido de Acción Nacional, la larga marcha, 1939–1994: Oposición leal y partido de protesta*, 1999.

Lomnitz-Adler, Claudio. *Exits from the Labyrinth: Culture and Ideology in the Mexican National Space*, 1992.

Melhuus, Marit. "Power, Value, and the Ambiguous Meanings of Gender." In Marit Melhuus and Kristianne Stoler, eds., *Machos, Mistresses, Madonnas: Contesting the Power of Latin American Gender Imagery*, 1996.

Meyer, Michael C., William Sherman. *The Course of Mexican History*, 1987.

Mraz, John. *Nacho López y el fotoperiodismo mexicano en los años cincuenta*, 1999.

Pansters, Wil, ed., *Citizens of the Pyramid: Essays on Mexican Political Culture*, 1997.

Paz, Octavio. *El laberinto de la soledad*, 1950.

Pilcher, Jeffrey M. *Que Vivan los Tamales! Food and the Making of Mexican Identity*, 1998.

Ramírez, Santiago. *El mexicano: Psicología de sus motivaciones*, 1977.

Ramos, Samuel. *El perfil del hombre y la cultura en México*, 1934.

Rothenstein, Julian. *J. G. Posada: Messenger of Mortality*, 1989.

Schryer, Frans J. *Ethnicity and Class in Rural Mexico*, 1990.

Street-Porter, Tim. *Casa Mexicana: La arquitectura, el diseño, y el estilo de México*, 1995.

Vasconcelos, José. *The Cosmic Race/La raza cósmica*, 1997. Originally published in 1925.

Womack, John. *Zapata and the Mexican Revolution*, 1968.

Zermeño, Sergio, ed. *Movimientos sociales e identidades colectivas: México en la década de los noventa*, 1997.

Zolov, Eric. *Refried Elvis: The Rise of Mexican Counterculture*, 1999.

Web Sites

General information about indigenous groups: http://www.sedesol.gob.mx/ini

Government institution for culture and arts: http://www.cnca.gob.mx

Hyperlink about the Zapatista uprising: http://www.eco
.utexas.edu/Homepages/Faculty/Cleaver/
zapsincyber.html

Informative hyperlink on Mexico: http://lanic.utexas
.edu/la/Mexico/

Mexican newspaper: http://www.jornada.unam.mx

Mexican weekly magazine: http://www.proceso
.com.mx

Official demographic information: http://www
.conapo.gob.mx

Statistical information: El Instituto Nacional de
Estadística, Geografía e Informática. Official Statisti-
cal Information. Web Site. Electronic document.
Available from http://www.inegi.gob.mx

—WIL G. PANSTERS

FEDERATED STATES OF MICRONESIA

CULTURE NAME

Micronesian

ALTERNATIVE NAMES

FSM

ORIENTATION

Identification. Formed in 1978, the Federated States of Micronesia (FSM) is an island nation in the Caroline archipelago of the western Pacific Ocean. Between 1947 and 1986, these islands were administered by the United States as part of the United Nations Trust Territory of the Pacific Islands. The United Nations trusteeship was terminated in 1986, when the FSM and the United States entered into a Compact of Free Association that guaranteed financial assistance to the FSM in exchange for U.S. authority over matters of security and defense through the year 2000. Communities throughout the FSM are culturally and linguistically heterogeneous. A shared national identity has been important for economic and political negotiations with outsiders, but sociocultural diversity within the FSM is more often the hallmark of islander identity.

Location and Geography. The Federated States of Micronesia consists of 607 islands with a total land area of 270 square miles (700 square kilometers) scattered across more than one million square miles (2.6 million kilometers) of the western Pacific Ocean. The islands are grouped into four geopolitical states: from west to east, Yap, Chuuk, Pohnpei, and Kosrae. The capital of the FSM is Palikir, which is located in a mountainous region of the main island of Pohnpei. Each state features both mountainous volcanic islands and low-lying coral atolls, with the exception of Kosrae, which has one mountainous island. Coral atolls consist of several small islets within a fringing reef, arranged around a central lagoon. Volcanic islands have a greater diversity of ecological zones, including an interior of dense rain forest and soaring mountains, a coastal plain of ridges and winding valleys, and thick mangrove swamps crowding the shoreline.

Demography. Virtually all of the islands in the FSM suffered severe depopulation following the introduction of diseases by the Europeans in the mid-1800s. Since the late 1800s, population figures have risen steadily. The 1999 population, estimated at 116,268, is up 19 percent from 1990. The annual growth rate of the nation's population is at 2 percent, down 1 percent from the growth experienced between 1950 and 1980. This drop in the population's growth rate can be attributed, in part, to emigration and the free movement of citizens between the FSM and the United States and its territories allowed by the Compact of Free Association. Despite international migration trends, the rapidly growing population of the FSM is expected to double in the next 36 years.

Linguistic Affiliation. English, the official language, is taught in schools and is widely known throughout the region. It is, however, a second language for most Micronesians. Virtually every inhabited island in the FSM is associated with a distinct language or dialect from the Austronesian (Malayo-Polynesian) language family. With the exception of a few Polynesian outliers, the languages spoken among the islanders of Chuuk, Pohnpei, Kosrae, and the coral atolls of Yap State are classified as Nuclear Micronesian. Yapese mainlanders speak a Western Micronesian language. The linguistic diversity among citizens of the FSM is a testament to the importance of local communities.

Symbolism. On the FSM's national flag, four white stars on a sea of blue represents the four unified states in a vast expanse of the western Pacific. The flag symbolically acknowledges that although each state is composed of a diversity of cultures over many miles of ocean, they are joined, not separated,

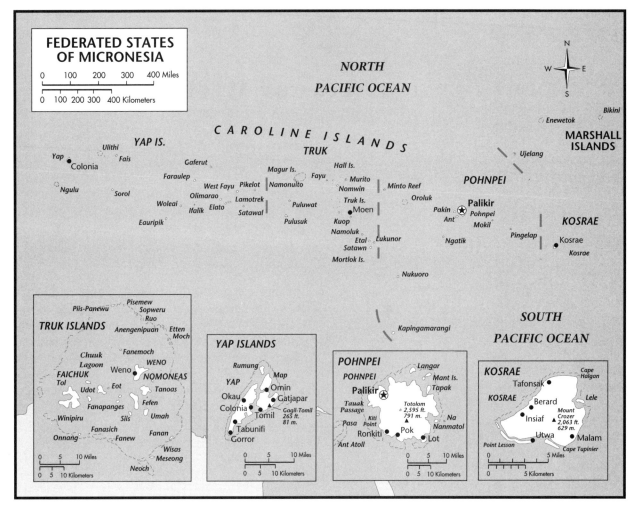

Federated States of Micronesia

by the sea. The sea and maritime themes associated with fishing and voyaging are employed as symbols of a pan-Micronesian identity. Island food and the land on which it is grown also figure prominently in discourse on national identity. Even so, gatherings of ethnically distinct Micronesians during national events feature performances and associated symbolism that highlight the rich cultural diversity of the nation. Dance forms are highly regionalized, often expressing the unique cultural histories of the performers. Images employed in paintings, decorations, and publications often emphasize the cultural heritage of individual states.

HISTORY AND ETHNIC RELATIONS

Emergence of the Nation. At the end of World War II, the United States assumed control over Micronesia. Prior to this time the islands were governed successively by Spain, Germany, and Japan. In 1947 the entire region became known as the

United Nations Trust Territory of the Pacific Islands (TTPI), a geopolitical entity administered entirely by the United States. The establishment of the Congress of Micronesia in 1964 was the first sign of the Micronesian movement towards autonomy. Dissatisfaction with the TTPI administration's inadequate development strategies and their own lack of control over economic planning compelled members of the congress to press for self-government. Micronesia's strategic location at the threshold of the Asian mainland gave the islanders leverage in their negotiations with the United States, which began in 1969.

A draft constitution for the FSM was crafted by delegates from each of the TTPI districts during the constitutional convention of 1975. The hope was to forge a national identity and unite all districts under a single, constitutional federation. The relatively greater U.S. military interests in the Marshall Islands, Northern Marianas, and Palau, however, provided leaders of these districts with the incentive to pursue separate negotiations. In a referendum held in 1978, the voters from the remaining four central districts (Yap, Chuuk, Pohnpei, and Kosrae) approved the constitution and became the FSM. The new government formally commenced operations in 1979, yet remained under the authority of the United States until 1986 when the Compact of Free Association took effect. The United Nations welcomed the FSM as a sovereign nation in 1991.

National Identity. The creation of a national identity has not been easy considering the differences between island sociocultural practices, languages, and resources. The continuing importance of the FSM's economic and political relationship with the United States and other foreign powers, however, has contributed to the emergence of a national identity. The identification of FSM's citizenry as a nation is largely a response to the economic and political dependency fostered by the United States. This supralocal identity is of recent origin and rarely supersedes the importance of local communities in day-to-day activities. Citizens of the FSM value their identity as members of distinct ethnic groups with diverse cultural traditions and values. This sense of ''unity in diversity'' is embedded in the preamble to the FSM constitution: ''To make one nation of many islands, we respect the diversity of our cultures. Our differences enrich us. The seas bring us together, they do not separate us. Our islands sustain us, our island nation enlarges us and makes us stronger.''

Ethnic Relations. Numerous ethnic groups are gathered within the FSM. Although these groups have, at times, assumed a pan-Micronesian identity when dealing with external powers, individuals maintain strong ethnic affiliations and a diversity of interests. The high degree of circular migration brings diverse cultures together and often contributes to the reification of ethnic identities. Ethnic differences are often at the heart of political contention between the states and also contribute to local disputes. Even so, other distinctions, including village, class, kinship, and religious affiliation, often take precedence over ethnicity in defining islander identity.

URBANISM, ARCHITECTURE, AND THE USE OF SPACE

Architecture in the FSM is a mixture of indigenous designs, colonial influences, and Western models. Open-sided houses made of wooden posts with thatch roofs and earthen floors have largely been replaced by homes made of cement block or poured concrete with corrugated steel roofs. In the urban centers, many homes feature modern kitchens, bathrooms, separate bedrooms, and driveways for automobiles. In rural areas, separate cook-, bath-, and boathouses are still the norm, but Western building materials are increasingly used in construction. Traditional feast houses and meetinghouses are still important places for social interaction in many rural communities, although churches are often the most prominent buildings.

The use of space is related to the relative importance of subsistence production in island communities. Urban residents who rely on the cash economy are settled in close proximity to government offices and places of employment. They generally own little arable land, though they often tend small gardens on house plots. Rural villages on high islands are located within a short distance of both the sea and extensive family gardens devoted to taro, yam, sweet potato, or cassava cultivation. Communities on the coral atolls are usually concentrated along the leeward shoreline of lagoons, not far from more centrally located taro pits, providing protection from storms and access to both marine and terrestrial resources.

FOOD AND ECONOMY

Food in Daily Life. The social and symbolic significance of food is one of the most salient aspects of life in Micronesia. Sharing food is an expression of solidarity that validates kinship ties and defines a host of rights, duties, and obligations between people. Meals usually consist of a starchy carbohydrate, and fish or chicken, and may include a variety of fruits. Taro, breadfruit, yams, sweet potatoes, and cassava are the primary starches. Meat, usually fish, is also considered to be an essential part of Micronesian meals. Hundreds of edible fish species are available to fishers in addition to an abundance of marine turtles, shellfish, and crustaceans. Locally-raised livestock, including chicken and pigs, is usually reserved for feasting. Fruits accompany mealtime, and are casually eaten throughout the day, or are incorporated into recipes; fruits include coconut, banana, papaya, pandanus, mango, and a variety of citrus.

Production and consumption of locally harvested produce has diminished throughout the FSM as a result of an increasing reliance on the cash economy and imported foods. Today, boiled rice, fried or baked bread, pancakes, and ramen noodles

Maritime and voyaging themes are major cultural symbols in Micronesia; the sea is viewed as joining the islands together, rather than separating them.

often constitute the starch component of meals. Canned meats have made similar inroads, but atoll residents and rural high-islanders still rely heavily on subsistence fishing.

Food Customs at Ceremonial Occasions. Food is the focal point of most ceremonial occasions. Feasts involving the distribution of enormous quantities of food are integral to religious ceremonies, government celebrations, and secular parties marking life-cycle events and changes in status. The distribution of food takes place in accordance with culture-specific rules of hierarchy and etiquette, and is often a sign of the host's wealth and generosity. Certain foods assume a special status during feasts and are considered essential. In Pohnpei, for example, pigs, yams, and *sakau* (a beverage, with psychoactive properties, made from *piper methisticum* root) are the most prestigious foods featured during feasts. Elsewhere, taro, sugarcane, and coconuts figure prominently. Although subsistence produce and "traditional" recipes are highlighted during feasts, foreign food imports are gaining currency as markers of wealth among those participating more fully in the market economy.

Basic Economy. The cash economy is almost entirely dependent on the flow of funds from the United States. Since 1986, the nation has received roughly $100 million per year from the United States in Compact of Free Association funds and supplementary grants. Sixty percent of compact disbursements support administrative costs of the government including salaries and benefits, and 40 percent are funneled into infrastructure projects and economic development. Thus, the FSM's public sector drives the cash economy and supports the small, service-oriented private sphere. The subsistence economy is based on small-scale horticulture, fishing, and the exploitation of resources in kin-based island territories. Participation in these two spheres of the economy is not mutually exclusive and many subsistence farmers and fishers move in and out of the cash economy. Remittances from family members participating in the cash economy also supplement the income of households primarily engaged in subsistence production. The prestige economy, based on indigenous forms of status, reciprocity, and exchange, intersects these two dimensions of the economy.

Land Tenure and Property. On the small islands in the FSM, land is scarce. Complex, diverse, and often competing tenure systems governing ownership and access rights to the precious land have developed throughout the islands. Many of these systems include aboriginal and postcolonial elements. On most islands access to land may depend upon membership in a lineage or clan. With the exception of Yap and a few atolls in the state of Pohnpei where patrilineal affiliation governed inheritance of land rights, matrilineages traditionally controlled estates in Micronesia. These estates were often subject to chiefly authority and control. In most cases, the oldest male member of the matrilineage managed the estate. After a century of colonial rule, systems of land tenure followed the path away from corporate, descent group ownership toward individualization of tenure. Furthermore, the nuclearization of the family and greater individual self-interest accompanying Westernization are weakening systems of land tenure based on lineage affiliation.

Commercial Activities. Commercial production, conducted on a very small scale in the FSM, is centered on subsistence produce. Fresh fruits, vegetables, and fish are sold in roadside markets throughout the region. The commercial sale of merchandise and food imports is the mainstay of the many mom-and-pop shops scattered across the islands and the larger retailers and wholesalers. Handicrafts made from local materials are also sold on a limited scale to tourists.

Major Industries. The FSM economy suffers from the impoverished state of the industrial sector. There are only two small garment factories in the entire nation. The agricultural industry is limited by the high costs of transshipment and a shortage of arable land. Fishing is the most successful and potentially lucrative industry in the FSM. The nation's exclusive economic zone (EEZ) contains 2.5 million square miles (6.5 million square kilometers) of ocean and vast schools of tuna. To date, local fishing companies and joint ventures have had limited success, but the sale of fishing licenses and access rights to the EEZ account for over half of the nation's internal revenue. Tourism attracts more than 20,000 visitors a year, but occupancy rates average only 30 percent throughout the FSM. Lack of infrastructure, inadequate hotel facilities, and limited air transportation hamper the development of a mass tourist market.

Trade. Import dependence is high in the FSM, and the trade balance deficit is equivalent to roughly 60 percent of gross domestic product (GDP). The export sector of the economy is small, averaging 5 percent of the GDP. Niche agricultural produce, including gourmet pepper, *sakau* (kava), betel nut, and citrus fruit, is exported in limited quantities. Copra (dried coconut flesh), once the region's main export, is now produced in limited supplies due to falling prices and competing markets. Marine products account for approximately 80 percent of the nation's commodity export market. Tuna, the principal marine export, is shipped to Japan, Guam, Taiwan, Korea, and the United States.

Division of Labor. Education is one of the principal bases upon which the division of labor in the cash economy is built. Employees of the state and federal governments are typically high school graduates and many hold postsecondary degrees. Mastery of the English language is another trait of salaried workers in the government sector. Among participants in the subsistence economy, labor is primarily divided on the basis of gender. Age and ability also influence the assignment of tasks. Children begin performing domestic chores at an early age, assisting in child care and other gender-specific work. In addition, experts with specialized knowledge may perform specific tasks related to healing, building, or divining.

SOCIAL STRATIFICATION

Classes and Castes. Social hierarchies in the Caroline Islands are a complex amalgam of indigenous ranking systems and income-centered socioeconomic stratification. Traditional ranking systems across the islands are diverse, but the greatest differences in status are typically found on the high islands where status is primarily determined by descent group affiliation, seniority, and the relationship between people and the land. Age, gender, achievement, and specialized knowledge, in addition to kinship affiliation and land claims, are typically important for determining status on the more egalitarian coral atolls. Achievement in the market economy, however, constitutes another dimension of stratification in the FSM that has, in some instances, eroded indigenous status distinctions.

Symbols of Social Stratification. Traditional hierarchies and income-based class distinctions are evident in behavior, language, and consumption practices. High ranking, in genealogy, age, or title, is acknowledged by acts of deference and displays of respect by those of lower rank. Respected elders or title holders may receive the first share of food at a feast, or may be seated in an honored position. Traditional stratification may be marked by the use of a special honorific language reserved for people of high title, the observance of taboos and ritual proscriptions, or displays of generosity that accom-

Men gather for a meeting outside the men's house, a community building where men eat, sleep, and store their canoes. Meetinghouses and feast houses are important places for social interaction among Micronesians.

pany feasts. The accumulation of goods and conspicuous consumption, hallmarks of income-based class distinctions, is growing in importance among participants in the market economy. Automobiles, appliances, food imports, and Western-style houses and dress have become symbols of economic success throughout the FSM.

POLITICAL LIFE

Government. The structure of the FSM's national government is modeled on U.S. political institutions. The president, head of the executive branch, is elected to a four-year term by the National Congress from among its members. The unicameral National Congress constitutes the legislative branch of the government and is composed of fourteen senators. The Supreme Court, consisting of trial and appellate divisions, is headed by a chief justice and no more than five associate justices appointed for life by the president with the advice and consent of the National Congress. Each of the four state governments includes executive, legislative, and judicial branches, while municipalities within each state govern at the village level.

Leadership and Political Officials. There are no political parties in the FSM. Elected officials repre-

sent a great diversity of cultures and interests. The tendency of leaders to vote in the interests of their state's constituents has, at times, hampered consensus and fostered a sense of disunity. Leadership on the national, state, and municipal levels is interwoven with a strong attachment to traditional forms of local leadership. Today, there is some crossover between traditional leadership and elective office. For example, two councils of chiefs constitute a fourth branch of the Yap State government. In Chuuk and Pohnpei many district magistrates also hold titles based on descent, and elected officials often have genealogical ties to traditional leaders.

Social Problems and Control. The structure of courts in the FSM is patterned after the judicial system of the United States with federal trial and appellate divisions and state supreme and district courts. Law enforcement is handled by both municipal and state police officers. Despite the existence of formal legal mechanisms, crime is often handled by local communities in accordance with customary practice. Societies throughout the FSM feature a variety of formal and informal social control mechanisms. Formal control may be conducted by a council of elders or persons of chiefly status who mediate between parties and levy fines. Informal control stems from the avoidance of actions that cause shame and embarrassment and the need to maintain one's personal and family status through honorable and respectful behavior. A sense of corporate responsibility among kin, coupled with the interdependence of island societies, curbs disruptive behaviors.

The most pressing social problems in the FSM are related to the sociocultural transformations occurring as a result of Westernization. The high rate of suicide among young males is related to the erosion of traditional authority, the declining significance of the extended family, and the displacement of young men seeking education and employment away from home communities. These factors, coupled with alcohol consumption and the lack of clearly defined roles, also contribute to the high frequency of youth violence and delinquency. Alcoholism and the declining influence of extended kin on nuclear family relationships appear to be factors in the increasing incidence of physical and sexual domestic abuse.

Military Activity. Under the provisions of the Compact of Free Association between the FSM and the United States, the United States is granted full authority and responsibility for the nation's security and defense. The FSM is obligated by the ''Military Use and Operating Rights Agreement'' to provide specified locations for the establishment of U.S. military sites.

SOCIAL WELFARE AND CHANGE PROGRAMS

The FSM has a generous system of social welfare. Health services are provided and medications dispensed for a nominal fee to all citizens. The government absorbs most costs, including the high cost of overseas referrals. Grants from the U.S. Department of Health and Human Services cover the cost of many immunization and disease prevention programs. Education is compulsory through eighth grade and is freely provided through twelfth grade. Free public education is made possible through direct U.S. financial assistance, grants from the U.S. Department of Education, and compact funds that also provide scholarships for college study in the United States. The nation also operates a social security system that provides monthly income to retirees.

NONGOVERNMENTAL ORGANIZATIONS AND OTHER ASSOCIATIONS

Activity of NGOs in the FSM is curtailed by the strong financial presence of the United States and its supporting agencies. Millions of dollars in grants are funneled into the FSM by a host of U.S. bureaucracies including the Departments of Agriculture, Education, Interior, Health and Human Services, and Labor. Relief from typhoons, droughts, landslides, and other natural disasters is provided by the Federal Emergency Management Agency.

GENDER ROLES AND STATUSES

Division of Labor by Gender. Among those who participate in the subsistence economy, gender is a major organizing principle in the division of labor. Women are the primary child-care providers and gardeners. They are responsible for many domestic chores including meal preparation and laundry. Women also harvest subsistence produce, weave mats, tend livestock, glean shellfish, and fish inshore. Men are the primary builders and carpenters. They do much of the heavy labor associated with subsistence horticulture and conduct the more dangerous fishing activities beyond the reef. High status positions in religious and traditional political hierarchies are primarily held by men, although women's church organizations provide a separate system of ranking among the women in some societies.

Participation in the market economy has blurred the strict demarcation of gender roles associated with subsistence production. Across the FSM, 52 percent of females 15 years of age and older participate in the cash economy compared to 66 percent of males. Men still hold the higher status jobs in government, but the increasing frequency of female employment in the labor force often requires men to perform domestic tasks traditionally performed by women.

The Relative Status of Women and Men. With the exception of Yap and a few coral atoll societies in Pohnpei, Micronesian societies emphasize matrilineal descent. Women, therefore, are the channels through which identity, titles, land rights, and property are acquired. This provides women with a level of status that is not found in more patriarchal societies, allowing women to exercise considerable influence over the conduct of domestic affairs, and even the allocation of use rights to land. Men typically control the political and economic affairs in the public sphere and have ultimate authority over domestic decisions, but the complementarity of tasks provides males and females with valued roles in society. The shift towards a market-oriented economy, however, has unsettled traditional gender relations. In many societies, the patrilineal emphasis of Western cultures is eroding matrilineal inheri-

A paved road in the coastal village of Kolonia, Pohnpei. Pohnpei is the main island in Micronesia.

tance practices, while greater female participation in the cash economy is challenging male roles and diminishing the complementarity of tasks performed by males and females.

MARRIAGE, FAMILY, AND KINSHIP

Marriage. Although polygamy was practiced traditionally, monogamy has been the norm since the arrival of Christianity in the mid-1800s. Marriages in many parts of the FSM are still arranged by families with the consent of prospective spouses. Marriage unions that create family alliances and concentrate land, wealth, and status, such as preferential cross-cousin marriage, are favored in many Micronesian societies. Clan exogamy is still a very important marriage requirement. A large majority of marriages take place under the auspices of Christian churches, but they are often preceded by common-law unions in which couples co-reside. Formal marriages typically involve the exchange of gifts between the spouses' families and feasting to mark the occasion, and may involve the transfer of land between families. Divorce can be initiated by either spouse, but it is less commonly practiced among couples with children.

Domestic Unit. Households are often composed of extended kin. On average, extended kin account for

18 percent of household membership. This is down from 30 percent in the 1970s, indicating a clear trend towards the nuclearization of the domestic group. Household composition is dependent on a variety of postmarital residence patterns. Where patrilocality is the norm (Pohnpei, Yap), the household may consist of a joint family of brothers, their wives, and children, or a stem family that includes multiple generations of father-son ties. Conversely, matrilocal residence (favored in Chuuk and Yap's outer islands) establishes a household composed of related women and in-marrying husbands. Neolocal residence, which encourages the creation of nuclear families, is gaining popularity due to Westernization and the influence of the market economy.

Inheritance. Customs governing the inheritance of land, corporeal property, and certain skills or lore are complicated by the rapid pace of Westernization. In general, individually owned corporeal property may be disposed of in accordance with the owner's wishes and is usually passed to children or siblings. Specialized knowledge may be owned by descent groups, but it is commonly inherited by children of the possessors who are deemed to be competent and adept students. Land is another issue. Where land is owned by a corporate descent group, usufruct rights are inherited either matrilineally or patrilineally upon birth or adoption into a lineage. Lifelong use rights to specific plots of land may be divided by the male lineage head among his sons (patrilineal) or sister's sons (matrilineal). As Western concepts of ownership and formal inheritance codes become more entrenched, individual ownership of land is becoming increasingly common. Heirship disputes between those claiming individual ownership and those claiming usufruct rights through descent are not uncommon given the competing forms of ownership. Formal legal codes and courts often handle these disputes and govern the disposal of property in cases of intestate succession.

Kin Groups. Kinship in Micronesia extends far beyond the confines of the domestic unit. Systems of descent vary considerably between and within states. On the main island of Yap, people have affiliations with both a localized, patrilineal land estate and a geographically dispersed matrilineal clan. Chuukese and outer islanders of Yap are organized into matrilineal lineages and clans that share rights to land. Matrilineal clans are also found on Pohnpei where their influence has diminished as a result of acculturation. In Kosrae, descent is reckoned bilaterally, creating ego-focused kindreds. Though built on principles of descent, these extended kinship ties are validated and legitimized by performance, including the sharing of land, food, and resources.

SOCIALIZATION

Infant Care. Children are highly valued in the FSM. They are considered to be a family's source of wealth and insurance for parents in old age. For this reason, parents create a nurturing environment and indulge infant needs. Although mothers are the primary caregivers, fathers and older siblings also tend to infants. They also receive a great deal of attention from extended kin and neighbors. Because of the importance of interaction in small island communities, infants are carried facing outwards, away from the holder. Infants typically nurse on demand and may be breast-fed for a number of years. Cosleeping with parents is the norm.

Child Rearing and Education. The transmission of cultural values and expectations begins early in the socialization of children. Children are taught to be cooperative, generous, sharing, and respectful. Discipline, in the form of shaming and ridicule, is often administered by family members and the community at large, but corporal punishment is the prerogative of parents. Education of children involves a combination of formal schooling and informal acquisition of gender-related knowledge and skills. In the past, the transmission of lore and skills was an important aspect of growing up in a subsistence household. Today, formal education is mandatory and most children attend grade school between the ages of five and fourteen.

Higher Education. Greater participation in the market economy places a premium on higher education in the FSM. More and more families are sending children to high school and college with the hopes of providing them greater access to employment. Since the 1980s, the percentage of citizens over 25 years of age with education beyond grade school has increased from 25 to 47 percent. High school enrollment is near 70 percent of both males and females between the ages of 14 and 17. College enrollment lags far behind elementary and high school rates. Only 27 percent of males and females between the ages of 18 and 21 attend college. Most of these students are enrolled at branch campuses of the College of Micronesia, while a limited number receive scholarships to study at colleges in the United States.

ETIQUETTE

Rules of etiquette among Micronesians focus on displays of respect related to kinship, gender, age, political rank, and religious title. Brothers and sisters should avoid one another in public and refrain from telling bawdy jokes or making sexual remarks in each other's presence. Among matrilineal societies, respect for one's mother's brother is marked by the use of polite language and physical avoidance on formal occasions. Women show respect for their husbands by walking behind them in public or serving them first during meals. Although members of the same sex may hold hands as a sign of friendship, public displays of affection between males and females are extremely rare. Further, men and women usually occupy separate social spaces during church services and community gatherings. Older members of society as well as titled persons enjoy an exulted position of respect, and may be given first shares of a feast distribution or special seats during public gatherings.

In addition to demonstrating age, gender, and political status, food etiquette illustrates the importance of generosity in Micronesian cultures. Sharing food with visitors is a must, and hosts take pride in providing sustenance to others. Guests are usually fed first and are expected to eat in moderation. Compliments paid to the host center on the host's generosity and the experience of satiation. In

A man with a small child in front of his house in Kolonia, Pohnpei, Caroline Islands. Fathers and mothers equally tend to children in Micronesian society.

general, Micronesian etiquette reflects the emphasis on harmonious, nonassertive, and respectful behavior. In public, people tend to speak cautiously and avoid confrontation with others. Gossip is an ever-present check on disrespectful or inappropriate public behavior.

RELIGION

Religious Beliefs. Missionization of the region began in the mid-1800s. Prior to the arrival of Christianity, beliefs focused on the activity of ancestral souls, a pantheon of deities, and the numerous spirits, both kind and malevolent, that inhabited the earth, sea, and sky. Today, roughly half of the population is Catholic and half belong to various Protestant sects, most notably the United Church of Christ (Congregational). Although Christianity has largely replaced the traditional animistic systems of belief, elements of pre-Christian belief systems are interwoven with ecclesiastical practice. Many Micronesians still believe in the power of deceased ancestors to influence events and the existence of spirits and spirit possession.

Religious Practitioners. Prior to Christian conversion, island societies relied on a variety of religious specialists to mediate between the natural and supernatural world. The men who held these positions were responsible for a variety of tasks including divination, healing, navigation, weather control, and bringing about propitious events such as victory in battle and abundant harvests. Although specialists with supernatural skills are still employed from time to time, the majority of formal religious practitioners are members of Catholic and Protestant churches. Practitioners in both faiths are ordained by the formal ecclesiastical organizations. Protestant churches feature a hierarchy of religious titles for which members of each congregation compete.

Rituals and Holy Places. The ritual cycle of Christian churches dominates the organization of community activity in many parts of Micronesia. Elements of traditional culture, such as competitive feasting and the harvest of first fruits, have been incorporated into church calendars. People can be found preparing for, or celebrating, a church-related event almost every day. Churches are the primary holy places and are often the most conspicuous buildings in Micronesian communities. Even so, many places associated with legendary or historical events are considered sacred. Such sites may have an inherent power relating to the past, or may be the abode of spirits.

Death and the Afterlife. Death is an occasion for great feasting in all island societies of the FSM. Each culture has specific mourning rites and observances that are integrated with Christian beliefs and rituals. In general, the first feast, associated with intense mourning and the burial itself, lasts between three and four days. The body is usually interred on ancestral land or in the church cemetery. On some islands, formal mourning among close kin and friends may continue for a number of months. At the end of this period another feast may be held by the immediate family to recognize the assistance of those who observed the mourning rites. Death anniversaries are commonly celebrated and may involve community-wide feasts or small family gatherings. The rich diversity of indigenous beliefs concerning the afterlife have largely been replaced by the Christian emphasis on heaven and hell. Even so, many believe in the ability of ancestral spirits to influence events and intercede on behalf of kin.

MEDICINE AND HEALTH CARE

In the past, island medical practice was intimately related to religious beliefs. Illness could result from the transgression of taboos, unprovoked spirit attack, or the loss of the soul, or be due to the malevolent work of sorcerers. Depending on the etiology of the illness, treatment by specialists could involve the use of herbal remedies with supernatural powers, massage, or spiritual mediation between human and supernatural domains.

Today, Micronesians rely on Western biomedicine in concert with indigenous remedies. Health care is subsidized by the government and provided to citizens for a nominal fee. There is a main hospital in each state and numerous dispensaries are scattered throughout the island communities, but the limited number of trained doctors places a heavy burden on existing services. There are approximately 3,500 citizens per doctor in the FSM. Western medicine is considered indispensable for the treatment of the nation's primary health problems including perinatal infection, tuberculosis, skin disease, venereal disease, intestinal parasites, and diseases related to the high consumption of unhealthy imported foods, including diabetes, obesity, and heart disease. Masseurs, midwives, and specialists in herbal remedies, however, are still employed for the treatment of a variety of ailments.

SECULAR CELEBRATIONS

National holidays include New Year's Day (1 January), Constitution Day (10 May), United Nations Day (24 October), and National Day (3 November). Christmas (25 December) is also nationally recognized. In addition to these federal holidays, each state and municipality has its own celebrations. Common among these are dates celebrating the signing of state and municipal constitutions, as well as Liberation Day (11 September), which commemorates the U.S. victory over Japan in WWII.

THE ARTS AND HUMANITIES

Support for the Arts. Arts and literature in the FSM receive very little government or private support. Exhibits of Micronesian art are rare and usually restricted to regional museums and universities. There is a trend, however, towards greater Micronesian participation in Pacific-wide art events, such as the Pacific Festival of Arts, held in various places in the South Pacific, and the Rarotonga Festival of Pacific Arts, held on Rarotonga, Cook Islands.

Literature. Oral literature occupies a special place among the arts in Micronesian societies. Stories told and retold through generations transmit historical understandings, specialized knowledge, and the mores of society. Besides the work of foreign scholars, a number of Micronesians have recorded indigenous histories, myths, and folklore. In addition, regional publications commonly feature indigenous poets and writers.

Graphic Arts. Many of the skills required for the production of indigenous graphic art in the FSM have been lost. Canoe carving, once a highly evolved and valued art form, is largely forgotten among the young men who prefer to fish from fiberglass outboard motorboats. Western models have largely replaced indigenous architectural detailing and design. Tattooing was abandoned as a form of artistic expression in the postcontact era. Many of the more elaborate textiles are no longer produced, although women still fashion a large variety of woven and plaited goods. The Kapingamarangi in Pohnpei and the Chuukese also produce finely carved wooden crafts, mostly for sale to tourists.

Performance Arts. Both music and dance are very important modes of expression in Micronesian societies and often serve to transmit islander identity and commemorate history. Forms of musical expression vary from pre-Christian chants to popular genres such as reggae, hip-hop, and pop. Choral hymns sung in four-part harmony by church choirs are commonly performed during secular and church-related events. Indigenous chants and songs featuring complex rhythms, harmony, and metaphorical language in conjunction with various dance movements are often favored ways of expressing cultural affiliation during public celebrations.

THE STATE OF THE PHYSICAL AND SOCIAL SCIENCES

Research conducted in the FSM is typically research on the FSM, funded by U.S. and foreign granting agencies. Three major scientific investigations involving more than 30 researchers were funded during the U.S. Naval Administration's tenure. Since that time hordes of foreign researchers, primarily from the United States, have descended on the islands. Regional physical and social science programs within the FSM are limited by inadequate financial support. The College of Micronesia, the only university in the nation, does not support extensive research programs. College-educated Micronesians often take their talents elsewhere, contributing to what has been called the region's "brain drain."

BIBLIOGRAPHY

Alkire, William H. *An Introduction to the Peoples and Cultures of Micronesia*, 1977.

Bernart, Luelen. *The Book of Luelen*, 1977.

Demmke, Andreas, et. al. *Federated States of Micronesia Population Profile: A Guide for Planners and Policy-Makers*, 1997.

Falgout, Suzanne. "Americans in Paradise: Custom, Democracy, and Anthropology in Postwar Micronesia." *Ethnology* 34 (2): 99–111, 1995.

Federated States of Micronesia. *Statistical Yearbook*, 1999.

Fischer, John L., and Ann M. Fischer. *The Eastern Carolines*, 1970.

Flinn, Juliana. *Diplomas and Thatch Houses: Asserting Tradition in a Changing Micronesia*, 1992.

Goodenough, Ward H. *Property, Kin, and Community on Truk*, 1951.

Hanlon, David. *Upon a Stone Altar: A History of the Islands of Pohnpei to 1890*, 1988.

———. *Remaking Micronesia: Discourses over Development in a Pacific Territory, 1944–1982*, 1998.

Hezel, Francis X. *Reflections on Micronesia*, 1982.

———. *The First Taint of Civilization: A History of the Caroline and Marshall Islands in Pre-Colonial Days, 1521–1885*, 1983.

———. *Strangers in Their Own Land: A Century of Colonial Rule in the Caroline and Marshall Islands*, 1995.

Hezel, Francis X., and M. Levin. "Micronesian Emigration: Beyond the Brain Drain." In J. Connell, ed., *Migration and Development in the South Pacific*, 1990.

International Monetary Fund Economic Reviews. Marshall Islands and Federated States of Micronesia, 1995.

Keating, Elizabeth. *Power Sharing: Language, Rank, Gender, and Social Space in Pohnpei, Micronesia*, 1998.

Kiste, Robert C., and Mac Marshall, eds. *American Anthropology in Micronesia: An Assessment*, 1999.

Labby, David. *The Demystification of Yap: Dialectics of Culture on a Micronesian Island*, 1976.

Lessa, William A. *Ulithi: A Micronesian Design for Living*, 1966.

Lingenfelter, Sherwood Galen. *Yap: Political Leadership and Culture Change in an Island Society*, 1975.

Lutz, Catherine, ed. *Micronesia as Strategic Colony: The Impact of U.S. Policy on Micronesia Health and Culture*, 1984.

———. *Unnatural Emotions: Everyday Sentiments on a Micronesian Atoll and Their Challenge to Western Theory*, 1988.

Marshall, Mac. *Weekend Warriors: Alcohol in a Micronesian Culture*, 1979.

Meller, Norman. *Constitutionalism in Micronesia*, 1985.

Peoples, James G. *Islands in Trust: Culture Change and Dependence in a Micronesian Economy*, 1985.

Perin, Dan. *Economic Use of Land in the FSM: A Review and Description of Land Tenure Systems in the FSM*, 1996.

Petersen, Glenn. *One Man Cannot Rule a Thousand: Fission in a Pohnpeian Chiefdom*, 1982.

———. "A Micronesian Chamber of Chiefs? The 1990 Federated States of Micronesia Constitutional Convention." In G. M. White and L. Lindstrom, eds., *Chiefs Today: Traditional Pacific Leadership and the Postcolonial State*, 1997.

Pinsker, Eve C. "Point of Order, Point of Change: Nation, Culture, and Community in the Federated States of Micronesia." Ph.D. dissertation, University of Chicago, 1997.

——— "Traditional Leaders Today in the Federated States of Micronesia." In G. M. White and L. Lindstrom, eds., *Chiefs Today: Traditional Pacific Leadership and the Postcolonial State*, 1997.

Poyer, Lin. *The Ngatik Massacre: History and Identity on a Micronesian Atoll*, 1993.

Rubenstein, Donald H. "Suicide in Micronesia." In F. X. Hezel, D. H. Rubenstein, and G. M. White, eds., *Culture, Youth, and Suicide in the Pacific: Papers from an East-West Center Conference*, 1985.

Ushijima, Iwao, and Ken-ichi Sudo, eds., *Cultural Uniformity and Diversity in Micronesia*, 1987.

Ward, Martha C. *Nest in the Wind: Adventures in Anthropology on a Tropical Island*, 1989.

—BRYAN P. OLES

MOLDOVA

CULTURE NAME

Moldovan

ALTERNATIVE NAMES

Moldavian, Romanian, Bessarabian. Moldavia is the Anglicized version of the Russian *Moldavija* and is not used by Moldovans. Many Moldovans consider themselves, their culture, and their language Romanian. Moldovans/Romanians in the region between the rivers Prut and Dniestr sometimes call themselves Bessarabians.

ORIENTATION

Identification. The principality of Moldova was founded around 1352 by the Transylvanian ruler (*voievod*) Dragoş in what today is the Romanian region of Bucovina. According to one legend, Dragoş successfully hunted a wild ox on the banks of the river Moldova and then chose to stay in the land, which he named after the river. The name "Moldova" probably derives from the German *Mulde*, "a deep river valley with high banks."

Location and Geography. The Republic of Moldova is a landlocked country between Romania and Ukraine that covers 13,199 square miles (33,845 square kilometers). It includes the Gagauz Autonomous Region in the south and the disputed Transdniestrian region in the east. The latter region separated from Moldova in 1991–1992 but did not gain official recognition. The capital, Chişinău, is in the center of the country and has 740,000 inhabitants. Chişinău was first mentioned in 1436 and was the capital of the Russian province of Bessarabia in the nineteenth century.

Moldova is on a fertile plain with small areas of hill country in the center and north. Only 9 percent of its territory is covered by forest, mostly in the middle. In the northern part, fertile black soil prevails and the primary crop is sugar beet. In the central and southern zones, wine making and tobacco growing are widespread. The temperate continental climate in the center of the country, with long warm summers, relatively mild winters, and high rainfall, is favorable for agriculture. The semiarid Budjak steppe in the south has drought problems. The main rivers are the Dniestr in the east and the Prut in the west. Both originate in the Carpathians; whereas the Dniestr flows directly into the Black Sea, the Prut joins the Danube at the southern tip of the country.

Demography. Moldova has 4.32 million inhabitants. In the 1989 census, 64.5 percent of the population was Moldovan, 13.8 percent Ukrainian, 13 percent Russian, 3.5 percent Gagauz (a Christian Orthodox Turkic people), 2 percent Bulgarian, 1.5 percent Jewish, and 1.7 percent other nationalities, mainly Belarussians, Poles, Greeks, Germans, and Rom (Gypsies). Although the official number of Rom is only 11,600, the real number probably is 100,000. There are few concentrated Rom settlements in Moldova, and the degree of linguistic assimilation (Russian or Moldovan) is high. The Ukrainian population traditionally settled in the north and east. Gagauz and Bulgarians have concentrated settlements in the southern Budjak region. The Russian population, for the most part workers and professionals brought to Moldova after World War II, is concentrated in Chişinău, Bălţi, and the industrial zones of Transdniestria. Jews have lived in Moldovan cities in great numbers since the early nineteenth century, but many have left. Between 1990 and 1996, Moldova experienced a total migration loss of 105,000 persons. Jews, Ukrainians, and Russians were the most likely to leave. Consequently, the Moldovan portion of the population was believed to have increased to 67 percent by 1998. The population density is the highest in the territory of the former Soviet Union.

Linguistic Affiliation. As a written language, Moldovan is classified as being Romanian, a Daco-

MOLDOVA

0   30   60 Miles

0   30   60 Kilometers

Mohyliv Podol's'kyy

Tul'chyn

Briceni

UKRAINE

Soroki

Rāşcani

Floreşti

Rybniţa

Bălţi

Raut

Falesti

Codri

Orhei

Mt. Balanesti
1,407 ft.
429 m.

Dubásari

Ungheni

Chişinău

Hills

Botna

Tiraspol

Cogalnic

Tighina

ROMANIA

Căuseniî

Leova

Steppe

Bacău

Basarabeasca

Comrat

Ialpug

Bugeac

Cahull

Prut

Bilhorod
Dnistrovs'kyy

Galaţi

Mouths
of the
Danube

Moldova

Black
Sea

Moldova

Romanian language in the family of eastern Romance languages. As a subdialect of Daco-Romanian, Moldovan is spoken not only in the Republic of Moldova but in the entire territory of the former principality. It displays dialectical features particular to its geographic region and exhibits influences on its grammar and vocabulary from Russian and Ukrainian, languages with which it has been in contact for centuries. Since the fourteenth century, Moldovan has been the traditional name of the language spoken by the population of this region. Until the early seventeenth century, Church Slavonic was used in official documents, but it was slowly replaced by Moldovan, which was written in Cyrillic at that time. When the principalities of Valachia and Moldova united in 1859, the Latin alphabet was introduced for Romanian. In the eastern part of Moldova, which became the Russian province of Bessarabia in 1812, the language continued to be called Moldovan and the Cyrillic alphabet was used until Bessarabia joined the Romanian kingdom in 1918. After the Soviet annexation of Bessarabia in 1940–1944, the Cyrillic alphabet was reintroduced. Intensive Russification and a policy aimed at showing that Moldovan and Romanian were different languages led to a deterioration in the "purity" of the language spoken by the majority of the population. Russian loan words were used widely, especially in technical fields, and Moldovan became a "kitchen language." Moldovans who were educated in Russian-speaking schools still have difficulty expressing themselves in areas other than daily encounters. Russification and "de-Romanization" were considerably more pronounced in urban than in rural areas, but those policies were resisted by Moldovan intellectuals, who upheld the use of their language. The national awakening that took place in the late 1980s led directly to the adoption of a language law on 30 August 1989 that defined Moldovan, written in the Latin script, as the state language. Although the language is still officially named "Moldovan," considerable re-Romanization has made the difference between Romanian and Moldovan virtually a distinction between a standard written language and a dialect. Cyrillic is used to write Moldovan only in the separatist region of Transdniestria. Ordinary Moldovans on the right bank of the Dniestr, however, may use Cyrillic for private notes or letters, especially if they are 40 to 60 years of age and uneducated. Despite the change of state language, very few non-Moldovan residents are fluent in Moldovan, and many have a negative attitude toward that language. Between 1940 and 1989, Russian was the lingua franca. The introduction of new requirements in 1989 aimed at fostering the use of Moldovan was widely regarded as forceful Romanization and conjured unhappy memories of Romanian rule in Bessarabia. Fears of possible unification with Romania also played a major role. The political battle over the future status of the Moldovan and Russian languages is deeply connected with the conflicts that arose in 1990 between the central government and separatist movements in Gagauzia and Transdniestria. The language issue remains highly politicized, and attitudes toward Moldovan, especially when it is called Romanian, continue to be largely negative among the non-Moldovan population. Moldovans who were born and brought up after 1980 tend to speak less and less Russian, a development that could lead to growing problems of interethnic communication.

Symbolism. The national symbols represent over six hundred years of history as well as a close connection to Romania. The state flag is composed of the traditional Romanian colors of blue, yellow, and red. In the center is the republic's seal, consisting of the Romanian eagle with the historical Moldovan seal on its breast. Since the fourteenth century, the seal has consisted of an ox's head with a star between its horns, a rose to the right, and a crescent to the left. The national anthem was the same as that of Romania in the early years of independence but was changed to "Our Language" (*Limba noastră*), which is also the name of the second most important secular holiday. Its name has a special integrating power in two respects: Language is the most important national symbol for Moldovans, and it evades the answer to the question of how this language should be labeled: Romanian or Moldovan. All these symbols, however, do not appeal to other ethnic groups and thus confine the idea of an "imagined community" to the titular nation.

In regard to the conflict over symbols between "Romanians" and "Moldovans," the ballad *Miorița* plays a crucial role. It tells the story of a Moldovan shepherd who is betrayed and murdered by two Romanian colleagues: For the Romanian side, this story is about an "incident in the family," while for the Moldovan side, it reproduces the distinction between the good, diligent, and peaceful Moldovan and the mean and criminal Romanian. Next to hospitality, diligence and peacefulness are the national characteristics Moldovans associate with themselves. When Moldovans want to show pride in their country, they refer mostly to the qualities of its wine and food and the beauty of its women. Wine is an especially powerful symbol, associated with quality, purity, and healing. The cellars of Cricova with their extensive collection of old wines are considered the state treasure. Moldovans are also eager to underscore their Latin heritage, expressed by the statue of a wolf feeding Romulus and Remus in front of the Museum of National History in Chişinău.

HISTORY AND ETHNIC RELATIONS

Emergence of the Nation. According to official historiography, the Republic of Moldova derives directly from the Moldovan principality that was founded by Dragoş and gained independence from the Hungarian kingdom under the Valachian voievod Bogdan I in 1359. The government thus celebrated the 640th anniversary of statehood in 1999. However, what is today the Republic of Moldova consists only of the central and eastern parts of the original principality. The Transdniestrian region was never part of the principality, but Moldovan colonists settled on the left bank of the Dniestr in the fifteenth century. At the beginning of the fifteenth century, the principality extended from the Carpathians to the Dniestr. Under Stephen the Great (1457–1504), who defended the principality successfully against the Ottoman Empire, Moldova flourished. Many churches and monasteries were built under his regency. Stephen is regarded as the main national hero of contemporary Moldova. His statue stands in the city center of Chişinău, the main boulevard is named for him, and his picture is printed on every banknote. However, soon after Stephen died, Moldova lost its independence and became, like the neighboring principality of Valachia, a vassal state of Constantinople.

In the Treaty of Bucharest of 1812, the Ottoman Empire was forced to cede the area between the Prut and the Dniestr to the Russian Empire under the name Bessarabia. In 1859, western Moldova and Valachia formed the united principality of Romania, which gained independence from the Ottoman Empire in 1878. Thus, the Moldovans in Bessarabia were excluded from the Romanian nation-building process and remained in an underdeveloped, remote, agricultural province of the Russian Empire. Only with the upheavals of the World War I and the October Revolution did the Moldovans of Bessarabia join the Romanian nation-state. The Moldovan parliament, the Sfatul Țării, declared the independence of the "Democratic Republic of Moldova" on 24 January 1918 but then voted for union with Romania on 27 March 1918. The unification was mostly due to the desperate circumstances the young, unstable republic faced and was not applauded by all sections of the population. The following twenty-two years of Romanian rule are considered by many Moldovans and non-Moldovans as a period of colonization and exploitation. The subsequent period of Sovietization and Russification, however, is regarded as the darkest period in the national history. Stalin annexed Bessarabia in June 1940 and again in 1944, when the Soviet Union reconquered the area after temporary Romanian occupation. The northern and southern parts of Bessarabia were transferred to the Ukrainian Soviet Socialist Republic (SSR), and in exchange the western part of what since 1924 had been the Moldovan Autonomous Socialist Republic on the territory of the Ukrainian

SSR was given to the newly created Moldovan Socialist Soviet Republic. Having been ruled by foreign powers since the sixteenth century, Moldova declared its independence on 27 August 1991.

National Identity. After sentiments ran high in favor of unification with Romania at the beginning of the 1990s, the tide turned, and in a 1994 referendum 95 percent of the voters elected to retain independence. As a result of their close historical, linguistic, and cultural ties with Romania, many Moldovans see themselves as Romanian. At the same time, the one hundred eighty years of separation from Romania and the different influences Bessarabia has experienced since the early nineteenth century have preserved and reinforced a distinctive Moldovan identity east of the Prut. Unlike Romanians, a high percentage of Moldovans have an ethnically mixed family background. Consequently, probably less than 5 percent of the people consider themselves to have a pure Romanian identity, whereas another 5 to 10 percent would identify themselves as Moldovan in the sense of being outspokenly non-Romanian. The existence of these two groups is reflected in a fierce debate between "Unionists" and "Moldovanists." Most inhabitants of the titular nation consider their Moldovan identity as their central political one but their Romanian identity as culturally essential. Since discussions on unification with Romania have disappeared from the public agenda, the question of how to form a multi-ethnic nation-state is growing in importance.

Ethnic Relations. Bessarabia has always been a multiethnic region, and ethnic relations generally are considered good. Especially in the north, Moldovans and Ukrainians have lived together peacefully for centuries and share cultural features. In recent history, Moldova has rarely experienced ethnic violence; in April 1903, for example, 49 Jews were killed and several hundred injured during the Chişinău pogrom, but mainly by Russians rather than Moldovans. In the late 1980s, when support for the national movement began to grow, ethnic tension between Moldovans and non-Moldovans increased, initially in Transdniestria and Gagauzia and later in Chişinău and Bălţi. Whereas the conflict between Gagauz and Moldovans was kept below the level of large-scale violence, the Transdniestrian conflict escalated into a full-fledged civil war in spring 1992. More than a thousand people were said to have been killed, and over a hundred thousand had to leave their homes. Although this conflict had a strong ethnic component, it was not ethnic by nature; it was fought mainly between the new independence-minded political elite in Chişinău and conservative pro-Soviet forces in Tiraspol. Moldovans and non-Moldovans could be found on both sides. On the right bank of the Dniestr, where the majority of the Russian-speaking community lives, no violent clashes took place. Since the war, additional efforts have been made to include non-Moldovans in the nation-building process. The 1994 constitution and subsequent legislation safeguarded the rights of minorities, and in the same year broad autonomous powers were granted to the Gagauz.

URBANISM, ARCHITECTURE, AND THE USE OF SPACE

Chişinău's city center was constructed in the nineteenth century by Russians. Official buildings and those erected by the early bourgeoisie are in a neoclassical style of architecture; there are also many small one-story houses in the center, and the outskirts are dominated by typical Soviet-style residential buildings. Small towns (mainly enlarged villages) also have examples of Soviet-style administration buildings and apartment blocks. Depending on their original inhabitants, villages have typical Moldovan, Ukrainian, Gagauz, Bulgarian, or German houses and a Soviet-style infrastructure (cultural center, school, local council buildings). Houses have their own gardens and usually their own vineyards and are surrounded by low metal ornamented bars. Interaction differs in urban and rural areas. In the villages, people are open and greet passersby without prior acquaintance; in the cities, there is a greater anonymity, although people interact with strangers in certain situations, for example, on public transportation.

FOOD AND ECONOMY

Food in Daily Life. *Mamaliga*, a hard corn porridge, is regarded as the national dish. It is poured onto a flat surface in the shape of a big cake and is served mainly with cheese, sour cream, or milk. Non-Moldovan inhabitants joke that Moldovans would be unhappy if they could not eat mamaliga once a week. The main foods in daily life are a mixture of vegetables and meat (chicken, goose, duck, pork, and lamb), but the availability of vegetables depends on the season. Filled cabbage and grape leaves as well as soups such as *zama* and the Russian *borsch* also form part of daily meals. *Plăcintă* is a pastry filled mainly with cheese, potatoes, or cabbage that often is sold on the streets.

Buildings and a church line a street in Chisinau. The city architecture was mostly constructed by the Russians in the nineteenth century.

Restaurants in Chişinău offer Russian, Moldovan, and Jewish dishes along with an increasingly international cuisine.

Food Customs at Ceremonial Occasions. Orthodox Christian baptisms, funerals, and weddings are accompanied by large gatherings where several meat and vegetable dishes, desserts, and cakes as well as wine are served. Homemade vodka and brandy also are offered. At Easter, a special bread, *pasca*, is baked in every household, and eggs are painted in various colors. Families go to the graveyard to celebrate their dead kin; they eat food at the graves while drinking wine and offering it to each other as they remember the dead.

Basic Economy. The national currency is the *leu* (100 *bani*). Besides gypsum and very small gas and oil reserves, the country has no natural resources and is totally dependent on energy imports, mainly from Russia. Moldova has experienced a sharp downturn in its economy in the last ten years. In 1998, the gross domestic product (GDP) was 35 percent of the 1989 level, and the state is unable to pay pensions and salaries on time. As a result, more people produce food and other necessities for themselves now than in the 1980s. This includes virtu-ally the entire rural population and many city dwellers who own small gardens in the countryside. The parallel economy is estimated to account for 20 to 40 percent of the GDP.

Land Tenure and Property. During the Soviet period, there was no private land, only state-owned collective farms. Since 1990, as part of the transition to a market economy, privatization of land as well as houses and apartments has taken place. However, the process is still under way and has faced fierce resistance from so-called agroindustrial complexes.

Commercial Activities. Moldova in general and Chişinău in particular have many traditional Balkan-style markets. There are mixed as well as specialized markets for food, flowers, spare parts, and construction materials. This ''market economy'' clearly outsells the regular shops. Besides foodstuffs, which are partially home-grown, all products are imported. These types of commercial activities are flourishing because of market liberalization and the economic downturn. Many educated specialists find it easier to earn money through commercial activities than by practicing their professions.

Major Industries. Industry is concentrated in the food-processing sector, wine making, and tobacco. Other fields include electronic equipment, machinery, textiles, and shoes. The small heavy industry sector includes a metallurgical plant in Transdniestria that produces high-quality steel.

Trade. The main trade partners are Russia, Ukraine, Belarus, Romania, and Germany. Russia and other Commonwealth of Independent States (CIS) countries accounted for 69 percent of exports and 58 percent of imports in 1998. Exports are mainly agroindustrial products (72 percent), especially wine, but also include shoes and textiles (12 percent). The main import goods are mineral products (31 percent), machinery and electronic equipment (19 percent), and chemical products (12 percent). To realign foreign trade away from Russia and toward Western European and other countries, Moldova has constructed an oil terminal on the Danube and is seeking closer economic ties with Romania and the European Union. It is expected to join the World Trade Organization.

SOCIAL STRATIFICATION

Classes and Castes. Large landowners (*boyars*) disappeared after the establishment of Soviet power. There is an emergent class of high-ranking officials

A worker supervising bottling at a winery in Chisinau. Wine is a symbolic drink used to honor the host at a meal.

and managers who had access to state enterprises or funds in the Soviet period and appropriated some of those resources during the transitional phase and young entrepreneurs who amassed wealth after the introduction of a market economy through new business ventures. Social stratification is determined mainly by economic and political power. After the breakup of the Soviet Union, those who had higher positions in the government tended to be Moldovans, while Russians dominated the private sector. Urban workers have maintained their rural connections and grow fruit and vegetables on small plots of land in the towns.

Symbols of Social Stratification. Newly built ornamented houses and villas, cars (especially Western cars with tinted windows), cellular telephones, and fashionable clothes are the most distinguishing symbols of wealth. Consumer goods brought from abroad (Turkey, Romania, Germany) function as status symbols in cities and rural areas.

POLITICAL LIFE

Government. Moldova is a democratic and unitary republic. Since the territorial-administrative reform of 1999, it has been divided into ten districts (*judeţe*) and the Autonomous Territorial Unit of Gagauzia. A special status is envisaged for the Transdniestrian region. The political system is mixed parliamentary-presidential, with the parliament (one hundred one representatives) and president both directly elected for a four-year period. The prime minister is appointed by the president only after the minister and his or her cabinet have received a vote of confidence from the parliamentary majority. The rights of the president to dissolve the parliament are very restricted. Some executive powers are vested in the president's hands: he or she can issue decrees and has special powers in defense and foreign policy. The delicate balance of power between parliament, government, and president is held to be responsible for the relatively high level of democracy as well as the blocking of important reform projects. Consequently, there have been discussions aimed at strengthening the powers of the president. Judicial powers are vested in the courts.

Leadership and Political Officials. Patrimonial structures and the Orthodox tradition of godfatherhood have strong political implications. Personal networks established over the years help people gain political posts, but such contacts also make them responsible for redistributing resources to the people who have backed them. Although kinship has a certain influence on these personal networks, relationships established in other ways during education and earlier work may be more important.

Today's political forces have their roots either in the Moldovan Communist Party or in the national movement of the 1980s. The national movement started with the creation of the Alexe Mateevici Cultural Club in 1988 as an intellectual opposition group. In less than a year, it evolved into a broad mass movement known as the Popular Front of Moldova. Although the party system has experienced striking fluctuations in the last ten years, the main political forces have in essence remained the same. The Communist Party, whose place was taken temporarily by the Agrarian Democratic Party, is still one of the strongest political players. It has a mixed ethnic background and is backed mainly by the agroindustrial complexes. It is opposed to privatization and other reforms and strongly favors the idea of ''Moldovanism.'' At the opposite end of the political spectrum are the Christian Democratic Popular Front and the Party of Democratic Forces. Both derive directly from the Moldovan national movement and have no former communists in their ranks. The Front favors unification with Romania and advocates liberal market reforms and democratization. The Party of Democratic Forces also favors stronger ties with Romania and the West but has abandoned the idea of unification; it too blends market reforms with social democratic ideas. The former president, Mircea Snegur (1992–1996), a previous Communist Party secretary and the ''father'' of Moldovan independence, has been joined in his Party for Rebirth and Reconciliation by other former communists who switched to the national movement early on. Petru Lucinschi, who was elected president in 1996, held high posts in the Communist Party of the Soviet Union and has extensive, well-established connections among the social-democrat-oriented former political elite. Unlike Snegur, he and the parties associated with him are widely trusted by non-Moldovan voters. In Moldovan politics everybody knows each other and personal interests, sympathies, and antipathies as well as tactical reshuffles play an important role.

Social Problems and Control. The economic crisis resulted in an increase in poverty, theft, and petty and large-scale racketeering. Illegal cultivation of opium poppies and cannabis takes place on a limited basis, with both being trafficked to other CIS countries and Western Europe. In the villages, where people relate to one another in a less anonymous way, hearsay and gossip are effective tools of social control.

Military Activity. The army consists of 8,500 ground and air defense troops and has no tanks. As a landlocked country, Moldova has no navy, and after it sold nearly its entire fleet of MIG-29 fighters to the United States in 1997, it was left practically without an air force. The 1999 budget allocated only $5 million to defense spending, 2 percent of the total budget. The Republic of Moldova takes part in the NATO Partnership for Peace Program but has no plans to join either NATO or the CIS military structure. Although it is a neutral country and the constitution rules out the stationing of foreign military forces on Moldovan soil, Russian troops are still stationed in Transdniestria.

SOCIAL WELFARE AND CHANGE PROGRAMS

A system of social security covering unemployment benefits, health care, and pensions for the elderly and the disabled as well as assistance for low-income families has been set up. However, the level of social benefits is very low, and they are not paid in time because of the socioeconomic crisis. National and international nongovernmental organizations (NGOs) aid orphans and street children.

NONGOVERNMENTAL ORGANIZATIONS AND OTHER ASSOCIATIONS

Several international NGOs are active, especially in the fields of human rights and development. There are several local NGOs, most of which are small and inefficient. A Contact Center tries to coordinate the activities of the Moldovan NGO community. NGOs are frequently politically biased and get involved in political campaigns. Many NGO activists often see their organizations principally as vehicles for the pursuit of their own interests.

GENDER ROLES AND STATUSES

Division of Labor by Gender. Women in both urban and rural areas carry the burden of domestic duties and child care in addition to working outside the home. As a result of tradition and economic necessity, women engage in domestic food-processing activities in the summer to provide home-canned food for the winter months.

The Relative Status of Women and Men. Although men seemingly have more decision-making power in the public and private spheres, women act as the organizers of daily and ritual life. They organize social gatherings, gift-giving relations, and the infrastructure of numerous official and semiofficial events. There are no moral restrictions on women's participation in public life, although

Women at a market in Chisinau. Many Moldovan women work both inside and outside of the home.

many women choose not to have executive positions and give priority to their domestic duties.

MARRIAGE, FAMILY, AND KINSHIP

Marriage. When a young couple decides to marry, it is not unusual for the girl to go to her boyfriend's house and stay there. The next day her parents are informed about this, and the families come together to agree on the marriage. It can take a couple of months before the civil and religious wedding ceremonies are held. Divorce is common, and many women have to earn a living on their own after being abandoned by their husbands without the marriage being officially dissolved.

Domestic Unit. Newlyweds usually live together with the groom's parents until they can build a house in the village or rent an apartment in town. In the villages, there is a general rule of ultimogeniture (the youngest son and his family live with the parents, and he inherits the contents of the household).

Inheritance. Inheritance is regulated by law. Children inherit equally from their parents, although males may inherit the house of their parents if they live in the same household.

Kin Groups. Relatives support each other in performing agricultural and other tasks as well as ceremonial obligations. The godparenthood system regulates the mutual obligations between the parties. Godparents are responsible for the children they baptize throughout life-cycle rituals, especially marriage and the building of a house. Godparenthood is inherited between generations; however, it is also common for this role to be negotiated independently of previous ties.

SOCIALIZATION

Infant Care. Babies are taken care of by their mothers and grandmothers. In villages, babies are wrapped in blankets during the very early months, and cloth diapers are used. Toddlers walk around freely, and their clothes are changed when they wet themselves.

Child Rearing and Education. Children generally grow up close to their grandparents, who teach them songs and fairy tales. Girls are expected to help their mothers from an early age and also take care of smaller siblings. A good child is expected to be God-fearing and shy and does not participate in adult conversations without being asked to do so.

Higher Education. A few universities remain from the Soviet period, together with about fifty technical and vocational schools. As a result of economic difficulties, people sometimes complete higher education in their late thirties, after establishing a family. The College of Wine Culture is a popular educational institution that offers high-quality training.

ETIQUETTE

It is proper to drink at least a symbolic amount of wine during a meal or in a ritual context to honor the host and toast the health of the people present. Occasionally in villages, toasting with the left hand may not be regarded as proper. It is improper to blow one's nose at the table. Smoking in private homes is an uncommon practice; both hosts and guests usually go outside or onto the balcony to smoke. In villages, it is highly improper for women to smoke in public. People usually acknowledge passersby in the villages irrespective of previous acquaintance.

Workers at a ceramic factory in Marginea.

RELIGION

Religious Beliefs. The majority of the population, including non-Moldovans, are Orthodox Christians (about 98 percent). There are a small number of Uniates, Seventh-Day Adventists, Baptists, Pentecostalists, Armenian Apostolics, and Molokans. Jews have engaged in religious activities after independence with a newly opened synagogue and educational institutions.

Religious Practitioners. During the interwar period, Moldovans belonged to the Romanian Orthodox Church, but they now belong to the Russian Orthodox Church. There is an ongoing debate about returning to the Bucharest Patriarchate. Priests play an important role in the performance of ritual activities. In the villages, there are female healers who use Christian symbols and practices to treat the sick.

Rituals and Holy Places. The Orthodox calendar dictates rules and celebrations throughout the year, such as Christmas, Easter, and several saints' days. Some of the rules include fasting or avoiding meat and meat fat as well as restrictions on washing, bathing, and working at particular times. Baptisms, weddings, and funerals are the most important lifecycle rituals and are combined with church attendance and social gatherings. Easter is celebrated in the church and by visiting the graveyards of kin. Candles are an inseparable part of rituals; people buy candles when they enter the church and light them in front of the icons or during rituals.

Death and the Afterlife. The dead are dressed in their best clothes. Ideally, the corpse is watched over for three days and visited by relatives and friends. A mixture of cooked wheat and sugar called *colivă* is prepared and offered to the guests. If possible, the ninth, twentieth, and fortieth days; the third, sixth, and ninth months; and the year after the death are commemorated. However, this usually depends on the religiosity and financial resources of the people concerned. Graveyards are visited often, wine is poured on the graves, and food and *colivă* are distributed in memory of the dead.

MEDICINE AND HEALTH CARE

Modern medicine is widely used. Health care is poor because of the state of the economy.

SECULAR CELEBRATIONS

Major holidays include New Year's (1 January), Women's Day (8 March), Worker's Day (1 May), Victory Day (9 May), Independence Day (27 Au-

Swimmers and sunbathers at a lake in Chisinau. The central portion of the country enjoys long, warm summers.

gust), and *Limba noastră* ("Our Language"), a celebration of the national language (31 August).

THE ARTS AND HUMANITIES

Support for the Arts. In the Soviet period, state funds provided workshops for painters and other artists, who were guaranteed a regular income. This practice has ceased, and funds for workshops and other financial support are very limited. However, artists have better opportunities to sell to foreigners and the new business elites. National and international sponsors provide more encouragement for artistic activity than does the state.

Literature. The most important work of early literature is the ballad *Miorița*. Oral literature and folklore were prevalent until the nineteenth century. This and the classical Moldovan literature of the nineteenth century can hardly be distinguished from Romanian literature. The greatest Romanian writer, Mihai Eminescu, was born in the western part of Moldova and is perceived by Moldovans as part of their national heritage. Other renowned Moldovan writers include Alexei Mateevici, the author of the poem "*Limba noastră*;" the playwright Vasile Alecsandri; the novelist Ion Creangă; and the historian Alexandru Hâjdeu. Ion Druța, Nicolae Dabija, Leonida Lari, Dumitru Matcovschi, and

Grigorie Vieru are regarded as the greatest contemporary writers and poets.

Graphic Arts. Besides the painted monasteries around Suceava (Romania), sixteenth-century icons are the oldest examples of Moldovan graphic arts. At the beginning of the twentieth century, the sculptor Alexandru Plămădeală and the architect A. Șciusev added their work to the heritage of Bessarabian arts. Bessarabian painters of the nineteenth and twentieth centuries concentrated on landscapes and rural themes as well as typical motifs of Soviet realism. Since the recent changes, however, young modern artists such as Valeriu Jabinski, Iuri Matei, Andrei Negur, and Gennadi Teciuc have demonstrated the potential and quality of Moldovan art.

Performance Arts. Folkloristic and classic music dominate, but Western music, especially jazz, is widely performed. The Soviet system helped popularize a systematic musical education, and people from all sections of society listen to and perform music of different styles. The opera singer Maria Bieşu, the folklore ensemble *LauŢării*, the folklore dance ensemble *Joc*, and the dance ensemble *Codreanca* have become famous outside the country. Folklore and classical concerts are relatively cheap and are attended by young and old people of differ-

Tobacco leaves hanging out to dry in a Moldovan village. Tobacco farming is one of the major industries.

ent social statuses. Rock and pop concerts are expensive but attract many young people.

THE STATE OF THE PHYSICAL AND SOCIAL SCIENCES

The Academy of Science was the traditional place for research in Soviet Moldova. In an agricultural country, particular stress was placed on agriculture-related sciences, and a special Agricultural University was established for the education of specialists and for research in that field. After the political transition, the State University was reorganized and private universities, focusing mainly on economic subjects, were established.

BIBLIOGRAPHY

Aklaev, Airat R. "Dynamics of the Moldova-Trans-Dniestr-Conflict (late 1980s to early 1990s)." In Kumar Rupesinghe and Valery A. Tishkov, eds, *Ethnicity and Power in the Contemporary World*, 1996.

Batt, Jud. "Federalism versus Nationbuilding in Post-Communist State-Building: The Case of Moldova." *Regional and Federal Studies* 7 (3): 25–48, 1997.

Bruchis, Michael. *One Step Back, Two Steps Forward: On the Language Policy of the Communist Party of the Soviet Union in the National Republics*, 1982.

———. "The Language Policy of the CPSU and the Linguistic Situation in Moldova." *Soviet Studies* 36 (1): 108–26, 1984.

———. *Nations-Nationalities-People: A Study of the Nationalities Policy of the Communist Party in Soviet Moldavia*, 1984.

———. *The Republic of Moldavia from the Collapse of the Soviet Empire to the Restoration of the Russian Empire*, 1997.

———. Chinn, Jeff. "The Case of Transdniestr." In Lena Jonson and Clive Archer, eds., *Peacekeeping and the Role of Russia*, 1996.

——— and Steve Ropers. "Ethnic Mobilization and Reactive Nationalism: The Case of Moldova." *Nationalities Papers* 23 (2): 291–325, 1995.

Crowther, William. "Ethnic Politics and the Post-Communist Transition in Moldova." *Nationalities Papers* 26 (1): 147–164, 1998.

———. "Moldova: Caught between Nation and Empire." In Ian Bremmer and Ray Tarasm, eds., *New States, New Politics—Building the Post-Soviet Nations*, 1997.

———. "The Construction of Moldovan National Consciousness." In Laszlo Kürti and Juliet Boulder Langman, eds., *Beyond Borders: Remaking Cultural Identities in the New East and Central Europe*, 1997.

———. "The Politics of Ethno-National Mobilization: Nationalism and Reform in Soviet Moldavia." *Russian Review* 50 (2): 183–202, 1991.

Dima, Nicholas. "Recent Ethno Demographic-Changes in Soviet Moldavia." *East European Quarterly* 25 (2): 167–178, 1991.

———. *From Moldavia to Moldova*, 1991.

———. "The Soviet Political Upheaval of the 1980s: The Case of Moldavia." *Journal of Social Political and Economic Studies* 16 (1): 39–58, 1991.

———. "Politics and Religion in Moldova: A Case-Study." *Mankind Quarterly* 34 (3): 175–194, 1994.

Dyer, Donald L., ed. *Studies in Moldovan: The History, Culture, Language and Contemporary Politics of the People of Moldova*, 1996.

———. "What Price Languages in Contact?: Is There Russian Language Influence on the Syntax of Moldovan?" *Nationalities Papers* 26 (1): 75–84, 1998.

Eyal, Jonathan. "Moldavians." In Graham Smith, ed., *The Nationalities Question in the Soviet Union*, 1990.

Feldman, Walter. "The Theoretical Basis for the Definition of Moldavian Nationality." In Ralph S. Clem, ed., *The Soviet West: Interplay between Nationality and Social Organization*, 1978.

"From Ethnopolitical Conflict to Inter-Ethnic Accord in Moldova." *ECMI Report #1*, March 1998.

Grupp, Fred W. and Ellen Jones. "Modernisation and Ethnic Equalisation in the USSR." *Soviet Studies* 26 (2): 159–184, 1984.

Hamm, Michael F. "Kishinev: The Character and Development of a Tsarist Frontier Town." *Nationalities Papers* 26 (1): 19–37, 1998.

Helsinki Watch. *Human Rights in Moldova: The Turbulent Dniester*, 1993.

Ionescu, Dan. "Media in the Dniester Moldovan Republic: A Communist-Era Memento." *Transitions* 1 (19): 16–20, 1995.

Kaufman, Stuart J. "Spiraling to Ethnic War: Elites, Masses and Moscow in Moldova's Civil War." *International Security* 21 (2): 108–138, 1996.

King, Charles. "Eurasia Letter: Moldova with a Russian Face." *Foreign Policy* 97: 106–120, 1994.

———. "Moldova." In *Eastern Europe and the Commonwealth of Independent States*, 1994.

———. "Moldovan Identity and the Politics of Pan-Romanianism." *Slavic Review* 53 (2): 345–368, 1994.

———. *The Moldovans, Romania, Russia and the Politics of Culture*, 2000.

———. *Post-Soviet Moldova: A Borderland in Transition*, 1995.

Kolstø, Pål. "The Dniestr Conflict: Between Irredentism and Separatism." *Europe-Asia Studies* 45 (6): 973–1000, 1993.

———. Andrei Malgin. "The Transnistrian Republic: A Case of Politicized Regionalism." *Nationalities Papers* 26 (1): 103–127, 1998.

Livezeanu, Irina. "Urbanization in a Low Key and Linguistic Change in Soviet Moldavia." *Soviet Studies* 33 (3): 327–351, 33 (4): 573–589, 1981.

Neukirch, Claus. "National Minorities in the Republic of Moldova—Some Lessons, Learned Some Not?" *South East Europe Review for Labour and Social Affairs* 2 (3): 45–64.

O'Loughlin, John, Vladimir Kolossov, and Andrei Tchepalyga. "National Construction, Territorial Separatism, and Post-Soviet Geopolitics in the Transdniester Moldovan Republic." *Post-Soviet Soviet Geography and Economics* 39 (6): 332–358, 1998.

Ozhiganov, Edward. "The Republic of Moldova: Transdniester and the 14th Army." In Alexei Arbatov, Abram Chayes, Antonia Handler Chayes, and Lara Olson, eds., *Managing Conflict in the Former Soviet Union: Russian and American Perspectives*, 1998.

Roach. A. "The Return of Dracula Romanian Struggle for Nationhood and Moldavian Folklore." *History Today* 38: 7–9, 1988.

Van Meurs, Wim P. "Carving a Moldavian Identity out of History." *Nationalities Papers*, 26 (1): 39–56, 1998.

———. *The Bessarabian Question in Communist Historiography: Nationalist and Communist Politics and History-Writing*, 1994.

Waters, Trevor. "On Crime and Corruption in the Republic of Moldova." *Law Intensity Conflict and Law Enforcement* 6 (2): 84–92, 1997.

—HÜLYA DEMIRDIREK
AND CLAUS NEUKIRCH

MONACO

CULTURE NAME

Monegasque; Monacan

ORIENTATION

Identification. Officially known as the Principality of Monaco, or the Principaute de Monaco.

Location and Geography. This small country is 0.8 square miles (1.95 square kilometers) in size, or approximately the same size as Central Park in New York City. It is the smallest state in the world after Vatican City. Located on the Mediterranean Sea, Monaco is surrounded by France on three sides. Nice, France, is the nearest large city at a distance of 11 miles (18 kilometers). Monaco is rocky and situated on steep hills that drop off into the Mediterranean. Part of the Côte d'Azur, Monaco's terrain and geography are typical of the northwestern area of the Mediterranean. The climate is mild year-round, with an average low temperature of 47 degrees Fahrenheit (8 degrees Celsius) and an average maximum high of 78 degrees Fahrenheit (26 degrees Celsius). Monaco is divided into four neighborhoods: Monaco-Ville, the old original city, which is on a rocky promontory extending into the sea; La Condamine, along the port; Monte-Carlo, the main resort, residential and tourist area; and Fontvieille, a newly constructed area on land reclaimed from the sea.

Demography. Recent surveys place the permanent population of Monaco at about 30,744. Approximately 22 percent are native Monegasque, 35 percent French, 18 percent Italian, and another 25 percent consist of various other nationalities. Roman Catholicism is the main religion, practiced by 95 percent of the population.

Linguistic Affiliation. French is the official language, but Italian and English are also spoken frequently. Monegasque, a language derived from both French and Italian, is spoken by native residents of Monaco, although only about 22 percent of the population claims direct Monegasque descent.

Symbolism. The Monegasque flag consists of two equal horizontal bands of red and white: red on top, white beneath. The state seal and emblem of the House of Grimaldi is made up of a shield with red and white diamonds flanked by two monks holding swords pointed upward, with a crown draped with red cloth in the background. The monks represent the legend of François Grimaldi, and who supposedly seized control of Monaco by disguising himself as a Franciscan monk, entering the fortress unnoticed during the night.

HISTORY AND ETHNIC RELATIONS

Emergence of the Nation. The first inhabitants of Monaco were the Ligurians, an ancient Indo-European tribe. Monaco was located near an important coastal path that stretched from Spain through southern France and into Italy. The peoples living in this area were eventually absorbed into the Roman Empire and became part of the province of Maritime Alps. With the fall of the Roman Empire, Monaco and the surrounding coastal areas were perpetually attacked by various invaders, including the Saracens, and the native population fled inland. It was only after the final expulsion of the Saracens in about 1000 C.E., that people returned to living on the coast.

Monaco's recorded history began in 1215 when the Ghibellines of Genoa, led by Fulco del Cassello, colonized it after receiving sovereignty over the area from Emperor Henry VI. Attracted by Monaco's strategic location and harbor, the Genoese immediately began to construct a fortress, known as the Rock of Monaco, and a walled city. To attract permanent residents, the Genoese granted land and tax exemptions. As a result, Monaco quickly became an important city and over the next three centuries was frequently contested by rival political factions.

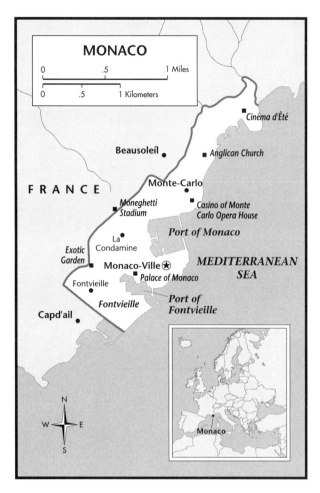

Monaco

In 1297 François Grimaldi, who was originally from a powerful Guelph family in Genoa, and a small army seized control of the Rock of Monaco. Although the Grimaldis were expelled in 1301, they returned thirty years later, and the House of Grimaldi has ruled Monaco uninterrupted (except from 1789 to 1814, when it fell under French rule) since then.

Charles Grimaldi, known as Charles I, succeeded in reinstating the House of Grimaldi on 12 September 1331 and is considered the founder of the principality. However, it was not until 1489 that Monaco gained complete autonomy from French control when Lambert Grimaldi convinced King Charles VIII of France to grant the principality its independence. Monaco's sovereignty was officially recognized in 1512 by Louis XII in a signed document that also declared a perpetual alliance with the king of France. In 1524 Monaco was placed under the protection of Spain for political reasons. This caused long-term financial difficulties for Monaco, since the occupying Spanish military force was entirely supported by the Monegasques. In the early 1600s Monaco once again flourished, under the reign of Honoré II, who strengthened his country's alliance with France. Over the next two hundred years Monaco prospered under France's protection. In 1861, with the Treaty of 2 February, Charles III ceded Monaco's authority over the towns of Menton and Roquebrune to France in exchange for total independence from French political influence. However, in July 1919, after the end of World War I, Monaco was placed once again under limited French protection according to the Treaty of Versailles, a relationship that still exists today.

National Identity. The native Monegasques are proud of their country's unique history and position in the world. The name Monaco is believed to derive from the word "monoikos" associated both with the ancient Greeks and the Ligurians. The Ligurians settled along the Mediterranean coast, from Spain to Italy, before the age of the Roman Empire. The coastal road used by the Ligurians later came to be known as "The Road of Hercules." In Greek, Hercules was often called "Heracles Monoikos," or "Hercules Along" but it is possible that "monoikos" derives from an older Ligurian word. The Monegasque have managed to maintain their traditions, institutions, and dialect through the centuries despite the influence of their much-larger neighbors. This cultural identity is reflected in many of the local festivals and in Monaco's world prominence, which is disproportionate to the principality's size. However, only a small part of the population, less that 20 percent, can claim direct Monegasque heritage. The majority of the principality's citizens are French or of French descent (47 percent). People of Italian origin make up about 16 percent with the rest of the population consisting of a variety of nationalities.

Ethnic Relations. Monaco has close ethnic ties with France and Italy, and nationals of these countries account for more than half of the population. Some one-quarter of the population consists of people from a variety of other nationalities, reflecting a tolerance of different ethnic groups. However, immigration is very limited due to the principality's size, and citizenship is not easy to acquire.

URBANISM, ARCHITECTURE, AND THE USE OF SPACE

The steep, rocky hills and narrow coastline have influenced architecture and urban planning in Monaco. Streets are narrow and steep, and buildings must be constructed into the hills in limited amounts of space. The architecture in general reflects a Mediterranean influence, and local materials, including granite, marble, and terra-cotta tiles, are common. Recent-twentieth-century residential construction included numerous high-rise apartment buildings. Like many Mediterranean communities, Monaco has public squares, and its mild climate is favorable to outdoor living. Many buildings have balconies or terraces that face the sea. Some medieval structures survive in the old fortified city of Monaco-Ville on the Rock, where the royal palace is located. Monaco's most famous building is the Casino in Monte Carlo, built in 1866 and designed by French architect Charles Garnier.

FOOD AND ECONOMY

Food in Daily Life. Access to fresh, local produce and the sea has led to the development of a local cuisine and appreciation for good food. Monaco has many restaurants, and seafood is featured in many dishes. Daily eating habits reflect a Mediterranean heritage, and both French and Italian influences can be found in the local recipes. Breakfast is very small, but lunch and dinner often have several courses.

Food Customs at Ceremonial Occasions. Holidays such as Christmas, Holy Week before Easter, and Carnival before Lent are occasions for special food. Some traditional Monegasque dishes include *brandamincium*, salt cod pounded with garlic, oil, and cream surrounded by cardoons, edible Mediterranean plants, in white sauce; *barba-Giuan*, or "Uncle John," stuffed fritters; and *fougasses*, flat, crunchy biscuits sprinkled with sugared anise seeds and flavored with rum and orange-flower water.

Basic Economy. Tourism and related businesses are the main components of the Monegasque economy today. The tourist industry began when the famous casino was opened in Monte Carlo. Banking and financial activities are the second most important part of the economy. The industrial sector is small but significant and includes pharmaceuticals, cosmetics, flour-milling, and food products. Investment in real estate and business services make up the fourth most important sector of the economy. Foreign companies receive special investment incentives that have led many to open offices in the principality. Monaco does not impose an income tax on its residents and consequently has attracted corporate and individual investment. A significant financial services industry has developed as a result.

Land Tenure and Property. Due to Monaco's small size, the availability of land and private space has always been limited. Significant economic growth and an increase in population since 1950 have greatly augmented this problem, forcing developers to build multistoried structures very close together. An increase in tourism and the necessity for hotels have put an added strain on available space. Property is expensive both to buy and maintain, but Monaco's real estate business continues to thrive. To create additional space, the Monegasque government has had to find innovative ways to satisfy the demand for construction: the use of land reclaimed from the sea. The most recent of these is the neighborhood of Fontvieille.

Commercial Activities. Business related to tourism accounts for the majority of commercial activities. Hotels, restaurants, shops, gambling, and services related to Monaco's port provide both employment and revenue for the principality. The real estate business has also become an important commercial concern since 1970.

Major Industries. Industry did not begin to significantly develop until the 1950s, and consists entirely of light industry, with no obvious adverse effects on other parts of the economy or Monegasque society. The first industries, which developed at the beginning of the twentieth century, included a brewery, a chocolate factory, and a flour mill. The chemical, pharmaceutical, parapharmaceutical, and cosmetics industries all developed after World War II and today consist of twenty-three separate businesses—many of which are leaders in their sectors in Europe. Plastics, electronics, printing, textiles, and construction also are significant industries.

Trade. Recent figures place the estimated value of Monegasque imports at U.S. $415,300 and exports at approximately the same figure. Monaco does not publish economic figures including gross domestic product, although recent estimates put it at about U.S. $800 million. Exports include a variety of Monegasque products, and imports include agricultural products and manufactured and consumer goods. Some of Monaco's most important exports include: cosmetics, pharmaceuticals, clothing, small electronics, and paper products.

Division of Labor. Of the estimated thirty thousand jobs existing in Monaco, two-thirds of them are held by workers commuting from neighboring French or Italian towns along the coast. Seasonal tourist work also accounts for an increase in non-

Contrasting old and modern architecture. The rocky, steep terrain of Monaco has influenced urban architecture; many buildings are constructed into the hills.

native Monegasque workers to the principality, including workers who have immigrated to Europe from other parts of the world. Women make up slightly less than half the workforce, and recent statistics place unemployment at about 3.2 percent.

SOCIAL STRATIFICATION

Classes and Castes. Monaco's high average income and individual wealth, as well as its very small size, make it a country with minimal class distinctions. The principality's status as a tax haven make it an attractive place to establish residence for wealthy people from all over the world. A significant number of residents are from a variety of nationalities, and several are celebrities, helping to make Monaco synonymous with wealth, power and prestige the world over.

Symbols of Social Stratification. Overall Monaco has one of the highest standards of living in the world. Differences in social stratification are not immediately obvious. The principality's popularity as an exclusive resort and tax haven has led to the development of a very wealthy social class. Material symbols of wealth such as luxury goods, expensive cars, and exclusive shops are visible everywhere. Monaco's coastal position has also made it a popu-

lar port for luxury yachts. The tourist industry necessitates a large workforce, as do Monaco's light industrial concerns, but more than half the people employed in these sectors do not live in Monaco.

POLITICAL LIFE

Government. Until 1910, the Principality of Monaco was governed by an absolute monarchy. In 1911 Prince Albert I promulgated the first constitution, which was modified in 1917. It was modified again in 1933 by Prince Louis II, and other reforms were made by Prince Rainier III in 1962. Monaco's refusal to impost tax on its residents and international businesses led to a severe crisis with France in 1962. This crisis led to a compromise in which it was agreed that French citizens with less than five years of residence in Monaco would be taxed at French rates and companies doing more than 25 percent of their business outside the principality. Another result of the crisis was the creation of a new, more liberal constitution ad the restoration of the National Council. The constitution provides that executive power is under the authority of the reigning prince. Succession to the throne passes to the direct and legitimate descendants of the prince, with male descendants taking precedence over female. The prince represents

Monaco in its foreign relations and signs and ratifies treaties. The prince nominates a Council of Government, consisting of a minister of state and three government councilors, one each for finance and economy, the interior, and public works and social affairs. The Minister of State is a French Citizen, appointed by the prince, and selected for a three-year term a from a group of senior French civil servants selected by the French government. The Minister of State is in charge of foreign relations and, as the prince's representative, directs executive services, the police and the Council of Government. Under the Council of Government's authority is the eighteen-member National Council. Members of the National Council are elected for five years by direct vote based on a system of proportional representation. Eligible voters must be over the age of twenty-one and hold Monegasque citizenship for more than five years. The new constitution of 1962 gave the right to vote to women, established a Supreme Court to guarantee fundamental rights, and abolished the death penalty.

Leadership and Political Officials. Local affairs are directed by the Communal Council which administers the principality's four quarters: Monaco-Ville, La Condamine, Monte Carlo, and Fontvieille. The Council of the Crown consists of seven members holding Monégasque nationality who are nominated by the prince. The president and three members are selected by the sovereign: the others are selected by the national Council. Current government officials include: the Chief of State, Prince Rainier III; the Minister of State, Michel Leveque; the Council of Government, ministers for: the Interior, Finance, and Economic Affairs, Public Works and Social Affairs, National Council President, President of the Supreme Court, and the Director of Judicial Services.

Social Problems and Control. Due to its small population and unique economic situation, Monaco does not face many of the social problems that larger countries must deal with, such as violent crime and poverty. After going through a period of economic growth and industrial development following World War II, a primary concern is the principality's ability to sustain its economy, attract new investments, and maintain the quality of life for its citizens. Current social problems include managing industrial growth and tourism, environmental concerns, and maintaining the quality of life. Alcoholism and illegal drug abuse are present but not widespread. Monaco has a very low crime rate, in part due to the high number of law enforcement officials in relation to the total population and the high standard of living. Widespread use of security cameras throughout the principality also further discourage open criminal activity. Excluding private security, there are around 400 permanent police officers, 95 percent of whom are French. Legal power belongs to the Sovereign, presently Prince Rainier III, who delegates full exercise of it to the courts and tribunals. The independence of the judges is guaranteed by the constitution. Monaco's legal organization includes all degrees of jurisdiction: a Court of First Instance, a Court of Appeal, a Higher Court of Appeal and a Criminal Court. There are also tribunals with specific competence, such as the Work Tribunal, the Rent Arbitration Commission, and the Higher Arbitration Court, for collective work disputes. The Supreme Court is at the top of the principality's legal organization.

Military Activity. Monaco does not have a military, although it does have a small police force. The French government is responsible for Monaco's defense.

SOCIAL WELFARE AND CHANGE PROGRAMS

The government efficiently manages several social welfare and change programs. Some current programs include creating more affordable housing for workers by reclaiming land from the sea for new construction and promotion of Monegasque culture, brought about by a revived interest in the principality's history. Consequently, Monegasque language classes have now been instituted in all elementary schools. The Monegasque government also ensures generous pensions, maternity leave, vacation time, and welfare programs for all citizens.

NONGOVERNMENTAL ORGANIZATIONS AND OTHER ASSOCIATIONS

Monaco has many nongovernmental organizations and cultural, academic, and professional associations. Among these are the Permanent International Association of Navigation Conventions, the International Committee of Military Medicine and Pharmacy, the Scientific Community for Oceanic Research, the International Music Council, the International Union for the Conservation of Nature, and the International Union of the History and Philosophy of Sciences. Monaco joined the United Nations in 1993 and is an active participant. Other intergovernmental organizations of which Monaco is a member include Interpol, UNESCO, and WHO. The International Hydrographic Bureau has its headquarters in Monaco.

Scenic view of the Port of Fontvieille. Tourism is the major industry in Monaco.

GENDER ROLES AND STATUSES

Monaco has a Mediterranean, Roman Catholic culture emphasizing the family. Until the second half of the twentieth century, women's roles revolved principally around family and household. Women were not active in politics until the 1960s when they first received the vote. Although fewer women than men are employed outside the home, Monegasque women work in a variety of fields and are politically active.

MARRIAGE, FAMILY, AND KINSHIP

Not withstanding its status as a cosmopolitan resort, Monegasque society is based on centuries-old traditions. Immediate and extended family are the basic social units. Marriage is considered an important family event and the divorce rate is low, with less than a quarter of marriages ending in divorce.

Marriage. Marriage is an important family event, Church weddings, held according to Roman Catholic traditions, are popular. A civil ceremony, held at the city hall, is also required even when a religious ceremony is organized. Some couples choose only to have the civil ceremony.

Domestic Unit. The domestic unit consists of immediate family members. Before industrialization after World War II, the domestic unit also included extended family such as grandparents and other elderly relatives. The low divorce rate and general affluence help contribute to a stable average domestic unit in Monaco. Monegasque social activities frequently revolve around family events and gatherings.

Inheritance. Inheritance laws are based on those of France.

SOCIALIZATION

Infant Care. Monaco provides excellent maternity and infant care. Women are guaranteed several months of maternity leave and there are high quality, low cost day care centers and nurseries available. National health and education programs ensure that Monegasque families have complete early childhood support and care.

Child Rearing and Education. A national health service and an excellent public education system provide Monegasque children with high-quality, low-cost education and with health care from infancy through adolescence. Monaco's small size, unique history, and high standard of living have helped the principality avoid many of the child social problems that face larger countries. The traditional Monegasque culture, based on family and kinship ties, has changed with twentieth-century industrialization and growth, but child welfare remains important. Grandparents often help in caring for young children, particularly when both parents work.

Education is compulsory from ages of six to sixteen. School curricula are identical to those of France but also include the study of Monegasque history, the institutions of the principality, and the Monegasque language. There are four public primary schools for study up to age fourteen and three specialized high schools: Lycée Albert I, the Technical Lycée of Monte Carlo, and the Charles II College. There are also four private schools through the high school level.

Higher Education. Monaco does not have a university, although there are several specialized institutions of higher learning, including the Rainier III Academy of Music and the Nursing School at the Princess Grace Hospital Complex. Monaco's literacy rate is 99 percent.

ETIQUETTE

Etiquette in Monaco is influenced by the country's unusual blending of roles as an international tax haven, exclusive resort destination in combination with the Monegasque traditions. The Monegasque are proud of the country's history and residents strive to maintain the quality of life that exists there. The principality attracts people from a variety of nationalities who are nevertheless united by a high level of personal wealth. The rules of etiquette are much like those found in France with an emphasis on respect for privacy. The royal family of Monaco, the Grimaldi, frequently attract the attention of the press. Monaco's royal family became a popular subject of tabloid journalism when the American actress Grace Kelly married Prince Rainier III. Discretion and privacy are still emphasized in Monaco.

RELIGION

Religious Beliefs. Roman Catholicism is the state religion, although freedom of worship is guaranteed by Article 23 of the Constitution. However, 95 percent of the population claims to be Roman Catholic.

Religious Practitioners. Most Monegasque are Roman Catholic and the church plays an important role in Monegasque traditions, particularly on feast days and special holidays. Church attendance is not as high as a century ago and it is difficult to estimate the exact number of practicing Catholics.

Rituals and Holy Places. There are several traditional festivals and rituals in Monaco. Saint Devote, the patron saint of Monaco, is venerated in a ritual held on 27 January every year. A torchlight procession, a religious ceremony and blessing mark the day that Saint Dévoe is believed to have arrived in Monaco. Other religious rituals and ceremonies are held during Holy Week before Easter, and on the feast days of Saint Roman, 9 August, Saint John, 23 June and Saint Blaise.

Death and the Afterlife. Monegasque beliefs about death and the afterlife are in accordance with the teachings of the Roman Catholic church.

MEDICINE AND HEALTH CARE

Monaco has a government-supported health system that provides high-quality medical care to all its citizens. Life expectancy is placed at 74 years for males and 81 for females. Infant mortality rate is approximately 7 per 1000 births. Monaco's birthrate exceeds the number of deaths per year. For specialized care of serious care of serious health problems Monaco's residents may seek care in larger medical centers, such as the hospital in Nice.

SECULAR CELEBRATIONS

National Day, 19 November, celebrates Monaco's independence as a principality. A parade, a thanksgiving Mass held in the cathedral, and special events are organized. Other important celebrations have religious origins. The Feast of Saint Devote, the patron saint of Monaco, is celebrated on 27 January. The festival of Saint John, on 24 June, is another important Monegasque holiday. Religious holidays are celebrated with the closing of businesses, special church services, and traditional customs. The National Committee of Monegasque Traditions, established in 1924, is dedicated to the preservation and revival of Monegasque folk traditions and festivals.

THE ARTS AND HUMANITIES

Support for the Arts. The Monegasque government actively supports the arts, cultural institutions, and the humanities through a variety of programs and events. The Prince Pierre Foundation was founded to encourage culture in the letters and the arts, by the creation and awarding of prizes. These

The Monaco Grand Prix. This Formula 1 car race is held in Monte Carlo.

awards include the Grand Literary Prize, created in 1951; the Prince Rainier III Prize for Musical Composition, founded in 1960; and the International Contemporary Art Prize, awarded for the first time in 1965. The Princess Grace Foundation was established in 1964 with the aim of promoting charitable activities and provides support for the Princess Grace Dance Academy. Recent investments in the arts and humanities include the creation of a Cultural and Exhibition Center, which will contain an auditorium and other performance and event areas on the site of the old Centenary Hall. The Monte Carlo Ballet and the Monte Carlo Opera are world-renowned. The Monte Carlo Ballet gained international fame in the 1920s when the choreographer Sergey Diaghilev was based there with his Ballets Russes. Monaco is also home to the International Circus Festival held every February and the International Fireworks held in July. The Grand Prix de Monaco, a Formula 1 car race held in the streets of Monte Carlo, is one of the principality's most famous cultural events and attracts thousands of spectators.

Literature. The Great Literary Prize recognizes outstanding literary works annually. The Princess Grace Irish Library was established recently to hold a collection of over 8,000 volumes related to Irish history, culture and writing, in both Irish and English languages.

Graphic Arts. The Prince Pierre Foundation annually awards the International Prize for Art, established in 1965, to recognize outstanding achievement in the visual arts. The Municipal School of Decorative Arts provides education in the visual arts.

Performance Arts. The Monte Carlo Philharmonic Orchestra was established in 1863 and found its permanent home in the Garnier Palace in 1879. The Monte Carlo Ballet and the Monte Carlo Opera are internationally acclaimed. Since 1892 the Monte Carlo Opera has occupied Garnier Hall, named after its architect, who also designed the Paris Opera House. Many premier performances have been staged at the Monte Carlo Opera, including Sergei Diaghilev's *Ballets Russes* in the 1920s. The International Circus Festival is also held annually in Monaco.

THE STATE OF PHYSICAL AND SOCIAL SCIENCES

Monaco is particularly well known for its activity in the marine science field. The Oceanographic Museum, formerly directed by Jacques Cousteau, is the most famous institution devoted to marine science in the world. The Scientific Community for Oceanic Research is based in Monaco, and numerous other scientific and academic societies also have branch offices in the principality. Monaco's history of supporting oceanic and scientific studies dates to the 1860s when Prince Albert pursued his scientific interests by conducting numerous maritime expeditions. Throughout the twentieth century, Monaco has promoted scientific research. The Prehistory and Speleological Association was formed in 1951 and in 1960 Prince Rainier III inaugurated the Museum of Prehistoric Anthropology. Prince Rainier is also the president of the International Commission for the Scientific Exploration of the Mediterranean. The Scientific Center of Monaco is host to a variety of activities including seismological, meteorological, and radioactivity studies. The Monaco Underwater Reserve, consisting of almost 50 hectares, was established by the Monégasque Association for the Protection of Nature to provide a protected environment for a wide variety of marine life. In 1971 the ''Albert I of Monaco'' Prize for Oceanography was created to recognize outstanding research.

BIBLIOGRAPHY

Campbell, Siri. *Inside Monaco*, 2000.

Doyle, Stanton, and Ewing, Debra; Kelly, Robert; and Youngblood, Denise, ed. *Country Review: Monaco 1998–1999*, 1998.

The Magic Principality, 1994.

Rogatnick, Joseph H. ''Little States in a World of Power: A Study of the Conduct of Foreign Affairs by Andorra, Liechtenstein, Monaco, and San Marino.'' Ph.D. dissertation, University of Pennsylvania, 1976.

Web Sites

Monaco Government Tourist Office. www.monaco.mc

United States Department of State, Bureau of European Affairs. ''Background Notes, Monaco.'' www.state .gov

—M. CAMERON ARNOLD

MONGOLIA

CULTURE NAME
Mongolian, Mongol

ALTERNATIVE NAMES
Formerly called Mongolian People's Republic (1921–1989)

ORIENTATION

Identification. Genghis Khan banded the Mongolian tribes together for the first time in 1206 and formed a unified state. The steppe empires and nomadic culture created by the ancient Mongols hold a unique place in world history, and modern Mongols are very proud of this particular heritage.

Location and Geography. Mongolia is a large landlocked country in Central Asia, and is bordered on the north by the Russian Federation and on the south by the People's Republic of China. Measuring 604,100 square miles (1,565,000 square kilometers) in area, the country is larger than Western Europe, encompassing several geographical zones: desert, steppe, and mountainous terrain. Mongolia's climate is extreme, with low precipitation and long harsh winters where temperatures can dip to −50 degrees centigrade. The capital city is Ulaanbaatar, meaning "Red Hero."

Demography. With only 2.6 million people as of July 2000, Mongolia is one of the world's most sparsely populated countries. The nation also has an extremely young population, with over 70 percent of people less than thirty years old.

Linguistic Affiliation. Khalkha Mongolian is the official language and is spoken by 90 percent of the people. Minor languages include Kazakh, Russian, and Chinese. Khalka Mongolian is part of the diverse Uralic-Altaic language family, which spread with the ancient Mongol Empire and also contains Korean, Manchu, Turkish, Finnish, and Hungarian.

Each of these languages features a highly inflected grammar. Khalkha Mongolian may be written in traditional Uighur (vertical) or Cyrillic script.

Symbolism. The national symbol is the soyombo, featured on the Mongolian flag. Each aspect of the complex design is meaningful and there are components representing fire, sun, moon, earth, water, and the yin-yang symbol. The soyombo dates to at least the 17th century, and is associated with Lamaism.

HISTORY AND ETHNIC RELATIONS

Emergence of the Nation. The name "Mongol" first appears in historical records in the 10th century C.E. Until the late 12th century, the Mongols were a fragmented group of warring clans. In 1162, a Mongol named Temujin was born who eventually became the leader of the Borjigin Mongol clan. After twenty years of warfare, he united most of the Mongol clans and was given the honorary title Genghis Khan ("Universal King") in 1206. The unparalleled conquests of the Mongols under Genghis Khan enabled them to expand their empire far beyond their own territories in Asia, as far as central Europe. The Mongol Empire lasted approximately 175 years, until internal conflicts caused its power to wane. In the 17th century, the former empire lost its independence and was ruled by the Manchus for 200 years. In 1911 the Manchu government was overthrown; the Mongols spent the next ten years freeing themselves from Chinese domination with Russian assistance. A decade of political and military struggles led to the Mongolian-Soviet treaty of 1921, which recognized Mongolia's independence. In 1924, the Mongolian People's Republic was officially established as the second socialist nation in the world after the U.S.S.R. Major democratizing political and economic reforms began in the late 1980s following the disintegration of the U.S.S.R. This democratic movement resulted in the emergence of

Mongolia

multiple political parties and the beginnings of a free market economy by 1990.

National Identity. National culture—including societal organization, governance, land management, cultural customs, and material culture—was largely shaped by the nomadic pastoral lifestyle. The legacy of Genghis Khan's empire is a rallying point for Mongol nationalist pride today.

Ethnic Relations. Approximately 78 percent of people are Khalkha Mongols. Minority groups include Kazakh, Dorvod, Bayad, Buriad, Dariganga, Zahchin, Urianhai, Oolld. and Torguud. The largest of these minority groups, Kazakhs make up 4 percent of the total population. Small numbers of Russians and Chinese permanently live in Mongolia. While relations between Mongols and Russians are generally warm, widespread resentment exists among Mongols for the growing presence of entrepreneurial Chinese in their country.

URBANISM, ARCHITECTURE, AND THE USE OF SPACE

Rapid urbanization and industrialization accompanied extensive Soviet aid following World War II and in the 1950s, the country adopted a new economic strategy that added industrial activities and more extensive farming to its mainstay of livestock production. Many people migrated from rural to urban areas to work in the new industrial centers, and a population that was 78 percent rural in 1956 was 58 percent urban by 1990. Many urban settlers continued to live in traditional nomadic *gers*, round tents made of folding wooden walls and heavy felt outer coverings.

FOOD AND ECONOMY

Food in Daily Life. Approximately twenty five million head of livestock supply the staples of the diet; meat and dairy products feature prominently in this cuisine. Mongolian cooking is generally very simple and does not use many spices, flavorings or sauces. Common dishes include steamed meat–filled dumplings (*buuz*), mutton soup with noodles (*guriltai shul*) and fried meat pasties (*huushuur*). Mongolians drink copious quantities of milk tea (*suutei tsai*), which frequently contains salt and a generous spoonful of fresh or rancid butter.

Food Customs at Ceremonial Occasions. Food is an important element of the Mongolian hospitality tradition. When guests arrive, each household sets out a special hospitality bowl containing home-made cheeses, flour pastries (*bordzig*), sugar cubes and candy. The fattest animals are slaughtered to be eaten. Meat-filled dumplings are traditionally served to guests. Vodka shots are served at regular intervals during a celebration.

Basic Economy. Primary to the economy are the "five types of animals:" sheep, goats, cattle (mainly yak), horses, and camels. From these livestock numerous animal products are harvested, including meat, dairy products, hides, and wool. Agricultural production takes place in some regions where grains (wheat, barley, oats), animal fodder, potatoes, and other vegetables are grown. The country is rich in natural resources including coal, copper, gold, fluorspar, and molybdenum, and has prospective areas for oil extraction that are currently being explored.

The national currency is the *tugrik*.

Land Tenure and Property. Before socialism, a quasi-feudal system existed in which local aristocratic families and monasteries primarily governed: they administered pastureland, settled disputes between herding households, and collected taxes. Herders mostly owned their animals but paid taxes to the nobility for using pastureland. In the 1920's, the U.S.S.R. forced rural collectivization of herds within the Soviet Union and encouraged the Mongolian government to follow suit. However, widespread resistance by herders delayed the implementation of nationwide herding collectives until after World War II. Under the socialist system, the numbers of private animals that could be owned was tightly restricted, but these restrictions began to be lifted in the late 1980's.

Major Industries. A number of manufacturing plants were built under socialism which continue to operate today. Industries include food and beverage processing, leather goods, textiles, carpets, chemicals, cement, and mining operations, especially coal mining.

Trade. Under socialism, the country participated in Comecon, the U.S.S.R.-led, Communist-bloc trade organization. Approximately 85 percent of foreign trade was with the Soviet Union. In the early 1990's, the abrupt loss of foreign aid from the U.S.S.R. along with new trade policies among the former Soviet satellite nations resulted in major economic disruption. Since then, the country has been developing its free market economy and products now being exported include livestock, animal products, cashmere, wool, hides, copper, and fluorspar and other nonferrous metals. The country maintains trade relations with over 25 countries and joined the World Trade Organization in 1997.

Division of Labor. In rural areas of the country, livestock production still predominates followed by crop production. In herding households, people of all ages are involved in safeguarding, caring for, and increasing the herds on which they subsist. While both young men and women participate in herding activities, older persons may help with caring for animals at the campsite and doing household chores including repairing tools, preparing hides, sewing, cooking, and childcare. By contrast, in urban areas manufacturing, industrial, and service-oriented jobs are the norm. For these jobs, specialized abilities and training are more frequently required.

SOCIAL STRATIFICATION

Classes and Castes. Like many nomadic pastoral cultures, the Mongols had a segmentary society, originally organized into a hierarchy of families, clans, tribes, and confederations. While social classes including nobility, herders, artisans, and slaves existed, the social structure was not completely rigid and social mobility was possible. Under socialism, economic and social equality increased as variation in herd size and wealth levels was reduced. Economic expansion and rapid industrialization also contributed to increasing social mobility. The post-socialist period has been marked by increasing wealth differentiation. While certain segments of the population, such as new entrepreneurs, have prospered in the 1990s, others have become rapidly impoverished.

Symbols of Social Stratification. In ancient times, material cultural objects including headdresses, clothing, horse-blankets and saddles, jewelry, and other personal objects were visual symbols of tribal affiliation and social status. Today emerging wealth is often shown by purchasing and dis-

Two cars travel up a street in the capital city of Ulan Bator. The population in 1990 was 58 percent urban.

playing expensive imported goods from Western countries.

POLITICAL LIFE

Government. As a socialist nation, Mongolia modeled its political and economic systems on those of the U.S.S.R. For seven decades, the Mongolian People's Revolutionary Party (MPRP) governed, working closely with the Soviet Union. A major transition in governmental structure and political institutions began in the late 1980s in response to the collapse of the U.S.S.R. Free elections in 1990 resulted in a multiparty government that was still mostly Communist. A new constitution was adopted in 1992. In 1996, the Communist MPRP was defeated for the first time since 1921 by an electoral coalition called the Democratic Alliance. However, after four turbulent years and a series of prime ministers, the MPRP regained control of the government in 2000.

The highest legislative body is a unicameral parliament called the State Great Hural with 76 elected members. A president serves as the head of state and a prime minister is the head of government. After legislative elections, the leader of the majority party is typically elected prime minister by the parliament. The president is elected to a four year term by popular vote. Local government leaders are elected at the *aimag* (provincial) and *soum* (district) levels.

Social Problems and Control. The original Mongolian legal code was the *yasa*, a body of laws created after Genghis Khan's death but greatly influenced by his system of state administration. This legal code dealt with military discipline, criminal law and societal customs and regulation. The modern legal system is closely related to that of the Soviet Union. Under socialism, crimes committed against the state and/or socialist owned property were treated particularly harshly. In the post socialist era, emerging poverty has resulted in an increase in crimes such as property theft and robbery, especially in the major cities.

Military Activity. Situated in the geographically strategic location between Russia and China, the country is deeply concerned with national security issues. Mongolian and Soviet troops have generally been closely allied throughout the 20th century. These armies fought together in the 1921 Mongolian Revolution and in the 1930s against Japanese border incursions. Under socialism, both Soviet and Mongolian military bases existed in the Gobi region where the Mongolian border with China was heavily guarded.

Mongolian nomads cook at a stove outside a yurt. Meat and dairy products are a predominant staple of the diet.

SOCIAL WELFARE AND CHANGE PROGRAMS

An elaborate social welfare system was established under socialism, providing all citizens with access to health care, education, and pensions. The government received significant subsidies from the U.S.S.R. to pay for these generous programs. Following the withdrawal of Soviet aid, funding these programs has been a major challenge. New social problems, such as the existence of several thousand street children, have arisen as fallout from the ongoing economic crisis.

GENDER ROLES AND STATUSES

Division of Labor by Gender. For many centuries, there was a customary gender division of labor in this nomadic pastoral society. Men typically handled external affairs including military, administrative, and trade matters. Men were primarily responsible for herding animals, hunting, slaughtering animals, and maintaining animal shelters. Repairing carts, tools, and weapons were also considered men's work. Women were mainly responsible for housework, milking animals, making dairy products, cooking, washing, sewing, and nurturing children.

Relative Status of Women and Men. Unlike their counterparts elsewhere in Asia, Mongolian women historically enjoyed fairly high status and freedom. Since fertility was valued over virginity, the Mongols did not place the same emphasis on female purity as found in the Islamic societies in Asia. Although women had legal equality with men under socialism, they were burdened with the responsibilities of housework and childcare as well as their labor for wages.

MARRIAGE, FAMILY, AND KINSHIP

Marriage. Traditionally, families were the main unit of production in this herding society. The kinship system was patrilineal and sons generally established households in a common camp with their fathers. Marriages were arranged by parents and a bridal dowry (usually consisting of animals) was negotiated based upon the social status of the families. The 20th-century norm became for children to choose their own marriage partners with less extensive parental involvement.

Domestic Unit. Several generations of families customarily live together in a nomadic camp known as a *khot ail* ("group of tents") and share herding tasks. This camp, generally consisting of two to seven households, serves as a way of pooling labor for herding and has numerous social and ritual functions. Besides the khot ail, a larger neighborhood group called *neg nutgiinhan* ("people of one place") generally consists of four to twenty khot ails that frequently move and work together.

Inheritance. Historically, the cultural pattern of old age support was ultimogeniture and the youngest son would typically inherit the largest share of the parent's animals. Today, there is greater variation in inheritance depending on personality considerations and the economic and living circumstances of different family members.

SOCIALIZATION

Child Rearing and Education. Children have always been treasured in Mongolian culture, and large families were historically the norm. Large families were considered desirable because many children ensured extra help and security in old age. Although family size is changing today, the country is still so sparsely populated that some people still believe it is advantageous to have "as many Mongolians as possible." Attitudes about child rearing are generally quite relaxed and all family members participate in the supervision and moral education of children. Under socialism, a high value was placed on elementary education and literacy. While education was limited to monks in Buddhist monasteries before the 20th century, under socialism the adult literacy rate rose to over 90 percent.

Higher Education. The Mongolian State University was founded in 1942. Much of the teaching was originally in Russian due to a lack of Mongol language texts in specialized fields. Under socialism, the higher education system provided opportunities for promising students from all regions of the country to participate in advanced study in the Soviet Union or in Eastern Europe and education was closely linked to upward social mobility.

ETIQUETTE

Hospitality has always been extremely important in Mongolian culture. Since visitors often travel great distances, there are many ritual ways of showing politeness, especially to guests. One such custom that remains from feudal times is the snuff bottle ritual— a guest and host offer each other their snuff bottles to examine as part of a greeting ritual. It is customarily expected that guests will be served the finest food possible and that vodka will also be plentiful.

RELIGION

Religious Beliefs. The main religion is Lamaism, which is the Yellow Sect of Tibetan Buddhism. Until the 16th century, shamanism was the dominant religion in Mongolia. Lamaism was introduced to the populace by the leader Altan Khan (1507–83). In the 18th century, the Manchus further encouraged Lamaism since they preferred Mongol males to become monks rather than warriors. Paralleling the Stalinist period in the Soviet Union, communists held massive religious purges in the 1930s. More than 700 monasteries were destroyed and thousands of monks were killed. In the post-socialist period, Buddhism is experiencing a resurgence and young people are again learning Buddhist practices from their elders who still remember them from their own childhoods. Approximately 5 percent of the total Mongolian population are Sunni Muslims, mainly ethnic Kazakhs in the western region. After 1990, Western missionaries arrived in Mongolia and began to proselytize; there may be as many as several thousand Mongolian Christians today.

Religious Practitioners. As the importance of Lamaist temples grew in the society, each Mongol

Women making felt in Undursant. Traditionally, women enjoyed high social status.

family was encouraged to provide one son to be raised in a temple and become a lama. Fewer women became nuns although there were some who pursued this career. Training for lamas focused on theological studies and learning to perform elaborate ceremonies to be carried out for the people. Since many temples had extensive libraries, some lamas were also trained in subjects including astronomy, astrology, mathematics, and medicine. While a small percentage of temples were preserved intact under socialism, the majority were dismantled and the lamas returned to the work force at large. In the post-socialist era, those who are familiar with Lamaist traditions are now in great demand to educate younger people who have received no formal religious training.

Rituals and Holy Places. For centuries, Lamaist temples played a central role in community life and were a major gathering place for nomads living considerable distances apart. Although many temples were destroyed under socialism, a number remained standing including three major temples that were preserved as showcases of traditional culture: Gandan Monastery (Ulaanbaatar), Erdene Zuu Monastery (Ovorkhangai), and Amarbayasgalant Monastery (near Darkhan).

Death and the Afterlife. Funerals were traditionally an important and costly event for Mongolian families. They would customarily give lamas substantial monetary gifts to pray for the well-being of the spirit of the deceased. Receiving the lamas' consultation about the handling and disposition of the body was considered very important to prevent future misfortune from occurring to the family. Others in the community would typically provide gifts of animals and money to assist the family at the time of the funeral.

MEDICINE AND HEALTH CARE

While basic healthcare became available nationwide under socialism, specialized care remained concentrated in cities. Along with Western-style medicine, herbal medicine, acupuncture, and massage are widely practiced in Mongolia. Based on the Soviet and Eastern European tradition, therapeutic spas became very popular. Although the primary healthcare system operated quite efficiently under socialism, providing adequate healthcare resources in the post-socialist era has proved challenging due to the ongoing economic crisis. Thus, the long-term impact of this major societal transition on health indicators is unknown. In 2000, the estimated life expectancy at birth for the total population was 67.25 years, with male life expectancy being 64.98 years and female life expectancy being 69.64 years.

SECULAR CELEBRATIONS

Major public holidays are New Year's Day (1 January); Lunar New Year or *Tsagaan Car*, meaning "White Month," a three-day holiday with variable dates in late January to early February); Women's Day (8 March); Naadam, anniversary of 1921 Mongolian Revolution (11–13 July); and Mongolian Republic Day (26 November).

THE ARTS AND HUMANITIES

Literature. Since the Mongols were always highly mobile, most art forms that became popular were portable and involved little or no equipment, such as epic poetry, literature, music, and dance. The most famous epic poem of all time is "The Secret History of the Mongols," a long poem describing Genghis Khan's rise to power and the creation of the Mongol Empire. This poem was written down in the mid- to late-13th century and was supposed to be hidden from non-Mongols. Folktales also played a major role in oral literature and their subject matter ranged from love to heroism to supernatural acts. Modern literature has been heavily influenced by Western literary styles, especially Russian literature.

Graphic Arts. The nature and types of graphic arts found in Mongolia were also influenced by the nomadic heritage. Articles of daily use including saddles, horse blankets, storage chests, and knives were often highly decorative. Painting and sculpture could be found in permanent buildings, such as temples, throughout the country. Religious themes dominated traditional painting and sculpture because these art forms were largely produced within Lamaist temples. The Museum of Fine Arts in Ulaanbaatar has an extensive collection of Lamaistic paintings, sculpture, and other religious objects from different periods. Scroll paintings called *tanka* that depicted the various gods and saints of Lamaist Buddhism decorated every temple. These paintings were both imported from Tibet and created locally by lamas. *Tanka* came in a variety of sizes and were often painted on cotton or silk. In the post-socialist period, it has become increasingly popular for Mongol families to own *tanka* and display them in their homes. Under socialism, local artists produced their own substantial body of Soviet-encouraged socialist art, which is less in favor today.

Performance Arts. Performing arts have been widely practiced in Mongolia for centuries. Today there are many professional and amateur theaters and musical organizations both in the capital and in other provincial towns. In both the socialist and post-socialist eras, the government has been supportive of performing arts and has subsidized traveling shows of operas, plays, ballets, folk music and dancing, and circuses. The most important folk instrument is the *morin khuur* (horse-head fiddle), a stringed instrument whose name comes from the horse head carved above the tuning pegs. The morin khuur has a trapezoid-shaped body, leather sounding board, and two strings that are played with a bow made of wood and horsehair. Playing from a seated position, the musician rests the morin khuur on his knee. In many areas of the country, men were traditionally expected to know how to play the morin khuur. It is often played together with the *tovshuur* and the *shudraga* (two banjo-like stringed instruments). Other instruments used in folk music include transverse and vertical flutes, drums, cymbals, gongs, and tambourines. Like poetry, vocal music is very important in this culture and there are multiple types of folk songs. Herding songs and work songs are most typical and these songs can have specific purposes (e.g., a herding song to call back animals that have strayed or a work song sung while setting up camp). Other types of folk songs include *yurol* (songs of blessing), *maatgal* (songs of praise), *urtyn duu* (''long songs'' performed by professional singers with operatic training), and *khoomei* (harmonic singing in which one performer combines humming and whistling to sound like several people singing at once). In the post-socialist era, the country's youth have embraced Western music and there are quite a few nightclubs in the major cities where one can dance to the same pop music topping the charts in the United States, Europe, and elsewhere in Asia. A growing number of local rock groups are now performing whose music is mainly sold in Mongolia but can also sometimes be found in other Asian countries.

THE STATE OF THE PHYSICAL AND SOCIAL SCIENCES

Based on the Soviet model, under socialism the country established specialized research institutes that were separate from the academic departments which taught science in universities. The Mongolian Academy of Science was founded in 1961 and had at least 14 working research institutes by the 1980s. In the post-socialist period, the Mongolian Academy of Science fell upon hard times during the national economic crisis. However, funding from a variety of international organizations enabled some Mongolian scientists to study abroad and have access to state-of-the-art equipment. The Academy also has Internet access, allowing scientists to easily communicate with their scholarly peers in other nations.

BIBLIOGRAPHY

Bawden, C. R. *The Modern History of Mongolia*, 1989.

Bruun, O. and O. Odgaard, eds. *Mongolia in Transition: Old Patterns, New Challenges*, 1996.

Cooper, L. *Patterns of Mutual Assistance in the Mongolian Pastoral Economy*, 1994.

———. *Wealth and Poverty in Pastoral Economy*, 1995.

De Hartog, L. *Genghis Khan: Conqueror of the World* 1989.

Dondog, L., ed. *Mongolia Foreign Investment Trade and Tourism*, 1996.

Goldstein, M., and C. Beall. *The Changing World of Mongolia's Nomads*, 1994.

Griffin, K., ed. *Poverty and the Transition to a Market Economy in Mongolia*, 1995.

Harper, C. *An Assessment of Vulnerable Groups in Mongolia*, 1992.

Jagchid, S., and P. Hyer. *Mongolia's Culture and Society*, 1979.

Major, J. S. D. *The Land and People of Mongolia*, 1990.

Mearns, R. *Pastoral Institutions, Land Tenure and Land Policy Reform in Post-Socialist Mongolia*, 1993.

Morgan, D. *The Mongols*, 1986.

Neupert, R. F. *Population Policies, Socioeconomic Development and Population Dynamics in Mongolia*, 1996.

Oyunchimeg, D. *Mongolian Economy and Society in 1995*, 1996.

Potkanski, T. *Decollectivisation of the Mongol Pastoral Economy (1991–92): Some Economic and Social Consequences*, 1994.

Rossabi, M. *China and Inner Asia: From 1368 to the Present Day*, 1975.

———. *Khubilai Khan: His Life and Times*, 1988.

Rupen, R. *How Mongolia Is Really Ruled: A Political History of the Mongolian People's Republic 1900–1978*, 1979.

Sneath, D. *Social Relations, Networks and Social Organisation in Post-Socialist Rural Mongolia*, 1994.

Storey, R. *Mongolia*, 1993.

Swift, J. *Rural Development: The Livestock Sector in Poverty and the Transition to a Market Economy in Mongolia*, 1995.

Templer, G., J. Swift, and P. Payne. *The Changing Significance of Risk in the Mongolian Pastoral Economy*, 1994.

World Bank. *Mongolia Poverty Assessment in a Transition Economy*, 1996.

World Factbook. *Mongolia*, 1999.

Web Sites

Permanent Mission of Mongolia to the United Nations. www.undp.org/missions/mongolia/mngstate.htm, 2000.

—SHERYLYN H. BRILLER

MONTENEGRO SEE SERBIA AND MONTENEGRO

MONTSERRAT

CULTURE NAME

Montserratian

ORIENTATION

Identification. Before 1995, this pear-shaped island had a population of about ten thousand and was lush, green, mountainous, isolated, and unspoiled. There are three green-clad mountain ranges and the island is edged by largely black sand beaches. Much of the land is fertile with a healthy tropical climate.

Location and Geography. Montserrat, covering 39.5 square miles (63.7 square kilometers), is a British Crown colony between Nevis and Guadeloupe. Christopher Columbus gave this Caribbean island its name. On his second voyage, Columbus noticed that the island resembled the land around the Spanish abbey of Santa Maria de Montserrati.

Montserrat occupies a region of the earth's crust that is geologically unstable, with volcanic activity and earthquakes an ever present reality. Hurricanes and other natural disasters have long plagued this otherwise idyllic "Emerald Isle" of the Caribbean. Economic issues and ecological necessity remain persistent features of the national culture and values. Although many people are impressed with the individuality of the island, Montserrat is a country looking for a national identity.

Demography. Montserrat has for some time been considering independence from Great Britain. It has a unique blend of Anglo-Irish and African cultures and thus is an example of a fairly successful blend of two very different cultures and races. Until recently, national self-image was a hot topic as a result of extensive outmigration. After Hurricane Hugo in 1989, the population dropped from 11,500 to slightly less than 10,000 people. After 1995, volcanic eruptions halved that number.

Linguistic Affiliation. The official language is English, but a dialect is widely spoken on informal occasions. Monserratians tend to use standard English in formal contexts and creole English in informal contexts.

Symbolism. The national emblem is a carved Irish shamrock adorning Government House, and the island's flag and crest show a woman with a cross and harp. Other cultural survivals, such as a value systems, codes of etiquette, musical styles, and an Irish recipe for the national dish called "goat water" stew, are considerably more problematic as cultural legacies.

HISTORY AND ETHNIC RELATIONS

Emergence of the Nation. Very little is known of the early history of Montserrat. The aboriginal population probably was made up of Arawak Indians who were killed off by Carib Indians by the time of Columbus's voyage in 1494. The Caribs left the island by the middle of the seventeenth century but continued to raid it. They named the island *Alliouagana* ("Land of the Prickly Bush"), perhaps after the aloe plant.

Montserrat is often referred to as "the Emerald Isle of the West" because the Irish figured prominently in its early history. Montserrat was first settled in 1632 by a British contingent from the mother colony of Saint Kitts. Although the original colonists were English and Irish, Montserrat quickly became a haven for Irish Catholics escaping from religious persecution. The Irish first came as indentured servants and later as slaves to work in the plantation system.

Later, Catholic refugees from Virginia came to escape from religious persecution. By 1648, there were one thousand Irish families on the island. The French occupied the country between 1644 and 1782 but ceded it to Britain in 1783.

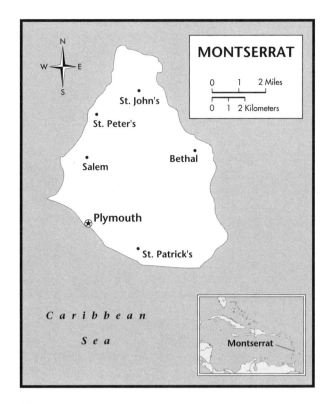

Montserrat

In 1649, Cromwell sent political prisoners to Montserrat, increasing the population and helping to preserve its Irish character.

National Identity. Irish cultural retentions are largely symbolic. Some claim that modern-day Montserratians have an Irish brogue, but linguistic evidence is not conclusive. Irish names abound, and the phenotype of the inhabitants seems "lighter" than it is in other Afro-Caribbean countries. Most of the inhabitants appear to be of an African heritage.

The national emblem is a carved Irish shamrock adorning Government House, and the island's flag and crest show a woman with a cross and harp. Other cultural survivals, such as a value systems, codes of etiquette, musical styles, and an Irish recipe for the national dish called "goat water" stew, are considerably more problematic as cultural legacies.

Montserrat's luxuriant vegetation, emerald hills, and fern-covered ravines have given it a striking resemblance to Ireland, and its history has left ruins of the plantation period as well as colorful houses in the capital city of Plymouth. However, the contemporary culture is pan-Caribbean with a heavy overlay of African and Anglo-Irish elements.

Sugar and slaves eventually changed both the economy and the culture. In the seventeenth century, after tobacco production waned, Montserrat developed into a typical plantation colony. The date of the arrival of the first slaves (1651) corresponded roughly with the start of the sugar industry. Slaves quickly outnumbered Irish indentured servants, and eventually there were more blacks than whites.

By 1705, a planter class, based on slave labor and sugar, was fully established. The planter class attempted to control and coerce the blacks, leading to several rebellions, including the Saint Patrick's Day rebellion of 17 March 1768.

Sugar fortunes began to disappear toward the end of the eighteenth century. Earthquakes, droughts, hurricanes, French raids, and the loss of slave labor after emancipation (1834) combined to end the "plantocracy." Cotton supported the economy until the 1960s, when tourism and an elaborate real estate construction scheme were instituted.

Montserrat has become an emigration society, with remittances being important sources of revenue. The recent volcanic eruptions have made Montserrat dependent on Britain for its survival.

URBANISM, ARCHITECTURE, AND THE USE OF SPACE

Some islanders are sensitive about the size of Montserrat. Its size of 30,000 acres, of which almost two-thirds are mountainous and barren, coupled with the recent economic and ecological crises, has created an "economics of scale." The industrial and commercial potential has been hampered by low population growth, mountainous terrain, poor air access, the high cost of energy, and a limited infrastructure. Choked by conditions of underdevelopment and poverty, nationalism is a sentiment held by a relatively small segment of the population. Lacking in this national self-image are emotionally charged symbols such as flag waving. Rather than chauvinistic political rhetoric, one is more likely to hear references to an unspoiled landscape, satisfaction with the customs and lifestyle, and sentiments of security derived from the safety of a home isolated from the rapidly changing world.

FOOD AND ECONOMY

Food in Daily Life. Native-grown breadfruit, mango, soursop, pawpaw, and cashews are regarded by some locals as less desirable food.

Basic Economy. Agriculture has not supported the population. To foster tourism, the government decided to avoid high-rise hotels and noisy nightclubs; instead, Montserrat was to be a model of "the way

A woman walks along a narrow street in the town of Plymouth.

the Caribbean used to be." In the 1960s, Montserrat embarked on a tourist venture called "residential tourism." In a country where 90 percent of the citizens are black, white North Americans and Europeans were encouraged to settle in a restricted part of the island as permanent or part-time residents. The result has been a concentration of prosperous white foreigners living in villas by the sea, with multiple servants and imported amenities.

Another economic factor was the establishment of an offshore medical school that catered to North Americans, mostly from the United States. Montserrat was a regional media center, broadcasting to the entire Antillean region. The most famous of the foreign studios, however, pulled out after the last hurricane.

Montserrat's agricultural history has been marked with repeated failures; the island has been plagued with charges of international banking frauds; and the trade deficit has been balanced only by overseas remittances and capital from foreign expatriates. When Hurricane Hugo struck in 1989, aid for reconstruction was provided by the United Kingdom.

Major Industries. The economy is based mainly on agriculture, real estate, building construction, tourism, and assembling industries. There is little manufacturing activity. There was, until the volcanic eruptions, an expanding tourist trade; and the island was beginning to build an integrated cotton industry (sea island cotton), although the island lacks the technology to handle large volumes of cotton. The off-shore medical school had to move to another island after the recent natural disaster.

Trade. The government had plans of reviving farming, creating a tourist industry, and supporting a real estate-and-home-construction scheme; but Montserrat has been for many years marginal in relation to overseas markets, compounded by a series of natural disasters to the island.

SOCIAL STRATIFICATION

Classes and Castes. The pattern of social stratification that emerged after the slavery period remains relatively unaltered. Lower classes predominate in this society.

The upper class includes resident owners and managers of the larger estates, expatriate colonial officials, professionals, religious leaders, bank managers, and larger merchants. Most are white or light-skinned. There are no poor whites. The upper classes generally live and work in the capital city of Plymouth, speak English, and adhere to legal forms

A fisherman untangles his net from his boat on the beach at Carr's Bay.

of marriage and a nuclear form of the family. They belong to the Anglican, Methodist, and Roman Catholic denominations.

The middle class consists of salaried employees or civil servants who work for the post office, hospitals, courts, or the police department. This is the class that aims for secondary schooling. With increased educational opportunities, there is a growing middle class, which tends to use "standard" English in formal contexts, and creole English in others. Many of these households employ at least one domestic servant. Mostly Anglican, Methodist, or Roman Catholic, this is the class most anxious about appropriate behavior. There is an emerging professional class.

The lower classes are primarily black and are characterized by sporadic employment, with many people dependent on remittances. Virtually all live outside Plymouth. Migration was predominantly a lower-class phenomenon before the 1995 evacuations. Most of the members of this class follow Pentecostal faiths. Relationship patterns perhaps represent the greatest institutional variation between classes.

POLITICAL LIFE

Government. Representative government was introduced in 1936; Montserrat got a new constitution in 1952, and Britain introduced a bicameral system of government in 1960. Virtually all effective political power has been in the hands of the few who control production (the monopoly of the wealthy). Montserrat has elected to remain a colony, although some have argued for a discontinuation of colonial status. There is almost total dependence on Great Britain.

Leadership and Political Officials. Montserrat has a representative government with a ministerial system, practicing parliamentary democracy rooted in the Westminster model. The head of state is represented by a governor, who exercises executive authority. Britain is still responsible for the island's external affairs, defense, and law and order, although Montserrat has a fairly autonomous local government. The chief minister is John Osborne, who has always favored independence for the country. The recent natural disasters effectively put this question to rest for now.

Social Problems and Control. A nation of emigration, with severe loss of population, Montserrat has choking conditions of underdevelopment, poverty, unemployment, declining productivity of abused space, unavailable markets, land problems, and insecure subsistence production, as well as fear, suspicion, and mistrust, especially since the natural disasters of Hugo and the volcanic eruptions. It is a nation suffering from a colonial past, a Caribbean laboratory with "infinitely limited alternatives." There have been various schemes proposed to eliminate some of the social problems, but to date all have failed, e.g., the geothermal project that did not take into account popular superstition about disturbing the dormant volcanoes. The present socioeconomic crises cannot be separated from the recent natural disasters. Great Britain has had to bail out the Montserratians once more.

NONGOVERNMENTAL ORGANIZATIONS AND OTHER ASSOCIATIONS

In a typical parish, there might be three rum shops, four small provision shops, a sub-post office, the Methodist church and smaller Holiness church, and a school. However, Rotary and Jaycees are both active on the island. Montserrat has a theater with plays that address Caribbean issues and at least two dance groups. Choral music groups and sports are also popular.

GENDER ROLES AND STATUSES

Gender roles vary by class, with more rigidity in the lower strata. Homosexuality is feared. Marriage is valued, being associated with socioeconomic standing and as a demonstration of ambition and the attainment of social adulthood.

MARRIAGE, FAMILY, AND KINSHIP

Marriage. Once a proposed marriage union is recognized, the couple are referred to as being "friendly" or as being "sweethearts." The migration of either party in such a union is regarded as terminating that union. Most lower-class Montserratians eventually legally marry, because marriage is associated with a higher socioeconomic standing. Legal divorce is fairly rare.

Domestic Unit. The major domestic unit is the household, which encompasses kinship, mating, land tenure, and inheritance. Migration has caused some unique problems for maintenance of the domestic unit in Montserrat.

Inheritance. About half the children born are technically illegitimate, but no stigma is attached to this fact. All children are entitled to an equal share of the parents' fixed property regardless of birth order or sex.

Kin Groups. Standard English kin terms apply in Montserrat, except for "niece" and "nephew," which are rarely used. Children are typically given the name of their genitors regardless of the type of mating arrangement.

SOCIALIZATION

Child Rearing and Education. Children are cared for within the domestic unit of family, which tends to be matrifocal. Children are given the name of their genitor. Pre-primary education is provided in nursery schools for 3-5 year-olds, while primary education for children of 7-11 years is provided in 15 primary schools. Religion has had a strong influence on education. Anglicans and Methodists broadened the base, and Quakers also played a vital role in education. Education, however, tended to render the educated unfit for life on the island.

Higher Education. Secondary education is fairly well developed throughout the island, but access to tertiary education is only through a school of continuing education sponsored by the University the West Indies.

Water cascades over the yellow rocks and soil of the Galway Soufriere volcanic vent. Montserrat depends on Britian for its survival, due to recent volcanic eruptions.

RELIGION

Religious Beliefs. Protestant sects have multiplied in recent times. Catholics were a strong religious group in the 1800s, but today the largest religious denomination is Anglican Protestant. The first church, built by Governor Anthony Brisket, was probably Anglican. Pentecostal churches are growing.

MEDICINE AND HEALTH CARE

Medical services are reasonably adequate on the island, with a number of private medical practitioners available as well as doctors in the government health service. Health centers are scattered throughout the island. Free medical attention and medication are provided for children and the aged.

SECULAR CELEBRATIONS

Saint Patrick's Day, March 17, is celebrated with feasts and festivities by the island's Irish inhabitants, and local scholars made it a national day on which to celebrate the freedom fighters of the abortive 1768 slave uprising. August 1 is Emancipation Day, and August Monday a national holiday, with picnics, bazaars, and dances. Many parishes have village days, beauty contests, and Calypso contests.

THE ARTS AND HUMANITIES

The arts and humanities are largely confined to folk representations. The trappings of black power, Afro clothing, and plaited hair have appeared and disappeared. However, there has been a new appreciation of self and a search for national identity. The new consciousness has found expression in research into local folk music, folktales, proverbs, riddles, and dialects. There has been an attempt to recognize and reconcile the African contributions to Montserrat's cultural mosaic.

BIBLIOGRAPHY

Berleant-Schiller, R. "Montserrat." *World Bibliographical Series* 134, 1991.

Fergus, H. A. "Montserrat: Paradise or Prison." *Bulletin of Eastern Caribbean Affairs* 12 (1): 1–10, 1986.

———. *History of Alliouaguana: A Short History of Montserrat*, 1975.

Fitzgerald, T. K., and H. A. Fergus, H. A. "National Self-Image on A Caribbean Island: Montserrat, W. I." *Journal of Eastern Caribbean Studies* 22 (2): 56–67, 1997.

Fitzgerald, T. K. *Metaphors of Identity: A Culture-Communication Dialoque*, 1993.

Irish, J. A. G. *Life in a Colonial Crucible: Labor and Social Change in Montserrat 1946–Present*, 1991.

Kurlansky, M. *A Continent of Islands: Seraching for the Caribbean Destiny*, 1992.

Messenger, J. C. "Montserrat: 'The Most Distinctively Irish Settlement in the New World.'" *Ethnicity* 2: 281–303, 1975.

Philpott, S. B. *West Indian Migration: The Montserrat Case*, 1973.

Schlesinger, P. *Media, State and Nation: Political Violence and Collective Identities*, 1991.

Smith, A. D. *National Identity: Ethnonationalism in Comparative Perspective*, 1991.

Williams, A. R. "Under the Volcano: Montserrat." *National Geographic* 192 (1): 58–75, 1997.

—THOMAS K. FITZGERALD

THE UNITED KINGDOM OF MOROCCO

CULTURE NAME
Moroccan

ALTERNATIVE NAMES
Local long form: Al Mamlakah al Maghribiyah; local short form: Al Maghrib

ORIENTATION

Identification. Al Maghrib, the Arabic name for Morocco, means ''far west'' or ''where the sun sets.'' When the Arabs first arrived in northern Africa in the seventh century C.E., Morocco was believed to be the westernmost point in the world. At that time, the Maghrib region included the countries that are today Morocco, Algeria, and Tunisia. The countries of the Maghrib share many common historical and cultural features. All have indigenous Berber populations and a strong Islamic base. Similarly, all were colonized by France, and remain largely bilingual, with both French and Arabic being spoken. Although European influence in Morocco is strong, it is still a country of distinctly Arabic tradition. The vast difference between the crude life on the streets and the hospitality and intimacy found in the home reflect the duality that is deeply ingrained in Moroccan culture. But one aspect of Moroccan life that is distinctly unified is religion. The king has declared that all citizens are born Sunni Muslims, and Islam is an important part of everyday ritual life. The Moroccan government is a constitutional monarchy, with a very powerful king. It is this mix of European and Arab influence, loyalty to the king and a strong Islamic base, that creates the uniquely Moroccan identity.

Location and Geography. Morocco is slightly larger than the state of California, covering approximately 174,000 square miles (447,000 square kilometers), and lies in northern Africa just south of the Strait of Gibraltar. Its bordering countries are

Spain to the north, Algeria to the east, and the disputed Western Sahara territory to the south. The northern portion of the country borders the Atlantic Ocean to the west and the Mediterranean Sea to the northeast, resulting in a moderate and subtropical coastal climate. Temperatures in the interior are more extreme, with very hot summers and cold winters. Morocco is comprised of four distinct geographic regions. The Rif Mountains lie in the northern part of the country parallel to the Mediterranean coast and rise to 8,000 feet (2,400 meters). The Rif are home to the Rifi Berbers, one of the largest indigenous tribes remaining in the country. A wide area of coastal plains extends across the western seaboard, a region of phosphate mining and the cultivation of citrus, olives, tobacco, and grains. Many of these resources are processed for export, making the western coast the economic center of the country. The majority of Morocco's heavily populated urban centers also lie in this region, including the capital city of Rabat. The Atlas Mountain region has three distinct ranges, known as the Middle, High, and Anti-Atlas. The High and Middle Atlas are home to the Amazigh Berbers, another of the major tribes, while the Soussi tribe lives in the Anti-Atlas. Vastly different from the bustling cities, the countryside allows these groups to maintain their tribal tradition as farmers. Finally, a corner of the Sahara desert lies in the southeastern part of Morocco, where few nomadic people remain and a desert climate prevails.

Demography. The current population of Morocco is approximately 30 million, half of whom are under the age of nineteen. Out of the total population, 99.1 percent are identified as Arab-Berber. The indigenous tribes who occupied much of northwestern Africa were given the generic title Berber, meaning simply non-Arab, by the Arabs. After centuries of intermingling, most Moroccans today are an Arab-Berber mix, although a few tribes in the countryside identify themselves as purely Berber. The remaining .09 percent of the population is com-

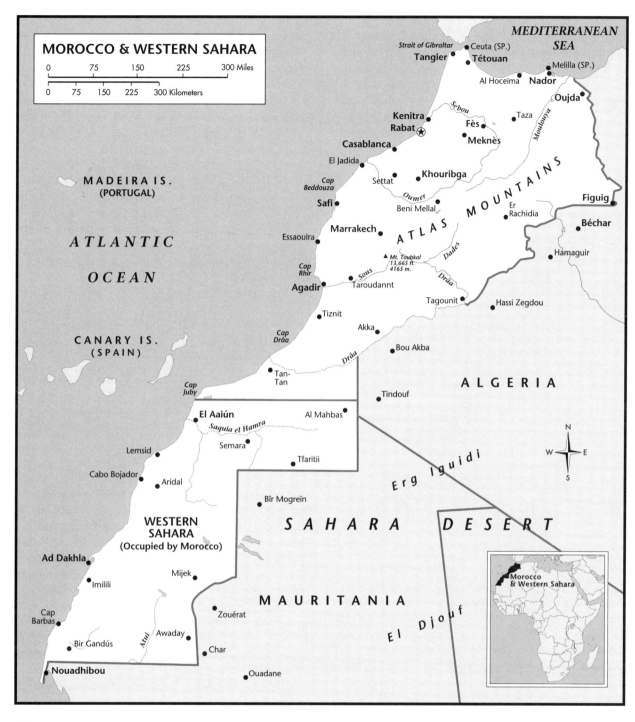

Morocco

prised of Jews, white Europeans, and black Africans. (Demographic and other statistics presented in this article do not include Western Sahara.)

Linguistic Affiliation. Moroccan Arabic is the official language of Morocco. It is spoken by roughly three-quarters of the population and differs slightly from modern standard Arabic and other dialects in

grammar and vocabulary. Although half a century has passed since the French colonial period in Morocco ended, French remains the official language in business, government, and diplomacy. Before the Arabs spread their language and culture across northern Africa, Berber dialects were spoken in Algeria, Morocco, and Tunisia. Although the dialects can still be heard in some rural areas, the Berber linguistic tradition is oral rather than literary, and there is no formal alphabet or standard written form of the language. There are three main Berber dialects in Morocco. Rifan is the dialect spoken in the Rif Mountains as well as in some rural areas of eastern Morocco along the Algerian border. In the High and Middle Atlas region the dialect spoken has many names; it may be called Amazigh, Zaran, or Tamazight. In the southwestern oasis and the Anti-Atlas region, the dialect may be called Soussi, Celha, Tashelhait, or Chleuh. Spanish is widely spoken in the northern parts of the country, and English is commonly spoken to international tourists. Multilingualism exists to such a degree that Moroccans may switch from one language to another midsentence.

Symbolism. Perhaps the most famous city in Morocco is Casablanca. Port activities by the French turned this city into the economic capital of the country in the early 1900s. In 1942 the city was the site of an Allied invasion, and in 1943 it was the host city for a conference between Franklin Delano Roosevelt and Winston Churchill. But it was the 1943 Hollywood classic film *Casablanca*, starring Ingrid Bergman and Humphrey Bogart, that transformed the city into an international symbol of romance and wartime struggle. The black-and-white film was the 1943 Academy Award winner for best picture. Other films with quintessential images of Morocco include *Lawrence of Arabia* and *The Jewel of the Nile*. A more eastern symbol of Morocco is the Hassan II Mosque, built in Casablanca in 1993. It is one of the largest and most extravagant mosques in the Arab world.

Dating back to the Alaouite Dynasty in the seventeenth century, a red flag was used as a symbol of the Moroccan state. In Rabat and Salé the flag was raised every morning and lowered every evening. When the French took control in 1912, a five-pointed linear known as Solomon's seal was placed on the flag in order to distinguish the nation's flag from others. Because green is the traditional color of Islam, the star on the flag is green.

HISTORY AND ETHNIC RELATIONS

Emergence of the Nation. The first people to have contact with the Berbers were probably the Phoenicians, who invaded northern Africa in the twelfth century B.C.E. The Phoenicians were essentially a maritime people who established trading posts and simple colonies along the northern coast. The Phoenician colonies were later taken over by the Carthaginians, and expanded as part of the Carthaginian Empire. In the second century B.C.E., the city of Carthage fell to the Romans, and the African Mediterranean coast came under Roman dominance for roughly six hundred years. Following the decline of the Romans, the Vandals, Visigoths, and Byzantine Greeks successively set up their own empires. Finally, in 682 C.E., the Arabs invaded northwestern Africa, and the first Muslim Arab dynasty, the Idrisid, came to power. Pagan and Christian inhabitants of the land were converted to Islam during this period. For centuries to follow, Arab and Berber factions fought a bitter civil war over control of the land. By the fifteenth century, European powers had become aware of the trading and economic potential of their southern neighbor. Britain, Spain, Portugal, and France took turns controlling various coastal areas of Morocco. Finally, at the Conference of Algeciras in 1906, France was recognized as the dominant European power in the area. This conference also established the northernmost city, Tangier, as an international free port, under control of the Spanish.

In 1912, Moroccan Sultan Moulay Hafid signed the Treaty of Fez, establishing Morocco as a protectorate of France. The treaty outlined roughly the same borders that define the country today.

As early as the 1920s, an Islamic fundamentalist movement arose in Fez. The goal of the movement was to create a stronger form of Islam and a central Moroccan government. After World War II, the independence movement began to gain momentum. In 1944, Istiqlal, the Moroccan Independence Party, sent an Independence Manifesto to the sultan and French authorities requesting independence. The French responded by arresting several Istiqlal leaders, and deporting the Moroccan royal family to Madagascar in 1953. The people reacted with violence toward French officials, and demanded the return of the king. In August 1955, Berber tribesmen attacked French troops in the village of Oued Zem, killing every French person in the town. Finally, in December 1956, the Moroccan sultan, Muhammad V, was taken to France where he signed a declaration promising to move the nation toward a democratic state with the establishment of a constitutional monarchy. During the same year, the Spanish signed an agreement to remove the international status of Tangier, making Morocco a completely independent and united nation.

National Identity. The civil war between the Arabs and the Berbers finally began to subside in the 1940s and 1950s. After World War II, the quest for independence from France unified the two groups behind a common cause, and the Arabs and Berbers

Entrance to a Moroccan market. Street markets, with local goods, are found in every major city.

began to share nationalistic feelings toward Morocco and its sultan. Widespread acceptance of Islam by both sides further strengthened the independence movement. The movement spread the idea that a stronger central government was needed to provide spiritual leadership to a Muslim population. In modern Morocco devotion to Islam and loyalty to the king are still cornerstones of national identity.

Ethnic Relations. Just south of Morocco lies a disputed territory known as the Western Sahara. The indigenous people that live inside the territory are the Saharawi. Because they are nomadic, their exact number is difficult to determine, although it is estimated to be around 250,000. Prior to the mid-1970s, Spain, Mauritania, and Morocco claimed ownership of all or part of the Western Sahara. In 1975, 350,000 Moroccan civilians backed by King Hassan II marched into the northern part of Western Sahara to claim the territory for Morocco. The massive demonstration is remembered as Green March Day. In an attempt to establish the Western Sahara as an independent nation, a guerilla group called the Polisario formed in 1973. The Polisario have historically received financial support from the Algerian government, which has economic interest in the valuable phosphates within the territory. In 1979, the Polisario convinced Mauritania to relin-

quish its claims on Western Sahara; Spain had already done the same. Morocco is now the only country that claims ownership of the territory. Since 1974 several United Nations referendums have been set to allow the Saharawi population to vote on whether they prefer independence or annexation to Morocco. Each time, the Moroccan government has found reason to postpone the vote, and the territory remains in dispute.

URBANISM, ARCHITECTURE, AND THE USE OF SPACE

The eclectic influence of many cultures is strikingly apparent in Moroccan architecture. Typical of all cities is the *medina*, a large walled area that encloses houses and shops. Medina structures with Arabic-style arches and crenellated walls are usually found in the oldest parts of town. Some buildings within the medina are centuries old, while others are relatively new. Units inside have a wide range of modernity in electricity, water, and sewage services. Other parts of town are constructed like French villages with European-style townhouses and modern plumbing. Also found in every city are traditional Arab mosques, most of which are tall buildings with ornamental geometric patterns covering the doors and walls. In homes, there is a drastic difference between the inside and outside of the building, reflecting the differences Moroccans perceive between public and private life. The outside may be a neglected cement block with a simple door, while inside lie beautiful, ornately decorated rooms. The furniture in homes is usually floor level with plush pillows lining the walls. People come here to eat and lounge, and choose a decorating style that shows the relaxed privacy and intimacy only available in the home.

FOOD AND ECONOMY

Food in Daily Life. Two of the most basic foods in Moroccan daily life are couscous and *harira* soup. Couscous, a dish made with granulated seminola grains, is usually topped with mutton, veal, or beef and a variety of vegetables such as tomatoes, turnips, and pimentos. It is eaten by all sectors of society, and may be referred to as the national dish. The national soup, harira, is a thick paste that comes in many varieties, although it is classically made from water, bouillon, beef or mutton, onions, saffron, walnuts, and salt. Figs and dates are among the most common fruits eaten on a daily basis. Breakfast in Morocco may consist of bread served with olive oil or butter, and coffee or mint tea. Schools and businesses close at noon each day for two to three hours for a midday meal. A traditional dish that may be served during this time is *tajine*, a steam-cooked stew made of meat and vegetables in a spicy broth. A light dinner of harira soup and bread is commonly eaten in the evening. Cakes and desserts made of fruits and marzipan, a sweet almond paste, are sold in pastry shops and on the streets. Imported foods that are not typically part of the traditional Moroccan diet are available in major cities at French-style street markets. As dictated by Islamic law, Muslims do not partake of any alcoholic beverages.

Food Customs at Ceremonial Occasions. Moroccans are famous for their hospitality and proudly serve their guests as much food as they can afford. It is considered disgraceful to allow guests to leave a meal unsatisfied. A specialty dish commonly prepared for ceremonial occasions is *pastilla*, a layered pastry filled with pigeon, eggs, and nuts, topped with cinnamon and sugar. Another specialty dish is *mechoui*, a whole roasted lamb or calf, usually stuffed with couscous or other fillings. In Moroccan homes, families and their guests eat from a communal bowl, usually without utensils, while seated on the floor. Hearty Moroccan eating habits come to a halt during the thirty days of Ramadan, when every Islamic person in the country must fast from dawn until dusk. Moroccans seen eating or drinking during daylight hours in Ramadan may be arrested. During this time, every house prepares harira soup to be eaten as the first meal when the sun goes down. Late at night, a main meal with several dishes is served.

Basic Economy. Agriculture and forestry form the basis of Morocco's economy. Barley, wheat, citrus, vegetables, olives, and livestock are produced for subsistence and for trade. Since gaining its independence, the state has owned most of Morocco's major industries. In 1993, however, Morocco started a new stage of privatization, attempting to encourage international investors. The government authorized the transfer of 112 enterprises—75 companies and 37 hotels—to the private sector. The International Monetary Fund and the World Bank are supporting steps to reform the economy; progress is slow, however, and Morocco remains a heavily indebted developing country.

Commercial Activities. Street markets with local foods and handicrafts, including carpets, traditional dress, pottery, jewelry, and carved wood, can be found in every major city. Intense haggling over the price of most of these goods is the local custom. Maintaining good personal relations with everyone is very important as favors, bribes, kickbacks, and connections all come into play when making the final deal. In the Rif Mountains, large quantities of marijuana, called *kif*, are grown for profit. Drug trafficking of marijuana and cocaine is on the rise for both domestic and international drug markets.

Major Industries. Morocco is the world leader in the production and exportation of phosphates, with three-quarters of the world's reserves. Other major industrial activities include rock mining, food processing, construction, and the manufacturing of leather goods, mineral ores, and textiles. A significant amount of foreign exchange revenue is brought in by Morocco's tourist industry. Because of the rich cultural and historic heritage and renowned hospitality of the people, tourism is growing rapidly.

Trade. Morocco's primary exports are phosphates and phosphoric acid, citrus fruit, wheat, fish, and minerals. The products go primarily to the members of the European Union (EU), Japan, the United States, Libya, and India. The primary imports are industrial machinery, foods, and fuel. Morocco's primary importers are the EU, the United States, Saudi Arabia, the United Arab Emirates, and Russia.

Fes-el bazaar on a holiday. Almost all Moroccans are Sunni Muslim.

Morocco is a member of the World Trade Organization and the Arab League and is an associate member of the EU.

Division of Labor. Unemployment and underemployment are big problems for the unskilled and uneducated. There are a large number of beggars, and 13 percent of all Moroccans fall below the poverty line. Uneducated individuals who have risen slightly above the poverty level have most likely learned a specific trade or skill. For example, a man who learns to become a stone carver provides himself with lifelong work. Uneducated women may find employment by providing domestic services to families other than their own. Those who are fortunate enough to receive university degrees may become doctors, lawyers, university professors, or other professionals. People of the middle and upper classes do not perform any physical labor, and would consider it lowering themselves to do any of their own housework. Physical work must be left to provide jobs for those who have no alternative source of employment.

SOCIAL STRATIFICATION

Classes and Castes. A wide gap exists between the very rich and the very poor. A strong belief in fatalism, that things are meant to be exactly as they are, and the Islamic principal of giving to those in need, lends to the acceptance of social and economic inequality. At the top level of the class system exists the monarch and royal family, members of the government, and a group of very wealthy Moroccans who do not work. They are joined by wholesale merchants and the owners of large manufacturing, industrial, or international trading companies. The upper class often claims to be Arab, although there are as few pure Arabs as there are pure Berbers remaining. An upper middle and middle class is comprised of professionals, mostly educated in Europe. Another group, called Sherfa, are those who claim descent from the prophet Muhammad. Sherfa typically do not work, and those who have no inherited wealth live off the alms of others. A relatively new class, referred to as the Muhajerin, or emigrants, is comprised of nearly 2 million Moroccans who live and work abroad, in order to send their wages back to support their families in Morocco. Many of the Muhajerin are not likely to ever return to their native country. Berber farmers in the countryside have little access to the education and social climbing available to those in larger cities. Most remain poor and are looked down upon. Jews and other foreigners generally prosper, while sub-Saharan black Africans are often discriminated against.

Symbols of Social Stratification. The number of languages spoken and the proficiency acquired are primary identifiers of social class in Morocco. Well-spoken French is perceived as a characteristic of a refined, sophisticated individual. The inability to speak any French usually signifies a lack of education. Fluency in Arabic is accepted, and rather expected of any respectable individual, while those who speak only Berber dialects are looked down upon. Other symbols of status are headgear and clothing. Moroccans have occasion to wear both traditional and Western clothing, therefore it is not the style of the clothes, but rather the quality of what is being worn that symbolizes one's status. For example, the *jellaba*, the traditional one-piece hooded garment worn by both men and women, comes in many varieties. Those of a higher class have theirs hand made by a tailor with intricate needlework and fine fabric. The jellaba is also available at corner shops at a much lower quality. Among the rural poor a knit cap is worn, which would never be placed on the head of an upper- or middle-class man. Turbans worn by Berber men are often white while those of Arab men are orange. A more traditional, perhaps ceremonial, hat is the fez, worn by older upper-class men. Women who wish to show that they are Islamic fundamentalist cover their heads to the hairline with a scarf or the hood of the jellaba when in public. Young women are increasingly challenging traditions such as this, some even daring to sit in public cafés and smoke cigarettes with uncovered heads.

POLITICAL LIFE

Government. The Kingdom of Morocco developed a constitutional monarchy based on Islamic law and French and Spanish civil law systems soon after receiving independence. The three branches of the government are the executive, the legislative, and the judicial. The executive branch includes the chief of state—the hereditary position held for life by the king—the prime minister, and a council of ministers, who are appointed by the king. The legislative branch consists of a bicameral parliament with a Chamber of Counselors and a Chamber of Representatives. The 270 members of the Chamber of Counselors are selected by local councils, professional organizations, and labor syndicates for nine-year terms. The 325 members of the Chamber of Representative are elected by popular vote for six-year terms. A judicial branch, consisting of a Supreme Court of Judges, is presided over by the monarch. Administration is further divided into thirty-seven provinces. Provincial governors are appointed by the king and answer to the central government.

Leadership and Political Officials. The successor to Mohammed V, the first king of the independent Morocco, was his son Hassan II. Upon taking the throne in 1961, Hassan II agreed to recognize the Royal Charter proclaimed by his father, which outlined steps for establishing a constitutional monarchy. Ruling for more than thirty-eight years, King Hassan II was one of the longest serving monarchs in the entire Arab world. In July 1999, King Hassan II died of heart failure at the age of seventy. Mohammed VI, the thirty-five-year-old son of Hassan II, took the throne in 1999 and became the eighteenth king of the Alaouite dynasty.

In Morocco today there are an abundance of political parties, most of which belong to one of two major groupings. The National Entete is the coalition of rightist political parties that was created in 1993 by the National Popular Movement, the Social Democratic Movement, and the Constitutional Union. The Democratic Bloc, the opposition or leftist coalition created in 1992, comprises the Istiqlal Party, the Socialist Union of Popular Forces, the Party of Progress and Socialism, and the Organization of Democratic Popular Action. There are about a dozen Islamic fundamentalist political parties. These groups are not legal although they are unofficially tolerated. Several independent parties also exist. Relations between the king and the many parties have often been stormy, resulting in several attempts at restructuring political control.

Social Problems and Control. The first constitution in 1962 favored a strong monarchy, subordination of all other political institutions to it, and minimal influence from political parties. This constitution was not well accepted and was followed by a period of civil unrest and student riots. In June 1965 the king responded by invoking a state of emergency and assumed all legislative and executive powers. A new government was created with no political parties. In July 1970 the state of emergency ended when the king submitted to referendum a new constitution with an even stronger monarchy. Following the political changes, two unsuccessful military coup attempts took place, one in 1971 and one in 1972. The king responded with another constitution, which increased the number of directly appointed parliamentary representatives. In the early 1990s opposition parties once again began calling for democratization of Morocco's political institutions. The king responded with yet another constitution, this time integrating the opposition parties to a greater degree than ever before. Nevertheless, requests for integration from the opposition have still not been met entirely.

Military Activity. The Moroccan Royal Armed Forces include the Army, Navy, Air Force, Gendarmerie, and Auxiliary Forces. The king is the commander in chief of all armed forces. In 1997–1998, military expenditures were about US $1.36 million, or 3.8 percent of the national gross domestic product. Since the mid-1970s the Moroccan military has been involved in the ongoing war with the Western Sahara guerilla group, the Polisario.

SOCIAL WELFARE AND CHANGE PROGRAMS

Pressure from the French and other European governments to investigate human rights violations against the Saharawi people in Western Sahara have yielded positive results. In eagerness to be accepted as an EU member country, and to divert international attention on the issue, the Moroccan government has taken action. In 1990 King Hassan II created a Consultative Council on Human Rights, composed of representatives from the government and opposition political parties. The council made an offer to provide compensation to the victims of abusive detention and the families of the disappeared. Since King Muhammad VI came to power in 1999, sixty-eight human rights abuse cases have been settled; the council, however, has taken nearly six thousand complaints. Compensation ranged from US $100,000 to US $250,000 per claimant. Many cases remain unresolved, but the council is reacting in a slow and careful manner, attempting to prevent a backlash from conservative forces in the government.

NONGOVERNMENTAL ORGANIZATIONS AND OTHER ASSOCIATIONS

Most of the nongovernmental organizations (NGOs) in Morocco came to the country in the early 1990s. The monarch's opening to human rights issues resulted in an inflow of NGOs, especially those concerned with the treatment of the Saharawi people. In 1994 the monarch allowed Human Rights Watch to conduct a fact-finding investigation on violations of human rights and to publicize the results. Some of the major NGOs active in the country include the Moroccan Organization of Human Rights, the Moroccan League for the Defense of Human Rights, and the Moroccan Association of Human Rights. Amnesty International has chapters located in Casablanca, Rabat, and Marrakech, al-

Dye vats in Fez, Morocco.

though it is not officially recognized by the central government.

GENDER ROLES AND STATUSES

Division of Labor by Gender. In the home, a gender-based hierarchy allows male children far greater freedom and opportunity than female children. Girls as young as four and five are expected to help with household chores and to care for their younger siblings. Cooking, cleaning, and child rearing are the traditional duties assigned to women. Men who are not formally educated find work in a range of positions from taxi driver to artisan to tour guide. Educated men are the rulers of the country and with the right connections may hold any position they wish. Women in higher socioeconomic sectors have greater access to education, resulting in a growing number of female doctors, lawyers, and university professors.

The Relative Status of Women and Men. In almost every aspect of Moroccan life, the status of men is higher than that of women. For the most part, women remain in private, domestic places, and are subject to ridicule and harassment by men in public life on the streets. Worship in mosques is generally reserved for men and all Muslim leaders are male. A few hours, however, are set aside each week to allow women to worship. Within the family, the maintained virginity of a young woman is guarded, as it is vital to her acceptance for marriage. On the other hand, male sexual activity before marriage is regarded as normal. Life is both socially and economically difficult for women with no husband and no education. Female prostitution in the country is widespread.

MARRIAGE, FAMILY, AND KINSHIP

Marriage. Parents still have considerable influence over the choice of their children's spouse, although in some less traditional families this practice is changing. Once a person with the appropriate economic and family background has been agreed upon, the groom offers a bride-price to the family of the bride-to-be. In return, the bride's family negotiates a dowry with the groom's family, and assures them that her virginity is intact. Weddings take place during summer months, and usually last for two or three days, depending on the financial circumstances. At traditional weddings, the bride is carried to the groom on a table, ornately decorated with henna-stained hands and feet. Islamic law dictates that Muslim women must marry Muslim men; it is acceptable, however, for a Muslim man to take a non-Muslim woman as his wife. If divorce occurs, it is likely to be instigated by the man, as a divorced woman has little chance to remarry and may have a difficult time providing for herself.

Domestic Unit. The extended family is of utmost importance as it is a source of status and reputation as well as financial support. One's personal dignity and honor are an extension of the family name. The concept of *hshuma*, or shame, is spread to the entire family if one member of the family is known to have misbehaved. Therefore, there is great pressure to protect the reputation of all members of the family. Moroccans view married life as the only normal way for adults to live, and the idea of living alone is abhorrent. Polygamy is allowed under Islam, although it is rarely practiced. In such cases, the wives may live together in one house, or depending on the family's economic status, each wife may reside in her own dwelling with her offspring.

SOCIALIZATION

Infant Care. Most women still give birth at home with the help of a midwife or other female family members. Modern-style births in hospitals and clinics are becoming available in major cities, but having a child at home is still the norm. Breast-feeding is practiced by almost all women as it is the healthiest and most economic source of nutrition.

Child Rearing and Education. Elementary schools teach subjects in Arabic until the third grade, when education becomes bilingual in both Arabic and French. Officially, education is mandatory from age seven to age thirteen for both girls and boys. Girls, however, are often taken out of school at a young age to assist the older women in their families with domestic duties, especially among the lower socioeconomic sectors. By the end of secondary school, more than three-quarters of the students enrolled are boys.

Higher Education. There are thirteen universities in Morocco with roughly 250,000 students enrolled in all. Both public and private education is available. Public education is free to all citizens through the first undergraduate degree. Wealthy Moroccans often send their children to be educated abroad, usually in Europe. University education is highly valued and is a means to allow individuals to raise their social status and standard of living.

ETIQUETTE

When greeting one another, Moroccans usually shake hands and touch their heart to show personal warmth. Segregation of the sexes is very important in almost every social situation outside the home. Only very modern, Westernized women are active in public life. In the Berber countryside, the appearance of women in public may be slightly more common than in major cities. Traditionally, elders are respected and honored by the entire community.

Moroccans have a very lax concept of punctuality. Dates, appointments, business meetings, and people tend to run behind schedule without concern. Saving face, especially in public, is of the utmost importance and may lead to white lies being told to cover any potentially embarrassing or shameful situation. When tensions do occur, yelling, expressing frustration, and generally creating a public scene is acceptable and quite ordinary.

RELIGION

Religious Beliefs. Nearly 99 percent of Moroccans are Sunni Muslim. Moroccans are tolerant of the small percentage of Christians and Jews living in the country, believing they worship the same God. The five main pillars observed by Muslims are: making a public profession of faith, praying five times a day according to the position of the sun,

Bedouins trade goods at a market in the Sahara Desert, Morocco.

fasting during the month of Ramadan, giving alms to those in need, and making a pilgrimage to Mecca once in a lifetime. Moroccans have added a few unique features of their own to traditional Islam. Two of these features, whose origins are likely attributed to Berber religious practices, are Baraka and Murabitin. Baraka refers to spiritual power that manifests in the form of a blessing or good fortune, similar to the concept of good karma in Buddhism. Murabitin are the individuals who possess good Baraka, similar to the concept of sainthood in Catholicism. Baraka may rub off on individuals who spend time with Murabitin. Also, most villages and medina neighborhoods have a fortune-teller who will charge to offer a vision, provide a remedy, or put a curse on someone. When news travels that pagan practices are taking place, Muslim missionaries will travel to the area to stop them and bring the people back to Islam.

Religious Practitioners. The king claims to be a descendant of the prophet Muhammad, the founder of Islam. He also holds the position of the religious head of state, and all local religious leaders are subordinate to his decisions.

Rituals and Holy Places. Small dome-shaped temples are constructed for the Murabitin after their death, as they are thought to continue exuding

spiritual power. Individuals seeking blessings, such as a woman who wishes to become pregnant, make pilgrimages to Murabitin temples. Muslim mosques are found nationwide. Traditionally, non-Muslim foreigners are not allowed inside mosques. The Mosque Hassan II in Casablanca, however, allows foreigners to tour some facilities.

Death and the Afterlife. Because of the low number of doctors and medical clinics in the country, families in Morocco frequently face death. According to Islam, a body must be buried within twenty-four hours after death. The family of the deceased prepares the body at home, perhaps with the help of an individual in the community experienced in caring for the dead. Men are designated to chant Muslim professions of faith as they carry the body to the burial site. Moroccan women wear white during the grieving period, and must, by Islamic law, abstain from sex for forty days following the death of a spouse. Bodies are buried on the in right side with the head facing south toward Mecca. In this position they are ready for resurrection by Allah on Judgment Day. It will then be decided if the soul will enter heaven or hell. A day or two after the funeral, a formal meal is served while passages from the Koran, the sacred book of Islam, are read aloud. A spirit of charity and giving are important to all during the condolence period.

Workers replacing tiles on a Moroccan street.

MEDICINE AND HEALTH CARE

Hepatitis A and B, intestinal parasites, and occasional outbreaks of cholera are all health problems in Morocco. HIV and AIDS are present and rapidly spreading. Both urban and rural areas suffer from a shortage of health-care centers, hospitals, and staff. Existing biomedical equipment is often inefficient or outdated. In 1987 a national vaccination project was launched with the goal of immunizing all children under one year of age and all women of procreating age. The Ministry of Health also launched the First Project of Social Priorities to set up health-care centers that would provide education in nutrition, hygiene, and birth control in the thirteen poorest provinces. In the late 1990s life expectancy at birth was seventy years for women and sixty-six for men. Morocco's health-care and life expectancy rates are the lowest in the three countries of the Maghrib, but higher than those of the sub-Saharan African countries to the south.

SECULAR CELEBRATIONS

Moroccans celebrate a number of national holidays and festivals each year. National Day is held on 3 March, in celebration of King Hassan II's accession to the throne in 1961. Independence Day is celebrated on 18 November, commemorating the end of the French Protectorate in Morocco. On 6 November, Green March Day is celebrated to commemorate the Moroccan march into Western Sahara in 1975. Among the most popular festivals are: the National Folklore Festival, held in Marrakech each June; a Festival of Roses, held in El Kelaa des M'Gouna each May; and a Date Festival, held in Erfoud each October.

THE ARTS AND HUMANITIES

Support for the Arts. International tourists are the primary supporters of most Moroccan arts, which include handcrafted pottery, rugs, jewelry, drums, and carved stone. A number of museums that exhibit Moroccan paintings and sculptures are supported by the state. Every year, the state awards the Moroccan Book Prize and the Grand Prize of National Merit.

Literature. Some of the most famous figures in Moroccan legends and literature are Aisha Qandisha and the Djinns, known in English as genies. The legend of Aisha Qandisha is that of a beautiful seductive woman with the legs of a goat, who lives in riverbeds and flames. Aisha often appears to men in dreams and may leave them impotent for life. Moroccan children fear her presence. According to genie legends, these spirits frequent places associated with water to create mischief in human affairs. The Berber tradition holds a long history of storytelling and song.

Performance Arts. Music making is very common at festivals or whenever people are gathered for social events. Men and women sing while drums and stringed instruments, such as the *lotar* and the *kamanja*, are played. Musical gatherings are often accompanied by group folk dancing. Women and girls are believed to be susceptible to slipping into a trance while dancing to the rhythm of the drum. Snake charmers perform for tourists in major cities.

THE STATE OF THE PHYSICAL AND SOCIAL SCIENCES

In the area of social sciences, Morocco excels in the area of linguistics and human languages. The Arabic Language Institute in Fez (ALIF) offers courses in Modern Standard Arabic as well as Colloquial Moroccan Arabic. ALIF also offers cultural tours, lectures, and classes on Maghreb literature, media, and Islam. The University of Mohamed V and the Al Akhawayn University have schools of humanities and social sciences that offer Master of Arts degrees in international studies and diplomacy as well as advanced language programs. Morocco's largest project in the area of physical sciences is a late-Pliocene vertebrate excavation site, located in Ahl al Oughlam. Ahl al Oughlam has yielded eighty species of vertebrates, mainly mammals and birds. The site was discovered in 1985 and has been under excavation since 1989; it is by far the richest late-Neogene vertebrate in North Africa. Excavations at Ahl al Oughlam are part of a Franco-Moroccan co-operation program between the Casablanca Program of the National Institute of Science and Archeology (INSAP) of Rabat, Morocco, and the Mission Littoral of the French Minister of Foreign Affairs.

BIBLIOGRAPHY

Abun-Nasr, Jamil. *A History of the Maghrib*, 1987.

Alemseged, Z. and D. Geraads. "*Theropithecus atlanticus* (Cercopithecidae, Mammalia) from the late Pliocene of Ahl al Oughlam, Casablanca, Morocco." *J. Hum. Evol.* 34: 609–621, 1998.

Bacon, Dan. *Lonely Planet Moroccan Arabic Phrasebook*, 1999.

Bendourou, Omar. "Power and Opposition in Morocco." *Journal of Democracy* 7 (3): 108–122, 1993.

Bentahila, Abdeli. *Language Attitudes among Arabic French Bilinguals in Morocco*, 1983.

Dwyer, Kevin. *Arab Voices: The Human Rights Debate in the Middle East*, 1991.

Fernea, Elizabeth. *A Street in Marrakech*, 1988.

Gibb, Hamilton A. R. *Mohammedanism: A Historical Survey*, 1969.

Hargraves, Orin. *Cultureshock: A Guide to Customs and Etiquette*, 1999.

Mernissi, Fatima. *Beyond the Veil*, 1987.

Munson, Henry. *Religion and Power in Morocco*, 1993.

Nydell, Margaret K. *Understanding Arabs: A Guide for Westerners*, 1996.

Rabinow, Paul. *Reflection on Fieldwork in Morocco*, 1978.

Wolfert, Paula. *Couscous and Other Good Foods from Morocco*, 1987.

Web Sites

ArabNet. Morocco Culture. Electronic document. Available from http://www.arab.net/morocco/culture/mo_people.html

Meda Democracy Evaluation. Human Rights and Democracy in Morocco. Electronic document. Available from http://www.usa.euromed.net/MED/EVALUATION/MDP/final-report-96-98-107.htm

University of Würzburg. Morocco Index: Constitutional Background. Electronic document. Available from http://www.uni-wuezburg.de/law/mo_indx.html

Virtual Tours of the Maghre: Morocco. Electronic document. Available from http://maghreb.net/countries/morocco/marrakech.html

—AMANDA JILL JOHNSTON

MOZAMBIQUE

CULTURE NAME

Mozambican

ORIENTATION

Identification. Arab traders who made their way down the East African coast mingled with African peoples, creating a hybrid culture and language called Swahili. This culture still predominates in several East African countries and exerts a strong influence in northern Mozambique. The name "Mozambique" is thought to come from the Swahili *Musa al Big*, the name of an ancient Arab *sheikh*, ("chief") who lived on the northern Ilha de Moçambique.

Location and Geography. Mozambique is on the southeastern coast of Africa, bordering Tanzania, Malawi, and Zambia to the north; Zimbabwe to the west; South Africa and Swaziland to the south; and the Mozambique Channel to the east. The capital, Maputo, is in the south, near the coast. The area of the country is 308,642 square miles (799,509 square kilometers). The terrain ranges from rain forests and swamps to mountains, grasslands, sand dunes, and beaches. The Zambezi River is an important natural resource, supplying power through the Cahora Bassa dam, one of Africa's largest hydroelectric projects. The Zambezi flows west to east and cuts the country into northern and southern regions that diverge, to some extent, in terms of culture and history as well as climate.

There are two main seasons: the wet season from November through March and the dry season from April through October. Drought is common, particularly in the south. However, the country also has experienced devastating floods, most recently in 1999. Mozambique a great diversity of animal life, including zebras, water buffalo, elephants, giraffes, lions, hippopotami, and crocodiles. The country has established national parks and game reserves where these animals are protected.

Demography. The estimated population in 1998 was 18,641,469. This figure represents a twofold increase since 1970. Mozambique once had the highest growth rate in southern Africa, but the rate of increase declined significantly from the mid-1970s through the 1990s as civil war caused losses from both death and emigration. There are about 1.1 million Mozambicans in Malawi and Zimbabwe. More than two-fifths of the population is under the age of fifteen.

The population is divided among roughly sixty different ethnic groups, including nine major ones. The largest group is the Makua-Lomwe in the north, who account for about half the population. Farther north are the Makonde near the coast and the Yao near Lake Malawi. Southern tribes include the Tsonga, the Karanga, the Chopi, the Shona, and the Nguni. Roughly 3 percent of the population is European, Indian, Chinese, Pakistani, or mestizo (mixed African and European). These people are concentrated in the coastal cities and usually work as doctors, teachers, shopkeepers, or industrial laborers.

Linguistic Affiliation. The official language is Portuguese, a legacy of the country's colonizers. When Mozambique gained independence in 1975, Frelimo wanted to evict the colonial language but was not successful in finding a replacement. No other language is spoken by a majority. In the north, the Bantu languages of Yao and Makua predominate; in the Zambezi Valley, it is Nyanja is the dominant languages; and in the south, Tsonga is spoken. Along the northern coast, many people speak Swahili. Portuguese is the language of education and government but is rarely spoken outside the cities. Because six of the neighboring countries are former British colonies, English is used occasionally, particularly in Maputo, in dealings with businesspeople and tourists from South Africa.

Symbolism. The flag consists of horizontal bands of green, black, and yellow with a red triangle at the

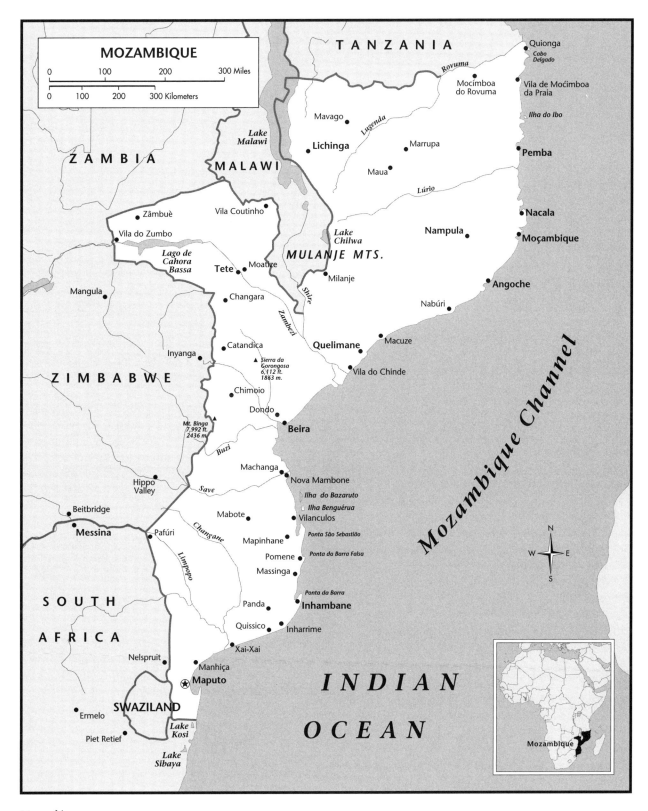

Mozambique

left border. In the center is a yellow star overlaid with a book, symbolizing education; a hoe, symbolizing agriculture; and a rifle, which stands for defense and vigilance.

HISTORY AND ETHNIC RELATIONS

Emergence of the Nation. The earliest inhabitants were small groups of hunters and gatherers such as the Khoi and the San. These groups were part of what is known as the Bushmen. These nomadic people eventually moved out or intermarried with Bantu-speaking tribes that came to the area around the third century C.E. In the eighth century, Arab traders began establishing trading posts along the coast. By the fourteenth century, those settlements had developed into independent city-states and were the main political and commercial centers in the area.

The Portuguese explorer Vasco da Gama was the first European to reach current-day Mozambique. When he arrived in 1498, the Maravi kingdom of the Mwene Matapa was in control of the central Zambezi Basin. Da Gama first landed in the Muslim island town of Moçambique, and by 1510 the Portuguese controlled trading from Sofala in present-day Mozambique north to Mogadishu in what is now Somalia. In 1515, they began to expand their explorations into the interior with the intention of further controlling trade and taking control of gold mines. They subdued the inhabitants and over the next century claimed rights to vast areas of land and to the people who lived there, whom they forced to work on their farms and in their gold mines. The Mwene Matapa recognized Portuguese rule in 1629. The Portuguese called the area *Terra da Boa Gente* ("Country of the Good People").

Portuguese rule was challenged by local landlords (*prazeiros*), who wanted power for themselves, and by fighting among the African tribes they were trying to subdue. In the late seventeenth century, the Rozwi kingdom defeated the Mwene Matapa and forced the Portuguese south of the Zambezi River. Portuguese supremacy continued to wane until the end of the eighteenth century, when Portuguese seized control of the port at Delagoa Bay in the south, later named Lourenço Marcos (today Maputo, the capital). In 1752, the first colonial governor was appointed. Slavery existed in the area before the Portuguese came, but they introduced the concept of exporting slaves, and by 1790 nine thousand people were being shipped out each year. The slave trade took the healthiest young people, sapping many cultures of their vitality and growth.

In the early 1800s, when the British began to pass laws against the slave trade in West Africa, this opened new opportunities for it to grow along the eastern coast of the continent. Even after the Portuguese outlawed slavery in 1878, it went on for many years.

The Zulu presented another challenge to Portuguese rule. Under the leadership of the warrior Shaka, the Zulu tribe expanded its domain by attacking villages throughout southern Africa. The Zulu also battled the Portuguese, capturing the fort at Lourenço Marcos in 1833.

European colonizers in nearby territories refused to recognize the Portuguese claim to Mozambique. The British in particular contested several areas in the south of the colony and actively ruled the areas to which they laid claim. In 1875, this dispute erupted into a major conflict that was settled in Portugal's favor.

A conference was held in 1885–1886 in Berlin in an attempt to divide the African continent peacefully among the European colonizers. Portugal claimed a territory that stretched from Angola on the west coast to Mozambique in the east. The British did not agree to this, and boundary wars were fought until Portugal relinquished Mashonaland, part of current-day Zimbabwe, in 1891. The Portuguese also had to subdue the African inhabitants of their colony, which was particularly difficult in the interior Zambezi region and the north.

In the late 1800s, Portugal chartered private companies to oversee inland territories, superseding the power of the local landlords. In 1907, in an attempt to consolidate and enforce its power and to combat local corruption, Portugal moved the administration of Mozambique from Lisbon to offices in the colony itself.

During World War I, Portugal conscripted thousands of Mozambican men to fight for the Allies; this resulted in a violent uprising in 1917. More than 130,000 Mozambicans died in the war.

With the establishment of the Colonial Act in 1930, Mozambique's limited autonomy was replaced by a more centralized Portuguese administration. In 1951, Portugal declared the colony an overseas province. Throughout the 1950s, the Portuguese government attempted to increase the white population. This, combined with atrocious treatment of the African population led to a steady migration out of Mozambique to the neighboring countries.

In the 1960s, Mozambique was swept up in the pan-African movement toward independence. The

Workers at a rice co-operative in Mozambique. Agriculture is the largest industry.

secret police suppressed the actions of the political organizers, who were forced to work in nearby African nations. In 1962, exiled leaders in Tanzania established Frelimo, the *Frente de Libertação de Moçambique* (the Mozambican Liberation Front). Frelimo, lead by Eduardo Mondlane, was strongest militarily in the north, from where it drew most of its guerrilla fighters. Fighting between Frelimo and Portuguese troops broke out in 1964, after which Portugal sent more than seventy thousand troops to subdue the uprising. However, it was a costly war, and when Portuguese army officers revolted in the mid-1970s, the colonial government collapsed. Mozambique gained independence on 25 June 1975. With the beginning of the independence movement, many Portuguese fled the country, and the white population fell from 200,000 to 30,000 in 1977.

Frelimo was declared the new ruler and established a government based on Marxist-Leninist ideology. However, conflict within Frelimo's leadership, both political and ethnic, was widespread. That conflict had already led to violence, including the assassination of Mondlane in the late 1960s. Frelimo also faced external opposition, most notably from the rebel group called Renamo the (Mozambican National Resistance). The ongoing civil war that resulted disrupted Mozambique's economy, caused tens of thousands of deaths, and forced large numbers of people out of their homes and villages.

In the late 1980s, Frelimo, under pressure from the International Monetary Fund, renounced its Marxist stance in order to receive foreign aid. In 1990, a new constitution was introduced that allowed for a multiparty democracy. On 4 October 1992, the civil war officially ended when a peace accord was signed by Frelimo and Renamo leaders.

National Identity. The country is divided along both ethnic and linguistic lines. Mozambicans often identify primarily with a tribe and/or linguistic group. However, the independence movement that began in the 1960s was a unifying force, causing these disparate elements to join together in resisting the Portuguese. Ironically, some of the main unifying factors in the country have been remnants of the colonial system, including the Portuguese language and the Roman Catholic religion. This is most evident in the central Zambezi Valley, where Portuguese influence was strongest.

Ethnic Relations. Despite ethnic and linguistic differences, there is little conflict among the various groups. The greatest cultural disparities are those which divide the north of the country from the south. The groups north of the Zambezi follow a system of matrilineal descent. Many of them are seminomadic, moving every few years to more fertile soil. Because they are far from the capital and other urban centers, these northern groups show less influence from the Portuguese. South of the river, in the Zambezi Valley, the people adopted Portuguese dress, language, and religion to a larger extent.

URBANISM, ARCHITECTURE, AND THE USE OF SPACE

All the main cities are located on the coast. Maputo was constructed on a European model and has wide streets, public gardens, and paved sidewalks inlaid with mosaic tiles. The city has two parts: the older residential area on a cliff overlooking the harbor and the newer industrial area below, where the factories, port facilities, and most office buildings are located. In the 1950s, the Portuguese architect Amancio d'Alpoim Guedes designed many of the city's office and apartment buildings, which combine shapes and symbols from traditional African art with a modern sensibility.

Aerial view of the capital city Maputo. It was constructed with wide streets, public gardens, and paved sidewalks inlaid with mosaics.

Most of the cities took in a large number of refugees from the countryside during the civil war. To cope with that sudden population increase, shantytowns were erected along the outskirts. Poor sanitation in those settlements led to the spread of disease. Government planners have been attempting to combat this problem by building low-cost apartments, but they have been unable to keep up with the growing population.

Beira, the second largest city, is primarily a port. Located several hundred miles north of Maputo, on the coast, it is the center of the commercial fishing industry and a center of trade with Malawi and Zimbabwe. Like Maputo, it took in a large number of refugees during the civil war. It is also a Portuguese-style colonial city.

Nampula in the north is the third largest city and was established in the late 1960s when the Portuguese drained a swamp and built it. The city grew even more rapidly than expected, partly as a result of its location along the commercial railway between Malawi and the port of Nacala. However, despite its harbor and modern facilities, Nampula has declined in importance because of the deterioration of the railroad line that leads from the city to the interior and to Malawi.

The oldest surviving settlement is Moçambique Island in the north. The Arab architecture of the twelfth and thirteenth centuries, including coral-block mosques and houses, is still standing. Fort Saint Sebastian, a huge stone fort built by the Portuguese in 1507, is another physical testament to the island's history. The fort has been preserved as a museum. The town continues to thrive with large Asian and Muslim populations.

The country also has the remains of several ancient cities, including Nhacangara near the border with Zimbabwe. This site has a stone fortress with paths and tunnels, and traces of terraces on the nearby hills indicate earlier settlement. Archaeologists speculate that the country has many more long-uninhabited cities that have not been discovered. However, research into them has been impeded by the civil war.

Much historic colonial architecture was destroyed in the civil war. Renamo's strategy was to destroy every building that Frelimo erected. That destruction extended to include even small structures in the countryside, until the whole country was virtually destroyed.

Despite the rapid growth of the cities, nine-tenths of the population is rural. Traditional village houses are round huts made of poles held together with mud, and thatched roofs made of palm leaves. However, most homes built today are made of cement blocks and have tin roofs. Each village erects a *boma* around its perimeter. This is a fence with sharpened posts, that provides protection against attacks by lions and other wild animals. The fields lie outside the *boma*. Villages are centered on a cattle pen called a *kraal*, or a community building.

FOOD AND ECONOMY

Food in Daily Life. Most of the crops originally cultivated in the region have been supplanted by European imports. The exception is millet, a grain that sometimes is made into beer. The diet of rural residents is based on the cassava root, which is called *mandioca* in Portuguese. Its importance is testified to by its name, which translates as "the all-sufficient." This malleable food source can be baked, dried in the sun, or mashed with water to form a porridge. In its most common form, it is ground into a coarse flour along with corn and then mixed with cassava leaves and water. The resulting dough is served in calabashes. Corn is the other staple food; both corn and cassava were introduced from the Americas by the Portuguese. Cashews, pineapple, and peanuts, which are other important foods, found their way to Mozambique in the same way.

Along the coast, the cuisine is more varied and Portuguese-influenced than it is in inland areas. The diet there includes more fruit and rice as well as seafood dishes such as *macaza* (grilled shellfish kabobs), *bacalhão* (dried salted cod) and *chocos* (squid cooked in its own ink). Food is seasoned with peppers, onions, and coconut. Palm wine (*shema*) is a popular drink.

Food Customs at Ceremonial Occasions. Food is a part of many celebrations. It is customary to serve a meal at parties, rituals, and other social gatherings. For the poor (who are the vast majority of the population), while ceremonial occasions often entail large feasts, the food served is the same as what is eaten everyday.

Basic Economy. The gross national product has nearly no growth rate and is one of the lowest in the world. Although only 5 percent of the land is arable, 80 percent of the people work in agriculture. The farming techniques are primitive, involving few tools and work animals. After independence, many farms were organized on the basis of Chinese and Cuban models; however, with the changes imposed by the International Monetary Fund in the late 1980s, a system of decentralization and private ownership was introduced. The main crops cultivated are corn, cassava, coconuts, peanuts, cotton, sugar, and cashews. However, the nation cannot meet its food needs, particularly for corn, and must import large quantities of food. Mozambique's currency is the *metical*.

Land Tenure and Property. There is no tradition of private land ownership. Land belongs to the community rather than to any individual. When the country won independence, the socialist Frelimo government took over ownership of all the land from the Portuguese and encouraged villagers to farm collectively, according to their traditions.

Commercial Activities. The main goods produced for sale within the country are agricultural. Farmers grow corn, cassava, peanuts, bananas, and citrus fruits for their own consumption. Some of these products are sold at local markets, and some are transported to the capital and other cities for sale there.

Major Industries. Agriculture is by far the largest industry. Fishing along the coast (particularly shrimp) accounts for one-third of the country's exports. The rivers also provide fish, and there are several fisheries that produce mackerel, anchovies, and prawns. Mining and manufacturing account for one-fifth of the gross domestic product. The principal products are coal, beryllium, limestone, and salt. There are also deposits of tantalite, iron ore, uranium, copper, gold, and diamonds. The country also manufactures textiles, plastics, beverages, food, cement, glass, and asbestos.

Trade. The main exports are shrimp, cashews, cotton, sugar, and timber, which go primarily to Spain, the United States, Japan, and Portugal. Imports of food, machinery, petroleum, and consumer goods come from South Africa, the United States, Portugal, and Italy. The country has an unfavorable trade balance, although it is alleviated somewhat by remittances sent by Mozambicans working in South Africa.

Division of Labor. The workforce is divided primarily along geographic lines. The majority of the population is rural, and these people are farmers. In cities, there are more skilled workers as well as street vendors and a small white-collar workforce. Professionals such as teachers, lawyers, and government officials constitute a small percentage of the population and generally come from a small number of middle-class or wealthy families.

Supporters turn out at an election rally in Chokwe, Mozambique. Citizens enjoy universal suffrage.

SOCIAL STRATIFICATION

Classes and Castes. During the time of Portuguese rule, the *prazeiros*, (Portuguese landowners) formed the wealthiest and most powerful class. Below them were the mestizos, those of mixed African and Portuguese descent; and at the bottom were Africans, who constituted the vast majority of the population. Despite the internal diversity of the population, which is composed of various cultural and linguistic groups, ethnicity has never been a major factor in social status. Since independence, most Portuguese have left the country. Today, with the exception of the tiny ruling elite, nearly everyone in the country is poor.

Symbols of Social Stratification. The way people dress reflects the confluence of different cultures as well as the individual's economic standing. In the cities, men wear Western-style suits to go to work. Women wear Western-style dresses made from fabric with brightly colored African patterns. Throughout the country men have, for the most part, replaced the traditional loincloth with T-shirts and dashikis. Women in rural areas, however, generally have kept their traditional garb of long strips of fabric that are wrapped around the body, under the arms, and over one shoulder. They also have retained the traditional head scarf or turban. Young

people almost exclusively wear Western clothing, except for the extremely indigent. Despite the European and American influence on fashion, some styles, such as blue jeans and short skirts, have not been adopted. Dress also can be a marker of ethnic identity. Muslims in the north wear traditional long white robes and head coverings; Asian men wear white two-piece cotton suits, whereas Asian women dress in black or colored silk dresses. Language also can be an indicator of socioeconomic standing. Portuguese is learned in school and is therefore the language of the privileged elite; it is almost entirely unheard outside the cities.

POLITICAL LIFE

Government. The constitution adopted in 1990 declared Mozambique a multiparty democratic republic. The 250 members of the unicameral Assembly of the Republic are elected by universal suffrage. The president is both chief of state and head of the government and is elected for a five-year term, with a maximum limit of three terms.

Leadership and Political Officials. While Mozambique is officially a multiparty democracy, the government is still dominated by the two main parties, Frelimo and Renamo. The third party, which did not win any seats in the legislature in the

1999 elections, is called the Democratic Union. Frelimo, the ruling political party from independence through the end of the civil war, suffered from infighting among its leaders. Both Frelimo and Renamo took their leaders from workers in the independence movement. While there are varying levels of education among politicians, almost all have studied abroad in Portugal or other European countries.

Social Problems and Control. Crime is a growing problem, particularly in the cities, which have been flooded with poor unemployed men from the countryside seeking work. The justice system was fashioned after the Portuguese model. However, without enough qualified judges and lawyers, this system could not function well, so Frelimo modified it. Because prison facilities could not accommodate the large number of criminals, the government established rehabilitation camps (usually farms) for minor offenders and alcoholics (Frelimo considered alcoholism a crime). Frelimo also set up vigilante groups of citizens to turn in alcoholics and antigovernment individuals. One of the most pressing problems is human rights violations on the part of law enforcement agents, and the mistreatment of criminals and suspects.

Military Activity. Under Frelimo, the police force was nationally controlled, with local divisions in each town. Frelimo also put in place the National Service of Popular Security, an arm of the police force that deals with terrorism and sabotage. When peace accords were signed in 1992, Frelimo had an estimated seventy thousand troops and Renamo had twenty thousand. Those fighters were compelled to turn in their weapons, and a new national force, the Mozambican Defense Force, was established, including fifteen thousand men from each party.

SOCIAL WELFARE AND CHANGE PROGRAMS

Social welfare comes primarily from within the family, which cares independently for its own elderly or ailing member. Other aid comes from international charitable organizations.

NONGOVERNMENTAL ORGANIZATIONS AND OTHER ASSOCIATIONS

Since the peace treaties were signed, the United Nations has played a large role in the peacekeeping process. It stationed almost eight thousand people who were responsible for supervising the dis-

A woman cooks over an open-air fire in Mozambique. Women often face obstacles when seeking nontraditional employment.

mantling and rebuilding of the armies, over the 1994 elections to ensure that they were fair and democratic, and helped return almost two million refugees to their homes. As part of the last project, the United Nations aided in the reconstruction of water systems, roads, schools, and clinics. The International Organization for Migration (IOM) also helped with the repatriation process. One of the biggest problems is the presence of land mines left over from the civil war. It is estimated that up to two million were buried. The United Nations collaborated with USAID and a Norwegian group to help find and defuse them.

The refugee situation has created another crisis in the form of legions of abandoned street children, particularly in Maputo, where they number an estimated half a million. Many volunteer aid organizations work with orphans and abandoned children to care for them and educate them to be self-sufficient. Among these groups are Save the Children and the Institute for International Cooperation and Development (IICD). The World Food Program buys grain grown in areas of the country where production exceeds use and redistributes it in other areas.

GENDER ROLES AND STATUSES

Division of Labor by Gender. The constitution guarantees all citizens the right to work, but women often face obstacles when they seek nontraditional employment. Women have historically been responsible for all domestic tasks. In the towns and cities, they generally are confined to the home, whereas in rural areas, they play an important role in the agricultural labor force. The Organizaçao de Mulheres de Mozambique (Organization of Mozambican Women, or OMM), which works to promote women's rights, has implemented programs to teach women to sew and crochet and sell the products they produce for cash.

The Relative Status of Women and Men. According to the constitution, men and women have equal rights. However, both traditional and colonial attitudes keep women in a somewhat subordinate position. Even within the ranks of Frelimo, which declared itself a proponent of women's rights, women have not attained positions of power.

MARRIAGE, FAMILY, AND KINSHIP

Marriage. Polygamy is traditionally practiced and until recently was quite common. In 1981, Frelimo instituted a law designed in conjunction with OMM that established monogamous marriage, and by which both spouses share ownership of property and decisions about where to live. The law also entitled women to a means of maintenance and specified the responsibilities of fathers in financially supporting their children. Marriage celebrations involve feasting, music, and dancing.

Domestic Unit. The traditional family includes several generations living together under one roof. However, in many areas, this family structure has been dismantled by the civil war, which took many lives, compelled many men to emigrate from rural areas to the cities or to neighboring countries, and left large numbers of children orphaned or abandoned.

Inheritance. Tribes north of the Zambezi River follow a matrilineal model of inheritance. They trace their ancestry through the mother's side, and at marriage the man becomes part of the woman's family. In the south, the model is patrilineal.

Kin Groups. South of the Zambezi River, tribes follow a patrilineal descent; to the north, kin ties are established through the mother's line.

SOCIALIZATION

Infant Care. Young children rarely are separated from their mothers. It is customary for women to tie their babies to their backs with a strip of cloth and take them along when they work in the fields.

Child Rearing and Education. Children are treated with affection but are expected to defer to their elders and often begin to work at a young age. After the civil war, as many as half a million children were left without families. Many of these children wander Maputo and other cities and stay alive by stealing or selling small items on the street. Relief organizations have alleviated the problem somewhat by caring for and educating children, and reuniting families.

Because of the Portuguese legacy of suppressing education in colonies, Mozambique was estimated to have a literacy rate of only 10 percent when it gained independence in 1975. The first postindependence government made raising this number a priority and instituted compulsory education for children between the ages of six and twelve. This program was largely disrupted by the civil war. When the war ended in 1995, the literacy rate was 40 percent and only 60 percent of primary-school-age children were in school. Only 7 percent of children were enrolled at the secondary level. Since the peace treaties were signed, these numbers have begun increasing, but the destruction of many school buildings and a lack of trained and educated teachers have left the country with a problem that will not be soon eradicated.

Higher Education. There are three institutes of higher education that enrolled a total of seven thousand students in 1995. Eduardo Mondlane in Maputo is the only university.

ETIQUETTE

Greetings are lengthy and involve inquiring into the health of each other's family. People generally stand close together and are physically affectionate.

RELIGION

Religious Beliefs. The native religion is animism. Arab traders brought Islam to the area, and the Portuguese brought Christianity. Historically, the introduction of Christianity by both Catholic and Protestant missionaries was a mixed blessing. While their teachings conflicted with the traditional way of life, they offered Mozambicans access to health

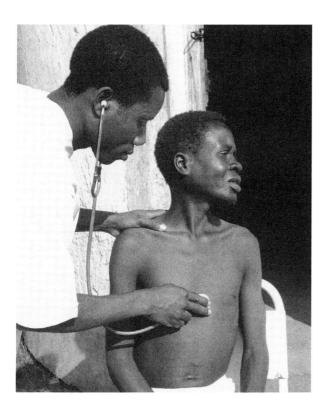

A doctor examining a TB patient in Morrumbala Hospital. The civil war took a heavy toll on medical care throughout the country.

care and an education, as the colonial Portuguese government did not provide those things.

Today the constitution ensures religious freedom and separation of church and state. However, when Frelimo took power, it expressed hostility toward Roman Catholicism, viewing it as a Portuguese tool of oppression. Twenty to 30 percent of the population is Christian, and 10 percent follows Islam; Islam is most prevalent near the northern coast. Many people who adhere to Christianity or Islam still practice traditional religion. About two-thirds of the population follows animist rituals and customs. The traditional belief system places a high importance on a connection with one's ancestors as well as with the spirit world.

Religious Practitioners. The animism practiced in Mozambique includes sorcerers, wise men and women, and witch doctors or traditional healers, who are capable of communicating with spirits and act as go-betweens for the rest of the people. The healers are well versed in the medicinal uses of local plants as well as spiritual healing.

Rituals and Holy Places. Many animist rituals involve music and dance. For example, Makonde men perform a dance that involves large masks called *mapicos*. The masks are carved in secret, and represent demons; women are not allowed to touch them. The dance, which is performed to the accompaniment of drums and wind instruments, enacts a repeated attack on villagers by the demons and is a ritual that lasts for many hours.

MEDICINE AND HEALTH CARE

When independence was won in 1975, the government created a free, nationalized health care system, at the same time banning private practice; this resulted in an exodus by the majority of the country's doctors. The government's goal was to improve health through preventive medicine, employing nurses to give vaccinations and educate the population about sanitation and other basic health care measures. Many of the clinics it established, however, were destroyed in the civil war. Since the war ended, it has invested a large amount of money in rebuilding those clinics and has done away with the law prohibiting private practice in an effort to increase the number of doctors. A shortage of supplies and trained personnel was exacerbated by the destruction caused by the civil war. The main health threats are sleeping sickness, transmitted by the tsetse fly, and malaria. Life expectancy is forty-seven years for men and fifty years for women. The infant mortality rate is 130 per thousand, the highest in the world.

Many people rely on traditional herbal medicines and healing methods under the guidance of village healers, in combination with what little health care and medicine the government provides.

AIDS is a growing problem. In Maputo and the other urban centers, the infection rate is about 10 percent. Outside the cities, the rate is 17 percent for low-risk groups and 27 percent for high-risk groups. While these numbers are lower than those in some surrounding countries, AIDS is a major concern and a threat to the nation's future.

SECULAR CELEBRATIONS

The major holidays are New Year's Day on 1 January, Heroes' Day on 3 February, Women's Day on 7 April, Workers' Day on 1 May, Independence Day on 25 June, the Anniversary of the End of Armed Struggle on 7 September, the Anniversary of the Opening of Armed Struggle on 25 September, and Family Day on 25 December.

THE ARTS AND HUMANITIES

Support for the Arts. There is a national performing arts company called the Nambu Productions as well as a national dance company, both of which perform contemporary productions based on traditional forms. The Frelimo government also established a National Institute of Culture that collects and preserves traditional music, crafts, stories, and myths.

Literature. Literary production has been limited because of poverty and a low literacy rate. There is a strong oral tradition of storytelling, and many of the country's contemporary writers draw on that tradition. Literary writing has historically been tied to resistance to Portuguese colonialism and for this reason was largely censored before independence. Writers such as Luis Bernardo Honwana were imprisoned for their work. Honwana is also a documentary filmmaker but is best known for the book *We Killed Mangy-Dog*, which combines personal and cultural autobiography. Virtually all the poets and writers use the colonial Portuguese language as their medium. The poet Jose Craveirinha sees Portuguese, particularly with the infusion of local African words, as an important part of the nation's cultural heritage and is a proponent of retaining it as the national language. Because of a lack of education and other disadvantages, women have been underrepresented in the literary realm. One exception is Noemia De Sousa, who is known as the mother of Mozambican writers. When she began writing in the 1950s and 1960s, she was the only *mestiça* writing in Portuguese in Africa. She takes on the subject of African women and their work and has become a voice for the women of her country.

Graphic Arts. Mozambique is known for the traditional sculpture and wood carving produced by the Makonde people in the north. Using hardwoods (primarily mahogany, ebony, and ironwood), the Makonde fashion masks and sculptures known as "family trees," large depictions of various figures that tell stories of generations. Mozambique also has produced several well known contemporary artists, including Malangatana Goenha Valente, whose large canvases depict conflict between colonial culture and native culture. Two contemporary sculptors are Nkatunga and Chissano.

Performance Arts. The country has a long musical tradition. Song serves several purposes, including religious expression, the relating of current events, and making fun of neighbors. It is customary for musicians to make their own instruments.

Drums have wooden bases covered with stretched animal skins. Wind instruments known as *lupembe*, used by the Makonde tribe, are made from animal horns, wood, or gourds. The *marimba*, a kind of xylophone that has been adopted in Western music, originated in Mozambique, where it is popular with the Chopi in the south. Chopi musicians also use the *mbira*, strips of metal attached to a hollow box and plucked with the fingers. The musical style is similar to West Indian calypso and reggae. A contemporary form of music called *marrabenta* has developed in the cities and draws on traditional complex rhythms.

There are elaborate, well-developed traditions of dance throughout the country. Dances often have religious significance. The Chopi perform a hunting dance in which they dress in lion skins and monkey tails, carry spears and swords, and act out battles. Makua men in the north dance on two-foot-tall stilts, hopping around the village for hours, bedecked in colorful outfits and masks. On Moçambique Island, a form of dance practiced by women combines complex steps and rope jumping.

Storytelling is another traditional art form. The national culture is rich in tales, proverbs, myths, and jokes that have been passed down from generation to generation.

THE STATE OF THE PHYSICAL AND SOCIAL SCIENCES

Facilities for the physical and social sciences are virtually nonexistent. However, Maputo has a Museum of Natural History that specializes in natural history and ethnography as well as the Freire de Andrade Museum for minerals and the History Museum for military affairs. The town of Ilha da Inhaca is home to a marine biology museum.

BIBLIOGRAPHY

Armon, Jeremy, and Dylan Hendrikson, eds. *Mozambican Peace Process in Perspective*, 1998.

Bowen, Merle L. *State against the Peasantry: Rural Struggles in Colonial and Postcolonial Mozambique*, 2000.

Chan, Stephen, and Moises Venancio. *War and Peace in Mozambique*, 1988.

Ciment, James. *Angola and Mozambique: Postcolonial War in Southern Africa*, 1997.

Earle, Deborah, ed. *From Conflict to Peace in a Changing World: Social Reconstruction in Times of Transition*, 1998.

Ferraz, Bernardo, and Barry Muslow. *Sustainable Development in Mozambique*, 2000.

Hall, Margaret. *Confronting Leviathan: Mozambique Since Independence*, 1997.

James, R. S. *Mozambique*, 1988.

Jouanneau, Daniel. *Mozambique*, 1995.

Landau, Luis. *Rebuilding the Mozambique Economy: Assessment of a Development Partnership*, 1998.

Lopes, Armando Jorge. *Language Policy: Principles and Problems*, 1997.

Newit, Mayn. *A History of Mozambique*, 1995.

Nordstrom, Carolyn. *A Different Kind of War Story*, 1997.

Reidy, Mary, ed. *Mozambique*, 1995.

—ELEANOR STANFORD

MYANMAR SEE BURMA

NAMIBIA

CULTURE NAME
Namibian

ORIENTATION

Identification. Namibia was colonized by Germany and South Africa and was named Südwestafrika or South West Africa. Those who opposed colonial rule preferred Namibia, from a Nama/Damara word meaning "shield" used for the coastal desert, the Namib, which long protected the interior from access by sea. During the colonial period, many indigenous peoples were dispossessed of their lands and relegated to reserves established for each ethnic group. The emphasis on ethnicity was opposed by growing nationalist sentiment, and Namibia became a unitary nation-state when it gained independence in 1990.

Location and Geography. Covering 318,500 square miles (825,000 square kilometers) on the southwest coast of Africa, Namibia is bordered by Angola and Zambia (north), Botswana (east), South Africa (south), and the Atlantic Ocean (west). The coast, with its productive fishing grounds and the deep water harbor of Walvis Bay, is edged by the dunes and gravel plains of the Namib desert. Inland, the hills and plains of the central plateau are predominantly scrub savannah, gradually transforming into the Kalahari semi-desert to the east. The flat north-central and northeastern regions have extensive flood plains and areas of dense vegetation. The driest country in sub-Saharan Africa, Namibia only has permanent rivers on its northern and southern borders.

Demography. With large expanses of arid and semi-arid land, Namibia has a small population—about 1.7 million—for its size. The population is youthful, with 44 percent aged fourteen and under and only 4 percent older than 65. About 60 percent live in the far north, where rainfall is sufficient for

grain farming. In 1996 Namibia's capital city, Windhoek, had a population of 183,000.

Linguistic Affiliation. Despite the small population, there is great linguistic variety. Most Namibians speak Bantu languages like Oshiwambo and Otjiherero as their first language. Others speak Khoisan languages (Nama/Damara and various Bushman languages), while a smaller percentage are native speakers of Indo-European languages like Afrikaans and English. Afrikaans was promoted as a language of wider communication before independence and is still widely spoken in southern and central Namibia. At independence, English was chosen as the primary language for government and education because it was not associated with any particular ethnicity and could facilitate interaction with the outside world. Urban dwellers, young people, and northerners are more likely to have learned it.

Symbolism. The colors on the national flag symbolize important natural and human characteristics of Namibia: sunlight and the desert (yellow), rain and the ocean (blue), crops and vegetation (green), the blood shed in war (red), and peace and reconciliation (white). Schoolchildren sing the national anthem daily; it is also heard on the radio and at national celebrations.

HISTORY AND ETHNIC RELATIONS

Namibia was originally inhabited by nomadic hunters, gatherers, and pastoralists (livestock herders), the ancestors of today's Bushman and Khoi-speaking people. Agriculturalists and pastoralists speaking Bantu languages, such as the Owambo and Herero, arrived in the fifteenth through seventeenth centuries and settled throughout northern and central Namibia. In the eighteenth and nineteenth centuries, Nama- and Afrikaans-speaking pastoralists, under pressure from white settlers in South Africa, moved into southern and central

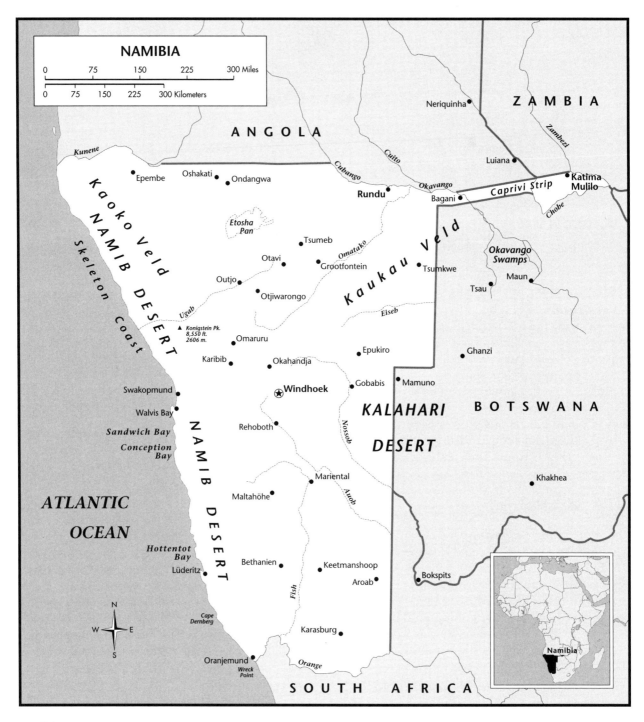

Namibia

Namibia. The different groups came into conflict over access to land and other resources, but they were linked by trade relationships.

European traders, missionaries, and settlers began arriving in significant numbers in the mid-1800s. Increasing expropriations of land and cattle by German settlers led Herero and Nama communi-ties to rebel. In a series of genocidal wars from 1904 to 1907, the German military killed three-quarters of the Herero population and nearly one-half the Namas. The survivors were settled on barren reserves and forced to work in mines and on commercial farms. Since labor was short, large numbers of men from the far north, a densely-populated area not subject to white settlement, were brought south as contract laborers. This pattern of eviction from the land and migrant labor continued when South Africa assumed control after World War I. In the 1960s and 1970s, South Africa formally extended its apartheid system to Namibia, creating ethnic homelands with their own administrations for each ethnic group. Movement outside one's own homeland was strictly controlled.

Emergence of the Nation. The boundaries defining present-day Namibia were European creations, and there was no prior sense of common identity among the many different groups inhabiting the area. Their common experience of oppression under colonialism, however, led to shared nationalist sentiment, first expressed in the 1940s during a letter-writing campaign by traditional leaders to the United Nations protesting South African rule. Initiated by the Herero Chiefs Council, the campaign grew throughout the 1950s to include leaders from other ethnic groups. In 1959, thirteen protestors were killed in Windhoek by South African forces as they demonstrated against the planned relocation of their community. The Windhoek Massacre and ensuing government repression stimulated the rise of new nationalist organizations. The most successful of these, the South West Africa People's Organization (SWAPO), was initially based among Owambo contract workers, but soon attracted broader support, took up armed struggle, and gained UN recognition as the "sole and authentic" representative of the Namibian people. The strongest and most enduring element of SWAPO ideology has been nationalism, seen as a necessary counter to the ethnic divisions perpetuated by apartheid. At independence on 21 March 1990, SWAPO became the first democratically elected ruling party of the new nation, a position it has held through two subsequent elections. The country was divided into thirteen new administrative regions, cross-cutting the boundaries of the former ethnic homelands.

National Identity. Despite significant cultural differences and considerable ethnic stereotyping, there is a widely shared orientation to the nation, particularly among young people, who are more likely to travel through the country for economic and educational reasons. Urban areas, large workplaces such as mines and fisheries, and secondary and tertiary schools are multi-ethnic sites where people are creating new ways of interacting across ethnic boundaries. Soccer is extremely popular among

men of all ethnicities, and the national team is followed closely and is widely discussed.

Ethnic Relations. Despite the emphasis on nationalism, ethnicity is still a force in Namibian society. Some groups have restored kings to power and made land claims since independence, and the official opposition party, the Democratic Turnhalle Alliance (DTA), is an alliance of ethnically-based organizations. Some members of smaller groups fear domination by the Owambos, who comprise about half the population of the country and provide most of SWAPO's electoral support.

URBANISM, ARCHITECTURE, AND THE USE OF SPACE

Most of central and southern Namibia, an area formerly known as the Police Zone, was appropriated for white settlement. Today it consists of large commercial farms and widely scattered towns with Western-style buildings, some distinctly German. In the rural communal areas (former ethnic homelands), there are a variety of architectural styles in addition to Western buildings. Construction materials include sticks and logs, earth, and thatch. Houses may be round, square, or beehive-shaped; in some areas, clusters of huts are enclosed in wooden palisades. Some dwellings and shops are also made of metal sheets or concrete blocks with metal roofs, a style also seen in some urban neighborhoods.

In urban areas under apartheid, whites lived in the town centers, while blacks and mixed-race people were clustered in outlying "locations," sometimes divided into sections by ethnicity. Although legislation enforcing this racial segregation was abolished in the late 1970s and 1980s, attitudes and economic barriers have changed more slowly and this pattern has persisted. Urbanization increased greatly after independence, especially in Windhoek, as the last restrictions on population movement were removed and exiles returned from abroad. The rapidity of urban growth has led to problems in the provision of basic services as well as higher unemployment and increased crime.

FOOD AND ECONOMY

Food in Daily Life. For agriculturalists, the staple foods are millet and sorghum; for pastoralists, dairy products. Beans and greens are eaten with millet in the north, but otherwise few vegetables are grown or consumed. Hunting and gathering, more important in the past, still provides a dietary supplement for some. Meat is highly desired and eaten

Himba woman next to a mud hut at a Nomadic People Camp in the Skeleton Coast. Namibia was originally inhabited by nomadic hunters, gatherers, and pastoralists.

as often as it is feasible—daily for some, on special occasions for others. Fish consumption is slowly increasing with government promotion of Namibian fish products.

Food Customs at Ceremonial Occasions. Important occasions are marked by the slaughter of cattle or goats, and the consumption of meat, home-brewed beer, purchased beverages, and other foods. In some cultures, leftover meat is sent home with the guests.

Basic Economy. The Namibian economy is divided between capital-intensive industry, which accounts for most of the gross domestic product, and labor-intensive subsistence agriculture, which employs over half of the population. With little access to financial or technical assistance, most subsistence farmers rely on small-scale commercial activity and/or family members who earn wages or pensions to make ends meet.

Land Tenure and Property. Land tenure in central and southern Namibia is based on private property. In the rural communal areas, land is not bought or sold; families have heritable rights to use specific plots or pay fees to traditional leaders for use rights. In pastoral communities, all members generally have access to grazing and water in the community's area. Recent sources of controversy include the illegal fencing of communal land for private use by the wealthy and the extensive ownership of land by whites.

Commercial Activities. Alongside Namibian retail stores and South African chains, informal, small-scale commercial activity is widespread. Home-brewed alcohol, freshly butchered meat, prepared foods, and crafts are the major products sold. Others buy small quantities of soap, fruit, watches, and other goods to resell along the roadside or in small shops.

Major Industries. Mining (diamonds and other gemstones, uranium), fishing and fish processing, and commercial agriculture (cattle and sheep) have long been the economic mainstays in terms of value produced. Earnings fluctuate greatly depending on world market prices and weather conditions. The manufacturing sector is growing with government promotion and incentives, although the small size of the skilled labor force and domestic market are limiting factors. Tourism has grown substantially since independence.

Trade. Diamonds and other minerals are the most important exports, followed by processed and unprocessed fish, other food products, and live animals. The main export destinations include the United Kingdom, South Africa, and Spain. Most imports are purchased from South Africa, and include food and beverages as well as a wide variety of manufactured goods. Imports slightly exceed exports.

SOCIAL STRATIFICATION

Classes and Castes. Namibia is characterized by great economic inequality; the wealthiest 1 percent consume more than the poorest half of the population combined. Segregation has continued since the end of apartheid, although more non-whites have joined the upper classes. Whites, only 7 percent of the population, own and manage most large businesses and commercial farms; in the civil service, the races are on more equal terms. In the rural communal areas, teachers, health care workers, government employees, and successful business people form a local elite, though they are still closely integrated into their communities through kinship ties and obligations.

Symbols of Social Stratification. The wealthier classes of all races are distinguished by expensive cars, large homes in exclusive neighborhoods, a command of English, attendance at private schools, and extensive travel.

POLITICAL LIFE

Government. Namibia has a parliamentary government with two houses (National Assembly and National Council), a president, prime minister, and cabinet. There is a clear separation of judicial, legislative, and executive powers, and the constitution is internationally acclaimed for its guarantees of fundamental rights and freedoms. Elections since independence have been judged "free and fair" by outside observers.

Leadership and Political Officials. Voters elect parties, rather than candidates, and the parties select representatives to fill the seats they win.

Social Problems and Control. Although crime levels are relatively low, recent years have seen an increase in violent crime and theft, along with complaints that the police lack the manpower and equipment to combat crime properly.

Military Activity. The major post-independence military accomplishment was merging the previously opposed People's Liberation Army of Namibia and the South West Africa Territorial Force into a single national army. Namibia's recent involvement in a civil war in the Democratic Republic of the Congo has been controversial.

NONGOVERNMENTAL ORGANIZATIONS AND OTHER ASSOCIATIONS

During a wave of grassroots organizing in the 1980s, dozens of community-based organizations (CBOs) were formed to deal with worsening social problems and to complement the political struggle for independence. Today numerous CBOs, nongovernmental organizations (NGOs), cooperatives, and religious groups provide housing assistance, legal advice, education, community media outlets, and self-help projects. The government has created a favorable climate for these groups, seeing them as valuable partners in the task of developing Namibia.

GENDER ROLES AND STATUSES

Division of Labor by Gender. In the rural communal areas, men and boys generally care for livestock, build and maintain homesteads, plow fields, and contribute some agricultural labor, while women and girls do most of the agricultural labor, food preparation, childcare, and household work.

The Relative Status of Women and Men. Women married to migrant laborers have taken on some traditionally male responsibilities, and women who fled the country to participate in the liberation struggle took on new roles as combatants, students, and refugee camp workers. They pushed SWAPO to support gender equality and helped ensure that the Constitution guarantees equal rights for men and women, however the process of changing discriminatory legislation is slow and ongoing. Women still have fewer economic opportunities than men, and the incidence of rape and domestic violence is extremely high.

MARRIAGE, FAMILY, AND KINSHIP

Marriage. Weddings are extremely important social events in Namibia, bringing family and friends together to sing, dance, and feast. Most weddings combine old and new elements. Many Owambo couples, for example, say their vows in a church ceremony accompanied by identically-dressed bridesmaids and groomsmen, then exit to a crowd of guests shouting praises, dancing, and waving horsetail whisks.

Domestic Unit. Most households are not nuclear families, but contain other kin as well. The head of the household manages domestic finances, makes important decisions, and organizes productive activities.

Kin Groups. Corporate kin groups are formed by ties traced through women (matrilineal), men (patrilineal), or both (bilateral), depending on ethnicity. These kin groups provide a support network for their members and control joint property, especially livestock; in the past, they also played significant roles in political and religious affairs. There has been a general shift from matrilinealism to patrilinealism. For example, wives and children in matrilineal communities can now assert rights to the property of deceased husbands and fathers, which has been traditionally inherited by the man's matrilineal relatives (his siblings and sisters' children).

SOCIALIZATION

Infant Care. Babies are breast-fed and carried on the mother's back until about the age of two. Most sleep with their mothers, and children usually share a bed or room with siblings.

Downtown Windhoek, Namibia's capital city, is a rapidly growing urban center.

Child Rearing and Education. Parents receive substantial help with child rearing from other family members. It is not unusual for children to live with other relatives if the parents have work obligations, the child needs to be closer to school, or a relative needs a child's help. Most boys and girls attend primary school, although sometimes they stay at home to help with the livestock or crops.

Higher Education. Education is highly valued, but the limited availability of places in secondary and tertiary schools, as well as the expense involved, hinders many students from continuing beyond primary school.

ETIQUETTE

Extended greetings and handshakes are very important in most Namibian cultures. When food and drink is offered, it is polite to accept. There is a general emphasis on emotional restraint in public, and public displays of affection between spouses or lovers are frowned upon, especially in rural areas.

RELIGION

Although a small percentage of the population practices traditional religions, the vast majority are Christian. The Lutheran Church is the largest; other major denominations include the Catholic, Dutch Reformed, and Anglican churches. Easter and Christmas are public holidays and especially popular times for travel so families can gather together.

MEDICINE AND HEALTH CARE

The health care system ranges from state-of-the-art private hospitals in Windhoek to small state- or church-run clinics in the rural areas. Traditional healers are sometimes consulted instead of or in addition to the biomedical system, particularly when biomedicine has been unsuccessful.

Although malaria is fairly common in the north and 10 percent of the population suffers from chronic malnutrition, the most serious health problem is HIV-AIDS—20 to 25 percent of the adult population is estimated to be infected, and the number is still rising. Life expectancy has dropped significantly, and analysts predict a major loss of economic productivity as most of those infected are young people. The number of AIDS orphans is already testing the ability of kinship networks to cope.

A Himba village in Kaokoland. In pastoral communities, all members generally have access to grazing and water in the community's area.

SECULAR CELEBRATIONS

Celebrations with national or political significance include Cassinga Day (4 May) which commemorates the deaths of hundreds of Namibian refugees in a 1978 attack, Independence Day (21 May), and Heroes Day (26 August). These occasions are marked by singing, dancing, and speeches by public officials. Other secular holidays include New Year's Day (1 January), Workers' Day (1 May), and Africa Day (25 May).

THE ARTS AND HUMANITIES

Support for the Arts. Before independence, European-influenced arts were relatively well-funded by private and governmental sources. Since independence, research on and promotion of indigenous music, dance oral literature, and other artistic forms has increased greatly with government support.

Literature. The literary community in Namibia is relatively small. Most literature in the indigenous languages consists of traditional tales, short stories, and novels written for schoolchildren. Published fiction, poetry, and autobiographical writings appear in both the English and Afrikaans languages.

Graphic Arts. Many craftspeople produce objects for local use and the tourist trade; wood carvings (containers, furniture, animals) from the Kavango and basketry from Owambo are the best known examples. Some craftspeople have formed organizations to assist each other with production and marketing.

Performance Arts. The National Theatre of Namibia serves as a venue for both Namibian and foreign musicians and stage actors, in addition to assisting community-based drama groups. School and church groups create and stage less formal productions. Traditional dance troupes representing the various ethnic groups of Namibia perform at local and national festivals and holiday celebrations, and also participate in competitions.

THE STATE OF THE PHYSICAL AND SOCIAL SCIENCES

The only university, the University of Namibia (UNAM), was founded in 1992. The largely foreign faculty is slowly being replaced as qualified Namibian candidates become available. Applied sciences are emphasized over theoretical sciences in an effort to meet Namibia's human resource needs. Agricultural, environmental, and health sciences are prominent, and numerous socioeconomic research reports have been produced by UNAM's Social Sciences Division and several independent social science research organizations.

BIBLIOGRAPHY

Bauer, Gretchen. *Labor and Democracy in Namibia, 1971–1996,* 1998.

Becker, Heike. *Namibian Women's Movement, 1980 to 1992: From Anti-Colonial Resistance to Reconstruction,* 1995.

Emmett, Tony. *Popular Resistance and the Roots of Nationalism in Namibia, 1915–1966,* 1999.

Gordon, Robert J. *The Bushman Myth: The Making of a Namibian Underclass,* 1992.

Hayes, Patricia, Jeremy Silvester, Marion Wallace, and Wolfram Hartmann, eds. *Namibia Under South African Rule: Mobility and Containment, 1915–1946,* 1998.

Katjavivi, Peter H. *A History of Resistance in Namibia,* 1988.

Leys, Colin, and John S. Saul. *Namibia's Liberation Struggle: The Two-Edged Sword,* 1995.

The Namibian. *the.namibian.com.na.*

Pendleton, Wade C. *Katutura, A Place Where We Stay: Life in a Post-Apartheid Township in Namibia,* 1996.

Sparks, Donald L., and December Green. *Namibia: The Nation After Independence,* 1992.

Tapscott, Chris. "National Reconciliation, Social Equity and Class Formation in Independent Namibia." *Journal of Southern African Studies* 19 (1): 29–39, 1993.

Ya–Otto, John. *Battlefront Namibia: An Autobiography,* 1981.

—WENDI A. HAUGH

Nauru

CULTURE NAME

Nauruan is the indigenous name used on official documents. Politically, the country is called the Republic of Nauru (RON).

ALTERNATIVE NAMES

Pleasant Islander. Other spellings have appeared, such as Naoero on the national crest.

ORIENTATION

Identification. The name Pleasant Island was used by the first Europeans in reference to the lush vegetation and friendly inhabitants. Nauruans are attempting to recreate that image after the devastation left by phosphate mining.

Location and Geography. Nauru is a single, almost circular island, 37 miles (60 kilometers) south of the equator. It is over 185 miles (300 hundred kilometers) from its nearest neighbor, Ocean Island, and nearly 500 miles (800 kilometers) from Kiribati to the east and the Marshall Islands to the northeast. The Solomon Islands are 744 miles (1,200 kilometers) to the southwest. Topographically, Nauru is shaped like a hat, with a coastal fringe forming the brim and the raised interior forming the crown. The interior, known as Topside, makes up four-fifths of the island; it has been mined for phosphate, and now is an almost impassable area of calcite pinnacles. Buada lagoon is in the raised interior. The island covers a total area of 13 square miles (21 square kilometers). The island is a raised reef consisting of calcite and phosphate on a volcanic base. Nauru has very steep sides that drop down to the ocean floor. This has made anchorage for shipping difficult and necessitated the use of a special mooring device.

Demography. The population has been estimated to be over nine thousand, of which indigenous Nauruans account for about six thousand. In the 1992 census, the population was projected to reach 8,100 by 1996, with a growth rate of 4.3 percent. The remainder of the population includes Pacific islanders from Kiribati, Tuvalu, and Fiji, along with Chinese, Filipinos, Indians, Australians, and New Zealanders. The population is relatively young, with 66 percent of the people under age 24. Population growth has been a major concern throughout the twentieth century. Attempts to reach a total of 1,500 were set back by the influenza epidemic of 1919, but that figure was reached in 1932, a date that now is celebrated as a national holiday. However, the population was severely reduced by starvation, disease, and bombing during World War II. In 1943, of the 1,201 Nauruans deported to Truk by the Japanese, 464 died, leaving 737 to return on 31 January 1946. The population reached 1,500 again in 1950 and has continued to grow. The nation continues to espouse a positive population policy. A very small proportion of Nauruans live overseas, but many visit Australia, New Zealand, and other countries for purposes of work or education or to visit family, and return home.

Linguistic Affiliation. Nauruan is classified as a Micronesian language but does not fit easily within subgroupings of Austronesian languages. It shares some words with Kiribati but is recognized as standing alone. Nauruans are writing their own dictionary. All Nauruans speak English as well as their own language.

Symbolism. The frigate bird is a major symbol; it is found on the fin of Air Nauru planes and appears as the official logo. The crest consists of two palm trees encircling an orb that includes a Christian cross above a resting frigate bird and a flower. Above the orb is a twelve-pointed star representing the twelve tribes of Nauru. Beneath the orb are the words "God's Will First," indicating the Christian basis of the community's way of life. Phosphate has become another symbol, forming the basis of the nation's wealth.

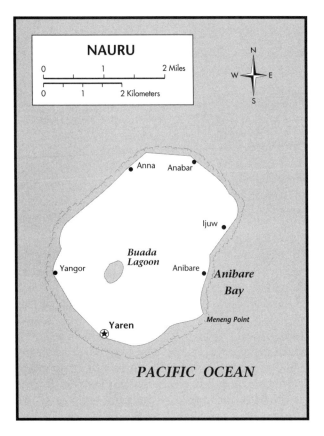

Nauru

and the Pacific islands, particularly Kiribati and Tuvalu. Nauruans chose not to work in the mine other than to hold administrative positions in the 1950s and 1960s. Today most of the administrators are Nauruan, and labor is brought in on contract from the Philippines and India as well as from Kiribati and Tuvalu. World War II left a major mark on the history of Nauru. In 1942, the Japanese invaded, bringing some seven thousand men and military installations and building three runways. Two-thirds of the population was deported to Truk, an atoll to the north, where one-third died of starvation and disease. Those left on Nauru suffered severe privation, including starvation and bombing by the Americans for two years. When Australian forces reclaimed Nauru at the end of the war, the island was a mass of military litter, almost totally lacking in food supplies.

In the 1800s, the island had been a playground for whalers and beachcombers who left behind many English-sounding surnames, as well as guns and gin that added to the damage caused by mining. Nauruans want to rehabilitate the island so that they can use the interior four-fifths that has been mined out. Rehabilitation will be funded by 1993 payments of $120 million by Australia and $12 million each by Great Britain and New Zealand as compensation for mining damage before 1968.

National Identity. National identity as Nauruan remains very strong. It can be claimed only by those born of a Nauruan mother. All Nauruans are registered at birth, or shortly thereafter in the Births Deaths and Marriages register of the Nauru government, under their mother's clan. Failure to register a child as Nauruan eliminates that person from the entitlements of being Nauruan, particularly access to land rights, and to shares in phosphate revenue. A child of a Nauruan father, but whose mother is of another nationality must seek special permission to be registered as Naruan.

Ethnic Relations. Ethnic relations between Naruans and other groups brought into the small island, such as Chinese, Filipinos, Kiribati, Tuvalu, and Fijians are marked by clear distinctions—the latter are grouped as Pacific Islanders. Each group is known for its particular place in the phosphate industry, and for the lifestyle adopted in Nauru. For example, the Kiribati men have brought their small canoes, from which they fish to sell to nauruans. All other groups work for Nauruans in one way or the other.

HISTORY AND ETHNIC RELATIONS

Emergence of the Nation. In 1968, Nauru took over the management of its people and affairs when independence was granted by the trusteeship committee of the United Nations. It took over the running of the phosphate mines in 1970 after paying $13.5 million (U.S.) to the British Phosphate Commission. Those two assertions of social and economic self-reliance released Nauruans from the dominance of outsiders who had exploited the phosphate and the people for seventy years. Mining for phosphate, which dominated Nauruan history in the twentieth century, began when the Pacific Phosphate Company based in Sydney found high-grade phosphate in 1906. This mineral was used to fertilize pasture in Australia and New Zealand. Control passed from Pacific Phosphate to the British Phosphate Commission (BPC) in 1919. BPC was owned by Australia, Great Britain, and New Zealand. In addition to running the mine, Australia became the administering authority under a League of Nations mandate after World War I. Thus, the lives of Nauruans became inextricably tied to Australia and BPC until they achieved independence in 1968. The mine was run using laborers from China

URBANISM, ARCHITECTURE, AND THE USE OF SPACE

Nauru lacks an urban space. Eighty-five percent of the population lives on the narrow coastal strip, with the rest living around the Buada lagoon. All nine thousand inhabitants are crowded alongside the phosphate-processing facilities and the port, mainly in the southwest corner of the island. The airport runway takes up much valuable flat land. Virtually no land is used for agriculture. Until Topside is rehabilitated, the expanding population will become increasingly crowded on the coastal strip. Before mining commenced, the people of Nauru used the interior of the island as a means of crossing from one coast to the other and as a source of food and recreation. The government intends to return Nauru to its status as Pleasant Island with vegetation and places for recreation.

FOOD AND ECONOMY

Food in Daily Life. Almost all food is imported, with the exception of fish caught by Kiribati fishermen. Nauru provided pandanus and fish in pre-mining times, and these were eaten with coconut meat. In times of drought, food shortages could last for two or more years. As a result of mining revenues, the people have a variety of supermarket foods, from turkey to milk. Rice is the basic staple, and fish with rice is the ideal meal. This diet is said to contribute to a high rate of obesity, which often is a precursor to diabetes.

Basic Economy. Phosphate revenues are the mainstay of the economy, together with investments made with revenues earned from earlier mining activities. An average per capita income of $14,400 (U.S.) per year covers up the two extremes: those who have a large number of investments offshore and those who have barely enough to live on. Nauru is an expensive place to live, as almost all necessities have to be imported, although water is now obtained from a desalinization plant. Until the mid-1980s, Nauruans had a strong welfare economy in which housing, education, and health were provided and government scholarships were available for tertiary education overseas. Major cutbacks in social welfare provisions have forced people to buy the materials for their houses and rely more on their personal incomes. Nauru Trust Funds are another potential source of income for all citizens who are recognized landowners and members of Nauruan matrilineage. Five funds were set up between 1920 and 1968, but payments have not been forthcoming as the trustees and the government

struggle to assess the amount of revenue in the funds. The Nauruan people will have to live off the proceeds of mining, which is almost finished. The government is looking for economic alternatives.

SOCIAL STRATIFICATION

Classes and Castes. Nauruans pride themselves on being a democratic society and denounce the two classes that formerly marked their society. The *temonibe* and *amenengame* classes consisted of the senior matrilineage as opposed to those in the junior matrilineages. These two classes were distinguished from the *itsio*, or slave class, which included those who arrived on Nauru from outside and had no land holdings. Heads of lineages were drawn from the temonibe class. A chiefly system instituted in 1927 was replaced in 1951 by the Nauru Local Government Council which consists of elected members.

Symbols of Social Stratification. Symbols of stratification are more latent than overt. Elites with large off-shore bank accounts are known by reputation, as it is not acceptable to flaunt wealth on the island. Trucks or motorbikes and large houses are the extent of manifestations of wealth.

POLITICAL LIFE

Government. Nauru is an active member of the South Pacific Forum and participates in the South Pacific Bureau of Economic Cooperation (SPBEC) and the Forum Fisheries Agency. As the chair of the forum in 1993, Nauru presented a strong case for sustainable development in the small Pacific island states. Its strength is derived from the struggles of its leaders to maintain recognition of Nauruans' rights in their own land. As early as 1921, concerns about Nauruans' returns from phosphate were raised by leaders such as Timothy Detudamo and Hammer de Roburt. Those leaders pressured the BPC and the Australian administration to grant greater shares of the phosphate returns to the Nauruan people and provide better living conditions. Administrative costs were taken out of phosphate profits rather than paid for by Australia as the administering authority under the League of Nations mandate. In 1927, the Australian administration instituted a system of chiefs for the twelve districts. In 1951, Nauruans chose to replace that structure by a more democratic elected body, the Nauru Local Government Council (NLGC), with elected councillors representing the districts. The NLGC was disbanded in 1992. The government now consists of a president

Queen Elizabeth II and Prince Philip visit Nauru. Great Britain helps fund rehabilitation for mining-damaged land.

and five cabinet ministers as well as a judiciary and a public service. Nauru maintains diplomatic relations with several countries. There is no military force.

Social Problems and Control. Drunk driving, particularly by young Nauruan men is a serious problem and the leading cause of death on the island. Families exercise social controls, though there is a police force for major social violations. Concerns about pay-outs from the Trust Funds led to a sit-in across the airport runway in 1993 at the time the Pacific Forum leaders were arriving. That reaction resulted in those women (it was a women's action) being fined, some lost their jobs, and the leaders were arrested. There is no jail as such on the island. Serious criminal offenders may be incarcerated in an Australian jail by arrangement.

SOCIAL WELFARE AND CHANGE PROGRAMS

Nauruans grew up under a broad welfare system in which all their welfare needs were met. Those funds came from the Australian administering authority out of a special Nauru Trust Fund whose money came from phosphate profits. Housing, education, health care, and the public service were all paid for under this administrative account. That system was terminated in 1986, and older Nauruans are finding it hard to live under the new regime, especially those whose lands were mined early. Nauruans have been asking the government for money from the trust funds, and this has caused political antagonism.

NONGOVERNMENTAL ORGANIZATIONS AND OTHER ASSOCIATIONS

Nongovernmental organizations are active mainly within church and youth activities. Both the Congregational and Catholic church have church committees amongst others that work with the Social Welfare department.

GENDER ROLES AND STATUSES

Division of Labor by Gender. A division of labor by gender is not easily defined. The matrilineal social system gives women a lot of power, so they lead behind the scenes, while men take the political roles in government. Civil Service consists of mostly male heads with women seeking these jobs in the past 20 years. Two of the diplomats in overseas postings have been women. Most of the primary school teachers are women, while men are active in phosphate management. The term "division of labor" is no longer appropriate.

Workers at a phosphate mine in Nauru. Phosphate revenues are the mainstay of the economy, however, the interior four-fifths of the island has been mined out.

The Relative Status of Women and Men. Nauruans maintain social ties through the mother (matrilineal ties). Mothers are the anchor persons of kin groups and residential groups, and ties between sisters and brothers are strong. Women are the main care givers within and between households, but they have entered the workforce in considerable numbers in the last fifteen years. Men predominate in political affairs and all senior government positions. Only two women have shared political office at any one time. Male leadership has dominated Nauru's external affairs. Women are active in the National Council of Women and in church committees.

MARRIAGE, FAMILY, AND KINSHIP

All Nauruans belong to a matrilineal group or clan. Each birth and death is publically identified by clan affiliation in a public document. That affiliation lasts the lifetime of the individual and is not altered by marriage. A marriage partner must be selected

Islanders with a tame frigate bird for catching fish. Almost all food is imported, with the exception of fish.

from another clan. Marriage today is largely a Christian affair, though there are concerns that some young people are opting not to marry; their children belong to the mother's lineage. Households center on the mother, who takes care of and then is cared for by her children. The nominal head of the household is the male, but the decision-making head is the mother, who is largely responsible for economic management as well as social care. Land and other properties are inherited by both sons and daughters, but only daughters can pass on their rights to their children without seeking extended

family consent. Modern properties such as motorbikes are passed on within extended families. All Nauruans belong to a district. That affiliation is inherited through the mother or father but may be changed during a person's lifetime for political reasons. District affiliation includes responsibility for participating in district activities.

SOCIALIZATION

Children belong to the mother's lineage but are cared for equally by their paternal kin. Adoptions, whether formal or informal, are fairly common. Children are indulged by Western standards; they can and do exercise a traditional right of demand for goods from the mother's brother. They are seldom left alone and form part of a large network of kin that extends around the island. A primary school is located in each village; from there students progress to government high school or the Catholic high school. A few are sent to Australia or New Zealand to study, especially if their parents received their secondary education overseas. Government scholarships for Nauruans are offered for tertiary study in Australia and New Zealand. The University of the South Pacific Extension Centre is offering opportunities for tertiary study.

ETIQUETTE

Nauru is a Christian country so a prayer opens most gatherings. Children are expected to honor and respect their elders. Mothers are particularly honored. Dress is usually European. Many elements of Australian etiquette are followed as public practice.

RELIGION

Religious Beliefs. Christianity arrived in the 1880s, introduced by both a Catholic missionary and a Congregational minister. Those two religions dominate today. The Catholic Church provides a secondary school, while the Congregational Church, which is the national church, has a major church in the center of the downtown area and smaller churches in the districts. Timothy Detudamo translated the Bible into Nauruan in the 1930s. Before Christian beliefs arrived and mining destroyed Topside, Nauruans believed in the primordial establishment of the island by two spirits that came from Kiribati and were manifest in two rocks, one on either side of Topside. Those rocks have disappeared, along with many of the other useful aspects of Topside. Buada lagoon is another site of spiritual strength for some Nauruans.

MEDICINE AND HEALTH CARE

Government concerns about health have led to programs of intervention, including encouraging more sports and physical activity by young people. Attempts are being made to reduce the high rate of road accidents, particularly among male motor-

cyclists. High alcohol use also is being addressed by educational programs. Two hospital exist on the island. One is run by the government for Naurans and a separate facility is run by the Nauru Phosphate Corporation for its contract workers.

THE ARTS AND HUMANITIES

Nauruans have revived their interest in their history. The Department of Education is producing a history from a Nauruan perspective as well as a Nauruan dictionary. Writers are being encouraged, mainly through the USP Extension Centre on Nauru, to produce stories, poems, and songs. Throughout the twentieth century, poems were written to commemorate special events. Those poems recorded not just historical events but also the culture of Nauru.

THE STATE OF THE PHYSICAL AND SOCIAL SCIENCES

The project to rehabilitate the interior (Topside) has generated considerable interest in the plants and animals of the island. The Committee for Rehabilitation of Nauru consisted of Australians supported by AIDAB and Nauru, working alongside Nauruans. It encouraged a number of young people to share their interest in and knowledge about plants as well as understanding of the social dynamics of the island.

BIBLIOGRAPHY

Dobson Rhone, R. "Nauru: The Richest Island in the South Seas." *National Geographic* 11(6):559–589, 1921.

Ellis, Albert F. *Ocean Island and Nauru*, 1935.

Fabricius, Wilhelm. *Nauru 1888–1900*, 1992.

Hambruch, Paul. *Nauru. Ergebnisse der Sudsee Expedition, 1908–1910*, 1915.

Kretzschmar, K. E. *Nauru*, 1913.

Pollock, Nancy J. *Nauru Report*, 1987.

———. "Social Fattening Patterns in the Pacific: A Nauru Case Study." In N. J. Pollock and I. de Garine, eds., *Social Aspects of Obesity*, 1995.

———. *Social Impact of Mining on Nauruans*, in press.

Viviani, Nancy. *Nauru, Phosphate and Political Progress*, 1970.

Weeramantry, C. *Nauru: Environmental Damage under International Trusteeship*, 1992.

—NANCY J. POLLOCK

NEPAL

CULTURE NAME

Nepalese

ALTERNATIVE NAME

Nepali

ORIENTATION

Identification. Nepal is named for the Kathmandu Valley, where the nation's founder established a capital in the late eighteenth century. Nepali culture represents a fusion of Indo-Aryan and Tibeto-Mongolian influences, the result of a long history of migration, conquest, and trade.

Location and Geography. Nepal is a roughly rectangular country with an area of 147,181 square miles (381,200 square kilometers). To the south, west, and east it is bordered by Indian states; to the north lies Tibet. Nepal is home to the Himalayan Mountains, including Mount Everest. From the summit of Everest, the topography plunges to just above sea level at the Gangetic Plain on the southern border. This drop divides the country into three horizontal zones: the high mountains, the lush central hills, and the flat, arid Terai region in the south. Fast-moving, snow-fed rivers cut through the hills and mountains from north to south, carving deep valleys and steep ridges. The rugged topography has created numerous ecological niches to which different ethnic groups have adapted. Although trade has brought distinct ethnic groups into contact, the geography has created diversity in language and subsistence practices. The result is a country with over thirty-six ethnic groups and over fifty languages.

Demography. The population in 1997 was just over 22.6 million. Although infant mortality rates are extremely high, fertility rates are higher. High birth rates in rural areas have led to land shortages, forcing immigration to the Terai, where farmland is more plentiful, and to urban areas, where jobs are available. Migration into cities has led to overcrowding and pollution. The Kathmandu Valley has a population of approximately 700,000.

Linguistic Affiliation. After conquering much of the territory that constitutes modern Nepal, King Prithvi Narayan Shah (1743–1775) established Gorkhali (Nepali) as the national language. Nepali is an Indo-European language derived from Sanskrit with which it shares and most residents speak at least some Nepali, which is the medium of government, education, and most radio and television broadcasts. For many people Nepali is secondary to the language of their ethnic group or region. This situation puts certain groups at a disadvantage in terms of education and civil service positions. Since the institution of a multiparty democracy in 1990, linguistic issues have emerged as hotly debated topics.

Symbolism. The culture has many symbols from Hindu and Buddhist sources. Auspicious signs, including the ancient Hindu *swastika* and Shiva's trident, decorate buses, trucks, and walls. Other significant symbols are the emblems (tree, plow, sun) used to designate political parties.

Prominent among symbols for the nation as a whole are the national flower and bird, the rhododendron and *danfe*; the flag; the plumed crown worn by the kings; and the crossed *kukhris* (curved knives) of the Gurkhas, mercenary regiments that have fought for the British Army in a number of wars. Images of the current monarch and the royal family are displayed in many homes and places of business. In nationalistic rhetoric the metaphor of a garden with many different kinds of flowers is used to symbolize national unity amid cultural diversity.

HISTORY AND ETHNIC RELATIONS

Emergence of the Nation. Mongolian tribes from the east called Kiratis brought Buddhism in the sev-

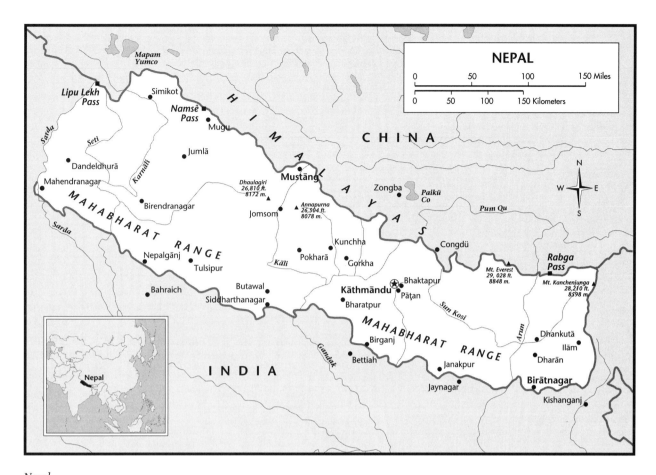

Nepal

enth or eighth century B.C.E. Hinduism flourished in the third and fourth centuries C.E. under the Licchavis, an Indo-Aryan people from northern India, and after the migration of Hindus from India during the Mughal period. The Hindu Malla dynasties reigned in the Kathmandu Valley between the thirteenth and fifteenth centuries, encouraging tolerance toward Buddhism and an orthodox, caste-oriented form of Hinduism. Since unification in the late eighteenth century and through the hundred-year period of Rana rule, the culture of hill Hindus, *Parbatiya*, has been dominant.

The birth of the nation is dated to Prithvi Narayan Shah's conquest of the Kathmandu Valley kingdoms in 1768. The expansionist reigns of Shah and his successors carved out a territory twice the size of modern Nepal. However, territorial clashes with the Chinese in the late eighteenth century and the British in the early nineteenth century pushed the borders back to their current configuration.

National Identity. To unify a geographically and culturally divided land, Shah perpetuated the culture and language of high-caste Hindus and instituted a social hierarchy in which non-Hindus as well as Hindus were ranked according to caste-based principles. Caste laws were further articulated in the National Code of 1854.

By privileging the language and culture of high-caste Hindus, the state has marginalized non-Hindu and low-caste groups. Resentment in recent years has led to the organization of ethnopolitical parties, agitation for minority rights, and talk about the formation of a separate state for Mongolian ethnic groups.

Despite ethnic unrest, Nepalis have a strong sense of national identity and pride. Sacred Hindu and Buddhist sites and the spectacular mountains draw tourists and pilgrims and give citizens a sense of importance in the world. Other natural resources, such as rivers and flora and fauna are a source of national pride.

Ethnic Relations. The population consists of numerous racial, cultural, and linguistic groups that often are divided into three broad categories: Indo-Nepalese, Tibeto-Nepalese, and indigenous Nepalese. The Indo-Nepalese migrated from India over several

The village of Siklis, in the Himalayas. Village houses are usually clustered in river valleys or along ridge tops.

centuries; they practice Hinduism, have Caucasian features, and speak Indo-Aryan languages. They have settled primarily in the lower hills and river valleys and the Terai. The Tibeto-Nepalese have distinctively Mongolian features and speak Tibeto-Burmese languages; these groups occupy the higher hills and mountainous areas. Different groups within this category practice Buddhism, animism, or Hinduism. There are scattered tribes of indigenous Nepalis, whose origins probably predate the arrival of Indo- and Tibeto-Nepalese peoples.

Hindu castes and Buddhist and animist ethnic groups were historically collapsed into a single caste hierarchy. At the top are high-caste Hindus. Below them are alcohol-drinking (*matwali*) castes, which include Mongolian ethnic groups. At the bottom are untouchable Hindu castes that have traditionally performed occupations considered defiling by higher castes. The Newars of the Kathmandu Valley have a caste system that has been absorbed into the national caste hierarchy.

Historically, members of the highest castes have owned the majority of land and enjoyed the greatest political and economic privileges. Members of lower castes have been excluded from political representation and economic opportunities. The untouchable castes were not permitted to own land, and their civil liberties were circumscribed by law. Caste discrimination is officially illegal but has not disappeared. In 1991, 80 percent of positions in the civil service, army, and police were occupied by members of the two highest castes.

URBANISM, ARCHITECTURE, AND THE USE OF SPACE

Nepal historically was one of the least urbanized countries in the world, but urbanization is accelerating, especially in the capital, and urban sprawl and pollution have become serious problems. Kathmandu and the neighboring cities of Patan and Bhaktapur are known for pagoda-style and *shikhara* temples, Buddhist *stupas*, palaces, and multistory brick houses with elaborately carved wooden door frames and screened windows. Although the largest and most famous buildings are well maintained, many smaller temples and older residential buildings are falling into disrepair.

At the height of British rule in India, the Rana rulers incorporated Western architectural styles into palaces and public buildings. Rana palaces convey a sense of grandeur and clear separation from the peasantry. The current king's palace's scale and fortress-like quality illustrate the distance between king and commoner.

Rural architecture is generally very simple, reflecting the building styles of different caste and ethnic groups, the materials available, and the climate. Rural houses generally have one or two stories and are made of mud brick with a thatched roof. Village houses tend to be clustered in river valleys or along ridge tops.

FOOD AND ECONOMY

Food in Daily Life. Many Nepalis do not feel that they have eaten a real meal unless it has included a sizable helping of rice. Most residents eat a large rice meal twice a day, usually at midmorning and in the early evening. Rice generally is served with *dal*, a lentil dish, and *tarkari*, a cooked vegetable. Often, the meal includes a pickle *achar*, made of a fruit or vegetable. In poorer and higher-altitude areas, where rice is scarce, the staple is *dhiro*, a thick mush made of corn or millet. In areas where wheat is plentiful, rice may be supplemented by flat bread, *roti*. Most families eat from individual plates while seated on the floor. Though some urbanites use Western utensils, it is more common to eat with the hands.

Villagers celebrate the end of the plowing season. Most Nepalese are subsistence farmers.

Conventions regarding eating and drinking are tied to caste. Orthodox high-caste Hindus are strictly vegetarian and do not drink alcohol. Other castes may drink alcohol and eat pork and even beef. Traditionally, caste rules also dictate who may eat with or accept food from whom. Members of the higher castes were particularly reluctant to eat food prepared by strangers. Consequently, eating out has not been a major part of the culture. However, caste rules are relaxing to suit the modern world, and the tourist economy is making restaurants a common feature of urban life.

Food Customs at Ceremonial Occasions.
At weddings and other important life-cycle events, feasts are generally hosted by the families directly involved, and numerous guests are invited. At such occasions, it is customary to seat guests on woven grass mats on the ground outside one's home, often in lines separating castes and honoring people of high status. Food is served on leaf plates, which can be easily disposed of. These customs, however, like most others, vary by caste-ethnic groups, and are changing rapidly to suit modern tastes.

Basic Economy.
The large majority of the people are subsistence farmers who grow rice, maize, millet, barley, wheat, and vegetables. At low altitudes, agriculture is the principal means of subsistence, while at higher altitudes agropastoralism prevails. Many households maintain chickens and goats. However, few families own more than a small number of cows, water buffalo, or yaks because the mountainous topography does not provide grazing land for large animals.

Nepal is one of the poorest countries in the world. This poverty can be attributed to scarce natural resources, a difficult terrain, landlocked geography, and a weak infrastructure but also to feudal land tenure systems, government corruption, and the ineffectiveness of development efforts. Foreign aid rarely goes to the neediest sectors of the population but is concentrate in urban areas, providing jobs for the urban middle class. The name of the national currency is rupee.

Land Tenure and Property.
Historically, a handful of landlords held most agricultural land. Civil servants often were paid in land grants, governing their land on an absentee basis and collecting taxes from tenant-farming peasants. Since the 1950s, efforts have been made to protect the rights of tenants, but without the redistribution of land.

Overpopulation has exacerbated land shortages. Nearly every acre of arable land has been farmed intensively. Deforestation for wood and animal fodder has created serious erosion.

Commercial Activities.
The majority of commercial activity takes place at small, family-owned shops or in the stalls of sidewalk vendors. With the exception of locally grown fruits and vegetables, many products are imported from India and, to a lesser extent, China and the West. Jute, sugar, cigarettes, beer, matches, shoes, chemicals, cement, and bricks are produced locally. Carpet and garment manufacturing has increased significantly, providing foreign exchange. Since the late 1950s, tourism has increased rapidly; trekking, mountaineering, white-water rafting, and canoeing have drawn tourists from the West and other parts of Asia. The tourism industry has sparked the commercial production of crafts and souvenirs and created a number of service positions, such as trekking guides and porters. Tourism also has fueled the black market, where drugs are sold and foreign currency is exchanged.

Major Industries.
There was no industrial development until the middle of the twentieth century. Much of earliest industrial development was accomplished with the help of private entrepreneurs from India and foreign aid from the Soviet Union,

China, and the West. Early development focused on the use of jute, sugar, and tea; modern industries include the manufacturing of brick, tile, and construction materials; paper making; grain processing; vegetable oil extraction; sugar refining; and the brewing of beer.

Trade. Nepal is heavily dependent on trade from India and China. The large majority of imported goods pass through India. Transportation of goods is limited by the terrain. Although roads connect many major commercial centers, in much of the country goods are transported by porters and pack animals. The few roads are difficult to maintain and subject to landslides and flooding. Railroads in the southern flatlands connect many Terai cities to commercial centers in India but do not extend into the hills. Nepal's export goods include carpets, clothing, leather goods, jute, and grain. Tourism is another primary export commodity. Imports include gold, machinery and equipment, petroleum products, and fertilizers.

Division of Labor. Historically, caste was loosely correlated with occupational specialization. Tailors, smiths, and cobblers were the lowest, untouchable castes, and priests and warriors were the two highest Hindu castes. However, the large majority of people are farmers, an occupation that is not caste-specific.

SOCIAL STRATIFICATION

Classes and Castes. Historically, caste and class status paralleled each other, with the highest castes having the most land, capital, and political influence. The lowest castes could not own property or receive an education. Although caste distinctions are no longer supported by law, caste relations have shaped present-day social stratification: Untouchables continue to be the poorest sector of society, while the upper castes tend to be wealthy and politically dominant. While land is still the principal measure of wealth, some castes that specialize in trade and commerce have fared better under modern capitalism than have landowning castes. Changes in the economic and political system have opened some opportunities for members of historically disadvantaged castes.

Symbols of Social Stratification. Caste and ethnic groups are often identifiable by both physical traits and styles of dress and ornamentation. These symbols of ethnic identity along with distinctive forms of music, dance, and cuisine, continue to be important. The culture of caste Hindus is the national

Herding cattle down a dirt road. Grazing land is limited by the mountainous topography.

"prestige culture." In a process of "Sanskritization," members of diverse groups have acquired the customs, tastes, and habits of the ruling elite. Westernization is vying with Sanskritization as a cultural influence, and the ability to speak English is a mark of prestige and an asset in the job market. In cities, most men and an increasing number of women wear Western clothes. In the past, status was vested in the ownership of land and livestock; modern status symbols include motorcycles, cars, fashionable clothing, televisions, and computers.

POLITICAL LIFE

Government. The Shah dynasty has ruled the country since its unification, except during the Rana period from the mid-nineteenth to the mid-twentieth century. During the Rana administration, the Shah monarchs were stripped of power and the country was ruled by a series of prime ministers from the Rana noble family. In 1950, the Shah kings were restored to the throne and a constitutional monarchy was established that eventually took the form of the *panchayat* system. Under this system, political parties were illegal and the country was governed by local and national assemblies controlled by the palace. In 1990, the Movement for the

Restoration of Democracy (People's Movement) initiated a series of popular demonstrations for democratic reforms, eventually forcing the king to abolish the panchayat system and institute a multiparty democracy.

The country is divided administratively into fourteen zones and seventy-five districts. Local and district-level administers answer to national ministries that are guided by policies set by a bicameral legislature made up of a House of Representatives and a National Council. The majority party in the House of Representatives appoints the prime minister. The executive branch consists of the king and the Council of Ministers.

Leadership and Political Officials. The government is plagued by corruption, and officials often rely on bribes to supplement their income. It is widely believed that influence and employment in government are achieved through personal and family connections. The king is viewed with ambivalence. He and his family have been criticized for corruption and political repression, but photos of the royal family are a popular symbol of national identity and many people think of the king as the living embodiment of the nation and an avatar of the god Vishnu.

Social Problems and Control. International attention has focused on the plight of girls who have been lured or abducted from villages to work as prostitutes in Indian cities and child laborers in carpet factories. Prostitution has increased the spread of AIDS. Foreign boycotts of Nepali carpets have helped curb the use of child labor but have not addressed the larger social problems that force children to become family wage earners.

Military Activity. The military is small and poorly equipped. Its primary purpose is to reinforce the police in maintaining domestic stability. Some Royal Nepal Army personnel have served in United Nations peacekeeping forces. A number of Nepalis, particularly of the hill ethnic groups, have served in Gurkha regiments. To many villagers, service in the British Army represents a significant economic opportunity, and in some areas soldiers' remittances support the local economy.

NONGOVERNMENTAL ORGANIZATIONS AND OTHER ASSOCIATIONS

Aid organizations are involved in health care, family planning, community development, literacy, women's rights, and economic development for low castes and tribal groups. However, many projects are initiated without an understanding of the physical and cultural environment and serve the interests of foreign companies and local elites.

GENDER ROLES AND STATUSES

Division of Labor by Gender. Only men plow, while fetching water is generally considered women's work. Women cook, care for children, wash clothes, and collect firewood and fodder. Men perform the heavier agricultural tasks and often engage in trade, portering, and other work outside the village. Both men and women perform physically demanding labor, but women tend to work longer hours, have less free time, and die younger. In urban areas, men are far more likely to work outside the home. Increasingly, educational opportunities are available to both men and women, and there are women in professional positions. Women also frequently work in family businesses as shopkeepers and seamstresses.

Children and older people are a valuable source of household labor. In rural families, young children collect firewood, mind animals, and watch younger children. Older people may serve on village councils. In urban areas and larger towns, children attend school; rural children may or may not, depending on the proximity of schools, the availability of teachers, and the work required of them at home.

The Relative Status of Women and Men. Women often describe themselves as "the lower caste" in relation to men and generally occupy a subordinate social position. However, the freedoms and opportunities available to women vary widely by ethnic group and caste. Women of the highest castes have their public mobility constrained, for their reputation is critical to family and caste honor. Women of lower castes and classes often play a larger wage-earning role, have greater mobility, and are more outspoken around men. Gender roles are slowly shifting in urban areas, where greater numbers of women are receiving an education and joining the work force.

MARRIAGE, FAMILY, AND KINSHIP

Marriage. Nepal is overwhelmingly patrilineal and patrilocal. Arranged marriages are the norm in the mainstream culture. Because marriages forge important social bonds between families, when a child reaches marriageable age, the family elders are responsible for finding a suitable mate of the appropriate caste, education level, and social stra-

brideprice substitutes for a dowry. In others, clan exogamy is an important feature of marriages. Until recently, polygyny was legal and relatively common. Now it is illegal and found only in the older generation and in remote areas. Child marriages were considered especially auspicious, and while they continue to be practiced in rural areas, they are now prohibited by law. Love marriage is gaining in popularity in the cities, where romantic films and music inform popular sentiment and the economy offers younger people economic independence from the extended family.

Domestic Unit. Among landholding Hindu castes, a high value is placed on joint family arrangements in which the sons of a household, along with their parents, wives, and children, live together, sharing resources and expenses. Within the household, the old have authority over the young, and men over women. Typically, new daughters-in-law occupy the lowest position. Until a new bride has produced children, she is subject to the hardest work and often the harshest criticism in her husband's household. Older women, often wield a great deal of influence within the household.

The emphasis in joint families is on filial loyalty and agnatic solidarity over individualism. In urban areas, an increasing number of couples are opting for nuclear family arrangements.

Inheritance. Fathers are legally obligated to leave equal portions of land to each son. Daughters do not inherit paternal property unless they remain unmarried past age thirty-five. Although ideally sons manage their father's land together as part of a joint family, familial land tends to be divided, with holdings diminishing in every generation.

Kin Groups. Patrilineal kin groups form the nucleus of households, function as corporate units, and determine inheritance patterns. A man belongs permanently to the kinship group of his father, while a woman changes membership from her natal kin group to the kin group of her husband at the time of marriage. Because family connections are critical in providing access to political influence and economic opportunities, marriage alliances are planned carefully to expand kinship networks and strengthen social ties. Although women join the husband's household, they maintain emotional ties and contact with their families. If a woman is mistreated in her husband's household, she may escape to her father's house or receive support from her male kin. Consequently, women often prefer to marry men from the same villages.

For Buddhist monks, Nepal is significant as the birthplace of Lord Buddha.

tum. The bride's family generally provides a substantial dowry to the groom's family, while the groom's family furnishes a much smaller gift of clothing, jewelry, and personal items to the bride. Both families are expected to host a feast during the wedding festivities, which generally last three days. The cost of a wedding, especially to the bride's family, is high and often puts families into debt.

Hindu castes do not generally approve of cross-cousin marriage, which is preferred among some Mongolian ethnic groups. Among some groups, a

Nepalese men in a wedding ceremony; arranged marriages are the norm in mainstream culture.

SOCIALIZATION

Infant Care. Infants are carried on the mothers' back, held by a shawl tied tightly across her chest. Babies are breast-fed on demand, and sleep with their mothers until they are displaced by a new baby or are old enough to share a bed with siblings. Infants and small children often wear amulets and bracelets to protect them from supernatural forces. Parents sometimes line a baby's eyes with *kohl* to prevent eye infections.

Child Rearing and Education. Mothers are the primary providers of child care, but children also are cared for and socialized by older siblings, cousins, and grandparents. Often children as young as five or six mind younger children. Neighbors are entitled to cuddle, instruct, and discipline children, who are in turn expected to obey and defer to senior members of the family and community. Children address their elders by using the honorific form of Nepali, while adults speak to children using more familiar language. Because authority in households depends on seniority, the relative ages of siblings is important and children are often addressed by birth order.

Certain household rituals mark key stages in child's development, including the first taste of rice and the first haircut. When a girl reaches puberty, she goes through a period of seclusion in which she is prohibited from seeing male family members. Although she may receive special foods and is not expected to work, the experience is an acknowledgment of the pollution associated with female sexuality and reproductivity.

From an early age, children are expected to contribute labor to the household. The law entitles both girls and boys to schooling; however, if a family needs help at home or cannot spare the money for uniforms, books, and school fees, only the sons are sent to school. It is believed that education is wasted on girls, who will marry and take their wage-earning abilities to another household. Boys marry and stay at home, and their education is considered a wise investment.

ETIQUETTE

The customary greeting is to press one's palms together in front of the chest and say *namaste* ("I greet the god within you"). Men in urban areas have adopted the custom of shaking hands. In the mainstream culture, physical contact between the sexes is not appropriate in public. Although men may be openly affectionate with men and women with women, even married couples do not demonstrate physical affection in public. Some ethnic groups permit more open contact between the sexes.

Hospitality is essential. Guests are always offered food and are not permitted to help with food preparation or cleaning after a meal. It is polite to eat with only the right hand; the hand used to eat food must not touch anything else until it has been thoroughly washed, for saliva is considered defiling. When drinking from a common water vessel, people do not touch the rim to their lips. It is insulting to hit someone with a shoe or sandal, point the soles of one's feet at someone, and step over a person.

RELIGION

Religious Beliefs. Eighty-six percent of Nepalis are Hindus, 8 percent are Buddhists, 4 percent are Muslims, and just over 1 percent are Christians. On a day-to-day level, Hindus practice their religion by "doing *puja*," making offerings and prayers to particular deities. While certain days and occasions are designated as auspicious, this form of worship can be performed at any time.

Buddhism is practiced in the Theravadan form. There are two primary Buddhist traditions: the Buddhism of Tibetan refugees and high-altitude ethnic groups with cultural roots in Tibet and the Tantric form practiced by Newars.

There is a strong animistic and shamanic tradition. Belief in ghosts, spirits, and witchcraft is widespread, especially in rural areas. Spiteful witches, hungry ghosts, and angry spirits are thought to inflict illness and misfortune. Shamans mediate between the human and supernatural realms to discover the cause of illness and recommend treatment.

Religious Practitioners. Many forms of Hindu worship do not require the mediation of a priest. At key rites of passage such as weddings and funerals, Brahmin priests read Vedic scriptures and ensure the correct performance of rituals. At temples, priests care for religious icons, which are believed to contain the essence of the deities they represent. They are responsible for ensuring the purity of the temple and overseeing elaborate *pujas*.

Buddhist monasteries train young initiates in philosophy and meditation. Lay followers gain religious merit by making financial contributions to monasteries, where religious rites are performed on behalf of the general population. Within Buddhism there is a clerical hierarchy, with highly esteemed *lamas* occupying the positions of greatest influence. Monks and nuns of all ranks shave their heads, wear maroon robes, and embrace a life of celibacy and religious observance.

Rituals and Holy Places. Nepal occupies a special place in both Hindu and Buddhist traditions. According to Hindu mythology, the Himalayas are the abode of the gods, and are specifically associated with Shiva, one of the three principal Hindu deities. Pashupatinath, a large Shiva temple in Kathmandu, is among the holiest sites in Nepal and attracts Hindu pilgrims from all over South Asia. Pashupatinath is only one of thousands of temples and shrines scattered throughout Nepal, however. In the Kathmandu Valley alone, there are hundreds of such shrines, large and small, in which the major gods and goddesses of the Hindu pantheon, as well as local and minor divinities, are worshiped. Many of these shrines are constructed near rivers or at the base of pipal trees, which are themselves considered sacred. For Buddhists, Nepal is significant as the birthplace of Lord Buddha. It is also home to a number of important Buddhist monasteries and supas, including Boudha and Swayambhu, whose dome-shaped architecture and painted all-seeing eyes have become symbols of the Kathamandu Valley.

Death and the Afterlife. Hindus and Buddhists believe in reincarnation. An individual's meritorious actions in life will grant him or her a higher rebirth. In both religions the immediate goal is to live virtuously in order to move progressively through higher births and higher states of consciousness. Ultimately, the goal is to attain enlightenment, stopping the cycle of rebirth.

In the Hindu tradition, the dead are cremated, preferably on the banks of a river. It is customary for a son to perform the funeral rites. Some Buddhists also cremate bodies. Others perform what are called "sky burials," in which corpses are cut up and left at sacred sites for vultures to carry away.

MEDICINE AND HEALTH CARE

Infant mortality is high, respiratory and intestinal diseases are endemic, and malnutrition is widespread in a country where life expectancy is fifty-seven years. Contributing to this situation are poverty, poor hygiene, and lack of health care. There are hospitals only in urban areas, and they are poorly equipped and unhygienic. Rural health clinics often lack personnel, equipment, and medicines. Western biomedical practices have social prestige, but many poor people cannot afford this type of health care. Many people consult shamans and other religious practitioners. Others look to Ayurvedic medicine, in which illness is thought to be caused by imbalances in the bodily humors. Treatment involves correcting these imbalances, principally through diet. Nepalis combine Ayurvedic, shamanic, biomedical, and other systems.

Although health conditions are poor, malaria has been eradicated. Development efforts have focused on immunization, birth control, and basic medical care. However, the success of all such projects seems to correlate with the education levels of women, which are extremely low.

THE ARTS AND HUMANITIES

Literature. Nepal's literary tradition dates only to the nineteenth century with Bhanubhakta Acharya's adaptation of the Hindu epic, *Ramayana*, for a Nepali readership. The development of literature in Nepal has been hindered by heavy government control and censorship, which led Nepali authors and poets to seek publication outside of Nepal until the 1930s, when Nepal's first literary journal,

A Nepalese person carrying a wicker basket filled with fuel.

Sharada, created a more open venue for literary expression. Among Nepal's greatest writers and poets are Lakshmi Prasad Devkota, Lekhnath Paudyal, Balkrishna Sama, and Guruprasad Mainali.

Graphic Arts. Much of Nepali art is religious. Newari artisans create cast-bronze statuary of Buddhist and Hindu deities as well as intricately painted *tangkas* that describe Buddhist cosmology. The creation and contemplation of such art constitutes a religious act.

Performance Arts. Dramatic productions often focus on religious themes drawn from Hindu epics, although political satire and other comedic forms are also popular. There is a rich musical heritage, with a number of distinctive instruments and vocal styles, and music has become an marker of identity for the younger generation. Older people prefer folk and religious music; younger people, especially in urban areas, are attracted to romantic and experimental film music as well as fusions of Western and Asian genres.

THE STATE OF THE PHYSICAL AND SOCIAL SCIENCES

Universities are underfunded, faculties are poorly paid, and library resources are meager. Nepalis accord less respect to degrees from universities than to degrees obtained abroad and many scholars seek opportunities to study overseas or in India. Despite these limitations, some fine scholarship has emerged, particularly in the social sciences. In the post–1990 period, political reforms have permitted a more open and critical intellectual environment.

BIBLIOGRAPHY

Acharya, Meena, and Lynn Bennett. "The Rural Women of Nepal: An Aggregate Analysis and Summary of Eight Village Studies." *The Status of Women in Nepal*, 1981.

Adams, Vincanne. *Tigers of the Snow and Other Virtual Sherpas: An Ethnography of Himalayan Encounters*, 1996.

Ahearn, Laura Marie. "Consent and Coercion: Changing Marriage Practices Among Magars in Nepal." Ph.D. dissertation. University of Michigan, 1994.

Allen, Michael, and S. N. Mukherjee, eds. *Women in India and Nepal*, 1990.

Bennett, Lynn. *Dangerous Wives and Sacred Sisters: Social and Symbolic Roles of High-Caste Women in Nepal*, 1983.

Bista, Dor Bahadur. *Fatalism and Development: Nepal's Struggle for Modernization*, 1991.

Blaikie, Piers, John Cameron, and David Seddon. *Nepal in Crisis: Growth and Stagnation at the Periphery*, 1978.

Borgstrom, Bengt-Erik. *The Patron and the Panca: Village Values and Pancayat Democracy in Nepal*, 1980.

Borre, Ole, Sushil R. Pandey, and Chitra K. Tiwari. *Nepalese Political Behavior*, 1994.

Brown, T. Louise. *The Challenge to Democracy in Nepal: A Political History*, 1996.

Burghart, Richard. "The Formation of the Concept of Nation-State in Nepal." *Journal of Asian Studies*, 1984.

Cameron, Mary Margaret. *On the Edge of the Auspicious*, 1993.

Caplan, Lionel. "Tribes in the Ethnography of Nepal: Some Comments on a Debate." *Contributions to Nepalese Studies* 17 (2): 129–145, 1990.

Caplan, Patricia. *Priests and Cobblers: A Study of Social Change in a Hindu Village in Western Nepal*, 1972.

Des Chene, Mary. "Ethnography in the *Janajati-yug*: Lessons from Reading *Rodhi* and other Tamu Writings." *Studies in Nepali History and Society* 1: 97–162, 1996.

Desjarlais, Robert. *Body and Emotion: The Aesthetics of Illness and Healing in the Nepal Himalaya*, 1992.

Doherty, Victor S. "Kinship and Economic Choice: Modern Adaptations in West Central Nepal." Ph.D. dissertation. University of Wisconsin, Madison, 1975.

Fisher, James F. *Sherpas: Reflections on Change in Himalayan Nepal*, 1990.

Fricke, Tom. *Himalayan Households: Tamang Demography and Domestic Processes*, 1994.

———, William G. Axinn, and Arland Thornton. "Marriage, Social Inequality, and Women's Contact with Their Natal Families in Alliance Societies: Two Tamang Examples." *American Anthropologist* 95 (2): 395–419, 1993.

Furer-Haimendorf, Christoph von. *The Sherpas Transformed*. Delhi: Sterling, 1984.

———, ed. *Caste and Kin in Nepal, India and Ceylon*, 1966.

Gaige, Frederick H. *Regionalism and National Unity in Nepal*, 1975.

Gellner, David N., Joanna Pfaff-Czarnecka, and John Whelpton. *Nationalism and Ethnicity in a Hindu Kingdom: The Politics of Culture in Contemporary Nepal*, 1997.

Ghimire, Premalata. "An Ethnographic Approach to Ritual Ranking Among the Satar." *Contributions to Nepalese Studie* 17 (2): 103–121, 1990.

Gilbert, Kate. "Women and Family Law in Modern Nepal: Statutory Rights and Social Implications." *New York University Journal of International Law and Politics* 24: 729–758, 1992.

Goldstein, Melvyn C. "Fraternal Polyandry and Fertility in a High Himalayan Valley in Northwest Nepal." *Human Ecology* 4 (2): 223–233, 1976.

Gray, John N. *The Householder's World: Purity, Power and Dominance in a Nepali Village*, 1995.

Gurung, Harka Bahadur. *Vignettes of Nepal*. Kathmandu: Sajha Prakashan, 1980.

Hagen, Toni. *Nepal: The Kingdom in the Himalayas*, 1961.

Hitchcock, John. *The Magars of Bunyan Hill*, 1966.

Hofer, Andras. *The Caste Hierarchy and the State in Nepal: A Study of the Muluki Ain of 1854*, 1979.

Holmberg, David. *Order in Paradox: Myth, Ritual and Exchange among Nepal's Tamang*, 1989.

Hutt, Michael. "Drafting the 1990 Constitution." In Michael Hutt, ed., *Nepal in the Nineties*, 1994.

Iijima, Shigeru. "Hinduization of a Himalayan Tribe in Nepal." *Kroeber Anthropological Society Papers* 29: 43–52, 1963.

Jones, Rex, and Shirley Jones. *The Himalayan Woman: A Study of Limbu Women in Marriage and Divorce*, 1976.

Justice, Judith. *Policies, Plans and People: Culture and Health Development in Nepal*, 1985.

Karan, Pradyumna P., and Hiroshi Ishii. *Nepal: A Himalayan Kingdom in Transition*, 1996.

Kondos, Alex. "The Question of 'Corruption' in Nepal." *Mankind* 17 (1): 15–29, 1987.

Kumar, Dhruba, ed. *State Leadership and Politics in Nepal*, 1995.

Landan, Perceval. *Nepal*, 1976.

Levine, Nancy. *The Dynamics of Polyandry: Kinship, Domesticity, and Population on the Tibetan Border*, 1988.

Levy, Robert I. *Mesocosm: Hinduism and the Organization of a Traditional Newar City in Nepal*, 1990.

Liechty, Mark. "Paying for Modernity: Women and the Discourse of Freedom in Kathmandu." *Studies in Nepali History and Society* 1: 201–230, 1996.

MacFarland, Alan. *Resources and Population: A Study of the Gurungs of Nepal*, 1976.

Manzardo, Andrew E. "To Be Kings of the North: Community, Adaptation, and Impression Management in the Thakali of Western Nepal." Ph.D. dissertation. University of Wisconsin, Madison, 1978.

Messerschmidt, Donald A. "The Thakali of Nepal: Historical Continuity and Socio-Cultural Change." *Ethnohistory* 29 (4): 265–280, 1982.

Molnar, Augusta. "Women and Politics: Case of the Kham Magar of Western Nepal." *American Ethnologist* 9 (3): 485–502, 1982.

Nepali, Gopal Singh. *The Newars*, 1965.

Oldfield, Henry Ambrose. *Sketches from Nepal, Historical and Descriptive*, 1880, 1974.

Ortner, Sherry B. *High Religion: A Cultural and Political History of Sherpa Buddhism*, 1989.

Pigg, Stacy Leigh. "Inventing Social Categories through Place: Social Representations and Development in Nepal." *Comparative Studies in Society and History* 34: 491–513, 1992.

Poudel, P. C., and Rana P. B. Singh. "Pilgrimage and Tourism at Muktinath, Nepal: A Study of Sacrality and Spatial Structure." *National Geographical Journal of India* 40: 249–268, 1994.

Regmi, Mahesh C. *Thatched Huts and Stucco Palaces: Peasants and Landlords in 19th Century Nepal*, 1978.

Rosser, Colin. "Social Mobility in the Newar Caste System." In Christoph von Furer-Haimendorf, ed. *Caste and Kin in Nepal, India, and Ceylon*, 1966.

Shaha, Rishikesh. *Politics of Nepal, 1980–1991: Referendum, Stalemate, and Triumph of People Power*, 1993.

Shrestha, Nirakar Man. "Alcohol and Drug Abuse in Nepal." *British Journal of Addiction* 87: 1241–1248, 1992.

Slusser, Mary S. *Nepal Mandala: A Cultural Study of the Kathmandu Valley*, 1982.

Stevens, Stanley F. *Claiming the High Ground: Sherpas, Subsistence and Environmental Change in the Highest Himalaya*, 1993.

Stone, Linda. *Illness Beliefs and Feeding the Dead in Hindu Nepal: An Ethnographic Analysis*, 1988.

Thompson, Julia J. "'There are Many Words to Describe Their Anger': Ritual and Resistance among High-Caste Hindu Women in Kathmandu." In Michael Allen, ed., *Anthropology of Nepal: Peoples, Problems, and Processes*, 1994.

Tingey, Carol. *Auspicious Music in a Changing Society*, 1994.

Vansittart, Eden. *The Gurkhas*, 1890, 1993.

Vinding, Michael. "Making a Living in the Nepal Himalayas: The Case of the Thakali of Mustang District." *Contributions to Nepalese Studies* 12 (1): 51–105, 1984.

—Marie Kamala Norman

THE NETHERLANDS

CULTURE NAME
Dutch

ALTERNATIVE NAMES
Netherlands culture, Hollandic culture. The Dutch use Nederlandse cultuur and Hollandse cultuur to describe their culture.

ORIENTATION
Identification. The English word "Dutch" derives from the German *deutsch* ("German"). "Dutch" referred originally to both Germany and the Netherlands but came to be restricted to the people and language of the Netherlands when that country became independent in the seventeenth century. "Holland" and "the Netherlands" often are used as synonyms even though "Holland" refers only to the provinces North and South Holland.

The Dutch distinguish between two major cultural subdivisions in their nation. The most important distinction is between the Randstad (Rim City) and non-Randstad cultures. Randstad culture is distinctly urban, located in the provinces of North Holland, South Holland, and Utrecht. The non-Randstad culture corresponds to the historical divide between the predominantly Protestant north and the Catholic south, separated by the Rhine River.

Significant local variations of Dutch culture include the Friesian culture in the extreme north and the Brabant and Limburg cultures in the south. The southern culture was subject to discriminatory policies until the nineteenth century. The Friesians prize their language and descent from the ancient Friesian people, while the Limburgers and Brabantines emphasize their southern culture and Catholic heritage.

The Netherlands has for centuries provided a safe haven for ethnic minorities fleeing from discrimination and persecution, with each minority influencing Dutch culture in its own way. Many Jews from Spain and Portugal and Protestant merchants from the Spanish-ruled southern Netherlands sought refuge in the Dutch Republic in the sixteenth and seventeenth centuries. The twentieth century was characterized by the influx of guest workers from the Mediterranean, migrants from the former Dutch colonies, and refugees from war-torn countries.

The Netherlands does not have a strong uniform national culture. Most Dutch people reject the notion and consider it to be tainted with an unacceptable form of nationalism. Instead, they emphasize the country's cultural diversity, tolerance of difference, and receptiveness to foreign influences. Nevertheless, the Randstad culture has been hegemonic in the Netherlands because of the concentration of political, economic, and cultural power in that densely populated region.

Location and Geography. The Netherlands is situated in northwestern Europe and borders on Germany to the east, Belgium to the south, and the North sea to the west and north. The name "Netherlands" means "Low Lands" in reference to the nation's topography as an alluvial plain. Differences in altitude are minimal. Almost one-quarter of the landmass is below sea level, protected from the encroaching sea by dikes and dunes. The Netherlands is also a relatively small country (13,297 square miles [34,425 square kilometers]) without surface water.

The Netherlands is divided in twelve provinces. Amsterdam (730,000 inhabitants) is the capital, but the government meets in The Hague (440,000 inhabitants). Utrecht (235,000 inhabitants) is the transportation hub, while the port city of Rotterdam (590,000 inhabitants) constitutes the economic heartland. These four cities together with a string of interconnected towns, form the Randstad, which has a population of 6,100,000.

The Netherlands

Demography. The Netherlands had a population of 15,898,331 in 2000. It is the most densely populated country in Europe (1,196 inhabitants per square mile [462 per square kilometer] in 1996). There are 2,700,000 foreign residents. The majority, approximately 780,000, originate from the European Union, including 432,000 Germans. Other sizable groups are Surinamese (297,000), Turks (300,000), Moroccans (252,000), and Antilleans (99,000).

The average life expectancy in 1996 was 75.2 years for men and 80.7 years for women, while the infant mortality rate was 5.1 per 1,000.

Linguistic Affiliation. The official language of the Netherlands is Standard Dutch. This language is used in all official matters, by the media, and at schools and universities. Dutch closely resembles German in both syntax and spelling. It freely borrows words and technical terms from French and especially English.

Dutch is also the official language in Flandres, Belgium, where it is called Flemish. Creole languages are increasingly replacing Dutch in Suriname and the Netherlands Antilles as decolonization progresses. Afrikaans, which is widely spoken in South Africa, is related to Dutch. Friesian is the second official language of the Netherlands; it is spoken by a half million Friesians. In addition, there are about twenty-five major dialects of Dutch.

Symbolism. The display of the national flag and the singing of the national anthem are important expressions of identity for a decreasing number of citizens. The flag consists of three horizontal strips in the colors red, white, and blue. The national anthem is the *Wilhelmus*. It was a rebel song during the independence war against Spain and was adopted as the national anthem in 1932.

The complex relationship of the Dutch people with the sea is notable. The sea has historically been both adversary and ally. The Dutch used to repel foreign invaders by deliberately piercing river dikes. However, if not for the extensive waterworks, 65 percent of the Netherlands would be flooded permanently. The Dutch take great pride in their struggle against the sea and reclaiming of land, which they view as mastery over nature.

Another source of national pride that sets aside regional and religious differences is sports, especially soccer and speed skating. Whenever the national team engages in international competitions, orangemania reigns. People dress in orange (in reference to the name of the royal family), raise national and orange flags, and decorate houses and streets as a patriotic feeling of athletic superiority floods the nation. The *Elfstedentocht* ("Eleven-City Tour") also raises national awareness. This speed-skating event in Friesland occurs only occasionally as it takes a prolonged period of frost to harden the 125 miles of lakes and canals that connect the eleven Friesian towns.

The clearest example of national symbolism is the Dutch royal family. The queen is regarded as the embodiment of the *Dutch* (nation) and a symbol of hope and unity in times of war, adversity, and natural disaster. Her popularity is manifested annually at the celebration of Queensday on 30 April. The capital, Amsterdam, in particular, is transformed into a gigantic flea market and open-air festival.

The 1940–1945 occupation by Nazi Germany provides a continued source of national identity. There are more than eight hundred World War II monuments and memorials, and the Dutch people still use the war years as the most important historical point of reference. The conflation of Jewish and non-Jewish Dutch suffering is a striking characteristic of national remembrance. The Dutch pride themselves on their fierce resistance to the Nazi regime and their sheltering of 25,000 Jewish and 300,000 non-Jewish Dutch, but there also was extensive collaboration with the Nazis. More than a hundred thousand Jews were deported to concentration camps. Anne Frank symbolizes this deeply ambiguous self-perception of the Dutch as victims, resisters, collaborators, and passive bystanders. The Frank family was harbored for two years by Dutch resisters before finally being betrayed by Dutch collaborators.

HISTORY AND ETHNIC RELATIONS

Emergence of the Nation. Dutch national identity emerged during the sixteenth and seventeenth centuries, especially in the struggle for independence from Catholic Spain during the Eighty Year War (1568–1648). The Dutch people received independence from the House of Habsburg in the Treaty of Munster in 1648. The Netherlands was temporarily unified with Belgium after the Congress of Vienna. The Catholic Belgian elite sought its freedom from the Protestant Dutch, and Belgium became independent in 1839.

National Identity. Dutch national identity emerged from the struggle for political sovereignty and religious freedom from the Catholic Habsburgs (Philip II). The Dutch merchant class formed an alliance with the House of Orange; the merchants supplied the funds to wage war, while the House of Orange provided political stability and military protection. Politics became more dependent on consensus and negotiation than on authoritarian rule as power rested in the hands of provincial viceroys.

The rapid expansion of the Dutch merchant fleet enabled the establishment of a worldwide network of trade relations that created naval dominance and increasing wealth for the merchant class. Handicapped by a small population (670,000 inhabitants in 1622) and besieged by growing English and French might, the Dutch Republic began to decline. Paradoxically, at that time, the conspicuous consumption of the wealthy merchant class re-

A woman selling cheese at the market in Alkmaar. The Netherlands has an advanced free market economy.

sulted in the so-called Golden Age. Stately canal houses were constructed in Amsterdam, and great works of art were commissioned.

The Netherlands was one of the poorest nations in northwestern Europe by 1750. In 1813, at the end of the French occupation (1795–1813), William I of the House of Orange-Nassau accepted the throne and became the first Dutch king. The Dutch nobility never had a position of prominence and influence in Dutch society. Only after constitutional reforms in 1851 did the nation begin its ascent to industrialization.

Rural–urban migration and especially the establishment of male suffrage in 1887 undermined traditional ways of life in the eyes of some politicians. The Anti-Revolutionary Party was founded in 1878 to reverse that trend. That party advocated autonomy for different political and religious communities. Its initiative resulted in the early twentieth century in a process of vertical segmentation or pluralism known as pillarization. Pillarization meant that each substantial subsection of the Dutch population was able to participate in social institutions and organizations (labor unions, schools, universities, political parties, social clubs, churches, newspapers, and radio stations) that catered to its specific needs. The four main pillars where Catholic, Protestant, socialist, and conservative. Intensive co-operation and negotiation between the pillars took place among national politicians. Secularization and emancipation in the late 1960s resulted in de-pillarization because of a greater vertical social mobility, growing intermarriage, and a declining identification with each of the four pillars.

A strong self-conscious national identity did not develop in the Netherlands because of these centrifugal historical processes, and this denial of a national identity became a hallmark of Dutch culture. Religious, cultural, and ethnic diversity are considered the essence of Dutch culture. The persistence of sizable religious and regional minorities and the decentralization of administrative power have allowed cultural diversity to survive. In the absence of a countrywide shared identity, the hegemonic Randstad culture has provided most of the markers of national identity.

Ethnic Relations. There is not much debate about racism or ethnic discrimination among the Dutch people, probably because of their self-ascribed tolerance. Nevertheless, the socioeconomic position of most non-European minorities is far worse than that of the indigenous population. The status of immigrant groups after World War II depended mainly on the moment and condition of their entry. Dutch-speaking Indonesians arrived at the height of the postwar economic upswing after Indonesia's independence in 1950. The Indonesians had ample time to secure a stable position in Dutch society. By contrast, the Mediterranean guest workers who arrived in the late 1960s and early 1970s regarded themselves and were viewed by the Dutch authorities as temporary residents and therefore did not familiarize themselves with Dutch culture. Guest workers were recruited principally from Spain and Italy and later from Turkey and Morocco. Those workers performed unskilled labor in the industry and service sectors. Many Dutch-speaking Surinamese arrived after Suriname became independent in 1975. Those immigrants and the poorly educated Turkish and Moroccan labor migrants were among the first to suffer from the economic decline of the 1970s. The position of the Surinamese improved during the 1980s and 1990s, but the Turks and Moroccans remained the most disadvantaged ethnic groups in Dutch society. Local residents of the Netherlands Antilles have been migrating to the Netherlands since the mid-1970s in search of work and schooling. The 1990s was marked by the immigration of substantial groups of refugees from west Africa, Somalia, Sri Lanka, Afghanistan, and the Balkans.

URBANISM, ARCHITECTURE, AND THE USE OF SPACE

Dutch cities are extremely compact and densely populated. Government intervention ensures that intercity areas are well kept and that ethnic ghettos and industrial wastelands do not emerge. The major cities are constantly subject to urban renewal projects. Much attention is given to fostering a sense of community by creating public places, such as parks and squares with benches and playgrounds. The country has an intricate network of railroads and an even denser web of bicycle paths.

Early Dutch architecture was influenced by a Calvinist ethos of uniformity and sobriety. This distinct style emerged after the Netherlands separated from Spain in 1581. Unlike their contemporaries in France and Great Britain, wealthy Dutch merchants built fairly modest yet stately canal houses in Amsterdam. Dutch cities lack the grandeur and flamboyance of Paris and London because the government meets in inconspicuous buildings.

Contemporary Dutch architecture is more cosmopolitan. The expressionist Amsterdam School and the cubist Stijl architects of the 1920s were inspired by international art movements. Modernism became the principal style of the post-World War II housing boom. The city center of Rotterdam is a typical example. Largely destroyed in World War II, the heart of this port city was rebuilt in an American style with steel and glass skyscrapers. At the end of the twentieth century, the Randstad cities began developing postmodern suburban business parks and indoor shopping malls.

The Dutch have a desire for spatial organization that is informed by Calvinist assumptions about order as a synonym for cleanliness and sinlessness. The Calvinist sense of space can be seen clearly from the air. The land is carefully divided in Mondrian-like squares and rectangles. In part, this is related to surface water management with its need for canals and dikes, but it also reflects the Dutch desire for order and uniformity. This can be seen most clearly in the undistinguished suburban housing development projects.

Dutch houses are relatively small and have prominent front doors and large windows. Homes are stacked with formidable amounts of furniture, indoor plants, and flowers. Dutch interiors are a reflection of the outside world, congested but orderly and clean.

FOOD AND ECONOMY

Food in Daily Life. The Netherlands does not have a distinct culinary culture because of its Protestant ethnic and the absence of a strong culinary tradition at the court due to an emphasis on Calvinist soberness. Food is seen as a necessary part of life, with no need for luxury. Traditional foods include pea soup, kale stew, hotchpotch (a thick stew), white asparagus, French fries with mayonnaise, meat croquets, and raw herring. In the morning, the Dutch consume several sandwiches with cheese, peanut butter, or chocolate sprinkles. Lunch consists of sandwiches, often with cold cuts and perhaps a small salad on the side. Dinner, which generally is served between five and seven P.M., is a two- or three-course meal that often begins with soup. The main dish usually contains a mixture of potatoes with vegetables and meat, fish, or poultry and is followed by dessert. Chinese–Indonesian, Surinamese, and Italian food have become part of the Dutch diet.

Food Customs at Ceremonial Occasions. The Dutch hardly ever invite people with whom they are not closely acquainted for dinner. Instead, coffee has a strong social significance. Neighbors often invite each other over for a cup of coffee with the invariable one cookie, and the morning coffee break at work is a sacred institution. Coffee-drinking

A drawbridge over a canal in Haarlem. Dutch cities are compact and densely populated.

rituals reveal the core meaning of the crucial Dutch word *gezelligheid* ("cozy," "sociable," or "pleasant").

Basic Economy. The Netherlands has an advanced free market economy. The Dutch pride themselves on having an economy that performs smoothly, known as the polder model, which hinges on periodic negotiations among labor unions, employers' associations, and the government to control wage scales and taxes. The labor force consisted of 7,097,000 persons in 1999; the unemployed numbered 292,000. The annual gross national product (GNP) amounted to 323 billion euros ($373 billion) in 1997. Imports totaled about 55 percent of GNP; and exports totaled 61 percent. The average income after taxes is 20,000 euros ($23,160). The Netherlands never had a major wave of industrialization but remained firmly oriented toward agriculture, trade, and service industries. Two percent of the Dutch population are employed in the highly mechanized agricultural sector (which includes the fishing industry), 24 percent are employed in the industrial sector, and 74 percent work in service industries.

Trade. Dutch exports can be divided into five main categories: agricultural products, 15 percent; natural or enriched fuels, 6 percent; chemical products,

17 percent; industrial products, 12 percent; and machinery, 24 percent. Germany is the principal trading partner. Two-thirds of Dutch exports go to five nations: Germany, Belgium, France, the United States, and the United Kingdom. Those five trading partners account for 61 percent of Dutch imports.

SOCIAL STRATIFICATION

Classes and Castes. Differences in wealth are relatively small in comparison to many other countries because of progressive taxation and the redistribution of fiscal funds to the unemployed and occupationally inactive. This equality of income is clearly shown when Dutch households are subdivided into four separate income categories. The lowest quartile has an average income of 8,730 euros ($10,105) after taxes, whereas the highest quartile has an average income of 38,365 euros ($44,420). An open discussion of class, income, and status differences is more or less taboo in a society that strongly emphasizes equality. Although Dutch society in general is firmly middle class, an estimated 5 to 10 percent of the population lives at a subsistence level. This income polarization and the ensuing social segmentation began in the 1980s. Low-skilled workers, the unemployed, the disabled, the aged, and single-parent households have been

Two windmills in the Netherlands.

hit hardest. Low-income households are concentrated in the Randstad cities and the two most northern provinces, Friesland and Groningen.

Symbols of Social Stratification. Class differences entail few visible signs of cultural differentiation, but those minor differences have a great symbolic value in creating social distinction. The most obvious differences can be observed in housing, consumption patterns, and community participation. Lower-class homes are small and tend to hold a large amount of furniture and decorative articles. Higher-class homes are more spacious and tend to hold less and often more sober furniture. The social participation of Dutch people does not depend entirely on class background, but higher-income households tend to have less involvement in community life than do low-income households. Lower class people are in general more rooted in community life and less restrained in contacts with neighbors and relatives.

Differences in clothing are relatively slight but important class markers. The Dutch dress with little eye for flamboyance. Even corporate dress codes are informal. Only the very rich and young urban professionals have a dress style that adheres to international clothing standards.

Speech patterns also may vary with class. Lower class people tend to speak in a local dialect, while the middle and upper classes speak Standard Dutch.

POLITICAL LIFE

Government. The Netherlands is a unitary state governed by a central body. The political system is a parliamentary democracy as well as a constitutional monarchy. The queen has little political influence; her role is largely symbolic. Political power lies in the hands of a cabinet of ministers headed by a prime minister. The cabinet is accountable to the parliament (*Staten-Generaal*), whose members are elected at four-year intervals. The Dutch Parliament consists of the First Chamber and the Second Chamber, which together constitute the legislative body. The Second Chamber initiates new legislation. Its members are directly elected by the people, who have had universal suffrage since 1919. The members of the Second Chamber are elected by proportional representation, which leads to a great number of political parties that together compete for 150 seats. The First Chamber either ratifies or rejects the new legislation proposed by the Second Chamber. Its members are elected by the members of the *Provinciale Staten*. Each of the twelve provinces has a local governing board (*Provinciale Staten*) whose chair is the commissioner to the queen, who is appointed by the government for a life term. Its members are elected by the inhabitants of the province. Each municipality has an elected council presided over by the mayor and elected aldermen. Commissioners and mayors are handpicked by the government for life terms.

Leadership and Political Officials. The main political parties are the PvdA (social democrats), VVD (conservatives), and CDA (Christian democrats). These parties are supplemented by a large number of smaller parties, ranging from socialist and nationalist to religious and green. Dutch cabinets are invariably coalitions of the major political parties. Open debate and negotiation toward consensus are part of Dutch political culture.

Most top level government positions are occupied by former members of the Second Chamber who have moved up in the party ranks. Most public functionaries at the ministries are career bureaucrats. Interactions between politicians and ordinary citizens are fairly limited, especially on the provincial and national levels. Only industrial associations, unions, nongovernmental organizations (NGOs), and political lobbies interact directly on political matters. These groups have a strong impact on political decision making.

Social Problems and Control. Traffic violations are the most common legal infraction. Violent crimes are low compared to other European countries and the United States; 273 murders were committed in 1996, amounting to 1.8 murders per 100,000 inhabitants. Dutch citizens worry mostly about muggings and burglaries. People hardly ever take the law into their own hands. There are very few neighborhood watches and no armed citizens' militias. The Netherlands has very strict gun control. Possession of small quantities of soft drugs (marijuana and hashish) is not prosecuted. The sale of soft drugs in so-called coffeeshops is not legal but is tolerated. The Netherlands has become a magnet for drug tourists because of its liberal stance toward drugs and its position as a major transport hub within Europe. The Netherlands has a great tolerance of prostitution. Randstad cities have red light districts in which women display themselves behind windows to potential customers.

Military Activity. The Dutch army was professionalized during the 1990s, when conscription was formally abolished. The defense budget declined substantially between 1989 and 1998 because of the end of the Cold War. In the absence of armed conflicts, the Dutch armed forces become only active during national disasters such as major floods and forest fires and in international peacekeeping operations under the auspices of the United Nations or NATO. Even though the Dutch hold the military in low esteem, their attitude toward peacekeeping missions is very positive.

SOCIAL WELFARE AND CHANGE PROGRAMS

The modern Dutch welfare state, with its elaborate system of laws and regulations, came into existence after World War II. The current array of welfare laws is impossible to summarize, but the main assumption is that people are entitled to a sufficient income to satisfy their basic needs and should not be at the mercy of charity.

The welfare system was created to provide for the aged and as a temporary safety net for unemployed breadwinners. However, in the present postindustrial economic system, this system has become a permanent source of income for a large and stable group, and this has created increasing dependency on the state. High economic growth at the turn of the twentieth century, tax incentives, and government reeducation programs had rapidly reduced long-term unemployment to record lows. Unemployment benefits are sufficient to maintain the recipients at a minimum standard of living.

NONGOVERNMENTAL ORGANIZATIONS AND OTHER ASSOCIATIONS

Nongovernmental organizations in the Netherlands consist mostly of charity funds and environmental and human rights organizations. Important organizations include Amnesty International, Greenpeace, the World Wildlife Fund, and *Natuurmonumenten* (an organization for the protection of the Dutch natural environment), which have a large middle and upper class following. They have a considerable impact on national politics. The Dutch contribute large sums to international disaster aid and consider themselves morally obliged to do so.

GENDER ROLES AND STATUSES

Division of Labor by Gender. Women constitute only 38 percent of the labor force and often work part-time. This low rate of participation has ideological and historical reasons. There is a prevailing belief that maternity care has great developmental benefits for children. Furthermore, the Dutch involvement in both world wars contributed to the

A worker cultivates the perfect rows of tulips growing in the Bollenstreek bulb-region of the Netherlands.

late entry of women in the labor force. Unlike in Great Britain and Germany, where many men fought in the war, the Dutch did not enter World War I. The German occupation during World War II kept the male labor force largely intact in spite of the hundreds of thousands of forced laborers who were deported to Nazi Germany, and women thus were not needed to take the place of male workers. Dutch women only slowly started entering the labor force after the pillarization of society crumbled in the late 1960s. They still lag behind men in terms of income and job status. The average annual income of men was 26,410 euros ($30,580) before taxes in 1997 versus only 13,455 euros ($15,580) for women. Women are found mostly in low-paying service jobs such as nursing and cleaning.

The Relative Status of Women and Men. Although women and men are equal before the law and the trend toward gender equality has been noticeable, women and men still occupy distinct functions in Dutch society. The differences between men and women are especially noticeable within the nuclear family, where the woman continues to perform the role of homemaker, while the man is seen as the breadwinner or provider. This is especially true among working-class families. Women are underrepresented in leadership positions in politics and the economy.

MARRIAGE, FAMILY, AND KINSHIP

Marriage. Dutch people are free to choose their spouses. The common basis for marriage is most often love. This does not mean that people marry independently of the constraints of class, ethnicity, and religion. The choice of a partner is often class-based. Monogamy is the only marriage form allowed. Many Dutch couples live in a consensual arrangement. Same-sex couples can marry and have the same rights as heterosexual couples.

The marriage ceremony may consist of two separate formal events: the municipal registration and a religious ceremony, with the latter being optional. The couple holds a wedding reception where friends and relatives gather to celebrate the nuptial engagement. Almost 45 percent of the Dutch population is married; about eighty thousand marriages are registered each year, while on average thirty thousand couples file for divorce.

Domestic Unit. The nuclear family is the most common household unit, although it is increasingly losing ground to single-parent families, couples without children, and single-person households. The principal authority in the household is generally the man, although there is a trend toward more equality of marriage partners. Extended family households are rare. Dutch couples have a neolocal postmarital residence pattern, as couples are free to choose where they live.

Kin Groups. The Dutch make a distinction between relatives by marriage and relatives by blood. Consanguineal relatives are considered more important than are affinal relatives. Solidarity and support (financial and emotional) are usually directed at the closest kin (parents, children, and siblings). This is also illustrated by prevailing inheritance patterns. Disinheritance is not permitted by law. Every child receives an equal share.

SOCIALIZATION

Infant Care. The average nuclear family is relatively small, with only one or two children. Toddlers receive much parental attention. Many children are cared for primarily by their parents in the parental home. Infants usually are put in playpens, where parents can leave them without restraining their own movement around the house. Since in many families both parents are employed, children aged 6 weeks and up are often placed in a nursery when their parents are at work. Children often enter play groups at age 2 and at age 4 are officially required to attend primary school.

Child Rearing and Education. Dutch childrearing practices are permissive. Children are encouraged to discover their surroundings individually or with other children. Corporal punishment is disapproved of by most parents. Instead, parents reprimand misbehaving children verbally. Peer groups are important among Dutch adolescents. Teenagers have developed a wide array of subcultures in which to explore their identity such as punks, headbangers, and in particular *gabbers* (Dutch slang for "mates") whose working-class members shave their heads, wear expensive training suits, and congregate at rave parties.

Higher Education. Dutch children are praised for successful performance at school. It is firmly believed that a good education and fluency in English are a sure road to success. Many children thus seek additional education after finishing high school. Approximately 70 percent of the adult population receives formal education after high school, and 20 percent of the adult population has received higher vocational training (HBO) or attended a university.

ETIQUETTE

Most traits of Dutch etiquette resemble those of the rest of the Western world, but there are several distinguishing national codes of behavior. The Dutch either shake hands when they meet and depart or, in the case of women and closely acquainted men and women, kiss each other three times on the cheek.

The Dutch have a strong desire to order their time in agendas and on calendars. Dutch children are given their first agenda at primary school to write down scheduled lessons and homework. A full agenda signifies a full life. The Dutch are very punctual, and showing up even five minutes late is considered inappropriate. As a result, everything has to be done at fixed times: There is a time to work, a time to clean the house, a time to drink coffee, and a time to visit friends.

The Dutch do not line up and show almost no consideration in public for a person's status, gender, or age. The use of the formal "you" (*U*) to address a person is becoming less common, whereas the growing importance of the informal "you" (*jij*) is meant to illustrate a commitment to equality.

Brick row houses in Haarlem have prominent front doors and large windows.

RELIGION

Religious Beliefs. The largest religious congregation in the Netherlands is Catholic (30 percent of the population), followed by Reformed Protestant (14 percent), Dutch Reformed (7 percent) and Muslim (4 percent). More striking, however, is the fact that 40 percent of the population are not religious or connected to a denomination. The extremely rapid secularization of the Netherlands after the 1960s has meant that religion plays a decreasing role in ordering people's social and cultural lives, with the notable exception of the small rural communities in the Dutch Bible Belt, which runs along the towns Zierikzee, Dordrecht, Utrecht, Zwolle, and Assen. Among the 60 percent who profess to being religious, an ever-increasing group either does not actively participate in religious ceremonies or is involved in New Age religions.

Religious Practitioners. Religious practitioners (priests, ministers, and imams) belong to the major religions in the Netherlands. The Roman Catholic ecclesiastical authority is represented by bishops who try to influence national debates about the family, social welfare, abortion, and euthanasia.

Rituals and Holy Places. The Catholic south of the Netherlands is rich in annual religious processions, some of which date back to the Middle Ages, such as the blood processions in Boxtel and Boxmeer, both in the province of North-Brabant. Shrines include those of Saint Gerardus in Wittem and Onze Lieve Vrouwekerk in Masatricht.

Death and the Afterlife. Beliefs about death and the afterlife correspond to the doctrines of the major religions. The deceased is either buried at a cemetery or cremated at a cremation center. All burials and cremations are arranged by professional undertakers.

MEDICINE AND HEALTH CARE

Health care is almost completely the responsibility of the state. The Dutch institutionalized, although they did not socialize, health care during the twentieth century to a much larger extent than did many other Western nations. Even care for the aged and the disabled takes place primarily in an institutionalized setting. Secularization and increasing wealth have compelled the government to take over care for the aged because traditional institutions such as church, community, and family are no longer able or willing to perform this task adequately. Almost everyone in the Netherlands carries medical insurance. The unemployed and low-income families are protected by public health insurance, while higher-income families have private insurance.

SECULAR CELEBRATIONS

Carnival celebrations the weekend before Ash Wednesday have become secular festivities that are spreading rapidly from the Catholic south to the Protestant north. The symbolic celebration of the Queen's birthday (Queen's Day) takes place on 30 April. Although Queen Beatrix was born on 31 January, the festivities are held on the former Queen Juliana's birthday. Remembrance of Dutch casualties in World War II is celebrated on Memorial Day, 4 May. The nation observes a minute of silence at eight P.M. to commemorate the dead. Liberation Day, the celebration of the end of the German occupation in 1945, occurs on 5 May. Most major cities stage elaborate festivities and music festivals. Family members and friends exchange gifts on the eve of Saint Nicolas Day (5 December), while children receive gifts on his birthday (6 December). On New Year's Eve, the Dutch reflect on the year that has passed and gather with friends rather than family members. The new year is welcomed with champaign and fireworks, and resolutions are made.

THE ARTS AND HUMANITIES

Support for the Arts. Graduates of art academies receive a four-year stipend of about 455 euros ($525) a month to start a professional art career. In addition, several public and private foundations provide modest funding for artists. An important source of support are the artworks for public places commissioned by national, provincial, and local governments.

Literature. Dutch oral literature dates back to at least 500 B.C.E. The earliest Dutch written literature goes back to the mid-1200s with the songs of the troubadour Heynric van Veldeken. The works on world history and the lives of saints written in verse by Jacob van Maerlant (1230–1300) mark the beginning of a truly national literature. Dutch literature bloomed during the Renaissance with playwrights such as Hooft, Cats, Huygens, Bredero, and Joost van den Vondel (1587–1679).

Dutch literature entered a period of relative decline after the seventeenth century, only to arise to world stature in the mid-nineteenth century with the publication of *Max Havelaar* by Multatuli (a pseudonym for Eduard Douwes Dekker), which describes the colonial exploitation of the Netherlands Indies. The Movement of the Eighties (1880–1894), led by the poets Kloos and Gorter, marked a new era in Dutch literature. The novels of Louis Couperus were the fin-de-sicle apotheosis of the national literature.

The breadth of twentieth-century Dutch literature is great; Slauerhoff, Roland Holst, Bordewijk, and Vestdijk are the most important authors of the inter-war period. The principal post-World War II poets and writers are Lucebert, Kouwenaar, Vroman, Haasse, Mulisch, Hermans, Reve, Wolkers, Nooteboom, and Van der Heijden.

Graphic Arts. Contemporary Dutch graphic arts have been dominated by the legacy of the seventeenth century with its emphasis on painting, drawing, and etching. The masterpieces of Dutch painting are displayed at the Rijksmuseum (Rembrandt and Vermeer), the Van Gogh Museum, and the Stedelijk Museum (contemporary art) in Amsterdam. In addition, there are important collections at the Kröller-Muller Museum (impressionism, expressionism) in Otterloo and the Haags Gemeentemuseum (Mondrian) and the Mauritshuis (Rembrandt and Vermeer) in the Hague. Museums are visited principally by the middle and upper classes, with the exception of major retrospectives of popular painters such as Vermeer, Rembrandt, and Van Gogh, which attract a wide audience.

Performance Arts. Classical music (notably the Concertgebouw Orchestra) and ballet (the National Ballet and the Netherlands Dance Theater) are the principal performance arts with international appeal. Cabaret has a long-standing national tradition and is still popular. The Early Music Festival of Utrecht is known for its concerts featuring medieval and Renaissance music. The North Sea Jazz Festival in the Hague is world-renowned. The Pinkpop and Low Lands festivals are two major events for popular music. The Holland Festival in Amsterdam is the most important annual presentation of the new programming season of contemporary Dutch performance arts. The performance arts attract mainly the middle and upper classes.

THE STATE OF THE PHYSICAL AND SOCIAL SCIENCES

Most scientific research in the Netherlands is conducted at universities and corporate research laboratories. There are thirteen universities. Twenty-four lower, middle, and higher polytechnic schools train students exclusively in applied work. The Netherlands Organization for Scientific Research (NWO) is the principal funding agency for the physical and social sciences. This foundation is under the authority of Ministry of Education, Culture and Science (OC&W) and finances seven areas of science (chemical sciences, earth and biological sciences, humanities, medical sciences, physical sciences, social and behavioral sciences, and technical sciences). The 1998 budget totaled 300 million euros ($345 million), of which 36 percent was allocated to the physical sciences and about 5.5 percent to the social and behavioral sciences. This amount is dwarfed by the 3.3 billion euros ($3.8 billion) spent in 1996 on research and development in corporate laboratories.

BIBLIOGRAPHY

Alpers, Svetlana. *The Art of Describing: Dutch Art in the Seventeenth Century*, 1983.

Bakvis, Herman. *Catholic Power in the Netherlands*, 1981.

Blom, J. C. H., and E. Lamberts, eds. *History of the Low Countries*, 1999.

Boissevain, Jeremy, and Jojada Verrips, eds. *Dutch Dillemas*, 1989.

Boxer, C. R. *The Dutch Seaborne Empire 1600–1800*, 1965.

Brachin, P. *The Dutch Language: A Survey*, 1985.

Central Bureau for Statistics. *Statistical Yearbook of the Netherlands*, annual ed.

Dekker, G., J. de Hart, and J. Peters. *God in Nederland: 1966–1996*, 1997.

Dieleman, F. M., and S. Musterd, eds. *The Randstad*, 1992.

Engbersen, Godfried. *Publieke Bijstandsgeheimen*, 1990.

Ginkel, Rob van. *Notities over Nederlanders*, 1997.

Goudsblom, Johan. *Dutch Society*, 1967.

Government Publishing Office. *Social and Cultural Report*, biennial report.

Horst, Han van der. *The Low Sky: Understanding the Dutch*, 1996.

Jong, Louis de. *Het Koninkrijk der Nederlanden in de Tweede Wereldoorlog*, 1991.

Jonge, Huub de red. *Ons Soort Mensen: Levensstijlen in Nederland*, 1997.

Kalb, Don. *Expanding Class: Power and Everyday Politics in Industrial Communities, the Netherlands, 1850–1950*, 1997.

Lambert, Audrey. *The Making of the Dutch Landscape: An Historical Geography of the Netherlands*, 1971.

Lijphart, Arend. *The Politics of Accommodation: Pluralism and Democracy in the Netherlands*, 1975.

Newton, Gerald. *The Netherlands: An Historical and Cultural Survey, 1795–1977*, 1978.

Presser, Jacob. *The Destruction of the Dutch Jews*, 1969.

Prüpper, Henk. *Waterlanders: Bespiegelingen over de Moraal van Nederland*, 1995.

Righart, Hans. *Het Einde van Nederland?* 1992.

Roelandt, Theo. *Verscheidenheid in Ongelijkheid*, 1994.

Schama, Simon. *The Embarrassment of Riches*, 1987.

———. *The Netherlands in Perspective*, 1987.

———. *In Care of the State*, 1988.

Ven, G. P. van de. *Leefbaar Laagland: Geschiedenis van de Waterbeheersinq en Landaanwinning in Nederland*, 1993.

White, Colin, and Laurie Boucke. *The Undutchables*, 1993.

Wouters, Cas. *Informalisering*, 1990.

Web Sites

Bureau for Long-Term Social and Cultural Prognosis: http://www.cpb.nl

Department of Justice: http://www.minjus.nl/

Dutch Census Bureau: http://www.cbs.nl/

Dutch newspapers: http://www.nrc.nl/

Dutch search engine: http://www.ilse.com/

University of Amsterdam: http://www.uva.nl/

Utrecht University: http://www.uu.nl/

—DENNIS MARES
AND ANTONIUS C. G. M. ROBBEN

NETHERLANDS ANTILLES

CULTURE NAME

Netherlands Antillean; Antiyas Hulandes (Papiamentu)

ORIENTATION

Identification. The Netherlands Antilles consists of the islands Curaçao ("Korsow") and Bonaire; the "SSS" islands, Sint Eustatius ("Statia"), Saba, and the Dutch part of Saint Martin (Sint Maarten); and the uninhabited Little Curaçao and Little Bonaire. The Netherlands Antilles is an autonomous part of the Kingdom of the Netherlands. From a geographic, historical, linguistic, and cultural point of view, Aruba, which seceded in 1986, is part of this group.

Location and Geography. Curaçao and Bonaire, together with Aruba, form the Dutch Leeward, or ABC, islands. Curaçao lies just off the Venezuelan coast at the southwestern end of the Caribbean archipelago. Curaçao and Bonaire are arid. Sint Maarten, Saba, and Sint Eustatius form the Dutch Windward islands, 500 miles (800 kilometers) north of Curaçao. Curaçao encompasses 171 square miles (444 square kilometers); Bonaire, 111 square miles (288 square kilometers); Sint Maarten, 17 square miles (43 square kilometers); Sint Eustatius, 8 square miles (21 square kilometers), and Saban, 5 square miles (13 square kilometers).

Demography. Curaçao, the largest and most populated of the islands, had a population of 153,664 in 1997. Bonaire had 14,539 inhabitants. For Sint Maarten, Sint Eustatius, and Saba the population figures were 38,876, 2,237, and 1,531 respectively. As a result of industrialization, tourism, and migration, Curaçao, Bonaire, and Sint Maarten are multicultural societies. On Sint Maarten, migrants outnumber the indigenous island population. Economic recession has caused a growing migration to the Netherlands; the number of Antilleans living there is close to 100,000.

Linguistic Affiliation. Papiamentu is the local language of Curaçao and Bonaire. Caribbean English is the language of the SSS islands. The official language is Dutch, which is spoken little in daily life.

The origins of Papiamentu are much debated, with two views prevalent. According to the monogenetic theory, Papiamentu, like other Caribbean Creole languages, originated from a single Afro-Portuguese proto-creole, that developed as a lingua franca in western Africa in the days of the slave trade. The polygenetic theory maintains that Papiamentu developed in Curaçao on a Spanish base.

Symbolism. On 15 December 1954, the islands obtained autonomy within the Dutch kingdom, and this is the day the Antilles commemorates the unity of the Dutch Kingdom. The Dutch royal family was an important point of reference to the Antillean nation before and directly after World War II.

The Antillean flag and anthem express the unity of the island group; the islands have their own flags, anthems, and coats of arms. Insular festive days are more popular than national festivities.

HISTORY AND ETHNIC RELATIONS

Emergence of the Nation. Before 1492, Curaçao, Bonaire, and Aruba were part of the Caquetio chiefdom of coastal Venezuela. Caquetios were a ceramic group engaged in fishing, agriculture, hunting, gathering, and trade with the mainland. Their language belonged to the Arowak family.

Christopher Columbus probably discovered Sint Maarten in 1493 on his second voyage, and Curaçao and Bonaire were discovered in 1499. Because of the absence of precious metals, the Spanish declared the islands *Islas Inutiles* ("useless islands"). In 1515, the inhabitants were deported to Hispaniola to work in mines. After an unsuccessful at-

Netherlands Antilles

tempt to colonize Curaçao and Aruba, those islands were used to breed goats, horses, and cattle.

In 1630, the Dutch seized Sint Maarten to make use of its large salt deposits. After the Spanish reconquered the island, the Dutch West India Company (WIC) took possession of Curaçao in 1634. Bonaire and Aruba were taken over by the Dutch in 1636. The WIC colonized and governed the Leeward

Islands until 1791. The English occupied Curaçao between 1801 and 1803 and 1807 and 1816. After 1648, Curaçao and Sint Eustatius became centers for smuggling, privateering, and the slave trade. Curaçao and Bonaire never developed plantations because of the arid climate. Dutch merchants and Sephardic Jewish merchants on Curaçao sold trade goods and slaves from Africa to the plantation colonies and the Spanish mainland. On Bonaire, the salt was exploited and cattle were bred for trade and food on Curaçao. Colonization on Bonaire did not take place until 1870.

Dutch administrators and merchants formed the white elite. Sephardim were the commercial elite. Poor whites and free blacks formed the nucleus of the small Creole middle class. Slaves were the lowest class. Because of the absence of commercial, labor-intensive plantation agriculture, slavery was less cruel when compared to plantation colonies like Surinam or Jamaica. The Roman Catholic Church played an important role in the repression of African culture, the legitimization of slavery, and preparations for emancipation. Slave rebellions occurred in 1750 and 1795 on Curaçao. Slavery was abolished in 1863. An independent peasantry did not arise because blacks remained economically dependent on their former owners.

The Dutch took possession of the Windward Islands in the 1630s, but colonists from other European countries also settled there. Sint Eustatius was a trade center until 1781, when it was punished for trading with the North American independents. Its economy never recovered. On Saba, colonists and their slaves worked small plots of land. On Sint Maarten, the salt pans were exploited and a few small plantations were established. The abolition of slavery on the French part of Sint Maarten in 1848 resulted in the abolition of slavery on the Dutch side and a slave rebellion on Sint Eustatius. On Saba and Statia, slaves were emancipated in 1863.

The establishment of oil refineries on Curaçao and Aruba marked the beginning of industrialization. The lack of local labor resulted in the migration of thousands of workers. Industrial laborers from the Caribbean, Latin America, Madeira, and Asia came to the islands, along with civil servants and teachers from the Netherlands and Surinam. Lebanese, Ashkenazim, Portuguese, and Chinese became important in local trade.

Industrialization ended colonial race relations. The Protestant and Sephardim elites on Curaçao maintained their positions in commerce, civil service, and politics, but the black masses were no longer dependent on them for employment or land.

The introduction of general suffrage in 1949 resulted in the formation of nonreligious political parties, and the Catholic Church lost much of its influence. Despite tensions between Afro-Curaçaoans and Afro-Caribbean migrants, the process of integration proceeded.

In 1969, a trade union conflict at the Curaçao refinery angered thousands of black laborers. On 30 May a protest march to the government seat ended in the burning of parts of Willemstad. After a request for intervention by the Antillean government, Dutch marines helped to restore law and order. Newly founded Afro-Curaçaoan parties changed the political order, which still was dominated by white Creoles. Within the state bureaucracy and the educational system, Antilleans replaced Dutch expatriates. Afro-Antillean cultural traditions were revalued, racial ideology was changed, and Papiamentu became recognized as the national language on Curaçao and Bonaire.

After 1985, the oil industry has declined and in the 1990s, the economy was in recession. The government is now the largest employer, and civil servants take up 95 percent of the national budget. In 2000, a series of agreements with the International Monetary Fund (IMF) concerning the restructuring of the government expenses and a new economic policy have paved the way for renewed Dutch financial aid and economic recovery.

National Identity. In 1845, the Windward and Leeward Islands (including Aruba) became a separate colony. The governor, appointed by the Dutch, was the central authority. Between 1948 and 1955, the islands became autonomous within the Dutch kingdom. Requests from Aruba to become a separate partner were refused. General suffrage was introduced in 1949.

On Sint Maarten, political leaders preferred separation from the Antilles. On Curaçao, the major political parties also opted for that status. In 1990, the Netherlands suggested a breakup of the colony into autonomous Windward and Leeward (Curaçao and Bonaire) countries. However, in a referendum in 1993 and 1994, a majority voted for the continuation of the existing ties. Support for an autonomous status was largest on Sint Maarten and Curaçao. Insularism and economic competition constantly threaten national unity. Despite economic setbacks, in 2000 the Island Council of Sint Maarten expressed the desire to separate from the Antilles within four years.

Ethnic Relations. The Afro-Antillean past is a source of identity for most black Antilleans, but

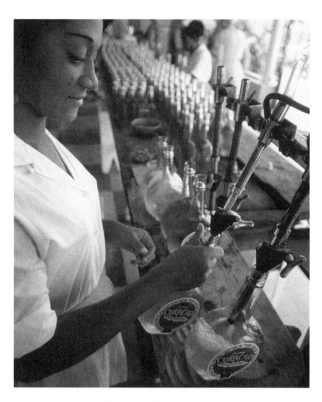

Women's participation in the labor market has increased since the 1950s.

different linguistic, historical, social, cultural, and racial backgrounds have strengthened insularism. To many people "yui di Korsow" (Child from Curaçao) refers only to Afro-Curaçaoans. White Creoles and Jewish Curaçaoans are symbolically excluded from the core population of Curaçao.

URBANISM, ARCHITECTURE, AND THE USE OF SPACE

Curaçao and Sint Maarten are the most densely populated and urbanized islands. Punda, the old center of Willemstad on Curaçao, has been on the United Nations World Heritage List since 1998. Plantation houses from the sixteenth to nineteenth centuries are spread over the island, next to the traditional *cunucu* houses in which poor whites, free blacks, and slaves used to live. Sint Maarten has residential areas on and between the many hillsides. The Bonairean cunucu house differs from the ones on Aruba and Curaçao in its ground plan. The cunucu house is built on a wooden frame and filled in with clay and grass. The roof is made of several layers of palm leaves. It consists minimally of one living room (*sala*), two bedrooms (*kamber*), and a kitchen, which is always situated downwind. The picturesque Saban cottage has style elements of traditional English cottages.

FOOD AND ECONOMY

Food in Daily Life. Traditional food customs differ between the islands, but all of them are variations of Caribbean Creole cuisine. Typical traditional foods are *funchi*, a maize porridge, and *pan bati*, a pancake made of maize flour. Funchi and pan bati combined with *carni stoba* (a goat stew) form the basis of the traditional meal. *Bolo pretu* (black cake) is prepared only for special occasions. Fast food and international cuisine have become more popular since the establishment of tourism.

Basic Economy. The economy centers on oil refining, ship repair, tourism, financial services, and the transit trade. Curaçao was a major center of offshore business but lost many clients after the United States and the Netherlands signed tax treaties in the 1980s. Efforts to stimulate tourism on Curaçao have been only partly successful. Market protection has resulted in the establishment of local industries for the production of soap and beer, but the effects have been limited to Curaçao. On Sint Maarten, tourism developed in the 1960s. Saba and Sint Eustatius depend on tourists from Sint Maarten. Bonairean tourism doubled between 1986 and 1995, and that island also has oil transshipment facilities. Underemployment climbed to 15 percent on Curaçao and 17 percent on Sint Maarten during the 1990s. Emigration by unemployed persons from the lower classes has caused social problems in the Netherlands.

Land Tenure and Property. There are three types of land tenure: regular landed property, hereditary tenure or long lease, and the renting of government land. For economic purposes, especially in the oil and tourism industries, government lands are rented in long renewable leases.

SOCIAL STRATIFICATION

Classes and Castes. In all the islands, racial, ethnic, and economic stratification are intertwined. On Saba, the relationship between black and white inhabitants is comfortable. On Curaçao, racial and economic stratification are more obvious. Unemployment is high among the Afro-Curaçaoan population. Trade minorities of Jewish, Arabian, and Indian descent and foreign investors have their own positions in the socioeconomic structure. Curaçao, Sint Maarten, and Bonaire have many immigrants from Latin America and the Caribbean, who hold the lowest positions in the tourism and construction sectors.

Symbols of Social Stratification. Luxury goods such as cars and houses express social status. In traditional celebrations of important life events such as birthdays and First Communion, conspicuous consumption takes place. The middle classes aspire to upper-class consumption patterns, which often puts pressure on a family's budget.

POLITICAL LIFE

Government. There are three levels of government: the kingdom, which consists of the Netherlands, the Netherlands Antilles, and Aruba; the Netherlands Antilles; and the territories of each of the five islands. The council of ministers consists of the complete Dutch cabinet and two ministers plenipotentiary representing the Netherlands Antilles and Aruba. It is in charge of foreign policy, defense, and the safeguarding of fundamental rights and freedoms. Since 1985, Curaçao has had fourteen seats in the national parliament, known as the Staten. Bonaire and Sint Maarten each have three, and Sint Eustatius and Saba have one each. The central government is dependent on coalitions of parties from Curaçao and the other islands.

Political autonomy in regard to internal affairs is almost complete. The governor is the representative of the Dutch monarch and the head of the government. The island parliament is called the Island Council. Representatives to each are elected for a four-year term. Political parties are island-oriented. A lack of synchronization of national and island policies, machine-style politics, and conflicts of interests between the islands are not conducive to efficient government.

Military Activity. Military camps on Curaçao and Aruba protect the islands and their territorial waters. The Coast Guard of the Netherlands Antilles and Aruba became operative in 1995 to protect the Netherlands Antilles and Aruba and their territorial waters from drug trafficking.

SOCIAL WELFARE AND CHANGE PROGRAMS

There is a social welfare plan called the Social Safety Net on Curaçao, to which the Netherlands contributes financially. The results have been meager and the exodus of young unemployed Antilleans to the Netherlands has increased.

A man cutting a wahoo. Curaçao, Netherlands Antilles.

NONGOVERNMENTAL ORGANIZATIONS AND OTHER ASSOCIATIONS

OKSNA (Body for Cultural Cooperation Netherlands Antilles) is a nongovernmental advisory board that advises the minister of culture on the allocation of subsidies from the Dutch development aid program for cultural and scientific projects. Centro pa Desaroyo di Antiyas (CEDE Antiyas) allocates funds to social and educational projects. OKSNA and CEDE Antiyas receive funds from the Dutch development aid program. Welfare organizations focus on areas ranging from day care centers to the care of the elderly. The government supports many of these activities.

GENDER ROLES AND STATUSES

Division of Labor by Gender. Women's participation in the labor market has increased since the 1950s, but men still hold the most important positions throughout the economy. Women work mostly in sales and as nurses, teachers, and civil servants. Unemployment is higher for women than for men. Since the 1980s, the Antilles has had two female prime ministers and several female ministers. Women from the Caribbean and Latin America work in the tourism sector and as live-in maids.

The Relative Status of Women and Men. Until the 1920s, the upper strata of society, especially on Curaçao, had a highly patriarchal family system in which men had social and sexual freedom and women were subordinate to their spouses and fathers. In the Afro-Antillean population sexual relations between men and women were not enduring and marriage was the exception. Many households had a female head, who often was the chief provider for herself and her children. Men, as fathers, husbands, sons, brothers, and lovers, often made material contributions to more than one household.

Mothers and grandmothers enjoy high prestige. The central role of the mother is keeping the family together, and the strong bond between mother and child is expressed in songs, proverbs, sayings, and expression.

MARRIAGE, FAMILY, AND KINSHIP

Marriage. Couples often marry at an older age because of the matrifocal family type, and the number of illegitimate children is high. Visiting relationships and extramarital relationships are prevalent, and the number of divorces is growing.

Domestic Unit. Marriage and the nuclear family have become the most common relationships in the middle economic strata. Salaried employment in the oil industry has enabled men to fulfill their roles as husbands and fathers. Women's roles changed after agriculture and domestic industry lost economic importance. Raising children and taking care of the household became their primary tasks. Monogamy and the nuclear family are still not as predominant as in the United States and Europe, however.

Inheritance. Inheritance rules vary on each island and between ethnic and socioeconomic groups.

Kin Groups. In the upper and middle classes, kinship rules are bilateral. In the matrifocal household type, kinship rules stress matrilinear descent.

SOCIALIZATION

Infant Care. The mother takes care of the children. Grandmothers and older children assist in the care of younger children.

Child Rearing and Education. The educational system is based on the Dutch educational reforms of the 1960s. At age four, children attend kindergarten and, after age six, primary school. After age twelve, they enroll in secondary or vocational schools. Many students go to Holland for further studies.

The picturesque Saban cottage has style elements of traditional English cottages.

Although Dutch is the language of only a small percentage of the population, it is the official language of instruction in most schools.

Higher Education. The Curaçao Teacher Training College and the University of the Netherlands Antilles, which has departments of law and technology, provide higher education. The university is located on Curaçao and Sint Maarten.

ETIQUETTE

Formal etiquette is adapted from European etiquette. The small scale of the island societies influences everyday interaction patterns. To outside observers, communication styles lack openness and goal orientation. Respect for authority structures and gender and age roles are important. Refusing a request is considered impolite.

RELIGION

Religious Beliefs. Roman Catholicism is the prevalent religion on Curaçao (81 percent) and Bonaire (82 percent). Dutch Reformed Protestantism is the religion of the traditional white elite and recent Dutch migrants who are less than 3 percent of the population. Jewish colonists who came to Curaçao in the sixteenth century account for less than 1 percent. On the Windward Islands Dutch Protestantism and Catholicism have had less influence, but Catholicism has become the religion of 56 percent of Sabans and 41 percent of the inhabitants of Sint Maarten. Methodism, Anglicanism, and Adventism are widespread on Statia. Fourteen percent of Sabans are Anglican. Conservative sects and the New Age movement are becoming more popular on all the islands.

Religious Practitioners. *Brua* holds a position similar to that of Obeah on Trinidad. Originating from the word "witch," brua is a mixture of non-Christian spiritual practices. Practitioners use amulets, magic waters, and fortune-telling. Montamentu is an ecstatic Afro-Caribbean religion that was introduced by migrants from Santo Domingo in the 1950s. Roman Catholic and African deities are revered.

Death and Afterlife. Opinions on death and afterlife are in accordance with Christian doctrine. Afro-Caribbean religions mix Christian and African beliefs.

MEDICINE AND HEALTH CARE

All the islands have general hospitals and/or medical centers, at least one geriatric home, and a pharmacy. Many people use medical services in the United States, Venezuela, Columbia, and the Netherlands. Specialists and surgeons from the Netherlands visit the Elisabeth Hospital on Curaçao on a regular basis.

SECULAR CELEBRATIONS

The traditional harvest celebration is called seú (Curaçao) or simadan (Bonaire). A crowd of people carrying harvest products parade through the streets accompanied by music on traditional instruments. The fifth, fifteenth, and fiftieth birthdays are celebrated with ceremony and gifts. The Dutch queen's birthday is celebrated on 30 April, and Emancipation Day on 1 July. The Antillean national festival day occurs on 21 October. The French and Dutch sides of Sint Maarten celebrate the feast day of Saint Martin on 12 November.

THE ARTS AND HUMANITIES

Support for the Arts. Since 1969, the Papiamentu and Afro-Antillean cultural expressions have influenced art forms. The white Creole elite on Curaçao leans toward European cultural traditions. Slavery and the pre-industrial rural life are points of reference. Few artists, with the exception of musicians, make a living from their art.

Literature. Each island has a literary tradition. On Curaçao, authors publish in Papiamentu or Dutch. In the Windward Islands, Sint Maarten is the literary center.

Graphic Arts. The natural landscape is a source of inspiration to many graphic artists. Sculpture often expresses the African past and African physical types. Professional artists exhibit locally and abroad. Tourism provides a market for nonprofessional artists.

Performance Arts. Oratory and music are the historical foundations of the performance arts. Since 1969, this tradition has inspired many musicians and dance and theater companies. Tambú and tumba, which have African roots, are to Curaçao what calypso is to Trinidad. Slavery and the slave rebellion of 1795 are sources of inspiration.

THE STATE OF THE PHYSICAL AND SOCIAL SCIENCES

The Caribbean Maritime Biological Institute has done research in marine biology since 1955. Since 1980, scientific progress has been strongest in the fields of history and archeology, the study of Dutch and Papiamentu literature, linguistics, and architecture. The University of the Netherlands Antilles has incorporated the Archeological Anthropological Institute of the Netherlands Antilles. The Jacob Dekker Instituut was founded in the late 1990s. It focuses on African history and culture and the African heritage on the Antilles. Because of a lack of local funds, scientific research relies on Dutch finances and scholars. The fact that both the Dutch and Papiamentu languages have a limited public hampers contacts with scientists from the Caribbean region.

BIBLIOGRAPHY

Broek, A. G. *PaSaka Kara: Historia di Literatura na Papiamentu*, 1998.

Brugman, F. H. *The Monuments of Saba: The Island of Saba, a Caribbean Example*, 1995.

Central Bureau of Statistics. *Statistical Yearbook of the Netherlands Antilles*, 1998.

Dalhuisen, L. et al., eds. *Geschiedenis van de Antillen*, 1997.

DeHaan, T. J. *Antilliaanse Instituties: De Economische Ontwikkelingen van de Nederlandse Antillen en Aruba, 1969–1995*, 1998.

Goslinga, C. C. *The Dutch in the Caribbean and in Surinam, 1791–1942*. 1990.

Havisser, J. *The First Bonaireans*, 1991.

Martinus, F. E. ''The Kiss of a Slave: Papiamentu's West African Connection.'' Ph.D. dissertation. University of Amsterdam, 1996.

Oostindie, G. and P. Verton. ''KiSorto di Reino/What Kind of Kingdom? Antillean and Aruban Views and Expectations on the Kingdom of the Netherlands.'' *West Indian Guide* 72 (1 and 2): 43–75, 1998.

Paula, A. F. ''Vrije'' Slaven: En Sociaal-Historische Studie over de Dualistische Slavenemancipatie op Nederlands Sint Maarten, 1816–1863*, 1993.

—LUC ALOFS

NEVIS SEE SAINT KITTS AND NEVIS

NEW CALEDONIA

CULTURE NAME

New Caledonian; Kanaks

ALTERNATIVE NAMES

The word "Caledonian" is used by the French and others who have settled in the islands. The term "Kanak" is used to designate native residents of this South Pacific archipelago and their culture.

ORIENTATION

Identification. The Kanak culture developed in this South Pacific archipelago over a period of three thousand years. Today, France governs New Caledonia but has not developed a national culture. The Kanak claim for independence is upheld by a culture thought of as national by the indigenous population.

Location and Geography. Kanaks have settled over all the islands officially indicated by France as New Caledonia and Dependencies. The archipelago includes the principal island, Grande Terre, Belep Island to the north, and Pines Island to the south. It is bordered on the east by the Loyalty Islands, consisting of three coral atolls (Mare, Lifou, and Ouvea).

Grande Terre, which is 250 miles (400 kilometers) long and at the widest point extends for 30 miles (50 kilometers), is divided by mountains averaging 2,600 feet (800 meters) in height. A coral reef approximately a mile from the coast surrounds the island with a shallow lagoon. Descending from the mountain chain, numerous rivers have created wide, green valleys with steep slopes. On the drier west coast great plains are separated by several large rivers. With rich soil limited to waterway banks, the Kanaks developed a system of slash-and-burn agriculture, which over centuries reduced the primary forest surface, shrunk marshes, and favored the extension of herbaceous savannah. Dense forest covering the Loyalty Islands has provided natural compost for agriculture.

The Kanaks occupy the Loyalty Islands entirely. Those on Grande Terre live on the northern half of the island in territories demarcated in the nineteenth century as "indigent reserves." Farther south, Kanaks are less numerous, although 30 percent of them live near the capital, Noumea.

Demography. In 1996, there were 196,836 inhabitants, up from 164,173 in 1989. Kanaks number 86,788, or 44 percent of the population; Europeans, 34 percent; Polynesians (Wallisians and Tahitians), 12 percent; and Asians (principally Indonesians and Vietnamese), 4 percent. The population is young; 47 percent of Kanaks are less than twenty years old, but that number falls to 31 percent among Europeans.

Linguistic Affiliation. French, the official language, is spoken by most residents; Indonesian, Vietnamese, Tahitian, Wallisian, and Chinese are among the twenty-eight languages spoken by Kanaks. Apart from the population of French origin, all the inhabitants are at least bilingual. Command of the French language varies with the academic and social status of individuals. Languages spoken by Kanaks, which are classified as Austronesian, belong to the linguistic family spoken by the Oceanians who progressively peopled the Pacific islands over ten centuries. Contact with the Anglo-Saxon navigators and traders who reached the archipelago in the nineteenth century led to the formation of a pidgin English, Bichelamar, that disappeared when French was established. For two decades Kanaks requested that their languages be recognized and taught. Four of those languages now can be studied to earn a Bachelor's degree, and in 1988 the French state authorized the study of regional languages in elementary schools. French, whose use has been protested by Kanak nationalists, is used in politics; vernacular languages are reserved for private life.

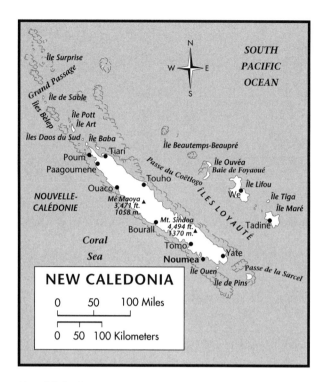

New Caledonia

Symbolism. The flag *Kanaky*, a yellow solar disk with a hut ridgepole set against three bands of color—green (vegetation), red (the people's blood), and blue (sea and sky)—signifies the desire for independence. The flag is tolerated by the administration, which recognizes the French flag. Since November 1998, Caledonians have been asked to seek symbols of a "new citizenship" with which all the communities can identify. The shared national reference is the land: ancestral land for Kanaks, a land of exile for settlers, or a land of welcome for recent immigrants.

HISTORY AND ETHNIC RELATIONS

Emergence of the Nation. For the population of French origin, "New Caledonia is France." Slowly, through the experience of colonialism, the native population formed the idea of a separate nation. Before colonization by the French in 1853, linguistic and territorial divisions separated Melanesian groups. Social and racial discrimination practiced by whites commingled all Pacific blacks and then only those of New Caledonia under the term "Kanak" (*kanaka* means "human being" in Hawaiian). In the 1970s, local nationalist movements took up this term as a symbol of the colonized people's unity.

National Identity. Common markers of national identity among the Kanak include the cultivation of

yams and taros, a hierarchy that differentiates high-ranking persons (masters of the soil and chiefs) from lower status persons, kinship relations, the practice of nonmercantile ceremonial exchanges between clans and chieftainships for marriages and funerals, and belief in ancestors' presence among the living.

Ethnic Relations. The introduction into the islands of colonized nation–states, borders drawn between archipelagos, and objections to "indigent" travel through boat destruction broke ancient bonds. However, over thirty years, independence in a number of Pacific countries has encouraged Oceanians to resume contact. The indigent peoples of Oceania have developed an ideology of a "Pacific way" that acknowledges a common culture that overcomes geographic and political divisions.

Kanaks and other ethnic groups form withdrawn communities that maintain functional connections (economic, educational, and administrative). The social universe is split in two: on one side are Kanaks with their "customs" and nationalistic claims; on the other side are communities that wish to keep New Caledonia as part of the French republic. This division led to violent conflict during the period of 1984–1988.

URBANISM, ARCHITECTURE, AND THE USE OF SPACE

Noumea, the capital created by early French colonists, is the only large city. Greater Noumea, including Paita and Mont Dore, holds 90 percent of non-Kanak population and 34 percent of Kanaks. Kanak cultural foundations are rural, and even in cities demands for "custom" are essential, although Kanaks born in Noumea are slowly building an urban culture.

Over the last twenty years, wooden colonial houses with verandas and gardens in Noumea have disappeared, replaced by styleless buildings. Kanaks have maintained a form of architecture (a round hut of wood and straw pitched against a central pole) found in the Loyalty Islands; the nationalist movement has revived traditional construction on Grande Terre. The most noteworthy local administration building is the Tjibaou Cultural Center in Noumea. The architect, although influenced by traditional Kanak houses, used modern construction techniques.

For Kanaks space is divided between premises reserved for important men and other residences placed closer to the women and children. This arrangement is still used during gatherings, but no official spatial discrimination exists between communities. Kanaks avoid being alone in empty spaces.

FOOD AND ECONOMY

Food in Daily Life. Kanaks traditionally eat yams, taros, bananas, and sweet potatoes, which until recently accounted for the bulk of their diet. A decline in horticulture, access to wage-earning jobs, the installation of electricity in villages, and travel to Noumea have altered eating habits. Rice has tended to replace yams and taro, and frozen food, beef, and mutton substitute for wild pork, deer, fish, and bats.

Food Customs at Ceremonial Occasions. Sea cow, turtle, and fish remain ceremonial dishes, along with *bougna*, a dish of steamed yams and meat cooked under hot stones. Introduced by Europeans, beer and whiskey are the inevitable drinks at festivities and on weekends.

Basic Economy. The economy is founded on nickel mining and import trade. Financial transfers that account for up to 50 percent of the budget are received from France; local production (agriculture, animal breeding, and fishing) accounts for 3 percent of the gross domestic product. A small coffee industry and subsistence farming counterbalance the poverty of the land reserves. The average income of Kanaks is seven times lower than that of Europeans.

Land Tenure and Property. Clan and lineage systems are patrilineal and form the basis of Kanak social units for private land ownership. Families that belong to these inclusive entities attain land. If a family has no descendant, property goes back to the lineage and clan and is redistributed to one of its members. French law recognizes only collective property on Kanak land reserves. To attain individual private property, Kanaks must buy land or real estate outside the reserves.

Commercial Activities. Most food products come from Australia, New Zealand, and France. Public services (health, schooling, justice, and administration) are managed by the French.

Major Industries. Nickel, the principal raw material, is sent semirefined to France. No manufactured object is made entirely in the archipelago.

Division of Labor. Mining industry labor power is supplied mainly by Wallisians and Kanaks. Com-

Man fishing from a rock ledge; fish is a national ceremonial food.

mercial activity is conducted exclusively by Europeans and Asians. Training and management are mainly in the hands of Europeans.

SOCIAL STRATIFICATION

Classes and Castes. Through the nickel industry, New Caledonia formed a working class that included people from all ethnic groups. European farmers settled on colonized lands in Noumea, forming a white bourgeoisie with a high standard of living. At the bottom of the social scale, Indonesians (farm workers) and Kanaks on reserves struggled with poverty. Today, the working class has increased as the nickel industry and trade have developed. The arrival of professionally qualified French people has enlarged the middle and upper classes. Kanaks have difficulty finding work.

POLITICAL LIFE

Government. The government consists of an authority representing the French state, an elected territorial assembly, and an executive council composed of eleven ministers.

Leadership and Political Officials. Members of the government are expected to adopt a collegial form of administration in the interests of all Caledonians, while political confrontations are limited to the territorial assembly. Elected members of the independence parties (minority) and anti-independence parties (majority) sit in these two political structures. Apart from these official mechanisms, Kanaks participate in other forms of political life. In this "customary" system, which is organized around chiefdoms recognized in the nineteenth century by the French administration, chiefs are named by notables and the state. Kanak independents in electoral proceedings (municipalities, provinces, and the territorial assembly, etc.) take into account the importance and influence of chiefs, who have been given an advisory capacity role in a "customary senate."

Social Problems and Control. The French judicial system applies to New Caledonia, but for matrimonial and landowning issues, Kanaks refer to traditional practices in accordance with the "specific rights" statute recognized by the Constitution. For criminal affairs concerning Melanesians, courts are aided by "customary assessors," Kanak men and women who explain their countrymen's behavior.

Although theft is rare, murder is three times more common than it is in metropolitan France. Penal sanctions are often misunderstood in an ancient warrior society that does not always side with victims. Numerous matters are settled outside the French justice system by "customary courts" or direct vengeance.

Military Activity. The French army ensures the regional security of New Caledonia. Kanak nationalists do not have an army.

SOCIAL WELFARE AND CHANGE PROGRAMS

Caledonian workers contribute to a social security fund. A Free Medical Aid organization helps the poor.

NONGOVERNMENTAL ORGANIZATIONS AND OTHER ASSOCIATIONS

Several Australian, New Zealander, and international organizations intervene marginally in the sanitary, environmental protection, and "aid to women" fields.

GENDER ROLES AND STATUSES

Division of Labor. In the Kanak culture, each member of a couple fulfills specific and complementary tasks for work in the fields. Women prepare meals, care for children, and carry wood.

The Relative Status of Women and Men. Men have a monopoly in public speaking, landowning rights, and religious rituals. Only aged or high-ranking women play a role in those areas.

MARRIAGE, FAMILY, AND KINSHIP

Marriage. It is common practice to take a spouse from outside the clan but inside the close parentela. The kinship system authorizes marriage between cousins of different clans (cross-cousins). Most of these monogamous matrimonial alliances are arranged by families to unite persons of similar rank and maintain an equilibrium between the women given and received by each clan. The husband's clan gives that of the wife matrimonial compensation in the form of food-producing goods, clothing, shell currency, and more. The number of marriages has diminished as the level of compensation has continued to increase. Kanak society tolerates divorce, but the wife returns home without the children, who remain in the husband's care. No official remarriage exists.

Domestic Unit. Familial residences are situated on the husband's clan site; often several generations live together. The master of the grounds, who is the father or grandfather of the children, generally has about ten persons under his authority. Men and women tend to group separately for meals and sometimes for sleep. Women handle the domestic tasks.

Inheritance. Land rights are transmitted from father to son, with daughters being excluded from inheritance. Otherwise, objects acquired in a lifetime are turned over to maternal uncles (the mother's brothers).

Kin Groups. A family fits into a lineage that is a segment of a wider patrilineal clan. Each region has a variable number of exogamic clans whose members are dispersed within territorial units made of several clans. They assemble for marriages and funerals or to assert landowning rights together.

SOCIALIZATION

Infant Care. Small children are carried by the mother or father and do not sleep in separate places. Very early they are informed of their rights and duties in the family and the political hierarchy. To pacify them, parents give in to their whims as long as children do not disobey kinship taboos.

Most New Caledonian women prepare meals, care for children, and carry wood.

Child Rearing and Education. Boys are given more freedom than are girls. Valued traits include the ability to defend oneself and face challenges, as well as the traditional indispensable know-how (knowledge of clan history, medicinal plants, and political relationships between groups). Children are considered to have the temperament of a grandparent. Children are all educated in either public or religious schools; however, the failure rate is high.

Higher Education. To attain skilled jobs, Kanak families now encourage children to receive a higher education. The proportion of Kanak students obtaining a bachelor's degree has increased.

ETIQUETTE

Kanaks show respect in personal interactions. Certain relationships involve compulsory familiarity. One respects maternal relatives, one's elders, and aged persons, but maintains a joking relationship with paternal aunts and cross-cousins. Women must respect men by maintaining spatial distance, keeping silent, and using special terms of politeness. Familiarity allows people to stand close together, touch, and talk together. In public places, Kanaks adopt a discreet and subdued attitude, avoiding excessive speaking or gesticulating, which are consid-

ered rude. Contact with strangers is marked by gifts and formal speech. Strangers are observed attentively from afar and judged on the basis of their behavior.

RELIGION

Religious Beliefs. Kanaks are all officially Catholic or Protestant but maintain a belief in an immanent ancestral presence under diverse forms or totems (animals, plants, minerals, and atmospheric phenomena).

Religious Practitioners. There is no priestly caste, but each lineage has a guardian of the magic that protects the clan.

Rituals and Holy Places. Rites that invoke ancestors are domestic. There are no collective religious rituals. Sacred places, old dwelling sites, and cemeteries exist, but propitiatory rites are made individually.

Death and the Afterlife. Kanaks believe the land of the dead is underwater. It receives the souls of those who have had funeral ceremonies that continue for one year after death; through those ceremonies, one becomes an ancestor.

A dancer performs a traditional dance in Moumea. Kanaks maintain a belief in an immanent ancestral presence under diverse forms or totems.

MEDICINE AND HEALTH CARE

Death and sickness seldom are considered natural; they are often attributed to witchcraft or vengeance from ancestors for insufficient respect. Sickness is healed by plants and invocations. Everyone has a well-developed knowledge of these remedies, but people sometimes employ a specialist. Healers provide treatment and identify persons considered guilty of witchcraft. Dispensaries and hospitals are used by Kanaks, who simultaneously resort to traditional cures.

SECULAR CELEBRATIONS

French Independence Day on 14 July is celebrated principally by the European community. Since 1984, Melanesian nationalists have tried to make 24 September, the day of the takeover by the French, a public holiday called Kanak Mourning Day.

THE ARTS AND HUMANITIES

Support for the Arts. Kanak and Caledonian artists are aided by the Kanak Culture Development Agency, which manages the Tjibaou Cultural Center. They also are members of independent associations that receive grants from the New Caledonia Territory and the French state.

Literature. Oral literature consists of poetry, epics, tales, myths, and historical accounts. There have been several publications, but the majority of texts collected in vernacular languages are unpublished. A written modern Kanak literature has emerged.

Graphic Arts. Sculptors, painters, and illustrators are inspired by ancient and modern art. They show their work at the Tjibaou Center, in galleries in the Pacific countries, and at international art festivals.

Performance Arts. Kanak music is marked by the *kaneka*, inspired by traditional rhythms, reggae, and rock. Dramatic art has begun to appear.

THE STATE OF THE PHYSICAL AND SOCIAL SCIENCES

Physical and social sciences are taught at the University of Noumea, created in 1986, which has courses only for the first and last years; therefore, students also must study in France. Research is done at public institutions such as the CNRS, the IRD, and the CIRAD.

BIBLIOGRAPHY

Bensa, A. *Chroniques kanak. L'ethnologie en Marche*, 1995.

———. *Nouvelle-Calédonie: Vers l'émancipation*, 1998.

———, with Antoine Goromido. "The Political Order and Corporal Coercion in Kanak Societies of the Past (New Caledonia)," *Oceania* 68 (2): 84–106, 1997.

——— and J. C. Rivierre. *Les Chemins de l'alliance: L'Organisation Sociale et ses Représentations en Nouvelle-Calédonie (région de Touho, Aire Linguistique Cèmuhî)*, 1982.

Bensa, A., and I. Leblic, eds. *En Pays Kanak: Nouvelle-Calédonie, Ethnologie, Linguistique, Archéologie, Histoire*, 2000.

Boulay, R., ed. *De Jade et de Nacre: Patrimoine artistique Kanak*, 1990.

Clifford, J. *Person and Myth: Maurice Leenhardt in the Melanesian World*, 1982.

Connell, J. *New Caledonia or Kanaky? The Political History of a French Colony*, 1987.

Dauphiné, J. *Les Spoliations Foncières en Nouvelle-Calédonie (1853–1913)*, 1989.

David, G., D. Guillaud, and P. Pillon. *La Nouvelle-Calédonie à la Croisée des Cemins*, 1999.

Douglas, B. *Across the Great Divide: Journeys in History and Anthropology: Selected Essays, 1979–1994*, 1998.

Dussy, D. "Les Suats de Nouméa: Des Occupations Océaniennes Spontanées à la Conquête Symbolique de la Ville en Nouvelle-Calédonie," *Journal de la Société des Océanistes* 103: 275–287, 1996.

Freyss, J. *Économie Assistée et Changement Social en Nouvelle-Calédonie*, 1993.

Leblic, I. *Les Kanak Face au Développement: La Voie Étroite*, 1993.

Leenhardt, M. *Notes d'Ethnologie Néo-Calédonienne*, 1930.

Maclellan, N., and J. Chesneaux. *After Moruroa: France in the South Pacific*, 1998.

Merle, I. *Expériences Coloniales: Nouvelle-Calédonie, 1853–1920*, 1995.

Naepels, M. *Histoires de Terres Kanakes: Conflits Fonciers et Rapports Sociaux dans la Région de Houaïlou (Nouvelle-Calé)*, 1998.

Ozanne-Rivierre, F. "Structural Changes in the Languages of Northern New Caledonia." *Oceanic Linguistics* 34 (1): 44–72, 1995.

Rivierre, J. C. "La Colonisation et les Langues en Nouvelle-Calédonie." *Les Temps Modernes* 464: 1688–1717, 1985.

Saussol, A. *L'Heritage. Essai sur le Problème Foncier Mélanésien en Nouvelle-Calédonie*, 1979.

Shineberg, D. *They Came for Sandalwood*, 1967.

Tjibaou, J. M. *La Présence Kanak*, 1996.

Wittersheim, E. with A. Bensa. "Nationalism and Interdependence: The Political Thought of Jean-Marie Tjibaou," *Contemporary Pacific* 9 (2):181–210, 1998.

—ALBAN BENSA

NEW ZEALAND

CULTURE NAME

New Zealander

ALTERNATIVE NAME

Kiwi

ORIENTATION

Identification. Originally discovered by Polynesians between 1200 and 1300 C.E., the country was settled by Maori ("the people") and areas were named after the *iwi* (tribes). In 1642, the Dutchman Abel Tasman named the land Staten Island. This was soon changed to Nieuw Zeeland, after Zeeland in Holland. Tasman was attacked and never landed, but in 1769, James Cook claimed sovereignty for George III of England.

Extensive European settlement did not begin until 1840, and New Zealand remained a Maori culture. Whalers from the United States and Britain frequently sailed New Zealand waters, married or had children with Maori women, and introduced trappings of Euro-American culture, especially muskets. Missionaries began their activities around 1814.

In the 1860s, gold was discovered, bringing Chinese miners from Australia as well as China and Hong Kong. The Chinese have remained, though they now are chiefly market gardeners and café owners and professionals. Business and banking were supported by a Jewish population. Other minorities who have retained much of their culture are Polish, Lebanese, Yugoslav, and Dutch.

Regional cultural distinctions tend to be between North Island and South Island, coinciding largely with population composition and size. Half a million Maori plus nearly two million Pakeha (Caucasians of Europeans descent) live in the north, and eight hundred thousand (mostly Pakeha) live in

the south, culturally subdivided between English (Canterbury) and Scottish (Otago).

The emerging culture leans increasingly on Maori symbolism in art and literature. Maori culture (*taonga*) is being reinvented, and parts of it are incorporated in ceremonies and other public events. Visiting dignitaries receive a Maori welcome, and the All Black Rugby Team (the national team) performs a *haka* (challenge) before games.

Location and Geography. New Zealand is in the southwest Pacific Ocean and has three main islands—North, South, and Stewart—separated by the Cook Strait and the Foveaux Strait. Several other islands are under New Zealand's jurisdiction.

The three main islands are 990 miles (1,600 kilometers) long and 280 miles (450 kilometers) wide and contain great topographic and climatic variation. The Southern Alps run the length of the western part of the South Island, with peaks over 9,840 feet (3,000 meters). North Island has three peaks over 6,560 feet (2,000 meters), and there are three active volcanoes. Moving glaciers, deep fjords, and large lakes are characteristic of South Island. The climate varies from subtropical in Northland to continental in Central Otago.

The country was two-thirds deforested by the time of the European settlement, and so the high country is largely tussock (South Island) and secondary bush (North Island) with extensive pine plantations.

Demography. In 1996, the population was 3,681,546, including 2,749,980 on the North Island and 931,566 on South Island. Eighty-five percent are urban dwellers, with Auckland, the largest city, approaching one million in population. Eighty percent of the population is of European origin, mainly from the United Kingdom, Holland, Yugoslavia, Poland, Germany, Sweden, and Austria; 14.5 percent claim Maori descent; and the remainder are Pacific Islanders. Along with descen-

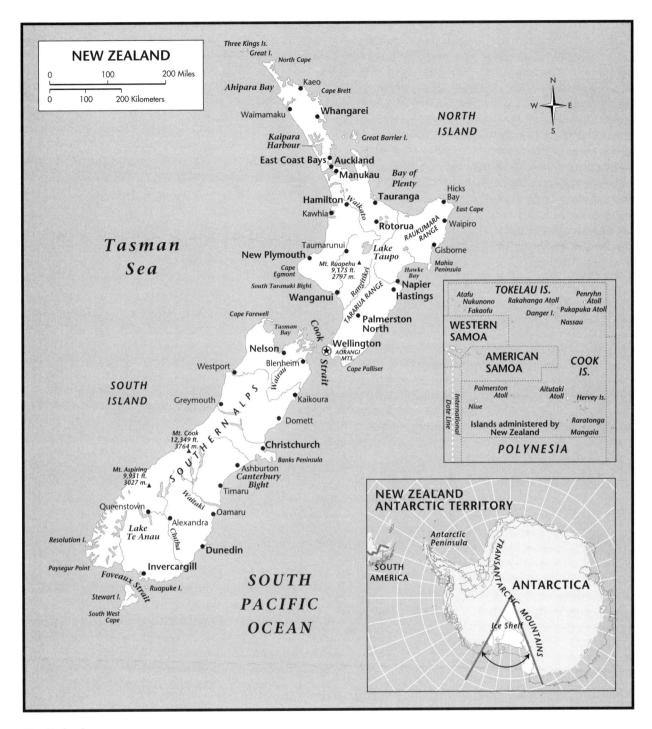

New Zealand

dants of the Chinese, recent immigrants have come from southeast Asia. The original Maori population has been estimated at two hundred thousand. By 1900, their decline as a result of war and disease to just over forty thousand was viewed as the signal of a dying culture or race. The population has risen steadily since then. The success of the campaign for Maori pride has allowed people to identify themselves without regard to skin color. This demographic and social phenomenon has been assisted by the setting up of the Waitangi Tribunal to hear the claims of iwi requesting redress of wrongs resulting from their ceding of sovereignty to Britain.

Linguistic Affiliation. The official language is English, but all government institutions and some private ones use Maori as well. While 99 percent of Maori speak English, few Pakeha speak Maori. Preschool Maori children attend *Kohanga-reo* (language nests) to learn Maori. Universities have Maori studies departments. Maori is a Malayo-Polynesian language.

Symbolism. A national flag, coat of arms, and anthem are important symbols. Other symbols tend to be commercial or cultural and are of Maori origin. The national airline has a stylized *Koru* (fern leaf), all the national sports teams have a fern leaf, the feathered cloak of a Maori chief is used on ceremonial occasions, and *haka* is performed before international rugby matches. The kiwi, a flightless, nocturnal bird unique to New Zealand, is the symbol for everything from New Zealand.

HISTORY AND ETHNIC RELATIONS

Emergence of the Nation. Maori have a commemorative and oral history whose major instrument of record is the genealogy (*whakapapa*), which is recorded in the structure of the *marae* (meeting house) and in the *moko* (tattoo) worn by many Maori. Maori history features ties with ancestors and with the land.

In 1819, east coast North Island tribes raided the west coast tribes. In 1820, the chief Hongi Hiki visited England, and secured muskets and ammunition. Upon his return, there began the "Musket Wars" on South Island. A state of tribal unrest and migration set in, and the 1820s was distinguished by the appearance of many Maori prophet-military leaders such as Te Rauparaha.

In 1823, Britons were extended protection by New South Wales (Australia), and ten years later, James Busby arrived as the first British resident. However, there were no plans for British settlement until 1839, when the New Zealand Company was ordered to establish British rule. The first settlers arrived in 1840, the year of the signing of the Treaty of Waitangi.

The treaty has been a great source of disharmony between Maori and Pakeha. It was drawn up by a European whose Maori was not fluent and read to chiefs who were unfamiliar with instruments of diplomacy. The greatest ambiguities turned on ideas of sovereignty and ownership alien to the Maori. The British understood themselves to be offering protection in return for sovereignty and the right to use or buy land at nominal cost. In 1975, the Waitangi Tribunal was established to hear claims of abuse of the treaty. Many claims have resulted in return of land, cash compensation, restoration of rights to natural resources, and the handing over of businesses to Maori.

In the 1840s, there were fierce battles between Maori and Europeans. Although the British had an advantage in arms, Maori had an advantage in tactics, and their *pa* (fortresses) of earth and wooden palisades absorbed artillery shells. The British infantry had to get past the palisades and grapple hand to hand with Maori warriors.

In 1854, the first General Assembly opened and the first governor was appointed. In 1856, Henry Sewell became the first prime minister. Wars broke out again in the 1860s on North Island, but they were quickly suppressed. In 1865, the capital was transferred from Auckland to Wellington, which was considered more central.

Outbursts of Maori resistance were led by charismatic prophets—military leaders such as Te Kooti. However, under the second term of Thomas Grey, a division of the country into provinces and districts and the formation of a parliament with four Maori seats created a stable and unified colony. The last British (Australian) troops left in 1870. That year a national university was established. Women were enfranchised in 1893.

Culturally, the ideals of Europe were adhered to. European craftsmen built mansions for newly enriched land holders, bankers, gold dealers, and politicians. The Mechanics Institute and lending libraries were established, and cities, such as Dunedin, were built.

National Identity. The ruling institutions were British in origin and conduct but were open to Maori, and scholar-politicians such as Te Rangi Hiroa (Sir Peter Buck) and Apirana Ngata achieved pre-World War II preeminence internationally. Maori have had their own parliamentary party, are members of parliament, and have sought to introduce elements of Maori culture into debates.

National identity involves icons more than institutions. Sportspersons in general are iconic national identities, with Sir Edmund Hillary at the summit.

Ethnic Relations. Intermarriage between Europeans and Maori has been common since the first contact. New Zealand used to boast that it was completely without racial prejudice. However, "Maori radicals," often with university training, saw the differentials in school conditions and funding, knew about living conditions in low-income state-assisted housing, and voiced their concerns.

A row of typical houses in Dunedin, of the colonial villa verandah style.

There were protests, marches, and sit-ins. Maori are still relatively underprivileged, but they are being given access to opportunities for education and high-profile jobs in politics and business. Many outstanding artists are Maori, from Kiri Te Kanawa to Ralph Hotere.

Pacific Islanders living in New Zealand include Cook Islanders, Samoans, Tongans, Tokelauans, Fijians, and Nieueans. Basically, they see themselves as being in New Zealand temporarily to earn money to send their children to school, but many remain permanently. Pacific Islanders tend to be concentrated in and around Auckland and Wellington. They are ghettoized and cling to their Christian views and cultural ways—Polynesian but not identical to each other or to Maori. Urban life, poverty, large families, and a large percentage of teenagers have led to ethnically based conflict in the cities. The recent high-profile immigration of Asians, many of them wealthy, has been accompanied by some ethnic tension.

Gang organization is a feature of the culture. The Mongrel Mob, Black Power, and the Nomads are the three prominent Maori gangs. Each gang, however, views each "chapter" as a family, or *whanau*. The White Knights is a Pakeha gang that tends toward machismo and racism. Leather jack-ets, patches, and motorcycles are the chief ritual objects.

URBANISM, ARCHITECTURE, AND THE USE OF SPACE

Despite the rural image, 86 percent of the people live in the five main urban centers: Auckland (one million people), Wellington (nearly 360,000), Christchurch (332,000), Hamilton (160,000), and Dunedin (112,000).

Vernacular architecture has involved the colonial villa verandah style: single-story, wooden, with a central hallway, but with the principal bedroom often in the front of the house. State housing provided a standardized bungalow-style house often made of brick and rented to low-income families. These houses have been privatized.

The only distinctive style of architecture is the Maori *marae*. Its elaborately carved timbers represent origin myths and genealogies. There, a communal sleeping area, and a strict etiquette of greeting, precedence, speechmaking, and farewell is preserved.

New Zealanders like close contact. People who go to pubs or cafés where a band is playing maintain close bodily contact, and open spaces, such as

A woman works at a factory for wool products in Dunedin, New Zealand.

parks and gardens have benches placed opposite to each other or in pairs.

As Europeans have become fifth-generation descendants, it has become increasingly important to them to represent their ancestors. Both Maori and Pakeha households are not complete without pictures of significant ancestors. Contemporary marae architecture derives from the elaborately carved storehouses and chiefs' houses of earlier times.

New Zealanders are inveterate trampers and campers. Countless tracks are maintained by the Department of Conservation or by local enthusiasts. The geometry of the landscape and the sense that it is very different from the city has been the most powerful influence on a unique style of painting.

New Zealanders try to have a hideaway cabin by the lake, the sea, or the stream. In North Island, this is known as a bach; in the South Island, as a crib. There is usually no running water or electricity.

FOOD AND ECONOMY

Food in Daily Life. Before 1975, the diet was based on meat, potatoes, temperate climate vegetables in season (cabbage, peas, beans, carrots, spinach, cauliflower, and broccoli), bread, fruits in season, dairy products, and fish. Chicken was a restaurant deli-

cacy, and the favorite fast food was the meat pie. Beverages were tea and beer. Since 1975, the cuisine has opened up to include a range of tropical and subtropical fruits, vegetables, and spices. It has taken advantage of its Mediterranean climate to produce wine. Food items are readily available in supermarkets. There are ubiquitous fast-food restaurants. However, there is no New Zealand cuisine. Christmas features the presentation of the turkey or ham, followed by the Christmas pudding. The Sunday roast is still served in the British tradition.

The Maori cuisine is based on seafood, mutton birds (young petrels), wild pork or fowl, fat lamb, and kumara. The method of cooking is the earth oven (*hangi*) in which stones are heated by fire, the fire is extinguished so that the stones steam, and a large sealed basket containing the food is buried over the stones and left to cook for several hours. When Maori gather for meetings on the marae, men and women jointly help prepare the food; men dig the hole, place the stones, and bury and remove the food.

Food Customs at Ceremonial Occasions. In the Burns Clubs, the Ceremony of Piping in the Haggis is observed. Otherwise, there is the availability of hot cross buns at Easter.

Basic Economy. New Zealand is an exporter of dairy, meat, fish, and fruit products, which now include processed foods such as wine, deer velvet, venison, smoked and pickled seafood, cheeses, and yogurt. Multinational food companies are moving their processing plants to Australia so that New Zealand-grown food often finds its way back via that country. Logging of plantation pine forests is a major industry, but relatively little processing is carried out. Thus, the food supply is in surplus, and imports are largely luxury items or processed items from Australia or ''fresh'' fruits and vegetables out of season. Reforms in the 1980s encouraged a reduction in the farming sector because of the weakening of the European and British markets for primary produce. It was proposed to industrialize New Zealand. Apart from oil and natural gas finds and one aluminum smelter, heavy industry is not viable. Manufacturing, assembly, and processing have been encouraged, but since they rely on imported machinery and services, this has not been successful. Motor car assembly and light engineering (especially electrical and electronic appliances) are the basis of the industrial sector.

The fastest growing sector of the economy is service: trade, hospitality, tourism, finance, consultancy, computer software, advertising and film, business services, and insurance.

Almost every household gardens and produces some fresh food for itself. Gardening is a universal hobby.

Land Tenure and Property. Under a clause in the Treaty of Waitangi, the Crown had the exclusive right to extinguish Maori title in land. Under these terms, the Crown had a monopoly over land purchases while bestowing title to land valid in English common law. The Crown became the largest landowner.

In Maori land tenure, tribal boundaries were defined by the putative area settled and utilized by the ancestors, modified by wars and invasions. An individual may claim the use of and the right to burial in the ancestral lands of either parent. The purchase of Maori land by the government created further fragmentation, and the Waitangi Tribunal has been set up to hear claims for compensation. Since the treaty was signed in 1840 and purchases were made until recently, and since Maori have become urbanized, the legitimacy of land claims is complex. Nevertheless, the sense of belonging to one area, the region of the ancestors, still is strong and is finding echoes among the Pakeha. Having reached a fifth generation of settlement, many families see themselves centered in the areas where they first arrived; as Maori have tribal *hui* (gatherings), Europeans have family reunions.

Other land can be bought and sold. Inheritance by individuals is entirely discretionary among both Maori and Pakeha, and all ownership follows the pattern of English common law. Crown land is managed by the relevant agencies (departments of conservation, forestry, agriculture, and fisheries); iwi lands are managed by elders (*kaumatua*), increasingly on a commercial basis.

Commercial Activities. New Zealand is a primary producer and exporter of meat, dairy products, wool, hides, fish and aquatic invertebrates, wood, fruit, aluminum, and fuels. Tourism is a growing industry.

Major Industries. Processing goods to a second stage or final stage occurs in the dairy industry. Alumina is processed to ingots for export. Cattle is processed for meat for export or for pet food. Wood converted to wood chips is exported for newsprint. Imported parts are assembled as automobiles and electrical and electronic goods. Chemicals are processed for fertilizers.

Trade. The primary export markets are the United States, the United Kingdom, Japan, Russia, Australia, Taiwan, and China. Markets are being developed in the Middle East (Saudi Arabia) and Southeastern Asia (Malaysia and Indonesia).

Division of Labor. The formerly powerful trade unions are now toothless. New Zealand is a monetarist economy that is ''restructuring'' industries and businesses through the increased use of electronic information and communications procedures and American-inspired management techniques. Jobs are increasingly specialized, requiring certification or on-the-job training. An emphasis on strategy in marketing, stock keeping, accounting, and management rather than on-the-floor production has emphasized and rewarded the managerial class. Computer skills are virtually mandatory.

In 1997, unemployment was 6.7 percent, overall; Maori 16.9 percent; Pacific Islander, 15.3 percent; and Pakeha, 4.7 percent.

SOCIAL STRATIFICATION

Classes and Castes. New Zealand no longer is considered a welfare state in which all are equal. Ethnic (Maori, Pacific Islander) poverty is evident in

A worker removes bird protection nets from wine grapes in a vineyard. New Zealand's Mediterranean climate is conducive to wine producing.

slum areas of the large cities, but there are also poor Pakeha.

New Zealand has a well-established class society based on income. Cities have developed a "first settler" elite of "old" families claiming prestige and status and occupying the inner ring of the city. Not all are wealthy. Maori maintain a status structure based on *mana* (inherited or earned) and respect (of older for younger, female for male), though this has largely broken down in the cities.

Symbols of Social Stratification. There are ostentatious houses and expensive cars in some areas. The Maori chiefly class (*rangatira*) and chiefs (*ariki*) wear a feathered cloak (as do honored Pakeha) on special marae occasions. Cultural performances of Maori dances include the traditional kilt (male) and apron (female).

POLITICAL LIFE

Government. New Zealand is a member of the British Commonwealth, and the sovereign is represented by a governor general. Within the Commonwealth, New Zealand is autonomous and is governed by a house of representatives with one hundred twenty elected members of parliament from six political parties. The present government is the first to be elected under a system of proportional representation. A clear majority under this system is unlikely, and the government usually is a coalition.

Leadership and Political Officials. The national government is divided between executive (elected) and administrative officers. It is headed by a prime minister, twenty cabinet ministers, and several ministers outside the cabinet. Below these are regional government bodies divided into cities and districts led by mayors and councillors. Government departments are run on a day-to-day basis by chief executives recommended by the state services commissioner.

Social Problems and Control. The Privy Council in London is the final court of appeal but may deliver only an opinion, not a judgment. The New Zealand Court of Appeal is the highest national appeals court. Its findings must be observed by the High Court. The High Court holds hearings in the main centers. There are district courts (local), employment courts, family courts, youth courts, Maori land courts, and environment courts. There are also over one hundred tribunals dealing with small claims and complaints.

Community law centers, originally set up by law students, give legal advice to those who cannot afford lawyers. There are also victim support groups. The most notable effort at informal social control has been the attempt by Maori to be allowed to exercise *whanau* (family) authority over accused and accuser in the context of the marae, where the whanau confront each other and elders seek a settlement.

The country is divided into four police region, and there are about 6,500 full-time officers. There are seventeen armed offenders squads that are called out when firearms are involved. There is also a search and rescue service. Other than the armed offenders squad, police do not carry firearms.

Accusations of "racial bias" by police toward Maori and Polynesians have become more frequent, but attitudes toward the police vary with the social and economic circumstances of a person's life. Drug and alcohol abuse seems to be a common ingredient in a large proportion of public and domestic violence and crime.

Military Activity. The armed forces are small and participate in peacekeeping exercises under United Nations or other multinational auspices or independently, including regional training search and rescue operations, fisheries protection, Antarctic support, hydrographic survey, and disaster relief.

SOCIAL WELFARE AND CHANGE PROGRAMS

New Zealand has a noncontributory income support scheme for the unemployed, disabled, and sick, for domestic purposes (low income/sole parent), and for retired persons. Numerous social services are government-funded but also rely on volunteers. The numerous services (school, church, club, victim support, etc.), are coordinated as the New Zealand Council of Social Services, which lobbies for changes in government welfare programs and agencies. It stresses biculturalism. There is a no-fault Accident Compensation Corporation funded by employer and employee levies.

NONGOVERNMENTAL ORGANIZATIONS AND OTHER ASSOCIATIONS

Numerous charitable trusts supported by individual donations or corporate profits fund community activities from bagpiping to creche care. There are neighborhood watch organizations. School boards serve voluntarily. There are chapters of worldwide associations such as the Red Cross, Salvation Army, Saint Vincent de Paul, Returned Services Association

(veterans), and numerous charitable societies for the blind, the deaf, and the disabled.

GENDER ROLES AND STATUSES

Division of Labor by Gender. The stereotype of women in the home and men in the workplace is slowly disappearing. There has been an increase in the number of de facto partnerships and a resulting lack of commitment of men financially and emotionally to children and domestic responsibility.

The Ministry of Women's Affairs seeks to enforce equal opportunity legislation. Shearing gangs are traditionally mixed (male shearers/female sorters), and trades and occupations are becoming less gender-based. There is one female bishop (Anglican), though congregations are overwhelmingly female. In 1996 there were forty women members of parliament, and in 1997 the first woman prime minister took office.

The Relative Status of Women and Men. New Zealand was shocked by the power of gender difference among Maori as shown in the movie *Once Were Warriors*. Many would argue that although those portrayed were Maori, the degree of domestic sexual abuse and violence is a feature of New Zealand society. Under law there is no gender discriminations. Though almost as many women as men graduate with doctorates, in 1997 there were 402 male professors and 46 female ones. All seven university vice-chancellors were male. Women have been most successful in business at the upper middle range of the executive level or as national magazine editors or heading their own niche companies. Some sports teams are mixed.

MARRIAGE, FAMILY, AND KINSHIP

Marriage. Except in Muslim, Hindu and a few Chinese groups, marriages are entered into by mutual choice. Marriage may be conducted by a celebrant, a Church priest, or a vicar. Parental consent is required if a partner is under 20 years of age. De facto relationships are officially recognized for inheritance and benefit purposes. In 1996, 43 percent of males and 41 percent of females over 15 years were married. The only ground for divorce is irreconcilable breakdown, signaled by the two parties living separately for two years. Traditional weddings are still in evidence, but more people plan their own, and minorities hew to their traditional forms.

Domestic Unit. The nuclear family predominates though there is an increasing number of single-

A view of Queen Street, the main thoroughfare of Auckland, the largest city, with a population approaching one million.

parent homes. Among Maori the extended family (*whanau*) live as neighbors or as a mixed and changing household of relatives. Job availability tends to determine the choice of a living place.

Inheritance. If there is a legally drawn up will, property is bequeathed by the estate holder. Maori inherit rights to ancestral land, tattoos, and burial places.

Kin Groups. Maori have revived their traditional social organization into *whanau* (extended family), *hapu* (lineage), and iwi (tribe) in an effort to reclaim their identity and negotiate under the Treaty of Waitangi. Quasi-tribes descended from a known ancestor as well as iwi celebrate periodic gatherings (*hui*). That pattern is also followed by Pakeha with family reunions based on genealogical research.

SOCIALIZATION

Infant Care. Pakeha use playpens and place an infant in a separate crib, often in a separate room. Maori, especially in low-income and rural areas, have all children sleep together. Children, including infants, may spend as much time at an ''aunty's'' house as at the house of the natural mother. An ''aunty'' is any close female relative or friend who may provide full- or part-time infant and child care.

Babies are usually put into prams, though commercial baby carriers also are used. Calming and stimulating are matters of individual philosophy.

Child Rearing and Education. New Zealand has a fully comprehensive education system. The Maori ''renaissance'' has resulted in special Maori education from preschools to middle schools. The Maori language is increasingly an option at all levels, and one aim is for a total education in Maori. Alternative schooling such as Montessori, Rudolph Steiner, home schooling, and state-run correspondence school is available and government-approved. Primary, intermediate, and high school are based on a British model, with uniforms from the intermediate level on and a prefect system with a head boy responsible for discipline. There are co-ed and single-sex schools. Obedience and being able to ''take it'' are still prized male values.

Higher Education. There are seven universities with 214,228 students and twenty-five polytechnics.

ETIQUETTE

The sacred feature of the Maori is the head and so touching it is avoided. In the marae, the *hongi* (touching of noses) is the accepted greeting. Otherwise the handshake, the hug, and the cheek kiss are used, depending on the degree of intimacy. Verbal greetings includes "Hello," "How are you?" "Gidday," and, especially, in North Island, *Kia Ora* ("Good health," "Are you well?"). Men enjoy "mateship," which involves close contact, but otherwise contact distance is arm's length. Behavior in public places is orderly, and good humor is expected. Depending on how recently they have arrived in the country, immigrants and refugees maintain their own customs but gradually adapt, especially in school.

RELIGION

Religious Beliefs. Sixteen religious sects are represented—with the Anglican Church (18.4 percent) the largest, followed by Catholic (13.8 percent) and Presbyterian (13.4 percent). Twenty-six percent of the people have no religious affiliation. The Pentecostal, Buddhist, and Muslim religions have had the greatest degree of increase.

Religious Practitioners. Archbishops, bishops, priests, presbyters, rabbis, imams, mullahs, elders, and pastors are office holders in New Zealand branches of worldwide churches. There is one Maori church (Ratana), and Maoridom makes wide use of the sacred-secular healing and counseling powers of the *tohunga*, a specialist in medicine and spirit belief.

Rituals and Holy Places. Rites of the Christian calendar are observed. Cathedrals are present in every major city, and many rural areas maintain small wooden parish churches. Cemeteries are controlled by local bodies, except for Maori burial grounds. Statues of nineteenth- and early twentieth-century Pakeha public figures and war memorials are universal. Their disfigurement has become a sign of Maori protest. Waitangi has become a national memorial, as has One Tree Hill in Auckland, both marking significant events in the evolution of early Maori–European relations. Birthdays, anniversaries, and deaths may be privately or publicly commemorated.

Death and the Afterlife. If embalming is not to take place, burial occurs within a day or two of death. Otherwise, funeral parlors embalm and show the body. Funeral services may be held in churches or funeral parlors. A Maori funeral (*tangi*) takes place in the marae and is a mixture of festivity and grief. Christians believe in a heaven for the afterlife (and a hell if Fundamentalist). Maori ancestors dwell after death in the ancestral lands and are

A boy and a wooden Maori sculpture. Maori tribes were among New Zealand's first settlers.

the reference point for political and economic as well as spiritual life.

MEDICINE AND HEALTH CARE

The former welfare state established a wide network of hospitals, clinics, visiting professionals, free medicine, and free treatment funded from taxes. Political reform led to a mixed system of care based on subsidization, along with legislation allowing for medical insurance and private hospitals. These reforms have generated considerable political debate.

Traditional medicine practiced by tohungas has always been resorted to by Maori, while some Pakeha utilize alternative medical system. All forms of medical practice emphasize a close interaction between the physical and the nonphysical. "Natural" medicines are widely available in health shops, and pharmaceutical medicines are available in licensed pharmacies.

SECULAR CELEBRATIONS

New Year's Day, Waitangi Day, a special assembly at Waitangi of public dignitaries, the queen's birthday, and the anniversary of a province are celebrated.

THE ARTS AND HUMANITIES

Support for the Arts. Profits from the state-run lottery are used by Creative New Zealand to provide funds for the arts. Individual and corporate trusts also support both arts and sport.

Literature. The art of oratory is highly prized among the Maori, who speak extemporaneously but use traditional formulas and references. The Montana Book Awards are a national competition for all categories of writing. Many authors have international reputations and have been winners of overseas competitions. There is a large collection in the national and city libraries of rare European manuscripts as well as private collections. Early missionary influence was the most influential force for Maori and Pakeha literacy.

Graphic Arts. Cities such as Dunedin have state-of-the-art public art galleries. All forms of graphic arts are practiced, and a national style has emerged, blending Maori and European elements. Training in traditional Maori carving has been widely taken up.

Performance Arts. There is a National Symphony Orchestra and at least two first-class city symphony orchestras. The National Youth Orchestra meets once a year. The Royal New Zealand Ballet tours the country. Other national arts organizations are the New Zealand Drama School, Chamber Music New Zealand, New Zealand Choral Foundation, and the New Zealand Film Commission. Local operatic, choral, drama, and orchestral groups are numerous, and New Zealanders perform in a large number of bands. European opera and classical music are the staple fare at one end, with New Zealand composers receiving regular performances, while pop music is locally generated. European drama and ballet prevail, but New Zealand producers and choreographers produce their own versions, and there are many dramatists. Traditional Maori dancing and singing (*waiata*) are presented widely. Most television programming is imported, but New Zealand produces a soap opera and nature documentaries.

THE STATE OF THE PHYSICAL AND SOCIAL SCIENCES

All universities have state-of-the-art laboratory equipment, as do the larger research hospitals. There are also Crown Research Institutes and private research institutes. There is a Ministry of Science and Technology. Much government-funded research is linked to agriculture and geology. Medical research is prominent. New Zealand has proved adept at computer software innovation, small electronic devices, and sporting innovations. Polytechnics train mechanics and tradespeople.

All universities and some polytechnics teach the social sciences. Social scientists are increasingly employed by government and private agencies and firms dealing with or employing multicultural districts and workforces. Private consultants carry out "social impact" studies of new industrial, agricultural, and developmental projects. Economists have a direct input into economic policy.

BIBLIOGRAPHY

Belich, James. *Making Peoples: A History of New Zealanders from Polynesian Settlement to the End of the Nineteenth Century,* 1996.

Duff, Alan. *Once Were Warriors,* 1993.

Kawharu, Hugh. *Maori Land Tenure: Studies of a Changing Institution,* 1977.

New Zealand Official Year Book 1998, 1998.

Salmond, Anne. *Between Worlds: Early Exchanges between Maori and Europeans 1773–1815,* 1997.

—PETER J. WILSON

NICARAGUA

CULTURE NAME

Nicaraguan

ALTERNATIVE NAMES

Nicas; formally known as the Republic of Nicaragua.

ORIENTATION

Identification. Officially identified as the Republic of Nicaragua, the origin of the country's name is attributed to more than one source. According to one story, it was Nicarao, an indigenous chief at the time of the Spanish invasion, for whom the Spaniards named their conquest. Nicarao is a Nahuatl name, Nahuatl being the language of the Aztecs. A related story traces the origin back further, saying that chief Nicarao took his name from his own people, who derived the name based on the geographic location of their land. Nicaragua may be a combination of *nic-atl-nahuac* meaning ''next to the water'' in the Arawak language.

Regardless of the origins of the country's name, the people's pride rings out in the national anthem which begins ''Hail to thee, Nicaragua,'' in acknowledgement of the country's independence from its centuries of colonizers.

Location and Geography. As the largest country in Central America with an area of 51,000 square miles (129,494 square kilometers), Nicaragua is about the size of New York State. The country is bounded by the Pacific Ocean and Caribbean Sea, with Honduras bordering it at the north and Costa Rica at the south. Nicaragua has three major geographic regions: the Pacific lowlands in the west, the Caribbean lowlands in the east, and the central highlands located between these two. Lake Managua and Lake Nicaragua are the country's largest lakes.

The climate varies more from elevation than from the seasons. Rainfall fluctuates greatly in Nicaragua and is seasonal; the rainy period runs from May through October. The Caribbean lowlands are the wettest section of Central America, receiving between 98 and 256 inches (250 and 650 centimeters) of rain annually. The east receives heavy annual rainfall and can even see serious flooding during the rainy season, while the west is drier year-round.

Demography. The Nicaraguan government has not conducted a national census since 1971, although since then it has collected demographic data through periodic sample surveys of the population. In 1990, an estimated 3.87 million people lived in Nicaragua. The population in 1993 was estimated at 4.08 million. Population growth rates have soared, and the median age is only about fifteen since so many adults were lost in the revolution and then in the hurricane of 1998. The population density in 1990 was 83 persons per square mile (32 per square kilometer), making it the lowest in Central America aside from Belize. The population is 55 percent urban, with most people concentrated in the Pacific lowlands because of the fertile land there. The Caribbean lowlands are more sparsely settled.

Linguistic Affiliation. When the Spaniards landed in western Nicaragua in the early 1500s, they encountered three main tribes each led by a chieftain, each with its own culture and language. Spanish is now the official language of Nicaragua and is spoken by more than 70 percent of the population. Most Spanish speakers live in the Pacific lowlands and central highlands. Grammar and usage follow Central American forms, which has some distinct differences from formal Spanish. The British presence in Nicaragua introduced many English words to the Spanish speakers, particularly in western Nicaragua. Likewise, American slang from the periods in which U.S. Marines occupied Nicaragua has made its way into the vernacular of Spanish speakers.

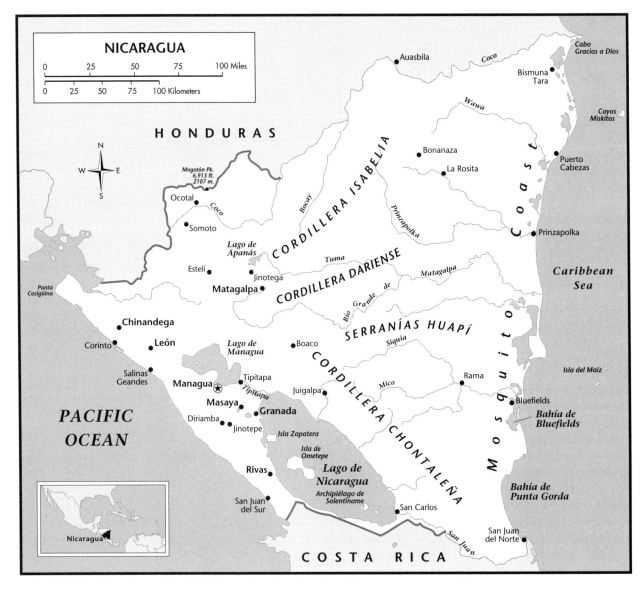

Nicaragua

The Creoles, the black people of the Caribbean region, are the descendants of colonial-era slaves, Jamaican merchants, and West Indian laborers. The Creoles are English-speaking, although many speak Spanish as a second language. Indigenous peoples of the Caribbean lowlands, the Miskito, Rama, and Sumu, preserve their own tribal languages. However, the English-speaking Miskito have resisted being absorbed into the Spanish culture. They refer to Spanish-speaking Nicaraguans as ''los Espanoles'' or ''the Spanish,'' clearly differentiating themselves from their western compatriots. The Creoles share this resentment of the western Hispanic culture. Black Carib, also known as Garifuna language, is an amalgam of an Arawak language, African vocabulary, and some English additions.

Symbolism. Volcanoes dominate the landscape of Nicaragua, as well as the art and consciousness of Nicaraguans. A volcano is featured in the country's coat of arms that is centered on its flag. From most places in Nicaragua, you can look up and see one, two, or three volcano cones. The most notable formation is the twenty-five major volcanoes in a line that runs parallel to the Pacific coastline in western Nicaragua.

One particular volcano captures the attention of Nicaraguans and dominates the Managua skyline. Momotombo, which means ''ruling above the waters'' stands at 4,100 feet (1,230 meters). Momotombo is an active volcano that smokes continuously. In fact, the gases have been harnessed by a geothermal power station erected on the side of the volcano; the station generates one-fifth of Nicaragua's electricity.

HISTORY AND ETHNIC RELATIONS

Emergence of the Nation. From 1823 until independence, Nicaragua had been included in Provincias Unidas del Centro de America, a federation of Central American provinces annexed to Mexico. Nicaragua formally declared independence on 30 April 1838.

In the 1850s, the nation's independence became vulnerable as a result of the gold rush in California. Thousands of hopeful prospectors from the United States made their way to California through Nicaragua; this route was quicker and safer than crossing the continental United States. At this time, Nicaragua became the subject of a rivalry between the United States and Britain. Both foreign powers wanted to control an interoceanic transit route, be it by land or via a new Caribbean to Pacific canal.

By 1852, the Accessory Transit Company of American tycoon Cornelius "Commodore" Vanderbilt was providing transportation for 20,000 United States citizens per month via Nicaragua. Soon after, he supported the expedition of William Walker who wanted to take over Nicaragua as a slave state annexed to the United States. William Walker was born in Nashville, Tennessee, and gained a reputation as a buccaneer and United States adventurer. In 1855 he entered Nicaragua with a small band of mercenaries armed with a new type of quick-action rifle. There, with the help of his Liberal allies, Walker was able to surprise and capture the conservative capitol of Granada and establish a coalition government. In June 1856, a new regime was formed and Walker was elected president. On 22 September, he suspended the Nicaraguan laws against slavery in order to gain support from the southern states in America and declared English to be the country's official language. His government was formally recognized by the United States that year. Then, in a reversal of alliance, Cornelius Vanderbilt backed a coalition of Central American states who fought against Walker. In 1857, Walker returned to Tennessee briefly and then sailed to Nicaragua again with more followers. There he was taken prisoner by the British and turned over to Honduran authorities, who tried and executed him on 12 September 1860.

Managua replaced the city of Leon as the capital in 1858, in an attempt to neutralize the vicious rivalry between Leon and Granada. Leon had served as the capital from its founding in 1610, but the capital was moved to Managua because it was halfway between the fervently liberal intellectual city of Leon and the ardently conservative city of Granada. Managua remains the capital city to this day.

In 1936 Anastasio Somoza, the head of the National Guard, staged a coup to bring down President Sacasa. Five months later, he became president of Nicaragua. He started a dictatorship, with the support of the United States, that lasted until his assassination in 1956. He was succeeded by his two sons Luis and Anastasio. The Somoza dictatorship ended in 1979 when the Frente Sandanista de Liberacion Nacional (FSLN) successfully waged a campaign against the National Guard, which was loyal to the Somoza family, and wrested control from the Somoza family. Because the Somoza family was plagued by corruption, many of their colleagues and beneficiaries, fearing prosecution for their actions, fled the country. The United States, concerned about the collectivization efforts of the Sandinistas and their acceptance of aid from Cuba and the Soviet Union, began to covertly arm the Contra opposition.

The Contra war of 1990 left Nicaragua highly divided. In the ensuing election, Violeta Barrios de Chamorro was elected president of Nicaragua that year. She had become a prominent leader after the 1978 assassination of her husband, Pedro Chamorro, a respected publisher and editor of the daily newspaper *La Prensa* who consistently investigated the corruption of the Somoza family. Violeta Chamorro founded her administration on the principle of national reconciliation. She is credited with leading the country through the transition from war to peace, stabilizing the economy, and initiating a market economy.

In 1997, Arnoldo Aleman Lacayo became the president of the Republic, running under the Liberal Alliance party.

National Identity. Like other Latin Americans, Nicaraguans place a great importance on family and the protection of personal *dignidad*, or dignity. This extends outward to a collective feeling of national pride among the Nicaraguan people. This nationalism is represented by heroes and martyrs in the history and folklore—especially the leader fighting against colonial influences.

Ethnic Relations. Three Indian cultures lived in pre-Columbian Nicaragua, each living in a distinct region and speaking an indigenous tongue. According to the Constitution of 1987 of the Republic of Nicaragua, all of the indigenous Atlantic coast communities enjoy the right to preserve and develop

Easter festival in Managua; most Nicaraguans are Roman Catholic.

their cultural identity within the nation. This speaks directly to the Miskito, the largest minority group, who have long enjoyed a greater autonomy than any of the other indigenous tribes. This law also applies to the Sumus living along the Caribbean just north of Bluefields, a port town founded by Dutch traders.

URBANISM, ARCHITECTURE, AND THE USE OF SPACE

Some of the most beautiful buildings in the major cities of Managua and Leon are the existing examples of colonial architecture, in particular the Roman Catholic cathedrals. Buildings illustrative of colonial architecture can be found in Managua, in the *Palacio de los Heroes de la Revolucion* (previously called the *Palacio Nacional*) and the old Cathedral; the Cathedral is currently in ruins. In Leon, the former capital of Nicaragua, the architecture is also colonial, with a traditional charm due to its narrow streets, red tiled roofs, and stout buildings.

A lack of city planning is apparent in the current development of Managua. Its business district was leveled in a 1972 earthquake, and much of the later development took place outside the city's center. This has resulted in the tremendous growth of suburbs, spreading out from the city without a long-term plan.

FOOD AND ECONOMY

Food in Daily Life. Nicaragua has a local cuisine that shares some flavors and ingredients with Mexican food, while it also bears a resemblance to the cuisines of Honduras and Guatemala. Corn and beans are staples of the diet, and garlic and onions season most dishes. Like other Central Americans, Nicaraguans consume corn tortillas with most meals. Nicaragua's version of the tortilla is large, thin and made of white corn. It is used as an edible utensil to wrap meat and beans. Beans are consumed daily as a necessary source of protein in a country where most people cannot afford to eat meat regularly. Nicaraguans are partial to a small red bean generally eaten refried in a dish called *gallo pinto*, or "spotted rooster." This is primarily a breakfast dish.

Nicaraguans also enjoy *tamales*, but their version—called *nacatamal*—has some unique characteristics. The entire meal of corn, rice, tomatoes, chili, potatoes, cassava root, and often a piece of meat, is wrapped in a leaf deriving from a banana-like plant.

The yucca root is a vegetable eaten for its vitamins; it is aptly named *vigoron* in Spanish, for its high percentage of nutrients. The yucca root is often served with pork rind and greens and sold at roadside stands. In addition, fruits such as mangos and plantains are popular in Nicaragua.

The favorite nonalcoholic drink is coffee. Nicaraguans drink coffee with hot milk at breakfast and black with sugar the rest of the day. *Pinol*, the national drink, is also nonalcoholic and is made from corn flour with water. *Tiste*, similar to pinol, is a beverage made from ground tortillas and cacao which can be served cool or at room temperature. Also popular is *chichi*, wine of the Indians, made from fermented corn. Beer is consumed as a typical light alcoholic beverage, while rum is the hard liquor of choice.

Food Customs at Ceremonial Occasions. At celebratory meals, Nicaraguans eat steak, either grilled steak called *bistec a la parrilla*, or grilled sirloin known as *lomo*.

Basic Economy. Nicaragua's Gross Domestic Product (GDP) for 1992 was $1.6 billion (U.S.). The Chamorro administration agreed to International Monetary Fund (IMF) and World Bank standards aimed at weaning the country off its dependency on foreign aid. One main aim of this plan was to halt the rampant inflation of the Nicaraguan currency, the *cordoba*. The plan was designed to stabilize the local currency, encourage foreign investment, and increase exports.

The economy began expanding in 1994 and grew 4.5 percent in 1996 (its best performance since before the Sandinista regime). As a result, GDP reached $1.969 billion. However, in the aftermath of political unrest as well as El Niño (1997) and Hurricane Mitch (1998), the GDP in Nicaragua has plunged. Nicaragua remains the second-poorest nation in the hemisphere with a per capita GDP of $438, which is lower than where it stood before the Sandinista conquest in 1979. Its economy suffers from persistent trade and budget deficits. Until agricultural efforts improve, the economy will continue to suffer and Nicaragua will remain dependent on foreign assistance (22 percent of GDP in 1996).

Land Tenure and Property. Much of the country's productive land was under the control of the Somoza family until 1979, when the Sandinistas redistributed land and organized farmers into cooperatives. However, the Sandinistas did not invest in improving farm equipment so harvests declined, leading many farmers to flock to urban centers in search of work. In 1981, the administration passed the Agrarian Reform Law, which defined the process of nationalization and stated what could be done with expropriated land. This law guaranteed property rights to those who continued to farm their land, but land that was underdeveloped or abandoned was subject to expropriation. Land ownership became an issue again in the 1990s as the Chamorro government redistributed the land, breaking up the state farms.

Commercial Activities. About 10 percent of Nicaragua's land is cultivated. The most fertile land is in the Pacific coast region, where volcanic ash has fertilized the soil. Coffee is grown in the Central Highlands and cotton is raised in the Pacific region. In addition, the country cultivates maize, sorghum, dry beans, soya beans and tobacco commercially. Rice is the country's most important food crop, while coffee, cotton, bananas, and beef are the country's principal exports.

Major Industries. There has been little urban industry in Nicaragua since the Sandinista revolution. In 1978, the industrial sector shrank due to political and economic problems. In the early 1980s, food processing plants, sugar mills, and vegetable oil refineries were operating at only 50 percent capacity. Prior to that, the country's industry was comprised of food

processing plants and the manufacture of animal by-products such as candles, soap, and leather.

The Miskito people generally eat the meat of the green turtle as a staple protein in their diet. But in the first half of the twentieth century, foreign demand for turtle meat increased and the Miskito discovered that they could earn more by selling the meat. Two foreign processing companies established operations in Bluefields and Puerto Cabezas in 1969. The industrialization and export of turtle meat quickly depleted the turtle population. Motivated by conservation of the turtle, in 1977 the Nicaraguan government suspended the operations of these companies.

Trade. Today Nicaragua's economy is based on agricultural efforts, since the nation has very fertile land and a low density of population on that land. Export crops such as coffee, cotton, bananas, and sugar rose steadily from 1950 to 1975. In 1992, the country's largest coffee crop was exported. The Nicaraguans also raise livestock for local consumption as well as trade. The Spanish brought the first cattle in the sixteenth century, and Nicaragua has been successfully raising and exporting beef since about 1950. In fact, forty-nine thousand tons of beef are produced each year.

Division of Labor. Traditional Hispanic divisions of labor are the standard in Nicaragua. Men work in the fields or factories, while women carry out the domestic chores. Children in rural communities help out with the farming, often missing school during harvest seasons. Most workers of the urban lower class are self-employed and unsalaried workers in small business ventures. Workers in this informal sector include tinsmiths, seamstresses, bakers, carpenters, and peddlers. In a family where the male works in this sector, the wife may take in laundry or sell food in the street to supplement the family income.

SOCIAL STRATIFICATION

Classes and Castes. Nicaragua has always been a society of classes in indigenous cultures, the priests and nobles ruled over the laborers and slaves. This is what the Spanish found when they arrived, and their domination didn't do much to affect this class system. For generations, there was no notion of social or economic mobility for Nicaraguans. Agricultural laborers were descendants of laborers, and expected their children to follow in this path. With few other options available, most did.

Only with the 1979 revolution of the Sandinistas was there a widespread attempt to level the

A man walks by a wall painted with political graffiti in Managua. The 1979 revolution of the Sandanistas was an attempt to eliminate the class system.

playing field and eliminate the class system. The Sandinistas deliberately took power and expropriated wealth from the rich and spread it evenly among the poor. The Sandinistas also began a national literacy campaign: they recruited young people from the upper classes to teach literacy skills to families in rural areas.

Symbols of Social Stratification. Land is the traditional basis of wealth and status in Nicaragua. Traditionally, landowners have prospered with the export of coffee, cotton, beef, and sugar, and land was concentrated in the hands of a few. Less than one-fifth of the population could be described as middle class or higher. Most Nicaraguans who have work still toil as migrants, following crops and working only during the harvest period. When the Sandinistas gained power, they seized the property of the Somoza family and instituted the Agrarian Reform Law, transferring land to peasant families and squatters on lands.

The telephone is another potent symbol of economic and social stratification, as evidenced by the number of telephones in the country and who has them. In 1993 there were approximately 60,000 telephones, only 1.5 per 100 inhabitants.

POLITICAL LIFE

Government. Modeled on the democratic system of the United States, the Nicaraguan government is divided into three branches: the executive, the legislative, and the judicial. The executive branch is made up of a president, vice president, and an appointed cabinet. The legislative branch, with a 92-member National Assembly, enacts the country's laws. As in the United States, the judicial branch is comprised of a supreme court and lower, local courts.

Leadership and Political Officials. Established by the Law on Municipalities in 1988 by the Sandinista National Assembly, the first municipal governments were selected in 1990. An effort was made to decentralize the political power which had been so abused in Nicaragua for decades. Under this system, citizens vote directly for council members in Nicaragua's nine regions; the number of members depends on the size of the city. The constitution details the responsibilities and powers of these municipal governments; they are primarily responsible for control of urban development, sanitation, environmental protection, construction and maintenance of roads, parks, and bridges, and the creation of museums and libraries.

Social Problems and Control. Poverty is the most pressing social problem in Nicaragua, and has been for decades. In 1994 the United Nations identified poverty and unemployment as the two reasons why Nicaraguans do not believe in the salve of democracy. The report asserted that 75 percent of Nicaraguan families live in poverty, and that unemployment hovered at 60 percent. Because of the uneven distribution of wealth, as well as the economic and political upheavals of recent decades, the poor have even suffered during periods of economic growth. In the 1970s, 30 percent of personal income flowed to the richest 5 percent of households. During the agricultural export growth in the Pacific lowlands and central highlands, many peasants were pushed off their land and ended up as low-wage migrant laborers.

The drug problem in Nicaragua was considered quite modest as of 1993, despite the country's position along a drug transit route from South American to the United States.

Military Activity. Nicaragua has a land force, a navy, and an air force. During the Sandinista regime, military service was mandatory but conscription was ended when Violeta Chamorro became president. As the country stabilized, the armed forces were downsized. The police organization, together with the Customs Organization, is considered to be exceedingly corrupt. Favors can easily be bought for the cost of a bribe.

SOCIAL WELFARE AND CHANGE PROGRAMS

The bulk of social welfare programs coincided with the 1979 Sandinista triumph. Declaring 1980 the year of literacy, the Sandinista government successfully launched a volunteer literacy campaign, focused on the countryside, to teach anyone over ten years old to read. At that time, this meant about 800,000 people. Young people of the more privileged class volunteered with parental permission to spend several months living and working with peasants, teaching entire families to read. The youth also taught political literacy based on Paulo Freire's concept of consciousness-raising.

NONGOVERNMENTAL ORGANIZATIONS AND OTHER ORGANIZATIONS

Nicaragua has long been dependent on foreign aid. Principle donors have been the United States, the USSR, and Canada, all of whom have been concerned about stabilizing Nicaragua because of its geopolitical positioning. From 1990 to 1998, the United States invested $983 million in economic assistance. In the 1960s, the United States Agency for International Development (USAID) funded local programs aimed at improving regional infrastructure, particularly improving highway routes that would assist industrial development by improving interregional trade routes.

After the 1972 earthquake, foreign aid poured in to Nicaragua. The corrupt Somoza regime, however, managed to extort a significant amount of that aid for themselves, rather than using it to rebuild the country.

USAID now has three program areas operating in Nicaragua: strengthening democracy, creating jobs for sustainable growth, and promoting primary education and nutrition classes for healthy families. In 1998, Hurricane Mitch brought additional foreign aid dollars to Nicaragua to help deal with the damage from the worst national disaster in two centuries in the region. The destruction of Hurricane Mitch, combined with the devastating drought of El Niño in 1997 and 1998, resulted in a dreadful economic setback for the country.

GENDER ROLES AND STATUSES

Division of Labor by Gender. The roles of most men and women in Nicaragua are shaped by traditional Hispanic values. Women are most respected in the role of mother, but more women have been entering the workforce since the 1980s. Men are typically not involved in childrearing.

Relative Status of Women and Men. The status of men and women has changed since the revolution of the 1980s. As the revolution sought to liberate poor Nicaraguans, it also managed to liberate women from their subordinate role in the Hispanic culture. Women established neighborhood committees to organize urban resistance. Women gained the respect of male soldiers when they fought, and died, alongside them. Estimates are that women comprised about 25 percent of the Sandinista Front of the National Liberation Army.

MARRIAGE, FAMILY, AND KINSHIP

Marriage. The minority of couples who are not Roman Catholic, outside of the upper and middle classes, formalize their marriages through ceremonies officiated by another church or the state. Many common-law unions exist, but Roman Catholics abide by the church's emphasis on marriage. Because of poverty and a shortage of affordable hous-

A woman teaches a man how to print letters as part of a literacy program in Nicaragua; the Sandanistas helped start these programs.

ing, newly married couples may live with one set of parents.

Domestic Unit. Like many Hispanic cultures, family relationships are highly valued and include relatives beyond the nuclear family unit. The word *compadrazago*, which literally means copaternity, indicates the bond among children, parents, grandparents, and godparents. With a high fertility rate, households are large—generally comprised of six to eight persons—and include grandparents and aunts and uncles. In rural areas, large families are regarded as a blessing: parents have help with chores and farm work. In urban settings, large families with extended kin allow for creative ways in which to house entire families, despite the space constraints of city living.

Inheritance. Land is the lifeblood of Nicaraguan farmers. It is a source of pride and dignity for a farmer to own the land he cultivates. And land can be a means of escaping the poverty that plagues so many Nicaraguans. Inheritance of land in Nicaragua has been complicated by the fact that most of the land was in the hands of a few privileged families. The peasant families who farmed this land had no claims to land ownership. This changed with the Sandinista government as it awarded and distrib-

uted land to rural families. Now, however, relatives and allies of the Somoza regime who emigrated in 1980 want to reclaim the thousands of acres they owned. Disputes over resettlements remain a controversial national issue, one that is being watched by the international community.

Kin Groups. Loyalty to kin is strong and extended families often reside together, sharing the childrearing duties as well as any resources of the household. The notion of kin may be extended to those not related by blood or marriage with the tradition of naming godparents.

SOCIALIZATION

Infant Care. Infants are raised principally by the mother with the help of extended kin. In agrarian communities, families tend to be large since more children increase the number of workers, thus raising the family's farming productivity. Infant mortality is high in Nicaragua. This figure was reduced in 1980 from 121 to 59 deaths per thousand, due to the Sandinista governments' increase in health clinics. Even the reduced infant mortality rate, though, is high when compared to that of neighboring countries.

Child Rearing and Education. Nicaragua's education system is underfunded and inadequate; access to education improved in the 1980s with the introduction of free education, but a large majority of the population had not completed primary schooling in 1993. Literacy was estimated at about 50 percent at the end of the Somoza regime, while a literacy campaign in the 1980s reportedly raised the literacy rate to about 77 percent. In 1981, approximately 1,500 Cuban teachers were teaching in Nicaragua, and 1,300 Nicaraguan students were attending schools in Cuba.

Schooling is now free and compulsory for children from ages seven to twelve, but only 70 percent of primary age students actually attend classes. By law all schooling is in Spanish, even in the West where Spanish is not spoken in the home.

Higher Education. The intellectual and cultural city of Leon gave birth to the country's first university. The National University of Nicaragua has approximately 7,000 students at campuses in Leon and Managua. The Central American University, located in Managua, is a Roman Catholic institution. The private Jesuit Universidad Centroamericana is also located in Managua. Two separate independent institutions, Universidades Nacionales Autonomas de Nicaragua, also operate as an alternative to the leading universities.

ETIQUETTE

Nicaraguans share a sense of respect and personal distance, which is apparent in language exchanges. Nicaraguans rarely use the familiar *tu* form of address, even though most other Latin Americans use this casual exchange. However, the Nicaraguans routinely address one another using the informal and nonstandard pronoun *vos*.

RELIGION

Religious Beliefs. Officially, Nicaragua is a secular state. Roman Catholicism arrived in Nicaragua with the Spanish conquest in the sixteenth century and remained the established faith until 1939. Most Nicaraguans are Roman Catholic, but many blacks along the coast, belong to Protestant denominations.

Practicing Roman Catholics, those who attend mass and receive the sacrament, tend to be women and members of the upper and middle classes residing in urban centers. With a paucity of priests to reach more potential members, the Roman Catholic Church is relatively inactive in rural communities.

Popular religion revolves around the saints, and prayers directed to them usually make requests for the saint's intervention in an illness or particular problem.

Along the coast, blacks largely belong to the Pentecostal and evangelical churches which have been growing in the 1990s. The largest of the Protestant congregations are the Moravian Church and Baptist Convention of Nicaragua. Virtually all Miskito and many Creoles and Sumn are Moravians. Other denominations in the west include churches established by missionaries from the United States, such as the Assemblies of God, the Episcopal Church, the Church of Jesus Christ of Latter Day Saints, Jehovah's Witnesses, and the Seventh Day Adventists.

Religious Practitioners. Roman Catholic priests lead mass and deliver the sacrament. In the mid-1980s there was only one priest for every 7,000 Roman Catholic Nicaraguans, approximately; this is a lower rate than in any of the other Latin American countries. The Roman Catholic bishops have sometimes offered tacit approval of the political leader, while at other times they allied themselves with the opposition. While started by foreign missionaries, most Protestant congregations are now lead by local Nicaraguan ministers who operate autonomously while maintaining a connection to their sister churches in the United States.

Rituals and Holy Places. As a predominantly devout Catholic country, Christian religious holidays are honored. Nicaraguans celebrate Holy Wednesday in March, Maundy Thursday, Good Friday, and Easter. Maundy Thursday marks the transition through death and into life as experienced on Good Friday and Easter. In December, Catholics honor the Immaculate Conception and Christmas. Holy Saint's days are celebrated regularly. Each city in Nicaragua has its own patron saint and some saints may be shared between towns. The people give gifts to these saints in exchange for blessings such as healing, a good crop, or a husband. Even more important than the miracles that the Nicaraguans request of the saints are the annual celebrations, known as fiestas, which are held for each saint. These fiestas are times of great joy and everyone in the city joins in the celebration. Fiestas may begin with a parade in which the statue of the saint is carried into the city, followed by a daylong party of eating, drinking, and dancing.

Death and the Afterlife. Traditionally, the spouse of the deceased prepares the body for burial. The

Nicaraguan children relax at their home in Managua. Households are generally comprised of six to eight persons, as an extended family.

body is laid out in the home for viewing, and anyone from the village can enter to view the body. Roman Catholics believe in the concept of heaven, and understand death as the passage to eternal life.

MEDICINE AND HEALTH CARE

During the 1980s, health care improved as the Sandinista regime built public clinics in both urban and rural areas. Nevertheless, the people of Nicaragua continue to suffer from malaria, poor diet, and unhealthy sanitary conditions caused by inadequate water and sewage systems. In the early 1990s the life expectancy of a Nicaraguan was 62 years, among the lowest in Central America. Enteritis and other diarrheal diseases were among the leading causes of death. Pneumonia, tetanus, and measles accounted for more than 10 percent of all deaths. A high incidence of infectious diseases remains, with malaria and tuberculosis being particularly endemic.

The Somoza regime tried to curb population growth by making contraceptives available through public health clinics. It is estimated that only about 5 percent of women of childbearing age use birth control devices.

SECULAR CELEBRATIONS

Nicaraguans celebrate New Year's Day on 1 January, Liberation Day on 18 July, and Independence Day on 15 September. The day before Independence Day, on 14 September, Nicaraguans commemorate the 1856 Battle of San Jacinto, in which Nicaraguans defeated William Walker and his Northern American mercenaries. Santo Domingo, the patron saint of Managua, is celebrated in a festival held from 1 to 10 August. This festival combines church ceremonies with horse racing, bullfights, cockfights, and a spirited carnival.

THE ARTS AND HUMANITIES

Since the early 1980s, the Ministry of Culture has worked to preserve folk art and train a new generation of artisans so that traditional crafts would not be lost.

Literature. Until the 1980s when the Sandinistas launched their literacy campaign, half of the Nicaraguan population was functionally illiterate. While few Nicaraguan writers have received international recognition, poet Ruben Dario is the noted exception. Dario is the pseudonym of Felix Ruben Garcia Sarmiento whose modernist poetry began a new movement in Nicaraguan literature. A nineteenth century poet, Dario lived from 1867 to 1916 and produced "*Azul*," or "Blue." Dario lived as an exile outside of his homeland, but visited Leon for long periods and served as a diplomat representing Nicaragua. Dario's birthplace has been renamed in his honor and is preserved as a national shrine. Another author, Pedro Joaquin Chamorro, published a volume of short stories and two novels before his assassination in 1978.

Graphic Arts. The Nicaraguan tradition of producing utilitarian and decorative ceramics and earthenware continues. Locally crafted earthenware still employs the shapes and motifs found in pre-Columbian pieces. Other local crafts include silverwork, woodcarving, embroidery, and sculpting. Gold filigree is practiced on the Atlantic coast.

Performance Arts. Folkloric dance is one of Nicaragua's enduring pre-Colonial art forms. Traditional dances are performed at festivals and fiestas, and children study this aspect of their heritage in after-school programs. Similar to folk dances in Mexico and Guatemala, Nicaraguan dance tradition features the *palo volador*, or flying pole, in which a performer is strapped to a rope wound around a pole and then unwinds, swinging farther into the air accompanied by the pounding rhythm of percussion instruments. The *marimba*, a kind of xylophone, is also part of Nicaragua's rich musical tradition. The city of Masaga is the primary performing arts center in the country.

Dances such as *Las Inditas*, *Los Diabilitos*, and *Las Negras* all involve masked characters. Another traditional dance theme is the re-enactment of the Spanish Conquest, parodying the conquerors by depicting them in pink masks with grotesque facial features. The farcical dance portrays the Spaniards and their conquest as clumsy, but inevitably triumphant.

THE STATE OF THE PHYSICAL AND SOCIAL SCIENCES

Nicaragua has several functioning research institutes despite the country's unrest. The *Observatorio Geofisico*, founded in 1980 in Managua, concentrates on the study of geophysics, geology, seismology, and volcanology. The National University of Agriculture in Managua was founded in 1929. About two thousand students attend the university and study agronomy, animal sciences, and natural resource management. The faculty employs a dean for each of these areas of study as well as for distance education, and the facilities include a botanical garden that is maintained by students and used for agricultural research. The Polytechnical University of Nicaragua, also in Managua, is a technical school that was founded in 1968 by the Nicaraguan Baptist Convention. This university offers vocational degrees in engineering, nursing, banking and finance, architecture, and industrial arts.

BIBLIOGRAPHY

Belli, Humberto. *Breaking Faith: The Sandinista Revolution and Its Impact on Freedom and Christian Faith in Nicaragua*, 1985.

Box, Ben. *Mexico and Central America Handbook*, 1997.

Cortazar, Julio. *Nicaraguan Sketches*, 1989.

Davis, Peter. *Where Is Nicaragua?*, 1987.

Dozier, Craig L. *Nicaragua's Mosquito Coast: The Years of British and American Presence*, 1985.

Edmisten, Patricia Taylor. *Nicaragua Divided: La Prensa and the Chamorro Legacy*, 1990.

Flora, Jan, and Edelberto Torres-Rivas, eds. *Sociology of Developed Societies of Central America*, 1989.

Freire, Paulo. *Pedagogy of the Oppressed*, 1970.

Gall, Timothy L., ed. *International Handbook of Universities*, 1997.

Lappe, Frances Moore, and Joseph Collins. *Now We Can Speak: A Journey through the New Nicaragua*, 1982.

Merrill, Tim L., ed. *Nicaragua: A Country Study*, 1993.

Parker, Franklin D. *The Central American Republics*, 1964.

Rosett, Peter, and John Vandermeer, eds. *Nicaragua: Unfinished Revolution*, 1986.

Rushdie, Salman. *The Jaguar Smile: A Nicaraguan Journey*, 1987.

Smith, Hazel. *Self-determination and Survival*, 1993.

Turner, Barry, ed. *The Statesman's Yearbook 2000: The Politics, Cultures, and Economics of the World*, 1999.

Vilas, Carlos M. *State, Class and Ethnicity in Nicaragua: Capitalist Modernization and Revolutionary Change on the Atlantic Coast*, 1989.

Walker, Thomas W. *Nicaragua: The Land of Sandino*, 1986.

Walker, William. *The War in Nicaragua*, 1985.

—S. B. DOWNEY

NIGER

CULTURE NAME

Nigerien, Nigerienne

ORIENTATION

Identification. From the early twentieth century until independence in 1960, the colony of Niger was part of French West Africa. Since the boundaries of the nation-state were imposed by European colonial powers, ethnic and cultural borders do not coincide with state boundaries. Since independence, there have been governmental efforts to promote a national culture.

Location and Geography. The area of this landlocked country is 490,000 square miles (1,267,000 square kilometers). One of the hottest countries of the world, Niger straddles the Sahara and Sahelian climate zones. Niger is essentially a flat country. Rainfall is rare north and east of the Air Massif but generally adequate in the west. The capital city is Niamey, with a 1998 population of approximately 500,000, located on the Niger River, which has a multiethnic population.

Demography. The population was approximately 9.2 million in 1998. The Hausa are numerically the predominant group, constituting approximately 53 percent of the population, followed by the Zarma-Songhai, 21 percent; the Fulani (Peul), 10 percent; the Tuareg, 10 percent; the Kanuri (Beri-Beri or Manga), 4.4 percent; and Arabs, Tubu, and Gourmantche, approximately 1.6 percent. In the precolonial era, Niger included regions of several "traditional" African kingdoms, empires, and states with varying degrees of stratification and centralization.

Linguistic Affiliation. There are five main ethnolinguistic groups, corresponding to the five national languages, in addition to French, the official language: Haussa, Anna-Songhai, Fulani or Fulbe, Tamajaq, and Kanuri or Beri-Beri. French is used primarily in official written governmental and international correspondence; the local vernacular languages are more often used in daily social interaction, markets, and trading.

Symbolism. The major groups share many Muslim beliefs and practices, including respect for Islamic/Koranic scholarship in Arabic. Much imagery comes from Islam, the major official religion. Most groups have retained elements of pre-Islamic cultural, symbolic, ritual, and political life, such as spirit possession, bilateral descent patterns, and spirit pantheons in local cosmological systems. Elements from nature also figure prominently in national symbolism. Millet stalks, for example, are popular motifs in embroidery on women's traditional blouses and appear on the emblem of a political party. The national flag's colors of green, orange, and yellow represent the different climate zones. In the increasingly important tourist industry, certain symbols and motifs have been adapted from local art forms, such as the Agadez Cross.

HISTORY AND ETHNIC RELATIONS

Emergence of the Nation. Several precolonial empires had an impact on Niger, including the Songhai to the west and the Bornu Empire to the east as well as the Fulani Empire of Sokoto. In the nineteenth century, the first European explorers came to the area, searching for the mouth of the Niger River. Although French efforts at subjugation began before 1900, dissident ethnic groups, especially the Tuareg, were not conquered until the early twentieth century. The new colony was considered lacking in resources, and no paved roads or railroads were built between 1922 and 1944. No efforts were made to encourage river transportation, and the literacy rate remained among the lowest in Africa. Higher education opportunities were limited. The French constitution of 1946 permitted Niger to elect a representative to the French National Assembly and provided for decentraliza-

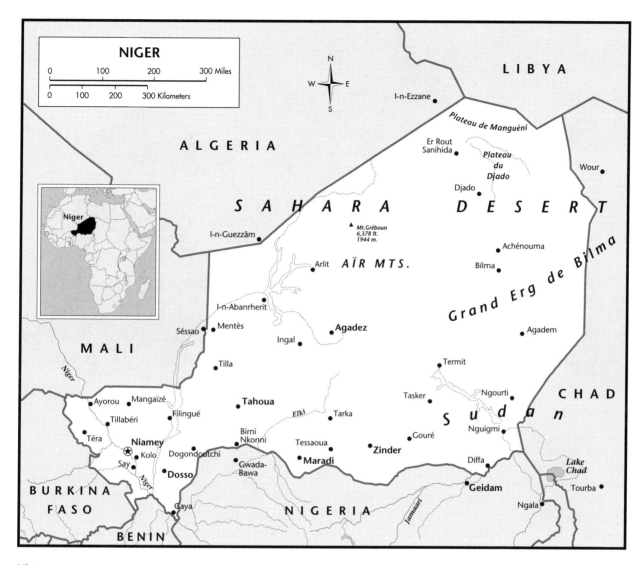

Niger

tion of power and limited participation in political life for local advisory assemblies. The law of 23 June 1956 gave Niger's politicians more of a voice in the management of their country by establishing a government council presided over by the governor. In addition to removing voting inequalities, these laws provided for the creation of governmental organs, giving individual territories a high degree of self-government. After the establishment of the Fifth French Republic in 1958, Niger became an autonomous state. Two years later, a new constitution adopted by referendum permitted the creation of a republic (18 December 1958). Independence was proclaimed on 3 August 1960.

National Identity. The population is affected by cultural elements from North Africa as well as Africa south of the Sahara. In general the ethnic

groups tend to be distributed according to region. While the national identity incorporates many elements from all the regional and cultural/ethnic influences, the recent tensions between north and south and east and west have been based on distinctive aspects of ethnic and geographic regional experience. Many of these tensions are rooted in uneven development of the different regions.

Ethnic Relations. Ethnicity is an important factor in disunity and conflict in contemporary Niger. Political tensions exist between sedentary peoples and nomads. However, apart from military antagonism between the Zarma-Songhai and the Tuareg in the nineteenth century, the people have little historical basis for exclusively ethnically rooted hostility and conflict. Contemporary ethnic conflict stems largely from deliberate decisions of the nation's

Tuareg camel-riders, Tamazlak. The Tuareg form 10 percent of the population.

colonial and postcolonial rulers and the different responses by the various groups to colonial economic and educational policies.

After independence, the new regime was dominated by educated Zarma, who were concerned with the demographic and economic imbalance between their group and the more numerous and commercially minded Haussa. In the first fifteen years after independence, the policies of the new regime intensified ethnic consciousness. Although the military government that took power in 1974 attempted to suppress that consciousness, ethnic identity has continued to mold political and economic demands. Subdivisions within each ethnolinguistic and cultural group also exist and occasionally are more salient than differences between ethnic groups. Precolonial societies often distinguished nobles and Islamic scholars from commoners and slaves; merchants from farmers herders, and fishers; and warriors from producers.

URBANISM, ARCHITECTURE, AND THE USE OF SPACE

Despite growing migration to the towns and the recent growth of the capital city, Niger remains overwhelmingly rural. Outside the capital city, architecture and the use of space reflect traditional regional and sedentarized-nomadic differences. In both rural and urban areas, architecture also reflects social stratification. Throughout much of the rural south, west, and east, there are adobe mud houses and a few concrete tin-roofed houses of functionaries and teachers. In much of the rural north, there are semi-sedentarized nomadic camps with tents of various materials (grass, animal hides) interspersed with adobe mud houses. Tents have portable walls, which are removed and transported for nomadic migration with herds. The greater degree of sedentarization in a community, the more common the adobe mud houses. In semi-nomadic Tuareg communities, women build and own the tent and men build and own the adobe house. In the tent, there is gender-based symbolism: for example, the left side of the interior of a Tuareg tent is associated with the married woman owner and her belongings and the right side is associated with her husband. As houses become more common as a result of sedentarization, there are corresponding changes in property relations between the sexes. In many communities, mosques are surrounded by the homes of traditionally aristocratic, chiefly, and Islamic scholar families. Homes of families of traditionally lower or ambiguous status are located farther from the mosque and its surrounding neighborhood. Another important feature in the countryside is the widespread opposition between the settled community (village or camp) and the wild. There is the idea of the settled community as a human habitation and center of civilization, as opposed to the unsettled, wild areas surrounding it that are believed to be inhabited by spirits. People are believed to be vulnerable to the influence of the spirits of the wild on certain specified occasions, such as during life transitions or during travel. The spirits of the ''wild'' spaces must be controlled before people engage in activities that alter their domain. In Niamey, most families' houses also tend to be of the standard adobe mud type, usually rented, although there is variation according to nationality and socioeconomic class. Many Europeans in Niamey inhabit buildings locally called ''villas,'' that are made of concrete and often have running water, electricity, and air-conditioning. In Niamey there have been increasing gaps between the standard of living, income, and comfort of most Nigeriens and that of many foreign residents. Europeans and a few well-to-do Africans tend to reside in neighborhoods high on a hill, called the Plateau, and near the river in European-colonial concrete villas and Western-style apartments. Also on the Plateau are government offices, ministries, the presidential palace, and the presidential guard as well as the offices of many international aid agencies and embassies.

FOOD AND ECONOMY

Food in Daily Life. Millet, sorghum, and beans are the major food crops, and peanuts and cotton are the major cash crops. Rice is grown along the banks of the Niger River. Millet is the basic daily staple for most rural people in all regions, followed in importance by corn, sorghum, rice, macaroni, beans, cowpeas, cassava, and wheat dishes such as couscous. Rice is a ''status'' food that is served at rites of passage, holidays, and other special occasions. Millet dishes vary in style but usually are prepared as a ''paste'' or stiff cooked porridge dough and covered with a vegetable sauce that occasionally contains small pieces of meat. However, most meat is served apart from sauces, grilled and eaten on the side on special occasions. In the northern Aïr region, millet often is also served with goat's or camel's milk. Also popular in the north is cheese made from goat's milk. Food taboos include a nationwide avoidance of pork and specific taboos observed by different groups.

Food Customs at Ceremonial Occasions. Important ceremonial occasions at which special meals

Despite growing migration to towns, Niger remains overwhelmingly rural.

are served include Muslim holidays. Ritual animal sacrifice and slaughter and communal consumption of meat are important at those holidays. Extended families, often residing in a few nearby household clusters in rural areas, normally consume the meat together after it is slaughtered by an Islamic scholar or the male household head. Men, women, and children usually eat apart. Other dishes include ''high-status'' foods such as rice, macaroni, and couscous with richer sauces. There are also liquid grain beverages resembling beers. Among the Tuareg, a special beverage called *eghajira* (or *eghale*) consists of pounded millet, goat cheese, and crushed dates blended with water and served from elaborately carved decorated wooden ladles.

Basic Economy. Niger is one of the world's poorest nations, with a per capita income of $220 (U.S.) in 1995. The northern zone is devoted primarily to pastoral nomadism involving camels, cattle, sheep, and goats. In the Aïr Massif there are pockets of oasis gardens that require constant irrigation. The southern Sahelian zone is devoted to agropastoralism, which at the fringe of the Sudanian zone becomes essentially agriculture. Despite efforts by the government to increase agricultural production and the development of uranium mining, the gross national product has declined sharply.

Niger has been plagued by ecological disaster, economic crises, and political uncertainty. After the drought of 1968–1974, the government attempted to make the country self-sufficient in food production. This was achieved in 1980, but another drought in 1984 caused food shortages. Austerity measures imposed by the World Bank and the International Monetary Fund further weakened the economy, bringing shortages and unemployment. In more arid regions, livestock production dominates with the raising of cattle, camels, sheep, and goats. There is fishing on the Niger River and Lake Chad, with dried fish sold widely.

Commercial Activities. There are permanent markets in the major towns and market days in rural communities. Much commerce is conducted by truck and traditional camel caravan trade between Niger and Nigeria. Goods in local markets include fresh produce such as fruits and vegetables, dried river fish, canned goods from Algeria, household supplies and tools and cloth from as far away as China, spices, perfumes, and traditional medicines from Algeria, Nigeria, and Mecca. Many Haussa and Zarma-Songhai women cook and sell snack foods by the side of the road. Some women manufacture knitted items and engage in leatherwork.

Major Industries. Mining accounts for nearly 20 percent of the gross domestic product. Uranium exports are a major source of national income. Uranium mines opened in 1971, and output reached a peak in 1981. Declining demand and falling world prices then led to a reduction in output. It is estimated that Niger has 10 percent of the world's uranium reserves. Coal is used to generate electricity for the mining towns. Other important minerals include tin-bearing cassiterite, iron, tin, coal, phosphates, gold, and salt. Manufacturing consists mainly of food processing, textile production, and leather tanning. Tourism has become important.

Trade. The traditional caravan trade, while it has diminished in importance, is still conducted by Tuareg men. The men go east to Bilma to trade millet for salt and dates and then go south to Kano and other parts of Nigeria to trade the salt and dates for household tools, luxury goods such as cloth and spices, and more millet.

Division of Labor. In rural communities, many work roles still correspond to traditional patterns of age, gender, and social class. The major cultural and ethnic groups are characterized by a marked degree of specialization in labor that derives from their complex precolonial hierarchical, stratified social organization. Those social orders featured hereditary, endogamous occupational groupings with traditionally performed distinct roles as well as relationships of fictive kinship and mutual dependence. In the past, slavery was important. Age-based roles cut across this system in the form of fictive kinship and apprenticeship. Because of their joking relationships with persons of aristocratic origin, smith-artisans and oral historians (*griots*) often are referred to metaphorically as their "cousins" or "little sisters (brothers)." Young children begin training for the specialized tasks of their social background, such as working the forge, in an apprenticeship, usually under the same-sex parent or another older close relative. Social strata with varying tributary and servile origins formerly served aristocratic or "noble" patrons, and even today in many rural areas, families of aristocratic origins are still attached to their inherited smiths and *griots*. However, prestigious descent no longer always corresponds to socio-economic prosperity, and many families of noble origin now have difficulty supporting their client families. In the towns, many of these "client-patron" relationships are breaking down. Particularly important today are arts and crafts specialists. Among the Haussa, there are metalworkers, leatherworkers, griots, and other specialized hereditary strata. Among the Tuareg, smith-artisans in the countryside manufacture jewelry, weapons, and household, gardening, and herding tools for nobles and serve as ritual specialists, providing music at nobles' name days, weddings, and other festivals as well as acting as go-betweens for marriage arrangements and as political intermediaries for traditional chiefs. In the towns, many Tuareg smith-artisans are active in the market trade, adapting their traditional silver, wood, and leather works for European tourist and African functionary tastes and sometimes working in gold. Griots and smith-artisans exert much informal power through their critical social commentary. Also important among all groups are Koranic or Islamic scholars, often called *marabouts*, who serve as religious scholars and scribes and, in the countryside, combine legal, medical, and religious professions.

SOCIAL STRATIFICATION

Classes and Castes. New classes are emerging, particularly in the towns. While marriages still tend to be endogamous in the countryside, there is increasing intermarriage in the towns and monetization has disrupted many old client–patron rights and obligations. Functionaries may be of di-

Granaries in a Niger village.

verse social origins. Within each cultural/ethnic group, there remain salient social stratum differences in rural communities, whereas in the towns, socio-economic status tends to operate more independently of traditional social origins. Some cultural and ethnic groups have not benefitted from economic development, although the government has attempted to narrow these gaps. After the Tuareg separatist rebellion ended, more Tuareg were integrated into the army, given functionary posts in semi-autonomous northern regions, and admitted to the university in Niamey.

Symbols of Social Stratification. Traditionally, aristocratic people were distinguished not by vast differences in wealth or standard of living but by exterior verbal and nonverbal symbols of body, dress, and ornamentation. These symbols included cultural values emphasizing reserved, dignified conduct such as controlled and indirect speech; bodily signs of ease such as soft hands and long fingers set off by ornate rings; a portly well-nourished body; layered, voluminous cloth and, for men, an elaborately wrapped headdress; and heavy and intricately worked silver and gold jewelry for women. Certain material items were forbidden to all but the aristocracy. Griots and smith-artisans in these societies were expected to lack reserve, dress less modestly; and say what nobles could not. Throughout

the country, however, there were minimal differences among the social strata: Within each group, all spoke the same language, ate similar foods, and lived in housing that, except for chiefs' residences, was not radically different. The external class and caste symbols, however, necessitated a relatively more comfortable lifestyle conspicuous consumption for high-status person. These distinctions also included greater monopoly over resources such as land, livestock, and trade. Despite these differences, there has always been the possibility of mobility. Today many external symbols no longer correspond to social origins, and wealth does not always coincide with prestigious status.

POLITICAL LIFE

Government. Niger is a republic, with recent alternations between military and transitional parliamentary governments. In principle, a president is elected for a five-year term through universal suffrage. The eighty-three-member *Assemblée Nationale*, which was inaugurated in 1993, was suspended in 1996. The next elections were scheduled for the years 2000 (legislative) and 2001 (presidential).

Leadership and Political Officials. The national government is headed by an appointed prime minister and the Council of Ministers. Local governmental organization is based on seven *departements*, or provinces, headed by *prefects* (similar to governors), thirty-two *arrondissements*, and one hundred fifty *communes*. The first president was overthrown by a military coup because of widespread discontent with the government's failure to distribute drought relief effectively from 1968 to 1974. After the adoption of a new constitution in December 1992, in early 1993 Niger conducted its first multiparty presidential and legislative elections since independence. The constitution provided for a semi-presidential system of government in which executive power is shared by the president of the republic, who is elected by universal suffrage for a five-year term and a prime minister named by the president. The unicameral legislature has eighty-three deputies elected for a five-year term under a system of proportional representation.

After a coup in 1999, the head of the presidential guard, Daouda Malam Wanke, was named president and head of the National Council for Reconciliation. This coalition was expected to lead Niger for a nine-month transition period. Following this period, Tandja Mamadou was sworn in as president, returning Niger to civilian rule.

Social Problems and Control. Although the main security forces consist of the army, the *gendarmerie* (rural paramilitary police), and the national police, there are alternative formal and informal mechanisms for dispute settlement and social control, particularly in rural areas. In the towns, there is a secular court system based on French law. Civil and criminal cases that do not involve security-related acts are tried publicly. Defendants have the right to be present, confront witnesses, examine the evidence against them, present evidence of their own, and choose a lawyer. Minors and defendants charged with crimes carrying a sentence of ten years or more are eligible to be defended at public expense. Defendants and prosecutors may appeal a verdict to the Court of Appeals and then to the Supreme Court. The Court of Appeals reviews questions of fact and law, while the Supreme Court reviews only the application of the law. Cases involving divorce or inheritance may be heard by a traditional chief or a customary court. Customary courts in large towns and cities are headed by a legal practitioner who is advised by an assessor who is knowledgeable about the society's traditions. The judicial actions of chiefs and customary courts are not formally regulated. Cases that are not resolved by chiefs or customary courts can be appealed to the formal court system. While there are no official religious courts, in the countryside plaintiffs first take disputes to local councils of Islamic scholars, elders, and chiefs, who arbitrate many local land disputes, marital conflicts, and thefts, sometimes referring to Koranic law. Additional, informal means of social control include gossip, praise songs, and certain "pollution beliefs" involving theft and divine retribution.

Military Activity. The president is commander in chief of the armed forces. There is a two-year period of conscription.

SOCIAL WELFARE AND CHANGE PROGRAMS

In the industrial sector, the labor federation, the National Union of Nigerien Workers (USTN), includes 423 unions representing 70 percent of the wage earners. Most of the workforce, however, is employed in subsistence agriculture and herding and artisan work and is not unionized or salaried. Thus, the majority of the USTN membership is made up of civil servants, teachers, and employees of state-owned corporations such as the national electrical utility (NIGELEC). The USTN and the Teachers Union have stated policies of political autonomy, but all unions have informal ties to political parties. There are a hundred or more trade associations. There is also an office approximating Social Security for retiring functionaries.

NONGOVERNMENTAL ORGANIZATIONS AND OTHER ASSOCIATIONS

The vast majority of people are more affected by customary informal organizations or foreign aid organizations, such as insurance-like pooling and "community chests," and by religious-sponsored charity or tithing.

GENDER ROLES AND STATUSES

Division of Labor by Gender. Although women traditionally do not take part in official political decision making and there is some division of men's and women's worlds, the local cultural ideology defines these conditions as complementary rather than unequal. Men tend to be characterized as the breadwinners and perform labor in the "public" and "official" domain as opposed to the "private and domestic" and "unofficial" domains. Men tend to travel more widely than women to do migrant labor and on caravan expeditions. Women tend to cook, act as the primary caregivers for children and aged persons, and do domestic work such as crush-

An aerial view of Agadez. Architecture reflects traditional regional and sendentarized-nomadic differences.

ing grain. In rural areas, women perform arduous physical labor such as gathering firewood hand-processing food, fetching water from the well, and building and tending cooking fires. Semi-nomadic women construct the tent, whereas men construct the adobe mud houses. Those Haussa women who are in seclusion can participate in economic activities covertly by sending cooked snacks and crafted items with children for sale at markets. Women can participate in economic activities covertly, from within their compound walls, by sending cooked snacks and crafted items with children for sale at markets. Women may become respected herbal healers.

The Relative Status of Women and Men. In 1993, the government appointed five women to ministerial positions in a twenty-eight-member cabinet. Women's organizations and other human rights groups conduct educational campaigns to increase the participation of women in the official political process. The traditional practice of husbands' casting their wives' proxies was widely used during the National Assembly elections and the first round of presidential elections. Human rights groups have tried to eliminate this practice. Despite variations among the different ethnic groups in the traditional status of women, women do not enjoy official equal legal status with men nationally.

While the head of household has certain legal rights, divorced or widowed women, even those with children, are not considered the heads of the households. Women's rights groups have been attempting to strengthen women's rights in inheritance, land tenure, and child custody and to end the practice of repudiation, which permits a husband to obtain an immediate divorce without having further responsibility for his wife and children. There is a small but increasing number of women professionals. In some regions, particularly the towns, domestic violence against women and children is widespread. Families often intervene, however, and divorce can be granted for physical abuse. In some towns, prostitution is the only economic alternative for a woman who wants to leave her husband. Some women own property: for example, some urban women own houses that they rent, and rural Tuareg women inherit, own, and manage livestock and date palms. Recently, there have been isolated incidents of violence against women for religious reasons.

MARRIAGE, FAMILY, AND KINSHIP

Marriage. First marriages are almost always arranged by the parents in both rural and urban communities. Usually, there are no "forced" unions;

A nomadic teacher uses a rock as a blackboard during a lesson at a temporary school near Arlit.

unwanted suitors may be vetoed by either potential partner, but youths cannot easily marry someone of whom their parents disapprove. Traditional parental preferences for social stratum endogamy and cousin marriage are breaking down in the towns. Men can have up to four wives, according to Islamic law. Not all men have the economic means to practice polygyny, which is slightly more prevalent in towns. It is rarer in more nomadic groups and more commonly practiced in sedentarized communities and among clans of Islamic scholars. Most people marry unless they are severely disabled. Divorce rates vary within ethnic groups. Remarriage varies with the age and local status of a divorced woman.

Domestic Unit. In general, the compound, either walled or fenced in, is the basic domestic unit; in rural areas, it is also the basic unit of production. Among the rural Haussa, compounds are organized around a postmarital residence pattern of a married father and his sons with their wives in a large extended household that is organized around traditional farming labor. Among the Tuareg, rural compounds tend to be somewhat smaller, ideally constituting more nuclear households, but adjacent to or near compounds of the married couple's parents. Initially, there are two to three years of uxorilocal residence, followed by possible virilocal

residence after the paying of the bride wealth and groom service and stable marriage if the couple chooses to move. In the major towns, compounds tend to be located farther from kin than they are in the countryside, and many unrelated persons may rent within the same compound.

Inheritance. Many groups practice patrilineal Islamic-influenced inheritance. There are also bilateral inheritance practices and much informal preinherited property in the form of gifts. Some groups have alternative, non-Koranic forms of inheritance.

SOCIALIZATION

Infant Care. Infants generally are not placed in separate spaces to sleep and play; they usually are kept in close proximity almost as an extension of the mother's body. The mother usually carries the infant on her back in a cloth or in a goat-hide sling over the shoulder. Most infants are breast-fed. As infants mature, older female siblings usually take over much of the child care. Parents often play with and sing songs to babies who cry. Other games include playing at "riding" camels or horses. Babies and toddlers are allowed to explore and wander widely. Weaning occurs at approximately two-and-a-half years of age in most groups.

Child Rearing and Education. Early childhood is characterized by rather lax discipline. Children are permitted considerable verbal license toward certain persons. Among the Haussa particularly, children act as important go-betweens and intermediaries for adults, often entering spaces where adults cannot go. Cultural values that are inculcated early in childhood include an emphasis on generosity and sharing, respect toward adult authority figures such as Islamic scholars and elders, and careful observation of adult tasks in apprenticeships. There are clearly demarcated rites of passage; name days, popularly called by the French term *bapteme*, are celebrated among all groups one week after a birth and the conferring of a Koranic name on the child. The child's hair is shaved to sever ties with the spirit world. In rural areas, male circumcision usually is performed by a specialist called a barber when boys are three to seven years old. The next important rite of passage is marriage. General similarities include the practice of secluding the bride, sharp social and ritual spatial segregation of the bride's and groom's families; and the use of henna on the hands and feet. Wedding rituals often include pre-Islamic as well as Islamic ritual phases.

Higher Education. In rural areas, many families discourage girls from pursuing an education beyond primary school. At the one university, the University of Niamey, males predominate. Among some groups, particularly the nomads in the north, many families opposed all secular schools until recently, fearing them as sources of government control and cultural change.

ETIQUETTE

General rules of conduct include the importance of greetings, many of which are elaborate. Among all ethnic and cultural groups, it is considered extremely rude to approach someone with a question or statement without a preliminary greeting. French business formats and salutations are the rule. Indirect expression is the ideal, particularly between high-status persons. It is considered rude to overtly refuse to do something or strongly contradict someone. Dress should be modest and neat among both men and women. Recently, there has been violence against women wearing clothing considered immodest by Islamic reformists. Among many persons, ideally some bodily distance is maintained, although close friends of the same sex frequently walk arm in arm.

A woman buying peppers at the market in Naimey; there are permanent markets in major towns and market days in rural communities.

RELIGION

Religious Beliefs. Islam is the religion of 98 percent of the population, followed by traditional religions and Christianity. There is a great deal of religious tolerance, and many Islamic beliefs and practices are strongly influenced and modified by the local cultures. Many local cosmologies and rituals have both Islamic and pre-Islamic elements. Haussa and Zarma-Songhai rituals feature particularly elaborate spirit pantheons. Pre-Islamic myths and rituals coexist in local historical consciousness with Koranic traditions.

Religious Practitioners. Islamic scholars combine medical-psychiatric and legal skills, particularly in rural communities. Marabouts also enact important Muslim rituals, such as animal sacrifice, naming, marriage, and funeral condolences. A specialist called an *imam* leads the call to prayer. In rural Tuareg society, smith-artisans play important ritual roles. Additional religious specialists include *zima* spirit mediums among the Zarma-Songhai, *bori* (possession) leaders among the Haussa, and some persons in all groups who are believed to bring rain.

Rituals and Holy Places. Rites of passage are prominent. Spirit possession exorcism and mediumship rituals also are widely practiced. Other ceremonies take place on official Muslim holidays. The Friday prayer takes place at a special prayer ground near the mosque. In parts of the northern Air Mountain region, there are sacred places associated with prominent marabouts and more specialized holy clans claiming descent from Muhammad called *icherifan*, and places of pilgrimage where marabouts travel for conferences. Throughout the countryside, designated places are demarcated as spaces for smith-artisans and herbalists to conduct ritual preparations and communicate with spirits, such as the ruins of ancestral houses and special natural features (rocks, medicinal trees). Tombs of prominent marabouts usually are set apart from ordinary cemeteries.

Death and the Afterlife. Islam influences beliefs and practices surrounding death. Mortuary ceremonies consist of preparation of the body, burial, and a series of ritual meals with Koranic readings and alms giving called condolences. Burial takes place soon after death. The body is washed and wrapped in a white shroud and then taken by men chanting Koranic liturgical music to the grave site. A marabout reads verses from the Koran and leads the prayer. Upon the internment, two lines are formed so that the angel of death may pass through. Women remain at home during this phase but are very active in mortuary rites. Condolences consist of ritual meals held one week after death and repeated at various intervals. At the initial condolence ceremony, the marabout officiates, transmitting his religious blessing or benediction (called *al baraka*) to the guests. Beliefs concerning the afterlife include pre-Islamic elements. It is believed that an angel weighs good and evil deeds at a final judgment and that the deceased subsequently enters paradise or various levels of hell. Alongside these beliefs, however, traditional beliefs regarding ancestors, souls, and spirits persist.

MEDICINE AND HEALTH CARE

There are two broad categories of health care. The first includes government-sponsored institutions with workers trained in Western biomedicine: several hospitals in the major towns and in the capital city of Niger, clinics in rural areas, mobile immunization health units, and traditional healing specialists. The second category consists of "traditional" or local healing specialists and practitioners: Koranic/Islamic scholars and a more specialized group who claim descent from the Prophet; non-Koranic healers whose means include divination and herbal medicine; bone setters; and various ritual adepts or cult leaders, such as musicians, in spirit possession and mediumship. Some patients alternate between and combine treatments from the various healers, and there are shortages of medicines such as antibiotics. Some rural people, particularly women, are hesitant to use hospitals and clinics. There have been sporadic efforts to integrate some traditional healers, such as herbal medicine women, into the Western biomedical establishment through training programs and certification. In Niamey, there has been a proliferation of private practices, but private medical insurance is not available to the vast majority of people. Many uncontrolled medical substances are hawked on the streets. The risk-sharing arrangements that exist are primarily employer-based programs in urban areas. In rural communities, traditional practitioners remain important. Islamic scholars heal with verses from the Koran and perform Koranic ritual divination and social and psychiatric counseling. Those healers, sometimes called "sorcerers," often divine with plants, perfumes, cowrie shells, and other means. Herbalists work with tree bark, leaves, and roots and conduct ritual incantations and sometimes serve more specialized functions such as marital counseling. Spirit possession specialists provide music that is believed to enhance communication with the spirits that possess the person in trance. Possession rituals are usually public events, with musicians, audience, and trance adepts all interacting in a form of group therapy.

SECULAR CELEBRATIONS

National holidays include New Year's Day, 1 January; Niger Independence Day, 8 August; and Niger Republic Day, 18 December. Government offices, including foreign embassies, are closed on those days, which feature parades, political speeches, and folkloric performances. There are also several Christian and Muslim holidays.

THE ARTS AND HUMANITIES

Support for the Arts. There is great appreciation for the arts and literature. Visual art, theater, and musical performances are connected to the traditional but changing roles of artisans and oral historians. The National Museum and several privately and publicly-funded artisan workshop and cooperatives support jewelry, leather work, pottery, and other art production. There are prominent modern literary authors, essayists, poets, and painters. A well-known Tuareg painter, Rissa Ixa, founded the Association for the Promotion and Development of Traditional Arts and Cultures in Niger. A Haussa painter in Maradi produces paintings that comment on local social and political issues, and there are many novelists.

Literature. Literary production includes both traditional oral and verbal art forms and contemporary written forms that appear both in French and in local vernacular languages. Niger has a vast repertoire of oral art, based on traditions of oral historians and smith-artisans, much of which has been transcribed and published by the national press through the support of artists and scholars connected to the University of Niamey. This repertoire includes battle and epic praise poetry, love poetry, current political songs, proverbs, and riddles. Zarma-Songhai and Haussa plays often address current events.

THE STATE OF THE PHYSICAL AND SOCIAL SCIENCES

Niger has a number of prominent researchers, particularly in history, sociology, ethnology, and literature. The *Centre National de Recherches en Sciences Humaines* conducts research, mostly in the humanities but also in the sciences and social sciences, and publishes *Etudes Nigeriennes*. The *Musee National* is also nominally the responsibility of the Centre. The University of Niamey was created in 1974, and the Centre, now known as *IRSH or l'Institut des recherches en sciences humaines* (Human Sciences Research Institute) was attached to it. CELTHO (Center for the Study of Oral History) is sponsored by the United Nations and the Organization of African Unity.

BIBLIOGRAPHY

Charlick, Robert. *Niger: Personal Rule and Survival in the Sahel*, 1991.

Decalo, Samuel. *Historical Dictionary of Niger*, 3rd ed., 1997.

Fuglestad, Finn. *A History of Niger 1850–1960*, 1983.

Human Rights Watch. *Niger: Human Rights Report*, 1993.

Masquelier, Adeline. "Narratives of Power, Images of Wealth: The Ritual Economy of Bori in the Market." In Jean Comaroff and John Comaroff, eds., *Modernity and Its Malcontents*, 1993.

Rasmussen, Susan. *Spirit Possession and Personhood among the Kel Ewey Tuareg*, 1995.

———. *The Poetics and Politics of Tuareg Aging: Life Course and Personal Destiny in Niger*, 1997.

Schmoll, Pamela. "Black Stomachs, Beautiful Stones: Soul-Eating among Haussa in Niger." In Jean Comaroff and John Comaroff, eds., *Modernity and Its Malcontents*, 1993.

Stoller, Paul. *Fusion of the Worlds: An Ethnography of Possession among the Songhay of Niger*, 1989.

———. *Embodying Cultural Memories: Spirit Possession, Power, and the Hauka in West Africa*, 1995.

———, and Cheryl Olkes. *In Sorcery's Shadow*, 1987.

U. S. Department of State, Bureau of African Affairs. *Niger: Background Notes*, 1994.

Weaver, Marcia, Holly Wong, Amadou Sekou Sako, Robert Simon, and Felix Lee. "Patient Fees in the Niamey Hospital." *Social Science and Medicine* 38: 563–574, 1994.

—SUSAN J. RASMUSSEN

NIGERIA

CULTURE NAME

Nigerian

ORIENTATION

Identification. Though there is archaeological evidence that societies have been living in Nigeria for more than twenty-five hundred years, the borders of modern Nigeria were not created until the British consolidated their colonial power over the area in 1914.

The name Nigeria was suggested by British journalist Flora Shaw in the 1890s. She referred to the area as Nigeria, after the Niger River, which dominates much of the country's landscape. The word *niger* is Latin for black.

More than 250 ethnic tribes call present-day Nigeria home. The three largest and most dominant ethnic groups are the Hausa, Yoruba, and Igbo (pronounced ee-bo). Other smaller groups include the Fulani, Ijaw, Kanuri, Ibibio, Tiv, and Edo. Prior to their conquest by Europeans, these ethnic groups had separate and independent histories. Their grouping together into a single entity known as Nigeria was a construct of their British colonizers. These various ethnic groups never considered themselves part of the same culture. This general lack of Nigerian nationalism coupled with an ever-changing and often ethnically biased national leadership, have led to severe internal ethnic conflicts and a civil war. Today bloody confrontations between or among members of different ethnic groups continue.

Location and Geography. Nigeria is in West Africa, along the eastern coast of the Gulf of Guinea, and just north of the equator. It is bordered on the west by Benin, on the north by Niger and Chad, and on the east by Cameroon. Nigeria covers an area of 356,669 square miles (923,768 square kilometers), or about twice the size of California.

Nigeria has three main environmental regions: savanna, tropical forests, and coastal wetlands. These environmental regions greatly affect the cultures of the people who live there. The dry, open grasslands of the savanna make cereal farming and herding a way of life for the Hausa and the Fulani. The wet tropical forests to the south are good for farming fruits and vegetables—main income producers for the Yoruba, Igbo, and others in this area. The small ethnic groups living along the coast, such as the Ijaw and the Kalabari, are forced to keep their villages small due to lack of dry land. Living among creeks, lagoons, and salt marshes makes fishing and the salt trade part of everyday life in the area.

The Niger and Benue Rivers come together in the center of the country, creating a ''Y'' that splits Nigeria into three separate sections. In general, this ''Y'' marks the boundaries of the three major ethnic groups, with the Hausa in the north, the Yoruba in the southwest, and the Igbo in the southeast.

Politically, Nigeria is divided into thirty-six states. The nation's capital was moved from Lagos, the country's largest city, to Abuja on 12 December 1991. Abuja is in a federal territory that is not part of any state. While Abuja is the official capital, its lack of adequate infrastructure means that Lagos remains the financial, commercial, and diplomatic center of the country.

Demography. Nigeria has the largest population of any African country. In July 2000, Nigeria's population was estimated at more than 123 million people. At about 345 people per square mile, it is also the most densely populated country in Africa. Nearly one in six Africans is a Nigerian. Despite the rampages of AIDS, Nigeria's population continues to grow at about 2.6 percent each year. The Nigerian population is very young. Nearly 45 percent of its people are under age fourteen.

With regard to ethnic breakdown, the Hausa-Fulani make up 29 percent of the population, followed by the Yoruba with 21 percent, the Igbo with

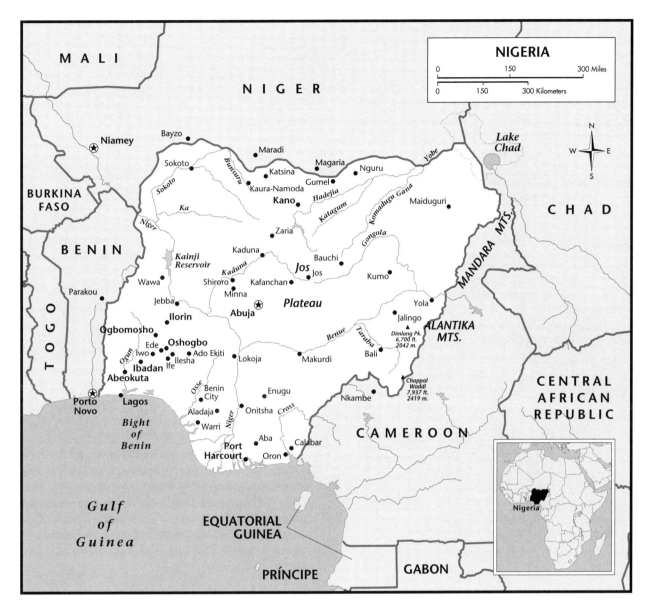

Nigeria

18 percent, the Ijaw with 10 percent, the Kanuri with 4 percent, the Ibibio with 3.5 percent, and the Tiv with 2.5 percent.

Major urban centers include Lagos, Ibidan, Kaduna, Kano, and Port Harcourt.

Linguistic Affiliations. English is the official language of Nigeria, used in all government interactions and in state-run schools. In a country with more than 250 individual tribal languages, English is the only language common to most people.

Unofficially, the country's second language is Hausa. In northern Nigeria many people who are not ethnic Hausas speak both Hausa and their own tribal language. Hausa is the oldest known written language in West Africa, dating back to before 1000 C.E.

The dominant indigenous languages of the south are Yoruba and Igbo. Prior to colonization, these languages were the unifying languages of the southwest and southeast, respectively, regardless of ethnicity. However, since the coming of the British and the introduction of mission schools in southern Nigeria, English has become the language common to most people in the area. Today those who are not ethnic Yorubas or Igbos rarely speak Yoruba or Igbo.

Pidgin, a mix of African languages and English, also is common throughout southern Nigeria. It basically uses English words mixed into Yoruban or Igbo grammar structures. Pidgin originally evolved from the need for British sailors to find a way to communicate with local merchants. Today it is often used in ethnically mixed urban areas as a common form of communication among people who have not had formal education in English.

Symbolism. Because there is little feeling of national unity among Nigeria's people, there is little in terms of national symbolism. What exists was usually created or unveiled by the government as representative of the nation. The main national symbol is the country's flag. The flag is divided vertically into three equal parts; the center section is white, flanked by two green sections. The green of the flag represents agriculture, while the white stands for unity and peace. Other national symbols include the national coat of arms, the national anthem, the National Pledge (similar to the Pledge of Allegiance in the United States), and Nigeria's national motto: Peace and Unity, Strength and Progress.

HISTORY AND ETHNIC RELATIONS

Emergence of the Nation. Every ethnic group in Nigeria has its own stories of where its ancestors came from. These vary from tales of people descending from the sky to stories of migration from far-off places. Archaeologists have found evidence of Neolithic humans who inhabited what is now Nigeria as far back as 12,000 B.C.E.

The histories of the people in northern and southern Nigeria prior to colonization followed vastly different paths. The first recorded empire in present-day Nigeria was centered in the north at Kanem-Borno, near Lake Chad. This empire came to power during the eighth century C.E. By the thirteenth century, many Hausa states began to emerge in the region as well.

Trans-Sahara trade with North Africans and Arabs began to transform these northern societies greatly. Increased contact with the Islamic world led to the conversion of the Kanem-Borno Empire to Islam in the eleventh century. This led to a ripple effect of conversions throughout the north. Islam brought with it changes in law, education, and politics.

The trans-Sahara trade also brought with it revolutions in wealth and class structure. As the centuries went on, strict Islamists, many of whom were poor Fulani, began to tire of increasing corrup-

tion, excessive taxation, and unfair treatment of the poor. In 1804 the Fulani launched a jihad, or Muslim holy war, against the Hausa states in an attempt to cleanse them of these non-Muslim behaviors and to reintroduce proper Islamic ways. By 1807 the last Hausa state had fallen. The Fulani victors founded the Sokoto Caliphate, which grew to become the largest state in West Africa until its conquest by the British in 1903.

In the south, the Oyo Empire grew to become the most powerful Yoruban society during the sixteenth century. Along the coast, the Edo people established the Benin Empire (not to be confused with the present-day country of Benin to the west), which reached its height of power in the fifteenth and sixteenth centuries.

As in the north, outsiders heavily influenced the societies of southern Nigeria. Contact with Europeans began with the arrival of Portuguese ships in 1486. The British, French, and Dutch soon followed. Soon after their arrival, the trade in slaves replaced the original trade in goods. Many of the coastal communities began selling their neighbors, whom they had captured in wars and raids, to the Europeans in exchange for things such as guns, metal, jewelry, and liquor.

The slave trade had major social consequences for the Africans. Violence and intertribal warfare increased as the search for slaves intensified. The increased wealth accompanying the slave trade began to change social structures in the area. Leadership, which had been based on tradition and ritual, soon became based on wealth and economic power.

After more than 350 years of slave trading, the British decided that the slave trade was immoral and, in 1807, ordered it stopped. They began to force their newfound morality on the Nigerians. Many local leaders, however, continued to sell captives to illegal slave traders. This lead to confrontations with the British Navy, which took on the responsibility of enforcing the slave embargo. In 1851 the British attacked Lagos to try to stem the flow of slaves from the area. By 1861 the British government had annexed the city and established its first official colony in Nigeria.

As the nonslave trade began to flourish, so, too, did the Nigerian economy. A new economy based on raw materials, agricultural products, and locally manufactured goods saw the growth of a new class of Nigerian merchants. These merchants were heavily influenced by Western ways. Many soon became involved in politics, often criticizing chiefs for keeping to their traditional ways. A new divide within

Central Ibadan, the second-largest city. Nigeria is the most densely populated country in Africa.

the local communities began to develop, in terms of both wealth and politics. Because being a successful merchant was based on production and merit, not on traditional community standing, many former slaves and lower-class people soon found that they could advance quickly up the social ladder. It was not unusual to find a former slave transformed into the richest, most powerful man in the area.

Christian missionaries brought Western-style education to Nigeria as Christianity quickly spread throughout the south. The mission schools created

an educated African elite who also sought increased contact with Europe and a Westernization of Nigeria.

In 1884, as European countries engaged in a race to consolidate their African territories, the British Army and local merchant militias set out to conquer the Africans who refused to recognize British rule. In 1914, after squelching the last of the indigenous opposition, Britain officially established the Colony and Protectorate of Nigeria.

National Identity. The spread of overt colonial control led to the first and only time that the ethnic groups in modern Nigeria came together under a commonly felt sense of national identity. The Africans began to see themselves not as Hausas, Igbos, or Yorubas, but as Nigerians in a common struggle against their colonial rulers.

The nationalistic movement grew out of some of the modernization the British had instituted in Nigeria. The educated elite became some of the most outspoken proponents of an independent Nigeria. This elite had grown weary of the harsh racism it faced in business and administrative jobs within the government. Both the elite and the uneducated also began to grow fearful of the increasing loss of traditional culture. They began movements to promote Nigerian foods, names, dress, languages, and religions.

Increased urbanization and higher education brought large multiethnic groups together for the first time. As a result of this coming together, the Nigerians saw that they had more in common with each other than they had previously thought. This sparked unprecedented levels of interethnic teamwork. Nigerian political movements, media outlets, and trade unions whose purpose was the advancement of all Nigerians, not specific ethnic groups, became commonplace.

As calls for self-determination and a transfer of power into the hands of Nigerians grew, Britain began to divest more power into the regional governments. As a result of early colonial policies of divide and conquer, the regional governments tended to be drawn along ethnic lines. With this move to greater regional autonomy, the idea of a unified Nigeria became to crumble. Regionally and ethnically based political parties sprang up as ethnic groups began to wrangle for political influence.

Ethnic Relations. Nigeria gained full independence from Britain on 1 October 1960. Immediately following independence, vicious fighting between and among political parties created chaos within the fledgling democracy. On 15 January 1966 a group of army officers, most of whom were Igbo, staged a military coup, killing many of the government ministers from the western and northern tribes. Six months later, northern forces within the military staged a countercoup, killing most of the Igbo leaders. Anti-Igbo demonstrations broke out across the country, especially in the north. Hundreds of Igbos were killed, while the rest fled to the southeast.

On 26 May 1967 the Igbo-dominated southeast declared it had broken away from Nigeria to form the independent Republic of Biafra. This touched off a bloody civil war that lasted for three years. In 1970, on the brink of widespread famine resulting from a Nigeria-imposed blockade, Biafra was forced to surrender. Between five hundred thousand and two million Biafran civilians were killed during the civil war, most dying from starvation, not combat.

Following the war, the military rulers encouraged a national reconciliation, urging Nigerians to once again become a unified people. While this national reconciliation succeeded in reintegrating the Biafrans into Nigeria, it did not end the problems of ethnicity in the country. In the years that followed, Nigeria was continually threatened by disintegration due to ethnic fighting. These ethnic conflicts reached their height in the 1990s.

After decades of military rule, elections for a new civilian president were finally held on 12 June 1993. A wealthy Yoruba Muslim named Moshood Abiola won the elections, beating the leading Hausa candidate. Abiola won support not only from his own people but from many non-Yorubas as well, including many Hausas. This marked the first time since Nigeria's independence that Nigerians broke from ethnically based voting practices. Two weeks later, however, the military regime had the election results annulled and Abiola imprisoned. Many commanders in the Hausa-dominated military feared losing control to a southerner. They played on the nation's old ethnic distrusts, hoping that a divided nation would be easier to control. This soon created a new ethnic crisis. The next five years saw violent protests and mass migrations as ethnic groups again retreated to their traditional homelands.

The sudden death of Nigeria's last military dictator, General Suni Abacha, on 8 June 1998 opened the door for a transition back to civilian rule. Despite age-old ethnic rivalries, many Nigerians again crossed ethnic lines when they entered the voting booth. On 22 February 1999 Olusegun Obasanjo, a Yoruba who ironically lacked support from his own people, won the presidential election. Obasanjo is seen as a nationalist who opposed ethnic divisions. However, some northern leaders believe he favors his own ethnic group.

Unfortunately, violent ethnic fighting in Nigeria continues. In October 2000, clashes between Hausas and supporters of the Odua People's Congress (OPC), a militant Yoruba group, led to the deaths of nearly a hundred people in Lagos. Many also blame the OPC for sparking riots in 1999, which killed more than a hundred others, most of them Hausas.

URBANISM, ARCHITECTURE, AND THE USE OF SPACE

With the influx of oil revenue and foreigners, Nigerian cities have grown to resemble many Western urban centers. Lagos, for example, is a massive, overcrowded city filled with traffic jams, movie theaters, department stores, restaurants, and supermarkets. Because most Nigerian cities grew out of much older towns, very little urban planning was used as the cities expanded. Streets are laid out in a confusing and often mazelike fashion, adding to the chaos for pedestrians and traffic. The influx of people into urban areas has put a strain on many services. Power cuts and disruptions of telephone service are not uncommon.

Nigerian architecture is as diverse as its people. In rural areas, houses often are designed to accommodate the environment in which the people live. The Ijo live in the Niger Delta region, where dry land is very scarce. To compensate for this, many Ijo homes are built on stilts over creeks and swamps, with travel between them done by boat. The houses are made of wood and bamboo and topped with a roof made of fronds from raffia palms. The houses are very airy, to allow heat and the smoke from cooking fires to escape easily.

Igbo houses tend to be made of a bamboo frame held together with vines and mud and covered with banana leaves. They often blend into the surrounding forest and can be easily missed if you don't know where to look. Men and women traditionally live in separate houses.

Much of the architecture in the north is heavily influenced by Muslim culture. Homes are typically geometric, mud-walled structures, often with Muslim markings and decorations. The Hausa build large, walled compounds housing several smaller huts. The entryway into the compound is via a large hut built into the wall of the compound. This is the hut of the father or head male figure in the compound.

FOOD AND ECONOMY

Food in Daily Life. Western influences, especially in urban centers, have transformed Nigerian eating habits in many ways. City dwellers are familiar with the canned, frozen, and prepackaged foods found in most Western-style supermarkets. Foreign restaurants also are common in larger cities. However, supermarkets and restaurants often are too expensive for the average Nigerian; thus only the wealthy can afford to eat like Westerners. Most urban Nigerians seem to combine traditional cuisine with a little of Western-style foods and conveniences. Rural Nigerians tend to stick more with traditional foods and preparation techniques.

Food in Nigeria is traditionally eaten by hand. However, with the growing influence of Western culture, forks and spoons are becoming more common, even in remote villages. Whether people eat with their hand or a utensil, it is considered dirty and rude to eat using the left hand.

While the ingredients in traditional plates vary from region to region, most Nigerian cuisine tends to be based around a few staple foods accompanied by a stew. In the south, crops such as corn, yams, and sweet potatoes form the base of the diet. These vegetables are often pounded into a thick, sticky dough or paste. This is often served with a palm oil-based stew made with chicken, beef, goat, tomatoes, okra, onions, bitter leaves, or whatever meats and vegetables might be on hand. Fruits such as papaya, pineapples, coconuts, oranges, mangoes, and bananas also are very common in the tropical south.

In the north, grains such as millet, sorghum, and corn are boiled into a porridge-like dish that forms the basis of the diet. This is served with an oil-based soup usually flavored with onions, okra, and tomatoes. Sometimes meat is included, though among the Hausa it is often reserved for special occasions. Thanks to the Fulani cattle herders, fresh milk and yogurt are common even though there may not be refrigeration.

Alcohol is very popular in the south but less so in the north, where there is a heavy Islamic influence. Perhaps the most popular form of alcohol is palm wine, a tart alcoholic drink that comes from palm trees. Palm wine is often distilled further to make a strong, ginlike liquor. Nigerian breweries also produce several kinds of beer and liquor.

Food Customs at Ceremonial Occasions. Food plays a central role in the rituals of virtually all ethnic groups in Nigeria. Special ceremonies would not be complete without participants sharing in a meal. Normally it is considered rude not to invite guests to share in a meal when they visit; it is even more so if the visitors were invited to attend a special event such as a marriage or a naming ceremony.

Basic Economy. Until the past few decades, Nigeria had been self-sufficient in producing enough food to feed the population. However, as petroleum production and industry began to boom in Nigeria, much of the national resources were concentrated on the new industries at the expense of agriculture.

Homes and market near the Lagos Lagoon. Nigerian cities have grown to resemble western urban centers.

Nigeria, which had previously been a net exporter of agricultural products, soon needed to import vast amounts of food it once was able to produce for itself.

Since the 1960s, Nigeria's economy has been based on oil production. As a leading member of the Organization of Petroleum Exporting Countries (OPEC), Nigeria has played a major role in influencing the price of oil on the world market. The oil-rich economy led to a major economic boom for Nigeria during the 1970s, transforming the poor African country into the thirtieth richest country in the world. However, falling oil prices, severe corruption, political instability, and economic mismanagement since then have left Nigeria no better off today than it was at independence.

Since the restoration of civilian rule in 1999, Nigeria has begun to make strides in economic reform. While hopes are high for a strong economic transformation, high unemployment, high inflation, and more than a third of the population living under the poverty line indicate it will be a long and difficult road.

Oil production has had some long-lasting ethnic consequences as well. While oil is Nigeria's largest industry in terms of output and revenue, oil reserves are found only in the Niger Delta region and along the coast. The government has long taken the oil revenues and dispersed them throughout the country. In this way, states not involved in oil production still get a share of the profits. This has led to claims that the minority ethnic groups living in the delta are being cheated out of revenue that is rightfully theirs because the larger ethnic groups dominate politics. Sometimes this has led to large-scale violence.

More than 50 percent of Nigeria's population works in the agriculture sector. Most farmers engage in subsistence farming, producing only what they eat themselves or sell locally. Very few agricultural products are produced for export.

Land Tenure and Property. While the federal government has the legal right to allocate land as it sees fit, land tenure remains largely a local issue. Most local governments follow traditional land tenure customs in their areas. For example, in Hausa society, title to land is not an absolute right. While communities and officials will honor long-standing hereditary rights to areas of land traditionally claimed by a given family, misused or abandoned land may be reapportioned for better use. Land also can be bought, sold, or rented. In the west, the Yoruban kings historically held all the land in trust, and therefore also had a say in how it was used for the good of the community. This has given local governments in modern times a freer hand in settling land disputes.

Traditionally, only men hold land, but as the wealth structure continues to change and develop in Nigeria, it would not be unheard of for a wealthy woman to purchase land for herself.

Major Industries. Aside from petroleum and petroleum-based products, most of the goods produced in Nigeria are consumed within Nigeria. For example, though the textile industry is very strong, nearly all the cloth produced in Nigeria goes to clothing the large Nigerian population.

Major agricultural products produced in Nigeria include cocoa, peanuts, palm oil, rice, millet, corn, cassava, yams, rubber, cattle, sheep, goats, pigs, timber, and fish. Major commercial industries in Nigeria include coal, tin, textiles, footwear, fertilizer, printing, ceramics, and steel.

Trade. Oil and petroleum-based products made up 95 percent of Nigeria's exports in 1998. Cocoa and rubber are also produced for export. Major export partners include the United States, Spain, India, France, and Italy.

Nigeria is a large-scale importer, depending on other countries for things such as machinery, chemicals, transportation equipment, and manufactured goods. The country also must import large quantities of food and livestock. Major import partners include the United Kingdom, the United States, Germany, France, and the Netherlands.

SOCIAL STRATIFICATION

Classes and Castes. The highest tier of Nigerian society is made up of wealthy politicians, businessmen, and the educated elite. These people, however, make up only a tiny portion of the Nigerian population. Many Nigerians today suffer under great poverty. The lower classes tend have little chance of breaking from the vicious cycle of poverty. Poor education, lack of opportunities, ill health, corrupt politicians, and lack of even small amounts of wealth for investment all work to keep the lower classes in their place.

In some Nigerian ethnic groups there is also a form of caste system that treats certain members of society as pariahs. The criteria for determining who belongs to this lowest caste vary from area to area but can include being a member of a minority group, an inhabitant of a specific village, or a member of a specific family or clan. The Igbo call this lower-caste group Osu. Members of the community will often discourage personal, romantic, and business contact with any member of the Osu group, regardless of an individual's personal merits or characteristics. Because the Osu are designated as untouchable, they often lack political representation, access to basic educational or business opportunities, and general social interaction. This kind of caste system is also found among the Yoruba and the Ibibios.

Symbols of Social Stratification. Wealth is the main symbol of social stratification in modern Nigeria, especially in urban areas. While in the past many ethnic groups held hereditary titles and traditional lineage important, money has become the new marker of power and social status. Today the members of the wealthy elite are easily identifiable by their fancy clothing and hairstyles and by their expensive cars and Western-style homes. Those in the elite also tend to have a much better command of English, a reflection of the higher quality of education they have received.

A man places skewers of meat in a circle around a fire. Rural Nigerians favor traditional foods and preparation techniques.

Wealth also can be important in marking social boundaries in rural areas. In many ethnic groups, those who have accumulated enough wealth can buy themselves local titles. For example, among the Igbo, a man or a woman who has enough money may claim the title of *Ozo*. For women, one of the requirements to become an *Ozo* is to have enough ivory, coral, and other jewelry for the ceremony. The weight of the jewelry can often exceed fifty pounds. Both men and women who want to claim the title must also finance a feast for the entire community.

POLITICAL LIFE

Government. Nigeria is a republic, with the president acting as both head of state and head of government. Nigeria has had a long history of *coups d'états*, military rule, and dictatorship. However, this pattern was broken on 29 May 1999 as Nigeria's current president, Olusegun Obasanjo, took office following popular elections. Under the current constitution, presidential elections are to be held every four years, with no president serving more than two terms in office. The Nigerian legislature consists of two houses: a Senate and a House of Representatives. All legislators are elected to four-year terms. Nigeria's judicial branch is headed by a Supreme Court, whose members were appointed by the Provisional Ruling Council, which ruled Nigeria during its recent transition to democracy. All Nigerians over age eighteen are eligible to vote.

Leadership and Political Officials. A wealthy political elite dominates political life in Nigeria. The relationship between the political elite and ordinary Nigerians is not unlike that between nobles and commoners. Nigerian leaders, whether as members of a military regime or one of Nigeria's short-lived civilian governments, have a history of doing whatever it takes to stay in power and to hold on to the wealth that this power has given them.

Rural Nigerians tend to accept this noble-peasant system of politics. Low levels of education and literacy mean that many people in rural areas are not fully aware of the political process or how to affect it. Their relative isolation from the rest of the country means that many do not even think of politics. There is a common feeling in many rural areas that the average person cannot affect the politics of the country, so there is no reason to try.

Urban Nigerians tend to be much more vocal in their support of or opposition to their leaders. Urban problems of housing, unemployment, health care, sanitation, and traffic tend to mobilize people into political action and public displays of dissatisfaction.

Political parties were outlawed under the Abacha regime, and only came back into being after his death. As of the 1999 presidential elections, there were three main political parties in Nigeria: the People's Democratic Party (PDP), the All Peoples Party (APP), and the Alliance for Democracy (AD). The PDP is the party of President Obasanjo. It grew out of support for opposition leaders who were imprisoned by the military government in the early 1990s. The PDP is widely believed to have received heavy financial assistance from the military during the 1999 elections. The APP is led by politicians who had close ties to the Abacha regime. The AD is a party led by followers of the late Moshood Abiola, the Yoruba politician who won the general election in 1993, only to be sent to prison by the military regime.

Social Problems and Control. Perhaps Nigeria's greatest social problem is the internal violence plaguing the nation. Interethnic fighting throughout the country, religious rioting between Muslims and non-Muslims over the creation of Shari'a law (strict Islamic law) in the northern states, and political confrontations between ethnic minorities and backers of oil companies often spark bloody confrontations that can last days or even months. When violence of this type breaks out, national and state police try to control it. However, the police themselves are often accused of some of the worst violence. In some instances, curfews and martial law have been imposed in specific areas to try to stem outbreaks of unrest.

Poverty and lack of opportunity for many young people, especially in urban areas, have led to major crime. Lagos is considered one of the most dangerous cities in West Africa due to its incredibly high crime rate. The police are charged with controlling crime, but their lack of success often leads to vigilante justice.

In some rural areas there are some more traditional ways of addressing social problems. In many ethnic groups, such as the Igbo and the Yoruba, men are organized into secret societies. Initiated members of these societies often dress in masks and palm leaves to masquerade as the physical embodiment of traditional spirits to help maintain social order. Through ritual dance, these men will give warnings about problems with an individual's or community's morality in a given situation. Because belief in witchcraft and evil spirits is high through-out Nigeria, this kind of public accusation can instill fear in people and cause them to mend their ways. Members of secret societies also can act as judges or intermediaries in disputes.

Military Activity. Nigeria's military consists of an army, a navy, an air force, and a police force. The minimum age for military service is eighteen.

The Nigerian military is the largest and best-equipped military in West Africa. As a member of the Economic Community of West African States (ECOWAS), Nigeria is the major contributor to the organization's military branch, known as ECOMOG. Nigerian troops made up the vast majority of the ECOMOG forces deployed to restore peace following civil wars in Liberia, Guinea-Bissau, and Sierra Leone. Public dissatisfaction with Nigeria's participation in the Sierra Leonean crisis was extremely high due to high casualty rates among the Nigerian soldiers. Nigeria pledged to pull out of Sierra Leone in 1999, prompting the United Nations to send in peacekeepers in an attempt stem the violence. While the foreign forces in Sierra Leone are now under the mandate of the United Nations, Nigerian troops still make up the majority of the peacekeepers.

Nigeria has a long-running border dispute with Cameroon over the mineral-rich Bakasi Peninsula, and the two nations have engaged in a series of cross-boarder skirmishes. Nigeria, Cameroon, Niger, and Chad also have a long-running border dispute over territory in the Lake Chad region, which also has led to some fighting across the borders.

SOCIAL WELFARE AND CHANGE PROGRAMS

Severe poverty, human rights violations, and corruption are some of the major social ills that have plagued Nigeria for decades. Because Nigeria is in the midst of major political change, however, there is great hope for social reform in the country.

President Obasanjo's administration has been focusing much of its efforts on changing the world's image of Nigeria. Many foreign companies have been reluctant to invest in Nigeria for fear of political instability. Obasanjo hopes that if Nigeria can project the image of a stable nation, he can coax foreign investors to come to Nigeria and help bolster the country's failing economy. The World Bank and the International Monetary Fund (IMF) are also working with Nigeria to develop economic policies that will revitalize the nation's economy.

Obasanjo also says that rooting out corruption in all levels of government is one of his top priori-

A man sells patterned cloth at a market. Nigerians are expert dyers, weavers, and tailors.

ties. He signed the Anti-Corruption Act in June 2000, creating a special commission for investigating charges of corruption brought by ordinary Nigerians against government officials.

According to Amnesty International's 2000 report, Nigeria's new government continues to make strides in improving human rights throughout the country, most notably in the release of political prisoners. However, the detention of journalists critical of the military and reports of police brutality continue to be problems. Foreign governments and watchdog organizations continue to press the Nigerian government for further human rights reforms.

GENDER ROLES AND STATUSES

Division of Labor by Gender. In general, labor is divided in Nigerian society along gender lines. Very few women are active in the political and professional arenas. In urban areas, increasing numbers of women are becoming involved in the professional workforce, but they are greatly outnumbered by their male counterparts. Women who do manage to gain professional employment rarely make it into the higher levels of management.

However, women in Nigeria still play significant roles in the economy, especially in rural areas. Women are often expected to earn significant portions of the family income. As a rule, men have little obligation to provide for their wives or children. Therefore women have traditionally had to farm or sell homemade products in the local market to ensure that they could feed and clothe their children. The division of labor along gender lines even exists within industries. For example, the kinds of crops that women cultivate differ from those that men cultivate. In Igbo society, yams are seen as men's crops, while beans and cassava are seen as women's crops.

The Relative Status of Women and Men. Modern Nigeria is a patriarchal society. Men are dominant over women in virtually all areas. While Nigeria is a signatory to the international Convention on Equality for Women, it means little to the average Nigerian woman. Women still have fewer legal rights than men. According to Nigeria's Penal Code, men have the right to beat their wives as long as they do not cause permanent physical injury. Wives are often seen as little more than possessions and are subject to the rule of their husbands.

However, women can exercise influence in some areas. For example, in most ethnic groups, mothers and sisters have great say in the lives of their sons and brothers, respectively. The blood relationship allows these women certain leeway and influence that a wife does not have.

MARRIAGE, FAMILY, AND KINSHIP

Marriage. There are three types of marriage in Nigeria today: religious marriage, civil marriage, and traditional marriage. A Nigerian couple may decide to take part in one or all of these marriages. Religious marriages, usually Christian or Muslim, are conducted according to the norms of the respective religious teachings and take place in a church or a mosque. Christian males are allowed only one wife, while Muslim men can take up to four wives. Civil official weddings take place in a government registry office. Men are allowed only one wife under a civil wedding, regardless of religion. Traditional marriages usually are held at the wife's house and are performed according to the customs of the ethnic group involved. Most ethnic groups traditionally allow more than one wife.

Depending on whom you ask, polygamy has both advantages and disadvantages in Nigerian society. Some Nigerians see polygamy as a divisive force in the family, often pitting one wife against another. Others see polygamy as a unifying factor, creating a built-in support system that allows wives to work as a team.

While Western ways of courtship and marriage are not unheard of, the power of traditional values and the strong influence of the family mean that traditional ways are usually followed, even in the cities and among the elite. According to old customs, women did not have much choice of whom they married, though the numbers of arranged marriages are declining. It is also not uncommon for women to marry in their teens, often to a much older man. In instances where there are already one or more wives, it is the first wife's responsibility to look after the newest wife and help her integrate into the family.

Many Nigerian ethnic groups follow the practice of offering a bride price for an intended wife. Unlike a dowry, in which the woman would bring something of material value to the marriage, a bride price is some form of compensation the husband must pay before he can marry a wife. A bride price can take the form of money, cattle, wine, or other valuable goods paid to the woman's family, but it also can take a more subtle form. Men might contribute money to the education of an intended wife or help to establish her in a small-scale business or agricultural endeavor. This form of bride price is often incorporated as part of the wooing process. While women who leave their husbands will be welcomed back into their families, they often need a justification for breaking the marriage. If the husband is seen as having treated his wife well, he can expect to have the bride price repaid.

Though customs vary from group to group, traditional weddings are often full of dancing and lively music. There is also lots of excitement and cultural displays. For example, the Yoruba have a practice in which the bride and two or three other women come out covered from head to toe in a white shroud. It is the groom's job to identify his wife from among the shrouded women to show how well he knows his wife.

Divorce is quite common in Nigeria. Marriage is more of a social contract made to ensure the continuation of family lines rather than a union based on love and emotional connections. It is not uncommon for a husband and wife to live in separate homes and to be extremely independent of one another. In most ethnic groups, either the man or the woman can end the marriage. If the woman leaves her husband, she will often be taken as a second or third wife of another man. If this is the case, the new husband is responsible for repaying the bride price to the former husband. Children of a divorced woman are normally accepted into the new family as well, without any problems.

Domestic Unit. The majority of Nigerian families are very large by Western standards. Many Nigerian men take more than one wife. In some ethnic groups, the greater the number of children, the greater a man's standing in the eyes of his peers. Family units of ten or more are not uncommon.

In a polygamous family, each wife is responsible for feeding and caring for her own children, though the wives often help each other when needed. The wives also will take turns feeding their husband so that the cost of his food is spread equally between or among the wives. Husbands are the authority figures in the household, and many are not used to their ideas or wishes being challenged.

In most Nigerian cultures, the father has his crops to tend to, while his wives will have their own jobs, whether they be tending the family garden, processing palm oil, or selling vegetables in the local market. Children may attend school. When they return home, the older boys will help their father with his work, while the girls and younger boys will go to their mothers.

Inheritance. For many Nigerian ethnic groups, such as the Hausa and the Igbo, inheritance is basically a male affair. Though women have a legal right to inheritance in Nigeria, they often receive nothing. This is a reflection of the forced economic independence many women live under. While their husbands are alive, wives are often responsible for providing for themselves and their children. Little changes economically after the death of the husband. Property and wealth are usually passed on to sons, if they are old enough, or to other male relatives, such as brothers or uncles.

For the Fulani, if a man dies, his brother inherits his property and his wife. The wife usually returns to live with her family, but she may move in with her husband's brother and become his wife.

Kin Groups. While men dominate Igbo society, women play an important role in kinship. All Igbos, men and women, have close ties to their mother's clan, which usually lives in a different village. When an Igbo dies, the body is usually sent back to his mother's village to be buried with his mother's kin.

If an Igbo is disgraced or cast out of his community, his mother's kin will often take him in.

For the Hausa, however, there is not much of a sense of wide-ranging kinship. Hausa society is based on the nuclear family. There is a sense of a larger extended family, including married siblings and their families, but there is little kinship beyond that. However, the idea of blood being thicker than water is very strong in Hausa society. For this reason, many Hausas will try to stretch familial relationships to the broader idea of clan or tribe to diffuse tensions between or among neighbors.

SOCIALIZATION

Infant Care. Newborns in Nigerian societies are regarded with pride. They represent a community's and a family's future and often are the main reason for many marriages.

Throughout Nigeria, the bond between mother and child is very strong. During the first few years of a child's life, the mother is never far away. Nigerian women place great importance on breast-feeding and the bond that it creates between mother and child. Children are often not weaned off their mother's milk until they are toddlers.

Children who are too young to walk or get around on their own are carried on their mother's backs, secured by a broad cloth that is tied around the baby and fastened at the mother's breasts. Women will often carry their children on their backs while they perform their daily chores or work in the fields.

Child Rearing and Education. When children reach the age of about four or five, they often are expected to start performing a share of the household duties. As the children get older, their responsibilities grow. Young men are expected to help their fathers in the fields or tend the livestock. Young women help with the cooking, fetch water, or do laundry. These tasks help the children learn how to become productive members of their family and community. As children, many Nigerians learn that laziness is not acceptable; everyone is expected to contribute.

While children in most Nigerian societies have responsibilities, they also are allowed enough leeway to be children. Youngsters playing with homemade wooden dolls and trucks, or groups of boys playing soccer are common sights in any Nigerian village.

In many Nigerian ethnic groups, the education of children is a community responsibility. For ex-

Nigerian people at a market. Food plays a central role in the rituals of all ethnic groups in Nigeria.

ample, in the Igbo culture the training of children is the work of both men and women, within the family and outside it. Neighbors often look after youngsters while parents may be busy with other chores. It is not strange to see a man disciplining a child who is not his own.

All Nigerian children are supposed to have access to a local elementary school. While the government aims to provide universal education for both boys and girls, the number of girls in class is usually much lower than the number of boys. Sending every child in a family to school can often put a lot

of strain on a family. The family will lose the child's help around the house during school hours and will have to pay for uniforms and supplies. If parents are forced to send one child to school over another, many will choose to educate boys before girls.

Higher Education. Historically, Nigerians have been very interested in higher education. The lack of universities providing quality education equal to that in Britain was a major component of the social reforms that led to Nigeria's independence. Today there are forty-three universities in Nigeria. The majority of these are government-run, but the government has recently approved the creation of three private universities.

While Nigeria's system of higher education is the largest in Africa, the demand for higher education far exceeds the capacity of the facilities. There simply are not enough institutions to accommodate the demand. In 1998 only thirty-five thousand students were accepted to Nigerian universities out of a pool of more than four hundred thousand applicants.

Nigeria also has 125 technical training schools. The majority of these focus on polytechnic and agricultural training, with a few specializing in areas such as petroleum sciences and health.

ETIQUETTE

Age is greatly respected in Nigeria. In an area where the average life expectancy is not very high, those who live into their senior years are seen as having earned special rights of respect and admiration. This is true of both men and women.

Socially, greetings are of the utmost importance. A handshake and a long list of well wishes for a counterpart's family and good health are expected when meeting someone. This is often true even if you have seen that person a short time earlier. Whether you are talking to a bank teller or visiting a friend, it is considered rude not to engage in a proper greeting before getting down to business.

Shaking hands, eating, or passing things with the left hand are unacceptable. The left hand is reserved for personal toiletries and is considered dirty.

RELIGION

Religious Beliefs. It is estimated that 50 percent of Nigerians are Muslim, 40 percent are Christian, and that the remaining 10 percent practice various indigenous religions.

While Muslims can be found in all parts of Nigeria, their strongest footholds are among the Hausa and the Yoruba. Islam in Nigeria is similar to Islam throughout the world. It is based on the teachings of the Prophet Muhammad, which are outlined in the Qur'an.

Christianity is most prevalent in the south of Nigeria. The vast majority of Igbo are Christians, as are many Yorubas. The most popular forms of Christianity in Nigeria include Anglican, Presbyterian, American Southern Baptist, and Methodist.

Also, there are large pockets of Seventh-Day Adventists and Jehovah's Witnesses.

Conflict with the way some missionaries administered the churches during colonial times also created several breakaway African-Christian churches. Most of these adhere to the doctrines of Western churches but have introduced African music and tradition to their Masses. Some have even eased Christian restrictions on polygamy.

Relations between Christians and Muslims are tense in many areas. Since late 1999, numerous clashes between the two have led to thousands of deaths. The northern city of Kaduna has been the flash point for many of these riots, as local leaders discussed whether to institute Shari'a law in the region. Demonstrations by Christians against the idea soon led to violent confrontations with Muslims. The debate over Shari'a law and the violence accompanying it continue in many of the northern states.

While Islam and Christianity are the dominant religions in Nigeria, neither is completely free of influence from indigenous religions. Most people who consider themselves good Muslims or good Christians often also follow local religious practices. This makes up for perceived shortcomings in their religion. Most indigenous religions are based on a form of ancestor worship in which family members who have passed into the spirit world can influence things in the world of the living. This mixing of traditional ways with Islam has led to groups such as the Bori cult, who use spirit possession as a way to understand why people are suffering in this life. The mixing of traditional ways with Christianity has led to the development of the Aladura Church. Aladura priests follow basic Christian doctrine but also use prophecy, healing, and charms to ward off witchcraft.

Many Nigerians follow the teachings of purely indigenous religions. Most of these religions share the idea that one supreme god created the earth and its people, but has left people to decide their own paths in life. Followers of the traditional Yoruban religion believe that hundreds of spirits or minor gods have taken the place of the supreme god in influencing the daily lives of individuals. Many Yoruban slaves who were taken to the Caribbean and the Americas brought this religion with them. There it was used as the basis of Santeria and voodoo.

Because the vast majority of Igbos converted to Christianity during colonialism, few practice the traditional Igbo religion, which is based on hundreds of gods, not a single creator.

A man sits in front of his farmhouse in Toro, Nigeria. Traditionally, only men own land.

Religious Practitioners. According to Muslim and Christian traditions, officials in these religions tend to be male. For most indigenous religions, priests and priestesses are common. Traditional priests and priestesses get their power and influence from their ability to be possessed by their god or by their ability to tell the future or to heal. In the Igbo religion men serve as priests to Igbo goddesses, and women serve as priestesses to Igbo gods. While both men and women can rank high in the Yoruban religion, women usually are among the most respected of traditional priests.

Rituals and Holy Places. Because many of the indigenous religions are based on various spirits or minor gods, each with influence over a specific area of nature, many of the traditional rituals are based on paying homage to these gods and spirits. Likewise, the area of control for a spirit also marks the places that are holy to that spirit. For example, a tribe's water spirit may have a specific pond or river designated as its holy place. The Kalabari, Okrika, and Ikwerre tribes of the Niger Delta region all have festivals in honor of water spirits sacred to their peoples. The Yoruba hold a twenty-day Shango festival each year to honor their god of thunder. Many Igbo consider it bad luck to eat yams from the new harvest until after the annual Yam Festival, a harvest celebration held in honor of the Igbo earth goddess Ani.

Death and the Afterlife. Christian and Muslim Nigerians believe that following death, a person's soul is released and judged by God before hopefully going on to Heaven. Many traditional religions, especially those of the eastern tribes, believe in reincarnation. In these tribes, people believe that the dead will come back as a member of his or her mother's or sister's family. Many in-depth ceremonies are necessary to prepare the body before burial. For example, if the person was inflicted with some physical disability, steps would be taken to prevent it from being passed on to him in the next life. An infertile woman may have her abdomen cut open before burial or a blind man may have a salve made from special leaves placed over his eyes.

Regardless of religion, Nigerians bury their dead. This is customary among Christians and Muslims, but it also is based on traditional beliefs that the body should be returned to the earth that sustained it during life.

Muslims are buried so that their heads face the holy city of Mecca in Saudi Arabia. For others, it is customary to bury a man with his head turned toward the east, so he can see the rising sun. A woman is buried facing west, so she will know when the sun sets and when it is time to prepare dinner for her husband in the next life. People also cover the body with black earth during burial because many believe that red earth will result in skin blemishes in the next life.

The ethnic groups in eastern Nigeria believe that the more music and dancing at a funeral, the better that person's chances of a successful afterlife. The size of funerals depends on the social standing of the deceased. Men are expected to set aside money that will be used to ensure they have a properly elaborate funeral. Women, children, and adolescents tend to have much less elaborate funerals.

MEDICINE AND HEALTH CARE

Nigerians, like people in many developing countries, suffer from widespread disease and a poor health care system. Malaria, HIV/AIDS, parasitic infections, and childhood diseases are rampant throughout the country. Widespread poverty also contributes to the poor level of health care, as many people shy away from modern treatments that are too expensive. Corruption at all levels of government makes it difficult for health care funding to trickle down to the average Nigerian. Underfunding and neglect have left many clinics and hospitals in poor physical condition and without modern equipment. Pharmacies, both state-run and private, regularly run out of medicines. Patients looking for cheaper remedies often turn to black-market vendors, who often sell expired or counterfeit drugs. There also is a shortage of qualified medical personnel to adequately treat the whole population.

In 2000, the estimated life expectancy of Nigerian men and women was fifty-one years. The estimated infant mortality rate was over 7 percent, or about seventy-four infant deaths for every thousand live births.

AIDS has extracted a devastating toll on Nigeria. The World Health Organization and UNAIDS estimated that 2.7 million Nigerian adults were living with AIDS or HIV in 1999. The vast majority of Nigerians who are HIV-positive do not know it. Some 1.7 million Nigerians had already died of the disease by the end of 1999. The primary mode of HIV transmission in Nigeria is through heterosexual intercourse.

Both Western and traditional forms of medicine are popular in Nigeria. Traditional medicine, also known as *juju*, is common at the rural level. Practitioners of juju use a variety of plants and herbs in their cures. Most families also have their own secret remedies for minor health problems.

Many rural people do not trust Western-style medicine, preferring instead to use traditional ways. In many instances the traditional medicine is very effective and produces fewer side effects than modern drugs. Most of modern medicine's prescription drugs grew out of traditional herbal remedies. However, there are conditions in which traditional medicine can do more harm than good. Sometimes this leads to conflict between the government-sponsored health care system and traditional ways. Some organizations are now looking at ways to combine the two in an attempt to coax people back into health centers.

The federal government is responsible for the training of health care workers and running nationwide health campaigns such as those aimed at fighting AIDS, Guinea worm infection, river blindness, and leprosy.

SECULAR CELEBRATIONS

Nigeria observes three secular national holidays and several officially recognized Muslim and Christian holidays when government, commerce, and banks are closed. The secular holidays are New Year's Day (1 January), Workers' Day (1 May), and National Day (1 October). The Christian holidays are Christmas (25 December), Good Friday, and Easter Monday. The Muslim holidays are Eid al-Fitr (the last day of Ramadan, the Muslim holy month of fasting), Tabaski, and Eid al-Moulid. Aside from Christmas, the religious holidays fall on different days each year.

THE ARTS AND HUMANITIES

Support for the Arts. Nigerian art traditionally served a social or religious purpose and did not exist for the sake of art per se. For example, dance was used to teach or to fulfill some ritualistic goal. Sculpture was used in blessings, in healing rituals, or to ward off bad luck. With increasing modernization, however, Nigerian art is becoming less oriented to a particular purpose. In some cases, Nigerians have abandoned whole forms of art because they no longer served a purpose. For example, the elaborate tombstones once widely produced by the Ibibio are becoming increasingly rare as Western-style cemeteries are replacing traditional burial grounds.

The government has recognized this decline in Nigerian art. In an attempt to promote Nigerian nationalism through art, it has launched some programs, such as the All-Nigeria Festival of Arts, to

Women engrave designs into yellow calabash gourds. Nigerian art traditionally served a social or religious purpose.

revitalize the Nigerian art world. Many wealthy Nigerians looking to recapture their roots, as well as Western tourists and collectors looking for an African art experience, are willing to spend money on Nigerian art. This has led to a slight revival of the art industry.

Literature. Nigeria has a long and incredibly rich literary history. Nigerians are traditionally story-tellers. Much of precolonial history in Nigeria is the result of stories handed down from generation to generation. With colonization and the introduction of reading, writing, and the English language, Nigerian storytellers soon began sharing their talents with a worldwide audience. Perhaps Nigeria's most famous writer is Wole Soyinka, who won the 1986 Nobel Prize for literature. His most famous works include *A Dance of the Forests*, *The Swamp Dwellers*, and *The Lion and the Jewel*. Other famous Nigerian authors include Chinua Achebe, whose *Things Fall Apart* is a favorite among Western schools as an example of the problems inflicted on African societies during colonization, and Ben Okri, whose novel *The Famished Road* won Britain's 1991 Booker Prize.

Graphic Arts. Nigeria is famous for its sculpture. The bronzework of the ancient cities of Ife and Benin can be found in museums all over the world. These areas in southern Nigeria still produce large amounts of bronze castings. Woodcarvings and terra-cotta sculptures also are popular.

Nigerians are expert dyers, weavers, and tailors. They produce massive quantities of beautiful, rich, and colorful textiles. However, the majority of these are sold primarily for everyday wear and not as examples of art.

Performance Arts. Dance and music are perhaps the two most vibrant forms of Nigerian art. Nigerian music is dependent on strong rhythms supplied by countless drums and percussion instruments. Highlife is a type of music heavily influenced by Western culture. It sounds like an Africanized version of American big band or ballroom music. Afrobeat combines African rhythms and melodies with jazz and soul. One of Nigeria's best-known Afrobeat artists, Fela Kuti, was heavily influenced by American artists such as James Brown. Palm wine music gets its name from the palm wine saloons where it is traditionally heard. Its fast-paced, frenzied rhythms reflect the rambunctious nature of many palm wine bars.

Perhaps Nigeria's most popular form of music is juju, which uses traditional drums and percussion instruments to back up vocals and complicated guitar work. Popular juju artists include King Sunny Ade, Ebenezer Obey, and Shina Peters.

The State of the Physical and Social Sciences

While Nigeria's system of higher education is better than most in Africa, many of its best and brightest students go to universities in the United States or Europe in search of better facilities and academic support. These students often stay abroad, where there are more opportunities to pursue their talents and to benefit economically. This loss of sharp and influential minds has left the physical and social sciences in a poorer state than they need be. The few sciences that are thriving in Nigeria, such as geology and petroleum sciences, are often headed by non-Nigerians, brought in by foreign companies that have contracts to exploit Nigeria's natural resources.

BIBLIOGRAPHY

Achebe, Chinua. *Things Fall Apart*, 1959.

Achu, Kamala. *Nigeria*, 1992.

Adeeb, Hassan. *Nigeria*, 1996.

Ajayi, Omofolambo S. *Yoruba Dance: The Semiotics of Movement and Body Attitude in a Nigerian Culture*, 1998.

Anifowose, Remi. *Violence and Politics in Nigeria: The Tiv and Yoruba Experience*, 1982.

Awosika, V. O. *A New Political Philosophy for Nigeria and Other African Countries*, 1967.

Babajuma, Malomo. *Nigeria, My Beloved Country*, 1975.

Barkindo, Bawuro M. *Studies in the History of Kano*, 1983.

Central Intelligence Agency. *CIA World Fact Book 2000*, 2000.

Ellah, Francis J. *Ali-Ogba: A History of the Ogba People*, 1995.

Falola, Toyin. *The History of Modern Nigeria*, 1999.

Falola, Toyin, and Adebayo, Akanmu. *Culture, Politics, and Money Among the Yoruba*, 2000.

Forman, Brenda-Lu. *The Land and People of Nigeria*, 1972.

Hauss, Charles. *Comparative Politics: Domestic Responses to Global Challenges*, 2000.

Hodgkin, Thomas. *Nigerian Perspectives*, 1960.

Ikime, Obaro. *The Fall of Nigeria: The British Conquest*, 1982.

Levy, Patricia. *Cultures of the World: Nigeria*, 1996.

Maier, Karl. *This House Has Fallen: Midnight in Nigeria*, 2000.

Nnoromele, Salome. *Life Among the Ibo Women of Nigeria*, 1967.

Ojaide, Tanure. *Great Boys: An African Childhood*, 1948.

Owhonda, John. *Nigeria: A Nation of Many Peoples*, 1998.

Ransome-Kuti, Olikoye. "Who Cares for the Health of Africans? The Nigerian Case." Transcript of lecture given in Kaduna, Nigeria, on March 19, 1998, as part of the International Lecture Series on Population Issues sponsored by the John D. and Catherine T. MacArthur Foundation, 1998.

Smith, Robert S. *Kingdoms of the Yoruba*, 1988.

Stremlau, John. "Ending Africa's Wars." *Foreign Affairs* (July/August 2000): 117–132.

Thomas, T. Ajayi. *A History of Juju Music: A History of an African Popular Music from Nigeria*, 1992.

Turtoe-Sanders, Patience. *African Tradition in Marriage: An Insider's Perspective*, 1998.

UNAIDS and World Health Organization. *Epidemiological Fact Sheet on HIV/AIDS and Sexually Transmitted Infections: Nigeria*, 2000.

Uwechue, Ralph. *Reflections of the Nigerian Civil War*, 1969.

Veal, Michael E. *Fela: The Life and Times of an African Musical Icon*, 2000.

Wall, L. Lewis. *Hausa Medicine: Illness and Well-being in a West African Culture*, 1988.

Williams, Jeff. "Nigeria." *The Lonely Planet: West Africa*, 1999.

—TIM CURRY

NIUE

CULTURE NAME

Niuean

ORIENTATION

Identification. The origin of the word "Niue" is obscure. Formerly, the island included two endogamous, warring factions that occupied separate territories: a northern region called Motu and a southern region called Tafiti.

Location and Geography. Sometimes affectionately called "the Rock," Niue Island is one of the world's largest coral islands and smallest self-governing states. Niue is a large coral island ten miles by seven miles (16 kilometers by 11 kilometers). Some 350 miles (600 kilometers) southeast of Samoa, Niue has no strategic or trade significance and was not annexed by one of the European powers until 1900, long after most other Pacific islands.

Formed by volcanic upheavals, the island sits atop 100-foot (30-meter) cliffs rising straight out of deep ocean. All fourteen villages are situated on a narrow terrace that encircles the island. The interior consists of a central saucer-shaped plateau, one hundred fifty feet (forty-five meters) higher than the terrace, covered in ferns, scrub, and second-growth trees. In the southeast quadrant, the remaining primary forest has been set aside as a conservation area protected by legislation and supernatural strictures.

There is no surface water except in a few caves with small, brackish pools. Rainwater is collected in tanks as run off from roofs. Despite fluctuation in annual rainfall, the tropical climate is conducive to agricultural production, although cultivation is difficult because of the terrain: a thin layer of fertile soil surrounding jagged limestone pinnacles. East-southeast trade winds give way during the wet season (November to March) to variable winds and occasional storms. Hurricanes have been massive forces of social change, occurring on average once every seven years and causing considerable damage to both buildings and agriculture.

There are no surrounding protective reefs or sheltered lagoons. The capital, Alofi, is on the western, lee side of the island at the only place where a wharf could be constructed. Until very recently, the monthly cargo ship had to anchor in deep water about a mile offshore and transfer goods to a barge or lighter for transport to the wharf.

Demography. Niue has always had a small population, probably never more than five thousand, because of the strenuous work involved in crop production and the periodic famines. The demographic concern is depopulation, not overpopulation. Spurred in large part by extremely adverse weather, outmigration on a massive scale has been a feature of life since the opening of the airport in 1971. Every five-year census since 1970 has recorded a decline in the population between 15 and 23 percent; in 1995, just over two thousand people remained on the island.

Most outmigrants are unmarried youths or adult couples with young children who intend to stay away permanently. Some fifteen thousand Niueans now live in New Zealand. The proportion of children in the population dropped from one-half in 1970 to about one-third in 1995, while the proportion of elderly people has increased from 6.4 to nearly 10 percent.

Linguistic Affiliation. The Niuean language is related to other western Polynesian languages, such as Samoan and Tongan, with slight pronunciation differences between the Motu and Tafiti moieties and different spelling conventions.

Most Niueans are bilingual. Niuean tends to be the language of family and village life, and English the language of business. Considerable switching between languages occurs in almost every setting.

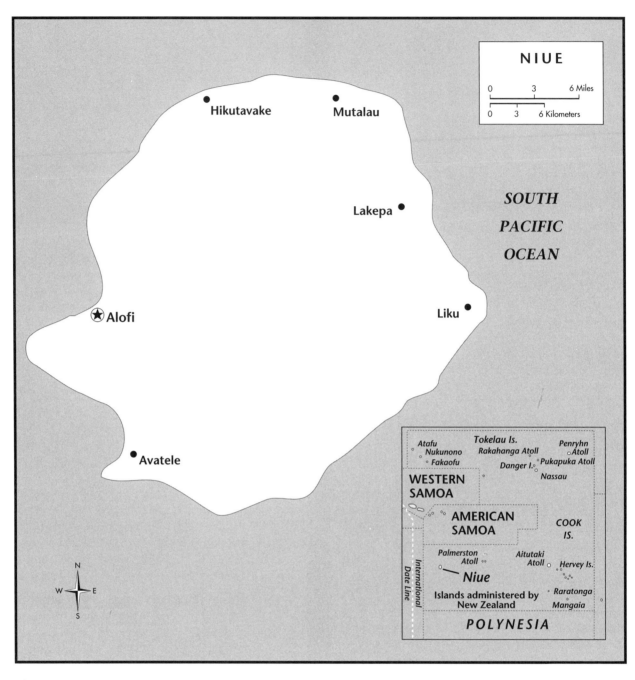

Niue

HISTORY AND ETHNIC RELATIONS

Emergence of the Nation. On attempting to land in June 1774, Captain James Cook and his crew were forcefully repelled by parties of fearsomely attired men uttering blood curdling screams and brandishing spears. Hastily leaving after little actual combat, Cook called the place "Savage Island," a name that appeared on maps into the twentieth century.

National Identity. Until around 1960, Niueans had a poorly developed concept of their island as constituting a distinct culture or nation. Between the mid-19th and 20th centuries, Niue was gradually but increasingly exposed to the outside world, resulting in inexorable change in ways of life and Niuean identity. External influences included mission activity, labor migration, colonization, development of a money economy based on agricultural exports and mercantile endeavors, service in foreign wars, and control by a rigid and rather unresponsive administration. People gradually began to develop an allegiance to a broader entity than their natal villages. That process began during encounters with colonial administrators. The process was accelerated in the early 1960s, when the general populace was able to work with and live next to a large and diverse group of white New Zealanders (*palagi*) brought to help the island recover from hurricanes. Those workers came from a wide range of socioeconomic positions with varying aspirations and experiences. Outmigration in the 1970s also heightened a sense of national identity, as Niueans arriving in New Zealand felt a need to distinguish themselves from other Pacific Islanders and the Maori.

Ethnic Relations. Few outsiders reside on the island, but those who do are generally well tolerated, although competition for scarce jobs can lead to resentment. Most foreigners are expatriates who provide technical advice to the government or have married Niueans. In the early 1980s, about one hundred people from Tonga, where pressure on land was intense, mobilized kin ties and moved to Niue. Also present were a few dozen high school children from the Tokelaus, receiving education not available in their homeland. In the 1990s, a handful of people from Tuvalu settled in a deserted village, escaping the threat that rising seawater posed to their homeland.

URBANISM, ARCHITECTURE, AND THE USE OF SPACE

No area can be described as urban, but nearly one-fifth of the population lives in the vicinity of Alofi, a typical Pacific port town-capital. Villages are laid out around a central, flat open space, the village green (*male*) which is used for meetings, sports events, and ceremonies. Most houses symbolically if not literally face the most socially important and visually dominant structures near the male: the church and the pastor's house. The church is a central feature of social organization, underpinning all social interaction, providing moral guidance, enabling the redistribution of goods and services from wealthy to less well-off members of the village, socializing children, and upholding traditions while spurring change.

Most buildings have been constructed within the past twenty years, using materials, styles, and furnishings imported mainly from New Zealand.

FOOD AND ECONOMY

Food in Daily Life. Despite the fact that many families can afford imported foodstuffs such as canned corned beef, frozen lamb or chicken, and rice, agriculture remains important. Subsistence activities not only raise food, especially highly prized ceremonial foods, but also symbolize the central values linked to work and identity. Enough surplus food is produced to sustain only one small market each week.

Fishing results in a variety of deep-sea catches, such as yellowfin tuna, red bass, and sailfish. Despite the difficult terrain, slash-and-burn (shifting) agriculture is a major crop-producing activity. Niueans cultivate both root crops such as *talo* (taro), yams, and tapioca, and tree crops such as coconut, breadfruit, papaya, and mango, as well as bananas. Planting also sustains the production of pigs. Hunting of fruit bats, birds, and land crabs, and gathering of fern shoots and other vegetation occurs regularly.

Food Customs at Ceremonial Occasions. A boy's first haircutting (*hifi ulu*) and a girl's ear-piercing ceremony (*huki teliga*) are occasions for displaying family solidarity, wealth, and status. Symbolically marking role transitions, these ceremonies involve the donation of cash or gifts to the celebrants. Such gifts are reciprocated by an elaborate and public presentation of feast foods. The extended family does extra work to procure sufficient quantities of these highly esteemed uncooked foods, such as pigs, fish, taro and other prized root crops such as *ufi* (yams), and barrels of salt pork or canned corned beef.

Celebrations of one's twenty-first birthday, weddings, graduation from college, or major community events are less ceremonially intricate. Feast foods are cooked in an earth oven (*umu*) and presented to guests along with other items. After the blessing, each guest gathers items for later consumption into a basket.

Basic Economy. The economic base of the island is foreign aid. In the early 1970s, the economic productive work base changed from agriculture to service provision. By the mid-1980s, more than 80 percent of employed adults worked for wages for the government. In 1990, restructuring and downsizing of the civil service took place. Despite the political and social upheaval this caused, the island's standard of living and economy did not plummet, in large part because of the aid still arriving from New Zealand and other international sources. Per capita aid remains among the highest in the world.

Land Tenure and Property. Land is inalienable and cannot be sold or deeded permanently to non-Niueans. There is a preference for patrilineal inheritance of real property such as land and an emphasis on primogeniture. Women have some rights, but these are not as strong as those of male claimants. Absentee landowners cause considerable tension in some families. The Land Court is probably the most important and contentious aspect of the judiciary. Major political struggles revolve around means to resolve the dilemmas posed by absentee landowners.

Commercial Activities. Tourism, based on deep-sea scuba diving and snorkeling, is the biggest money earner, with the two thousand people who visit annually contributing around $1 million to the economy. Like the export trade, tourism is vulnerable to disruption because of bad weather.

Other commercial activity is heavily agriculture-based: the manufacture for export of coconut cream, taro, passion fruit, limes, and honey. Plaited ware such as hats and baskets and other handicrafts are important export items. Earlier attempts to assemble hand-sewn soccer and rugby balls and similar light industries failed largely because of transportation problems. A small but significant proportion of government revenue is generated through the sale of postage stamps to collectors.

Trade. Niue generally imports approximately fifteen times as much as it exports. Usually, the primary trade item, taro, accounts for 85 percent of export earnings but is highly vulnerable to disruption from weather. In 1996, Niue experienced a 40 percent reduction in exports because of a severe drought; taro brought in only $90,000. In that year, imports reached a five-year high of $3.4 million. Along with food products and alcohol and tobacco, the major imported goods are consumer durables such as outboard motors, aluminum dinghies, refrigerators, and motorcycles.

Division of Labor. Men, especially young men, are expected to undertake physically strenuous or dangerous tasks such as deep-sea fishing. Older men and educated younger men represent the family or village in civic and spiritual affairs. Women generally are assigned tasks focused on the domestic domain, such as caring for old people or children, cooking, sewing, and weaving.

SOCIAL STRATIFICATION

Niue is characterized by a lack of hereditary rulers, a very flexible social hierarchy, an individualistic achievement orientation, and a strong work ethic. More than by speech patterns, dress styles, comportment, or social interaction, differentiation into fluid socioeconomic strata depends on personal charisma or accomplishment and material wealth, such as ownership of aluminum fishing dinghies or outboard motors.

POLITICAL LIFE

Government. There is a democratically elected parliamentary government. The premier is chosen by a vote by the twenty elected representatives in the *Fale Fono* (Niuean Assembly). The formation of distinct political parties has been more discussed than realized. Political cleavage exists between those who do and those who do not wish to change the infrastructure initially set up by the New Zealand administration.

Niueans over age 18 get two votes. One vote is to elect the village representative. These politicians tend to be older men with prestigious backgrounds, such as pastors, government officials, and successful planters and merchants. The second vote is used to elect six island-wide representatives or Common Roll members. These politicians often include women and tend to be younger than village representatives who have been educated abroad as teachers, doctors, or administrators. Hence, modern politics both conforms to a Polynesian tradition of gerontocracy by having elders represent individual villages and deviates from that convention by rewarding individual achievement and expertise in new arenas.

Social Problems and Control. A small police force consisting of a chief and a constable assigned to each village maintains law and order. Most criminal acts are relatively minor misdemeanors (petty theft, unsafe driving, allowing pigs to wander) and are dealt with locally by warnings or small fines. More serious crimes, such as assault, are prosecuted in the magistrate's court and may result in large frees or imprisonment.

SOCIAL WELFARE AND CHANGE PROGRAMS

Basic social welfare programs exist. For example, free nutrition supplements are available to ensure the health and well-being of young children, and older people receive a modest pension.

Girls in school uniforms walk along the street. Schooling is compulsory, secular, and free for all children ages 5 to 14.

NONGOVERNMENTAL ORGANIZATIONS AND OTHER ASSOCIATIONS

Various voluntary associations include a trade union for government employees, women's groups, sports teams, church choirs, dance groups, and youth groups.

GENDER ROLES AND STATUSES

Although women are not automatically accorded the sociopolitical status that men achieve after marriage, women can achieve positions of authority and influence, especially at older ages, through education and by demonstrating effective leadership.

As important as gender in assigning tasks and respect is chronological age. Those who are older are respected and deferred to not just because of family background, experience, and accomplishments but because they are older. Attention to relative age is linguistically signaled and bolstered by the social, religious, economic, and political organization of life.

MARRIAGE, FAMILY, AND KINSHIP

Domestic Unit. In the past, villages were endogamous, somewhat matrifocal units. The mixing of youth from all villages at the high school has

caused the breakdown of this tradition, and that of the Motu-Tafiti rivalry.

People live in extended family groups called *magafaoa*, which oversee land ownership and use. Villages are composed of related magafaoa. Households within a magafaoa occupy clusters of nearby dwellings. The head of a household is usually a married man (*patu*) who represents his domestic unit in church and village politics. Also living in his household are his wife and unmarried children, any recently married children and their spouses, and some grandchildren. Frequently, a household includes a sibling of the patu or of his spouse, a widowed older relative, or a niece or nephew who goes to a nearby school.

SOCIALIZATION

Infant Care. Mothers are the primary caregivers for infants. Grandmothers are crucial resources, especially for firstborn children, because they teach new mothers how to parent properly. A child who crawls and begins to talk is thought to be capable of understanding. When a child is around one year old, the indulgent period of infancy gives way to intense training in social behaviors and a heightening of the role that fathers play in the lives of their children.

A child is the responsibility of all members of a magafaoa and may be fed, clothed, chastised, and cared for by any family member; the child thus may end up living in a different household temporarily or permanently. While at play, toddlers and young children are usually in the care of older siblings.

Child Rearing and Education. There are six elementary schools and one high school. Schooling is compulsory, secular, and free for all children age 5 to 14. At more advanced grades, instruction is delivered in English. The curriculum is modeled on that used in New Zealand schools but includes materials especially designed for a Pacific Islander context.

Higher Education. Postsecondary education at the university or technical college level is available only overseas. Students are selected for further training and supported by government scholarships and then return to take up government jobs, such as physicians or nurses, engineers, technicians, administrators and managers, teachers, and mechanics.

ETIQUETTE

Niuean society is a gerontocracy based on obedience to and respect for those who are older than oneself, with special accord being given to males and those who are first-borns. Gifts (e.g., food, shell necklaces, money) are frequently exchanged informally as well as formally, signaling esteem and friendship, and are expected to be reciprocated at some later time.

RELIGION

The first missionaries to arrive in the mid-nineteenth century were Samoan. They were followed in 1861 by English representatives of the London Missionary Society. Most Niueans are Christian, with the majority (75 percent) being affiliated with the Protestant Church of Niue (Ekalesia Niue). In general, pastors are men trained in seminaries in Samoa or elsewhere who play a central role in village life as spiritual and civic leaders.

To varying degrees, most Niueans still embrace older religious ideas, believing in a supernatural world inhabited by aitu, spirits of dead ancestors or ghosts. Aitu keep a close eye on behavior and punish with misfortune, illness, or even death upon individuals who transgress social norms or flout cultural conventions. Death implies movement from this world to a parallel supernatural world inhabited by ghosts and ancestral spirits. Death is not necessarily instantaneous but rather a gradual transition, as implied by use of the same word, mate, to denote states distinguished in other cultures as delirious, unconscious, dying, and dead.

Any location at which an unexpected or violent death occurs will have a fono or prohibition placed on it, distancing the living from the revenge of ancestral sprits. Until the appropriate time for a pastor to lift this tapu (supernatural edict), people will not visit or will behave there in a very circumspect fashion. Caves or chasms with a history of importance in human affairs are named and treated with respect because of supernatural associations.

MEDICINE AND HEALTH CARE

High-quality (Western) biomedical care is available free of charge. Emergency services and in-patient care for surgical conditions are provided at Lord Liverpool Hospital in Alofi. Patients requiring specialist care are sent by air to nearby countries. Outpatient care is available at several clinics, including a mobile one that regularly visits each village. Public health surveillance and the prevention of disease are a key aspect of health service delivery. This is accomplished through sanitary disposal of wastes, provision of potable water, rodent and mosquito control, and well-baby clinics and childhood vaccination programs.

Herbalists and traditional healers (taulaatua) address psychosocial issues that do not always respond well to other therapies as well as diseases that are deemed to be uniquely Niuean in origin and manifestation. Despite an official ban, there is underground support for and provision of this kind of care.

SECULAR CELEBRATIONS

There are two official days of celebration: Peniamina's Day and Independence Day. Peniamina was a Niuean who went to Samoa in the mid-nineteenth century and later returned with Samoan missionaries. He is credited with bringing the Bible and beginning the modernization of Niue. Independence from New Zealand was granted on 19 October 1974, a process begun fourteen years earlier. Niueans resisted being hurried to independence even when the United Nations applied pressure. At stake was the fashioning of the world's first Compact of Free Association—a model used subsequently in independence agreements by other Pacific societies—

which gave Niueans self-determination but continued New Zealand citizenship, monetary aid, and military protection.

THE ARTS AND HUMANITIES

Niueans do not have a strong interest in preserving their history by collecting artifacts or through oral storytelling or the recitation of genealogies. Traditional dances and songs are featured at important events such as weddings and official ceremonies. A recent surge of interest in history has resulted in the establishment of a small museum in Alofi and the revival of several handicrafts, such as the building of canoes by hand and the making of *hiapo*, a mulberry bark cloth.

Some returned migrants make a living through the arts, such as sculpture, writing, painting, and composing music. Such endeavors, however, are aimed more at an overseas commercial art market than at the local community. Most funding for the arts comes from overseas; the New Zealand government is interested in fostering and maintaining traditional Pacific arts and crafts.

BIBLIOGRAPHY

Barker, Judith C. *Social Organization of Health Services for Preschool Children on Niue Island, Western Polynesia,* 1985.

———. ''Health and Functional Status of the Elderly in a Polynesian Population.'' *Journal of Cross-Cultural Gerontology* 4: 163–194, 1989.

———. ''Home Alone: The Effects of Out-Migration on Niuean Elders' Living Arrangements and Social Support.'' *Pacific Studies* 17 (3): 41–81, 1994.

———. ''Between Humans and Ghosts: The Decrepit Elderly on a Polynesian island.'' In Jay Sokolovsky, ed., *The Cultural Context of Aging: Worldwide Perspectives,* rev. 2nd ed., 1997.

———. ''Road Warriors: Driving Behaviors on a Polynesian Island.'' In Robert A. Hahn, ed., *Anthropology in Public and International Health: Bridging Differences in Culture and Society.* New York: Oxford University Press, 1999.

Chapman, Terry M. *The Decolonization of Niue,* 1976.

Connell, John C. *Migration, Employment and Development in the South Pacific: Country Report Number 11—Niue,* 1983.

Loeb, Edwin M. ''History and Traditions of Niue.'' *Bernice P. Bishop Museum Bulletin* no. 32, 1926.

McBean, Angus. ''Niue Today . . .'' *South Pacific Bulletin* October 1962, pp. 33–37, 60–64.

McLachlan, Sue. ''Savage Island or Savage History? An Interpretation of Early European Contact with Niue.'' *Pacific Studies* 6: 26–51, 1982.

Niue Government. *Niue: A History of the Island,* 1982.

Pollock, Nancy J. ''Work, Wages and Shifting Cultivation on Niue.'' *Pacific Studies* 2: 132–143, 1979.

Scott, Dick. *Would a Good Man Die? Niue Island, New Zealand and the Late Mr. Larsen,* 1993.

Yarwood, Vaughn, with photographs by Glenn Jowitt. ''Life on the Rock.'' *New Zealand Geographic* 37: 56–86, 1998.

—JUDITH C. BARKER

NORTHERN IRELAND

CULTURE NAME

Northern Irish

ALTERNATIVE NAMES

Ulsters, Ulster Unionists, Protestant Ulsterites, Loyalists; Republican, Nationalist

ORIENTATION

Identification. The island of Ireland is known as *Eire* in Irish Gaelic. The name of the capital city, Belfast, derives from the city's Gaelic name, *Beal Feirste*, which means "mouth of the sandy ford," referring to a stream that joins the Lagan River.

The state of conflict in Northern Ireland is manifested in the names by which the Northern Irish identify themselves. Ulsters or Ulster Unionists identify themselves by ethnicity, religion, and political bent. These residents are generally Protestants from England who colonized the country in the nineteenth century and earlier supported William of Orange when he wrested the throne of England from the Catholic James II. The Nationalists are native Irish who were ruled by Irish chiefs. They are Roman Catholics who want Northern Ireland to be reunited with the Republic of Ireland, removing the northern counties from the sovereignty of England. The Ulster Unionists remain politically, religiously, and culturally loyal to England, yet feel that Northern Ireland is their homeland. Nationalists believe that the land is theirs, and their loyalty is to their compatriots in the Free State of Southern Ireland.

Location and Geography. Northern Ireland is the smallest country in the United Kingdom, situated on the second largest island of the British Isles. It occupies one-sixth of the island it shares with the independent Republic of Ireland. Northern Ireland is composed of six of the twenty-nine counties of Ireland, covering about 5,452 square miles (14,120 square kilometers). It is separated from the Republic

of Ireland by a three-hundred-mile-long artificial boundary. Northern Ireland makes up the northwestern corner of the island; the entire island is bordered on the west by the Atlantic Ocean, on the east by the Irish Sea, and on the south by the Celtic Sea. The waters around Northern Ireland's coast are shallow.

The climate is mild as a result of Atlantic Ocean breezes and the Gulf Stream, with comfortable summers and temperate winters. Snow is uncommon, and temperatures dip below freezing only a few times a year. However, rainfall is heavy. Low mountains with steep cliffs dropping off to the sea and fertile lowlands are the principal topographic features. The two major mountain ranges are the Sperrin Mountains and the Mourne Mountains. Most of the farmable land, in the middle of the country, is used as grazing pastures for livestock. Lough Neagh, in central Northern Ireland, is the largest lake in the British Isles.

Until seven thousand years ago, Ireland was linked to Europe by a land bridge, but the ocean eroded that bridge and separated Ireland from the continent. Scotland lies just thirteen miles east of the island across the English Channel.

The Upper Bann River begins in the Mourne Mountains and flows northwest for twenty-five miles before entering Lough Neagh. The Erne River, which is seventy-two miles long, starts in the Republic of Ireland and flows northward into Northern Ireland. The Foyle River, marking the northwestern boundary with the Republic of Ireland, passes through Londonderry and empties into the Atlantic Ocean, becoming a bay called Lough Foyle.

Soggy areas called peat bogs have developed in parts of the country. The bogs contain layers of vegetation that have partly decayed in the moist earth. As the layers build up, they form a thick crust of turf that is called peat. This turf, originally cut by hand, is now cut by machine. The resulting

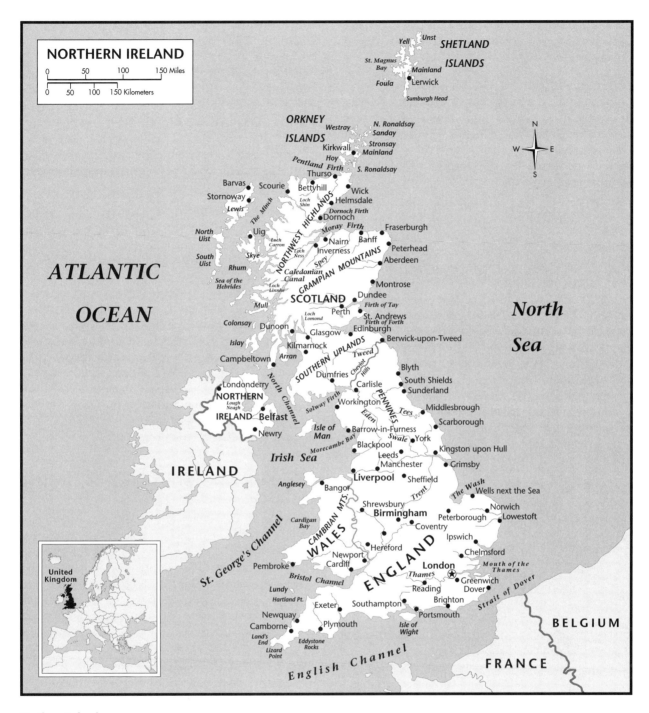

Northern Ireland

briquettes are burned for fuel and remain the major source of heat and electricity in rural areas.

Demography. In 1998, the Annual report of the Registrar General for Northern Ireland reported the population of Northern Ireland to be 1,668,000. The population is most dense in the east. In the 1980s, the population was described as being 70

percent Protestant and 30 percent Catholic, but 60 percent Protestant and 40 percent Catholic may be more accurate. The population breakdown is difficult to ascertain because many residents are reluctant to indicate their religion.

Catholic families have a higher birthrate because of their religious beliefs and their desire to surpass the population of the Unionists. Stability in the population has resulted from the fact that many Catholics were forced to go to London to escape unemployment.

Linguistic Affiliation. English is spoken throughout the country, and the native language of Gaelic, or Gaeltacht, is disappearing. Many Gaelic speakers died in the Great Famine of the 1840s, and Gaelic was replaced by English, which was needed to achieve social mobility. Gaelic still carries a stigma as the language of the poor.

Gaelic is a Celtic language that probably was introduced by Celts in the last few centuries B.C.E. Similar to Scottish Gaelic, it shares common structures with Welsh and Breton. It is an idiomatic language with a complex grammatical system that is considered rich in terms of warmth and expressiveness. Irish is required at some schools but is taught with an emphasis on grammar rather than conversation. The Gaelic League, formed in 1893, is a revivalist organization, that attempts to propagate the Irish language and culture. In the 1920s, the Gaelic League attempted to deanglicize the country by gaelicizing the schools. It wanted to require that all teachers at teacher training colleges have a background and proficiency in Irish. However, the league realized that Gaelic would languish if it was not also used in the home environment.

Symbolism. The Union Jack flag and the British crown are associated with the Unionists both by their Protestant supporters and by their Catholic opponents. Members of the Orange Order have a picture of the crown on the huge drums that are used in the parades in which Orangemen celebrate the victory of William of Orange over James II at the Battle of the Boyne in 1690. Another image associated with the rivalry between Loyalists and Nationalists is the Ulster emblem of a right hand severed at the wrist from which no blood should flow.

Northern Ireland is recognizable by its lush green countryside and stout mountains leading down to a steep and craggy shoreline. The flag of the Free State of Ireland, which has equal vertical bands of green, white, and orange is a symbol of the Irish nation.

HISTORY AND ETHNIC RELATIONS

Emergence of the Nation. Prior to 1920 the island of Ireland was part of the United Kingdom of Great Britain and Ireland. The Government of Ireland Act of 1920 founded the Irish Free State and allowed six Ulster counties to remain part of the United Kingdom, becoming Northern Ireland. The Irish Republi-

can Army (IRA) opposed the establishment of the Irish Free State. In 1925, an agreement among the Irish Free State, Northern Ireland, and Great Britain partitioned Ireland and defined the borders. Catholic residents of Ulster did not want to see Ireland divided, but Protestant business leaders wished to remain linked to England. In 1936, the Irish Free State proclaimed its complete independence, and in 1949 it renamed itself the Republic of Ireland. Since 1974, the United Kingdom has ruled Northern Ireland directly.

National Identity. The Northern Irish see themselves as distinct from the English but connected to their compatriots in the Republic of Ireland. The Northern Irish see the British of Northern Ireland as interlopers and oppressors.

Ethnic Relations. Violent antagonism between Catholics and Protestants developed in the nineteenth century and resulted from history and religion. The influx of settlers from England and Scotland was not welcomed by the native Irish, since the newcomers were awarded the best parcels of land. At first, the minority Ulster Protestants could not dominate the Catholic majority, but after the victory of the Protestants supporting William of Orange at the Battle of the Boyne, they prevailed.

URBANISM, ARCHITECTURE, AND THE USE OF SPACE

Particularly in Belfast, most decisions involving public planning are made to preserve public security in the midst of "the Troubles." Many of the busiest streets in that city have control zones where only pedestrians can travel. Automobiles are not allowed in those zones to reduce the risk of car bombings. Cars that are parked in commercial parking lots are given a quick inspection for potential bombs. The boundaries that separate Catholic and Protestant neighborhoods are enforced by the police.

Graffiti and wall murals appear throughout urban areas, depicting the sentiments of Unionists and Nationalists. In the case of the Nationalists, IRA propaganda and images of men with guns tell supporters to "fight back" and state that "we will meet force with force." Catholic children learn from graffiti the strong views and potential for violence held by the Nationalists.

In a sign welcoming travelers to the County of Londonderry, Nationalists have expressed their anti-British feelings by scratching out the word "London" and identifying the county as Derry, as it is known among Catholics. At Free Derry Corner, two large murals commemorate the events of

PATRICK J DOHERTY. — AGED 31 YEARS.
GERARD V DONAGHY. — AGED 17 YEARS.
JOHN F DUDDY. AGED 17 YEARS.
HUGH P GILMORE. — AGED 17 YEARS.
MICHAEL G KELLY. — AGED 17 YEARS.
MICHAEL M McDAID. — AGED 20 YEARS.
KEVIN G McELHINNEY. — AGED 17 YEARS.
BERNARD McGUIGAN. AGED 41 YEARS.
JAMES G McKINNEY. — AGED 34 YEARS.
WILLIAM A McKINNEY. — AGED 27 YEARS.
WILLIAM N NASH. — AGED 19 YEARS.
JAMES J WRAY. AGED 22 YEARS.
JOHN P YOUNG. AGED 17 YEARS.
AND TO JOHN JOHNSTON. AGED 59 YEARS.
WHO DIED LATER AS A RESULT OF INJURIES RECEIVED THAT
WHO WERE MURDERED BY BRITISH PARATROOPS ON BLOODY SUNDAY 30TH JA

A memorial to fourteen unarmed marchers who were shot by British paramilitary troops during a civil rights march in Derry on Sunday 30 January 1972. Since 1974, the United Kingdom has ruled Northern Ireland directly.

Bloody Sunday, in which thirteen people were killed and another fourteen were injured, after British soldiers opened fire during an illegal demonstration in 1972.

The Ulster Architectural Heritage Society is an organization that educates the public and lobbies for historic buildings in nine counties in Northern Ireland.

FOOD AND ECONOMY

Food in Daily Life. The diet is rather simple. Porridge or oatmeal often is eaten at breakfast. At midmorning, one stops for a cup of tea or coffee with cookies or biscuits. Most people eat the main meal at midday. This meal generally is meat-based, featuring beef, chicken, pork, or lamb. Fish and chips are eaten for a quick meal, and a rich soup with plenty of bread can be bought in taverns at lunchtime. Potatoes are a staple, but onions, cabbage, peas, and carrots are eaten just as frequently. Irish stew combines the chief elements of the cuisine with mutton, potatoes, and onions.

Bakeries carry a variety of breads, with brown bread and white soda bread served most often with meals. White sliced bread is called *pan* in Irish. Belfast's soda bread enjoys an excellent reputation; made of flour and buttermilk it is found throughout the country. In the evening, families eat a simple meal of leftovers or eggs and toast.

A drink generally means beer, either lager or stout. Guinness, brewed in Dublin, is the black beer most often drunk. Whiskey also is served in pubs, and coffee is also available.

Food Customs at Ceremonial Occasions. Food customs of the Northern Irish are not really different from the practices of the Irish in the Republic of Ireland. Christmas supper includes meat such as chicken and ham followed by plum pudding. Being a strongly Catholic country, the Friday night prohibition of meat is observed by Catholics. Since fish is permitted, the Friday evening meal generally features trout or salmon.

Basic Economy. The economy of Northern Ireland is based on agriculture and manufacturing. The agriculture sector benefits from rich farming soil. Agriculture contributes to manufacturing through processing of livestock and dairy products. Northern Ireland's principle industries are textiles, shipbuilding, and engineering.

Unequal resources and unequal opportunities resulting from colonization have created conflict.

The ethnic and religious strife is really a matter of an uneven distribution of economic resources and opportunities.

Land Tenure and Property. The current distribution of land between Catholics and Protestants can be traced back to the settlement patterns of the seventeenth century. The eastern counties of Antrum and Down were settled by the Scottish because of their proximity to Scotland. The settlers who later came from the north of England got land in Monaghan. In the 1600s, the incoming Protestants took the best land for farming, leaving the Catholics with less fertile and more mountainous parcels. As a result, a majority of Protestants established roots in Antrum and Down as well as Armagh and Londonderry.

Commercial Activities. The Industrial Revolution occurred in Belfast during the twentieth century and made the country the world's major linen center and the home of two flourishing shipyards. The success of shipbuilding spawned related industries in engineering and rope making.

Major Industries. Northern Ireland, Belfast in particular, has always been an industrial center. Early in the twentieth century, the major industries were shipbuilding and rope making. The success of Belfast's industries kept it inextricably bound to Great Britain, from which it imported its raw materials. The owners and managers of most industries were Protestants, reinforcing the paternalistic relationship to England.

Trade. As much as 80 percent of external trade is with England. Textiles, in particular linen, are the major export. Grain also is exported; during the Great Famine, grain and foodstuffs were exported to England, with little done to relieve the starving Irish people.

Division of Labor. Catholics generally are excluded from skilled and semiskilled jobs in shipyards and linen mills. They historically were restricted to menial jobs on the docks, earning lower wages than the Protestants who worked in skilled jobs and management positions. Ulster Unionists tend to own businesses. Many Catholic Republicans are unemployed.

SOCIAL STRATIFICATION

Classes and Castes. The class structure renders Protestants superior in that they dominate the professional and business classes, tending to own the majority of businesses and large farms. Catholics tend to be unskilled workers or work small farms. Catholics tend to be poorer than Protestants as a result of economic inequality that often is attributed to ethnic and religious roots. The general enmity between the two groups is exacerbated by long standing prejudices. Protestants generally believe that Catholics are lazy and irresponsible. Social separation contributes to these perceptions. Protestant and Catholic families live in separate enclaves and worship separately, and their children study in segregated schools.

Irish Catholics may tend to drink, whereas Protestants are viewed as more British and puritanical. On Sundays, Catholics often engage in leisure or recreation activities after mass, while Protestants scorn Sunday leisure activities, often choosing not to garden in deference to the sabbath.

Symbols of Social Stratification. Protestants tend to comport themselves as British, members of the United Kingdom. In regard to owning land and businesses, Protestants constitute the economic, social, and political elite. Their accent and manners are in keeping with those of Great Britain. Catholics, who tend to be poorer and have larger families, speak Gaelic, although not fluently. Most Protestants belong to the Orange Order, which is dedicated to maintaining the Protestant religion and Protestant social superiority.

POLITICAL LIFE

Government. Northern Ireland is symbolically headed by the British monarch but it is governed by an elected parliament. The Ireland Act of 1920 established a parliament that was suspended in 1972 because of the ethnic violence. The makeup of the parliament is intended to include fifty-two delegates in the Northern Ireland House of Commons who serve five-year terms. The House selects twenty-four Senate members who serve eight-year terms. House members choose the prime minister from the political party that holds the most seats.

The judicial system is similar to that of England, in which the courts base decisions on parliamentary legislation and common law. A magistrate hears minor cases, and more serious cases are heard by the Crown Court, which is made up of a judge and jury. Any appeals go before a nine-judge court in the British House of Lords.

There is no written constitution. The three viable political options are the continuance as part of the United Kingdom, association with the Republic of Ireland, and independence. The country has the

Farmhouse in mountains of Mourn. Northern Ireland has lush green countryside and stout mountains leading to a steep and craggy shoreline.

right to self-determination under the Northern Ireland Constitution Act of 1973, but unless there is a majority vote for independence or a formal alliance with Ireland, it will remain part of the United Kingdom.

Leadership and Political Officials. Each of the twenty-six districts has an elected council. Belfast and Londonderry have their own councils, which focuses on education, public works, local planning and public health. Protestants tend to hold most elected positions, and this has led to an uneven distribution of resources.

In the 1830s, the Catholic Emancipation Act allowed Catholics to seek election to the British legislature. However, Protestant leaders in Northern Ireland gerrymandered the voting districts so that the Catholics were always a minority in every district.

Social Problems and Control. Most violence results from the civil unrest between Catholics and Protestants. Bombings and individual attacks generally are motivated by the politically charged atmosphere and segregation. Nonpolitical crimes are generally based on socioeconomic inequity. Burglary and theft accounted for nearly three-quarters of all recorded crime in Northern Ireland in 1995.

Between 1990 and 1995, the number of arrests for drug-related offenses more than tripled.

Military Activity. The presence of British police and military personnel is pervasive. There are police checkpoints, and citizens must carry documents routinely. The Ulster Volunteer Force is a Unionist military organization that is highly secretive and has been labeled a terrorist group since it is openly anti-Catholic. The Ulster Defense Association was a legal organization until 1991. The Royal Ulster Constabulary and the British Army are responsible for keeping the peace; the Royal Ulster Constabulary employs a special branch of army intelligence to anticipate and prevent all terrorist attacks.

The Irish National Liberation Army is composed of older, more experienced members. The Provisional Irish Republican Army is a descendant of the original IRA. In this secretive group, which is a military wing of the IRA, each member knows only the names of his immediate colleagues. The IRA has detonated bombs under cars, striking at the moment a police patrol passes. The IRA has killed twenty to thirty soldiers and police officers per year since the 1980s.

Young Nationalists are recruited for paramilitary service. First they join Fionna Eireann as a scout or recruit. To prove themselves, young initiates must participate in the beating or kneecapping of a Protestant.

The military carries out regular security patrols in Unionist and Loyalist areas on foot or in police or army vehicles. The 1974 Prevention of Terrorism Act was passed to prevent the IRA from extending its attacks to Great Britain; it authorizes detention for up to seven days for anyone seemingly engaged in terrorism in Northern Ireland, Great Britain, or the Republic of Ireland.

SOCIAL WELFARE AND CHANGE PROGRAMS

Social insurance benefits exist for orphans, widows, pensioners, and persons on disability or maternity leave. The state, the employer, and the employee all contribute to the fund that provides these benefits. Health services and medicines are free to all persons with long-term illnesses. Beyond that, there are two kinds of entitlements: free health services for those who have a low income and a lower level of services for people with higher incomes.

NONGOVERNMENTAL ORGANIZATIONS AND OTHER ASSOCIATIONS

Most nongovernmental organizations operating in the country, including the Northern Ireland Human Rights Commission and the Northern Ireland Assembly, are concerned with human rights and human rights violations resulting from violent attacks by the IRA and the British Army. The Northern Ireland Human Rights Commission, which was established by the Northern Ireland Act of 1988, has the duty and power to ensure the human rights of all residents and to counter human rights violations.

GENDER ROLES AND STATUSES

Division of Labor by Gender. The position of women in the economic structure shifted during the period of direct rule, with more women entering the workforce between 1952 and 1995 as the number of jobs expanded. Typically, women work in low-paid, part-time jobs in the service sector, and even though their participation in the workforce has increased, it has remained below that of men.

The most dramatic increase in women's employment was that of married women after a constitutional revision. In 1937, the constitution reflected religious bias by stating that a working woman who married had to resign from her job. It was not until 1977 that an Employment Equality Act made that practice illegal.

The Relative Status of Men and Women. Women have become increasingly involved in the peace movement. The Northern Ireland Peace Movement, which began in 1976, allied Protestant and Catholic women who marched together through both Loyalist and Republican parts of Belfast. Two of the founders, Mairead Corrigan and Betty Williams, received the Nobel Peace Prize in 1976 for their efforts to unite Catholics and Protestants to halt the violence.

MARRIAGE, FAMILY, AND KINSHIP

Marriage. Premarital chastity is valued by both religions, especially in rural areas. Young people are expected to abstain from sex until after they are married in a religious ceremony in a church. Marriages often are brokered by a matchmaker since the economic aspects of marriage require experienced calculation. In the 1920s, postfamine marriages were infrequent, with many young people abstaining from marriage; there were more single than married people in the age range of twenty-five to thirty. Farmers who had small plots of land wanted to keep it and they discouraged early marriages of their children to avoid the need to subdivide the land.

In the 1970s, marriage rates increased, but Ireland was joining the West in embracing the nuclear family model. While more marriages occurred, married couples were having smaller families. By 1977, the birthrate had declined by one-third. This trend toward nuclear families applied to both Catholics and Protestants, although Catholics still had larger families. Even after marriage, contraception, which is forbidden by the Roman Catholic Church, is not legally obtainable in much of the country.

Since the 1600s, when the Scots and English arrived, very little intermarriage between those ethnic groups and the original Irish inhabitants has occurred. However, it is said that as many as one-fifth of marriages in Belfast today are between a Catholic and a Protestant; this figure may be exaggerated.

Domestic Unit. Families tend to live together in nuclear units in government housing projects that reinforce the separation of Catholics and Protestants. Catholics get smaller, older houses, while Protestant government officials award new or upgraded dwellings to other Protestants. Catholics tend to have larger families, making their homes more crowded. The government once talked about altering family assistance to favor smaller families but decided that move would lead to charges of religious discrimination from Catholics.

Inheritance. Inheritance customs changed after the 1920s. After the famine, farmers felt betrayed by the land, and the generations of birthright to a family's land stopped. Farmers who had small plots wanted to hold on to what they had and were reluctant to subdivide their parcels to hand down to their sons.

Generally the father would give his land to one son, not necessarily the oldest. Only then could that son take a bride. Often this did not take place until the father reached the age of seventy, at which time an old age pension allowed him to bequeath his land. In the meantime, the grown children who were not going to inherit land had no place in the home and usually emigrated or looked for work as craftsmen in a neighboring town.

Parents enjoy a patriarchal status and the father claims the best chair near the fire. Historically, when parents retired and passed their land to a son, they stopped sleeping in the kitchen and moved to a smaller room in the back of the house, where they would display heirlooms and religious pictures that previously were kept in the main hearth area.

Kin Groups. Kinship is reinforced by religion, class, and socioeconomic status. Catholics feel a kinship among themselves as the minority as well as links to their coreligionists in the Republic of Ireland. Protestants associate with their British heritage and identify with their compatriots in Great Britain in terms of religion, socioeconomic status, and class. Nuclear families are the main kin group, with relatives involved as kin in the extended family. Children generally adopt the father's surname. The first name is generally a Christian name, usually the name of a saint.

Main street of Enniskillen. Families tend to live together in nuclear units in government housing projects.

SOCIALIZATION

Infant Care. Infant mortality as measured in the 1926 Dublin census was high. In the 1990s the infant mortality rate fell to a level lower than that in Europe as a whole.

Child Rearing and Education. The mother raises younger children. However, when a boy makes his first communion, generally at age seven, his father rears him alongside his older brothers. Education is compulsory from ages six to fifteen. Schools are segregated, with Catholics attending parochial schools and Protestants attending public schools.

Higher Education. Queen's University in Belfast, which was founded in 1845 and originally was called Queen's College, is the most prestigious university. About eight thousand students study there, mostly in the sciences. The Union Theological College was founded in 1853. In 1968, the New University of Ulster opened in Colraine; two thousand students are enrolled. Vocational schools include the

Belfast College of Technology, Ulster Polytechnic in Newtownabbey, and the Agricultural College. Assembly College, founded in 1853, is a Presbyterian training school.

ETIQUETTE

Rules of etiquette are situational and are affected by status and class. While political conversations in pubs may be intense, political discussions occur only among friends and people with similar views. People are reluctant to discuss their political, religious, social, and economic views with outsiders.

RELIGION

Religious Beliefs. For Catholics, Good Friday, Easter, and Christmas are the most holy days and are observed by attending church services and spending time with the family. While Catholic-Protestant conflict has worsened in the last century, the religious and political history between the two groups goes back centuries. In 1534, King Henry VIII of England established himself the leader of a new church of Protestantism that he tried to impose in Ireland. He offered to increase the landholdings of Irish nobles who would recognize the new church. However, few of the Irish, and none in Ulster, accepted the offer. In 1541, Henry declared himself king of Ireland and outlawed monasteries. In 1547, Edward VI, his son and successor, declared Protestantism the official religion of Ireland and dispatched troops to enforce the new law. Those troops arrested Irish nobles and seized the property of those who refused to convert. Edward gave the confiscated land to the English Protestants who were settling there. Elizabeth I continued that policy and enforced Protestantism. In 1560, she was named head of the Irish Church and insisted that English, not Gaelic, be used in religious services.

Religious Practitioners. The Catholic clergy provide a link between God and the Catholic congregants. This represents a significant difference between Roman Catholics and Protestants. Catholic clergy participate in the civil rights movement in an attempt to equalize the volatile conflict. However, Protestants complain that the Catholic clergy exacerbate the situation by interfering with politics when they support Nationalist candidates and participate in demonstrations against the British Army.

Rituals and Holy Places. The headquarters of the Catholic and Protestant churches are located in Armagh. Each religion has a cathedral named for Saint Patrick, a fifth century missionary who brought Christianity to the Celts of the island.

Death and the Afterlife. Protestants believe that the Catholic Church teaches that salvation is found only in their religion, which means that the Protestants are heretics damned to eternal damnation. Catholics killed in "the Troubles" are venerated as martyrs.

MEDICINE AND HEALTH CARE

A national health care program was started in the 1950s. The Department of Health and Social Services administers the health care system by using tax revenues. Many services are free, such as hospitalization and maternity coverage.

SECULAR CELEBRATIONS

Saint Patrick's Day is the most widely celebrated secular holiday and is characterized by vigorous parades. New Year's Day is celebrated on 1 January. The controversial annual pride parade of the Orange Order is held on Orange Day on 12 July to celebrate and commemorate the victory of Prince William of Orange over King James II. This Protestant organization had about ninety thousand members in the 1990s. The public parade and celebration evoke tension in Belfast, often provoking Nationalists to violence.

THE ARTS AND HUMANITIES

Support for the Arts. Since the partition of Ireland is artificial, there is no real distinction between the two cultures.

Established in 1962, the Arts Council of Northern Ireland is the prime distributor of public support for the arts. Its mission is to develop and improve the knowledge, appreciation, and practice of the arts; to increase public access to and participation in the arts; and to encourage and assist artists.

Literature. Most Irish literature has been written by authors in and around Dublin. However, Northern Ireland produced the Nobel Prize-winning poet, Seamus Heaney, who has published many collections of poems. His career parallels the violent political struggles of his homeland, but he is fascinated primarily by the earth and the history embedded there. His verse incorporates Gaelic expressions as he explores the themes of nature, love, and mythology. His poems use images of death and dying, and he has written elegiac poems to friends and family members lost to "the Troubles." Northern Ireland is also the birthplace of C. Day Lewis, who wrote novels and verse and taught and translated classical literature. Lewis was named poet laureate of the United Kingdom in 1970.

Graphic Arts. Celtic designs can be seen in artistic and everyday images. The Celtic influence appears in the lettering on shop signs, letterheads, jewelry, and tombstones.

Performance Arts. Irish music incorporates fiddles, bagpipes, drums, flutes, and harps. Folk music is performed in pubs and parades. The Ulster National Orchestra in Belfast and the Philharmonic Society are the leading classical musical groups. Traditional Irish music has grown very popular outside the country in the last decade.

THE STATE OF THE PHYSICAL AND SOCIAL SCIENCES

Queen's University has a strong reputation in the sciences. Many of the eight thousand members of the student body receive undergraduate and postgraduate degrees in agriculture, food science, and horticulture. The university has research programs in livestock production and crop and grass production as well as food quality and processing to improve the competitiveness of the beef, sheep, and pig livestock sectors.

BIBLIOGRAPHY

Barritt, Denis P., and Charles F. Carter. *The Northern Ireland Problems: A Study in Group Relations*, 2nd ed., 1972.

Boyle, Kevin, and Tom Hadden. *Northern Ireland: The Choice*, 1994.

Brown, Terence. *Ireland: A Social and Cultural History, 1922 to the Present*, 1985.

Buckland, Patrick. *A History of Northern Ireland*, 1981.

Callaghan, James. *A House Divided: The Dilemma of Northern Ireland*, 1973.

Coogan, Tim Pat. *The Troubles: Ireland's Ordeal 1966–1996 and the Search for Peace*, 1997.

Darby, John, ed. *Northern Ireland: The Background to the Conflict*, 1983.

Finnegan, Richard B. *Ireland: The Challenge of Conflict and Change*, 1983.

Harkness, David. *Ireland in the Twentieth Century: Divided Island*, 1996.

Hennessey, Thomas. *A History of Northern Ireland 1920–1996*, 1997.

Hughes, Michael. *Ireland Divided: The Roots of the Modern Irish Problem*, 1994.

Mullan, Don. *Bloody Sunday: Massacre in Northern Ireland*, 1997.

Murphy, John A. *Ireland in the Twentieth Century*, 1975.

Murray, John, Sean Sheehan, and Tony Wheeler. *Ireland: A Travel Survival Kit*, 1994.

Robertson, Ian. *Blue Guide: Ireland*, 1992.

Ruane, Joseph, and Jennifer Todd. *The Dynamics of Conflict in Northern Ireland: Power, Conflict and Emancipation*, 1996.

See, Katherine O'Sullivan. *First World Nationalisms: Class and Ethnic Politics in Northern Ireland and Quebec*, 1986.

Shivers, Lynne, and David Bowman. *More Than the Troubles: A Common Sense View of the Northern Ireland Conflict*, 1984.

Taylor, Peter. *Loyalists: War and Peace in Northern Ireland*, 1999.

—S. B. DOWNEY

SEE ALSO: UNITED KINGDOM

COMMONWEALTH OF THE NORTHERN MARIANA ISLANDS

CULTURE NAME

The original inhabitants and dominant ethnic group of the Commonwealth of the Northern Mariana Islands (all the Marianas except Guam) in western Micronesia refer to themselves as Chamorros (*tsa-'mor-os*). The term *chamorri* was used to designate the upper caste at the time of Magellan's arrival in 1521. The Spaniards heard this as *chamurres* and understood it to mean "friend." By 1668, the term had shifted to *chamorro* ("bold"), because Chamorro men often wore a topknot of hair on an otherwise shaved scalp.

ALTERNATIVE NAMES

A more general designation of the people of the Northern Marianas is Mariana Islanders, but residents frequently use the acronym CNMI.

ORIENTATION

Identification. Ferdinand Magellan claimed the islands for Spain in 1521 and first named them *Las Islas de las Velas Latinas* ("The Islands of the Lateen Sails") after the triangular sails on the native canoes. Later, angered by the islanders' penchant for stealing from his ships, he renamed the archipelago *Las Islas de los Ladrones* ("The Islands of the Thieves"). In 1668, the name was changed to Las Marianas in honor of Mariana of Austria, widow of Philip IV of Spain.

Location and Geography. The CNMI is in western Micronesia, about three-quarters of the way from Hawaii to the Philippines. The fourteen islands stretch like beads on a five hundred-mile string, from Farallon de Pajaros in the north to Rota in the south. The climate is tropical. Temperature varies only slightly between a December–June dry season and a July–November rainy season. Typhoons are a threat from August through November.

The Marianas are high islands, largely limestone terraced in the south and volcanic in the north. The 176 square-mile (458 square kilometers) land area (21 percent of it arable) is concentrated in the three southern islands of Rota, Tinian, and Saipan. Only three other islands (Agrigan, Pagan, and Anatahan) are larger than ten square miles (26 square kilometers) in area. Culturally integrated but politically separate, the United States Territory of Guam lies thirty miles farther south at the bottom of the chain. Garapan is the capital of the CNMI, located on Saipan, the site of the commonwealth's only urbanized population.

Demography. The population grew from 16,780 in 1980 to an estimated 66,000 in 1998. Most of this nearly 400 percent growth was in the form of labor pools from Asia migrating in response to unprecedented economic growth. The 1995 breakdown of the population by ethnicity was Filipino, 19,868 (33.75 percent); Chamorro, 17,120 (29.1 percent); Chinese, 6,837 (11.6 percent); Micronesian, 4,818 (8.2 percent); Carolinian, 3,041 (5.2 percent); Korean, 2,325 (3.95 percent); white, 2,013 (3.4 percent); Japanese, 1,047 (1.8 percent); and all others, 1,777 (3.0 percent).

Linguistic Affiliation. The official languages are English, Chamorro, and Carolinian, an Eastern Malayo-Polynesian language that is a combination of dialects from atolls in the area of Truk. Chamorro is closely related to Tagalog (Pilipino). After more than four hundred years of Western (Spanish, German, and English) and Asian (Japanese) colonial domination, Chamorro is untouched in its grammar, although major portions of the vocabulary have been transformed into variants of Spanish and English. The Chamorros and Carolinians are largely multilingual, speaking their native tongues, English, and Japanese. Carolinian is spoken mostly in the home and the immediate neighborhood, while Chamorro is used widely in communities through-

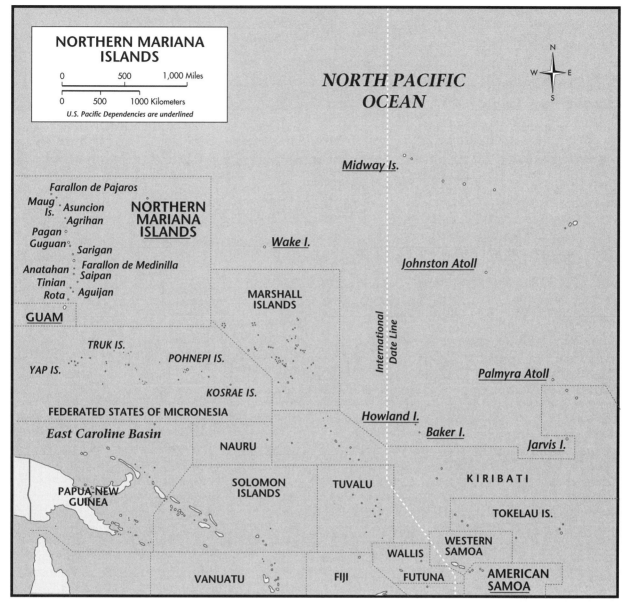

Northern Mariana Islands

out the islands. Guamanians consider the Chamorro of the CNMI, especially on Rota, a picturesque, almost sing-song dialect of their self-proclaimed standard language. Chamorros of the Northern Marianas generally are proud of their distinctive way of speaking.

Symbolism. The Catholic Church and its calendar dominate Chamorro symbolic rituals. Every community has a saint's day, and the major seasonal holidays are occasions for family and community feasting. The most important identifying symbol, displayed on the flag, is the Latte stone. These carved limestone columns in their most modest form are four- to five-foot-tall supports designed to provide a raised foundation for living and ceremonial structures. Parallel double rows of eight to twelve much taller Latte pillars topped by separate capstones are all that is left of what must have been huge structures throughout the archipelago. Much about the Latte stones remains unknown. Whatever their actual significance to those who hewed them from the islands' limestone deposits, these stones have emerged as one of the most visible links to the Chamorros' past.

HISTORY AND ETHNIC RELATIONS

The cultural history of the CNMI can be divided into a precontact period and successive periods of Spanish, German, Japanese, and American political hegemony.

Emergence of the Nation. The early history of the Marianas is little known, but they appear to have been first settled 3,500 years ago by people who sailed northward and eastward from southeastern Asia via the Philippines. The archaeological record and the little that can be gleaned from early Spanish accounts suggest that Chamorro society had developed a two-tiered system of stratification roughly based on differences of wealth stemming from richer coastal holdings as opposed to a more subsistence-level economy of inland horticulture. This was especially apparent on the larger southern islands (especially Guam), as attested by the size and distribution of Latte structures and patterns of human burial there.

Villages were small and scattered, and there is little evidence of major ceremonial centers. Kinship and descent may have been organized around matrilineal clans, a common pattern in Micronesia. However, both patrilineal and cognatic (bilateral) systems are widespread in southeastern Asia, and the Chamorros did not move further into the Pacific. The rapid replacement of Chamorro with Spanish naming practices after contact is of little note since the cultural history of the islands after 1521 was one of initial population decimation followed by massive Hispanic acculturation.

Magellan sighted the islands and claimed them for Spain in March 1521, when he made his landfall at Guam. The estimated Chamorro population at that time was nearly seventy-five thousand. By the time of the first official census in 1710, that number had plummeted to about 3,500. The disease, forced labor, and harsh treatment introduced by the Spaniards took a toll. The resulting collapse of Chamorro society and culture left a vacuum that was filled by the Catholic Church and other Hispanic institutions. Chamorro culture today, with the exception of the language structure, is largely the product of 350 years of forced inclusion in and adaptation to the Spanish Empire.

Spain sold the islands to Germany in 1899, and at that time Guam became a possession of the United States. The Germans had little impact on Chamorro culture, though they did introduce new forms of education, bureaucracy, and governance. In 1919, after Germany's defeat in World War I, Japan administered the Mariana Islands (except for Guam) and most of the rest of Micronesia under a mandate from League of Nations.

Throughout the Japanese period, the Chamorros remained isolated from their masters. Intensive agricultural development in copra and then sugarcane was carried out largely by thousands of Japanese nationals. Education and other trappings of modernization enhanced some aspects of Chamorro life, and some Chamorros look back on that period as a golden age of economic prosperity and stability. However, other than an acquired taste for imported rice, little that was Japanese remained after the battles on Saipan and Guam in 1944.

In July 1947, the area was recognized as a United Nations Trust Territory administered by the United States, beginning a period of American acculturation and modernization. The traditional Hispanic nature of Chamorro culture was infused with Yankee economic and political energy. Tourism and the reopened markets on Guam encouraged the people of the Northern Marianas to look beyond their island borders. The stage was set for confrontation with the wider world.

National Identity. In 1978, after years of debates and plebiscites, the Northern Marianas entered into a commonwealth association with the United States. Though still under foreign control, the new Commonwealth of the Northern Mariana Islands reintroduced in modern form a measure of autonomy missing from Chamorro culture for over four hundred years.

Ethnic Relations. Except for colonizers, for most of their history the Chamorro lived in ethnic isolation. The arrival of refugees from the Caroline Islands in the late nineteenth century did little to change that situation. Only since the creation of the CNMI and its attendant economic opportunities have Chamorros had to deal with large immigrant populations from Asian countries. The exposure of recent cases of labor exploitation may result in an improvement of social and economic relations in the growing multiethnic populations, especially in the urbanizing areas of Saipan.

URBANISM, ARCHITECTURE, AND THE USE OF SPACE

The urban pattern in the CNMI (essentially only on Saipan) is one of small towns growing rapidly in response to new economic opportunity in the form of tourism and light manufacturing. Areas with a denser population are characterized by a low, rectangular architecture, the product of simple plans

A man holds a green fish he caught using Daiwa tackle. A subsistence economy of farming and fishing remains fundamental.

and construction blocks. While some resort areas and golf courses take advantage of the tropical landscape and sweeping shorelines, street life tends to be defined by the glow of neon lights.

FOOD AND ECONOMY

Food in Daily Life. Rice dominates the diet, which is now built on a base of vegetables and marine resources. Most food purchased at local markets is imported from Japan, Australia, and the United States. Three meals a day, eaten at home, are the norm. Even those working in towns are usually close enough to go home for lunch, as do farmers.

Food Customs at Ceremonial Occasions. Food at religious and secular ceremonies is characterized primarily by being eaten communally. Families bring prepared food and additional food and drink for preparation on site. While the dishes and settings are generally more elaborate, the meals do not differ markedly from those for everyday consumption.

Basic Economy. While a viable subsistence economy of farming and fishing remains fundamental, the people of the CNMI look increasingly to employment in tourism and government.

Land Tenure and Property. Many families, especially among the Chamorros, own or homestead small farm parcels. In general, only native residents of the CNMI can own property. Leasing land to outside commercial interests is a major source of income for many citizens.

Commercial Activities and Major Industries. Tourism is by far the largest sector of the economy, followed by government activities and light industry, especially garment manufacturing.

SOCIAL STRATIFICATION

Classes and Castes. Economic differentiation is emerging along with the commercial economy in general. However, there are no large class differentials with the exception of the migrant labor populations, which live in poor economic conditions relative to the native residents. The subsistence economy is stable and substantial. Increases in wealth and population size are beginning to take a toll, but the CNMI, though not egalitarian, is relatively homogeneous both socially and economically.

POLITICAL LIFE

Government. The CNMI is a commonwealth that has a political union with the United States. It is self-governing with a locally elected governor, lieutenant governor, and bicameral legislature.

Leadership and Political Officials. The CNMI has a two-party system modeled after that of the United States. With a relatively small population concentrated on a few of the larger islands, politics are very personal and family-centered. Nearly everyone are related to the political leaders, and family loyalty is fierce. Fistfights and shouting matches occur at some political rallies.

Social Problems and Control. Until recently, crime was not a major problem, and it is still not common outside the urbanizing towns. Informal sanctions of disapproval and ostracism remain effective controls in most areas of social life. Rising population densities on the three largest islands have been accompanied by increased rates of juvenile delinquency, drug trafficking, and immigrant labor abuses. Nevertheless, there are few displays of public violence, and violent crime remains rare.

Women tend to hold more importance in home roles, rather than outside the household.

GENDER ROLES AND STATUSES

Chamorro culture is deeply Hispanicized with overtones of American individualism. Men play dominant roles outside the household, where women tend to hold sway.

MARRIAGE, FAMILY, AND KINSHIP

Marriage. Chamorro culture is heavily influenced by its commitment to Catholicism. Marriage is largely a matter of personal romantic love and is monogamous. Few adults remain unmarried, and large families are favored.

Domestic Unit. Newly married couples may remain with the bride's family until children are born, at which time an independent nuclear household is established neolocally. Larger extended family households develop occasionally, but the goal is for the married couple and children to live independently.

Inheritance. As islanders, Chamorros must deal with restricted land allocation to heirs. This problem has been ameliorated by the lessening need for land as a result of the growing cash economy in the

Workers in a taro field. Migrant labor populations live in poor economic conditions, compared to native residents.

towns. A form of primogeniture is practiced in which an oldest brother acts as a kind of corporate head of a sibling group that works its farming parcels collectively until other opportunities draw siblings away to other ventures. Distinctions among subsistence parcels, pastureland, government-issued homesteads, and residential lots provide additional options for distribution decisions, which typically are made public and implemented at a formal family meeting.

Kin Groups. Kinship is cognatic and bilateral. There are no corporate kin groups beyond the household and family, but extended kindreds permeate the society and shape social relationships to a large degree. Rarely does one travel to another island and not stay with relatives. The Catholic system of godparenthood further ramifies kinship networks by creating ritually defined fictive kinship relationships between children and the friends and colleagues of their parents.

SOCIALIZATION

Infant Care. Infant care is diffused throughout the household and the community, with siblings and neighbors forming an open network of caregivers. Young children are rarely left alone; they are nearly always in the company—and usually in the arms—of someone from the family or neighborhood.

Child Rearing and Education. Chamorros place a high value on formal education. Obedience to authority and a capacity for independent living go hand in hand. School age in the Marianas is from six to sixteen (first through twelfth grades). Schools operate on the American model. There are Head Start programs and preschool opportunities for the child under six years old.

Higher Education. The Northern Marianas College on Saipan is a two-year school that offers degrees in education, liberal arts, and business. Students who wish continue their education attend the University of Guam or the University of Hawaii. Young people who leave the CNMI to complete their higher education often do not return.

ETIQUETTE

Chamorros are on intimate terms with one another. They are used to being close together and often do not have to speak to communicate. When one encounters an older Chamorro, one need not say much, but one is expected to at least nod with a bow or to kiss the elder's hand briefly as a sign of respect. Casual "hellos" in the neighborhoods often consist of no more than a raising of the eyebrows in recognition. Especially at public social events, an arm around a male or female friend is a sign of casual good feeling.

RELIGION

Since the coming of the Spanish, Chamorro culture has been Catholic and Hispanic, and the Chamorro world continues to revolve around the Church calendar. The most distinctive buildings, events, customs, and ideas are Catholic, from the many community churches and chapels, to the saints' days' feasts, to the week-long wakes in the homes of the dead.

MEDICINE AND HEALTH CARE

Generally the CNMI is a healthy place to live. There are no poisonous snakes or insects and no malaria. The leading cause of death is heart disease. Automobile accidents are the fifth leading cause of death. The infectious diseases usually associated with a tropical climate are not present. Influenza has been the leading cause of illness, followed by gastroenteritis. There are health centers with dental facilities on Rota and Tinian. Medicaid and other federal health programs are available.

SECULAR CELEBRATIONS

Commonwealth Day is celebrated on 8 January, and holidays celebrated by other groups, such as the Fourth of July, are gala occasions for everyone.

BIBLIOGRAPHY

Cordy, Ross. "Social Stratification in the Mariana Islands." *Oceania* 53: 3, 272–276, 1983.

Gale, Roger William. *The Americanization of Micronesia: A Study of the Consolidation of U.S. Rule in the Pacific*, 1979.

Rogers, Robert F. *Destiny's Landfall: A History of Guam*, 1995.

Spoehr, Alexander. *Saipan: The Ethnology of a War-devastated Island*, 1954.

Thompson, Laura. *Guam and Its People*, 1947.

Web Sites

Central Intelligence Agency. *The World Factbook: Northern Mariana Islands*. [http://www.odci.gov/cia/publications/factbook/cq.html]

Economic Service Council. *The CNMI Guide*. [http://www.cnmi-guide.com]

—J. JEROME SMITH

NORWAY

CULTURE NAME
Norwegian

ALTERNATIVE NAMES
Norsk (in Norwegian), Norse (historical)

ORIENTATION

Identification. The name *Norge* ("the Northern Way") originally pertained to a region of the country before political consolidation under Harald the Fair-Haired around 900 C.E. In later use, the country's name indicates its location on the northern periphery of Europe. Some of the northerly sections of the country are home to at least two main groups (coastal and mountain) of an indigenous population of Sami (previously called Lapps) with a separate language and distinct cultural traditions. Some groups of Sami practice reindeer nomadism and range across northern Sweden and Finland. A smaller Gypsy population also was part of the otherwise homogeneous population. For humanitarian reasons, in the late twentieth century, the country welcomed asylum seekers and immigrants from other countries. Norwegians have an acute sense of identity fostered by a nineteenth century national romantic movement and by the country's emergence in 1905 as an independent constitutional monarchy. The small scale of Norwegian society, with a population of little more than four million, also promotes cultural sharing.

Location and Geography. Norway is situated on the western side of the Scandinavian peninsula, which it shares with its eastern neighbor, Sweden. The North Sea borders the country on the west, and the Barent Sea lies to the north. Spitsbergen, a group of islands four hundred miles to the north in the Arctic Ocean, is a Norwegian dependency. The country also shares borders with Finland and Russia in its northern regions. A long and narrow landmass, Norway extends more than 1,100 miles from north to south and varies in width between 270 miles and 4 miles. One-third of the country lies north of the Arctic Circle. The dominant feature of the topography is a backbone of mountains extending down the Scandinavian peninsula, with fjords, or long inlets of the sea, penetrating inland on the west and south. With a total area of 125,181 square miles (324,200 square kilometers), much of the country is dominated by rugged mountainous or coastal landscapes that have made tourism an important industry. Only about 3 percent of the land area is suitable for raising crops, and nearly half of that land is situated in the east, near Oslo, the capital, where broad, open valleys produce grain and root crops. The west coast traditionally has supported smaller farms perched along the fjords or nestled in mountain valleys. Farming and fishing have always been major occupations in this region. Trondheim, a medieval cathedral city on the west coast, also has an agricultural hinterland. The northern region constitutes the largest part of the country, with 35 percent of the land area and only 12 percent of the population. Fishing has been the major traditional occupation in this region. Oslo, which was called Kristiania before the nation gained independence, has long been associated with major governmental functions.

Demography. In January 2000, the total population was 4,478,497. Approximately thirty thousand to forty thousand of those residents self-identify as Sami. The first census which was taken in 1769, recorded 723,618 residents. For most of the nineteenth century, the population grew at an average annual rate of 1.7 percent in spite of substantial migration to the United States during the second half of that century. The post–World War II growth rate declined to about 0.2 percent annually.

Immigrants constitute just under 6 percent of the total population. The largest number of immi-

Norway

grants came from Sweden and Denmark, with the third largest contingent coming from Pakistan.

In 1999, the population grew by 0.7 percent, the largest annual rate of growth since the first half of the 1950s. This unusual growth is accounted for by the arrival of 19,300 persons from abroad. Approximately 67,200 persons with a political refugee background lived in Norway at the beginning of 1999. Among the recent refugees, the largest groups are from Bosnia (11,000), Vietnam (10,500), and Iran (8,100). Refugees are concentrated in and around the largest cities, with approximately one-third living in the Oslo area.

Linguistic Affiliation. The major languages of the indigenous minority and majority populations are

Samisk (Lappish), a Finnic language, and two official Norwegian languages, Bokmål and Nynorsk, both of which are Germanic languages. Bokmål, or ''book language,'' is derived from the Danish-influenced Norwegian used in the eastern region. A product of the national romantic movement, Nynorsk, or ''New Norwegian,'' was constructed in the nineteenth century from peasant dialects to create a genuinely Norwegian written language. Formulated by Ivar Aasen, a self-taught linguist from the west coast, Nynorsk was consciously constructed to reveal a clear relationship to Old Norse, linking contemporary Norway with the Viking age.

Symbolism. The flag, folk costumes, the land (or landscape), and the home are the major symbols of national unity. The flag (a red background with blue stripes outlined in white) is owned and flown not only by public agencies but by many private individuals. On Constitution Day (17 May), citizens appear at public celebrations carrying small flags and wearing red, white, and blue streamers pinned to their clothing. In the year 2000, there were thirteen official flag days. Folk or national costumes (bunad) are owned by large numbers of both men and women. Based on local traditional peasant apparel, women's costumes include elaborate skirts, blouses, jackets, stockings, and shoes adorned with silver pins and decorations. Because of increased affluence in recent decades, more individuals own costumes, which are considered correct attire for any festive or formal occasion. The design and colors of the costumes vary according to locality so that each large fjord or valley has a distinctive costume. Fostered by national romanticism, folk costumes are partially constructed traditions, with some historically authentic elements and some new elements. The costume for the city of Bergen, for example, was designed in 1956.

The national anthem affirms a love for the land and the importance of the home as symbols of nationhood. Festive days in this home-centered society often feature a public celebration followed by gatherings of families and relatives in people's homes. Entertaining is done at home, not at restaurants or bars. Homes are comfortable refuges and are decorated to express the identity of the family. Because there is less geographic mobility than is the case in some other countries, family members and relatives tend to live in the same region over a number of generations and identify with the local area. This attachment to place is also apparent in people's relationship to nature. Half the nation's families have access to nearby ski huts, cabins, or boats, and virtually everyone engages in outdoor pursuits such as skiing, hiking, and boating. In a variety of ways, Norwegians aim to preserve rather than transform the local natural landscape. At the same time, they attempt to preserve the cultural traditions of the locality through numerous folk museums and other specialized heritage organizations.

HISTORY AND ETHNIC RELATIONS

Emergence of the Nation. Norway claims the heritage of early Norse seafarers, raiders, colonizers, explorers, and merchants for whom the ''Viking Age'' (793 to 1050 C.E.) was named. In the ninth century Harald Fairhair became the first king of all of Norway, consolidating smaller kingdoms through alliance and conquest. Harald's descendant, Olaf Tryggvesson (Olaf I), converted to Christianity while in England and came to Norway in 995 to force conversion of the country from the Norse religion. Killed in 1030 at the Battle of Stiklestad, Olaf II (Saint Olaf) was the first king to organize an administration for church and state. His brother, Harald III, was killed invading England in 1066. The Black Death devastated the country in 1349–1350, killing at least one-third of the population. A weakened Norway was politically joined with Sweden and Denmark at the Union of Kalmar, in 1397. Danish kings ruled Norway until 1814.

The emergence of the nation-state can be traced to the development of a national culture, then to that of a national identity, and finally to the political events that led to the country's final emergence as an independent nation in 1905. The Napoleonic Wars resulted in the dissolution of the union between Denmark and Norway in 1814, the year in which the Norwegian constitution was established. Norway had been a province of Denmark for nearly four hundred years before it was ceded to Sweden. The union with Sweden was dissolved in 1905.

The foundation for the development of a national culture can be traced to the national romanticism of an intellectual elite. In the late eighteenth century, Norway was predominantly rural, with a tiny elite of religious and government officials under the king of Denmark. Those administrators began to collect information about the topography and landscape of the national regions and the natural history of the land. Later, the educated bourgeoisie wrote about the history of the country, tracing the connection between the present and the Icelandic sagas, the Viking period, the medieval period, and the decline of Norway in the period before the union with Denmark (1380–1814). Those intellectuals also began recording and describing rural culture,

A collection of houses built for coal miners and painted colorful tones to reduce suicide rates in the long, dark winters of Spitsbergen.

including folktales, architecture, customs, clothing, mythology, music, and peasant dialects. From a national romantic perspective, this information helped make the case for a distinct Norwegian land, culture, and history quite different from those of other Nordic countries. Rural culture became identified as Norwegian culture, a culture that could be traced back to Viking times.

National Identity. The idea of a distinct Norwegian culture piqued the interest of writers, painters, dramatists, musicians, and religious leaders. The culture of the rural peasants was not the culture of the intellectual elite, but the elites reinterpreted and identified with that tradition. By the middle of the nineteenth century, schoolbooks reflected the theme of a distinct, rural Norwegian culture, as did a variety of popular journals. Writers conveyed the notion that everything of true value was found close to home, in the everyday life of simple people. In the second half of the century, voluntary organizations that promoted popular enlightenment helped shape the consciousness of a common culture and history. In the national dialogues that followed, a national identity was formed, contributing to the eventual dissolution of the union with Sweden.

Ethnic Relations. Relations between the majority population and the indigenous Sami peoples have been problematic on occasion. In 1999, the United Nations Human Rights Commission asked Norway to explain the delay in giving the Sami population self-determination. Defining the population has been difficult in that many people in that population who were not engaged in reindeer nomadism chose or felt compelled to assimilate into mainstream Norwegian culture. The establishment in Karasjok, north Norway, of a Sami parliament to coordinate relations with local, regional, and national government offices has helped draw attention to the needs of that population. The Sami parliament and the governments of Norway, Sweden, and Finland are beginning to coordinate Sami issues across national boundaries.

Because immigration has been tightly controlled, immigrants from non-Scandinavian countries have not constituted a large or visible minority until recently. In the 1980s, as the attitude toward asylum seekers became somewhat less sympathetic, survey data showed that about half the respondents felt that those newcomers were given too much special treatment.

Surveys have shown that outside of business dealings, relatively few Norwegians have contact with the immigrant populations. Those who have had informal contact with immigrants tend to be sympathetic and positive toward them, but those who have not had such contact tend to be less positive. In a survey in 2000, 64 percent of residents agreed that the country should continue to take in as many immigrants and asylum seekers as it does currently. Over 90 percent of the surveyed population agreed that immigrants should have the same job opportunities as native residents, affirming a basic belief in equality of opportunity.

URBANISM, ARCHITECTURE, AND THE USE OF SPACE

The national culture is informed by an anti-urban bias that idealizes the natural environment and rural life. Regional policies are aimed at providing a high level of services and amenities in less populated regions to encourage people to remain there rather than migrate to urban centers. Cities such as Oslo, Bergen, and Trondheim have low population densities since they incorporate substantial areas of undeveloped "natural" forests within their boundaries that are used by the residents for recreation. In Oslo, streetcars run through the city to the edge of the forest, where they empty their cargo of hikers and skiers. While all the cities have parks for relaxation and enjoyment, those manicured urban environments are not as culturally important as the wilder and less regulated woods, mountains, and seashores. A walk in the woods on Sunday morning, either on a challenging trail or on the "family path" suitable for baby buggies and wheelchairs, is considered almost essential for coping with urban stress. In the winter, these paths become cross-country ski trails. Cities, thus, attempt to incorporate natural areas to counterbalance the built environment. Similarly, residential dwellings usually have their own mode of indoor-outdoor living. Single-family homes and apartment houses usually have a deck, balcony, or porch that gives residents convenient access to the outdoors.

While many older residences have straight sidewalks and broad, open lawns, many newer houses are nestled into their own miniature woods of closely planted trees and evergreen shrubs. The distinction between the built environment and the natural environment is often blurred as these two areas are made to interpenetrate.

Except perhaps for Oslo's City Hall, which serves as a landmark for ships coming up the fjord to the harbor, government architecture is usually less awe-inspiring and intimidating than inviting and approachable. The *Storting*, or parliament hall, in Oslo is built to a human scale and is embedded within a busy downtown area with considerable foot traffic. The Royal Palace, which is situated on a small hill overlooking a busy street, is the destination for thousands of cheerful marchers in the Constitution Day parade as they greet and are greeted by the royal family waving from the balcony.

Seating in parks and public places is not conducive to conversation among strangers. Acquaintances can find seating next to each other, but not in an arrangement that encourages eye contact and conversation. This configuration allows people to use public space without drawing attention to themselves or invading the personal space of others. In homes, in contrast, furniture often is arranged to encourage conversation among family members and friends. Homes should be furnished to reflect the good taste of their owners, often with the clean simplicity of Scandinavian design, using natural materials such as wood and wool.

FOOD AND ECONOMY

Food in Daily Life. The food considered by many to be most typically Norwegian is brown cheese that is thinly sliced with a cheese plane (a Norwegian invention) and eaten on bread. Breakfasts (*frokost*) usually consists of coffee, breads (including flatbread or crisp bread), pickled or smoked fish, cold meats, perhaps boiled eggs, and milk products such as cheese, butter, yogurt, and varieties of sour milk. Breakfast may be more substantial than the noon meal (*lunsj*) which may consist of an open-faced sandwich of bread, cheese, paté, or cold meat, perhaps accompanied by a piece of fruit and coffee. Fish and meat (pork, beef, lamb, chicken, and whale) and boiled potatoes, usually served with gravy or melted butter, traditionally have defined the late afternoon meal (*middag*). Root vegetables such as carrots often supplement potatoes. Beer or wine is drunk occasionally in the evening. Pizza and hamburgers are popular occasional meals and often are served at fast-food restaurants. Cafés and cafeterias serve open-faced sandwiches with cold meats, smoked fish, or cheese as well as simple but substantial meals of meat or fish and boiled potatoes. Chinese, Indian, and other ethnic restaurants often occupy the medium-price niche, while restaurants with seafood and continental cuisine are the most expensive. In the last several decades, the cuisine has become more diversified and international. The consumption of fats has gone down in the last twenty years, the consumption of meat has never been higher, and the consumption of fish has gone down

Women work in a Rabol, a traditional farm kitchen. Hafjell, Norway.

and is much lower than recommended by the Nutritional Council. The popularity of potatoes has declined, while that of rice and pasta has gone up. Cereal consumption is stable. Norway has continued to hunt minke whales along its coast. Whale meat is eaten as steaks or in a stew.

Food Customs at Ceremonial Occasions. For Constitution Day, many families traditionally eat a meal of flat bread, thinly sliced dried meats, and milk porridge, with beer or aquavit as a beverage. Christmas meal traditions vary by region and may include roast pork, other meat, or lutefisk. On festive occasions, both restaurants and family meals may feature a *kaldt bord* with a large array of cold meats, cheeses, shrimp, smoked or pickled fish, salads, jams, and soft and crisp breads. Cloudberries and lingonberries, both of which grow wild on mountain plateaus, are particular favorites.

Basic Economy. The country is highly dependent on international trade for manufactured consumer goods but has a trade surplus. Most employment is in highly specialized services and manufacturing, with only a small workforce in the traditional occupations of forestry, farming, and fishing. In a labor force of more than two million workers, approximately 72 percent are in services, 23 percent work in industry, and 5 percent engage in agriculture,

forestry, and fishing. The currency is the Krone (Crown).

Land Tenure and Property. The allocation of farmland is regulated carefully to encourage the continuity of ownership within the family line. Farms are not divided among heirs, thus avoiding the fragmentation of farms into small, economically nonviable units. The lineal descendants of a farmer have the first right to purchase a farm. Conflicts over farm boundaries and the surreptitious movement of boundary stones are part of the folklore of most agricultural districts. Hikers have the right to walk on unplanted farmland.

Commercial Activities. Firms produce, package, distribute, and sell food products, beverages, textiles, clothing, footwear, wood products, furniture, and chemicals for domestic consumption. Printing, publishing, and media production are important enterprises for a highly literate nation that is a world leader in the consumption of newspapers, magazines, and books per capita.

Major Industries. As a consequence of the discovery and exploitation of North Sea oil in the 1970s, Norway has become the world's second largest exporter of oil and natural gas. Much of this production is managed by Statoil, a government enterprise. Since 1993 the country has exported hydroelectricity, which it produces in excess of domestic needs. Although shipbuilding has declined, Norway has one of the leading merchant fleets, with approximately 762 ships. Other exports include transportation equipment, electrometallurgical products, electrochemical products (processed with hydroelectric power), paper and pulp from the extensive forests, and fish, increasingly produced in fish farms in coastal waters. For the home market, the country produces equipment, furniture, and textiles. About half the manufacturing firms are located along the Oslo fjord. Livestock are the most important products of the subsidized agricultural sector.

Trade. Norway exports goods to its main trading partners: the European Union, Sweden, Germany, the United Kingdom, Netherlands, France, and the United States. Exports include petroleum and natural gas, hydroelectric power, metals, chemicals, paper pulp, and fish. The United States is a significant importer of smoked salmon. Manufactured goods, machinery, and chemicals are imported from the trading partners.

Division of Labor. Government, labor, and management are integrated into a centralized industrial planning system. Since the 1970s, the principle of codetermination has meant that labor and management increasingly share the determination of daily operations and longer-term planning. Workers typically have a great deal of autonomy. As a consequence of this trend in industrial democracy, emphasis is placed on training and the upgrading of workers' skills. In contrast to countries where labor is cheap and training is limited, decision making frequently is delegated to lower-level workers. The division of labor is based more on skills than on status and seniority.

SOCIAL STRATIFICATION

Classes and Castes. The ethos of egalitarianism is reflected in the highly progressive marginal tax rate on personal incomes. While income differences are relatively flat, there is a small proportion of extremely rich owners and managers of merchant fleets. Although the affluent are likely to own ski huts in the mountains, their huts may not be better furnished than those of less affluent workers. Conspicuous consumption is not admired. Leisure time is an important resource for industrial workers, who in 2002 will have five weeks of vacation annually. Counting national holidays, this brings the

number of working hours in the year down to 1,703 for industrial workers. Immigrant populations have tended to move into some of the less desirable and less well-paid occupations such as cleaners and fast food workers.

Symbols of Social Stratification. Affluent individuals signal their wealth by driving a luxury car, wearing expensive clothing, and taking expensive vacations. They may have a posh Oslo accent. However, these differences in possessions and advantages do not symbolize differences in moral worth. The author Aksel Sandemose, in *En Flyktning krysser sitt spor* (1953), described the law of the fictional village of Jante, which warns that "you should not believe that you are better than we are." The Law of Jante expresses a widespread cultural belief in egalitarianism.

POLITICAL LIFE

Government. Norway is a constitutional monarchy that divides responsibility between the parliament *(Storting)* and the King's Council of State, which consists of a prime minister and other ministers of state. The *Storting*, which consists of 165 representatives, is the supreme authority and controls finances. Representatives are elected by direct vote for a four-year term. One-quarter of the representatives serve in the upper chamber *(Lagting)*, and the rest form the lower chamber *(Odelsting)*. Local government is represented by 450 municipalities in eighteen counties.

Leadership and Political Officials. Leaders are supposed to be articulate and dedicated spokespersons for the policies of their parties. The major parties, listed roughly in order of their popularity in recent elections, are the Norwegian Labor Party *(Arbeiderpartiet)*, a socialist party affiliated with labor unions; the Progress Party *(Fremskrittspartiet)*, a nationalistic party; the Conservative Party *(Høyre)*; the Christian People's Party *(Kristelig Folkepartiet)*, which supports the use of the principles of Christianity in politics; the Center Party *(Senterpartiet)*, which originally focused on agrarian issues; the Socialist Left Party *(Sosialistisk Venstrepartiet)*; and the Liberal Party *(Venstre)*, a reform party. Coalition governments that rely on the cooperation of two or more parties are not uncommon. Party leaders receive considerable media attention and are supposed to be accessible to the electorate. They are not likely to respond to offers of gifts or special privileges.

Social Problems and Control. The judicial system has three levels: the district *(Herredsrett)* and city

A young Lapland boy and girl wearing traditional dress in Kautokeino. Each large fjord or valley has a distinctive costume.

courts *(Byrett)*, the High Court *(Lagmannsrett)* with six jurisdictions in the nation; and the Supreme Court *(Høyesterett)*. Each municipality has a conciliation council *(Forliksråd)*, where civil cases go first for mediation and possible out-of-court settlement. If this effort fails, the case can be taken to the district or city court. An "ombud" system has been established to hear complaints about actions by government agencies and private firms. The crime rate is about ten reported crimes per hundred thousand population. While the rate of crimes against persons is increasing, most crimes involve property.

Military Activity. National military service is required, with the option of community service for conscientious objectors. The nation has an army, navy, and air force; is a member of the North Atlantic Treaty Organization (NATO); and participates in peacekeeping operations. Norway spends 3 percent of the gross national product on defense.

Social Welfare and Change Programs

After 1945, the National Insurance Scheme was developed to manage and allocate resources for health, old age, disabilities, widows, widowers, children, and single parents. Approximately 15 percent of government expenditures are for health services. Nongovernmental organizations play an important role in supplementing this welfare system in partnership with the government. Special attention is given to organizations that support disadvantaged citizens through subsidies granted by local governments.

Nongovernmental Organizations and Other Associations

Approximately 62 percent of the population belonged to at least one voluntary organization in 1995. Historically, voluntary organizations were first developed in the middle of the nineteenth century as agents of change to support the social movements that were sweeping the country. Voluntary organizational life has been based on unpaid participation, personal membership, and commitment to egalitarian democratic principles. While participation in religious and temperance organizations has declined, membership has increased in organizations devoted to recreation and outdoor sports.

Gender Roles and Statuses

Division of Labor by Gender. In the contemporary period, Norway has followed an ideology, if not always the practice, of gender neutrality in access to economic, political, social, and religious roles. Women entered the workforce in larger numbers during the 1970s but continued to be involved in unpaid work to a greater degree than were men. There are few women in the upper levels of management of businesses and industries. According to the United Nations Development Programme, which created a "Gender-Related Development Index" to measure achievements in increased life expectancy, educational attainment, and income equality for men and women in 146 countries, Norway ranked second behind Canada and ahead of Sweden.

The Relative Status of Women and Men. The cause of gender equality was advanced by the women's movement of the 1960s. At that time, nine of ten women with small children did not work outside the home. Women began to enter the labor force in greater numbers with the increase in industrialization. Now nearly eight of ten women are employed outside the home.

Education is deliberately gender-neutral, with the goal of giving everyone an equal opportunity for self-realization. In the 1980s, women entered

Sod roofs of old houses in Roros, a mining town founded in 1646. Norway.

higher education in larger numbers, and constituted approximately 55 percent of the students at universities in 2000. In law and administration, men and women are accorded equality, with parental leaves available for both. Many of the roles traditionally reserved for men, such as the military and politics, are now integrated. In 1981, at age forty-one, Dr. Gro Harlem Brundtland first served as the prime minister, the youngest person and the first woman to do so. Several political parties follow the "sixty/forty" rule in establishing committees, with women constituting at least 40 percent of the membership.

The armed services are sexually integrated, although the majority of service personnel are men. In 1998, the commander of a coastal defense submarine was a woman, with a crew of twenty men and one other woman. Some women's organizations regard this as tokenism and state that when the critical mass of 30 percent women is achieved, they will be pleased with the progress of integration of the armed forces.

MARRIAGE, FAMILY, AND KINSHIP

Marriage. Marriages are supposed to be romantic love matches between two individuals with similar values and perspectives. Marrying for economic, social, or political reasons would seem improper to most people. When King Harald, then the crown prince, wished to marry a commoner rather than seek a bride among the royal families of Europe, the nation approved.

Currently, 38 percent of residents are married, compared with 47 percent in 1978. The divorce rate has doubled in the last twenty years. In this generation, married women have worked for pay outside the household to a greater degree than was the case in earlier generations.

Domestic Unit. Currently, families usually consist of a husband, a wife, and no more than two children. Single-parent families are increasingly common. Two major urban family cultures, with a rural variant, exist. These cultures include the urban middle-class family, which may focus on a fair exchange of services and an equal sharing of tasks, and the urban working-class family, which may focus on the common good of the family rather than the needs of the individual members. Urban families often create symbolic boundaries between themselves and others; internally, they value "peace and quiet" as a theme of family life. The typical rural farm family focuses on maintaining a committed, harmonious unit. Divorce seems to be more common in the first type of family.

Inheritance. At marriage all material goods become joint property. A couple may enter into a contract specifying that, in case of divorce, each will retain the goods they brought to the marriage. This may be important in the case of farms and other significant property. Surviving spouses have a right to continue living in the family house until death. Children inherit equally from the parents.

Kin Groups. Three-generation family households exist most commonly in rural areas. Parents and children often choose to live close to each other. Relatives on both sides of a marriage are invited for life-crisis ceremonies such as baptism, confirmation, marriage, and death.

SOCIALIZATION

Infant Care. With the institutionalization of parental leave from employment, both parents can be available to provide care for infants. Traditionally, infants were regarded as defenseless and in need of constant care. Infants sleep in separate beds or cribs, either in their parents' bedroom or in a separate room. Breastfeeding on demand is now usual, but in previous generations was scheduled about every four hours. Fresh air is considered important and often babies are allowed to sleep outdoors in a pram. Stimulation, exploration, and play, both indoors and outdoors, are now emphasized. Some mothers carry infants close to their breast in carrying slings, but the use of prams is more common. Many parents use day care facilities for one to six year olds, although this form of institutional care for the youngest ages is controversial. For older toddlers, the social experience of interacting with others in day care facilities is highly valued.

Child Rearing and Education. The national culture tends to be extremely child-centered. A national welfare system for children was enacted as early as 1896, and in 1981, a national ombudsperson for children was established. Ideally, children should be cooperative and independent. However, socialization tends to be permissive since children are not taught boundary-setting rules and manners early. Childhood lasts longer than it does in many European countries, with adolescence not ending before graduation from high school. Since numerous mothers are employed, many children are socialized in child care facilities, either privately or through the local authority. Paid babysitters, usually young

girls, may provide child care in cities when grandmothers are not available.

Confirmation as a member of the church is an important rite of passage. The ceremony is followed by a party to which neighbors and relatives are invited. Girls usually are given a *bunad*, or folk costume.

In traditional rural society, children were transformed into responsible adults, participating in adult economic activities, without going through a culturally recognized stage of adolescence. In the late twentieth century, adolescence became much more important for developing an identity separate from one's parents.

Higher Education. Vocational training or higher education for the majority of citizens is emphasized. After ten years of compulsory schooling, students may go on to an upper secondary school and then to one of the four universities or many colleges. Education accounts for approximately 14 percent of government expenditures.

ETIQUETTE

Residents tend to be egalitarian, private, and noncompetitive. Gender equality is observed in most social settings. People rarely use the polite or formal form of address; the use of the informal pronoun for personal address is almost universal. Independence and self-sufficiency are valued. Being indebted by borrowing or receiving favors makes people uncomfortable. Individuals generally do not call attention to themselves through loud speech or flamboyant behavior. Personal space is respected, and so individuals stand well apart from each other when conversing. Punctuality is expected both in business and in social life.

People may be reserved among strangers but are warm and friendly once a relationship has been established. One should not inquire about personal issues unless one is well acquainted with a person. Respect for each individual's dignity is expected.

Competition is downplayed in most settings, Even the victors in sports contests are supposed to be humble and not obviously proud. After the 1994 Winter Olympics in Lillehammer, King Harald worried that perhaps the nation had not been a good host since its athletes had won so many medals.

RELIGION

Religious Beliefs. The Norwegian-born Viking Olav Tryggvason was baptized as a Christian in

A classical-style building along Karl Johans Gate in downtown Oslo, Norway.

London in 994 C.E. Soon afterward, King Olav brought Christianity to his homeland, converting first the leaders and later the farmers. In 1536, the Reformation came to the area, with the consequence that a greater emphasis was placed on personal faith. In 1814, the Evangelical Lutheran religion was named the official religion of the state, but the constitution also guaranteed freedom of religion. The pietist movement, which was particularly strong in the country in the late eighteenth and early nineteenth centuries, posed an alternative to the state church and contributed to an individual sense of religious commitment unmediated by the clergy. The state church subscribes to a belief in God, Jesus Christ, and the Holy Ghost. The main religious holidays celebrate belief in the birth, death, and resurrection of Christ. Other religious groups such as Roman Catholics, Pentecostalists, Seventh Day Adventists, Baptists, and Methodists, receive state subsidies. In recent years, immigrant populations have brought Islam to the nation.

Religious Practitioners. The king is the head of the state church, which employs a system of bishops and priests in the administrative structure. Local priests hold religious services and perform baptisms, confirmations, weddings, and funerals. The king appointed the first woman priest in 1961 and the first woman bishop in 1993. More than seventy nationally organized Christian voluntary organizations reinforce religious beliefs and practices. Those organizations also carry out missionary work at home and abroad and help with youth work and welfare.

Rituals and Holy Places. During the medieval period, the holy shrine of Saint Olav in the cathedral at Trondheim was a destination for pilgrims. In the contemporary period, 87 percent of the population belongs to the state church. While about seven million church visits are recorded annually, many people are more likely to be found on ski slopes or hiking trails than in church on Sunday. Religious services in the state church occur weekly and on the major religious holidays, including Holy Thursday, Good Friday, Easter, Ascension, and Whitmonday.

Death and the Afterlife. According to the doctrine of the state church, souls reside in heaven with Jesus after death. After the funeral, the body of the deceased is cremated or interred in a graveyard, usually adjacent to a church.

MEDICINE AND HEALTH CARE

Norway is one of the healthiest countries in the world, with an average life expectancy of nearly seventy-eight years. Modern medicine replaced folk

A church in Bud, a fishing village near Molde. The constitution guarantees freedom of religion.

medical beliefs in the eighteenth and nineteenth centuries. Currently, there are over fifteen thousand doctors and nearly sixty thousand nurses. The compulsory National Insurance Scheme provides free hospital care and modest charges for medicines and primary care. Approximately 15 percent of government expenditures go for health care.

SECULAR CELEBRATIONS

The major holidays are New Year's Day (1 January), Labor Day (1 May), Constitution Day (17 May), Christmas (25 December), and Boxing Day (26 December). Labor Day is celebrated by the labor unions, with parades in the larger towns. The most important celebration of nationhood is on Constitution Day, which is an occasion for massive public parades by voluntary organizations, bands, unions, schools, and other civic groups. Christmas and Boxing Day are focused on family visits and gift giving.

THE ARTS AND HUMANITIES

Support for the Arts. Because of the small population base, the artistic community is challenged to earn a living. Government subsidies coordinated by thirty nationwide artists' organizations have pro-

vided a particularly Norwegian solution. Professional artists receive a minimum income until retirement. Through a variety of cooperative arrangements with counties and municipalities, the government has sponsored the creation of touring cultural organizations, bringing concerts, theater, and art exhibitions to smaller towns.

Literature. The Icelandic sagas of Snorri Sturlusson (1178–1241) often are considered the beginning of Norwegian literature, followed by *The King's Mirror*, a thirteenth century work. Pedar Clausson Friis (1545–1614) wrote descriptive works about the country and translated the sagas into Norwegian. *The Trumpet of the Northland* (1700) by Petter Dass details life in Norway. In the early eighteenth century, Ludvig Holberg wrote in a variety of forms, including satire and comedy. Henrik Wergeland (1808–1845) inspired the national romantic movement. As their contribution to the discovery of a national culture, Peter Asbjørnsen and Jørgen Moe collected the *Norwegian Folktales* (1841–1844). In the nineteenth century, the dominant figure was Henrik Ibsen (1828–1906), whose psychological dramas remain important in world literature. Knut Hamsun wrote powerful novels in the twentieth century. Later writers include Sigurd Hoel, Nordal Grieg, Tarjei Vesaas, and the Nobel Prize winner Sigrid Undset. Significant postwar writers include Jens Bjørneboe, Bjorg Vik, and Kjartan Flagstad.

Graphic Arts. Painters in the nineteenth century helped establish a national romantic vision. Edvard Munch's (1863–1944) symbolist works have been influential internationally. In sculpture, Gustav Vigeland's Frogner Park sculptures are well known. Pottery, glass, jewelry, metalsmithing, and textiles are central to Scandinavian design.

Performance Arts. The nation's greatest musician, Edvard Grieg (1843–1907), was inspired by the folk themes of his homeland, as was the violinist Ole Bull. Many cities have festivals for the performing arts. Perhaps the most famous is Bergen's annual festival featuring music, drama, and dance. Molde's jazz festival is notable. The National Theater and National Opera in Oslo are important institutions.

THE STATE OF THE PHYSICAL AND SOCIAL SCIENCES

The universities at Oslo, Bergen, Trondheim, and Tromso have extensive science and social science departments. Many of the regional colleges are strong in one or both areas. A variety of research institutes focus on applied knowledge, in fields as diverse as fish farming and petroleum extraction.

BIBLIOGRAPHY

Aarebrot, Frank. "Norway: Center and Periphery in a Peripheral State." In Stein Rokkan and Derek Urwin, eds., *The Politics of Territorial Identity: Studies in European Regionalism*, 1982.

Alvestad, Marit, and Ingrid Pramling Samuelsson. "A Comparison of the National Preschool Curricula in Norway and Sweden." *Early Childhood Research and Practice* 1 (2): 1999.

Anderson, Myrdene. "Transformations of Centre and Periphery for the Saami in Norway." *Anthropologica* 29 (2): 109-130, 1987.

Burgess, J. Peter. *Ivar Aasen's Logic of Nation: Toward a Philosophy of Culture*, 1999.

Caulkins, Douglas. "Norwegians: Cooperative Individualists." In Carol Ember, Melvin Ember, and David Levinson, eds., *Portraits of Culture: Ethnographic Originals*, 1994.

———. "Are Norwegian Voluntary Organizations Homogeneous Moralnets? Reflections on Naroll's Selection of Norway as a Model Society." *Cross-Cultural Research* 29 (1): 43–57, 1995.

Christiansen, Peter Munk, and Hilmar Rommetvedt. "From Corporatism to Lobbyism: Parliaments, Excecutives, and Organized Interests in Denmark and Norway." *Scandinavian Political Studies* 22 (3): 195–220, 1999.

Dobbin, Frank, and Terry Boychuk. "National Employment Systems and Job Autonomy: Why Job Autonomy Is High in the Nordic Countries and Low in the United States, Canada, and Australia." *Organizational Studies* 20 (2): 257–291, 1999.

Fitzhugh, William, and Elisabeth I. Ward. *Vikings: The North Atlantic Saga*, 2000.

Grønlund, Inga Lena. "Restructuring One-Company Towns: The Norwegian Context and the Case of Mo I Rana. *European Urban and Regional Studies* 1 (2): 161–185 1994.

Gullestad, Marianne. *Kitchen-Table Society*, 1984.

———. "Small Facts and Large Issues: The Anthropology of Contemporary Scandinavian Society." *Annual Review of Anthropology* 18: 71–93, 1989.

———. Gullestad, Marianne. *The Art of Social Relations: Essays on Culture, Social Action and Everyday Life in Modern Norway*, 1992.

———. *Everyday Life Philosophers: Modernity, Morality, and Autobiography in Norway*, 1996.

Hellevik, Ottar. *Nordmenn og det Gode Live: Norsk Monitor 1985–1995*, 1996.

Hodne, Bjarne. *Norsk Nasjonalkultur: En Kulturpolitisk Oversikt*, 1995.

Hylland, Thomas Eriksen, ed. *Flerkulturell forståelse*, 1997.

Jenssen, Anders Todal. "All That Is Solid melts into Air: Party Identification in Norway." *Scandinavian Political Studies* 22 (1): 1–27, 1999.

———. 'Jo Mere vi er Sammen, dess Gladere Blir Vi'? Kontakt, Vennskap og Konflikt Mellom Nordmenn og Innvandrere. *Tidsskrift for Samfunnsforskning* 32 (1): 23–52, 1991.

Jonassen, Christen T. *Value Systems and Personality in a Western Civilization: Norwegians in Europe and America*, 1983.

Keil, Anne Cohen, ed. *Continuity and Change: Aspects of Contemporary Norway*, 1993.

Klausen, Arne Martin, ed. *Den Norske Væremåten: Antropologisk Søklys på Norsk Kultur*, 1984.

Martinson, Floyd. *Growing Up in Norway: 800 to 1990*, 1992.

Rasmussen, Bente, and Tove Hapnes. "Excluding Women from the Technologies of the Future? A Case Study of the Culture of Computer Science." *Futures* 23 (10): 1107–1119, 1991.

Reed, Peter, and David Rothenberg. *Wisdom in the Open Air*, 1993.

Selbyg, Arne. *Norway Today: An Introduction to Modern Norwegian Society*, 1986.

Selle, Per. *Frivillige Organisasjonar i Nye Omgjevnader*, 1996.

Stiles, Deborah, Judith Gibbons, Suzanne Lie, Therese Sand, and Jodie Krull. "'Now I Am Living in Norway': Immigrant Girls Describe Themselves." *Cross-Cultural Research* 32 (3): 279–298, 1998.

Su-Dale, Elizabeth. *Culture Shock! Norway*, 1995.

Sundberg, Jan. "The Enduring Scandinavian Party System." *Scandinavian Political Studies* 22 (3): 221–241, 1999.

Ugland, Thorbjørg Hjelmen. *A Sampler of Norway's Folk Costumes*, 1996.

Vanberg, Bent. *Of Norwegian Ways*, 1984.

—D. DOUGLAS CAULKINS

OMAN

CULTURE NAME

Omani

ALTERNATIVE NAMES

Various peoples in Oman use regional names such as Dhofari, which identifies them as being from the southern region of Oman, or Zanzibari, which identifies them as having close links with East Africa and at one time Zanzibar.

ORIENTATION

Identification. Although Oman has existed as a distinct nation for several thousand years, the modern state—the Sultanate of Oman—is a creation of the last two centuries. The traditional territorial concept of Oman was altered in this period by the independence of the northwestern part of Oman as the United Arab Emirates and the absorption into the sultanate of the southern region of Dhofar. Although the names of both Oman and Dhofar are clearly of great antiquity, their original meanings and sources are uncertain. While most northern Omanis share a common Arab, Muslim, and tribal culture, the people of Dhofar remain culturally distinct and often feel culturally closer to neighboring regions in Yemen to the west.

Location and Geography. The Omani culture owes much to the geography of the country. The cultural heartland lies in the interior, in the valleys of the mountainous backbone which parallels the coastal plains and the interior plains. Seas to the north and east and deserts to west and south have served to isolate the country from the outside world. At the same time, Oman's presence on the Indian Ocean has fostered a long maritime tradition which has enriched the culture through the settlement of many Baluchis (the Indo-Iranian people of Baluchistan) along the northern coast and the interaction with East African cultures. Traditionally,

Oman's capital was located in the interior but Muscat (Masqat), now the principal seaport, has served as the capital since the beginning of the nineteenth century. Northern Oman is separated from southern Dhofar by several hundred miles of desert, which results in the cultural distinctiveness of the Dhofaris.

Demography. Oman's only census (1993) revealed a total population of 2 million, of which 1.5 million were Omanis. There were 175,000 residents of Dhofar. Census figures were not broken down into ethnic or linguistic categories, although it can be estimated that several hundred thousand Omanis were of Baluchi origin. About half the Omani population belongs to the Ibadi sect of Islam and a similar number belong to mainstream Sunni Islam. There are several small communities of Shia Muslims. Population growth is estimated at nearly 4 percent per year.

Linguistic Affiliation. Arabic is the principal language spoken by Omanis, who have spoken it since the immigration of Arab tribes nearly two millennia ago. The Omani dialect generally is close to modern standard Arabic, although coastal dialects employ a number of loanwords from Baluchi, Persian, Urdu and Gujarati (two Indo-Aryan languages), and even Portuguese. The mountain peoples of Dhofar, as well as several small nomadic groups in the desert between Dhofar and northern Oman, speak a variety of unique South Arabian languages that are not mutually intelligible with modern Arabic. Minority groups speak Arabic as well as their own languages at home, and English is widely spoken as a second language.

Symbolism. The national symbol employs a pair of crossed *khanjars*, the traditional daggers that all Omani men wore until recently (and still wear on formal occasions). This symbol is integrated into the national flag and appears in nearly all government logos.

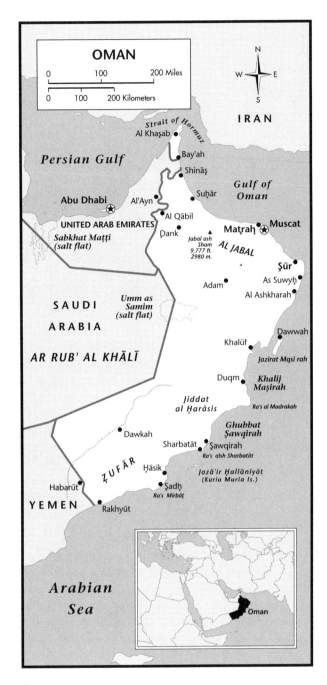

Oman

HISTORY AND ETHNIC RELATIONS

Emergence of the Nation. Oman has a very long history and was known as Magan to ancient Persian and Mesopotamian civilizations and was an important producer of copper and ornamental stone. The Arab tribes in Oman adopted Islam during the lifetime of the prophet Muhammad (c.570–632) and forced the Persian colonizers to leave. Since then, Oman has generally remained an independent Arab and Ibadi/Sunni Muslim entity.

National Identity. The Omani national identity has evolved from its predominant Arab language and culture, its tribal organization, and Islam. Oman withstood attempts by classical Islamic empires to subdue the country, and the Portuguese invasion of the sixteenth century was confined to coastal ports and was terminated by national Omani resistance in the mid-seventeenth century.

Ethnic Relations. Although the dominant cultural group in Oman is Arab and Ibadi/Sunni Muslim, the culture has been very tolerant of other groups. Ethnic, sectarian, or linguistic conflict rarely occurs in Oman although tribal disputes are not unknown.

URBANISM, ARCHITECTURE, AND THE USE OF SPACE

The contemporary urban character of Omani culture has strong ties to Indian Mogul architectural style. This is manifested in the seafront white-washed two- and occasionally three-story residential buildings that line the road along the harbor of Matrah (Muscat's sister city). It is also seen in the style of some mosques and minarets with their slim and ornate shapes, as well as in public buildings such as the Ministry of Foreign Affairs building in Qurm. Other contemporary constructions are more eclectic in style.

Earlier architectural styles found in the towns and interior cities of Oman, such as Nizwa, Ibri, Ibra, and Bahla, reflected a pared down and simpler cultural expression and use of space that was consistent with Ibadism, a relatively austere form of Islam.

Private residences reflect the culture's concern for gendered space. Most Omani homes have formal rooms for men and their visitors, while women generally socialize in each other's private quarters. When people meet to mark various rites of passage, such as births, marriages, and deaths, the celebrations are marked by clear gendered space. It is women who visit other women on the occasion of a birth in a family. Marriage rituals entail elaborate celebrations for women only, for men only, and, when space is open, with segregated sitting areas. Deaths are similarly marked by gendered use of space, with only men attending the actual burial of a body.

FOOD AND ECONOMY

Food in Daily Life. Omani cuisine revolves around rice. The morning meal is not significant, often consisting of bread or leftovers from the day before, and tea. The main meal of the day is in early to mid-afternoon. It is generally a large dish of rice with a thin sauce often based on tomato or tomato paste and meat or fish. Pork does not exist in the Omani diet as it is prohibited by Islam. The evening meal is generally very light, sometimes consisting only of fruit or bread and tea. The influence of Indian cooking is very strong. A variety of Indian restaurants are found throughout the country. In the capital area, there are a number of Western fast-food establishments, as well as a variety of French, Italian, Japanese, and Chinese restaurants.

Food Customs and Ceremonial Occasions. Dates, fresh or dried, are important to the diet and to the ritual of hospitality. Equally important is *helwa*, a sweet confection based on clarified butter, honey, and spices. Both are served to guests with strong, bitter, and often cardamom-scented coffee. During Ramadan, the Islamic month of fasting, Omanis refrain from eating or drinking between sunrise and sunset. They break their fast with coffee and dates followed shortly thereafter by a ritual meal, often shared with family and close friends, of elaborate foods heavy in oils and spices.

Basic Economy. A large percentage of Omanis live in rural areas and many others own land and property in the countryside even though they live and work in the towns. Many of those in the countryside are self-sufficient farmers and fishermen. Livestock production is the basis of agricultural activity in the center and south of Oman, with fishing along Oman's long coastline coming a close second. Nearly one-third of Omani's nonoil exports come from agriculture and fisheries. Oman imports more than half the vegetables and dairy products it needs and just under half the beef, eggs, and mutton.

Land Tenure and Property. All land is officially owned by the state. Some land has been recognized as privately held and in the late twentieth century the government pursued a policy of providing all Omanis with private parcels of land for residences and farms. Shared property rights or land use rights are held by custom and are generally tribal in origin. Hence much of the interior semiarid and arid lands are used by nomadic pastoral tribes. Although their territory is no longer recognized as theirs by the state, it remains uncontested by local inhabitants and other tribes.

Commercial Activities. Agriculture and fishing are the traditional economic activities in Oman. Dates and limes, make up most of the country's exports. Coconut palms, wheat, and bananas are also grown. Cattle are raised in Dhofar. Fish and shellfish exports create a steady income of roughly $40 million (U.S.).

Major Industries. Oman is an oil-producing nation and revenues from petroleum products have been the backbone of Oman's dramatic development over the last three decades of the twentieth century. But oil resources are not extensive and natural gas reserves are becoming more prominent, with liquified natural gas exports expected to provide significant new income in the early twenty-first century.

Trade. After oil, petroleum, and liquified gas, fish and shellfish account for the majority of Oman's export trade. The fish and shellfish are sold mainly to Saudi Arabia and the United Arab Emirates, although some of this fresh product finds its way in refrigerated trucks further north. Dates and limes are also exported.

Division of Labor. Both men and women engage in agricultural activities: men work the date gardens, while women tend to the fields of wheat, barley, and alfalfa. Men go out in fishing boats or dive from the shore, while women often mend fishing nets. Children take on domestic agricultural and fishing tasks at an early age, nine being a common age for starting. The elderly are greatly respected and are often relieved from any physical work, but their opinions and ideas are eagerly sought by the middle-aged and young.

SOCIAL STRATIFICATION

Classes and Castes. Omani culture does not have a caste system, but it does operate in a hierarchy based on family connections (tribal ties), relative wealth, and religious education. At the top of the pyramid is the sultan and his immediate family, the Al-Sa'id. This is followed by a large tribal group, the Al-Bu Sa'id. Prior to the discovery of oil in the country, the wealthiest group (class) was arguably made up of the merchant families, many of them Indian in origin, language, and culture; a particular Omani community, mainly of Hyderabadi origin, also accumulated some wealth through trade in foodstuffs. Certain families and tribes had built reputations for religious learning and mediation skills, and they often represented the government in the interior of the country. In the late twentieth century, wealth spread somewhat and a few more Omani families joined the ranks of the extremely wealthy. Oman has a small but growing middle class while the vast majority of its population out-

A crowded market in Fanja. The vast majority of the population outside of the capital area are engaged in subsistence agriculture, fishing, or animal husbandry.

side of the capital area are engaged in subsistence agriculture, fishing, or animal husbandry.

Symbols of Social Stratification. Dress in Omani culture is a ''badge,'' one highly visible and prominent marker of ethnic identity. Among Omani nationals, dress is finely tuned to reflect each person's region of origin or ethnic background. Women's clothing and, in particular, the choice of face covering and head cloth advertises membership in a particular tribal, ethnic, or language group. Men's clothing, consisting of a long, ankle-length shirt (locally called a *thawb* or *dishdashah*), is also amenable to the expression of tribal and regional belonging through variations in the style of the collars and sleeves. Head covering is required of men as well as women.

POLITICAL LIFE

Government. Oman is a sultanate (a type of monarchy) with a sultan as the head of state and head of government. His position is hereditary within the Al Bu Sa'id family. There are few checks on the power of the sultan and his decrees form the basis of law. He appoints a council of ministers and can dismiss ministers without reason. There is no prime minister.

Leadership and Political Officials. Senior members of the sultan's family routinely receive important government positions. More distant members of the family serve as ministers, other government officials, and the equivalent of governors throughout the country. Other ministers and senior government officials are chosen by merit and family or tribal connections; Muscat merchant families are overrepresented. There are no political parties and a limited electorate chooses candidates for the Majlis al-Shura, an indirectly elected consultative council dealing with social issues.

Social Problems and Control. The legal system is derived from a combination of Western and Arab civil codes with the *Shari'ah* (Islamic law) used in family matters such as marriage and inheritance. The Royal Oman Police covers the entire country and is responsible for traffic, criminal investigation, firefighting, the coast guard, and immigration. Crime is infrequent although the capital area has seen a modest increase in burglaries and there is some drug and alcohol abuse. Civil disobedience is unknown and there is complete respect for the law and state institutions.

Military Activity. The armed forces of Oman were created to counter several insurrections beginning in the 1950s. Since the mid-1970s, however, there has been no unrest in Oman and the security forces are geared to protect against potential external threats. Oman continues to maintain a relatively large military establishment in part to provide employment for its people.

SOCIAL WELFARE AND CHANGE PROGRAMS

Social welfare is still basically a family and kin network business. The old, the handicapped, the disabled, and the disadvantaged are looked after by a network of relatives. Since the 1970s, the government has worked hard to establish a social welfare service to promote stability and security for families in a rapidly changing social environment. The Ministry of Social Affairs, Labor, and Vocational Training takes responsibility for making monthly payments to the elderly, the widowed, the divorced, and the disabled. Special attention has been given to training the mildly disabled, especially the young, through special government centers.

NONGOVERNMENTAL ORGANIZATIONS AND OTHER ORGANIZATIONS

Oman has very few nongovernmental organizations (NGOs). Perhaps as a reflection of security concerns, it remains very difficult to acquire formal government recognition of NGO status. The first NGO to be created in Oman in the 1970s, the Omani Women's Association, was integrated into the Ministry of Social Affairs and Labor in the early 1980s. The Association for the Welfare of Handicapped Children, which was founded in 1990, runs a number of centers for the care and rehabilitation of disabled children and has acquired a semiofficial status. The Oman Charitable Organization (also known as the Oman Benevolent Society), was created in the late 1990s by royal decree to provide assistance to the needy. Other NGOs include sports clubs, literary associations, and university cultural centers.

GENDER ROLES AND STATUSES

Division of Labor by Gender. Gender roles are shaped by the demands of the economic realities of peoples' lives. In the desert interior of the country, women contribute very actively to economic activities associated with livestock raising and have significant social and political power. In the agricultural oasis settlements, the economic role of women is not as active and this is reflected in reduced social and political power. Women's roles in religion reflect the formal restrictions of Islam. In urban centers and towns, however, many women serve as teachers in Islamic pre-schools, the *kuttaib*.

The Relative Status of Women and Men. Women have significant authority within the family unit and make strong contributions toward family decisions regarding various rites of passage. Outside the kin group, however, women have little authority or privilege. From the early 1990s, the government has made great efforts to include women in government. Women were nominated to run for election to the consultative council in 1997, with two obtaining seats, and several speeches of the sultan emphasized the importance of integrating women into public life.

MARRIAGE, FAMILY, AND KINSHIP

Marriage. Marriages are normally arranged. The preferred marriage is to a cousin. First choice is to a patrilateral cousin, and second choice is to a matrilateral cousin. Even the well-educated elite of the country, university medical students, express a preference for their families to arrange marriages for them. Love matches are very infrequent, as marriage is viewed more as a contract between two families with the major aim being to produce offspring for the next generation. In polygamous households (more common among the wealthy, but not restricted to them), the first wife tends to be a close cousin and the second wife a younger, less-close relative. In the past, men tended to take on additional wives—Islam permits up to four—but in recent years, men have tended to divorce first wives and remarry, often leaving divorced women destitute and reliant on the government for support.

Domestic Unit. The domestic unit is generally an extended three-generation nuclear family; residence is usually patrilocal, with the husband's family. Although many nuclear family units reside in single residences, individual family members keep in constant contact with each other through either daily visits or regular telephone calls. It is not unusual to find families of eight, nine or ten persons living in one household. The eldest male has the greatest authority in the family while an elderly female usually takes responsibility for allocating tasks within the household.

Inheritance. The rules of inheritance are entirely governed by the *Shari'ah* (Islamic law), which lays down the percentage of an estate that each relative may inherit. In descending order of shares, this moves from the direct descendants (sons, wives,

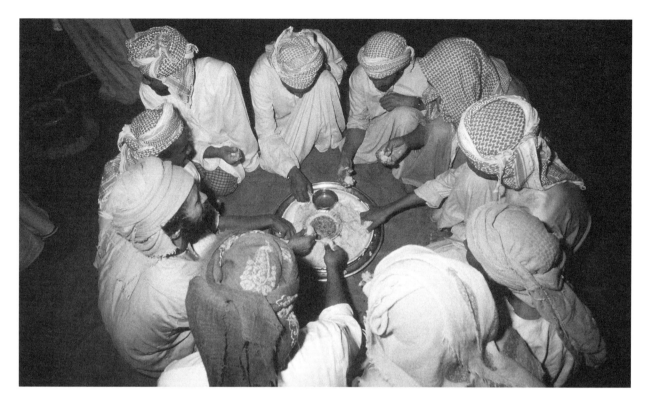

A group of Bedouin eat a meal. Omani cuisine revolves around rice.

daughters, and husbands) to cousins and more distant relatives. These rules apply to fixed property and capital. In the interior among the pastoral tribes, women often pass on their share of certain large livestock (camels) to brothers or sons, in exchange for informal welfare security in their old age.

Kin Groups. Omani culture is organized around the kin group as a large extended family or tribe inhabiting a particular valley or set of hamlets. There are also dispersed kin groups, the pastoral tribes, who move around with their livestock in search of grazing land in a territory normally regarded as theirs to use. Life revolves around the kin group in the interior of the country, while in the urban centers the extended family or tribe is the hub and locus of much activity and networking.

SOCIALIZATION

Infant Care. Omanis do not separate the infant or child from family rhythm or routine. The newborn child remains exclusively with her or his mother for the first forty days after birth. After that the infant sleeps, eats, and plays at her side, and is nursed on demand for two years. Infants are not offered particular stimulation, but soothed and calmed and encouraged to watch rather than interact.

Child Rearing and Education. After the age of two, Omani children are encouraged to behave like miniature adults, taking on duties or hospitality toward guests at a very young age. They are only reprimanded, ever mildly, occasionally with a tap across the back of the legs. They are socialized to look to their peer group. Punishment for unusual or unacceptable behavior is often offered as: ''What would your friends say?'' Girls are circumcised with little ceremony at or just after birth and boys are circumcised in later childhood with some celebration of their entering an age of ''reason.''

Primary education for both boys and girls is encouraged. In the later intermediary and high school years, however, attendance by girls, particularly in rural areas, declines, largely due to a persistent pattern of early marriage. Many boys also leave school before the end of their secondary education in order to seek jobs, thus contributing to a large low-skill sector of the workforce. The government also operates a number of vocational training institutes.

Higher Education. In 1986, Oman opened its first university. Built upon a combination of American and English models of higher education, the first colleges were of medicine, engineering, science, Islamic studies and education, and agriculture. In the

1990s, several more colleges were opened including a faculty of commerce and economics and a faculty of *Shari'ah* and law. Enrollment in the university is nearly equally split between male and female students. It was only in 1993 that, under pressure from elements in the private sector and the government, the university administration decided to deny women admission to two colleges, engineering and agriculture. In the late 1990s, the government sanctioned several private colleges that emphasized business curricula.

ETIQUETTE

Omanis are very polite and formal in public. Upon meeting, formulaic greetings must be exchanged before a discussion can ensue. To do otherwise would be considered rude. Although men and women may interact in public, their contact should always be chaperoned or in the open. Even educated elite women often find it necessary to be chaperoned by a male relative at public events, parties, or receptions. Omanis tend to stand close to one another as Arabs do, and it is common for friends and relatives of the same sex to hold hands. Two or more men or women entering a doorway at the same time always try to persuade the others to enter first, although a man always invites a woman to enter first. On the other hand, forming lines in shops, banks, and other public places is not a cultural trait, although women invariably are encouraged to go first.

RELIGION

Religious Beliefs. Nearly all Omanis are Muslim, divided nearly equally into Sunnis and Ibadis with a small percentage of Shia. A few families of Indian origin are Hindu but there are no Omani Christians or Jews. Omanis tend to be careful in their observance of religious obligations. Most carry out the prescribed five prayers per day and many men go to nearby mosques to perform them. Most Omanis observe the dawn–to–dusk fasting required during the Islamic month of Ramadan, and it is against the law to eat, drink, or smoke in public during daylight hours in Ramadan. In addition to formal religious beliefs and practices, superstitions are common and some folk rituals are practiced.

Religious Practitioners. There is little formal religious hierarchy. The government appoints the *mufti* who serves as the country's highest Islamic authority. Traditional religious educators, known as sheikhs, are trained by the Ministry of Awqaf

View of Muscat city buildings along the Gulf of Oman. Oman is a sultanate, with a sultan as the head of state and government.

and Religious Affairs and teach in Koranic schools throughout the country. Religious judges (*qadi*) are appointed by the state to serve in *Shari'ah* courts. There are also religious healers (*mutawi'*) whose services are called upon by the population, often to deal with mental illnesses.

Rituals and Holy Places. All Omani Muslims are obliged to fast during Ramadan. One of the pillars of Islam, this period of abstinence lasts twenty-nine or thirty days. This month is also one of celebration and prayer and is followed by two important festivals, one immediately after the period of fasting, *Eid-il-Fitr*, and one sixty-six days later, *Eid -il Adha.* Many Omanis undertake the *hajj*, or pilgrimage to the holy city of Mecca (in Saudi Arabia), if they are physically and financially able. Because of the austerity of Ibadi Islam, there are no specific holy places in northern Oman; there are, however, some venerated tombs of "saints" in Dhofar.

Death and the Afterlife. Omanis are pragmatic when it comes to dealing with sickness. They will try modern medicine but if that fails will turn to traditional healers. Traditional herbalists, bonesetters, and exorcists have a thriving practice, especially in the interior of the country. Many look to the cold and hot properties of foods for curing sickness (a common practice in Islamic belief). Spirit possession, often among women, is addressed through *zar*, or exorcism, ceremonies, which frequently involve the community in the curative process.

SECULAR CELEBRATIONS

National Day takes place on 18 November, the birthday of the sultan, Qabus ibn Sa'id. This is the principal nonreligious celebration of the year and includes a major pageant, a profusion of fireworks around the country, and the sultan's annual policy speech. Armed Forces Day (11 December) is the occasion for a large banquet hosted by the sultan for his officers, senior government officials, and the diplomatic corps. The Islamic, but not the Christian, New Year's Day is an official holiday.

THE ARTS AND HUMANITIES

Support for the Arts. The government provides some limited assistance for the arts through subsidies to such organizations as the Omani Arts Society. Most artists, however, either hold full-time jobs or come from well-to-do families.

Literature. In the past, literature was confined to religious treatises and histories. Like other Arabs, Omanis gave great importance to oral traditions, including poetry and an emphasis on genealogical roots. The Ministry of Information has sought to revive these traditions through folk programs on radio and television. In the last decades of the twentieth century, a small number of authors published works of fiction and poetry.

Graphic Arts. Traditional Omani handicrafts are in decline although periodic attempts are made to encourage their production. Notable handmade products include silver and gold jewelry, woven baskets, goat- and camel-hair rugs, swords and *khanjars* (daggers), and large pottery water jugs. Drawing, painting, and photography have become popular forms of expression in educated circles, although artists still tend to avoid representation of the human form as per Islamic convention.

Performance Arts. Local instrumental and vocal music is very popular, as are songs from other Arab countries. Traditional performers still provide songs and dances at events such as marriages. The Ministry of National Heritage and Culture maintains a small national theater. Arab entertainers are well known throughout the country and many educated Omanis enjoy Western performance arts.

THE STATE OF THE PHYSICAL AND SOCIAL SCIENCES

Physical sciences, particularly earth sciences such as geology and hydrology, are popular subjects for study and research in Oman's university and in a number of government ministries. The social sciences, however, are not as well represented. Economics and sociology are taught at the university, but anthropology, political science, and psychology are not.

BIBLIOGRAPHY

Allen, Calvin H., Jr. *Oman: The Modernization of the Sultanate*, 1987.

———, and W. Lynn Rigsbee II. *Oman under Qaboos: From Coup to Constitution, 1970-1996*, 2000.

Bannerman, J. P. "The Impact of the Oil Industry on Society in the Arabian Peninsula." In R. I. Lawless, ed., *The Gulf in the Early Twentieth Century: Foreign Institutions and Local Responses*, 1986.

Barth, Fredrik. *Sohar: Culture and Society in an Omani Town*, 1983.

Chatty, Dawn. "The Bedouin of Central Oman." *Journal of Oman Studies* 6 (1): 149–162, 1983.

———. *Mobile Pastoralists: Development Planning and Social Change in Oman*, 1996.

———. "A Women and Work in Oman: Cultural Constraints and Individual Choice." *International Journal of Middle East Studies* 32 (2): 241–254, 2000.

Costa, Paolo M., et al. *Musandam: Architecture and Material Culture of a Little Known Region of Oman*, 1991.

Damluji, Salma Samar. *The Architecture of Oman*, 1998.

Eickelman, Christine. "Women and Politics in an Arabian Oasis." In Farhad Kazemi and R. D. McChesney, eds., *A Way Prepared: Essays on Islamic Culture in Honour of Richard Bayly Winder*, 1988.

Eickelman, Dale F. "Omani Village: The Meaning of Oil." In J. E. Peterson, ed., *The Politics of Middle Eastern Oil*, 1983.

———. "From Theocracy to Monarchy: Authority and Legitimacy in Inner Oman, 1935–1957." *International Journal of Middle East Studies* 17 (1): 3–24, 1985.

———. "National Identity and Religious Discourse in Contemporary Oman." *International Journal of Islamic and Arabic Studies* 6 (1): 1–20, 1989.

Hawley, Donald. *Oman and Its Renaissance*, jubilee ed., 1995.

Janzen, Jorg. *Nomads in the Sultanate of Oman: Tradition and Development in Dhofar*, 1986.

Kechichian, Joseph A. *Oman and the World: The Emergence of an Independent Foreign Policy*, 1995.

Kervran, Monique, and Vincent Bernard. "Mihrab/s omanais du 16e siècle: Un curieux exemple de conservatisme de l'art du stuc iranien des époques seldjouqide et mongole." *Archéologie islamique* 6: 109–156, 1996.

Le Cour Grandmaison, Colette. "La société rurale omanaise." In Paul Bonnenfant, ed., *La Péninisule Arabique d'aujourd'hui*, 1982.

Oman, Sultanate of. Diwan of Royal Court. Office of the Advisor for Conservation of the Environment. *The Scientific Results of the Royal Geographical Society's Oman Wahiba Sands Project 1985–1987*, 1988.

Pelletreau, Robert H., Jr., John Page, Jr., Joseph A. Kechichian, Georgie Anne Geyer, and Christine Eickelman. "Symposium: Contemporary Oman and U.S.-Oman Relations." *Middle East Policy* 4 (3) 1–29, 1996.

Peterson, J. E. *Oman in the Twentieth Century: Political Foundations of an Emerging State*, 1978.

———. "Legitimacy and Political Change in Yemen and Oman." *Orbis* 27 (4): 971–998, 1984.

———. "The Political Status of Women in the Arab Gulf States." *Middle East Journal* 43 (1): 34–50, 1989.

Pridham, B. R., ed. *Oman: Economic, Social, and Strategic Developments*, 1987.

Skeet, Ian. *Oman: Politics and Development*, 1992.

Tabuki, Salim Bakhit al-. "Tribal Structures in South Oman." *Arabian Studies* 6: 51–56, 1982.

Townsend, John. *Oman: The Making of a Modern State*, 1977.

Wikan, Unni. *Behind the Veil in Arabia: Women in Oman*, 1982.

Wilkinson, J. C. *Water and Tribal Settlement in South-East Arabia: A Study of the Aflaj of Oman*, 1977.

———. *The Imamate Tradition of Oman*, 1987.

—Dawn Chatty
and J.E. Peterson

PAKISTAN

CULTURE NAME

Pakistani

ALTERNATIVE NAMES

While the official name of the nation is the Islamic Republic of Pakistan, generally the country has been referred to as Pakistan since 1971.

ORIENTATION

Identification. As part of India's independence from Great Britain in 1947, a partition took part of their land and created Pakistan as a separate Islamic nation. It is estimated that approximately 95 percent of the population are Muslim, but members of several minority religions live there, including some Hindus, Christians, Parsis, Sikhs, and Buddhists. Although the modern nation of Pakistan was but fifty-three years old in 2000, it has territorial areas and tribal populations whose histories date back many centuries; thus Pakistan has both an ancient and a relatively new identity.

Location and Geography. Pakistan is in South Asia and is 339,697 square miles (879,815 square kilometers) in area. It was created from what had been the northwest side of India. All of the country except the southern portion is landlocked, with Afghanistan to the northwest, Jammu and Kashmir to the northeast, India to the east and southeast, and Iran to the west. In the southern portion, along the shores of the city of Karachi, which was the original capital when the nation was formed in 1947, is the Arabian Sea. Karachi is well known for its shorelines. Most of the northern section of the country consists of mountains and also the famous Khyber Pass, whose history goes back several thousand years. It is in this northern section where most of the ancient tribes still live and where many ancient tribal cultures and customs still exist.

Pakistan consists of several provinces, including Punjab, Sind, North-West Frontier, Baluchistan, and the Federally Administered Tribal Areas (FATA).

The city of Islamabad, which is centrally located in the country, was officially named the capital of Pakistan in 1961, and construction began on government buildings in addition to others. Islamabad became the active capital in 1966. In addition to modern government buildings it also features a wide variety of modern hotels, an international airport, and the nearby famous ancient city of Rawalpindi.

In addition to being known for a number of mountains, including K-2, which is the second-highest mountain in world, Pakistan also has several lakes and rivers, including the Indus River, which is 1,800 miles (2,896 kilometers) long. Pakistan also has several deserts, in Punjab and Sind. Pakistan is also home to Taxila, the oldest known university in the world. In the north, leading from China, through Tammu and Kashmir, is a famous ancient silk road.

Pakistan is diverse. There are snowcapped mountains in the north, sunny beaches in the south, and a wide variety of geographically and culturally interesting sites elsewhere.

Demography. The population of Pakistan is estimated to be 135 million. An estimated 40 million live in urban areas, with the balance in rural areas. In addition to the residents of the major cities of Islamabad, Karachi, Lahore, and Peshawar, which is the city at the edge of the Kybher Pass gateway, a number of tribal residents live in valleys. These include Chitral Valley, at an elevation of 3,800 feet (1,158 meters), where the majority of the people are Muslims but that also is home to the Kafir-Kalash (wearers of the black robe), a primitive pagan tribe. In Swat Valley, which was once the cradle of Buddhism, Muslim conquerors fought battles and residents claim to be descendants of soldiers of Alexander the Great. In the Hunza Valley, people are noted

Pakistan

for longevity, which they claim is because of diet and way of life. The people of Hunza Valley are Muslims and also are believed to be descendants of soldiers of Alexander the Great. In North-West Frontier Province is Kaghan Valley, which is bounded on the west by Swat Valley, on the north by Gilgit, and on the east by Azad Kashmir. The people of Kaghan Valley are Muslim-Pathans as well as Kohistanis and Gujars. Shardu Valley is the capital of the district of Baltistan and is known as "Little Tibet" because the lifestyle there is similar to that in Tibet itself. The people of each of these valley areas are well known for their tribal cultures, hand-

icrafts, and for fascinating clothing, most of which is woven and handmade there and unique to their particular area.

Linguistic Affiliation. The official language of Pakistan is Urdu, but most public officials, people, and others in Pakistan also speak English; English is referred to as the informal official language of Pakistan. Urdu was created by combining the languages of early invaders and settlers, including Arabic, Persian, and Turkish. The spoken form of Urdu is the same as that of Hindi but it is written in a different script than Hindi.

While Urdu and English are prevalent throughout Pakistan, a number of other languages are spoken in different valleys and areas. These include the Punjaki, Sindhi, Pushto, Balochi, Brahvi, Saraiki, and Hindko dialects, among others.

Symbolism. The design of Pakistan's flag was officially adopted by the country's Constituent Assembly in July 1947, it was flown for the first time on their independence day, 14 August l947. The flag was designed by Ali Jinnah, the man acclaimed as the founder of Pakistan. There is a thick white strip on the left side of the flag; the rest of the flag has a dark green background with a white crescent and a five-pointed star centered on it. The white represents peace, and the dark green represents prosperity. The crescent stands for progress, and the star stands for light, guidance, and knowledge. Pakistan also has a national emblem. In the middle of a circled wreath of jasmine flowers is a shield that has four sections, each of which shows a major product of the country from when the country was created. One section shows cotton, another shows wheat, one tea, and one jute. Above the four sections are the crescent and star, as on the national flag. On a scroll beneath the wreath is written in Urdu "Faith, Unity, Discipline."

HISTORY AND ETHNIC RELATIONS

Emergence of the Nation. For many years India sought independence from Great Britain. During most of those years the Muslim League of India was also striving to establish an independent Islamic nation. The Muslim leader was Ali Jinnah from as early as 1916; in 1940 he began advocating and working for a separate Muslim state. When the British finally agreed to India's independence and withdrew in 1947, Pakistan became a Muslim nation, with Ali Jinnah as its first governor-general. Originally it was divided into two parts. The nation now called Pakistan was then called West Pakistan, and on the opposite side of India, some 1,000 miles (1,609 kilometers) away, was another Muslim area, designated East Pakistan. In 1956 Pakistan became a republic. In 1971 East Pakistan waged a successful war of independence from West Pakistan and became the independent nation of Bangladesh.

While the history of Pakistan as an independent nation dates only to 1947, the history of the territory it encompasses dates back many thousands of years, during the period when the territory was a portion of the Indian subcontinent. In addition, the land is home to the famous Khyber Pass, which is the route that many invaders into India used. These include Mogul invaders and Alexander the Great. Many centuries ago a number of Buddhists also used that northern section as a route, so Pakistan today has many interesting Buddhist sites and historical notes as part of its history. Punjab is also a portion of the country; it was the home of the founder of the Sikh religion, and it continues to play a significant role in Pakistan. Lines of demarcation between India and Pakistan in northern border areas are unclear in places or in dispute, and controversy continues to surround these lines.

National Identity. The national identity of Pakistan today is that of an Islamic nation; it was created as such. However, because the territory that is now Pakistan has a history that goes back several thousand years, the area has a history that forms part of the present identity of Pakistan. That is one of the reasons why both residents and visitors find the relatively young nation of Pakistan historically interesting and why the national identity includes many sites and stories that are centuries older than the nation itself.

Ethnic Relations. There are at least five ethnic groups within Pakistan. In general, there are not continuous or frequent problems between the different ethnic groups other than ethnic tensions in Sind, which occur somewhat regularly.

URBANISM, ARCHITECTURE AND THE USE OF SPACE

Because of the relative newness (1966) of the capital city of Islamabad, it features modern architecture arrayed under a master plan. In addition to modern capital buildings, Islamabad is also home to the famous Shah Faisal Mosque, which is so large that the prayer hall can accommodate ten thousand persons, while verandas and porticoes can hold more than twenty-four thousand worshipers. It also has a courtyard that has enough space for forty thousand people.

Islamabad also has a sports complex, art galleries, a museum of natural history, and four universities.

Other sites in and near Islamabad include Rawal Lake; the Rose and Jasmine Garden, the Murghzar Mini Zoo and Children's Park; and the Shakarparian Hills, whose terraced garden features views of other hills, Rawal Lake, and the cities of Rawalpindi and Islamabad.

The ancient city of Rawalpindi, on the border of Islamabad, has a history that dates back three thousand years. While many new modern buildings have been added to this city, it has retained much of its historical look and is well known for its bazaars that specialize in handicrafts. Rawalpindi is home to Linquat Memorial Hall with a large auditorium and library; Ayub National Park; and the Rawalpindi Golf Course, which was completed in 1926 but is still in regular use.

Another well-known urban area is Lahore, founded four thousand years ago. Lahore was the cultural center of the Mogul Empire, which glorified it with palaces, gardens, and mosques. It is the second-largest city in Pakistan and the capital of Punjab. Some of its historical sites include the Royal Fort, which was built in 1566 by Akbar the Great, and Wazir Khan's mosque, which was built in 1683 and is still considered one of the most beautiful mosques in all of South Asia.

Another ancient but still famous site in Lahore is the Shalimar Gardens, which were originally laid out in 1642 by Mogul emperor Shah-Jehan. The garden is surrounded by high walls and a watchtower at each of the four corners. The garden is used as the site of regular special state receptions. Lahore is also home to several other well-known mosques, museums, and parks.

A more recent historical site in Lahore is the Minar-e-Pakistan, where a resolution was passed in 1940 demanding creation of a separate homeland for the Muslims. The minar is an estimated 197 feet (60 meters) high.

Another equally well-known urban area is the city of Karachi, which was the first capital of Pakistan. Karachi is in the south of the nation and in addition to being a modern city on the shores of the Arabian Sea, it has a number of interesting sites, including the Masjid-e-Tooba which is said to be the largest single-dome mosque, and several art galleries and bazaars. It has a wide variety of water sports and remains the center of commerce and industry.

There are a number of other urban areas throughout Pakistan, but one of the best known is the city of Peshawar, which is the northernmost major city and is home to the gateway to the Khyber Pass. Peshawar is a city of Pathan tribals who are also Muslims. Alexander the Great and parts of his army stayed in this city for forty days in 327 B.C.E. Balahissar Fort is on both the eastern and western approaches to the city, and it is from near here that one can take a train along the mountain routes of the Khyber Pass. While the city is centuries old, the modern Peshawar is well known for its bazaars and for several colleges and a university.

FOOD AND ECONOMY

Food in Daily Life. Because at least 95 percent of the Pakistani population is Muslim, there are two food customs that are followed almost universally. One is that Muslims do not eat pork (therefore beef, chicken, lamb, and fish are the basic foods), and the other is that during the month of Ramadan, fasting is a daily activity.

Spices and curry are an essential part of any Pakistani recipe. The most prevalent spices include chili powder, tumeric, garlic, paprika, black and red pepper, cumin seed, bay leaf, coriander, cardamom, cloves, ginger, cinnamon, saffron, nutmeg, and poppy seeds, among others. Using yogurt to marinate meats is another typical recipe. Because of the use of spices and curry for the main dish, the usual side dish is plain rice. Lentils are another common specialty. The food in the south is more exotic and highly spiced, while that in the north often features plain barbecued meat as the main dish. Usually any meat, fowl, or seafood is curried, and frying is the typical method of cooking. Ghee, which is clarified butter, is another commonly used recipe item and is often used for frying.

Wheat and flour products are considered mainstays of the daily diet, and the use of pickles, chutneys, preserves, and sauces along with curried meats, seafood, vegetables, and lentils and are why Pakistani cuisine has such a unique flavor.

Green tea is the typical drink served at all meals.

Food Customs at Ceremonial Occasions. Fasting is an important part of the Muslim observance of Ramadan, but food does play a role on many other occasions. One such event is the Eid-ul-Azha (Feast of Sacrifice) in the last month of the Muslim calendar, commemorating the occasion when the prophet Abraham was about to sacrifice his son in response to an order from God. Muslims who can afford it are required to sacrifice a sheep, goat, camel, or cow symbolizing Abraham's submission to God. The meat of the sacrificed animal is divided into three equal parts, with the first donated to the poor, the second given to relatives and/or friends, and the third cooked at the home of the person who made the sacrifice. Eating the meat is part of the festival celebration activity.

The important religious festival Shab-I-Barat involves a special type of pudding known as *halwa* and unleavened bread known as *nan* being distributed among the poor. The halwa and nan dishes are specially decorated with silver or gold leaves and also are sent to relatives and neighbors.

Workers on a community sanitation project examine the pipes for a new sewer in Faisalabad.

Food also plays a role in the celebration of the end of the Ramadan fasting period. This starts with a special breakfast of *sheer kharma* (a sweet dish), which is vermicelli cooked in milk with dried dates, raisins, almonds, and other nuts. In addition, crowds hurry to local bazaars to purchase fruit, meat, and sweets as well as new clothes and jewelry.

Sweets are distributed as part of the celebration of the birth of a new baby in a family, and an animal sacrificial offering is also made—one goat for a girl and two for a boy, with the animal meat distributed among the poor or among friends and relatives. Food also is involved in a ceremony celebrating a child becoming six or seven months old. Sisters and relatives place rice pudding in the infant's mouth using a silver spoon, and a drop of chicken broth is also put in the mouth. After this ceremony the adults then hold an elaborate dinner concluded with a special dessert called *kheer*.

Basic Economy. Pakistan is a poor country and its economic outlook is bleak. It relies heavily on foreign loans and grants, and debt obligations take nearly 50 percent of the government's expenditures. The average per capita income per person in Pakistan is estimated at $460 (U.S.). A large number of Pakistanis, estimated at 35 percent, live below the poverty line.

Land Tenure and Property. An estimated 54.69 million acres (22.14 million hectares) of land are used for agriculture. The major crops are cotton, wheat, rice, and sugarcane. A large amount of land in Pakistan has archaeological sites, such as Moenjo Daro, Harappa, Taxila, Kot Dijji, and Mehr Garh.

Commercial Activities. A large percentage of the commercial activities include the sale of handicraft items such as the carpets for which Pakistan is well known.

Major Industries. Major industries of Pakistan include textiles, cement, fertilizer, steel, sugar, electric goods, and shipbuilding.

Trade. Pakistan's major exports include cotton, textile goods, rice, leather items, carpets, sports goods, fruit, and handicrafts. Major imports include industrial equipment, vehicles, iron ore, petroleum, and edible oil. Trade partners include the United States, Hong Kong, Japan, Germany, the United Kingdom, and the United Arab Emirates.

A caravan along the Silk Road.

Division of Labor. Forty-eight percent of workers are in the service sector, 27 percent are in industry, and 25 percent are in agriculture.

SOCIAL STRATIFICATION

Classes and Castes. There is no caste system in Pakistan. There are high-income, middle-income and a large number of low-income persons throughout the country. Locale makes an important difference in the quality of life; a low-income person in an urban area has more problems than one living in a tribal, mountainous area.

Symbols of Social Stratification. There have been and continue to be a number of social development shortcomings in Pakistan, but in recognition of them, the government in 1992–1993 initiated the Social Action Program (SAP) to make social development and social services available to all levels of the Pakistanis. Reports show that while some had benefited, the rural people who were meant to benefit mostly did not. Some of the program's expenditures were for elementary education, primary health, welfare, and rural water supply and sanitation. It is believed that many people do not understand the purpose and scope of the SAP and that substantial changes must be made in the program if it is to be successful.

POLITICAL LIFE

Government. The government of Pakistan consists of an elected prime minister, a president, and a Parliament that consists of the Senate (Upper House) and the National Assembly (Lower House). There are 57 members of the Senate and 217 members of the National Assembly. The prime minister is the head of government, and the president, who is elected by the legislature, is the head of state. There are also ministers in charge of government divisions such as education and tourism. These are appointed by the prime minister. They in turn appoint the governors of the different states within the country. Also appointed by the prime minister are the chief justices of the Supreme Court.

Leadership and Political Officials. Each individual state within the country has a governor, and each city has its own mayor. Additionally, most tribal groups have a head chief.

Social Problems and Controls. The greatest social problem in Pakistan is drug use. There are both governmental and non-government programs

Women gathered together at a wedding in Islamabad. Muslin marriages unite not only a couple but also their families.

working toward rehabilitation of drug users and ending drug use.

Military Activity. Branches of the military are the army, navy, air force, civil armed forces, and national guard. The military of Pakistan consists of members from all ethnic groups within the country. Their duties have included participation in United Nations (UN) peacekeeping and nation-building activities in different areas of the world. Soldiers in the Pakistani Army are regular participants in the long-running dispute, sometimes resulting in violence, with India regarding sovereignty over Kashmir.

Military activity in Pakistan has included four military coups. After those in 1955, 1969, 1977, the government was returned to civilian control via popular election. The most recent coup took place in October 1999, and toward the end of 2000 a general was still acting as the head of the government, although he has promised a democratic election for a new prime minister in the near future.

NONGOVERNMENTAL ORGANIZATIONS AND OTHER ASSOCIATIONS

There are a number of nongovernmental organizations (NGOs) within Pakistan, including the Aurat

and Behood women's organizations, as well as international Lions and Rotary clubs, to which a large number of men belong. The World Bank and its various agencies have been active in Pakistan since 1952.

The Aga Khan Rural Support Program has worked to build up village organizations with separate groups for men and women and then, through their groups, to launch a number of development activities. The Orange Pilot Project, headquartered in Karachi, has been active in urban development, including working to improve one of Karachi's worst slum areas, with the first focus being on sanitation, followed by a range of community development activities.

GENDER ROLES AND STATUSES

Division of Labor by Gender. The majority of Pakistani women are homemakers, and men are generally referred to as the breadwinners. The largest percentage of working women in Pakistan are nurses or teachers. Women are represented in government as ministers in Parliament and ambassadors. Benazir Bhutto was the first female prime minister and served from 1988 to 1990.

The Relative Status of Women and Men. The women of Pakistan are regular voters as are the men, and women also are regular attendees at colleges. Islam gives women rights to child custody, to alimony, and to inheritance, and they also have the right to conduct business and enter any profession. Women are engaged in agriculture production and the services sector. Women judges have been appointed to four high courts as well as several lower courts and a 10 percent quota was established for women to become police officers.

There are growing numbers of violent crimes against or involving women and the government has introduced the concept of women police stations, which have been opened in Rawalpindi, Karachi, and Abbottabad in the North West Frontier.

A number of computer training centers have been established for women and the government has opened "women development centers" that specialize in training community development workers in family planning, hygiene, sanitation, adult literacy, community organization, and legal rights.

MARRIAGE, FAMILY AND KINSHIP

Marriage. One form of a Muslim marriage involves a *nikah*, a formal legal document signed by the bride and groom in front of several witnesses; this establishes that the couple is legally married.

There are other Muslim marriage traditions as well. One includes the *mayun* or *lagan* which takes place three or four days before the marriage and starts with the bride retiring to a secluded area of her home. On the day before the marriage there is a *menhdi* ceremony, when the bride's hands and feet are painted with henna. When the marriage ceremony takes place it is required that at least two witnesses be there, and all the guests offer a short prayer for the success of the marriage. After the ceremony, dried dates are distributed to the guests. Wedding customs vary somewhat among provinces, but the Muslim marriage is seen as uniting both families as well as the couple.

Each tribal group also has certain ceremonies that are an important part of the marriages within that group.

Inheritance. Women have inheritance rights in Pakistan, so that inheritance benefits can go to women and children after the death of the husband and father.

Kin Groups. A Muslim marriage is seen as uniting the families of both the bride and groom, so the kin group is expanded after a marriage. In some tribes there can be neither a cross-cultural marriage nor a dual ethnic one, so therefore the kin groups are and basically remain identical ethnically and culturally.

SOCIALIZATION

Infant Care. The addition of a new baby to a Muslim family is seen as a great blessing and there are a wide variety of ceremonies that take place both at the birth and throughout the different stages of infancy. To help families with infant care there are a number of child health centers throughout the country.

Child Rearing and Education. Most Pakistani families consider it the privilege of the grandfather to name the baby. Another tradition is that the first garment for a baby's layette is made from an old shirt that had belonged to the grandfather. The child is usually named within forty days after birth and thus is generally known by a nickname until then. A baby boy's hair is shaved off, with the belief that this will then ensure thick growth throughout life. The shorn hair is weighed and balanced against silver, and that silver is then given to the poor.

In February 1998 the prime minister announced a draft for a new education policy from 1998 to 2010, to increase the number of elementary and secondary schools to meet the projected enrollment of twelve million children, including about six million female children in the primary schools by 2003. The draft also suggested establishment of community-based nonformal schools to fill the school gap and to help minimize the cost of primary schools. The new education policy also proposed training about thirty-six thousand teachers each year from 1998 to 2003 to maintain a pupil-teacher ratio of forty to one, with most new teachers to be females. A reduction in military spending was also proposed so funds could be channeled toward countrywide primary education for all children.

Higher Education. Higher education is seen as having an important role in preparing an individual for a successful career. There are nearly one thousand colleges and universities located throughout almost the entire country.

RELIGION

Religious Beliefs. Pakistan was formed as an Islamic nation, and Islam continues to be the religion of approximately 95 percent of the population. There are also small groups of Buddhists, Christians, Parsis, and Hindus. The Muslim religion was

Houses in Baltit. Pakistan's landscape includes snowcapped mountains and valleys such as this, as well as sunny beaches.

founded by the prophet Muhammad in the seventh century, when, according to Islamic belief, he received messages from God and wrote them down in what became the Qur'an, the Islamic book that instructs Muslims on how to conduct their lives.

Rituals and Holy Places. One of the prevalent rituals for Muslims is the month of Ramadan, during which time they are required to fast from dawn to sunset (this is not required of very young children, the elderly, or pregnant women). Ramadan is also a time when Muslims thank Allah for his blessings during the past year. An additional requirement during Ramadan is that all Muslims must help the less fortunate with both cash and food gifts. The Eid, or day ending Ramadan, starts with an elaborate breakfast; then Muslims go to a mosque or special park for prayer.

An equally important Muslim celebration is Eid-I-Milad-un-Nabi, the birth of the prophet Muhammad, on the twelfth day of Rabi-uh-Awwal, which is the third month of the Muslim calendar. In addition to special gatherings in mosques, where the story of the life and mission of Muhammad is told, large groups of Muslims parade through the streets singing praise to Muhammad. Even private homes are decorated (as are the mosques) in celebration and praise of Muhammad.

Another important Muslim religious festival is Shab-I-Barat, which is held on the fourteenth day of Shaban, the eighth month of the Muslim year. The belief is that on this day the lives and fortunes of mankind are registered in Heaven for the coming year. During Muharram, which is the first month of the Muslim calendar, the martyrdom of Imam Husain, the grandson of Muhammad, is commemorated. For the first nine days of the month the death is recounted, and then on the tenth day, which is the day he was murdered, there are barefoot processions with persons carrying banners relating to the tragedy of his death.

Other religions in Pakistan also have special festivals/rituals and holidays, with Christmas and Easter being the special ones of the 750,000 Pakistani Christians. Christmas coincides with the birthday of the Ali Jinnah, acclaimed as Pakistan's founder, so both Muslims and Christians celebrate on this day.

The main festival of the Buddhist community is Baisakhi Purnima, the day on which Buddha was born; it is the same calendar date when later in his life he is believed to have attained his great wisdom of enlightenment.

Parsi residents of Pakistan celebrate their New Year (Naoroz) on 21 March. Approximately fifty-five hundred Parsis live near Karachi.

View over central Karachi, Pakistan's first capital. Set on the shore of the Arabian Sea, it is a center of commerce and industry.

Pakistani Hindus also have a number of festivals; the two most special ones are Diwali (Festival of Lights) and Holi (Festival of Colors). The Festival of Lights is held in Lahore at the Shalimar Gardens, which are filled with multicolored lights and where folk music and dances are performed.

A colorful and interesting festival is held in North-West Frontier Province in April, in the Peshawar stadium. Events include the Khattak famous dance of the Pathans and musical concerts; tribal people participate in colorful costumes.

During Eid, tribesmen gather around the shrine of Baba Kharwari in Ziarat Valley, and wrestling and marksmanship contests are held. A large number of people visit it regularly to offer sacrifices in memory of the saint.

The Quaid-I-Azam Residency in Ziarat Valley was Ali Jinnah's residence during his last illness and now houses relics of him and is a highly revered sacred site. It was originally built in 1882 by the British and used by the agent to the governor as his summer headquarters.

Takht Bhai is one of the holy places of Buddhism. The Buddhist monastery of Takht Bhai stands 500 feet (152 meters) above the plain on the hill. The Buddhists selected this spot to construct a religious complex where the monks and students could pursue their rituals and studies. The main stupa is surrounded on three sides by chapels in which images of both the Buddha and Buddhisattva were installed.

Makli Hill, near Thatta town is where more than one million graves of kings, queens, saints, scholars, philosophers, and soldiers are located. Gravestones and mausoleums are considered masterpieces in stone carving representing different eras and dynasties.

Death and the Afterlife. Shab-I-Barat is also celebrated as a remembrance day of deceased family and friends. Special illumination of the mosques takes place and food is distributed among the poor. It is also a time when children participate in fireworks. After distribution of the food the Qur'an is read and prayers are said; then most Muslims visit cemeteries and put flowers and lights on the graves of deceased family and friends.

MEDICINE AND HEALTH CARE

At a seminar at Aga Khan Medical University in September of 1998, medical experts reported that perinatal mortality rates in Pakistan were alarmingly high, with an estimated 54 deaths per thousand births. A 1990–1994 national health survey reported that eighty-nine children per thousand under age five died in Pakistan from pneumonia, diarrhea, vaccine prevention diseases, or a combination of them, with most of these deaths occurring in the first week after birth.

A number of programs have been undertaken to attack polio; the World Health Organization and Japan have participated. At the end of the twentieth century, there were one hundred thousand deaths from and at least twenty thousand new cases of paralytic polio each year.

A survey by the Federal Bureau of Statistics in Pakistan indicated that about 50 percent of the basic health units were without doctors and that about 70 percent of government health facilities are without any female staff. Only about 56 percent of the country's people have safe drinking water and just 24 percent have good sanitation.

Programs are underway to expand basic health services for women, develop a women-friendly district health system, and both strengthen and improve human resource capacity to sustain women's health development.

SECULAR CELEBRATIONS

Official national holidays include: Pakistan Day, 23 March; May Day, 1 May; Independence Day, August 14; Defense of Pakistan Day, 6 September; death of Ali Jinnah, 11 September; and birth of Ali Jinnah, 25 December.

The Awami Mela or People's Festival of Lahore held annually each March, is a six-day pageant that features equestrian sports, cattle displays, and enormous crowds of people. Special events include polo, animal dances, large band displays, acrobatics by camels, dancing horses, parades, and folk dances.

Another festival in Lahore is Basant, when the sky is filled with thousands of colored kites in celebration of the coming of spring. The color yellow is associated with the festival, everyone dresses in yellow and mostly yellow foods are cooked.

Often a national holiday is declared when Pakistan's national cricket team wins a major international match.

THE ARTS AND THE HUMANITIES

Support for the Arts. The Pakistan National Council of the Arts (PNCA) has established the National Gallery, the Sadequinn Gallery, and the National Music and Dance Center. They also regularly hold exhibitions, seminars and theater workshops.

In the early 1970s the National Film Development Corporation was formed to use film to make people aware of social and cultural values. The corporation holds film festivals regularly.

Literature. Faiz Ahmad Faiz is considered to have been Pakistan's greatest poet, and there is a national holiday celebrating his birth. Pakistan has been referred to as a land of poetry, and it is said that nearly every Pakistani has written some poetry.

Graphic Arts. There are a wide variety of graphic art examples, including handpainted clay products, the hand design for batik products, and block printing called Ajrak. Glazed pottery with handpainted designs is common throughout the country, and artistic work in clay goes back thousands of years.

Pakistani handicrafts are as varied as the ethnic backgrounds of the craftsmen and include work in wood, beaten brass and copperware, pottery, and jewelry, a wide variety of fabrics that feature embroidery, and the hand-designed carpets for which Pakistan is internationally recognized.

Performance Arts. There are so many dance and music performance arts in Pakistan—many unique to the ethnic culture of the performer—that they are almost considered common rather than unique. Music and dance are done in the both classical and folk form. Usually the performer wears a costume that features ethnic design.

Just as the costume worn by the performer identifies the tribe or ethnic group, so does the music or performance. For example, while dancing in a circle is the basic formation for Pakistani folk dances, there are also many versions of the Pathans' *khattak*, but they all begin with dancers in two columns accompanied by pipe and drum music. There is the *Jhoomer* in Baluchistan, which involves spinning around at top speed, as men do on dark nights by the light of flickering torches. The women of Punjab do the *jhoomer* in what is referred to as a romantic fashion. Also in Punjab, the *juddi* starts with girls singing to the beat of a drum; then they join in a circle and start to dance. Still another dance of Punjab is the *bhangra* which is described as being like rock and roll and which is always done at the beginning of the harvest season. The *Ho Jamalo* originated in Sind but is popular throughout Pakistan. It is a dance that is performed as part of a victory or celebration.

There are four main families of musical instruments in Pakistan and more than six hundred Pakistani musical instruments; the most well known are the *sitar*, *veena*, *rabab*, *sur mandal* and *tanpura*.

The most popular of all the instruments is the sitar but a two-piece drum, the *tabla* is reputedly the most important accompaniment for all Pakistani music and dancing. Nearly all the instruments are used primarily for solo performances; the Western concept of orchestral music is not part of the Pakistani musical heritage. However, Western instruments such as the piano, violin, and accordion are now often included in Pakistani concerts because they are adaptable to Pakistani music.

Several other musical instruments are used, particularly the *dhol*, a double-sided drum that is usually hung around the neck and played with sticks, while the *dholkit* is smaller and played by hand. In addition, the flute is often used.

THE STATE OF THE PHYSICAL AND SOCIAL SCIENCES

In the social sciences, one of the major concerns is the low rate of literacy in Pakistan. Efforts are being made and outside the educational establishment to address this concern. Another social concern is that frequently young children must work—most often in carpet manufacturing jobs—to supplement the family's income and sometimes to provide the sole income in the family. As a result, the children do not have time to attend school. Efforts made to address this problem have often involved trying to find work for the parents.

In the physical sciences one of the largest problems is that because of ever-increasing population growth, natural resources are often misused, with land being lost to desertification, waterlogging, and soil erosion. There is increasing contamination of groundwater and surface water from agricultural chemicals as well as from industrial and municipal wastes. Because of the important role of agriculture in the overall economy of the country, agricultural production is and will continue to be greatly threatened by land degradation unless solutions can be found rapidly.

BIBLIOGRAPHY

Alichin, Bridget, and Alichin, Raymond. *The Rise of Civilization in India and Pakistan*, 1982.

Cohen, Stephen. *Pakistan Army 1998*, 1999.

Harrison, Selig. *India and Pakistan: The First Fifty Years*, 1998.

Hussain, Ishrat. *Pakistan: The Economy of an Elitist State*, 1999.

Mayhew, Bradley. *Lonely Planet Pakistan*, 1998.

Mirza, Humayun. *From Plassey to Pakistan: The Family History of Iskander Mirza, the First President of Pakistan*, 1999.

Mittman, Kevin, and Mittman, Karin. *Culture Shock/Pakistan*, 1991.

Mumtax, Khawar, and Mitha, Yameema. *Pakistan: Tradition and Change*, 1996

Shaw, Isobel. *Pakistan Handbook*, 1996

Sisson, Richard, and Rose, Leo, *War and Secession: Pakistan, India and the Creation of Bangladesh*, 1991.

Talbot, Ian. *Pakistan: A Modern History*, 1998.

Williams, Penny; Farooqi, Mukarram; Anis, Rafea; and Khan, Rizwanullah. *Social Development in Pakistan*, 1999

—CONNIE HOWARD

PALAU

CULTURE NAME
Palauan (Belauan)

ALTERNATE NAMES
Pelew (archaic English), Los Palaos Islands (Spanish)

ORIENTATION

Identification. The name Palau may be derived from the Palauan word for village, *beluu* (Pelew). Some trace the name to the Spanish word for mast, *palao*.

Palau comprises several cultures and languages. Ethnic Palauans predominate, inhabiting the main islands of the archipelago. Descendants of the Carolinean atolls, especially Ulithi, settled on Palau's southern atolls of Hatohobei, Sonsorol, Fannah, Pulo Anna, and Merir. Southwest Islanders, as these Carolineans are called, speak Nuclear Micronesian languages. Today most live on Koror and also speak Palauan and English.

Palauans recognize a series of expanding identities, from the village of one's father, one's mother, one's village, or one's island, to the Palauan nation as a whole. Overseas, Palauans retain strong links and identification to their homeland, while developing their own variations on Palauan identity. Shared schooling and work experiences have resulted in some elites considering themselves Micronesian.

Location and Geography. Located in the western Pacific, the Palauan archipelago is the westernmost portion of the Caroline Islands, which are in turn part of the Micronesian geographical subdivision of Oceania. East of Mindanao in the Philippines, Palau is 722 nautical miles (1,340 kilometers) southwest of Guam. Palau's three hundred volcanic and raised coral islands and atolls rise up from the Philippine Plate, with the highest stone outcrops reaching about 720 feet (2,220 meters) on the largest island, Babel thuap. The islands have a total land area of 191 square miles (495 square kilometers). The weather is hot and humid, with annual rainfall around 150 inches (3,800 milimeters). The flora and fauna are tropical, but Palau is best known for its 70-mile-long (113-kilometer-long) barrier reef which encloses spectacular coral reefs and a lagoon of approximately 560 square miles (1,450 square kilometers), a divers' paradise.

The capital and major population center is Koror, the small set of islands to the south of the main island of Babelthuap. In 2004 the capital will be relocated to Melekeok on Babelthuap.

Demography. As of 1995 the resident population of Palau was 17,225. It was 71 percent urban. The demography of Palau must be understood in historical perspective. Estimated at fifty thousand prior to European contact, the number dropped to about thirty-seven hundred people by 1900. The population then began a slow growth that finally accelerated from 1945 through the 1960s.

Fertility has stabilized at 2.1 children per woman, with a death rate of 7.4 per thousand. In the late twentieth century, the natural population growth has been counterbalanced by outmigration. While the number of Palauans has been relatively stable at about thirteen thousand, including the peoples of Hatohobei and Sonsorol, an estimated seven thousand Palauans today reside overseas for a total population of around twenty thousand.

The most important demographic shift of the late twentieth century was the increase in resident foreigners, from 4 percent of the population in 1973 to 25.5 percent in 1995. The largest and longest-standing community was then Filipinos (2,654 workers and their dependents), followed by other Asians (738), Americans (535), other Micronesians (467) and Pacific islanders (232). By 1999 Asian workers had increased to 5,250.

Linguistic Affiliation. Palauan is considered an Austronesian language of a Western subgroup,

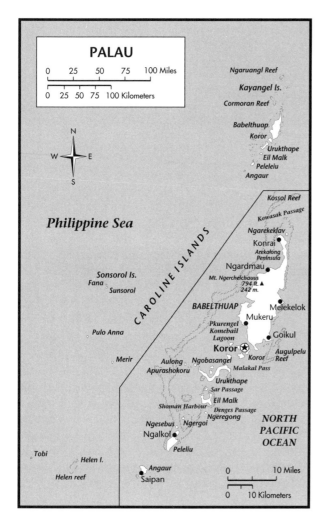

Palau

which along with Chamorro (Mariana Islands) is considered separate from the other Micronesian and Pacific languages grouped under the label "Oceanic." English and Palauan are official languages; elders also read and speak Japanese. The Palauan language incorporates Spanish, German, Japanese, and English loanwords.

Symbolism. Most of Palau's important cultural symbols are derived from its chiefly past, in particular the gable of the community meetinghouse, bai. This impressive thatched building was the center of political, social, and artistic life. Today the decorated bai gable is used in most national and state seals and to decorate Palauan buildings. Other important symbols include the circle subdivided in four, representing wealth, and the half shell symbol of the giant clam shell, which also represents the foundation of Palau and the creation of humanity from the sea. The image of the traditional Palauan mother at the time of her first child ceremony symbolizes the

wealth and fertility of this matrilineal society. Symbols of nationhood include the national flag, a full golden moon on a blue background, and the national anthem.

HISTORY AND ETHNIC RELATIONS

Emergence of the Nation. Archaeologists estimate that the islands were first settled approximately 4,000–4,500 years ago. Palauans participated in the wide-ranging Micronesian trade system, with some interaction with Malay traders. In the nineteenth century Palau was loosely part of the Spanish Pacific. After the Spanish-American War in 1898, Palau was among the islands sold to Germany. In 1914 the islands were occupied by the Japanese, a control later confirmed as a League of Nations Class C Mandate. The United States took possession of the islands in 1944, during World War II. Starting in 1947, Palau was part of the United Nations Trust Territory of the Pacific Islands, under the administration of the United States. Palauans chose not to affiliate with the remaining islands of the territory in the Federated States of Micronesia, instead establishing their own constitutional government in 1981.

While the majority of Palauans preferred free association with the United States, ratification of a Compact of Free Association was delayed by constitutional nuclear-free clauses, which required a 75 percent suspension vote of the people to conform with the compact. Palauans also feared U.S. military land use. Between 1983 and 1991 Palau conducted seven plebiscites and experienced escalating violence, including the assassination of the first elected president. After a three-year cooling-off period, and clarifying statements by the United States on the conditions under which the U.S. military might be present on the islands, the compact was approved, the trusteeship terminated, and the nation formally recognized by the United Nations in 1994.

National Identity. The concept of being "Palauan" grew during the century of colonial administration, drawing together those previously separated by villages, clans, and cultures. While the disruptions of the compact plebiscites pitted Palauans against one another, the plebiscites also cemented support for the national constitution.

Ethnic Relations. Palauans are inclusive in their conceptualization of being Palauan, incorporating long-term residents according to Palauan custom. The constitution confirms the citizenship of all those of Palauan heritage. Ethnic differences between Palauans and Southwest Islanders are declining in importance in the face of increasing numbers of Asian foreign workers.

URBANISM, ARCHITECTURE, AND THE USE OF SPACE

Palau is highly urbanized, with 71 percent of its population residing in Koror and Airai on the south of Babelthuap. Those without land rights on Koror live on land leased from the government, generally in single- or two-story houses of wood or cement with tin roofs.

The bai gable is a common architectural feature. Village communities still have bai meeting houses, a few in traditional styles. Today's government buildings are large air-conditioned cement structures. The future capital, Melekeak, is influenced by classical architecture. The national congress, named the Olbiil era Kelulau (House of Whispers), symbolizes the process of quiet consensus rather than open public debate of issues.

FOOD AND ECONOMY

Food in Daily Life. Palauans enjoy a strong domestic economy based on the dual importance of protein (odoim) provided by men and starch (ongraol) foods produced by women. Each clan has certain recognized food taboos, and there are special foods for titled individuals and for pregnant and lactating women. The extended family system was organized around a series of clan exchanges of food and related valuables—at the time of the building of a house, taking of a title, birth, and death.

Today, imported rice is a staple food that has been integrated into the exchange cycle. A basic meal comprises a starch food, preferably soft or hard taro, tapioca, or rice, and a protein food, normally fish. Coffee and breads or cereal may instead provide a fast breakfast. While starch and protein foods still comprise the basic categories, the Palauan diet is strongly enriched by Japanese and American foods, and more recently by the various cuisines of China, the Philippines, and Korea. There are many restaurants, and local markets feature both Palauan and imported food. Beer is commonly consumed and a local brewery has been established.

Food Customs at Ceremonial Occasions. Special foods vary by state, village, and occasion. In the past a special drink made from a molasses derived from coconut sap was served to chiefs and elders; it was valued for its medicinal benefits and its religious meanings.

Nearly every weekend Palauan kin groups gather in the modern equivalents of clan exchanges for house parties and funerals, and to celebrate a woman's first child. Classmates and workmates also join in the festivities and exchanges. Rice and store-bought foods predominate in these exchanges, in addition to taro, fish, and pork.

Basic Economy. The production of root crops and fishing still provide a strong basis for the Palauan economy. Large taro swamps are worked by women in each of the villages, and men fish primarily from large outboard motorboats. Foreign workers are now employed in the farming and fishing industries and also work in household food production.

On this subsistence basis there is a strong wage economy. Of the Palauan population sixteen years of age and older, 58 percent are engaged in wage labor, with a male participation rate of 68 percent and female rate of 51 percent. About 40 percent work in the government sector.

Payments associated with the Compact of Free Association between the United States and Palau accounted for 55 percent of 1999 revenues. These payments began in 1994 and are front-loaded within the fifteen-year agreement. Major infrastructural development projects are funded by the compact and by international aid.

Land Tenure and Property. In the past, lands, titles, and wealth were held by the clans and controlled by senior female and male elders; in this matrilineal society, however, those related through a senior female had a stronger say in such areas than those related through a man. Each clan controlled taro fields, a named house plot, and other lands. There were certain village lands: those for the chiefly meetinghouses, men's clubs, and dock houses, as well as some public lands. Certain lands could also pass individually from a father to his children.

The majority of lands were alienated during colonial control; these lands were returned to Palau in the 1980s. Certain lands were retained by the new nation for public buildings such as the hospital and government edifices. Otherwise, land may be owned only by Palauan citizens.

Commercial Activities. The traditional Palauan economy was an integrated system of trade and exchange. One could earn Palauan money by performing certain tasks, such as house and canoe building, or through the preparation of certain foods. One also earned wealth for one's clan by participating in the food exchanges, with taro the

Men building a wooden boat. Fish are Palau's main export, and the annual catch may be up to 780,000 pounds (291,000 kilograms).

standard for Palauan money. Commercial activities have been added to the traditional economy. Raw and cooked foods are prepared for sale in markets and stores. Carved storyboards are produced for sale mainly to visitors. A full range of contemporary commercial occupations have been added, mainly in retail sales, construction, and housing services.

Major Industries. The major industry at present is the construction of public infrastructure, funded by the Compact of Free Association and foreign aid. Tourism and fisheries are major export earners; agricultural production is primarily for local consumption.

Trade. Importation of capital goods associated with infrastructural development constitutes over half of all imports, with imports of foods and live animals at 13 percent. Imports are primarily commercial, totaling $65.9 million (U.S.) in 1998 (a decline from $79.6 million [U.S.] in 1996). Total exports, composed of predominantly fish, were $3 million (U.S.)in 1996. The annual fish catch fluctuates between 500,000 and 780,000 pounds (186,500 and 291,000 kilograms).

Tourism is the country's fastest growing industry, with foreign visitors increasing nearly threefold from 23,398 in 1990 to 54,745 in 1999. It is estimated that tourism contributed $65 million (U.S.) to the economy in 1995.

Division of Labor. Except for certain highly specialized tasks such as master builder, master fisher, or master farmer, men and women of all ages traditionally performed basic productive tasks, moving into management positions in the clan and village as they aged. The main division of labor at this time is by nationality, with Palauans and Southwest Islanders holding the primary positions in the governmental sector—in management and the professions—with increased participation by foreigners in private sector positions. Filipino and Chinese workers are primarily engaged in production and service occupations.

SOCIAL STRATIFICATION

Class and Castes. In the past, members of the highest ranking clans of the village were also the wealthiest, controlling state and village as well as clan monies and resources. Leaders were responsible for caring for their descendants and dependents.

The chiefly system is declining as new systems of stratification based on educational attainment and wealth develop in concert with increased participation in the world economy. Foreigners generally fit into the stratification system according to the level and status of their wage-paying job.

Symbols of Social Stratification. In the past there were few symbols of social stratification, other than women wearing Palauan money pieces around their necks, chiefly men wearing a dugong (sea cow) vertebrae bracelet or adze. Today fine clothing, houses, fast speedboats, and four-wheel-drive cars are signals of personal achievement.

POLITICAL LIFE

Government. The Palau national constitution was ratified in 1981. It is modeled on the United States constitution with a popularly elected president and vice president, two-house National Congress, and a judiciary. There are sixteen states based on historical village-states, each with a governor and state constitution.

Leadership and Political Officials. The president and vice president are the highest recognized elected officials. There are no political parties. The Ibedul of Koror and the Reklai of Melekeok continue to be recognized as paramount chiefs of Palau. The states are comprised of a number of villages, each of which has its own male and female chiefly councils. A council of chiefs from each state advises the national government. At the state level both elected governors and traditional leaders are recognized. The level of integration of the elected and traditional leadership varies by state.

Social Problems and Control. There is a national police and judiciary. Palau is experiencing many of the social problems of societies undergoing rapid transformation. High consumption of alcohol contributes to accidents and assaults especially involving young men. Marijuana is grown and sold in the islands, and imported drugs such as ''ice'' (cocaine) are a problem among the young. The paramount chiefs are working with government officials on youth programs and programs that aim to control alcohol and drug use.

Military Activity. Palau does not have a national military, although the young men's clubs of the village-states are still active; in the civil unrest of the 1980s these clubs were often called in to establish and maintain order. Some Palauans do volunteer for service in the various branches of the U.S. military.

SOCIAL WELFARE AND CHANGE PROGRAMS

The constitution mandates a strong program of health and educational support. Education is free and mandatory through high school (grade twelve), with support services for those who do not graduate. Private religious elementary and high schools (including Catholic, Protestant, Seventh Day Adventist, and Palauan Modekngei) are supported by school fees as well as government contributions. Medical services are provided at low cost through the Belau National Hospital and clinics, and there are several private medical clinics. There is a national social security system for those who have contributed through taxes upon their wages, and there are both government and private retirement programs.

NONGOVERNMENTAL ORGANIZATIONS AND OTHER ASSOCIATIONS

Semigovernmental nonprofit organizations include a community action agency, head start programs, and the Belau National Museum. Environmental concerns are strongly represented by the Palau Conservation Society, and local offices of the Nature Conservancy.

GENDER ROLES AND STATUSES

Division of Labor by Gender. In the past there was a strongly gendered division of labor in daily work tasks, with men in charge of fishing and the construction of houses and community buildings, and women in charge of farming and shellfish collection. Today both men and women are active in wage labor, and gender is of little importance except in national political offices, which are rarely held by women. There are women physicians, lawyers, and business managers, and the first Palauan woman serves on the Palau Supreme Court.

The Relative Status of Women and Men. Palauan society recognizes complementary roles for men and women. The traditional governing village council was male, with a female chiefly counterpart council. Senior women were integrally involved in leadership: they selected (and could remove) the male titleholders. Senior women still have strong voices in clan decisions on property and wealth controlled by the matrilines, because money from exchanges enters the clan through the woman. Changes in legal inheritance, however, are eroding women's power.

The Ngardmaun State Office Building in Babeldaob Island. Palau's government is modeled on that of the United States.

MARRIAGE, FAMILY, AND KINSHIP

Marriage. In the past marriages were arranged, with intermarriage among members of the high clans, but at present, individuals may select their own partners. Within the clan marriage is not permitted to relatives reckoned through either the father or mother to four generations. Marriage may be formalized through the court, church, and/or traditional ceremonies involving the exchange of prescribed foods and wealth between the clans. Divorce is common, especially among younger couples with few children, and may be initiated by either husband or wife. In the past most adults would marry; today, there are increasing numbers of single or widowed individuals.

Domestic Unit. The basic unit is the *telungalek*— people descended from one woman. In the past households were comprised of three- or four-generation extended families. Today, there are increasing numbers of nuclear family households, particularly among the young.

Inheritance. Lands, titles, and wealth traditionally passed through the matriline, with decisions made by senior female and male elders. Today, social security payments and intestate estates pass to the wife and children of the deceased, a major transformation of inheritance practices.

Kin Groups. Beyond the *telungalek* are recognized lineages and clans that may extend beyond the village or state. Certain clans are associated by past histories.

SOCIALIZATION

Infant care. At the time a woman's first child is born there are special ceremonies: her female elders gather, organize a series of hot baths, and present the young woman to the community in a public ceremony. During this time the infant is cared for primarily by female relatives, who bring the child to the mother for nursing. Care of infants is dispersed among family members, and it is common for children to be adopted by their grandparents. Men are active in caring for their young children, especially boys.

Child Rearing and Education. In the past, children learned through observation and working alongside adults. Today there is a formal education system beginning generally with head start or kindergarden classes, followed by elementary and secondary schools.

Higher Education. Secondary education is universal, with most Palauans bilingual in Palauan and English. There is a two-year Palau Community College which trains students from throughout the region and also feeds into four-year systems predominantly in Guam and the United States. Palauans enjoy high standards of education and literacy.

ETIQUETTE

Respect toward elders and leaders is still pronounced. In particular the head is considered sacred and should not be touched.

RELIGION

Religious Beliefs. Christianity has been established in Palau for the past century, with Catholic (44 percent) and Protestant (29 percent) churches predominating. There is also a syncretic Palauan religion, Modekngei, which in 1995 accounted for 11 percent of the people.

Palauans still recognize Palauan gods and their totemic embodiments, refraining from eating clan totems. Christian beliefs and indigenous practices often coexist.

Religious Practitioners. Ordained priests, pastors, and Modekngei leaders are highly respected leaders of religious ceremonies, and there is strong lay and community involvement in the churches.

Rituals and Holy Places. Major Christian rituals and holy places are recognized, in addition to indigenous village-based shrines.

Death and the Afterlife. Funerals remain one of the most important of all Palauan rituals. As in the past this is the occasion for a major gathering of the lineages and clans, organized primarily by the female elders. Transfers of food and wealth are made to settle the affairs of the deceased and for a deceased man, the obligations to his wife and children, who return to the woman's natal house. Although general graveyards were established in the nineteenth century by colonial administrations, it is still common for an individual to be buried in the stone platform of the house or lineage.

MEDICINE AND HEALTH CARE

Local Palauan medicines of leaves and herbs and Palauan medicinal and massage practitioners are still valued, although Palau has also fully incorporated Western medicine. The Belau National Hospital provides a high standard of services, relying in some cases on medical referrals to the Philippines and the United States. There are male and female trained physicians and surgeons, as well as nurses. There is an active dental service and village-based public health services.

SECULAR CELEBRATIONS

Palau celebrates a range of national holidays including Constitution Day (9 July) and Independence Day, many American holidays, as well as an extended Christmas/New Year's period.

THE ARTS AND HUMANITIES

Support for the Arts. The Belau National Museum, which opened in 1955, was begun privately with strong local support. The government of Palau is considering funding a new national museum as part of the capital relocation project. Palau has twice sent delegations to the Pacific Festival of Arts and will host the 2004 festival.

Literature. Poetry is the most developed of Palauan literary arts (in Palauan and in English), with several well-known poets; little is available, however, in published form.

Graphic Arts. The graphic arts are highly developed in Palau. In the past the village meetinghouse was the center of both visual and performance arts. The end gables (bai) of these houses and the interior beams were decorated with low-relief painted carvings, depicting histories of the village and its relationships with other villages. Most of the older houses (depicting sailing ships and planes as well as Palauan scenes) were destroyed during World War II or by typhoons, and the few extant and newly constructed gables today depict pre-European Palauan styles.

Carved wooden storyboards, derived from the beam carvings, are a highly developed art form, primarily for sale to foreigners. Carvers of storyboards, shell jewelry makers, and weavers may earn considerable income. Watercolors of traditional village scenes by the late Charlie Gibbons are highly prized. Palauan artists also work in oils and linocuts.

Performance Arts. Dancing is a highly developed art form. Traditional dances are performed by village groups. The women's dances are stately and performed by two lines of women, while the men's line dances often include war stances and stick dances. Oratory is highly developed, with senior elders performing historical chants and pieces from

Palm trees surround a traditional men's house. The bai *gable is an important cultural symbol.*

a number of musical genres. In village meetings there are also informal theatrical skits and clowning in informal dancing. Contemporary Palauan music is composed and performed in nightclubs and on public occasions, with local diskettes and CDs offered for sale.

THE STATE OF THE PHYSICAL AND SOCIAL SCIENCES

Palau has long been a site of research in marine biology, building upon the scientific skills of Palauan master fishermen. Scientists at the Micronesian Mariculture Demonstration Center were the first to successfully spawn giant clams in a laboratory environment, and to develop programs to build stocks of endangered hawksbill turtles. The Palau International Coral Reef Center for scientific research, coral reef management, and educational programs, funded by Japan, is due to open in 2001. A private Coral Reef Research Foundation studies the biochemical properties of marine invertebrates, especially sponges, in cancer research.

The Palau Ministry of Community and Cultural Affairs—which includes the Palau Historic Preservation Office, Belau National Museum, and Ministry of Education—operates aggressive programs in cultural conservation, counteracting strong American influences in education. In conjunction with the construction of the Babelthuap road, major archaeological and oral history projects are under way.

BIBLIOGRAPHY

Nero, K. L. ''The Breadfruit Tree Story: Mythological Transformations in Palauan Politics.'' *Pacific Studies* 15 (4): 199–209, 1992.

—— and N. Thomas. *An Account of a Voyage to Pelew*, 2001.

Parmentier, R. J. *The Sacred Remains: Myth, History, and Polity in Belau*, 1987.

Ramarui, D. *The Palauan Arts*, 1980.

Republic of Palau. Office of Planning and Statistics. *Statistical Yearbook, 1999*, 1999.

Smith, D. R. *Palauan Social Structure*, 1983.

Yamaguti, O. *The Music of Palau: An Ethnomusicological Study of the Classical Tradition*, 1967.

Zobel, E. *The Position of Chamorro and Palauan in the Austronesian Family Tree: Evidence from Verb Morphology and Morphsyntax*. Paper presented at the Eighth International Conference on Austronesian Linguistics, Taipei, December 1997.

—KAREN L. NERO

PALESTINE, WEST BANK, AND GAZA STRIP

CULTURE NAME

Palestinian

ORIENTATION

Identification. Palestine is the name the Romans gave in the second century C.E. to a region of the present-day Middle East situated on the eastern shore of the Mediterranean Sea west of Jordan. The name is derived from the Greek *Palaestina*, or ''Land of the Philistines,'' a seafaring people who settled a small coastal area northeast of Egypt, near present-day Gaza, around the twelfth century B.C.E. Also known as the Holy Land, Palestine is held sacred by Christians, Jews, and Muslims, some of the most important events in each religion having taken place there, especially in the city of Jerusalem.

Location and Geography. Palestine's geographical area has varied greatly over the centuries, as the land was conquered repeatedly by the great empires that came to power in the Mediterranean and the Middle East. Israel, the West Bank and the Gaza Strip, and parts of Egypt, Jordan, and Syria were once part of Palestine.

The Gaza Strip is a narrow sliver of land about eighteen miles long (twenty-nine kilometers)and five miles wide (eight kilometers) on the Mediterranean Sea between Egypt and Israel. It is mostly flat and sandy, with little fertile soil. The West Bank is about ninety miles long (one-hundred-forty-five kilometers) and thirty miles wide (forty-eight kilometers) and is surrounded on all sides by Israel except to the east, where it abuts the Jordan River and the Dead Sea. The West Bank is fertile in the north and mostly barren in the south.

Demography. The estimated 2000 population of Gaza was 1,132,063, approximately 99.5 percent of whom were Palestinian Arab. The West Bank estimate was 2,020,298, with approximately 83 percent Palestinian Arab and 17 percent Jewish. About half of the population of the West Bank is under age fifteen.

Linguistic Affiliation. Like the Jews, the Palestinians are a Semitic people, and the languages of the two groups are similar. Palestinians speak primarily Arabic and Jews speak a Hebrew derived from that of the Bible. The two languages have some of the same words and sound similar to people unfamiliar with the languages.

Symbolism. The Palestinian flag, consisting of three bands of (top to bottom) black, white, and green with a red triangle on the flagstaff side pointing to the center of the white band, is a symbol of Arab unity.

Another popular symbol in Palestine and the rest of the Arab world is the eagle of Saladin, named for a twelfth-century warrior who united Arabs to defend Islamic territories against the Crusaders. It was depicted on Egypt's 1954 Liberation Flag, which was a variation of the Arab Revolt Flag of 1917.

HISTORY AND ETHNIC RELATIONS

Emergence of the Nation. Because of its location at the crossroads of Africa, Asia, and Europe, Palestine has been the battleground of the great powers in the region throughout its history. Conquerors of the region included Egypt, Assyria, Macedonia, Rome, Byzantium, Arabia, and Turkey. Settlement in the area is believed to date back to about 8000 B.C.E., to the village of Jericho in the West Bank.

By about 1000 B.C.E. the Hebrews had established the kingdom of Israel, which later split into two kingdoms, Judah and Israel. The area later changed hands among Assyrians, Babylonians, and Greeks. In the first century B.C.E. the Romans conquered the region and drove out most of the Jews.

Around 640 C.E. as the Islamic religion spread across the Middle East, the area fell to Arab Muslim armies. Many historians believe that modern-day

Palestinian Authority

With the World War I (1914–1918) defeat of the Ottoman Empire, Britain was mandated by the League of Nations to govern Palestine. During the war, both Jews and Arabs had been given conflicting assurances regarding control of Palestine. The British had given their support for Arab control over a region that the Arabs believed included Palestine. Britain had also pledged to support a Jewish homeland in Palestine, however.

Also, during the late nineteenth century, Jewish immigrants had been returning to Palestine in increasing numbers as they fled European and Russian persecution and sought to return to their homeland. Jewish immigration steadily increased after World War I, increasing tensions between the Jews and the Arabs and often resulting in violence.

With the coming of World War II and the Holocaust, there was a surge in Jewish immigration, exacerbating the problem and forcing Britain to relinquish its mandate and turn the problem over to the United Nations in 1947. That same year, the UN voted to partition Palestine into separate Arab and Jewish states, a plan the Arabs did not accept because they wanted all of the territory. The Jews did accept the proposal. Naming their state Israel, they declared its independence on 15 May 1948. Five Arab armies immediately attacked Israel. After the war, the West Bank was controlled by Jordan, and the Gaza Strip came under Egyptian rule, but Israel controlled the rest of Palestine. More than half a million Palestinians were displaced from their homes during the turmoil, many fleeing to the West Bank, the Gaza Strip, and other Arab countries. Nineteen forty-eight thus marks the beginning of an ongoing struggle to build a Palestinian nation, as those displaced by the war have since that time agitated to return to a Palestinian homeland. The Palestine Liberation Organization (PLO), formed in 1964 under Egyptian leadership and led by Palestinian politician Yasser Arafat beginning in 1969, emerged as the main voice of the Palestinian people.

Israel and its Arab neighbors have endured many wars since 1948. In the 1967 Six Day War, Israel captured the West Bank and the Gaza Strip, among other areas. The West Bank and the Gaza Strip are often called the Occupied Territories, and most of the residents are Palestinian Arabs. Many have been refugees in the Occupied Territories since the 1948 war. Israel also annexed East Jerusalem, a revered holy site of Jews, Muslims, and Christians, in 1967.

Another major milestone on the road to statehood was reached in December 1987 when a traffic accident in the Gaza Strip sparked the *intifada*, an

Palestinians are descended from these Arabs. Except for brief periods during the Crusades, Palestine remained in Muslim hands almost continuously, becoming part of the Ottoman Empire in the sixteenth century.

often violent, twenty-year-long campaign of civil disobedience and nationalism in which militant Palestinians vowed to extinguish Israel and the Israelis. The PLO used this time of turmoil to engage in negotiations in which it renounced terrorism, recognized Israel's right to exist, and proposed the creation of a Palestinian state.

The intifada intensified peace talks, and in 1993 Arafat and Israeli prime minister Yitzhak Rabin signed a historic peace accord calling for eventual Palestinian self-rule in the Gaza Strip and the West Bank town of Jericho. The Palestinian National Authority (PNA), a new governing body created to assist in self-rule for Palestinians in Gaza and the West Bank, began administering these areas in 1994, achieving yet another breakthrough in the creation of a Palestinian state. Palestinians in Gaza and the West Bank reached another milestone in 1996 when Israel withdrew its troops from most of the area and they elected Arafat as president of the Palestinian National Authority.

Ethnic Relations. The modern-day conflict between Israel and the Palestinians dates back to World War I and the conflicting promises to Arabs and Jews regarding a homeland in Palestine. The years since the war have been marked by enmity, violence, and terrorism as each group seeks to assert its claim to a Palestinian homeland.

After decades of violence between the two factions—and decades of international attempts to bring stability and normalcy to the region—peace seemed no closer at hand in the early days of the twenty-first century. Amid ongoing peace talks, fierce violence erupted in October 2000, claiming more than three hundred lives and leaving thousands wounded.

URBANISM, ARCHITECTURE, AND THE USE OF SPACE

Thousands of Palestinians in the West Bank and the Gaza Strip live in refugee camps that have gradually become permanent settlements, while many others live in comfortable homes in modern towns.

In a traditional village, one-story houses made of white stone predominate. They usually have a kitchen, a sitting room, bathing room, and small bedrooms. Many homes have gardens and are surrounded by a high wall with a gate. Wealthier families sometimes have two-story homes, the top used for living quarters and entertaining, the bottom for utilities and storage. Some homes have indoor plumbing and electricity.

The crowded refugee camps are equipped with small cement-block huts with corrugated metal doors and roofing. Food is prepared on a metal grate placed over a container of charcoal. Thin mats placed on the floor serve as beds. People bathe and wash clothes in metal drums filled with water from a community well.

FOOD AND ECONOMY

Food in Daily Life. Palestinians often buy snacks or light meals from street vendors as they go about their daily business. It is customary to eat the main meal between two and three o'clock in the afternoon. Many dine on *falafel*, sandwiches made with balls of deep-fried hummus, or grilled lamb sandwiches, called *shwarma*. Pita bread is usually a part of every meal. Other popular dishes include lamb, eggplant, chicken, and rice. Also popular are pastries, usually made with honey and almonds or pistachios.

Drinking coffee or tea is a major social activity for Palestinian men, and conversations and business deals often end with several cups.

Food Customs at Ceremonial Occasions. A favorite dish served at weddings, feasts, and funerals is *mensaf*, a large platter of rice covered with a rich lamb or goat stew and pine nuts.

Basic Economy. The Palestinian economy is based almost completely on agriculture, with livestock, fishing, and some small industry making a smaller contribution. Palestinians depend on Israel for about 90 percent of their external trade.

The West Bank is largely a region of small villages where agriculture is the mainstay of the economy. The chief crop is olives, which are produced on about half of the cultivated land. Other important crops are grains, fruits, and vegetables. Agriculture also dominates the economy of the Gaza Strip, the main crops being citrus fruits and vegetables.

Both the West Bank and Gaza are heavily dependent on Israel and oil-producing Arab states for jobs. Forty percent of Gazans commute to jobs in Israel, earning more than one-third of Gaza's gross national product. After the Israeli occupation in 1967, the West Bank became heavily dependent on service-sector jobs generated by the strong Israeli economy, and Palestinians came to dominate the construction industry in Israel.

The Palestinian economy was dealt serious setbacks in recent years. Jobs in Israel became much more difficult to obtain after the *intifada* began in 1987 and as tensions between Israelis and Palestin-

Palestinians farming land near Efrata, West Bank. Agruculture is the foundation of the Palestinian economy, especially in the northern part of the West Bank.

ians increased in recent years. The Palestinians went on frequent strikes and Israel barred them from the country, hiring workers from other countries to replace them. The Palestinians also lost another major source of income when many lost their jobs in Arab oil nations because they supported Iraq in the Persian Gulf War in 1991. High unemployment plagues both Gaza and the West Bank.

Palestinians are hoping the new Gaza International Airport, opened in 1998, will boost the economy. Produce can now be shipped directly to Europe rather than having to go through Israel first. Also, in the late 1990s foreign investment began flowing into new industrial zones in an attempt to create more jobs within the Occupied Territories.

Major Industries. The West Bank supports a few small industries, including textiles, food processing, cement manufacturing, and the manufacture of toys, furniture, clothing, and shoes.

Trade. Since the Israeli occupation of the West Bank and the Gaza Strip in 1967, the Palestinian economy has become very dependent on Israel's, especially for jobs and as a market for agricultural products. Most of Palestine's exports—consisting of fruits, vegetables, and cooking oil—are exported to Israel.

SOCIAL STRATIFICATION

Classes and Castes. For the most part, Jewish Israeli settlements in the West Bank are separated from Palestinian communities. Most of the best roads, shopping facilities, jobs, and services are found in the Israeli areas, and Palestinians resent this.

Adding to the frustration and anger of ordinary Palestinians is the fairly recent emergence of two distinct cultures within the Palestinian community. At one extreme are the Palestinians who were educated in private schools and often lived in the United States or Europe before their parents returned to their homeland in Palestine, many after the 1993 Oslo accords, carrying their children with them. Many of the returnees get the best jobs through social or political connections, and many flaunt their money and automobiles. At the other extreme are the majority of Palestinians, those who have lived in Palestine throughout the Israeli occupation and who spend their days doing menial chores in poverty.

Symbols of Social Stratification. Elite Palestinians often sport the trappings of privilege and political connection. They live in nice homes, often have two cars, and frequently employ maids. With their

Haradar settlement on the West Bank.

connections, they can easily move freely in and out of the Palestinian territories, an extremely difficult proposition for the poor. To many, the gulf between rich and poor may pose a bigger problem than achieving the goals sought in negotiating the final sovereignty status of the territories.

POLITICAL LIFE

Government. In 1993 Israel and the PLO, in their first direct talks, signed a historic agreement calling for limited Palestinian autonomy in Gaza Strip and Jericho in the West Bank as a first step to Palestinian sovereignty in the Occupied Territories. The Palestinian National Authority (PNA) was set up as an instrument of Palestinian interim self-rule. By early 1996, most of the rest of the West Bank had come under Palestinian administration.

The PNA includes the eighty-eight-member Palestinian Legislative Council, an elected body, and Yasser Arafat, elected president in 1996. There is also a twenty-member cabinet appointed by the president. At the beginning of 2001, however, Arafat alone was the de facto "government" of the Occupied Territories.

The PNA has set up a judicial system. It is also responsible for local government, education, commerce, industry, agriculture, labor, health, taxation, and tourism, among other matters.

Leadership and Political Officials. The leading figure in the Palestinian fight for statehood has been Yasser Arafat. At the beginning of 2001, he was the chairman of the Executive Committee of the PLO, the president of the Palestinian Authority, and the head of the Central Committee of Fatah, the major political faction within the PLO.

Social Problems and Control. The biggest problem for the Palestinians at the beginning of the twenty-first century was the ongoing struggle for a homeland in Palestine and the right to self-determination. Unemployment and poverty are also huge problems. Many young Palestinians—who constitute a majority of the population of Gaza and the West Bank—have never experienced life outside a refugee camp. Their lives have been shaped by conflict and violence, rampant unemployment, and continual unrest.

With ongoing violence continually shattering hard-won peace accords, however, a Palestinian state—and peace and stability in the Middle East—still seemed elusive at the beginning of the twenty-first century.

Military Activity. Established in May 1994, the Palestinian Police Force includes the Palestinian National Security Force, the Palestinian civil police, the civil defense force, the Preventive Security Force, and the General Intelligence Service. Quasi-military security organizations include the coast guard and military intelligence.

NONGOVERNMENTAL ORGANIZATIONS AND OTHER ASSOCIATIONS

The Palestinians receive substantial international aid, and the United Nations Relief and Works Agency (UNRWA) handles most of the needs of the refugees, about half a million of whom still live in camps. In addition to health centers and hospitals, which provide free basic health care, the UNRWA supplies educational and social services, as well as money for the unemployed needy. The UNRWA also supports special groups such as people with disabilities and the elderly.

GENDER ROLES AND STATUSES

Division of Labor by Gender. Many Palestinian men consider it unacceptable for women to work outside the home, so women are usually restricted to homemaking or local cottage industries. They also frown on women wearing Western-style dress, preferring them to dress in the traditional Muslim *jilbab*, a long jacketlike dress, with a scarf to cover their hair.

The Relative Status of Women and Men. As in other Arab cultures, men are at the center of Palestinian life. The family patriarch makes all decisions regarding living arrangements, children's marriages, and money. Obedience to one's father or husband is one of the highest indicators of honor in an Arab woman's life.

MARRIAGE, FAMILY, AND KINSHIP

Marriage. Although polygamy is a common practice among Arab men, with as many as four wives allowed, most Palestinian men have only one or two wives.

Traditionally, when a man and woman wish to marry, the man approaches the woman's family as a prospective husband. After declaring their engagement, the couple and their families get to know one another before the wedding. In urban areas and among university students, couples may marry without the older family traditions. A wedding calls for a big celebration, with singing, dancing, and feasting. The couple exchanges vows in a simple Muslim ceremony called the Katb al-Kitab.

Domestic Unit. Extended families tend to live together in the same household. It is unusual for young people to have their own place before they marry and have children. Frequently, married children also live with their parents. Elderly parents are nearly always cared for at home by the families of their children.

If a man has more than one wife and can afford a large house, each wife gets a separate set of rooms. More often, the houses are small and afford little privacy.

Kin Groups. Family clans dominated by the patriarchs of each group once played a major role in Palestinian society, but these were based on land ownership that no longer exists, so clans have lost their importance. The extended family remains, however, as the strongest social unit.

SOCIALIZATION

Infant Care. A people with one of the world's highest birth rates, the Palestinians care for their children with pride. An infant boy's circumcision is

an occasion for celebration. Extended families help in caring for infants and young children.

Child Rearing and Education. Because about half of the Palestinian population is under age fifteen, education is a prime concern. The school system in Gaza is based on Egypt's and the West Bank's system is based on Jordan's, and there are numerous literacy and cultural centers at all learning levels. Schools vary, but most children get a free public education, from kindergarten through high school. Children from well-to-do families may attend an Islamic or a Christian school.

Higher Education. Obtaining a university degree is a high priority for Palestinians. Palestine boasts eight universities and four colleges, all of which grant bachelor's degrees in arts and sciences. A few also offer graduate programs, and Al-Najah University awards a doctorate degree in chemistry.

ETIQUETTE

Palestinian men shake hands on meeting, and women kiss one another on the cheeks. Palestinians are friendly and hospitable, and neighbors pay one another frequent short visits at which coffee, tea, and sweets are shared. It is considered polite to turn down a dinner invitation to avoid imposing, but the host will continue to insist on the guest's company. Proper dress is essential in displaying good manners. Both men and women cover their heads, and women must always cover their shoulders and upper arms.

RELIGION

Religious Beliefs. Muslims are the predominant religious group in Palestine, comprising around three quarters of the population, and Islamic practices prevail in the territories. Most Palestinian Muslims belong to the Sunni sect.

The word Islam means "submission," to the will of Allah (God) and obedience to his commands. Muslims believe that the prophet Muhammad (c. 570-632 C.E.) received Allah's commands from the angel Gabriel and that these revelations are recorded in the Koran (or Quran), the Islamic holy book. The Koran sets forth rules for everyday behavior as well as religious doctrine. Islam is inseparable from day-to-day life, so religion, politics, and culture are all bound together in Muslim communities.

Religious Practitioners. An *imam* (spiritual leader) delivers the weekly sermon at a mosque.

An official inspects magnetic identifications at the checkpoint between the Gaza Strip and Israel. Conflict between Israelis and Palestinians has resulted in decades of violence and created a need for tight security.

Islam has no priests, and the imam usually has a full-time job in the secular world.

Rituals and Holy Places. Devout Muslims pray five times a day, bowing toward the city of Mecca in Saudi Arabia, the birthplace of Muhammad. They are summoned to prayer by the call of a *muezzin* (crier) issuing from the minarets of the many mosques that dot the Palestinian skyline. Daily prayer is one of the "five pillars of Islam." The other four are the testimony of faith ("there is no God but Allah, and Muhammad is Allah's messenger"), giving to the poor, making at least one *hajj* (pilgrimage) to Mecca, and fasting during Ramadan and other religious holidays.

Palestine contains many sites that are holy to Muslims (as well as many that are holy to Christians and Jews, hence much of the religious conflict in the region). The most revered to Muslims are the Dome of the Rock and al-Aqsa mosques, built in Jerusalem on the site at which Muhammad is believed to have ascended to heaven on a night's journey known as *al-Isra' wa al-Mi raj.*

Death and the Afterlife. Palestinians observe a three-day mourning period when someone dies. Family and friends offer condolences and recite the Koran. Neighbors serve meals to the deceased's family and their guests throughout the three-day period. The deceased's death is observed again at the forty-day anniversary.

Medicine and Health Care. In the West Bank, with its vast refugee population of more than half a million, the United Nations Relief and Works Agency provides health, educational, and social services. More than thirty health centers and hospitals provide free basic health care. Special services are also provided for the elderly and people with disabilities.

THE ARTS AND HUMANITIES

Literature. Like most Arabs, Palestinians regard verse more highly than prose. The work of the highly esteemed poet and writer Mahmoud Darwish, like that of many Palestinian writers and artists, is highly political and deals with the Israeli occupation and the plight of the Palestinians. Darwish's "Identity Card," which graphically paints the Palestinians' dilemma, is one of the best-known works by a Palestinian. Darwish's work has been translated into the major languages. He also composed Palestine's Declaration of Independence. In *The Wind-Driven Reed and Other Poems*, Fouzi al-Asmar evokes the Palestinian longing for a homeland.

Palestinian-Israeli writer Emile Habibi, a long-time representative in the Israeli Knesset, began writing in response to a leading Israeli politician's statements that the Palestinians did not exist; otherwise, they would have produced their own literature. Habibi went on to write a series of short stories and novels, one of which was translated into sixteen languages.

Many Palestinian writers and artists live outside Palestine as émigrés. Palestinian-American Edward Said is a well-known historian and essayist. Said's *Peace and Its Discontents* and other books explore Palestinians' problems and aspirations. Other highly regarded émigré writers include Liana Badr and Hassan al-Kanafani.

One of the greatest Palestinian fiction writers is Ghassan Kanafani, whose short stories in *All That Remains: Palestine's Children* depicts the aimlessness and desperation of Palestinian refugees.

The works of many leading Palestinian writers are translated in Salma Khadra Jayyusi's *Modern Palestinian Literature*.

Graphic Arts. Because Islam forbids the portrayal of people and animals, most Arab designs feature plants, leaves, or geometric shapes. Many Palestinians are skilled in calligraphy and illustrate verses from the Koran in beautiful designs and sell them at art shows. In larger tourist cities such as Jerusalem, Bethlehem, and Ramallah, craftsmen sell woven rugs and tapestries, leather goods, pottery, and ceramic jars. Also available are crafts made from olive wood and ivory: jewelry boxes, scenes of the Last Supper, crosses, camels, and mosques.

BIBLIOGRAPHY

Aburish, Said. *Cry Palestine: Inside the West Bank*, 1991.

Ciment, James. *Palestine/Israel: The Long Conflict*, 1997.

Gall, Timothy L., ed. *Worldmark Encyclopedia of Cultures and Daily Life*, vol. 3, 1997, s.v. "Palestinians."

Gerner, Deborah. *One Land, Two Peoples: The Conquest over Palestine*, 1991.

Gluck, Sherna Berger. *An American Feminist in Palestine: The Intifada Years*, 1994.

Grossman, David. *Sleeping on a Wire: Conversations with Palestinians in Israel*, 1993.

Hellander, Paul, Andrew Humphreys, and Neil Tilbury. *Israel & the Palestinian Territories*, 1999.

Khalidi, Walid. *Palestine Reborn*, 1992.

Kimmerling, Baruch, and Joel Migdal. *Palestinians: The Making of a People*, 1994.

Lughod, Abu. "Palestinian Higher Education." *Boundary 2*, Spring 2000, pp. 80–95.

Oz, Amos. *Israel, Palestine and Peace: Essays*, 1995.

Said, Edward. *The Politics of Dispossession: The Struggle for Palestinian Self-Determination, 1969–1994*, 1994.

Shipler, David. *Arab and Jew: Wounded Spirits in a Promised Land*, 1986.

Stefoff, Rebecca. *West Bank/Gaza Strip*, 1999.

Szulc, Tad. "Who Are the Palestinians?" *National Geographic*, June 1992, pp. 84–113.

—ROBERT H. GRIFFIN

PANAMA

CULTURE NAME

Panamanian

ALTERNATIVE NAMES

Panameño (Spanish)

ORIENTATION

Identification. The Republic of Panama is a former Spanish colony in Central America with a mixed population of Creoles, mestizos, European immigrants, Africans, and indigenous Indians.

Location and Geography. The country is a natural land bridge connecting the South American continent with Central America. The isthmus runs east-west in the form of an inverted "S." Low mountains run through most of the country, leaving a gap in the center that is nearly at sea level. The Pacific coastline, with the Azuero Peninsula jutting south to define the Gulf of Panama, is longer than the Atlantic coastline. The area of the country is 25,590 square miles (74,046 square kilometers).

Demography. In 2000, Panama had approximately 2.816 million inhabitants, 700,000 of whom lived in Panama City, with another 300,000 in the immediate suburbs. The urban elite is primarily Creole, mostly of Spanish descent. There are also populations of Spanish, Italian, Greek, and Jewish origins. There is a longtime Chinese community, and a small Hindu community lives in the capital, Panama City. The largest demographic group is the *interioranos* ("interior people"), who are classified as "Hispano-Indians." This group is largely mestizo (mixed European and native American), and its members consider themselves the "real Panamanians." Some interioranos grade imperceptibly into an acculturated native American population known pejoratively as *cholos*, who refer to themselves as *naturales* ("natives"). Together, these two groups constitute 70 percent of the population. There are

four officially recognized Indian ethnic groups (the Kuna, Guaymi or Ngawbe, Embera, and Waunan), which number fewer than 200,000. People of African descent account for 15 percent of the population. These "Afro-colonials" descend from slaves who were imported in colonial times. They speak Spanish and are Roman Catholic. The "Afro-Antillean" group descends from Caribbean residents who came to work on the construction of the Panama canal. They speak English, French, or an English patois at home and are mostly Protestant.

Linguistic Affiliation. The official language is Spanish, but English is used widely in business, especially banking and tourism, and by some people of African descent.

Symbolism. Some coins bear the image of Urraca, an Indian chief who resisted the Spanish conquests, but most coins depict Vasco Nuñez de Balboa, the discoverer of the Pacific Ocean.

HISTORY AND ETHNIC RELATIONS

Emergence of the Nation. Panama became an autonomous nation because of its function as the custodian of the transisthmus shipping route—the "path between the seas." It gained independence in 1903 as part of an American-sponsored revolt against Colombia that led to the signing of a treaty granting the United States the right to build the Panama Canal.

The Spanish discovered and conquered Panama between 1502 and 1519. At that time, it was referred to as the *Castilla de Oro*, a source of gold and potential converts. From 1519 through 1538, the area that is now Panama was a base for soldiers sent to conquer the Andean civilizations in South America. After 1538, it was used as a land route to Spain's South American colonies and a transshipment point for Andean gold. From 1568 to 1671 there was series of pirate raids, and in 1671 Panama City was sacked by buccaneers under the command

1719

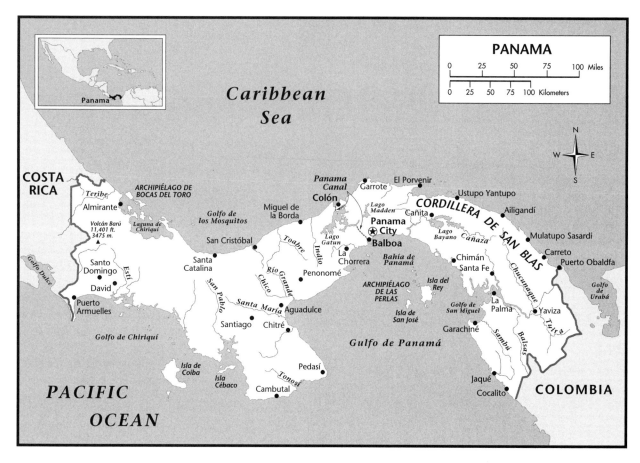

Panama

of Sir Henry Morgan. Local traders engaged in smuggling until Spain shifted the official gold route to Cape Horn, and the area entered a period of commercial decline.

After independence from Spain and union with Colombia in 1821, the isthmus again became an important transit route. Slavery was abolished in 1852. The United States completed a railroad across the area in 1855 to expedite movement to the gold fields in California. After failing to build a sea-level canal in the 1880s, the French sold their concession to the United States, which conspired with the elite in Panama City to declare independence when they could not obtain a favorable treaty from Colombia.

From 1903 to 1978, the United States controlled the Canal Zone, a five-mile strip on both sides of the canal. Residents of that area were called ''Zonians'' and remained American citizens even after three generations of residence. These mostly white employees of the Canal Company lived an isolated life and were prejudiced against the Panamanian population. In 1977, after lengthy negotia-

tions, President Jimmy Carter signed a treaty that abolished the Canal Zone as a colonial enclave, arranged for Panamanian ownership of the canal in the year 2000, and provided for the closing of American military bases.

In 1925, the United States intervened in a revolt by Kuna Indians on the northeast Atlantic coast and established a tribal reserve. The Kuna enclave has been successful. In the 1930s, the United States' military hired Kuna laborers to work at army bases. After the transfer of sovereignty over the canal, those workers migrated to Panama City.

National Identity. Panamanians do not consider themselves former Colombians. From 1578 to 1751, Panama was the seat of a Spanish *real audiencia* (court of chancery), with Spanish lawyers and a governor or captain general. The presence of this judicial-legislative-executive government body led to the building of a sense of independent nationhood.

Ethnic Relations. Unlike the former Canal Zone, the government has always repudiated racism and segregation. Because of its nationalistic policies, the government also forbade the use of English in public schools, thus discriminating against the black population.

URBANISM, ARCHITECTURE, AND THE USE OF SPACE

Survivors of the burning of Panama City in 1671 rebuilt a walled bastion on a rocky promontory to the west. This became the home of the colonial administration and the Creole elite, who lived in two-story mansions. Outside the city walls was a neighborhood of free blacks living in thatched structures. Farther out were the cattle ranches and farms of the elite, which were staffed by slaves. The walled city survives as the Casco Viejo, and the areas adjacent to it are now densely populated slums. Because the former Canal Zone abuts the old city on the north and west, the growing population was forced to fan out along the bay to the north and east. On the Panamanian side, city blocks were plotted along radial avenues. Bella Vista, a gracious area of Art Deco mansions for the elites grew up in the 1920s along the bay. Farther inland there were working-class tenements. On the "Zone" side there was parkland, with occasional housing clusters. The government is transferring that housing to private owners but is committed by treaty to conserve the natural rainforest areas of the former Zone to prevent the canal from silting.

A few neighborhoods of upper-class walled villas have appeared. Large middle-class subdivisions are being built away from the city center. There are scattered apartment blocks of public housing for workers. Several shopping malls cater to the needs of a city with heavy traffic and an extensive bus system. The major downtown center is the banking district along Via España just past the old aristocratic Bella Vista and next to the first luxury hotels. This and nearby areas have high-rise offices, hotels, and apartments.

Colon on the Atlantic side is now a lower- and underclass settlement abutting the free trade zone. The largely Jewish, Italian, and Arabic entrepreneurs of that zone live in Panama City high-rises and commute daily in small airplanes.

The dominant architectural structure remains the Panama Canal. Inaugurated in 1914, it is still an engineering wonder in which Panamanians take pride.

FOOD AND ECONOMY

Food in Daily Life. Unlike other Spanish colonies, Panama's subsistence agriculture never depended on corn. Game and fish were always sources of protein, and corn is eaten mainly in the form of thick cakes called *arepas* and maize gruel. The Kuna roast bananas and boil them in a soup dish that consists of water squeezed through grated coconut meat, fish, and fowl or a game meat. This dish resembles the *sancocho* eaten by many non-Indian Panamanians—a soup of poultry or meat cooked with root vegetables and corn. All the towns and cities have Chinese restaurants, a legacy of the Chinese who came to work on the railroad in the 1850s.

Food Customs at Ceremonial Occasions. Upper class families are likely to serve fresh seafood at weddings, baptisms, and other celebrations. Their cooking style tends to be continental. Interioranos, in contrast, value beef. Their traditional Sunday meal is *tasajo*, smoked and cured beef with the flavor of ham.

Basic Economy. Before 1502 the native populations practiced slash-and-burn agriculture, growing a variety of root crops. When the urban elite bought rural property, they turned to cattle raising and exported the meat and hides. Livestock production is still an important economic activity, even on very small landholdings, and parts of the rain forest have been converted into pastureland. The naturales and Indian groups still practice slash-and-burn agriculture and do not raise cattle. Afro-colonials engage in coastal horticulture and fishing, as do the Kuna. The unit of currency is the balboa, which is pegged to the United States dollar.

Land Tenure and Property. The San Blas Kuna have had a tribal land reserve since the 1930s. The government is in the process of setting up large reserves for the Guaymí, the Embera, and the Kuna of the Bayano. Interioranos tend to divide up their holdings among many heirs, so that over time properties become quite small, intensifying migration to the cities and to northern and western frontier areas to clear the rain forest and to claim government forest lands through "squatters' rights." Urban migrants are similarly involved in large scale land invasion in idle lands on the periphery of the city. Some of these are planned, others are spontaneous.

Commercial Activities. Interioranos have a system of rural markets and fairs in which locally-owned shops are tied to Chinese shopkeepers and

A Kuna woman applies paint to her face in the San Blas Islands. Four Indian ethnic groups are officially recognized, including the Kuna.

wholesalers in the towns. Since the 1960s, Panama has become an international banking center.

Major Industries. Panama never had a plantation economy. Today agribusiness specializes in the production of sugar and bananas.

Trade. The economy relies on transit, transhipping, and banking to earn foreign currency. Panama exports coffee, bananas, beef, and tropical hardwoods. As a major international transshipping center, all types of the world's industrial goods pass through Panama, which keeps or imports electronics, automobiles, and a wide variety of luxury goods. Panama also imports petroleum, as it has no oil fields.

Division of Labor. As of 1997 estimates put 18 percent of the labor force in agriculture, another 18 percent in industry, and 67 percent in service. Of these sectors agriculture is the least productive, accounting for only 8 percent of the gross national product, with industry at 25 percent and services at 67 percent.

SOCIAL STRATIFICATION

Classes and Castes. The urban Creole upper class, known as the *rabiblancos* ("white butts"), mingles socially with Americans, Spaniards, Italians, and the oldest segment of the Jewish community, the Sephardic Jews, who came to the country in the 1890s. Prosperous merchants in the small Hindu community worship at a prominent hilltop temple. The Chinese community includes a few wealthy commercial families, members of the professions, a middle class of shopkeepers, and a few very poor recent immigrants. It is perceived as monolithic. People from the interiorano community, other mestizos, and some blacks have also risen to wealth and prominence through the professions, government, and business and services. These people do not intermarry with the old elite. The large urban middle classes consist of interioranos, mestizos, blacks, and educated Indians, especially Kunas.

Symbols of Social Stratification. Class division is not rigid, and the elite is not resented. It is closely linked to the symbols of the republic through its descent from illustrious ancestors and the founding fathers of independence from Spain and Colombia, many of whom have streets named after them.

POLITICAL LIFE

Government. The republic is a constitutional democracy. Panama inherited from Colombia a binary system of liberals versus conservatives, both of which agreed on opposition to the presence of the United States in the Canal Zone. In 1940, these were eclipsed by a nationalist movement led by Arnulfo Arias, who employed fascist rhetoric and methods and was deposed during World War II. Elected again decades later, Arias was deposed again. Omar Torrijos, a military leader, instituted a corporatist, welfare-oriented state with a new constitution that declared him as head of government above a subservient president and cabinet. Although there was a legislative assembly and local councils throughout the republic, the regime was largely a command structure. It borrowed funds from abroad to build an infrastructure, including electrification and education, and united the public behind its effort to gain control of the canal. Torrijos died in a plane crash in 1981, and shortly after his death the military leader Manuel Noriega took over the civil government. After refusing to recognize the results of the 1989 elections, Noriega had the legislature declare him president. Five days later, the United States invaded to protect the Canal, restore democracy, and eventually arrest Noriega for drug trafficking.

Leadership and Political Officials. In the aftermath of the invasion, the Defense Forces were abolished, and Panama has come to have a lively and openly debated political life. Political leaders include members of the old elite. Most persons in public life tend to be middle class, of urban or interiorano origin.

Social Problems and Control. Crime is scarce outside of certain slums in Panama City and Colon, where robberies are common. International drug smuggling is a problem in jungle areas near the border with Colombia. Drug cartels, however, are not reputed to maintain bases within the republic. Panama has never had a leftist guerrilla movement. All the regimes have been able to contain social tensions without endemic violence.

Military Activity. The armed forces have become a police force with a limited defense role. Although the United States vacated its bases, it retains the right to defend the canal against an attack from any source.

SOCIAL WELFARE AND CHANGE PROGRAMS

Many social welfare programs were initiated by the Torrijos regime in the 1970s. Today there is a social security system of public hospitals and rural clinics, and the bureaucracy encourages local people to seek outside aid for development projects. The retirement policy for civil servants is very liberal, providing a modest pension after age fifty. The current trend has been to favor privatization and self-help programs.

NONGOVERNMENTAL ORGANIZATIONS AND OTHER ASSOCIATIONS

Many international organizations, including the United Nations Educational, Scientific, and Cultural Organization (UNESCO), the Food and Agricultural Organization of the United Nations (FAO), and the World Health Organization (WHO), operate locally. Fundación Dobbo Yala was founded by indigenous professionals to represent the native American groups and channel foreign aid funds for educational and development projects. Native Lands attempts to protect indigenous land holdings and reserves.

GENDER ROLES AND STATUSES

Division of Labor by Gender. The current president is a woman, and women have reached the top levels of all the professions, especially government service and education. However, there is almost no feminist movement, and relations between the sexes are traditionally Hispanic, with a double standard for sexual relations. Prostitution is legal, and workers in highly visible urban brothels claim to have been secretaries or schoolteachers from other republics whom hard times forced to emigrate in search of economic survival.

Relative Status of Women and Men. In the role of *Carnaval* Queens, young unmarried women enjoy the very highest symbolic status in almost every municipality in the republic, since all celebrate carnival. Similarly the Kuna Indians revere adolescent girls, and celebrate their coming of age in an elaborate three day ceremony, the *inna suid*, which culminates in the young woman's hair being cut off down to the scalp. Women enjoy public equality with men, and are seen on the job and in public places such as restaurants, mingling freely with male family members, while being accorded deference and respect.

MARRIAGE, FAMILY, AND KINSHIP

Marriage. Although Guaymí Indian leaders may have more than one wife, other Panamanians marry only one spouse at a time. Divorce is permitted under liberal terms by the Civil Code. Couples of African descent on the Atlantic coast tend to live together without marrying. These unions frequently dissolve as men and women may find new partners during the weekly pre-carnival *Congo* dances.

Domestic Unit. The ideal family unit for most Panamanians is the nuclear family of a married couple and their children. The Kuna Indians, however, prefer to have new husbands go to live with their brides in the latter's house. These then become extended families around a grandmother, her husband, and her married daughters and their husbands.

Inheritance. Kuna Indians inherit their houses from their mothers. All other property is inherited equally among all heirs from both parents. In the rest of Panama the Civil Code provides for a similar system. In the absence of a will, a deceased widowed man's property goes equally to all his children, male or female.

Kin Groups. Kindreds, networks of related nuclear families, are very important to the urban elites. Upper class persons are likely to give parties, for exam-

View of the Panama Canal. Opened in 1914, the canal is an engineering marvel and a source of pride among Panamanians.

ple, attended only by relatives. Interioranos and naturales also value similar extended family networks. One man will be a pioneer in frontier areas, for example and his and his wife's relatives will follow. Such extended families are opening up the frontier areas.

SOCIALIZATION

Infant Care. Increased rural-to-urban migration has emptied some villages, especially those of coastal blacks and some interioranos, of young adults. Children live with their grandparents; in extreme cases, there are villages that skip a generation. Among the Kuna, male labor migration has left wives behind in matrilocal households to raise children.

Child Rearing and Education. The educational system is effective through the primary school level. Official literacy rates are as high as 90 percent, and an assumption of literacy prevails in daily interactions in the cities.

Higher Education. The University of Panama is state-supported and has a long history. The Catholic University of Santa Maria la Antigua is its major competitor.

ETIQUETTE

Panamanians are formal in dealings with strangers. There is a minimum of greeting behavior in public, and manners tend to be stiff and not courtly. Once included in family and friendship groupings, a stranger can be incorporated into a party-going network quickly. Dress tends to be formal despite the tropical climate.

RELIGION

Religious Beliefs. Panama is 85 percent Roman Catholic. Traditional beliefs and practices have been maintained among the native American groups despite a history of missionization.

Rituals and Holy Places. The most important ritual is Carnaval. The capital closes down the five days before Ash Wednesday, and a young queen chosen by charitable organizations presides. A competing "more authentic" celebration takes place in Las Tablas in the interior. Coastal blacks celebrate the *Congo*, which starts in January and also is presided over by a queen in each community. Its male and female dance groups perform each weekend. The colonial port city of Potrobelo on the Atlantic coast is the site of a shrine to an icon of the Black

Men surround a bull and spectators watch from behind a fence on the Plaza Colonial as they prepare for a bullfight.

Christ, an object of great veneration and of an annual pilgrimage that attracts great numbers during Holy Week.

MEDICINE AND HEALTH CARE

The construction of the canal led to the conquest of yellow fever and advances in public health. A legacy of that period is safe drinking water throughout the republic. Gorgas Memorial Hospital specializes in tropical medicine. There is one world-class private hospital, Clinica Paitilla, and several crowded public hospitals.

SECULAR CELEBRATIONS

Panama celebrates two independence days, on 3 November from Colombia and on 28 November from Spain. Festivities tend to be low-key, however, although school children parade in most localities. New Year's Eve and New Year's Day are occasions of much merriment, with children burning effigies of Father Time at midnight in many areas. Larger towns in the central provinces hold rodeos for cowboys almost every Sunday.

THE ARTS AND THE HUMANITIES

Support for the Arts. Funding from banks has helped art galleries thrive, and local artists are in great demand. The National Institute for Culture (INAC) and the school system both support graphics arts education. Other than that support mainly stems from the open market in art and native and local crafts. A private group, the National Association for Concerts, contracts with local and foreign performers for classical music concerts. The best museum is the Museo del Hombre Panameño in the former railroad station.

Literature. Panama has a number of writers producing short stories, novels, and poetry. Rogelio Sinán is a successful poet and novelist who has acquired an international reputation, but most writers produce for the local market, where they are well received.

Graphic Arts. The Kuna Indians are world-famous for their *molas*, applique textile panels in geometric or representational designs. The Embera Indians produce basketry of very high quality, as well as wood carvings in tropical hardwoods.

THE STATE OF THE PHYSICAL AND SOCIAL SCIENCES

Smithsonian Tropical Research Institute runs Barro Colorado Island, a wildlife station inside the canal waterway. There are numerous social scientists, but none has fully described the overall national culture.

BIBLIOGRAPHY

De St. Malo, Guillermo and Godfrey Harris. *The Panamanian Problem: How the Reagan and Bush Administrations Dealt with the Noriega Regime*, 1993.

Doggett, Scott. *Panama*, 1999.

Drolet, Patricia Lund. "The Congo Ritual of Northeastern Panama: An Afro-American Expressive Structure of Cultural Adaptation." Ph.D. dissertation, University of Illinois, Urbana, 1980.

Figueroa Navarro, Alfredo. *Dominio y Sociedad en el Panamá Colombiano (1821–1903)*, 1978.

Gasteazoro, Carlos Manuel. *Introducción al estudio de la Historia de Panamá. I: Fuentes de la Época Hispana*, 1956.

Howe, James. *A People Who Would Not Kneel: Panama, the United States, and the San Blas Kuna*, 1998.

Joly, Luz Graciela. "One Is None and Two Is One: Development from Above and Below in North-Central Panama." Ph.D. dissertation, Gainesville, 1981.

McCullough, David. *The Path between the Seas: The Creation of the Panama Canal, 1870–1914*, 1977.

Moore, Alexander. "From Council to Legislature: Democracy, Parliamentarianism, and the San Blas Cuna." *American Anthropologist* 86 (1): 28–42, 1984.

Salvador, Mari Lynn, ed. *The Art of Being Kuna: Layers of Meaning among the Kuna of Panama*, 1997.

Wali, Alaka. *Kilowatts and Crisis: Hydroelectric Power and Social Dislocation in Eastern Panama*, 1989.

Young, Philip D. *Ngawbe: Tradition and Change among the Western Guaymi of Panama*, 1971.

Web Site

U.S. State Department, Central Intelligence Agency. *World Factbook: Panama* http://www.cia.gov/cia/publications/factbook/pm.html

—ALEXANDER MOORE

PAPUA NEW GUINEA

CULTURE NAME

Papua New Guinean

ALTERNATIVE NAMES

Niugini (Pidgin English)

ORIENTATION

Identification. Papua is probably derived from the Malay word *papuwah* ("fuzzy hair"). In 1545, a Spanish explorer called the island *Nueva Guinea*. In 1884, the western half of New Guinea was officially recognized as Dutch New Guinea, the northeastern section became German New Guinea, and the southeastern quarter became British New Guinea. In 1905, Australia took over the territory, renaming it the Territory of Papua. After World War II, the British and German territories were combined and jointly administered by Australia as the Territory of Papua and New Guinea. In 1975, the country became Papua New Guinea or, officially, the Independent State of Papua New Guinea.

Location and Geography. Papua New Guinea consists of eastern New Guinea along with New Britain, New Ireland, Bougainville, and six hundred small islands and archipelagoes. The land area is over 178,000 square miles (462,000 square kilometer), with the mainland accounting for 80 percent. The western half of the island is the Indonesian province of Irian Jaya. To the south is Australia, and to the east and southeast are the Solomon Islands and other Melanesian countries. To the north and northwest are the Philippines, South Korea, and Japan.

The central mountain chain extends the length of the island and is covered in tropical rain forest. Upland valleys and the headwaters of fast-flowing rivers descend to the coast through some of the world's largest swamps.

Papua New Guinea has a tropical monsoon climate and is generally hot and humid, although the climate varies from one area to another.

Over 75 percent of the nation is covered in rain forest. Swamp forest is found in the poorly drained lowlands, and sago palm is a staple food of the people living there. Around Port Moresby and in drier areas to the west are grassy plains and savanna woodlands.

Demography. The 1990 census showed a population of 3,761,954. Over half the population was under age 20. With an annual growth rate of 2.3 percent, the population topped four million by 1992 and is expected to grow to more than five million by the year 2000. Around 85 percent of the population lives in small villages and rural outposts; the other 15 percent is concentrated in ten major urban areas where most of the non-Melanesian population of about 25,000 resides. The largest cities are Port Moresby with a population over 220,000, Lae (90,000), Madang (30,000), Mt Hagen (45,000), Wewak (23,000), and Goroka (25,000).

Linguistic Affiliation. Well over one thousand languages are spoken throughout New Guinea. After Colonization, Papua New Guineans needed to communicate with one another and with outsiders. On German (and later Australian) plantations and wherever individuals speaking different languages met, a pidgin language referred to as Neo-Melanesian or Melanesian Pidgin developed. Now known as *Tok Pisin* ("talk pidgin"), Melanesian Pidgin is spoken throughout Papua New Guinea. While English is taught in school and is the official language of business and government, Tok Pisin is a symbol of national identity and a preferred means of communication. Hiri Motu, a trade language that originated on the south coast in Papua among participants in a traditional trade network, is spoken only in that area.

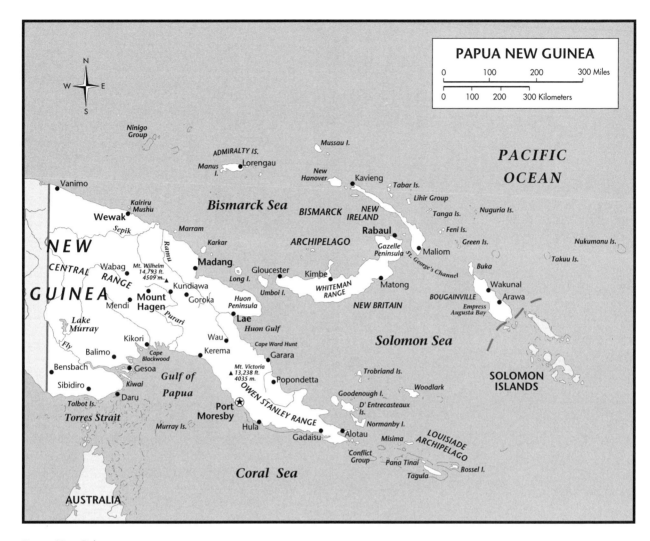

Papua New Guinea

Symbolism. While preparing for independence and attempting to promote national identity, leaders and artists drew on symbols reflecting the nation's unique cultural and natural diversity and continuing traditions. The national flag is a rectangle divided diagonally from the top left corner to the bottom right. The upper triangle is red with a yellow bird of paradise; the lower triangle is black with five white stars representing the Southern Cross. Black, red, and yellow are traditional colors in many Papua New Guinean societies. Items of traditional exchange (*kina* shells, pigs) are prominent on the currency. The Southern Cross symbolizes the country's close relations with other South Pacific nations. The national song, "O Arise All You Sons," reflects a commitment to Christianity in its references to God and the "Lord".

HISTORY AND ETHNIC RELATIONS

Emergence of the Nation. Before colonization, an individual's identity was grounded in his or her kin group and rarely extended beyond the kin groups of close relatives and in-laws. While an individual may have shared a language and culture with tens of thousands of persons, only leaders and other unusual individuals spent time outside the villages nearest to his or her "place." After colonization, Papua New Guineans experienced political, social, and economic integration. Missionaries and administrators suppressed "tribal" warfare to allow freedom of movement and integrated villagers into the colonial economy as plantation workers and mission helpers. Missionary activities also led to the spread of Christianity and Western education; the building of roads, airstrips, and radio stations; and the shared experience of racial prejudice directed at local peoples by many whites.

Colonization and change were uneven, with island and coastal areas colonized before the interior and some groups resisting change for decades. Outsiders did not visit the highlands until the 1930s, and some areas were first contacted as late as the 1970s. Differences in education and economic development contributed to ethnic and class differences.

National Identity. In the 1960s, Australia moved toward liberating Papua New Guinea by establishing self-government and a House of Assembly and building institutions of higher learning to train an educated elite to serve the country.

The focus on higher education was matched by efforts to foster closeness and national pride among the students that would cut across ties with *wantoks* (those in the same language group) and flow outward to the rest of the country. Students were taught to express their experiences in poetry, music, stories, and art that dealt with the ''beauty of village life,'' the opposite sex, pride in their cultures, and the question of how they could lead the country into the modern world without becoming selfish. Regardless of this soul-searching, class differences are emerging as educated parents with good jobs provide for their children's future, and there is increasing intermarriage between persons of different cultural background who mingle in school and at work. Communicating in English or Tok Pisin, many couples fail to pass on their mother tongues to their children, alienating their village kin.

Ethnic Relations. Before independence on 16 September 1975, a number of micronationalist movements threatened secession from a nation that many felt was a colonial invention. Papua Besena emerged in 1973 under the leadership of Josephine Abaijah. Its objective was to free Papua from Australian colonial rule and unification with the more heavily populated New Guinea. In March 1975, Papua Besena declared Papuan independence but did not go beyond that symbolic act.

In 1964, the discovery of copper in Bougainville resulted in the construction of a giant copper mine. It was argued that the profits from the mine would benefit all of Papua New Guinea. Bougainvilleans were suspicious of the motives of the Australians and the expatriate company and resentful of the mainland Papua New Guineans who were brought in to build the mine. In November 1988, a guerilla operation began that became the Bougainville Revolutionary Army (BRA). The conflict continued throughout the 1990s and has been difficult for the police and defense forces that have been pitted against fellow citizens.

URBANISM, ARCHITECTURE, AND THE USE OF SPACE

Before European settlement, there were no towns. Thousands of villages and hamlets were connected by narrow paths, customs, and networks of marriage and trade partners. Bush material houses were temporary as people moved with their new gardens and as alliances dissolved and re-formed. Men spent their nights with other men and boys in elaborate men's houses, while their wives and female relatives slept and ate in smaller women's houses. Most villages were home to more than one kin group. With colonization, dispersed settlements were combined into larger villages for easier administration and the provision of education and health care. The first towns grew up around mission and administrative centers, near airstrips, or on hillsides overlooking good harbors. Towns were small, and homes and nonresidential structures were simple one-story buildings. The first Papua New Guineans to live in towns were men. Many workers were chosen from nearby villages to which they were expected to return at night, but some lived in servants' quarters (*boi haus*) or company barracks. The exclusion of New Guineans from areas of European settlement was maintained almost up until independence. After World War II, there was an expansion of economic opportunities for both colonizers and local peoples, resulting in a rapid growth of towns and an increase in urban migration as men, and later their wives and children, came to town seeking employment, education, and excitement. The Australians tried to control the influx by building company housing for workers and their families and denying residency rights to other migrants, but that policy was only partly successful. ''Squatter'' settlements became stepping-stones for migrants who came to test the waters in town and migrants who wanted to save money to invest in their villages. They have become islands of safety in crime-filled towns as wantoks band together, apart from other groups.

In preparing for independence, colonial and Papua New Guinean officials built institutions such as the National Arts School, where students and other artists and architects used traditional and modern elements in designs for buildings in the capital and elsewhere.

Papua New Guineans continue to be ambivalent about the expense and violence of town life. Markets, parks, and shopping centers draw thousands

Three men in a bachelor house in Omarakana, Kiriwina, Trobriand Island. Traditionaly, even married men lived in separate houses from their wives.

of visitors every day, most of whom are interested in observing the spectacle and meeting up with wantoks to gossip or plan group events. Airports are crowded with travelers' friends and families, onlookers, and unemployed youths observing the movements of people from around the world.

FOOD AND ECONOMY

Food in Daily Life. Staples include starchy vegetables (wild sago, breadfruit, yams, taro, sweet potatoes, and rice) complemented by wild greens, several varieties of bananas, and coconuts, mango, and other fruits. Domestication of animals and hunting provide fowl, pork, and meat from birds, marsupials, turtles, and cassowaries. In riverine and coastal areas, fish and shellfish may form a significant part of the diet. Villagers cook two meals a day, boiling or roasting the food. Earth ovens are dug on ceremonial grounds for special occasions. Leftovers, sugarcane, and coconut milk are consumed while people work in their gardens. Tea is drunk at all times. Urban restaurants provide international cuisine to those who can afford it. *Kai* bars (fast-food stands) are popular. Food taboos vary and are often temporary, as with restrictions on pregnant women and initiates. Others are totemic, involving plants or animals that are

symbolic of kin groups. Still others are relational; for example, a son-in-law may not consume food in the presence of his mother-in-law.

Food Customs at Ceremonial Occasions. Papua New Guinea is renowned for ceremonial occasions at which hundreds of pigs or other valuables are distributed to guests. Competitive feasting ("fighting with food") between big men and chiefs features oratory, dancing, singing, drumming, and feasting that go on for days, along with the payment of bride-prices and other exchanges. Special drinks were rarely part of such ceremonies in the past, but now beer and alcohol are often part of major exchanges. Papua New Guineans celebrate nontraditional holidays such as Christmas and Easter, but rarely with the exuberance or expense involved in a traditional feast.

Basic Economy. Villagers produce most of their own food, and many townspeople plant gardens and rely on open-air markets for fruits and vegetables sold by village women using *kina* for currency. Urban supermarkets import an array of expensive foods and other items. Most residents rely on small trade stores for rice, sugar, tea, and tinned fish, as well as soap, clothing, blankets, kerosene lanterns, and matches.

A group of people gather in front of a store in Mount Hagen.

Land Tenure and Property. Most land is vested in kin groups and allocated according to need. Individual land ownership is not common; individuals may own a grove of banana trees but not the land they grow on. While land normally passes from father or mother's brother to children or nieces and nephews, the intended recipients provide much assistance and gifts to the "owners" before the land passes to their care. Migrants who fail to participate in village exchanges risk being "dispossessed" in favor of people who have supported local landowners.

Commercial Activities. Commerce is centered in the towns. Papua New Guinea developed its own television station in the late 1980s, and radio news and entertainment shows reach most villages. Tourism brings forty thousand visitors a year, mostly to the Sepik River and Trobriands. The road system is limited. Port Moresby is cut off from the rest of the country except by air and ship. With most places being difficult to reach, there are many undeveloped areas and labor migration is high.

Major Industries. The major industries are extractive. In addition to gold mining and oil drilling, major industries include coffee, copra, cocoa, cattle, oil palm, timber and wood-chip mills, and tuna canneries.

Trade. Traditional artifacts and carvings are sold throughout the world but provide only a small income. Important exports are copper, gold, coffee, cocoa, copra, coconut oil, and timber. Imports include machinery and transport equipment, food and live animals, manufactured goods, and pharmaceuticals.

Division of Labor. Outside the cities there is little specialization. The village division of labor is by age and gender, with men and women cooperating to feed their families from gardening and other subsistence activities and children and older persons assisting in a variety of ways. Cash crops generally are owned by men, but men and women tend and harvest them. Urban specialization is served by local schools, and few residents are educated abroad.

SOCIAL STRATIFICATION

Classes and Castes. There are no castes and only recent evidence of the slow emergence of classes. Economic inequality, however, cuts across ethnic and cultural boundaries. The common perception is of a country divided into "elites" and "grassroots," with the grassroots including most villagers and low-income earners in town and the elites being educated, higher-income persons, "coffee millionaires," and other entrepreneurs. Social interaction is intense as elites attend clan affairs and are expected to open their homes to wantoks at any hour.

There is evidence of growing disparities in the lifestyles and opportunities of elites versus grassroots and of the emergence of a middle class. Most villagers are not poor. Daily life is simple with few of the expenses of urban life. Villagers invest their cash income and traditional wealth in the social and political relations that maintain their place in village society. The elites and the middle class, however, must balance the expenses of living in town with investments in larger kin groups. While the demands of wantoks can act as a powerful leveling force, higher-income families are investing in productive businesses and ensuring that their children have the same class privileges they do.

Symbols of Social Stratification. There are many expensive restaurants and night spots in Port Moresby and other big cities, and the highways are jammed with imported cars. While some elites dress down for work and social occasions in clothes bought at secondhand stores or wear the grassroots fashion for women, the *laplap* and the *meri* blouse, many buy their clothes from fashionable boutiques and department stores or overseas. Wealthy citizens have invested in properties outside the country in anticipation of retirement or a people's revolution.

POLITICAL LIFE

Government. Papua New Guinea is an independent Commonwealth nation that achieved independence on 16 September 1975 from the Australian-administered United Nations trusteeship. It is a parliamentary democracy with a governor general representing the British Crown, a prime minister and cabinet, and a 109-member unicameral, popularly elected parliament. The legal system is based on English common law. There is a Supreme Court in which the chief justice is appointed by the governor general on the recommendation of the National Executive Council. Other judges are appointed by the Judicial and Legal Services Commission. There is universal suffrage, and the voting age is 18 years. In 1977, the Organic Law on Provincial Government resulted in decentralization. There are nineteen provinces (former colonial districts), each with an elected assembly, premier, and cabinet. There is also a National Capital District. At the local level there are local government councils that lost power as provincial governments gained government resources and funds. Corruption and other difficulties led to the abolition of provincial governments in 1995 and their replacement with a local government structure headed by governors in each province.

Leadership and Political Officials. Most traditional leaders achieved influence by building extensive networks of exchange partners and supporters. The characteristic "big man" was hardworking, skilled in oratory, personable, intelligent, generous, and the husband of more than one wife. Big men still exist, but their influence has lessened because they cannot control the global forces affecting their communities. Candidates for higher office must build multiple local power bases, an expensive and delicate political operation that often results in questionable campaign practices and eventual electoral disappointment and single terms of office. There are many political parties, and prime ministers must forge coalitions. Parties are unstable and hard to distinguish on the basis of substantive issues. Prime ministers rarely stay in office for the

A man splitting a sago palm trunk using traditional tools.

full five years, and parliament members switch parties frequently.

Social Problems and Control. There are both village and national court systems. Village courts use custom rather than English law, a situation that sometimes results in injustice from the point of view of the larger society. A chief ombudsman can resolve some conflicts between the two systems, but his reach rarely extends beyond Port Moresby. Policing a large and thinly populated country is difficult, and many citizens fear the police. Rural police sometimes compensate for inadequate manpower by using excessive force with lawbreakers; and urban police can be equally brutal. Crimes go unreported because citizens fear police brutality or prefer to handle the offenders, who are often kin, themselves. The police have been known to take the law into their own hands, as has the Papua New Guinea Defense Force. The nation's "law and order" problem is multifaceted, but the depredations of youthful gangs, outbreaks of rioting and looting, and the resurgence of tribal warfare are major sources of disorder and misery.

Military Activity. The nation's only major military action has been the ongoing conflict with the Bougainville Revolutionary Army. In the late 1970s and 1980s, there were fears of an Indonesian invasion across the border with Irian Jaya. A small guerilla freedom movement of no more than four hundred men used the sparsely populated border area to stage attacks against the Indonesian army and then flee to the Papua New Guinea side. Unwilling to contemplate war with the much larger Indonesia, Papua New Guinea used its armed forces to send refugees back across the border and capture rebels.

SOCIAL WELFARE AND CHANGE PROGRAMS

There is little support for social welfare and change programs. There is no social security system, few institutions to help the mentally ill or handicapped, and no welfare programs or food stamps. Part of the problem is the government's need to spend money on roads, schools, and basic infrastructure for a population thinly spread over a rugged countryside. Another problem is the belief that the extended family or village will always care for its own. Nonetheless, Papua New Guinea has supported offensives against several social problems, including wife beating and the rise in AIDS and other sexually transmitted diseases (STDs).

Houses in Eware Village in Morobe.

NONGOVERNMENTAL ORGANIZATIONS AND OTHER ASSOCIATIONS

Nongovernmental organizations and voluntary associations help residents confront rapid social and economic changes. Organizations with multiple aid programs include the Australian International Development Assistance Bureau (AIDAB), the United Nations Development Programme (UNDP), and the International Red Cross. AIDAB's Women in Development Fund targets women as beneficiaries of financial and educational support, teaching business and management training, giving women start-up funds, and encouraging family planning and women's political involvement. The UNDP office in Port Moresby officially opened in 1975.

Voluntary organizations include Canadian University Services Overseas (CUSO), Japan International Cooperation Agency (JICA), the U.S. Peace Corps, and British Voluntary Service Overseas (VSO). Community Aid Abroad (Australia) and Ecological Enterprises support or enhance the work of the Papua New Guinea Integral Human Development Trust, a literacy and awareness resource group with twenty-three member organization that is involved in programs for progressive social change. It has trained over two thousand young men and women as village literacy teachers and runs an AIDS awareness program and the Cross-

Cultural Awareness Program for immigrant workers and volunteers.

GENDER ROLES AND STATUSES

Division of Labor by Gender. Village subsistence centers on horticulture, with men clearing forests and bush so that their wives can plant gardens and tend pigs. Some crops, such as bananas, sugarcane, and cash crops (such as coffee and cocoa) are planted and tended by men. While women often help pick cash crops, most of the income goes to men. Men build houses and fences, while women make grass skirts and net bags (*bilums*). Women do the daily cooking, while men butcher pigs for feasts. Both men and women look after small children, with a father tending his infant while the mother weeds her gardens. In town, most women do domestic chores and child care while their husbands are at work. Women with jobs employ extended kin to do chores. In both towns and villages, men who do women's work are stigmatized as "rubbish men." Working women do not experience the same stigma, although they suffer prejudice and sexual harassment if they appear too independent and assertive.

The Relative Status of Women and Men. Trobriand chiefs and others who go on open seas

A decorative wood carving on a village hut in Kaminabit Village, near the Sepik River.

Kula (exchange) expeditions and give away yam harvests at the annual yam festival gain authority and privilege, and a chief may have many wives and expect commoners to bow in his presence. However, without female relatives to participate in female exchange events and redeem matrilineage lands and honor, those men's power would evaporate. Among the Gende and many other societies, big men achieve their positions by investing in feasts, bride-prices, and other exchange needs of their partners and followers. To do this, big men need many wives and female helpers to raise food and pigs to give away. Hardworking women are a man's most valuable asset, and husbands who do not consider their wives' interests risk losing them to other men. Women's procreative power induces men to go to great lengths in initiation and other rituals to strengthen themselves for contact with women and achieve a balance or edge in gender relations. In the towns, men and women are redefining their relations. With less education and fewer job opportunities, women do not contribute much income to urban households and as a consequence suffer the infidelities and physical abuses of men who feel burdened by the demands of family and the high expectations extended kin place on employed men, especially those who earn high salaries. Village women help pay back their own bride-prices and assist men in raising cash crops. Some rural women earn money by selling vegetables in urban markets.

Marriage, Family, and Kinship

Marriage. The choice of a marriage partner is rarely left to the individual. After initiation into adult society, young men and women spend time with the opposite sex in supervised courtship sessions. Ideal marriage partners are hardworking and attractive. Clan exogamy is a must, and parents hope their daughters will marry prosperous suitors whose kin pay large bride-prices and who will be good allies in exchange and war. Women pressed into incompatible marriages can return home or threaten suicide. If those strategies fail, young women may run away with lovers or commit suicide.

Men are more likely to be unmarried, as polygyny is practiced and big men attract a greater share of wives. In Gende society, as many as 10 percent of adult males are polygynous at some time. Divorce occurs even in areas where Catholicism is practiced. Often it is the women who initiate it, as men are loath to lose a female worker. After divorce, most adults remarry unless they are very old and living with children or grandchildren.

As Papua New Guineans become more involved in the cash economy and urbanization, marriage patterns are being transformed. Bride-price inflation is one response to economic inequality. The practice of women competing for men rather than men trying to attract women is having an impact on marital politics throughout the nation. Women are in an insecure position, especially urban women who must tolerate domestic abuse and infidelity to hold on to their husbands.

Domestic Unit. The basic village household consists of a husband, a wife, their unmarried children, and perhaps the husband's parents. Extended families live in adjacent houses, gathering frequently for meals, companionship, work parties, and ceremonies. Men's houses are no longer common, although young men may live with other bachelors. Household decisions involve consensus between able-bodied adults, although young wives defer to older members. Residence is usually patrilocal. Less common is matrilocality and avunculocality. Neolocality occurs only in towns. Even then, a couple may be joined by their parents and other kin.

Inheritance. Land and property rights generally pass from parents to children or from uncles to

Wife of Papua New Guinea chief applies face paint. Marriages are usually arranged, but women in poor marriages may return home or commit suicide.

nieces and nephews. These kin relations are extended to other members in an individual's kin group. All these persons have an interest in the prosperity of the kin group, and those of the younger generation who contribute the most to that prosperity are likely to receive the most. Reciprocity is a key element, and nonkin can become "sons" and "daughters" of a group if they contribute generously to group affairs. While women generally do not use clan or lineage lands, they retain the option to do so by contributing to group exchanges.

Kin Groups. The important kin groups are patrilineal and matrilineal lineages and clans, Clan members do not necessarily live on clan land. Women marry out, and migrants move far from their ancestral territories to find wage employment and other benefits in town. All the members of a kin group, however, must participate in clan affairs, contributing to bride-prices and other exchanges and helping with initiation and mortuary ceremonies. Clans and lineages can shrink and disappear through deaths and indifference. Persons join other clans, allying themselves with their wives' clans or being adopted as children. An important asset is the

land a clan's members hold in common. Land is valuable and a way of life for 85 percent of the population. It is also a form of social security for persons living in towns, most of whom actively engage in kin group affairs to maintain their rural option.

SOCIALIZATION

Infant Care. Most babies are born outside the village in a birth hut or garden house, where mother and child spend the first few days or weeks after the birth in relative isolation, gathering strength and hiding from malevolent forces. For the next several years, mothers nurse their babies, and the babies are carried everywhere and played with by adoring relatives. In many societies, there is a small feast when the baby, especially a first child, is around a year old to celebrate its existence and let the parents show their appreciation to all those who made its birth possible, including the mother's family and the bride-price supporters.

Child Rearing and Education. Child rearing is indulgent until age five or six for girls and a few years older for boys. Children explore their environment and run free most of the day. Corporal punishment is rare as people believe a child's spirit may leave its body if the child is hit or frightened. A troublesome child is left alone or ignored. If necessary, such children may be taken to the bush or a garden house to act out or sulk. Children are taught by example. Little girls follow in their mothers' and older sisters' footsteps, at first doing child minding or running errands, and later helping in the gardens. Boys spend a longer time playing with other boys but eventually collect firewood and carry water and, later, clear bush and hunt or fish with their fathers. Older boys and girls may go through separate initiation or puberty ceremonies to prepare them for marriage and adulthood. Rituals and taboos are elaborate, arduous, and sometimes terrifying. Young men and women are taught the meanings and responsibilities of their genders to prepare them for social responsibilities and marriage, including sexuality. Badness in children is not something parents blame themselves for; evil spirits may cause a child to be selfish and cruel, in which case, the parents hire a medium.

Higher Education. Higher education is a goal of many parents, especially for their sons. Many parents worry about the physical dangers urban life holds for women. The urban job market is competitive, and some parents are not impressed with the value of a high school or college education, knowing that education does not guarantee a job. Many school leavers and unemployed graduates cause trouble in towns and villages. Parents spend their education dollars on only the brightest, most socially responsible children.

ETIQUETTE

In village society, etiquette centers on reciprocity and being hospitable to guests and unexpected visitors, Feasting exchange partners has an urban equivalent in parties where workmates and wantoks are welcome along with their spouses and children. Reciprocity is expected but is not always possible, putting barriers between individuals of different income levels. One custom that everyone can participate in is sharing betel nut (buai). Relations between older and younger and male and female are relaxed. On meeting, men and women of different ages clasp hands or clasp one another around the waist. Couples do not openly express affection in public, but friends of the same sex may hold hands while walking. It is not rude to stare or for persons to crowd one another at counters or stand very close. In chiefly societies, commoners must bow before chiefs and are prohibited from eating foods reserved for the chief and his family.

RELIGION

Religious Beliefs. The first mission in eastern New Guinea was the London Missionary Society, which in 1871 set up mission teachers from the Loyalty Islands on islands adjacent to and on the Papuan mainland. Some New Guineans resisted the changes missionaries represented, while others accepted opportunities for new forms of wealth, power, and age and gender relations. Working for the mission sometimes provided young men with an income that allowed them to support and choose brides. Schooled in Christian ethics, young women often refused to have bride-prices paid for them. More often, Papua New Guineans have sought to blend old and new religions. Cargo cults aimed at acquiring the wealth and power of outsiders through blends of Christian and local rituals have been common. Today, indigenized forms of Christianity seek to control the human condition in a period of insistent and significant change.

Most societies have stories telling how superhuman beings created the natural world and society, inventing food plants, pigs and pig exchanges, male and female cults, sorcery, and other aspects of culture. In some societies, such deities are important in

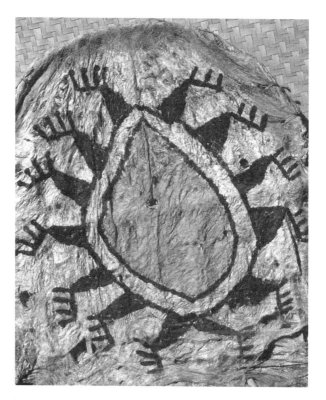

Tapa cloth stretched onto a cane framework is decorated by a painting of an insect.

male and female cults; in others, they have little to do with present fortunes. Instead, sorcerers and witches, the spirits of deceased ancestors, nonhuman forest spirits, and monsters command the attention of the living. Another common belief is that the physical and nonphysical worlds are intertwined and that the well-being of living humans is directly related to the maintenance of proper social ties, adherence to taboos, and the propitiation of spirits. Except in the case of infants and the very old, death is not natural but results from wrongdoing or oversights on the part of the living.

Religious Practitioners. The pragmatic focus of their religions and the absence of a hierarchy is reflected in the intense involvement of Papua New Guineans in the ritual maintenance of their own spiritual and physical well-being. Only in a few chiefly societies do hereditary chiefs and their henchmen act as religious specialists. More generally, it is expected that all adults will acquire magic spells used in gardening, healing or preventing minor illnesses, and love magic. Many people possess a knowledge of sorcery or witchcraft. Big men often purport to be powerful spirit mediums and to possess both healing powers and deadly war sorcery. Witches are deviant or marginalized individuals who are suspected of using their relations with spirits and other cosmic forces to harm members of their own groups.

Rituals and Holy Places. Many rituals focus on health and fertility, such as male and female initiation rituals. Aimed at bringing about the maturation and future success of the initiates, initiation involves seclusion in the forest or a menstrual hut, fasting and food taboos, and body mutilation. Initiates seek contact with spirit guides who will help them throughout their lives and even marry spirit women on occasion. Initiation and other ceremonies focus on eliciting the help of ancestors and the living and are accompanied by the exchange of valuables and food. In preparation for war or in compensation for war deaths, a group may sacrifice hundreds of pigs to call forth the aid of the ancestors. Cannibalism and head-hunting—not universally practiced—were often aimed at rejuvenation or acquiring the bravery and good characteristics of the deceased, with wives eating a portion of their husbands' dead bodies to incorporate their virility and young warriors displaying enemies' heads as symbols of their own magic and efficacy.

Death and the Afterlife. When a person is near death or has died suddenly, mediums are called in to discover the causes and the identity of the sorcerer or witch who may have been involved. Appropriate rituals and sacrifices are performed to prevent death or free the deceased's spirit. Once death has occurred, relatives gather to express their sorrow, wailing and sometimes chopping off fingers, pulling teeth, shaving hair, or pulling out facial hairs. Burial is now common. In the past a corpse might be cremated, thrown in a river or buried at sea, or left in a tree to rot. The dry bones might be buried under a house floor to provide protection to the living with the jawbone worn around the neck of a relative or leader. Rituals believed to help the deceased accommodate to their new state occur at the funeral and at later mortuary ceremonies. Spirits may be encouraged to stay near the living. Some are sent off to a "place of spirits" not far from the living, on mountaintops or in the forest. Funerals and mortuary ceremonies are times to pay off the deceased's debts, recognize his or her accomplishments, and restore friendly relations among the living by exchanging wealth.

MEDICINE AND HEALTH CARE

Along with plant medicines and traditional therapies for treating physical symptoms, patients and caregivers use rituals designed to overcome or ascertain the causes of sickness and mental illness, such as

ruptured social relations, sorcerers, and ghost attacks. People make use of both Western and traditional treatments in dealing with symptoms while turning to traditional medicine to cure the underlying social and cultural causes of illness. Urban areas have adequate medical staffing in hospitals and clinics. Rural areas are serviced by a thinly spread system of aid posts and small health centers. Aid post workers have only the barest knowledge of first aid. Some village women are trained in midwifery and community-based family-planning services. Trained nurses and paramedics are rare, and doctors even more so. In 1992, there was one doctor for every six thousand persons. In rural areas, health care focuses on first aid and treating chronic diseases such as malaria and pneumonia. Attempts are made to deal with the special health concerns of women and children, including family planning, pregnancy and childbirth, and nutrition and growth. Infant and child mortality rates have dropped, with the most recent figures showing sixty-seven of every one thousand infants dying before the age of twelve months, but women's nutritional needs are not as well met. In many areas, women and girls are fed significantly less than men and boys, resulting in weight loss, anemia, osteoporosis, and greater susceptibility to illness. AIDS, gonorrhea, and syphilis are spreading. Urban use of alcohol, tobacco, sugar, and fatty foods has resulted in increased rates of disease. Medical, sports, and nutrition services and exercise classes are springing up in towns.

SECULAR CELEBRATIONS

There are many local and provincial celebrations, including New Year's Day (1 January), Easter, the Port Moresby Show in mid-June, Remembrance Day (23 July) to commemorate World War II, the Highlands Show in August or September, Independence Day (16 September), and Christmas.

THE ARTS AND HUMANITIES

Support for the Arts. In 1972, the government established the Creative Arts Centre (CAC) to train and support individuals, stage exhibitions, and commission work for national and private projects. In 1976, the CAC became the National Arts School. After Independence, the government supported the arts to promote a national culture. The completion of the parliament building in 1984 marked the apex of national artistic culture.

Literature. After the 1960s, historians and others took a greater interest in oral history and folklore.

Oral traditions relating to clan genealogies, initiation and mortuary chants, magic and sorcery, and the teaching of children about their cultures were collected and analyzed, and some were published. In the 1960s and 1970s, there was also an interest in modern Papua New Guinea writing in English. Publishing outlets include the journals *Bikmaus*, *Ondobondo*, and *The PNG Writer*. Autobiographies have been published by overseas companies and by the National Research Institute.

Graphic Arts. The National Arts School offers courses in graphic design, textile design, fine arts, and music. Students are encouraged to generate contacts and income for themselves and the school. In addition to helping with large-scale projects such as the National Parliament, the National Museum, and the Papua New Guinea Banking Corporation building in Port Moresby, students have been involved in designing publicity for the Port Moresby Show, and making murals, carved screens, and sculptures for shopping centers. Pottery is enjoying a renaissance as potters combine modern techniques with traditional designs. Tourists buy replicas or actual artifacts in local markets and several shops in Port Moresby. Tourism and the international art market fuel cottage industry production of wood carvings. Colorful string bags are produced and sold by women.

Performance Arts. In 1975, the National Cultural Council funded the Raun Raun Theatre, a popular theater movement that attempts to transpose traditional cultural forms into contemporary theater and address the concerns of rural society.

THE STATE OF THE PHYSICAL AND SOCIAL SCIENCES

With the development of institutions such as the University of Papua New Guinea (UPNG), the National Research Institute (formerly the Institute of Applied Social and Economic Research), and the PNG Institute of Medical Research in the 1960s and 1970s, Papua New Guinea has become a place where local and foreign scientists and academics engage in long-term interdisciplinary research. Perhaps the social science that has gained the most has been anthropology. Other subjects taught at UPNG include biology, business and economics, education, law, and medicine. In recent years, the UPNG's law faculty, the Law Reform Commission, NRI, and other national bodies and visiting researchers have focused on a number of pressing law and order issues, including violence against women, rioting and political corruption, the resurgence of tribal fighting, gangs, and

conflicts over compensation for resource development. The Papua New Guinea Institute of Medical Research in Goroka and Madang sponsors research on a range of topics, including sexuality, STDs, nutrition, growth and development, infant mortality, and the epidemiology of health and disease.

BIBLIOGRAPHY

Abaijah, Josephine. *A Thousand Coloured Dreams: The Story of a Young Girl Growing Up in Papua*, 1991.

Ahlburg, Dennis A. "Demographic and Social Change in the Island Nations of the Pacific." *Asia-Pacific Population Research Reports* No. 7, February 1996.

Beier, Ulli, ed. *Voices of Independence: New Black Writing from Papua New Guinea*, 1980.

Boutilier, James A., Daniel T. Hughes, and Sharon W. Tiffany, eds. *Mission, Church, and Sect in Oceania*, 1978.

Bray, Mark, and Peter Smith, eds. *Education and Social Stratification in Papua New Guinea*, 1985.

Connolly, Bob, and Robin Anderson, Directors. *First Contact*, video, 1983.

—— *First Contact: New Guinea's Highlanders Encounter the Outside World*, 1987.

Dickerson–Putman, Jeanette, ed. *Women, Age, and Power: The Politics of Age Difference among Women in Papua New Guinea and Australia*, special issue, *Pacific Studies* 19 (4): 1996.

Dinnen, Sinclair. *Crime, Development, and Criminological Research in Papua New Guinea*, 1992.

Dorney, Sean. *Papua New Guinea: People, Politics and History since 1975*, 1990.

Eri, Vincent. *The Crocodile*, 1970, 1981.

Gewertz, Deborah B. and Frederick K. Errington. *Emerging Class in Papua New Guinea: The Telling of Difference*, 1999.

Goddard, Michael. "The Rascal Road: Crime, Prestige, and Development in Papua New Guinea" *The Contemporary Pacific* 7 (1): 55–80, 1995.

Hays, Terence E., ed. *Ethnographic Presents: Pioneering Anthropologists in the Papua New Guinea Highlands*, 1992.

Herdt, Gilbert H., ed. *Rituals of Manhood: Male Initiation in Papua New Guinea*, 1982.

Kilage, Ignatius. *My Mother Calls Me Yaltep*, 1980, 1984.

Kituai, August Ibrum. *My Gun, My Brother: The World of the Papua New Guinea Colonial Police, 1920–1960*, 1998.

Langmore, Diane. *Missionary Lives: Papua, 1874–1914*, 1989.

Lawrence, Peter, *Road Belong Cargo: A Study of the Cargo Movement in the Southern Madang District New Guinea*, 1964.

Lutkehaus, Nancy C., and Paul B. Roscoe, eds. *Gender Rituals: Female Initiation in Melanesia*, 1995.

Marksbury, Richard A., ed. *The Business of Marriage: Transformations in Oceanic Matrimony*, 1993.

May, R. J., ed. *Micronationalist Movements in Papua New Guinea*, 1982.

———, and Hank Nelson, eds. *Melanesia: Beyond Diversity*, 1982.

Mell, Michael Yake. *The Call of the Land*, 1993.

Mennis, Mary R. *Hagen Saga: The Story of Father William Ross, Pioneer American Missionary to Papua New Guinea*, 1982.

Mihalic, F. *The Jacaranda Dictionary and Grammar of Melanesian Pidgin*, 1971.

Narokobi, Bernard. *The Melanesian Way*, 1980.

Papua New Guinea National Statistical Office. *Population Trends in Papua New Guinea*, 1991.

Pomponio, Alice. *Seagulls Don't Fly into The Bush: Cultural Identity and Development in Melanesia*, 1992.

Powell, Ganga, ed. *Through Melanesian Eyes: An Anthology of Papua New Guinean Writing*, 1987.

Robbins, Joel. "Dispossessing the Spirits: Christian Transformations of Desire and Ecology among the Urapmin of Papua New Guinea." *Ethnology* 34: 211–24, 1995.

Rosi, Pamela. "Papua New Guinea's New Parliament House: A Contested National Symbol." *The Contemporary Pacific* 3 (2): 289–323, 1991.

———, and Laura Zimmer–Tamakoshi. "Love and Marriage among the Educated Elite in Port Moresby," in R. Marksbury, ed., *The Business of Marriage: Transformations in Oceanic Matrimony*, 1993.

Sexton, Lorraine. "Wok Meri: A Woman's Savings and Exchange System in Highland Papua New Guinea." *Oceania* 52: 167–198, 1982.

Smith, Michael French. *Hard Times on Kairiru Island: Poverty, Development, and Morality in a Papua New Guinea Village*, 1994.

Soaba, Russell. *Wanpis*, 1978.

———. *Maiba*, 1985.

Stephen, Michele, ed. *Sorcerer and Witch in Melanesia*, 1987.

Strathern, Andrew. *Ongka: A Self-Account by a New Guinea Big Man*, 1979.

———. "Violence and Political Change in Papua New Guinea." *Pacific Studies* 16 (4): 41–60, 1993.

Stratigos, Susan, and Philip J. Hughes, eds. *The Ethics of Development: Women as Unequal Partners in Development*, 1987.

Swadling, Pamela. *Papua New Guinea's Prehistory: An Introduction*, 1986.

Toft, Susan, ed. *Domestic Violence in Papua New Guinea*, 1985.

Turner, Mark. *Papua New Guinea: The Challenge of Independence*, 1990.

Webb, Michael. *Lokal Musik: Lingua Franca Song and Identity in Papua New Guinea*, 1993.

Weiner, Annette B. *The Trobrianders of Papua New Guinea*, 1988.

White, Osmar. *Parliament of a Thousand Tribes: Papua New Guinea: The Story of an Emerging Nation*, 1972, orig. 1965.

Wormald, E., and A. Crossley, eds. *Women and Education in Papua New Guinea and the South Pacific*, 1988.

Worsley, Peter. *The Trumpet Shall Sound: A Study of "Cargo" Cults in Melanesia*, second ed., 1968.

Zimmer–Tamakoshi, Laura. "Bachelors, Spinsters, and Pamuk Meris." In R. Marksbury, ed., *The Business of Marriage: Transformations in Oceanic Matrimony*, 1993.

———. "Nationalism and Sexuality in Papua New Guinea". *Pacific Studies* 16 (4): 20–48, 1993.

———. "Passion, Poetry, and Cultural Politics in the South Pacific." In R. Feinberg and L. Zimmer–Tamakoshi, eds., *Politics of Culture in the Pacific Islands*, Special Issue of *Ethnology* 34 (2 & 3): 113–128, 1995.

———. "Empowered Women." In W. Donner and J. Flanagan, eds., *Social Organization and Cultural Aesthetics: Essays in Honor of William H. Davenport*, 1996.

———. "The Last Big Man: Development and Men's Discontents in the Papua New Guinea Highlands." *Oceania* 62 (2): 107–122, 1997.

———, ed. *Modern Papua New Guinea*, 1998.

Web Sites

Barry, Glen. *Papua New Guinea Rainforest Conservation*, http://forests.org/forests/useinfo.html

Burton, John. *Papua New Guinea Virtual Library*, http://coombs.anu.edu.au/SpecialProj/PNG/WWWVL-PNG.html

Grimes, Barbara F., ed. *Ethnologue: Languages of the World*, 13th ed., 1996, http://www.sil.org/ethnologue/

Jenkins, Carol and the National Sex and Reproduction Research Team. *National Study of Sexual and Reproductive Knowledge and Behavior in Papua New Guinea*, 1994. Johns Hopkins University Health Information: Health News, http://www.intelihealth.com/enews?232763

McCall, Grant. *Papua New Guinea: General Information on Papua New Guinea*, 1998, http://www.arts.unsw.edu.au/Centres/SouthPacific/APNGFA_PNG_Gen_Information.html

United Nations Development Programme in Papua New Guinea, http://www.undp.org.pg/undppng.htm. University of Papua New Guinea, http://www.upng.ac.pg/

Zimmer–Tamakoshi, Laura. *Fieldwork: The Anthropologist in the Field*, 1996, http://www.truman.edu/academics/ss/faculty/tamakoshil/intro.html

—Laura Zimmer–Tamakoshi

PARAGUAY

CULTURE NAME

Paraguayan

ORIENTATION

Identification. The name "Paraguay" derives from the river that divides the eastern half of the nation from the western Chaco region. The vast majority of the population (95 percent) shares a Paraguayan identity, but several other cultural identities exist. The indigenous population is composed of seventeen ethnic groups from five linguistic families. Most immigrants have blended into the national population, but several groups have maintained distinct identities and cultures. Those groups include Mennonites, who settled in the western (Chaco) and the northern regions early in the early twentieth century; Japanese, who settled in agricultural colonies primarily during the 1950s and 1960s; and more recent Korean, Lebanese, and ethnic Chinese immigrants, who have settled in the urban centers of Asunción and Ciudad del Este since the 1970s. In the 1960s and 1970s, large numbers of Brazilian immigrant farmers moved to the eastern frontier region and became the backbone of the soybean export sector. By the 1990s, a second generation of Brazilians had been born and raised in Paraguay, and a few intermarried with the local population. These *brasiguayos* form a distinct subgroup.

Location and Geography. Paraguay is a landlocked nation of 157,047 square miles (406,752 square kilometers) in South America, surrounded by Brazil, Argentina, and Bolivia. The inhospitable and semiarid Chaco forms the western part of the nation. Flat and infertile, much of it covered by scrub forests, the Chaco contains approximately 61 percent of the national land area but less than 3 percent of the population. In contrast, eastern Paraguay has rolling hills, richer soils, lush semitropical forests, and grassy savannas. The re-

gion so impressed early explorers that they called it a "second Eden." Temperatures are high in a humid subtropical climate in the summer months of October to March, while in the winter months of July to September night frosts may occur. Rainfall occurs throughout the year but is usually heaviest between October and April; annual variations can be extreme.

The capital, Asunción, lies on the Paraguay River at the point dividing eastern and western Paraguay. The city was founded in 1537 by Juan de Salazar y Espinoza, a Spanish explorer who led an expedition upriver from the fort at Buenos Aires. Befriended by the local Guarani, he established the fort of Nuestra Señora de la Asunción overlooking the bay where Asunción now stands. The Asunción *cabildo* (city council) was established in 1541. Asunción has dominated national society and politics since that time.

Demography. In 1999 the population was estimated to be 5,222,000. Approximately 95 percent of the population is mestizo. The population has more than tripled since 1950 and is growing 2.5 percent annually, with a total fertility rate of 3.8 children per woman. The growth rate has declined slightly from the period preceding 1975. The population is relatively young; 40 percent is under age 15, and only 5 percent is sixty or older.

Population figures for the ethnic populations are disputed. Estimates place the indigenous population at less than 3 percent of the national population. The largest groups are the Enxet Lengua, Pai-Tavyter, Nivaclé (Chulupí), Chiripá, and Mbyá. The Japanese settlers and their descendants are estimated to number about eight thousand, and the Mennonites approximately fifteen thousand. There are no reliable estimates for Korean, Chinese, and Brazilian immigrants and their offspring. The 1992 census counted only several thousand Korean and Chinese immigrants, but observers place their numbers between thirty thousand and fifty thousand.

Paraguay

Most observers estimate that between 300,000 and 350,000 Brazilians settled in eastern Paraguay in the 1960s and 1970s.

Linguistic Affiliation. The majority of the people speak an indigenous language, although they do not self-identify ethnically as indigenous. Guarani, a Tupi Guarani language and the language of eastern Paraguay's dominant precolonial indigenous population, is recognized as an official national language along with Spanish. Spanish is the language of business and government, and Guarani is spoken in everyday life. According to the 1992 census, nearly half the population speaks both Guarani and Spanish in the home and 39 percent speaks only Guarani. In rural areas and among the lower social classes, Guarani is the dominant language. Although most schooling is conducted in Spanish, children are required to study Guarani as well. There is considerable lexical borrowing and linguistic code switching in informal conversation.

The use of Guarani Language does not imply indigenous ethnicity; it is the language of the national culture. The form of Guarani spoken in the national culture is somewhat different from that used by indigenous Guarani speakers, and many indigenous people speak non-Guarani languages. Religion, residence, and community affiliation—not language—are the cultural markers of indigenous identity. Historians attribute the prominence of the Guarani language in the national culture to extensive interbreeding between Spanish men and Guarani women from the earliest colonial times.

Symbolism. The most powerful symbols of the national culture are the Guarani language and imagery derived from Paraguay's national history, especially its wars. More than a means of communication, Guarani is a powerful marker of national identity that can be used to assert unity among Paraguayans of disparate social classes and political persuasions, especially in contrast to foreigners. Related images of Paraguay's indigenous heritage that also symbolize the national culture include traditional harp music, certain foods, and crafts.

The national territory and sovereignty and the great sacrifices Paraguayans made historically to defend that territory and sovereignty figure prominently in the national imagery and tradition. The War of the Triple Alliance (1865–1870), in which Paraguay fought against Brazil, Argentina, and Uruguay, continues to haunt the national consciousness and remains a potent national symbol. The Chaco War (1932–1935)also symbolizes the sacrifices Paraguayans have made to defend their homeland. Key battles are commemorated with national holidays. The dominant imagery is that of blood shed to defend the national patrimony.

HISTORY AND ETHNIC RELATIONS

Emergence of the Nation. The origins of the modern population lie in the cultural and biological mixing that occurred in the earliest period of Spanish contact. The Guarani were horticulturists organized in chieftainships based on extended kinship. Although they traced descent patrilineally, they had matrilocal settlement patterns and alliances were formalized through the exchange of women. Few women came with the handful of Spanish explorers who established the fort of Nuestra Señora de la Asunción in 1537. The Guarani *caciques* (chiefs) exchanged women to formalize their alliance with the Spanish against the hostile peoples of the Chaco. The Paraguayan people trace their origins to the children of those unions.

National traditions of autonomy and pride also have their origins in the early colonial years. Distant from colonial centers and lacking the mineral wealth of other regions, the colony remained isolated and impoverished. The Spanish landowners and *encomenderos* (recipients of Colonial grants to the labor and other tribute of specified indigenous groups) sometimes overruled and even overthrew the appointed governor. Colonial politics were tumultuous, with intense rivalry among the early conquerors and between the settlers and their economic rivals, notably the Jesuit missions. Colonists also chafed under the economic dominance of Buenos Aires and taxation of their exports by the Argentinians. The colony faced military threats from hostile indigenous peoples, Brazilian slave hunters, and Portuguese attempts to annex part of the colony. Left to their own devices by the Spanish, the colonists had to defend themselves against those threats by raising citizen militias and arming themselves as best they could, and as a result the colony has been described as the most militarized in Latin America. The colony was so impoverished and isolated that visitors commented on the obsolescence of the colonists' arms. Until the final years of the colonial period, barter was the normal means of exchange and the economy was based largely on subsistence activities. This period thus established the tradition of ethnic mixing, local self-sufficiency based on isolation and poverty, the need to defend life and land against continuous threat, and resentment of economic exploitation by Brazil and Argentina.

These orientations were reinforced by the experiences of the nineteenth century. After Argentinians deposed the Spanish viceroy in 1810, they attempted to extend their control to include the territory of Paraguay. Paraguayans resisted and in 1811 defeated the Argentinian army at the battle of Paraguari. In May of that year, Paraguayans overthrew the last Spanish governor. After several years of political maneuvering, José Gaspar Rodríguez de Francia emerged as the leader of the new republic and was elected perpetual dictator by the Popular Congress in 1816. Popular, iron-fisted, and fiercely nationalistic, Francia implemented policies that benefitted ordinary residents while limiting or destroying the power of the Spanish and creole elites, the Catholic Church, the mercantile houses, and the landed estates. Although he was derided by foreign critics and enemies as an isolationist madman who drove his country into poverty, scholars now argue that Francia expanded internal and external trade. However, he permitted trade only under his supervision, guaranteeing that the nation reaped the benefits, and strictly controlled the movements of foreigners in the national territory.

After Francia's death in 1840, the presidency was assumed by Carlos Antonio López and then, in 1862, by López's son, Francisco Solano. In 1864, Francisco Solano López declared war on the powerful Triple Alliance of Brazil, Argentina, and Uruguay. The events that provoked López's declaration of war are debated. Although his motivations were long dismissed as megalomaniacal pretensions, some recent analysts have argued that López was forced into declaring war to preempt Brazilian and Argentinian designs to assume dominion over their smaller neighbors, including Paraguay. This disastrous war resulted in the death of most Paraguayan men and many women and children and destroyed the nation's economy. It also ended Paraguay's brief period of self-determination and relatively egalitarian prosperity. Only the intervention of the U.S. president, Rutherford B. Hayes, in 1878 prevented Argentina from claiming a large part of western Paraguay. Argentina became the middleman for most of Paraguay's international trade, and foreigners acquired vast expanses of the nation's land.

The War of the Triple Alliance left Paraguay a nation largely of small farmers engaged in the production of basic food crops for subsistence and local trade. Ethnically and culturally, the population was homogeneous, with the family serving as the basic socioeconomic unit. Although the small political elite that emerged after the war emulated European styles, the vast majority of the population spoke Guarani and led a subsistence lifestyle based on indigenous and Spanish customs interwoven by the hardships of life on an isolated and impoverished frontier.

National Identity. The national identity derives from these historical antecedents. Although the Guarani language is its most salient symbol, that identity is not based on an actual or mythologized pre-Columbian Guarani past. Instead, it has its origins in the fusion of indigenous and Spanish peoples in colonial times and was shaped by threats to territory and sovereignty from the earliest colonial times. The strong sense of national identity also has been nurtured by the homogeneity of the population throughout the country's modern history.

Ethnic Relations. Despite the alliance of the Guarani and Spanish peoples that gave rise to the nation, Paraguayan relations with indigenous peoples typically have been marked by hostility and exploitation. Spanish colonists faced continual threats from the indigenous groups in the Chaco and repeatedly launched armed campaigns against them. Although the Guarani gave women to the Spanish to cement their alliance, the Spanish took many more women, as well as food and other goods, by force. The Spanish also quickly organized to establish their control over Guarani labor through the *encomienda* system. While Francia recognized the land claims of some indigenous villages, Paraguayans later appropriated indigenous land through force, fraud, and bureaucratic maneuvers. Indigenous peoples remain at the fringes of the national society.

Relations with Mennonite and Japanese settlers have been limited to occasional bureaucratic and economic transactions. These immigrant enclaves, located primarily in remote rural areas, maintain their own economic, social, and cultural institutions and in most cases have greater economic resources than do the surrounding Paraguayan communities made up primarily of small farmers. Intermarriage is rare and is disapproved. Paraguayans perceive the immigrants as disdaining and rejecting the national culture.

In the 1970s and 1980s, critics charged that the influx of Brazilian immigrants threatened Paraguayan culture and national sovereignty in the eastern frontier region. However, most of those immigrants settled in ethnically homogenous communities, and there was little direct contact between them and the local population. Although there have been some confrontations between Paraguayan and Brazilian farmers over land, most conflicts have involved large tracts of land claimed by absentee owners rather than land farmed by immigrant settlers.

URBANISM, ARCHITECTURE, AND THE USE OF SPACE

Until the mid-1970s, the majority of residents lived in rural areas, nearly all in the central region surrounding Asunción. Most lived on farmsteads in small adobe houses with palm-thatched roofs, with their fields surrounding the house. Towns were of typical Spanish colonial design, built around a central plaza and home to a few administrative, craft, and professional workers and shopkeepers. The central institutions of the national government as well as religious and educational institutions, commerce, and industry were and still are in Asunción.

Since the 1970s, the population has become increasingly urban, and by 1992, just over 50 percent lived in urban areas. Asunción is the largest urban center, with an estimated population of 550,000. The extension of roads, the construction of massive

A brick kiln. The towns of Aregua and Tobatí both produce ceramic and clay work.

hydroelectric works on the eastern border, and agricultural colonization programs drew people from the central regions to the sparsely populated border regions, especially along the eastern border with Brazil. Ciudad del Este, founded in 1963, is now the second largest city and a major commercial center, with an estimated population of 234,000.

FOOD AND ECONOMY

Food in Daily Life. Corn, *mandioca* (cassava), and beef form the basic diet. Typical dishes include *locro* (a corn stew), *sopa paraguaya* (a rich corn flour and cheese bread), *chipa guazú* (a cross between *sopa paraguaya* and a corn soufflé), and *mbaipy so'ó* (corn pudding with beef chunks). *Mandioca* root is commonly served boiled, and its starch is a main ingredient of several traditional foods, including *chipa* (a dense, baked bread of *mandioca* starch and cheese) and *mbejú* (an unleavened fried bread). The main meal of the day is eaten at noon and usually includes corn- or *mandioca*-based food. A wide variety of tropical and semitropical fruits also are eaten. Drinks made of *yerba maté* (Paraguayan tea) are ubiquitous. The tea may be drunk hot (*maté*) or cold (*tereré*), and medicinal herbs often are added. The leaves also may be toasted and boiled to make a tea

that is served at breakfast or for a late afternoon snack.

Food Customs at Ceremonial Occasions. Special family celebrations and social gatherings call for an *asado*, or barbecue, with beef roasted over open fires and accompanied by boiled mandioca and sopa paraguaya. Chipa traditionally is prepared for the major religious holidays of Christmas and Holy Week. Special meals during these holidays also may include an *asado* of beef or a pit-roasted pig.

Basic Economy. Paraguay's currency is the guarani, with an exchange rate of approximately 3500 guarancies to one U.S. dollar in 1999. Until recently the economy was primarily rural and agricultural. The majority of the population, peasant farmers, produced subsistence crops as well as cash crops of cotton or tobacco. Approximately 40 percent of the population is still involved in agriculture, and the majority are small farmers who engage to some degree in subsistence production. Agriculture, together with forestry, hunting, and fishing, accounts for 25 percent of the gross national product (GDP) and nearly all exports. Paraguay has few mineral resources, but its rivers have made hydroelectric power generation a major source of revenue. The manufacturing sector is small (15 percent of

GDP). The economy also has a very large informal sector composed of thousands of urban street vendors, domestic workers, and microenterprises. An estimated 10 percent of the labor force was unemployed in 1996, and almost half was underemployed. Despite government promises of reform, public sector employment, long a major source of political patronage, has continued to grow, increasing 17 percent from 1989 to 1995.

Although the country is largely self-sufficient in the basic foodstuffs of corn, mandioca, and wheat, it depends on imports for processed foods, other consumer goods, capital goods, and fuels. Although many small farmers continue to rely on their own production for food, they have been drawn into the market economy to purchase processed goods such as soap, cooking oil, clothing, medicine, and other basic consumer items.

Land Tenure and Property. Land distribution is among the most unequal in Latin America. According to the 1991 agricultural census, 77 percent of the agricultural land was owned by barely 1 percent of the population. At the other extreme, small farms of less than 49.4 acres (20 hectares), accounting for over 80 percent of all agricultural holdings, occupied only 6 percent of the agricultural land.

Although the system of land tenure is based on private property, common practice and historical tradition play an important role in shaping notions of land rights. Peasants have long claimed the right to occupy unused public lands for agricultural purposes. Mechanisms for formalizing occupation rights were specified in twentieth century legal codes and the 1967 constitution, which recognized the right of every citizen to a plot of land. The right to own land for investment or speculation is viewed by the majority of the rural population as secondary to the right of peasants to use land for subsistence. While some peasants own clear title to the land they cultivate and some rent or sharecrop, informal occupation of land is widespread.

The private property regimen is complicated by a long history of bureaucratic fraud and ineptitude. During the Stroessner dictatorship (1954–1989), large tracts of land were illegally transferred to Stroessner's relatives and cronies, and some peasant and indigenous communities were violently displaced as powerful military figures took over their lands. Although most land claims have been regularized in central Paraguay, conflict over land continues to be a source of unrest in the eastern and northern frontier regions, where many titles are of questionable origin. Indigenous groups have lost vast expanses of their land and face legal and physical threats as a result of their efforts to gain recognition of their claims.

Commercial Activities. Agriculture and hydroelectric power account for the majority of commercial production. Major agricultural goods produced for sale include grains, oilseeds (soybeans), cotton, sugarcane, tobacco, meat and poultry, mandioca, fruits and vegetables, lumber, eggs, and milk. Large estates and immigrant settlers produce most of the grains, oilseeds, and beef. The Mennonites are known for dairy production. Small farmers produce mandioca, cotton, tobacco, and sugarcane as well as fruits and vegetables for sale on the domestic market. A multitude of microenterprises and artisans produce bricks for construction, clothing, furniture, and other small consumer items.

Because of lax border controls and low tariffs, resale and transshipment of goods account for a significant part of the commercial economy. These activities range from illicit transshipment of cocaine and other drugs from producing countries to the markets of North America and Europe to the resale of clothing, vegetables, and other inexpensive consumer items by individuals who purchase them in Brazil or Argentina and bring them into the country without paying import duties.

Major Industries. Aside from hydroelectric power generation, the major industries are heavily dependent on the agricultural sector. Small industries process flour, beer, cigarettes, soap, shoes, and furniture. There is some oilseed processing, meatpacking, and textile production, but most of the beef, cotton, and soybeans are exported in their raw state rather than being processed domestically.

Trade. No reliable figures on international trade exist because a large part of that trade consists of the reexportation and transshipment of licit and illicit goods. The major recorded exports include soybeans and cotton, meat products, and timber. Half of Paraguay's international trade is with nations in the Southern Cone Common Market (Brazil, Argentina, and Uruguay). Brazil is the most important trade partner, followed by the Netherlands, which imports soybeans for crushing. Unrecorded reexports include a wide variety of goods that range from cigarettes to automobiles, contraband compact discs, and drugs. Paraguay's major imports include machinery, vehicles, spare parts, fuels and lubricants, and alcoholic beverages and tobacco, much of which is reexported. Brazil and

An enclosed yard in Asunción. The capital is the center of religious and educational institutions, commerce, and industry as well as government.

Argentina provide most of Paraguay's imports, followed by the United States and Japan.

Informal international trade centers on Ciudad del Este, which depends heavily on shopping "tourism." Brazilians and Argentinians travel to Ciudad del Este to take advantage of the low import duties to purchase consumer electronics, office equipment, perfumes, whiskey, cigarettes, and other consumer items. This trade, along with illicit trade through the area, has earned Ciudad del Este notoriety as a smuggler's paradise. Shopping tourism declined in 1997 and subsequent years, because of weakening economic growth in Brazil and Argentina and stricter controls by Brazilian authorities.

Division of Labor. A person's economic position depends primarily on education and social status, with access to many positions in the government bureaucracy and state enterprises and sometimes private enterprises also dependent on a personal connection with politically powerful benefactors. Among the poor and working classes, young children are expected to help assure family survival by assisting in agricultural production or working outside the home. Among small farmers, most agricultural labor is provided by family members.

However, peasant farmers still practice a form of cooperative labor known as *minga*, in which at critical times in the agricultural cycle neighbors or kin work together to prepare or harvest each other's fields.

SOCIAL STRATIFICATION

Classes and Castes. Wealth and income distribution are extremely unequal. A small elite owns most of the land and the commercial wealth and reaped most of the benefits of economic growth in recent decades. Recent surveys indicate that 20 percent of the population of the greater Asunción metropolitan area and 60 percent of the population in rural areas live in poverty. Indigenous peoples are the most impoverished. Mennonite and Japanese immigrants have established thriving agricultural colonies, while the more recent Korean, Chinese, and Arab immigrant groups are concentrated in urban commercial activities and reexportation. Brazilian immigrants are disproportionately concentrated in midsize commercial farming enterprises but also include extremely impoverished small farmers and laborers as well as wealthy landowners and middle-class entrepreneurs.

Symbols of Social Stratification. Language is an important marker of social status. Members of the upper classes primarily speak Spanish in public and in private, although they may understand Guarani. Members of the poorer social groups speak Guarani primarily or exclusively, and may have only a limited understanding of Spanish. The social distance between classes has traditionally been extreme, and peasants or workers were expected to show deference toward members of the political and landowning elite.

POLITICAL LIFE

Government. Paraguay is a republic consisting of the city of Asunción and seventeen additional departments, which are further subdivided into local administrative units known as *municipios*. The executive branch consists of the president and vice president, who are directly elected to five-year terms, and a council of ministers appointed by the president. The legislative branch is made up of the Senate and the Chamber of Deputies, which also are directly elected for five-year terms. The judiciary, including the Supreme Court, is appointed. In 1991, Paraguay initiated direct election of departmental and municipal executives and councils.

Contemporary political life has been shaped by General Alfredo Stroessner's thirty-five year dictatorship. After assuming power in a military coup in 1954, Stroessner ensured his control by fusing the ruling Colorado Party, government bureaucracies, and the military. Compliance to his personable authoritarian rule was achieved through a combination of brutal repression and patronage. Stroessner assured the allegiance of top military leaders and political cronies through grants of land, lucrative state contracts, and control of profitable smuggling activities. Benefits ranging from government posts to seeds were distributed to Colorado Party supporters, with the patron-client chains extending down to the poorest neighborhoods and rural towns. Although a formal judicial system existed, de facto adjudication was by the law of *mbareté* (the rule of the strong), in which the more powerful party or the party with the more powerful benefactor prevailed, thus ensuring the dominance of Stroessner's allies.

In February 1989, Stroessner was removed from power in a coup led by General Andrés Rodríguez. Although Rodríguez was a longtime Stroessner ally, he carried out his promise to lead the nation to a more democratic government. Freedom of the press, freedom of association, and other basic rights are recognized, and civilian officials have gained office through open elections. However, the Colorado Party remains strongly entrenched, and many of Stroessner's top allies and officials are still in high government and party posts.

Leadership and Political Officials. Paraguay's two major political parties, the Colorados (National Republican Association), and the Liberals (Authentic Radical Liberal Party, have their roots in the period of the Triple Alliance. Affiliation with a political party commonly is based on family and personal ties. Both parties have hierarchical organizations with competing internal factions. In 1993, a new party, the Encuentro Nacional, was formed to challenge the traditional parties. Its strongest support is among younger, more educated urban voters. Several smaller parties also exist. There is little substantive difference among the major parties. Access to leadership positions is through the party hierarchy and personal ties.

Social Problems and Control. Paraguay has a civilian police force responsible for public order and a legal system based on French and Roman law. At the local level, justices of the peace and magistrates are responsible for administrative and criminal proceedings. There are also courts of appeal, the Tribunal of Jurors and Judges of First Instance, and judges of arbitration.

Street crime and violence increased during the 1990s with worsening economic conditions. The police force is widely perceived as corrupt and complicit in some crime. The judiciary has been the least affected among all the branches of government by the post-Stroessner political reforms, and local magistrates and justices of the peace are seen by many people as available for purchase, especially in rural areas. Government corruption at all levels is pervasive and contributes to widespread public cynicism toward politics and government.

Conflict over land intensified dramatically in the 1990s, especially in the north and the eastern border region. While there have been reports of peasant farmers taking up arms, most of the violence has been directed against them. Landowners (whether or not they have legitimate title) have employed private gunmen to defend their claims and have forcibly and illegally evicted occupants and destroyed their homes and crops. In the early 1990s, a number of peasant leaders were assassinated. The government has made no significant moves toward land reform and has acted slowly to resolve conflicting claims.

A muchacho herding cattle into a corral.

Military Activity. Under Stroessner, Paraguay was one of the most heavily militarized nations in the world, with an extremely high ratio of police and military personnel to civilian population. Military personnel enjoyed great benefits and power. Efforts to depoliticize the military since 1989 have been tenuous, and military privileges remain considerable. In April 1996, General Lino Oviedo led an attempted coup against then–president Guillermo Wasmosy. Although most of the military remained loyal to Wasmosy and the coup was unsuccessful, Oviedo later ran for and the won the Colorado Party's nomination for president. His candidacy eventually was nullified and he was imprisoned, but the resultant political uncertainty immobilized the government. Although the military has refrained from intervening directly in recent political affairs, it is never far from the halls of power.

SOCIAL WELFARE AND CHANGE PROGRAMS

The government runs a system of underfunded and understaffed public health posts and hospitals and provides retirement benefits for employees of the government and state enterprises and veterans of the Chaco War. Nominal government programs to benefit peasants and indigenous peoples are ineffective and corrupt. Religious organizations and nongovernmental agencies provide some social services and play a central role in promoting change.

NONGOVERNMENTAL ORGANIZATIONS AND OTHER ASSOCIATIONS

Workers are represented through four major unions. Currently, three confederations of peasant organizations work to promote peasants' interests in national public policy discussion and occasionally intervene to support peasants in land conflicts. A number of regional peasant organizations assume similar roles at the local level and promote local development initiatives. A number of trade and business associations exist, the most powerful of which represent the interests of rural landowners and ranchers, cotton exporters, and grain enterprises. Since 1989, a large number of nongovernmental organizations and associations have been formed, with interests ranging from the promotion of sustainable development to advocacy for women, street children, and indigenous peoples. Although the number of people directly involved in these organizations is small, they play an important role defending human rights and promoting social change.

GENDER ROLES AND STATUSES

Division of Labor by Gender. Although the dominant conception of gender roles gives responsibility for the domestic sphere to women while men dominate in the public sphere, women have long had a central role in providing for their families and are economically active outside the home. They played a critical role as workers in national reconstruction after the War of the Triple Alliance. They have always played an important role in agriculture, both in subsistence production and in the production of cash crops on small peasant farms. However, the economic contributions of women frequently go unrecognized because their agricultural work, and informal sector work performed within the household, are difficult to distinguish from domestic activities. Recent surveys in urban areas indicate that women constitute at least one-third of the economically active population. Women are employed predominantly in domestic service and sales and as office workers, while men are employed across a wider range of activities. Women also are more heavily involved in the informal sector than are men.

Women assumed more active roles in political parties and government after the fall of the Stroessner dictatorship in 1989, and several women now have high-level positions in political parties, the legislature, and government ministries. However, positions of power are still held overwhelmingly by men. Although men dominate the formal bureaucracy of the Catholic Church, women are important in the practice of folk Catholicism.

The Relative Status of Women and Men. Paraguay is a conservative and male dominated society in which formal rights and privileges in many spheres were until recently denied to women. It was the last Latin American nation to grant women the right to vote (1961). Before the constitutional reforms of 1992, married women could not work outside the home, travel, or dispose of their own property without the consent of their spouses. Husbands had the right to dispose of conjugal property, including property the wife brought to the union, as they saw fit. The 1992 reforms modified those provisions, formally granting women equal rights and interests within the marriage. Women are also disadvantaged economically. A 1990 survey in the Asunción metropolitan area found that women earned only 56 percent as much as men. The earnings gap was larger for more highly educated and trained workers. Female-headed households are among the poorest in the society.

MARRIAGE, FAMILY, AND KINSHIP

Marriage. Marriages are formed by the choice of the couple and may be church, civil, or consensual unions. According to the 1992 census, 68 percent of women above age nineteen were in unions, of whom 78 percent were married in a church or civil ceremony. Legal divorce is rare, although unions are often unstable, especially among the poor. Although it is a conservative Roman Catholic society, Paraguay has long been characterized by unstable consensual unions and a high illegitimacy rate. Men's extramarital behavior draws little criticism as long as it does not impinge on the family's security, but women's behavior reflects on the family, and women are expected to be faithful if they are in a stable union.

Domestic Unit. Most people live in a nuclear family that consists of a married couple and their unmarried children or a single woman and her children. In 1992, 20 percent of households were

A sub-tropical rainforest in the Mbaracayu Reserve. Only about one-third of Paraguay consists of rainforest; the other two-thirds is semiarid and infertile.

headed by women. Extended households are rare, although relatively well-off urban families may take in the children of poorer rural relatives or those of an unwed female relative. The man holds formal authority within the family and is treated with respect by the children. The woman is responsible for managing the household, caring for the children, maintaining ties with extended kin, and often earning an income outside the home.

Inheritance. Land and other property pass by inheritance to a surviving spouse and then to biological or adopted children. The right to specify an alternative disposition of property is granted to the husband, but his wife may legally contest his decision.

Kin Groups. Family and extended kin are the most important center of loyalty and identity for individuals, and the ideal is an extensive and strong extended kin network. Kin may be called on to provide essential support and assistance in times of need, and the wealthy may mobilize extended kin to support their political ambitions. In addition to kinship ties by marriage and birth, great importance is placed on fictive kin ties established through godparenthood. Parents select godparents for their children's baptism, confirmation, and marriage. Those

godparents have special rights and responsibilities toward their godchildren and are expected to assist in meeting a child's needs if necessary. Children are expected to show their godparents special deference and respect, but ties to the godchild's parents (coparents) may be even more important and extend beyond the death of the godchild. Social equals and extended kin are preferred as godparents, although poorer parents may seek more influential benefactors as godparents for their children.

SOCIALIZATION

Infant Care. Infants are showered with affection and attention by both women and men of all ages. A crying infant will be comforted instantly by the nearest adult or older child. Infants typically are carried in the arms rather than in a sling or stroller. They usually are left to play on the ground or floor or are placed on a bed to sleep, although the use of playpens and cribs is common among the urban middle and upper classes. Parents expect infants to be active and responsive.

Child Rearing and Education. While middle-class and upper-class children are indulged and expected to devote themselves to studying and playing, the children of poorer urban and rural families

1751

are expected to assume productive work roles at a very young age. These children assist in agricultural work, household chores, and the care of younger siblings. It is not unusual for very young children to work as street vendors. Physical discipline is common, and children are controlled through the threat of physical punishment.

Formal education consists of six years of primary schooling followed by six years of secondary schooling. Primary education is compulsory from ages six to twelve, but there are not enough schools, especially in rural areas. Although poor families value education, their children often must miss classes or drop out an early age to help the family financially. In 1994, 90 percent of primary age children were enrolled, while only 34 percent of secondary age children were.

Higher Education. Possession of a university degree is an important source of social prestige and access to higher-status jobs but is available to only a small proportion of the population.

ETIQUETTE

Greetings vary by social class, gender, and the level of intimacy of the parties. Except in formal business situations, upper-class and middle-class women who are social equals greet each other with a kiss on each cheek, whether they are acquaintances or are meeting for the first time. Male and female acquaintances in these social classes greet each other the same way. Men in all social classes shake hands in formal situations. Leave-taking follows the same rules.

RELIGION

Religious Beliefs. Paraguay is overwhelmingly Roman Catholic. There are also several Protestant sects and small groups of the Baha'i, Buddhist, and Jewish faiths.

Rituals and Holy Places. In addition to Roman Catholic holy days and rituals, Paraguay honors the Virgin of the Immaculate Conception on 8 December. This day is celebrated with a pilgrimage led by religious and government officials to the holy shrine in Caacupé.

Death and the Afterlife. Beliefs and practices concerning death follow Roman Catholic tradition. The dead are interred in mausoleums, and the novena is traditionally observed, although this practice is declining in urban areas. Traditionally, All Saints' Day

is celebrated on 1 November by decorating deceased family members' tombs and gathering in cemeteries to honor the dead.

MEDICINE AND HEALTH CARE

Modern biomedical practices are combined with herbal and folk remedies. Public health clinics and hospitals are inaccessible to many people, especially in rural areas, and the urban and rural working classes and the poor often depend on self-medication or private pharmacies for medical treatments. Herbal remedies are used simultaneously with pharmaceuticals. Some herbal specialists exist, but most people are knowledgeable about the medicinal uses of common plants or resort to relatives or neighbors for advice on their use.

SECULAR CELEBRATIONS

National holidays include 1 January (New Year's Day), 3 February (Ban Blas, patron saint of the nation), 1 March (Heroes' Day), 1 May (Labor Day), 14–15 May (Independence Day), 12 June (Peace of Chaco), 15 August (Foundation of Asunción), 25 August (Constitution Day), 29 September (Battle of Boquerón, the anniversary of a key victory in the Chaco War), 12 October (Day of the Race, the anniversary of the discovery of America), 1 November (All Saints' Day), 8 December (Immaculate Conception), and 25 December (Christmas). Maundy Thursday, Good Friday, Easter, Ascension Day, and Corpus Christi are recognized as national holidays and are observed according to the religious calendar.

THE ARTS AND HUMANITIES

Literature. The internal market for literature was constrained until recently by the poverty and the limited education of the majority of the population and by repression and censorship under Stroessner's dictatorship. Nonetheless, there is an active literary tradition. Most literature is in Spanish, although contemporary authors may include Guarani phrases and dialogue in their works. The most renowned contemporary authors are Augusto Roa Bastos and Josefina Plá.

Graphic Arts. Traditional folk arts include ñanduti (a spider web-like lace made in the town of Itaugua), ao poí (embroidered cloth), several kinds of ceramic and clay work (especially in the towns of Aregua and Tobatí), and silver filigree jewelry (centered in the town of Luque). Paintings by contem-

A forest cleared for farming in eastern Paraguay.

porary artists are displayed in a number of galleries in Asunción.

Performance Arts. The country is known for slow and often melancholy harp and guitar music. Although European in origin, that music usually is performed in Guarani and reflects national themes. Music is performed by ordinary people for entertainment at social gatherings and celebrations as well as by professional musicians. Performances of traditional dance, including the bottle dance (so called because the performers balance bottles on their heads) and polkas are popular. Theater was introduced by Francisco Solano López, and in 1863 the first Italian opera by a touring company was performed in Asunción's National Theater. Theater today is centered in Asunción, and works occasionally are performed in Guarani as well as Spanish.

THE STATE OF THE PHYSICAL AND SOCIAL SCIENCES

The physical and social sciences as well as the humanities are taught at the two major universities (National University and Catholic University), as are applied sciences (agriculture and engineering) and the professions. Funding for basic research and teaching is limited, and the faculties were under close surveillance during the Stroessner years. The independent Paraguayan Center for Sociological Studies was established in 1963, and has been the most important center for social science research. In the last years of Stroessner's dictatorship, other private social science institutes were established, and the number of private research organizations grew rapidly after Stroessner's fall. These institutes obtain most of their funding from international sources.

BIBLIOGRAPHY

Galeano, Luis. *Ensayos Sobre Cultura Campesina*, 1984.

———. "Las Transformaciones Agrarias, las Luchas y los Movimientos Campesinos en el Paraguay." *Revista Paraguaya de Sociología.* 28: 80, 1991.

Kleinpenning, J. M. G. *Man and Land in Paraguay*, 1987.

Lewis, Paul. *Paraguay under Stroessner*, 1980.

López, Adalberto. *The Revolt of the Comuneros: A Study in the Colonial History of Paraguay*, 1976.

Nickson, R. A. *Historical Dictionary of Paraguay*, 1993.

Pastore, Carlos. *La Lucha Por la Tierra en el Paraguay*, 1972.

Pottthast-Jutkeit, Barbara. "The Ass of a Mare and Other Scandals: Marriage and Extramarital Relations in Nineteenth-Century Paraguay." *Journal of Family History* 16, (3): 215–239, 1991.

Riquelme, Marcial. *Negotiating Democratic Corridors in Paraguay: The Report of the Latin American Studies Association Delegation to Observe the 1993 Paraguayan National Elections*, 1994.

Roett, R., and R. S. Sacks. *Paraguay: The Personalist Legacy*, 1991.

Service, Elman R., and Helen Service. *Tobatí, A Paraguayan Town*, 1954.

Warren, Harris G. *Paraguay and the Triple Alliance: The Postwar Decade, 1869–1878*, 1978.

———. *Rebirth of the Paraguayan Republic: The First Colorado Era, 1878–1904*, 1985.

Whigham, Thomas. *The Politics of River Trade: Tradition and Development In the Upper Plata, 1780–1877*, 1991.

White, R. A. *Paraguay's Autonomous Revolution, 1810–1840*, 1978.

Williams, John Hoyt. *The Rise and Fall of the Paraguayan Republic, 1800–1870*, 1980.

—Beverly Nagel

PERU

CULTURE NAME
Peruvian

ORIENTATION

Identification. Peru has a long and rich history. The Spanish conquistadors Francisco Pizarro (c.1475–1541) and Diego de Almagro (1475–1538) received news of a mighty and rich empire lying just south of the present territory of Central America. The indigenous population of Panama referred to this powerful state as the land of Piru or Peru (word meaning "land of abundance" in the region's native Quechua tongue). The northern and central part of the South American continent was described as such in all the early chronicles and ethnohistoric accounts. Although the name Peru was used by foreigners to describe the indigenous Inca population, they called themselves the Tahuantinsuyu (meaning "the four-quarters" in Quechua). To this day, one of the most powerful groups to challenge Peruvian national identity is that of the contemporary Indian population, which at different times in history has seen itself as the rightful heirs of the Inca empire and has resisted European influence on its culture. The name Peru was pervasive during the colonial period and was used to denominate the larger sections of the powerful viceroyalty of Lima. Upon independence, Peru was the name given to the country.

Location and Geography. Peru has an approximate land area of 496,225 square miles (1,285,223 square kilometers) and is located in the central western section of the South American continent. It borders Ecuador and Colombia to the north, Brazil and Bolivia to the east, Chile to the south, and the Pacific Ocean to the west. Peru's capital, Lima, is located on the coast, about 8 miles (13 kilometers) from the Pacific Ocean. Lima is home to almost a third of Peru's total population, with a total of two-thirds of the country's population living in the coastal region.

Peru is divided into three major regions. The western coast contains dry, desertlike regions to the north as well as to the south, with more agriculturally productive lands along the major valleys formed by the western-draining Andean rivers. The Central Andes run as the backbone of Peru and are comprised of two large mountain ranges with spectacular snow-capped volcanoes and temperate mountain valleys. The Andean mountains were the traditional home of the ancestral Inca kingdom. To this day, the Andes support many of the current surviving indigenous populations, some still claiming a direct Inca ancestry. Finally, in the northeast, the large region of Amazonian tropical forest has recently been the scene of oil exploration and political colonization projects. Peru's tropical forest basin also is the source of three of the major tributaries of the Amazon River, the Ucayali, Huallaga, and Marañón Rivers.

Since the 1980s, there has been the growing of impact of the *El Niño* (the child) current. This strong southern current, called El Niño because it occurs around Christmas, is responsible for a warming of the water temperature off the Peruvian coast that leads to great rainfalls, large-level floods along the coast, and periods of drought along the southern highlands.

Demography. Peru's population in 2000 was approximately 25 million. At the moment of conquest (mid-1500s), the original indigenous population numbered around 12 million. Only in the last forty years of the twentieth century was Peru once again able to reach that initial number, since the indigenous population had been almost completely decimated. Two-thirds of Peru's population is concentrated along the major urban centers of the coast and the rest is in the Andes, making the Amazon the least populated of its regions. There are four major ethnic groups in Peru: (1) whites (of European an-

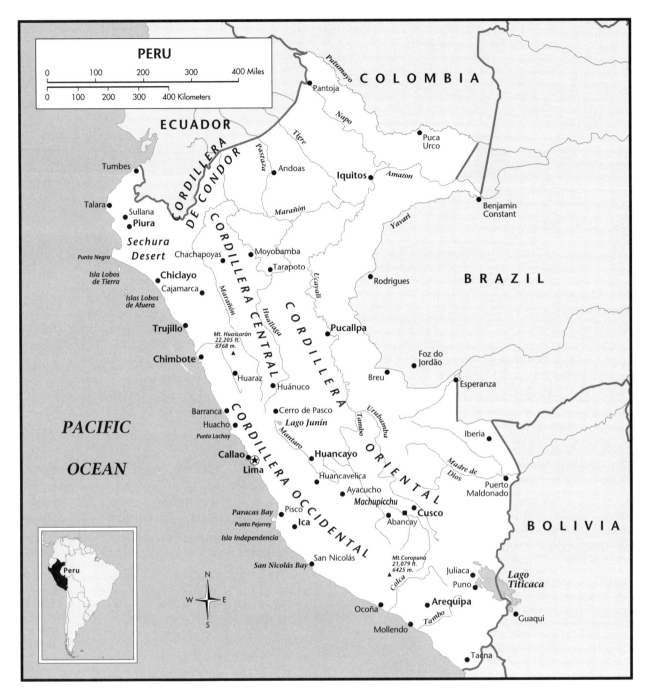

Peru

cestry); (2) mestizos (of mixed European and Indian ancestry—pejoratively referred to as *cholos*); (3) Indians (of Native American ancestry); and (4) Afro-Peruvians (of African descent). Accurate statistics for each of these four populations are difficult to collect because of the fluidity and arbitrariness in defining people as members of each community. The following rough estimates are usually given for each group: the Indian population is the largest, comprising almost 45 percent of the overall popula-

tion; the mestizo population is second, with around 40 percent; and whites and blacks are a distant third and fourth with 10 percent and 5 percent, respectively.

In the late twentieth century, the Asian-Peruvian community (mainly of Chinese and Japanese descent) gained greater public recognition, especially with the election of a Peruvian president of Japanese ancestry (Alberto Fujimori). Both Asian populations have similar migration histories starting in the late 1800s and tend to be incorporated into the same racial/ethnic category.

Linguistic Affiliation. Spanish and Quechua are both recognized as official languages in Peru. Spanish, however, is the language enforced by both the education system and the government. Introduced by the Spaniards, Spanish was forced upon the indigenous population throughout the colonial period by the Spanish Crown. This enforced linguistic practice continued throughout Peru's republic period (from the 1830s to the present). The Spanish spoken in Peru is also unique to the region, combining the Castillian tongue with many native Quechua and Aymara terms.

Although Quechua is spoken by most of Peru's Indian population, a significant amount of the Indian population speak Aymara as their native language. Aymara speakers are typically located in the southern region of the country along the shores of Lake Titicaca, which Peru shares as a border with Bolivia. Because of large migration within the country, Aymara and Quechua speakers are also found throughout the major urban centers of Peru.

Originally spoken by the Incas, Quechua was imposed upon all the populations conquered by them, allowing the Incas an easier medium of communication and domination. After the Spanish conquest, Quechua gained recognition as the indigenous lingua franca and also took on a characteristic of resistance rather than domination. There are also several other dozen languages spoken by other indigenous groups, most of which live in Peru's Amazon basin. The rich African influence also has contributed to a culturally and stylistically distinct variation of Peruvian Spanish.

Symbolism. The archaeological remains of the royal Inca estate of Machu Picchu is one of the most striking images emblematic of Peruvian culture. The majestic image of this ancient ruin perched high in the Andes is used to symbolize the resilience of Peruvian traditions. The fact that Machu Picchu lies on an 8,000-foot (2,440 meter) mountaintop and that it escaped destruction by the Spaniards looms large in the imaginations of Peruvians and tourists. The ruins evoke the nation's Indian past and legitimizes both Peru's historical heritage and cultural tradition.

Other emblematic figures of Peru are that of the Lake Titicaca and the island of the sun. The island of the sun is the largest of the islands in Lake Titicaca and was considered sacred by the Incas. As a result of this sacred status, the Incas maintained a temple to the sun on the island and a group of religious servants including celibate women (called *acllas*) year round. The highest navigable lake in the world at 12,500 feet (3,810 meters) above sea level and with an extension of 3,200 square miles (8,300 square kilometers), Titicaca is a natural border between Peru and Bolivia. The temperate waters of Lake Titicaca, as well as the different Indian communities that still make their livelihood off the lake's resources, are reminders of Peru's ancient traditions. Like other South American countries, Peru also imbues its flag, national anthem, and national coat of arms with sacred value. These three national symbols are held in enormous esteem and provide a common ground for Peruvians to memorialize their country's political and military struggles.

HISTORY AND ETHNIC RELATIONS

Emergence of the Nation. The current configuration of Peru took form on 28 July 1821 when it declared its independence from Spanish rule. The declaration followed the occupation of Lima by the Argentinian general José de San Martín and the fleeing of the royalist forces to the interior of the country. But it really was not until 1824 and the battles of Ayacucho and Junín that the royalists were defeated and Spanish power in the whole continent was finally overthrown. These final battles were led not by San Martín, but rather by the Venezuelan generals Simón Bolívar and Antonio José de Sucre. San Martín had already retired to Europe after seeking Bolívar's support to secure Peru's independence. In this manner, Peruvian independence was obtained a couple of years later than most other South American states. This tardiness was due to the politically and religiously more conservative nature of the Peruvian aristocracy, the large presence of Spaniards in the territory, and the solid Spanish military stronghold of Lima.

National Identity. Peruvians maintain a very strong sense of national identity supported by a series of common characteristics such as language, religion, food, and music. Spanish and Catholicism have historically provided a zealous sense of national belonging and cultural identity. These national characteristics have also enabled a national ethos to withstand the regional and ethnic differences inherent in the Peruvian population. Before the advent of roads or railways, the sheer difficulty in traversing Peru's geography was one of the greatest obstacles to solidifying a national identity. Since the 1960s, and especially due to a large internal migration toward the major urban centers, regional differences have seemed to present less of a destabilizing peril. This same migration phenomenon also has provided some relief to the divisive hierarchical structure of racial and ethnic differences. Since independence, mainly Indians and blacks, and mestizos to a lesser degree, have suffered the brunt of racial discrimination. This uneven ethnic structure has made it difficult for these groups to fully participate as national citizens and to identify solely as Peruvians. Nevertheless, even with these regional and ethnic differences, a national identity is still solidly in place, most probably also due to the centralized nature of the education system and bureaucratic structures.

Ethnic Relations. A Peruvian identity is most firmly found among the white elite and large mestizo communities. The three other ethnic groups—Indians, blacks, and Asians—tend to have much more complex identity formations as Peruvians. Indians above all have faced five centuries of ethnically discriminatory and genocidal practices against its population. Even after independence their general treatment was not radically different. Indians are still portrayed as backwards and inferior and perform the hardest and less remunerative forms of labor. The more than sixty Amazon Indian groups still face cultural extinction as a result of oil exploration, agricultural production, and mining colonizing campaigns.

Afro-Peruvians also have suffered the brunt of racial and cultural discrimination since their emancipation in 1854. Through the lack of opportunities to improve their social situations, most Afro-Peruvians have been limited to rural work or domestic labor. The black community has traditionally occupied the coastal parts of the nation and has its major concentrations along the areas of Chincha (three hours south of Lima) and the neighborhoods of La Victoria and Matute within Lima. Meanwhile, black men in Peru have been particularly enabled to excel as national icons within both local and national soccer teams. This iconization of Afro-Peruvian athletes as national sports heroes stands in sharp contrast with the friction that the community has on the whole encountered as part of Peruvian culture.

Chinese and Japanese immigrants came to Peru in the late nineteenth and early twentieth centuries. Both groups were brought in to work as rural laborers in the large hacienda/estate holdings. Japanese migrants have experience a more difficult integration because of their lesser tendency to marry outside their culture. The election of a Peruvian president of Japanese ancestry, however, has brought into question many of the traditional assumptions regarding the friction between Asian-Peruvians and their national counterparts. Some analysts have argued that Fujimori was voted into power by Indians and mestizos who saw themselves being closer to an Asian-Peruvian candidate than to one representing the traditional white elite.

Urbanism, Architecture, and the Use of Space

There are three major architectural traditions in Peru. The pre-Hispanic tradition represents all those indigenous architectural traits existing in the territory before the Spanish conquest. The ruins of places such as Machu Picchu in Ayacucho, the temple of the sun in Cuzco, and the ruins of Sacsahuamán, also in Cuzco, solemnly stand as testimonials to a non-Western form of architecture and space dynamics. Pre-Hispanic buildings are made out of stone masonry and are fitted expertly with each other, to such a degree that not even a needle can be pushed in between them. The main constructions of all Inca urban centers are the Inca's palace, the main temple of the sun, and the house for the Acllaconas (females virgins selected for religious service).

The Spanish conquest brought with it a completely different architectural sensibility. In most places pre-Hispanic buildings were destroyed and Catholic churches were built on top of the major Indian temples, such as the convent of Santo Domingo that was built over the temple of the sun in Cuzco. This colonial architecture brought with it many of the styles in vogue in the European courts of the sixteenth, seventeenth, and eighteenth centuries, including that of the Baroque. Some of the best examples of this colonial period are the cathedrals in both Lima and Cuzco, as well as the Church of San Agustín and the residence of the Marqués de Torre Tagle in Lima. Traditionally, the colonial architectural sensibility impacted the whole urban space, creating a central plaza surrounded by the most important buildings in the administration of the city, such as the government palace, the cathedral, the archbishop's palace, and the city government building. The oldest Peruvian cities such as Arequipa, Cuzco, and Lima are the best examples of this colonial style.

Since the nineteenth century, however, a wider notion of modernist tradition has become popular in Peruvian culture. This has meant the expansion of the urban space and the construction of much more architecturally modern buildings and housing

Lima residents wait to vote for a new mayor. Peruvian voters tend to vote for the most charismatic candidates, not those of a particular party or ideology.

though both rely heavily on soups and rice as dietary staples. In this manner seafood and plantains are typical of the coastal diet, while different kinds of meat, corn, and potatoes are much more frequently consumed in the highlands. *Ceviche*, fish marinated in *ají*, a hot sauce made mainly from spicy peppers, tomato, onions and lemon, is an example of a particular Peruvian delicacy. African dishes such as the *cau cau* (tripe casserole) and the *mazamorra* (*chicha* drink made from maize) are particular Peruvian dishes that reflect this tradition more than others. Meanwhile, roasted guinea pig is also an Andean delicacy dating most probably to pre-Hispanic days.

Food Customs at Ceremonial Occasions. All Peruvian festivities are accompanied by large levels of eating and drinking, a practice that seems to have a long tradition in both indigenous and Spanish cultures. Typical indigenous celebrations, such as the Inti Raymi (summer solstice), are accompanied by large roasting of meats (such as llama, guinea pig, pork, and lamb) and the ritual drinking of *chicha de jora* (maize beer). Another Peruvian ceremonial occasion, the observation of holy week, has strong food restrictions. During this time the consumption of meat is religiously restricted, providing for a whole array of seafood-based dishes. High on this list of alternative foods are fish and bean dishes, mainly the consumption of cod fish (*bacalao*), as well as *fanesca*, and the infamous *humitas* (corn and cheese cakes). Humitas are highly regarded since they were originally made only for the holy week observation, but in the last couple of years have become part of the national cuisine found at restaurants and food shops.

Basic Economy. Peru is traditionally portrayed as a country with a developing economy dependent upon the export of raw materials and the import of manufactured goods. It is also one of the leading fishing countries in the world and ranks among the largest producers of bismuth, silver, and copper. Traditionally, Peru has also been an agricultural-based society with almost a third of its workforce involved in farm labor. Until the 1980s, Peru had been able to be more or less self-sufficient in terms of food; since then, however, the nation began the large-level importation of wheat, corn, rice, vegetable oils, dairy products, and meat to feed its population. Since the 1980s there also has been a concerted effort, with limited success, to create nontraditional export industries (such as fish meal, shrimp, minerals, and oil) and to manufacture certain consumer goods rather than importing them.

throughout Lima, but more strikingly in the adjacent city of Miraflores. Banks and other financial institutions throughout the country also are reflective of this modernist trend. These financial towers and their glass constructions are very much indicative of a dramatic shift in the architectural style of Peru.

The urban space, especially that of Lima, changed rapidly in the last three decades of the twentieth century. Lima has experienced a significant increase of its population as a result of inner migrations and the creation of shanty towns (*pueblos jóvenes*) around its perimeter. People take over abandoned lands just outside the city limits and overnight construct flimsy homes of aluminum steel, plywood, and other malleable materials. Only after the pueblos jóvenes have survived possible forceful removal at the hands of the police will cement and sturdier materials be used for reconstructing the residences.

FOOD AND ECONOMY

Food in Daily Life. Peru is known for its distinct cuisine. The daily food customs are marked regionally between the coast and the highlands even

Land Tenure and Property. After independence, land ownership remained in the hands of the traditional family elites that had governed the colonial territory. These large landholders maintained the traditional hacienda structure in which the indigenous population and other rural workers labored almost as indentured servants. Since the 1960s large projects of agrarian reform have been implemented, and these radical land transformations have significantly altered the traditionally skewed land accumulation practices. The lack of modern agricultural techniques as well as the limited size of the land plots, however, have impacted negatively on the overall production of these new farming strategies.

Commercial Activities. Hernando De Soto's book, *The Other Path* (1989), was quite influential in making explicit the large place occupied by the informal economy in Peru. According to some, over half of Peru's population is part of this informal economy as noncontractual workers making a living off the streets or in nonregulated small business ventures in addition to street vendors who sell anything from food to flowers, with some of the most typical jobs in the informal sector include car cleaning, windshield wiping, and working in family-owned stores and businesses. But even the other half of the workforce that labors under signed legal contracts must also rely on informal labor (such as selling jewelry, and driving taxis) in their spare time to make enough for themselves and their families to survive.

Major Industries. Most of Peru's industries are located within the greater radius of the capital, Lima, even after concerted efforts from the state to disperse their location. Traditionally Peru had provided the labor force and minor raw materials for its assembly industry. However, the recent state tendency has been to provide wider support for industries that meet the national demand for consumer goods, as well as in the laws that regulate the production of cement, steel, fertilizers, processed food, textiles, and petroleum. The support has come in the form of tax relief and trade protection policies that have allowed manufacturing to become one of the fastest growing segments of the economy. The demand for increased manufacturing has been met to some degree, although the fact that many of these incipient industries still fall within the ranks of the informal economy makes it quite difficult for the state to regulate their growth and secure the complete benefits.

Trade. Because of Peru's colonial past, trade has always played a major role in the economy—mainly the export of raw materials and the importing of manufactured goods. The United States is by far Peru's most important trading partner, accounting for-one third of all its imports and exports. Western Europe, Japan, Colombia, and Brazil comprise most of the rest of the country's trading relationships. The main products sold to these countries are minerals (silver, lead, copper, bismuth, and zinc) and agricultural products (cotton, sugar, and coffee). Oil has also become a major export item since the 1980s when a large reserve was found in the Amazon basin along with the reserves already being exploited along Peru's northern coast. Both shrimp and other types of fish (anchovies and tuna, for example) also figured high in Peru's exports in the late twentieth century.

Division of Labor. In general, the most menial forms of labor in rural and urban settings are reserved for those populations with the lowest social status: Indians, blacks, and mestizos. It is not a coincidence that these populations are the ones with the least amount of formal schooling or secondary education. Meanwhile, political office and high-level financial positions are traditionally occupied by both the white and mestizo elite. These individuals tend to have at least a secondary school education, although the majority of the time the positions are much more a result of family relationships than personal merit. Peru also suffers from a ''brain exodus'' (*fuga de cerebros*) since many of its most capable and educated professionals have left the country for better paying and more secure jobs abroad.

SOCIAL STRATIFICATION

Classes and Castes. Peru does not recognize any official form of caste system but in fact its treatment of the indigenous population can be seen in many ways as an implicit caste arrangement. In this implicit caste system, race and/or ethnicity is the major variable to divide the population into strongly (and after five centuries, voluntarily) enforced groupings. In Peru's racial hierarchy, very much a remnant of its colonial past, whites occupy the highest rung of the ladder while the rest of the population clings to the lowest part depending on their skin color and implied cultural status. Class also plays a significant role in the social structure, superimposing itself upon the skewed racial hierarchy of the country. Not surprisingly, whites tend to occupy the highest positions in the country and also posses the greatest amount of schooling. The class arrangement, however, is somewhat more fluid and

Apartments in suburban Lima. The architecture of the city is strongly influenced by the Spanish colonizers.

has allowed for traditionally discriminated individuals to occupy high status positions either in politics or in the arts (nationally recognized writers such as César Vallejo and José María Arguedas were of Indian ancestry). But to a great degree these are individual exceptions that testify to, rather than question, the harsh caste and class arrangement present in Peru.

Symbols of Social Stratification. Language and dress are the most common symbols to designate either caste or class differences in Peru. Native American communities still maintain their indigenous languages such as Quechua, Aymara, and the lesser known Indian languages spoken by the Amazon groups. Many of these Indian communities have also maintained some form of traditional dress that identifies them as belonging to their group of origin. Both the colonial legacy and the contemporary market economy have contributed to widespread competition for Western status markers. The ownership of cars, expensive clothing, knowledge of English or other foreign languages, and modern appliances are typical markers of elite status in contemporary Peru. Meanwhile lower-class Peruvians can be seen wearing secondhand clothes and battling to survive almost on a day-to-day basis.

POLITICAL LIFE

Government. The constitution decrees a popularly elected president serving a five-year term. The president selects the prime minister who presides over the rest of the ministers, who comprise the cabinet. The country also possesses a unicameral legislature of 120 senators, popularly elected to five-year terms. Meanwhile judges are elected to the Supreme Court by the president himself from a list of nominees submitted by the National Justice Council. The judges must be approved by the Senate before they are sworn into office and are allowed to serve until they reach seventy years of age.

Leadership and Political Officials. Peru, not unlike most other South American nations, is very prone to populism, that is, to vote for and support the most charismatic figures of the political leaders. In the last three decades of the twentieth century alone, there were four such figures who were able to achieve the presidency: Alberto Fujimori (both reelected president and ousted of power in 2000), Alan García Pérez, Fernando Belaúnde Terry, and Víctor Raúl Haya de la Torre. Haya de la Torre founded the APRA party (Alianza Popular Revolucionaria Americana), which was also the party of the socialist García, who gained the presidency in 1985. Candidates rather than parties or ideologies, however, are the key voting elements in electing people into office. It is also typical for parties to be formed or rallied around individuals considered to have good chances of being elected.

Social Problems and Control. Peru has faced the serious challenge of one of the most ruthless guerrilla groups on the continent, popularly known as the Shining Path (Sendero Luminoso). Since erupting in the early 1980s, the armed struggle between the Shining Path and the Peruvian state has cost over thirty thousand lives and has helped to justify the increasing police and military repression. This has meant a greater military presence in the cities and a significant increase in the incarceration of both males and females. In the 1990s jails also became a target of military crackdowns since in several prisons their educational administrations were controlled by the inmates rather than by the police. Also during this decade, because of the increasingly violent threats made on judges, secret trials (where the judges remained hooded) were carried out.

The increase of the cocaine drug trade also contributed to a greater United States presence in the country and more military activity in the eastern Andean slopes where 80 percent of the world's coca used in cocaine production is harvested. Between the guerrilla presence (including that of other groups, such as the Tupac Amaru), drug trafficking, and general conditions of poverty, the judicial system is continuously under attack for its real deficiencies and questionable practices.

Military Activity. The Peruvian military is composed approximately of 180,000 persons, divided as follows: the army, 75,000; the navy, 18,000; the air force, 15,000; and paramilitary personnel, 70,000. Almost 2 percent of the gross domestic product is spent on defense. Peru has had major wars with two neighboring countries: Chile and Ecuador. Its first war with Chile (called the Pacific War) in the late 1800s was a great reversal and resulted in a loss of territory for Peru. Its more recent armed struggles with Ecuador in the 1940s, 1980s, and 1990s had a much more positive territorial and diplomatic outcome for Peru. Because of the unstable social conditions, guerrilla warfare, and the drug trade, however, Peru's military in the late twentieth century concentrated more on maintaining internal order than in fighting national wars.

SOCIAL WELFARE AND CHANGE PROGRAMS

The Peruvian government has traditionally been involved with national health and social security benefits; however, the government has had very limited success in providing Peruvian citizens with adequate care in both areas. In terms of national health programs, the lack of sufficient doctors and nurses, adequate hospital facilities, competent rural medicine agenda, and general funding has contributed to a deficient health system. Meanwhile, shortages of affordable housing, stable labor conditions, and retirement benefits has also impacted negatively with the increase of informal economy and the construction of shanty towns (pueblos jóvenes) around Lima. Modernization, which looks to privatize many of the social services provided by the Peruvian state, has also had a negative impact on social welfare programs.

NONGOVERNMENTAL ORGANIZATIONS AND OTHER ASSOCIATIONS

The main nongovernmental organizations (NGOs) in Peru are strongly linked to human rights, ethnic identity, and women's issues. There has also been concerted efforts to encourage and support social welfare programs but they have met with limited results. Among these programs the three most successful have been the *comedores populares* (soup kitchens), *vaso de leche* (glass of milk), and *wawa wasis* (child care centers). There have also been social organizations such as the *asentamientos humanos* linked to the pueblos jóvenes (shanty towns) around Lima. Guerrilla activities (mainly from the Shining Path), however, have seriously limited these organizations' activities by threatening and killing several of its most popular leaders, including María Elena Moyano, an Afro-Peruvian grassroots activist. These scare tactics have even impacted international NGOs making them less willing to support development programs in Peru.

GENDER ROLE AND STATUSES

Division of Labor by Gender. Men and women have traditionally occupied different labor roles. Since Incan times, women customarily (but not exclusively) were in charge of weaving and minor agricultural obligations while men took care of road construction, farming, and military obligations. A division of labor by gender is even further reinforced today. There are also areas, however, where this division is being blurred. As women gain more training and formal education, traditional occupa-

A farm worker stands in a harvested field holding a threshing fork. About one-third of Peru's workforce traditionally consisted of farmers.

tions such as in business, politics, and the police are becoming viable options. At the same time the large local and international migration has left women in charge of households and forced them to get involved in social movements and in the fight for progressive change.

The Relative Status of Women and Men. Although some would argue otherwise, Peru could be described as a patriarchal society. Men are preferentially treated in most, if not all, aspects of society. Sons are preferred over daughters, are given more freedom, and are less burdened with household chores and family obligations. In theory men are expected to marry and provide for their families. There are, however, large numbers of female-run households where the mother has to work and provide for her children. Meanwhile, it is a common social practice for men to have other female lovers and children outside of their initial marriage.

MARRIAGE, FAMILY AND KINSHIP

Marriage. In general, Peruvians have free choice about who they can or cannot marry, with class and money being the two most significant variables in terms of marriage decisions. Many couples decide to live together (as opposed to getting married) be-

cause of their lack of resources for carrying out both the legal and religious ceremonies. Lack of economic resources is also a key reason for couples to continue to live with one of the spouses' families until they are financially secure enough to move out on their own. Heterosexual and monogamous marriages are the only ones sanctioned by the state and the Catholic Church, although men having more than one household is tolerated and even expected. Divorce and remarriage are very much a legal possibility but the Catholic Church and the conservative society strongly frowns upon remarriage following a Catholic (or other) religious ceremony.

Domestic Unit. The Peruvian model for a domestic unit is the Western nuclear family. Nevertheless, because of traditional indigenous traditions and scant resources, extended kin can also be the norm. Men in general have the highest authority within the house, although women also have much of the decision-making power, especially concerning children and family matters, even though it tends not to be explicitly recognized.

Inheritance. Males and females have equal legal rights in regard to inheritance, although in some instances women must either work harder or get

1763

Market in the Sacred Valley. In Peru's informal economic sector, street vendors sell anything from food to flowers.

legal representation because their claims might not be taken seriously.

Kin Groups. Unlike most urban Peruvians (over two-thirds of the country), the rural populations still maintain strong ties to their extended kin. Many rural populations, even when they have moved to urban centers, recognize their ties to large extended kin groups known as *ayllus*. Since pre-Hispanic times ayllus have defined land distributions, social obligations, and authority figures within each kin group. At present, ayllus still play a powerful part in defining people's roles and obligations in village social structures.

SOCIALIZATION

Infant Care. The greatest differences in child rearing practices are between the indigenous and white/mestizo populations. Indian mothers tend to carry their infants in colorful slings upon their backs even while performing trying agricultural labor. Indian mothers also openly nurse their children in public places, seeing it as a natural function, a practice that is shunned by the more Westernized mestizo and white mothers.

Child Rearing and Education. Boys and girls are strongly encouraged to attend grade and high school although either lack of money or the need for a child's labor at home persuades many lower-class families to keep their children from attending public schools. In general children are brought up to be respectful of their elders, obedient, and hard working.

Higher Education. The oldest university in South America is located in Peru. The Universidad Nacional de San Marcos in Lima was founded 12 on May 1551. Public universities have recently suffered from a credibility crisis because of their large graduation numbers and the increasing infiltration of leftist political groups. This has also contributed to the emergence of several private (including Catholic) universities, which have developed much more discriminating characteristics for admissions and graduation.

ETIQUETTE

Possibly as a legacy of the strongly hierarchical pre-Hispanic cultures or European colonialism, self-discipline is strongly advocated among Peruvians. The control of one's emotions and feelings is highly valued among all Peruvians, but especially among men. Respect for elders, shown through such actions as giving up one's seat for elderly people on buses, also has a strong place among public values. These values of discipline and respect for others are in sharp contrast to a political scene marked with great levels of authoritarianism and widespread corruption. Youths are also responsible for providing a strong alternative counterculture to main normative values. This counterculture is mainly expressed through musical outlets, such as the national adaptation of rock and punk music, and North American tastes in fashion and popular culture. Public expressions of sexuality, including that of homosexual behavior, is strongly discouraged.

RELIGION

Religious Beliefs. Peru prides itself on being a Catholic country since the late 1500s. At present, about 90 percent of the population are Catholics while the other 10 percent belong to Protestant faiths, the most important being Evangelists, Adventists, and Mormons. Indigenous communities have also created a symbiotic form of religion not really recognized with any other name than a popular form of Catholicism. Indian groups have mixed Catholic saints with pre-Hispanic traditions, thus allowing them to maintain ancient forms of worship under the guise of Catholic rituals. For example, the indigenous feast of the Inti Raymi (summer solstice) is celebrated in many communities as the feast days of Saints Peter and Paul.

Religious Practitioners. In the Catholic tradition male priests, especially bishops and archbishops, still demand an enormous amount of respect and authority. Nuns come in second place and are well respected for their religious commitment to sexual abstinence, obedience, and poverty. Among Indian communities the shamans, or *brujos/curanderas* are deemed the local counterparts of priests in terms of religious and spiritual authority.

Rituals and Holy Places. *Huacas* (sacred mountain places) are still deemed sacred deity dwellings that demand the respect and veneration of the indigenous populations. The Spanish Catholic missionaries were very aware of these Andean practices, which is why many Catholic churches were built on top of huacas and other pre-Hispanic temples.

Death and the Afterlife. Peruvians' notion of an afterlife very much follows Catholic notions of heaven, purgatory, and hell. Even indigenous groups have been heavily influenced by the Christian notions of Armageddon and rebirth. In Indian communities there are long-standing traditions of millenarians and of the second coming of the Inca ruler to punish the white colonizers. This symbiotic Christian/Andean second-coming myth initially gained strength in the resistance movement of Tupac Amaru that initially challenged Spanish colonialism in the seventeenth century.

MEDICINE AND HEALTH CARE

Life expectancy in Peru is sixty-seven years, which is quite high considering the serious deficiencies in the country's public health systems. Only two-thirds of its population has access to public medical attention, and only 25 percent of those living in conditions of extreme poverty. In general, misinformation, poverty, and malnutrition are the greatest impediments to improving the country's health conditions. Since the mid-1980s there has been a concerted effort to combat infant mortality and to implement national infant vaccination campaigns that have proven quite successful. Along with Western medicine there is still a tradition of *curanderos* (natural healers), and *parteras* (midwives) who are still regularly consulted, especially by the rural and Indian population.

Remaining structures of the ruined city of Machu Picchu, built by the Incas in the Andes.

SECULAR CELEBRATIONS

The major secular Peruvian celebrations are National Independence Day (celebrated three consecutive days, 28, 29, and 30 July); the Battle of Arica (7 June); and Carnival (a movable holiday celebrated on the three days just before Catholic Lent). Religious festivities with the exception of Christmas used to have a greater level of public celebration than they do in modern times. All holidays tend to be celebrated with large quantities of food, alcoholic beverages, sports (mainly soccer and volleyball), and general gaiety and relaxation.

THE ARTS AND HUMANITIES

Support for the Arts. Because of the difficult economic conditions of the country, the arts in general are one of the areas the government least supports.

Literature. Peru boasts a world-class literary selection of authors, starting with writers such as Ricardo Palma (1833–1919) who was the first to utilize Peruvian themes in his writing. In the twentieth century alone Peru produced such accomplished authors as Ciro Alegria, José María Arguedas, Alfredo Bryce Echenique, and probably the country's best-known literary figure, Mario Vargas Llosa. Meanwhile César Vallejo is hailed as Peru's most gifted poet, and is for many second on the continent only to the Chilean nobel laureate, Pablo Neruda.

Graphic Arts. Peru has a long artistic tradition, starting with the famous colonial painting and sculpture schools of Lima, one of the most accomplished schools on the continent. Contemporary artists, such as Fernando de Szyszlo (a painter) and Joaquín Roca Rey (a sculptor), have continued a more abstract tradition.

Performance Arts. Theater had an early start in the colonial period and the country also maintains a National Symphony Orchestra, a national ballet company, as well as folk dance companies. Meanwhile, the popular music genre has offered such singing giants as Lucho Barrios, Jesús Vasquez, Chabuca Granda, and Susana Baca, to mention a few.

THE STATE OF THE PHYSICAL AND SOCIAL SCIENCES

The sciences in Peru had an early development closely tied to the foundation of the Universidad Nacional de San Marcos in Lima. The social sciences more than the physical have had a more prestigious development, with the work of intellectuals such as Gustavo Gutiérrez (liberation theologist and philosopher), Julio C. Tello (archaeologist), and José Carlos Mariátegui (political philosopher). The country's difficult political conditions as well as the limited resources of the universities have seriously limited the general advancement of the physical and social sciences.

BIBLIOGRAPHY

Alegría, Ciro. *The World Is Broad and Alien*, 1973.

Americas Watch. *Untold Terror: Violence against Women in Peru's Armed Conflict*, 1992.

Arguedas, José María. *Deep Rivers*, 1978.

———. *Yawar Fiesta*, 1985.

Brown, Michael, and Eduardo Fernández. *War of Shadows: The Struggle for Utopia in the Peruvian Amazon*, 1991.

Bryce Echenique, A. *A World for Julius*, 1992.

———. *Permiso para vivir (Antimemorias)*, 1993.

Classen, Constance. *Inca Cosmology and the Human Body*, 1993.

"Coca and Cocaine: Effects on People and Policy in Latin America," *Cultural Survival*, Report #23, 1986.

Cotler, Julio. *Clase, estado, y nación en el Perú*, 1978.

Crabtree, J. *Peru Under García: An Opportunity Lost*, 1992.

Deere, Carmen Diana. *Household and Class Relations: Peasants and Landlords in Northern Peru*, 1990.

Degregori, Carlos Iván. *Ayacucho, 1969–1979: El surgimiento de Sendero Luminoso*, 1990.

Durand, F. *Business and Politics in Peru: The State and the National Bourgeoisie*, 1994.

Flores Galindo, Alberto. *Buscando un Inca: Identidad y utopía en los Andes*, 1987.

———. *La agonía de Mariátegui*, 1989.

Glave, Luis Miguel. *Trajinantes: Caminos indígenas en la sociedad colonial, siglo XVI–XVII*, 1989.

Gootenberg, Paul. *Imagining Development: Economic Ideas in Peru's "Fictitious Prosperity" of Guano 1840-1880*, 1993.

Gutiérrez, Gustavo. *Las Casas: In Search of the Poor in Jesus Christ*, 1993.

Holligan de Díaz-Límaco, Jane. *Peru in Focus: A Guide to the People, Politics, and Culture*, 1998.

Isbell, Billie Jean. *To Defend Ourselves: Ecology and Ritual in an Andean Village*, 1985.

Jenkins, D. *Peru: The Rough Guide*, 1997.

Kennedy, Joseph. *Coca Exótica*, 1985.

Kirk, Robin. *Grabado en piedra: Las mujeres de Sendero Luminoso*, 1993.

Klaren, Peter. *Modernization, Dislocation, and Aprismo: The Origin of Peru's Aprista Pary, 1870–1932*, 1973.

Kristal, Efraín. *The Andes Viewed from the City: History and Political Discourse on the Indian in Peru, 1848–1930*, 1987.

Lowenthal, Abraham, ed. *The Peruvian Experiment*, 1975.

Lumbreras, Luis. *The Peoples and Cultures of Ancient Peru*, 1974.

MacCormack, Sabine. *Religion in the Andes*, 1992.

Mallon, Florencia. *Peasant and Nation: The Making of Post-colonial Mexico and Peru*, 1995.

Manrique, Nelson. *Campesinado y nación: Las guerrillas indígenas en la guerra con Chile*, 1981.

Mariátegui, José Carlos. *Seven Interpretive Essays on Peruvian Reality*, 1971.

Matos Mar, José, and José Carlos Mejía. *La reforma agraria en el Peru*, 1980.

Morales, Edmundo. *Cocaine: White Gold Rush in Peru*, 1989.

Mosely, Michael. *The Incas and their Ancestors*, New York: Thames and Hudson, 1992.

Noble, David Cook, and Alexandra Parma Cook. *Good Faith and Truthful Ignorance: A Case of Transatlantic Bigamy*, 1991.

Palmer, David Scott, ed. *Shining Path of Peru*, 1992.

———. "Archaeology, History, Indigenismo, and the State in Peru and Mexico." In Peter R. Schmidt and Thomas C. Patterson, eds., *Making Alternative Histories*, 1995.

Patterson, Thomas. *The Inca Empire*, 1992.

Poole, Deborah, and Gerardo Renique. *Peru: Time of Fear*, 1992.

Reid, M. *Peru: Paths to Poverty*, 1985.

Rostworowski, María. *Historia del Tahuantinsuyu*, 1988.

Silverblatt, Irene. *Moon, Sun and Witches: Gender Ideologies and Class in Inca and Colonial Peru*, 1987.

Spalding, Karen. *Huarochirí: An Andean Society under Inca and Spanish Rule*, 1984.

Stark, Orin, Carlos Iván Degregori, and Robin Kirk, eds. *The Peru Reader: History, Culture and Politics*, 1995.

Stein, Steve. *Populism in Peru: The Emergence of the Masses and the Politics of Social Control*, 1980.

Stern, Steve J. *Peru's Indian Peoples and the Challenge of Spanish Conquest: Huamanga to 1640*, 2nd ed. 1993.

———, ed. *Resistance, Rebellion, and Consciousness in the Andean Peasant World*, sixteenth-nineteenth Centuries, 1989.

Vallejo, César. *Collected Poems of César Vallejo*, 1970.

Varese, Stefano. *La Sal de los Cerros*, 1968

Vargas Llosa, Mario. *Conversations in the Cathedral*, 1975.

———. *Aunt Julia and the Scriptwriter*, 1982.

———. *A Fish in the Water*, 1994.

Wise, Carol, and Manuel Pastor. "Peruvian Economic Policy in the 1980s: From Orthodoxy to Heterodoxy and Back." *Latin American Research Review* 27 (2): 83–118.

—O. HUGO BENAVIDES

THE PHILIPPINES

CULTURE NAME

Filipino

ORIENTATION

Identification. The Republic of the Philippines was named the Filipinas to honor King Philip the Second of Spain in 1543. The Philippine Islands was the name used before independence.

Location and Geography. The Republic of the Philippines, a nation of 7,107 islands with a total area of 111,830 square miles (307,055 square kilometers), is located on the Pacific Rim of Southeast Asia. Two thousand of its islands are inhabited. Luzon, the largest island with one-third of the land and half the population, is in the north. Mindanao, the second largest island, is in the south. The Philippines are 1,152 miles (1,854 kilometers) long from north to south. The width is 688 miles (1,107 kilometers). There are no land boundaries; the country is bordered on the west by the South China Sea, on the east by the Philippine Sea, on the south by the Celebes Sea, and on the north by the Luzon Strait, which separates the country from its nearest neighbor, Taiwan. The closest nations to the south are Malaysia and Indonesia. Vietnam and China are the nearest neighbors on the mainland of Asia.

The islands are volcanic in origin. Mount Mayon in southern Luzon erupted in 2000. Mount Pinatubo in central Luzon erupted in 1991 and 1992. Both eruptions caused destruction of villages and farms and displaced thousands of people from their tribal homelands. Because the country is volcanic, the small islands have a mountainous center with coastal plains. Luzon has a broad central valley in the northern provinces along the Cagayan River and plains in the midlands near Manila, the capital. Mindanao and Panay also have central plains. Northern Luzon has two major mountain ranges: the Sierra Madres on the eastern coast and the

Cordilleras in the center. The highest peak is Mount Apo in Mindanao at 9,689 feet (2,954 meters).

The weather is hot because of the country's closeness to the equator. The temperatures are constant except during typhoons. The dry season is from January to June; the wet season with monsoon rains is from July to December. Temperatures are cooler in November through January, dropping below 30 degrees Celsius (85 degrees Fahrenheit). The summer months of April and May have temperatures in excess of 39 degrees Celsius (100 degrees Fahrenheit). Typhoons occur from June through November.

Demography. The estimated population in July 2000 was eighty-one million. The average life expectancy is sixty-seven years. Four percent of the population is over age sixty-five. The most populous area is Metropolitan Manila, where eight million to ten million people live.

Linguistic Affiliation. The official languages are Filipino, which is based on Tagalog with words from other native languages, and English. Since only 55 percent of residents speak Filipino fluently, English is used in colleges, universities, the courts, and the government. The country's seventy to eighty dialects are derived from Malay languages. Three dialects are of national importance: Cebuano in the southern islands, Ilocano in the north, and Tagalog, the language of the National Capital Region. When Tagalog was chosen as the basis for a national language, Cebuanos refused to use Filipino. ''Taglish,'' a mixture of Filipino and English, is becoming a standard language. Filipinos are proud that their country has the third largest number of English speakers in the world. Filipino English includes many Australian and British terms. It is a formal language that includes words no longer commonly used in American English. Spanish was taught as a compulsory language until 1968 but is seldom used today. Spanish numbers and some Spanish words are included in the dialects.

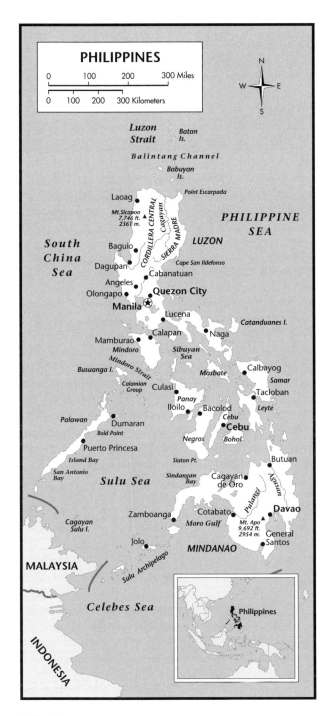

Philippines

eagle in the world, is the national bird. Doctor Jose Rizal is the national hero. Rizal streets and statues of Rizal are found in most towns and cities. Several municipalities are named for Rizal. The most prominent symbol is the flag, which has a blue horizontal band, a red horizontal band, and a white field. The flag is flown with the blue band at the top in times of peace and the red band at the top in times of war. Flag ceremonies take place once a week at all governmental offices. Schools have a flag ceremony each morning. All traffic stops while the flag is being honored. The national anthem is sung, a national pledge is recited in Filipino, and the provincial hymn is sung.

HISTORY AND ETHNIC RELATIONS

Emergence of the Nation. Early inhabitants are believed to have reached the area over land bridges connecting the islands to Malaysia and China. The first people were the Negritos, who arrived twenty-five thousand years ago. Later immigrants came from Indonesia. After the land bridges disappeared, immigrants from Indo-China brought copper and bronze and built the rice terraces at Benaue in northern Luzon. The next wave came from Malaysia and is credited with developing agriculture and introducing *carabao* (water buffalo) as draft animals. Trade with China began in the first century C.E. Filipino ores and wood were traded for finished products.

In 1380, the "Propagation of Islam" began in the Sulu Islands and Mindanao, where Islam remains the major religion. The Muslim influence had spread as far north as Luzon when Ferdinand Magellan arrived in 1521 to claim the archipelago for Spain. Magellan was killed soon afterward when a local chief, Lapu-Lapu, refused to accept Spanish rule and Christianity. Miguel Lopez de Legazpi landed in the Philippines in 1564 and consolidated Spanish power, designating Manila as the capital in 1572. Roman Catholic religious orders began Christianizing the populace, but the Sulu Islands and Mindanao remained Muslim. The Spanish governed those areas through a treaty with the sultan of Mindanao. The Spanish did not attempt to conquer the deep mountain regions of far northern Luzon.

The occupation by Spain and the unifying factor of Catholicism were the first steps in creating a national identity. Filipinos became interested in attaining independence in the middle of the nineteenth century. In the 1890's, the novels of José Rizal, his exile to a remote island, and his execution by the Spaniards created a national martyr and a rallying

The dependence on English causes concern, but since Filipino does not have words for scientific or technological terms, English is likely to remain in common use.

Symbolism. National symbols have been emphasized since independence to create a sense of nationhood. The Philippine eagle, the second largest

point for groups seeking independence. Armed attacks and propaganda increased, with an initial success that waned as Spanish reinforcements arrived. The Spanish-American War of 1898 and the defeat of the Spanish fleet in Manila Bay led the Filipino leader Emilio Aguinaldo to declare independence from Spain. The United States paid twenty million dollars to the Spanish for the Philippines under the Treaty of Paris. Aguinaldo did not accept United States occupation and fought until the Filipino forces were defeated. In 1902, the Philippines became an American territory, with the future president William Howard Taft serving as the first territorial governor. Over the next two decades, American attitudes toward the Philippines changed and the islands were given commonwealth status in 1933. Independence was promised after twelve years, with the United States retaining rights to military bases.

The Japanese invaded the Philippines early in 1942 and ruled until 1944. Filipino forces continued to wage guerrilla warfare. The return of U.S. forces ended the Japanese occupation. After the war, plans for independence were resumed. The Republic of the Philippines became an independent nation on 4 July 1946.

The new nation had to recover economically from the destruction caused by World War II. Peasant groups wanted the huge land holdings encouraged by the Spanish and Americans broken apart. In 1955, Congress passed the first law to distribute land to farmers.

Ferdinand Marcos governed from 1965 to 1986, which was the longest period for one president. From 1972 to 1981, he ruled by martial law. Marcos was reelected in 1982, but a strong opposition movement emerged. When the leader of the opposition, Benigno Aquino, was murdered after his return from exile in the United States, his wife, Corazon Aquino, entered the presidential race in 1986. Marcos claimed victory but was accused of fraud. That accusation and the withdrawal of United States support for Marcos led to "People Power," a movement in which the residents of Manila protested the Marcos regime. The Filipino military supported Aquino, who was declared president, and the Marcos family went into exile in Hawaii.

The Aquino years saw the passage of a new constitution with term limits and the withdrawal of U.S. military forces in 1991, when the government did not grant a new lease for United States use of military bases.

Fidel Ramos, the first Protestant president, served from 1991 to1998. Major problems included a fall in the value of the peso and the demands of Muslim groups in Mindanao for self-determination and/or independence. The government offered self-governance and additional funds, and the movement quieted.

Joseph "Erap" Estrada was elected for one six-year term in 1999. The demands of the Muslim rebels escalated, culminating with the kidnaping of twenty-nine people by the Abu Sayyaf group in April 2000. Late in the year 2000, impeachment proceedings were brought against Estrada, who was charged with financial corruption.

National Identity. Filipinos had little sense of national identity until the revolutionary period of the nineteenth century. The word "Filipino" did not refer to native people until the mid-nineteenth century. Before that period, the treatment of the islands as a single governmental unit by Spain and the conversion of the population to Catholicism were the unifying factors. As a desire for independence grew, a national flag was created, national heroes emerged, and a national anthem was written. A national language was designated in 1936. National costumes were established. The sense of a national identity is fragile, with true allegiance given to a kin group, a province, or a municipality.

Ethnic Relations. Ninety-five percent of the population is of Malay ancestry. The other identifiable group is of Chinese ancestry. Sino-Filipinos are envied for their success in business. They have maintained their own schools, which stress Chinese traditions.

Seventy to eighty language groups separate people along tribal lines. Approximately two million residents are designated as cultural minority groups protected by the government. The majority of those sixty ethnic groups live in the mountains of northern Luzon. People whose skin is darker are considered less capable, intelligent, and beautiful. Descendants of the Negritos tribe are regarded as inferior.

Urbanism, Architecture, and the Use of Space

The architecture of the islands shows Spanish influence. Spanish brick churches built during the colonial era dominate the towns. The churches are large and different from traditional construction. It is difficult to imagine how the indigenous population in the seventeenth century was able to build them.

Filipino families enjoy close kin bonds, and extended families living together are the norm.

Seaports and government centers had a larger proportion of Spanish buildings with wide verandas and tiled roofs. Towns destroyed during the liberation campaign in World War II, especially in central and northern Luzon, were rebuilt using wood. Areas of Manila destroyed during World War II have been restored to their historical Spanish appearance. Newer buildings in Manila range from standard multistory offices to Western-style gated housing areas for the affluent, to tenements and shacks.

Traditional houses in rural areas are *nipa* huts constructed of bamboo and roofed with leaves from palm trees or corrugated metal. Cinder blocks are the most commonly building material used. The blocks are plastered and painted on the inside and outside when funds permit. Plasterers add decorative touches to the exterior. Older houses have a "dirty" open-air kitchen for food preparation. Newer, larger houses designate a room as a dirty kitchen in contrast to the "clean" kitchen, which has an eating area where utensils are stored. Enclosed kitchens provide a roof over the cook and keep dogs and chickens from wandering into the cooking area. The roof is pitched so that rain will run off. Middle-class houses and commercial buildings have tiled roofs.

FOOD AND ECONOMY

Food in Daily Life. Filipinos do not consider it a meal if rice is not served. Plain steamed rice is the basis of the diet. Three crops a year are harvested to provide enough rice for the population, and the government keeps surpluses stored for times of drought. Salt water and freshwater of fish and shellfish are eaten daily, served either fresh or salted. Fish, chicken and pork are usually fried, although people are becoming more health-conscious and often choose alternative methods of cooking. Garlic is added to food because it is considered healthful. Filipino food is not spicy. All food is cooked on gas burners or wood or charcoal fires and is allowed to get cold before it is eaten. Rice is cooked first, since it takes longer. When it is ready, rice will be placed on the table while the next items of the meal are prepared and served.

Table knives are not used. Forks and spoons are used for dining. The food is eaten from a spoon. The traditional method of placing food on a banana leaf and eating with one's hands is also used throughout the country. It is acceptable to eat food with one's hands at restaurants as well as in the home.

Breakfast is served at 6 A.M. and consists of food left over from the night before. It is not reheated. Eggs and sausage are served on special occasions.

Small buns called *pan de sol* may be purchased from vendors early in the morning.

At midmorning and in the afternoon, people eat *merienda*. Since Filipinos are fond of sweet foods, a mixture of instant coffee, evaporated milk, and sugar may be served. Coca-Cola is very popular. Sweet rolls, doughnuts, or a noodle dish may be available. Lunch is a light meal with rice and one other dish, often a fish or meat stew. Fish, pork, or chicken is served at dinner with a soup made of lentils or vegetables. Fatty pork is a favorite. Portions of small cubes of browned pork fat are considered a special dish.

Fruits are abundant all year. Several kinds of banana are eaten, including red and green varieties. Mangoes, the national fruit, are sweet and juicy. A fruit salad with condensed milk and coconut milk is very popular on special occasions.

Vegetables are included as part of a soup or stew. Green beans and potatoes are commonly eaten foods. The leaves of *camote*, a sweet potato, are used as a salad and soup ingredient. *Ube*, a bland bright purple potato, is used as a colorful ingredient in cakes and ice cream. *Halo-halo*, which means "mixture," is a popular dessert that consists of layers of corn kernels, ice cream, small gelatin pieces, cornflakes and shaved ice. *Patis*, a very salty fish sauce, is placed on the table to be added to any of the dishes.

Fast food has become part of the culture, with national and international chains in many towns. All meals at fast-food restaurant include rice, although French fries also tend to be on the menu. Banana ketchup is preferred, although the international chains serve tomato ketchup. A national chain, Jollibee, has entered the U.S. market with a restaurant in California, where many Filipino immigrants live. The company plans to expand to other cities with Filipino populations.

Food Customs at Ceremonial Occasions.

Léchon, a suckling pig that has been roasted until the skin forms a hard brown crust, is served at important occasions. The inside is very fatty. Strips of the skin with attached fat are considered the best pieces. The importance of the host and the occasion are measured by the amount of *léchon*. served. Blood drained from the pig is used to make *dinuguan*

Sticky rice prepared with coconut milk and sugarcane syrup is wrapped in banana leaves. Glutinous rice is grown especially for use in this traditional dessert.

Gin and beer are available for men and are accompanied by *balut*, a duck egg with an embryo.

Dog meat is a delicacy throughout the country. It is now illegal to sell dog meat at markets because cases of rabies have occurred when the brains were eaten.

Basic Economy.

Agriculture, forestry, and fishing are the occupations of 40 percent of the thirty million people who are employed. Light manufacturing, construction, mining and the service industries provide the remainder of employment opportunities. The unemployment rate is over 9 percent. Fifty percent of the population lives below the poverty line. The Asian financial crisis resulted in a lack of jobs, and the drought period of the El Niño weather cycle has reduced the number of agricultural positions. It is not uncommon for people to "volunteer" as workers in the health care field in hopes of being chosen to work when a position becomes available. People work seven days a week and take additional jobs to maintain or improve their lifestyle or pay for a child's education. Eight hundred thousand citizens work overseas, primarily as merchant seamen, health care, household, or factory workers in Saudi Arabia, Hong Kong, and Taiwan. Over Seas Workers (OSWs) have a governmental agency that looks after their interests. Laws govern hours of work, insurance coverage, and vacation time, but workers may be exploited and mistreated. Recruitment centers are found in all large municipalities. OSWs send $7 billion home each year, providing 4 percent of the gross domestic product.

Land Tenure and Property.

Nineteen percent of the land is arable and 46 percent consists of forests and woodlands. Deforestation by legal and illegal loggers with no tree replacement has reduced the number of trees. Large amounts of arable land remain in the hand of absentee landowners who were given land grants during the Spanish colonial period. Although land reform legislation has been passed, loopholes allow owners to retain possession. Those responsible for enacting and enforcing the legislation often come from the same families that own the land. Peasant groups such as the HUKs (People's Liberation Army, or *Hukbong Magpapayang Bayan*) in the 1950s and the NPA (New People's Army) at the present time have resorted to guerrilla tactics to provide land for the poor. There is an ongoing demand to clear forests to provide farmland. The clearing technique is slash and burn. Environmentalists are concerned because timber is destroyed at random, eliminating the homes of endangered species of plants and animals.

Commercial Activities.

The local market is a key factor in retail trade. Larger municipalities have daily markets, while smaller communities have

Philippine children playing on Guimaras Island. Young children typically live with grandparents or aunts for extended periods.

markets once or twice a week. Trade at the market is conducted in a barter system. *Suki* relationships are established at the marketplace so that the buyer returns to the same vendor. Markets are divided into "dry" markets where clothing and household items are sold and "wet" markets where food is sold. *Sari-sari* establishments are small neighborhood stores. They are convenient since they have packaged products and are in the neighborhood, but no fresh foods are available there. In larger towns, supermarkets with fixed prices are adjacent to the market. Electronic equipment, furniture, and clothing have fixed prices and are sold in stores or at kiosks. Shopping malls are found in most provincial capitals. Malls with Western shops are found throughout metropolitan Manila.

Major Industries. Metropolitan Manila is the primary manufacturing area, with 10 percent of the population living there. Manila and the adjacent ports are the best equipped to ship manufactured goods. Manufacturing plants produce electrical and electronic components, chemicals, clothing, and machinery. The provinces produce processed foods, textiles, tobacco products, and construction materials. Manufacturing in the home continues to be common in remote areas.

Trade. Rice, bananas, cashews, pineapple, mangoes, and coconut products are the agricultural products exported to neighboring countries. Exported manufactured products include electronic equipment, machinery, and clothing. The United States, members of the European Union, and Japan are the major trading partners. Imports consists of consumer goods and fuel. The country has mineral and petroleum reserves that have not been developed because of the mountainous terrain and a lack of funding.

Transportation of products is difficult since the highway system beyond metropolitan Manila consists of two-lane roads that are under constant repair and sometimes are washed out by typhoons. Interisland shipping costs add to the expense of manufacturing. Congress, governmental agencies, and the financial community are attempting to find solutions to these problems. The rate of road construction is accelerating and a light rail system is planned. Filipino membership in the Association of South East Asian Nations (ASEAN), a regional trade organization, is an important factor in the development of trade policies.

Division of Labor. In rural areas, lack of mechanization causes the entire family to work in the rice fields. Planting rice seedlings, separating them, replanting, and changing water levels in the fields are done by hand and are labor-intensive. Crops such as tobacco, corn, and sugarcane demand full family participation for short periods during the planting and harvest seasons.

In the cities, traditional roles common to industrialized countries are followed. Men perform heavy physical tasks, while women work as clerks and teachers and in health care.

SOCIAL STRATIFICATION

Classes and Castes. Filipinos believe in the need for social acceptance and feel that education can provide upward mobility. Color of skin, beauty, and money are the criteria that determine a person's social position. Light coloring is correlated with intelligence and a light-skinned attractive person will receive advancement before his or her colleagues. Family position and patron–client associations are useful in achieving success. Government officials, wealthy friends, and community leaders are sponsors at hundreds of weddings and baptisms each year. Those connections are of great importance.

There is a gap between the 2 percent of the population that is wealthy and the masses who live in poverty. The middle class feels too obligated to those in power to attempt to make societal changes.

The people of the Philippines enjoy watching professional basketball played by American professional teams and teams in Filipino professional leagues. Basketball courts are the only sport-site found in every *barangay* and school. Cockfights are a popular sport among men. Cocks have metal spurs attached to the leg just above the foot. The contest continues until one of the cocks is unable to continue fighting or runs away. Cuneta Astrodome in metropolitan Manila is used for both professional basketball and cockfights. Mah-jongg, a Chinese game played with tiles, is very popular, especially with women.

Symbols of Social Stratification. Money to buy consumer goods is an indicator of power. Wealthy people lead western lifestyles. They travel abroad frequently and pride themselves on the number of Westerners they have as friends. Since few people outside Manila have a family car, owning a vehicle is a clear statement of a high social level. Houses and furnishings show a person's social position. Upholstered furniture instead of the traditional wooden couches and beds, rows of electrical appliances that are never used and area rugs are all important.

Women above the poverty level have extensive wardrobes. Sending one's children to the best schools is the most important indicator of social position. The best schools often are private schools and are quite expensive.

POLITICAL LIFE

Government. The country has a republican form of government that was developed during the commonwealth period. It contains three branches: executive, legislative, and judicial. The first constitution, based on the United States Constitution, was written in 1935. When President Marcos declared martial law in 1972, that constitution was replaced by another one providing for a head of state, a prime minister, and a unicameral legislature. The president had the power to dissolve the legislature, appoint the prime minister, and declare himself prime minister. A new constitution was approved in a national referendum in 1987. It was similar to the 1935 constitution but included term limitations. The 221 members of the House may serve three consecutive three-year terms, which is also the case for provincial governors. The twenty-four senators, who are elected at large, may serve two consecutive six-year terms. The president serves one six-year term, but the vice president may serve two consecutive six-year terms. The president and vice president do not run on the same ticket and may be political opponents.

The seventy provinces have governors but no legislative bodies. Over sixty cities have been created by legislation. Cityhood is desirable since cities are funded separately from the provinces so that additional federal money comes into the area. Each province is divided into municipalities. The smallest unit of government is the barangay, which contains up to two hundred dwellings and an elementary school. The barangay captain distributes funds at the local level.

Leadership and Political Officials. Charges of corruption, graft, and cronyism are common among government officials at all levels. People accept cronyism and the diversion of a small percentage of funds as natural. Rewriting the constitution to eliminate term limits and establishing a strong two-party system are the reforms that are discussed most often. Politicians move from party to party as the needs of their constituencies dictate because the political parties have no ideologies.

Many of the people who are currently active in politics were politically active in the commonwealth era. Men of rank in the military also move into the

A house belonging to a family of the Igorot tribe in Bontoc. The Philippines are home to approximately sixty ethnic groups in seventy to eighty language groups.

political arena. Joseph Estrada, whose term as president is 1998–2004, entered the public eye as a popular film star. He then became the mayor of a large city and went on to become vice president in the Ramos administration. Previous presidents have had political or military backgrounds, with the exception of Corazon Aquino, the president from 1986 to1992, who became politically active after her husband was assassinated.

Social Problems and Control. The formal system of law mirrors that of the United States. A police force, which has been part of the army since 1991, and a system of trials, appeals, and prisons are the components of the apparatus for dealing with crime. Theft is the most common crime. Because the Philippines has a cash economy, thieves and pickpockets can easily gain access to thousands of pesos. Petty thieves are unlikely to be apprehended unless a theft is discovered immediately. Another common crime is murder, which often is committed under the influence of alcohol. Guns are readily available. Incest is punished severely if the victim is younger than fifteen years old. Capital punishment by lethal injection was restored during the Ramos administration. Six executions of men convicted of incest have taken place since 1998. Illicit drugs are found throughout the archipelago but are more common

in the capital area and the tourist centers. Marijuana and hashish are exported.

An ongoing concern is the desire for autonomy among tribal groups. Mindanoao and the Cordilleras Autonomous Region, where indigenous groups are located, are allowed a greater degree of local control and receive additional funds from the government. Muslim Mindanao has a strong separatist movement. Terrorist groups have developed in support of the movement. In the year 2000, terrorists engaged in acts of kidnaping for ransom, a crime that is common in the country. The government deployed additional military forces to attack terrorist strongholds.

Military Activity. The armed forces consist of an army, a navy, a coast guard, and an air force. The army includes the Philippines National Police; the navy includes the marines. Military service is voluntary. Public respect for the military is high. Military expenditures account for 1.5 percent of the gross domestic product. Current military activity is focused on terrorist activity in Mindanao. The oil-rich Spratly Islands in the South China Sea are an area of concern that is monitored by the navy. The Spratlys belong to the Philippines but are claimed by several other countries, and the Chinese have unsuccessfully attempted to establish a base there. In 1998, the Philippines signed a visiting forces agreement that allows United States forces to enter the country to participate in joint training maneuvers.

SOCIAL WELFARE AND CHANGE PROGRAMS

Land reform has been a concern since independence. Spanish and American rule left arable land concentrated in the hands of 2 percent of the population and those owners will not give up their land without compensation. Attempts made to provide land, such as the resettlement of Christian farmers in Mindanao in the 1950s, have not provided enough land to resolve the problem. Until land reform takes place, poverty will be the nation's primary social problem. Eighty percent of the rural population and half the urban population live in poverty. Governmental organizations provide health clinics and medical services, aid in establishing micro businesses such as craft shops and small factories, and offer basic services for the disabled. The number of beggars increases in times of high unemployment. People consider it good luck to give money to a poor person, and so beggars manage to survive.

NONGOVERNMENTAL ORGANIZATIONS AND OTHER ASSOCIATIONS

While nongovernmental organizations (NGOs) work throughout the country to solve social problems, they are most visible in metropolitan Manila, where they work with squatters. The rural poor gravitate to urban areas, cannot find a place to live, and settle in public areas, riverbanks and garbage dumps. It is estimated that one of every four residents of metropolitan Manila is a squatter. Shanty towns are so large that in 2000, when rains from two successive typhoons made garbage dumps collapse, over two hundred people were buried alive as their homes were swept away. Nongovernmental organizations exert pressure on the government for land on which squatters can build permanent housing. Forced evictions are another target of NGOs, since an alternative place to live is not provided.

Volunteer agencies from the United States, the United Kingdom, the Netherlands, Germany, Denmark and Japan work with NGOs and governmental agencies. Projects to help children and meet environmental needs are the focus of volunteer efforts. Volunteer agencies are supervised by the Philippine National Volunteer Service Coordinating Agency.

A farmhouse overlooks vegetables growing on a terraced field. In these volcanic islands, mountains are common.

GENDER ROLES AND STATUSES

Division of Labor by Gender. Traditional roles prevail in rural areas, where men cultivate the land but the entire family is involved in planting and harvesting the crops. Women work in gardens and care for the house and children as well as barnyard animals. In urban areas, men work in construction and machine upkeep and as drivers of passenger vehicles. Women work as teachers, clerks, owners of *sari-sari* stores, marketers of produce and health care providers. Occupational gender lines are blurred since men also work as nurses and teachers. In the professions, gender lines are less important. Women attorneys, doctors and lawyers are found in the provinces as well as in urban areas.

The Relative Status of Women and Men. While families desire male children, females are welcomed to supply help in the house and provide a home in the parents' old age. Women's rights to equality and to share the family inheritance with male siblings are firmly established and are not questioned. The oldest daughter is expected to become an OSW to provide money for the education of younger siblings and for the needs of aging family members. Women are the familial money managers. The wedding ceremony can include the gift of a coin from the groom to the bride to acknowledge this role.

Since personal relationships and wealth are considered the road to success, women have an equal opportunity to achieve. Winners of beauty pageants are likely to succeed in the business and professional world, especially if the pageant was at an international level.

MARRIAGE, FAMILY AND KINSHIP

Marriage. Marriage is a civil ceremony that is conducted city offices. A religious ceremony also is performed. The ceremony is similar to those in the United States with the addition of sponsors. Principal sponsors are friends and relatives who have positions of influence in the community. The number of principal sponsors attests to the popularity and potential success of a couple. It also reduces a couple's expenses, since each principal sponsor is expected to contribute a substantial amount of cash. Members of the wedding party are secondary sponsors who do not have to provide funds.

Arranged marriages have not been part of Filipino life. However, men are expected to marry and if a man has not married by his late twenties, female relatives begin introducing him to potential brides. The median age for marriage is twenty-two. Young professionals wait until their late twenties to marry, and engagements of five to seven years are not uncommon. During this period, the couple becomes established in jobs, pays for the education of younger siblings, and acquires household items. A woman who reaches the age of thirty-two without marrying is considered past the age for marriage. Women believe that marriage to a wealthy man or a foreigner will guarantee happiness. Divorce is illegal, but annulment is available for the dissolution of a marriage. Reasons for annulment include physical incapacity, physical violence, or pressure to change one's religious or political beliefs. Interfaith marriages are rare.

Domestic Unit. The extended family is the most important societal unit, especially for women. Women's closest friendships come from within the family. Mothers and daughters who share a home make decisions concerning the home without conferring with male family members. One child remains in the family home to care for the parents and grandparents. This child, usually a daughter, is not necessarily unmarried. The home may include assorted children from the extended family, and single aunts and uncles. Several houses may be erected on the same lot to keep the family together.

Childcare is shared. Fathers carry and play with children but are unlikely to change diapers. Grandparents who live in the home are the primary care givers for the children since both parents generally work. Preschool grandchildren who live in other communities may be brought home for their grandparents to raise. Indigent relatives live in the family circle and provide as household and childcare help. Young people may work their way through college by exchanging work for room and board. Family bonds are so close that nieces and nephews are referred to as one's own children and cousins are referred to as sisters and brothers. Unmarried adult women may legally adopt one of a sibling's children.

Inheritance. Inheritance laws are based on those in the United States. These laws provide that all children acknowledged by a father, whether born in or out of wedlock, share equally in the estate. Females share equally with males.

Kin Groups. Because of the closeness of the immediate family, all familial ties are recognized. Anyone who is remotely related is known as a cousin. Indigenous tribes live in clan groups. Marriage into another clan may mean that the individual is considered dead to his or her clan.

People have a strong sense of belonging to a place. A family that has lived in metropolitan Manila for two generations still regards a municipality or province as its home. New Year's Day, Easter, and All Saint's Day are the most important family holidays. Bus traffic from Manila to the provinces increases dramatically at these times, with hundreds of extra buses taking people home to their families.

SOCIALIZATION

Infant Care. Infants are raised by family members. Young children are sent to live with their grandparents or aunts for extended periods. People who live outside the country leave their children with the family for the preschool years.

Infants spend their waking time in someone's arms until they can walk. They are part of every activity and learn by observation. Someone will remain in the room with them when they sleep. Infant mortality is high, and so great care is taken of babies. Helpers and older sisters assist with the day-to-day care of babies.

Child Rearing and Education. Children are seldom alone in a system in which adults desire com-

Workers spread rice on palm mats to dry in the midday sun. Filipinos do not consider a meal complete without rice.

pany and do not understand the need for privacy. Children have no pressure to become toilet trained or to learn to eat at the table. They are spoon fed or eat from a parent's plate until the age of six. They must learn respect for authority, obedience, and religious faith. Self-esteem is fostered. A child's first birthday is celebrated with a party.

Filipinos regard education as the path to upward mobility. Ninety percent of the population over ten years of age is literate. The Department of Education, Culture and Sports (DECS) is the largest governmental department. Approximately twelve million elementary school pupils and five million secondary students attended school in 1999 and 2000. Education is compulsory until age twelve. Statistics indicate that children from the poorest 40 percent of the population do not attend school. Elementary education is a six-year program; secondary education is a four-year program. Pre-schools and kindergartens are seldom available in public schools but are in private schools. Children are grouped homogeneously by ability. First grade students begin being taught in Filipino; English is added after two months. In elementary and secondary schools, reading, science, and mathematics are taught in English while values, social studies, and health are taught in Filipino. Children learn some Filipino and English words from the media. "Linga

franca" is an experimental approach in which students are taught in the native dialect and Filipino for the first two years and English in the third grade. This program came about as a response to concerns that English was being used more than were the native languages.

Elementary school, secondary school, and college students are required to wear uniforms. Girls wear pleated skirts and white blouses. Public school pupils wear dark blue skirts. Each private school has its own color. Boys wear white shirts and dark pants. Women teachers are given a government allowance to purchase four uniforms to wear Monday through Thursday. Men wear dark pants and a *barong*, a lightweight cotton shirt, or a polo shirt. Female teachers are addressed as ma'am (pronounced "mum"). Male teachers are addressed as sir. These titles are highly prized and are used by teachers in addressing one another.

Class sizes range from twenty to more than fifty in public schools. The goal is to keep class size below fifty. Pupils may have to share books and desks. Schools may lack electricity and have dirt floors or be flooded in the rainy season. The walls may not be painted. The Japanese, Chinese, and Australians have provided new classrooms, scientific supplies, and teacher training for the public schools. Private schools charge fees but have smaller class sizes. They have a reputation of providing a better education than do the public schools.

Computers are not readily available in elementary or secondary schools although DECS is stressing technology. President Estrada met with Bill Gates of Microsoft to procure computers and software for use in the schools.

Classrooms in both public and private schools have a picture of the Virgin Mary and the president at the front of the room. Grottoes to the Virgin Mary or a patron saint are found on school campuses. School days begin and end with prayer.

The school year runs from June to March to avoid the hot months of April and May. School starts at seven-thirty and ends at four-thirty with a break of one and a half hours for lunch. No meals are served at the school, although the parent-teacher association may run a stand that sells snacks for break time.

Dropping out is a serious concern. In 1999 and 2000, the high school dropout rate increased from 9 percent to 13 percent. The increase is attributed to the need to provide care for younger siblings or to get a job to enable the family to survive the high inflation and the currency devaluation that followed the Asian financial crisis. The DECS has a Non-Formal Education Division to meet the needs of out-of-school youth as well as the needs of uneducated adults. Programs include adult literacy, agriculture and farm training, occupational skills, and training in health and nutrition. Programs for at-risk youth are being added at the high school level. The Open High School System Act of 2000 is designed to provide distance learning via television for youths and uneducated adults.

Higher Education. A college degree is necessary to obtain positions that promise security and advancement. Approximately two million students attend colleges and universities. Each province has a state college system with several locations. The University of the Philippines, located in Manila, is a public university that is regarded as the best in the country. Private colleges are found in the major municipalities. The University of Santo Tomas in Manila is a private school that was established in 1611; it is the oldest site of higher education in the country. English is the primary language of instruction at the college level. Colleges and universities have large enrollments for advanced degrees since a four year degree may not be sufficient to work in the higher levels of government service.

ETIQUETTE

People believe that it is one's duty to keep things operating smoothly. It is very important not to lose face. Being corrected or correcting another person in public is not considered acceptable behavior. People want to grant all requests, and so they often say yes when they mean no or maybe. Others understand when the request is not fulfilled because saying no might have caused the individual to lose face. When one is asked to join a family for a meal, the offer must be refused. If the invitation is extended a second time, it is permissible to accept. Time consciousness and time management are not important considerations. A planned meeting may take place later, much later, or never.

Filipinos walk hand in hand or arm in arm with relatives and friends of either sex as a sign of affection or friendship. Women are expected not to cross their legs or drink alcohol in public. Shorts are not common wear for women.

People pride themselves on hospitality. They readily go out of their way to help visitors or take them to their destination. It is of the highest importance to recognize the positions of others and use full titles and full names when introducing or referring to people. Non-verbal language, such as pointing to an object with one's lips, is a key element in communication. One greets friends by lifting the eyebrows. A longer lift can be used to ask a question.

RELIGION

Religious Beliefs. The Philippines is the only Christian nation in Asia. More than 85 percent of the people are Roman Catholic. The rosary is said in the home at 9 P.M., just before the family retires for the night. Children are introduced to the statue of "Mama Mary" at a very early age.

Protestant missionaries arrived in 1901 and followed the Catholic example of establishing hospitals, clinics, and private schools. The Church of the Latter Day Saints (Mormons) is currently the most active missionary group.

Sunni Muslims constitute the largest non-Christian group. They live in Mindanao and the Sulu Islands but have migrated to other provinces. Muslim provinces celebrate Islamic religious holidays as legal holidays. Mosques are located in large cities throughout the country. In smaller communities, Muslims gather in small buildings for services. Animism, a belief that natural objects have souls, is the oldest religion in the country, practiced by indigenous peoples in the mountains of Luzon.

A roundabout with a fountain sits between old buildings in Manila. Some areas of the city were destroyed during World War II, when the country was invaded by Japan and then liberated by the United States.

Freedom of religion is guaranteed by the constitution. The disagreement between the Muslim population of the southern provinces and the federal government is not so much about religion as it is about political goals. Non-Catholics do not object to Catholic symbols or prayer in public venues.

Each barangay has a patron saint. The saint's day is celebrated by a fiesta that includes a religious ceremony. Large amounts of food are served at each house. Friends and relatives from other barangays are invited and go from house to house to enjoy the food. A talent show, beauty contest, and dance are part of the fun. Carnival rides and bingo games add to the festivities.

Religious Practitioners. Religious leaders are powerful figures. Business and political leaders court Cardinal Jaime Sin because of his influence with much of the population. Local priest and ministers are so highly respected that requests from them take on the power of mandates. A family considers having a son or daughter with a religious career as a high honor. Personal friendships with priests, ministers, and nuns are prized. Clerics take an active role in the secular world. An example is Brother Andrew Gonzales, the current secretary of DECS.

Faith healers cure illness by prayer or touch. "Psychic" healers operate without using scalpels or drawing blood. The several thousand healers are Christians. They believe that if they ask for a fee, their power will disappear. Patients are generous with gifts because healers are greatly respected.

Rituals and Holy Places. The major rituals are customary Christian or Muslim practices. Sites where miracles have taken place draw large crowds on Sundays and feast days. Easter is the most important Christian observance. On Easter weekend, the entire Christian area of the country is shut down from noon on Maundy Thursday until the morning of Black Saturday. International flights continue and hospitals are open, but national television broadcasts, church services, and shops and restaurants are closed and public transportation is sparse. People stay at home or go to church. Special events take place on Good Friday. There are religious processions such as a parade of the statues of saints throughout the community.

Death and the Afterlife. A twenty-four-hour vigil is held at the deceased person's home, and the body is escorted to the cemetery after the religious ceremony. The tradition is for mourners to walk behind the coffin. A mausoleum is built during the lifetime of the user. The size of the edifice indicates the position of the builder.

Mourning is worn for six weeks after the death of a family member. It may consists of a black pin worn on the blouse or shirt of the mourner or black clothing. Mourning is put aside after one year. A meal or party is provided for family members and close friends one year after the burial to commemorate recognize the memory of the deceased.

All Saint's Day (1 November) is a national holiday to honor the dead. Grave sites are cleared of debris and repaired. Families meet at the cemetery and stay throughout the twenty-four hours. Candles and flowers are placed on the graves. Food and memories are shared, and prayers are offered for the souls of the dead. When a family member visits a grave during the year, pebbles are placed on the grave to indicate that the deceased has been remembered.

MEDICINE AND HEALTH CARE

Life expectancy is seventy years for females and sixty-four years for males. The Health Care Law of

Painted Jeepneys on a city street.

1995 provides citizens with basic health care at no cost through subsidies. The working poor are given financial assistance when necessary. Children receive inoculations at no cost. The World Health Organization (WHO) declared the Philippines to be polio-free in 2000. It is the first nation in the world to be recognized for the elimination of polio.

Regional public hospitals provide service to everyone. People who live far away ride a bus for hours to reach the hospital. Funds for ambulances are raised by lotteries within each barangay or are provided by congressmen and are used only for the people who live in that area. Private hospitals are considered superior to public hospitals. Paying patients are not discharged from hospitals until the bill is paid in full. Patients have *kasamas* (companions) who remain with them during the hospital stay. Kasamas assist with nursing chores by giving baths, getting food trays, taking samples to the nurses' station and questioning the doctor. A bed but no food is provided for the kasama in the hospital room.

The infant mortality rate is 48.9 percent, and one-third of the children are malnourished. Over 13 percent of preschool and elementary school children are underweight. A government program provides nutritious food for impoverished pupils at the midmorning break. This is only offered to schools in the poorest areas. National test scores are examined to see if improvement has occurred. If the scores are better, the program is expanded.

The most prevalent health problem is "high blood" (hypertension). One in ten persons over the age of fifteen has high blood pressure. Tuberculosis is another health concern; The country has the fourth highest mortality rate in the world from that disease. Malaria and dengue fever are prevalent because there is no effective program for mosquito control. The number of deaths attributed to dengue increased in the late 1990s.

Herbal remedies are used alone or in conjunction with prescribed medications. A dog bite treated with antibiotics and rabies shots also may be treated with garlic applied to the puncture. The study of herbal remedies is part of the school health curriculum. Many elementary schools have herb gardens that are planted and cared for by the students.

SECULAR CELEBRATIONS

New Year's Day is more of a family holiday than Christmas. It is combined with Rizal Day on 30 December to provide time for people to go home to their province. Midnight on New Year's Eve brings an outburst of firecrackers and gunfire from randomly aimed firearms.

Other national secular holidays are Fall of Bataan Day, an observation of the Bataan Death March in 1942 on 9 April. Labor Day is celebrated on 1 May. Independence Day on 12 June celebrates freedom from Spanish rule. It is celebrated with fiestas, parades, and fireworks. Sino-Filipinos celebrate the Chinese New Year, which is not a national holiday, in January or February. In Manila, fireworks and parades take place throughout Chinatown. Muslims celebrate Islamic festivals.

ARTS AND HUMANITIES

Support for the Arts. The government provides support for institutions such as the National Museum in Manila. Libraries exists in colleges and universities. The best collections are in Manila. Museums are located in provincial capitals and in Manila. The Cultural Center of the Philippines in Manila is a center for the performing arts that opened in 1970. It is a multibuilding complex created under the direction of former first lady Imelda Marcos, who encouraged musicians to enter the international community and receive additional training. Nongovernmental organizations preserve the folk heritage of the indigenous groups.

Literature. Literature is based on the oral traditions of folklore, the influence of the church and Spanish and American literature. Filipino written literature became popular in the mid-nineteenth century as the middle class became educated. The greatest historical literature evolved from the independence movement. José Rizal electrified the country with his novels. During the early years of American control, literature was written in English. The English and American literature that was taught in the schools was a factor in the kind of writing that was produced. Writing in Filipino languages became more common in the late 1930s and during the Japanese occupation. Literature is now written in both Filipino and English. Textbooks contain national and world literature.

Graphic Arts. The Filipino Academy of Art, established in 1821, shows early art reflecting Spanish and religious themes. Juan Luna and Felix Hidalgo were the first Filipino artists to win recognition in Europe at the end of the nineteenth century. Contemporary artists use a variety of techniques and mediums to reflect social and political life. Crafts reflect the national culture. Each area of the country has specialties that range from the batik cotton prints of the Muslim areas to the wood carvings of the mountain provinces of Luzon. Baskets and mats are created from rattan. Textiles are woven by hand in cooperatives, storefronts, and homes. Banana and pineapple fiber cloth, cotton, and wool are woven into textiles. Furniture and decorative items are carved. Silver and shell crafts also are created

Sex and violence are major themes in films, which are often adaptations of American screen productions. American films are popular and readily available, and so high-quality Filipino films have been slow to develop.

Performance Arts. Drama before Spanish colonization was of a religious nature and was intended to persuade the deities to provide the necessities of life. The Spanish used drama to introduce the Catholic religion. Filipino themes in drama developed in the late nineteenth century as the independence movement evolved. Current themes are nationalistic and reflect daily life.

Dance is a mixture of Filipino and Spanish cultures. Professional dance troupes perform ballet, modern dance, and folk dance. Folk dances are performed at meetings and conferences and reflect a strong Spanish influence. Indigenous dances are used in historical pageants. An example is a bamboo dance relating a story about a bird moving among the reeds. People enjoy ballroom dancing for recreation. Dance instructors are available at parties to teach the waltz and the cha-cha.

Music performance begins in the home and at school. Amateur performances featuring song and dance occur at fiestas. Popular music tends to be American. Guitars are manufactured for export; folk instruments such as the nose flute also are constructed.

THE STATE OF THE PHYSICAL AND SOCIAL SCIENCES

The physical sciences focus on the needs of the country. Aquaculture, the development of fish and shellfish farms in coastal areas, is a rapidly growing field. Centuries of fishing and dynamiting fish have changed the balance of nature. Hormonal research to stimulate the growth of fish and shellfish is a priority. Control of red tide, an infestation that makes shellfish unsafe to eat, is another area of concentration. Agricultural research and research into volcano and earthquake control are other areas of study. The development of geothermal and other energy sources is ongoing. Other environmental research areas of importance are waste resource management, water resource management, and forest management. The social sciences are focused on the needs of the country with the primary emphasis on resolving the problems of poverty and land reform.

BIBLIOGRAPHY

Department of Education, Culture and Sports. *Fact Sheet*, 2000.

Europa World Factbook, 1999.

Goodno, James R. *Philippines: The Land of Broken Promises*, 1991.

Karnow, Stanley. *In our Image: America's Empire in the Philippines*, 1989.

Oleksy, Walter. *The Philippines*, 2000.

Peters, Jens. *Philippines*, 1997.

Roces, Alfredo. *Culture Shock: Philippines*, 1999.

Schirmer, Daniel B., ed. *The Philippines: A History of Colonialism*, 1987.

Sonneborn, Liz. *The Philippines*, 1988.

Sullivan, Margaret W. *The Philippines: Pacific Crossroads*, 1993.

Thompson, W. Scott. *The Philippines in Crisis*, 1992.

Timberman, David G. *Philippines Today: The Challenge*, 1996.

Tope, Lily Rose. *Philippines*, 1991.

U.S. Department of the Army. *Philippines: A country study*, 1991.

Web Sites

Country Watch *Philippines*, 2000, http://www.countryside.com

National Statistics Office, Income and Employment Statistics. *Annual Poverty Indication Survey*, 1999, http://www.nso.census.gov.ph

U.S. Department of Health.*Health Care Law of 1995*, 1999, http://www.doh.gov.ph

U.S. Department of State. *Background Notes: Philippines*, 1998.

U.S. Department of State, Central Intelligence Agency. *World Factbook 2000*, http://www.odci.gov/cia/publications/factbook/geos/rp.html

U.S. Library of Congress. *Philippines: A country study*, 1999, http://lcweb2.loc.gov

—SALLY E. BARINGER

POLAND

CULTURE NAME
Polish

ALTERNATIVE NAMES
Polanie, Polen, Poliane, Pologne, Polonia, Polska, Republic of Poland, and Rzeczpospolita Polska

ORIENTATION

Identification. Polanie was derived in the tenth century from the name of a Slavonic tribe near Poznan. It means dwellers or people of the field, meadow, or plain.

There are five Polish regional cultural traditions with associated dialects. Poles residing abroad could be considered as a sixth group. Regional cultural differences, identification, and dialects are becoming increasingly less noticeable and less important.

Location and Geography. Poland is located in Central Europe. It covers 120,700 square miles (312,680 square kilometers). On the north Poland is bordered by the Baltic Sea, Russia, and Lithuania; on the east by Belarus and Ukraine; on the south by Slovakia and the Czech Republic; and on the west by Germany. Originally, the capital was Cracow (Kraków), but in 1611 it was moved to Warsaw (Warszawa), the current seat of government.

Seventy-five percent of the land lies below 650 feet (200 meters). The Baltic Sea forms a natural northern border, and the Sudetes and Carpathians form the southern border. Poland does not have any natural borders on the east or west. Polish wars and large scale changes in the borders, both ethnically and politically, have been to the east and west while the northern and southern borders have changed little over the past one thousand years.

Demography. In 2000, the estimated population was about 39.4 million. Of this, 38.1 to 38.5 million were ethnic Poles. Worldwide there are an addi-

tional 13 million Poles who live abroad. Due to Poland's history of shifting borders and the changes over time in the ethnic policies pursued by both foreign and Polish governments, it is difficult to establish the exact size of ethnic groups. Many individuals have the right to claim membership in several groups while others may not wish to have their ethnic affiliation recorded.

The largest ethnic minorities include approximately 400,000 Germans and perhaps an equal number of Ukrainians, followed by 275,000 Belarussians, then 25,000 Roma (Gypsies), and 13,500 Lithuanians. The over three million people of the Jewish population that inhabited Poland before World War II has been reduced to some six thousand to ten thousand people.

Linguistic Affiliation. Polish belongs to the west Slavic group of languages of the Indo-European language family, which in turn is part of the Nostratic macrofamily. Poles use the Latin alphabet. Literary Polish developed during the sixteenth century and is based on the speech of educated city people, upper class usage, and the Great Polish and Little Polish Dialects. Starting in the nineteenth century, technological and cultural changes introduced a new vocabulary. During the 1920s and 1930s, there was an attempt to coin and introduce a Polish-derived vocabulary for the newly diffused technology. Otherwise, the new vocabulary is taken from German, Latin, Russian, and English. The spelling of diffused words is changed to reflect the Polish alphabet.

Geographical areas have distinct speech patterns. Most Poles can identify people's places of origin by their speech. The major dialects are: Great Polish in the northwest centered on Poznań; Kuyavian, east of "Great Poland"; and Little Polish, around Cracow. Kashubian, with about 200,000 speakers along the Baltic coast, has its own orthography and literature. The Slovincian dialect of Kashubian could be considered a separate language.

Poland

A similar linguistic separation can be made regarding the Górale, or ''Highlanders,'' of Podhale. The Mazurians and Silesians, in areas that before World War II were politically separated from Poland, spoke an archaic Polish with many words and expressions borrowed from German. Starting in 1918 with the regaining of Polish independence, the leveling influences of school, the military, mass media, urbanization, and mass migration of population have reduced the differences between regional dialects so that spoken and written language is nearly standardized.

Symbolism. Poland's flag consists of two equal-sized horizontal bars. The upper bar is white and the lower red. The coat-of-arms is a white eagle on a red field. Legend has it that while hunting the first king of the Poles encountered a huge white eagle making a strange cry and hovering over a nest of young. Such white birds were not known in the land and

the King took it as an omen. The national anthem, *Jeszcze Polska nie Zginęła* (''Poland Has Not Yet Perished''), was written in 1797 by an émigré soldier-poet, Józef Wybicki, serving in the Polish legions of Napoleon Bonaparte's army in Italy. It was adopted in 1918.

Polish identity is rooted in its past. Some see Poland as the bulwark of Christendom. If the Poles had not defeated the Muslim Crimean Tatars and Turks during King Jan III Sobieski's raising of the Turkish siege of Vienna in 1683, Christianity would have been supplanted by Islam. Poland's role as guardian of western European civilization against the Russians and later the Bolsheviks is commemorated by the Tomb of the Unknown Soldier in the center of Warsaw.

Others view Poland as the suffering Christ among nations raising the torch of liberty and independence for themselves and others. This position is exemplified in the slogan "For your freedom and ours" and popularized by Polish romantics such as authors Zygmunt Krasiński, Adam Mickiewicz, and Juliusz Słowacki, as well as musician Frédéric Chopin and political leaders such as Józef Piłsudski.

There is an emotional bond between the Catholic Church and Poles. This bond was formed because for the last several centuries Poland's main enemies were Orthodox Russians and Protestant Germans. In this context, a Pole was a Catholic and a Catholic was a Pole. The bond was strengthened because individuals persecuted by the authorities could seek succor and solace from the Church. Further, during communist times, the Church was the one institution that presented an independent voice.

HISTORY AND ETHNIC RELATIONS

Poland is an example par excellence of the imagined community and of the ability of nationalism to shape the world. Poland exists because individuals voluntarily fought for a free and united Poland. History is one of the themes used to create a commonality and a feeling of pride. Poles consider themselves to be members of a community.

Emergence of the Nation. No one knows when or where the ancestors of modern Poles originated. It is clear that they were living somewhere on the Eurasian continent and diverged from other Slavs. However, there is no certainty regarding their presence east of the Elbe and Oder Rivers before the eighth century.

The traditional date for the founding of the Polish state is the beginning of written Polish history in 956 C.E., when Prince Mieszko I married a Bohemian princess and accepted Christianity. Mieszko's son, Bolesław Chrobry (Bolesław the Brave), was the first crowned Polish king. His armies reached Prague and Kiev and exemplified the next one thousand years of Polish history. At times, the Poles fought with the Swedes and Balts to the north, and the Czechs and Turks to the south, but there was almost constant strife with the Germans to the west and the Russian states to the east. Sometimes the wars were between only two enemies, and sometimes two would join in attacking the third. In 1226, Prince Conrad of Mazovia, Poland, invited the Teutonic Knights, a primarily German crusading order, to help fight the Prussians, a group of Balts living in what eventually became East Prussia. In 1382, the Lithuanian Grand Duke Jagiello (Jogailo) married Jadwiga of Anjou, a Polish princess who was crowned king [sic] in Cracow in 1385. This marriage joined Lithuania and Poland in a personal union, wherein one individual rules two states. The Treaty of Lublin, 1569, created the Republic of Poland-Lithuania. At its peak in 1634–1635, the Polish-Lithuanian Commonweath stretched from the Baltic to the Black Seas and encompassed Latvia, Lithuania, and much of present day Poland, Belarus, Ukraine, and Estonia, as well as scattered territories in some other countries. Political and territorial decline then set in.

The nobility held absolute power of life and death over the serfs tied to their land. The clergy, merchants in the cities (the burghers), and the Jews were protected by royal charters, but were a minuscule portion of the population. After 1572, Poland's kings were elected *viritim*; that is, they were voted upon directly by the mounted assembly of the entire nobility. The kings acted more like managers than rulers. In 1652, the *Sejm*, Poland's parliament, introduced the *liberum veto*, which mandated that all legislation had to pass unanimously. The country lost independence and unity when Austria, Prussia, and Russia divided the Polish-Lithuanian Commonwealth among themselves. The country was divided on three occasions, in 1772, 1793, and 1795.

For brief periods, there were two small Polish states under foreign domination. The first Polish state was the Duchy of Warsaw, 1807–1813, created by Napoleon from Prussian territory inhabited by Poles. The second, with limited territory and sovereignty, was established at the Congress of Vienna. The Congress Kingdom, 1815–1864, was ruled by the Russian czar in a personal union. After an unsuccessful insurrection, it was incorporated into Russia as a province.

Poland declared independence in 1918. World War I was ending and the partitioning powers were collapsing. Austria disintegrated and Imperial Germany was weakened. Russia had survived two revolutions and was in the midst of a civil war. The Poles defeated the Germans and the Federal Socialist Republic of the Russian Soviets, the precursor of the Soviet Union. Between 1918 and 1939, the Polish government worked to unify the country economically, politically, socially, and ethnically.

On 1 September 1939, Germany attacked Poland and, seventeen days later, so did the Soviet Union. The zones of occupation had been demarcated in the Hitler-Stalin Pact of 23 August 1939. Most of the Polish military personnel became prisoners of war. However, some escaped to neutral countries, and others were able to reach England or France where they continued fighting against the Germans. Some stayed in Poland and became guerilla fighters, forming the nucleus of the Home Army (AK) with allegiance to the government in exile in London.

Both occupying powers ruled harshly. The Germans attempted to kill all Roma, Jews, and educated Poles. The Nazi intent was to reduce Poles to unskilled laborers. The Soviet killed twenty-two thousand Polish officers and deported 1.5 million civilians, primarily the educated and business people, to Siberia.

After Germany attacked the Soviet Union on 22 June 1941, the Soviets raised a Polish army. Two divisions totaling seventy-five thousand men transferred to the Middle East in 1942 and eventually fought in Italy. Others founded the army of Communist Poland.

In 1944, the Polish Home Army staged an uprising in Warsaw. Receiving no Soviet assistance, the uprising was crushed. The Germans then razed much of Warsaw, singling out structures of historical importance.

In 1945, Poland regained political unity, albeit as a Soviet satellite. The country had to cede some of its eastern territory to the Soviet Union and, as compensation, acquired territory that had been German in 1939. Poland, for the first time in its history, did not have significant ethnic and religious minority populations. In 1989, the Soviets no longer supported the Polish Communist government, and the Poles began a shift to democracy and a market economy.

National Identity. Polish nationalism fed on the country's history of deprivation and want. It has a militant and even truculent attitude. There is a feeling that Poles have been suffering unduly.

The first manifestation of Polish nationalism was during the Confederation of Bar in 1768 when there was an attempt to reform the political system. In the Constitution of 3 May 1791, the burghers were enfranchised to expand the definition of the nation. General Tadeusz Kościuszko's Manifesto of Polaniec in 1794 took the first steps to include the largest group of the population, the peasants.

Until 1795, the Polish-Lithuanian Commonwealth had to integrate and unify a state made up of many ethnic and religious groups. The term nation was used to refer only to the politically powerful multi-ethnic nobility. Since the nobles constituted some 8 to 12 percent of the population, this meant that the vast majority was excluded.

In 1795, the issue became how to leave multiethnic empires, on what basis to form and deter-mine the boundaries of the reconstituted state, and how to govern it. Because of repression and unsuccessful revolts, many Poles, in order to escape imprisonment or to obtain a university education, went abroad and were exposed to French and German ideas. Many adopted the position that a nation is like a kin group with common descent, language, and culture, and that it has a right by primordial occupancy to its native soil. They adopted the ideology that ethnic groups have a right to an independent state, that a state's population should be composed of members of a single nation, and that a state should encompass all members of the ethnic group.

The Nationalists, led by Roman Dmowski, conceived the nation as a distinct ethnic community which had an inalienable right to its ancestral territory. They saw the German empire as the principal enemy and were prepared to accept national autonomy under Russian suzerainty. Domestically they were strident, harsh, and intolerant, especially to other ethnic groups.

The independence camp, led by Piłsudski, conceived the nation as a spiritual community united by culture and history. They were prepared to fight all who stood in the way of Polish independence. They saw Russia as the principal enemy and were prepared to cooperate with Austria and Germany. Domestically they were relatively mild and tolerant.

Today the popular feeling is that a Pole is anyone who has Polish ancestry and exhibits Polish cultural traits, speaks Polish, and acts according to Polish norms.

Ethnic Relations. After 1939, due to the Soviet and German genocides, changes in the country's boundaries, migration, and the expulsion of ethnic peoples by the Communist government of Poland, the country became an almost monoethnic society. Current estimates of the combined non-Polish ethnic populations range between less than one million to more than two million, or between 2 and 5.5 percent of the country's inhabitants.

Some fifteen ethnic groups are numerous enough to be recognized and to appear in statistics. The Germans, Belarussians, Ukrainians, Lithuanians, and Jews have states where members of their nationality are the majority and can be appealed to for political help.

The Belarussians and Lithuanians are the indigenous people in Poland's northeast. Both groups have adjacent states where their ethnic group constitutes the majority. Both groups have schools that teach in their respective languages. Because of a

In the center of Krakow's main market square is the mid-16th century Cloth Hall, built in the middle of the Renaissance.

history of emigration, many Lithuanians have relatives in the United States.

For the past one thousand years, Germans and Poles have at times fought wars and ruled one another. In 1945, the Poles expelled five million Germans living in areas which were formerly part of Germany. The Germans remaining in Poland are the largest physical presence and most important political minority in the country.

For centuries, the Poles have ruled territories inhabited by the Ukrainians. In 1947, as a way of crushing the Ukrainian resistance movement, the majority of the population was transferred from their homeland in southeastern Poland to scattered locations in the western territories taken over from Germany. As a result, many Ukrainians assimilated into Polish society.

The Roma came to Poland in the sixteenth century. They were one of the groups the Nazis attempted to exterminate. In 1994, the Association of the Roma in Poland organized an observance of the Nazi actions at the Auschwitz concentration camp. A growing number of Roma have entered Poland since 1990.

The earliest record of a Jew in Poland is in a letter written in 977 C.E. from the Pope instructing the king not to be overly friendly to a Jew. The first ghetto in Poland was created in the fourteenth century when Jews from Spain and Western Europe immigrated and asked for a sector of the city where they could live according to their religion and laws. The request was granted by King Kazimierz III. Until the beginning of the seventeenth century, the Polish-Lithuanian Commonwealth was tolerant toward the Jews and even invited them to come and settle. The relationship deteriorated as the fortunes of the Commonwealth declined, and there was a massive immigration of Jews from Germany, and later, from Lithuania and Russia. Relations were exacerbated by the Russian czarist policy of discrimination against Jews and stirring up ethnic antagonisms. The first organized anti-semitic pogrom was in 1881. The last one was on 4 July 1946 in Kielce when forty-two Jews were killed. During World War II, the Soviet Union deported people to central Asia and the Nazis operated death camps. Of the more than three million Jews in Poland in 1939, ninety thousand were left by the end of the war. The government-sponsored anti-semitic campaign of 1968–1969 drove out most of those who remained.

Prior to 1989, the Communist government at times denied the very existence of national minorities in Poland. When minorities were recognized, each acknowledged minority could be represented by only one organization and with one publication. As a result, between 1956 and 1981, there were only six organizations. After 1989, the right to free association resulted in the establishment of approximately two hundred ethnic organizations. There is legislation establishing the right to study and be taught in one's native language. Likewise, minorities have the right to access mass media, including local public radio and television, and to use their native language in broadcasting.

Since 1993, minority parties are exempt from the requirement that political parties must get a specified percentage of votes to obtain membership in the Sejm. On the local level, minorities have the right to participate in self-government. Little is known about how the laws and regulations are actually implemented.

As of 1995, there are a half million illegal aliens in Poland. Most of them came from eastern Europe and the former Soviet Union.

URBANISM, ARCHITECTURE, AND THE USE OF SPACE

The vast majority of the urban population lives in apartments and relies on mass transportation. The increasing ownership and use of private automobiles has produced associated traffic and parking problems.

In most Polish cities, there are three types of areas or "cities." The "socialist city" was constructed after World War II to accommodate the influx of people caused by industrialization. The general appearance of this city was heavily influenced by what was in practice in the Soviet Union. The city has broad streets and large public spaces. Housing consists of four- or five-story apartment buildings. Typically, construction was shoddy. Apartments commonly consist of two or three rooms plus a kitchen and a bathroom. All apartments have access to gas, electricity, and municipal water and most have central heating. There is minimal space for parking and children's play. The center of the city is devoted to government buildings, not to commercial outlets and the service sector. Places of employment, especially industry, are located some distance from dwellings.

The "capitalist/industrial city" was constructed during the nineteenth century and up to 1939. Architecturally, western European influences are noted. One difference from the "socialist city" is that the buildings represent a great variety of archi-

tectural characteristics. The interior space is much less standardized. Much space is devoted to commercial activities and, in the older parts of the city, industrial plants abut residential areas.

The "medieval city" was built during the feudal period. Building styles and town plans reflect practices and theories current in western Europe at that time. Most of the surviving structures are palaces or public buildings. Only a very few houses of merchants or people of modest means still exist.

Polish cities suffered heavy damage during World War II. Some, such as Gdańsk, Szczeczin, and Wrocław, were heavily damaged by fighting, and the Germans deliberately razed most of Warsaw. Consequently, buildings and areas that appear ancient are often products of post-World War II construction. This was done by the Communist government to emphasize the nation's will to survive despite attempts to destroy it.

FOOD AND ECONOMY

Food in Daily Life. The mainstays of the Polish diet are meat, bread, and potatoes. For many Poles, dinner is not dinner without meat, primarily pork. Bread is consumed and treated with reverence. In the past, if a piece of bread fell on the ground, it was picked up with reverence, kissed, and used to make the sign of a cross. Peasants trace a cross on the bottom of a loaf of bread with a knife before slicing it. Poles consume three-hundred pounds of potatoes per capita per year. Vegetables consumed are local cool weather crops such as beets, carrots, cabbage and legumes (beans, peas, lentils). Another important source of nutrition is milk in various forms such as fresh or sour milk, sour cream, buttermilk, whey, cheese, and butter.

The Polish daily meal sequence is dependent upon the family and the season; however, typically it starts with a substantial breakfast eaten between five and eight A.M.. Eggs, meat, bread, cheese, and cold cuts may be served. Between nine and eleven in the morning, people may have a second breakfast similar to an American bag lunch. Dinner, the main meal of the day, is served between one and five in the afternoon and contributes 40 to 45 percent of the calories for the day. It consists of a large bowl of soup, a main course, and dessert. Salads, when served, are eaten with the main course. On Sundays, appetizers may start the meal. The last meal of the day is a light supper eaten between six and eight in the evening. It may be a repeat of the breakfast menu or include cold fresh water fish, aspic dishes, and cooked vegetable salads. Addition-

A wooden house in Czerwinsk.

ally, there may be a sweet dish such as pancakes or rice baked with apples or other fruit.

Tea and coffee are served after meals. People differentiate between tea made from tea leaves and that made from herbs or fruits. In many dialects, the two types of teas have different names. Tea is consumed more frequently and coffee is viewed as slightly special. Vodka was first distilled in Poland in the sixteenth century and is consumed with food, commonly sausage, dill pickles, or herring, as a chaser.

Food Customs at Ceremonial Occasions. Namedays and weddings center on individuals. Because common first names are noted in published calendars along with holidays, people know when to acknowledge an individual's nameday. Such celebrations typically feature poultry, cakes, and other party foods. At weddings, the bride and groom are greeted with bread and salt (the essentials of life) upon their return from church.

The Christmas season is the traditional time for baking cookies, honey-spice cakes, and cheese-dough apple cakes. Among the oldest and most traditional Christmas treats are honey-rye wafers and poppy seed or nut crunch. *Babka*, a cake, is another traditional dish that must be taller than it is wide and it must be narrower at the top than at the bottom.

The most solemn family gathering of the year is the Christmas Eve supper. Family gather to share the *opłatek*, a thin white wafer sometimes called angel bread, followed by an odd number of meatless dishes. However, fish is permitted. Traditional dishes include noodles with poppy seeds and wheat pudding.

For Christmas Day dinner, many feel that game adds a special touch of the outdoors and make a special effort to obtain half a hare for the pâté.

Pączki (Polish style donuts) are the traditional pastry eaten on Shrove Tuesday and on Fat Thursday (the beginning of the pre-Lenten Mardi Gras season). At Easter the tradition is to consume food blessed on Holy Saturday. One standard item is hard-boiled eggs. Easter breakfast features fresh meat, game, and smoked meats. There is a tradition of roasted suckling pig with a red egg in its snout.

During fall harvest festivals, the fruits of the fields are blessed, and cereals and bread made from freshly threshed wheat are eaten as well as placed on graves on All Saint's Day. On Saint Martin's Day, the traditional food is a goose.

Basic Economy. Poland is changing from an economy where the state sector, dominated to one where the economy is controlled privately. In 1989, 95 per-

Produce and shoe merchants at a market in Plock.

cent of those employed were in the state sector, which generated 90 percent of the gross domestic product (GDP) and received 85 percent of individuals' investment funds. By 1997, 67 percent of those employed were in the private sector, which was producing 63 percent of the GDP. In 1999, the private sector, generated about 70 percent of economic activity.

In 1996, 44 percent of those employed were in service occupations, 30 percent in industry and construction, and 26 percent in agriculture. The latter produces only 5 percent of the GDP. Polish farms are small, inefficient, lack capital, and have surplus labor. The main products are potatoes, fruits, vegetables, wheat, poultry, eggs, pork, beef, milk, and cheese. The average farm sells most of its products and buys about a fourth of the food consumed by the family.

Land Tenure and Property. While a few state farms remain, the vast majority of farm land is privately owned. City apartments are being privatized. Most of the industrial enterprises in the politically "sensitive sectors" such as coal, steel, telecommunications, aviation, and banks are still owned by the government.

Commercial Activities. Poland produces agricultural products, minerals, coal, salt, sulfur, copper,

manufactured, goods, glass, textiles, beverages, machinery, and ships.

Major Industries. Between 1945 and 1989, the government's centralized planning system mobilized resources but could not ensure their efficient use. It made huge strides in helping to develop heavy industry but neglected farming, consumer goods, and housing. Their efforts also hurt the environment. After 1989, there was a reduction of the state-owned sector balanced by the development of the private. Poland has privatized medium and small state-owned enterprises and passed a liberal law for the establishment of new companies. The major industries are machine building, iron and steel, coal mining, chemicals, shipbuilding, food processing, glass, beverages, and textiles.

Trade. Since 1989, the main effort has been to shift Poland's international trade from countries that were part of the Soviet Union and its erstwhile satellites to other countries, especially member states of the EU.

By 1997, Poland exported mainly to Germany, Russia, Italy, Ukraine, the Netherlands, and France. Its main exports are manufactured goods, chemicals, machinery and equipment, food, and live animals, and mineral fuels. It imports primarily from

Germany, Italy, Russia, France, United Kingdom, and the United States. Poland's main imports are manufactured goods, chemicals, machinery and equipment, mineral fuels, food, and live animals.

Division of Labor. In the cities, both men and women are employed outside the home. However, there is a male bias in employment. Proportionately, more women are unemployed than men. In rural areas, women participate fully in farm work, both in the fields and in the house. Additionally, women operate a large number of farms.

Polish women perform "the second shift"; the phenomenon of simultaneously managing an external job and a household. Shopping, especially for groceries, and housework are considered women's jobs. A man will do almost anything not to cook, wash dishes, or clean house.

SOCIAL STRATIFICATION

The strong and rigid social stratification that marked Poland prior to 1939 has all but disappeared. This has happened because during World War II, both the Nazis and the Communists deliberately killed educated Poles. At the end of the war, the intelligentsia was greatly reduced in numbers. For forty-five years, the Communist government pursued policies intended to reduce social classes. They fostered education and the economic and educational advancement of peasants and workers. With the government's success in creating industrial jobs, there has been a great movement of rural people to cities.

Classes and Castes. Currently there are six strata or groupings: peasants, workers, intelligentsia, *szlachta* (nobles or gentry), the *nomenclatura* (the ruling group during the existence of the communist government), and a nascent middle class. The workers and intelligentsia have increased both numerically and proportionately. The ruling class that held power during Communist rule is fighting to regain political power and maintain economic power. The szlachta may still constitute some 10 to 15 percent of the population, but their significance has been practically eliminated. People starting businesses are just beginning to differentiate themselves.

Symbols of Social Stratification. During Communist rule, the general population assumed many of the customs of the szlachta. Thus, the common way of addressing someone is as *pan* (male) or *pani* (female), terms that formerly were used among and toward members of the szlachta. For people who are

above the peasant and worker classes, men kiss women's hands and follow current fashions in dress. Since social status does not necessarily correlate with high income, there is a discrepancy between status and consumption. The educated and the szlachta stress politeness and social graces to differentiate themselves from the uneducated and the newly rich.

POLITICAL LIFE

Government. The highest law is the Constitution of 16 October 1997. The Polish government is divided into three branches: executive, legislative, and judicial. The executive branch includes a president, a prime minister, two deputy prime ministers, and a cabinet or council of ministers. The president, who is the chief of state, is elected by a popular vote for a five-year term. The prime minister and the deputy prime ministers are appointed by the president and confirmed by the *Sejm*. The prime minister nominates and the president appoints the members of the council of ministers who are then approved by the Sejm.

The legislative branch consists of two houses: the one hundred seat Senate whose members are elected for four-year terms by a majority vote from the provinces, and the four hundred sixty-seat Sejm whose members serve four years and are elected to ensure proportional representation. Four seats are constitutionally reserved for ethnic German parties.

Leadership and Political Officials. There are a great many political parties. Most of them are still in the process of being formed, developing ideologies, and establishing a solid basis among the voters. Ideologically some are successor parties of the Communist party and others are post-Solidarity parties. In addition, there are a great many minor parties; some have an ideological basis and some reflect the ambitions of a popular individual.

Social Problems and Control. The Polish legal system is a combination of the continental system of law (Napoleonic Code) and holdovers from Communist legal theory. Under the continental civil law, interpretation of the law by judges is not a major factor and the rule of precedent is not an important element.

Since 1989, the Polish legal system has undergone significant transformation as part of a larger democratization process. There is some judicial review of legislative acts and court decisions can be appealed to the European Court of Justice in Strasbourg, France. Poland has a commercial code that

Polish farms tend to be small and inefficient; they produce only 5 percent of the nation's gross domestic product.

meets the European Union (EU) standards and, on 26 May 1981, Poland ratified The United Nations Convention on Contracts for the International Sale of Goods (CISG).

A still controversial issue is the treatment of former Communist government officials, especially the members the secret police. Debate centers around barring them from holding public office or positions of trust and whether Communist government officials who committed crimes should be held accountable now.

An issue gaining in importance is the treatment of people with different sexual orientation. The legal system, the society, and especially the Catholic Church are intolerant toward them. Yet there is a world-wide trend to legitimize these types of minorities and incorporate them into society with full civil and legal rights.

Military Activity. Poland is a member of the North Atlantic Treaty Organization (NATO). It has an army, a navy, and an air defense force. In 1998, Poland spent 2.2 percent of its GDP (3.3 billion dollars) on the military. At the end of the twentieth century Poland had no serious military threats or international disputes.

SOCIAL WELFARE AND CHANGE PROGRAMS

The government's social welfare system is insufficiently funded and needs a comprehensive overhaul to adjust to changing political and economic conditions.

NONGOVERNMENTAL ORGANIZATIONS AND OTHER ASSOCIATIONS

Nongovernmental organizations (NGOs) are involved in aiding children, family and general social welfare. In 1984, Poland was the first central/eastern European country to pass a law making NGOs possible. They have about two million members. By 1998, about twenty-six thousand NGOs were operating. NGOs may register as either associations or foundations. Both types of organizations may provide services.

There is a NGO support industry. In 1993, an informal coalition of Polish NGOs, the Forum of Nongovernmental Initiatives (FIP), was created, and the Network of Information and Support Center for the Nongovernmental Organizations (SPLOT) was established in 1994.

In general, NGOs try to satisfy local needs. More than 90 percent of Poland's NGOs are active in education (including social as well as general education); social welfare; and family, children and young people. Most of their funding comes from donations by corporations and individuals, the central government, international NGOs, and their own business activities.

GENDER ROLES AND STATUSES

Division of Labor by Gender. Traditionally, the woman's place was in the home, and her rule in household matters was absolute. By 1979, women were 43.4 percent of the work force, in 1988, 45 percent, and in 1996, 46 percent. According to a study, women employed outside the home averaged 6.5 hours on the job and 4.3 hours on housework, while women without jobs spent 8.1 hours on housework.

The socialist government offered women opportunities for higher education and employment. In 1990, for every 100 males who completed higher education there were 89 women. On average, women and men have accumulated the same 11.1 years of education. However, women's earnings are lower. Between 1982 and 1993, women earned only 66 to 67 percent of men's wages. This was due in part to women choosing careers in badly paid sectors of the economy. Seventy percent of the women worked in health, social security, finance, education, and retail sales, but only 15 percent of graduates in technical subjects were women. Even in the better paid sectors of the economy, women were primarily in administration or worked as semiskilled workers.

Women operate a significant percentage of farms; in 1992 they operated 20 percent of farms. Almost 70 percent of female farmers were single and more than 40 percent were age 60 or older. Usually the children have moved away and the husband has died or is unable to farm.

The reorientation of Poland's economy from a socialist command model to a capitalistic market driven one has had a disproportionate impact on women. Despite the fact that women make up less than 50 percent of the workforce, 55 percent of the unemployed are women.

The Relative Status of Women and Men. Women live in a male-oriented society with few groups working to change the national attitudes. They are subject to family violence at home and sexual harassment in the work place. They also have less access to credit and jobs. Very few women have achieved top leadership positions in politics, business, and the professions. They are excluded from leadership in the Catholic Church.

Among the peasants and workers, there is a strong patriarchal ideology and the husband is apt to regard himself as superior and the master. The wife is expected to make it clear that her husband is the head of the family. However, a man will not make important decisions without consulting his wife. In upper class and intelligentsia families the relationship is more equal, and a man places great value on his wife's opinions and counsel.

One area where there is significant disagreement and change is regarding women's reproductive rights. Under socialist governments, sex education in schools was minimal and, while contraceptive devices and medication and abortions were available, their accessability varied over time and from place to place. During socialist times abortions were common and, at times, their numbers approached those of live births. After 1989, severe restrictions were imposed, especially on abortions. The law of 20 November 1996 allows abortions in the first trimester and beyond the twelfth week in cases of rape or incest, provides for free abortions to women meeting specified conditions, and enjoins the Ministry of Education to enforce sexual education programs in schools.

MARRIAGE, FAMILY, AND KINSHIP

Marriage. People typically married before age twenty. Unmarried women over twenty were considered spinsters, and bachelors in their late twenties were subjected to public censure and mockery. Both men and women expect to marry, have children, and have only one spouse for a lifetime. Marriage has always been viewed as a holy responsibility, and it is commonly believed that the unmarried or the never married cannot be really happy and will have difficulty obtaining salvation.

Traditionally, most marriages were arranged to improve family fortunes. Love was not important. Formal divorce was difficult. However, one way to escape was for one member of the couple to move, ostensibly to earn money in a distant locale, and to not return.

Domestic Unit. Ideally, the domestic unit is a three-generation extended family consisting of the married couple, their children and the husband's parents. However, in 1991, over 6 percent of families consisted of a single mother with one or more

Musicians in traditional Polish costume perform folk music during Swieto Ludowe. The festival commemorates the founding of the town of Narweka.

children. Ten percent of all mothers are single, and many of them have never been married.

Inheritance. Traditionally, a father could divide the inheritance any way he saw fit. Now there are legal restrictions, especially on the division of real estate. The rural inheritance system does not work well. Often properties are inherited by several heirs. One heir takes possession and is expected to make cash payments to the others. Because of frequent changes in governments and in legal and monetary systems, this generates ill will and interminable arguments regarding equitable division of inheritances.

Kin Groups. Poles recognize kinship through both genders and use the same kin terms for both father's and mother's relatives, but differentiate between genders and generations. When individuals attempt to manipulate the formal economic and political systems, they try to utilize kin ties to do so. Groups of relatives assemble for formal occasions, especially for funerals and weddings.

SOCIALIZATION

Infant Care. According to Polish tradition, a pregnant woman should not look at the disabled, mice, or fire in order not to damage the infant. Pregnancies are hidden as long as possible, and people avoid talking about them to guard against jealousy, witchcraft, and the evil eye. There are no professional midwives. An older respected woman—*babka* or *baba*—aids in the delivery. Breast-feeding is seen as beneficial and healthy. In the Lublin area, boys are fed for three years, and in Kujawy, all infants for two. Newborns sleep with the mother until they are christened, usually three or four weeks, with six weeks being the usual maximum. Afterwards infants sleep in a cradle. Selection of godparents is important, because the child is assumed to acquire the characteristics of the same sex godparent. The godfather provides the swaddling cloth. The infant is clothed in a shirt, cap, and diapers and then wrapped in the cloth. For boys, an important event is the first haircut, usually at about three years.

Child Rearing and Education. Poles emphasize good manners and etiquette. Children who misbehave are called "impolite." Boys, in particular, are raised to be brave, independent, self-reliant, and tough. Patriotism is also stressed. Farming people and workers use physical punishment while upper classes tend to rely on psychological sanctions. The father is the stern disciplinarian, an authoritarian

Traditionally, the women's place was in the home, but a significant number of women run their own farms, particularly after children move out or if the husband dies or becomes disabled.

who should be respected and obeyed. In the middle and upper class, the mother is in charge of the children's education, and the development of their patriotism. Ideally, the mother is kind and nurturing, and mediates between the father and the children. In many urban families both parents are employed outside the home and the grandparents play an important role in raising the children.

Having established the National Education Commission in 1770, Poland has a long tradition of formal schooling. Education suffered after the country was partitioned. The partitioning powers tried to impose their culture and language on the Poles. The Germans devoted the most attention to education and, by 1911, illiteracy had been eliminated in their territory. In the Russian-controlled areas, schools were relatively few, children were taught in Russian, and Polish was treated as a foreign language.

With the reestablishment of independence in 1918, there was a concerted effort to educate the population. By 1939, illiteracy had been reduced to 12 percent and was less than 1 percent in 2000. There are nursery schools, eight-year primary schools, secondary schools, and universities. Secondary schools offer basic vocational training, voca-

tional and technical training, and general college preparatory education. State schools at all levels are free and attendance to age eighteen is obligatory.

Higher Education. The Cracow Academy was founded in 1364 (called the Jagiellonian University after 1400) and is one of the oldest universities in Europe. By 1939, Poland had six universities, including the Catholic University in Lublin, which later became the only private university in the Communist block. By 1989, the country had ten universities and a number of specialized schools geared to the needs of agriculture, industry, medicine, and teaching.

ETIQUETTE

There is great stress on being polite and courteous. Men are expected to kiss ladies' hands and to behave with decorum. An acceptable gift for women is an odd number of flowers, regardless of whether a woman is the recipient or presenter. Most men consider themselves judges of a fine drink, and for men the standard gift is alcohol. One must always drink from a glass, never directly from a bottle.

RELIGION

Religious Beliefs. Approximately 95 percent of Poland's inhabitants are Roman Catholics, with about 75 percent attending church services regularly. The other 5 percent are Eastern Orthodox, Protestants and other Christian religions. Judaism and Muslim are the largest non-Christian religions.

Religious Practitioners. There is a hierarchy of priests, monks, and nuns as appropriate in the Roman Catholic Church along with ministers of other Christian denominations. On rare occasions, one may still encounter witches and fortune tellers.

Rituals and Holy Places. The Catholic church has formal religious services and practices, and it encourages preservation of folk culture, such as the common roadside shrines built and maintained by the people and the large annual pilgrimages to shrines such as Częstochova, Kalwaria, Lanckorona, and Piekarnie Śląskie. Traditionally on the Feast of the Purification, 2 February, the priests bless the *gromnica*, the candle used to ward off lightning, sickness, and general misfortune.

In rural areas, there are religious practices based on the annual cycle of the growing seasons and associated farming practices and to ensure good luck. When cleaning house in preparation for Christmas, a corner is left unswept lest some happiness is thrown out. There are many local variations of Christmas activities, but one common thread is bringing samples of crops into the house and sharing food with animals. The ubiquitous custom is the evergreen, or fir tree, found even in Orthodox Jewish homes during the feast of Hanukkah.

Easter was the time of Resurrection both of Christ and of nature. A common rural custom is to sprinkle water on the ground to ensure a bountiful harvest. A popular extension of this practice is the dousing of people with water. In many areas, there are follow-up festivities on Easter Monday, *dyngus* day.

In celebration of the shortest night of the year on Saint John's Eve, 23 June, people build bonfires and jump over them to gain purification and protection from evil. In many areas, people float flower garlands in rivers. Traditionally, haying also starts about this time and 29 June was a time for fairs.

In the fall, 28 October is devoted to Saint Jude, the patron of things most difficult to achieve and solutions to problems that seem hopeless. During World War II, Saint Jude was the patron of Underground Poland and is still considered the protector of Polish exiles and homeless wanderers worldwide.

On All Saints' Day, 1 November, and All Souls' Day, 2 November, people place candles in cemeteries and at places of torment and execution.

Death and Afterlife. Death is visualized as a tall, slender woman dressed in a white sheet and carrying a scythe. Nothing could stop her, but animals could warn of her approach. People preferred that death be speedy and painless and that it come as a result of illness rather than without warning. The dying individual was placed on the ground, and doors and windows were opened so that the soul could go to heaven. The dead may be buried in their Sunday best.

Traditionally, a house where someone died was considered unclean and was marked with a cloth nailed to the door, black if the deceased was an older married man or woman, green if a young man, and white if a young girl. White cloth and flowers were considered symbols of mourning. Survivors did not wear red. The casket was made from boards with no knots from an evergreen tree. The deceased was placed on a plank or in the coffin between two chairs in the main room of the house. Coins were placed in the hand, mouth, or left armpit so that the deceased has been paid and has no reason to return. Candles were lit and left burning, especially the first night. It was believed that the soul stays around the body so food and drink were left in the open. The wake *pusta noc* involved singing and wailing to keep away any bad spirits. It was the beggars' job to do the majority of lamenting. If an enemy came to the wake, it was considered to be a pardon.

At the funeral, people said goodbye, women by putting their hand on the coffin and men by placing their cap on it. The coffin was closed with wooden pegs. The coffin was taken out of the house feet first, and the cattle and bees had to be notified of their master's demise. Once the coffin was in the grave those present (except family members) threw dirt in the grave. The soul went to the Creator then returned to the body until the priest threw dirt on the coffin. At that point, the soul went to Saint Peter to find out its fate—heaven or hell.

Tombstones were for important people. The common marker was a birch cross giving the name, date, and prayer requests as well as a shrub or a plant. *Kasza* (porridge) was featured at the funeral feast along with vodka with honey. Beggars were fed as well. Masses were said for the dead on the third, seventh, ninth, and fortieth day after death. On the first anniversary of death, there was a large meal for relatives, friends, and beggars.

Horse-drawn carriages await passengers in a square in Old Town Warsaw. Warsaw has been Poland's capital since 1611, when it succeeded Cracow.

MEDICINE AND HEALTH CARE

In cases of illness, people use both modern and folk medicine and seek help from practitioners of both. Reliance on folk medicine has been lessening, and modern medicine with physicians, nurses, clinics, pharmacies, and sanatoria is the norm. A recent development is the addition of the speciality of family physician.

Formally, there are two types of modern health care. One is provided by dentists and physicians in private practice on a fee basis to those able to pay. The other is by the national and regional governments. This system is in trouble due to insufficient and shrinking resources and is considered unsatisfactory by the patients, the health care workers, and the state. Patients complain of no continuity of treatment and care, difficult access to specialists, and problems meeting various legal requirements. All health care workers, from the physicians to the lowest employee, complain of low salaries and prestige.

SECULAR CELEBRATION

The national holidays are Constitution Day, 1 May (1791) and Independence Day, 11 November (1918).

THE ARTS AND HUMANITIES

Support for the Arts. In the last ten years, there has been a fundamental shift in the constraints faced by artists. Before 1989, art was heavily subsidized by the state, but demands were made on artists to produce propaganda materials. In addition, art was subject to political censorship. Certain topics and ways of presenting works of art were forbidden and, if violated, could expose the artist to legal sanctions, including prison sentences. Some artists never displayed their art publicly. With the fall of socialism, both state support and censorship, except in certain areas such as pornography, have disappeared. Consequently, artists are more politically free but have fewer resources.

Literature. Oral literature was the earliest genre. In the preliterate days and among the peasants much later, folk songs, legends, poetry, jokes, and riddles were important artistic expressions. Folk songs dealt with universal themes such as love, sorrow, and lack of freedom. Tales and legends dealt with the doings of kings, contests between knights and dragons, and the exploits of ancient robbers and bandits as well as with the lives of saints. Political jokes and stories and urban legends deal with current events and circulate nationwide.

Initially, Polish literature was written in Latin and can be said to have begun with the annals of the tenth century. Literature in Polish began and enjoyed a "golden age" in the sixteenth century with the writing of Mikołay Rej, who wrote exclusively in Polish and has been called the father of Polish literature, and Jan Kochanowski, the first genuine and great Polish poet. In the seventeenth century, Wespazjan Kochowski wrote the first messianic interpretation of Poland's destiny, a theme developed during the romantic period by Adam Mickiewicz, Juliusz Słowacki, and Zygmunt Krasiński. In the twentieth century, three Polish writers were awarded Nobel prizes: Henryk Sienkiewicz, 1905; Władysław Reymont, 1924; and Czesław Miłosz, 1980. Between 1940 and 1989, there were severe political restrictions on what could be published. At the end of the twentieth century the main constraint is economical, based on what the public will buy.

Graphic Arts. The Poles have participated in all the great art movements of Western culture. One of Poland's early notable sculptors, Wit Stwosz (Veit Stoss), lived during the fifteenth century. The wooden altar tryptich in the Church of the Virgin Mary in Cracow is his most famous work. The first noted painter was the Italian, Bernardo Bellotto, who in the late eighteenth century painted Polish life. Painting developed in the second half of the nineteenth century with Jan Matejko and Henryk Siemiradzki being the best known. The portraitist Stanisław Wyspiański was also active in drama and design.

Performance Arts. Theater and movies have a special potency in Polish society. People tend to see their own life and history as filled with drama and romance, and they love theater. Attending a performance, whether a play, a movie, a concert or ballet, is an important social activity, and people tend to see it as a serious and edifying experience rather than mere entertainment.

The first public theater in Poland was established in 1763. This spurred great popularity of drama and especially comedy in the second half of the eighteenth century. There were some very influential and important playwrights. Franciszek Zablocki produced very high level comedies. His best known is the "Flirting Dandy." Mickiewicz's *Dziady* ("Forefathers' Eve") combined folklore and mystic atmosphere to create a new kind of romantic drama and offered a new formula for national destiny. Its visionary third part was published in 1832. Franciszek Bohomolec satirized the aristocracy and

Wojciech Boguslawski wrote a popular national comic opera. During the nineteenth century almost all poets wrote poetry in dramatic form. Some of the most important dramatists were Aleksander Fredro, Slowacki, and Stanislaw Wyspianski. During the twenty years between the world wars, there were no major dramatic developments. The best plays were written by novelists. After World War II, the Communist government attempted to use the theater for propaganda purposes, with indifferent success. There has been a revival since 1989.

Polish ballet was built on folk dances but is primarily an urban enjoyment. Between the world wars, it generally had low standards. After World War II, it received considerable state support and much was done to improve it. It emphasizes classical and folk dancing, but some modern ballet themes are present.

Music has had few official constraints. It is founded on the rhythms and melodies of folk music adapted for performance in gentry homes and reaches back to the middle ages. A distinctive Polish church music was flourishing during the Renaissance. The first major Polish opera was staged in 1794. The famous composer Frederic Chopin is considered the musical embodiment of Polishness. After World War II, there was a lively revival of music in Poland. All branches of music are well represented. Popular music is strongly influenced by western styles. Polish jazz is excellent and has a reputation for experiment.

Polish cinema goes back to 1909, but it began to attract international attention only after World War II. The directors best known abroad are Andrzej Wajda and Roman Polanski. After 1989, people tended to curtail consumer spending and movie audiences shrank. In the 1970s, there were two-thousand five hundred movie theaters but by 1992, there were fewer than one thousand. Foreign films have great appeal. In 1992, of 122 new titles shown, fifteen were Polish and eighty-nine were recent American films. The remainder were of Australian, English, Finnish, French, German, and Japanese productions. Since 1989, about one half of the films have been co-productions with foreign partners.

Radio and television are attractive sources of entertainment and information. Television provides quality cinema and a wide variety of programs in several languages through cable, local channels, and satellite hookups. Most families own a VCR. In 1990, over 6,000 companies sold and rented video cassettes. There is legislation to curb video piracy and an association has been formed to protect copyrights.

THE STATE OF THE PHYSICAL AND SOCIAL SCIENCES

Over the centuries, Poles have made notable contributions to the sciences, including the astronomer Nicolaus Copernicus (Mikołaj Kopernik); Alfred Korzybski, the founder of general semantics; economists Oscar Lange and Michael Kalecki; Nobel Prize winner Maria Curie-Skodowski; and the anthropologist Bronislaw Malinowski.

Between 1945 and 1989, the social sciences were subjected to severe restrictions and neglect. There was censorship of publications and restrictions were placed on travel and research topics. Topics of research were circumscribed and certain areas could not be investigated. Since 1989, the political constraints have been lifted and the main problem is to obtain funding for research and publication.

BIBLIOGRAPHY

Biskupski, M. B. *The History of Poland*, 2000.

Bugajski, Janusz. "Poland." In *Ethnic Politics in Eastern Europe: A Guide to Nationality Policies, Organizations, and Parties*, 359–397, 1994.

Curtis, Glenn E., ed. *Poland: A Country Study*, 1994.

Davies, Norman. *Heart of Europe: A Short History of Poland*, 1984.

Dunn, Elizabeth. "Employee Reciprocity, Management Philosophy: Gift Exchange and Economic Restructuring in Poland." *The Anthropology of East Europe Review: Central Europe, Eastern Europe and Eurasia*, 18 (1): 73–79, 2000.

Erdmann, Yvonne. "The Development of Social Benefits and Social Policy in Poland, Hungary and the Slovak Republic Since the System Transformation." *East European Quarterly*, 32 (3): 301–314, 1998.

Knab, Sophie Hodorowicz. *Polish Herbs, Flowers & Folk Medicine*, 1995.

——— *Polish Customs, Traditions and Folklore*, 1993.

Lemnis, Maria, and Henryk Vitry. *Old Polish Traditions: In the Kitchen and at the Table*, 1996.

Mucha, Janusz. "Getting out of the Closet: Cultural Minorities in Poland Cope with Oppression." *East European Quarterly*, 31 (3): 299–309, 1997.

Simoncini, Gabrielle. "National Minorities of Poland at the End of the Twentieth Century." *The Polish Review*, 43 (2):173–193, 1998.

Sosnowski, Alexandra. "Polish Cinema Today: A New Order in the Production, Distribution, and Exhibition of Film." *The Polish Review* 40 (3): 315–329, 1995.

Titkow, Anna. "Polish Women in Politics: An Introduction to the Status of Women in Poland." In *Women in the Politics of Postcommunist Eastern Europe*, 24–32, 1998.

Wierzbicka, Anna. *Understanding Cultures Through Their Key Words: English, Russian, Polish, German, and Japanese*, 1997.

Wierzbicki, Zbigniew T. "Monographs on the Rural Community in Poland." *Eastern European Countryside*, 3: 23–38, 1997.

Zuzowski, Robert. "Poland: Spin-Doctors' State." *Political Change in Eastern Europe Since 1989: Prospects for Liberal Democracy and a Market Economy*, 71–95, 1998.

—ANDRIS SKREIJA

PORTUGAL

CULTURE NAME

Portuguese

ORIENTATION

Identification. The name "Portugal" derives from a Roman or pre-Roman settlement called Portus Cale (the modern city of Porto) near the mouth of the Douro River. The Romans referred to this region as the province of Lusitania, and the prefix *Luso* (meaning "Portuguese") is still used in some contexts. In the ninth century, during the reconquest (714–1140 C.E.), Christian forces dominated the area between the Minho River, which forms the border of modern Portugal in the north, and the Douro River, and the region became known as *Territorium Portucalense*. In 1095, the king of Castile and Leon granted Portucale (northern Portugal) to a Burgundian count. Despite the diversity of invading populations and distinct regional economies and ways of living, Portugal is a homogeneous nation with a single national cultural identity and no ethnolinguistic groups.

Location and Geography. Continental Portugal at 35,516 square miles (91,986 square kilometers) occupies approximately a sixth of the Iberian peninsula. Since the majority of the population was rural until the 1960s, geography has been an important factor in cultural adaptations and worldview. The northwest (the province of Minho) is lush, green, densely populated, and the major source of emigrants. The northeast (the province of Trás-os-Montes) is more mountainous and is divided into a northern region (*terra fria*) with long cold winters and a warmer region (*terra quente*) to the south. The central part (including the provinces of Beira Alta, Beira Baixa, and Beira Litoral) varies from high and desolate mountain plateaus (the Serra da Estrela) to low coastal areas. The provinces of Ribatejo and Estemadura are low-lying regions near Lisbon and the Tagus River. Much industry is concentrated in this area. Southern Portugal, drier and more Mediterranean in climate, includes the provinces of the Alentejo and the Algarve. The Alentejo, an undulating plain with cork trees and wheat fields, was traditionally an important cash-crop area. The Algarve is semitropical with almond, fig, and citrus trees. It is also a region of tourism and fishing.

Portuguese inhabit the Azores and Madeira in the Atlantic. As a result of colonial expansion and massive emigration in the nineteenth and twentieth centuries, there are Portuguese-speaking people in Asia, Africa, South America, the United States, Canada, Australia, and northwestern Europe. The capital is Lisbon, located on a number of hills on the northern shore of the Tagus River estuary. The original name for Lisbon, an important Roman city, was *Olisipo*. Lisbon, which became the capital in 1298, is also the political, cultural, economic, educational, and social center.

Demography. In 1999, the population of continental and island Portugal was estimated at 9.9 million. The population increased until the 1960s, when it declined by more than 200,000 as a result of emigration to northern Europe. In the 1970s, the population rose by more than a quarter million as *retornados* returned from Africa after decolonization. Portugal has been receiving immigrants, primarily from former overseas territories such as the Cape Verde Islands. This immigrant population, which has settled primarily in the greater Lisbon area, is estimated to be approximately 200,000.

Linguistic Affiliation. Portuguese is a Romance language with Latin roots, although some words are Arabic in origin. Emerging as a language distinct from Latin and Castilian in the ninth century, Portuguese was made the official language under King Dinis (1279–1325). Dialects are found only in regions near the border with Spain and are disappearing. French was widely used by the aristocracy in the nineteenth century. Spoken in Brazil, Angola,

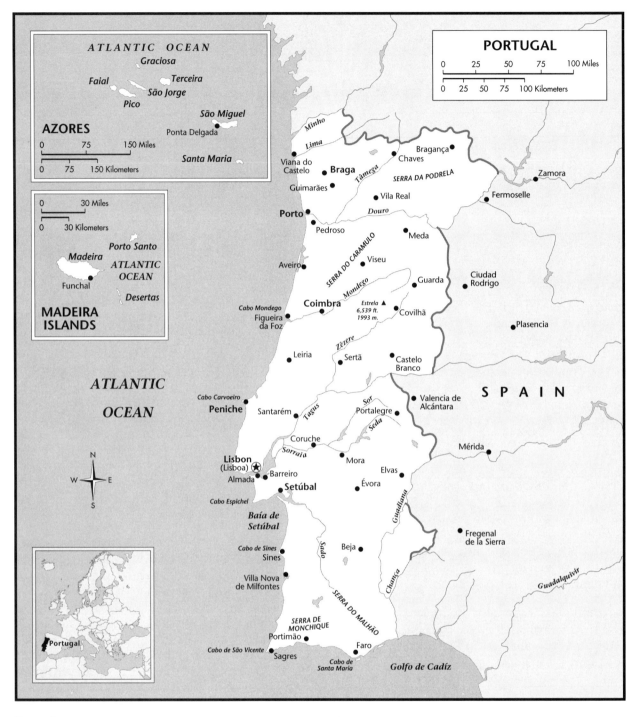

Portugal

Mozambique, Guinea-Bissau, the Cape Verde Islands, São Tomé, Príncipe, and Macão, Portuguese is the world's fifth largest language in terms of number of speakers.

Symbolism. Many cultural symbols of national identity focus on the Age of Discovery and an imagined community that extends beyond the political frontiers of the nation. The national flag, adopted on 19 June 1911 during the First Portuguese Republic (1910–1926), includes an ancient astronomical device (the armillary sphere) used for maritime navigation and represents Portugal's role in global exploration. "*A Portuguesa*," the national anthem, officially adopted in 1911, has as its central symbol a female figure modeled after "La Marseillaise" (the

Woman of Marseilles), the French symbol of republicanism. It expresses the nationalism that emerged in late nineteenth-century Anglo-Portuguese conflicts over African territory.

Nostalgia for the past and for the homeland is represented in the sentiments of *Sebastianismo* and *saudade* and in the lyrics of the *fado*. Sebastianismo is a messianic belief in the return of King Sebastian, who died in Morocco in 1578 or 1579. Sebastian was expected to drive out the Spaniards (who ruled from 1580 to 1640) and restore the nation to glory. Until recently, 1 December was a national holiday commemorating the overthrow of the Spaniards in 1640. Sebastianism is present in a worldview that expresses a hope that what one wants will happen and a feeling that it will never happen. Saudade refers to a melancholic and hopeful nostalgia for a homeland that is far away. The fado, derived from the Latin word for "fate," is a popular urban song form that generally expresses sadness, longing, and regret. The fado is thought to date back to the late eighteenth or early nineteenth century and to combine Moorish, African, and indigenous elements.

HISTORY AND ETHNIC RELATIONS

Emergence of the Nation. Portugal has been inhabited since Paleolithic times. Various peoples settled in the region, though the modern Portuguese trace their descent to the Lusitanians, who spread over the peninsula in the third millennium B.C.E. Lusitanians made contact with Celtic peoples who moved into the region after 900 B.C.E. Roman armies invaded the peninsula in 212 B.C.E. and established towns at the present-day sites of Braga, Porto, Beja, and Lisbon. Successive invasions of Germanic tribes in the fifth and sixth centuries C.E. and Moors in the eighth century C.E. added new elements to the population, particularly in the south. Portugal emerged as an independent kingdom in 1140 with its capital in the northern city of Guimarães. Early statehood, the expulsion of the Moors, and the expulsion or conversion of the Jews laid the foundation for a unified national culture.

In the fifteenth century, the Portuguese inaugurated the Age of Discovery and for three centuries built and expanded a seaborne empire. This imperial enterprise gave the nation a reputation for racial tolerance that is still invoked as the foundation of Portugal's comfort with cross-cultural diversity despite homogeneity at home. The loss of Brazil in 1822 and a series of economic and political crises led to a decline in the world position of the nation in the nineteenth century. The monarchy was eliminated in 1910 with the establishment of the First Portuguese Republic, which was replaced by the authoritarian dictatorship of António Salazar in 1926. Salazar formed his New State (*Estado Novo*) in 1932 on a corporatist political model and emphasized God, family, and work as the central values of the national culture. He limited access to higher education and, in emphasizing the Catholic faith, promoted humility, routine, and respect for authority as guiding principles of social life. He also celebrated the rural way of life by sponsoring a national competition in 1938 for the most Portuguese village.

The Salazarist regime survived until 1974, when it was overthrown by military men frustrated by the hopelessness of the colonial wars in Africa. The African colonial system was dismantled after 1974. In the late 1980s, Portugal became a member of the European Community, and in 1994, Lisbon served as the European cultural capital.

National Identity. The population of Portugal, the first unified national-state in Western Europe, has been extremely homogeneous for most of its history. A single religion and a single language have contributed to this ethnic and national unity. Portugal was the last western European nation to give up its colonies and overseas territories, turning over the administration of Macau to China as recently as 1999. Its colonial history has been fundamental to national identity, as has its geographic position at the margin of Europe looking out to the Atlantic.

Ethnic Relations. Portugal has retained linguistic and other cultural ties with former colonies, including Brazil. In 1996 the Community of Portuguese-speaking Countries was created. A recently-arrived population of immigrants, most from former colonies in Africa and Asia, has introduced some ethnic diversity, particularly in the Lisbon metropolitan area. These populations are residentially segregated in neighborhoods with poor housing and a general absence of public amenities. They are subjected to a form of subtle racism within a society that views itself as anti-racist.

Portugal's gypsy population, estimated at about 100,000, offers another element of ethnic diversity. The gypsies live apart, and primarily in the south. They can often be found at rural markets selling clothing and handicrafts. Portugal also has small Protestant and Jewish communities, largely composed of foreigners.

URBANISM, ARCHITECTURE, AND THE USE OF SPACE

In 1930, 80 percent of the population lived in rural villages, and thirty years later, 77 percent of the population was still rural. Since 1960, urbanization has been fueled by extensive internal migration from the countryside to the cities, but only 35.8 of the population was defined as urban in 1996. The two large cities of Lisbon and Porto are both on the coast.

The hallmark of Portuguese architecture are *azulejos*, glazed ceramic tiles that cover the facades and interiors of churches, government buildings, and private homes. Azulejos were introduced by the Moors. Both geometric and representational patterns are used, the latter often depicting historical events or religious scenes. The azulejos style was taken to colonial Brazil and to India, and has been adopted by returned emigrants who have built new houses across the landscape of northern and central Portugal as social statements of their success abroad. Akin to azulejos are the mosaics used on the sidewalks of major walking avenues in Lisbon and Porto as well as in provincial towns. These avenues, lined with cafés and teahouses, are important public spaces where people stroll and converse. Stucco in various pastels is used on buildings, including the main government buildings in Lisbon. The other distinctive style of architecture is known as Manueline, after King Manuel I. It is a form of ornamentation that mixes elements of Christianity with ropes, shells, and other aquatic imagery, reflecting the nation's seafaring past.

Vernacular buildings in rural areas use local materials. In the north, traditional peasant houses, often with two stories and a red tubular clay tile roof, were built with thick granite walls. Animals were kept on the ground floor, which also was used for storage. Many of these houses had verandas. All had a big hearth in the kitchen with an overhanging chimney used to smoke hams and sausage as well as to cook and heat. The kitchen is the center of private family space; these houses often also contain a parlor (*sala*) for receiving guests. In the south one-story, whitewashed, flat-roofed houses with blue trim around the windows and doorways are common. This form of architecture evokes the Moorish past. These houses, which are built to keep out the summer heat, have huge chimneys and hearths. Since the 1970s, new housing and large apartment complexes have been built to accommodate the growing urban population.

FOOD AND ECONOMY

Food in Daily Life. The cuisine varies by region. The north is known for *caldo verde*, a kale and potato soup generally flavored with a slice of *chouriço* (spicy sausage). Also important are grilled sardines. The traditional bread, especially in the northwest, is *broa*, a grainy corn bread with a thick crust. In Minho, the traditional wine is *vinho verde*, a young wine made from grapes that grow on arbors that often serve as property markers. In the northeastern region of Trás-os-Montes, fresh and cured pork, is used in a number of dishes. A stew of mixed meats and vegetables called *cozida à portuguesa* originated in this region and has become a national dish. In central Portugal, cheeses are more common because of pasturing in the Serra da Estrela and fish (including octupus, squid, and eel) is abundant. In the south, the most popular soup is a form of *gazpacho* with bread and smoked pork. A pork and clam stew cooked in a *cataplana* (a tightly sealed steamer) is the regional dish of the Alentejo. Olive oil (*azeite*) is used throughout the country.

Bacalhau (salt cod) has been a national dish since the fifteenth century, when the Portuguese began fishing off the coast of Newfoundland. *Pastéis de bacalhau* (codfish croquettes) are a popular appetizer. An important seasoning is cumin; equally important is *piri-piri*, a hot red chili often used to season barbecued chicken. Cinnamon is a common flavoring for desserts, such as the traditional rice pudding (*arroz doce*).

Port, a fortified wine produced in the region of the upper Douro River, is a major export. In rural households on ceremonial occasions, port is offered to celebrated guests, including the parish priest.

The noon meal (*o almoço*) is served at about twelve thirty, and dinner (*o jantar*) at 8 P.M. Breakfast (*o pequeno almoço*) is Continental style. In rural regions, it was traditional for men to stop at the local café before heading to the fields to have their *pinga* (a shot of stiff brandy) to *matar o bicho* (kill the beast).

Food Customs at Ceremonial Occasions. One of the most important ceremonies in rural households is the annual killing and preserving of the pig. This event occurs in late December or January and usually takes two days, since it involves making sausage, smoking ham (*presunto,*), and salting several other parts of the pigs, including the belly (*toucinho*). The noon meal on the first day is called *sarrabulho* and consists of rice, innards, and the blood of the pig.

Azulejos, blue glazed tiles, are made into pictorial panels throughout Portugal. Ceramics and architecture are the country's greatest art forms.

The traditional family meal on Christmas Eve is *bacalhau* with *molho verde* (a green sauce made with virgin olive oil), cabbage (*couve*), and boiled potatoes. On Twelfth Night, a *bolo rei* (kings' bread) is served, often with a lucky coin in it. On the occasion of the village *festa*, some families roast a goat (*cabrito*).

Coffehouses are places to meet friends, talk business, and study. Various styles of coffee are served, each with a special label.

Basic Economy. According to 1998 estimates agriculture constitutes 4 percent of the gross domestic product, industry 36 percent, and services 60 percent. Twelve percent of the population works in agriculture (compared with 40 percent in 1960), 32 percent in industry (32 percent in 1960), and 56 percent in services, commerce, and government (28 percent in 1960). Tourism is an important component of the service sector. Few families are wholly subsistence farmers, having relied traditionally on cash from the sale of surplus produce or from emigration of family members. Remittances from workers abroad are important to the economy, as are European Union transfers. Competition in the context of the European Union is changing the face

of subsistence agriculture. Oil and gas are imported, and hydroelectric power is underdeveloped.

Land Tenure and Property. Patterns of land tenure vary by region. In the Algarve, landholdings are small and are cultivated by owners, tenants, or sharecroppers. The Alentejo has traditionally been a region of low population density, latifundia that originated in the Roman estate system, and landless day laborers. Before 1974, approximately five hundred absentee landlords owned the bulk of the land. After 1974, the agrarian reform movement altered the system of land tenure in this region, although some of the early "revolutionary" expropriations have been restored to their original owners. The north has a much higher population density, land fragmentation, *minifúndia* that originated with the system brought by the Germanic invaders of the fifth and sixth centuries, and subsistence farming. These peasants (*lavradores*) own, rent, and/or sharecrop several fields scattered throughout a village as well as neighboring villages. Although not as numerous as in the south, there is a population of landless day laborers (*jornaleiros*) in northern Portugal, many of whom are women. Jornaleiros provide supplemental labor to the peasant household. In the much less densely populated northeastern region, a form of communal property ownership and communal farming survived into the twentieth century.

Commercial Activities. Commercial activities vary regionally. The peasants in the north cultivate corn (rye in the northeast), potatoes, wine grapes, and vegetables to sell at regional markets. Many also raise milk cattle, and the milk is sold to local cooperatives. Along the coastline, populations engage in fishing. Fish canning is an important export industry. The local economies in the north have been supplemented by centuries of emigration, and as a result, men have developed artisanal skills as masons and carpenters. Around Braga, Porto, and Guimarães there is a population of worker-peasants employed in the textile industry. The people of the Algarve engage in agriculture, fishing, and tourism. Cash-crop agriculture (wheat, olives, cork) predominates in the Alentejo. In central continental Portugal, a variety of irrigated grains (wheat, corn, and rice) are cultivated on medium-sized family farms for commercial sale. The Azores are largely agricultural, with some islands depending primarily on dairy and meat production and others on a combination of cattle raising, whaling, fishing, and small-scale agriculture (sugar beets, tea, tobacco, and vegetables). Madeira relies on agriculture (wine, bananas, sugarcane), fishing, and whaling in addition to small-scale cottage industry and tourism. The embroidery industry is a major employer of female workers.

Major Industries. Furniture, food processing, wineries, and pulp and paper are among the major industrial activities in the north. Heavier industry (steel working, shipbuilding, iron production, transport equipment, electrical machinery) and the bulk of the industrial working class are concentrated in the Lisbon-Setubal region in the south. In recent years, the construction industry has become important, and tourism is growing. Other important manufacturing industries are leather products, textiles, porcelain, and glassware.

Trade. Portugal's major exports are textiles, clothing and footwear, cork and paper products, machinery, transport equipment, and chemicals, and agricultural products. More than 80 percent of this trade is with other member states of the European Community. The most important trading partners are Germany and Spain.

SOCIAL STRATIFICATION

Classes and Castes. At the end of World War II, Portugal had a small upper class, a small middle class, a small urban working class, and a mass of rural peasants. The upper class included leaders of industry, financiers, top military personnel, the Catholic episcopate, the large landholders of the Alentejo, some professionals, and some government officials. The middle class included smaller rural landowners, secondary-level military officers, small business operators and shopkeepers, civil servants, and schoolteachers. The lower class (*o povo*) consisted of the urban and rural working poor. There was little social mobility, and a distinction was made between those who worked with their hands and those who did not. Social status was ascribed and sustained by class endogamy. Before 1974, the State was based on corporative bodies representing different interest groups (the military, the Church, landholders, workers' syndicates, etc.). In theory, the Corporate State channeled class interests but in practice these were often circumvented by personal contacts.

The rural south with its massive population of landless day laborers was more hierarchical than the rural north, explaining the strength of the Communist Party and class consciousness in the south after the 1974 "revolution." Social stratification in the villages of the north was more fluid. Exposure to the very wealthy elites was also more limited. The 1976 constitution defined Portugal as a republic engaged in the formation of a classless society. While the Marxist tones of the constitution have largely been eradicated, Portugal is less socially rigid than in the past and education, which is more widely accessible as the country moves toward a service-oriented economy, is an avenue to social mobility. The middle class has grown and the peasant population has declined, but the distance separating the social, economic, and political elites from the bulk of the population remains.

POLITICAL LIFE

Government. Portugal has moved from an authoritarian regime, to a provisional military government, to a parliamentary democracy. The president, representing the executive branch, is elected by universal suffrage for a five-year term and appoints the prime minister. In 1982, a constitutional revision put the military under civilian control, with the president as the commander in chief. A unicameral Assembly of the Republic, with two hundred thirty members elected by universal suffrage for four-year terms, constitutes the legislative branch. Center-right leadership predominated between 1985 and 1995 and the Socialist Party assumed leadership in 1995. Portugal has had regional voting patterns

A commercial building in the Amoreiras district of Lisbon. Services and industry account for 96 percent of the GDP.

since the nineteenth century, with urban voting trends opposed to rural trends and the north voting more conservatively than the south.

At the local level, villages are run by a parish council (*junta da frequesia*) whose members are elected by village households. Throughout the Salazar period, the juntas had little real power and few economic resources, though the members had local prominence. They depended on the *câmara*, the administrative body in the county seat, and the câmara is still an important unit of political organization and administration. After 1974, political parties and agricultural cooperatives assumed importance, though participation varies by region.

Regionalization has become increasingly important, in part mandated by constitutional provisions for administrative decentralization.

Leadership and Political Officials. Although there was only one legal political party under Salazar (the União Nacional), today there are a wide variety of political parties with varying political viewpoints that stretch from the far right to the far left. The four major parties are the Portuguese Communist Party (PCP), The Portuguese Socialist Party (PS), the Social Democratic Party (PSD), and the Popular Party (PP; formerly the Center Democratic Party or CDS).

Before 1974 local people were not engaged with the political process but since then public debate and voting have both increased dramatically. In some rural communities, particularly in the south, a system of patronage prevailed, but this also changed after the 1974 revolution. Cultural elites have been replaced by officeholders and *politicos*, ambitious men who are part of the village bourgeoisie. Today office and positions of leadership are an achieved rather than an ascribed status, based on personal achievement rather than on whom one knows or the family of one's birth.

Social Problems and Control. There is a national Supreme Court and several administrative, military, and fiscal courts. Under the Estado Novo, the PIDE (political police) was a powerful mechanism for repression. Known to have scores of informants, the PIDE had the authority to arrest and detain without charge or trial and served not only as an internal investigative arm but also as an institution of border and customs control. The PIDE was abolished in 1974, but there is a police force (*Polícia de Segurança Pública*) in the main cities and towns. In rural areas, order is maintained by the *Guarda Nacional Republicana* (GNR). Violent crime is rare. Drugs and theft have become a problem, primarily in large metropolitan areas. In small communities, shame is still a powerful mechanism of social con-

Vineyards above the upper Douro River. This region produces port, a major export.

trol, and throughout the country, parents use shame to discipline children.

Military Activity. The three military branches are the Army, Navy, and the Air Force. In 1997 military expenditures were 2.6 percent of the GDP. The military age is 20. The Portuguese military was heavily involved in the Colonial Wars in Africa and by 1974, 80 percent of Portugal's military forces were committed to that region. Military service was extended to as long as four years during the 1960s, a phenomenon that resulted in a sharp increase in clandestine emigration to France during that decade. The military, under the title of the Armed Forces Movement (Movimento das Forças Armadas/MFA), instigated the bloodless coup of 25 April 1974 that overthrew the *Estado Novo* dictatorship. Portugal was a founding member of NATO. The United States maintains use of the Lajes Air Base on the island of Terceira in the Azores.

SOCIAL WELFARE AND CHANGE PROGRAMS

Prior to the twentieth century, the Roman Catholic Church and other charitable institutions such as the Santa Casa de Misericórdia were the primary mechanisms of social welfare in Portugal. During the Salazar regime, a system of Casas do Povo were established in local places, primarily to regulate the Corporate State, but also to take care of individual needs. Their impact was limited. State-operated systems of welfare did not emerge until the 1960s and they have improved with the growth of parliamentary democracy and greater economic stability and prosperity. Even so, in the early 1990s welfare benefits, financed through employee and employer contributions, were low by comparison with other European nations. Welfare programs include benefits for the ill and disabled, old-age pensions, maternity leaves, and small family allowances. After 1975 Portugal introduced a national health care system that paid all medical and pharmaceutical expenses.

NONGOVERNMENTAL ORGANIZATIONS AND OTHER ASSOCIATIONS

The Church is the major nongovernmental association that organizes social relationships. At the local level, people belong to a range of confraternities (*confrarias*) that are under the auspices of their parish church. In the past confraternities were important mutual aid societies, sources of loans and the organizations responsible for proper burials. At the local level there has also been an important increase in folkloric dance groups (*ranchos*) that involve adolescents and young adults in the reinvention of traditions. These ranchos are under the auspices of the national Federation for Portuguese Folklore. Portuguese people participate in a variety of other urban and national associations, many of them professionally based. Recently new associations for particular social groups, for example the gay and lesbian community and various immigrant communities, have also been formed.

GENDER ROLES AND STATUSES

Division of Labor by Gender. Labor force statistics frequently underestimate the participation of women, particularly in the rural economy of the north. Some anthropologists view these activities as the basis of the significant economic and political power of peasant women. Middle- and upper-class women were at one time restricted to the domestic sphere, but this has changed as women have received advanced education and professional training, and full legal equality. Factors such as an interventionist state, low wages, flexibility in the allocation of labor resources of family members, a rigid social structure, and incipient economic and technological development explain the low rate of labor market segregation by gender.

Since the 1960s, women have outpaced men in higher education, although class factors are ultimately more important in shaping these trends. Portugal has had one woman serve as president. Local attitudes are more conservative, and women have been slower to win political positions in municipal elections.

Women still perform the major domestic chores, although men are involved in child care. Among the elites, women rely on inexpensive domestic help. Important religious positions are still primarily in the hands of men.

The Relative Status of Women and Men. Under the Salazar regime, women were subordinate to men and had few personal, political or economic rights. After 1974, the status and roles of women changed. The 1976 constitution outlawed discrimination by sex, and divorce and abortion became legal under certain circumstances. Women were given control over their economic lives and gained the right to carry their own passports and vote.

MARRIAGE, FAMILY, AND KINSHIP

Marriage. The marriage rate rose in the twentieth century. People generally marry later in the north than in the south, though the differences are disappearing. In the south, consensual unions have been common, and the north has had high rates of permanent spinsterhood. Although it has declined since 1930, illegitimacy was high in rural northern Portugal and remains high. Marriage has generally been class endogamous, and there is a tendency for villages to be endogamous.

Domestic Unit. Households in the north tend to be complex, many of them composed of a three-generation stem family. Some villagers in the northeast follow a custom of natalocal residence for many years after marriage. In the south, households are simpler, generally composed of a nuclear family. Obligations between friends are sometimes felt to be more important than those between kin. Headship of the household is held jointly by a married couple, who in the rural north are referred to as *o patrão* and *a patroa*. Among urban middle-class groups and in the south, the concept of a dominant male head of household is more prevalent.

Inheritance. The Civil Code of 1867 called for partible inheritance, but parents can dispose freely of a third share (*terço*) of their property, and women have the right to receive and bestow property. Among the peasants of the north, where inheritance is generally postmortem, parents use the promise of the terço as a form of old age security by marrying a child into the household. At their death, that child becomes the owner of the house (*casa*); the rest of the property is divided equally among all heirs. *Partilhas* can cause friction between siblings since land is variable in quality. Some peasants hold land under long-term lease agreements that traditionally was passed on in one piece to one heir. The 1867 Civil Code eliminated the system of entailed estates (*vínculos*) that made it possible for wealthier classes to pass on property to a single heir, usually by male primogeniture. Wealthier landowners have been able to keep property intact by having one heir buy out the siblings.

Kin Groups. Kinship is reckoned bilaterally, but the structure of domestic groups and the kinship links that are emphasized vary by region and social class. In northern Portugal, nicknames (*apelidos*) are extremely important as terms of reference that connote moral equivalence in otherwise socially stratified rural communities. In the northwest, nicknames identify localized kin groups linked through females. In this region, there is a preference for uxorilocality and uxorivicinality, both of which can be linked to male emigration. Spiritual kinship ties are established at baptism and marriage. Kin frequently are chosen to serve as godparents (*padrinhos*). In the absence of government-based in-

Portraits of the deceased ornament their grave markers in an Azorean cemetery.

stitutions of childcare, eldercare, etc. the support networks based on kinship are extremely important in both rural and urban areas.

SOCIALIZATION

Child Rearing and Education. Socialization is an important aspect of education. A child who is *"bem educado"* has good manners and is respectful toward adults. The Portuguese are indulgent toward their children, who are welcome everywhere. Life cycle ceremonies for children are in accordance with Catholic ritual. Baptisms are important events for the extended family. First communion can be an occasion for a family celebration.

ETIQUETTE

Although Portugal has become more informal in its rules of etiquette, polite terms of address are still used. People with education are still addressed with phrases such as *Senhor Doutor* (Mr. Dr.) and an upper class and/or educated women still garners the title *Dona*, often coupled with a first name as in "Dona Maria." Like Spanish, Portuguese makes a distinction between the more formal and courteous "o senhor/a senhora" and the more informal and intimate *tu*. Strangers generally greet each other with a handshake. In more informal environments men who know one another will embrace and women greet one another with a kiss on both cheeks. Urban Portuguese of the middle and upper classes dress quite formally and there is a powerful sense of propriety about appropriate public dress.

RELIGION

Religious Beliefs. The majority of the citizens are Catholic, nominally if not in practice. Portugal has experienced waves of political anticlericalism throughout its history. Under Salazar, Portugal experienced a religious revival and the position of the local priest in the villages was greatly enhanced. Only after 1974 was this position challenged, and in recent years there has been a decline in the number of clergy. Religiosity is generally weaker in Lisbon and the south and stronger in the center, the north, and the islands. People develop personal relationships with particular saints. Magical practices, sorcery (*feitiço*), witchcraft (*bruxaria*) associated with notions of illness and healing, and notions of envy (*inveja*) that invoke the evil eye are still part of the belief system of many people.

Rituals and Holy Places. Local village life is marked by celebrations honoring the saints and the Virgin Mary. *Romarias* (pilgrimages) to regional

A group of people wait for a bus in Angro Do Heroismo. Urban Portuguese have a powerful sense of propriety about appropriate public dress.

shrines are a central feature of religious practice, especially in the north. Villagers also celebrate an annual festa (generally to honor the patron saint) that includes a procession and combines sacred and secular elements.

The famous religious shrine Fátima is in the province of Ribatejos northeast of Lisbon, where the Virgin of the Rosary appeared to three small shepherd children in 1917. In 1932, devotion to Our Lady of Fátima was approved by the Catholic Church and a large basilica was built. Fátima is now a place of international pilgrimage. Pilgrims often walk there from the remotest corners of northern Portugal for the May and October observances. Among the other important pilgrimage sites are Bom Jesus do Monte in Braga and Nossa Senhora dos Remedios in Lamego.

Death and Afterlife. Death is a fundamental part of village life. Church bells toll to send the message that a neighbor (*vizinho*) has passed away. In some areas, the gates and doors of the dead person's house are opened to allow anyone to enter and relatives begin to wail around a body prepared for viewing. Burial is in local cemeteries, and family graves are well tended. Each village has several burial societies (confrarias). All Saints Day is an occasion for reverence for those who have departed. Mourning is signified by the wearing of black; a widow generally will wear black for the rest of her life, while other kin remain in mourning for varying lengths of time. Portugal has various cults of death. Such beliefs are not confined to rural areas; in the cities there is a network of spirit mediums who claim to contact the dead.

MEDICINE AND HEALTH CARE

The death rate and infant mortality have declined, and life expectancy has increased. Since 1974, medical education has been improved and there are more medical personnel and hospitals. Health care is better in the cities than in the countryside, although women in rural areas no longer give birth at home. Good health often is associated with what is natural, and changes in diet are frequently cited as the cause of disease. The leading causes of death are malignant neoplasms, diseases of the circulatory and respiratory systems, and death from injuries and poisons. Portugal has a low suicide rate but high motor accident fatalities. Folk medical practices are still prevalent in some parts. Curers use a combination of prayer, religious paraphernalia, and traditional and modern medicines.

SECULAR CELEBRATIONS

25 April has been an official holiday since 1974, commemorating the overthrow of the *Estado Novo* by the Armed Forces Movement. On 1 May, the Portuguese celebrate Labor Day. Portugal Day (10 June) commemorates the death of Luis de Camões, the national epic poet. 15 August, celebrating the Assumption of the Virgin, is observed. 5 October is Republic Day, commemorating the collapse of the monarchy in 1910. Since 1974 it has assumed more significance as a national holiday, while 28 May, a commemorative day complete with military parades that in the Salazar regime honored the 1926 military coup, is no longer a day of national celebration.

THE ARTS AND HUMANITIES

Literature. The most famous work of national literature is *Os Lusíadas*, an epic poem about the voyage of Vasco da Gama by Luís de Camões (1525?–1579?). Of importance during the seventeenth century, when Portugal regained autonomy, were the *Lettres Portugaises* (*Portuguese Letters*) written by Sister Mariana Alcoforada. In the early 1970s, Alcoforada's work stimulated the *Novas Cartas Portuguesas* (*New Portuguese Letters*), a statement of feminism written by the so-called three Marias. The greatest period for literature was the nineteenth century, when Júlio Dinis, Camilo Castelo Branco, and José Maria Eça de Queirós used a social realist and sometimes satirical style to write about class relations, family, inheritance, and religion. Realism was revived during the twentieth century with the short stories of rural life by Manuel Torga, the novels of Aquilino Ribeiro, and epic tales such as Ferreira de Castro's *Emigrantes*. Perhaps the greatest Portuguese modernist is Fernando Pessoa. Modernism attacked the values of the middle classes of the liberal period. Contemporary realists include Lobo Antunes and José Saramago, who won the Nobel Prize in 1998.

Graphic Arts. The greatest art forms are architecture and ceramics. Painting has not been particularly important. Folk arts are well developed, and craftspeople are found throughout the country. Rugs made in Arraiolas are well-known internationally. Women in the north and the island of Madeira produce embroidered goods that are sold to tourists. Pottery varies in style according to geographic region. Artistic expression is also evident in the items produced for decorating the floats carried in religious processions and in the filigree jewelry made in the Porto region, which also is worn at festivals.

Performance Arts. The fado is one of the most important performing traditions. *Ranchos folklóricos* (folkloric dance groups) are being revived, supported by the tourist industry. Dancers dress in traditional regional costumes and perform dances that have historical and regional origins. Bullfighting is also an important performance art.

THE STATE OF THE PHYSICAL AND SOCIAL SCIENCES

Since 1974, the social sciences have emerged strongly, with programs in most universities. Of importance are the Institute of Social Sciences of the University of Lisbon and the Instituto Superior de Ciências Sociais in Lisbon. Portugal publishes two major journals of social science.

BIBLIOGRAPHY

Barreto, António, ed. *A Situação Social em Portugal, 1960-1995*, 1996.

Brettell, Caroline. *Men Who Migrate, Women Who Wait: Population and History in a Portuguese Parish*, 1986.

Brito, Joaquím Pais de. "O Estado Novo e a Aldeia mais Portuguesa do Portugal." In *O Fascismo em Portugal*, 1982.

Cabral, João de Pina. *Sons of Adam, Daughters of Eve: The Peasant Worldview of the Alto Minh*, 1986.

Cole, Sally. *Women of the Praia*, 1991.

Cutileiro, Jose. *A Portuguese Rural Society*, 1971.

Downs, Charles. *Revolution at the Grassroots: Community Organizations in the Portuguese Revolution*, 1989.

Feldman-Bianco, Bela. "Multiple Layers of Time and Space: The Construction of Class, Ethnicity, and Nationalism among Portuguese Immigrants." In Nina Glick Schiller, Linda Basch, and Cristina Blanc Szanton, eds., *Towards a Transnational Perspective on Migration*, 1992.

Ferreira, Virginia. "Women's Employment in the European Semiperipheral Countries: Analysis of the Portuguese Case." *Women's Studies International Forum* 17: 141–155, 1994.

Gallagher, Thomas. *Portugal: A Twentieth Century Interpretation*, 1983.

Herr, Richard, ed. *The New Portugal: Democracy in Europe*, 1992.

Lourenço, Nelson. *Família Rural e Indústria*, 1991.

Maxwell, Kenneth. *The Making of Portuguese Democracy*, 1995.

Opello, Walter. *Portugal: From Monarchy to Pluralist Democracy*, 1991.

Pinto, António Costa, ed. *Modern Portugal*, 1998.

Reed, Robert. "From Utopian Hopes to Practical Politics: A National Revolution in a Rural Village." *Comparative Studies in Society and History* 37: 670–691, 1995.

Robinson, Richard. *Contemporary Portugal*, 1979.

Wheeler, Douglas L. *Historical Dictionary of Portugal*, 1993.

—CAROLINE B. BRETTELL

PRÍNCIPE SEE SÃO TOMÉ AND PRÍNCIPE

PUERTO RICO

CULTURE NAME

Puerto Rican

ALTERNATIVE NAMES

Borinquen, Borincano, Borinqueño

ORIENTATION

Identification. Christopher Columbus landed in Puerto Rico in 1493, during his second voyage, naming it San Juan Bautista. The Taínos, the indigenous people, called the island *Boriquén Tierra del alto señor* ("Land of the Noble Lord"). In 1508, the Spanish granted settlement rights to Juan Ponce de León, who established a settlement at Caparra and became the first governor. In 1519 Caparra had to be relocated to a nearby coastal islet with a healthier environment; it was renamed Puerto Rico ("Rich Port") for its harbor, among the world's best natural bays. The two names were switched over the centuries: the island became Puerto Rico and its capital San Juan. The United States anglicized the name to "Porto Rico" when it occupied the island in 1898 after the Spanish-American War. This spelling was discontinued in 1932.

Puerto Ricans are a Caribbean people who regard themselves as citizens of a distinctive island nation in spite of their colonial condition and U.S. citizenship. This sense of uniqueness also shapes their migrant experience and relationship with other ethnoracial groups in the United States. However, this cultural nationalism coexists with a desire for association with the United States as a state or in the current semiautonomous commonwealth status.

Location and Geography. Puerto Rico is the easternmost and smallest of the Greater Antilles, bordered by the Atlantic Ocean to the north and the Caribbean Basin to the south. Puerto Rico is a crucial hemispheric access point. It was thus a valuable acquisition for European powers and the United States. Puerto Rico retains its strategic importance, housing the U.S. Army Southern Command and other military facilities. Since the 1940s, the U.S. Navy has used its offshore islands for military maneuvers that have damaged their ecology, economy, and quality of life.

Puerto Rico includes the surrounding small islands, including Culebra and Vieques to the east and Mona to the west. Mona is a nature reserve and wildlife refuge under government jurisdiction. The total land area, including the smaller islands, is 3,427 square miles (8,875 square kilometers).

The tropical island ecosystem is unique and diversified in spite of industrialization and urban sprawl. Beside Mona, the government has established several other nature reserves. There are twenty forest reserves, such as El Yunque Rain Forest and the Caribbean National Forest, which are under federal jurisdiction.

A rugged central mountain range constitutes two-thirds of the island and separates a northern coastal plain noted for karst formations from a drier southern plain. The Taínos recognized the power of the seasonal hurricanes that affect the island. The Spanish word *huracán* originated from the Taíno *juracán*, the sacred name for this phenomenon.

Spain turned Puerto Rico into a military stronghold. San Juan was walled and fortified to house military forces, but the other settlements were neglected until the eighteenth century; isolated by the scarcity of roads, they subsisted on contraband, with little official management. The impenetrable highlands became a refuge in which settlers, runaway slaves, Taínos, and deserters produced a racially mixed population.

Demography. Puerto Rico is densely populated and urbanized. Census projections for 2000 place the population at 3,916,000, not including the estimated 2.7 million Puerto Ricans in the mainland United States. Almost 70 percent of the island is

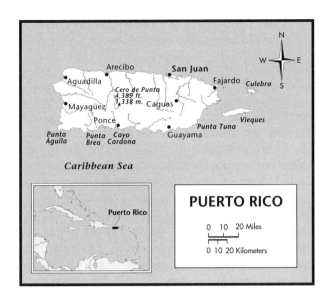

Puerto Rico

urban, in contrast to its rural character up to the 1940s. Sprawl has integrated formerly distinct *barrios* (rural and suburban neighborhoods), cities, and towns. The San Juan metropolitan area extends almost to Fajardo in the east and west to Arecibo. Ponce in the south and Mayagüez in the west also have become sprawling metropolitan areas.

Puerto Ricans self-define as a homogenized Taíno, African, and Spanish mixture. Taínos were Amerindians who occupied the island before European domination. Then estimated at thirty thousand, they were reduced to two thousand by the seventeenth century through exploitative labor, disease, native uprisings, and emigration to the other islands. But many fled into the highlands or intermarried: Spanish immigration to the island was mostly male and interracial relations less stigmatizing than among Anglo settlers. The contemporary revival of Taíno identity is partially based on the survival of Taíno highland communities.

Although the Spanish introduced slavery to replace a dwindling Taíno labor force, slavery never reached large proportions until the plantation system was fully implemented in the nineteenth century. However, there was a significant African influx of slave, indentured, and free labor.

Chinese labor was introduced in the nineteenth century, and immigrants came from Andalusia, Catalonia, the Basque provinces, Galicia, and the Canary Islands. Threatened by Latin America's nineteenth century revolutions, Spain facilitated immigration through economic incentives, attracting other nationalities as loyalists fled republican uprisings. The nineteenth century also brought Corsican, French, German, Lebanese, Scottish, Italian, Irish, English, and American immigration.

The U.S. occupation increased the American presence, and the 1959 revolution in Cuba brought an estimated 23,000 Cubans. Many Dominicans immigrated in search of economic opportunities; some use Puerto Rico as a port of entry into the United States. Tension and prejudice against these two groups have emerged. Americans, Cubans, and Dominicans tend to consider their presence in Puerto Rico temporary.

Linguistic Affiliation. Spanish and English are the official languages, but Puerto Rico is overwhelmingly Spanish speaking, despite government efforts to eradicate Spanish or foster bilingualism. Puerto Rican Spanish is a dialect of standard Spanish that has its own particularities. The influence of Taíno is evident in descriptions of material objects ("hammock" and "tobacco"), natural phenomena ("hurricane"), place names and colloquialisms. However, Africans gave Puerto Rican Spanish defining nuances. African speech contributed words and also influenced phonology, syntax, and prosody.

Language is a significant cultural marker of national identity for a people whose culture has always been under siege because of colonialism. U.S. officials disdained Puerto Rican Spanish as an unintelligible "patois" that had to be eradicated; they also believed that by learning English, Puerto Ricans would be socialized into "American values." The U.S. government imposed educational policies prescribing schooling in English through the first half of the twentieth century; language became part of the long-standing struggles over Puerto Rico's culture and colonial condition.

Although "English-only" policies were abrogated after the establishment of the commonwealth in 1952, debates about language have intensified. Purists decry the loss of the "mother tongue," advocating vigilance and "correctness," yet the "deterioration" of Puerto Rican Spanish through English "interference" has been exaggerated. Puerto Ricans in the United States have developed a linguistic repertoire that involves mixing English and Spanish in everyday talk. This code switching has been stigmatized as "Spanglish" and condemned by language purists, but is actually culturally significant as an identity marker.

Symbolism. The most powerful cultural symbol is the island itself. Idealized in a variety of media, its image resonates even among members of U.S. migrant communities. Natural and human-made features associated with the island are imbued with great value. The *coquí* (a tiny indigenous tree frog), royal palms, Taíno petroglyphs, Luquillo Beach and El Yunque, *bomba* and *plena* (music and dance forms of African origin), literature, and native food are some of these features. Puerto Ricans in New York City have built *casitas*, copies of the traditional rural wooden houses painted in vibrant colors and decorated with Puerto Rican objects.

The *jíbaro*, the highland rural folk, has become a controversial symbol because jíbaros are depicted as descendants of white Spanish settlers in a way that casts Puerto Rico as a backward rural society and negates Puerto Rico's African roots.

HISTORY AND ETHNIC RELATIONS

Emergence of the Nation. The Taínos received the Spanish with civility but were quickly farmed out in *encomiendas*, a system of indentured labor, to work at mining and cultivation. By mid-century, African slaves were imported for labor, and both slaves and Taínos soon rose in armed rebellion.

Spain realized that the island's wealth did not lie in gold and silver, yet it was attacked repeatedly by European powers that recognized its strategic location. Puerto Rico survived on contraband and piracy, trading cattle, hides, sugar, tobacco, and foodstuffs directly with other nations.

In the eighteenth century, the Spanish initiated a series of improvements, reforming the system of land tenure and in effect initiating private ownership. Overhauled policies allowed trade with other nations. These measures fostered development and increased settlement, urbanization, and population growth; they also facilitated the emergence of a sense of culture. By the eighteenth century, Puerto Ricans had developed a definite creole identity, distinguishing themselves from the *hombres de la otra banda* ("men from the other side"), who were transient colonial administrators, military personnel, or exploiters.

The nineteenth century fostered increased political consciousness and claims for autonomy or incorporation as an overseas province. In liberal times, Puerto Rico was granted civil liberties, which were abrogated upon the return to conservatism and repression.

The independence movement culminated in the Grito de Lares of 1868, an armed rebellion that was reported to the Spanish by an infiltrator and suppressed. Some of its leaders were executed, and those who were exiled continued their struggle from Europe, Latin America, and New York City, where they worked alongside Cuban patriots.

National Identity. Cultural nationalism generated political activism, literary and artistic production, and economic development. In 1897, Spain granted Puerto Rico an Autonomic Charter that recognized its right to internal self-government. The first autonomous government was constituted in April 1898, but its accession was postponed when the United States declared war on Spain.

The national consciousness that emerged under Spanish rule survived into the twentieth century under U.S. control. The United States saw itself as exercising a benign modernizing function, but Puerto Ricans saw it as eroding their culture and curtailing their autonomy. This tension was aggravated by U.S. capitalistic practices. The government facilitated the economic exploitation of the island's resources by absentee corporations and fostered the exportation of local workers as cheap migrant labor. Claiming that the island lacked resources and was overpopulated, the U.S. government encouraged migration, with the consequent formation of diasporic communities across the United States.

Americanization efforts included English-only education and the implementation of an American educational system, the appointment of pro-U.S. officials, the incorporation of Anglo-Saxon common law principles and practices into the island's legal system, the grant of U.S. citizenship on the eve of World War I, and the introduction of U.S. currency and the devaluation of the local peso.

The advent of the commonwealth in 1952 did not end debates over Puerto Rico's culture and colonial status. Many people view the changes over the last century as modernization and the introduction of a corporate capitalist culture that has spread around the world without erasing cultural differences.

Ethnic Relations. Cultural identity is commonly defined in terms of nationality rather than ethnicity. Puerto Ricans in the United States have been defined as an ethnoracial group in spite of their nationalism.

URBANISM, ARCHITECTURE, AND THE USE OF SPACE

Old San Juan is a world-class example of Spanish urban architecture adapted to a tropical environment. After the commonwealth government initiated its renovation, it became a tourist attraction and a handsome residential and commercial area. Its

A man hand-rolls cigars for the Bayaman Tobacco Corporation, the last family-owned cigar producer in Puerto Rico. They produce five thousand cigars per day.

landmarks and fortifications, such as the Castle of San Felipe del Morro, are regarded as international treasures. The greater San Juan metropolitan area is a congested mix of undistinguished building styles that contains functionally distinct areas: Condado and Isla Verde are tourist enclaves, Santurce is a mix of commercial and residential spaces, Hato Rey has become the financial and banking center, and Río Piedras is the site of the University of Puerto Rico. Sprawl has eroded the sense of community and precluded pedestrian use, and an excellent network of modern highways has fostered car dependency to the detriment of the environment.

The Spanish plan of cities organized in a grid pattern of intersecting streets with central plazas bordered by public buildings recurs throughout the older sectors of the island's towns and cities. Residential architecture is eclectic. The U.S. occupation brought about a revival of the Spanish colonial style. Grillwork is ubiquitous because it offers security against criminality. Elite families built Art Nouveau and Art Deco houses, some luxurious and deserving of their designation as private "castles." The 1950s brought good examples of contemporary architecture.

Puerto Ricans have a strong cultural preference for owning their own houses. Housing develop-

ments (*urbanizaciones*) are the norm; shopping centers and strip malls have partially replaced the old marketplaces. Public housing projects (*caseríos*) have supplanted the old urban slums; people initially resisted them because they violated cultural expectations of individual housing and community. High-rise condominiums were constructed in the 1950s and have become desirable housing choices. In the few remaining rural areas, wooden and straw huts have been replaced by cement block houses.

FOOD AND ECONOMY

Food in Daily Life. Food preferences were shaped by the island's cultural diversity and predominantly rural lifestyle. Taíno and African influences are seen in the use of tropical fruits and vegetables, seafood, condiments, and legumes and cereals (the ubiquitous rice and beans). The Spanish contributed culinary techniques and wheat products and introduced pork and cattle. The tropical climate required the importation of preserved food; dried codfish was long a dietary mainstay. Candied fruits and fruits preserved in syrup are also traditional. Rum and coffee are the preferred beverages.

Traditionally, meals were patterned after Spanish custom: a continental breakfast, a large midday

A street scene in Ponce's historic district. Almost 70 percent of the island is urban.

meal, and a modest supper. Many people now eat a large breakfast, a fast-food lunch, and a large dinner. Puerto Ricans tolerate fast-food, but prefer native food and home cooking. There are fast-food establishments that serve rice and beans, and other local dishes. The island boasts restaurants and eating places across the economic and gastronomic spectrums; San Juan, in particular, offers international choices.

Food Customs at Ceremonial Occasions. Although American holidays are legally celebrated, the foods associated with them are prepared according to local tastes and culinary techniques. Thus, the Thanksgiving turkey is done with *adobo*, a local seasoning mix. The traditional holiday menu includes *pernil* or *lechón asado* (spit-roasted pork), *pasteles* (plantain or yucca tamales), and *arroz con gandules* (rice with pigeon peas); typical desserts are *arroz con dulce* (coconut rice pudding), *bienmesabe* (coconut pudding), and *tembleque* (coconut milk pudding). *Coquito* is a popular coconut and rum beverage.

Basic Economy. Industrialization has eroded the viability of agriculture as an important economic activity and the island is dependent on food imports. Local products are considered of higher quality.

Land Tenure and Property. Most Puerto Rican land is in private hands. Owning a home holds important cultural value. The emphasis placed on owning one's own home led to agrarian reform in the 1940s and the *parcela* program, a local homesteading effort by which the government appropriated land held by corporations for exploitative agribusiness and sold it for minimum prices. The only period within the twentieth century when private property was affected was precisely between 1898 and the 1940s when the whole island was literally carved up among a handful of absentee U.S. sugarproducing corporations and their local subsidiaries.

The government holds portions and there are protected nature reserves.

Commercial Activities. Beginning in the 1950s, Operation Bootstrap, the commonwealth's developmental program, fostered rapid industrialization. Tax incentives and cheap skilled labor brought many U.S. industries to the island, but by the late 1960s, the social costs and the ending of tax incentives eroded the economy. The flight of industry to cheaper labor markets in Asia and Latin America and the rise of transnational business have reduced the process of industrialization.

Major Industries. Restrictive U.S. laws and policies and U.S.-dominated banking and finance have limited Puerto Rico's ability to develop its own markets and conduct international business. The island is now dependent on manufacturing and services. The government remains a major employer. It has fostered petrochemical and high-technology industries that capitalize on an educated labor force. Pharmaceuticals, chemicals, electronics, medical equipment, and machinery are the leading products. Tourism is the most important service industry.

Trade. Major imports include chemicals, machinery, food, transport equipment, petroleum and petroleum products, professional and scientific instruments, and clothing and textiles.

Major exports include chemicals and chemical products, food, and machinery.

Division of Labor. There is a professional class in Puerto Rico. It is a full-fledged Westernized society, with the government being a major employer. Unemployment rates average at 12.5 percent. Agriculture is a waning labor source.

A doorway painted to represent a Puerto Rican flag.

SOCIAL STRATIFICATION

Classes and Castes. A capitalist class structure is organized by access to wage labor and means of production. During the colonial period, small farms and subsistence agriculture prevailed. This prevented the emergence of a privileged *hacendado* class as in other latin societies. In the nineteenth century, with the implementation of an economy dependent on sugar, tobacco, and coffee, landowning and merchant classes emerged, along with a small class of urban professionals. Most political leaders came from those classes, but the bulk of the population remained artisans, sharecroppers, and laborers. Families that retained their assets under U.S. control made the transition to the professional, business, banking, and industrialist class. The economic changes of the 1950s produced an expanded middle class of government employees, administrators, and white-collar workers and an industrial working class replaced the rural one.

Symbols of Social Stratification. A "good" family and education are considered more important than wealth, but class distinctions increasingly are based on the ability to purchase and consume certain goods and commodities such as cars, electronic media, clothes, and travel.

POLITICAL LIFE

Government. The official head of state is the president of the United States even though Puerto Ricans can not vote in presidential elections. A local governor is elected every four years through universal suffrage. An elected resident commissioner represents the island in the U.S. Congress but has no vote. Puerto Rico has its own constitution. A bicameral legislature is elected every four years. The Senate is composed of two senators from each of eight senatorial districts and eleven senators at large; the House of Representatives consists of eleven representatives at large and one each from forty representative districts. Minority party representation is guaranteed in both chambers regardless of election returns.

Leadership and Political Officials. Political parties are based on the three traditional positions on status: autonomy in an enhanced commonwealth status, statehood, and independence. Currently, these positions are represented by the Popular Democratic Party (PPD), the New Progressive Party (PNP), and the Independence Party of Puerto Rico (PIP). The PPD was founded in the late 1930s by the architect of commonwealth status, Luis Muñoz Marín, who became the first elected governor in 1948. The PNP emerged in 1965, succeeding an old pro-statehood party. The PIP was established in 1948 when a PPD faction split off because of Muñoz's failure to support independence. Its popularity peaked in 1952 but has decreased. However, the PIP plays an important opposition role.

Over the last forty years, government control has alternated between the PPD and the PNP. Puerto Ricans vote politicians in and out for their governing abilities rather than their position on status. Concerns about the economy and the quality of life predominate.

Several plebiscites have been held to allow residents to exercise their right to self-determination by expressing their status preference. However, the United States has not honored any plebiscite results.

Social Problems and Control. The unified court system is administered by the island's Supreme Court, which is appointed by the governor. But Puerto Rico is also subject to federal law and constitutes a district within the U.S. federal court system, with a local district court that has jurisdiction over federal law cases. Legal practice incorporates elements from Anglo-American common law and the continental civil code law inherited from Spain. There is no "customary" law.

The island has its own police force, though the FBI also exercises jurisdiction. The correctional system has been plagued by overpopulation, lack of rehabilitation programs, poor physical facilities, undertrained correctional officers, and violent inmate gangs. Criminality is a major problem. Some attribute it to the flight of Cuba's organized crime, which shifted operations to Puerto Rico after 1959. Others blame modernization and the alleged deterioration of traditional values. Many crimes are committed by drug addicts. Drug addiction has also brought the spread of AIDS.

Military Activity. The island is fully integrated into the U.S. military system. Puerto Ricans serve in the U.S. forces. There is also a local national guard. Many residents object to U.S. military control and the military use of Culebra and Vieques. The U.S. ceased maneuvers in Culebra in the mid-1970s, but intensified them in Vieques. It has faced resistance and civil disobedience from many Puerto Ricans.

SOCIAL WELFARE AND CHANGE PROGRAMS

Ongoing economic difficulties have produced high rates of unemployment. Puerto Rico receives federal aid but does not get equal coverage or qualify for most welfare programs. The local government is the main welfare provider. Although it has man-aged to sustain a relatively high standard of living, the cost of living is steep and Puerto Ricans accumulate high levels of debt. However, Puerto Rico's achievements in reducing mortality, increasing literacy, improving medical services, and raising life expectancy have placed it on a par with many U.S. states.

NONGOVERNMENTAL ORGANIZATIONS AND OTHER ASSOCIATIONS

The list of organizations and associations in Puerto Rico is vast, since the number and kind of them there parallel those found in any state of the U.S. They include international (the Red Cross), national (YMCA, Boy and Girl Scouts), and local groups (Puerto Rico Bar Association).

GENDER ROLES AND STATUSES

Division of Labor by Gender. Gender relations have become increasingly egalitarian. When the island had a subsistence lifestyle, women were important economic producers in rural households and outside the home. The ideal of the home-tending housewife has been honored among the middle and upper classes but has become impractical. In an ideal male world, women are expected to do the double duty of workplace and household labor, but this is changing because of the need to maintain double-salary households.

The Relative Status of Women and Men. There is a long-standing tradition of women being active in public life as intellectuals, writers, activists, politicians, and professionals. When women's suffrage was approved in 1932, Puerto Rico elected the first woman legislator in the Western Hemisphere.

MARRIAGE, FAMILY, AND KINSHIP

Marriage. Puerto Ricans consider family life a core cultural value; family and kin are viewed as the most enduring and reliable support network. Despite a high divorce rate and an increase in serial monogamy, most people prefer marriage to living together, although female virginity is not as important as it was in the past. Today courting is based on group or individual dating rather than chaperoned outings. Wedding ceremonies may be religious or secular but preferably include receptions for relatives and friends. Although remaining single is increasingly acceptable, marriage is an important marker of adulthood.

A Taino Indian in tiger-striped body paint.

are preferred to outsiders, and professional infant care providers are regarded with ambivalence. Puerto Ricans have adopted most modern child raising practices, such as separate beds and bedrooms, medical care, toys, and equipment. From infancy, children are socialized toward family and communal participation. Traditionally, they are expected to learn through observation rather than instruction. Children must learn *respeto*, the most valued trait in the culture. Respeto refers to the belief that every person has an intrinsic dignity that must never be transgressed. One must learn to respect others by learning to respect oneself. All other valued qualities, such as obedience, industriousness, and self-assurance, follow when a child internalizes *respeto*.

Child Rearing and Education. Elementary education is legally mandated, but the youth of the population has strained the public education system. Those who can afford it prefer private schooling, which better prepares children for college.

Puerto Ricans distinguish between *instrucción* (schooling) and *(educación)* (education). Education transcends schooling. Education is within the province of the family, since an educated person is not someone who has achieved "book learning" but a person who is respectful, cordial, courteous, polite, and "cultured."

Higher Education. Credentialism is on the rise, and a college degree is required for most positions and for upward mobility. The rates of high school and college graduation have increased in recent decades. The newly acquired importance of higher education sustains the university system, which includes the public University of Puerto Rico and the private Interamerican University, Sacred Heart College, and Catholic University. All these institutions have multiple campuses. People have access to professional training in law, medicine, engineering, and other fields.

ETIQUETTE

Respeto and educación are indispensable components of social interaction. Indirection is also an important strategy. People believe that directness is rude and use a variety of euphemisms and hedges to avoid it. Close friends are allowed directness but maintain the boundaries of respect. Puerto Ricans prefer people who are publicly expressive but not excessively so. Friends customarily greet by kissing each other, and engaging in animated conversation is viewed as a social asset. Although social drinking is approved, drunkenness is not. Relajo is a joking

Domestic Unit. The nuclear family is prevalent, but relatives socialize often. Having children is preferable to childlessness, but it is increasingly the couple's choice. Working spouses who share household chores are becoming common, but socializing children is still predominantly a female role even among family-oriented men. Male authority is invoked and appealed to, but women's authority over many domains and activities is recognized.

Kin Groups. Relatives are expected to support each other materially and emotionally. Support is legally prescribed and required along descent, ascent, and collateral lines. Elders are respected. Kinship is bilateral, and people commonly use both the father's and the mother's family name as surnames.

Inheritance. Civil law requires that a third of an estate must be bequeathed equally among all the legal heirs. Another third may be used to improve an heir's lot, and the last third may be disposed of freely by the testator. The estate of a person who dies without a will is divided equally among all the legal heirs.

SOCIALIZATION

Infant Care. People try to rear children within the family. When the mother is unavailable, relatives

A young woman holds a banner during a pro-statehood demonstration. A U.S. commonwealth since 1952, Puerto Rico has maintained a strong sense of nationalism.

form of indirection that is similar to teasing. It is used to criticize others indirectly, convey problematic aspects of their behavior, stress absurdities, and impart potentially negative information.

RELIGION

Religious Beliefs. The U.S. occupation brought Protestant missions to a predominantly Catholic society. An estimated 30 percent of the population is now Protestant. All major denominations are represented, and there is a synagogue in San Juan but no mosque. Revivalism is quite popular.

The Catholic Church had much power under Spain, but Catholics are prone to a populistic kind of religion that is wary of the established church and its hierarchy. Many people are nonobservant, yet consider themselves devout because they pray, are faithful, treat others with compassion, and communicate directly with God.

African slaves introduced *brujería* (witchcraft practices). In the nineteenth century, European spiritualism became popular. It is the most important alternative practice and coexists with established religions. Many people consider both forms equally legitimate and practice both. Spiritualist mediums are predominantly women who hold divinations and seances in their homes; many have become successful and even wealthy. Cuban immigrants brought *santería*, a blend of Yoruba and Catholic religions. Spiritualism and santería have merged into *santerismo*. Both posit a spirit world, worship a hierarchy of guiding saints and deities from the sacred and secular worlds, and practice divination.

Religious Practitioners. Most religious life in Puerto Rico is enacted in terms of a populist style, in the case of established religions, and engages espiritismo and santería as culturally-specific systems of belief that co-exist with mainstream religious practices.

MEDICINE AND HEALTH CARE

Until the second half of the twentieth century, Puerto Rico suffered from the dire health conditions that are typical of poor, underdeveloped countries. Tropical diseases and parasites contributed to high mortality rates and low life expectancy. Progress in health care has been dramatic, and the island now has modern medical facilities. Mortality rates and life expectancy have improved, and many diseases have been eradicated.

SECULAR CELEBRATIONS

People celebrate both United States and Puerto Rican holidays and feast days. Major local holidays include New Year's Eve (1 January), Three Kings Day (6 January), Hostos Day (11 January), Constitution Day (25 July), Discovery Day (19 November), and Christmas Day (25 December). Easter Thursday and Friday are observed. Cities and town celebrate the patron saint's feast day, usually with carnivals, processions, masses, dances, and concerts. These celebrations are local, except for the eve of the island's patron saint, Saint John (23 June).

The government sponsors civic and military parades for political holidays such as the Fourth of July and Constitution Day. Christmas, New Year's Eve, and Three Kings are the high points of a holiday party season that extends from mid-December to mid-January. Easter brings religious processions.

THE ARTS AND HUMANITIES

Support for the Arts. The arts are important as expressions of cultural nationalism. The government has contributed to their institutionalization through the establishment of the Instituto de Cultura Puertorriqueña, which sponsors and funds artistic activities and programs. Although the institute has been criticized for fostering an essentialistic notion of national identity and favoring ''high'' culture, it has been instrumental in recovering the artistic past and fostering new arts production. Local artists have access to support from U.S. institutions. Universities and colleges are also sources of work, support, and facilities. There are museums in Ponce and San Juan and art galleries all over the island. A performing arts center in Santurce has facilities for theater, concerts, opera, and dance.

Literature. Puerto Rican literature is usually dated to the nineteenth century publication of *El Gíbaro*, a collection of pieces on the island's traditions, because the book represents the first self conscious expression of a native culture. Literary production is diverse, locally valued, and internationally acknowledged. Puerto Rican authors work in all genres and styles.

Graphic Arts. Graphic arts production is diverse and prolific. The pictorial tradition dates back to the eighteenth century with José Campeche, who specialized in religious painting and portraiture and is acknowledged as the island's first artist. Francisco Oller's impressionist work hangs in Paris museums. Twentieth century artists have been particularly successful in print media.

Performing Arts. Music ranges from popular and folk genres to classical works. Salsa, the island's most recent contribution to world music, is rooted in African rhythms. Puerto Rico has classical composers and performers and has been the site of the international Casals Festival since the 1950s. There are established ballet companies and groups that perform modern, folk, and jazz dance. Efforts to establish film production companies have floundered.

THE STATE OF THE PHYSICAL AND SOCIAL SCIENCES

Most social and physical science research is conducted in institutions of higher learning. The social sciences have been instrumental in documenting and analyzing Puerto Rican society and culture. Because of its uniqueness, Puerto Rico is among the most intensely researched places in the world.

BIBLIOGRAPHY

Berman Santana, Deborah. *Kicking Off the Bootstraps: Environment, Development, and Community Power in Puerto Rico*, 1996.

Cabán, Pedro. *Constructing a Colonial People*, 1999.

Carr, Raymond. *Puerto Rico: A Colonial Experiment*, 1984.

Carrión, Juan Manuel, ed. *Ethnicity, Race, and Nationality in the Caribbean*, 1970

Fernández García, Eugenio, Francis Hoadley, and Eugenio Astol eds. *El Libro de Puerto Rico*, 1923.

Fernández Méndez, Eugenio. *Art and Mythology of the Taíno Indians of the Greater West Indies*, 1972.

———. *Historia cultural de Puerto Rico, 1493-1968*, 1980.

———. Eugenio ed. *Crónicas de Puerto Rico*, 1958.

Fernández de Oviedo, Gonzalo *The Conquest and Settlement of the Island of Boriquén or Puerto Rico*, 1975.

Flores, Juan. *The Insular Vision: Pedreira's Interpretation of Puerto Rican Culture*, 1980.

———. *Divided Borders: Essays on Puerto Rican Identity*, 1993.

González, José Luis. *Puerto Rico: The Four-Storeyed Country and Other Essays*, 1993.

Guinness, Gerald. *Here and Elsewhere: Essays on Caribbean Culture*, 1993.

Harwood, Alan. *Rx: Spiritist as Needed: A Study of a Puerto Rican Community Mental Health Resource*, 1977.

Lauria, Antonio. ''''Respeto,' 'Relajo' and Interpersonal Relations in Puerto Rico.'' *Anthropological Quarterly*, 37 (1): 53–67, 1964.

López, Adalberto, and James Petras, eds. *Puerto Rico and Puerto Ricans: Studies in History and Society*, 1974.

Maldonado Denis, Manuel. *The Emigration Dialectic: Puerto Rico and the USA*, 1980.

Mintz, Sidney W. *Caribbean Transformations*, 1974.

———. *Worker in the Cane: A Puerto Rican Life History*, 1974.

Morris, Nancy. *Puerto Rico: Culture, Politics, and Identity*, 1993.

Osuna, Juan José. *A History of Education in Puerto Rico*, 1949.

Steiner, Stan. *The Islands: The Worlds of Puerto Ricans*, 1974.

Steward, Julian, Robert Manners, Eric Wolf, Elena Padilla, Sidney Mintz, and Raymond Scheele. *The People of Puerto Rico: A Study in Social Anthropology*, 1956.

Trías Monge, José. *Puerto Rico: The Trials of the Oldest Colony in the World*, 1997.

Urciuoli, Bonnie. *Exposing Prejudice: Puerto Rican Experiences of Language, Race, and Class*, 1995.

Wagenheim, Karl, ed. *Cuentos: An Anthology of Short Stories from Puerto Rico*, 1978.

——— and Olga Jiménez de Wagenheim. eds. *The Puerto Ricans: A Documentary History*, 1993.

Zentella, Ana Celia. *Growing Up Bilingual: Puerto Rican Children in New York City*, 1993.

—Vilma Santiago-Irizarry

QATAR

CULTURE NAME

Qatari

ORIENTATION

Identification. Residents of Qatar can be divided into three groups: the Bedouin, Hadar, and Abd. The Bedouin trace their descent from the nomads of the Arabian Peninsula. The Hadar's ancestors were settled town dwellers. While some Hadar are descendants of Bedouin, most descend from migrants from present-day Iran, Pakistan, and Afghanistan and occasionally are referred to as lrani-Qataris. *Al-abd*, which literally means "slaves," are the descendants of slaves brought from east Africa. All three groups identify themselves as Qatari and their right to citizenship is not challenged, but subtle sociocultural differences among them are recognized and acknowledged.

Location and Geography. Qatar is a small peninsula on the western shore of the Arabian Gulf that covers approximately 4,247 square miles (6,286 square kilometers). The landmass forms a rectangle that local folklore describes as resembling the palm of a right hand extended in prayer. Neighboring countries include Bahrain to the northwest, Iran to the northeast, and the United Arab Emirates and Saudi Arabia to the south. Qatar and Bahrain both claim the uninhabited Hawar Islands just west of Qatar. Until recently, only small semipermanent seasonal encampments existed in the interior desert. Water resources near the coast combined with opportunities for fishing, pearl diving, and seagoing trade have supported larger, more permanent settlements. These settlement patterns have contributed to the social differentiation between Bedouin and Hadar.

Demography. In 1998, the population was estimated at 579,000. Most estimates agree that only about 20 percent of the population are Qatari, with the remainder being foreign workers. A total of 91.4 percent live in urban areas, mostly in the capital. Because male foreign laborers come without their families, there is an imbalance of males and females in the total population. The foreign workers, mostly from India and Pakistan, cannot obtain citizenship and reside in the country on temporary visas.

Linguistic Affiliation. The official language is Arabic. English, Farsi, and Urdu are widely spoken. Arabic is closely associated with the Islamic faith; thus, its use reinforces the Islamic identity of the nation and its citizens. The Qatari dialect of Arabic is similar to the version spoken in the other Gulf States and is called Arabic. The adjective *khaleeji* ("of the Gulf") that is used to describe the local dialect also distinguishes citizens of the six Gulf States from north African and Levantine Arabs.

Farsi, the official language of Iran, is also widely spoken by families that trace their descent from that country. As a result of the influx of foreign workers, many other languages are commonly spoken, including English, Urdu and Hindi, Malalayam, and Tagalog. While many Qataris speak more than one language, it is very rare for immigrants to learn Arabic. Interactions between Arabs and foreign workers are conducted in English or the language of the expatriate.

Symbolism. Symbols of national identity include the family, items associated with the nation's past, and images of the ruler. Qataris often employ an idiom of kinship and/or tribalism, referring to compatriots as "brother," "sister," or "cousin." This linguistic convention signals the inclusion of those sharing citizenship while excluding foreign workers. Images and ideas associated with desert nomadism and maritime trade that are used to evoke Qatar's past include Bedouin tents and carpets, falcons used for hunting, camels, weapons, sailing vessels, and pearls and pearl diving equipment. Traditional architectural features also serve as national symbols, such as the wind towers that cooled

Qatar

HISTORY AND ETHNIC RELATIONS

Emergence of the Nation. In the 1760s, members of the Al-Khalifa of the Utub tribe migrated to Qatar from Kuwait and central Arabia and established a pearling and commercial base in Zubarah in the north. From there the Al-Khalifa expanded their territory by occupying Bahrain, which they have ruled ever since. The Al-Thai, the current ruling family, established themselves after years of contention with the Al-Khalifa, who still held claims to the Qatar peninsula through most of the nineteenth century. In 1867, Britain recognized Mohammad bin Thani as the representative of the Qatari people. A few years later, Qasim Al-Thani (Mohammad's son) accepted the title of governor from the Ottoman Turks, who were trying to establish authority in the region. Qasim Al-Thani's defeat of the Turks in 1893 usually is recognized as a confirmation of Qatar's autonomy. In 1916, Abdullah bin Qasim Al-Thani (Qasim's son) entered an agreement with Britain that effectively established the Al-Thani as the ruling family. That agreement provided for British protection and special rights for British subjects and ensured that Britain would have a say in Qatar's foreign relations. The increase in state income from oil concessions strengthened the Al-Thani's position.

When Britain announced its intention to withdraw from the region, Qatar considered joining a federation with Bahrain and the seven Trucial States. However, agreement could not be reached on the terms of federation, and Qatar adopted a constitution declaring independence in 1971. The constitution states that the ruler will always be chosen from the Al-Thani family and will be assisted by a council of ministers and a consultative council. The consultative council was never elected; instead, there is an advisory council appointed by the ruler. Despite periodic protests against the concentration of power and occasional disputes within the ruling family, the Al-Thani's size, wealth, and policies have maintained a stable regime.

URBANISM, ARCHITECTURE, AND THE USE OF SPACE

Doha, the capital, houses more than 80 percent of the population. Its parks, promenade, and award-winning waterfront architecture are considered as the centerpiece of Doha. The large-scale land reclamation project undertaken by the government to create those waterfront properties is recognized as a major engineering feat and a symbol of the country's economic and technological advancements.

homes before the introduction of electricity and the carved gypsum panels on buildings erected before 1940.

The date on which Qatar received independence from Great Britain in 1971 and the anniversary of the ruler's accession to office are celebrated as national holidays. The nation's flag, the state seal, and photographs of the rulers are displayed prominently in public places and local publications. Qataris also celebrate Islamic holidays.

Smaller towns such as Dukhan, Um Said, and Al Khor have become centers of the oil industry, and Wakrah, Rayyan, and Um Slal Mohammad have grown as suburban extensions of Doha. Smaller villages are spread throughout the desert interior. Village homes often are kept as weekend retreats for urban residents and as links to the tradition of desert nomads.

Doha's cityscape represents an attempt to fuse the modern with the traditional. At the start of the building boom in the 1960s, little thought was given to aesthetics; the objective was to build as quickly as possible. As the pace of development slowed, more consideration was given to developing a city that symbolized Qatar's new urban character and global integration. Designs were solicited that used modern technologies to evoke the nation's past. The main building of the university has cube-shaped towers on the roof. Those towers, with stained glass and geometric gratings, are a modernist rendition of traditional wind towers. The university towers are decorative rather than functional; however, they are highly evocative of Qatar's commitment to the lifestyles of the past while encouraging economic and technological development. Similar examples are found in government and private buildings. Many building designs incorporate architectural elements resembling desert forts and towers or have distinctively Islamic decorative styles executed in modern materials.

Homes also symbolize people's identities. The homes of Qatari citizens are distinct from the residences of foreign workers. The state provides citizens with interest-free loans to build homes in areas reserved for low-density housing. Foreign workers live in rental units or employer-provided housing and dormitories.

FOOD AND ECONOMY

Food in Daily Life. The presence of foreign workers has introduced foods from all over the world. Qatar's cuisine has been influenced by close links to Iran and India and more recently by the arrival of Arabs from North Africa and the Levant as well as Muslim dietary conventions. Muslims generally refrain from eating pork and drinking alcohol, and neither is served publicly.

Foods central to Qatar's cuisine include the many native varieties of dates and seafood. Other foods grown locally or in Iran are considered local delicacies, including sour apples and fresh almonds. The traditional dish *machbous* is a richly spiced rice combined with meat and/or seafood and traditionally served from a large communal platter.

The main meal is eaten at midday, with lighter meals in the morning and late evening. However, with more Qataris entering the workforce, it is becoming more common to have family meals in the evenings. The midday meal on Friday, after prayers, is the main gathering of the week for many families. During the month of Ramadan, when Muslims fast from dawn to dusk, elaborate and festive meals are served at night.

Coffee is a central feature of the cuisine. Arabian coffee made of a lightly roasted bean that is sweetened and spiced with cardamon is served in small thimble-shaped cups to guests in homes and offices. Most households keep a vacuum jug of coffee and sometimes tea ready for visitors. Another beverage, *qahwa helw* (sweet coffee), a vivid orange infusion of saffron, cardamom, and sugar, is served on special occasions and by the elite.

In recent years, restaurants and fast-food franchises have opened. Those establishments primarily serve foreign workers. Qataris, especially women, are reluctant to eat in public places; but will use the drive-through and delivery services of restaurants. Qatari men sometimes socialize and conduct business in restaurants and coffeehouses.

SOCIAL STRATIFICATION

Classes and Castes. The primary axes of social stratification are the nationality and occupation. The practice of hiring foreign workers has created a system in which certain nationalities are concentrated in particular jobs, and salaries differ depending on nationality. The broadest division is between citizens and foreigners, with subdivisions based on region of origin, genealogy, and cultural practices.

Despite this inequality, the atmosphere is one of comfortable and tolerant coresidence. Foreign workers retain their national dress. Their children can attend school with instruction in their native languages. Markets carry a broad range of international foods, music, and films. Foreigners are permitted to practice their religion publicly, and many expatriate religious institutions sponsor community activities and services.

Qataris are internally stratified according to factors such as tribal affiliation, religious sect, and historical links to settlement patterns. For example, Qataris with genealogical links to Arabia are likely to identify with Bedouin cultural values and be adherents of Sunni Islam, whereas Qataris with genealogical links to the northeastern side of the Gulf are

Fishing boats off the coast of Qatar. Seafood is a central part of Qatar's cuisine.

likely to identify with settled townsfolk and may be adherents of Shi'a Islam. Genealogical and geographic subdivisions among citizens correlate with occupational categories. The crafts are viewed as the province of Irani-Qataris, and freed slaves are disproportionately represented in certain professions, such as entertainment and the police force.

POLITICAL LIFE

Government. Qatari is technically an "Emirate," ruled by an Emir. Since independence the country's rulers have been of one particular family, the Al Thani. The Emir and many of the cabinet of ministers, as well as other high ranking officials are members of the Al Thani family (a large patrilineally related kin group) and are overwhelmingly male. However, some high level appointments have been made outside of the ruling family. Because of the concentration of power within the Al Thani, divisions or disputes among members of this large kin group will influence political relations. In 1998, Qatar held open elections for a "municipal council." This was the first election ever held in Qatar, and the campaigning was not only lively but drew in large portions of Qatar's citizenry. While a number of women ran for office, none were elected in this first vote. Both women and men turned out

to vote for representatives from their residential sectors. The Municipal Council represents local residential sectors to other governmental bodies.

SOCIAL WELFARE AND CHANGE PROGRAMS

After independence, Qatar developed extensive social welfare programs, including free health care, education through university, housing grants, and subsidized utilities. Improvements in utility services, road networks, sewage treatment, and water desalination have resulted in a better quality of life. In recent years, institutions have been established to support low-income families and disabled individuals through educational and job training programs.

NONGOVERNMENTAL ORGANIZATIONS AND OTHER ASSOCIATIONS

A number of international NGO's have offices and operations in Qatar, such as UNESCO, UNICEF, and the Red Crescent Society. Since 1995, the Emir's wife Shaikh Mouza, has been instrumental in encouraging and facilitating the establishment of organizations to serve women, children, family and the disabled. These service organizations have made significant headway particularly in the areas of health and education.

A young girl stands in a doorway beside an old merchant house in Qatar.

GENDER ROLES AND STATUSES

Division of Labor by Gender. Schooling is gender-segregated. After completing schooling, men and women can obtain employment in government agencies or private enterprise. Qatari women tend to take government jobs, particularly in the ministries of education, health, and social affairs. High-level positions are held predominantly by men. While the presence of the foreign workforce has put more women in the public sphere, those women work primarily in occupations that reinforce the division of labor by gender. Foreign females are hired mostly as maids, nannies, teachers, nurses, and clerical or service workers.

The Relative Status of Women and Men. Gender roles are relatively distinct. Men engage in the public sphere more frequently than do women. Women have access to schooling and employment and have the right to drive and travel outside the country. However, social mores influenced by Islam and historical precedent leave many women uncomfortable among strangers in public. Instead, their activities are conducted in private spaces. To provide women with more access to public services, some department stores, malls, parks, and museums designate "family days" during which men are allowed entry only if they accompany their families.

MARRIAGE, FAMILY, AND KINSHIP

Marriage. Most marriages are arranged. Usually the mother and sisters of the groom make initial inquiries about prospective brides, discuss the possibilities with the young man, and, if he is interested, approach the family of the prospective bride. That woman has the opportunity to accept or refuse the proposal. Marriages often are arranged between families with similar backgrounds, and it is common for several members of two lineages to be married to each other. Marriages between Qataris and other Gulf Arabs are common, but the government discourages marriage to non-Gulf citizens. One must get official permission to marry a noncitizen, and the citizen may have to give up the promise of government employment and other benefits.

Polygyny is religiously and legally sanctioned. While it remains common among the ruling family, the number of polygynous marriages has dropped in recent years. A wife can divorce her husband if he takes another wife, and with more education and economic options, women are more likely to do that now than they were in the past. Another reason for the decrease in polygyny may be the rising cost of maintaining more than one household.

The divorce rate has risen sharply since 1980. Both women and men may seek a divorce, and custody is granted in accordance with Islamic law. Young children are kept with the mother; once they reach adolescence, custody reverts to the father.

Domestic Unit. Extended, joint, and nuclear households are all found today. The preference is to live with or at least near the members of the husband's family. This patrilineal proximity is accomplished by means of a single extended household, walled family compounds with separate houses, or simply living in the same neighborhood.

Kin Groups. "Family" in Qatar refers to a group larger than the domestic unit. Descent is reckoned through the male line, and so one is a member of his or her father's lineage and maintains close ties to that lineage. After marriage, women remain members of the father's lineage but are partially integrated into the lineages of their husbands and children. Children of polygynous marriages often identify most closely with siblings from the same mother. As children mature, such groups sometimes establish separate households or compounds.

SOCIALIZATION

Child Rearing and Education. Children are important in family life. If a marriage is barren, the couple may resort to medically-assisted conception, polygyny, or divorce. Child care is the province of adult females, although children have close ties to their male relatives as well. The employment of foreign nannies has introduced new child care practices and foreign influences.

Higher Education. Public schooling has been available since the 1950s. In 1973, a teacher's college was opened and in 1977 the colleges of Humanities and Social Sciences, Science, and Sharia and Islamic were added to form the University of Qatar. Subsequently the College of Engineering, College of Administrative Sciences and Economics, and the College of Technology were added to the original four. Qataris can attend kindergarten through university for free. Students who qualify for higher education abroad can obtain scholarships to offset the costs of tuition, travel, and living abroad.

ETIQUETTE

Social behavior is conducted in a manner respectful of family privacy, hospitality, and the public separation of genders. Visits with unrelated persons occur outside the house or in designated guest areas separate from the areas regularly used by the family. One does not inquire unnecessarily about another person's family. Despite this strong sense of family privacy, it is considered rude not to extend hospitality to strangers. Tea, coffee, food, and a cool place to sit should be offered to any visitor. Conversely, it is rude not to accept hospitality. When greeting a member of the opposite sex, it is best to act with reserve, following the Qatari's lead. Some Qatari women feel comfortable shaking hands with a man, but others refrain. Similarly, men may refrain from extending the hand to women or sitting beside them.

RELIGION

Religious Beliefs. The majority of the citizens and the ruling family are Sunni Muslims, specifically Wahhabis. There is, however, a large minority of Shi'a Muslims. Recent events such as the Iranian Revolution, the Iran–Iraq War, and alleged discrimination against Shi'a Muslims have exacerbated sectarian tensions. These divisions are rarely discussed openly.

BIBLIOGRAPHY

Crystal, Jill. *Oil and Politics in the Gulf: Rulers and Merchants in Kuwait and Qatar,* 1990.

Ferdinand, Klaus. *The Bedouins of Qatar,* 1993.

Field, Michael. *The Merchants: The Big Business Families of Saudi Arabia and the Gulf States,* 1985.

Grill, N. C. *Urbanisation in the Arabian Peninsula,* 1984.

Kanafani, Aida. *Aesthetics and Ritual in the United Arab Emirates,* 1983.

Kay, Sandra, and Dariush Zandi. *Architectural Heritage of the Gulf,* 1991.

Lawless, R. I. *The Gulf in the Early 20th Century: Foreign Institutions and Local Responses,* 1986.

Lorimer, J. G. *Gazetter of the Persian Gulf, Oman and Central Arabia,* 1970 [1915].

Metz, Helen Chapin, ed. *Persian Gulf States: Country Studies,* 1993.

Montigny-Kozlowska, A. "Les lieux de l'identite des Al-Na'im de Qatar." *Maghreb-Machrek* 123: 132–143, 1989.

———. "Les Determinates d'un fait de la notion de territorie et son evolution chez les Al-Naim de Qatar." *Production Pastorale et Societe* 13:111–113, 1983.

Nagy, Sharon. "Social Diversity and Changes in the Form and Appearance of the Qatari House." *Visual Anthropology* 10:281–304, 1997.

———. *Social and Spatial Process: An Ethnographic Study of Housing in Qatar,* 1997.

Palgrave, B. W. *Personal Narrative of a Year's Journey through Central and Eastern Arabia*, 1868.

Peck, Malcolm. *Historical Dictionary of the Gulf Arab States*, 1997.

Schofield, R., and G. Blake, eds. *Arabian Boundaries Primary Documents*.

Zahlan, Rosemarie. *The Creation of Qatar*, 1979.

—SHARON NAGY

REUNION ISLAND

CULTURE NAME
Reunion Islander

ORIENTATION
Identification. Reunion Island (in French, *La Reunion*) is a multicultural society composed of people originally from France, Mozambique, India, China, Madagascar, and the Comores. Islanders use their ethnic origins to define themselves as *Cafres* (African ancestry) *Z'oreilles* (born in mainland France), *malabars* or *Tamouls* (from Tamil Nadu southern India), *Z'arabes* (from Gujarat in northern India), *Chinois* (from China), *Malgaches* (from Madagascar), *Comores* (from Comores), *Petits blancs* (poor rural whites living in the highlands), or *Creoles blancs* (white landowners). The term *Creole* today also applies to people with a mixed ethnic background. All the residents of the island are administratively French citizens.

Location and Geography. Reunion Island lies in the Indian Ocean, off the eastern coast of Madagascar. At 970 square miles, (2,512 square kilometers), it is the largest of the Mascarene islands. High plains separate two volcanic systems. Climatic variations range from humid to dry tropical to Mediterranean. More than half the land is not suitable for cultivation. Periodic cyclones can be devastating. The capital is Saint Denis.

Demography. In 1999, the population was over 717,000. It is difficult to categorize the population by ethnic background, but estimates indicate that approximately twenty percent of the population is of Indian ancestry, and around five percent is born in mainland France.

Linguistic Affiliation. Although French is the official language, Creole is the language of everyday life. Based on French, with a mixture of Malagasy and Tamil words, it is used with relatives and for informal interactions. French is generally used in formal situations. Although everybody understands it, many people cannot speak it; therefore, its use is a marker of educational achievement and social status.

Symbolism. Economic and cultural ties are almost exclusively with mainland France; Reunion is officially called "the France of the Indian Ocean." Since the development of tourism in the 1970s, the image the island tries to project to the outside world is that of a multicolored society where people with different ethnic backgrounds live together peacefully.

HISTORY AND ETHNIC RELATIONS
Emergence of the Nation. Discovered at the beginning of the sixteenth century, the island was reached by the French in 1643. Reunion (then called *Mascarin*) was devoid of inhabitants. The French sent twelve convicts into exile there. In 1649 they officially claimed the island in the name of the king and named it *Bourbon*. Colonization started in 1665, when the French East India Company sent the first twenty settlers. After 1715, settlers produced coffee and spices, which ultimately were replaced by sugarcane. In 1792, France renamed the island *La Reunion*.

The labor force needed on the sugarcane plantations was supplied by slaves from Mozambique and Madagascar. At the end of the seventeenth century, the population could be divided into white French landowners and African and Malagasy slaves. A great number of white settlers arrived too late to gain access to the land and, excluded from the plantation system, retired in the highlands, where they constituted a poor white population (*Petits blancs*).

The abolition of slavery in 1848 led white landowners to recruit indentured laborers for their plantations, particularly Tamils. Most Tamils stayed at the end of their five-year contracts and continued to work for the white landowners. At the turn of the century, some Chinese and Muslim Gujaratis ar-

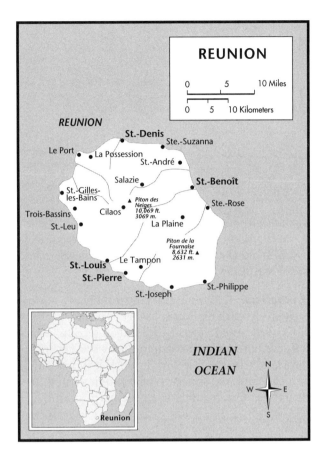

Reunion

rived to sell food and textiles. In 1946, Reunion became one of the four overseas department of France, and it became an administrative region in 1974.

Having lost their cultural links with their societies of origin, African and Maslagasy slaves were subject to deculturation and pauperization. By contrast, whites, Chinese, Muslim Gujaratis, Tamils, and French from the mainland have been able to maintain most of their original systems of value while adapting it to the local context.

National Identity. Since the beginning of immigration, the French government has stressed assimilation of the populations under its control, exploiting the resources of the island while pressuring immigrants to become "French." As a result, all members of this multicultural society are officially "French citizens." However, many descendants of Tamil immigrants have maintained their ancestral beliefs and patterns of behavior. Although Chinese residents were also converted to Christianity, they are less westernized than are residents of south Indian ancestry. Most still speak Chinese and have kept links with relatives in China. Gujaratis Muslims also have been able to preserve their culture and religion.

Ethnic Relations. Whites and people of African, Tamil, and mixed ancestry consider themselves the original inhabitants of the island, in contrast to Gujaratis and Chinese. However, all native residents feel a strong difference between themselves and people from mainland France. The French, who generally do not stay more than three or four years on the island, are rarely considered full members of the society. Both populations live close to each other but inhabit different cultural worlds.

FOOD AND ECONOMY

Basic Economy. The economy was traditionally based on agriculture. During the eighteenth and nineteenth centuries, the most important crops were coffee and cloves and then sugarcane.

Major Industries. The labor force consists of workers in services (seventy-three percent), industry (nineteen percent), and agriculture (eight percent). Major industries include sugar, rum, handicrafts, and flower oil extraction.

Trade. The major exports are sugar, rum vanilla, and perfume essences. Imported commodities include manufactured goods, food, beverages, tobacco, raw materials, machinery and transportation equipment, and petroleum products. The economy depends on financial assistance from mainland France, which is also the principal trading partner. Around 100,000 people born in Reunion work and live in mainland France. Massive importation of goods has led to a large deficit in the balance of trade. The government has promoted tourism to reduce unemployment, which affects more than a third of the labor force.

SOCIAL STRATIFICATION

Classes and Castes. The transformation of Reunion into a French department slowly substituted a pseudo-industrial and consumer society for a colonial and rural society. There are large disparities in wages and deep social inequalities between workers. The minimum wage is around ten percent lower than it is in mainland France, while the wages of those in the public sector are approximately forty percent higher. The gap between rich and poor accounts for the current social tensions. The white and Indian communities are substantially better off than are other segments of the population. Immigrants from France hold the key positions in admin-

A sugar factory in Saint Louis. Sugar is one of Reunion Island's major exports.

istration, and in the private sector, their wages are higher than are those of other groups. People of African descent are still at the bottom of the social scale. The outbreak of rioting in February 1991 reflected the seriousness of socioeconomic tensions.

Symbols of Social Stratification. Use of the French language characterizes social stratification. As most of the population learns Creole at home and French at school, the ability to speak French is a sign of education and high status.

POLITICAL LIFE

Government. The political system is French. The representative of the French state is the prefect, who is appointed by the French president. There are one general council and one regional council, whose presidents are elected by their members, that finance development projects. City mayors are popularly elected, along with five deputies to the French National Assembly.

Social Problems and Control. The legal system is French. Homicide and rape are relatively numerous and are committed mostly by men under the influence of alcohol. Court judgments take into account the social background of criminals.

Military Activity. Defense is the responsibility of France. The military is absent in Reunion, and men serve their military terms in France.

SOCIAL WELFARE AND CHANGE PROGRAMS

Because unemployment is a major problem, state programs of social welfare are important. More than sixty percent of the population receives welfare benefits.

SOCIALIZATION

Infant Care. The care of infants varies with the family's ethnic and cultural background. Regarding sleep practices, for instance, among families from the mainland France, a child is put in a separate room very early and may have stories, toys, and a night lamp to accompany him or her in the sleep. On the other side, among families of Indian origin, children consider sleep a positive and auspicious event, and children go to bed without reluctance. Most of these children share bedrooms with siblings of the same sex.

Child Rearing and Education. Children of Tamil ancestry learn to separate the world into two basic spheres of action: that of the family and the community, in which the Indian value system predomi-

Fishermen haul a boat onto one of Reunion's rocky beach heads.

Hikers gaze on the beauty of Cirque de Malfate from the peak of Piton Meido on Reunion Island.

nates, and that where the cultural models of the larger society are dominant.

Higher Education. In 1954, fifty-seven percent of the population was illiterate, but today the rate is less than 10 percent. Education is valued in families of Tamil, Gujarati, and Chinese ancestry. For the lower and middle classes, school is a democratic institution that allows one to achieve a better future. Pupils with African and mixed origin who frequently grow up in a family with a single mother, often experience failure at school. In contrast, education is particularly valued in families of Tamil, Gujarati, and Chinese ancestry. For the lower and middle classes, school is a democratic institution that allows one to achieve a better future. There are seven thousand students at the ever-expanding University of La Réunion.

RELIGION

Religious Beliefs. The dominant religion is Roman Catholicism, totaling eighty-six percent of the population. Christianity was established by the first settlers. Although indentured contracts specified that a laborer's religion be respected, the Catholic Church and the authoritarian administration attempted to convert newcomers. Tamils were obliged to go to church, wear French clothes, and give Christian names to their children. Contract workers had to express Christian attitudes and practice Christian rites to be accepted by their employers and the larger society. In the eighteenth century, Catholic priests attempted to prevent the construction of Hindu temples and the public practice of Hinduism. When it was finally authorized, the priests continued to spread a negative perception of the Hindu religion as "pagan."

Religious Practitioners. Although they have been largely christianized, people of Indian origin refer to Hindu Gods in important matters. While it has been adapted to a new social context, folk Hinduism has been maintained almost as it was in India at the time of emigration more than one century ago. Among the expressions of this religion are fire walking, animal sacrifices, and rituals of possession by a deity or ancestor. This Hinduism is strongly connected with the idea of protection against bad luck, the evil eye, and the negative forces of the visible and invisible world.

MEDICINE AND HEALTH CARE

In rural areas, modern medicine is complemented by traditional local practices based on a mixture of different beliefs (Hindus, Christian, and Malagasy).

A worker at a sugar processing factory.

Many people consult *devineurs* who can predict the future and give advice about their problems.

SECULAR CELEBRATIONS

The major holidays are the same as those in France (National Day, Bastille Day, Christmas, New Year's Eve), supplemented by local celebrations such as the anniversary of the abolition of slavery on 21 December and the Tamil and Chinese new years.

THE ARTS AND HUMANITIES

Literature. A local literature that has existed for the last twenty years celebrates the culture of Reun-

ion. Most writers who use the Creole language emphasize a global identity (that of being *réunionnais* and neglect the cultural heterogeneity of the population.

THE STATE OF THE PHYSICAL AND SOCIAL SCIENCES

In the 1970s a local university was created, and French scholars received funding to conduct research on the island. Numerous studies, focused primarily on the Creole language and culture, have since been published. Undertaken by researchers or students from mainland France or natives of the island, they mostly see the society as an integrated unit or a place of culturally distinct subcultures. An outward perspective—still awaited—should allow a better analytic distanciation.

BIBLIOGRAPHY

Ghasarian, Christian. *Honneur, Chance et Destin: La Culture Indienne à La Réunion*, 1991.

———. "Interpreting a Hindu Rite: A Critique of a Psychoanalytic Reading." *Berkeley Journal of Asian Studies* 7: 79–, 1996.

———. "We Have the Best Gods! The Encounter between Hinduism and Christianity in La Réunion." *Journal of Asian and African Studies* 23 (3–4): 286–295, 1996.

———. "Language Strategies in La Réunion." *Cahiers* 4(3): 7–18, University of Hull, England, 1998.

———. "Patrimoine et Ethnicité à La Réunion: Dynamiques et Dialogismes." *Ethnologie Francaise*, 3: 365–374, 1999.

Leguen, M. *Histoire de l'île de La Réunion*, L'Hartmattan, 1979.

Scherer, André. *La Réunion*, "Que sais-je?," 1980.

—CHRISTIAN GHASARIAN

ROMANIA

CULTURE NAME

Romanian

ORIENTATION

Identification. The name "Romania," which was first used when the three regions of the country were united in 1859, reflects the influence of ancient Rome on the nation's language and culture. The three regions—Walachia, Moldavia, and Transylvania—are relatively culturally uniform. An exception is the Hungarian community in Transylvania, which has its own language and traditions and considers itself Hungarian. The Roma (Gypsies), who are scattered throughout the country, mostly in small camps on the outskirts of towns and cities, are in many ways culturally unassimilated.

Location and Geography. Romania is in southeastern Europe at the north end of the Balkan peninsula, bordering Ukraine and Moldova to the north, Hungary to the northwest, Serbia to the southwest, Bulgaria to the south, and the Black Sea to the east. The land area is 91,699 square miles (237,500 square kilometers). The Carpathian Mountains cover about one-third of the country; they surround the Transylvanian Plateau and divide it from the other two main regions: Moldavia in the northeast and Walachia in the south. The Transylvanian Alps in the central region contain the highest peak, Mount Moldoveanu. The eastern and southern regions are characterized by rolling plains.

The Danube River stretches through the country for six hundred miles, forming its southern border with Serbia and Bulgaria and emptying into the Black Sea in the east. It is a source for irrigation and hydroelectric power.

Serious environmental problems include soil erosion and water and air pollution from unregulated industrial development. Because of economic hardship, the government has been slow to enforce laws that place restraints on industry.

Demography. The population was estimated to be 22,411,121 in 2000. Ninety percent of the people are Romanian, 7 percent are Hungarian, and 2 percent are Roma. The remainder is made up of Germans, Ukrainians, and others. Estimates of the Roma population range from 400,000 to one million; it is difficult to pinpoint because of the Roma's nomadic lifestyle. Before World War II, there was a large Jewish population, but almost 400,000 Jews were killed during the Nazi years, and many of the remaining Jews emigrated to Israel after the war. Today the Jewish population is estimated at less than 10,000. The German population has also decreased significantly. In the 1980s, Ceaucescu's government charged citizens large sums for permission to leave the country, a policy Germans felt was aimed specifically at them. Since Ceaucescu's regime fell in 1989, many Germans have emigrated.

Linguistic Affiliation. The official language is Romanian, which has Latin roots that date back to the Roman occupation of the area but also contains words from Greek, Slavic languages, and Turkish. In the fourteenth century, the country adopted the Cyrillic alphabet, but it later reverted to Roman lettering. Magyar (the language of ethnic Hungarians) and German are spoken, as are Serbian, Ukrainian, Slovak, Czech, Bulgarian, and Turkish. The language of the Roma population is Romany, although many Roma combine that language with Romanian.

Symbolism. The flag consists of blue, yellow, and red vertical stripes that symbolize Transylvania, Moldavia, and Walachia, respectively. The coat of arms, adopted in 1992, consists of a gold eagle against a blue background holding a cross in its beak, a sword in one claw, and a scepter in the other. Emblazoned on the eagle's chest are the symbols of the five provinces: Walachia, Moldavia, Transylvania, Banat, and Dobruja.

Romania

HISTORY AND ETHNIC RELATIONS

Emergence of the Nation. The first known inhabitants of present-day Romania were called Dacians. They were conquered by the Roman Empire in 106 C.E. Roman domination of the region lasted only until 271 but had a formative and long-lasting influence. Many Romans stayed and intermarried with the Dacians, helping to shape the customs and language of the region.

From the 200s through the 1100s, there was a series of invasions by various tribes from the north, including the Magyars and the Saxons. The northern region developed into a principality called Transylvania, the south into a principality called Walachia, and the east into Moldavia. Throughout

the fourteenth and fifteenth centuries, Walachia and Moldavia battled repeated invasions by the Ottoman Empire. They eventually succumbed around 1500 and spent more than three hundred years under Turkish rule. In 1601, the principalities of Moldavia, Walachia, and Transylvania were united for the first time under Prince Michael the Brave. During Michael's reign, Romania maintained a degree of sovereignty, but after his death, the Turks again dominated the region. They ruled through Greek officials who abused their power to exploit the peasants.

In the late 1700s and early 1800s, the Ottoman Empire was weakened by a series of defeats to the Russians. In 1821, an uprising in Walachia against the Greek rulers ended in the execution of the Romanian leader Tudor Vladimirescu, which further fanned desires for independence. The 1829 Treaty of Adrianpolie replaced Greek rule with Russian. In 1834, the Russians withdrew. In 1859, Prince Alexander Cuza was elected ruler of a united Moldavia and Walachia; three years later, the country was renamed Romania (then spelled Rumania). Cuza attempted to redistribute land and improve the living conditions of the poor, but those policies were unpopular with the upper class; in 1866, Cuza was forced to resign and was replaced by Prince Carol. In 1877, Carol led a successful joint revolt of Romanian and Russian troops against the Turks. The Congress of Berlin of 1879 marked the end of Turkish domination. Romania became a kingdom in 1881, and Prince Carol was crowned king.

Despite the nation's independence, the situation of the majority of the people remained unchanged. In 1907, increasing discontentment gave rise to a peasant revolt, in which the country estates of the nobility were burned. The army suppressed the uprising, killing ten thousand people.

In 1914, King Carol died and Ferdinand I took his place. Two years later, Romania entered World War I, joining the Allies in their fight against the Axis powers (Austria-Hungary and Germany in particular). After the war, the Trianon Treaty doubled the size of the country, uniting Moldavia and Walachia with Transylvania, Banat, Bessarabia (present-day Moldova), and Bucovina (today in southern Ukraine). In the years after World War I, a fascist movement called the Iron Guard won a large following in response to threats from the communist Soviet Union and rising unemployment.

Ferdinand died in 1927 and was succeeded by his son, Carol II, in 1930. Carol II resorted to military suppression of the opposition. In 1938 he outlawed political parties, and the head of the Iron Guard was executed.

At the outbreak of World War II, Carol II was forced to give up significant portions of the country to Russia and Hungary. His son Michael took the throne in 1940, but the real power fell to Marshal Ion Antonescu. In an effort to recoup Soviet-occupied territories, the country aligned itself with the German forces, participating in the invasion of the Soviet Union in 1941.

In August 1944, King Michael took power back from Antonescu. Romania joined the Allied forces but was soon occupied by Russia. After the war ended in 1945, most of the occupied territories were returned, but the Russian communists retained control. They abolished the monarchy in 1947, replacing King Michael with a puppet government under the leadership of Petru Groza. Business and industry were nationalized, and farmland was taken from the peasants and reorganized into government-run collectives. The communist leadership also imposed harsh penalties for expressing opposition to the government, imprisoning dissidents or putting them to work in extremely dangerous labor projects. Gheorghe Gheorghiu-Dej served as chief of state throughout the 1950s and was responsible for many of the Stalinist policies. In the early 1960s, he worked to distance Romania more from Soviet influence.

In 1965, Nicolae Ceausescu assumed the presidency and presented a new constitution. He initiated large-scale development projects, mainly with money borrowed from other countries. Many of those projects failed, sinking the country into debt that Ceaucescu attempted to pay off by exporting virtually everything the country produced, leading to severe shortages of food and fuel. The secret police kept the people in line through terror while Ceaucescu and his family, who controlled most of the government, continued to plunder the country for personal gain.

In the 1980s, worsening food shortages, along with the toppling of other communist regimes in Eastern Europe, stirred unrest. Protests in 1987 were put down with a combination of military force and extra food distribution. In December 1989, protests in the city of Timisoara were met with gunfire, and hundreds of citizens died. Other protests broke out across the country, and the situation escalated until troops refused to follow orders and joined the protesters. Ceaucescu and his wife attempted to flee the country but were halted by the army and brought to trial. Both were found guilty of murder and put to death by firing squad on Christmas Day 1989.

A party called the National Salvation Front assumed power, and in 1990 free elections were held. Ion Iliescu, the leader of the National Salvation Front and a former Communist Party member, won the presidency, and a new constitution was adopted in 1991. Iliescu put down student protests against the government by calling in twenty thousand coal miners to create a counter demonstration and later used the same tactic to force Petre Roman, a liberal prime minister, from office. Despite widespread dissatisfaction with Iliescu's leadership, he won reelection in October 1992. Four years later, voters replaced him with the reform-touting Emil Constantinescu of the Democratic Convention of Romania. Despite positive changes during his term, the December 2000 elections were a contest between Iliescu and Corneliu Vadim Tudor of the right-wing Greater Romania Party, who espoused a hard-line fascist ideology. Iliescu won the vote of a disillusioned, bitter, and frightened populace.

National Identity. The majority of residents share a common culture and history dating back to the Dacians. National identity is informed by pride in the country's resilience and ability to withstand attacks from the Austro-Hungarian Empire and the Turks and later from the Soviet Union. Many Hungarians living in Transylvania consider themselves more Hungarian than Romanian, and some consider the region a part of Hungary.

Ethnic Relations. Transylvania was once under Hungarian control, and parts of the region still have an ethnic Hungarian majority. Relations between Hungarians and Romanians are tense and have resulted in political conflict and occasional violence. In 1976, the communist government outlawed the use of the Hungarian language in education and the media in what it claimed was an effort to assimilate minorities into the national culture. Since 1989, the government has softened its stance, but discrimination still exists.

Romania has one of the world's largest populations of Roma. The Roma have a long history of persecution throughout Europe and still face discrimination. They have high rates of poverty, unemployment, and malnutrition, and many have left in an attempt to better their conditions.

During World War II, Jews were persecuted by both the government and the German military, and many were deported to Nazi concentration camps. Most of those remaining emigrated to Israel after World War II. Today, most of the country's Jews are concentrated in northern Moldavia and Bucharest.

URBANISM, ARCHITECTURE, AND THE USE OF SPACE

Bucharest is the capital and largest city, located in the center of the southern region of Walachia. Some old architecture still remains—there are several seventeenth- and eighteenth-century churches and a university dating to 1864—but the communists replaced most of the old buildings with concrete apartment complexes and skyscrapers. Between the two world wars, Bucharest was also a cultural center called "the Paris of the East," but its character has become more industrial and commercial. It is still home to some cultural attractions, including the National Art Museum, national theater and opera companies, and the country's largest university.

Other important cities include Brasov, an industrial center in the Transylvanian Alps; Constanta, a port on the Black Sea; Cluj-Napoca in central Transylvania; and Timisoara in the eastern Banat region.

In the cities, most people live in high-rise apartment buildings. Housing is limited, and conditions are cramped. Heating is often inadequate. In the countryside, most houses are old-fashioned two- or three-room wooden structures without plumbing or electricity. Traditional rural houses have roofs of red tiles, corrugated tin, or wooden shingles. In Moldavia and Walachia, they are usually white, while in Transylvania, they are painted different colors. In previous centuries, people often built houses almost entirely underground to protect themselves from Turkish attacks.

FOOD AND ECONOMY

Food in Daily Life. Breakfast is usually a small meal of bread with butter and jam and tea. The largest meal is eaten in the early afternoon. *Mititei*, grilled sausage seasoned with garlic, is a common appetizer. *Borsch*, cabbage soup with bran, or *ciorba*, a soup of lamb, mushrooms, and other meats and vegetables, is often served as a first course. Main dishes are usually meat-based, such as *tocana*, a pork stew flavored with garlic and onions. Other popular dishes include *sarmale*, cabbage leaves stuffed with rice and meat, and *mamaglia*, a cornmeal dish often served with poached eggs. Vegetables are served as side dishes. Typical desserts include *placinte*, a kind of pie, and *baclava*, a pastry made of nuts and honey.

Local wines produced in Moldavia and along the Black Sea coast are widely consumed. *Tuica*, a strong plum brandy, is also popular, as are beer and soft drinks.

Food Customs at Ceremonial Occasions. Wedding feasts include kegs of wine and *tuica* and an enormous round loaf of bread shared by the bride and groom. The annual sheep feast, *Simbra Oilor*, a traditional holiday marking the moving of the herds to the high pastures, is celebrated with a large community meal of cheese, meat dishes, and *tuica*.

Basic Economy. The labor force consists of 9.6 million people, of whom 37 percent work in agriculture, 34 percent in industry, and 29 percent in services. The unemployment rate is 11 percent, and

Fishermen in boats on the Danube near a fishing village. All fishermen officially work for the state, though they survive by selling 70 percent of their catch on the black market.

22 percent of the population lives below the poverty line.

After World War II, the communists built up the industrial sector and introduced a nationalized economic system. Large building projects left the country with debts; to pay them off, the government exported much of what it produced and imported little, creating shortages of consumer goods and food. Since 1989, the government has introduced reforms to create a free-market economy, privatizing some businesses and removing price controls. Although prices have gone up, wages have not; while more consumer goods are now available, many people cannot afford to buy them. Romania's currency is the leu.

Land Tenure and Property. When the communists came to power, they nationalized industries, transportation, and stores as well as private farms. The new government has begun to allow more private ownership of land, a change that has resulted in increased agricultural output. The new laws allow citizens to claim land that had been taken from their ancestors as long ago as four generations. The number of people reclaiming land is in the millions.

Commercial Activities. Many of the products produced for domestic sale are agricultural. The main crops are wheat, corn, sugar beets, sunflower seeds, and wine grapes. Farmers also raise cows, pigs, sheep, and chickens. Despite some improvement under the new government, shortages continue to be a problem, and consumers often wait in long lines to buy whatever the stores have in stock.

Major Industries. The primary industries include mining, timber, construction materials, metallurgy, chemicals, and machine building. Many industries have foundered in recent years, as they use old-fashioned equipment and are unable to compete with those of other countries. Since the early 1990s, tourism has become a growing industry.

Trade. Under communism, the Soviet Union was the primary trade partner. The Soviets sent raw materials that were processed in Romanian factories and then sold back to the Union of Soviet Socialist Republics (U.S.S.R.). Russia and the former Soviet republics remain important trading partners; others are Germany, Italy, France, and the United States. Exports include textiles and shoes, metals and metal products, and machinery and equipment.

The main imports are coal, natural gas, and crude oil as well as machinery and consumer goods.

Division of Labor. In an effort to build up the industrial base, the communist government moved some of the rural population to the cities, creating a shortage of farmers. Most of those who left were younger males, and the agricultural sector came to be composed primarily of women and older men.

The communist state valued science much more highly than the humanities and other fields and pushed young people to pursue careers in those areas. In the early 1990s, a significant number of people switched jobs as more opportunities arose; it was not uncommon to see former doctors and scientists entering fields such as journalism and sales.

The poor often have little choice of profession. Education is expensive, and the children of farmers and factory workers do not have much opportunity for advancement.

SOCIAL STRATIFICATION

Classes and Castes. The majority of the people are poor, and the overall standard of living is low compared to that of Western Europe. Under communism, a small elite had access to luxuries unthinkable to most of the population. Ceaucescu, for example, lived in a forty-room palace where walls were hung with artwork taken from churches and museums. Some of the old elite have managed to hold onto their wealth and power in the government after Ceaucescu's ouster. In general, however, few rise above the generally low standard of living.

Symbols of Social Stratification. Cars are rare, and people who own them are usually part of the elite. Other imported consumer goods and household appliances are also expensive and difficult to come by and represent another symbol of high economic standing. It is also a mark of wealth to be able to send one's children to the best day–care centers and provide them with private tutoring.

In the cities, the majority of the people wear Western-style clothing. In rural areas, some people still wear traditional garb. For women, this consists of wool skirts and vests whose embroidery varies from region to region. For men, it is a white blouse and pants cinched with a wool or leather belt and a cap or hat.

Throughout the country, Roma stand out in their brightly colored clothes. Women wear long flowing skirts, and men dress in white shirts with colorful sashes.

Hairstyles are often an indication of a woman's region of origin and marital status. Unmarried women wear their hair in braids, while married women cover their heads with cloths called *naframa*.

POLITICAL LIFE

Government. The president is the head of state and is elected by popular vote for a four-year term. He appoints the prime minister, who serves as the head of government. The prime minister appoints a cabinet called the Council of Ministers. The legislature is bicameral. The Senate (*Senat*) has 143 members, and the Chamber of Deputies (*Adunarea Deputatilor*) has 343 members. All legislators are elected by direct popular vote for four-year terms.

On the local level, the country is divided into forty districts administered by mayors and councils elected by the people. The head of each region is a prefect appointed by the central government.

Leadership and Political Officials. The 1991 constitution established a multiparty system. Sixteen parties are represented in the government, and there are several smaller ones that have not won seats. These parties are composed of former communists who favor gradual change, democrats pushing for faster reform, and groups representing the interests of the different ethnic minorities. After the corrupt and often brutal policies of Ceaucescu and other leaders, the people are wary of government officials in general.

Social Problems and Control. The majority of the crimes committed are nonviolent. Economic crimes are a significant problem; corruption, speculation, hoarding, and black market activities are all prevalent. Juvenile crime is also a concern. The legal system, previously a combination of civil law and communist legal theory, is now based on the constitution of France's Fifth Republic.

Military Activity. The military consists of the Army, the Navy, the Air and Air Defense Forces, the Paramilitary Forces, and Civil Defense. In 1996, Romania spent $650 million annually on the military, or 2.5 percent of the gross domestic product. During Ceaucescu's reign, paramilitary forces often were used to suppress uprisings or dissenting activity, and the security police tapped telephones, persecuted religious authorities, and instilled fear in the populace.

A young boy stands near his mother as she washes vegetables. The cloth covering a married woman's head is called a naframa.

SOCIAL WELFARE AND CHANGE PROGRAMS

The communist government instituted a system of social welfare under which assistance was provided only to employees of the state. These workers are still entitled to pensions for retirement, disability, and survivors as well as insurance in case of sickness or injury. The state also has programs for orphans, the mentally and physically handicapped, and the elderly. Many of these programs are inadequate; in the 1980s, older people were discouraged from going to hospitals because of a lack of staff and supplies. The responsibility for caring for the elderly often falls to the family.

NONGOVERNMENTAL ORGANIZATIONS AND OTHER ASSOCIATIONS

Various human rights and professional associations are active in the country. Many, such as the Children's Relief Network and Aid for Romanian Children, direct their efforts toward improving conditions in orphanages and helping thousands of abandoned children find homes. Some of these groups have a religious affiliation; others, such as the United States Agency for International Development (USAID), are funded by the governments of foreign countries.

GENDER ROLES AND STATUSES

Division of Labor by Gender. The communists attempted to get women into the work force in large numbers. While the majority of women work outside the home, they tend to occupy lower-level positions and generally are in traditional female fields, such as primary school education. Women also make up a large proportion of agricultural workers; as men left farming in the 1950s and 1960s, women were left behind in those jobs, which had come to be considered undesirable. While the definition of women's work has expanded, that of men's work has not, and women who work full-time outside the home are still expected to do all the cooking and housekeeping.

The Relative Status of Women and Men. After World War II, the communists succeeded in raising women's legal status, giving them equal rights in marriage and the workplace. Ceaucescu's regime was in many ways a step backward for women. His efforts to increase the population burdened women with either bearing children they did not want and could not afford or seeking illegal and dangerous abortions. The government also enforced mandatory gynecological examinations of women of

A Romanian town and the Transylvanian Alps. The highest peak in the country, Mount Moldoveanu, is located in these Alps.

childbearing age to prove that they had not had abortions.

Marriage, Family, and Kinship

Marriage. Traditionally, marriages were arranged by the couple's parents through a matchmaker. The bride's family was expected to contribute a dowry that usually consisted of linen and embroidery. Traditional rural weddings were large festivities to which the entire village was invited. The ceremony included not just the couple and their parents but grandparents, godparents, the matchmaker, attendants, speakers, cooks, and numerous other people.

Today it is customary for young people to choose their own spouses, but certain elements of the traditional ceremony are preserved. The bride's hair is braided in an elaborate style, and she dons a crown of flowers, jewels, and ribbons. The groom wears a white leather vest and a hat decorated with feathers, flowers, and leaves. The best man shaves the groom's beard to symbolize his departure from his previous lifestyle. In the ceremony, both the bride and the groom ask their parents to forgive them for leaving the family.

In their effort to undermine religion, the Communists made civil ceremonies a legal requirement and discouraged church weddings. They also gave

women greater rights in marriage, including equal control of children and property. When divorce laws were liberalized, the rates of divorce skyrocketed. To stem that trend, stricter laws were imposed in the 1960s, and divorce rates fell somewhat but remain high.

Domestic Unit. It is not uncommon for several generations to live together. Housing shortages force many people to live in close quarters. In the 1980s, the national average was ten square meters of living space per person; this has improved slightly, but not nearly to the goal set by the government of fourteen square meters per person by 2000.

Inheritance. Traditionally, an estate passes to the oldest son. Today, however, women are legally allowed to inherit property.

Kin Groups. The national culture places a high value on helping extended family members. An example of this was Ceaucescu's government, which was largely staffed by his relatives. Traditional families were large patriarchal units, as extra hands were always needed in the fields. Urbanization has led to smaller families, however, and to a decrease in the importance of family ties.

SOCIALIZATION

Infant Care. Ceaucescu made childbearing a priority in an effort to increase the population. He outlawed abortion and birth control and declared that each woman should have at least five children. While his policies were successful in producing more children, this was in many cases to the detriment of the children. Already poor families could not afford to feed or clothe them, and the orphanages filled with abandoned babies.

Child Rearing and Education. The communist government encouraged women to work outside the home and established state-run day-care centers called *crèches*. From a very young age, children are left in these centers all day while their parents work. Many *crèches* are overcrowded and insufficiently staffed. The largest day-care center is at Scinteia in Bucharest, which is exclusively for children of the elite.

School is free and mandatory from the ages of six to sixteen. From ages six to fourteen, children attend elementary school; after this, they must pass examinations to enter secondary school. About half these students go on to vocational schools; others continue their education at technical institutes or teacher-training programs.

Higher Education. Only 5 percent of students take a college preparatory course in secondary school. To study at a university, it is necessary to pass a rigorous examination that often requires expensive tutoring outside of school. The largest and most prestigious university is the University of Bucharest, founded in 1864. Other centers of higher education include Babes-Blyai University in Cluj-Napoca and the Polytechnic Institute in Bucharest.

ETIQUETTE

Romanians are known for hospitality and generosity. Guests are always fed. Men indicate their respect for women by a tip of the hat, a kiss on the hand, or standing to offer them a seat. It is also customary for younger people to defer to their elders.

RELIGION

Religious Beliefs. Seventy percent of the population is Romanian Orthodox, 6 percent is Roman Catholic (of which 3 percent is Uniate), 6 percent is Protestant, and 18 percent professes no religious affiliation. Under communism, religion was suppressed; churches were destroyed, and clergy were arrested. The government restricted religious practice but did not forbid it. The Romanian Orthodox Church as a whole did not oppose the government, and in many instances priests were used as tools of the administration.

Romanian Orthodoxy traces its history back to the Great Schism between Eastern and Western Christianity of 1054. The Eastern Orthodox Church, of which the Romanian Orthodox Church is one branch, has developed a more mystical slant than Roman Catholicism. Icons—images representing Christ, angels, saints, and other holy figures—hold an important place in Orthodox practice. They are considered a connection between the earthly and spiritual realms; it is believed that the saint is incarnated in the physical materials of the icon.

Religious Practitioners. The highest figure in Eastern Orthodox religion is the Patriarch of Constantinople. He is not considered infallible. Many Romanian priests lost the trust of their parishioners by working with the secret police during the communist regime. Some resisted, such as Laszlo Tokes, whose opposition to government intimidation led to popular acts of rebellion that ultimately led to Ceaucescu's ouster.

Rituals and Holy Places. Romanian Orthodox churches follow a specific pattern in the placement of icons. On the door there are usually life-size representations of the archangels Gabriel and Michael, above which there are several rows of other icons, including saints, martyrs, and apostles. Inside the church, there is a wall called an iconostasis where the images are displayed. On the feast day of a saint, that icon is placed on the altar for worshipers to kiss. It is customary for a family to have an icon in the home as well. When entering a house, guests cross themselves and bow to the icon before greeting the hosts.

Eucharist, or Holy Communion, is the central ritual in Orthodox services. During services on Sunday mornings, hundred of candles are lit and the smell of incense fills the church. Worshipers do not sit or kneel but stand erect.

Easter is the most important holiday in the Eastern Orthodox calendar. Its observation begins on Palm Sunday, when palm leaves or pussy willows are brought home from church. This is followed by the forty-day period of atonement of Lent, which ends on Good Friday. Easter Sunday, three days later, is celebrated with elaborately decorated eggs, feasting, and a midnight mass.

Roma women standing near their motor homes. Many Roma are not culturally assimilated into modern Romanian culture.

Christmas celebrations begin on 6 December (Saint Nicolas's Day), with family feasts. On the night before Christmas, young people wear costumes and perform *colinde*, traditional songs expressing hopes for good luck.

Death and the Afterlife. The belief in vampires popularized in the late 1800s by the story of Dracula has a long history in folk culture and is still followed in more traditional rural communities. It is believed that sometimes the soul does not leave the body after death, in which case the corpse does not decay but haunts the village of the deceased and can claim victims with a touch or even a glance. Garlic is thought to be helpful in keeping vampires away, as are food offerings made on Saint George's Day (23 April) and Saint Andrew's Day (29 November). The custom of covering mirrors in the home of the deceased has its origin in vampirism and the fear that the spirit of the dead person will see its reflection and not be able to leave.

MEDICINE AND HEALTH CARE

The health care system improved under the communist government, which provided free medical services to all citizens. Development was uneven, and while conditions in the cities improved mark-

edly, rural villages continued to suffer from a lack of doctors and facilities.

Environmental degradation has had negative effects on the health of the populations. Air pollution causes eye and lung disease, and many people do not have access to clean drinking water.

Many of the country's health problems are related to reproductive health and child care. Under Ceaucescu, abortion and birth control were banned; illegal abortions were common and often resulted in health problems. Many women were compelled to have children they could not support. Poor prenatal care and lack of food meant that many of those children were born prematurely and underweight; many were fed intravenously in hospitals with contaminated needles and contracted the AIDS virus. AIDS is a growing health concern, although the government has been slow to act and wary to release statistics. The main causes of death are cancer, cardiovascular disease, and alcoholism.

SECULAR CELEBRATIONS

New Year's Day is celebrated on 1 and 2 January. In Moldavia, the new year is brought in by a procession of people dressed as goats. In a rural tradition called *plugusorul*, a plow is decorated with green leaves and pulled throughout the village. Labor Day

1847

An overview of Bucharest's varied architecture. In the 1920s and 1930s, Bucharest was called "the Paris of the East."

is celebrated on 1 and 2 May, and Independence Day on 23 and 24 August, and the National Day of Romania on 1 December.

Different regions have traditions of spring and summer festivals, including the Pageant of the Juni in the city of Brasov, which is celebrated with parades, and *sinzienele*, which is observed throughout the country near the time of the summer solstice.

THE ARTS AND HUMANITIES

Support for the Arts. Under communism, the government forced artists to join unions, which supported them but censored their work. Today there is less state support for artists but more creative freedom.

Literature. The national literature traces its roots back to early ballads and folklore. The ballad form, which was most popular between the sixteenth and nineteenth centuries, often involved pastoral tales sung to the accompaniment of a lute or zither. The best-known folktale is that of Dracula, which was made famous by foreign authors. Ion Creanga, a nineteenth-century writer, was famous for his use of traditional storytelling techniques in fiction and memoirs. More contemporary writers are known for mixing politics, history, and literature. In the

late nineteenth century, the Moldavian poet Mihai Eminescu celebrated the country's history and culture. In that period, Ion Luca Caragiale wrote comic plays that dealt with political issues.

Romanian writers have made considerable contributions abroad. Tristan Tzara, who left for France during World War I, was one of the founders of the Dadaist movement. Eugene Ionesco (1912–1994), another expatriate who lived in France and wrote in French, composed the famous absurdist dramas *The Rhinoceros* and *The Bald Soprano*.

Graphic Arts. Traditional art forms include woven wool rugs, pottery, and wood carving. More folk art is preserved in the northwest region of Maramures than anywhere else in the country. Doorways, gates, and windows are carved with elaborate designs. Traditional costumes are also works of art, often displaying elaborate embroidery and a trimming of tiny glass beads.

Several painters rose to prominence in the nineteenth century after studying in Western Europe, including Nicolae Grigorescu, known for landscapes and depictions of rural life, and the portraitist Theodor Aman. Social realism dominated in the post–World War II period as the communist government compelled artists to produce works that glorified industrial workers and political leaders.

The most famous modern artist was Constantin Brancusi (1876–1957), a sculptor who made his home in France. He worked in wood and metal, creating abstract representations of people and nature. Late in his career, he was invited to create several sculptures for display in Tirgu-Jiu, the village of his birth. His works *The Kissing Gate* and *Table of Silence* are in a public park there.

Performance Arts. Romanian folk music is often mournful, such as the *doina* of the northwest. Common instruments include *nai* (panpipes), *tembal* (dulcimer), *bacium* (a long wooden wind instrument), *gorduna* (small double bass), and violins. Many folk musicians are Roma.

The national dance is the *hora*, a circle dance performed at festive occasions. Different regions have unique dances performed in pairs and groups.

Several Romanians have achieved prominence in classical music, including the pianist and conductor Dinu Lipatt and Georges Enesco, a violinist and composer whose work was influenced by traditional folk songs.

Drama companies in Bucharest and other cities' stage productions of classical Romanian works as well as contemporary pieces by national and foreign playwrights.

Early in the twentieth century, Bucharest became one of the centers of Eastern European filmmaking. In 1957, Ion Popescu-Gopo won an award at the Cannes Film Festival for an animated allegorical film called *Brief History*. Romanian filmmakers dealt with the repressive political environment of the 1970s in "iceberg movies" in which they disguised social and political statements in ostensibly innocent stories.

THE STATE OF THE PHYSICAL AND SOCIAL SCIENCES

The communist government gave science and technology priority over the humanities and social sciences. Subjects such as history and literature were tightly censored and viewed as vehicles for ideological indoctrination. Since communism fell, these fields have benefitted from more freedom of expression. The Department of Comparative Literature at the University of Bucharest reopened in the early 1990s after having been defunct for twelve years.

The center of academic research is the Romanian Academy. It has a library of over seven million volumes and a publishing house called Editura Academiei that prints academic papers and journals.

BIBLIOGRAPHY

Balas, Egon. *Will to Freedom: A Perilous Journey through Fascism and Communism*, 2000.

Bran, Mirel. "Romania: Computer-Generated Freedom." *UNESCO Sources*, February 2000.

Davies, Alan I. "The Secret of Fast Food in Romania." *Contemporary Review*, October 1, 1998.

"An Ex-President, the 'Less Bad' of Two Candidates, Wins Romania." *Philadelphia Inquirer*, December 11, 2000.

Lewy, Guenter. "The Travail of the Gypsies." *National Interest*, Fall 1999.

Michelson, Paul E. *Romanian Politics 1859–1871: From Prince Cuza to Prince Carol*, 1998.

Pop, Ioan Aurel. *Romanians and Romania: A Brief History*, 1999.

Rodina, Mihaela. "Bucharest Blues." *UNESCO Sources*, March 1997.

Roper, Steven D. *Romania: The Unfinished Revolution*, 2000.

Shen, Raphael. *Restructuring of Romania's Economy: A Paradigm of Flexibility and Adaptability*, 1997.

Siani-Davis, Peter, and Mary Siani-Davis, compilers. *Romania*, 1998.

"The Tortoise and the Hare." *The Economist*, August 7, 1999.

Treptow, Kurt W., ed. *History of Romania*, 1997.

U.S. Department of State, Bureau of Democracy, Human Rights, and Labor. *Human Rights Report on Romania*, February 28, 1999.

Web Sites

U.S. Department of State, Central Intelligence Agency. *Romania*, http://www.odci.gov/publications

—ELEANOR STANFORD

RUSSIA

CULTURE NAME

Russian

ORIENTATION

Identification. "Rus" may derive from the name of a tribe that gained political ascendancy in Kiev and other Slavic towns and lent its name to the language, culture, and state. Some scholars believe this to have been a Varangian (Viking) clan from Scandinavia, and others hold that it was a Slavic tribe. Some historians believe that "Rus" derives from an ancient name for the Volga River.

People ethnically identified as Russians have been politically and culturally dominant in a vast area for five hundred years of tsarist and Soviet imperial expansion. However, despite repression of their cultural autonomy, minority cultures have survived within the Russian Federation; including the peoples of the North Caucasus, numerous indigenous groups in Siberia, the Tatars in the Volga region, and the East Slavic Ukrainians and Belorusians. The last three groups are widely dispersed throughout the federation. All but the youngest citizens share a Soviet cultural experience, since under Communist Party rule the state shaped and controlled daily life and social practice. Much of that experience is being rejected by Russians and non-Russians who are reclaiming or reinventing their ethnic or traditional pasts; many communities are asserting a specific local identity in terms of language and culture. There is a broad cultural continuity throughout the federation and among the millions of Russians in the newly independent republics of Central Asia, the Baltic region, and the Caucasus.

Location and Geography. In addition to being the largest, the Russian Federation is one of the world's northernmost countries. It encompasses 6,592,658 square miles (17,075,000 square kilometers), from its borders with Finland, Estonia, Latvia, Belarus, and Ukraine on the west to the Bering Strait in the far northeast and from its borders with Georgia, Azerbaijan, Kazakhstan, Mongolia, and China in the south to the Arctic Ocean in the north.

European Russia, the most densely populated, urbanized, and industrialized region, lies between the Ukraine-Belarus border and the Ural Mountains. Seventy-eight percent of the population lives in this area. Two large industrial cities are located above the Arctic Circle: Murmansk on the Kola Peninsula and Norilsk in Siberia.

The great plains are divided by six ecological bands. In the northeast, above the Arctic Circle, lies a huge expanse of frigid, occasionally marshy tundra, a nearly unpopulated region where much of the land is permanently frozen and little grows but moss and shrubs. Below that is the taiga, a vast expanse of coniferous forest, which gradually blends with a band of mixed coniferous and deciduous forest to cover half the country. The capital, Moscow, is in the center of this region, where much agriculture has been located despite the thin, poor soil. A line of mixed forest and prairie with more arable soil characterizes the central areas, followed by Russia's "breadbasket," the black earth belt that constitutes less than a tenth of the national territory. Below that, the relatively arid steppe, with grasslands and semidesert and desert regions, runs along the northern edge of the Caucasus Mountains and north of the Caspian Sea beyond the Volga River basin into Central Asia.

The climate of much of European Russia is continental, with long, cold winters and short, hot summers. In the northern areas, winter days are dark and long; in the summer, the days are long and the sun barely sets. With the exception of the black earth belt, Russia has fairly poor soil, a short growing season, low precipitation, and large arid steppe regions unfit for agriculture except with extensive irrigation. These factors limit agricultural production and account for the frequency of crop failures; what is produced requires substantial labor. The

Russia

huge forests provide for foraging, hunting, and logging.

Many great rivers transect the country, such as the Dvina, Don, Oka, and Volga in the European heartland and the Ob, Yenisei, and Lena in Siberia; most of these rivers are linked by subsidiary waterways. Until the advent of railways and roads, the rivers were the only efficient way to travel, and they remain a significant form of transport for people and materials. Limited access to year-round seaports has always been a military and commercial problem. A lack of natural borders has meant vulnerability to invasion, a danger offset by the size of the country and its harsh, long winters.

These environmental factors have affected the demographic profile and shaped cultural, social, and political institutions, influencing colonizing projects, settlement patterns, household configurations, village politics, agricultural systems, and military technologies. Bold defiance of these natural limitations include Peter the Great's founding of

Saint Petersburg on northern swamplands in 1703, and the twentieth-century plan to reverse the northerly flow of some of Siberia's rivers to facilitate the movement of natural resources. Equally important is the ability of rural and urban dwellers to survive challenging conditions of land, climate, and politics. Tens of millions of families depend on food they grow for themselves.

Demography. In July 1999, the population was estimated at 146,393,000, a decline of more than two million since the end of the Soviet Union in 1991. The current figure includes several million immigrants and refugees from newly independent former Soviet republics. Since 1991, a stark drop in the birthrate has combined with a dramatic rise in the mortality rate. Average life expectancy for both men and women has declined since the 1980s.

This population decline is expected to worsen in the next decade. It is largely the result of the economic and social upheavals of the postsocialist period, which have impoverished the population and caused a decay of social services. Growing unemployment, long-term nonpayment of wages and pensions, paid wages that are below the poverty line, unsafe working and road conditions, the spread of infectious diseases, and the impoverishment of public health care systems have caused stress, depression, family breakdown, and rising rates of alcoholism, suicide, homicide, and domestic violence. Circulatory diseases, accidents, and suicides attributable to alcohol abuse are the leading causes of death among men. Malnutrition, disease, industrial pollution, poor health care, and reliance on abortion for birth control have reduced fertility rates and increased maternal and infant mortality.

In 1999, Russians accounted for 81 percent of the population and were the dominant ethnic group in all but a few regions. Other major ethnic nationalities are Tatars (4 percent), Ukrainians (3 percent), Chuvash (1 percent), Bashkir (1 percent), Belarussian (1 percent), and Mordovians (1 percent). Dozens of other ethnic nationalities make up the remaining 8 percent. There has been a significant rate of intermarriage between ethnic populations.

Until the twentieth century, the population grew steadily. The population of Rus' in the twelfth century is estimated at seven million. By 1796, Russia had a population of thirty-six million, to which territorial annexation had contributed greatly. In the 1850s, the population was sixty-seven million. The abolition of serfdom, accompanied by urbanization, industrialization, and internal migration in the second half of the nineteenth century, led to significant population growth, and by 1897 the population was 125 million. By 1917, the year of the Russian Revolution, the population had grown to 170 million. Famines, largely caused by civil war and the Soviet collectivization of agriculture, decimated the rural population in the 1920s and 1930s. In 1941, the population was around two hundred million. World War II caused the deaths of more than twenty million Soviet citizens. After the 1940s, population growth was slowed by the gender disparity and devastation of infrastructure caused by war.

Linguistic Affiliation. Russian is one of three East Slavic languages of the Slavic branch of the Indo-European language family. It is the most widely spoken Slavic language, with 1.39 million people speaking it as their native language and tens of millions more using it as a second language. Many people in non-Russian ethnic groups speak Russian as their native or only language, partly as a result of tsarist and Soviet campaigns to suppress minority languages. The collapse of the Soviet Union opened the way for linguistic revival movements in many ethnic communities.

There are three major dialects (northern, southern, and central), but they are mutually intelligible. Russian has been influenced by other languages, particularly Greek (Byzantine Christian) in the Kievan period, French in the eighteenth and nineteenth centuries, and English in the twentieth.

The Cyrillic alphabet was brought to Kievan Rus' along with Christianity in the tenth and eleventh centuries by the followers of Saint Cyril and Saint Methodius, who invented the first Slavic alphabet, Glagolitic, in the ninth century. Along with Old Russian, Church Slavonic was the primary literary language until the early eighteenth century, when it was reformed as part of Peter the Great's westernization and secularization campaigns. Many important texts were written in Church Slavonic and the more vernacular Old Russian, including historical chronicles, epic poems, folklore, and liturgical and legal works.

Symbolism. A popular visual symbol is Moscow's Saint Basil's cathedral with its colorful cupolas. Images of Saint Basil's and those of hundreds of other churches and cathedrals are key symbols of the country's long Orthodox history. Calendars, posters, and postcards with images of Orthodox churches are common in apartments and offices.

Bread symbolizes key aspects of the national self-image. It is the mark of hospitality, as in *khleb-sol* ("bread-salt"), the ancient custom of welcoming a visitor with a round loaf with a salt cellar on top. This tradition can be observed at political and diplomatic events when a host receives an important guest. In broader terms, bread is the symbol of life; in times of hardship it is the primary food, and being "without bread" signals starvation. Other foods are also important symbols: black caviar, which signifies luxury and plenty as well as the bounty of the rivers and seas; mushrooms and berries, the gifts of the forest and dacha; *bliny*, pancakes served before Lent; the potato, staple of the diet; and vodka, a symbol of camaraderie and communication.

Forest plants, creatures, and objects are widely used in symbolic ways. The white birch conjures the romance of the countryside; the wolf, bear, and fox are ubiquitous in folktales and modern cartoons; and the peasant hut *izba* signifies the cozy world of the past. Inside the *izba* are three other cultural symbols: the plump clay or tiled stove; the samovar, and the Orthodox icon in its corner shrine. While most people live in urban apartments images of traditional life still have great power and meaning.

Everyday conversation is filled with metaphors summarizing a highly complex view of shared cultural identity. Russians talk of soul *dusha* to refer to an internal spiritual domain that is the intersection point of heart, mind, and culture. True communion depends on an opening up of souls that is accomplished through shared suffering or joy. Communal feasting and drinking also can help open up the soul. Soul is said to be one of the metaphysical mechanisms that unite Russians into a "people" *narod*. Stemming from ancient Slavic words for clan, kin, and birth, and meaning "citizens of a nation," "ethnic group," or simply a "crowd of people," *narod* is used to refer to the composite identity and experience of the people through history. It often is invoked by politicians hoping to align themselves with the population. Leaders of the Soviet Union, trying to unite ethnic groups under a single multinational identity, ritualistically employed the term "Soviet people" (*sovietskii narod*). People still speak in terms of belonging by "blood"; a person is seen to have Russian blood, Jewish blood, Armenian blood, or a mixture of ethnic bloods. Nationalist discourse uses this concept to stress the purity of one's own people and disparage those with "foreign" blood.

After the collapse of the Soviet Union, the calendar of national holidays was altered. The compulsory celebration of the Great October Revolution (7 November) was diminished in scale, although it is still officially marked. The Day of Victory (9 May), the Soviet capture of Berlin that ended World War II, still provokes strong feelings. Cemeteries, parks, and public places are filled every year with people gathering to memorialize the war, and the media celebrate the heroism of the Soviet peoples. Even though these tributes are tempered by revisionist history, a core of patriotic feeling remains. A new political holiday is Russian Independence Day (12 June), marking the establishment of the Russian Federation in 1991. New Year's Eve is the most widely observed holiday. The observance of Christmas and Easter and other Orthodox holidays has grown since the end of the Soviet repression of religious observance.

HISTORY AND ETHNIC RELATIONS

Emergence of the Nation. The area now called Russia has always been multicultural. The Eastern Slavic tribes, the ancestors of modern Russians, traditionally are thought to have originated in the Vistula River valley in what is now Poland and to have migrated eastward in the seventh to the ninth centuries. Other evidence suggests that Eastern Slavic pastoral peoples were widespread in the central and eastern portions of the plain that stretches across the northern half of the Eurasian continent a thousand years earlier, coexisting with Finnic and Lithuanian tribes to the north and enduring recurring waves of conquest.

For more than a millennium, people sharing cultural traits, social structures, and religious beliefs have occupied present-day Russia, Ukraine, and Belorusia. Eastern Slavic society was culturally distinct and highly developed in terms of agriculture, technology, commerce, and governance by the tenth century. By the eleventh century a huge expanse had come under the nominal rule of the Kievan princes; at that time, the city-state of Kiev on the Dniepr River in present-day Ukraine was rivaled in size and splendor only by Novgorod far to the north. Prince Vladimir I, who ruled Kievan Rus' from 980 until 1015, brought Byzantine (Orthodox) Christianity to Kiev in 988 and sponsored the widespread baptism of the peoples of Rus'. A gradual process of the melding of pre-Christian practices with those of Orthodoxy consolidated the population under one political and cultural system. An intricate written code of customary law, the *Pravda Russkaia*, was in place by the eleventh century.

Wars after the death of Prince Yaroslavl the Wise in 1054 caused the gradual disintegration of Kievan Rus' until 1240, when Kiev fell under the domination of the Mongol Empire. The fall of Kievan Rus' and the political fragmentation that followed divided the Eastern Slavs into three distinct cultural-linguistic groups: Ukrainian, Belorusian, and Russian. The Mongols destroyed many cities and towns, and created a complex administrative system to exact tribute from its peoples and princes; Mongol control lasted until the late fifteenth century, although with less impact after 1380. The political power and territorial control of Muscovy expanded greatly under the four-decade reign of Ivan III, who died in 1505 after routing the Mongol armies. From that time on, the Russian state developed and expanded, with Moscow at its center. Ivan IV (the Terrible) was the first to crown himself tsar in 1546. He ruled in an increasingly arbitrary and absolutist fashion, brutalizing the aristocratic boyars in a decade-long period of terror known as the *oprichnina*. The century's end brought the "Time of Troubles"—fifteen years of political instability and civil and class strife that resulted in widespread impoverishment and famine, enserfment of the peasantry, and waves of migration of peasants to the edges of Russian territory.

Under Peter the Great, the Romanov tsar who ruled from 1682 to 1725, Russia began a period of imperial expansion that continued into the Soviet period. Peter attempted to modernize and westernize the country militarily, administratively, economically, and culturally, often through the use of force. His reforms changed society irrevocably, particularly through his introduction of new military and agricultural technologies, a formal educational system, a tight system of class ranking and service, and the founding of the European-style city of Saint Petersburg. Peter moved the capital from Moscow to Petersburg, where it remained until after the 1917 revolution.

After Peter's reign, Russian imperial rule expanded southward into the Crimea, southeast along the Volga River, and eastward across the Siberian forests to the Pacific Ocean. Through further expansion during the Soviet period (1917–1991), Russians achieved political and demographic dominance over a territory equal to one-sixth of the world's land surface. After 1991, Russian geopolitical power declined, but the federation remains the largest country in the world.

National Identity. Russia has had a thousand-year history of growth and contraction, political consolidation and disintegration, repression and relaxation, messianism and self-definition, and varying forms of socioeconomic interdependence with other nations. This history has had far-reaching effects on the other populations of Eurasia as well as on every aspect of the national culture.

For many centuries, the question of whether Russian culture is more ''eastern'' or ''western'' has been a burning issue. Situated at the crossroads of important cultures and civilizations in every direction, the Slavic groups and other peoples of Russia have profoundly influenced and been influenced by them all in terms of trade, technology, language, religion, politics, and the arts.

Ethnic Relations. Inter-ethnic relations are fraught with tensions spawned over centuries of Russian and Soviet colonial domination and activated in the aftermath of the collapse of the Soviet state. Most conflicts are multidimensional, simultaneously involving struggles for political control, rights over natural resources, migration and relocation, and the revitalization of national or ethnic cultures, religions, languages, and identities. Soviet policies—which compelled the use of the Russian language on all peoples, organized massive changes

in livelihood and lifestyle for tens of millions, forcibly moved whole populations (such as Crimean Tatars and Meshketian Turks), installed ethnic Russian political elites and managers in non-Russian regions, and extracted the wealth from local production into central coffers without sufficient economic return to the peripheries—have set the stage for the conflicts of today.

Conflicts over resources are heated in parts of Siberia and the Far East. The Sakha (Yahut) are trying to claim rights to some economic benefits from the vast diamond, oil, gold, and other mineral wealth in their republic. This struggle to reap even marginal benefits from their own territories has long been blocked by Russian central control over the resource extraction industries, and by the strategic relocation of tens of thousands of Russians to Yakutia in the Soviet period. This battle over resources is associated with a growing nationalist movement. Other Siberian peoples are engaged in similar struggles over oil and gas revenues, and rights to traditional fisheries, forest products, and reindeer-grazing lands. Environmental issues play a significant role, too, as people fight to prevent or reverse the spoiling of rivers, lakes, and soils by the oil and mining industries.

Occupation of the North Caucasus has been a cause of conflict for three centuries. Russia waged devastating wars with Chechnya from the mid-1990s on, attempting to repress local independence movements, stem a pan-Islamic movement from taking hold there, and maintain access to the oil wealth of the Caspian sea. There are few signs that this conflict will be resolved peacefully, and relations are characterized by intense hatred, prejudice, and propagandizing on both sides. Roots of this conflict lie in a long history of violent repression and impoverishment in Chechnya.

Internal migration and displacement has contributed greatly to ethnic tensions and prejudice, as several million Russians have returned from newly independent states in Central Asia, the Caucasus, and the Baltics, feeling themselves unwanted guests in those places, or in some cases (Tajikistan, Armenia, and Azerbaijan) escaping civil wars. Border regions between Russia and former Soviet republics, which often contain highly mixed and intermarried Russian and non-Russian populations, present a significant problem.

In general, unflattering and insulting stereotypes of Siberian natives, Koreans, Central Asians, peoples of the Caucasus, Ukrainians, Jews, and other ethnic nationalities are widely shared among Russians and circulate unimpeded in print media.

Ivan the Great's Bell Tower in the Kremlin.

One effect of the wars in Chechnya has been constant police harassment and public suspicion of the Caucasian residents of Moscow, Saint Petersburg, and other cities.

URBANISM, ARCHITECTURE, AND THE USE OF SPACE

In 1851, 92 percent of the population lived in rural villages, and at the time of the 1917 revolution, the population was more than 80 percent rural. The Soviet period brought movement to the cities as people tried to escape the harsh conditions on state-run collective farms. More than half of the rural population today is over age 65, because young people continue to migrate to the cities. Although there are still tens of thousands of small villages, many are disappearing as people die or depart.

By 1996, 73 percent of the population was urban, with most people living in high-rise apartment blocks constructed after the 1950s. Much of the urban population retains strong material and psychological ties to the countryside. Many people own modest *dachas* within an hour or two of their apartments and on weekends or in the summer work in their gardens, hike, hunt or gather in the forests, and bathe in lakes and rivers. Many other people retain ties to their natal villages or those of their parents or grandparents.

The largest cities are Moscow, nine million people; Saint Petersburg, nearly five million, Nizhnii Novgorod and Novosibirsk, 1.4 million each; Yekaterinburg, 1.3 million; and Samara, 1.2 million. After the end of the communist era, many places were rededicated with their prerevolutionary names.

Cities such as Moscow, Novgorod, Pskov, and Yaroslavl grew around the old fortresses (kremlins) and monasteries that formed their centers and near the gates where artisans and traders peddled their goods. The old cities reflect their complex and often violent histories through the coexistence of multiple styles. In the European regions, Byzantine churches from the thirteenth and fourteenth centuries stand in the shadows of modernist high-rises, with Renaissance, Baroque, or Neoclassical architecture nearby. These variegated cityscapes may be covered with grime, reflecting the proximity of industrial enterprises and the lack of funds for maintenance. In the wealthiest city centers, the post-Soviet years have brought varying degrees of urban revitalization.

Other cities were built almost from scratch and reflect a passion for grandiose urban planning. Saint Petersburg was built to secure access to the Gulf of Finland and the Baltic Sea. Catherine the Great saw to it that Petersburg became a European city, with streets, avenues, and plazas, designed in an elegant Venetian style. In the Soviet era, ambitious building projects led to the founding and construction of industrial cities such as Magnitogorsk, Russia's "Steeltown," in the 1930s.

The central parts of most cities have important governmental, commercial, and religious buildings. Intermingled with these edifices are multistoried nineteenth-century town houses now used for commercial purposes or housing, and neighborhoods of walk-up apartment blocks. Farther out from the center stand rows of white apartment towers dating from the 1960s. Reaching from ten to thirty stories, these mammoth buildings house the majority of the population in small apartments. Although they are often distant from city centers and industrial areas, these apartments have provided privacy and security to millions of families. They are spacious compared to the barracks or communal apartments in which many families lived until the 1950s. Almost all the cities share this general layout, although some have avoided the fires and demolition campaigns that destroyed millions of traditional wooden structures in the past.

A modern grandiosity characterizes the state buildings constructed in Soviet cities from the 1930s to the 1950s. As the capital, Moscow was virtually transformed, but other cities were also reshaped by Stalinist architectural projects, which juxtaposed monumentalist neoclassicism with revolutionary modernism and industrial futurism. In the 1930s, subway systems were constructed beneath the largest cities, including the vast Moscow Metro.

Immensity in architecture and wide boulevards and plazas often result in inhospitable urban spaces. In the Soviet period, many amenities were unavailable or overburdened. Commercial venues were organized in a top down fashion through state planning, and shopping was a challenge. Some goods and services were located in distant neighborhoods, although day care centers and schools were always close. The commercial privatization of the post-Soviet years has brought new stores, restaurants, and cafés that offer a variety of food and manufactured goods. This has occurred to a lesser extent in provincial towns and villages, many of which have experienced a decline in public services.

An important element of urban life are the enormous public parks and forested areas within or adjacent to city boundaries. The result of this prerevolutionary and Soviet urban planning remains a source of pleasure and recreation. People spend hours strolling or sitting on benches to talk, smoke, play chess, or read. Smaller urban parks sometimes center on a statue of a writer or political leader; ten years after the end of communist rule, statues of Lenin still anchor parks and plazas. Statues often serve as meeting places, and a park may have a special identity as the gathering place for a subcultural group such as hippies, punks, gays, or literati.

The huge public plazas in many cities have been central to political life for centuries. Moscow's Red Square and Manezh are historically significant spaces used for government ritual, revolutionary protest, parades, concerts, holiday celebrations, and state funerals.

Until recently, when new wealth has allowed a small proportion of the population to build private homes and mansions on urban fringes, domestic existence has meant living in small apartments. Because of limited space, the largest room serves as living room, bedroom, and dining room for many families. Domestic furnishing is highly consistent, in part because until the 1990s all furniture was purchased from state stores, where variation was limited. Among the characteristics of Russian taste are functional furniture, of oriental-type carpets on the walls, and large wardrobes instead of closets. The bath and toilet are commonly located in small separate rooms side by side. Narrow balconies are used for storage, tools, laundry, and sitting.

Family members spend much of their time at the kitchen table, eating and drinking tea while talking, reading, watching television, cooking, or working on crafts. When guests come, all sit around one table for the entire gathering, which may continue for hours. Wedding parties usually take place at the home of the family of the bride or groom, and everyone squeezes around an extended table.

Although public spaces within and around apartment blocks are often decrepit and dirty, the threshold to a family's apartment marks a crucial transition zone to private space, which is clean and tidy. Shoes are remain just inside the doorway to keep dirt from the interior of the home.

FOOD AND ECONOMY

Food in Daily Life. The most common food is bread. Potatoes, cabbage, carrots, and beets are the standard vegetables; potatoes are a staple. Onions and garlic are used liberally, especially in soups, stews, and salads.

Russians generally love meat. Starvation means having no bread, while poverty means going without hard sausage *kolbasa*. Sausage, pork, beef, mutton, chicken, and dried or salted fish are widely available and relatively cheap. Only some can afford to buy delicacies such as veal, duck, sturgeon, and salmon. Traditional aristocratic fare included such fancy foods, many of which are popular among the newly wealthy classes today.

For most people, breakfast is a quick snack of coffee or tea with bread and sausage or cheese. Lunch is a hot meal, with soup, potatoes, macaroni, rice or buckwheat kasha, ground meat cutlets, and peas or grated cabbage. This meal may be eaten in a workplace cafeteria at midday or after people return home from work; a later supper may consist of boiled potatoes, soured cabbage, and bread or simply bread and sausage.

People eat a wide range of dairy products, such as *tvorog*, a kind of cottage cheese, and *riazhenka*, slightly soured milk. These items can be purchased from large shops or private farmers' markets or made at home. In provincial cities and towns, unpasteurized milk is sold from tanker trucks, although bottles and cartons of pasteurized milk are available everywhere, as is sour cream. Hard and soft cheeses are also popular.

Fruits are widely loved and cultivated. In late summer, fruits and berries are harvested and made

Two Russian shoppers walk along the Moika Embankment in Saint Petersburg. Saint Petersburg is the second largest city in Russia, with about five million people.

into preserves, compotes, cordials, and concentrates for the winter months. Mushroom picking is an art, and many people can identify edible local varieties, which they salt, dry or can. Cabbage, cucumbers, garlic, and tomatoes are preserved by salting or pickling.

Russians are connoisseurs of tea. Coffee has grown in popularity and is often served thick and strong. Although wine, beer, cognac, and champagne are popular, vodka is the most common drink. Home-brewed vodka is a mainstay and serves as a crucial form of currency in rural areas.

Restaurants were not highly developed under communism, but the post-Soviet period has seen an explosion of restaurants, cafés, and fast-food places in the cities. The majority of people never eat out, for economic reasons and because they feel that restaurants do not provide food as good as that prepared at home. Restaurants and cafés cater largely to the new business classes. Workplace cafeterias and buffets still serve rudimentary midday meals for workers, but even these inexpensive meals are out of reach for many people.

Food Customs at Ceremonial Occasions. Communal feasting is central to marking birthdays, weddings, anniversaries, achievements, sig-

nificant purchases, and major public holidays. The table is laden with salads, appetizers, sausage and cheese, and pickled foods, followed by hot meat, potatoes, and *pirozhki* (meat or cabbage pies). Vodka and wine are drunk throughout the meal, which may last six to ten hours. Although table manners and hosting rituals are complex, the most important concern the rituals around vodka drinking. Toasting is elaborate and can be sentimental, humorous, poetic, ribald, or reverential. Vodka is always drunk straight, accompanied by a pickled or salty food.

Many people observe Lenten fasts, at which they consume no meat, butter, or eggs and occasionally do without vodka. Easter provides an opportunity for a fast-breaking celebration with special foods.

Basic Economy. The Soviet command economy provided a secure living standard for the entire population. Production systems were highly developed, technologically specialized, and spread strategically throughout the country. Almost all consumer and industrial products were produced within the nation or in the Soviet bloc countries. With the end of state support in 1991, many production enterprises declined or collapsed, and imports of higher-quality products reduced the market for domestic goods. This is true of consumer goods such as electronics, fashion, housewares, and automobiles as well as industrial, scientific, medical, construction, and agricultural equipment. As a result of collapsing markets, poor management, and ill-conceived privatization processes, many factories sit idle, while others have been dismantled and sold off. Some sectors, such as the food processing and distribution industries, are staging a slow comeback through modernization and a commitment to providing affordable local products.

The chronic shortages of the Soviet era led many people to produce for themselves. The current impoverishment has increased the importance of this practice, with a significant portion of the population partially dependent on their own produce. Many rural people raise food products for sale, and up to 80 percent of the vegetables consumed are produced in small private plots. The major crops grown by large agricultural enterprises are grain, sunflower seeds, and sugar beets. Livestock production has declined because of reduced government subsidies for feed and falling demand.

Land Tenure and Property. Under communism, all land, enterprises, and urban housing were state property, although there were several different forms of state control and individuals could hold long-term and inheritable use rights to land and apartments. The postcommunist period has seen an ongoing struggle over privatization and the commodification of land. While family apartments can now be privatized, legal reform of land ownership has been held up in the parliament (Duma), because of opposition by communist politicians. Some regions have instituted local land reform, and there is pressure to legislate coherent federal land reform to improve agricultural efficiency. Traditional views that land and natural resources cannot be owned but are collective resources have complicated the privatization process. This view is strengthened by many people's experience of watching privatization benefit only the existing elites.

Commercial Activities. Russia still manufactures a large range of consumer products, including food, clothing, automobiles, and household durables. The construction, banking, publishing, telecommunications, transport, and computer service industries are highly developed.

The unofficial economy, which grew out of the black market of the Soviet period, is huge and intricate and may account for over 50 percent of total economic activity. This shadow economy includes whole industries owned or controlled by organized crime, unreported trading activity, wages paid under the table to avoid taxes, wages and interenterprise payments made by barter, and rent-seeking and bribery schemes on the part of government officials. Attempts to end these entrenched systems have been ineffective.

Major Industries. European Russia was semi-industrialized by 1917, and Soviet modernization campaigns fully industrialized the country and spurred the development of mining, energy production, and heavy manufacturing. The Soviet Union was a major extractor of oil, natural gas, coal, and ferrous and nonferrous metals and a large producer of steel, chemicals, and paper products. Along with the automotive industry, the Soviet aircraft, truck, shipbuilding, railway, agricultural, road-building and construction machinery, military, and space industries produced for exportation as well as domestic use, although quality was often not up to world standards and plants were inefficient. Production levels in all these industries have declined significantly since 1991 as domestic and international demand has dropped, state subsidies have diminished, and new capital investment has been scarce.

Trade. Fuel and energy products constitute the major exports. Imports of foodstuffs, machine equipment, computers and other electronics, and chemicals are substantial. Major trading partners are the countries of the CIS (former Soviet republics, especially Ukraine, Belarus, and Kazakhstan) as well as Germany, Italy, Poland, the United States, the Netherlands, Britain, and Japan.

Division of Labor. Under the Soviet system, training for professional, academic, artistic, management, and other "intelligentsia" careers was highly developed in universities. Working-class students were taught the necessary skills in specialized institutes. The system was designed to ensure an adequate supply of workers in all sectors of the economy, and one of its results was a well-trained and stable workforce. Many aspects of this system have collapsed as whole industries have declined or shifted away from Soviet-era priorities. Huge numbers of personnel have left their original fields for careers in banking and finance, advertising, marketing, commerce, tourism, telecommunications, and security. Regions that offered steady employment for millions now house outdated, stagnant industries; high levels of unemployment in these areas force people to migrate or hunt for jobs. This has led to a confusing variety of choices for young people

A statue of poet Alexander Pushkin in front of the Russian Museum in Saint Petersburg. Pushkin inaugurated the "golden age" of Russian literature.

and the challenge of retooling in an uncertain economic landscape for the older generations. The predictable structures of industries and professions have been replaced by a more flexible system with opportunities for entrepreneurs from any social background. Success can be elusive, because of imperfect commercial laws and law enforcement, the difficulty of securing capital, criminality and corruption, and cutthroat competition.

SOCIAL STRATIFICATION

Classes and Castes. For centuries, the aristocratic and merchant classes were nearly castelike, with endogamous marriage, a strict social hierarchy, and highly codified behaviors. Peasants and serfs constituted a largely impoverished rural population. After emancipation in 1861, as Russia developed slowly along capitalist lines, peasants migrated to factories in urban areas, where they formed an impoverished industrial working class. Strikes and protests and the radicalization of the intelligentsia led to the revolution of 1905, which prompted limited constitutional and social reform along with a reactionary crackdown on political opposition.

Widespread destitution, the ravages of World War I, and ineffective political leadership set the stage for the revolutionary activity of February 1917 in which the government was overthrown; this was followed by the political revolution of October 1917, in which the Bolsheviks took power and introduced communist ideology and social transformation. In the civil war of 1917–1921 and under Stalin in the 1930s, aristocrats, merchants, and well-off peasants were killed, imprisoned, exiled, or forced to emigrate and their property was confiscated.

The Soviet Union was supposed to be ruled by councils (Soviets) formed from the working masses. The creation of social and economic equality was the goal of early communist ideologues. However, Soviet society evolved into a class-stratified and class-conscious state where communist elites and some professionals had special access to goods, services, and housing. Bureaucratic workers and shop clerks used their control of services or goods to benefit themselves through a set of practices known as *blat*. However, education, health care, and other social services were available to all.

Although they had special privileges, most Communist Party officials did not accrue wealth. Postsocialist privatization has allowed many of them to build large fortunes, by parlaying their political status into direct ownership of state resources and industries. A new entrepreneurial class has developed, some of whose members have become fabulously wealthy. More slowly, a middle class is emerging in the cities, formed of intellectuals newly employed in business ventures and midlevel management and service personnel. Most of the population is impoverished, because of industrial collapse, inflation, financial crises, and privatization structures that benefit only the powerful. In 2000, 37 percent of the population lived below the minimum subsistence level of $34 per month. In some regions of Siberia and the Far East, the provision of critical services such as heating, fuel, and water has collapsed. Coal miners and industrial workers have faced severe shortages of critical supplies such as soap, long-term wage arrears, and the collapse of medical clinics and schools.

Symbols of Social Stratification. "New Russians" are all presumed to drive late-model Mercedes or Jeeps, live in fancy new red brick *dachas*, dress in designer clothes, speak on cell phones, and wear heavy gold chains and rings with diamonds. There is some truth to this image, which reflects a popular sense that wealth is vulgar.

POLITICAL LIFE

Government. The years under Boris Yeltsin (1991–1999), were characterized by the reorganization of governmental structures and functions, with conflict over the balance of power between the president and the parliament, and between central and regional powers. A constitution approved by referendum in 1993 provided for a democratic federation with executive, legislative, and judicial branches. The parliament is divided into upper and lower houses. The lower house is the Duma, with 450 elected members; the upper house was to consist of local governors and legislators from the eighty-nine administrative regions, although the newly elected president, Vladimir Putin, replaced the governors with centrally appointed members, giving the president greater control over that house. Putin also changed the electoral and party system to remold the structure and power of the Duma. Economic issues have been at the heart of many political conflicts; battles over fiscal policy, privatization, control of key resources, tax collection, and social welfare provisions have been fierce and sometimes violent.

Leadership and Political Officials. The state has always been prone to authoritarian rule with censorship and strong government control over the media; oppression of political opposition, partly through the secret police; bureaucratic centralization; and legislation by decree. In the Soviet era, political purges killed millions and sent millions more to hard labor or internal exile. Although overt repression ended with Gorbachev and democratization has become a proclaimed political value, the mechanisms of democratic practice are far from universal.

With the end of communism, control over enterprises and whole industries was up for grabs, and top political leaders secured state resources for themselves, their families, and their colleagues, leading to cynicism among the public. Cronyism, bribe taking, inside deals among political and business leaders, a lack of transparency in decision making, and contradictory legislation have further alienated the populace from the political process.

There are over twenty-five registered political parties, although only five are substantial in size. Political fragmentation has been a problem, and coalitions between parties have been unstable.

Social Problems and Control. The rate of violent crimes grew steadily after the end of Stalin's repressive regime. The ubiquity of state authority in the form of the KGB, the police, the Communist Party, and the military created an atmosphere of surveillance and control. Drug abuse was relatively low because of the strong control of border regions, although it increased during the war in Afghanistan (1979–1989).

Economic crime, corruption and bribe taking, black market activity, and theft of state property were normal daily practice for many citizens and officials. An informal culture of networking facilitated the exchange of favors, access, and information and allowed many people to accrue privileges and material benefits. These activities were illegal but rarely prosecuted. One effect of widespread participation in shadow networks and black marketeering was a general disdain for legality.

The economic and social liberalization of the late 1980s set the stage for an explosion of criminal activity. Extortion through the offering of "protection" services became a fact of life for businesses and financed the expansion of mafia activity. The mafia has infiltrated every branch of industry: up to 70 percent of all banks may be mafia-owned, and organized crime plays a substantial role in raw material exports. In little more than a decade, the mafia created vast local and international networks for drug trafficking, prostitution, arms smuggling, nuclear materials smuggling, counterfeiting, money laundering, and auto theft. Mafia-organized contract killings have become common in the cities, and thousands of political leaders, businesspeople, and journalists have been murdered. Because law enforcement is weak and corrupt and because the mafia has close ties with government and business leaders, efforts to reduce its influence have been ineffective. Weak legislation, a judiciary that is underfunded, overwhelmed by cases, and plagued by corruption and overcrowded jails has created a society whose regulatory mechanisms cannot deal with the current conditions. Most people see no point in appealing to the law for assistance or protection.

Juvenile delinquency has grown substantially, along with narcotic abuse, prostitution, the spread of AIDS, and homelessness among teens and children. A number of dramatic terrorist acts have occurred—possibly connected to the war in Chechnya, which also has created opportunities for gun running, extortion, and kidnapping.

Military Activity. After the disintegration of the Soviet Union, Russia experienced a blow to its national pride and identity. Without a Cold War to legitimize a military presence in client states, few fiscal resources, and no longer the center of a superpower state, Russia's military forces contracted, and its military doctrine was revised to focus on national defense and the maintenance of political stability (particularly in border regions). Military issues today include the expansion of NATO, the need for multilateral nuclear disarmament, and separatist movements in the northern Caucasus.

Although military expenditure has decreased and the number of personnel in the armed forces has fallen, sizable forces are stationed in Georgia, Armenia, Moldova, and Tajikistan; these are nominally peacekeeping forces, but one of their functions is to protect Russian strategic interests.

Russia has waged two wars with Chechnya to repress independence movements in that republic. Russia wants to maintain access to the Caspian Sea's rich oil reserves, hopes to prevent the spread of Moslem fundamentalist movements in its territory, and fears that other ethnically based republics and autonomous regions will pursue independence if Chechnya succeeds. Russian forces invaded Chechnya in 1994 and in the following two years nearly leveled the capital city, Grozny, and killed at least thirty thousand of its citizens, including many ethnic Russians. Several thousand Russian forces were killed, and public opinion turned against the war. Russian forces began to withdraw in 1996. In 1999, Chechen rebels in Dagestan gave Russia a justification to renew its attacks; in this second war, Grozny was destroyed, thousands more were killed, and tens of thousands became refugees. Publicity about young men returning home maimed or dead spurred a movement of mothers against the war. Ferocious propaganda stimulated the populace to virulent nationalism and racism against those Russians called "blacks."

SOCIAL WELFARE AND CHANGE PROGRAMS

Soviet paternalism has given way to a weak welfare state. Soviet citizens were guaranteed free schooling, free comprehensive medical care, housing, maternity leave, and annual vacations, and there was an extensive system of pensions and special subsidies for retired persons, invalids, and war veterans. Although the level of access to social provisions was not uniform, most citizens' basic needs were met and people were largely satisfied with the services they received.

Budgetary difficulties have made it increasingly difficult for the postsocialist government to provide the services mandated by law, and new legislation has expanded the range of services. The result is the overall crumbling of social welfare systems. Hospitals and schools are in bad condition, especially outside the largest urban centers. International lending agencies such as the International Monetary Fund have pressed Russia to privatize social welfare and curtail subsidies. Government officials have delayed dismantling the welfare state for political reasons and a widely held view that people should be protected from poverty.

NONGOVERNMENTAL ORGANIZATIONS AND OTHER ASSOCIATIONS

Until Gorbachev, the only legal organizations and associations were those created and managed by the government bureaucracy and the Communist Party. The nongovernmental sector consisted of underground dissident groups, networks, and clubs. Although there was a wide range of unofficial activity, independent political and religious groups were persecuted by the KGB and legal authorities. Since the late 1980s, civil society has grown dramatically and includes organizations that span the country and cover major areas of concern. Groups in every region are dedicated to humanitarian, environmental, medical, cultural, religious, feminist, pacifist, and other causes. Groups focusing on the development and democratization of technical, commercial, legal, and political institutions are active. Scarce resources force many groups to operate on a shoe-

A woman places teapots and teacups in a cabinet, possibly for drying, at the Lomonosov Porcelain Factory. Unemployment for women has increased in the 1990s, especially in the manufacturing sector.

string budget, although partnerships with international foundations have provided start-up funds and strategic support.

GENDER ROLES AND STATUSES

Division of Labor by Gender. Traditionally, society was structured around gendered divisions of labor and authority. Rural communities were exogamous, patrilocal, and patriarchal, with newly married women subservient in the families of their husbands until they had borne sons. Among the gentry, every detail of household management was prescribed and encoded in laws that addressed even the most intimate details of family life.

A key part of communist ideology was the freeing of women from oppressive norms and structures. Women were trained for and encouraged to take up what was previously male-only labor, such as operating agricultural machinery, working in construction, and laying and maintaining roads and railbeds. Nurseries and day care centers were established to free women from child rearing. Women's increased participation in medicine, engineering, the sciences, and other fields was supported. "Liberated" to work in public jobs, women often retained the burden of all household

work as people held to customary notions of domestic propriety. Also, their equal employment status was not reflected in the workplace, where women faced several forms of discrimination. Nevertheless, in a number of domains, particularly in medicine and education, Soviet women gained authority and status. By the 1980s, one-third of the deputies to the Supreme Soviet were female, and women accounted for over 50 percent of students in higher education.

Much of the hard-earned status of women has eroded. As unemployment grew in the 1990s, the first to be discharged from lifelong positions were women; management jobs in the new commercial sector were reserved for men, and a traditionalist view of work and family reasserted itself throughout society. In part, this was a backlash against the "double burden" of employment and household labor; some women whose husbands had succeeded in the new economy were glad to leave their jobs and take up full-time household and family care. For women who want or need to work, recent trends toward devaluing women's work have been demoralizing and financially devastating. Some women have become entrepreneurs, although they face gender prejudice in setting up businesses and often are not taken seriously. The percentage of women holding political office has declined, and women's participation in high levels of industry, the sciences, the arts, and the government has shrunk, especially in big cities. Significant numbers of young women have been lured into prostitution, which appears to be the only way to escape poverty for many impoverished women from provincial regions.

The Relative Status of Women and Men. Many people have an inflexible image of gender roles and skills: men cannot cook, clean house, or perform child care, whereas women are bad at driving cars, managing finances, and supervising others. Men are valued for patriarchal and stern leadership, bravery, physical strength, and rationality; women are valued for beauty, intuition, emotional depth, and selfless generosity. Women are disproportionately represented among the devout, but the priesthood and hierarchy of the Orthodox Church are strictly male. Some new religious groups have women in leadership roles. Women are held in high regard as mothers, nurturers, and bearers of the most sacred dimensions of the culture. Many people value this conception of femininity and fear that it will be spoiled by feminists. Women's movement activists struggle against this viewpoint.

MARRIAGE, FAMILY, AND KINSHIP

Marriage. Romantic love is considered the only acceptable motivation for marriage, and there is a long tradition in literature, poetry, and song of idealizing lovers' passion, usually with tragic overtones, although bawdy approaches to the topic are also popular. Contemporary practice also highlights more pragmatic and cynical aspects of marital relationships, such as improving one's economic status or housing prospects. People frequently meet partners at school, university, or at work, although discotheques and clubs in the cities have become popular meeting places. Premarital sex is generally accepted, and marriages arising from unplanned pregnancies are not uncommon. Since the 1930s, twenty-three years has been the average age at marriage. Cohabitation is tolerated, but legal marriage is greatly preferred. Although economic uncertainty has led many to marry later or not at all, 97 percent of adults marry by age forty, and most before age thirty. Approximately one-half of all marriages end in divorce. Economic hardship and alcohol abuse are major contributing factors. Ethnic intermarriage became fairly common in Soviet times, and most people have at least one ancestor of a different nationality.

Domestic Unit. The multigenerational extended family living with the husband's family characterized peasant life until the twentieth century although household size varied by region. Among the aristocracy, the size and structure of the household unit was more flexible, although strict patriarchal control over the labor and behavior of the household was standard across social classes. One goal of the revolution was to replace traditional family practices with non-authoritarian communal living units. This experiment was short-lived, and after the 1930s, the values of family autonomy and privacy survived state intrusion.

The nuclear family is the most important domestic unit, and most married couples want an apartment of their own, away from their parents. The housing shortage and the high cost of new housing have made this a challenge, and families often live in apartments holding three generations, sometimes in stress-provoking conditions. Many couples with children live with a widowed parent of one spouse, most often the grandmother, who provides child care and food preparation. A grandparent's monthly pension may contribute significantly to the family budget.

Inheritance. Among the gentry, before the revolution, property was divided among all the living sons; as a result, large estates often were dissipated through fragmentation. Among the peasantry, household property included tools, clothes, and domestic items, while arable, pasture, and forest lands were held in common by the village and regularly repartitioned to provide adequate land for each family. Families with more married sons were allotted larger pieces of land. An ethos of egalitarianism with regard to property inheritance has remained strong.

In the Soviet period and for most families today, the most important real property consists of apartments and *dachas*. Ensuring that children have legal title to their parents' or grandparents' housing requires officially registering of the children as residents of those places before the death of the title holder. Otherwise, the title can revert to the government. With the advent of new wealth, inheritance laws are being reformulated, but there is controversy about taxes and legal procedures.

Kin Groups. Kinship is reckoned bilaterally, including consanguineal and affineal relations, although among the gentry recorded genealogies usually stressed the paternal. Until the midnineteenth century, kin terms for over sixty specific relations were in common use; with the social

A man is gathering mushrooms in Saint Petersburg. About 80 percent of vegetables consumed are grown in private plots.

criticized for crying or complaining. Women stay in the hospital for at least a week after a birth, during which time fathers are allowed to see the mother and baby only through a glass window. It is feared that fathers may spread germs or will be repulsed by the "female business" involved in birthing. After the birth, women are encouraged to nurse, although maternal malnutrition often causes failure at breast-feeding and formula is given instead. State maternity benefits and laws on maternity leave are generous, although they often are not observed by private businesses, and pregnant women may be fired. Infants used to be swaddled at birth and are still wrapped and bundled tightly except during bathing and diapering. It is thought that they will injure themselves otherwise. Many customary beliefs about the evil eye and other natural or supernatural dangers surround pregnancy, birthing, and new babies. Although they are coddled, very young babies can be spoken to as if they understood "civilized" behavior and may be scolded for crying, grabbing, or hair pulling. Babies are kept very warm but also get fresh air; it is common to see parents or grandmothers walking in a park on a frigid day with a heavily bundled infant, its face peeking out from the blankets in its carriage.

transformations of the last century, the number of terms has decreased. Even across distances, close relations are maintained between a person and his or her siblings, grandparents, aunts and uncles, cousins and their families, and nieces and nephews, and many people stay in touch with more distant relatives. Among the factors that account for the sustaining of close ties are a lack of geographic mobility, the importance of networks of support in hard times, and regular visits to relatives in ancestral villages in the summer to rest, work, or visit family graves.

There has been a resurgence of interest in aristocratic roots. The exploration and celebration of one's genealogical background has become quite popular, and some members of aristocratic families abroad have returned to visit their families' former estates and re-assert their rank. Many people are intrigued by the romance and drama of the great families of the past.

SOCIALIZATION

Infant Care. Most women give birth in often overcrowded and understaffed maternity hospitals. Childbirth practices reflect traditional ideologies: birthing mothers are supposed to be stoical and are

Child Rearing and Education. The Soviet state provided nurseries and preschools for children, from the smallest infants through seven-year-olds starting elementary school. There were never enough places to go around, and so mothers going back to work after maternity leave might rely on grandmothers or other female relatives. A range of methods ensured that children were inculcated with the values of communal responsibility and proper social behavior. Learning to follow instructions and rules was valued over developing creativity and initiative. Very little has changed, although funding for public child care and education has diminished, forcing teachers to provide services with reduced resources in aging and inadequate facilities. Major changes have been made in school curricula, but most schools rely on teaching materials prepared by centralized federal committees, ensuring widespread standardization of education. Progressivism in education is not highly developed. Academic standards remain high, and students are well trained in world history, foreign languages, music, mathematics, and science. In Soviet times, the values of internationalism were stressed, and the Soviet Union's role in modeling a multiethnic nation was highlighted; that has been replaced by an emphasis on the importance of citizenship and the nation's achievements in the arts and sciences.

Many nonacademic activities and expectations may be structured in terms of gender. Girls and boys are dressed in very different ways and given different responsibilities. Girls are encouraged to be quiet, friendly, and mutually supportive, while boys are expected to be noisy, boisterous, and competitive.

The school year is highly ritualized from the opening day of classes to graduation, with celebrations and performances, some of which involve parents. Many students spend their entire educational career in one school. A sense of identification with the school and lifelong friendships develop in these institutions, and students commonly keep in touch with each other and with their teachers and principals well into adulthood. Schools may commemorate the accomplishments of their graduates.

Higher Education. The Soviet Union had a world-class system of higher education, with forty universities and hundreds of institutions specializing in academic, scientific, professional, and technical disciplines. Business education, especially in management, finance, and marketing, has been developed only since 1991, but there are more than one thousand business training schools, including some at the most prestigious universities, such as Moscow State University. More than 90 percent of the population has completed secondary education, and around 12 percent have received a higher education. Ninety-nine percent of the adult population is literate, although literacy and completion rates are declining among educationally disadvantaged ethnic groups in the North Caucasus, southern Siberia, and the Far East. Higher education has come to be valued as a mark of social prestige and is regarded as critically important for economic success.

ETIQUETTE

The most significant elements of etiquette are the verbal markers of social status. People use the second person plural pronoun when addressing elders except for parents and grandparents, persons of higher status, strangers, and acquaintances. The informal second person singular is used only among close friends, within the natal family, and among close coworkers of equal status. The more distant two people are socially, the more likely it is that they will address each other with full formality. Addressing someone formally also entails using the person's full name and patronymic. Misuse of the informal mode is extremely insulting.

Table behavior is circumscribed by a code of manners. Hosts and hostesses must show unfailing generosity, even with unexpected guests, and guests must receive that hospitality with a show of willingness to be served, fed, and pampered. Drinking together and toasting are important aspects of these rituals.

The filthiness of urban surfaces means that one never sits on the ground or puts shod feet on a table. Proper feminine behavior requires the observance of a number of specific practices: clothes must always be immaculately clean and pressed, fastidious grooming is critical, and comportment should be elegant and reserved. However, in crowds, lines, and public transport, active shoving and pushing are the norm.

In Soviet times, being demure and not drawing attention to oneself through dress or behavior were highly valued, but this norm has vanished with the explosion of fashion and attention-getting subcultural identities.

The word ''uncultured'' is used by grandmothers and older people as a reprimand for behavior on the part of their charges or total strangers that are considered uncouth or inappropriate. The use of this reprimand has diminished as the social status of elders has fallen and as blatantly offensive behavior in the cities has become a mark of the power and ''coolness'' of youthful traders and ''toughs.''

RELIGION

Religious Beliefs. Although Prince Vladimir converted the East Slavs to Orthodox Christianity in 988, pre-Christian polytheism persisted for hundreds of years among the people, alongside Christian practices and beliefs. Many animistic elements, rites, and feasts associated with the agricultural calendar have persisted. Christian practices such as the curative application of ''holy water'' from a church are structured along the lines of pre-Christian customs. Churches frequently were constructed on ancient sacred sites. Traditional beliefs about forest and house spirits and metaphysical healing practices still exist among urbanized intellectuals and the working classes, especially among rural populations. A number of behavioral prohibitions stem from old beliefs: whistling indoors summons ill fortune and evil spirits are attracted by bragging or calling attention to good fortune or health. Telling people they have a lovely child may cause discomfort and necessitate warding off the evil eye.

The Soviet Union promoted ''scientific atheism,'' severely repressed all religious organizations, and destroyed or took over many religious

A house and the surrounding hills near Irkutsk, Siberia. The expense and lack of new housing has made for difficult living conditions in Russia.

properties and sacred objects. The recent revitalization of religious identification and practice has been swift and strong among adherents of Orthodoxy, Islam, Buddhism, Protestantism, Catholicism, and Judaism, although many Jews have emigrated. Indigenous shamanism is also being revived among many Siberian and Mongolian peoples. The state has returned thousands of churches, mosques, and temples as well as icons and other religious objects appropriated during the Soviet period to their respective communities. Monasteries and religious schools and training centers for all faiths have sprung up or reopened, and the number of religious practitioners has more than doubled since the 1970s. There has also been an explosion of alternative and New Age spiritual movements, publications, and practitioners.

A majority of ethnic Russians identify themselves as Orthodox Christians. A much smaller number are active participants in church activities, but the observance of key holidays is increasing. The Russian Orthodox Church has always been institutionally powerful, aligned with the state since Kievan times and even in the Soviet period, when it was allowed to function within strict limits. The control and reach of the state have often

been secured through the administrative networks and ideological influence of the Orthodox church.

Islam has been important throughout Russian history. It has been the major religion in the northern Caucasus since the eighth century and in the Volga region since the tenth. Today, Islam is the second largest religion, after Russian Orthodoxy, with at least 19 million practitioners, and among ethnic minorities most Tatars, Bashkirs, Kazakhs, Chechens, and Avars, are Sunni Muslim. Moscow is a center of Islam in Russia, with many active mosques and organizations to serve the one to two million Muslims in Moscow. There are significant populations in many other large cities as well.

Before the revolution, most of Russia's Jews were confined to rural settlements and endured constant persecution. In addition to facing both popular and official anti-Semitism in the Soviet period, Jewish populations were repressed and secularized to the point where the majority were nonpracticing and Judaism was regarded as an ethnicity but not a religious identity. From the 1970s, a slow rediscovery of Jewish tradition, both sacred and secular, has occurred, while major waves of emigration have reduced the numbers of Jews. A few synagogues functioned nominally during the Soviet period, and these have been somewhat revitalized in recent years as some of the several million Jews remaining in Russia rediscover lost traditions and rituals.

Buddhism was officially recognized in Russia in 1741. It is the primary religion of ethnic Buryats, Kalmyks, and Tuvans. Harshly persecuted under Stalin, when most temples and monasteries were destroyed and lamas murdered or sent to the Gulag, Buddhism has made a steady revival, and today claims several million adherents, among ethnic Slavs as well as traditionally Buddhist populations.

Roman Catholicism is practiced mainly be ethnic Poles, Germans, and Lithuanians. Various Protestant sects are long established, especially among ethnic Ukrainians, and in the years since perestroika foreign evangelical sects have sought adherents among nonbelievers and members of other religious groups. In 1997, the controversial "Law on Freedom of Conscience and Religious Associations" was passed, granting full rights of organization and association to only four religions: Orthodoxy, Islam, Judaism, and Buddhism. Others have to go through a complex registration process and their activities are restricted.

Religious Practitioners. The administrative head of the Russian Orthodox Church is the Moscow patriarchate. Bishops and metropolitans lead the 128 dioceses. Parish priests, who are trained in seminaries and are obliged to marry, serve the 19,000 parishes. The number of parishes and monasteries has grown substantially with the restoration of religious freedom. Islamic muftis lead the Muslim Spiritual Boards, with a variety of jurisdictions, but the hierarchical and regional structure of Islam in Russia is in flux, as numerous religious and religious-political organizations, institutes, and cultural centers vie for authority and followers. Mullahs are the local teachers and interpreters of Islam; many are hereditary, but some young mullahs are challenging existing structures of authority. Among Buddhists, lamas are the most important spiritual leaders and teachers.

Rituals and Holy Places. For most Orthodox believers, religious practice centers on the emotive experience of liturgy, which is chanted daily, on Sundays, and in long, elaborate services on holy days. Icons depicting the Virgin Mary and the saints are widely venerated, and the faithful light candles, pray, bow, and sometimes weep before these sacred images. The peasant hut of the last century always centered on the "red corner" where the family's icon hung, and many urban apartments have a table or shelf set aside for an icon. Churches and cathedrals are the most important sites of Orthodox worship. Local parishes across the country have raised funds to rebuild and restore churches destroyed by the Soviets, with some support from the Moscow patriarchate. Tens of millions of dollars are being spent to restore cathedrals in the large cities. Some, like the enormous Cathedral of Christ the Savior in Moscow, torn down in 1931, have been rebuilt from scratch and are widely venerated as symbols of the rebirth of Russian Orthodoxy.

A similar rebuilding and reclamation of older sites of worship has occurred among Russia's Islamic, Jewish, and Buddhist communities.

Death and the Afterlife. Proper care for and remembrance of the dead are considered very important. Around the time of death, it is crucial to do certain things to prevent the dead from staying or returning: mirrors are covered with black cloth, the body is laid out in ways that facilitate the ushering out of the spirit, and mourners accompany the deceased from home to church and from church to cemetery. In the church or hall where the body is displayed, mourners circle the open coffin counterclockwise and may kiss or lay flowers on the body. After burial, mourners return to the family's home, where certain foods are served with vodka and the deceased is remembered with stories and anecdotes. Food and vodka may be set at his or her place for nurturance of the soul. The soul remains on earth for forty days, at which time the family holds a second gathering to bid farewell as the soul departs for heaven. The anniversary of a death is memorialized every year; some people travel great distances to visit their loved ones' graves.

MEDICINE AND HEALTH CARE

Socialized medicine was a cornerstone of Soviet society. The medical sciences were well developed, with particular success in cardiology, oncology, and laser surgery. However, demand for medical services was often greater than the system could handle, and many hospitals and clinics were understaffed, underequipped, and lacking in supplies. Party officials and other elites had access to world-class, special clinics while the majority received the basic level of care available in the public clinics. Rural and provincial areas were especially ill served.

A secondary system of private medicine has developed alongside the state system. These privatized medical services are affordable by a limited proportion of the population; private insurance programs are in the early stages of development. Occasionally, private businesses pay for the medical care of their employees. Medicines and services are not available at prices all people can afford because funding for public health services have declined.

Social changes have been accompanied by the spread of communicable diseases. Tuberculosis has swept through prisons and other institutions, and the rates of venereal disease, hepatitis, and AIDS have grown. Poverty, poor living conditions, lack of adequate sanitation, drug abuse, and industrial pollution have contributed to a widespread decline in public health.

Folk medicine has traditionally been utilized, and hundreds of herbal and alternative remedies are commonly used; people grow herbs at their *dachas* for healing purposes. The practice of folk or alternative medicine has been legalized, and tens of thousands of practitioners advertise their services. Herbal medicine, homeopathy, the application of leeches, spiritual healing, mineral baths, light therapy, and other exotic forms of treatment are widely used. Professional physicians often prescribe folk therapies such as herbal teas or tinctures and mustard plasters.

SECULAR CELEBRATIONS

International Women's Day on 8 March, celebrating the contributions and role of women in social life, is a legal holiday and a day off from work; men bring flowers to the women in their lives, or call or send cards to congratulate female friends, wives, and relatives. Television features special shows dedicated to women, femininity, and the "female virtues." May Day, or Labor Day (1 May), the day of international labor solidarity, previously marked with parades, is now an occasion to celebrate the coming of spring. The Day of Victory on 9 May commemorates the Soviet capture of Berlin and the end of World War II. This holiday is taken seriously by older people, who gather to remember family members, friends, and comrades lost in the war. Television runs solemn tributes to veterans and war heroes. The Day of Russia on 12 June marks independence from the Soviet Union in 1991. It features parades and fireworks. The Day of the October Revolution, on 7 November is celebrated only by communists and people nostalgic for Soviet power. New Year's Eve is the most lavishly celebrated secular holiday. Grandfather Frost and his helper the Snow Maiden leave gifts under a decorated New Year's Tree, and people gather to await midnight with laughter, song, feasting, and vodka and champagne. These parties often last through the night.

Architectural view of Sveto Nikoski Church in Vladivostok. Orthodox Christianity is the religion with which most ethnic Russians identify.

THE ARTS AND HUMANITIES

Support for the Arts. State support for the arts was provided by the Soviet government because literature, art, theater, and music were perceived as media through which political ideologies could be conveyed. The state nourished the production of the arts through organizations such as the Composer's Union and the Writer's Union, which provided monetary support and social services, while monitoring and guiding creative output. After 1991, federal funding diminished greatly, just as artists were experiencing creative freedom for the first time. While private publishing houses, galleries, and theaters have appeared, the public has turned away from this art to enjoy detective, romance, adventure, and horror novels and films. Popular culture has enjoyed a renaissance, and artists struggle to support themselves.

Literature. Russia has always been primarily an oral culture in which a wide range of folkloric genres and traditions has flourished and provided the primary form of entertainment. Pre-Christian epic ballads, agricultural songs, laments, and tales dating back to before the tenth century were recorded for the first time in the seventeenth century.

Folktales and epic poems were carried by itinerant storytellers; riddles, jokes, and verbal games were popular in every village; and there was a broad spectrum of folk poetry, from sacred ritual verse to ribald ditties. Most great writers incorporated folkloric themes and genres in their work, and folklore is still widely known and shared.

The first written literature dates from the eleventh century, with the production of religious texts, including translations from Byzantine works, original sermons and other didactic works, and hagiographies. Chronicles such as the *Russian Primary Chronicle* are among the most important medieval literature in Old Russian. The *Song of Igor's Campaign*, a saga of the twelfth century campaign of Prince Igor against the Polovtsy, is a work of outstanding poetic beauty, metaphoric sophistication, and political commentary.

With the rise of Muscovy in the fifteenth century, a new literary tradition began to take shape with many historical, biographical, and instructional works, most with a religious character, along with ecclesiastical texts. More secular and popular literature appeared in the sixteenth century. A period of classicism in the eighteenth century saw the development of political and social satire, comedy, and romanticism.

The golden age of literature began in the early nineteenth century with the poet Aleksandr Pushkin, whose narrative poem, *Eugene Onegin*, transformed Russian literature with its shrewd depiction of social life and romantic love. The poetry and prose of Mikhail Lermontov; the stories, longer prose, and plays of Nikolai Gogol; and the stories and novels of Ivan Turgenev opened new paths in terms of language, psychological insight, and sociopolitical commentary. The works of the novelists Fyodor Dostoevsky and Lev Tolstoy took the novel to new levels of psychological realism, philosophical contemplation, and epic tragedy. Anton Chekhov's stories and plays were profoundly innovative. Most Russians know their national literature well.

The turn of the twentieth century ushered in a renewal of poetry, with competing schools of symbolism, acmeism, and futurism. For a brief period before and after the revolution, experimentation and utopianism in all the arts existed alongside realistic and satirical fiction. Many of the greatest literary figures of this period were imprisoned, exiled, or killed during the 1930s. A few key figures such as Boris Pasternak, Anna Akhmatova, and Marina Tsvetaeva, managed to survive but suffered great personal losses.

Socialist realism became the only officially sanctioned and supported mode of artistic production. It was supposed to present a realistic picture of workers and peasants building a socialist utopia. Thousands of paintings, sculptures, novels, plays, poems, songs, and motion pictures were created to accord with socialist realist doctrine; the vast majority were stilted and didactic. Works of art that diverged from the socialist realist mold were frequently repressed. Writers such as Aleksander Solzhenitsyn and Joseph Brodsky were hounded, and ultimately expelled. Except for the time of "the thaw" under Krushchev in the early 1960s, much creative work took place underground or was not published. Gorbachev's policy of glasnost opened the way for previously repressed work to be made public. In the late 1980s, dozens of works critical of Soviet politics or revealing the contradictions of Soviet life were openly published for the first time.

The post-Soviet years have brought writers of dark and droll social realism, such as Tatyana Tolstaya and Liudmilla Petrushevskaya, to the fore. The modern parables of Vladimir Makanin and Viktor Pelevin have become popular among literati and the young reading public.

Graphic Arts. Folk arts are ancient and varied. Animal, bird, plant, solar, and goddess motifs, and a palette of reds and golden yellows with traces of black and green favored by peasant artists prevail across a range of folk art media, particularly in painted wooden objects and embroidered textiles. There have been several periods of decline and revitalization as animist expressions were repressed under Christianization a thousand years ago and then under the Soviet regime. In both cases, peasant artists changed their output to accord with the dominant ideology. Soviet state-run studios kept many folk media alive, and the postsocialist period has seen independent craftspersons return to traditional mythological motifs, such as that of the Sirin, a bird with a woman's head and breasts.

With the adoption of Christianity in 988, Byzantine religious architecture and icon painting were brought to Russia. Several indigenous schools took root in Muscovy after ties with Byzantium were cut under the Mongols. Even though much of his work was destroyed by fire, Andrei Rublev (ca.1360–1430) is Russia's most renowned icon painter; the subtle color, harmonious composition, and spiritual serenity of his images are still revered.

After the sixteenth century, the tsar's court, the gentry, and wealthy merchants supported metalworking, jewelry, textile, and porcelain workshops.

An array of these crafts is on display in the Kremlin's Armory.

Secular painting, particularly portraiture and cityscapes, developed in the eighteenth century, spurred by the Empress Elizabeth's founding of the Academy of Fine Arts in Petersburg in 1757 and the collections amassed by Catherine the Great. The nineteenth century brought romanticism and realism. Realism characterized the work of the so-called Wanderers Society, a socially progressive movement of the 1870s; Ilia Repin is the most famous of the movement's artists. A folk art movement began later in the nineteenth century. The World of Art movement in the early twentieth century produced the theater designer and ballet impresario Serge Diaghelev, the abstract impressionist Vasilii Kandinsky, and the inspiration for a Symbolist movement. Abstraction dominated after 1910, especially in the form of neoprimitivism, Cubism, Suprematism, Futurism, and Constructivism. After the revolution, the abstract works of Constructivists such as Malevich, Tatlin, and Rodchenko were supported by the head of the People's Commissariat of Enlightenment. These artists had an industrial aesthetic that valued a proletarian utilitarianism, but their art was abstract and formalistic, out of synch with the development of Socialist Realism. After 1953, pluralism in the arts grew quietly until the blossoming of unofficial art movements from the 1960s on, with artistic circles rediscovering and experimenting with abstraction, expressionism, magic realism, and other suppressed genres. Underground exhibits often were held in artists' apartments and studios and in city parks, and some were important cultural and political events.

With the relaxation of censorship in the mid-1980s, new waves of performance art, postmodernism, and minimalism occurred, but there was also a surge of both harsh and critical realism and romantic longing for a spiritually whole Russia. In the 1980s, avant-garde painting gained popularity worldwide.

Performance Arts. The performing arts include those seen as "high culture"—symphonic music, opera, ballet, and theater—and the popular forms, encompassing everything from gypsy ballads to folk choruses, rock music to raves. In the first category are the composers of the nineteenth and twentieth centuries, such as Piotr Tchaikovsky, Modest Mussorgsky, Nikolai Rimsky-Korsakov, Sergei Rachmaninoff, Sergei Prokofiev, Igor Stravinsky, and Dmitry Shostakovich; opera greats such as Fedor Chaliapin; the ballet impresario Sergei Diaghilev and the dancers Vaslav Nijinsky, Anna Pavlova, Rudolph Nurieyev and Mikhail Baryshnikov; and the theatrical producer and acting teacher Konstantin Stanislavsky. Russians are still foremost in many areas of music and dance. Classical music and dance performances were state-subsidized so that tickets were relatively inexpensive and attendance was very high. Ballets and orchestras toured even in remote regions in an attempt to "bring culture to the masses." The level of appreciation for and amateur performance of music remain high.

Western rock music became popular in the 1960s largely through illegal copies of albums that circulated from hand to hand. Rock flourishes today among tens of thousands of rock groups and dozens of famous bands. Estrada, an often vulgar or campy form of pop singing and performance, has been popular since the prerevolutionary period. The singer Alla Pugacheva is the most famous artist in this genre. Folk choruses sing traditional and contemporary folk songs, either a capellà or accompanied by a balalaika and other native instruments. Bard singing arose in the postwar period as a quiet mode of protest but became enormously popular, with "secret" festivals in the countryside attracting thousands of fans. No social gathering is complete without impassioned singing and guitar playing. Most people know the words to many songs. Many young people are devoted to contemporary musical forms such as techno, hip-hop, and rap. Raves and other participatory musical events are very popular in the cities.

THE STATE OF THE PHYSICAL AND SOCIAL SCIENCES

The Soviet Union fostered the development of the physical sciences, and although hampered by the slow development of the computer industry and outdated laboratory equipment, many of its scientists and scientific institutions did important work. Fields with potential military application, such as physics, chemistry, and mathematics, along with other disciplines, were supported. Much of the money for the sciences has vanished. Where it exists, private or foundation funding can provide only minimal resources. Dozens of prestigious institutes are nearly closed, lacking funds even for essentials such as electricity and water.

The social sciences were organized around Marxist-Leninist theory and thus were forced to frame research in terms of dialectical materialism. Until the mid-1980s, social problems were not freely discussed and research that might portray living conditions or social attitudes in a negative light was restricted. Since the era of Gorbachev's reforms, the social sciences have flourished even though financing for pure research has been limited. Applied sociology has benefited, as polling has become a mainstay of business.

BIBLIOGRAPHY

Balzer, Marjorie Mandelstam. *Russian Traditional Culture: Religion, Gender, and Customary Law*, 1992.

Billington, James H. *The Icon and the Axe: An Interpretive History of Russian Culture.* 1970.

Boutenko, Irene A., and Kirill E. Razlogov, eds. *Recent Social Trends in Russia 1960–1995*, 1997.

Boym, Svetlana. *Common Places: Mythologies of Everyday Life in Russia*, 1994.

Buckley, Mary. *Redefining Russian Society and Polity*, 1993.

Colton, Timothy J. *Moscow: Governing the Socialist Metropolis*, 1995.

Curtis, Glenn E., ed. *Russia: A Country Study*, 1998.

Cushman, Thomas. *Notes from Underground: Rock Music Counterculture in Russia*, 1995.

Dallin, Alexander, and Gail W. Lapidus, eds. *The Soviet System from Crisis to Collapse*, 1991.

Dukes, Paul. *A History of Russia c. 882–1996*, 1998.

Dunn, Stephen P., and Ethel Dunn. *The Peasants of Central Russia*, 1988.

Eklof, Ben, and Stephen P. Frank. *World of the Russian Peasant: Post-Emancipation Culture and Society*, 1990.

Fedotov, George P. *The Russian Religious Mind*, vol. 1: *Kievan Christianity*, 1975.

Friedrich, Paul. "Semantic Structure and Social Structure: An Instance from Russia." In *Language, Context, and Imagination*, 1979.

Gerhart, Genevra. *The Russian's World: Life and Language*, 2nd ed. 1994.

Gregory, James S. *Russian Land, Soviet People: A Geographical Approach to the U.S.S.R.*, 1968.

Handelman, Stephen. *Comrade Criminal: Russia's New Mafiya*, 1995.

Hilton, Alison. *Russian Folk Art*, 1995.

Hubbs, Joanna. *Mother Russia: The Feminine Myth in Russian Culture*, 1988.

Humphrey, Caroline. *Marx Went Away—But Karl Stayed Behind*, updated edition of *Karl Marx Collective: Economy, Society and Religion in a Siberian Collective Farm*, 1998.

Ivanits, Linda. *Russian Folk Belief*, 1989.

Kaiser, Daniel H., and Gary Marker, eds. *Reinterpreting Russian History: Readings, 860–1860s*, 1994.

Khazanov, Anatoly M. *After the USSR: Ethnicity, Nationalism, and Politics in the Commonwealth of Independent States*, 1995.

Kingston-Mann, Esther, and Timothy Mixter, eds. *Peasant Economy, Culture and Politics of European Russia 1800–1921*, 1991.

Kotkin, Stephen. *Steeltown, USSR: Soviet Society in the Gorbachev Era*, 1991.

Laitin, David D. *Identity in Formation: The Russian-Speaking Populations in the Near Abroad*, 1998.

Ledeneva, Alena V. *Russia's Economy of Favours: Blat, Networking, and Informal Exchange*, 1998.

Lincoln, W. Bruce. *Between Heaven and Hell: The Story of a Thousand Years of Artistic Life in Russia*, 1998.

Mandel, David. *Rabotyagi: Perestroika and after Viewed from Below*, 1994.

Markowitz, Fran. *Coming of Age in Post-Soviet Russia*, 2000.

Millar, James R., and Sharon L. Wolchik, eds. *The Social Legacy of Communism*, 1994.

Pesmen, Dale. *Russia and Soul: An Exploration*, 2000.

Pilkington, Hilary. *Migration, Displacement, and Identity in Post-Soviet Russia*, 1998.

Pipes, Richard. *Russia under the Old Regime*, 1974.

Riasanovsky, Nicholas V. *A History of Russia*, 6th ed., 2000.

Ries, Nancy. *Russian Talk: Culture and Conversation during Perestroika*, 1997.

Rose, Richard. "Getting by without Government: Everyday Life in Russia." *Daedalus*, 123 (3): 41–62, 1994.

Ruffin, M. Holt, et al. *The Post-Soviet Handbook: A Guide to Grassroots Organizations and Internet Resources*, 1999.

Rzhevsky, Nicholas, ed. *The Cambridge Companion to Modern Russian Culture*, 1998.

Shalin, Dmitri N., ed. *Russian Culture at the Crossroads: Paradoxes of Post-Communist Consciousness*, 1996.

Shlapentokh, Vladimir. "Bonjour, Stagnation: Russia's Next Years." *Europe–Asia Studies*, 49 (5): 865–881, 1997.

Smith, Kathleen E. *Remembering Stalin's Victims: Popular Memory and the End of the USSR*, 1996.

Sokolov, Y. M. *Russian Folklore*, translated by Catharine Ruth Smith, 1971.

Stites, Richard. *Revolutionary Dreams: Utopian Vision and Experimental Life in the Russian Revolution*, 1989.

———. *Russian Popular Culture: Entertainment and Society since 1900*, 1992.

Thompson, Terry L., and Richard Sheldon. *Soviet Society and Culture: Essays in Honor of Vera S. Dunham*, 1988.

Toomre, Joyce. *Classic Russian Cooking*, 1992.

Tumarkin, Nina. *The Living and the Dead: The Rise and Fall of the Cult of World War II in Russia*, 1994.

—NANCY RIES

RWANDA

ALTERNATIVE NAMES

Banyarwanda, Banyamulenge, Bafumbira

ORIENTATION

Identification. The Rwandan culture includes not only the population of Rwanda but people in neighboring states, particularly Congo and Uganda, who speak the Kinyarwanda language. The important ethnic divisions within Rwandan culture between Hutu, Tutsi, and Twa are based on perceptions of historical group origins rather than on cultural differences. All three groups speak the same language, practice the same religions, and live interspersed throughout the same territory; they are thus widely considered to share a common culture, despite deep political divisions. The Rwandans in Congo and Uganda include both refugees, who generally maintain a strong identification with the Rwandan national state, and Kinyarwanda speakers who have lived outside Rwanda for generations and therefore have a distinct cultural identity within the wider national culture.

Location and Geography. Known as the "land of a thousand hills," Rwanda is a mountainous country located on the far western edge of the Rift Valley, bordering on Burundi, the Democratic Republic of Congo, Uganda, and Tanzania. Rwanda rises from relatively flat plains in the east along the Tanzania border to steep mountains in the west along the continental divide between the Congo and Nile rivers. From the continental divide, the land drops sharply to the shores of Lake Kivu, which forms most of Rwanda's border with Congo. A range of high volcanoes forms Rwanda's northwest border. The mountainous topography continues in the North Kivu region of Congo, where almost half of

the population identifies as Rwandan. A concentration of Kinyarwanda-speaking Tutsi, known as the Banyamulenge, lives in the high plains and mountains above Lake Tanganyika in South Kivu. The Bufumbira region of southwest Uganda is also Kinyarwanda speaking. The difficulty of travel and isolation resulting from the mountainous topography historically encouraged largely self-sufficient local communities and many local variations of the culture, but the modern centralized state implemented during the colonial period has encouraged a degree of cultural homogenization, at least within the borders of Rwanda.

Demography. War and political turmoil have led to radical population shifts in Rwanda in the past decade. According to the 1991 census, the total population of Rwanda was 7.7 million, with 90 percent of the population in the Hutu ethnic group, 9 percent Tutsi, and 1 percent Twa, though the actual percentage of Tutsi was probably higher. During the 1994 genocide, an estimated 80 percent of the Tutsi population living in Rwanda was killed, perhaps 600,000 people, but after a Tutsi-dominated government came to power in Rwanda in 1994, an estimated 700,000 Tutsi refugees returned from abroad. Meanwhile, several hundred thousand Hutu also died in the genocide and war and from diseases like cholera that spread in refugee camps when, at the end of the war, several million Hutu fled to Tanzania and Congo. Several million more were internally displaced within Rwanda. War that broke out in Congo in 1996 killed thousands more Hutu and drove most Hutu refugees back into Rwanda. As a result, the size and ethnic breakdown of the population are thought to be roughly comparable today to that before the 1994 war.

Rwanda is the most densely populated country in Africa. Prior to the 1994 war, Rwanda was among the most rural countries in the world, but the war precipitated rapid urbanization, with many

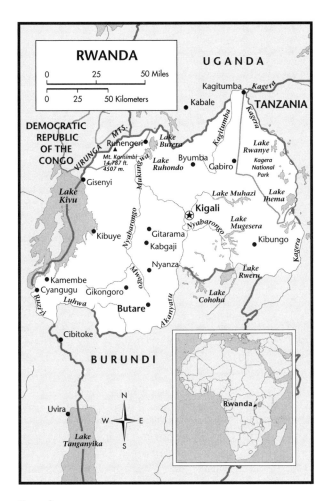

Rwanda

terest of all three ethnic groups. Hutu and Tutsi were also linked together throughout much of the territory in a system of cattle vassalage, in which Tutsi patrons provided cattle to Hutu clients. During the colonial period, however, the monarchy lost much of its legitimacy as it became increasingly identified with the Tutsi minority, and the system of cattle vassalage became viewed as a system of exploitation of Hutu by Tutsi. The cattle vassalage system was abolished in the 1950s and Hutu politicians deposed the king in 1961. After independence in 1962, the all-Hutu government sought to portray Rwanda as a Hutu country, emphasizing agrarian cultural symbols. Christianity became an important source of national symbols, with almost all national leaders openly identifying as Christians, the large majority as Catholic. Since the Tutsi retook power in 1994, historic symbols such as cattle have been revived, and a strong political faction has called for the reinstallation of the monarchy as a means of reunifying the country's ethnic groups.

HISTORY AND ETHNIC RELATIONS

Emergence of the Nation. Rwanda traces its origins to one of the many small kingdoms that emerged in the Great Lakes region of Central Africa beginning five hundred years ago. Land pressures throughout the densely populated region encouraged increasing political centralization, particularly among cattle-raising people, who feared the loss of pasture land to encroaching cultivation. The kingdom of Rwanda was founded in the sixteenth century in what is today eastern Rwanda, then moved west to modern central Rwanda, where it developed a unifying social system and a strong army and began to expand, incorporating neighboring kingdoms and chieftaincies through conquest or alliance. A complex system emerged, based on political and economic ties rather than shared cultural identity. In the central kingdom, power was centralized and an ethnic division between Hutu, Tutsi, and Twa became well developed. A system of cattle vassalage bound local communities together and tied them to the monarchy. Areas outside the central kingdom retained their distinct political and social organizations to varying degrees, with some chieftaincies merely paying tribute to the Rwandan king, but remaining otherwise autonomous. During this period, some Rwandans who resented the increasing political control emigrated from the kingdom, resettling in Congo, where they formed a distinct Rwandan community later known as the Banyamulenge.

refugees choosing not to return to their rural homes but to settle instead in the cities, primarily Kigali.

Linguistic Affiliation. Kinyarwanda is a unifying factor within Rwanda, since it is spoken almost universally. Closely related to Kirundi (spoken in Burundi), Mashi (spoken in the South Kivu region of Congo), and Kiha (spoken in northwestern Tanzania), Kinyarwanda is a Bantu language. Less than 10 percent of Rwanda's population also speaks French, and a small portion speaks English, primarily refugees returned from Uganda and Kenya. Kinyarwanda is the primary cultural identifier for Rwandans living outside Rwanda.

Symbolism. Historically, Rwanda's three ethnic groups have been identified with distinct aspects of the economy: the Tutsi with cattle, the Hutu with the land, and Twa with the forests. Each group had distinct roles in public rituals, and each group had a distinctive mode of dress. The monarchy served as an important unifying symbol, representing the in-

National Identity. Colonial rule, which began in 1895, was the primary force leading to the emergence of the Rwandan national identity. German colonial authorities and the Belgians who replaced them in 1916 actually regarded the Tutsi, Hutu, and Twa as three distinct national groups, but colonial policies led to a greater identification with the Rwandan national state for all groups, even as they also created greater ethnic identification and polarization. The colonial overlords helped the Rwandan monarchy to centralize its control and extend its social system throughout the territory that is contemporary Rwanda, eliminating the local social and political variations that had existed in the precolonial period. By establishing modern state institutions in Rwanda, the colonial administrators also imported the ideas of nationality associated with the modern nation-state. Subsequent social and political conflicts have revolved around how exactly Rwandan nationality should be defined (for example, which ethnic groups should be included as "true" Rwandans) rather than over the validity of Rwandan as a national identity, as in many African states.

Ethnic Relations. The three ethnic groups in Rwanda emerged through a complex process of immigration and social and economic differentiation that took place over several centuries. Tradition holds that Twa were the original inhabitants; Hutu came second in a wave of migration from the west, and Tutsi came much later from the northeast. Archeological and anthropological research, however, indicates that in fact patterns of migration were much more complex, as populations moved into Rwanda over many centuries. Each new group of migrants adopted the local language and most local customs, although they also added some of their own beliefs and practices to the local culture. Modern ethnic identities emerged fairly recently and therefore could not derive primarily from migration. In fact, the differentiation throughout the region into three fully distinct ethnic groups occurred only during the colonial period and grew much more from European ideas about race and identity than from historic cultural patterns.

German and Belgian policies were based on the concept of indirect rule which sought to administer colonies through existing structures of power. Colonial administrators mistakenly believed power in Rwanda to be organized primarily along ethnic lines, and thus they instituted policies that subjugated the Hutu and favored the Tutsi, whom they saw as the natural rulers. The colonial rulers did not, in fact, maintain local power structures un-

changed but centralized the political system, eliminating local political variations, including abolishing autonomous Hutu chieftaincies. In strengthening the rule of the Rwandan monarch throughout the territory, the colonials and their Tutsi allies in the royal court helped to extend the culture of central Rwanda to the rest of the territory. Many of the myths, practices, and beliefs of central Rwanda were spread to the rest of the territory, as were the system of cattle vassalage and the clear distinction between Hutu, Tutsi, and Twa. The northern region of the country, which was least integrated into pre-colonial Rwanda, has remained somewhat politically distinct from the rest of the country, and competition between the north and the rest of the country has remained an important political factor.

With the establishment of colonial borders, some Kinyarwanda-speaking people were situated outside Rwanda. The Rwandan populations of Bufumbira in southwest Uganda and the border regions of North Kivu, as well as the Banyamulenge population in South Kivu, had little connection to the Rwandan court even before colonial rule. Under separate colonial authorities, these groups developed distinctive cultural identities, even as the populations of Uganda and Congo associated them with Rwanda. Meanwhile, thousands of Rwandans migrated to Congo and Uganda for economic purposes, creating large Rwandan communities with a stronger identification with Rwanda in places such as Masisi in North Kivu. In the Rwandan community outside Rwanda, the distinction between Hutu and Tutsi remained less significant than it became within Rwanda, as most Kinyarwanda-speakers were collectively known as Banyarwanda.

Within Rwanda the myth that Tutsi were a distinct race that arrived recently and established its dominance over Hutu and Tutsi through conquest came to be embraced by most of the population. It served the interests of the Tutsi elite who used it to reinforce German and Belgian prejudice that regarded Tutsi as natural rulers. During the colonial period, Rwanda was administered jointly with its neighbor to the south, Burundi, which had a closely related language and a similar social structure. With Hutu, Tutsi, and Twa in Burundi as well, the ethnic politics in the two countries tended to develop in tandem, with events in one country inspiring a response in the other.

In the 1950s, as independence approached, a movement of Hutu ethno-nationalism arose in response to the growing impoverishment of Hutu and the dominance of Tutsi. The Hutu ethno-nationalists claimed that Hutu were the true Rwandans and that Tutsi were foreign interlopers. A peasant uprising in 1959 drove Tutsi chiefs from office and led thousands of Tutsi to flee the country, most of them to Uganda, Congo, and Burundi. Anti-Hutu violence in 1972 in Burundi, where Tutsi remained in charge, inspired anti-Tutsi violence in Rwanda in 1973 and led thousands more Tutsi to flee into exile. Hutu ethno-nationalism remained an important ideology in Rwanda and ultimately Hutu leaders used the idea that Tutsi were not "true" Rwandans to inspire Hutu soldiers and militia to slaughter the country's Tutsi population in 1994 along with moderate Hutu who challenged the exclusivist national ideology.

Although they embraced an exclusivist notion of identity during the colonial period, Tutsi since independence have sought to promote a more inclusive conception of national identity that regards Hutu, Tutsi, and Twa as one nationality. In 1990, the Rwandan Patriotic Front (RPF), a group of Tutsi refugees based in Uganda, invaded northern Rwanda to attempt to force the government to allow Tutsi refugees to return to Rwanda. Although hundreds of thousands of Tutsi were killed in the 1994 genocide—in part because Hutu were frightened by the RPF invasion—the RPF was ultimately successful on the battlefield, and in July 1994, they took control of the country. The current RPF-dominated government now promotes a multi-ethnic idea of Rwandan national identity.

Urbanism, Architecture, and the Use of Space

Rwanda is among the most rural countries in the world. Most people live in individual family compounds surrounded by banana groves and fields and scattered across the hillsides. The hill—the collection of families living on a single hill—has historically been the central social and political unit. Each hill had a chief who linked the population to the monarch. Although chieftaincies were abolished in the 1960s, the new administrative units generally preserved the hill divisions.

The extreme violence that swept the country in 1994 devastated Rwanda's rural social structure. With millions of people uprooted from their homes, hundreds of thousands killed, and hundreds of thousands more returned from long exile, Rwandan society underwent rapid social change. Most of the returned Tutsi refugees chose to settle in urban areas, while most Tutsi in the countryside were killed or chose to move to the cities. As a result,

urbanization took on a new ethnic character, even as the rate of urbanization jumped dramatically. Meanwhile, the government instituted a program of villagization in the countryside, forcing peasant farmers to leave their isolated homesteads to live together in small overcrowded villages. While the government claimed that these villages were intended to facilitate the administration of social services, many critics believed that the program was designed to facilitate social control.

Food and Economy

Food in Daily Life. Rwandan food is quite simple, with beans, bananas, sweet potatoes, potatoes, and sorghum being the most common foods. Dairy products are also widely consumed, particularly a traditional drink of curdled milk. Those who can afford to do so also eat meat, primarily beef, goat, and chicken. Sorghum and banana beers are common as well.

Rwandans traditionally eat food in public settings only for ceremonial purposes, but otherwise eat only in the home. In recent years, the taboo on eating in public has diminished significantly, and restaurants have appeared in most urban areas. While the system of clans has diminished sharply in importance in Rwanda, most Rwandans will still not eat the totemic animals associated with their clans.

Food Customs at Ceremonial Occasions. Important occasions in Rwanda always involve the ceremonial consumption of alcohol and food, but full meals are never served. People in attendance at a wedding or funeral are formally served a piece of meat and something else to eat, usually a roasted potato. A pot of sorghum beer is placed in the center of the room with numerous reed straws, and participants come forward to partake. Calabashes of banana beer are passed through the crowd.

It is also customary to serve people food and drink when they visit a home. Refusing to partake of offered food or drink is considered a grave insult. Hosts typically sip from drinks and taste the food first before passing them to the guests to show that they are safe for consumption and have not been poisoned. Visitors are often presented with food as gifts to take with them at the conclusion of their visits.

Basic Economy. Rwanda has an overwhelmingly agrarian economy. Most residents live largely from subsistence farming, growing some coffee on the side as a means of earning income. The level of industrialization remains extremely low.

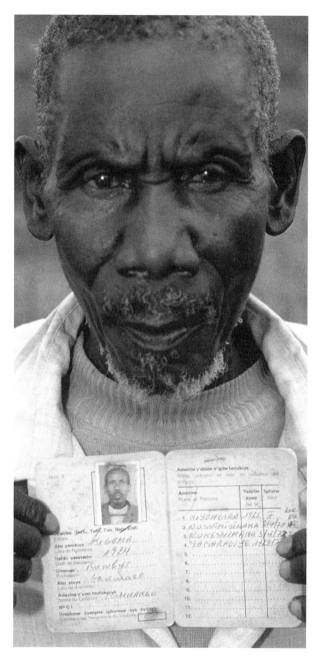

A Batwa holds up his identity card, which notes his ethnic origin. The Batwa have been subject to much discrimination in Rwanda.

Land Tenure and Property. Most Rwandans own the land that they work. Traditionally, all land was formally held by the king and rights to the land were distributed to subjects by the local chiefs, but in practice, Rwandans controlled their own land and passed it down as an inheritance to their male children. Private land ownership was formalized during the colonial period and continued as a general practice. Overpopulation and related poverty have led to

land accumulation by a limited elite and the emergence of a class of landless poor, but most rural residents, even the very poor, own at least some of the fields they work.

Commercial Activities. With almost no natural resources other than land, no access to the ocean, and extremely dense population, Rwanda's economic possibilities are extremely limited. Coffee has been the most important export, followed by other agricultural products such as tea and pyrethrum. Since the 1970s, Rwanda's economy has been heavily dependent upon foreign economic assistance. Foreign aid has financed the construction of roads, water and electrical systems, and the development of new economic ventures, most recently flowers for export. These ventures have generally benefitted only a limited elite associated with the government, while doing little to address the growing poverty of the masses.

Major Industries. Rwanda has developed a few small industries to meet local demands for products such as bottled beer, soap, and fabric, but these provide little employment and contribute little to the economy.

Trade. Coffee is the country's primary export, along with tea, which is grown on large estates in areas of high elevation, and pyrethrum, a type of chrysanthemum grown as a natural insecticide. Since the 1990–1994 war, Rwanda has become more involved in international trade with Uganda and Congo. Rwanda has become a major transport center for gold, diamonds, and other commodities mined in Congo.

SOCIAL STRATIFICATION

Classes and Castes. Historians have described the pre-colonial division between Hutu, Tutsi, and Twa as both a class and a caste division, though neither term is wholly accurate. Like caste divisions, one's group determined to some extent one's occupation, with Hutu engaged more in cultivation, Tutsi in raising livestock, and Twa in hunting and a few other activities such as making ceramics. The occupational lines were not, however, strictly enforced, as Hutu could own cattle and goats and most Tutsi engaged in at least some cultivation. The terms may be somewhat closer to class labels, because there clearly was a status distinction between Hutu, Tutsi, and Twa, with Tutsi at the top of the social hierarchy and Twa at the bottom. Each group had a specific socially proscribed public role, symbolized by distinct functions in public rituals.

The association between ethnic identity and class has broken down since independence. Since Hutu took control of the government, those Hutu with access to power were able to use their positions to enrich themselves and accumulate cattle and land, traditional signs of wealth. While most Hutu remained poor, a small Hutu elite was able to flourish. Without access to political power, Tutsi lost most opportunities for enrichment. With the change in government in 1994, Tutsi once again gained access to economic opportunities. Many Tutsi returning from Uganda or elsewhere were able to bring capital with them, and they have been able to use their international connections to engage in trade and other economic activities.

Despite the changing position of Hutu and Tutsi, the Twa have remained fixed at the bottom of the social hierarchy. Twa have almost no political power and remain the poorest segment of society. Twa are generally despised by Hutu and Tutsi alike, who regard them as dirty and dishonest. Whereas intermarriage between Hutu and Tutsi is common, it is extremely rare between Twa and other groups.

Symbols of Social Stratification. Historically, social status was symbolized through the possession of cattle, the primary sign of wealth in Rwanda. In fact, Hutu families that acquired sufficient cattle and were able to take clients in the cattle vassalage system would eventually have their status changed and come to be known as Tutsi, whereas Tutsi who lost their cattle and clients would eventually be considered Hutu. Although ownership of cattle is no longer associated with ethnic identity, it remains an important symbol of status. Other historic symbols of high social status, such as elaborate hair styles and distinctive dress, are no longer in practice. Social status in contemporary Rwanda is reflected in the knowledge of French or English, which demonstrates a degree of education, and in the possession of consumer goods such as vehicles and televisions. Twa are identified in part by their distinctive patterns of speech; while Kinyarwanda is generally spoken using three tones, Twa speak Kinyarwanda with two.

POLITICAL LIFE

Government. Rwanda has a powerful president, assisted by a multiparty cabinet and a prime minister. The national assembly and the judiciary have little independent power in practice. The country is divided into twelve regions, known as prefectures, each led by a prefect named by the president. The prefectures are divided into communes, led by burgomasters, and the communes into sectors. In 1999, local elections were held throughout Rwanda for the first time in a decade, but the level of competition was constrained by continuing political repression. The government promised presidential and legislative elections within five years.

The current political system evolved from the single-party state implemented by President Habyarimana in 1975. Under pressure from a prodemocracy movement and from the Rwandan Patriotic Front (RPF), multiparty politics was legalized in 1991, the office of prime minister implemented, and a multiparty "government of national unity," including ministers from all the major political parties, installed. The August 1993 Arusha Peace Accords between the RPF and the government stipulated a continuation of the system of coalition government. The Arusha Accords are the basis for the current government structure, though the current government excludes Habyarimana's political party because of its involvement in the 1994 genocide.

Leadership and Political Officials. With its long history of royal rule and social status divisions, Rwanda has strong hierarchical political traditions. Relations with politicians, like other social relations, are highly regulated by status roles. Common Rwandans are expected to show deference to their politicians, whose positions give them social status. In exchange for deference and loyalty, politicians are expected to provide their constituents with services and opportunities. Political officials must in turn show deference and loyalty to their political superiors and help to create popular support for the government or risk losing their positions.

While public political relations are formal and deferential, behind the scenes Rwandan politics has long been an arena of clandestine plotting and intrigue. Various clans competed for power in the royal court as alliances shifted and groups sought to increase their power through spying and assassination. These traditions of political intrigue have continued under the republican regimes, with rivals for power secretly plotting the demise of rulers and coup attempts common. Such duality can be seen at the grassroots level, where public deference by citizens may mask private resistance and disobedience.

Social Problems and Control. Traditionally in Rwanda, the local community played the primary role in maintaining social order. When crimes were committed or disputes arose, a council of elders would convene to reach a fair settlement in a process known as *agacaca*.

A member of the RFP loads a mortar as crowds watch the frontline. The Rwandan political system is dominated by the military.

The colonial rulers suppressed this system, while implementing a Western legal system. Nevertheless, informal local controls on behavior remained important, in part because the use of the legal system for political purposes undermined public confidence in it. Political authorities have frequently used informal means of repression against opponents, such as civilian militia, to maintain their power. In the early 1990s, for example, as the Habyarimana regime lost public support, soldiers, police, and civilian groups targeted opposition groups for arrest, torture, and assassination. The regime promoted anti-Tutsi rhetoric in the hopes of attracting support from Hutu. The regime arrested Tutsi and began to organize anti-Tutsi violence, which ultimately culminated in the genocide that took place from April to July 1994.

The Rwandan Patriotic Front took power through force in July 1994, leaving problematic legacies of the ethnic violence and war. As a mostly Tutsi movement, the RPF had difficulty gaining the support of the mostly Hutu population and thus used extensive force to maintain order. Immediately after taking power, the RPF began to arrest people suspected of involvement in the genocide and within a few years placed over 100,000 people in prison. Many critics claimed that many of those in prison were innocent and that the regime was more inter-ested in establishing control than in honestly seeking justice. The RPF, like its predecessor in power, also used force against the civilian population. The government recently initiated a program to renew the *agacaca* system, but the program did not receive substantial local support.

Military Activity. At least since the 1973 coup by army chief Juvénal Habyarimana, the military has been a dominant force in Rwandan political life. The prominence of the military increased markedly after the 1990 RPF invasion. Since the victory of the RPF rebel movement in the war in 1994, the military has dominated the political system, even though it remains officially a civilian regime.

Many RPF military officials hold positions in government ministries, and most observers consider them the real power in government offices. (Paul Kagame, who served simultaneously as head of the army and vice president, became president in 2000.) Officials who disagree with the RPF leadership, particularly the core of Tutsi officers around Kagame, are removed from office.

SOCIAL WELFARE AND CHANGE PROGRAMS

Social assistance in Rwanda has traditionally been provided by family members and neighbors,

Rwandan mothers and their children in Kigali. Children are a symbol of wealth.

though Christian churches have gradually taken on an increasing role in providing welfare assistance. Beginning in the 1970s, Rwanda began to receive substantial bilateral and multilateral development assistance. Since the 1994 war, hundreds of international nongovernmental organizations have also become involved in relief and development efforts. Despite these programs, Rwanda remains among the ten poorest countries in the world.

NONGOVERNMENTAL ORGANIZATIONS AND OTHER ASSOCIATIONS

Many of Rwanda's historic social organizations were eliminated either by the colonial regime or the collapse of the monarchy. Today, religious groups are the most important nongovernmental organizations in Rwanda. Christian churches sponsor not only many religious associations but also other social groups, such as women's groups, youth organizations, and farmers' cooperatives. Numerous economic groups, such as rotating credit societies, have been founded in the past two decades to help people cope with the serious poverty in the country. Since the 1994 genocide, a number of organizations for widows and orphans also have been created.

While nongovernmental organizations have become increasingly important in recent years, the level of group membership and activity in Rwanda remains relatively low.

GENDER ROLES AND STATUSES

Division of Labor by Gender. Agricultural work is divided between women and men. Men clear the land and assist women in breaking the soil, while women engage in most of the day-to-day farming activities, such as planting, weeding, and harvesting. Men bear the primary responsibility for overseeing livestock, assisted by youths who act as shepherds. Men also do heavy jobs around the house, such as construction, while women are responsible for maintaining the household, raising children, and preparing food. Formal nonfarm employment in Rwanda is dominated by men, while women often participate in informal nonfarm economic activities, such as market trading.

The Relative Status of Women and Men. In precolonial Rwanda—even as most positions of public authority were reserved for men—women enjoyed a modicum of political and economic power, as exemplified by the powerful position of queen mother. The relative position of women eroded during the colonial period and never fully recovered. Women in contemporary Rwanda hold few political positions and have limited economic power, as seen in the difficulties women have in inheriting land and property. Many women's associations have attempted to increase the status of women in recent years, with little apparent success.

MARRIAGE, FAMILY, AND KINSHIP

Marriage. Marriage is considered the most basic social institution in Rwanda, and the pressure to marry and have children is quite heavy. Unlike in the past, most couples today select their own mates, though approval of the family is expected. Marriage across ethnic lines between Hutu and Tutsi is relatively common.

Polygamy, once extensively practiced, has become uncommon except in some rural areas, such as the northwest. The decline in polygamy has been accompanied with a sharp increase in levels of divorce and remarriage.

Women bearing children out of wedlock were once punished by banishment or death. Illegitimacy remains strongly stigmatized, though it is also relatively common.

Produce for sale at the Cyangnu Market. Potatoes, beans, bananas, and sorghum are the most common Rwandan foods.

Domestic Unit. Rwandans consider children a sign of wealth, and bearing children is an important social duty. As a result, Rwanda has the highest rate of fecundity in the world, and Rwandan families are generally quite large. Rwandan families typically live in single-family compounds consisting of several buildings surrounded by a hedge or fence. Each wife (if there is more than one) typically has her own house in the compound, as do elderly parents. The husband's extended family typically lives in close proximity on the same hill or on a nearby hill. The wife's family may also live nearby or may be from further away, but both the husband's and wife's kin have important socially defined relations with the family.

Inheritance. Upon a father's death or retirement from active labor, his land and property are traditionally divided between his sons. The eldest surviving son is expected to take care of his mother and any unmarried sisters after his father's death. While wives and daughters have not formally been forbidden from inheriting, in practice inheritance by women has been difficult. In recent years, inheritance law has been revised to allow women to inherit more easily.

Kin Groups. Clan groupings historically have been important social relationships in Rwanda, but their significance has declined over the past century. Clan affiliations were passed down from father to children and cut across ethnic lines, with each clan including Hutu, Tutsi, and Twa. Competition between clans for political power was a major source of conflict in pre-colonial Rwanda. Today, clans serve little purpose beyond helping to define marriage partners, since people continue to be expected to marry outside their clans.

SOCIALIZATION

Infant Care. The mother plays the primary part in caring for infants, but she is assisted by other female relatives and by her older female children. Women generally carry their children on their backs for at least the first year, or until they bear another child.

Child Rearing and Education. The mother has the primary responsibility for child rearing and education. Her eldest brother, the maternal uncle, also plays an important part in overseeing the moral development and socialization of the children, ensuring that they learn social traditions. The state has assumed the responsibility for providing formal education for children, though only about 60 percent of children ever attend school. Even the small required fees are too much for many families to afford.

Children continue to be named in a public ceremony eight days after their births, but many other initiation rites are now rare. Tutsi children were once sent to the royal court for training and initiation, but this practice was abolished along with the monarchy. Few children are now initiated into the Lyangombe and Nyabingi sects.

Higher Education. Rwanda puts little emphasis on higher education. Less than 10 percent of Rwandans attend high school, and another small portion attends technical training schools. A very small percentage of the population continues on to university. Rwanda has one national university based in Butare, with branches in Kigali and Ruhengeri. In the past decade, several small private colleges have also been established.

ETIQUETTE

With its long history of hierarchical social relations, Rwandan culture puts great emphasis on practices of etiquette that demonstrate respect and emphasize social rank both inside and outside the family. Within the family, chairs are traditionally reserved for men, while other family members sit on mats on the floor. Men eat first, with women and children eating after. Visitors are given the best chairs and the first choice of food and drink.

Rwandans have an elaborate system of salutation that varies depending on the relative social rank and familiarity of the greeters. Rwandans almost always shake hands upon encountering someone. When greeting someone of higher rank, a person extends his or her right hand while placing the left hand on the right arm in a sign of deference. Close friends and others of equal rank may embrace, holding one another by the shoulders and brushing their heads together first on one side then on the other.

RELIGION

Religious Beliefs. Christianity has become a central part of Rwandan culture. More than 60 percent of the population are Catholics, and another 30 percent are Protestants, with the largest Protestant churches including Pentecostals, Seventh Day Adventists, Anglicans, Presbyterians, Free Methodists, and Baptists. Many Rwandans credit the Catholic Church with having supported the Hutu rise to power in the late 1950s and early 1960s, and the church has thus gained great influence and public support among Hutu. With the demise of the monarchy, most of the associated religious rituals ended, and Christian rituals have come to take their places.

At the same time, most Rwandan Christians continue to participate in certain indigenous religious practices as well. Veneration of ancestors remains widespread, with most Rwandans continuing to have traditional funerals and other traditional rites for the dead. Indigenous healers remain common as well. Two secret societies that worship ancestral heroes, known as Kubandwa sects, are less common today than in the past but are nevertheless widespread. The Nyabingi sect is found in the north of the country near the Ugandan border, while the Lyangombe sect is found in other parts of the country.

Religious Practitioners. Both Nyabingi and Lyangombe have priests associated with their worship, but these figures have little public importance today. Instead, the main religious leaders of Rwanda are Christian clerics. The Catholic bishops and leaders of Protestant churches are prominent national figures with considerable political influence, and pastors and priests are important local figures.

Rituals and Holy Places. The Kubandwa sects of Nyabingi and Lyangombe are secret societies that induct new members through initiation. Families experiencing difficulties of some sort will often choose to have a child initiated into the sect. The Lyangombe ceremonies are conducted outdoors in a clearing around a type of tree whose red flowers, tradition holds, represent Lyangombe's blood. Nyabingi ceremonies are also practiced outdoors. The level of secrecy of both sects has been increased because of the hostility they have faced first from colonial authorities and subsequently from Christian officials. Many Christian churches penalize members they find to have participated in one of the Kubandwa ceremonies.

Death and the Afterlife. Rwandans believe that the spirit continues after death, and they see their families as including not only the living, but those who have come before and those who will come in the future. Showing respect to dead family members is considered extremely important. Failing to appease the spirits of dead ancestors through appropriate rituals and offerings can lead the ancestors to neglect their families and allow evil spirits to inflict harm.

MEDICINE AND HEALTH CARE

Rwandans practice both Western and indigenous forms of health care. Christian churches have built numerous hospitals and health centers, but many Rwandans continue to visit indigenous healers, who combine herbal medicines with spiritual cures.

Rwandan refugees cross the Kagera River from Tanzania. In 1999 about 700,000 Tutsi refugees returned to Rwanda from abroad.

Rwandan indigenous medicine emphasizes the flow of bodily fluids. In Rwandan culture, no conceptual distinction is made between physical poisoning and enchantment, and poisoning is regarded as a major cause of illness.

SECULAR CELEBRATIONS

Prior to the 1994 genocide, Rwanda had holidays celebrating the 1959 revolution and the 1973 coup that brought President Habyarimana to power. These celebrations involved public gatherings and military parades. Since the rise of the Rwandan Patriotic Front, these holidays have been discontinued and new holidays have been created to commemorate the genocide and honor those killed. The most important holiday for Rwandan families is New Year's Day. Families traditionally gather for a meal and exchange of gifts on New Year's Day.

THE ARTS AND HUMANITIES

Support for the Arts. The Rwandan government provides very little support for the arts. The government supports a national dance troop based in Nyanza, but there are few other nationally funded artistic groups.

Literature. Rwanda has little literary tradition. The royal court had a tradition of oral history, but this tradition has not been continued.

Graphic Arts. Rwanda has few graphic arts. The main ones are decorative arts, primarily baskets and pottery. There are no traditions of carving or painting.

Performance Arts. Music and dance have been the most important artistic expressions in Rwanda. Both instrumental and vocal music have strong traditions in Rwanda. While traveling instrumentalists are no longer common as they once were, recorded music and public performances in clubs have become common.

The tradition of dance in Rwanda is particularly rich. The training of young Tutsi men at the royal court included training in a form of martial dance that involved drumming and demonstrations of prowess by individual dancers. This *intore* dancing has been preserved since the demise of the monarchy through a national dance troupe, and the tradition is widely taught in schools. Other types of dances were important in public ceremonies and continue to be performed at weddings and other celebrations.

THE STATE OF THE PHYSICAL AND SOCIAL SCIENCES

The physical and social sciences were weak in Rwanda even before the genocide, but they were completely decimated by the violence. Rwanda is heavily dependent upon foreign scholars and researchers for scientific advances and social analysis.

BIBLIOGRAPHY

Des Forges, Alison. *Leave None to Tell the Story: Genocide in Rwanda*, 1999.

Freedman, Jim. *Nyabingi: The Social History of an African Divinity*, 1984.

Lemarchand, René. *Rwanda and Burundi*, 1970.

Linden, Ian, and Jane Linden. *Church and Revolution in Rwanda*, 1977.

Longman, Timothy. "Nation, Race, or Class? Defining the Hutu and Tutsi of East Africa." In *The Global Color Line: Racial and Ethnic Inequality and Struggle from a Global Perspective. Research in Politics and Society*, vol. 6, 1999.

——— "State, Civil Society, and Genocide in Rwanda." In Richard Joseph, ed. *State, Conflict, and Democracy*, 1999.

Newbury, Catharine. *The Cohesion of Oppression: Clientship and Ethnicity in Rwanda, 1860–1960*, 1988.

———. "Ethnicity and the Politics of History in Rwanda." *Africa Today*, January–March, 1999.

Newbury, David, and M. Catherine Newbury. "Rethinking Rwandan Historiography: Bringing the Peasants Back In." *American Historical Review*, June 2000.

Prunier, Gérard. *The Rwanda Crisis: History of a Genocide*, 1995.

Reyntjens, Filip. *L'Afrique des Grands Lacs en crise: Rwanda, Burundi, 1988–1994*, 1994.

———. *Pouvoir et Droit au Rwanda: Driot Publique et Evolution Politique, 1916–1973*, 1985.

Sirven, Pierre. *La sous-urbanization et les villes du Rwanda et du Burundi*, 1984.

Taylor, Christopher C. *Milk, Honey, and Money: Changing Concepts in Rwandan Healing*, 1992.

Uvin, Peter. *Aiding Violence: The Development Enterprise in Rwanda*, 1998.

Vansina, Jan. "The Politics of History and the Crisis in the Great Lakes." *Africa Today*, January–March 1999.

van't Spijker, Gerard. *Les Usages Funeraires et la Mission de l'Eglise*, 1990.

Vidal, Claudine. *Sociologie des passions*, 1991.

—TIMOTHY LONGMAN